MILITARY JUSTICE CASES AND MATERIALS

EUGENE R. FIDELL

President, National Institute of Military Justice

ELIZABETH L. HILLMAN

Professor of Law
Rutgers University School of Law, Camden

DWIGHT H. SULLIVAN

Colonel, United States Marine Corps Reserve

LexisNexis Law School Publishing Advisory Board

MILITARY JUSTICE
CASES AND MATERIALS

EUGENE R. FIDELL

President, National Institute of Military Justice

ELIZABETH L. HILLMAN

Professor of Law
Rutgers University School of Law, Camden

DWIGHT H. SULLIVAN

Colonel, United States Marine Corps Reserve

LexisNexis and the Knowledge Burst logo are trademarks of Reed Elsevier Properties Inc, used under license. Matthew Bender is a registered trademark of Matthew Bender Properties Inc.

NOTE TO USERS

To ensure that you are using the latest materials available in this area, please be sure to periodically check the LexisNexis Law School web site for downloadable updates and supplements at www.lexisnexis.com/lawschool

Library of Congress Cataloging-in-Publication Data

Fidell, Eugene R.
  Military justice : cases and materials / Eugene R. Fidell, Elizabeth L. Hillman, Dwight H. Sullivan.
      p. cm.
  Includes index.
  ISBN 1-4224-1710-7 (hard cover)
  1. Courts-martial and courts of inquiry — United States. 2. Courts-martial and courts of inquiry —United States — Cases. 3. Military discipline — United States. 4. Military offenses — United States. I. Hillman, Elizabeth Lutes,
1967- II. Sullivan, Dwight Hall. III. Title.
  KF7620.F53 2007
  343.73'0143 — dc22

                    2007028352

744 Broad Street, Newark, NJ 07102 (973) 820-2000
201 Mission St., San Francisco, CA 94105-1831 (415) 908-3200
701 East Water Street, Charlottesville, VA 22902-7587
(804) 972-7600
www.lexis.com

ACKNOWLEDGMENTS

Assembling the materials in this book would have been impossible without the assistance of many officials, scholars and practitioners around the world. We are indebted to Dean and Professor Harold Hongju Koh and Senior Judge and Professor Robinson O. Everett, Sr. for kindly agreeing to write the preface and foreword; to Professor Michael F. Noone, Jr., who helped launch this book; and to those listed below, who assisted us in a variety of ways, including suggesting, providing, and translating materials, as well as sharing ideas and serving as sounding boards:

Major R.A. Allen, British Army; Gilbert Blades; Commander Philip D. Cave, JAGC, USN (Ret); Dean Alfred C. Aman, Jr., Suffolk University School of Law; Colonel R.S.B. Bello-Fadile, Nigerian Army (Ret); Biblioteca Juridica Digital, Colombia; Centro de Documentacion del Consejo General del Poder Judicial, Madrid; Niels Christansen, Deputy Judge Advocate General, Copenhagen; Hagay Cohen; Prof. Guido M. Coolen; Arne Willy Dahl, Judge Advocate General, Oslo; Agustina Del Campo, Washington College of Law, The American University; Kathleen M. Duignan, Executive Director, National Institute of Military Justice; M. Miguel Fobe, International Society for Military Law and the Law of War; Jacob Frisch; Prof. Robert K. Goldman, Washington College of Law, The American University; Steven Wiles and Jean Hannon, Harvard Law Library; Matias Hernandez, Washington College of Law, The American University; Commander Gordon Hook, RNZN; Stanislas Horvat, formerly Director, Military Law and Law of War Review, Brussels; Human Rights Watch; Prof. Peter A. Jaszi, Washington College of Law, The American University; Captain Abdullah Kaya, Turkish Army; Chief Justice J.L. Kheola, Lesotho; James R. Klein, The Asia Foundation, Bangkok; Major Gregory W. Kruse, USAF; Susan Lewis-Somers, Pence Law Library, Washington College of Law, The American University; Boonthip Pongjit Landgraf; L. Charles Landgraf, LeBoeuf, Lamb, Greene & MacRae L.L.P.; Philip Luther, Amnesty International; Prof. Ann E. Lyon, University of Swansea; John K. Mackenzie; Lieutenant Commander Sandra N. Macleod, Canadian Forces; Manuel Michel, Office of the Military Attorney General, Bern; James Morgan; Albert E. Moses; Judge Oded Mudrik, Tel Aviv District Court; Krishan S. Nehra, Law Library of Congress; Mr. Justice Devendra Pathik, Court of Appeal, Fiji; Ivan Y. Pavlov, The Bellona Foundation, St. Petersburg, Russia; Major-General (Ret) Jerry S.T. Pitzul, former Judge Advocate General of the Canadian Forces; Colonel Andrew C. Pratt, USAF; Matthew S. Freedus, Marina S. Barannik and Maria Helena Price, Feldesman Tucker Leifer Fidell LLP; Dott.ssa Debora Provolo, University of Padua; His Honour Judge James W. Rant, O.B.E., Q.C., late Judge Advocate General, London; Bruce C. Rashkow, formerly of the United Nations; Prof. Silvio Rondato, University of Padua; Peter Roudik, Law Library of Congress; Royal New Zealand Armed Forces; Rutgers University Law School, Camden; Stefan Ryding-Berg, Chief Legal Advisor, Armed Forces Headquarters, Stockholm; Brigadier General Dov Shefi, IDF (Ret); Kersi B. Shroff, Law Library of

Congress; Lucrecia Molina Theissen, Centro de Documentacion, Institute Interamericano de Derechos Humanos; Dean Glen Weissenberger, De Paul University College of Law.

We are also, of course, heavily indebted to Sean Caldwell and Keith Moore, of LexisNexis, whose patience we have tested and from whose wisdom and advice we have benefited beyond measure; and to our editors, families, professional colleagues, and secretaries (Allie Bernardo, Barbara Bayles-Roberts, and Debbie Carr) for their unstinting support of this effort — and for their patience — as we have attempted to juggle work on this book with other responsibilities. Debbie was especially helpful in securing permission for materials included in the book.

We gratefully acknowledge permission to reprint excerpts from many materials, including those from the following copyrighted materials:

Amnesty International, Human Rights Watch, and Washington Office on Latin America, *Colombia Human Rights Certification II* (2004). Copyright © 2004 Human Rights Watch. Reprinted with permission.

Diane Marie Amann, *Abu Ghraib*, 153 U. Pa. L. Rev. 2085, 2092-93 (2005). Reprinted with the permission of the *University of Pennsylvania Law Review*.

Captain Richard J. Anderson & Keith E. Hunsucker, *Is the Military Nonunanimous Finding of Guilty Still An Issue?*, Army Law., Oct. 1986, at 57, 58-59. Reprinted from *The Army Lawyer,* Department of the Army Pamphlet 27-50-series. The opinions and conclusions expressed herein are those of the individual author, and do not necessarily represent the views of the Judge Advocate General's Legal Center and School, the United States Army, or any other governmental agency.

Federico Andreu-Guzmán, Military Jurisdiction and International Law: Military Courts and Gross Human Rights Violations (International Commission of Jurists 2004). Reprinted with the permission of the International Commission of Jurists.

Kevin J. Barry, *A Face Lift (and Much More) for an Aging Beauty: The Cox Commission Recommendations to Rejuvenate the Uniform Code of Military Justice*, L. Rev. Mich. State u. — detroit C. L. 57 (2002). Reprinted with the permission of the author.

Major Christopher W. Behan, *Don't Tug on Superman's Cape: In Defense of Convening Authority Selection and Appointment of Court-Martial Panel Members*, 176 Mil. L. Rev. 190, 269-76 (2003). Reprinted from the *Military Law Review*, Department of the Army Pamphlet 27-100-series.

Frederic L. Borch, Judge Advocates in Combat: Army Lawyers in Military operations from Vietnam to Haiti 189-90 (2001). Reprinted with the permission of the U.S. Army Center of Military History, U.S. Army.

Paul W. Brosman, *The Court: Freer Than Most*, 6 Vand. L. Rev. 166, 167-68 (1953). Reprinted with the permission of the *Vanderbilt Law Review*.

Carol Chomsky, *The United States-Dakota War Trials: A Study in Military Injustice*, 43 Stan. L. Rev. 13, 15-22 (1990). Republished with the permission of the *Stanford Law Review*; permission conveyed through Copyright Clearance Center, Inc.

Major Steve Cullen, *Starting Over — The New Iraqi Code of Military Discipline*, ARMY LAW., Sept. 2004, at 44. Reprinted from *The Army Lawyer,* Department of the Army Pamphlet 27-50-series. The opinions and conclusions expressed herein are those of the individual author, and do not necessarily represent the views of the Judge Advocate General's Legal Center and School, the United States Army, or any other governmental agency.

Draft Principles Governing the Administration of Justice through Military Tribunals, E/CN.4/2006/58 (2006), by United Nations Commission on Human Rights. Copyright © 2006 United Nations. Reprinted with the permission of the United Nations.

Lieutenant Colonel Theodore Essex & Major Leslea Tate Pickle, *A Reply to the Report of the Commission on the 50th Anniversary of the Uniform Code of Military Justice (May 2001): "The Cox Commission,"* 52 A.F. L. REV. 233, 236-40, 248-50 (2002). Reprinted with the permission of the *Air Force Law Review.*

Thomas J. Feeney & Captain Margaret L. Murphy, *The Army Judge Advocate General's Corps, 1982-1987*, 122 MIL. L. REV. 1, 27 (1988). Reprinted from the *Military Law Review*, Department of the Army Pamphlet 27-100-series.

EUGENE R. FIDELL GUIDE, TO THE RULES OF PRACTICE AND PROCEDURE FOR THE UNITED STATES COURT OF APPEALS FOR THE ARMED FORCES (13th ed. 2007). Reprinted with the permission of the author.

Eugene R. Fidell, *Military Judges and Military Justice: The Path to Judicial Independence*, 74 JUDICATURE 14, 14-20 (June-July 1990). Reprinted with the permission of *Judicature.*

Eugene R. Fidell, *A Worldwide Perspective on Change in Military Justice*, 48 A.F. L. REV. 195 (2000). Reprinted with the permission of the *Air Force Law Review.*

Eugene R. Fidell & Jay M. Fidell, *Loss of Numbers,* 48 NAVAL L. REV. 194, 194-99 (2001). Reproduced with permission from the *Naval Law Review*; Reprinted from *Proceedings* with permission; Copyright © 2001 U.S. Naval Institute/www.usni.org.

Colonel Francis A. Gilligan, *The Bill of Rights and Service Members,* ARMY LAW., Dec. 1987, at 3. Reprinted from *The Army Lawyer,* Department of the Army Pamphlet 27-50-series. The opinions and conclusions expressed herein are those of the individual author, and do not necessarily represent the views of the Judge Advocate General's Legal Center and School, the United States Army, or any other governmental agency.

Lieutenant Colonel Patricia A. Ham, *Still Waters Run Deep? The Year in Unlawful Command Influence,* ARMY LAW.,JUNE 2006, 53, 54. Reprinted from *The Army Lawyer,* Department of the Army Pamphlet 27-50-series. The opinions and conclusions expressed herein are those of the individual author, and do not necessarily represent the views of the Judge Advocate General's Legal Center and School, the United States Army, or any other governmental agency.

ELIZABETH LUTES HILLMAN, DEFENDING AMERICA: MILITARY CULTURE AND THE COLD WAR COURT-MARTIAL 11, 30-31 (2005). Reprinted with the permission of the Princeton University Press.

Elizabeth Lutes Hillman, *The "Good Soldier" Defense: Character Evidence and Military Rank at Courts-Martial*, 108 YALE L.J. 879, 881 (1999). Reprinted by permission of the Yale Law Journal Company and William S. Hein Company from the *Yale Law Journal*, Vol. 108, pp. 879-911.

C. Quince Hopkins, *Rank Matters But Should Marriage?: Adultery, Fraternization, and Honor in the Military*, 9 UCLA WOMEN'S L.J. 177, 203-05 (1999). Reprinted with the permission of the author (originally published in 9 UCLA Women's Law Journal 1999).

Major Walter M. Hudson, *Racial Extremism in the Army*, 159 MIL. L. REV. 1, 30-40 (1999). Reprinted from the *Military Law Review*, Department of the Army Pamphlet 27-100-series.

Informal Opinion 1235, American Bar Association Committee on Ethics and Professional Responsibility, August 24, 1972. Reprinted with the permission of the American Bar Association. Copyright © 1972 American Bar Association.

Major Keven Jay Kercher, *Time for Another Haircut: A Re-Look at the Use of Hair Sample Testing for Drug Use in the Military*, 188 MIL. L. REV. 38, 38-39 (2006). Reprinted from the *Military Law Review*, Department of the Army Pamphlet 27-100-series.

Lieutenant Colonel Paul E. Kantwill & Major Sean Watts, *Hostile Protected Persons or "Extra-Conventional Persons:" How Unlawful Combatants in the War on Terrorism Posed Extraordinary Challenges for Military Attorneys and Commanders*, 28 FORDHAM INT'L L.J. 681, 736-39 (2005). Reprinted with the permission of the *Fordham International Law Journal*.

RAYMOND LECH, BROKEN SOLDIERS 39-42 (2000). From Broken Soldiers. Copyright © 2000 by The Board of Trustees of the University of Illinois. Used with permission of the University of Illinois Press and the author.

Major Kevin Lovejoy, *Abolition of Court Member Sentencing*, 142 MIL. L. REV. 1, 7-8 (1994) Reprinted from the *Military Law Review*, Department of the Army Pamphlet 27-100-series.

PETER MAGUIRE, LAW AND WAR: AN AMERICAN STORY 22, 139 (2000). Copyright © 2000. Reprinted with the permission of the Columbia University Press.

Lieutenant Colonel J. McClelland MBE, *Starting from Scratch: The Military Discipline System of the East Timor Defence Force*, 7 J. CONFLICT & SEC. L. 253, 253-73 (2002). Reprinted with the permission of the Oxford University Press and the *Journal of Conflict & Security Law*.

Professional Responsibility Notes, *Judge Advocate General of the Army, Standards of Conduct Office*, ARMY LAW., Dec. 1995, at 101. Reprinted from *The Army Lawyer*, Department of the Army Pamphlet 27-50-series. The opinions and conclusions expressed herein are those of the individual author, and do not necessarily represent the views of the Judge Advocate General's Legal

Center and School, the United States Army, or any other governmental agency.

STEPHEN A. SALTZBURG, LEE D. SCHINASI & DAVID A. SCHLUETER, MILITARY RULES OF EVIDENCE MANUAL (4th ed. 1997), *"Executive Order 12198 of March 12, 1980 Editorial Comment."* Reprinted from Military Rules of Evidence Manual, Fourth Edition, with permission. Copyright © 1997 Matthew Bender & Company, Inc., a member of the Lexis Nexis group. All rights reserved.

2 STEPHEN A. SALTZBURG, LEE D. SCHINASI & DAVID A. SCHLUETER, MILITARY RULES OF EVIDENCE MANUAL at p. 5-6 (5th ed 2003), *Rule 501 Editorial Comment* pp. 5-6. Reprinted from Military Rules of Evidence Manual, Fifth Edition, with permission. Copyright © 2003 Matthew Bender & Company, Inc., a member of the Lexis Nexis group. All rights reserved.

Harry N. Scheiber & Jane L. Scheiber, *Bayonets in Paradise: A Half-Century Retrospect on Martial Law on Hawai'i, 1941-1946*, 19 U. HAW. L. REV. 477, 487-520 (1997). Copyright © Jane L. and Harry N. Scheiber. All rights reserved. Reprinted with the permission of the University of Hawai'i Law Review and the authors. Excerpted from an article on the subject of the Scheibers' forthcoming book under the same title, BAYONETS IN PARADISE.

Gary D. Solis, *Military Justice, Civilian Clemency: The Sentences of Marine Corps War Crimes in South Vietnam*, 10-1 TRANSNAT'L L. & CONTEMP. PROBS. 59-84 (Spring 2000). Reprinted with the permission of *Transnational Law and Contemporary Problems*.

Robert C. Stacey, *The Age of Chivalry*, THE LAWS OF WAR: CONSTRAINTS ON WARFARE IN THE WESTERN WORLD 27-31 (Michael Howard, George J. Andreopoulus & Mark R. Shulman eds. 1994). Copyright © 1994, Yale University. Reprinted with the permission of the Yale University Press.

Robert N. Strassfeld, *The Vietnam War on Trial: The Court-Martial of Dr. Howard B. Levy*, 1994 WIS. L. REV. 839, 845-53. Copyright 2005 by The Board of Regents of the University of Wisconsin System. Reprinted with the permission of the Wisconsin Law Review.

Ryan Swift, *Occupational Jurisdiction: A Critical Analysis of the Iraqi Special Tribunal*, 19 N.Y. INT'L L. REV. 99, 100-105 (2006). Reprinted with permission from *New York International Law Review,* Spring 2006, Vol. 19, No. 2, published by the New York State Bar Association, One Elk Street, Albany, New York 12207.

THE UNITED KINGDOM MINISTRY OF DEFENSE, THE MANUAL OF THE LAW OF ARMED CONFLICT 16.35-.38 (2005). Reprinted with the permission of the UK Ministry of Defense, PSI Licence No. C2007001038.

Patricia M. Wald, *General Radislav Krstic: A War Crimes Case Study*, 16 GEO. J. LEGAL ETHICS 445 (2003). Reprinted with permission of the publisher, *Georgetown Journal of Legal Ethics* © 2003.

Earl Warren, *The Bill of Rights and the Military*, 37 N.Y.U. L. REV. 181, 181-85 (1962). Reprinted with the permission of the *New York University Law Review.*

Major Sean M. Watts & Captain Christopher E. Martin, *Nation-Building in Afghanistan: Lessons Identified in Military Justice Reform*, ARMY LAW., May 2006, at 1, 10-11. Reprinted from *The Army Lawyer,* Department of the Army Pamphlet 27-50-series. The opinions and conclusions expressed herein are those of the individual author, and do not necessarily represent the views of the Judge Advocate General's Legal Center and School, the United States Army, or any other governmental agency.

Major Emmett G. Wells, Book Review of ROBERT J. LIFTON & GREG MITCHELL, HIROSHIMA IN AMERICA: FIFTY YEARS OF DENIAL, 150 MIL. L. REV. 465 (1995). Reprinted from the *Military Law Review*, Department of the Army Pamphlet 27-100-series.

RUSSELL F. WEIGLEY, EISENHOWER'S LIEUTENANTS: THE CAMPAIGNS OF FRANCE AND GERMANY, 1944-45, 370-72, 568-69 (1981). Reprinted with the permission of the Indiana University Press.

Working paper on the Accountability of International Personnel taking part in Peace Support Operations, E/CN.4/Sub.2/2005/42 (7 July 2005), by Françoise Hampson, United Nations Commission on Human Rights, Sub-Commission on the Promotion and Protection of Human Rights,. Copyright © 2005 United Nations. Reprinted with the permission of the United Nations.

Steven D. Zansberg, Matthew S. Freedus, & Eugene R. Fidell, *The First Amendment in the Military Courts: A Primer for the Civilian Attorney*, 23 COMM. LAW 10, 13-16 (Fall 2005). Reprinted with the permission of the American Bar Association and the authors. Copyright © 2006 American Bar Association.

INTRODUCTION

Few fields of law have experienced as dramatic and abrupt an increase in public and professional attention over as short a time as has military justice. The reasons for this are not hard to sort out, and they help to explain why the authors have brought these materials together in a casebook for the first time.

First, of course, is the increased tempo of military operations around the world. This includes not only operations associated with hostilities (including but not limited to the "Global War on Terrorism"), but also operations of a peacekeeping or humanitarian character. These operations have involved a remarkable number of nations, with extremely diverse political and military cultures. Moreover, these operations have often called for joint activities, thereby bringing the armed forces of many countries together to an extent that has not been seen since World War II.

Second, in country after country, high profile military cases have arisen that have gripped the attention of the public, rather than — as was long the case — being an object of study only within narrow professional circles. These cases have involved issues ranging from maltreatment of women and prisoners to the expression of unpopular political and religious views to operational mishaps such as when a submarine attempts to surface under a fishery training ship or a jet fighter severs a ski gondola cable or bombs friendly forces. Questions of personal autonomy with respect to issues such as sexual orientation or resistance to mandatory vaccination programs have also arisen around the globe. The years-long controversy over military commissions in the United States, when added to the parade of other issues, has contributed powerfully to heightened public interest in the military legal field as a whole.

Third, military justice has increasingly tended to look across national boundaries. This is a result of the simple increased availability of information about other national systems of law thanks to such developments as the internet, but also because of the increased availability of supranational sources of law such as the Convention for the Protection of Human Rights and Fundamental Freedoms. Cases arising under the European Convention and comparable agreements in other parts of the world have repeatedly touched on the administration of military justice, and the decisions of the European Court of Human Rights in particular have become sufficiently numerous that it can now be said that an international body of military justice jurisprudence is emerging.

Coupled with all of these is, at least in some countries, the increasing willingness of judges and lawyers concerned with military justice to take into account, if not necessarily embrace, developments in other countries as they perform their functions in trying cases and arguing and deciding appeals. These judges and lawyers are increasingly availing themselves of opportunities to "compare notes" with their opposite numbers from other countries not only through meetings of organizations such as the International Society for Military Law and the Law of War, but also through the professional literature. Inessential reference to foreign legal materials continues to encounter resistance in the United States, the United Kingdom, and other countries, and is likely to remain a source of controversy in the coming decades.

Finally, in some countries the very idea of having a separate military justice system has been put in issue, sparking lively debate and occasional legislative action for reform and, on occasion, abolition or severe restriction. Consider the following from a member of the Swiss National Council in 1996:

> It is true that, at the time of submission of my initiative a year ago, public opinion was strongly shaken by the lenient verdict pronounced by a military court against an officer who was responsible for the death of a recruit. This verdict appeared deeply unjust. Military justice was again shown to be partial and to protect its own.

> But, well before this event and very regularly, many voices were raised seeking abolition of military courts. I will quote first of all the proposal contained in the report of November 1990 of the committee chaired by Mr. Schoch, state counselor, and vice-chaired by Mr. David and myself, a committee made up of 21 members, including many career soldiers, university professors, lawyers and people who were not committed under a political label, but of whom a large majority leaned to the right.

> This committee proposed to replace military courts with civil cantonal courts. It noted that for some time military courts have been an object of controversy, that they are especially faulted for being partial, and that, consequently, their replacement by civil courts would improve relations between the population and the army. The committee added that many countries have renounced military courts. For Switzerland, such a renunciation is all the more compelling — the army, on principle, should not fight beyond the borders.

> Swiss military justice, a jurisdiction called specialized, appears today to a good many citizens as corporate justice, achieving in the first place esprit de corps and the defense of its own. Such an exceptional arrangement is less and less understood. Every verdict raises a flood of criticisms. This situation is prejudicial not only for military justice itself, but also for the army. This situation keeps the army on the fringe of ordinary law, distances it from the rules of common law and causes the thesis of a State within the State to be believed.

> Military justice is an unnecessary parallel justice. Since the decriminalization of refusal to serve and the transfer of examinations of conscientious objection cases to civilian committees, military tribunals have seen their activities decrease by half.

> In view of this situation and taking into consideration the fact that a large majority of the crimes and offenses defined by the Penal Code are repeated just as they are in the Military Penal Code, military justice can all the more be transferred to civil courts. This transfer would

allow moreover savings roughly estimated at approximately 10 million francs if the entire cost is taken into account.

By a large majority, European countries have abandoned military justice, a clear trend takes shape in Europe since the 1980s. The Northern and Central European countries have abandoned military justice, in any event in peacetime. That is the case in France, Germany, Austria, the Netherlands, Denmark, Sweden, Norway and Finland. Likewise, in Eastern Europe, Hungary, the Czech Republic and Slovenia no longer have military courts. They survive only in the countries of Southern Europe, with an oftentimes dictatorial political tradition.

I come now to some arguments against this initiative. . . .

The principal argument is that military justice is specialized justice, better able to judge than civil courts. To that I reply that military courts are not perceived in this manner by the populace in particular. One thinks it is more as a question of privilege. Moreover, there is a strong similarity between the Swiss Penal Code and the Military Penal Code. The civil courts are entirely capable of deciding with full knowledge of the case and having resort to experts if need be, and one cannot fear a dissimilar practice.

I would like to quote an extract from the testimony of Colonel Ott in the newspaper of the Swiss Officers Society: "The handing over of serious cases to the civil courts in time of peace could remove an unnecessary source of conflict with the military. The sought-after expert knowledge could be assured, as in other cases, by specific experts or assistant defence counsel. That the civil courts generally handle in a satisfactory way the cited special cases — e.g. policemen, doctors — could in fact encourage one to assure the primacy of civilian control in this sector, too, analogously to many other countries."

It is clear that there will remain some procedural problems to work out with the cantons, but they are not particularly insoluble.

To conclude, I would like to point out a quotation which I recently found in an article in the *Journal de Genève et Gazette de Lausanne*, last September, which passed along the words of young people, in particular a youth who spoke vehemently against retaining military justice. He said in particular, and it will be my conclusion:

> With due respect to the *auditeur en chef* [judge advocate general], the defense of military justice is a rearguard action. It falls on our elected officials in Parliament, who will soon have to debate it, to transfer the powers of this jurisdiction to civil justice and to abolish purely and simply an antiquated institution which will seem like a cruel stupidity to our descendants.[1]

---

[1] Conseil National: Session d'hiver 1996, Dec. 13, 1996, AMTLICHES BULL. at 95.425 (Switz.) (remarks of Francine Jeanprêtre). The proposal ultimately failed.

These are strong words, and suggest the depth of feeling military justice can evoke despite the accelerating progress made since World War II. This book takes no position on the basic question of whether to have a separate system of military justice, but we note the issue as one many countries have faced and will continue to face as their institutions, values, and view of their role in the world evolves.

This book recognizes the proliferation of national systems of military criminal law; the interconnectedness of military justice systems because of worldwide deployments, multinational operations, and global terrorism; the growth of international bodies of law; and, we believe, the inclination of lawyers to inform themselves regarding the possibility of shared solutions to common problems of law and governance. Our hope is to illuminate some of the critical issues that shape national and international policy and legal decisions about the proper sphere and substance of military law, to increase the availability of military justice source materials from around the world, and to provide a framework through which students of military law and history can begin to assess various approaches to issues of military discipline and punishment.

This book does not attempt to present a treatise on military justice. Rather than a comprehensive review of the field, we have selected what we believe are among the most important aspects of contemporary military justice in order to stimulate thinking about how military justice relates to core values in a democratic society. Similarly, we have not tried to be exhaustive in the sense of trying to incorporate materials from every country or even every language, cultural or political affinity group among nations. It is our hope that continued progress will be made towards a global appreciation of this field as legal information systems continue to improve.

Learning about foreign military justice developments is of value not simply for its own sake or to better understand events elsewhere. It is of practical value because, by showing that what we do is not necessarily the only way to do things, it helps us to understand our own system and to conduct what ought to be a periodic, if not continual, conscious process of reevaluation so that we can be sure our system reflects the best thinking in order to achieve our national goals. The same impulse that leads us to view the states' role as laboratories for testing new ideas as part of the genius of the American federal system, or to view the various branches of the service in something of the same light, ought to cause us to welcome any opportunity to know and potentially learn from the experience of other democratic countries in the administration of military justice. That experience should be discounted where the other country's political or value system, strategic role, or other distinguishing features suggest a poor fit. But that discount can only be applied intelligently if we have first considered the pertinent data.[2]

The book presents these rich materials in five Parts. Part I, Foundations, sets the stage by exploring the origins and purposes of military justice; pointing out the many sources of law that govern; analyzing the unique and critical

---

[2] Eugene R. Fidell, *A World-Wide Perspective on Change in Military Justice*, 48 A.F. L. REV. 195, 201-02 (2000).

role of the commander in military justice; exploring the use of summary discipline; and assessing professional responsibility rules for military lawyers. Part II, Principles, steps further into legal analysis to study the jurisdiction of military courts, identify crimes and defenses that apply only in a military context, and analyze the extent to which the obligations of military service alter the protection of fundamental rights. Part III, Trials, brings students into the court-martial to meet military judges and juries, and to study the rules of procedure, evidence, sentencing, and appeal. Part IV, Special Contexts, assesses the challenges of multinational, peacekeeping, and humanitarian operations as well as military commissions. Part V, The Future, gives students a glimpse into the changes that lie ahead by focusing on the processes of legal reform and globalization. This material is especially important. It is our hope that students who have used this book for a course will, at the end, feel motivated to consider what changes, if any, ought to be made in their country's military justice system, and beyond that, will possess a new awareness for the interconnectedness of developments in the field. To state it directly, it is our conviction that in a democratic society, the more lawyers, judges, law professors, legislators, and public officials charged with responsibility for national defense and the administration of justice who concern themselves with such matters, the better. While it is inevitable that the lion's share of learning in this field will be possessed by the military bench and bar, it would be unhealthy if they had a monopoly over that learning.

These materials are presented to provoke discussion of the fundamental issues of military justice. These include: must the military be a separate society with its own governance and disciplinary procedures? How do the exigencies of war and military duty alter the balance of rights for servicemembers? What role should a commanding officer play in criminal investigation, prosecution, and appeal? How do personnel policies that require conscription, integration (along lines of race, gender, or sexual orientation), or behavioral modification (such as "zero tolerance" for sexual harassment) affect military criminality and criminal prosecution? How should military justice draw the line between misconduct that warrants the full panoply of procedural protections and that which can be summarily addressed? Are there unusual policy and fairness issues when a military criminal conviction means not only punishment as witnessed in the civilian courts, but also loss of employment and possibly vested pension benefits? Can military justice be administered fairly where several nations cooperate in a single mission? During emergencies, does (and must) due process fall before concerns of national (or human) security? Our hope is that this book will become a new and powerful tool to introduce the dilemmas of military law while deepening our understanding of criminal law and procedure, comparative law, international law, constitutional law, and democratic governance.

PREFACE
*Harold Hongju Koh**

"Military justice is to justice," Clemenceau reportedly said, "what military music is to music."[1] Yet the basic chords of military music have not transformed nearly as much over the last few decades as has the burgeoning legal field of military justice.

Since September 11, nations around the world have confronted a kaleidoscope of complex, high-profile military lawsuits, which until recently would have been comprehensible only to a tiny band of military legal specialists. Discussions of Common Article Three of the Geneva Conventions, the Uniform Code of Military Justice (UCMJ), admissibility of evidence obtained through coercion, and military commissions now fill the front pages of the daily newspapers.

Until now, American law schools have lacked a single, systematic casebook treatment of these topics, suitable for ready research by journalists and historians or classroom adoption by law teachers. Thanks to three skilled and experienced military law scholars — Eugene Fidell, Beth Hillman, and Dwight Sullivan — the important casebook you now hold in your hands fills that void.

The three authors enjoy unusually broad individual and collective expertise in military law and justice. A Coast Guard veteran and a graduate of Harvard Law School, Eugene Fidell is President of the National Institute of Military Justice and head of the Military Practice Group at Feldesman Tucker Leifer Fidell LLP. One of our country's leading commentators on military law, he has lectured and taught widely on military justice issues, and is now my colleague on the faculty at Yale Law School. Professor Beth Hillman of Rutgers-Camden School of Law holds a bachelor's degree from Duke, where she was the highest-ranking Air Force ROTC cadet on campus, a master's degree in history from the University of Pennsylvania, and a law degree and Ph.D. in history from Yale. She recently authored "Defending America: Military Culture and the Cold War Court-Martial" (Princeton University Press, 2005). As an Air Force veteran who served as an orbital analyst at the U.S. Space Command in Colorado Springs, Colorado, she directly experienced the injustices caused by the "don't ask, don't tell policy" regarding gays and lesbians in the military. Dwight H. Sullivan, a Colonel in the United States Marine Corps Reserve, is the country's leading expert on the military death penalty. He formerly worked as an attorney with the Maryland office of the American Civil

---

* Dean and Gerard C. & Bernice Latrobe Smith Professor of International Law, Yale Law School; U.S. Assistant Secretary of State for Democracy, Human Rights and Labor, 1998-2001.

[1] *See* FRESNO BEE, Oct. 17, 1968, at 17-A (attributing this statement to French statesman Georges Clemenceau). I am reliably informed by Fred Shapiro, Yale Law School's librarian, that this saying was later popularized by comedian Groucho Marx and *Washington Post* reporter Robert Sherrill, who used it as the title of his book, Robert Sherrill, MILITARY JUSTICE IS TO JUSTICE AS MILITARY MUSIC IS TO MUSIC (1970).

Liberties Union, and served with distinction as chief defense counsel for the
Guantánamo Bay detainees at the Office of Military Commissions of the U.S.
Department of Defense. Professors Fidell and Hillman are associated with the
National Institute of Military Justice (http://www.nimj.org) (NIMJ), a District
of Columbia non-profit corporation organized in 1991 by private lawyers, law
professors and former active duty military officers (now affiliated with
American University's Washington College of Law) with the mission of
advancing the fair administration of military justice and fostering improved
public understanding of the military justice system.

In this book, these accomplished authors do not attempt to present an ency-
clopedic overview of the field of military justice. Rather, three features make
this casebook both unique and thematically cohesive. First, the authors have
selected a number of key themes that pervade the contemporary military justice field to test the relationship between core principles of military justice and
the enduring values of a democratic society. Second, the book draws upon comparative legal materials from a number of other countries' military justice systems to illuminate the proliferation of national systems of military discipline
and criminal punishment, and the growing interconnectedness of military justice systems as a result of worldwide deployments, multinational operations,
the global "war against terrorism," and an emerging international law governing military justice. As the authors put it, "[t]he same impulse that leads
us to view the states' role as laboratories for testing new ideas as part of the
genius of the American federal system, or to view the various branches of the
service in something of the same light, ought to cause us to welcome any
opportunity to know and potentially learn from the experience of other democratic countries in the administration of military justice." Third, the book
throughout poses both legal and policy questions about the proper scope and
sphere of military law. When should a criminal case leave the civilian realm
and enter a military system of justice, and what values are enhanced or sacrificed by making that transition?

The book opens with an overview of the history and purposes of military justice, the sources of law, and the role of the commander, summary discipline,
and professional responsibility as coordinate loci of order and ethics within the
military justice system. Several chapters then address how doctrines of *in personam* and subject-matter jurisdiction patrol the boundaries of U.S. military
justice as a specialized jurisdiction, and highlight crimes and defenses that are
distinctive to military law. Chapters 10 to 17 highlight what could be called
the "constitutional law of military justice": substantive issues involving freedom of speech, religion, association, privacy and sexual orientation, as well as
structural issues surrounding the military jury and independence of military
judges, the requirement of a speedy trial, and the evidentiary issues usually
encountered in civilian law courses on criminal investigation. These chapters
ask: how much personal autonomy must one give up to serve one's country?
When, if ever, do considerations of military necessity and unit cohesion really
require mandatory vaccination, surrender of freedom of speech and religion,
and release of intimate personal information about sexual orientation?

The final three chapters are particularly innovative and timely. Chapter 18
discusses how military justice is carried out in delicate operational settings,

especially combat and peacekeeping operations. Chapter 19 explores the knotty issue of the use of military commissions before and after September 11, 2001, including cases which at this writing are currently on the Supreme Court's docket. And the final, thoughtful chapter asks important policy questions about how the inexorable process of globalization should prompt reform of national military justice systems in light of emerging international standards of human rights and humanitarian law.

As this book proceeds, it shifts increasingly away from doctrine toward cutting-edge questions of military and legal policy. The final chapters ask: how do we preserve military justice when a nation's armed forces are engaged in peacekeeping and humanitarian operations with many other nations? When do emergency situations properly call for the use of military tribunals to try non-uniformed suspects? And what changes, if any, should be made in our country's military justice system to take full account of the interconnectedness of global developments in this field.

To put it bluntly, is military justice too important a subject to be left to military lawyers? In a democratic society, where the military operates under civilian command, why shouldn't all informed citizens — including the media, students, lawyers, judges, law professors, legislators, nongovernmental organizations and public officials — understand the critical choices involved in seeking to balance effective national defense with the administration of justice?

Sixty years before the birth of Christ, Cicero famously remarked "inter arma enim silent leges," often translated as "[i]n a time of war, the law falls silent." This idea has sometimes been read as creating a false dichotomy between war and law, suggesting that, in a time of war, law can have little or no force. In its recent decision invalidating President Bush's military commissions order, *Hamdan v. Rumsfeld*,[2] the U.S. Supreme Court rebuffed that notion, holding that in the UCMJ, Congress had authorized the President to use military commissions, but had specified that, wherever practicable, the executive must follow the same procedural rules in military commissions as are applied in ordinary courts-martial. Rather than embracing ad hoc, crisis solutions, Justice Kennedy argued in concurrence, "[r]espect for laws derived from the customary operation of the Executive and Legislative Branches gives some assurance of stability in time of crisis. The Constitution is best preserved by reliance on standards tested over time and insulated from the pressures of the moment."[3] Significantly, the *Hamdan* Court rejected the government's attempted dichotomy between law and war by requiring consistent application of the law of war to Hamdan's case. The majority stated, "regardless of the nature of the rights conferred on Hamdan, they are, as the Government does not dispute, part of the law of war. And compliance with the law of war is the condition upon which the authority set forth in [the UCMJ] is granted."[4] As Justice Kennedy noted tersely in concurrence, "If the military commission at

---

[2] 126 S. Ct. 2749 (2006).

[3] *Id.* at 2799 (Kennedy, J., concurring).

[4] *Id.* at 2794.

issue is illegal under the law of war, then an offender cannot be tried 'by the law of war' before that commission."[5]

In short, as this important book vividly illustrates, the term "military justice" cannot and must not be an oxymoron. When war and military operations begin, law and justice do not simply evaporate. Rather, they shift into a different, more complex register, whose chords remain closely attuned to the values and needs of a democratic society governed under the rule of law.

---

[5] *Id.* at 2802 (Kennedy, J., concurring).

FOREWORD
Robinson O. Everett, Sr.

For many years there has been a need to expand the study of military justice beyond national borders to include developments in other countries and the growing body of international human rights law. This timely volume, prepared by acknowledged experts in military justice, will go far to meet that need. The authors' service in three branches of the United States armed forces (Air Force, Marine Corps, and Coast Guard) as well as their teaching experience in both civilian and service law schools uniquely qualifies them for the task.

Having a better understanding of military justice in other countries enables us to obtain a better understanding of their military cultures. This is especially helpful at a time when our own armed forces are often deployed in joint peace-keeping operations with troops from other nations. Even more important is that learning about other systems of military justice provides a sounder basis for evaluating and improving our own system.

Readers may even be led to ask whether a separate system of military justice is really necessary. If it is, what should be the jurisdiction of military tribunals? At one time our Supreme Court's view was that service members could not be punished by court-martial for conduct that was not service connected; but less than twenty years later, the Court changed its position and ruled that under our Constitution, status as a service member is sufficient to confer jurisdiction on a court-martial. Nonetheless, the question remains where the line should be drawn as a matter of policy, and in this regard the new book provides useful information. Furthermore, after looking at foreign systems, we may conclude that various offenses now in our Uniform Code of Military Justice should be deleted or amended and that new offenses should be added.

When the Code took effect in 1951, it authorized courts-martial to try certain civilians who were closely connected with the armed forces. However, the Supreme Court later ruled that military jurisdiction hinges on military status — at least in peacetime. To what extent does that view conform with the position taken in other countries? Also, it is helpful to consider the views of foreign countries as to the extent of military jurisdiction over civilians in time of emergency or martial law. On several issues — such as whether consensual sodomy can be punished — the Supreme Court has considered the practices of foreign countries in interpreting and applying our own Constitution and statutes; this approach might be helpful in future cases concerning military justice.

The book addresses a variety of other topics. For example, the authors deal not only with some of the peculiarly military offenses, but also with some of the defenses that may be asserted — such as condonation, necessity, obedience to orders, and the "good soldier" defense. They examine the free speech, associational and other rights of service members, which vary substantially from country to country.

The major role of commanders in military justice is a key focus of the book. Also, trial procedure is compared — which inevitably raises the question of who should preside over military trials. One alternative — now used in American courts-martial — is to have military judges who are legally trained members of the armed forces. Another possibility is to use civilians — either as presiding judges or as advisors for courts-martial. Of course, in some systems military courts still operate under the direction of military officers without legal training.

The extent of civilian involvement in administering military justice also varies with respect to the appellate process. In the United States, there was no direct civilian review of military trials until 1951. Then a civilian court of military appeals was established with the sole task of reviewing courts-martial; and in 1983 the decisions of that court were made subject to direct review by the Supreme Court. In some other countries, there also are courts of military appeals composed of civilian judges — who, unlike the American system, usually serve also on other courts or in other legal capacities. Of course, in some countries, review by civilian courts is either totally lacking or confined to collateral review.

Of special interest is the treatment of sentencing by military courts. What punishments are authorized? Is the death penalty permitted and, if so, under what circumstances? Information relevant to such questions may be found in this outstanding book.

The authors have done a remarkable job of assembling cases and materials about military justice. One result of their extraordinary efforts is to provide a better understanding of the function of military justice and of the alternatives available in administering it. Hopefully, this understanding will lead to improvements of military justice — both in the United States and elsewhere. Therefore, profound thanks are due to the authors for their valuable contribution.

ROBINSON O. EVERETT, SR.

Duke University School of Law
Durham, North Carolina
July 2007

SUMMARY OF CONTENTS

Acknowledgments . . . . *v*
Introduction . . . . *xi*
Preface, *Harold Hongju Koh* . . . . *xvii*
Foreword, *Robinson O. Everett, Sr.* . . . . *xxi*
Contents . . . . *xxv*
Editors' Note . . . . *xxxix*

PART I Foundations

Chapter 1. The Origins and Purposes of Military Justice   1
Chapter 2. Sources of Law   37
Chapter 3. The Role of the Commander   79
Chapter 4. Summary Discipline 133
Chapter 5. Professional Responsibility 199

PART II Principles

Chapter 6. Jurisdiction over the Person 235
Chapter 7. Jurisdiction over the Offense 327
Chapter 8. Military Crimes 401
Chapter 9. Military Defenses 457
Chapter 10. Freedom of Speech and Conscience 491
Chapter 11. Rights of Association and Identity 543

PART III Trials

Chapter 12. Judicial Independence 611
Chapter 13. The Military Jury 681
Chapter 14. Speedy and Public Trial 727
Chapter 15. Evidence 767
Chapter 16. Punishment 813
Chapter 17. Review and Appeal 851

PART IV Special Contexts

Chapter 18. Military Justice in Operational Settings 909
Chapter 19. Military Commissions 945

PART V The Future

Chapter 20. Law Reform and Globalization 1009

Table of Cases **TC-1**

Index **I-1**

TABLE OF CONTENTS

Acknowledgments .... *v*
Introduction .... *xi*
Preface, *Harold Hongju Koh* .... *xvii*
Foreword, *Robinson O. Everett, Sr.* .... *xxi*
Summary of Contents .... *xxiii*
Editors' Note .... *xxxix*

PART I. FOUNDATIONS

CHAPTER 1.   THE ORIGINS AND PURPOSES OF MILITARY JUSTICE

I. Contexts

   A. War 1

      Peter Maguire, Law and War: An American Story 1

      Carol Chomsky, The United States-Dakota War Trials 2

      Peter Maguire, Law and War: An American Story 6

      Major Emmett G. Wells, Book Review, Robert J. Lifton & Greg Mitchell, Hiroshima in America 7

      Russell F. Weigley, Eisenhower's Lieutenants 9

      Elizabeth Lutes Hillman, Defending America 10

      Barraza Rivera v. Immigration and Naturalization Service 11

   B. Occupation 15

      Harry N. Scheiber & Jane L. Scheiber, Bayonets in Paradise .. 15

      Ryan Swift, Occupational Jurisdiction 23

   C. Detention 24

      Raymond Lech, Broken Soldiers 24

      Lt. Col. Paul E. Kantwill & Maj. Sean Watts, Hostile Protected Persons or "Extra-Conventional Persons" 27

II. Objectives 29

   A. Early Codes of Conduct 29

      Robert C. Stacey, The Age of Chivalry 29

      Code of Articles of King Gustavus Adolphus of Sweden 31

   B. Modern Codes 33

      Joseph W. Bishop, Jr., Justice Under Fire 33

      Elizabeth Lutes Hillman, Defending America 34

CHAPTER 2.   SOURCES OF LAW

I. Constitutional, Statutory, and Regulatory Provisions   37

   United States Constitution, Article I, §§ 8 & 9; Article II,
   § 2; amend. II, III, V   37

   Uniform Code of Military Justice, Article 36   39

   Preamble, Manual for Courts-Martial, United States (2005 ed.) . .   39

   Military Rules of Evidence, Rule 101 & 1102   39

II. The Constitution and Military Justice   40

   Earl Warren, The Bill of Rights and the Military   40

   Davis v. United States   43

   United States v. Tulloch   44

   United States v. Mizgala   48

III. Statutes and Regulations   57

   Hamdan v. Rumsfeld   57

IV. Custom of the Service   62

   United States v. Pratt   62

V. International Law   68

   Federico Andreu-Guzmán, Military Jurisdiction and
   International Law   68

   The Nuremberg Principles   69

   Patricia M. Wald, General Radislav Krstic: A War Crimes
   Case Study   70

CHAPTER 3.   THE ROLE OF THE COMMANDER

I. Accountability and Liability   79

   In re Yamashita   79

   The Manual of the Law of Armed Conflict,
   United Kingdom Ministry of Defense   87

   Criminal Code, Ukraine   88

   United States v. Shearer   89

II. Prosecutorial Functions   92

   Queen's Regulations for the Army, United Kingdom   92

   Boyd v. Army Prosecuting Authority   94

   Potsane v. Minister of Defence   97

   Uniform Code of Military Justice, Articles 1, 22-25, 60   98

United States v. Dinges 104

III. Improper Influence over Proceedings 109

Uniform Code of Military Justice, Article 37 109

Manual for Legal Administration, United States Marine Corps . . 110

United States v. Thomas 112

IV. Pretrial Investigations 121

United States Constitution, amend. V 121

Uniform Code of Military Justice, Article 32 121

Rule for Courts-Martial 405 122

Colonel Francis A. Gilligan, The Bill of Rights and Service
Members 129

MacDonald v. Hodson 130

CHAPTER 4. SUMMARY DISCIPLINE

I. International Human Rights 133

Engel v. The Netherlands 133

A.D. v. Turkey 148

Canády v. Slovakia 150

II. Nonjudicial Punishment and Summary Courts-Martial 153

Uniform Code of Military Justice, Articles 15 & 20 153

Middendorf v. Henry 157

Tzufan v. Judge Advocate General 173

III. Justice at Sea 190

Herman Melville, White-Jacket, or The World in a Man-of-War . 190

United States v. Edwards 191

CHAPTER 5. PROFESSIONAL RESPONSIBILITY

I. Licensing 199

Uniform Code of Military Justice, Articles 26 & 27 199

Judge Advocate General of the Army, Standards of
Conduct Office 200

United States v. Steele 201

II. Regulation 205

Professional Responsibility for Lawyers 205

Army Rules of Professional Conduct for Lawyers 210

Informal Opinion 1235, American Bar Association Committee
on Ethics and Professional Responsibility 213

United States v. Cain 218

United States v. Meek 231

PART II. PRINCIPLES

CHAPTER 6.   JURISDICTION OVER THE PERSON

I. Statutory Provisions 235

Uniform Code of Military Justice, Articles 2 & 3 235

Canada, National Defence Act § 60 238

Singapore, Armed Forces Act, §§ 5 & 109 239

Morocco, Code of Military Justice, Articles 3 & 4 241

Switzerland, Military Penal Code, Article 2(9) 241

France, Code of Military Justice, Articles 59-66, 68, 70 241

Luxembourg, Revised Code of Military Procedure,
Articles 7-10 242

Interim Regulations of the People's Republic of China 243

Angola, Military Jurisdiction Act, Article 27 243

Uganda People's Defence Forces Act, § 119(1)(g) 243

United Kingdom, Armed Forces Act 2006 (c. 52), § 55 244

II. Former Soldiers 244

Lord Sackville's Case 244

*Neiman v. Military Governor of the Occupied Area of
Jerusalem* 245

United States ex rel. *Toth v. Quarles* 251

III. Dependents 262

Reid v. Covert 262

The Queen v. Martin 271

Martin v. United Kingdom 278

IV. Reservists 280

Willenbring v. Neurauter 280

H.M. The Queen v. Brady 295

*Sommacal v. Chief Auditor of the Army and Confederal Military
Department* 299

V. Civilians 304

   Duncan v. Kahanamoku 304

   Military Extraterritorial Jurisdiction Act 317

VI. International Human Rights 319

   Office of the High Commissioner for Human Rights 319

   Human Rights Report on Terrorism and Human Rights 320

CHAPTER 7. JURISDICTION OVER THE OFFENSE

I. Statutory and Regulatory Provisions 327

   Rule for Courts-Martial 203 327

   Model Code of Military Justice, Article 4 327

   Statement of Policy on Military Justice 328

   Philippines, Republic Act 328

   Cambodia, Law of Feb. 8, 1993 328

   Code of Service Discipline, Canada 329

   Military Discipline Supplementary Measures Act, South Africa . . 329

   Military Justice Law, 1955, Israel 329

II. Service Connection 330

   Solorio v. United States 330

   Re Colonel Aird; Ex parte Alpert 347

   Navales v. Abaya; In re Reaso 375

III. International Human Rights 381

   Draft Principles Governing the Administration of Justice 381

   Mora v. Colombia 383

   Colombia Human Rights Certification II, 2004 384

   Nineteen Merchants v. Colombia 389

   Letter to Bolivian President Carlos Mesa Gisbert 395

CHAPTER 8. MILITARY CRIMES

I. Unauthorized Absence: AWOL and Desertion 401

   National Defence Act (Canada) 401

   State v. Lance Corporal (Res) Poon Chee Seng 403

   Convening Authority v. Private Doyle 405

   United States v. Taylor 406

II. Dereliction, Disobedience, and Negligence 408

   Uniform Code of Military Justice, Article 90 408

   Military Discipline Code, South Africa 408

   Naval Discipline Act, Australia 408

   Defence Force Discipline Act, New Zealand 408

   Quinn v. Chief of Army 410

   United States v. Carson 413

III. Disorderly and Discrediting Acts 419

   Defence Force Discipline Act, New Zealand 419

   Uniform Code of Military Justice, Article 134 419

   Parker v. Levy 420

   Stuart v. Chief of General Staff 431

   United States v. Rogers 435

   Re Anning 437

IV. A Case Study: Adultery 441

   Manual for Courts-Martial, United States,
   Part IV, ¶ 62(c) 441

   Comments to Department of Defense on Adultery Policy 442

   United States v. Johanns 443

   United States v. Green 448

CHAPTER 9.   MILITARY DEFENSES

I. Crimes of Disobedience 457

   Thakur v. Union of India 457

   In re Hlongwane 458

   R. v. Kipling 459

II. The Defense of Superior Orders 463

   Military Penal Code, Austria 463

   Military Criminal Code, Denmark 463

   Nwaoga v. State 463

   United States v. Calley 465

III. Other Special Defenses 475

   A. Condonation 475

      Armed Forces Act, Malaysia 475

Queen's Regulations and Orders for the Canadian Forces 475

Attorney General ex rel. *Royal N.Z. Navy v. Lawrence* 476

B. Necessity and Duress 478

United States v. Washington 478

C. The Good Soldier Defense 485

United States v. Clemons 485

CHAPTER 10. FREEDOM OF SPEECH AND CONSCIENCE

I. Freedom of Speech 491

Parker v. Levy 492

United States v. Wilson 499

United States v. Mason 502

II. Free Exercise of Religion 507

Manual for Courts-Martial, Pt. IV, ¶14 507

United States v. Burry 507

Lieutenant (N) G.D. Scott v. Her Majesty the Queen 511

III. Conscientious Objection 514

United States v. Walker 514

Zonschein v. Judge Advocate General 523

Yoon v. Republic of Korea 530

CHAPTER 11. RIGHTS OF ASSOCIATION AND IDENTITY

I. Freedom of Association 543

United States Code 10 U.S.C. §976: Membership in military
unions prohibited 543

Right to Association for Members of the Professional Staff of
the Armed Forces 545

Guidelines for Handling Dissident and Protest Activities 553

Major Walter M. Hudson, Racial Extremism in the Army 556

II. The Right to Privacy 562

Repp v. United States 562

United States v. Stevenson 564

United States v. Roberts 569

III. Sexual Orientation 575

    United States v. Jameson 575

    Lustig-Prean & Beckett v. United Kingdom 581

    Homosexuality in the Armed Forces 589

    Armed Forces Code of Social Conduct 591

    United States Code 10 U.S.C. § 645: Policy Concerning
    Homosexuality 592

    Brief of *Amici Curiae, Cook v. Gates* 595

PART III. TRIALS

CHAPTER 12. JUDICIAL INDEPENDENCE

I. Statutory and Regulatory Provisions 611

    Uniform Code of Military Justice, Article 6a & 37 611

    Rule for Courts-Martial 109 612

    Model Code of Military Justice, Article 2 613

II. Military Judges 613

    Eugene R. Fidell, Military Judges and Military Justice 613

    Regina v. Généreux 626

    Dunphy v. Her Majesty the Queen 645

    Weiss v. United States 648

    Army Regulation 27-10, Legal Services: Military Justice 655

III. International Human Rights 658

    Draft Principles Governing the Administration of Justice 658

    Findlay v. United Kingdom 659

    Cooper v. United Kingdom 672

CHAPTER 13. THE MILITARY JURY

I. The Court-Martial Panel 682

    Uniform Code of Military Justice, Article 25 682

    United States v. Kirkland 683

II. Differences Between the Court-Martial Panel and the
    Civilian Jury 687

    Loving v. Hart 687

III. Selection of the Members by the Convening Authority 689

United States v. Smith 689

Findlay v. United Kingdom 699

United States v. Wiesen 708

IV. Court-Martial Size and Voting Requirements 723

Uniform Code of Military Justice, Article 16 723

United States v. Guilford 724

CHAPTER 14. SPEEDY AND PUBLIC TRIAL

I. Post-Trial Delays and Judicial Remedies 727

United States v. Tardif 727

Diaz v. Judge Advocate General of the Navy 733

Toohey v. United States 739

II. Public Access 742

Defence Force Discipline Appeal Act, 1982 742

Barry v. Chief of Naval Staff 743

United States v. Lonetree 744

Le Petit v. United Kingdom 750

Sutter v. Switzerland 752

Truskoski v. The Queen 756

Armed Forces Act, Singapore 758

ABC, Inc. v. Powell 758

CHAPTER 15. EVIDENCE

I. Introduction 767

A. Adopting the Military Rules of Evidence 767

Maj. Thomas J. Feeney & Capt. Margaret L. Murphy,
The Army Judge Advocate General's Corps, 1982-1987 767

Stephen A. Saltzburg, Lee D. Schinasi & David A.
Schlueter, Military Rules of Evidence Manual 768

B. Amending the Military Rules of Evidence 768

Military Rule of Evidence 1102 768

United States v. Parker 769

II. Self-Incrimination 771

Uniform Code of Military Justice, Article 31 771

United States v. Loukas 773

III. Search and Seizure 784

    Military Rules of Evidence 315 & 313 784

    United States v. Gardner 786

IV. Privileges 789

    United States v. Rodriguez 789

    Stephen A. Saltzburg, Lee D. Schinasi & David A. Schlueter,
    Military Rules of Evidence Manual 792

V. Classified Evidence 794

    United States v. Duncan 794

VI. Polygraph Results 795

    Military Rule of Evidence 707 795

    United States v. Scheffer 796

VII. Hearsay 804

    Military Rule of Evidence 803 804

    United States v. Broadnax 807

CHAPTER 16. PUNISHMENT

I. Sentencing Procedures 813

    A. Sentencing Authority 813

        Maj. Kevin Lovejoy, Abolition of Court Member
        Sentencing 813

    B. Adversarial Sentencing 815

        United States v. Green 815

        Rule for Courts-Martial 1001, Drafters' Analysis 815

    C. Principles 816

        United States v. Lania 816

    D. Pretrial Agreements 818

        Rule for Courts-Martial 901(f) 818

        United States v. Jobson 819

        United States v. McCants 819

II. Authorized Punishments 821

    Uniform Code of Military Justice, Article 56 821

    Rule for Courts-Martial 1003(b) 821

III. Unique Military Punishments 823

    United States v. Rush 823

    Uniform Code of Military Justice, Article 55 829

    United States v. Yatchak 829

    Eugene R. Fidell & Jay M. Fidell, Loss of Numbers 831

IV. Death Penalty 834

    Loving v. United States 834

    Loving v. Hart 845

V. Administrative Sanctions and Collateral Consequences 847

    Clinton v. Goldsmith 847

CHAPTER 17. REVIEW AND APPEAL

I. Command Review and Executive Clemency 851

    United States v. Davis 851

    Gary D. Solis, Military Justice, Civilian Clemency 855

    Letter from Captain Aubrey M. Daniel 3d to President
    Richard M. Nixon 864

II. Sentence Review 868

    Draft Principles Governing the Administration of Justice 868

    United States v. Durant 868

    Regina v. Love 876

    Case of Corporal Feni 883

III. Direct Appellate Review 886

    Draft Principles Governing the Administration of Justice 886

    Constitutional Interpretation, Republic of China Council of
    Grand Justices 886

    Clinton v. Goldsmith 887

    Eugene R. Fidell, Guide to the Rules of Practice and
    Procedure for the United States Court Appeals for the Armed
    Forces 892

    Notice of Proposed Rule Change 894

IV. Collateral Review 900

    United States ex rel. New v. Rumsfeld 900

    McKinney v. White 903

PART IV. SPECIAL CONTEXTS

CHAPTER 18. MILITARY JUSTICE IN OPERATIONAL SETTINGS

I. Portability 909

Uniform Code of Military Justice, Article 5 909

Stevens v. Warden, U.S. Penitentiary, Leavenworth, Kansas 910

Criminal Expo 2001, 5th International Military Criminal Law Conference 911

Françoise Hampson, Working Paper 913

II. Combat Operations 917

United States v. Bryant 917

United States v. Finsel 921

United States v. Manginell 924

III. Peacekeeping Operations 928

A. International Law and Domestic Military Law 928

United States v. Rockwood 928

B. Constitutional Challenges to Disobedience of Domestic Military Law 932

United States v. New 932

C. Peacekeeping and Military Justice Reform 935

R. v. Lieutenant-Colonel Joseph Carol Aristide Mathieu 935

R. v. Brown 939

Statement of Thierry Giet, Belgian House of Representatives 941

CHAPTER 19. MILITARY COMMISSIONS

I. Historical Background 945

Ex parte Milligan 945

Ex parte Quirin 952

II. Post-September 11, 2001, Military Commissions 964

Hamdan v. Rumsfeld 964

PART V. THE FUTURE
CHAPTER 20.   LAW REFORM AND GLOBALIZATION

I. International Human Rights 1011

    Draft Principles Governing the Administration of Justice 1011

II. Statutory and Regulatory Provisions 1011

    Uniform Code of Military Justice, Article 146 1011

    Review of the Manual for Courts-Martial 1013

III. Voices of Reform 1018

    Report of the Cox Commission 1018

    Kevin J. Barry, A Face Lift (and Much More) for an Aging
    Beauty 1029

IV. International Assistance in Reform 1038

    Lt. Col. J. McClelland MBE, Starting from
    Scratch 1038

    Maj. Steve Cullen, Starting Over—The New Iraqi Code of Military
    Discipline 1053

    Maj. Sean M. Watts & Capt. Christopher E. Martin,
    Nation-Building in Afghanistan: Lessons Identified in Military
    Justice Reform 1058

V. Globalization 1060

    Eugene R. Fidell, A Worldwide Perspective on Change in
    Military Justice 1060

    Lord Chief Justice of England and Wales, Practice
    Direction on the Citation of Authorities 1073

Table of Cases TC-1

Index I-1

EDITORS' NOTE

For easier reading and to conserve space, we have eliminated without notation many citations and footnotes, as well as most parallel citations, from excerpted materials. For citation format, we have relied on A UNIFORM SYSTEM OF CITATION (18th ed. 2005). Our footnotes are consecutively numbered throughout each chapter, but the footnotes we have selectively preserved from the original text show the original note number in brackets. Our additions to quoted material appear in brackets.

Views expressed in this book are those of the editors and individual authors, and do not necessarily represent the views of any government agency.

Chapter 1

THE ORIGINS AND PURPOSES OF MILITARY JUSTICE

In the United States and around the world, nations and multi-national coalitions have long relied on military justice to restrain the horrors of war and allocate the burdens and privileges of military service. This opening chapter sets the stage for the exploration of military justice that follows by sketching a framework for the origins and purposes of military justice. It introduces, or perhaps simply reminds, readers of the reasons that many nations have developed separate systems of military justice. The first section, Contexts, uses a series of historical vignettes to reveal the demands of the environments in which military justice has operated and to suggest the extent of military justice's challenge. The second, Objectives, briefly outlines the history of military commanders' efforts to establish military justice systems and the goals those systems have pursued. Throughout, the reader should keep in mind the balance and synergy between the primary objectives of military justice: to preserve discipline and to seek justice, often amidst the danger, deprivation, and high stakes of military operations.

I. CONTEXTS

No legal system operates in a vacuum. Criminal justice systems, perhaps more than any other legal regimes, are acutely sensitive to the social, political, and cultural contexts in which they are implemented. The investigation and prosecution of crime is heavily influenced not only by statutes and regulations, but by social norms, cultural practices, and community objectives. In military justice systems, these norms and objectives differ markedly from those that shape the procedures and outcomes of civilian criminal justice. This section provides a brief overview of some of these distinctive contexts. It focuses on revealing the challenges, risks, and fears that characterize the environments in which military crimes are committed, investigated, and prosecuted.

A. War

Peter Maguire, *Law And War: An American Story*
22 (2000)

Colonial leaders [in North America] had no qualms about slaughtering those tribes that resisted the colonists' "civilizing" influence. As early as 1675, colonists nearly wiped out the Algonquin Indians for attacking and destroying colonial settlements in what would come to be known as King Philip's War. In the end, King Philip, the Algonquin Indian leader, was captured and killed. His head was exhibited in Plymouth for the next twenty years, and his wife and children were sold as slaves in the West Indies. Reprisal would become the key word in America's emerging Indian policy. Tribes that refused American demands were subjected to harsh punitive measures.

America's first President, George Washington, ordered Major General John Sullivan to "chastize" hostile Iroquois in a May 31, 1779 letter. President Washington wanted the Indian villages "not merely overrun but destroyed. But you will not by any means, listen to any overture of peace before the total ruin of their settlements is effected." Washington wanted to establish a precedent of terror and believed that American national security demanded it: "Our future security will be in their inability to injure us . . . and in the terror with which the severity of the chastizement they receive will inspire them." Major General Sullivan shared his commander-in-chief's view that "the Indians shall see that there is malice enough in our hearts to destroy everything that contributes to their support."

In 1792, George Hammond, the first British ambassador to the United States, asked Thomas Jefferson what he "understood as the right of the United States in Indian soil?" Jefferson responded, "We consider it as established by the usage of different nations into a kind of jus gentium (Law of Nations) for America," arguing that while the United States would treat the invasion of Indian territory by "any other white nation" as an act of war, America assumed "no right of soil against the native possessors." Hammond was utterly unconvinced by Jefferson's earnest claims and told him that the British believed the United States planned to "exterminate the Indians and take their lands."

Carol Chomsky, *The United States-Dakota War Trials: A Study in Military Injustice*
43 STAN. L. REV. 13, 15-22 (1990)

The Dakota people are part of what is often identified as the Sioux Nation, a group comprised of seven politically distinct tribes — the Seven Council Fires — that share family ties and a cultural value system, social organization, and language. The four tribes principally involved in the war — the Mdewakanton, Wahpekute, Sisseton, and Wahpeton — are among those that refer to themselves as Dakota.

The Dakota people had once inhabited and controlled large areas of land in the upper Midwest. By 1862, however, the seven thousand Dakota occupied only a narrow strip of land — about one hundred twenty miles long and ten miles wide — along the Minnesota River in the southwestern part of Minnesota. The remainder of their land had been ceded to the United States in a series of treaties between 1805 and 1858 in return for cash payments and for money allocated to build facilities such as schools and mills. The Sisseton and Wahpeton tribes lived on the northwestern side of the reservation, with the Mdewakanton and Wahpekute tribes residing on the southeastern side. The reservation also contained two administrative centers established by the federal government, the Yellow Medicine or "Upper Sioux" Agency in the northwest and the Redwood or "Lower Sioux" Agency in the southeast.

Despite the pledges of eternal peace and friendship in the treaties, by the summer of 1862 serious tension existed between the Dakota and American communities, fueled by a lengthening list of Dakota grievances against the United States. The treaties of 1851 had promised the Dakota lump sum payments in exchange for land, but eleven years later the Dakota people still had not received the funds. After 1851, American settlers began to move onto reservation land north of the Minnesota River; in the treaties of 1858, a largely unwilling Dakota community was forced to relinquish that land. Restricted as they were to a small area, the Dakota could no longer support themselves in their traditional manner and so became increasingly dependent on the goods, services, and annuity payments promised in the treaties. When payments and delivery of goods were delayed, the Dakota suffered hunger and hardship.

In 1857, the Indian Agent [of the federal government] withheld the annuities in order to force the Dakota to pursue and capture an outlaw band of Dakota, thereby punishing the whole group for the actions of a few individuals who were not part of the community. Later, the Agent began to divide the payments unequally among the Dakota to reward those who adopted American ways at the expense of those who maintained a traditional Dakota lifestyle. When annuities were distributed, the Agent often paid most or all of the money directly to the traders for goods already sold to the Dakota on credit, based on unverified claims that were probably padded and were viewed with great — and justified — suspicion by the Dakota.

In the summer of 1862, the annuity payments were late once again. Rumors spread that, because of the American government's preoccupation with the Civil War, payments might be made in paper money rather than the stipulated gold, or might not be made at all. The traders were reported to have said that the payments, if ever made, would be the last. Because of past abuses by the traders, the Dakota made plans to demand payment of the annuities directly to the people rather than to the traders; when the traders learned of this, they refused to sell any more provisions on credit, though many of the Dakota were starving. When Indian Agent Thomas Galbraith met with the traders to try to resolve the impasse, Andrew Myrick, the spokesman for the traders, responded, "So far as I am concerned, if they are hungry, let them eat grass."

Thus, longstanding grievances over treaty violations and trader abuses, combined with worsening economic conditions and pressures created by the American drive to assimilate the Dakota, set the stage for war. An incident on Sunday, August 17, 1862, finally precipitated the conflict. Four young Dakota men returning from a hunting expedition killed five American settlers on two homesteads in Acton, Minnesota. The attack, apparently unprovoked by any immediate act, was fueled by the increasing tensions between the Dakota and the American settlers. If serious grievances against the Americans had not built up over the previous several years, the Dakota might have delivered the four men to the Americans for punishment, and peace would have prevailed, at least temporarily. The incident then might have remained an isolated occurrence, one of many so-called "Indian depredations" on the frontier.

Instead, many of the young Dakota men urged their leaders to initiate war against the American settlers to try to drive them from the Minnesota Valley. Councils were held among the Dakota that night. Many of the leaders expressed reluctance or even opposition to war. Some felt sympathy with or had ties to the American community; others realized that a war against the superior numbers and firepower of the Americans could not be won, even though many of the Minnesota men had been sent east to fight the Civil War. The young men, however, hoped to recapture their lost land, drive the American settlers away, and return to their traditional way of life.

Many also believed that the Americans would stop payment of the annuities and take vengeance upon the whole tribe in retaliation for the Acton killings, particularly because women were among the victims. They argued that the Dakota should strike first rather than wait for the inevitable. The Council decided on war.

The fighting began the next morning when a group of Dakota attacked the Redwood (Lower) Agency, a settlement populated by traders, the Indian agent, various government personnel and their families, farmer-Indians, and some other mixed and full bloods. Thirteen Americans were killed in the attack on the Agency, seven more were killed while fleeing from the settlement, and ten were captured.

Forty-seven settlers escaped from Redwood to Fort Ridgely, a federal army outpost garrisoned by Minnesota volunteer regiments that the United States government had mustered into federal service while the regular troops fought in the Civil War. After hearing the news of the attack, Captain John S. Marsh, the commander at Fort Ridgely, set out for the Redwood Agency with forty-six enlisted men and an interpreter. Despite warnings from fleeing settlers that he would be outnumbered, he continued toward the Agency. The Dakota attacked him and his men at the Redwood Ferry, killing twenty-four. The remaining soldiers retreated with some difficulty to Fort Ridgely.

In the days that followed, the Dakota fought several different kinds of engagements with Americans. The Dakota fought two battles at New Ulm, a German settlement in a strategically significant location in the Minnesota Valley. In both battles, the town was defended by men who had volunteered to serve in the fight against the Dakota; these "citizen-soldiers" fought to protect themselves and more than a thousand women, children, and unarmed men barricaded in the center of town. Other battles involved only the military: attacks on Fort Ridgely, an attack on a party of soldiers at Birch Coulee, skirmishes in Meeker County, and the final battle at Wood Lake. The American forces were led by Colonel Henry H. Sibley, appointed on August 19 by Minnesota Governor Ramsey to be commander of the volunteer forces and named on September 29 by President Lincoln to be Brigadier General of United States Volunteers in charge of the U.S. Military District of Minnesota.

From the outset the Dakota also attacked other American settlements and settlers who had not yet taken shelter behind the fortifications being constructed by the citizens of the towns. Many of the settlers were reportedly unarmed and taken by surprise. In most cases, the Dakota killed the men and took the women and children prisoners. Wild stories of mutilation by the Dakota in these encounters spread among the settlers, but historians have concluded that these reports were probably exaggerations of isolated instances of atrocities.

Meanwhile, the disagreements evident at the initial Council continued, dividing those Dakota who supported the war from those who opposed it. The Sisseton and Wahpeton located at the Yellow Medicine (Upper) Agency at first declined to join the war, and some of them helped American settlers and missionaries escape attacks on the Agency. Some Mdewakanton opposed continuing the war and urged return of the women and children hostages. Colonel Sibley contacted Taoyateduta (Little Crow), the reluctant leader of the war, to attempt negotiation, but Sibley demanded the return of the hostages before beginning any discussions. The Dakota held Councils to decide whether to negotiate. Taoyateduta was loath to do so, believing that no mercy would be shown the Dakota, but two other leaders, Chiefs Wabasha and Taopi, who had opposed the war from the outset, contacted Sibley to discuss a surrender.

On September 23, scarcely a month after the war had begun, the Dakota fighting men returned to camp after the battle at Wood Lake to discover that the Dakota who opposed continuation of the war had taken control of the white captives. Support for the war was rapidly diminishing, and those who wished to continue fighting or opposed surrender moved out of camp with their families and belongings, leaving the others behind. Among those who fled north were three of the leaders of the war effort, Taoyateduta, Shakopee (Little Six), and Wakanozanzan (Medicine Bottle). The remaining Dakota then sent word to Sibley that he and his soldiers could "come up," which he proceeded to do. On September 26, Sibley set up Camp Release opposite the Dakota camp. He entered the Dakota camp later that day and took some 1200 Dakota men, women, and children into custody. About 800 more surrendered in small groups over the next several weeks.

In thirty-seven days of fighting, 77 American soldiers, 29 citizen-soldiers, approximately 358 settlers, and an estimated 29 Dakota soldiers had been killed.

NOTES AND QUESTIONS

1. What crimes, if any, are revealed by these descriptions of United States-Native American armed conflict? Who was responsible? What legal forum could have prosecuted any crimes? Chomsky reports on what actually happened when the Dakota were tried by military commission: "[N]early four hundred Dakota men were tried for murder, rape, and robbery. All but seventy were convicted, and 303 of these were condemned to die. After an official review of the trials, the sentences of thirty-eight were confirmed and, on December 26, 1862, these thirty-eight were hanged in Mankato, Minnesota, in the largest mass execution in American history. On November 11, 1865, after three additional trials, two more Dakota followed them to the gallows." 43 STAN L. REV. 13.

2. The brutality of the United States' campaign against Native Americans is well known, from outright wars like King Philip's War to the 19th-century policy of forced removal. On the "trail of tears," the most infamous example of military action in support of removal, the U.S. Army forcibly marched 18,000 Cherokee Indians out of Georgia and into Oklahoma in 1838, leaving 4,000 Cherokee dead of exposure, starvation, disease, and violence. Less well known are the legal arguments that supported such aggressive military action. During the 1830s, two decisions of Chief Justice John Marshall's Supreme Court addressed the plight of Indians in the state of Georgia. In the first, *Cherokee Nation v. Georgia*, 30 U.S. 1 (1831), the Court held that Cherokees could not sue Georgia because they lacked the status of a sovereign nation and were instead a "ward" to the U.S.'s "guardian;" in *Worcester v. Georgia*, 31 U.S. 515 (1832), the Court upheld the doctrine of discovery, recognizing U.S. rights to lands previously held by Indians and asserting the supremacy of federal over state power, thus rejecting Georgia's extension of state law over Cherokee land as unconstitutional. The official response to the Court's ruling in Worcester, as Justice Breyer has explained, was swift: "The first thing the Georgia legislature did was pass a law that said anyone who comes to Georgia to enforce this ruling of the Supreme Court will be hanged. Andrew Jackson, President of the United States, supposedly said (and he said enough such things that it is probably true): 'John Marshall, the Chief Justice, has made his decision. Now let him enforce it.' Nobody did a thing." Stephen G. Breyer, *Reflections of a Junior Justice*, 54 DRAKE L. REV. 7, 9 (2005).

In the excerpt above, President George Washington advocates "terrorism" as a means to eliminate the threat that Indian tribes posed to U.S. interests. Was such "chastizement" or total destruction, of Indian tribes a legitimate goal for the young United States? If so, why? How was this practice justified under American law? *See, e.g.*, Nell Jessup Newton, *Federal Power Over Indians: Its Sources, Scope, and Limitations*, 132 U. PA. L. REV. 195 (1984); Robert A. Williams, Jr., *The Algebra of Federal Indian Law: The Hard Trail of Decolonizing and Americanizing the White Man's Indian Jurisprudence*, 1986 WIS. L. REV. 219; Robert J. Miller, *The Doctrine of Discovery in American Indian Law*, 42 IDAHO L. REV. 1 (2006).

Peter Maguire, *Law And War: An American Story*
139 (2000)

With the surrender of Japan came the discovery of the Japanese special warfare Units 731, 100, and 112. In a laboratory in Manchuria they conducted medical experiments on Chinese, Korean, and Russian POWs, similar to those the Nazis conducted at Dachau for the *Luftwaffe*. Prisoners were frozen alive, infected with syphilis, given transfusions of horse blood, subjected to vivisection with no anaesthesia, and given numerous x-rays to test the effects of radiation. Although the Soviets captured the laboratories in Manchuria, most of the 3,600 doctors and technicians made their way back to Japan. The head of Unit 731, Lieutenant General Shiro Ishii, traded his research results to American authorities in exchange for immunity from prosecution for himself and his staff.

Major Emmett G. Wells, *Book Review of Robert J. Lifton & Greg Mitchell, Hiroshima In America: Fifty Years of Denial*
150 Mil. L. Rev 465, 466-68 (1995)

[The year 1995] marked the fiftieth anniversary of the close of World War II. Tragically, the year also witnessed continuing acts of genocide around the world [in Rwanda and Bosnia] and a failure on the part of the international community to heed the lessons of Nuremberg. Perhaps it is symptomatic of this worldwide failure that our own nation persisted during 1995 in its attitude of denial toward the final horror of World War II: the atomic bombing of Hiroshima and Nagasaki. While the United States Postal Service attempted to commemorate the bombing with a stamp featuring a mushroom cloud, a conservative outcry prevented the Smithsonian Institution from displaying photographs of the carnage caused by the bombing. This national refusal to come to terms with the reality of Hiroshima is the theme of HIROSHIMA IN AMERICA.

All too often, debate on this subject is shrouded in references to the countless Japanese atrocities and the unquestionable justice of the Allied cause. Those arguments lose sight of the moral principle that combat — even combat for a just cause — should be waged against combatants. The bombing of Hiroshima and Nagasaki violated this principle, notwithstanding the evil nature of our Axis adversaries. The authors, Robert J. Lifton and Greg Mitchell show that our refusal to recognize that violation betrays our own values as a nation and undermines our ability to prevent future nuclear wars — even in the wake of the collapse of the Soviet Union.

Defenders of the bombing of Hiroshima and Nagasaki frequently accuse critics such as Lifton and Mitchell of "hindsight" and "Monday-morning quarterbacking." Ironically, it was the "official narrative" formulated by the Truman Administration to justify the bombing that was largely an afterthought. The Manhattan Project that produced the bomb had long since taken on its own "technological and organizational dynamism" and created what the authors term an atrocity-producing situation — "a psychological and political environment structured so as to motivate the average person to engage in slaughter." There was little discussion within the administration prior to dropping the bomb, and President Harry Truman would repeatedly insist years later that he had lost no sleep over the decision.

Moreover, Lifton and Mitchell show that a government cover-up began on August 6, 1945, when President Truman made a public announcement that the atomic bomb had been dropped on what he described as "an important Japanese Army base" even though the bomb had been aimed at the center of a city with a population of 300,000. From that point on, the government attempted to suppress information about civilian casualties and radiation poisoning. Reporters were banned from Hiroshima and Nagasaki, and film footage was suppressed until 1968. The deaths of more than a dozen United States prisoners of war in the Hiroshima explosion were covered up until 1979.

Meanwhile, the authors show that the government was propagating an "official" Hiroshima narrative. In November 1945, Hollywood granted the right of script approval to President Truman and General Leslie Groves for *The Beginning or the End*, a film version of the Hiroshima story. The Truman Administration ordered several revisions of the script, resulting in a film that, among other things, falsely depicted Truman ordering the showering of warning leaflets on the Japanese population prior to the bombing. Characteristically, the film changed the name of one of the four bombers from Bock's Car to Necessary Evil.

Public awareness, however, began to emerge with the publication of John Hersey's article "Hiroshima" in the New Yorker on 31 August 1946, describing the human effects of the attack. In 1947, amidst growing public doubts about the morality of the bombing, the Truman Administration literally commissioned Secretary of War Henry L. Stimson to write an article defending the action. To this day, this article continues to influence debate on the subject, even though it was false, or misleading, in many respects.

For example, Stimson characterized the bombing as "our least abhorrent choice" given the sole alternative of an invasion "expected to cost over a million casualties, in American forces alone." Leaving aside that the "million casualties" estimate was a complete fabrication, invading Japan had not been the only alternative. The sole impediment to Japanese surrender prior to the bombing had been Japan's insistence on keeping her emperor, and the bombing of Hiroshima did nothing to change that. The anticipated Soviet entry into the war against Japan (scheduled for August 15, 1945) would have been the coupe de grace. Yet, recommendations on the part of some scientists for a warning or a demonstration on uninhabited territory fell on deaf ears, notwithstanding that a secret demonstration before United States administrators at the Trinity test site had proven successful three weeks earlier.

The "official narrative" was designed to obscure the painful truths about Hiroshima. The atomic bomb dropped on that city immediately killed 100,000 people and fatally injured at least 50,000 others. At least sixty percent of the city was wiped off the map, yet less than ten percent of Hiroshima's manufacturing, transportation, and storage facilities — that portion having military significance — was damaged. The bomb was detonated at 1800 feet to "maximize the area that would be devastated by the blast and burn effects." This bombing violated everything for which this nation stands; consequently, our national response has been, and continues to be, one of denial. . . .

NOTES AND QUESTIONS

1. If the decision to drop the atomic bomb violated the law (what law?), in what court should those responsible be judged? Did the U.S. government act wrongfully in failing to disclose accurate information at the time to the public? If not, did it later become necessary to release such information? At what point does an obligation to release accurate information to the public arise?

2. "Indiscriminate" weapons, or those that cause disproportionate civilian casualties or destruction because their impact is uncontrollable, are generally considered unlawful. *See, e.g.,* U.S. DEP'T OF THE AIR FORCE, AIR FORCE

PAMPHLET 110-31, INT'L LAW — THE CONDUCT OF ARMED CONFLICT AND AIR
OPERATIONS 6-3 (1976). In 1996, the International Court of Justice issued an
Advisory Opinion on "The Legality of the Threat or Use of Nuclear Weapons."
35 I.L.M. 809 (1996); *see also* THE CASE AGAINST THE BOMB (Roger S. Clark &
Madeleine Sanns eds. 1996); CHARLES J. MOXLEY, JR., NUCLEAR WEAPONS AND
INTERNATIONAL LAW IN THE POST COLD WAR WORLD (2000). Does the atomic age
pose fundamental challenges to lawful conduct of war? If nuclear weapons
transform the nature of war, is their impact similar to other technological
advancements in weapons?

3. World War II pitted the Allied powers against the Axis powers, which
included Japan and Nazi Germany, two of the most feared, repressive, and
aggressive governments in modern history. Does the nature of that conflict
change the legal framework on which it was fought?

Russell F. Weigley, *Eisenhower's Lieutenants: The Campaigns of France and Germany, 1944-45*
370-72, 568-69 (1981)

[An esteemed military historian explores the difficulties created by high
casualty rates during the U.S. military campaign in France and Germany during the last two years of World War II.]

The casualties that dangerously thinned the combat ranks, as well as the
fatigue that drained the efficiency of the survivors, fell always disproportionately upon the infantry, and yet more disproportionately upon the
riflemen. . . . Before D-Day, American planning had modestly anticipated that
infantry would incur about three out of four casualties suffered in Europe.
More precisely, in April 1944 the War Department yielded to the pleas of the
European Theater of Operations [ETO] that the proportion of infantry in the
replacement pool must be raised from 64.3 to 70.3 percent. The first month of
combat in Normandy promptly demonstrated that the modesty of this expectation was excessive, for infantry losses proved to comprise 85 percent of the
casualties. By mid-July . . . the commander of the ETO Ground Forces
Replacement System, Brigadier General Walter G. Layman, lifted the estimate of infantry casualties to 90 percent of the total. . . .

Of the first three months' casualties after D-Day, about 30 percent were
killed, captured, or missing, 70 percent wounded. Of the 70 percent who were
wounded, 45 percent could be expected to recover and return to general assignment duty, while 11 percent could be placed in limited assignment duty. Forty-
six percent of the wounded could return to some kind of duty within 120 days,
and thus could figure importantly in replenishing losses. It was significant
that most of them expressed a strong desire to return to their old units, so
strong that many took the risk of going AWOL, leaving the replacement
pipeline when they felt trapped in it, to find their way back to their former
companies. . . .

The United States Army has never in its long history discovered a satisfactory method of [maintaining] the fighting strength, integrity, and morale of
units long exposed to the hard attrition of combat. In its first war requiring

massive forces, the Civil War, the United States Army simply held a regiment's nose to the grindstone of combat until that regiment was no more. With minor and usually ineffective exceptions, there was no replacement system. Union army regiments with a table of organization strength of 845 to 1025 were down to an average of 375 by the time of Gettysburg, only halfway through the war. New regiments were raised to take the place of depleted ones, an unconscionable waste of the experience of veteran officers and enlisted men. To avoid such waste, in the world wars the army gave depleted units infusions of individual replacements. . . . While units did not simply fade away as they had in the Civil War, there remained the Civil War problem, aggravated by the more continuous combat of the twentieth century, that once a unit entered the lines it stayed there until the end of the war. Divisions occasionally went to quiet sectors to rest and refit, but not often enough or according to any system. The Germany army almost until its final extremity rotated units out of the line of fire more frequently and regularly than the American army. The effect was to undermine an effective American division's asset of experience by sheer weariness.

Once an individual soldier was committed to combat, he had to count on remaining under fire until the war ended or he was so badly wounded he could not return — or until he was dead. For all its faults, nevertheless, this system was preferable to the British practice, followed in North Africa and fortunately less evident in Europe, of rotating units out of the line so frequently that relatively raw or rusty British formations were forever being chewed to pieces by veteran German divisions. The American replacement system of World War II was also far superior to the Korean and Vietnam War systems, which rotated individuals, officers as well as men, out of both their units and combat as soon as they had served under fire for a stipulated time. . . . [T]he World War II replacement system had the great virtue of sustaining unit integrity as well as numbers; the later Korean and Vietnam replacement system practically destroyed unit cohesion. . . .

[In order to address a near-desperate situation in France after the Battle of the Bulge — a surprise German attack in December of 1944 that took the lives of 19,000 American troops and led to the infamous Malmedy massacre and trial,] [t]he theater command considered a sweeping withdrawal of combat-trained men from engineer battalions and general service regiments. For the time being, Eisenhower settled for the less drastic expedient of sending his own representatives through the Communications Zone to select men qualified to fight and to hasten them to the front. He also promised a pardon and a clean slate to soldiers under court-martial sentences who would go to the front and fight; everyone who faced fifteen years or more of hard labor volunteered.

Elizabeth Lutes Hillman, *Defending America: Military Culture and The Cold War Court-Martial*
11 (2005)

[Meeting the personnel needs of an army at war is always a challenge for military and civilian leaders. Sometimes the political and social climate in which military personnel policies are made creates special challenges for commanding officers. For example, the 1948 executive order that required "equality of treatment" across racial lines forced the services to change their practices of assigning, training, and deploying service members, and the 1975 order to admit women to the national service academies forced changes in facilities, equipment, and administration. During the Vietnam War, the United States implemented a special program designed to increase the number of young men available for military service. Called Project 100,000, it did not work out as planned.]

Project 100,000 was a Great Society program intended to augment the armed forces with recruits previously rejected because of low scores on preadmission intelligence tests. This plan, which Senator Daniel Patrick Moynihan viewed as a means of rescuing young African American men from a destructive, matriarchal culture, brought over 400,000 young men, most from poverty, into the service between 1966 and 1972. Moynihan's rationale for the program combined two popular perspectives on military service: that it built character and made men and that the modern armed forces could be an instrument of social change. The additional training that was supposed to accompany the induction of these underprepared men did not materialize, and the consequences were dire, as historian Christian Appy has shown in his study of Vietnam soldiers. Half were sent to Vietnam, where they died at a rate twice that of other troops. Although African Americans comprised only 10 percent of the military in the late 1960s, they were 40 percent of the Project 100,000 inductees. A prime reason for the disproportionately high casualty rate among these troops was the high percentage sent into combat occupations, which made up most of the military occupations deemed suitable for "Project 100,000" men. Halfhearted social engineering efforts like Project 100,000, even coupled with sophisticated recruiting campaigns and extensive testing of potential inductees, failed to repair the military's deficit in skilled servicemembers.

BARRAZA RIVERA v. IMMIGRATION AND NATURALIZATION SERVICE
United States Court of Appeals for the Ninth Circuit
913 F.2d 1443, 1445-53 (9th Cir. 1990)

PREGERSON, CIRCUIT JUDGE:

Jose Antonio Barraza Rivera ("Barraza") petitions for review of a decision of the Board of Immigration Appeals ("BIA" or "the Board"). The BIA dismissed Barraza's appeal and upheld the immigration judge's denial of Barraza's requests for political asylum and withholding of deportation under the Immigration and Nationality Act. 8 U.S.C. §§ 1158 and 1253(h). The Board also upheld the immigration judge's denial of Barraza's motions for remand of his case to the Bureau of Human Rights and Humanitarian Affairs ("BHRHA") and for discovery of the basis of the BHRHA advisory opinion. We have jurisdiction over Barraza's petition under 8 U.S.C. § 1105a. We grant the petition, reverse the BIA order, and remand for further proceedings.

In December 1983, Barraza was forcibly recruited into military service in El Salvador, his home country. He entered training in January 1984 at a military headquarters in the city of La Union, and was trained in weaponry and self-defense for about 20 days. On or about January 13, 1984, Barraza took one or two hours off from training and went into town to apply for a passport. He applied for the passport on the advice of his mother, who was concerned about unlawful acts committed by the military. He changed from military to civilian clothing to apply for the passport, and did not indicate military service on his passport application. After training, Barraza was sent to the city of Morazan for two weeks, where he backed up troops fighting guerrillas. He never engaged in battle. Barraza returned to military headquarters in La Union on January 31, 1984. He and approximately one-half of the 100 soldiers in his unit were given a three-day leave to visit family.

Before being dismissed for leave, Barraza was pulled aside from the group by a man he identified in his testimony as Lieutenant Calbo. According to Barraza:

> [H]e said prepare yourself when you return, because we have a commission. We're going to take two men to . . . assassinate. And then I said why, it's an order he said, because they have paid me and I need the money. And then he said, what do you prefer, that they kill you or kill them? And then I said okay, as you say, lieutenant. . . .

Barraza returned to formation and was dismissed for leave. He then picked up his passport. On February 4, 1984, he left El Salvador for the United States because, he testified, "it wasn't correct what I was going to be doing." Barraza was apprehended by the INS near Brownsville, Texas, and was placed in deportation proceedings. He applied for political asylum. The BHRHA prepared an advisory opinion on his application and sent it to the INS pursuant to applicable regulations. A hearing on his asylum and withholding of deportation claims was held on December 18, 1985.

At the hearing, Barraza testified that he left El Salvador because he did not want to participate in killing the two men, and that he fears that, if returned to El Salvador, he faces persecution by both the military and the guerrillas. First, Barraza fears being punished for refusing to participate in paid assassinations. Second, he fears that the military will suspect that he is an informant for the guerrillas and will kill him for that reason. To support this claim, he testified that an uncle was beaten severely by soldiers in 1982 for suspected pro-guerrilla activity, and that another uncle and cousin were killed by soldiers, also in 1982. Also, Barraza stated that in December 1983, a friend and fellow soldier was killed by a colonel in Barraza's unit at headquarters in La Union after being held for several days by guerrilla captors. The colonel apparently accused this friend of being a guerrilla informant. Third, Barraza fears that the guerrillas will kill him if he is returned to El Salvador because he was a member of the military. To support this claim, he testified that a friend was killed by guerrillas after being identified as a member of the national guard.

Barraza also stated that his family informed him that anonymous threats against him had been attached to the door of his family's home, beginning approximately two months after he entered the United States. Barraza received two letters from his family just days before his asylum hearing in December 1985 that warned him not to return to El Salvador because of recent anonymous threats. The letters' authenticity was not challenged at the asylum hearing, and the letters were admitted into evidence.

Finally, Barraza submitted background documentation regarding El Salvador's civil war, death squad activities, and the military. In particular, he submitted newspaper and magazine articles on increased levels of violence from both sides of the civil war and an Amnesty International report on widespread human rights violations. The Amnesty International report stated that military officials were known to work in "close conjunction" with certain repressive civilian paramilitary groups. Barraza also submitted to the Board on appeal an article that appeared in the March 1986 edition of *The Progressive*. The article described in detail the extensive involvement of the Salvadoran military in death squad activities, and included specific accounts of military officers ordering soldiers to participate in assassinations requested by wealthy private citizens. The immigration judge denied Barraza's requests for political asylum and withholding of deportation. The BIA dismissed Barraza's appeal. . . .

[The court holds that "Barraza proved his asylum eligibility" because "he faces persecution by the Salvadoran military because he abandoned military service and fled the country to avoid participating in an inhuman act," explaining:]

Barraza was ordered by a military officer, under threat of death, to participate in the paid killing of two men. Barraza abandoned military service and fled El Salvador because he did not want to participate in the killings. He asserts that, if returned to El Salvador, he will be persecuted by the Salvadoran military because he refused to participate in the murders and deserted and because he will be suspected of pro-guerrilla activity. The BIA found that Barraza failed to establish a well-founded fear of persecution by the government, and, a fortiori, a clear probability of government persecution. The Board found that Barraza's fear of being persecuted as a suspected guerrilla sympathizer was not well-founded and also rejected Barraza's claim of persecution based on objection to military service.

We hold that the BIA's finding that Barraza failed to demonstrate a well-founded fear of persecution for his refusal to participate in paid assassinations is not supported by substantial evidence. Barraza demonstrated a well-founded fear of persecution based on his objection to participating in the murders under orders from a Salvadoran military officer, and is eligible for political asylum on that basis. . . .

In deciding Barraza's case, the BIA held that "a claim to conscientious objector status should be sustained and refugee status granted if an individual establishes that he will be forced to participate in activities which are contrary to the basic rules of human conduct." The Board, however, found that: (1) Barraza was not actually threatened by Lieutenant Calbo, the military officer who ordered him to participate in the assassinations; (2) Lieutenant Calbo was dead; and (3) Barraza failed to establish that the murders were sanctioned by the Salvadoran government or military. The BIA concluded that Barraza failed to establish a well-founded fear that if returned to El Salvador he would be forced, through military service, to participate in unconscionable acts, or would be punished for refusing to participate in the acts.

Assuming, as we must, that Barraza's testimony was credible, we cannot doubt that Barraza satisfied the subjective component of the "well-founded fear" standard. He testified that he opposed participating in paid assassinations because he believed they were wrong and illegal, and that he feared being forced to participate in the murders or being killed for refusing to participate. We conclude, based on the record before us, that Barraza has shown "genuine fear." *See Diaz-Escobar v. INS,* 782 F.2d at 1492. . . .

The issue, then, is whether substantial evidence supports the BIA's conclusion that Barraza did not show a reasonable possibility that the persecution he feared would occur if he was returned to El Salvador. We hold that the BIA's conclusion is not supported by substantial evidence.

The BIA's findings that Barraza was never threatened and that the military officer who threatened Barraza was dead are not supported by substantial evidence. The BIA explained:

> [T]he respondent states . . . that he would be killed by the lieutenant if he failed to take the action. The transcript indicates that the respondent was told that if he did not kill the intended victims . . ., they would kill him.

This is a strained reading of the transcript, which states in relevant part:

> A: There was a lieutenant that told me to come over here.
>
> Q: What was his name?
>
> A: They called him Calbo, Lieutenant Calbo.
>
> Q: Calbo?
>
> A: And he said prepare yourself when you return, because we have a commission. We're going to take two men to . . . assassinate. And then I said why, it's an order he said, *because they have paid me and I need the money. And then he said, what do you prefer, that they kill you or kill them?* (Emphasis added.)

When taken in context, the meaning of the exchange is clear: the lieutenant told Barraza that either Barraza helped kill the two men or whoever had hired the lieutenant to do the job would have Barraza killed.

Under the circumstances, Barraza could reasonably expect that, in either case, Lieutenant Calbo would be involved in the killing. . . . Reversed and remanded.

NOTES AND QUESTIONS

1. Was Eisenhower wrong to offer amnesty to convicted criminals during the campaign to liberate France and Germany from Hitler's control? What impact would such an action have on the morale of law-abiding infantrymen? On the disciplinary problems facing commanders of front-line forces?

2. Does the law place limits on who can serve in the military? Should it? Should the military be limited by law in assigning and training service members?

3. Was Project 100,000 fundamentally flawed or was its execution simply botched? How do the demographics of military personnel affect the disciplinary challenges of military commanders? Should military leaders, rather than civilian government officials and politicians, make decisions about recruiting tactics and personnel policies?

4. To what lengths can (and should) a government go in order to compel military service? Should opposition to forced wartime service constitute sufficient "persecution" to sustain a request for political asylum? In a footnote to *Bazzara-Rivera*, the Ninth Circuit addressed the legal definition of persecution, noting

> Requiring military service and punishing deserters does not, per se, constitute persecution. *See Rodriguez-Rivera v. United States INS,* 848 F.2d 998, 1005 (9th Cir.1988); *Kaveh-Haghigy v. INS,* 783 F.2d 1321, 1323 (9th Cir.1986) (per curiam). We have, however, recognized conscientious objection to military service as grounds for relief from deportation. *See Canas-Segovia v. INS,* 902 F.2d at 726. The Board also has addressed the conscientious objector issue. *In re A-G-,* Interim Dec. 3040 (B.I.A.1987) (persecution when conscriptee would be required to engage in internationally condemned conduct), *aff'd sub nom. M.A. v. United States INS,* 899 F.2d 304, 312 (4th Cir.1990) (en banc); *In re Salim,* 18 I. & N. Dec. 311 (B.I.A.1982) (forced military service against compatriots may be grounds for asylum eligibility).

B. Occupation

Harry N. Scheiber & Jane L. Scheiber, *Bayonets in Paradise: A Half-Century Retrospect on Martial Law on Hawai'i 1941-1946*
19 U. HAW. L. REV. 477, 487-520 (1997)*

[Securing borders and controlling territories, hostile and friendly, during times of war creates additional disciplinary and law enforcement burdens for military troops. The imposition of martial law is most often associated in the United States with the Civil War and President Lincoln's suspension of habeas corpus. During World War II, however, the territory of Hawai'i was under martial law for almost three years. Below, historians Harry and Jane Scheiber explain:]

Within hours of the early morning attack on December 7, 1941, Joseph P. Poindexter, the territorial governor of Hawai'i, issued a proclamation placing the entire territory under martial law. He suspended the writ of habeas corpus and requested the commanding general of the Hawaiian Department to exercise all governmental functions, including judicial powers, "until the danger of invasion is removed." In a simultaneous proclamation, the commanding general, Lieutenant General Walter C. Short, declared himself the "Military Governor" of Hawai'i — a self-assumed title that was to become a point of great controversy in later months — and he warned that citizens who disobeyed his orders would be "severely punished by military tribunals" or held in custody until the civil courts were once again able to function. . . .

Thus was the entire civilian population of the Hawaiian Islands placed under the control of a military governor whose discretionary powers were absolute. This comprehensive suspension of constitutional guarantees was destined to last for nearly three years, until October 1944. . . .

Although the wide scope of martial law brought the activities of all civilians in the Islands under Army rule, the declaration of martial law and the actual administration of military government had some uniquely harsh consequences for residents of Japanese ancestry — both alien residents and citizens-in Hawai'i, and to some degree for other residents of Asian ancestry. In marked contrast, however, to the drastic policy of forcibly evacuating and then interning the 110,000 Japanese-American residents of California, Washington, and Oregon, the Army did leave most Japanese-Americans in Hawai'i free to continue their lives in their own homes (and in most cases, their prewar employment), as best they could — but, like the rest of Hawai'i's civilian population, under Army rule. After initially being prevented from enlistment in the armed forces, they were finally invited to form a Hawai'i fighting unit; and, as is well known, their combat team became one of the most decorated units in American military history. . . .

This is not to say that Hawai'i residents of Japanese ancestry were regarded by the military government as beyond suspicion. Approximately 159,000 persons out of a total civilian population of 465,000 were of Japanese descent. Of these, 124,000 were citizens and another 35,000 aliens. Both military and civilian security officials had long believed that there was substantial danger of "fifth column" activity from within this group if the Islands were invaded by Japan; and after the Pearl Harbor attack, such an invasion appeared to be an immediate danger. As happened on the mainland, therefore, the Army and the FBI moved quickly to round up aliens and other individuals who previously had been investigated and were suspected of being disloyal or dangerous in a war situation. Eventually 1569 persons were detained on suspicion of disloyalty. Of these, 1466 — less than 1 percent of their ethnic group — were of Japanese descent. The detainees included almost all Shinto and Buddhist priests, teachers of Japanese language schools, other leaders of the Japanese community, and many Japanese fishermen whose offshore activities had become the subject of unsubstantiated rumors and suspicions.

These measures were deemed insufficient, however, by some prominent haoles [caucasians] and by many junior uniformed officers and their families in the Islands, who were a principal source of what a confidential FBI report in 1942 dismissed as "the million false and fantastic rumors" of disloyalty among the Japanese-Americans in Hawai'i. Colonel Green confided to his diary in February, not quite two months after the Pearl Harbor attack, that the Japanese-American residents had "simply shut up" and were "scared to death," in fear of "a local uprising and a slaughter." Green added, ominously: "I am afraid of it too." . . . [The Army eventually interned hundreds of

Hawai'ians of Japanese descent but successfully resisted the federal government's pressure for even harsher measures, such as mass evacuation.]

In the early weeks of the war, there was no public challenge to martial law. It was accepted as an emergency measure with practically no resistance in Hawai'i and indeed with obvious relief and enthusiasm in many segments of the civilian population. Most residents of the Islands apparently also believed that the civilian courts and the civilian government would resume their basic functions as soon as the acute emergency situation had passed — in a few months at most. Any assumption that the Army would willingly relinquish its control over civilian life, however, proved wholly unwarranted. For more than fifteen months — until March 1943, when some of the civilian government's authority and individual civil liberties were restored — the military would rule Hawai'i with virtually an unchecked authority, suspending constitutional guarantees on a wholesale basis. Although the Army did permit the civil courts to re-open for non-criminal, non-jury cases early in 1942, the jurisdiction of those courts was strictly limited; hence, nearly all misdemeanors and all felonies continued to be tried before military tribunals. The general orders issued by the Army recognized no residual or controlling powers in the governor, the legislative officers of the territory or its municipalities, or the civilian courts at any level. Indeed, the Army thereafter formally regarded the civilian courts, when they were allowed to resume functioning in a limited way, as "agents of the Military Governor."

Martial law was not lifted entirely until October 1944, more than two years after the Battle of Midway had ended any real danger of invasion or massive strike against Hawai'i. During the period of most comprehensive military rule in Hawai'i, from Pearl Harbor to March 1943, some 181 general orders were issued under the name of the commanding general. As the territorial attorney general recounted at the time, these orders represented a "military regime with . . . stringent controls over the civilian population." Control was administered by the person who had planned the takeover of control: Lt. Colonel Green, who assumed for himself the title of "Executive, Office of the Military Governor," and who appropriated the Iolani Palace offices that had been the seat of territorial government. . . . And so Lt. Colonel Green (soon to be jumped to Colonel, then a year later to Brigadier General) became, in effect, the czar of Hawai'i's civilian life — including civil and criminal law enforcement: he was effectively a dictator with vast power, overseeing every aspect of comprehensive martial law, both administrative and judicial. "My authority was substantially unlimited," Green wrote in his recollections of his Hawai'i assignment.

The scope of the Army's general orders reached into every corner of daily life, often with the imposition of policies that deviated dramatically from the norms of peacetime American communities — and in many ways from the rules that were established during the wartime emergency in the forty-eight mainland states. The Army controlled not only the civil and criminal law, but nearly the entire range of federal administrative law that on the mainland was under jurisdiction of the War Production Board, the Office of Price Administration, the War Labor Board, and other "alphabet agencies." Japanese alien residents were subjected to additional special regulations, to guard against subversion. They were prohibited from meeting in groups of ten or more (even for religious ceremonies); or carrying flashlights, portable radios and cameras; or possessing radio transmitters and other items, even road maps, that could be used in espionage. Areas of Oahu, especially in and near the military bases and airfields, were ruled off limits for all enemy aliens; and Japanese-American workers in the shipyards or other government installations were required to wear large badges that set them apart from others on those jobs. As a result many permanent residents who had been born in Japan, and who therefore were legally ineligible for U.S. citizenship, lost their jobs after decades of working in Hawai'i.

The 5000 residents of Korean ancestry also found themselves subjected to these restrictions, simply because Army police and sentries claimed to be unable to differentiate them by appearance from the Japanese. . . .

Other, far broader, restrictions applied to all civilians. Early measures instituted by the Army included the compulsory registration and fingerprinting of all civilians except infants, and strict censorship of the press and broadcasting as well as of the civilian mails. Hospitals and other emergency facilities were placed under direct military control. Within a few months of the outbreak of war, the Army was also busily regulating gambling (forbidding use of marked cards and dice), sale of alcoholic beverages, traffic and parking, prostitution, and even dog-leash requirements. Among the most intrusive, and, in the long run, most resented incursions on freedom were the curfew that kept civilians off the street at night and the blackout orders that kept their homes dark after sunset; these orders were kept in effect for two-and-a-half years. . . .

The Army also encouraged women and children in civilian families to relocate to the mainland for their safety. Consequently, several thousand were evacuated from the Islands, taking up temporary homes mainly in California and the State of Washington. Within two years after Pearl Harbor, however, the increasingly difficult circumstances in which many of these evacuees found themselves had become a severe embarrassment for the Army. Finding places for passage on ships going eastward from Hawai'i was one thing; it was another matter to make space available for their return when thousands of troops were being loaded on every available vessel departing the West Coast for the Islands, then the staging area for the entire Pacific war. As many of the evacuated women and children began to encounter severe economic deprivation, the issue became known as the "strandee" problem. Some 3000 Hawai'i residents in this status still remained on the West Coast in late 1943, denied places on Pacific-bound ships and focusing their anger on General Green and the Army command in Honolulu, which controlled space allocations. Secretary Ickes made it a policy priority for his department to press for return of the civilian strandees, but his office reported in March 1944 that after repeated appeals to the War Department, the Navy Department, and the War Shipping Agency "the upshot was flat failure." . . .

A particularly onerous and eventually much-criticized aspect of martial law was the Army's control over labor, including wartime wages, working conditions, and allocations of workers to industries and firms. At the outset of martial law, the military suspended all labor contracts, froze prevailing wages, and required all civilians working for public utilities, civilian agencies, or government contractors — an estimated total of 80,000 workers — to remain in their positions. Much more sweeping control was instituted three months later, however, when job-switching and absenteeism from work without an employer's permission were made criminal offenses: under terms of General Orders No. 91 (March 3, 1942), these designated workers were made subject to prosecution in the provost courts and to fines or imprisonment of up to two months' time for unauthorized absences from work or attempts to change jobs without permission. According to civilian leaders on the Islands, absenteeism was one of the crimes most frequently punished with jail sentences. What the General Orders termed a "failure to report to work" was interpreted by the provost judges as giving them authority to convict and punish for absences of even only a few hours. The harsh treatment received by "flagrant absentees" before the military tribunals was probably encouraged by the top Army legal officers, as evidenced by the advice given the provost officers at a May 1944 conference of all the provost judges: Because his office sought to "rehabilitate" such delinquents, the supervisor of the provost courts advised the judges, the typical defendant had already "had every chance" to correct his work habits before being prosecuted. . . . Under pressure from the Department of the Interior, General Robert Richardson, Jr. (then in command in Hawai'i) amended the general orders shortly after this May 1944 conference, to abolish jail sentences for absentees unless the convicted party could not pay the fine. But even that move, as Under Secretary of Interior Abe Fortas pointed out, could be fairly characterized as "still a far cry from restoration of an American system of values in Hawai'i." . . .

Thus, with "military security" as its justification, martial law pervaded every aspect of civilian life. Throughout the first two years of the war, every violation of the military's general orders — from the most violent crime to the most trivial misdemeanor, and including labor relations issues basic to workplace conditions — was prosecuted in military courts, with no provisions for the usual constitutional guarantees of due process. It is little wonder, then, that Army-administered justice, with its sweeping effects on civil liberties and everyday life, eventually became a storm center of political controversy both in the Islands and in the Roosevelt Administration's civilian leadership in Washington. . . .

A key legal and constitutional issue was the suspension of the writ of habeas corpus — a fundamental constitutional right, by which persons taken into custody could seek to have a court of law determine the legality of the proceedings that had led to their detention. At the outbreak of the war, when the civilian courts were first suspended, the Army had created a "military commission" of civilians and Army officers to try serious criminal offenses, including capital crimes, and to try crimes of war such as sabotage. Shortly after the Pearl Harbor attack, Colonel Green summoned to his office some leading members of the bar, the federal district judges, and the chief justice of the territorial supreme court; and he sought their support for the creation of this commission, as well as for the general takeover of the civilian courts. The lawyers and judges extended less than enthusiastic support, however, especially after Garner Anthony (a partner in one of the Islands' leading law firms and counsel to at least two of the "Big Five" companies that controlled much of Hawai'i's economy) expressed concern regarding the legality of the commission. In

Anthony's view, any civilian who served on such a commission might later be found liable in civil suits for wrongful imprisonment and other harms to defendants. . . .

Thus conceived in controversy, the commission went into operation with a mixed board of civilians and military officers, but the Army soon decided to drop the civilian members. The commission in fact tried only a handful of cases during the entire war period, and so was of small significance as measured by the number of individuals its operations touched. In one respect, however, the commission's operation proved to be of critical importance politically: It tried and convicted for murder, which the Army had designated a capital crime, a Maui Hawaiian resident named Saffrey Brown. In March 1942, Brown — the 32-year-old father of seven children — was arrested by the authorities after shooting his wife during a domestic dispute in Honolulu, where she had gone to live, apparently gone lalau (astray), in this instance reportedly with a lover, and Brown had visited to beg her to return. Local civilian officials in Maui believed that the gun had gone off during a struggle set off by "a fit of jealousy," and there was some testimony that the gun might even have been set off when one of the children hit Brown's hand. They did not believe that premeditated murder was at issue. They were outraged when the military commission passed a death sentence after denying Brown the right to a jury trial, reportedly permitting him to be represented by a non-lawyer (against a highly qualified Judge Advocate General lawyer for the Army's prosecution team), and failing to recognize explicitly any distinction between first and second degree murder. "This is the first time that the death sentence has ever been inflicted upon anyone living in the County of Maui," the county treasurer wrote to the Hawai'i territorial delegate to Congress, Samuel Wilder King, asking King to intercede if for no other reason than all who had attended the trial felt that premeditation had never been considered as a factor and that Brown's counsel had been unqualified.

Delegate King was appalled by the information that came to him from trusted political associates concerning what seemed a serious abuse of Army authority, and he called upon Secretary of the Interior Harold Ickes to ask the War Department to head off the prisoner's impending execution. After study of the record by the Judge Advocate General, Secretary of War Stimson decided to order General Emmons in Hawai'i to hold the execution order "in abeyance;" and within a month's time — under continuing political pressure from Washington — Emmons formally commuted Brown's sentence to a life term.

The controversy over the Saffrey Brown trial served, however, to dramatize the extent to which the Army had taken control of civilian governance and justice — and had set aside normal constitutional guarantees. . . .

Far more important institutionally than the Military Commission were the provost courts, established to enforce the whole range of military regulations; they also conducted trials for felonies and misdemeanors under territorial and federal laws, which were continued in effect by military orders. The provost courts were for more than three years the principal institutions of justice in Hawai'i. . . . [T]he provost judges were also the harsh enforcers of the notorious general orders against "chronic absenteeism" and job-switching by workers.

Civilians brought before the provost courts were denied virtually all of the basic constitutional guarantees of due process contained in the Bill of Rights, including the right to trial by jury and freedom from unreasonable searches and seizures without a warrant. Often no written charges were presented, and defendants were not permitted to cross-examine witnesses against them nor to call witnesses in their own behalf. In the few trials that were appealed, the trial record that was kept often proved to be crude and inaccurate. A single officer (often wearing a sidearm) presided in the provost court, and he directly examined prisoners and any witnesses. Many of the judges were without legal training, at least in the first year of the war. Although defendants were formally allowed the right to counsel, the provost judges commonly told them that lawyers were neither necessary nor desirable. Word soon spread that contrite acceptance of the court's verdict was likely to yield a lighter sentence than appearing with counsel — an important piece of common wisdom, since the verdict could not be appealed.

An investigation in Hawai'i conducted by the Solicitor of the Department of the Interior in late 1942 reported "defendants . . . convicted of violating 'the spirit of martial law' or 'the spirit' of general orders when the text has been found inadequate;" and that the sentences meted out were much more severe than those handed down by military courts against uniformed personnel for identical violations. Members of the Hawai'i bar who represented those defendants who decided to risk appearance with counsel had some memorable experiences before the provost judges. For example, one Honolulu lawyer, Samuel Patterson, reported that a provost judge threatened him with contempt simply because he had requested reduction of a client's bail. Authors of the Army's own official history of military government in Hawai'i would later conclude that "an orderly trial was practically unknown;" and they remarked upon serious "excesses" in the abusive way that hapless defendants were treated by the provost judges and other personnel of the provost courts, especially during the first year of the war. . . .

As a result of these practices, trial in a provost court only superficially resembled a civil court trial operating under constitutional rules of procedure. Their trials were "among the worst features of the military conquest of the civilian government," amounting to nothing more than "drum-head justice," an Interior Department lawyer charged in a report written just a year after Pearl Harbor. If the jurisdiction of the courts was challenged by a defendant, the provost judges were advised by the command, they should "arbitrarily deny the claim, and if they want to contest the matter let them get out a writ of habeas corpus." The average trial in provost courts took five minutes or less, and of the 22,480 trials conducted in Honolulu's provost court in 1942-43, some 99 percent resulted in convictions! Several hundred persons were sentenced to prison, at least two hundred of them for terms between six months and life; and more than $500,000 in fines were imposed in the first eight months of the war alone. No distinction was made between juveniles and adults, and defendants as young as fourteen years of age were tried by provost judges. Little wonder, then, that the administrator of the provost courts, Captain John Wickham, advised the judges at a 1944 conference that they should avoid publicity: "I would be very careful getting into the papers under any circumstances. . . . If there are any reporters in your courtroom, edit their stories. Establish a relationship with the reporter. If something pops up of unusual interest with dynamite in it request to see the story before [it is] published." . . .

Sentencing policy was an especially egregious feature of military justice. Punishments almost invariably were stiffer than those prescribed by civil law on conviction for similar offenses; and although the Army did establish procedures for review and for grants of clemency, no review was instituted before a prisoner had been incarcerated for three months or more (six months in the case of those sentenced for terms of a year or longer). Many persons who were jailed were forced to do hard labor, whether or not the sentence had specifically required it. The Army also authorized the provost courts to exact compulsory purchases of war bonds from prisoners in lieu of fines (a practice that the Treasury Department later disallowed), and often persons convicted by these courts were required to donate blood, or else were given a choice between serving time or donating blood. . . .

For most of the war period, however, public criticism of the provost courts was muted; private mail was censored by the Army, as were newspapers and radio broadcasts. To be critical of Army rule was to risk a suspicion of "disloyalty" that could all too easily lead to summary internment. . . . [T]he Solicitor of the Department of Interior reported from Hawai'i that he found the press being "rigidly censored," with a licensing system imposed by the Army. An editor had been warned, he wrote, against publishing any outright criticism of Army rule: "The press cannot report murders and rapes, and cannot discuss prostitution, and cannot even say that prostitution is under Army control. A complete, rigid and entirely illegal [sic] censorship is imposed over all mail to the mainland. Telephones are tapped, and recordings made, at will."

Doubtless many (perhaps most, at least at first) civilians in Hawai'i were thoroughly convinced that the Army's control of the justice system was justified, and that sacrifice of some traditional liberties was a reasonable price to pay for military security, as memories of the devastating Pearl Harbor attack did not fade quickly. The Army's decision to try nearly all civilians charged with significant civil and criminal violations in the provost courts was based in the first instance on the premise that "civil judges could not be sufficiently severe under existing civil law, and they could not be given appropriate powers [to exercise sanctions] by us." What the Army deemed appropriate severity in the administration of justice became evident soon enough. When the full record of the provost courts was reviewed in 1946 by a leading authority on military law who was then serving as special counsel to the Army, he concluded: "From all I have been able to learn, they were unfair, unjudicial, and unmilitary. If any officer ever ran a summary court the way these people ran a provost court you would fire them out to Canton Island or a little farther. . . . It's a very, very nasty, unpleasant picture, and you just cannot justify it in any way." A federal district court judge in Hawai'i put it rather more bluntly, characterizing the military regime in Hawai'i as simply "the antithesis of Americanism."

Ryan Swift, *Occupational Jurisdiction: A Critical Analysis of the Iraqi Special Tribunal*
19 N.Y. INT'L L. REV. 99, 100-05 (2006)

On March 19, 2003, a U.S.-led coalition invaded and occupied Iraq. On May 1, 2003, President Bush announced the end of major combat operations, and the military occupation of Iraq began. The United States and the United Kingdom announced the end of their formal occupation on June 30, 2004, pursuant to Security Council Resolution 1483. This resolution affirmed the application of international humanitarian law and its binding obligations on the occupying power until the establishment of an interim government.

In May 2003, a heated debate took place in the U.N. Security Council over the direction of post-conflict Iraq. In the end, the United States retained its hold on international legal authority. With the enactment of S.C. Res. 1483, the U.S.-led CPA [Coalition Provisional Authority] became the internationally recognized transitional occupation government of Iraq. The CPA occupation became subject to the international law of occupation, specifically The Hague Regulations of 1907 and the Geneva Conventions of 1949.

The CPA was created by the United States on June 16, 2003, as an organization under the control of the Department of Defense. Its stated purpose is to administer Iraq, in accordance with S.C. Res. 1483. In July 2003, the CPA created the IGC [Iraqi Governing Council] to serve as a transitional Iraqi governmental body. The IGC would be subject to the CPA's approval of its orders, directives, and personnel appointments. In effect, the IGC became a subordinate entity, operating under the authority of an occupying power.

Since March 2003, the United States, the United Kingdom, and other foreign forces have formed an occupying power. Security Council Resolution 1511 affirms the coalition's obligations as an occupying power. The occupying power, no matter what name it takes on, is bound by the Geneva Conventions and other sources of customary international humanitarian law.

Article 42 of the Annex to the 1907 Hague Convention IV Respecting the Laws and Customs of War on Land affirms: "Territory is considered occupied when it is actually placed under the authority of the hostile army. The occupation extends . . . where such authority has been established and can be exercised." As recognized in a U.S. Army text addressing this provision, "Article 42 . . . emphasizes the primacy of fact as the test of whether or not occupation exists." The Army text adds: "Article 43 of the Hague Regulations continues the theme of the traditional law with its provision for a clear transfer of authority: 'The authority of the legitimate power having in fact passed into the hands of the occupant . . . .'"

NOTES AND QUESTIONS

1. Is the long-term imposition of martial law ever a military necessity? Under what conditions?

2. Are wartime suspensions of civil liberties protections always suspect after the fact? The Army and Navy considered Hawai'i a "fortress" on which civil juries and courts could not be trusted because, in large part, of the majority non-white population, including substantial groups of Japanese, Chinese, Korean, and Philippine aliens and U.S. citizens. If you were an elected or appointed government official, what evidence, if any, would you require before giving credence to such claims?

3. The international law that applies during military occupations remains subject to dispute. *See, e.g.,* EYAL BENVENISTI, THE INTERNATIONAL LAW OF OCCUPATION (2d ed. 2004). Why has it proved difficult to define and enforce a body of law to govern occupying forces and territories? What political and military issues complicate this area of law? What disciplinary challenges face commanding officers in occupied territories?

C. Detention

Raymond Lech, *Broken Soldiers*
39-42 (2000)

[The prisoner of war camps controlled by North Korean and Chinese troops during the Korean War (1950-53) were characterized by some of the worst conditions in modern warfare. Death rates among U.S. troops surpassed forty percent, with starvation the most frequent killer. Under these conditions, military discipline sometimes faltered as prisoners fought for survival. After being repatriated after the war, several U.S. POW's were prosecuted at courts-martial for committing crimes while imprisoned.]

During World War II, the Japanese, who had occupied the Korean peninsula since 1905, established a number of mining camps throughout the northern half of the country. After the war, many of those camps were abandoned, and some of the deserted shanty towns were used as collection points for prisoners. Because Americans tend to nickname everything, one camp was appropriately given the sobriquet "Death Valley."

It was located about twenty-five miles above P'yŏngyang, near the western town of Usan close to the narrow waist of North Korea. The camp was situated in a deep, north-south ravine flanked by two high mountains. It was rare indeed when sunlight touched the floor of the chasm. A narrow dirt road ran through the middle of the camp, and at the southern half of the ravine were three rows of long, barracks-type buildings on each side of the dirt street, four buildings per row. A few hundred yards to the north was the upper compound, which had two rows, three buildings to a side. It was a typical mining camp of Japanese architecture, common throughout Korea. The long, narrow buildings contained a number of rooms as well as an end room that housed the kitchen. Each separated living compartment in the building was ten feet square, and there were between six and eight rooms in each barrack. No windows broke the sides; occasionally, Japanese-style sliding doors divided the rooms. Most important, the rooms were unheated. All winters in Korea are extremely severe, but during the last month of 1950 and the early months of the following year North Korea suffered the harshest winter in twenty-five years.

Death Valley housed approximately three thousand men. Until they were moved in late January 1951, the only clothing they had was what they wore when captured. Nearly fifty were without trousers or jackets. Meanwhile, the temperature often plummeted to thirty degrees below zero.

No matter how uncomfortable the crowding, the extremely cramped conditions at Death Valley saved many because they could share the only heat available — each others' bodies. The average living space, about the size of a small dining room, held thirty men. During the day, a man would sit grasping his spread knees tightly to his chest, then another man would slide back between the first man's knees and grab his own. This would be repeated twenty-eight more times until all were tightly squeezed into the same position. At night in some rooms, sleeping was carried out in shifts, with a third standing, a third sitting, and the final third lying down.

Occupants of each room developed their own system of how to sleep. Lt. Jeff Erwin slept next to Capt. Robert Wise, and the captain woke the lieutenant about six times a night for two months so Erwin would turn over and allow him to do the same. Another prisoner from Portsmouth, Ohio, Joel Adams, had a similar problem and remembers, "We laid on the floor and there would be so many men on each side of the room and the room was so small and crowded that we were forced to sleep on our side; if you wanted to change from your right to your left side you had to wake up all the men in the room and change over from the right side to the left side or vice versa."

The foulest sanitary conditions imaginable prevailed at Death Valley. Only a few half-full latrines were available for thousands of men. No shovels were available to dig new holes. Even if they had been, the ground was so frozen that a weak man with a spade wouldn't have been able to dent it. The call of nature was absolute, and Dr. (Capt.) William Shadish described the situation: "The men defecated on the ground at will, a lot of them because they couldn't help it. Diarrhea was very severe at that time, and explosive, so it was a very marked picture of not being able to find a square yard of ground without material on it. This was all frozen, of course, but it was a very potentially dangerous situation and I am sure the men walked in this material and took it into the rooms, and it was bad. Some of the men with severe diarrhea never made it out of the room."

Prisoners tried to stay in the crowded rooms at all times. If they did go out into the frigid daylight, they returned as quickly as possible. Boredom was not a problem, however, because men were busy watching for, picking, and killing lice. This parasite survived the dreadful winter by clinging to the grubby bodies of the men. There were thousands upon thousands of them, and, Doctor Shadish recalled, "You could see [a man's] collar just walking away with lice." In Lieutenant Erwin's room, POW's removed their clothing twice a day, according to the lieutenant, "to pick the lice off to keep them from eating you up. They would take blood out of you which we all knew and realized could not be replaced on the diet that we were on."

The food given to the three thousand confined Americans was cracked corn and only cracked corn, the same thing put into bird feeders or fed to chickens. Every man received about ten ounces a day. At the end of each building was a small sunken kitchen, where the corn was prepared for the several hundred people in that building. Jeff Erwin, the volunteer cook for his barrack, would awaken about 3:30 every morning to get it started. A couple of GIs helped, but no one was really anxious to assist. It seemed to Erwin that "everyone had the idea that they had to husband their strength in order to survive."

In the kitchen was an iron pot, and the first thing that had to be done was fill that rusted receptacle with water. About a hundred yards away from the building was a very small, polluted stream, and they would take two old gourds from the kitchen and walk to the water. The frozen stream was used by many prisoners as a latrine. A space would be cleared of the waste, and with whatever as available they would pick through the ice, fill the gourds, and return to the kitchen. Brush would be gathered from around the barracks area and used to build a smoky fire under the pot. When the water eventually came to a boil, the corn was tossed in and cooked for about four hours or until it became soft enough to chew and digest.

The mush was served by Erwin, and he made certain that everyone received exactly the same amount. In that abandoned mining camp, there was nothing to eat from and nothing to eat with. Men used whatever they could find to contain their food — often their caps — and they picked at it with their fingers. Those without any head covering cupped their hands, brought the soft pulp to their bearded faces, and slurped.

Ten ounces of corn mush a day was starvation fare, and every particle was precious. As captives ate, they guarded themselves and their food. "The men were more or less down to an animal stage," Erwin remembered. "They would sit and watch with a wolfish look and if a man was unable to eat — or anything like that, they would always grab it away from him." As many as twenty Americans died daily. Death Valley, North Korea, is the graveyard of perhaps five hundred young U.S. soldiers.

As for health care, the camp had two captured doctors, although, according to Erwin, "there is nothing in God's world they could do for anyone except give them a little sympathy." Doctor Shadish had a few rolls of bandages that he washed and used again and again, a hundred aspirin, a hundred sulfaguanidine tablets for diarrhea, and 150 sulfadiazine tablets. That was it. The camp also had a nominal hospital, but prisoners sent there were as good as dead (the POWs called it the "death house"). The long, mud-covered former cowshed had paper-draped windows and no heat. . . .

Bodies were stacked in the camp like cordwood, and all were naked. The moment someone died, the corpse would be stripped of everything. As Erwin pointed out, "We were facing reality." There was no point in leaving dead men with any item of clothing that the living could use to remain alive. Death Valley not only stripped men of their clothing but also of their civilization, and, finally, their lives. Death Valley was not unique. The same thing was occurring at numerous collection points throughout North Korea during the winter of 1950 and 1951.

Lt. Col. Paul E. Kantwill & Maj. Sean Watts, *Hostile Protected Persons or "Extra-Conventional Persons": How Unlawful Combatants in the War on Terrorism Posed Extraordinary Challenges for Military Attorneys and Commanders*
28 FORDHAM INT'L L.J. 681, 736-39 (2005)

[The United States was much criticized for failing to plan adequately for the challenges of dealing with detainees in the wars launched after the 9/11 terrorist attacks. This excerpt reveals some of the legal preparation that did take place, and some of the military and political difficulties that faced judge advocates in planning for lawful management of detainees and interrogation.]

As early as the fall of 2002, judge advocates began to prepare for what they anticipated to be a belligerent occupation of Iraq. In preparation for this eventually, they set about acquiring as many legal resources and as much legal history as they could find: they went so far as to contact the JAG School Librarian in order to acquire documents related to World War II occupation experiences in Germany and Japan. They included occupation issues in the military exercises preceding their deployment into the Iraqi theater and, based on assumptions that they would encounter common criminals and other detainees in addition to enemy prisoners of war, judge advocates wrote one of the first orders issued by the U.S. Army's Fifth U.S. Corps, establishing a detention system.

Among other provisions, this order specifically applied the Geneva Conventions, and borrowing from approaches previously used by U.S. judge advocates in Kosovo, also established a magistrate review requirement within twenty-one days of detention. This order grew eventually into a much more comprehensive effort that, in August 2003, established capture/detention cards, created Article 78, Geneva Convention IV review and appeal boards, produced internment orders, and implemented a criminal review board that effectively functioned as a provost court (by establishing maximum time served limits for administrative release). It appears that this was the first time that Article 78 boards and processes had ever been implemented.

If actual combat operations with a high contracting Party to the Conventions were not enough to raise the prospect of application of the Fourth Geneva Convention, then a de facto occupation, coupled with the prospect of processing, detaining and interrogating thousands of Iraqi and other captured personnel, certainly brought the Fourth Convention to the fore. At this point, the questions raised by failure to address the Fourth Geneva Convention at policy levels, such as whether unlawful combatants should be regarded as extra-conventional persons, became too large to ignore. They manifested themselves overtly within the context of detainee operations. Judge advocates, with no guidance from within the theater of operations or from outside, sought to provide the answers.

Since the majority of Fourth Geneva Convention-related issues manifested themselves in the area of detainee operations, judge advocates chose affirmatively to insert themselves into the process through attempts at the formulation of local policies regarding detainees. It is of paramount importance to note that, prior to judge advocates' involvement in policy formulation, there were no such policies in place. It is also important to note that they were not requested or tasked to formulate such policies. Rather, they noted an absence of guidance and were therefore concerned that some limitations should be placed on prospective detention activities. Lastly, it appears that legal personnel in theater did not review or employ several of the more controversial documents, such as the "Gonzales Memo" and the DOD Working Group Report.

Perhaps more important than anything else, however, were the legal premises from which they began their efforts. From all available evidence, it was clear that judge advocates took the view from the outset of operations in Iraq that the nature of the conflict was international armed conflict and that the Third and Fourth Geneva Conventions were therefore applicable. Indeed, the senior military attorney for Combined Joint Task Force 7 in Iraq testified that, in his view, the totality of the Third and Fourth Geneva Conventions applied to occupation operations in Iraq. As a consequence of this determination, individuals who failed to meet the criteria to be accorded POW status under Article 4 of the Third Geneva Convention remained protected persons under the Fourth Convention.

Because no preexisting policies or guidance reflected these views, judge advocates began to draft policies for their commanders and supported units. In a series of draft internal memoranda, judge advocates articulated clearly that operations were being conducted in a theater of war in which the Geneva Conventions were applicable. The policies expressly advised that Coalition forces treat all persons under their control humanely, ensuring that the rights of protected persons were preserved. Exhibiting an appreciation of the law regarding protected persons under the Fourth Geneva Convention, draft policies also contained language regarding derogations under Article 5 of the Fourth Convention, providing, in essence, that detainees who posed security risks to the Coalition may be regarded as having forfeited rights of communication.

By the time that these drafts were finally approved, the local policies bore little resemblance to public perceptions of their contents. As noted above, the policies, as approved, invoked specifically the application of the Geneva Conventions, going so far as to cite specific articles of the Fourth Geneva Convention. The policies opined exactly that detainees were protected persons under the purview of the Fourth Geneva Convention and discussed the possible use of derogations under Article 5.

Lastly . . . the policies attempted to set clear controls and limits on interrogation approaches and techniques — limiting approved techniques to those approved by Army Field Manuals (after extensive legal review at the highest levels long before the instant conflict) for use on prisoners of war, who receive the highest protections under international law. Ultimately, the policies employed from October 2003 through May 2004, were much more conservative in approach and protections than even the Field Manual, which, as noted above, contemplated application to prisoners of war. They also installed unprecedented oversight and control measures.

NOTES AND QUESTIONS

1. Sociologist Donald Black famously wrote that "[l]aw is stronger where other social control is weaker. Law varies inversely with other social control." DONALD BLACK, THE BEHAVIOR OF LAW 107 (1976). What sort of social control is at work during times of war? What kind of justice system ought to operate during military operations? Should the system differ from that in effect during periods of relative peace?

2. Who should make legal decisions regarding the treatment of detainees: military or civilian lawyers? Who should review such decisions? What happened in World War II Hawa'i? On recent U.S. conflicts and detention, see Srividhya Ragavan & Michael S. Mireles, Jr., *The Status of Detainees from Iraq and Afghanistan*, 2005 UTAH L. REV. 619.

3. Legal scholar Louis Henkin argued in an influential book that by the late 20th century, the idea of rights had attained more universal acceptance than any other "idea of the good" in the history of ideas. LOUIS HENKIN, THE AGE OF RIGHTS (1990). What impact does this growing consensus on international human rights have on war and other military operations?

II. OBJECTIVES

The laws governing armed conflict and the behavior of armed persons evolved in response to shifts in society, culture, and politics. As models of governance and social norms changed, the status of soldiers and officers and the relationship of warriors to the state also changed. This section briefly historicizes the development of disciplinary codes and the laws of war. These selections reveal the tension between a desire to protect human rights and an imperative for victory, between aspirational codes of military conduct and the essential violence of armed conflict.

A. Early Codes of Conduct

Robert C. Stacey, *The Age of Chivalry,* in *The Laws of War: Constraints on Warfare in the Western World*
27-31 (Michael Howard, George J. Andreopoulus & Mark R. Shulman eds. 1994)

The Age of Chivalry . . . [is] an appropriate label for the years between roughly 1100 and 1500. Even the Age of Chivalry, however, began in Rome. . . . In Roman eyes, "every war needed justification. The best reason for going to war was defence of the frontiers, and almost as good, pacification of the barbarians living beyond the frontiers. Outside these reasons one risked an unjust war, and emperors had to be careful." But within these limits, the conduct of war was essentially unrestrained. Prisoners could be enslaved or massacred; plunder was general; and no distinction was recognized between combatants and noncombatants. Classical Latin, indeed, lacked even a word for a civilian. The merciless savagery of Roman war in this sense carried on into the invasion period of the fifth and sixth centuries. . . . This was a style of warfare that was appropriate only against a non-Roman enemy, and in the Middle Ages this came to mean that Christians ought only employ it against pagans, like the Muslims in the Holy Land or, in the sixteenth century, the aboriginal peoples of the New World. . . . [This philosophy celebrated] war by God's people for God's own purposes. . . . [S]o long as it was fought for pious ends, such warfare knew no effective limits. The wars of conquest which Charlemagne waged against the pagan Saxons during the eighth century thus qualified perfectly as a Roman war. After thirty years of plunder, massacre, mass enslavement, and mass deportations the Saxons finally saw the reasonableness of Christianity and agreed to accept Baptism at the hands of the Franks. . . .

Ecclesiastical efforts to restrain intra-Christian violence during the tenth and eleventh centuries did bear some fruit, however, and it is with them that we begin to see the modern outlines of the laws of war as these would emerge in the Age of Chivalry. Carolingian church councils issued a number of decrees which demanded that noble miscreants give up their belt of knighthood, their *cingulum militare*, as part of the punishment for their crimes. We see in these measures our first evidence that the bearing of arms was seen as a noble dignity connected with a code of conduct, the violation of which might cost a man his status as a warrior. . . .

[Changes in the society, politics, and the advent of the cavalry intensified warfare during the eleventh century.] With respect to the laws of war, two consequences followed from these developments. First, long-established but only dimly perceptible codes of noble conduct on the battlefield began to be applied to the knights as well. A greater number of fighters were now covered by these standards of honorable conduct. In 1066, for example, William the Conqueror expelled from his *militia* a knight who struck at the dead Harold's body on the battlefield with his sword. . . . [K]nighthood had clearly emerged by 1100 as an indissoluble amalgam of military profession and social rank that prescribed specific standards of behavior to its adherents in peace and war. The laws of war would develop in the Age of Chivalry as a codification of these noble, knightly customs on the battlefield. Second, however, the sharp division which this knightly elite now drew between itself as an order of *bellatores* and the rest of society made up on *oratores* or *laboratores* meant that the laws of war themselves applied only to other nobles. In theory, peasants and townspeople ought not to fight at all. . . . If such common men did fight — and in practice they did, regularly — then no mercy was owed them on the battlefield or off. In the ordinary circumstances of battle a knight ought not kill another knight if it was possible instead to capture him for ransom. Armed peasants and townsmen, however, could be massacred at will. . . .

As an enforceable body of defined military custom, the laws of war as we are discussing them emerged [] out of the interplay of knightly custom with Roman law as this was studied and applied in court from the twelfth century on. By the fourteenth century this combination of knightly practice and legal theory had given rise to a formal system of military law, *jus militaire*, the law of the *milites*, the Latin word for knights. The enforceability of this law, at least in the context of the Hundred Years War, needs to be stressed. Charges brought under the laws of arms were assigned to special military or royal courts — the Court of Chivalry in England, the Parlement of Paris in France — where lawyers refined and clarified its precepts in formal pleadings. Knights and, of course, heralds remained the experts in the laws of arms. Their testimony was sought both in defining the law and in applying it to specific cases, a reflection of the status of *jus militaire* as a body of international knightly custom. From the fourteenth century on several attempts were made to record these customs in writing, the most famous being Honoré Bouvet's *Tree of Battles*. Like all medieval lawbooks these were partial and tendentious with a bias toward kings. The real history of the laws of war in the Age of Chivalry is buried in the hundreds of court cases brought under it and in the scores of chroniclers accounts of the conduct of actual war . . .

Code of Articles of King Gustavus Adolphus of Sweden, 1621
William Winthrop, Military Law and Precedents
907-18 (2d ed. reprint 1920)

[The brilliant and powerful Gustavus Adolphus, who led Sweden in the Thirty Years War until his death on the battlefield in 1632, is often called the father of modern warfare for his legal, administrative, and strategic innovations. His code of military laws — 167 articles long — is often cited as the first example of a comprehensive code of soldierly conduct. It specified crimes, established two levels of courts and detailed their composition, permitted review of convictions, and required a record of proceedings be maintained. A few articles follow:]

Imprimis. No commander nor private Souldier whatsoever, shall use any kind of Idolatry, Witchcraft, or Inchanting of Armies, whereby God is dishonored, upon pain of death.

2. If any shall blaspheme the name of God, either drunk or sober, the thing being proven by two or three witnesses, he shall suffer death without mercy. . . .

19. Whosoever behaves not himself obediently unto our great Generall, or our Ambassador coming in our absence, as well as if we our selves were there in person present, shall be kept in irons or in prison until such time as he shall be brought to his answer, before a Council of Warre, where being found guilty, whether it were wilfully done or not, he shall stand to the order of the Court, to lay what punishment upon him they shall thinke convenient, according as the person and fact is.

20. And if any shall offer to discredit these great Officers by word of mouth or otherwise, and not be able by proof to make it good, hee shall be put to death without mercy. . . .

46. No Colonell or Captaine shall command his soldiers to doe any unlawful thing; which who so does, shall be punished according to the discretion of the Judges. Also if any Colonell or Captaine or other Officer whatsoever, shall by

rigour take any thing away from any common souldier, he shall answer for it before the Court. . . .

50. He that is taken a sleepe upon the watch, either in any strength, trench, or the like, shall be shot to death.

51. He that comes off his watch where he is commanded to keepe his Guard, or drinkes himself drunke upon his watch or space of Sentinell, shall be shot to death.

52. He that at the sound of Drumme or Trumpet repaires not to his Colours, shall be kept in irons.

53. When any march is to be made, every man that is sworn shall follow his Colours; who ever presumes without leave to stay behind shall be punished.

54. And if it be upon mutiny that they doe it, be they many or be they few, they shall die for it. . . .

76. Whosoever giveth advice unto the enemy any manner of way, shall die for it. . . .

85. He that forceth any woman to abuse her, and the matter bee proved, hee shall die for it. . . .

92. They that pillage or steal either in our Land or in the enemies, or from any of them that come to furnish our League or Strength, without leave, shall bee punish'd as for theft. . . .

144. All these Judges [of the military courts] shall under blue skies thus swear before Almighty God, that they will inviolably keep this following oath unto us: I.R.W. doe here promise before God upon his holy Gospell, that I both will and shall judge uprightly in all things according to the Lawes of God, of our Nation, and these Articles of Warre, so farre forth as it pleaseth Almighty God to give me understanding; neither will I for favour nor for hatred, for good will, feare, ill will, anger, or any gift or bribe whatsoever, judge wrongfully; but judge him free that ought to be free, and doom him guilty, that I finde guilty; as the Lord of Heaven and Earth shall help my soule and body at the last day. I shall hold this oath truly.

NOTES AND QUESTIONS

1. "I believe that it has always been understood that the defenders of a fortress stormed have no claim to quarter." The Duke of Wellington (British Field Marshal during the Napoleonic Wars), *quoted in* Geoffrey Parker, *Early Modern Europe, in* THE LAWS OF WAR: CONSTRAINTS ON WARFARE IN THE WESTERN WORLD 48 (Michael Howard, George J. Andreopoulus & Mark R. Shulman eds. 1994). "The soldier, be he friend or foe, is charged with the protection of the weak and unarmed. It is the very essence and reason for his being. When he violates his sacred trust, he not only profanes the entire cult but threatens the very fabric of international society." General Douglas MacArthur, *quoted in* PETER MAGUIRE, LAW AND WAR 139 (2000). Can these statements be reconciled?

2. Under the Geneva Conventions, the "rule of distinction" is a fundamental aspect of lawful warfare. This rule requires that a combatant harm only other combatants and that combatants distinguish themselves from non-combatants. Can you discern the origins of this rule in the code of chivalry to which knights subscribed? What are its limitations as a means of protecting innocents during armed conflict?

3. Who is least protected under these early codes? Who is most protected? What punishments can misbehaving soldiers expect?

4. What role does religious faith play in the legal system established by King Gustavus Adolphus? How does that role limit or enhance its effectiveness? For more background on Gustavus Adolphus and early military law, see JOSEPH W. BISHOP, JR., JUSTICE UNDER FIRE: A STUDY OF MILITARY LAW 1-19 (1974); Christopher W. Behan, *Don't Tug on Superman's Cape: In Defense of Convening Authority Selection and Appointment of Court-Martial Panel Members*, 176 MIL. L. REV. 190, 190-202 (2003).

B.   Modern Codes

Joseph W. Bishop, Jr., *Justice Under Fire: A Study of Military Law*
21-25 (1974)

[Reforms in civilian criminal procedure led some to doubt whether modern law still had room for a separate system of military justice. After the Vietnam War, criticism of the military was at a peak in the United States. That criticism led many to defend the separate system of U.S. military law. The following eloquent summary by a yale Law School professor typifies these responses; his arguments for preserving a military justice system are numbered, in the original, from 1 to 4.]

1. Military discipline cannot be maintained by the civilian criminal process, which is neither swift nor certain. . . . An army without discipline is in fact more dangerous to the civil population (including that of its own country) than to the enemy. The public interest in discipline is therefore entitled to greater weight, and the rights of the accused to lesser weight, in the military than in the civilian context. . . .

The best statement of the "military discipline" argument today might be that its demands justify a procedure that does not lessen the chance of unjust acquittal, while it need not, and should not, increase the possibility of unjust conviction. In civilian jurisprudence the number of guilty men who are not punished is far, far greater than the number of innocent men who are, and few of us would have it otherwise. But the doctrine that it is better that ninety-nine (or nine hundred and ninety-nine) guilty men go free than that one innocent be convicted is not easily squared with the need to maintain efficiency, obedience, and order in an army, which is an aggregation of men (mostly in the criminally prone age brackets) who have strong appetites, strong passions, and ready access to deadly weapons. Moreover, there are some types of conduct — desertion and insubordination, for example — which are not crimes at all in the civilian life but whose deterrence is essential to the very existence of an army. . . .

2. Another aspect of the discipline argument: Since discipline is a responsibility of the military commander, he should have some control of the machinery by which it is enforced — to decide, for instance, whether a particular offender should be prosecuted and what degree of clemency will best promote the efficiency of his command.

3. Military offenses — absence without leave, desertion, insubordination, cowardice, mutiny, and the like — have no civilian analogues: The adjudication of guilt or innocence and the assessment of appropriate punishment may require experience and knowledge not commonly possessed by civilian judges and jurors.

4. Soldiers may be stationed and commit crimes in places outside the jurisdiction of American civilian courts. There is probably no constitutional reason why federal district courts could not be given jurisdiction to try soldiers for offenses committed in foreign countries. . . . But Congress has never attempted to exercise its power to give the federal courts jurisdiction over crimes committed by American servicemen outside the United States. One obvious reason is the difficulty of bringing before a court sitting in this country witnesses who live thousands of miles away. Both the ends of justice and of the public fisc are better served if a trial can be held in the place where the crime was committed.

Elizabeth Lutes Hillman, *Defending America: Military Culture and the Cold War Court-Martial*
30-31 (2005)

[In the United States, the greatest reform of military law occurred with the adoption of the Uniform Code of Military Justice (UCMJ) in 1950. The UCMJ's reforms were both welcomed and resisted; the following excerpt suggests some of the barriers to justice even under modernized military codes.]

Perhaps the most fundamental barrier to military legal reform was the violence and disorder of armed conflict. Attending to the niceties of due process during the heat of combat seemed misguided, if not ridiculous, to many commanders. Summary justice — written out of military legal practice by the UCMJ — rarely seemed more appropriate than in punishing crime in the midst of war, especially crime that rose to the level of wartime atrocities. Like other modern legal systems, procedural justice under the UCMJ did not make exceptions for crimes of war. Commanding officers and military lawyers had to abide by the rules set out in the UCMJ any time a court-martial was convened, even in theaters of combat. The tension between war and law — between battlefield necessity and due process, between the order to kill and the act of murder, between the serial use of a prostitute and a gang rape — structured the military's attempts to mark the fine line that separates crime from duty.

The demands of war made upholding the standards of military due process more difficult for both judge advocates and commanding officers. . . . Combat units faced the most pressure to conserve resources, but finding the time and effort required to follow legal procedures was difficult even for units far from the front lines. Shortages of personnel and materiel, rapid increase in troop strength, and the stress and danger of war competed with the UCMJ's emphasis on legal counsel, record-keeping, and other accoutrements of procedural justice.

The chaos of wartime also created disciplinary problems that were difficult to address with criminal prosecution. For example, a staggering criminal docket overwhelmed the brand-new military justice system during the Korean War. . . . Nearly one million courts-martial were held between 1950 and 1953, including 48,000 general courts. During wartime, soldiers were more likely to lack military experience and more likely to face extreme stress, both of which created more disciplinary problems. The deprivations and indignities of war led to unauthorized absence, alcohol and drug abuse, and minor disciplinary offenses. Crimes as well as tragic accidents occurred when soldiers, bored and lonely, fought among themselves. . . . As awkward as criminal prosecution could become during war, it was more needed than ever.

NOTES AND QUESTIONS

1. Sun Tzu wrote in THE ART OF WAR that "[t]he Commander stands for the virtues of wisdom, sincerely, benevolence, courage and strictness." Modern systems of military justice often limit the commander's ability to control the process and outcomes of military justice. What is lost when the commander is constrained by the demands of due process of law? What is gained?

2. Do you agree with Professor Bishop's arguments about the unsuitability of civilian criminal courts to enforce military justice? Would efficiency and justice both be served if military courts tried all military offenses plus civilian crimes committed outside the United States, leaving civilian jurisdictions to prosecute ordinary crime among servicemembers?

3. Some U.S. military leaders lamented the UCMJ's impact on military discipline and effectiveness. In a law journal article published after the war in Vietnam ended, General William C. Westmoreland and Major General George S. Prugh, former commander of Military Assistance Command-Vietnam and former Judge Advocate General of the Army, respectively, concluded "that the Uniform Code of Military Justice is not capable of performing its intended role in times of military stress. . . . It is presently too slow, too cumbersome, too uncertain, indecisive, and lacking in the power to reinforce accomplishment of the military mission, to deter misconduct, or even to rehabilitate." *Judges in Command: The Judicialized Uniform Code of Military Justice in Combat*, 3 HARV. J. L. & PUB. POL'Y 1, 53 (1980); *see also, e.g.*, GARY D. SOLIS, MARINES AND MILITARY LAW IN VIETNAM: TRIAL BY FIRE 241-44 (1989). Should the perspectives of senior military leaders (and lawyers) be heeded by the civilian legislators responsible for military codes? Should due process carry a different meaning in the midst of battle than it does in the miles of office corridors at the Pentagon? Does it? "[I]t will be a grave error if by negligence we permit the military law to become emasculated by allowing lawyers to inject into it principles derived from their practices in the civil courts which belong to a totally different system of jurisprudence." William Tecumseh Sherman, general in the U.S. Army during the Civil War, quoted in John S. Cooke, *Manual for Courts-Martial 20X, reprinted in* EVOLVING MILITARY JUSTICE 177 (Eugene R. Fidell & Dwight H. Sullivan, eds. 2002).

Chapter 2

SOURCES OF LAW

Military justice rests on sources of law that are at least as diverse as those found in the civilian courts. While the precise reach of the Constitution in courts-martial has not been charted, it is now beyond dispute that important areas of constitutional doctrine do apply in courts-martial. On the other hand, it is also generally recognized that at least some constitutional rules may apply in different ways in a military setting. For example, what constitutes a reasonable expectation of privacy for purposes of the Fourth Amendment's protection against unreasonable search and seizure may be quite different in a barracks than in a law school dormitory.

Below the constitutional level, Congress has enacted comprehensive military justice legislation — the Uniform Code of Military Justice — and has provided in other statutes that their provisions do or do not apply to courts-martial. The UCMJ, however, leaves a great deal of the specifics required for the administration of military justice to Executive Branch regulation. The Manual for Courts-Martial fills in many of the blanks, but much remains for interstitial lawmaking by the service secretaries through separate regulations. To make matters even more complicated, a plethora of service regulations must be consulted, since the military is a pervasively regulated society in which countless officials enjoy the power to make rules. These can be as lofty as the Secretary of Defense or as lowly as the commanding officer of a small unit or vessel.

Nor is this all, for military justice also at times requires resort to the statutes, rules and case law applied in the federal district courts; to customs of the service that are nowhere written down; to foreign and state law; and to treaty-based and customary international law, including but not limited to international humanitarian law and human rights law.

I. CONSTITUTIONAL, STATUTORY, AND REGULATORY PROVISIONS

United States Constitution
Article 1, Section 8

The Congress shall have power to . . . provide for the common defense and general welfare of the United States . . .

To declare war, grant letters of marque and reprisal, and make rules concerning captures on land and water;

To raise and support armies, but no appropriation of money to that use shall be for a longer term than two years;

To provide and maintain a navy;

To make rules for the government and regulation of the land and naval forces;

To provide for calling forth the militia to execute the laws of the union, suppress insurrections and repel invasions;

To provide for organizing, arming, and disciplining, the militia, and for governing such part of them as may be employed in the service of the United States, reserving to the states respectively, the appointment of the officers, and the authority of training the militia according to the discipline prescribed by Congress; . . . .

To make all laws which shall be necessary and proper for carrying into execution the foregoing powers, and all other powers vested by this Constitution in the government of the United States, or in any department or officer thereof.

Article I, Section 9

. . . The privilege of the writ of habeas corpus shall not be suspended, unless when in cases of rebellion or invasion the public safety may require it.

. . . No state shall, without the consent of Congress . . . keep troops, or ships of war in time of peace, enter into any agreement or compact with another state, or with a foreign power, or engage in war, unless actually invaded, or in such imminent danger as will not admit of delay.

Article II, Section 2

The President shall be commander in chief of the Army and Navy of the United States, and of the militia of the several states, when called into the actual service of the United States; he may require the opinion, in writing, of the principal officer in each of the executive departments, upon any subject relating to the duties of their respective offices, and he shall have power to grant reprieves and pardons for offenses against the United States, except in cases of impeachment.

He . . . by and with the advice and consent of the Senate, shall appoint ambassadors, other public ministers and consuls, judges of the Supreme Court, and all other officers of the United States, whose appointments are not herein otherwise provided for, and which shall be established by law: but the Congress may by law vest the appointment of such inferior officers, as they think proper, in the President alone, in the courts of law, or in the heads of departments.

Second Amendment

A well regulated militia, being necessary to the security of a free state, the right of the people to keep and bear arms, shall not be infringed.

Third Amendment

No soldier shall, in time of peace be quartered in any house, without the consent of the owner, nor in time of war, but in a manner to be prescribed by law.

Fifth Amendment

No person shall be held to answer for a capital, or otherwise infamous crime, unless on a presentment or indictment of a Grand Jury, except in cases arising in the land or naval forces, or in the Militia, when in actual service, in time of War, or public danger. . . .

Uniform Code of Military Justice, Article 36, 10 U.S.C. § 836

Article 36. President may prescribe rules.

(a) Pretrial, trial, and post trial procedures, including modes of proof, for cases arising under this chapter triable in courts-martial, military commissions and other military tribunals, and procedures for courts of inquiry, may be prescribed by the President by regulations which shall, so far as he considers practicable, apply the principles of law and the rules of evidence generally recognized in the trial of criminal cases in the United States district courts, but which may not, except as provided in chapter 47A of this title, be contrary to or inconsistent with this chapter.

(b) All rules and regulations made under this article shall be uniform insofar as practicable, except insofar as applicable to military commissions established under chapter 47A of this title.

Manual for Courts-Martial, United States (2005 ed.)

Preamble ¶ 1. Sources of military jurisdiction

The sources of military jurisdiction include the Constitution and international law. International law includes the law of war.

Military Rules of Evidence

Rule 101. Scope

. . . .

(b) Secondary sources. If not otherwise prescribed in this Manual or these rules, and insofar as practicable and not inconsistent with or contrary to the code or this Manual, courts-martial shall apply:

(1) First, the rules of evidence generally recognized in the trial of criminal cases in the United States district courts; and

(2) Second, when not inconsistent with subdivision (b)(1), the rules of evidence at common law.

Rule 1102. Amendments

(a) Amendments to the Federal Rules of Evidence shall apply to the Military Rules of Evidence 18 months after the effective date of such amendments, unless action to the contrary is taken by the President.

(b) *Rules Determined Not To Apply.* The President has determined that the following Federal Rules of Evidence do not apply to the Military Rules of Evidence: Rules 301, 302, 415, and 902(12).

II. THE CONSTITUTION AND MILITARY JUSTICE

Earl Warren, *The Bill of Rights and the Military*,
37 N.Y.U. L. REV. 181, 181-85 (1962)

It is almost a commonplace to say that free government is on trial for its life. But it is the truth. And it has been so throughout history. What is almost as certain: It will probably be true throughout the foreseeable future. Why should this be so? Why is it that, over the centuries of world history, the right to liberty that our Declaration of Independence declares to be "inalienable" has been more often abridged than enforced?

One important reason, surely, is that the members of a free society are called upon to bear an extraordinarily heavy responsibility, for such a society is based upon the reciprocal self-imposed discipline of both the governed and their government. Many nations in the past have attempted to develop democratic institutions, only to lose them when either the people or their government lapsed from the rigorous self-control that is essential to the maintenance of a proper relation between freedom and order. Such failures have produced the totalitarianism or the anarchy that, however masked, are the twin mortal enemies of an ordered liberty.

Our forebears, well understanding this problem, sought to solve it in unique fashion by incorporating the concept of mutual restraint into our Nation's basic Charter. In the body of our Constitution, the Founding Fathers insured that the Government would have the power necessary to govern. Most of them felt that the self-discipline basic to a democratic government of delegated powers was implicit in that document in the light of our Anglo-Saxon heritage. But our people wanted explicit assurances. The Bill of Rights was the result.

This act of political creation was a remarkable beginning. It was only that, of course, for every generation of Americans must preserve its own freedoms. In so doing, we must turn time and again to the political consensus that is our heritage. Nor should we confine ourselves to examining the diverse, complicated, and sometimes subordinate issues that arise in the day-to-day application of the Bill of Rights. It is perhaps more important that we seek to understand in its fullness the nature of the spirit of liberty that gave that document its birth.

Thus it is in keeping with the high purposes of this great University that its School of Law sponsor a series of lectures emphasizing the role of the Bill of Rights in contemporary American life. And it is particularly appropriate, after the splendid lectures of Mr. Justice Black and Mr. Justice Brennan on the relationship of the Bill of Rights to the Federal and State Governments, respectively, that you should delegate to someone the task of discussing the relationship of the Bill of Rights to the military establishment. This is a relationship that, perhaps more than any other, has rapidly assumed increasing importance because of changing domestic and world conditions. I am honored to undertake the assignment, not because I claim any expertise in the field, but because I want to cooperate with you in your contribution to the cause of preserving the spirit as well as the letter of the Bill of Rights.

Determining the proper role to be assigned to the military in a democratic society has been a troublesome problem for every nation that has aspired to a free political life. The military establishment is of course, a necessary organ of government; but the reach of its power must be carefully limited lest the delicate balance between freedom and order be upset. The maintenance of the balance is made more difficult by the fact that while the military serves the vital function of preserving the existence of the nation, it is, at the same time, the one element of government that exercises a type of authority not easily assimilated in a free society.

The critical importance of achieving a proper accommodation is apparent when one considers the corrosive effect upon liberty of exaggerated military power. In the last analysis, it is the military — or at least a militant organization of power — that dominates life in totalitarian countries regardless of their nominal political arrangements. This is true, moreover, not only with respect to Iron Curtain countries, but also with respect to many countries that have all of the formal trappings of constitutional democracy.

Not infrequently in the course of its history the Supreme Court has been called upon to decide issues that bear directly upon the relationship between action taken in the name of the military and the protected freedoms of the Bill of Rights. I would like to discuss here some of the principal factors that have shaped the Court's response. From a broad perspective, it may be said that the questions raised in these cases are all variants of the fundamental problem: Whether the disputed exercise of power is compatible with preservation of the freedoms intended to be insulated by the Bill of Rights.

I believe it is reasonably clear that the Court, in cases involving a substantial claim that protected freedoms have been infringed in the name of military requirements, has consistently recognized the relevance of a basic group of principles. For one, of course, the Court has adhered to its mandate to safeguard freedom from excessive encroachment by governmental authority. In these cases, the Court's approach is reinforced by the American tradition of the separation of the military establishment from, and its subordination to, civil authority. On the other hand, the action in question is generally defended in the name of military necessity, or, to put it another way, in the name of national survival. I suggest that it is possible to discern in the Court's decisions a reasonably consistent pattern for the resolution of these competing claims, and more, that this pattern furnishes a sound guide for the future. Moreover, these decisions reveal, I believe, that while the judiciary plays an important role in this area, it is subject to certain significant limitations, with the result that other organs of government and the people themselves must bear a most heavy responsibility.

Before turning to some of the keystone decisions of the Court, I think it desirable to consider for a moment the principle of separation and subordination of the military establishment, for it is this principle that contributes in a vital way to a resolution of the problems engendered by the existence of a military establishment in a free society.

It is significant that in our own hemisphere only our neighbor, Canada, and we ourselves have avoided rule by the military throughout our national existences. This is not merely happenstance. A tradition has been bred into us that the perpetuation of free government depends upon the continued supremacy of the civilian representatives of the people. To maintain this supremacy has always been a preoccupation of all three branches of our government. To strangers this might seem odd, since our country was born in war. It was the military that, under almost unbearable conditions, carried the burden of the Revolution and made possible our existence as a Nation.

But the people of the colonies had long been subjected to the intemperance of military power. Among the grievous wrongs of which they complained in the Declaration of Independence were that the King had subordinated the civil power to the military, that he had quartered troops among them in times of peace, and that through his mercenaries he had committed other cruelties. Our War of the Revolution was, in good measure, fought as a protest against standing armies. Moreover, it was fought largely with a civilian army, the militia, and its great Commander-in-Chief was a civilian at heart. After the War, he resigned his commission and returned to civilian life. In an emotion-filled appearance before the Congress, his resignation was accepted by its President, Thomas Mifflin, who, in a brief speech, emphasized Washington's qualities of leadership and, above all, his abiding respect for civil authority. This trait was probably best epitomized when, just prior to the War's end, some of his officers urged Washington to establish a monarchy, with himself at its head. He not only turned a deaf ear to their blandishments, but his reply, called by historian Edward Channing "possibly, the grandest single thing in his whole career," stated that nothing had given him more painful sensations than the information that such notions existed in the army, and that he thought their proposal "big with the greatest mischiefs that can befall my Country."

Such thoughts were uppermost in the minds of the Founding Fathers when they drafted the Constitution. Distrust of a standing army was expressed by many. Recognition of the danger from Indians and foreign nations caused them to authorize a national armed force begrudgingly. Their viewpoint is well summarized in the language of James Madison, whose name we honor in these lectures:

> The veteran legions of Rome were an overmatch for the undisciplined valor of all other nations, and rendered her the mistress of the world. Not the less true is it, that the liberties of Rome proved the final victim of her military triumphs; and that the liberties of Europe, as far as they ever existed, have, with few exceptions, been the price of her military establishments. A standing force, therefore, is a dangerous, at the same time that it may be a necessary, provision. On the smallest scale it has its inconveniences. On an extensive scale its consequences may be fatal. On any scale it is an object of laudable circumspection and precaution. A wise nation will combine all these considerations; and, whilst it does not rashly preclude itself from any resource which may become essential to its safety, will exert all its prudence in diminishing both the necessity and the danger of resorting to one which may be inauspicious to its liberties.

Their apprehensions found expression in the diffusion of the war powers granted the Government by the Constitution. The President was made the Commander-in-Chief of the armed forces. But Congress was given the power to provide for the common defense, to declare war, to make rules for the Government and regulation of the land and naval forces, and to raise and support armies, with the added precaution that no appropriation could be made for the latter purpose for longer than two years at a time — as an antidote to a standing army. Further, provision was made for organizing and calling for the state militia to execute the laws of the Nation in times of emergency.

Despite these safeguards, the people were still troubled by the recollection of the conditions that prompted the charge of the Declaration of Independence that the King had "effected to render the military independent and superior to the civil power." They were reluctant to ratify the Constitution without further assurances, and thus we find in the Bill of Rights Amendments 2 and 3, specifically authorizing a decentralized militia, guaranteeing the right of the people to keep and bear arms, and prohibiting the quartering of troop in any house in time of peace without the consent of the owner. Other Amendments guarantee the right of the people to assemble, to be secure in their homes against unreasonable searches and seizures, and in criminal cases to be accorded a speedy and public trial by an impartial jury after indictment in the district and state wherein the crime was committed. The only exceptions made to these civilian trial procedures are for cases arising in the land and naval forces. Although there is undoubtedly room for argument based on the frequently conflicting sources of history, it is not unreasonable to believe that our Founders' determination to guarantee the pre-eminence of civil over military power was an important element that prompted adoption of the Constitutional Amendments we call the Bill of Rights.

DAVIS v. UNITED STATES
Supreme Court of the United States
512 U.S. 452 (1994)

[Davis claimed that his court-martial conviction was invalid because Navy investigators continued to interrogate him after he stated "Maybe I should talk to a lawyer." The Court, in an opinion by Justice O'Connor, affirmed the decision of the Court of Military Appeals, applying garden-variety constitutional rules on custodial interrogations. The following appeared in a footnote.]

We have never had occasion to consider whether the Fifth Amendment privilege against self incrimination, or the attendant right to counsel during custodial interrogation, applies of its own force to the military, and we need not do so here. The President, exercising his authority to prescribe procedures for military criminal proceedings, *see* Art. 36(a), UCMJ, 10 U.S.C. § 836(a), has decreed that statements obtained in violation of the Self Incrimination Clause are generally not admissible at trials by court martial. Mil. Rules Evid. 304(a) and (c)(3). Because the Court of Military Appeals has held that our cases construing the Fifth Amendment right to counsel apply to military interrogations and control the admissibility of evidence at trials by court martial, *see, e.g., United States* v. *McLaren*, 38 M.J. 112, 115 (1993); *United States* v.

Applewhite, 23 M.J. 196, 198 (1987), and the parties do not contest this point, we proceed on the assumption that our precedents apply to courts martial just as they apply to state and federal criminal prosecutions.

UNITED STATES v. TULLOCH
United States Court of Appeals for the Armed Forces
47 M.J. 283 (C.A.A.F. 1997)

[The Army Court of Criminal Appeals held that the military judge erred by failing to establish a proper record before overruling Pvt. Tulloch's objection to trial counsel's peremptory challenge of an African-American member of the court-martial panel. One of the issues the Judge Advocate General certified to the Court of Appeals was whether the lower court erred in shifting to the government the ultimate burden of persuasion as to discriminatory intent and thereby violated the principle that the burden in such challenges rests with, and never shifts from, the opponent of the strike under *Purkett v. Elem*, 514 U.S. 765 (1995).]

EFFRON, JUDGE:

A. The Constitutional Framework

In *Swain v. Alabama*, 380 U.S. 202 (1965), the Supreme Court addressed the tension between the prosecution's historic privilege to exercise peremptory challenges unfettered by "judicial control" and "the constitutional prohibition on exclusion of persons from jury service on account of race." *See Batson v. Kentucky*, 476 U.S. 79, 91, *citing* 380 U.S. at 214-24; U.S. Const., amend. 14 (Equal Protection Clause). The Court held in *Swain* that it was appropriate to presume that a prosecutor had properly exercised the State's challenges, and it declined to examine the prosecutor's actions in the case under review. The Court noted, however, that a defendant could rebut the presumption through proof that the prosecutor had used challenges to exclude persons on the basis of race by showing, for example, a repeated pattern "in case after case." 380 U.S. at 223-24.

Twenty-one years later, the Court in *Batson* concluded that *Swain* had "placed upon defendants a crippling burden of proof" that had rendered prosecutors' use of peremptory challenges "largely immune from constitutional scrutiny." 476 U.S. at 92-93. The Court, in light of evolving standards of proof in other areas of the law involving allegations of discrimination, established new procedures for considering an alleged discriminatory use of peremptory challenges by the prosecution.

First, the "defendant may establish a *prima facie* case of purposeful discrimination" based "solely on evidence concerning the prosecutor's exercise of peremptory challenges at the defendant's trial." The defendant "must show that he" or she "is a member of a cognizable racial group, . . . that the prosecutor has exercised peremptory challenges to remove" members of that group from the jury, and that "these facts and any other relevant" circumstances "raise an inference that the prosecutor" excluded persons from the jury on account of race, such as "a 'pattern' of strikes" or the prosecutor's statements and questions during *voir dire* and while exercising challenges. 476 U.S. at 96-97.

Second, once the defendant has established a *prima facie* case, "the burden shifts to the" Government "to come forward with a neutral explanation" for the challenge, related to the particular case to be tried. The "explanation need not rise to the level" of justification for a challenge for cause, but the prosecutor may not merely deny "that he had a discriminatory motive" or affirm that the challenges were exercised in "good faith." 476 U.S. at 97-98.

Third, the trial court must determine whether "the defendant has established purposeful discrimination." *Id.*

The Supreme Court declined to formulate specific procedures to implement its holding "[i]n light of the variety of jury selection practices followed in our state and federal trial courts. . . ." *Id.* at 99 n.24.

B. Application of the Constitutional Framework to Trials under the Uniform Code of Military Justice

"[T]he protections in the Bill of Rights, except those which are expressly or by necessary implication inapplicable, are available to members of our armed forces." *United States v. Jacoby*, 11 U.S.C.M.A. 428, 430-31, 29 C.M.R. 244, 246-47 (1960). In *United States v. Santiago-Davila*, 26 M.J. 380 (1988), we considered whether the prohibition against discriminatory use of peremptory challenges in jury selection, as set forth in *Batson*'s equal-protection analysis, should be applied to use of peremptory challenges in courts-martial. *Cf. Frontiero v. Richardson*, 411 U.S. 677, 680 (1973) (the concept of equal protection of the laws applies to members of the armed forces through the Due Process Clause of the Fifth Amendment). We recognized that servicemembers do not have the right in a court-martial to a jury panel drawn from a representative cross-section of the population, 26 M.J. at 389, *citing* Art. 25, UCMJ, 10 U.S.C. § 825, but we noted that *Batson* was based on the "equal-protection right to be tried by a jury from which no 'cognizable racial group' ha[d] been excluded," not on the Sixth Amendment right to trial by jury. *Id.* at 389-90. We found no reason to exclude members of the armed forces from the protections of *Batson*, observing that

> even if we were not bound by *Batson*, the principle it espouses should be followed in the administration of military justice. In our American society, the Armed Services have been a leader in eradicating racial discrimination. With this history in mind, we are sure that Congress never intended to condone the use of a government peremptory challenge for the purpose of excluding a "cognizable racial group."

26 M.J. at 390. . . .

C. Nature of the Explanation

In *Purkett v. Elem*, 514 U.S. 765 (1995), the Supreme Court set forth the standard for reviewing whether a prosecutor has provided a permissible race-neutral explanation for a peremptory challenge after the defense has established a *prima facie* case of racial discrimination. The Court noted that the prosecutor was not required to offer an explanation that "is persuasive or even plausible." *Id.* at 768, *citing Hernandez v. New York*, 500 U.S. 352, 360 (1991) (plurality opinion). The Court held that any race-neutral explanation, such as the prospective juror's long hair, was permissible and that there is no requirement for the prosecutor to offer "a reason that makes sense." *Id.* at 769. According to the Court, it is inappropriate to focus on "the reasonableness of the asserted nonracial motive" rather than on "the geniuneness of the motive." *Id.* at 769.

The issue before us in the present case is how to apply *Purkett*, a rule fashioned for a civilian jury system, in the military context. As the Court of Military Review noted in *Moore*, a civilian jury is derived from a representative, randomly selected cross-section of the population. Few, if any, of the prospective jurors are likely to be known by counsel. In civilian trials, numerous peremptory challenges are provided to each party as a means of selecting the final composition of the jury.

In military life, the court-martial panel is selected by the convening authority on the basis of a best-qualified standard. All members selected by the convening authority serve on the panel unless removed through a challenge for cause, exercise of the one peremptory challenge generally permitted to each party (*see* Art. 41(b), UCMJ, 10 U.S.C. § 841(b)), or under the military judge's limited power to excuse a member.

In contrast to a prospective civilian juror, who is not required to possess any significant degree of education, experience, or judicial temperament, the military member comes to the court-martial panel cloaked with the designation by a senior commander, the convening authority, that the member is "best qualified for the duty by reason of age, education, training, experience, length of service, and judicial temperament." Art. 25(d)(2).

Purkett reflects the Supreme Court's sensitivity to the fact that in civilian life — where there are virtually no qualifications for jury service — instinct necessarily plays a significant role in the use of peremptory challenges to ensure that both the Government and the accused are able to present the case to jurors capable of understanding it and rendering a fair verdict. While instinct serves any counsel, civilian or military, who is seeking to shape a jury, there is a less compelling need for counsel in courts-martial to exercise such challenges in order to ensure that panel members are qualified, because the convening authority already has taken that into account in exercising his responsibilities under Article 25 to select members on the basis of a "best-qualified" standard.

The Court of Military Review in [*United States v.*] *Moore* [28 M.J. 366 (C.M.A. 1989)] carefully considered the differences between military and civilian tribunals and held that trial counsel must offer "a reasonable, racially neutral explanation." 26 M.J. at 701. To the extent that *Purkett* suggests that unreasonable or implausible explanations may suffice in civilian society, we adhere to the analysis of the differences in military and civilian tribunals in both the lower court opinion and our own opinion in *Moore*.

In *Moore*, we declined to apply the Supreme Court's *Batson* procedure for determining whether there is a *prima facie* case of discrimination. Today we hold that the same reasons require us to apply a different standard for assessing the validity of trial counsel's proffered race-neutral explanation. Once the convening authority has designated a servicemember as "best qualified" to serve on a court-martial panel, trial counsel may not strike that person on the basis of a proffered reason, under *Batson* and *Moore*, that is unreasonable, implausible, or that otherwise makes no sense. . . .

The decision of the United States Army Court of Criminal Appeals ordering a rehearing is affirmed.

CRAWFORD, JUDGE (dissenting):

This case raises the question of when this Court is bound by Supreme Court precedent. The majority holds that *Purkett v. Elem*, 514 U.S. 765 (1995), does not apply in the military context when the prosecutor sets forth a race-neutral explanation for a peremptory strike against an African-American which is not objectively verifiable by the trial judge and is disputed by the parties. In support of its view, the majority cites the differences between civilian juries and military court panels. However, noticeably lacking from the majority's discussion is any evidence of past patterns of discrimination in the military community such as existed in the civilian community. The reasons set forth by the majority for not applying *Elem* are really reasons for not applying *Batson v. Kentucky*, 476 U.S. 79 (1986), in the military in the first instance. With all due respect to my colleagues in the majority, when examined in this context, the fallacy of the majority's reasoning is readily apparent. Because the majority refuses to follow Supreme Court precedent and continues this Court's practice of fashioning a different rule for the military without adequate justification,[1] I dissent.

The majority correctly recognizes that *Batson* is based upon the Fifth Amendment "equal protection right to be tried by a jury from which no 'cognizable racial group' ha[d] been excluded." 47 M.J. at 285. Surely, there can be no dispute that this important equal-protection right applies to servicemembers accused of crimes as well as to their civilian counterparts. The issues, however, are (1) whether there was a deprivation of this right in the military as there was in many civilian systems, and, (2) whether the prophylactic measures of *Batson*, and especially its more restrictive progeny in this Court, *United States v. Moore*, 28 M.J. 366 (C.M.A. 1989), and *United States v. Santiago-Davila*, 26 M.J. 380 (C.M.A. 1988), were necessary in the military context to remedy a phantom deprivation. This Court in *Moore* eliminated the requirement for the opponent to make out a *prima facie* case of racial discrimination. Now the Court eliminates soft data for both sides, such as tone of voice, body language, or blinking as a race-neutral explanation under *Batson*.

---

[1] [n.1] *Some* examples include the following:

Right to counsel. *Compare Nichols v. United States*, 511 U.S. 738 (1994) (holding uncounseled misdemeanor conviction may be sentence enhancer) *with United States v. Kelly*, 45 M.J. 259 (1996) (holding uncounseled Article 15s and summary courts-martial may not be used as sentence enhancers).

Counsel's conflict of interest. *Compare Burger v. Kemp*, 483 U.S. 776, 783 (1987) (holding defendant must demonstrate "an actual conflict of interest adversely affected his lawyer's performance"), *with United States v. Smith*, 36 M.J. 455, 457 (C.M.A. 1993) (establishing a "rebuttable presumption that there is an actual conflict of interest whenever there is multiple representation and the military judge has not conducted a suitable inquiry on the record").

Implied bias. *See e.g., United States v. Youngblood*, 47 M.J 338, 345 (1997) (Crawford, J., dissenting).

One wonders whether the majority even leaves intact the third step in *Batson*, because here they did not even require the opponent to prove purposeful racial discrimination. . . .

The majority goes to great lengths to describe the differences between the military and the civilian jury systems while discussing the history of the application of *Batson* to the military. I have no dispute with the accuracy of the majority's discussion. I do, however, question why the majority does not follow that discussion to its logical conclusion and consider why it is necessary to apply a more stringent standard to the military where there is no evidence of a present or historical equal-protection deprivation in the military's jury-selection process than, in contrast, to the civilian system which is replete with historical equal-protection violations. This Court does not have the luxury that state courts have to expand rights as a matter of state law under a state constitution (*California v. Greenwood*, 486 U.S. 35, 43 (1988) (acknowledging that "[i]ndividual States may surely construe their constitution as imposing more stringent constraints . . . ."). Thus, I would conclude that the majority has not demonstrated adequate grounds or justification to fashion a more restrictive rule in the military context.

UNITED STATES v. MIZGALA
United States Court of Appeals for the Armed Forces
61 M.J. 122 (C.A.A.F. 2005)

[Airman First Class Mizgala pleaded guilty to a variety of offenses. On appeal, the question presented was whether his guilty plea waived his claim that he was denied a speedy trial and, if not, whether that claim was meritorious.]

JUDGE ERDMANN delivered the opinion of the court.

Article 10, Uniform Code of Military Justice (UCMJ), 10 U.S.C. § 810 (2000), assures the right of a speedy trial to military members by providing that "[w]hen any person subject to this chapter is placed in arrest or confinement prior to trial, immediate steps shall be taken to inform him of the specific wrong of which he is accused and to try him or to dismiss the charges and release him."

Mizgala was initially held in pretrial confinement for 117 days. His timely motion to dismiss for lack of a speedy trial under Article 10 was denied by the military judge and Mizgala entered unconditional guilty pleas to all of the charges. We granted review to determine whether Mizgala's unconditional guilty pleas waived appellate review of the speedy trial motion and, if not, whether Mizgala was denied his Article 10 right to a speedy trial. We find that Mizgala's unconditional guilty plea did not waive his right to appellate review of his litigated speedy trial motion, but find that his Article 10 right to speedy trial was not violated. . . .

Speedy Trial under the UCMJ

Congress enacted various speedy trial provisions in the UCMJ to address concerns about "the length of time that a man will be placed in confinement and held there pending his trial;" to prevent an accused from "languish[ing] in a jail somewhere for a considerable length of time" awaiting trial or disposition of charges; to protect the accused's rights to a speedy trial without sacrificing the ability to defend himself; to provide responsibility in the event that someone unnecessarily delays a trial; and to establish speedy trial protections under the UCMJ "consistent with good procedure and justice." *Uniform Code of Military Justice: Hearings on H.R. 2498 Before a Subcomm. of the House Comm. on Armed Services*, 81st Cong. 905-12, 980-983, 1005 (1949). *See United States v. Tibbs*, 15 C.M.A. 350, 359, 35 C.M.R. 322, 331 (1965) (Ferguson, J., dissenting); *United States v. Hounshell*, 7 C.M.A. 3, 7-8, 21 C.M.R. 129, 133-34 (1956).

Where an accused is incarcerated pending disposition of charges under the UCMJ, Congress has placed the onus on the Government to take "immediate steps" to move that case to trial. Article 10, UCMJ. "Particularly, [Congress] indicated that delay cannot be condoned if the accused is in arrest or confinement." *United States v. Wilson*, 10 C.M.A. 337, 340, 27 C.M.R. 411, 414 (1959).

While our cases have sometimes adopted different approaches to Article 10 speedy trial issues, they have consistently stressed the significant role Article 10 plays when servicemembers are confined prior to trial. We have referred to the right to a speedy trial as a "fundamental right" of the accused, *United States v. Parish*, 17 C.M.A. 411, 416, 38 C.M.R. 209, 214 (1968), and as "[u]nquestionably . . . a substantial right," *Hounshell*, 7 C.M.A. at 6, 21 C.M.R. at 132. A number of our earlier cases included speedy disposition of charges under the concept of "military due process." *United States v. Prater*, 20 C.M.A. 339, 342, 43 C.M.R. 179, 182 (1971) (citing *United States v. Schlack*, 14 C.M.A. 371, 34 C.M.R. 151 (1964)). *See also United States v. Williams*, 16 C.M.A. 589, 593, 37 C.M.R. 209 (1967).

The Government urges us to find that an unconditional guilty plea effectively waives a servicemember's Article 10 speedy trial rights in all instances. In support of their argument the Government directs our attention to Sixth Amendment jurisprudence, Rule for Courts-Martial (R.C.M.) 707(e), and the Speedy Trial Act of 1974, Pub. L. No. 93-619, 88 Stat. 2070, and points out that the speedy trial protection under each of those provisions is waived by an unconditional guilty plea. We will examine each of these areas in turn.

Sixth Amendment

The Sixth Amendment to the United States Constitution contains the constitutional guarantee to a speedy trial. Although the text of the amendment does not address waiver, courts have held that the Sixth Amendment right is waived by a voluntary guilty plea. *See Cox v. Lockhart*, 970 F.2d 448, 453 (8th Cir. 1992) ("A voluntary plea of guilty constitutes a waiver of all non-jurisdictional defects[,] . . . [and] the right to a speedy trial is non-jurisdictional in nature.") (citation omitted); *Tiemans v. United States*, 724 F.2d 928, 929 (11th Cir. 1984) ("[A] guilty plea waives all non-jurisdictional defects occurring prior to the time of the plea, including violations of the defendant's rights to a speedy trial and due process.").

We have consistently noted that Article 10 creates a more exacting speedy trial demand than does the Sixth Amendment. *United States v. Cooper*, 58

M.J. 54, 60 (C.A.A.F. 2003); *United States v. King*, 30 M.J. 59, 62 (C.M.A. 1990) (citing *United States v. Powell*, 2 M.J. 6 (C.M.A. 1976); *United States v. Marshall*, 22 C.M.A. 431, 47 C.M.R. 409 (1973)). Not only is the demand for a speedy trial under the UCMJ more exacting, by virtue of Article 98, UCMJ, 10 U.S.C. § 898 (2000), unreasonable delay in disposing of criminal charges in the military is unlawful. *See Powell*, 2 M.J. at 8; *United States v. Mason*, 21 C.M.A. 389, 393, 45 C.M.R. 163, 167 (1972). While the full scope of this "more exacting" Article 10 right has not been precisely defined by this court, it cannot be "more exacting" and at the same time be "consistent" with Sixth Amendment protections.

Rule for Courts-Martial 707

Rule for Courts-Martial 707 contains the speedy trial provision in the Rules for Courts-Martial. Rule for Courts-Martial 707(e) provides that "a plea of guilty which results in a finding of guilty waives any speedy trial issue as to that offense." We have found, however, that the language of Article 10 is "clearly different" from R.C.M. 707 and have held that Article 10 is not restricted by R.C.M. 707. *Cooper*, 58 M.J. at 58-60 (holding that the protections of Article 10 extend beyond arraignment); *Kossman*, 38 M.J. at 261 ("[I]n the area of subconstitutional speedy trial, Article 10 reigns preeminent over anything propounded by the President.").

The protections afforded confined or arrested servicemembers under Article 10 are distinct and greater given the nature of other speedy trial protections. *See United States v. Reed*, 41 M.J. 449, 451 (C.A.A.F. 1995) (listing sources for the right to a speedy trial in the military); *United States v. Vogan*, 35 M.J. 32, 33 (C.M.A. 1992) (also listing military speedy trial right sources). Rule for Courts-Martial 707(e) therefore does not act as a limitation on the rights afforded under Article 10.

Speedy Trial Act

Courts have uniformly held that a guilty plea "constitutes a waiver of [an accused's] rights under the [Speedy Trial] Act." *United States v. Morgan*, 384 F.3d 439, 442 (7th Cir. 2004). While the Speedy Trial Act does not apply to offenses under the UCMJ, there is a further distinction in the allocation of burdens under the two statutes. The Speedy Trial Act imposes the burden of proof upon an accused to support a motion to dismiss. 18 U.S.C. § 3162(a)(2) (2000). Under Article 10, the Government has the burden to show that the prosecution moved forward with reasonable diligence in response to a motion to dismiss. *United States v. Brown*, 10 C.M.A. 498, 503, 28 C.M.R. 64, 69 (1959). This distinction is additional proof of the importance of Article 10 to the incarcerated servicemember.

We therefore find nothing in the comparisons to the Sixth Amendment, R.C.M. 707 or the Speedy Trial Act that would compel our application of their speedy trial waiver rules to Article 10. It falls to this court then to determine whether an unconditional guilty plea waives a litigated Article 10 speedy trial motion. . . .

We take this opportunity to revisit our examination of whether an Article 10 claim is waived by an unconditional guilty plea or whether it may be reviewed by an appellate court in cases where the accused unsuccessfully raises an Article 10 issue at trial and then enters an unconditional guilty plea. In view of the legislative importance given to a speedy trial under the UCMJ and the unique nature of the protections of Article 10 discussed above, we believe that where an accused unsuccessfully raises an Article 10 issue and thereafter pleads guilty, waiver does not apply. Such a rule for Article 10 rights properly reflects the importance of a servicemember's right to a speedy trial under Article 10. Preservation of the right to appeal adverse Article 10 rulings is not only supported by the congressional intent behind Article 10, it also maintains the high standards of speedy disposition of charges against members of the armed forces and recognizes "military procedure as the exemplar of prompt action in bringing to trial those members of the armed forces charged with offenses." *United States v. Pierce*, 19 C.M.A. 225, 227, 41 C.M.R. 225, 227 (1970). *See also United States v. Hatfield*, 44 M.J. 22, 24 (C.A.A.F. 1996) ("[T]he mandate that the Government take immediate steps to try arrested or confined accused must ever be borne in mind."). A fundamental, substantial, personal right — a right that dates from our earlier cases — should not be diminished by applying ordinary rules of waiver and forfeiture associated with guilty pleas.

We therefore hold that a litigated speedy trial motion under Article 10 is not waived by a subsequent unconditional guilty plea. Thus, Mizgala's unconditional guilty plea did not waive his right to contest the military judge's denial of his Article 10 motion on appeal.

Having concluded that Mizgala did not waive review of his Article 10 claim by entering an unconditional guilty plea, we proceed to the merits of that claim.

Article 10 Speedy Trial

The standard of diligence under which we review claims of a denial of speedy trial under Article 10 "is not constant motion, but reasonable diligence in bringing the charges to trial." *Tibbs*, 15 C.M.A. at 353, 35 C.M.R. at 325. *See also Kossman*, 38 M.J. at 262; *United States v. Johnson*, 1 M.J. 101 (C.M.A. 1975). Short periods of inactivity are not fatal to an otherwise active prosecution. *Tibbs*, 15 C.M.A. at 353, 35 C.M.R. at 325 (citing *United States v. Williams*, 12 C.M.A. 81, 83, 30 C.M.R. 81, 83 (1961)). Further, although Sixth Amendment speedy trial standards cannot dictate whether there has been an Article 10 violation, the factors from *Barker v. Wingo* [407 U.S. 514 (1972)] are an apt structure for examining the facts and circumstances surrounding an alleged Article 10 violation. *Cooper*, 58 M.J. at 61; *Birge*, 52 M.J. at 212. . . .

We agree with the Court of Criminal Appeals that the military judge plainly erred in the manner in which he reviewed Mizgala's Article 10 motion. His ruling was erroneous as a matter of law in three regards. First, Article 10 and R.C.M. 707 are distinct, each providing its own speedy trial protection. The fact that a prosecution meets the 120-day rule of R.C.M. 707 does not directly "or indirectly" demonstrate that the Government moved to trial with reasonable diligence as required by Article 10. *See United States v. Edmond*, 41 M.J. 419, 421 (C.A.A.F. 1995); *Kossman*, 38 M.J. at 260-61.

Second, the military judge erred in determining that he was required to find gross negligence to support an Article 10 violation in the absence of Government spite or bad faith. An Article 10 violation rests in the failure of the Government to proceed with reasonable diligence. A conclusion of unreasonable diligence may arise from a number of different causes and need not rise to the level of gross neglect to support a violation. *Kossman*, 38 M.J. at 261. Finally, the military judge erred by limiting his consideration of the *Barker v. Wingo* factors to a Sixth Amendment speedy trial analysis. We have held that "it is 'appropriate' to consider those factors 'in determining whether a particular set of circumstances violates a servicemember's speedy trial rights under Article 10.'" *Cooper*, 58 M.J. at 61 (quoting *Birge*, 52 M.J. at 212).

Turning to the substance of Mizgala's claim, our framework to determine whether the Government proceeded with reasonable diligence includes balancing the following four factors: (1) the length of the delay; (2) the reasons for the delay; (3) whether the appellant made a demand for a speedy trial; and (4) prejudice to the appellant. *See Barker*, 407 U.S. at 530. *See also Birge*, 52 M.J. at 212. Applying those factors to Mizgala's case, we remain mindful that we are looking at the proceeding as a whole and not mere speed: "[T]he essential ingredient is orderly expedition and not mere speed." *United States v. Mason*, 21 C.M.A. 389, 393, 45 C.M.R. 163, 167 (C.M.A. 1972) (quoting *Smith v. United States*, 369 U.S. 1, 10 (1959)).

The processing of this case is not stellar. We share the military judge's concern with several periods during which the Government seems to have been in a waiting posture: waiting for formal evidence prior to preferring charges and waiting for a release of jurisdiction for an offense that occurred in the civilian community. There are periods evidencing delay in seeking evidence of the off-post offense and seeking litigation packages to support prosecution of the drug offenses. Nevertheless, constant motion is not the standard so long as the processing reflects reasonable diligence under all the circumstances. Our evaluation must balance the delay against the reasons for these periods of delay (such as the need to investigate offenses and obtain evidence), with the need to coordinate investigation and jurisdiction with civilian authorities. Once these necessary steps were completed, the Government moved expeditiously to refer the charges.

As to the consideration of possible prejudice, we find no material prejudice to Mizgala's substantial rights. In this regard, we note the test for prejudice set forth by the Supreme Court:

> Prejudice, of course, should be assessed in the light of the interests of defendants which the speedy trial right was designed to protect. This Court has identified three such interests: (i) to prevent oppressive pretrial incarceration; (ii) to minimize anxiety and concern of the accused; and (iii) to limit the possibility that the defense will be impaired. Of these, the most serious is the last, because the inability of a defendant adequately to prepare his case skews the fairness of the entire system.

Barker, 407 U.S. at 532 (footnote omitted). Mizgala experienced 117 days of pretrial confinement, which necessarily involves some anxiety and stress, but there is no evidence in the record that the conditions of that confinement were harsh or oppressive. Finally, there is no indication that his preparation for trial, defense evidence, trial strategy, or ability to present witnesses, on both the merits and sentencing, were compromised by the processing time in this case. Balancing those factors identified by the Supreme Court, we find that prejudice, if any, was minimal.

We hold that Mizgala was not denied his Article 10 right to a speedy trial and, after our de novo review of the speedy trial issue, we find there was no prejudice from the military judge's application of an erroneous standard of law. . . .

CRAWFORD, JUDGE (dissenting in part and concurring in the result):

While the majority notes that Article 10, Uniform Code of Military Justice (UCMJ), 10 U.S.C. § 810 (2000), is a "more exacting" right, it overlooks the history behind the UCMJ provisions of the *Manual for Courts-Martial, United States* (2002 ed.) (*MCM*), and mainstream jurisprudence in this area. Thus, I respectfully dissent from the majority opinion that an unconditional plea of guilty does not waive Appellant's rights to a speedy trial whether asserted under the Sixth Amendment, the UCMJ, or the *MCM*. The congressional history underlying Article 10 has not altered what a majority of the courts have held concerning unconditional guilty pleas.

History Behind the UCMJ. When Congress passed the UCMJ in 1950, there was some question as to the applicability of the Bill of Rights to members of the Armed Forces. Fifty-five years later, the Supreme Court still has never expressly held that the Bill of Rights applies to servicemembers. In *United States ex rel. Innes v. Crystal*, 131 F.2d 576, 577 n.2 (2d Cir. 1943) (citing *Ex parte Quirin*, 317 U.S. 1 (1942)), the court stated, "The Fifth and Sixth Amendments are, of course, inapplicable to courts-martial." This question about the application of the Bill of Rights to the military resulted in Congress passing Articles 10, 27, 31, 44, 46, and 63, UCMJ.

Early in the Court's history, when examining the question of speedy trial, it "bottom[ed] those [constitutional] rights and privileges" on the Due Process Clause of the Fourteenth Amendment rather than on the specific provisions in the Bill of Rights. *United States v. Clay*, 1 C.M.A. 74, 77, 1 C.M.R. 74, 77 (1951). In one of our earlier cases, *United States v. Hounshell*, this Court stated, "[t]he United States Constitution guarantees to a person protected under federal law 'the right to speedy and public trial.' Article 10 of the Uniform Code . . . reiterates that guarantee. . . ." 7 C.M.A. 3, 6, 21 C.M.R. 129, 132 (1956) (quoting U.S. Const. amend. VI). Indeed, the legislative history behind Article 10 strongly suggests it was intended only to remedy delays concerning pretrial restraint. *See Uniform Code of Military Justice: Hearings on H.R. 2498 Before a Subcomm. of the House Comm. on Armed Services*, 81st Cong. 905-12 (1949) [hereinafter *UCMJ Hearings*]. That subcommittee viewed Article 10 solely as a tool to terminate lengthy pretrial confinement. *Id.*

The right to counsel guaranteed under Article 27 was not applicable through the Bill of Rights to state proceedings until 1963. It was not until that year, in *Gideon v. Wainwright*, 372 U.S. 335 (1963), that the Supreme Court extended the right to appointment of counsel in state cases to all indigent felony defendants. Prior to that, Congress had ensured some right to counsel for military members by passing Article 27, but that right was limited to general courts-martial. Congress extended this right to special courts-martial in 1968. Of course, it is not enough to have counsel; counsel must zealously represent the accused, starting with a full investigation of the case. *See, e.g., House v. Balkcom*, 725 F.2d 608 (11th Cir. 1984). The right to counsel is one of the most valuable rights that a defendant possesses, but certain decisions are for the defendant to control while the remainder are left with counsel. The Supreme Court has recognized that counsel has the authority to manage most aspects of the defense without obtaining the defendant's approval. *See, e.g., Nixon v. Florida*, 125 S. Ct. 551 (2004). In *New York v. Hill*, the Supreme Court stated: "[D]efense counsel's agreement to a trial date outside the time period required by [the Interstate Agreement on Detainers] bars the defendant from seeking dismissal because trial did not occur within that period." 528 U.S. 110, 111 (2000). Moreover, the *Hill* Court said, "only counsel is in a position to assess the benefit or detriment of the delay to the defendant's case," *id.* at 115, and "only counsel is in a position to assess whether the defense would even be prepared to proceed any earlier." *Id.*

Feeling that the self-incrimination clause did not apply to military members, Congress enacted Article 31 to protect the right against self-incrimination in the military setting. Additionally, in enacting Article 31(b), Congress was concerned that the interrogation environment in the military and the interplay between military relationships and following orders deserved protection. *See UCMJ Hearings* at 984-85. As this Court stated, "[u]ndoubtedly it was the intent of Congress in this division of the Article to secure to persons subject to the Code the same rights secured to those of the civilian community under the Fifth Amendment to the Constitution of the United States — no more and no less." *United States v. Eggers*, 3 C.M.A. 191, 195, 11 C.M.R. 191, 195 (1953). In his testimony on the UCMJ, Mr. Felix Larkin, Assistant General Counsel in the Office of the Secretary of Defense, expressed the desire to "retain the constitutional protections against self-incrimination." *UCMJ Hearings* at 988. The UCMJ was enacted to ensure those constitutional rights because of the deep division as to the applicability of those rights in different factual scenarios. The commentary to Article 31(a) also underscores the intent to "extend [the] privilege against self-incrimination to all persons under all circumstances." H.R. Rep. 81-491 at 19 (1949).

Likewise, Congress enacted Article 44 because "the application of [the Fifth Amendment] is in doubt. . . . The matter could be clarified by extending the protection of the fifth amendment rather than granting protection by means of different or new statutory enactment." *Uniform Code of Military Justice: Hearings on § 857 and H.R. 4080 Before a Subcomm. of the Senate Comm. on Armed Services*, 81st Cong. 111 (1949) (statement of Sen. Pat McCarran, Chairman, Senate Judiciary Comm.). House commentary on the UCMJ observed: "The question is whether the constitutional provision of jeopardy follows a person who enters military service." H.R. Rep. 81-491 at 23.

As to the double jeopardy provision, this Court reiterated the theme that the Constitution did not apply, stating, "The constitutional privilege against former jeopardy, applicable to the civilian community, is granted to offenders against military law by Article 44. . . ." *United States v. Ivory*, 9 C.M.A. 516, 519-20, 26 C.M.R. 296, 299-300 (1958).

In the past, this Court applied a due process examination before it had announced that the Bill of Rights applies "except those [rights] which are expressly or by necessary implication inapplicable." *United States v. Jacoby*, 11 C.M.A. 428, 430-31, 29 C.M.R. 244, 246-47 (1960). Because the Supreme Court has not held that the Bill of Rights applies to servicemembers, our Court, in its early years, did not rely upon speedy trial rights.

The question of the application of the Fourth Amendment as to the right to privacy, the self-incrimination clause of the Fifth Amendment, speedy trial, or the right of confrontation cross-examination under the Sixth Amendment is moot based on congressional and presidential actions.

MCM Provision. The majority also overlooks R.C.M. 707(e), which states that: "Except as provided in R.C.M. 910(a)(2) [conditional pleas], a plea of guilty which results in a finding of guilty waives *any* speedy trial issue as to that offense." (Emphasis added.) This provision by the President does not violate any constitutional provision — there is certainly none prohibiting this waiver, and many federal courts provide for such a waiver.

Because the majority overlooks mainstream jurisprudence and the *MCM* provisions, I respectfully dissent.

NOTES AND QUESTIONS

1. Early in its existence, the Court of Military Appeals referred repeatedly to "military due process." *E.g., United States v. Clay*, 1 U.S.C.M.A. 74, 1 C.M.R. 74 (1951), as a shorthand for the process to which accused personnel were entitled. "As is clear from a close reading of the opinion, however, 'military due process' meant no more than an acceptance of the doctrine, suggested in early federal court decisions, that servicemen are entitled to the full protection of statutory rights granted to them by Congress. . . . [I]t did not mean that their trials were independently governed by any or all of the constitutional protections afforded their civilian counterparts." HOMER E. MOYER, JR., JUSTICE AND THE MILITARY § 2-105, at 236 (1972); *see generally id.* at 236-38 (collecting cases).

2. One of the leading military justice treatises observes that "[a]lthough disturbing, the [Supreme] Court's silence [on the application of the Bill of Rights to courts-martial] is only of academic interest, given that the Court of Military Appeals held in 1960 in *United States v. Jacoby*, [29 C.M.R. 244, 246-47 (1960)], that 'the protections of the Bill of Rights, except those which are expressly, or by necessary implication inapplicable, are available to members of the armed forces.'" 1 FRANCIS A. GILLIGAN & FREDRIC I. LEDERER, COURT-MARTIAL PROCEDURE § 1.52.00, at 1-26 & n.134 (3d ed. 2006). In what sense is the Court's silence disturbing? Is an across-the-board answer feasible or conceivable? See Chapter 17, § III, *infra*, on direct appellate review of courts-martial.

3. Judging by *Mizgala*, isn't it clear that judicial ways of thinking about statutory issues can be heavily influenced by constitutional jurisprudence even if the court is applying a nonconstitutional source of law? Were you persuaded by Judge Crawford's argument that "mainstream jurisprudence" compelled a finding that Mizgala had waived his speedy trial argument?

4. According to one of its judges, the Court of Appeals for the Armed Forces' "general approach is to apply the Bill of Rights' protections to servicemembers absent a specific exemption for the military justice system or some demonstrated 'military necessity that would require a different rule.'" H.F. "Sparky" Gierke, *The Use of Article III Case Law in Military Jurisprudence*, ARMY LAW., Aug. 2005, at 25, 35 & n.168 (quoting *Courtney v. Williams*, 1 M.J. 267, 270 (C.M.A. 1976)). Judge Gierke notes that despite "putting the burden on a party urging a military exception, the [court] has not been reluctant to find that military conditions do require a different rule," *id.* at 36, and concludes based on his survey of the cases, that "adjustments to constitutional rights in the military justice system are not made with a one-way ratchet. In some cases, military accused enjoy greater protections than their civilian counterparts." *Id.* at 39.

5. Article III jurisprudence can certainly exert a powerful influence over military jurisprudence, as Judge Gierke has noted, but the reverse is not true.

> Civilian jurisprudence has occasion to refer to military law in three types of cases. The first category includes those cases where a military personnel action such as a court-martial, nonjudicial punishment or administrative discharge is the subject of collateral attack. The second includes those occasional cases in which the subject matter of civilian litigation — civil or criminal — is such that it directly or indirectly requires or suggests the consideration of issues of military law. The third includes all those infinite other cases in which military jurisprudence might — like the jurisprudence of any common law jurisdiction — be referred to for whatever persuasive value or precedential merit it might possess. This latter category is potentially the broadest of the three, but to date it is in reality the one where civilian reference to military jurisprudence has fallen most short of the possible level of interaction. . . . Despite the opportunities thus presented, in the more than three decades since the Court of Military Appeals decided its first case, it has had little influence on the development of American law, either federal or state.

Eugene R. Fidell, *"If a Tree Falls in the Forest . . .": Publication and Digesting Policies and the Potential Contribution of Military Courts to American Law*, 32 JAG J. 1, 3-4 (1982). "[I]t would be regrettable if military jurisprudence were to continue to grow in a hothouse environment — influenced, to be sure, by outside stimuli, but scarcely influencing the outside." *Id.* at 11.

III.   STATUTES AND REGULATIONS

HAMDAN v. RUMSFELD
Supreme Court of the United States
126 S. Ct. 2749 (2006)

[Hamdan, a Yemeni national captured in Afghanistan and held as an enemy combatant at Guantánamo Bay, Cuba, sought habeas corpus and mandamus to block his trial by military commission on a conspiracy charge.]

[Justice Stevens was joined by Justices Souter, Ginsburg, Breyer and Kennedy in the following part of the opinion of the Court.]

The uniformity principles [of article 36(b), UCMJ] is not an inflexible one; it does not preclude all departures from the procedures dictated for use by court-martial. But any departure must be tailored to the exigency that necessitates it. . . .

Article 36 places two restrictions on the President's power to promulgate rules of procedure for courts-martial and military commissions alike. First, no procedural rule he adopts may be "contrary to or inconsistent with" the UCMJ — however practical it may seem. Second, the rules adopted must be "uniform insofar as practicable." That is, the rules applied to military commissions must be the same as those applied to courts-martial unless such uniformity proves impracticable.

Hamdan argues that Commission Order No. 1 violates both of these restrictions; he maintains that the procedures described in the Commission Order are inconsistent with the UCMJ and that the Government has offered no explanation for their deviation from the procedures governing courts-martial, which are set forth in the Manual for Courts-Martial, United States (2005 ed.) (Manual for Courts-Martial). . . .

The Government has three responses. First, it argues only 9 of the UCMJ's 158 articles — the ones that expressly mention "military commissions" — actually apply to commissions, and Commission Order No. 1 sets forth no procedure that is "contrary to or inconsistent with" those 9 provisions. Second, the Government contends, military commissions would be of no use if the President were hamstrung by those provisions of the UCMJ that govern courts-martial. Finally, the President's determination that "the danger to the safety of the United States and the nature of international terrorism" renders it impracticable "to apply in military commissions . . . the principles of law and rules of evidence generally recognized in the trial of criminal cases in the United States district courts." November 13 Order § 1(f), is, in the Government's view, explanation enough for any deviation from court-martial procedures. . . .

Hamdan has the better of this argument. Without reaching the question whether any provision of Commission Order No. 1 is strictly "contrary to or inconsistent with" other provisions of the UCMJ, we conclude that the "practicability" determination the President has made is insufficient to justify variations from the procedures governing courts-martial. Subsection 36(b) of

Article 36 was added after World War II, and requires a different showing of impracticability from the one required by subsection (a). Subsection (a) requires that the rules the President promulgates for courts-martial, provost courts, and military commissions alike confirm to those that govern procedures in Article III courts, "so far as *he considers* practicable." 10 U.S.C. § 836(a) (emphasis added). Subsection (b), by contrast, demands that the rules applied in courts-martial, provost courts, and military commissions — whether or not they conform with the Federal Rules of Evidence — be "uniform *insofar as practicable.*" § 836(b) (emphasis added). Under the latter provision, then, the rules set forth in the Manual for Courts-Martial must apply to military commissions unless impracticable.[2]

The President here has determined, pursuant to subsection (a), that it is impracticable to apply the rules and principles of law that govern "the trial of criminal cases in the United States district courts," § 836(a), to Hamdan's commission. We assume that complete deference is owed that determination. The President has not, however, made a similar official determination that it is impracticable to apply the rules for courts-martial.

Nothing in the record before us demonstrates that it would be impracticable to apply court-martial rules in this case. There is no suggestion, for example, of any logistical difficulty in securing properly sworn and authenticated evidence or in applying the usual principles of relevance and admissibility. Assuming *arguendo* that the reasons articulated in the President's Article 36(a) determination ought to be considered in evaluating the impracticability of applying court-martial rules, the only reason offered in support of that determination is the danger posed by international terrorism. Without for one moment underestimating that danger, it is not evident to us why it should require, in the case of Hamdan's trial, any variance from the rules that govern courts-martial.

The absence of any showing of impracticability is particularly disturbing when considered in light of the clear and admitted failure to apply one of the most fundamental protections afforded not just by the Manual for Courts-Martial but also by the UCMJ itself: the right to be present. *See* 10 U.S.C.A. § 839(c) (Supp. 2006). Whether or not that departure technically is "contrary to or inconsistent with" the terms of the UCMJ, 10 U.S.C. § 836(a), the jettisoning of so basic a right cannot lightly be excused as "practicable."

Under the circumstances, then, the rules applicable in courts-martial must apply. . . .

---

[2] [n.50] JUSTICE THOMAS relies on the legislative history of the UCMJ to argue that Congress' adoption of Article 36(b) in the wake of World War II was "motivated" solely by a desire for "uniformity across the separate branches of the armed services." *Post*, at 2842. But even if Congress was concerned with ensuring uniformity across service branches, that does *not* mean it did not also intend to codify the longstanding practice of procedural parity between courts-martial and other military tribunals. Indeed, the suggestion that Congress did *not* intend uniformity across tribunal types is belied by the textual proximity of subsection (a) (which requires that the rules governing criminal trials in federal district courts apply, absent the President's determination of impracticability, to courts-martial, provost courts, and *military commissions alike*) and subsection (b) (which imposes the uniformity requirement).

THOMAS, J., dissenting.

. . . The vision of uniformity that motivated the adoption of the UCMJ, embodied specifically in Article 36(b), is nothing more than uniformity across the separate branches of the armed services. *See* ch. 169, 64 Stat. 107 (preamble to the UCMJ explaining that the UCMJ is an act "[t]o unify, consolidate, revise, and codify the Articles of War, the Articles for the Government of the Navy, and the disciplinary laws of the Coast Guard."). There is no indication that the UCMJ was intended to require uniformity in procedure between courts-martial and military commissions, tribunals that the UCMJ itself recognizes are different. To the contrary, the UCMJ expressly recognizes that different tribunals will be constituted in different manners and employ different procedures. . . . Thus, Article 36(b) is best understood as establishing that, so far as practicable, the rules and regulations governing tribunals convened by the Navy must be uniform with the rule and regulations governing tribunals convened by the Army. But, consistent with this Court's prior interpretations of Article 21 and over a century of historical practice, it cannot be understood to require the President to conform the procedures employed by military commissions to those employed by courts-martial.[3]

Even if Article 36(b) could be construed to require procedural uniformity among the various tribunals contemplated by the UCMJ, Hamdan would not be entitled to relief. Under the Court's reading, the President is entitled to prescribe different rules for military commissions than for courts-martial when he determines that it is not "practicable" to prescribe uniform rules. The Court does not resolve the level of deference such determinations would be owed, however, because, in its view, "[t]he President has not . . . [determined] that it is impracticable to apply the rules for courts-martial." . . . This simply not the case. . . . The Court provides no explanation why the President's determination that employing court-martial procedures in the military commissions established pursuant to Military Commission Order No. 1 would hamper our war effort is in any way inadequate to satisfy its newly minted "practicability" requirement. On the contrary, this determination is precisely the kind for which the "Judiciary has neither aptitude, facilities nor responsibility and which has long been held to belong in the domain of political power not subject to judicial intrusion or inquiry." *Chicago & Southern Air Lines, Inc. v. Waterman S.S. Corp.*, 333 U.S. 103, 111 (1948). And, in the context of the present conflict, it is exactly the kind of determination Congress countenanced when it authorized the President to use all necessary and appropriate force against our enemies. Accordingly, the President's determination is sufficient to satisfy any practicability requirements imposed by Article 36(b). . . .

---

[3] [n.17] . . . [T]he only legislative history relating to Article 36(b) would confirm the obvious — Article 36(b)'s uniformity requirement pertains to uniformity between the three branches of the Armed Forces and no more. When that subsection was introduced as an amendment to Article 36, its author explained that it would leave the three branches "enough leeway to provide a different provision where it is absolutely necessary" because "there are some differences in the services." Hearings on H.R. 2498 before Subcommittee No. 1 of the House Committee on Armed Services, 81st Cong., 1st Sess., 1015 (1949). A further statement explained that "there might be some slight differences that would pertain as to the Navy in contrast to the Army, but at least [Article 36(b)] is an expression of the congressional intent that we want it to be as uniform as possible." *Ibid.*

NOTES AND QUESTIONS

1. Do you agree that Hamdan had the better of the argument on the meaning of the uniformity clause in Article 36(b) of the UCMJ? How much weight would you put on the fact that there was no uniformity clause in Article of War 38, the rule making provision that preceded the UCMJ for the Army and covered both courts-martial and military commissions? *See* Eugene R. Fidell, Dwight H. Sullivan & Detlev F. Vagts, *Military Commission Law*, ARMY LAW., Dec. 2005, at 47, 48 & n.10 ("better reading is that the uniformity referred to is uniformity among the various armed forces").

2. Justice Kennedy concurred in the result in *Hamdan*, finding that the military commission constituted by President George W. Bush's 2001 Military Order "exceeds the bounds Congress placed on the President's authority" in the UCMJ. In his view, "the Government has made no demonstration of practical need for these special rules, either in this particular case or as to the military commissions in general, . . .; nor is any such need self-evident. For all the Government's regulations and submissions reveal, it would be feasible for most, if not all, of the conventional military evidence rules and procedures to be followed." 126 S. Ct. at 2808. "[T]he term 'practicable' cannot be construed to permit deviations based on mere convenience or expedience. 'Practicable' means 'feasible,' that is 'possible to practice or perform' or 'capable of being put into practice, done, or accomplished.' WEBSTER'S THIRD INTERNATIONAL DICTIONARY 1780 (1961). Congress' chosen language, then, is best understood to allow the selection of procedures based on logistical constraints, the accommodation of witnesses, the security of the proceedings, and the like. Insofar as the '[p]retrial, trial, and post-trial procedures' for military commissions at issue deviate from court-martial practice, the deviations must be explained by some such practical need." *Id.* at 2801.

3. A few months after *Hamdan* was decided, Congress passed the Military Commissions Act, Pub. L. No. 109-366, 120 Stat. 2600 (2006), and in the process amended Article 36(b) so that it no longer required uniformity as between court-martial rules and military commission rules. *See id.* § 4(a)(3)(B), 120 Stat. 2631. Nonetheless, the Court's treatment of presidential determinations of "practicability" under Article 36 remains of interest from the standpoint of weighing departures in the *Manual for Courts-Martial* from district court norms. After *Hamdan*, would you expect courts to review such determinations with increased or decreased deference? *See generally* Gregory E. Maggs, *Judicial Review of the* Manual for Courts-Martial, 160 MIL. L. REV. 96 (1999). Should the level of deference be a function of the extent to which a military rule departs from the rule generally applied in the district courts; *i.e.*, the greater the departure, the greater the need to justify it? *See* Eugene R. Fidell, *Judicial Review of Presidential Rulemaking Under Article 36: The Sleeping Giant Stirs*, 4 MIL. L. RPTR. 6049 (1976).

4. In 1953, one of the first judges of the Court of Military Appeals wrote:

Authoritative sources developed during congressional hearings on the Code indicate clearly that the Morgan Committee's several drafts were aimed at — and the statute, as adopted, reflects — a thoughtful balancing of the two essential ingredients of military justice: the *justice* element and the *military* element. Within the first of these terms, of course, I mean to include those safeguards and other legal values which are a part of informed criminal law administration in the civilian community. And by use of the second I mean principally to comprehend acute considerations of discipline in an abnormal social situation, limitations growing out of the burdens, realities and necessities of military operations, and the like. The scales of this process constitute a recognizable and direct legacy to the Court of Military Appeals — and thus its members are enjoined to select from among the juristic principles of civilian forums only those which it believes — in the exercise of the very fullest judicial responsibility — to be consonant with the needs of justice as administered against a military background. This does not at all mean that they are to make short shrift of civilian legal doctrine. Quite the reverse. Certainly the civilian rule must ever furnish the guide in the usual case. It does connote, however, that the judges of the Court of Military Appeals — in this respect at any rate — enjoy greater freedom to choose than any I know.

Thus far I have been speaking of the delicate task of option between civilian legal principles, on the one hand, and requirements peculiar to the military on the other. However, the Court's freedom of choice does not end with the limits of this important area. Turning to a consideration of its position as a federal tribunal of appellate jurisdiction, we must recognize that it is a member of no civilian judicial hierarchy. As a *national* agency of adjudication, it is perforce free from the compulsive — and frequently noxious — influence of narrow, timorous and precedent-ridden state systems. Moreover, and by the same token, as well as by virtue of its assimilated status in the federal judicial scheme, it is similarly untrammeled by strict *stare decisis* even with that organization — save as the Supreme Court may enter the picture. True it is that the system of service jurisprudence — of which the Court of Military Appeals is a part — is explicitly remitted to federal doctrine, substantive and procedural, for guidance. However, at the same time it is undeniably accurate to say that the directive to this effect is framed in terms of "as near as may be." It could not with logic be stated in others. The net of all this, as I see it, is that this Court is freer than any in the land — save again the Supreme Court — to find its law where it will, to seek, newfledged and sole, for *principle*, unhampered by the limiting crop of the years. This is not to suggest, of course, that the new tribunal is licensed to act in an unjudicial manner. Indeed, it *must* look for its law in the sources of law — but it may do so, I believe, relatively unburdened by precedents demonstrated by the test of time and experience to be unrealistic, ill-devised, or outmoded.

Paul W. Brosman, *The Court: Freer Than Most*, 6 VAND. L. REV. 166, 167-68 (1953). How defensible was Judge Brosman's claim that the court was "freer than most"? Have subsequent developments such as the availability of direct review in the Supreme Court or the codification of the military law of evidence in the Military Rules of Evidence eroded his premises? As you study the court's subsequent opinions, do you detect any residue of the Brosman Doctrine?

5. Before *Hamdan* was decided, the Defense Department had announced that the military commissions would be bound by "military commission law," a phrase that was defined in a way that seemed to narrow the sources of law that would apply. In fact, it did not have that effect; those involved in the process were expansive in their reference to external sources of law, as one would have expected, since the participants were all accustomed to the diverse sources of law applied in courts-martial. *See generally* Eugene R. Fidell, Dwight H. Sullivan & Detlev F. Vagts, *Military Commission Law*, ARMY LAW., Dec. 2005, at 47. In the Military Commissions Act, Congress took steps to prevent the use of military commission law in courts-martial, and to provide that military justice jurisprudence would not be binding in military commissions. *See generally* Military Commissions Act § 3(a), 120 Stat. 2600, 2602 (2006) (adding 10 U.S.C. §§ 948b(c) ("judicial construction and application" of UCMJ "not binding on military commissions") and 948b(e) ("findings, holdings, interpretations, and other precedents of military commissions . . . may not be introduced or considered in" courts-martial and "may not form the basis of any holding, decision, or other determination of a court-martial")). Why did Congress decide to erect a barrier between military commission jurisprudence and court-martial jurisprudence? For further discussion of military commissions, see Chapter 19 *infra*.

IV. CUSTOM OF THE SERVICE

UNITED STATES v. PRATT
Coast Guard Board of Review
34 C.M.R. 731 (C.G.B.R. 1963)

The accused, a chief petty officer at the time of trial, was found guilty of five offenses and sentenced to be confined at hard labor for 12 months and to be reduced to the grade of seaman. The convening authority approved the reduction, but only six months of the confinement. On 18 June 1963 the unexecuted portion of the confinement was remitted on six months' probation by the General Counsel of the Treasury.

All of the offenses involved conduct of the accused while officer in charge of the Hampton Beach Lifeboat Station, New Hampshire, between 5 January and 25 August 1962. In brief, he was convicted of failing to go to the rescue of a boat in distress; of being found drunk on duty during the period 5 March to 25 August; of two disorderly conduct incidents; and of violating a station order restricting visitors aboard the station. We shall refer to these offenses in more detail in discussing the errors assigned.

Our initial concern is with the charge of failing to undertake a rescue and the contention that the accused's guilt was not established. The specification set forth that on 18 August 1962, the accused

   . . . was derelict in the performance of his duties while assigned as Officer in Charge, in that, when he was awakened and informed that a boat was in distress in the vicinity of the Isle of Shoals, he said "fuck it," or words to that effect, went back to sleep, and failed to initiate search and rescue procedures, as it was his duty to do.

The offense is charged as a violation of Article 92(3), UCMJ, making punishable any person who "is derelict in the performance of his duties." The prosecution's proof showed that the tower watch at the station had been informed via radio at 1:00 P.M., on 18 August that a 20-foot cabin cruiser was sinking one-half mile southeast of the Isle of Shoals, a place within the station's operational area. Two witnesses testified as to the accused's non-action. First, Lockard, BM2 [Boatswain's Mate, Second Class] testified: . . .

TC [Trial Counsel]: Q. Directing your attention to 18 August 1962, did you have occasion on that day to become aware of a distress report?

A. Yes.

Q. What did you do when you received the report?

A. I went to inform the chief at the time.

Q. And what happened then?

A. The chief was in his rack, I tried to awaken him by telling him of the distress with negative results. I reached over the second time and pulled him over on his back and told him again of the distress.

Q. Will you please speak up, speak louder, please. Continue.

A. I in turn turned around with negative results from trying to awaken him and went on the job myself.

Q. Was anything said to you during the period involved?

A. Yes.

Q. Who said it?

A. Chief Pratt.

Q. And what did he say?

A. "Oh, fuck it."

Q. Was anyone else present at this time?

A. In the room there wasn't, in the doorway there was.

On cross examination Lockard stated that he smelled alcohol on the accused on the occasion of August 18; the witness left the room right after the accused uttered the words and did not observe him further.

The testimony of Chevalier, [Seaman], who was not cross-examined on the point, included the following:

TC: Q. Directing your attention to the 18th of August 1962, did you have occasion to take part in an assistance case on that day?

A. Yes, sir.

Q. Will you describe what happened?

A. Well, from the time the boat. . . .

Q. Before the boat departed the station.

A. Well, I'd come down the stairs when I heard about the job and I asked if I could go on it and I stood in the doorway of the office and Lockard, the second class boatswain's mate, had already been in there and I was in the door and he yelled to the chief and told the chief that there was a boat sinking out at Isle of Shoals Light Station and he got no reply and he grabbed the chief by the shoulder and rolled him over and yelled it again and the chief looked up and he swore and he said "ah, fuck it." At that Lockard and I and the fireman that was there at the time departed.

Another witness, Judson Carver, [Boatswain's Mate First Class], testified that on the morning of 18 August, before he departed on liberty, he turned the charge of the station over to the accused who had just returned from liberty, and that the accused was not steady on his feet, his eyes looked foggy, his speech was not fully clear, and the odor of alcohol was on his breath.

The defense produced evidence tending to show that the accused was suffering from certain conditions and had been taking antihistamine drugs and sedatives prescribed for him at the Naval Hospital, Portsmouth. The defense contended that the accused was unable to act in response to the distress call because he was incapacitated by the medication. In his closing argument the defense counsel asked:

> Was he awake? Did he reach a sufficient level of consciousness so that the words . . . meant that he knew what was going on? (R 105)

It is plain that the officer in charge of a Coast Guard Lifeboat Station has a legal duty to initiate rescue procedures when it is reported to him that there is a boat in distress. The existence of such a duty was conceded by the defense counsel. The First Coast Guard District's operations plan covering lifeboat stations expresses the duty. Moreover it is deeply rooted in Coast Guard tradition. In M. E. Gilchrist's "Story of the United States Coast Guard" (1938) we read:

> The special motto of the lifesaving crews is: You have to go, but you don't have to come back.

The pamphlet, "Coast Guard History," published by the service, carries a section on lifeboat stations, headed "They have to go out, don't have to come back."[4] While it is clear enough as a general proposition of law, that the accused had a legal duty to render assistance to a boat in distress in the area, it is not so clear, under the evidence here adduced that a criminally punishable omission to act was established. For while the general duty to undertake a rescue plainly existed, the duty of a particular person to go to the rescue of

---

4 [n.1] The story goes that a young surfman once expressed misgivings about launching a boat in heavy surf. They could get out to the wreck alright, he said, but how were they going to get back? "Young feller" answered the old Hatteras boatswain, "the regulations say we got to go out there; there ain't nothing in the regulations about getting back." (Powell, What the Citizen Should Know About the Coast Guard, page 88.) See especially: "The United States Coast Guard — A Definitive History" by Stephen H. Evans.

a particular boat in distress at a particular time could exist only if the person had been made aware of the occasion for action on his part. It would seem to be elementary that a person ought not to be punished for failing to do something that he did not know he was supposed to do, when he was not reasonably chargeable with such knowledge.

In his work on General Principles of Criminal Law (2d Ed 1960) Prof. Jerome Hall refers to the case of a man charged with manslaughter of his wife, who died in childbirth, in which the court declared:

> One cannot be said in any manner to neglect or refuse to perform a duty unless he has knowledge of the condition of things which require performance at his hands. (*Westrup v Commonwealth,*123 Ky 95, 93 SW 646).

Prof. Hall writes:

> A duty to perform an overt act, of course, implies a duty to know the relevant facts. . . . The penal law does not require that a person actually know he is under a legal duty to act to prevent serious harms; it requires only that there be such a duty. On the other hand, the penal law does require that the defendant know the facts to which his duty refers as well as the facts which make it necessary to perform the duty.

Id., pages 204 and 205.

The relevant evidence in this case is insufficient to convince us that the accused knew the facts which made it necessary for him to initiate rescue procedures. We cannot say that the proof establishes beyond a reasonable doubt that the accused was actually made aware of the information which was shouted at him.

Furthermore this question required pointed submission to the triers of the facts. The defense counsel had requested the law officer to give the following instruction to the court:

> If you find that the accused failed to respond to a distress call on 18 August 1962 and you further find that this failure was due to his lack of conscious awareness of the said distress call, for whatever reason, then you must find him not guilty.

The law officer denied the request. In outline, he instructed the court that they must find (1) that Pratt had a certain prescribed duty to institute rescue procedures "when he was awakened and informed" that a boat was in distress at Isle of Shoals; (2) "that Pratt knew of this duty" and (3) that at the time and place alleged he was derelict in the performance of that duty in failing to institute rescue procedures "when he was awakened and informed." . . .

The evidence required more precise tailoring of the instructions than was done here. *Cf. United States v Smith* (No. 16,124), 13 U.S.C.M.A. 471, 33 C.M.R. 3; *United States v Acfalle* (No. 14,789), 12 U.S.C.M.A. 465, 31 C.M.R. 51. As we have seen, Pratt had to know the facts which made it necessary for him to act, before it could be said that his non-performance of duty was criminal. The instruction "that Pratt knew of this duty" was insufficient; it did not go far enough. Although the law officer stated that the accused's duty was to institute search and rescue procedures, "when he was awakened and informed that a boat was in distress," this fell far short of instructing the court that it was for them, the court, to say whether or not he had been awakened, and to say whether or not the information had penetrated. It could be argued that the law officer's references to the duty were misleading in stating as a matter of law that the accused "was awakened and informed." The accused was entitled to have this crucial issue of fact plainly and unmistakably submitted for decision to the members of the court. The failure to do so was prejudicial error. *United States v Kuefler*, 14 U.S.C.M.A. 136, 33 C.M.R. 348; *United States v Shanks*, 12 U.S.C.M.A. 586, 31 C.M.R. 172; *United States v Odenweller*, 13 U.S.C.M.A. 71, 32 C.M.R. 71. *See also United States v Heims*, 3 U.S.C.M.A. 418, 12 C.M.R. 174. Likewise, it was error to have denied the requested instruction. Accordingly, irrespective of our non-concurrence in the court's conclusion of guilt, the instructional deficiency requires reversal of the finding. Therefore the finding of guilty of Specification 2 of Charge I is set aside. . . .

[The board of review affirmed Chief Pratt's conviction on the other charges. Reassessing the sentence, it approved a reduction in rate only to pay grade E-4, and the confinement portion of the sentence as mitigated by the Judge Advocate General.]

NOTES AND QUESTIONS

1. Custom plays a pervasive but little studied role in military justice. It governs: construction of *Manual for Courts-Martial* provisions, R.C.M. 103 (Drafters' Explanation), at A21-4 (to be construed "in accordance with their plain meaning, with due deference to previous usage of terms in military law or custom"); pleading, R.C.M. 307(c)(3) (Discussion); functions of counsel, arts. 38(d)-(e), UCMJ; R.C.M. 502(d)(5), (d)(6); particular offenses, MCM ¶¶ 13.c.(3) (disrespect by neglecting to salute), 14.c.(2)(a)(ii) (authority to issue orders), 34.c.(2)-(3) (hazarding a vessel), 59.c.(2) (conduct unbecoming an officer); art. 105(1), UCMJ, and MCM ¶¶ 29a.(1), 29c.(3)(a)-(b) (behavior as a prisoner), 27.c.(2)(a) (reporting of captured or abandoned property); and punishment, R.C.M. 1003(c)(1)(B)(ii) ("unlisted" offenses); MCM pt. V, ¶ 5.c.(5) (permissible extra duties).

2. The *Manual's* treatment of dereliction of duty under Article 92(3) notes that "[a] duty may be imposed by treaty, regulation, lawful order, standard operating procedure, or custom of the service." MCM ¶ 16.c.(3)(a). Members of the service are afforded actual notice of the punitive articles, article 137, UCMJ, and general orders must be properly disseminated in order to serve as a basis for prosecution of members without actual knowledge of their terms. *United States v. Tolkach*, 14 M.J. 239 (C.M.A. 1982). Was Chief Pratt tried for violation of a duty imposed by custom? If so, did he have fair notice of the custom? Can you think of any context in which civilian criminal law penalizes violations of custom? *See* Chapter 8, § II, for further discussion.

3. Violation of a custom of the service can form the basis of charges under other punitive articles as well. Under the so-called "General Article" (Article 134), the Manual explains:

(b) *Breach of custom of the service*. A breach of a custom of the service may result in a violation of clause 1 of Article 134 ["all disorders and neglects to the prejudice of good order and discipline in the armed forces"]. In its legal sense, "custom" means more than a method of procedure or a mode of conduct or behavior which is merely of frequent or usual occurrence. Custom arises out of long established practices which by common usage have attained the force of law in the military or other community affected by them. No custom may be contrary to existing law or regulation. A custom which has not been adopted by existing statute or regulation ceases to exist when its observance has been generally abandoned. Many customs of the service are now set forth in regulations of the various armed forces. Violations of these customs should be charged under Article 92 as violations of the regulations in which they appear if the regulation is punitive. . . .

Manual ¶ 60.c.2(b). If you were defense counsel, how would you prove that a particular custom had fallen into desuetude?

4. Under ¶ 83.b.(4) of the *Manual*, it is an element of the Article 134 offense of fraternization "[t]hat such fraternization violated the custom of the accused's service that officers shall not fraternize with enlisted members on terms of social equality." What if the customs of one branch of the service are out of step with those of the other branches? *See Johanns v. United States*, 20 M.J. 155 (C.M.A. 1985). Typically these matters are now governed by service regulations. Given the increasing reliance on joint activities that transcend service lines, are disparate standards on fraternization defensible?

5. In *United States v. Simmons*, 63 M.J. 89 (C.A.A.F. 2006), the accused conceded that he had a duty to intervene when he saw one Marine assaulting another because he was the platoon's noncommissioned officer. The court noted that "applicable Navy and Marine Corps regulations evidence 230 years of the custom and tradition of the service creating the type of duty" Cpl. Simmons espoused at trial and on appeal. In *United States v. Wilson*, 33 M.J. 797, 798 & n.1 (A.C.M.R. 1991), a soldier was convicted of dereliction of duty in that he "willfully failed to ensure that the United States flag was treated with proper respect by blowing his nose on the flag when it was his duty as a military policeman on flag call to safeguard and protect the flag." The court observed that the government's theory was that Pvt. Wilson's duty arose from service custom. To prove the custom, the government asked the military judge to take judicial notice of various Army regulations. To prove knowledge, it "presented the testimony of the unit first sergeant, a former drill sergeant, who described the standard flag call instruction given to recruits in basic training and the training for flag call provided within the military police company." *Id.* at 798 n.1.

6. "Customs of the service are 'sometimes called common law of the Army' and signify 'generally a right or law not written, but established by long usage.'" JASON A. MOSS, OFFICER'S MANUAL 227 (1917), *quoted in* Joseph B. Berger III, *Making Little Rocks Out of Big Rocks: Implementing Sentences to Hard Labor Without Confinement*, ARMY LAW., Dec. 2004, at 1, 4 n.37. The Supreme Court recognized the role of "customary military law" that would govern "in the absence of positive enactments" in *Martin v. Mott*, 25 U.S. (12 Wheat.) 19, 35 (1827). "A custom's validity is established by a number of factors, including (1) habitual or long-established practice; (2) continuance without interruption; (3) continuance without dispute; (4) reasonableness; (5) certainty; (6) compulsoriness; (7) inherent consistency between customs." Berger, *supra*. Occasionally courts refer to "the common law of the Army." *E.g.*, *R. v. Durkin*, [1953] 2 Q.B. 364 (noting counsel for the Crown's reference to "common law of the army" in sustaining power to dissolve court-martial even without express statutory or regulatory authority). *Durkin* was followed in *Re Johnston's Appeal*, (1960) 9 F.L.R. 31, 37-38 (Austl. Cts.-Martial App. Trib.) (rejecting argument "that even if it could be assumed that there was 'a common law of the army' under which Army courts-martial had from time immemorial claimed and asserted the power to dissolve a court-martial and convene a second court-martial if the interests of justice so required, no such common law could be imputed to the [Royal Air Force] in view of its comparatively modern origin and of the fact that from its inception it had been regulated by statute and regulations made thereunder"). In *Johnston*, counsel argued in vain "that a court-martial is a tribunal of limited jurisdiction and that it is unsafe to seek to argue by analogy from the inherent powers possessed by superior courts of record as he said had been done by Lord Goddard C.J. in *Durkin's Case*." *Id*. at 38. As regulations and rules proliferate, is there still a proper role for any "common law" in the administration of military justice?

V. INTERNATIONAL LAW

Two bodies of international law serve as primary sources of military law: the law of armed conflict and international humanitarian law. International agreements, customary principles and rules, judicial opinions, and resolutions of international bodies constitute these fields of law. The excerpts below suggest the depth and breadth of international sources of military law.

FEDERICO ANDREU-GUZMÁN, MILITARY JURISDICTION AND INTERNATIONAL LAW: MILITARY COURTS AND GROSS HUMAN RIGHTS VIOLATIONS
International Commission of Jurists 2004

With the exception of the Declaration on the Protection of All Persons from Enforced Disappearance and the Inter-American Convention on Forced Disappearance of Persons, there are no specific norms, of either a treaty-based or declaratory nature, within international human rights law relating to military offences, military jurisdiction or military "justice." Other fields of international law do contain provisions on military jurisdiction, most of them relating to aspects of international, military, or judicial cooperation, or extradition. In the case of extradition, several treaties talk about the notion of a "purely military offence" or "essentially military crimes" while others talk about "offences under military law which are not offences under ordinary criminal law." While in multi-lateral treaties extradition does not apply in principle to military offences, this principle has become somewhat tempered with the emergence of a large number of bilateral and multi-lateral treaties which include military offences on the list of extraditable offences. The same can be said for judicial cooperation where all texts remit to domestic legislation whenever the treaty in question does not define what is to be understood by a "military offence."

The starting point for addressing the practice of trying military or police personnel who have committed human rights violations in military courts should [] be the international principles and standards which apply to the international obligations States have with regard to human rights matters. This means analyzing military jurisdiction in light of their international obligations which come into play whenever human rights are violated. The latter concern the State's legal duty to investigate human rights violations, bring to trial and punish the perpetrators, award compensation and provide the victims and their families with an effective remedy and the right to know the truth. . . .

Military jurisdiction is often used as a means of escaping the control of civilian authorities and of consolidating the military as a power within society, as well as a tool though which the military authorities can exert supremacy over civilians. The Human Rights Committee [of the United Nations] has repeatedly stated that States must take steps to ensure that military forces are subject to civilian authority. For its part, the General Assembly of the Organization of American States stressed that: "the system of representative democracy [enshrined both in the Charter of the Organization of American States and in the American Convention on Human Rights] is fundamental for the establishment of a political society in which human rights can be fully realized and one of the essential elements of such a system is the effective subordination of the military apparatus to the civilian authorities." Similarly, the United Nations Commission on Human Rights pointed out that promoting, protecting, and respecting human rights and fundamental freedoms mean that States must ensure that "the military remains accountable to democratically elected civilian government."

THE NUREMBERG PRINCIPLES

["On December 11, 1946, the U.N. General Assembly adopted a resolution in which it 'reaffirm[ed] the principles of international law recognized by the Charter of the Nürnberg Tribunal and the judgment of the Tribunal' and directed the International Law Commission (then called the Committee on the Codification of International Law) to 'formulate' those principles. G.A. Res. 95 (I), U.N. Doc. A/64/Add.1, at 188 (1946). The International Law Commission produced its distillation of the Nuremberg Principles in 1950." EDWARD M. WISE, ELLEN S. PODGOR & ROGER S. CLARK, INTERNATIONAL CRIMINAL LAW, CASES AND MATERIALS 640 (2d ed 2004).]

Principle I. Any person who commits an act which constitutes a crime under international law is responsible therefore and liable to punishment.

Principle II. The fact that internal law does not impose a penalty for an act which constitutes a crime under international law does not relieve the person who committed the act from responsibility under international law.

Principle III. The fact that a person who committed an act which constitutes a crime under international law acted as Head of State or responsible government official does not relieve him from responsibility under international law.

Principle IV. The fact that a person acted pursuant to order of his Government or of a superior does not relieve him from responsibility under international law, provided a moral choice was in fact possible to him.

Principle V. Any person charged with a crime under international law has the right to a fair trial on the facts and law.

Principle VI. The crimes hereinafter set out are punishable as crimes under international law:

(a) Crimes against peace:

(i) Planning, preparation, initiation or waging of a war of aggression or a war in violation of international treaties, agreements or assurances;

(ii) Participation in a common plan or conspiracy for the accomplishment of any of the acts mentioned under (i).

(b) War Crimes: Violations of the laws or customs of war which include, but are not limited to, murder, ill-treatment or deportation of slave-labour or for any other purpose of the civilian population of or in occupied territory, murder or ill-treatment of prisoners of war or persons on the seas, killing of hostages, plunder of public or private property, wanton destruction of cities, towns, or villages, or devastation not justified by military necessity.

(c) Crimes against humanity: Murder, extermination, enslavement, deportation and other inhumane acts done against any civilian population, or persecutions on political, racial, or religious grounds, when such acts are done or such persecutions are carried on in execution of or in connection with any crime against peace or any war crime.

Principle VII. Complicity in the commission of a crime against peace, a war crime, or a crime against humanity as set forth in Principle VI is a crime under international law.

Patricia M. Wald, *General Radislav Krstic: A War Crimes Case Study*
16 GEO. J. LEGAL ETHICS 445-72 (2003)

This article will focus on one major war crimes trial in which I participated as a judge of the International Criminal Tribunal for the former Yugoslavia (ICTY). In microcosm, I believe it raises and perhaps helps to answer many questions surrounding war crimes tribunals, their achievements and shortcomings. Among those questions are: Should major military exercises and the chaotic and anarchistic behaviors by soldiers and their leaders they so often spawn be justiciable at all or better left to the settlement negotiations? Is it fair for the international community to impose war crimes tribunals on some countries engaged in armed conflicts but not others? Do international courts operate in too cocoon-like an atmosphere, remote from the cultural milieu of the countries involved? Is case law interpreting international humanitarian principles so sparse and embryonic that it amounts to a violation of the universal maxim — *nulle crimen sine lege* (no crime without law) — which forbids trying an individual for something he could not have known was a crime at the time of commission? Finally, does it offend basic notions of justice to convict and imprison a middle-level officer of war crimes while his superior — the principal offender — walks free because the court has no authority to secure the arrest of the top leader?

The Fall of Srebrenica

In July 1995, the fourth year of the Bosnian war, and only months before the Dayton Accords ending the hostilities, what United Nations Secretary General Kofi Annan called "a massacre on a scale unprecedented in Europe since the Second World War" took place in a remote valley of Southeastern Bosnia-Herzegovina. A later United Nations report detailed the systematic slaughter of thousands of young men who had been supposedly protected by the U.N.-created safe haven of Srebrenica:

> The tragedy that occurred after the fall of Srebrenica is shocking [for two reasons:] first and foremost, for the magnitude of the crimes committed . . . [second] because the enclave's inhabitants believed that the authority of the United Nations Security Council, the presence of [U.N.] peacekeepers, and the might of NATO air power, would ensure their safety.

In 1998, the International Criminal Tribunal for the former Yugoslavia arrested General Radislav Krstic, the former Commander of the elite Drina Corps of the Bosnian Serb Army in 1995, on an indictment charging him with genocide, crimes against humanity, and war crimes arising out of the events following the downfall of Srebrenica. . . .

The Tribunal

The International Criminal Tribunal for the former Yugoslavia (the Tribunal) was established in 1993 by a United Nations Security Council Resolution to prosecute and try war crimes, crimes against humanity and genocide committed on the territory of the former Yugoslavia from January 1, 1991 onward. It represented a response by the international community to the steady stream of horror stories emanating from that beleaguered region in 1992-93. The prime mover in its establishment was the United States.

General Krstic was forcibly arrested in December 1998 by NATO soldiers in an ambush on a Bosnian road and detained at the U.N. detention unit on the outskirts of the Hague; his case was assigned to Trial Chamber I which began trial in March 2000. The three trial judges were myself; Judge Fouad Riad of Egypt, an international law professor, author and arbitrator, and Tribunal member since 1995; and Judge Almiro Rodrigues, the presiding judge, a former Deputy Attorney General of Portugal, professor of law, and member of the Tribunal since 1997. . . .

The Accused

On March 3, 2000, when his trial began, General Krstic was the most senior military officer to stand trial at the Hague. He was indicted for genocide, war crimes, and crimes against humanity based on the Srebrenica events. . . . Six months before Srebrenica, Krstic had lost a leg in a land mine accident; his prior record was unblemished; and he had been a valuable and cooperative partner with the Western powers in the implementation of the Dayton Accords since 1995. One reporter described him later as "a mild mannered man [who] oversaw the worst atrocity committed in Europe since the Nazis." . . .

Highlights of the Trial

The trial lasted for ninety-eight days over a period of seventeen months; 118 witnesses testified; over 1000 exhibits were introduced. . . . Chief Prosecutor Mark Harmon opened dramatically: "This is a case about the triumph of evil, about men who professed to be professional soldiers . . . [who] organized, planned and willingly participated in the genocide, or stood silent in the face of it." . . . Krstic, on the other hand, maintained that he did not become Commander of the Drina Corps until weeks after the executions, that he spent the crucial week of July 11-18 many miles away from the scene of the alleged massacres, preparing for and executing a separate military campaign against Zepa, the other "safe enclave" in the region. . . .

The Law

General Krstic was charged with war crimes, crimes against humanity, and genocide, all based upon the same factual scenario. The most serious charge, of course, was genocide — "the crime of crimes." Krstic's trial would be the first in the Yugoslav Tribunal to try the charge of genocide through to completion.

There was sparse judicial precedent construing the Genocide Convention of 1948; only a few prosecutions of Nazi leaders in national courts — including [Adolf] Eichmann in Israel — and several Hutu leaders in the Rwandan Tribunal, including the Prime Minister of Rwanda who pled guilty to the genocide charge. The Hutu slaughter of over 800,000 Tutsis, however, lent itself much more naturally than the Bosnian killings to the prototypal genocide perpetrated by the Nazis against the Jews that gave rise to the 1948 Convention.

From the beginning of the Bosnian war, there had been disputes among international scholars as to whether the Serbian-type "ethnic cleansing" of Bosnian Muslims constituted genocide. One respected judge on the International Court of Justice had said in a preliminary opinion that the "forced migration of civilians, more commonly known as 'ethnic cleansing,' is, in truth, part of a deliberate campaign by the Serbs to eliminate Muslim control of, or presence in, substantial parts of Bosnia-Herzegovina. Such being the case, it is difficult to regard the Serbian acts as other than acts of genocide," and several U.N. Resolutions had referred to "the abhorrent policy of 'ethnic cleansing' which is a form of genocide."

But the drafters of the Genocide Convention had deliberately resisted including forcible transfers or deportation per se in the definition of genocide. They feared that unless strictly construed "the idea of genocide [could] be expanded indefinitely to include the laws of war, protection of minorities or respect for human rights," thereby diluting its stigma which must be reserved for the "most heinous crimes of intentional group destruction."

The definition of genocide in the Convention and in the Tribunal Statute contains two essential requirements. First, the actions constituting genocide must fall within five specific categories only the first three of which are relevant here: (1) killing members of a targeted group; (2) causing members of the group serious bodily and mental harm; or (3) deliberately inflicting upon members of the group conditions of life calculated to bring about its physical destruction, in whole or in part.

In Krstic's case, the prosecution charged, and the proof easily showed, that "all of the military-aged Bosnian/Muslim males [from Srebenica] that were captured or fell otherwise in the hands of the Serb forces were systematically executed," and serious bodily and mental harm was inflicted on those few who survived.

The harder job was to prove the second element of genocide; that these acts were done with the specific intent to destroy a protected ethnic, racial or religious group in whole or in part, rather than as a military objective to advance the war, or even as revenge by a frustrated Serb army led by General Mladic, who was enraged because the Muslim army had not surrendered at Potocari as he demanded.

Unlike Rwanda and some earlier genocides, there had been no public calls in Bosnia for the killing of any group; the court therefore had to infer the required genocidal intent from the pattern of the executions and deportations themselves. From such evidence, it did find that "a decision was made . . . to capture and kill all the Bosnian/Muslim men indiscriminately. . . . No efforts thereafter were made to distinguish the soldiers from the civilians." The captured men had been stripped of their identifications; their belongings piled up and burned; their annihilation had to have been the only goal. Nor did the mass executions bespeak of unplanned or uncontrolled rampage by furious troops. They were carefully planned and orchestrated — dozens of holding places, hundreds of blindfolds, ligatures, burials on-site, and reburials.

But was an intent to kill the young men from Srebrenica — civilians and military alike — sufficient to meet the Convention's requirement that there be an intent to destroy "a national, ethnical, racial or religious group in whole or in part, as such." These words, as it turned out, have a long and tortured history.

In the Srebrenica case, the indictment originally named all Bosnian Muslims as the targeted group, but the prosecution later changed its position to argue only the Srebrenica Muslims constituted the group. The defense argued, on the other hand, that the Bosnian Muslims of Srebenica were not a specific national, ethnical, or religious group with characteristics distinguishable from the rest of Bosnian Muslims. On this issue the court sided with the defense — that meant the 1.5 million Muslims in Bosnia, not the 37,000 Muslims in Srebrenica were the relevant protected "group" for purposes of the genocide definition.

The next question, then, was whether it had been sufficiently shown that the Srebrenica Muslims were a distinct enough "part" of the larger group of Bosnian Muslims for the genocide definition to apply, since no one was claiming the Serbs had set out to destroy all the Muslims in Bosnia. Here the prosecution relied on proof that a strategic objective of the Serbs was to unite in a single state all the Serbs in this predominantly Serb region of Bosnia and by so doing to erase the border which separated Serbia from Eastern Bosnia. In this campaign only a few small enclaves like Srebrenica, where the population was predominantly Muslim, stood in the way. The permanent removal of the Muslim population of Srebenica was essential to that goal. The Srebrenica Muslims were, in short, a distinct "part" of the total Bosnian Muslim population the Serbs had slated for destruction.

There was one last bridge to cross: not all the Bosnian Muslim inhabitants of Srebrenica had been targeted for killing, only the military-aged men. The women and children had been transported unharmed to Muslim territory. So how, the defense argued, could one say that this even smaller fraction of Bosnian Muslims could qualify as a substantial enough "part" of the entire group to meet the definition? Here, in what I believe to be a novel interpretation, the court reasoned, based on testimony of social science experts who appeared before it, that the Serbs fully realized that the Muslim society in Srebrenica was a patriarchal one and that by depriving family units of their principal breadwinners and male authority figures, "they would profoundly disrupt the bedrock social and cultural foundation of the group." The women would not return to Srebrenica alone — ever. In the words of the prosecutor, "by killing the leaders and defenders and deporting the remainder, the VRS and General Krstic assured the Bosnian/Muslim community of Srebenica and its surrounds would not return to Srebenica nor would it reconstitute itself in that region or indeed anywhere else." Which is indeed what has actually happened. The widespread destruction of Muslim homes and mosques in that town added to the evidence of such an intent. . . .

The Sentencing

The prosecution asked for a life sentence, arguing that nothing less would be justified on a conviction of genocide. The defense made no submission on a sentence. In its judgment of conviction, the court cited prior decisions stressing the gravity of offense, individual circumstances, and deterrence as primary criteria in determining a sentence, but also noted that the statute instructed sentencing courts to take into account "the general practice regarding prison sentences by the courts of the former Yugoslavia." Although Yugoslav courts had at one time been authorized to hand down the death penalty for genocide, the Bosnian Code in 1998 abolished the death penalty and set twenty to forty years as the range for long-term imprisonment "for the gravest forms of criminal offenses." In pronouncing its sentence of forty-six years imprisonment, the court said:

> The [court's] overall assessment is that General Krstic is a professional soldier who willingly participated in the forcible transfer of all women, children and elderly from Srebrenica, but would not likely, on his own, have embarked on a genocidal venture; however, he allowed himself, as he assumed command responsibility for the Drina Corps,

to be drawn into the heinous scheme and to sanction the use of Corps assets to assist with the genocide. . . . General Krstic remained largely passive in the face of his knowledge of what was going on; he is guilty, but his guilt is palpably less than others who devised and supervised the executions all through that week and who remain at large. . . . His story is one of a respected professional soldier who could not balk his superiors' insane desire to forever rid the Srebrenica area of Muslim civilians, and who, finally, participated in the unlawful realisation of this hideous design.

The press in attendance at the sentencing described Krstic as "looking drawn and grey"; they said [he] "swallowed hard at the verdict." In Serbia a reporter wrote the reaction to Krstic's conviction and sentence was not a high-decibel one. "People want to get on with their lives, put these the bad days behind them." Krstic's counsel told reporters, "we expected this judgment from the very start of the trial." Bosnian Muslim women refugees from Srebrenica interviewed were outraged that he did not receive a life sentence. However, the lead prosecutor, Mark Harmon, said in an interview: "What happens to someone . . . who gets 45 [*sic*] years has got to give pause to any rational commander in the future who envisions, or who wants to participate in the commission of war crimes." Most reporters agreed that, "Even by the standards of the war crimes tribunal, this trial was harrowing."

Conclusion

Answers to those perplexing questions I posed earlier do not come easily. In concluding, I will underscore only a few key points:

(1) The factual scenarios of war crimes are complex — especially those committed by leaders far distant from their victims. The more powerful and highly placed the leader, the harder it may be to trace his trail down to the atrocities at the battlefield or village level. We are seeing some of that at the Milosevic trial now. Contemporary tyrants have learned valuable lessons from their Nazi predecessors; they put little on paper; they give few direct orders to kill or abuse. The proof of their involvement at trial is usually circumstantial and their complicity inferential. For those schooled in Western norms of criminal justice, this can turn out to be a risky — and very time-consuming — undertaking. Krstic was an appealing defendant in some respects: his sin — moral and legal — consisted of not standing up to the evil of his own superiors. He does not wholly fit the model of the bloodthirsty, wildly ambitious and reckless war criminal. Yet, because of the vicissitudes of international arrests, his superiors walk free. That basic paradox will not change with the new International Criminal Court though States Parties to that Court are required to turn over charged suspects in their custody or to apprehend those in their jurisdiction. But to some degree, international justice will always be a hostage of international diplomacy and national sovereignty.

(2) However, many believe individual accountability for grievous crimes against innocent victims is just as much an urgent imperative for international as for national self-respect and the integrity of legal order. There was no other forum in which General Krstic's case could have been heard; Bosnian court structures were in tatters after the war; Serbia, then under Milosevic,

certainly would not have done it. We may all agree that the preferable solution is for war crimes to be tried in the native country of the suspects, if those countries are truly committed to fair and open trials. And, indeed, the new International Criminal Court embraces that principle, making provision for the accused's home country to conduct the trial if it is willing and able to do so. But even today major nations and wartime countries admit openly they are not so willing or able. We need this permanent international forum to fill that void, lest the advances made in international criminal and humanitarian law during the past century deteriorate into mere rhetoric.

(3) "Command responsibility" and "criminal enterprise" are useful doctrines in an international criminal jurisprudence that deals with far-flung military campaigns, serial massacres, and nationwide strategies, such as ethnic cleansing; Milosevic's current trial covering five years and hundreds of activities in several countries is based on a criminal enterprise theory. But the way in which such theories are applied must be carefully monitored lest they escape legitimate limits and provide too easy an escape from the burden of proving guilt beyond a reasonable doubt in individual cases, especially in special intent crimes like genocide. There are arguments that military, and even civilian leaders should be presumed knowledgeable of and responsible for what goes on in their commands or jurisdictions, but such a presumption makes many Western criminal scholars uncomfortable, especially given the geographical scope and uncertain command structures that characterize many current wars. As for criminal enterprise, our own United States experience with overreaching under conspiracy doctrines should give us pause in too facilely globalizing those doctrines. Where precisely the line should be drawn needs further exploration and refinement.

(4) The procedural rules under which international courts operate are inevitably a mixture of different legal systems; the pieces do not always fit neatly, yet these rules, especially rules of evidence, can control the outcome of trial. The draft rules of the new International Criminal Court represent an improvement over those of the two ad hoc Tribunals but undoubtedly can themselves be improved with experience. The goal is a fair trial, not a familiar one.

(5) War crimes trials provide a unique service in documenting wartime crimes and atrocities and giving such records the imprimatur of international factfinding. In this way they pose a barrier not only to future denials that the crimes ever took place but to the phenomenon of war fatigue that envelops nations in the decades following the wars and impels them to ignore their own documentation efforts. "Those who do not heed the past are condemned to repeat it," George Santayana said, and a thorough record of wartime misdeeds compiled in the immediate aftermath is a contribution to history and hopefully to deterrence.

(6) The War Crimes Tribunals represent a maiden effort at defining and enforcing international humanitarian law which had previously been the exclusive sphere of diplomats and scholars. This application has required a tremendous effort to flesh out bareboned, sometimes vague, sometimes conflicting, definitions and doctrines within an overriding principle that no one must be punished for something that was not clearly recognized as a crime at

the time he did it. There is much more work to be done to establish a complete and coherent body of international humanitarian law, and my fervent hope is that eventually the United States will rejoin the community of nations to make its proper contribution to that development in the International Criminal Court. We were pioneers in this effort at Nuremberg and the Hague; it is sad to see the United States now in retreat. Nothing worthwhile — in the law or outside — comes easy and the fledgling efforts at international justice of the current Tribunals richly deserve attention, assessment, and, I personally like to think, even modest applause.

NOTE AND QUESTION

"There is a very high degree of international consensus on the basic rules of the laws of war." DOCUMENTS ON THE LAWS OF WAR 27 (ADAM ROBERTS & RICHARD GUELFF eds 3d ed. 2004). This is not the case with other aspects of military law. Why is the law of war universal? Is this an overstatement of the level of consensus?

Chapter 3

THE ROLE OF THE COMMANDER

Distinctive to military justice is the role of the commander in the legal process of identifying and prosecuting crimes. A commanding officer has no correlate in civilian criminal justice; the commander's role as leader, mentor, evaluator, and legal superior of her troops gives her a unique set of qualifications and biases in the process of investigating and prosecuting crimes. Apart from the involvement of the commander in the administration of military justice, international law and the laws of many states hold commanding officers criminally liable for the crimes of subordinates. This chapter explores the legal terrain of command. It begins with a study of individual accountability and state liability for military crimes. It turns then to the commanding officer's role in military justice, addressing first the prosecutorial function of the commander, then the need to limit that function, and finally the role of the commander in pretrial investigations.

I. ACCOUNTABILITY AND LIABILITY

IN RE YAMASHITA
Supreme Court of the United States
327 U.S. 1 (1946)

MR. CHIEF JUSTICE STONE delivered the opinion of the Court.

. . . From the petitions and supporting papers it appears that prior to September 3, 1945, petitioner was the Commanding General of the Fourteenth Army Group of the Imperial Japanese Army in the Philippine Islands. On that date he surrendered to and became a prisoner of war of the United States Army Forces in Baguio, Philippine Islands. On September 25th, by order of respondent, Lieutenant General Wilhelm D. Styer, Commanding General of the United States Army Forces, Western Pacific, which command embraces the Philippine Islands, petitioner was served with a charge prepared by the Judge Advocate General's Department of the Army, purporting to charge petitioner with a violation of the law of war. On October 8, 1945, petitioner, after pleading not guilty to the charge, was held for trial before a military commission of five Army officers appointed by order of General Styer. The order appointed six Army officers, all lawyers, as defense counsel. Throughout the proceedings which followed, including those before this Court, defense counsel have demonstrated their professional skill and resourcefulness and their proper zeal for the defense with which they were charged.

On the same date a bill of particulars was filed by the prosecution, and the commission heard a motion made in petitioner's behalf to dismiss the charge on the ground that it failed to state a violation of the law of war. On October

29th the commission was reconvened, a supplemental bill of particulars was filed, and the motion to dismiss was denied. The trial then proceeded until its conclusion on December 7, 1945, the commission hearing two hundred and eighty-six witnesses, who gave over three thousand pages of testimony. On that date petitioner was found guilty of the offense as charged and sentenced to death by hanging. . . .

The Charge. Neither Congressional action nor the military orders constituting the commission authorized it to place petitioner on trial unless the charge preferred against him is of a violation of the law of war. The charge, so far as now relevant, is that petitioner, between October 9, 1944 and September 2, 1945, in the Philippine Islands, "while commander of armed forces of Japan at war with the United States of America and its allies, unlawfully disregarded and failed to discharge his duty as commander to control the operations of the members of his command, permitting them to commit brutal atrocities and other high crimes against people of the United States and of its allies and dependencies, particularly the Philippines; and he * * * thereby violated the laws of war."

Bills of particulars, filed by the prosecution by order of the commission, allege a a series of acts, one hundred and twenty-three in number, committed by members of the forces under petitioner's command, during the period mentioned. The first item specifies the execution of a "a deliberate plan and purpose to massacre and exterminate a large part of the civilian population of Batangas Province, and to devastate and destroy public, private and religious property therein, as a result of which more than 25,000 men, women and children, all unarmed noncombatant civilians, were brutally mistreated and killed, without cause or trial, and entire settlements were devastated and destroyed wantonly and without military necessity." Other items specify acts of violence, cruelty and homicide inflicted upon the civilian population and prisoners of war, acts of wholesale pillage and the wanton destruction of religious monuments.

It is not denied that such acts directed against the civilian population of an occupied country and against prisoners of war are recognized in international law as violations of the law of war. Articles 4, 28, 46, and 47, Annex to Fourth Hague Convention, 1907, 36 Stat. 2277, 2296, 2303, 2306, 2307. But it is urged that the charge does not allege that petitioner has either committed or directed the commission of such acts, and consequently that no violation is charged as against him. But this overlooks the fact that the gist of the charge is an unlawful breach of duty by petitioner as an army commander to control the operations of the members of his command by "permitting them to commit" the extensive and widespread atrocities specified. The question then is whether the law of war imposes on an army commander a duty to take such appropriate measures as are within his power to control the troops under his command for the prevention of the specified acts which are violations of the law of war and which are likely to attend the occupation of hostile territory by an uncontrolled soldiery, and whether he may be charged with personal responsibility for his failure to take such measures when violations result. That this was the precise issue to be tried was made clear by the statement of the prosecution at the opening of the trial.

It is evident that the conduct of military operations by troops whose excesses are unrestrained by the orders or efforts of their commander would almost certainly result in violations which it is the purpose of the law of war to prevent. Its purpose to protect civilian populations and prisoners of war from brutality would largely be defeated if the commander of an invading army could with impunity neglect to take reasonable measures for their protection. Hence the law of war presupposes that its violation is to be avoided through the control of the operations of war by commanders who are to some extent responsible for their subordinates.

This is recognized by the Annex to Fourth Hague Convention of 1907, respecting the laws and customs of war on land. Article I lays down as a condition which an armed force must fulfill in order to be accorded the rights of lawful belligerents, that it must be "commanded by a person responsible for his subordinates." 36 Stat. 2295. Similarly Article 19 of the Tenth Hague Convention, relating to bombardment by naval vessels, provides that commanders in chief of the belligerent vessels "must see that the above Articles are properly carried out." 36 Stat. 2389. And Article 26 of the Geneva Red Cross Convention of 1929, 47 Stat. 2074, 2092, for the amelioration of the condition of the wounded and sick in armies in the field, makes it "the duty of the commanders-in-chief of the belligerent armies to provide for the details of execution of the foregoing articles [of the convention], as well as for unforeseen cases." And, finally, Article 43 of the Annex of the Fourth Hague Convention, 36 Stat. 2306, requires that the commander of a force occupying enemy territory, as was petitioner, "shall take all the measures in his power to restore, and ensure, as far as possible, public order and safety, while respecting, unless absolutely prevented, the laws in force in the country."

These provisions plainly imposed on petitioner, who at the time specified was military governor of the Philippines, as well as commander of the Japanese forces, an affirmative duty to take such measures as were within his power and appropriate in the circumstances to protect prisoners of war and the civilian population. This duty of a commanding officer has heretofore been recognized, and its breach penalized by our own military tribunals. A like principle has been applied so as to impose liability on the United States in international arbitrations. *Case of Jenaud*, 3 Moore, International Arbitrations, 3000; *Case of "The Zafiro*," 5 Hackworth, Digest of International Law, 707. . . .

We do not make the laws of war but we respect them so far as they do not conflict with the commands of Congress or the Constitution. There is no contention that the present charge, thus read, is without the support of evidence, or that the commission held petitioner responsible for failing to take measures which were beyond his control or inappropriate for a commanding officer to take in the circumstances.[1] We do not here appraise the evidence on which petitioner was convicted. We do not consider what measures, if any, petitioner took to prevent the commission, by the troops under his command, of the plain violations of the law of war detailed in the bill of particulars, or whether such measures as he may have taken were appropriate and sufficient to discharge the duty imposed upon him. These are questions within the peculiar competence of the military officers composing the commission and were for it to decide. *See Smith v. Whitney*, 116 U.S. 167, 178. It is plain that the charge on which petitioner was tried charged him with a breach of his duty to control the operations of the members of his command, by permitting them to commit the specified atrocities. This was enough to require the commission to hear evidence tending to establish the culpable failure of petitioner to perform the duty imposed on him by the law of war and to pass upon its sufficiency to establish guilt.

Obviously charges of violations of the law of war triable before a military tribunal need not be stated with the precision of a common law indictment. *Cf. Collins v. McDonald, supra*, 258 U.S. 420. But we conclude that the allegations of the charge, tested by any reasonable standard, adequately allege a violation of the law of war and that the commission had authority to try and decide the issue which it raised. *Cf. Dealy v. United States*, 152 U.S. 539; *Williamson v. United States*, 207 U.S. 425, 447; *Glasser v. United States*, 315 U.S. 60, 66, and cases cited. . . .

Mr. Justice Murphy, dissenting.

. . . I find it impossible to agree that the charge against the petitioner stated a recognized violation of the laws of war.

It is important, in the first place, to appreciate the background of events preceding this trial. From October 9, 1944, to September 2, 1945, the petitioner was the Commanding General of the 14th Army Group of the Imperial Japanese Army, with headquarters in the Philippines. The reconquest of the Philippines by the armed forces of the United States began approximately at the time when the petitioner assumed this command. Combined with a great and decisive sea battle, an invasion was made on the island of Leyte on October 20, 1944. "In the six days of the great naval action the Japanese position in the Philippines had become extremely critical. Most of the serviceable elements of the Japanese Navy had become committed to the battle with disastrous results. The strike had miscarried, and General MacArthur's land wedge was firmly implanted in the vulnerable flank of the enemy * * *. There were 260,000 Japanese troops scattered over the Philippines but most of them might as well have been on the other side of the world so far as the enemy's ability to shift them to meet the American thrusts was concerned. If General MacArthur succeeded in establishing himself in the Visayas where he could stage, exploit, and spread under cover of overwhelming naval and air superiority, nothing could prevent him from overrunning the Philippines." Biennial Report of the Chief of Staff of the United States Army, July 1, 1943, to June 30, 1945, to the Secretary of War, p. 74.

---

[1] [n.4] In its findings the commission took account of the difficulties "faced by the accused, with respect not only to the swift and overpowering advance of American forces, but also to errors of his predecessors, weakness in organization, equipment, supply * * *, training, communication, discipline and morale of his troops," and "the tactical situation, the character, training and capacity of staff officers and subordinate commanders, as well as the traits of character of his troops." It nonetheless found that petitioner had not taken such measures to control his troops as were "required by the circumstances." We do not weigh the evidence. We merely hold that the charge sufficiently states a violation against the law of war, and that the commission, upon the facts found, could properly find petitioner guilty of such a violation.

By the end of 1944 the island of Leyte was largely in American hands. And on January 9, 1945, the island of Luzon was invaded. "Yamashita's inability to cope with General MacArthur's swift moves, his desired reaction to the deception measures, the guerrillas, and General Kenney's aircraft combined to place the Japanese in an impossible situation. The enemy was forced into a piecemeal commitment of his troops." *Ibid*, p. 78. It was at this time and place that most of the alleged atrocities took place. Organized resistance around Manila ceased on February 23. Repeated land and air assaults pulverized the enemy and within a few months there was little left of petitioner's command except a few remnants which had gathered for a last stand among the precipitous mountains.

As the military commission here noted, "The Defense established the difficulties faced by the Accused with respect not only to the swift and overpowering advance of American forces, but also to the errors of his predecessors, weaknesses in organization, equipment, supply with especial reference to food and gasoline, training, communication, discipline and morale of his troops. It was alleged that the sudden assignment of Naval and Air Forces to his tactical command presented almost insurmountable difficulties. This situation was followed, the Defense contended, by failure to obey his orders to withdraw troops from Manila, and the subsequent massacre of unarmed civilians, particularly by Naval forces. Prior to the Luzon Campaign, Naval forces had reported to a separate ministry in the Japanese Government and Naval Commanders may not have been receptive or experienced in this instance with respect to a joint land operation under a single commander who was designated from the Army Service."

The day of final reckoning for the enemy arrived in August, 1945. On September 3, the petitioner surrendered to the United States Army at Baguio, Luzon. He immediately became a prisoner of war and was interned in prison in conformity with the rules of international law. On September 25, approximately three weeks after surrendering, he was served with the charge in issue in this case. Upon service of the charge he was removed from the status of a prisoner of war and placed in confinement as an accused war criminal. Arraignment followed on October 8 before a military commission specially appointed for the case. Petitioner pleaded not guilty. He was also served on that day with a bill of particulars alleging 64 crimes by troops under his command. A supplemental bill alleging 59 more crimes by his troops was filed on October 29, the same day that the trial began. No continuance was allowed for preparation of a defense as to the supplemental bill. The trial continued uninterrupted until December 5, 1945. On December 7 petitioner was found guilty as charged and was sentenced to be hanged.

The petitioner was accused of having "unlawfully disregarded and failed to discharge his duty as commander to control the operations of the members of his command, permitting them to commit brutal atrocities and other high crimes." The bills of particular further alleged that specific acts of atrocity were committed by "members of the armed forces of Japan under the command of the accused." Nowhere was it alleged that the petitioner personally committed any of the atrocities, or that he ordered their commission, or that he had any knowledge of the commission thereof by members of his command.

The findings of the military commission bear out this absence of any direct personal charge against the petitioner. The commission merely found that atrocities and other high crimes "have been committed by members of the Japanese armed forces under your command * * * that they were not sporadic in nature but in many cases were methodically supervised by Japanese officers and noncommissioned officers * * * that during the period in question you failed to provide effective control of your troops as was required by the circumstances."

In other words, read against the background of military events in the Philippines subsequent to October 9, 1944, these charges amount to this: "We, the victorious American forces, have done everything possible to destroy and disorganize your lines of communication, your effective control of your personnel, your ability to wage war. In those respects we have succeeded. We have defeated and crushed your forces. And now we charge and condemn you for having been inefficient in maintaining control of your troops during the period when we were so effectively beseiging and eliminating your forces and blocking your ability to maintain effective control. Many terrible atrocities were committed by your disorganized troops. Because these atrocities were so widespread we will not bother to charge or prove that you committed, ordered or condoned any of them. We will assume that they must have resulted from your inefficiency and negligence as a commander. In short, we charge you with the crime of inefficiency in controlling your troops. We will judge the discharge of your duties by the disorganization which we ourselves created in large part. Our standards of judgment are whatever we wish to make them."

Nothing in all history or in international law, at least as far as I am aware, justifies such a charge against a fallen commander of a defeated force. To use the very inefficiency and disorganization created by the victorious forces as the primary basis for condemning officers of the defeated armies bears no resemblance to justice or to military reality.

International law makes no attempt to define the duties of a commander of an army under constant and overwhelming assault; nor does it impose liability under such circumstances for failure to meet the ordinary responsibilities of command. The omission is understandable. Duties, as well as ability to control troops, vary according to the nature and intensity of the particular battle. To find an unlawful deviation from duty under battle conditions requires difficult and speculative calculations. Such calculations become highly untrustworthy when they are made by the victor in relation to the actions of a vanquished commander. Objective and realistic norms of conduct are then extremely unlikely to be used in forming a judgment as to deviations from duty. The probability that vengeance will form the major part of the victor's judgment is an unfortunate but inescapable fact. So great is that probability that international law refuses to recognize such a judgment as a basis for a war crime, however fair the judgment may be in a particular instance. It is this consideration that undermines the charge against the petitioner in this case. The indictment permits, indeed compels, the military commission of a victorious nation to sit in judgment upon the military strategy and actions of the defeated enemy and to use its conclusions to determine the criminal liability of an enemy commander. Life and liberty are made to depend upon the biased will of the victor rather than upon objective standards of conduct.

The Court's reliance upon vague and indefinite references in certain of the Hague Conventions and the Geneva Red Cross Convention is misplaced. Thus the statement in Article 1 of the Annex to Hague Convention No. IV of October 18, 1907, 36 Stat. 2277, 2295, to the effect that the laws, rights and duties of war apply to military and volunteer corps only if they are "commanded by a person responsible for his subordinates," has no bearing upon the problem in this case. Even if it has, the clause "responsible for his subordinates" fails to state to whom the responsibility is owed or to indicate the type of responsibility contemplated. The phrase has received differing interpretations by authorities on international law. In Oppenheim, International Law (6th ed., rev. by Lauterpacht, 1940, vol. 2, p. 204, fn. 3) it is stated that "The meaning of the word 'responsible' * * * is not clear. It probably means 'responsible to some higher authority,' whether the person is appointed from above or elected from below; * * *." Another authority has stated that the word "responsible" in this particular context means "presumably to a higher authority," or "possibly it merely means one who controls his subordinates and who therefore can be called to account for their acts." Wheaton, International Law (14th ed., by Keith, 1944, p. 172, fn. 30). Still another authority, Westlake, International Law (1907, Part II, p. 61), states that "probably the responsibility intended is nothing more than a capacity of exercising effective control." Finally, Edwards and Oppenheim, Land Warfare (1912, p. 19, par. 22) state that it is enough "if the commander of the corps is regularly or temporarily commissioned as an officer or is a person of position and authority." It seems apparent beyond dispute that the word "responsible" was not used in this particular Hague Convention to hold the commander of a defeated army to any high standard of efficiency when he is under destructive attack; nor was it used to impute to him any criminal responsibility for war crimes committed by troops under his command under such circumstances.

The provisions of the other conventions referred to by the Court are on their face equally devoid of relevance or significance to the situation here in issue. Neither Article 19 of Hague Convention No. X, 36 Stat. 2371, 2389, nor Article 26 of the Geneva Red Cross Convention of 1929, 47 Stat. 2074, 2092, refers to circumstances where the troops of a commander commit atrocities while under heavily adverse battle conditions. Reference is also made to the requirement of Article 43 of the Annex to Hague Convention No. IV, 36 Stat. 2295, 2306, that the commander of a force occupying enemy territory "shall take all the measures in his power to restore, and ensure, as far as possible, public order and safety, while respecting, unless absolutely prevented, the laws in force in the country." But the petitioner was more than a commander of a force occupying enemy territory. He was the leader of an army under constant and devastating attacks by a superior re-invading force. This provision is silent as to the responsibilities of a commander under such conditions as that.

Even the laws of war heretofore recognized by this nation fail to impute responsibility to a fallen commander for excesses committed by his disorganized troops while under attack. Paragraph 347 of the War Department publication, Basic Field Manual, Rules of Land Warfare, FM 27-10 (1940), states the principal offenses under the laws of war recognized by the United States. This includes all of the atrocities which the Japanese troops were alleged to have committed in this instance. Originally this paragraph concluded with the statement that "The commanders ordering the commission of such acts, or under whose authority they are committed by their troops, may be punished by the belligerent into whose hands they may fall." The meaning of the phrase 'under whose authority they are committed' was not clear. On November 15, 1944, however, this sentence was deleted and a new paragraph was added relating to the personal liability of those who violate the laws of war. Change 1, FM 27-10. The new paragraph 345.1 states that "Individuals and organizations who violate the accepted laws and customs of war may be punished therefor. However, the fact that the acts complained of were done pursuant to order of a superior or government sanction may be taken into consideration in determining culpability, either by way of defense or in mitigation of punishment. The person giving such orders may also be punished." From this the conclusion seems inescapable that the United States recognizes individual criminal responsibility for violations of the laws of war only as to those who commit the offenses or who order or direct their commission. Such was not the allegation here. *Cf.* Article 67 of the Articles of War, 10 U.S.C. § 1539, 10 U.S.C.A. § 1539.

There are numerous instances, especially with reference to the Philippine Insurrection in 1900 and 1901, where commanding officers were found to have violated the laws of war by specifically ordering members of their command to commit atrocities and other war crimes. . . . And in other cases officers have been held liable where they knew that a crime was to be committed, had the power to prevent it and failed to exercise that power. . . . In no recorded instance, however, has the mere inability to control troops under fire or attack by superior forces been made the basis of a charge of violating the laws of war.

The Government claims that the principle that commanders in the field are bound to control their troops has been applied so as to impose liability on the United States in international arbitrations. *Case of Jeannaud*, 1880, 3 Moore, International Arbitrations (1898) 3000; *Case of The Zafiro*, 1910, 5 Hackworth, Digest of International Law (1943) 707. The difference between arbitrating property rights and charging an individual with a crime against the laws of war is too obvious to require elaboration. But even more significant is the fact that even these arbitration cases fail to establish any principle of liability where troops are under constant assault and demoralizing influences by attacking forces. The same observation applies to the common law and statutory doctrine, referred to by the Government, that one who is under a legal duty to take protective or preventive action is guilty of criminal homicide if he willfully or negligently omits to act and death is proximately caused. *State v. Harrison*, 107 N.J.L. 213, 152 A. 867; *State v. Irvine*, 126 La. 434, 52 So. 567; Holmes, The Common Law, p. 278. No one denies that inaction or negligence may give rise to liability, civil or criminal. But it is quite another thing to say that the inability to control troops under highly competitive and disastrous battle conditions renders one guilty of a war crime in the absence of personal culpability. Had there been some element of knowledge or direct connection with the atrocities the problem would be entirely different.

Moreover, it must be remembered that we are not dealing here with an ordinary tort or criminal action; precedents in those fields are of little if any value. Rather we are concerned with a proceeding involving an international crime, the treatment of which may have untold effects upon the future peace of the world. That fact must be kept uppermost in our search for precedent.

The only conclusion I can draw is that the charge made against the petitioner is clearly without precedent in international law or in the annals of recorded military history. This is not to say that enemy commanders may escape punishment for clear and unlawful failures to prevent atrocities. But that punishment should be based upon charges fairly drawn in light of established rules of international law and recognized concepts of justice. . . .

THE MANUAL OF THE LAW OF ARMED CONFLICT
United Kingdom Ministry of Defence (2005)

Individual criminal responsibility

16.35 Individuals are responsible for the war crimes that they commit themselves or which they order or assist others to commit.

16.35.1 Article 7 of the Statute of the International Criminal Tribunal for the former Yugoslavia provides that "a person who planned, instigated, ordered, committed, or otherwise aided and abetted in the planning, preparation or execution of a crime . . . shall be individually responsible for the crime."

16.35.2 The Rome Statute of the International Criminal Court also confirms that an individual is responsible for a war crime if he:

a. commits the crime himself, on his own or jointly with others, or

b. orders, solicits, or induces a crime which is committed or attempted, or

c. aids, abets, or otherwise assists in the commission of the crime, including providing the means for its commission, or

d. contributes to the commission or attempted commission of the crime by a group of persons acting with a common purpose.

16.35.3 The fact that a subordinate was ordered to do an act, or make an omission, which was illegal does not, of itself, absolve the subordinate from criminal responsibility.

Responsibility of commanders

16.36 Military commanders are responsible for preventing violations of the law (including the law of armed conflict) and for taking the necessary disciplinary action. A commander will be criminally responsible if he participates in the commission of a war crime himself in one of the ways set out in paragraph 16.35.2, particularly if he orders its commission. However, he also becomes criminally responsible if he "knew, or owing to the circumstances at the time, should have known" that war crimes were being or were about to be committed and failed "to take all necessary and reasonable measures within his or her power to prevent or repress their commission or to submit the matter to the competent authority for investigation and prosecution."

16.36.1 The concept of command responsibility was first enunciated in the case of General Yamashita. In that case, General Yamashita was held to have failed to exercise "effective control" of his troops who were carrying out widespread atrocities in the Philippines. The Tribunal held that the nature of the crimes themselves provided *prima facie* evidence of knowledge and laid down a test that was reflected in the text of the *Manual of Military Law* Part III of 1958. According to that test, a commander was considered responsible if "he has actual knowledge or should have knowledge, though reports received by him or through other means". . . .

16.36.4 Despite the various formulations of the [command responsibility] test, there is general agreement on the nature of command and the degree of knowledge required.

16.36.5 The test of command in this context is one of "effective control" over a subordinate. There need not be proof of command in the sense of formal organizational structure "so long as the fundamental requirement of an effective power to control the subordinate, in the sense of preventing or punishing criminal conduct is satisfied."

16.36.6 Similarly, it is now accepted that an element of knowledge has to be proved, as command responsibility is not a form of strict liability. . . .

Responsibility of civilian authorities

16.37 Civilian superiors will also be liable for the acts of their subordinates in the same way as military commanders, though the difference in the command relationship means that a court is likely to require evidence of actual knowledge or a conscious disregard of information which would have enabled him to know.

Responsibilities of states

16.38 Parties to a conflict are obliged to instruct military commanders to prevent breaches to the law of armed conflict and ensure that their subordinates know of their obligations under that law. This provision is based on the principle that an effective disciplinary system to prevent breaches is the best way of ensuring compliance with the law of armed conflict. But failure to do so does not give rise to criminal responsibility.

16.38.1 Heads of state and their ministers are not immune from prosecution and punishment for war crimes. Their liability is governed by the same principles as those governing the responsibility of civilian authorities.

Criminal Code
Ukraine (2001)

Article 426. Omissions of military authorities

1. Willful failure to prevent a crime committed by a subordinate, or failure of a military inquiry authority to institute a criminal case against a subordi-

nate offender, and also willful failure of a military official to act in accordance with his/her official duties, if it caused any significant damage, shall be punishable by a fine of 50 to 200 tax-free minimum incomes, or service restrictions for a term up to two years, or imprisonment for a term up to three years.

2. The same acts that caused any grave consequences is punishable by imprisonment for a term of three to seven years.

3. Any such acts as provided by paragraph 1 or 2 of this Article, if committed in a state of martial law or in battle, shall be punishable by imprisonment for a term of seven to ten years.

NOTES AND QUESTIONS

1. The case of General Yamashita is infamous for the procedural unfairness of his trial, which General Douglas MacArthur controlled to the extent of selecting the judges and drafting the rules for trial, and for the Supreme Court's post-war review. *See, e.g.,* PETER MAGUIRE, LAW AND WAR: AN AMERICAN STORY 135-40 (2000). How strong is the precedent established by *In re Yamashita*? Why haven't military commanders since 1946 been charged under its rule for criminal culpability?

2. THE MANUAL OF THE LAW OF ARMED CONFLICT (2005) is an official reference work for members of the United Kingdom's armed forces and officials within the Ministry of Defence and other government departments. It follows in the steps of prior guidance, published in 1914 and 1958, on the law of armed conflict. Does it succeed in clarifying the standards to which commanding officers will be held? Does the Ukranian code meet international standards as set out in the UK MANUAL?

UNITED STATES v. SHEARER
Supreme Court of the United States
473 U.S. 52 (1984)

[A mother sued after the death of her son at the hands of a fellow soldier. Private Shearer was murdered near Fort Bliss in Otero County, New Mexico, by Andrew Heard, another private stationed at Fort Bliss. In 1977, Heard had been convicted of manslaughter and sentenced to four years of confinement by a German court; in February of 1979, he was released to the Army by German authorities and transferred to Fort Bliss; in June of 1979, he killed Private Shearer. Prior to the murder, several of his Army superiors at Fort Bliss recommended that Private Heard be discharged. New Mexico convicted Heard of murder and sentenced him to 15 to 55 years of confinement.]

CHIEF JUSTICE BURGER delivered the opinion of the Court. . . .

We granted certiorari to decide whether the survivor of a serviceman, who was murdered by another serviceman, may recover from the Government under the Federal Tort Claims Act for negligently failing to prevent the murder.

I

Respondent is the mother and administratrix of Army Private Vernon Shearer. While Private Shearer was off duty at Fort Bliss and away from the base, he was kidnapped and murdered by another serviceman, Private Andrew Heard. A New Mexico court convicted Private Heard of Shearer's murder and sentenced him to a term of 15 to 55 years' imprisonment.

Respondent brought this action under the Federal Tort Claims Act, 28 U.S.C. §§ 1346(b) and 2671 *et seq.,* claiming that the Army's negligence caused Private Shearer's death. Respondent alleged that Private Heard, while assigned to an Army base in Germany in 1977, was convicted by a German court of manslaughter and sentenced to a 4-year prison term. Upon his discharge from that confinement in Germany, the Army transferred Private Heard to Fort Bliss. Respondent alleged that, although the Army knew that Private Heard was dangerous, it "negligently and carelessly failed to exert a reasonably sufficient control over" him and "failed to warn other persons that he was at large." App. 14.

The United States District Court for the Eastern District of Pennsylvania granted summary judgment in favor of the Government. The Court of Appeals reversed. 723 F.2d 1102 (3d Cir. 1983). The court held that *Feres v. United States,* 340 U.S. 135 (1950), did not bar respondent's suit because "[g]enerally an off-duty serviceman not on the military base and not engaged in military activity at the time of injury, can recover under FTCA." 723 F.2d, at 1106. The court also held that respondent's suit was not precluded by the intentional tort exception to the Act, 28 U.S.C. § 2680(h). The Court of Appeals noted that respondent's complaint alleged negligence and reasoned that "if an assault and battery occurred as a 'natural result' of the government's failure to exercise due care, the assault and battery may be deemed to have its roots in negligence and therefore it is within the scope of the FTCA." *Id.,* at 1107. . . .

II

B

Our holding in *Feres v. United States,* 340 U.S. 135 (1950), was that a soldier may not recover under the Federal Tort Claims Act for injuries which "arise out of or are in the course of activity incident to service." *Id.,* at 146. Although the Court in *Feres* based its decision on several grounds,

> "[i]n the last analysis, *Feres* seems best explained by the 'peculiar and special relationship of the soldier to his superiors, the effects of the maintenance of such suits on discipline, and the extreme results that might obtain if suits under the Tort Claims Act were allowed for negligent orders given or negligent acts committed in the course of military duty." *United States v. Muniz,* 374 U.S. 150, 162 (1963), quoting *United States v. Brown,* 348 U.S. 110, 112 (1954).

The *Feres* doctrine cannot be reduced to a few bright-line rules; each case must be examined in light of the statute as it has been construed in *Feres* and subsequent cases. Here, the Court of Appeals placed great weight on the fact that Private Shearer was off duty and away from the base when he was murdered. But the situs of the murder is not nearly as important as whether the suit requires the civilian court to second-guess military decisions, *see Stencel Aero Engineering Corp. v. United States,* 431 U.S. 666, 673 (1977), and whether the suit might impair essential military discipline, *see Chappell v. Wallace,* 462 U.S. 296, 300, 304 (1983).

Respondent's complaint strikes at the core of these concerns. In particular, respondent alleges that Private Shearer's superiors in the Army "negligently and carelessly failed to exert a reasonably sufficient control over Andrew Heard, . . . failed to warn other persons that he was at large, [and] negligently and carelessly failed to . . . remove Andrew Heard from active military duty." App. 14. This allegation goes directly to the "management" of the military; it calls into question basic choices about the discipline, supervision, and control of a serviceman.

Respondent's case is therefore quite different from *Brooks v. United States,* 337 U.S. 49 (1949), where the Court allowed recovery under the Tort Claims Act for injuries caused by a negligent driver of a military truck. Unlike the negligence alleged in the operation of a vehicle, the claim here would require Army officers "to testify in court as to each other's decisions and actions." *Stencel Aero Engineering Corp. v. United States, supra,* 431 U.S., at 673. To permit this type of suit would mean that commanding officers would have to stand prepared to convince a civilian court of the wisdom of a wide range of military and disciplinary decisions; for example, whether to overlook a particular incident or episode, whether to discharge a serviceman, and whether and how to place restraints on a soldier's off-base conduct. But as we noted in *Chappell v. Wallace,* such "'complex, subtle, and professional decisions as to the composition, training, . . . and control of a military force are essentially professional military judgments.'" 462 U.S. at 302, at 2366, quoting *Gilligan v. Morgan,* 413 U.S. 1, 10 (1973).

Finally, respondent does not escape the *Feres* net by focusing only on this case with a claim of negligence, and by characterizing her claim as a challenge to a "straightforward personnel decision." Tr. of Oral Arg. 37. By whatever name it is called, it is a decision of command. The plaintiffs in *Feres* and *Stencel Aero Engineering* did not contest the wisdom of broad military policy; nevertheless, the Court held that their claims did not fall within the Tort Claims Act because they were the *type* of claims that, if generally permitted, would involve the judiciary in sensitive military affairs at the expense of military discipline and effectiveness. Similarly, respondent's attempt to hale Army officials into court to account for their supervision and discipline of Private Heard must fail. . . .

[The Court reversed the decision of the Court of Appeals.]

NOTES AND QUESTIONS

1. What distinguishes a "decision of command" from a decision that can be construed as negligent by a court? To what degree should courts be involved in allocating the burdens of the costs of military decisions?

2. Does barring actions by family members of injured servicemembers protect the morale and effectiveness of military units? Consider Richard S.

Lehmann, Note, *The Effect of the* Feres *Doctrine on Tort Actions Against the United States by Family Members of Servicemen*, 50 FORDHAM L. REV. 1241, 1264 (1981-82): "Courts should . . . recognize that when members of a serviceman's family bring suit, the effect, if any, on military discipline is insignificant. The spouse and children of a soldier are civilians, they are neither parties to the special relationship that exists between the soldier and his superiors nor are they subject to military orders. For them to assert in a public forum that military officers were negligent is less offensive to the military's system of discipline than it would be for those subject to it to make the same charge."

3. Commanders may be held accountable in court, but they are also held accountable by their subordinates. A commander's perceived errors or unfairness can cause her to lose the support of her troops, which can, in extreme circumstances, provoke a violent confrontation. Angry soldiers can organize resistance in an attempt at mutiny or strike back by themselves at individual officers. During the Vietnam War, hundreds of American officers were threatened, injured, or killed by rebellious troops. Fragging, so-called for the fragmentation grenades that were sometimes used for this purpose, reached a peak late in the war as morale eroded and discipline faltered. As one court explained in reviewing the appeal of a soldier convicted of the November 1970 attempted murder of an officer in Vietnam: "Appellant's threats against his superior officer strike at the very heart of military discipline in a combat zone and at a time when the incident rate of 'fragging' of superiors by subordinates is on the increase. It takes little imagination to visualize the chaos and utter breakdown in discipline that would ensue if superiors are subjected to the continuing terror of assassination by subordinates who do not believe they are amenable to orders or otherwise resent authority." *United States v. Creek*, 44 C.M.R. 908, 911 (A.C.M.R. 1972). For further discussion of fragging during the Vietnam War, see GARY D. SOLIS, MARINES AND MILITARY LAW IN VIETNAM: TRIAL BY FIRE 133-38, 168-70 (1989). How does "fragging" affect the administration of military justice?

II. PROSECUTORIAL FUNCTIONS

Queen's Regulations for the Army
United Kingdom

Definition of Command

2.001. The term 'Command' is used in different ways in these regulations and it is therefore necessary to explain how these may apply according to the context in which they appear. The different uses of this term are:

   a.   As a military order by any person whose rank, position, appointment or duty entitles him to give it.

   b.   As applied to the authority of an officer, warrant officer or non-commissioned officer (NCO) deriving from his military status. This is normally expressed as 'power of command.'

    c.   To describe a geographical area, of given boundaries, in which troops are stationed. It may contain districts, areas, or further subdivisions. In practice this covers those units and formations grouped together under a commander in chief (CinC) or general officer commanding (GOC) who is himself not subordinate to another general officer. In peace time geographical commands should not be referred to as 'theatres' (which is an abbreviation for 'theatres of war').

    d.   To refer to a body of troops over which an individual has direct authority, e.g. in the case of a battalion commander, his unit.

Higher Commanders

2.002. Under the existing organisation, the higher commanders of the Army are as follows:

    a.   *CinCs.* General officers who in conjunction with their other duties are operationally responsible to the Defence Council for the command of all British Army personnel in their area. For administrative matters, they are responsible through the Army Board. In certain respects, as members of a commanders in chief committee, they are directly responsible to the Chiefs of Staff.

    b.   *GOCs.* GOCs corps, divisions and districts, responsible to a superior commander.

    c.   *Commanders.*

        (1)   Commanders (general or other officers) of independent overseas commands, responsible to the Army Board.

        (2)   General and other officers, commanding British Army or multi-Service staffs in certain overseas territories, who are responsible directly to the Defence Council, such as Commander British Forces Cyprus.

        (3)   Officers, not above the rank of brigadier, in command of brigades, field forces, groups, areas or garrisons normally responsible to a GOC.

Directions, Guidance and Opinions of Higher Commanders

6.063. Higher commanders (*see* paras. 2002a, *b* and *c*(1)) may on their own initiative issue guidance on disciplinary matters whenever they consider it necessary to do so in the interests of military discipline. For example, a commander in chief may recommend as a matter of policy that certain offences committed within his command, such as the loss of arms, should usually be considered for trial by court-martial and may issue guidance on the appropriate levels of punishment for particular types of offence, for example alcohol-related motoring offences. Such guidance will normally be with the prior agreement of the Ministry of Defence (PS2(Army)) and the Director of Army Legal Services.

6.063A. A commanding officer or appropriate superior authority may at any time seek the opinion of a higher commander on disciplinary matters. Where a charge is preferred against an officer or warrant officer, his commanding officer has power [under the Army Act of 1955 and existing law] to dismiss the charge but, if he decides not to exercise this power, he is required [by law] to submit the case to higher authority in accordance with [appropriate regulations] and it is for the higher authority to decide how the case is to proceed. If the charge is one which appears to reflect adversely on the integrity or reputation of the officer or warrant officer (e.g. dishonesty, indecency or drug abuse), so as to bring into question his fitness for retention in the Army, it should usually be considered for trial by court-martial. If, in a particular case, the higher authority to which it is referred is of the opinion that there are exceptional and compelling reasons for dealing with it summarily, he is to consult the officer next superior to him in the chain of command before finally deciding how the case should be dealt with. It is open to that officer to refer higher for guidance if he feels it is in all the circumstances desirable. . . .

6.063C. Any opinion or guidance on policy matters given by or on behalf of a higher commander is not to inhibit a commanding officer or an appropriate superior authority in the exercise of any of the powers given him under the Army Act 1955, e.g. the commanding officer's power to dismiss a charge under . . . that Act where he is of the opinion that it ought not to be further proceeded with.

BOYD v. ARMY PROSECUTING AUTHORITY
House of Lords (2002)
[2002] UKHL 31

20. The appeals before the House challenge the compatibility of the appellants' trials by court-martial with article 6 of the European Convention on Human Rights and Fundamental Freedoms. In particular on behalf of the appellants Lord Thomas of Gresford QC based his challenge on their right to the determination of the charges against them by "an independent and impartial tribunal" in terms of the first sentence of article 6(1):

> In the determination of his civil rights and obligations or of any criminal charge against him, everyone is entitled to a fair and public hearing within a reasonable time by an independent and impartial tribunal established by law. . . .

29. The present appeals are by no means an isolated phenomenon. They are the latest in a series of challenges to the system of trial by court-martial under United Kingdom law which has been going on for a number of years. These challenges have borne fruit in the shape of substantial reforms to the court-martial system. Particularly important was the judgment of the European Court of Human Rights ("the European Court") in *Findlay v. United Kingdom* (1997) 24 EHRR 221 which criticised the system as it stood before the Armed Forces Act 1996 introduced a number of very significant changes, in particular the abolition of the institutions of "the convening officer" and "the confirming officer." The changes were designed to ensure the independence of the prosecuting authority and of its decision-making and also to make the courts-martial themselves independent of both the prosecuting authority and the wider Service command structure. The effects of the reforms were accurately summarised by the Appeal Court in *R v. Spear* [2001] QB 804, 812-813, para

18. In *Morris v. United Kingdom* (2002) 34 EHRR 1253, 1275, para 61 the European Court noted that these reforms had gone a long way to meeting its concerns in *Findlay*. All the appeals before the House arise from cases conducted in accordance with the reformed procedures. Despite the reforms, challenges to the system continue to come before the European Court. It was indeed only after leave to appeal to this House had been granted in the present cases that the European Court gave judgment in *Morris v. United Kingdom*. . . .

36. Under the existing system, an allegation that a person subject to military law has committed an offence must be reported to his commanding officer in the form of a charge and the commanding officer must investigate the charge: section 76(1) and (2) of the Acts. After investigation, the commanding officer may decide to refer the charge to higher authority under section 76(5)(b) and, if he does so, then the higher authority must usually refer the case to the prosecuting authority (section 76A(1)). For these purposes "the prosecuting authority" is an officer, appointed by Her Majesty, who has been legally qualified for at least 10 years (section 83A). If the prosecuting authority considers that court-martial proceedings should be instituted, he must determine any charge to be preferred and whether it is to be tried by general or district court-martial, and he must also prefer the charge (section 83B(4)). The prosecuting authority must notify the accused's commanding officer and a court administration officer (section 83B(6)). The prosecuting authority has the conduct of any subsequent court-martial proceedings against the accused and has power to make all the decisions relating to the prosecution (section 83B(7) and (8)). The prosecuting authority may delegate any of his functions to officers whom he appoints as prosecuting officers, but they too must be legally qualified (section 83C).

37. When the prosecuting authority notifies a court administration officer of a prospective court-martial, that officer must by order convene a court-martial of the required description (section 84C(1)). . . .

41. Lord Thomas's submission that the appellants' rights under article 6(1) had been infringed did not depend on any specific circumstances relating to their trials or to the individuals who had made up the courts-martial: rather, his was a general challenge to the system of trial of civil offences allegedly committed in the United Kingdom by courts-martial duly set up in accordance with the legislation. In such cases courts-martial did not constitute an independent and impartial tribunal. In support, Lord Thomas cited the dissenting opinion of Laskin CJC in *MacKay v. The Queen* 114 DLR (3d) 393, 401-402 where he was considering the case of a serviceman who had been tried by court-martial for various drugs offences under the Narcotic Control Act 1970. The Chief Justice said:

> In the present case, the charges against the accused were laid by the accused's commanding officer. The standing court martial was ordered by a senior commander and a member of the armed forces, a lieutenant-colonel, was appointed from an approved list as the standing court martial pursuant to section 154 [of the National Defence Act 1970]. Both the officer constituting the standing court martial and the prosecutor were part of the office of the Judge Advocate-General. In

short, the accused, who was tried on charges under a general federal statute, the Narcotic Control Act, was in the hands of his military superiors in respect of the charges, the prosecution and the tribunal by which he was tried. It is true that the Court Martial Appeal Court, consisting under section 201 . . . of the National Defence Act, of judges of the Federal Court of Canada and additional superior court judges appointed by the Governor in Council, exhibits independence and the appearance of independence in its composition but the same cannot be said of the constitution of a standing court martial when trying an accused for breach of the ordinary criminal law. Needless to say, there is no impugning of the integrity of the presiding officer; it is just that he is not suited, by virtue of his close involvement with the prosecution and with the entire military establishment, to conduct a trial on charges of a breach of the ordinary criminal law. It would be different if he were concerned with a charge of breach of military discipline, something that was particularly associated with an accused's membership in the armed forces. The fact that 'service offences' are so broadly defined as to include breaches of the ordinary law does not, in my opinion, make a standing court martial the equivalent of an independently appointed judicial officer or other than an ad hoc appointee, having no tenure and coming from the very special society of which both the accused, his prosecutor and his 'Judge' are members: cf *Committee for Justice and Liberty et al. v. National Energy Board et al.* (1976) 68 DLR (3d) 716, [1978] 1 SCR 369, 9 NR 115.

In my opinion, it is fundamental that when a person, any person, whatever his or her status or occupation, is charged with an offence under the ordinary criminal law and is to be tried under that law and in accordance with its prescriptions, he or she is entitled to be tried before a court of justice, separate from the prosecution and free from any suspicion of influence of or dependency on others. There is nothing in such a case, where the person charged is in the armed forces, that calls for any special knowledge or special skill of a superior officer, as would be the case if a strictly service or discipline offence, relating to military activity was involved.

The Chief Justice went on to conclude that the trial of the appellant for a contravention of section 3 of the Narcotic Control Act offended section 2(f) of the Canadian Bill of Rights 1960 in that he was not tried by an independent and impartial tribunal. . . .

98. Lord Thomas originally presented a separate argument to the effect that the decisions of the prosecuting authority to prosecute the appellants before a court-martial were themselves an infringement of the appellants' article 6 rights. In their judgment in *R v Saunby* paras 34-37, the Appeal Court rejected that argument and accepted the respondents' opposing argument that such decisions by a prosecutor lie outside the scope of article 6(1). Before the House Lord Thomas modified the appellants' contention and argued that the infringement of article 6 arose out of the congruence of unfair factors influencing the decision to prosecute and unfair factors influencing the court-martial's decisions on conviction and sentence. He therefore accepted that he could not

succeed on the prosecution point unless he succeeded in persuading the House that the courts-martial had not themselves been independent and impartial — in which event, of course, on his own submission, the appeals would have to be allowed anyway. On that approach any point relating to the decision to prosecute was subsumed in the issue relating to the fairness of the court-martial proceedings. That being so, since I have found that the court-martial proceedings did not infringe the appellants' article 6 rights, I would also reject the appellants' article 6 argument relating to the decisions to prosecute them. . . .

POTSANE v. MINISTER OF DEFENCE
Constitutional Court of South Africa
2002(1) SAI (CC) (2001)

. . . The common constitutional point [between the two cases combined here, *Potsane* and *Legal Soldier*] is whether the provisions of the Military Discipline Supplementary Measures Act 16 of 1999 (the Act) conferring authority on military prosecutors to institute and conduct prosecutions in military courts are to be struck down for their inconsistency with the provisions of section 179 of the Constitution (section 179). This section creates the office of the National Director of Public Prosecutions (the NDPP) and governs its powers and functions. The respondent in *Potsane* and the applicants in *Legal Soldier* (collectively referred to as "the soldiers") contend that section 179 invests the NDPP with exclusive prosecutorial authority, which is infringed by the competing authority conferred on military prosecutors by the Act. . . .

It is not the principle of a separate military justice system with jurisdiction to try soldiers and punish them (for both civilian and military transgressions) that is being questioned; nor is it the hierarchical structure of military courts and appellate tribunals created by the Act. The soldiers do not contend that it is constitutionally impermissible to establish such military courts. It should therefore be remembered the at the constitutional challenge here is directed at only one component of the military justice system, namely the prosecuting branch. . . .

The Act, containing not only the statutory authority for the impugned powers of military prosecutors but a whole new system of military justice, was enacted in order to harmonise the country's military justice system with a new wave of constitutionalism. While it was being drafted, a full bench of the Cape High Court struck down key provisions of the previous system of military justice. Foundational to this judgment was that courts martial lacked the essential attributes of independence and legal training necessary for them to pass muster as "ordinary courts" for the purposes of a fair trial. . . . Mindful of these strictures, the drafters of the Act made a clean break with the past, establishing a radically different military courts system "to provide for the continued proper administration of military justice and the maintenance of discipline." The emphasis shifted sharply from an essentially military system with forensic trappings to a system far closer to the ordinary criminal justice process. . . .

Counsel [for the Minister of Justice] mounted a forceful argument that the SANDF [South African National Defence Force] could not fulfill its constitutional obligations without the requisite capacity, competence, discipline and professionalism. These qualities, in turn, demand that military commanders at all times have ready access to services for the investigation and prosecution of crimes and MDC [military disciplinary code] transgressions by soldiers. . . .

Counsel for the Minister also underlined that military justice is concerned not so much with the prosecution of crime but with the maintenance of discipline. For that reason alone it was essential to read section 179 together with the section 200 [which calls for the SANDF to be "a disciplined military force"] so as not to undermine the capacity of the SANDF. . . . The conditions in which the SANDF must operate in times of war — and in which its soldiers must therefore be trained in peacetime — are such that quick and efficient investigation of infractions must be possible, as well as prompt decisions on and institution of prosecutions. . . .

Extra-territoriality is . . . essential to the functioning of military discipline, the jurisdiction of the SANDF over its members extending to wherever in the world they may be serving. It follows that there would have to be some agency clothed with the requisite authority to investigate alleged offences by South African soldiers abroad and to prosecute them if it deems it appropriate. . . .

Soldiers live and work in a culture of their own. This is recognised and accepted by acknowledging the constitutional validity of a separate military justice system with its own unique rules, offences, and punishments. . . . Military discipline . . . is about having an effective armed force capable and ready to protect the territorial integrity of the country and the freedom of its people. . . .

Modern soldiers in a democracy, those contemplated by chapter 11 of the Constitution, are not mindless automatons. Ideally they are to be thinking men and women imbued with the values of the Constitution, and they are to be disciplined. Such discipline is built on the reciprocal trust between the leader and the led. The commander needs to know and trust the ability and willingness of the troops to obey. They in turn should have confidence in the judgment and integrity of the commander to give wise orders. This willingness to obey orders and the concomitant trust in such orders are essential to effective discipline. At the same time discipline aims to develop reciprocal trust horizontally, between comrades. Soldiers are taught and trained to think collectively and act jointly, the cohesive force being military discipline built on trust, obedience, loyalty, *esprit de corps* and camaraderie. Discipline requires that breaches be nipped in the bud — demonstrably, appropriately, and wisely. . . . The appeal by the Minister of Defence is upheld . . .

Uniform Code of Military Justice
Article 1. Definitions

(9) The term "accuser" means a person who signs and swears to charges, any person who directs that charges nominally be signed and sworn to by another, and any other person who has an interest other than an official interest in the prosecution of the accused.

Article 22. Who May Convene General Courts-Martial

(a) General courts-martial may be convened by —

    (1) the President of the United States;

    (2) the Secretary of Defense;

    (3) the commanding officer of a unified or specified combatant command;

    (4) the Secretary concerned;

    (5) the commanding officer of a Territorial Department, an Army Group, an Army, an Army Corps, a division, a separate brigade, or a corresponding unit of the Army or Marine Corps;

    (6) the commander in chief of a fleet; the commanding officer of a naval station or larger activity of the Navy beyond the United States.

    (7) the commanding officer of an air command, an air force, an air division, or a separate wing of the Air Force or Marine Corps;

    (8) any other commanding officer designated by the Secretary concerned; or

    (9) any other commanding officer in any of the armed forces when empowered by the President.

(b) If any such commanding officer is an accuser, the court shall be convened by superior competent authority, and may in any case be convened by such authority if considered desirable by him.

Article 23. Who May Convene Special Courts-Martial

(a) Special courts-martial may be convened by —

    (1) any person who may convene a general court-martial;

    (2) the commanding officer of a district, garrison, fort, camp, station, Air Force base, auxiliary air field, or other place where members of the Army or the Air Force are on duty;

    (3) the commanding officer of a brigade, regiment, detached battalion, or corresponding unit of the Army;

    (4) the commanding officer of a wing, group, or separate squadron of the Air Force;

    (5) the commanding officer of any naval or Coast Guard vessel, shipyard, base, or station; the commanding officer of any Marine brigade, regiment, detached battalion, or corresponding unit; the commanding officer of any Marine barracks, wing, group, separate squadron, station, base, auxiliary air field, or other place where members of the Marine Corps are on duty;

(6) the commanding officer of any separate or detached command or group of detached units of any of the armed forces placed under a single commander for this purpose; or

(7) the commanding officer or officer in charge of any other command when empowered by the Secretary concerned.

(b) If any such officer is an accuser, the court shall be convened by superior competent authority, and may in any case be convened by such authority if considered advisable by him.

Article 24. Who May Convene Summary Courts-Martial

(a) Summary courts-martial may be convened by —

(1) any person who may convene a general or special court-martial;

(2) the commanding officer of a detached company other detachment of the Army;

(3) the commanding officer of a detached squadron or other detachment of the Air Force; or

(4) the commanding officer or officer in charge of any other command when empowered by the Secretary concerned.

(b) When only one commissioned officer is present with a command or detachment he shall be the summary court-martial of that command or detachment and shall hear and determine all summary court-martial cases brought before him. Summary courts-martial may, however, be convened in any case by superior competent authority when considered desirable by him.

Article 25. Who May Serve on Courts-Martial

(d) (2) When convening a court-martial, the convening authority shall detail as member thereof such members of the armed forces as, in his opinion, are best qualified for the duty by reason of age, education, training, experience, length of service, and judicial temperament. No member of an armed force is eligible to serve as a member of a general or special court-martial when he is the accuser or a witness for the prosecution or has acted as investigating officer or as counsel in the same case.

Article 60. Action by the Convening Authority

(a) The findings and sentence of a court-martial shall be reported promptly to the convening authority after the announcement of the sentence.

(b) (1) The accused may submit to the convening authority matters for consideration by the convening authority with respect to the findings and the sentence. . . .

(c) (1) The authority under this section to modify the findings and sentence of a court-martial is a matter of command prerogative involving the sole discretion of the convening authority. Under regulations of the Secretary concerned, a commissioned officer commanding for the time being, a successor in command, or any person exercising general court-martial jurisdiction may act under this section in place of the convening authority.

(2) Action on the sentence of a court-martial shall be taken by the convening authority or by another person authorized to act under this section. Subject to regulations of the Secretary concerned, such action may be taken only after consideration of any matters submitted by the accused under subsection (b) or after the time for submitting such matters expires, whichever is earlier. The convening authority or other person taking such action, in his sole discretion, may approve, disapprove, commute, or suspend the sentence in whole or in part.

(3) Action on the findings of a court-martial by the convening authority or other person acting on the sentence is not required. However, such person, in his sole discretion, may —

(A) dismiss any charge or specification by setting aside a finding of guilty thereto; or

(B) change a finding of guilty to a charge or specification to a finding of guilty to an offense that is a lesser included offense of the offense stated in the charge or specification.

(d) Before acting under this section on any general court-martial case or any special court-martial case that includes a bad-conduct discharge, the convening authority or other person taking action under this section shall obtain and consider the written recommendation of his staff judge advocate or legal officer. . . .

(e) (1) The convening authority or other person taking action under this section, in his sole discretion, may order a proceeding in revision or a rehearing.

(2) A proceeding in revision may be ordered if there is an apparent error or omission in the record or if the record shows improper or inconsistent action by a court-martial with respect to the findings or sentence that can be rectified without material prejudice to the substantial rights of the accused. In no case, however, may a proceeding in revision —

(A) reconsider a finding of not guilty of any specification or a ruling which amounts to a finding of not guilty;

(B) reconsider a finding of not guilty of any charge, unless there has been a finding of guilty under a specification laid under that charge, which sufficiently alleges a violation of some article of this chapter; or

(C) increase the severity of some article of the sentence unless the sentence prescribed for the offense is mandatory.

(3) A rehearing may be ordered by the convening authority or other person taking action under this section if he disapproves

the findings and sentence and states the reasons for disapproval of the findings. If such a person disapproves the findings and sentence and does not order a rehearing, he shall dismiss the charges. A rehearing as to the findings may not be ordered where there is a lack of sufficient evidence in the record to support the findings. A rehearing as to the sentence may be ordered if the convening authority or other person taking action under this subsection disapproves the sentence.

NOTES AND QUESTIONS

1. In 2005, Australia established a statutorily independent Office of Director of Military Prosecutions so that its Director could operate "independently and free from perceptions of command influence" and created a new position, Director of Defence Counsel Services, to improve the availability and management of defence counsel services to ADF [Australian Defence Force] personnel." *See* GOVERNMENT RESPONSE TO THE SENATE, FOREIGN AFFAIRS, AND TRADE REFERENCES COMMITTEE, REPORT ON THE EFFECTIVENESS OF AUSTRALIA'S MILITARY JUSTICE 2-4 (Department of Defence, October 2005). *See also* REPORT OF AN INQUIRY INTO MILITARY JUSTICE IN THE AUSTRALIAN DEFENCE FORCE (July 2001). What are the advantages of a distinct, centralized prosecutor's office within a military justice system? What are its disadvantages as compared to a system in which prosecutorial authority is dispersed among many commanding officers? *See* Lindsy Nicole Alleman, *Who Is in Charge, and Who Should Be? The Disciplinary Role of the Commander in Military Justice Systems*, 16 DUKE J. COMP. & INT'L L. 169 (2006) (comparing U.S., Canadian, and Israeli systems).

2. Article 17.1(a) of the Rome Statute of the International Criminal Court (1998) states that "a case is inadmissible" to the court's jurisdiction if it "is being investigated or prosecuted by a State which has jurisdiction over it, unless the State is unwilling or unable genuinely to carry out the investigation or prosecution"; art. 17.1 (b) states that a case is also inadmissible if it "has been investigated by a State which has jurisdiction over it and the State has decided not to prosecute the person concerned, unless the decision resulted from the unwillingness or inability of the State genuinely to prosecute." U.S. officials have been wary of supporting the ICC because of concern that U.S. servicemembers would be subjected to its jurisdiction. What sort of action by a commanding officer would constitute evidence of a genuine unwillingness or inability to prosecute a case?

3. A challenge to exclusive military jurisdiction over complaints against Dutch police (a system described as lacking "independent control") was rejected because the International Covenant on Civil and Political Rights "does not provide for the right to see another person criminally prosecuted." Does military, rather than civil, jurisdiction over military personnel place civilians who suffer at the hands of military personnel at a disadvantage compared to those who are the victims of civilian criminal acts? Should civilian victims have a say in deciding which legal forum will prosecute an offender?

See H.C.M.A. v. The Netherlands (213/1986), ICCPR, A/44/40 (30 March 1989) 267 at ¶¶ 2.3, 11.6; *see also Tzufan v. Judge Advocate General*, Chapter 4, § II.

4. The following passage appears in *Our Legal System Is Much More Independent than the Legal System in the US Military Structure: Conversation with Brigadier General Uri Shoham, IDF*, Int'l Ass'n of Jewish Lawyers & Jurists, JUSTICE, No. 18, at 18 (Autumn 1998):

> Q: Comparing the military legal system of Israel, Britain, and the US, where do the distinctions lie?

> Brig. Gen Shoham: There are many points which are common to all three military legal systems. All operate an adversary system; there is involvement on the part of the commander in initiating proceedings; the judges are legally qualified and officers may sit beside them and possess the same powers in passing judgment and sentence. There are many points of similarity but the process as a whole is not identical. One important difference is that in Israel, although the commander participates in the process, his involvement is very small in comparison to the situation in the United States . . . our legal system is much more independent than the legal system in the US military structure. [In Israel, many of the functions of the commander in American military justice, including ordering the pre-trial investigation and adjusting an unlawful sentence, are the province of an independent legal authority, the Military Attorney General.]

Is General Shoham's conclusion correct? If so, can you justify the U.S. lack of independence? If not, what ensures the independence of the justice process in the U.S.? On the Israeli system, see Menachem Finkelstein & Yifat Tomer, *The Israeli Military Legal System — Overview of the Current Situation and a Glimpse into the Future*, 52 A.F. L. REV. 137, 144 (2002).

5. A case that reached the Republic of Korea's Constitutional Court involved a petty officer who was providing "bayonet training" to a sergeant (who outranked the petty officer) and a corporal. Because he was not "participating in the training diligently," the petty officer ordered the men to race each other continuously between two points, with one able to rest only when he finished the race first. The sergeant disobeyed the order and a fight ensued; his eye was injured and he was discharged as a result. Later, the military police arrested him for disobeying the order of the petty officer; the prosecutor did not dismiss the charge but instead disposed of it "by exemption of prosecution," which was effectively a presumption of guilt and "damaged [the sergeant's] reputation and made him ineligible for injured veterans' benefits and disability compensation guaranteed under the Veterans' Pension Act on grounds that he himself was responsible for his injury." It also deprived him of the chance to prove himself innocent. The Constitutional Court held:

> [S]ince exemption is tantamount to a finding of sufficient basis for suspicion, it may put the accused at disadvantages, legal or factual, and cause him harms, tangible or intangible, in his life. . . . The exercise order of the bayonet training instructor was not only beyond the scope of his authority as a bayonet instructor but also violated the procedures applicable to discipline maintenance exercises in contravention

of due process of law. Even its substance was not something permitted under discipline maintenance exercises and amounted to cruelty. That particular order does not constitute a lawful order of a superior officer, one of the elements of the crime of insubordination. In short, the military prosecutor's decision to exempt, and not dismiss, the charge of insubordination on the basis that any order from a superior officer satisfies the element of the charge violates the rule against arbitrariness, violating the complainant's equality and his right to pursue happiness.

Military Discipline Maintenance Exercise, 1 KCCR 309, 89 HunMa 56 (Rep. of Korea Const. Ct. Oct. 27, 1989). Under the U.S. Constitution, would the category of "exemption of prosecution" be a legal way to dispose of a case? Are there advantages to military discipline in creating a category in between pressing charges and dismissing them? What are the risks created by civilian review of a military decision regarding prosecution?

UNITED STATES v. DINGES
United States Court of Appeals for the Armed Forces
55 M.J. 308 (C.A.A.F. 2001)

CHIEF JUDGE CRAWFORD delivered the opinion of the Court.

. . .

Colonel (Col) M, the special court-martial convening authority, testified at the *DuBay* hearing [held to determine whether the convening authority had an "other than official interest" in the prosecution of appellant] that he was stationed at Tinker Air Force Base (AFB) from 1991 to 1996, first as the Vice Commander, then as the Wing Commander. As the Vice Commander, he had little contact with the Boy Scouts. When he became Wing Commander, he was asked and accepted, like his predecessor, to be the District Chairman of one of eight Boy Scout districts in Oklahoma.

The Wing Commander has a prominent position at Tinker AFB. He is the individual on base who interfaces with the community, including the Chamber of Commerce, the Oklahoma City Neighborhood Initiatives Program, and the Oklahoma Military Advisor Committee. Col M also formed the Oklahoma City Bombing Disaster Control Group. He was deeply involved with that Control Group for nearly 24 hours a day from April 19, 1995, for 10 days, and 12 hours a day for 6 weeks thereafter.

Prior to becoming District Chairman, an unsalaried position, Col M's only contact with the Boy Scouts was as a Scout when he was a child, and a parent of a Scout from 1986-91. Personally, he was not overly involved with the Boy Scouts as a youth. He reached the rank of Star (two levels below Eagle Scout) and was also a member of the Order of the Arrow. The district chairmanship did not consume a tremendous amount of time — meeting less than once a quarter. Col M learned of the allegations against appellant from Mr. Moore, a full-time paid Scout employee, at a district meeting. Col M contacted the Staff Judge Advocate (SJA) and took actions similar to any case reported to him, initiating an investigation, appointing an Article 32 investigating officer, nominating a slate of court members as per standard operating procedure, and forwarding the charges to the general court-martial convening authority. Col M never told Mr. Moore what actions he took; nor did Mr. Moore ask or pressure him in any way. Furthermore, Col M did not know any of the Scouts who had made allegations against appellant, and was not contacted by any family member.

Appellant's transfer to Tinker AFB from Wright Patterson AFB, where he was administratively assigned but not physically located while attending college, was solely to ease the investigation and potential trial and not out of any personal interest. Since appellant was a Doctor of Philosophy candidate in Chemistry at the University of Oklahoma, his transfer to the Wing at Tinker AFB resulted in him being gainfully employed by the Director of Environmental Management at the Air Logistics Center. Prior to assigning appellant to the Environmental Management Director, Col M met with appellant and told him that he should take all the time necessary to work on his defense because this would be a very stressful time in his life. When not working on his defense, Col M told appellant to work hard for the Director because character evidence makes a difference at trial. He then personally drove appellant over to meet the Director.

At the *DuBay* hearing, the SJA described Col M's Boy Scout role as an "honorary and nominal position[] in his relations in the community." He was merely a figurehead. When asked by the defense if being District Chairman was an appointment duty, he responded: "[I]t was like many of his other duties, an honorary or a very nominal duty."

Col M was not even sure he told the SJA of his position with the Boy Scouts. . . .

Article 1(9), Uniform Code of Military Justice, 10 USC § 801(9), defines an "accuser" as a person who signs and swears to charges, any person who directs that charges nominally be signed and sworn to by another, and any other person who has an interest other than an official interest in the prosecution of the accused.

This provision was first enacted as an amendment to Article of War 65. This Article has been described as disqualifying a person from convening a court-martial who, "by reason of having preferred the charge or undertaken personally to pursue it, . . . might be biased against the accused, if indeed he had not already prejudged his case." William Winthrop, *Military Law and Precedents* 62 (2d ed. 1920 Reprint); *see* Arts. 22(b) and 23(b), UCMJ, 10 U.S.C. §§ 822(b) and 823(b). Moreover, Professor Davis describes an accuser as one who "*initiates* a charge out of a hostile *animus* toward the accused or a personal interest adverse to him. . . ." George B. Davis, *A Treatise on the Military Law of the United States* 20 (3d ed. Revised 1913).

Similarly, this Court has found that there is a personal interest when the convening authority is the victim of the accused's attempted burglary, *United States v. Gordon,* 1 U.S.C.M.A. 255, 2 C.M.R. 161 (1952); where the accused tries to blackmail the convening authority by noting that his son was a drug abuser, *United States v. Jeter,* 35 M.J. 442 (C.M.A. 1992); and where the accused has potentially inappropriate personal contacts with the convening authority's fiancée, *United States v. Nix,* 40 MJ 6 (CMA 1994). However, a convening authority is not disqualified because of "misguided prosecutorial zeal,"

United States v. Voorhees, 50 M.J. 494 (1999), or where the convening authority issues an order that the accused violates. *United States v. Tittel,* 53 M.J. 313 (2000).

Col M had no animus towards appellant and sought to ensure his gainful employment at Tinker AFB while the investigation was ongoing. Col M's role with the Boy Scouts has been properly described as titular and "an honorary and nominal" position. The initiation of charges was what any commander would do, and this is demonstrated by the fact that there were no further communications after the initial report made by Mr. Moore. Certainly, Col M was not the victim, was not an individual being blackmailed, and in fact, took less action than the commander in *Tittel.* For these reasons, we hold that Col M did not have "an interest other than an official interest" in appellant's case. . . .

EFFRON, JUDGE, with whom SULLIVAN, JUDGE, joins (dissenting):

The majority opinion concludes that it was permissible for Col M to act as the special court-martial convening authority in the present case. Col M, however, was subject to conflicting interests which precluded him from exercising the prosecutorial discretion of a special court-martial convening authority under applicable statutes, rules, and case law. *See* Arts. 1(9), 22(b), and 23(b), UCMJ, 10 U.S.C. §§ 801(9), 822(b), and 823(b); R.C.M. 401(c)(2)(A), Manual for Courts-Martial, United States (2000 ed.); *United States v. Gordon,* 1 U.S.C.M.A. 255, 261, 2 C.M.R. 161, 167 (1952); *United States v. Nix,* 40 M.J. 6 (C.M.A. 1994). I respectfully dissent.

I. Background

A. The exercise of prosecutorial discretion by court-martial convening authorities

The special court-martial convening authority plays a pivotal role in the military justice system, with broad discretion over the disposition of allegations and charges. Under RCM 306 and RCM 404, Manual, *supra,* Col M had virtually unfettered authority to choose among a variety of options, including: (1) follow the lead of civilian authorities and take no action; (2) dismiss any charges that may have been preferred; (3) take administrative action; (4) institute nonjudicial punishment proceedings; (5) refer the charges to a summary court-martial; (6) refer the charges to a special court-martial; or (7) order an investigation under Article 32, UCMJ, 10 U.S.C. § 832. After receiving the report of the Article 32 investigating officer, Col M had the authority to take any of the actions available to him prior to the investigation, as well as the option — which he exercised — of forwarding the matter to a superior commander for consideration of referral to a general court-martial. *See* R.C.M. 404(c). Although a servicemember's fate ultimately rests with the forum in which a case is considered, the exercise of prosecutorial discretion by the special court-martial convening authority is a critical decision point, particularly in terms of the severity of possible punishment.

To ensure that court-martial convening authorities exercise their considerable discretion with objectivity and without influence of personal interest, Articles 22(b) and 23(b) prohibit a commanding officer from convening a general or special court-martial when that officer is an "accuser." The definition of "accuser" under the Code includes a "person who has an interest other than an official interest in the prosecution of the accused." Art. 1(9); *see also* R.C.M. 401(c)(2). A commanding officer who is disqualified from functioning as a convening authority because he or she is an accuser must forward the charges for disposition by a superior convening authority. *See* Arts. 22(b) and 23(b); R.C.M. 504(c)(3), Manual, *supra*.

B. The relationship between Col M's interests and the investigation of appellant

As we noted in our initial review of this case, "At the heart of the granted issue is the following question: Was Col M so closely connected with this offense that a reasonable person would conclude that he had a personal interest in this case?" 49 M.J. at 234. The factual background concerning Col M's interest is detailed in the record of the proceedings we ordered under *United States v. DuBay,* 17 U.S.C.M.A. 147, 37 C.M.R. 411 (1967). When Col M assumed command of the 72nd Air Base Wing at Tinker Air Force Base (AFB) in July 1994, local Boy Scout officials asked him to be Chairman of the Big Teepee District of the Boy Scouts, one of eight districts in Oklahoma. Col M initially declined the request, but he reconsidered and decided to serve as Chairman because "he thought he could get good people to pay attention to them [the Boy Scouts organization] and to help them raise money[.]" The Council held 6 bimonthly meetings each year, and Col M attended "approximately 4" of the 6 meetings.

As Chairman of the Big Teepee District, Col M "was automatically also a member of the Board of Directors for the Last Frontier Council . . . a separately incorporated local Boy Scout council serving central, western, and southwestern portions of the State of Oklahoma." The Board of Directors exercised responsibility over the annual fundraising campaign. As a member of the Board, Col M "was responsible for contacting 10 to 12 fairly prominent people in the community and giv[ing] each of them a list of names to call and ask for money on behalf of the Boy Scouts."

Mr. Paul Moore, a central figure in the events that led to appellant's court-martial, was the Executive Director of the Last Frontier Council. As a salaried employee of the Boy Scouts, he was responsible for the day-to-day operations of the Council and accountable to the Council's Board of Directors. In November 1994, Mr. Moore heard of alleged sexual relationships between appellant, who then was an assistant scoutmaster of a troop, and several Boy Scouts. After "verif[ying] the information in his own mind," Mr. Moore confronted appellant, who confirmed one such relationship. Mr. Moore thereupon suspended appellant's involvement in the Boy Scouts.

After this meeting, Mr. Moore contacted civilian "local law enforcement officials to explore possible investigation concerning Captain Dinges' conduct." The civilian officials advised Mr. Moore that because appellant's alleged relationship involved an individual who was older than 16 years of age, the age of consent in Oklahoma, the civilians "were not interested in prosecuting" appellant.

On June 3, Col M attended the Last Frontier Council meeting at the Scout Service Center in Oklahoma City. Mr. Moore approached Col M, who was wearing his Air Force uniform, and "indicated that he had received information about an improper relationship between Captain Dinges and a Boy Scout." Mr. Moore asked "if this was something that the Air Force should be aware of," and Col M responded that "he was not sure, but that it was something the Air Force should look into and an investigator would contact Mr. Moore."

Later that day, Col M contacted his Staff Judge Advocate, who confirmed that the matter fell "within the scope of matters for investigation." The following day, Col M provided the Air Force Office of Special Investigations (OSI) with the information he received from Mr. Moore. The OSI, in turn, obtained permission to open an investigation from appellant's commander at the Air Force Institute of Technology (AFIT).

C. Col M's exercise of prosecutorial discretion

In August, appellant's commander was advised that the investigation was complete, that there was "sufficient information to disenroll Captain Dinges" from the PhD program in which he was a full-time student, and that the "recommended approach" was to transfer control of appellant from the AFIT to Tinker AFB. The commander agreed and called Col M to determine whether it was possible to transfer appellant to an organization at Tinker AFB "while the court process was being facilitated." Col M agreed to the reassignment of appellant. Appellant was designated as a "special assistant" to Col M, and he was assigned to work in the Environmental Management Directorate.

Col M directed an Article 32 investigation into the allegations, and the investigating officer recommended that charges be referred to trial by a general court-martial. Col M forwarded this recommendation to the general court-martial convening authority with his concurrence and recommended the names of possible court-members. Col M did not disclose his affiliation with the Boy Scouts of America when he forwarded his recommendation to the general court-martial convening authority.

II. Discussion

Col M held high-level positions of responsibility in the Boy Scout organization. He was a District Chairman and, in that capacity, served as a member of the Council's Board of Directors. As such, he owed a fiduciary duty of loyalty to the Boy Scouts. *See* Okla. Stat. Ann. tit. 18, § 1006B.7.a; *Resolution Trust Corp. v. Greer*, 911 P.2d 257, 261 n. 9 (Okla.1995); *Wilson v. Harlow*, 860 P.2d 793, 798 (Okla.1993). This was more than a nominal position. An important element of his responsibilities involved using his influence to persuade persons of means to financially support the Boy Scouts.

The subject of homosexuality is a highly charged matter for both the Boy Scouts, *see Boy Scouts of America v. Dale*, 530 U.S. 640, 644 (2000) (sustaining the Boy Scouts' First Amendment right to eject an admitted homosexual assistant scoutmaster from adult membership), and for the armed forces, *see* 10 USC § 654 (policy concerning homosexuality in the armed forces). With respect to the allegations against appellant, the impact on each entity was not necessarily the same. Because the impact could vary, there was a reasonable possibility that each organization's assessment of the proper disposition of the charges, and the factors considered in that process, would differ.

The potential conflict between Col M's personal interest in the impact the allegations might have on his fundraising and other activities with the Boy Scouts, on the one hand, and his role as appellant's Air Force commander, on the other, is precisely the type of situation that Congress sought to avoid when it disqualified an accuser from serving as a special or general court-martial convening authority. We need not question Col M's good faith, self-assessment of impartiality to find that his personal interest disqualified him from serving as a special court-martial convening authority. The majority finds it noteworthy that Col M was not the victim of appellant's conduct, and that he was not blackmailed by appellant. The test, however, is not whether a commander exhibited bias or prejudice, but simply whether the commander had "an interest other than an official interest in the prosecution of the accused." Art. 1(9). Because Col M had such an interest, he was disqualified from exercising authority over appellant's case and should have notified the general court-martial convening authority under RCM 401(c)(2). Under these circumstances, the findings and sentence should be set aside and the case should be returned to the Judge Advocate General with authority to order a rehearing. *See Nix,* 40 MJ at 8.

QUESTIONS

This case divided the Court of Appeals for the Armed Forces 3-2. Why was it so close? Whose argument do you find more compelling, Chief Judge Crawford's for the Court or Judge Effron's in dissent?

III. IMPROPER INFLUENCE OVER PROCEEDINGS

Uniform Code of Military Justice

Article 37. Unlawfully influencing action of court

(a) No authority convening a general, special, or summary court-martial, nor any other commanding officer, may censure, reprimand, or admonish the court or any member, military judge, or counsel thereof, with respect to the findings or sentence adjudged by the court, or with respect to any other exercises of its or his functions in the conduct of the proceedings. No person subject to this chapter may attempt to coerce or, by any unauthorized means, influence the action of a court-martial or any other military tribunal or any member thereof, in reaching the findings or sentence in any case, or the action of any convening, approving, or reviewing authority with respect to his judicial acts. The foregoing provisions of the subsection shall not apply with respect to (1) general instructional or informational courses in military justice if such courses are designed solely for the purpose of instructing members of a command in the substantive and procedural aspects of courts-martial, or (2) to statements and instructions given in open court by the military judge, president of a special court-martial, or counsel.

(b) In the preparation of an effectiveness, fitness, or efficiency report or any other report or document used in whole or in part for the purpose of determining whether a member of the armed forces is qualified to be advanced, in grade, or in determining the assignment or transfer of a member of the armed forces or in determining whether a member of the armed forces should be retained on active duty, no person subject to this chapter may, in preparing any such report (1) consider or evaluate the performance of duty of any such member as a member of a court-martial, or (2) give a less favorable rating or evaluation of any member of the armed forces because of the zeal with which such member, as counsel, represented any accused before a court-martial.

Manual for Legal Administration
United States Marine Corps (1999)

1003. Command Influence

1. Courts-martial are instruments of leadership and command that have been balanced to ensure fairness to accused servicemembers. The UCMJ preserved a substantial amount of command control over military justice proceedings, but the UCMJ requires independent discretion and judgment on the part of court-martial participants. This is how the UCMJ seeks to ensure fairness while preserving the Code as an instrument of command. Unlawful command influence occurs when senior personnel, wittingly or unwittingly, act to influence court-martial members, witnesses, defense counsel, or the military judge in a court-martial case. Unalwful command influence not only jeopardizes the validity of the judicial process, it undermines the morale of military members, their respect for the chain of command, and public confidence in the military.

2. While some types of influence are unlawful and prohibited by the UCMJ, other types of influence are lawful, proper, and a necessary part of command and leadership. The prohibition against unlawful command influence does not necessarily mean that a commander may abdicate responsibility for correcting disciplinary problems or administering justice. Rather, the commander must be vigilant to ensure that command action does not encroach upon the independence of the other participants in the military justice system.

3. *Lawful Command, Control, and Influence.* A commander may:

a. Personally dispose of a case at the level authorized for that commander.

b. Send a case to a lower level commander for that subordinate's independent action.

c. Send a case to a higher commander with a recommendation for disposition.

d. Withdraw subordinate court-martial convening authority in whole or for particular classes or categories of cases.

e. Order charges pending at a lower level transmitted up for further consideration, including, if appropriate, referral.

f. Mentor and train subordinates in military justice, but must do so recognizing that there exists the potential for misinterpreting the commander's intentions.

4. *Unlawful Command Influence.* A commander may not:

a. Order a subordinate to dispose of a case in a certain way. The law gives independent discretion to each commander at every level possessing authority to convene courts-martial.

b. Select or remove court-martial members in order to obtain a particular result in a particular trial. Selection of members must be based on the criteria contained in UCMJ, Article 25. Those criteria include age and experience, education and training, length of service, and judicial temperament.

c. Pressure the military judge or court members to arrive at a particular decision or harass defense counsel.

d. Intimidate or discourage witnesses from testifying or retaliate against a witness for testifying.

e. Criticize military judges, court members, witnesses, or defense counsel in a manner that may influence them or other military judges, court members, witnesses, or defense counsel in future cases.

f. Consider or evaluate, in a fitness report, the court-martial performance of any court member or give a less favorable rating or evaluation to a defense counsel because of the zeal with which the defense counsel represented an accused servicemember.

5. Though not, strictly speaking, unlawful "command influence," commanders should not have an inflexible policy on the disposition of a court-martial case or the punishment to be imposed. A convening authority must consider each case individually on its own merits. When a convening authority considers the post-trial submissions of the accused and acts on the sentence of a court-martial, s/he may not have an inflexible attitude toward clemency.

6. A commander who is an "accuser" may not thereafter act as a convening authority. A commander who is an accuser is disqualified to act as a convening authority and must forward the charges to a superior convening authority. A commander is considered to be an accuser when s/he:

a. Formally signs and swears to charges on the a charges sheet,

b. Directs that charges be signed and sworn to by another, or

c. Has an interest, other than an official interest, in the prosecution of the accused.

UNITED STATES v. THOMAS
United States Court of Military Appeals
22 M.J. 388 (C.M.A. 1986)

EVERETT, CHIEF JUDGE:

These four cases, all argued on the same day, are among many received by this Court and by the United States Army Court of Military Review which question the fairness of the court-martial proceedings because of certain acts and comments of Major General Thurman E. Anderson, the Commanding General of Third Armored Division, and members of his staff.

During one or more briefings conducted among officers and noncommissioned officers within his command, General Anderson addressed the subject of testifying at an accused's court-martial. He stated that he found it paradoxical for a unit commander, who had recommended that an accused be tried by a court-martial authorized to adjudge a punitive discharge, to later appear as a defense character witness at the sentencing stage of the trial, testify as to the accused's good character, and recommend that the convicted soldier be retained in the service. Some of General Anderson's remarks were elaborated upon and possibly distorted by his subordinates. Be that as it may, his comments were later interpreted, or misinterpreted, to reflect an intent that a commander, first sergeant, or other person from an accused's unit, should not give favorable presentencing testimony on behalf of an accused. This interpretation may have also extended to findings.

Based on the record of trial in appellant Giarratano's case and on the special findings by the military judge in that case, the Court of Military Review concluded that command influence was present at the Third Armored Division. *United States v. Treakle,* 18 M.J. 646 (A.C.M.R.1984). Depending on the facts of each case, the Court of Military Review fashioned several different remedies. These included sentence rehearings, if the record failed to show affirmatively that, in sentencing, the court members had not in fact been influenced by General Anderson's comments, *United States v. Treakle, supra* at 658-59; rehearings or reassessment of the sentence, if the record failed to show why the defense had not produced any character witnesses or if one or more witnesses who testified appeared to have been negatively influenced by General Anderson's remarks, *United States v. Schroeder,* 18 M.J. 792 (A.C.M.R.1984); *United States v. Hill,* 18 M.J. 757 (A.C.M.R.1984); and limited hearings to determine whether the accused had been deprived of character witnesses at the sentencing stage of the trial, *United States v. Abelon,* 19 M.J. 767 (A.C.M.R.1984); *United States v. Thompson,* 19 M.J. 690 (A.C.M.R.1984).

When additional information came to the attention of the Court of Military Review in the form of affidavits prepared by two officers from the Third Armored Division, that court first began to take remedial action at both the findings and post-trial review stages of the proceedings. . . .

With this background, we now turn to the central issue of these cases: Were the remedial actions taken by the Court of Military Review appropriate and adequate, under the circumstances of each case, to eliminate the prejudicial impact of unlawful command influence found to have been exercised within the Third Armored Division, or did General Anderson's comments have such a deleterious effect on the judicial process that even more drastic action, such as automatic reversal of the findings and sentence, is required? In answering this question, we will begin by considering the general's actions at the referral stage of the trial, proceed through the findings and sentence, and end with the final review and action by the convening authority.

I. Preliminary Observations

Command influence is the mortal enemy of military justice. Therefore, in the Uniform Code of Military Justice, Congress specifically prohibited such activity. Art. 37, 10 U.S.C. § 837; *see also* Art. 98, UCMJ, 10 U.S.C. § 898. Subsequently, the Military Justice Act of 1968 expanded the command-influence prohibitions of Article 37. Pub. L. No. 90-632, § 2(13), 82 Stat. 1338. Indeed, a prime motivation for establishing a civilian Court of Military Appeals was to erect a further bulwark against impermissible command influence. *See* Hearings on H.R. 2498 Before a Subcomm. of the House Committee on Armed Service, 81st Cong., 1st Sess. 608 (1949).

The exercise of command influence tends to deprive servicemembers of their constitutional rights. If directed against prospective defense witnesses, it transgresses the accused's right to have access to favorable evidence. U.S. Const. amend. VI; *cf.* Art. 46, U.C.M.J., 10 U.S.C. § 846. If directed against defense counsel, it affects adversely an accused's right to effective assistance of counsel. *Johnson v. Zerbst,* 304 U.S. 458 (1938); U.S. Const. amend. VI; *cf.* Art. 27, UCMJ, 10 U.S.C. § 827, and Art. 37. If the target is a court member or the military judge, then the tendency is to deprive the accused of his right to a forum where impartiality is not impaired because the court personnel have a personal interest in not incurring reprisals by the convening authority due to a failure to reach his intended result. *Cf. Tumey v. Ohio,* 273 U.S. 510 (1927); *United States v. Accordino,* 20 M.J. 102 (C.M.A.1985). . . .

A commander who causes charges to be preferred or referred for trial is closely enough related to the prosecution of the case that the use of command influence by him and his staff equates to "prosecutorial misconduct." Indeed, recognizing the realities of the structured military society, improper conduct by a commander may be even more injurious than such activity by a prosecutor. Likewise, as was perfectly clear to Congress when it enacted the Uniform Code of Military Justice and the Military Justice Act of 1968 — and as the judges of this Court have always understood — command influence "involves 'a corruption of the truth-seeking function of the trial process.'"

Consequently, in cases where unlawful command influence has been exercised, no reviewing court may properly affirm findings and sentence unless it is persuaded beyond a reasonable doubt that the findings and sentence have not been affected by the command influence.

II. Referral for Trial

Articles 22-24, UCMJ, 10 U.S.C. §§ 822-824, respectively, prescribe who may convene various types of courts-martial. If a court-martial is convened by someone who is not in one of the categories set forth in those articles, then its action can be set aside for lack of jurisdiction. Articles 22(b) and 23(b) also direct that an officer shall not convene a general or special court-martial, if he "is an accuser." According to Article 1(9), UCMJ, 10 U.S.C. §801(9), an "accuser" is "a person who signs and swears to charges . . . and any other person who has an interest other than an official interest in the prosecution of the accused."

Despite General Anderson's misguided zeal, his initial interest in the various prosecutions was official, rather than personal. Unlike the convening authority in *United States v. Gordon,* 1 U.S.C.M.A. 255, 2 C.M.R. 161 (1952), whose house had been broken into by the accused, General Anderson had not suffered an injury to his person or property. Unlike the convening authority in *United States v. Crossley,* 10 M.J. 376 (C.M.A.1981), and in *United States v. Shepherd,* 9 U.S.C.M.A. 90, 95-100, 25 C.M.R. 352, 357-62 (1958), his ego was not directly assailed by the accused's actions. Unlike the convening authority in *United States v. Corcoran,* 17 M.J. 137 (C.M.A.1984), and in *United States v. Marsh,* 3 U.S.C.M.A. 48, 11 C.M.R. 48 (1953), his authority was not willfully flouted. . . .

[In this case, General Anderson's remarks] were directed chiefly towards conduct of prospective witnesses after charges had been preferred, and they tended to cut off testimony in an accused's behalf only after a recommendation for his court-martial had been made. Thus, during processing of charges before referral, General Anderson's comments would not have adversely affected an accused. Conceivably, those remarks might even have benefited an accused because if his unit commander entertained a favorable opinion of him, that commander might have utilized nonjudicial punishment or administrative action, instead of seeking trial by court-martial where the results might prove to be too harsh.

III. Findings Based on Pleas of Guilty

In many of the cases referred by General Anderson, guilty pleas were entered — usually pursuant to pretrial agreements. Now it is contended that these accused should be allowed to withdraw these pleas and that the findings based thereon should be vacated. One rationale for this argument is that the pleas were involuntary because evidence available to such an accused was curtailed by General Anderson's actions, so guilty pleas were entered merely by reason of the hopeless predicament in which the accused had been placed. Another argument is that the actions of General Anderson were so pernicious that, *per se,* they tainted every proceeding with which he had any contact. *Cf. United States v. Treakle, supra* at 663 (Yawn, J., concurring in part and dissenting in part).

We are not persuaded by these arguments. In the first place, we are unable to find in the records before us any accused who entered a guilty plea because of the unavailability of witnesses who, in the absence of General Anderson's interference, might have testified at trial. Certainly, no such claim has been brought to our attention. *Cf. Hill v. Lockhart,* 474 U.S. 52 (1985). . . . In view of the safeguards surrounding the entry of guilty pleas by accused servicemembers, we perceive no unfairness in letting stand the guilty pleas entered in cases from the Third Armored Division. The possibility that, if General Anderson had not interfered, an accused who entered pleas of guilty might have pleaded not-guilty, introduced evidence, and obtained an acquittal is so remote that it does not disturb us — especially where no specific claim to this effect has been made. In these cases, we are persuaded beyond a reasonable doubt that the findings based on these provident guilty pleas were not affected by command influence. . . .

IV. Findings Based on Pleas of Not Guilty

In determining whether an accused's trial in a contested case before court members was adversely affected by command influence, we first consider the impact that such activities and communications may have had on the court members. In this regard, we place the burden upon both defense and trial counsel, as well as the military judge, to fully question the court members during voir dire and to determine thereby whether any of the members had knowledge of the commander's comments and, if so, whether the comments had an adverse impact on the member's ability to render an impartial judgment. When required, witnesses may be called to testify on this issue. *United States v. Karlson,* 16 M.J. 469 (C.M.A.1983). However, we are not prepared to disqualify members of a court-martial panel simply because they were assigned or were in close proximity to the command where the comments were made. To do so would ignore the members' oath to adhere to the military judge's instructions and to determine the facts in accordance therewith. *Cf. United States v. Garwood,* 20 M.J. 148 (C.M.A.1985).

In cases tried by military judge alone, we have no reason to believe that the command influence would have had any impact on the judges, who were completely independent of General Anderson and of other commanders in the field. Moreover, absent some specific claim to the contrary, we shall not assume that an accused chose trial by judge alone because of concerns about the impartiality of the court members.

In contested cases tried by members or by judge alone, a second question is whether the commander's comments so impeded the accused's access to defense witnesses that he was deprived of his sixth-amendment right to have witnesses called on his behalf. As already noted, the standard we shall use in testing for prejudice in this regard is that of *Chapman v. California,* [386 U.S. 18 (1967)]. *Cf. United States v. Remai,* [19 M.J. 229 (C.M.A.1985)].

In view of this high standard, if an accused properly raises the issue that his ability to secure favorable evidence has been impaired, the Government obviously bears a heavy burden in establishing that defense access to witnesses (character or otherwise) was not impeded by command influence to the extent that it affected the results of trial. Indeed, appellate defense counsel might well argue that the Government can never overcome this heavy burden because there will always be a possibility that a witness might have been available who could have tipped the scales in the defense's behalf.

In this connection, we draw a distinction between two classes of witnesses: (a) character witnesses, and (b) witnesses who will testify on matters other than an accused's character. As to the former, there was the greater likelihood that testimony would be inhibited by General Anderson's remarks. It is questionable whether his remarks could have been construed to apply to the latter class of witnesses. . . . To satisfy its burden of demonstrating that an accused was not deprived of favorable character witnesses, the Government might elect to proceed in one of several ways. The first would be to show that appellant had offered extensive favorable character evidence at trial, so that it could be inferred that General Anderson's remarks had not inhibited the availability of character witnesses. A second way would be to demonstrate from the accused's military records and otherwise that there simply was no evidence of good character available or that readily available rebuttal evidence of bad character would have been so devastating that, as a tactical matter, the accused could not have afforded the risk of putting his character in evidence. A third way for the Government to meet its burden might be to demonstrate that the prosecution evidence at trial was so overwhelming that there was no way in which the character evidence could have had an effect. This latter alternative should be used very sparingly, however: First, we recognize that character evidence can be very effective in creating reasonable doubt at trial; and, second, we do not wish to create even an appearance of condoning command influence on findings. . . .

V. Sentencing

In gauging the effect of command influence on an accused's sentence, the same approach should be used as for findings in contested cases. If the issue is properly raised, the burden is on the Government to establish beyond a reasonable doubt that favorable evidence in extenuation and mitigation was not curtailed by General Anderson's command activities. To satisfy this burden, the Government may demonstrate by an accused's military records or otherwise that no favorable evidence relevant to an accused's service in the Third Armored Division was available, as evidenced by his military records and otherwise, or that the defense made an informed decision not to present such evidence because it would have opened the door to damaging rebuttal evidence readily available to the prosecutor. If the record fails to show that the Government has met its burden, a rehearing on sentence or meaningful reassessment of the sentence, if possible, would be the appropriate remedy.

We note that there is no indication that, in appointing court members, General Anderson sought to name persons who were predisposed to adjudge heavy sentences. *Cf. United States v. McClain,* 22 M.J. 124 (C.M.A.1986). Of course, if he had followed this policy, resentencing would be in order because of the violation of Article 37.

VI. Review and Action

The Court of Military Review has directed new post-trial reviews in cases where the initial review was performed by General Anderson. Avoidance of any appearance of evil provides ample justification for requiring this procedure. Moreover, in many of the cases he reviewed, General Anderson was confronted with claims that his command influence had prejudiced the accused at trial and necessitated major remedial action. He could hardly be expected to review impartially contentions that his own acts had transgressed Article 37 and had violated the rights of the accused. . . . [The court proceeds to dismiss arguments of appellants in each of the four combined cases.]

VIII. Epilogue

In all four of these cases, we have upheld the decision of the Court of Military Review. Lest our action be construed as a tacit acceptance of illegal command influence in military justice, we emphasize that the decisions of the court below were preceded by extensive remedial action at that level. Indeed, we commend that court for recognizing the inherent dangers caused by illegal command influence and for deciding each case in a manner consistent with legislative intent and prior case law.

This Court understands the desire of military commanders to assure that the members of their commands adhere to high standards of discipline. Certainly, we do not wish to inhibit lawful zeal in achieving this end. However, Congress, in its wisdom and pursuant to powers conferred upon it by the Constitution, has placed limits on the means that can be employed by commanders in seeking to maintain discipline. Moreover, we are convinced that most commanders understand full well the reasons why in our democratic society Congress considered these limitations to be appropriate.

One of the most sacred duties of a commander is to administer fairly the military justice system for those under his command. In these cases, the commander, for whatever reason, failed to perform that duty adequately. Likewise, it is also apparent either that his legal advisor failed to perceive that a problem was developing from General Anderson's stated policies or that he was unable or unwilling to assure that the commander stayed within the bounds prescribed by the Uniform Code of Military Justice. The delay and expense occasioned by General Anderson's intemperate remarks and by his staff's implementation of their understanding of those remarks are incalculable. Several hundred soldiers have been affected directly or indirectly — if only because of the extra time required for completing appellate review of their cases. In addition, the military personnel resources — as well as those of this Court — required to identify and to surgically remove any possible impact of General Anderson's overreaching have been immense. Finally, and of vital importance, the adverse public perception of military justice which results from cases like these undercuts the continuing efforts of many — both in and out of the Armed Services — to demonstrate that military justice is fair and compares favorably in that respect to its civilian counterparts.

A primary responsibility of this Court in its role as civilian overseer for the military justice system is to ensure that commanders perform their military-justice responsibilities properly and that they are provided adequate guidance by their legal advisors in performing those responsibilities. Merely remedying the error in the cases before us is not enough. Instead, we wish to make it clear that incidents of illegal command influence simply must not recur in other commands in the future.

Recognizing that military commanders and judge advocates usually exert themselves in every way to comply with both the spirit and the letter of the law, we are confident that events like those involved here will not be repeated. However, if we have erred in this expectation, this Court — and undoubtedly other tribunals — will find it necessary to consider much more drastic remedies.

NOTES AND QUESTIONS

1. Command influence is a vexing reality in military legal systems. So long as military success depends on obedience and deference to authority, military culture will promote a social and professional hierarchy that works against the independent judgment and participation (as witnesses as well as panel members) of servicemembers. Given its relatively frequent appearance in military justice, judges often face the difficulty of fashioning the proper remedy to improper command influence. In *United States v. Gore*, 60 M.J. 178 (C.A.A.F. 2004), the Court of Appeals for the Armed Forces rejected the government's appeal of a dismissal ordered by a military judge after a Navy commander had ordered a chief petty officer not to testify in the trial. The dismissed charges included two counts of desertion and one of unauthorized absence; the chief had initially agreed to be a character witness for the accused. The court said of the chief, "He was a man desperate to please his commanding officer." *Id.* at 188. Do you think such an attitude is common among career-oriented sailors? What challenges does that attitude pose for accused servicemembers and their defense counsel? *See also* MANUAL FOR COURTS-MARTIAL, U.S. (2005), Rule for Courts-Martial 104.

2. Is the convening authority's mere presence in or near the courtroom a form of improper command influence? *See United States v. Harvey*, 64 M.J. 13 (C.A.A.F. 2006); *R. v. Sullivan*, 1 N.Z.C.M.A.R. 207, 216-17 (C.M.A.C. 1994) (noting "convention that convening authorities are not normally present during a court-martial hearing. We think this is a wise convention because of the appearance of justice requiring to be done").

3. The issue of command influence is often intertwined with that of pre-trial publicity. Consider, for example, the case of Lieutenant William L. Calley, Jr., charged with and convicted of crimes related to the My Lai massacre, the most notorious war crime of U.S. soldiers during the Vietnam War. Calley's defense counsel took the case to federal district court to challenge the impartiality of his trial. Quaere: can a war criminal whose crimes are widely acknowledged be afforded a fair and impartial trial? *See Calley v. Callaway*, 382 F. Supp. 650 (M.D. Ga. 1974).

4. Lt. Col. Patricia A. Ham, *Still Waters Run Deep? The Year in Unlawful Command Influence*, ARMY LAW., JUNE 2006, 53, 54: "[Command influence] remains the 'mortal enemy of military justice'" — the single most dangerous assault on the fairness, and appearance of fairness, of the system. Due to the preeminent role of the commander in the military justice system — he decides what cases go to trial, selects the members of the panel who decide guilt or innocence and, where necessary, an appropriate sentence, and he acts on cases after trial by bestowing mercy if he so chooses — improper use of command authority to interfere with the court-martial process potentially impacts servicemembers' most cherished fundamental rights. Depending on the form of interference involved in a particular case, unlawful command influence could affect the presumption of innocence, the right to a fair trial embodied in the Due Process Clause of the Fifth Amendment, the right to present a defense, the right to compulsory process of witnesses, and the right to effective assistance of counsel guaranteed by the Sixth Amendment, or the right to a fair and impartial panel guaranteed by Article 25 of the UCMJ. Simply stated, unlawful command influence turns 'military justice' into an oxymoron." Do you agree with this assessment of "command influence" as the primary threat to military justice? If so, what measures would help to control it? If not, what issues constitute a greater threat to fairness in military courts? *See, e.g., United States v. Stephens*, 21 M.J. 784 (A.C.M.R. 1986) (holding that a hearing must be convened to determine whether a battalion command sergeant major's statement to a panel member about sentencing any noncommissioned officer found guilty of accused's offenses to at least 30 days of confinement constituted unlawful command influence); *United States v. Littrice*, 13 C.M.R. 43 (1953) (involving trial for theft and a circular distributed by a group commander that included an admonition to panel members about the dangers of retaining thieves in the Army and the importance of respecting a commander's prerogatives in military justice); *United States v. Kitchens*, 31 C.M.R. 175 (C.A.A.F. 1961) (reminding that commanders must be wary of advising panel members about excessive leniency in recent cases); *United States v. Stoneman*, 57 M.J. 35 (C.A.A.F. 2002) (remanding for further proceedings a case in which a brigade commander sent inflammatory emails, including one stating that "My New Years Resolution is to CRUSH all leaders in this Brigade who don't lead by example, on and off duty. Leaders must focus on developing their REFERENT power, the power given to them by subordinates who respect them because of caring competent leadership, rather than their LEGAL power, which is the power they have by virtue of their rank.").

5. In *United States v. Simpson*, 58 M.J. 368 (C.A.A.F. 2003), the Court of Appeals heard the appeal of an Army drill sergeant from his conviction for sexually assaulting trainees. The investigation and trial provoked extensive media coverage at Aberdeen Proving Ground, Maryland, and Simpson argued that he was prejudiced by the pre-trial publicity and by unlawful command influence. Judge Effron's opinion for the court rejected both claims, holding that under *United States v. Biagase*, 50 M.J. 143, 150 (C.A.A.F. 1999), Simpson had not shown the required intent or appearance of command influence to "cause unfairness in the proceedings." Among other issues, Simpson raised the "zero tolerance" policy of the Army toward sexual harassment as a source of command influence. Does such a policy pose risks to the fair administration of military justice?

6. In *United States v. Bartley*, 47 M.J. 182 (C.A.A.F. 1997), a unanimous court rejected a pre-trial agreement in which a motion alleging unlawful command influence was dropped as part of the negotiation. The motion was based on the poster that appears below. Under what circumstances might such a poster constitute unlawful command influence?

WHO'S KIDDING WHOM?

Myths die hard. Those who cling to myths often are unencumbered by knowledge or insight. I am deeply concerned that many of our people persist in espousing a number of myths incompatible with Air Force concepts of discipline and justice. Seven of the most persistent myths are:

1. DUTY PERFORMANCE REPRESENTS THE PREEMINENT CRITERION IN EVALUATING SUBORDINATES

In fact, duty performance is only one of many important criteria. Others include military bearing and behavior, adherence to military standards and acceptance of responsibility consistent with rank. An undisciplined, unprincipled collection of workers, however individually talented, cannot sustain a military organization.

2. OFF-DUTY ACTIVITIES SHOULD NOT AFFECT EPR EVALUATIONS

An alarmingly large number of supervisors claim "I don't like my subordinate away from the job, I can't evaluate their off-duty activities and shouldn't consider those activities in my evaluation." That rationale is a convenient excuse to ignore a wide, unacceptable off-duty behavior, from drunk driving to drug abuse, from fraternization to financial irresponsibility. Military members are on duty 24 hours a day and judged by the civilian community on that basis. Performance ratings in the area of "adaptability to military life" and "bearing and behavior" both contemplate a after-duty performance as well.

3. DRUG ABUSERS STILL CAN BE CONSIDERED WELL ABOVE AVERAGE MILITARY MEMBERS

Some drug abusers may be among the best of their peers in performance of duties, professional appearance and working relationships. Bear in mind, however, that these same drug abusers also have made a conscious decision to flout military authority and violate the law. They jeopardize the safety of their coworkers and national security. Nonetheless, some supervisors continue to rate personnel involved in drug-related offenses as deserving a "5" EPR and among the top 10 percent of their peers. By its definition, drug abuse should preclude such high ratings.

4. ABUSES INVOLVING SMALL AMOUNTS OF DRUGS ARE NOT SERIOUS OFFENSES

Some of our people believe that the Air Force overreacts to "minor" drug offenses involving "small amounts" of marijuana or "experimentation" with drugs. Unfortunately, a "small amount" of any illicit drug, including marijuana, can severely compromise military readiness. The minor drug abuser is no less subject to censure than the petty thief.

22 AFVA 111-1   August 1990
Supersedes 22 AFVA 111-1, 1 May 88
Distribution: X (As determined by OPR)

5. DRUG ABUSERS CAN BE TRUSTWORTHY, DEPENDABLE AIRMEN

Whatever their possible merits, drug abusers are not trustworthy. Each instance of drug abuse is a knowing, deliberate decision to violate Air Force regulations and military law. A person who swears allegiance to laws of the land and then violates them at his or her convenience is unworthy of our trust.

6. SKILLED AIRMEN ARE TOO VALUABLE TO LOSE DUE TO OFF-DUTY MISCONDUCT

"Sergeant ———— is my best worker. I need Sergeant ———— here or I just may fall apart." In truth, no one is indispensable. Many bright, loyal, young Americans are waiting for a turn to enter the Air Force. We can ill afford to keep them willing to be under to spare criminals in our organization.

7. ANYONE WHO CAN BE REHABILITATED SHOULD BE

Rehabilitation is a proper goal of our justice system, but is is not the "only" goal. We should try to return to duty members who show real promise for further service. However, the military does not provide a guaranteed rehabilitation service for troublemakers. Our overall mission is one of national security. We have neither the time nor the resources to restore every member who has chosen to violate our laws, then wants to remain in the Air Force.

SUMMARY.

In summary, a number of dangerous myths have permeated the ranks of our "middle managers." The Air Force has standards which must be enforced in order to protect our country. When we decline to enforce these standards, discipline collapses and inevitably our mission is jeopardized.

RICHARD L. TREASKOMA, Major General, USAF
Commander

IV.　PRETRIAL INVESTIGATIONS

The Fifth Amendment exempts military justice cases from the grand jury indictment requirement. In place of the grand jury, the Uniform Code of Military Justice provides for a pretrial proceeding that is usually called an "Article 32 investigation." Commentators and practitioners are in virtually complete accord that the military's Article 32 hearing is far more beneficial to the accused than a civilian grand jury proceeding.

With only rare exceptions, a convening authority may not refer a case to a general court-martial unless an Article 32 investigation has been held or the accused has waived such an investigation. The investigation itself is a trial-like proceeding, though without all of the same rights to witnesses and evidentiary rules that would apply at a court-martial. After the proceeding is complete, the investigating officer prepares a report recommending disposition of the charges.

U.S. Constitution, Fifth Amendment

No person shall be held to answer for a capital, or otherwise infamous, crime, unless on a presentment or indictment of a Grand Jury, except in cases arising in the land or naval forces, or in the Militia, when in actual service, in time of War, or public danger. . . .

NOTE

The Fifth Amendment is generally construed as exempting all courts-martial from the grand jury provision. But Justice Marshall, joined by Justices Brennan and Blackman, argued:

> The language of this exception could be understood to mean that "cases arising in the land or naval forces," as well as in the militia, are only excepted from the requirement of grand jury indictment or presentment "in actual service in time of War or public danger." This Court, however, has interpreted the "time of war" provision as referring only to cases arising in the militia, not the land or naval forces. *Johnson v. Sayre*, 158 U.S. 109, 114 (1895). I am not convinced this reading of the Fifth Amendment is correct, but need not rely on a different interpretation here.

Solorio v. United States, 483 U.S. 435, 452 (1987) (Marshall, J., dissenting).

Uniform Code of Military Justice
Article 32. Investigation

(a) No charge or specification may be referred to a general court-martial for trial until a thorough and impartial investigation of all the matters set forth therein has been made. This investigation shall include inquiry as to the truth of the matter set forth in the charges, consideration of the form of charges, and a recommendation as to the disposition which should be made of the case in the interest of justice and discipline.

(b) The accused shall be advised of the charges against him and of his right to be represented at that investigation by counsel. The accused has the right to be represented at that investigation as provided in section 838 of this title [article 38] and in regulations prescribed under that section. At that investigation full opportunity shall be given to the accused to cross-examine witnesses against him if they are available and to present anything he may desire in his own behalf, either in defense or mitigation, and the investigation officer shall examine available witnesses requested by the accused. If the charges are forwarded after the investigation, they shall be accompanied by a statement of the substance of the testimony taken on both sides and a copy thereof shall be given to the accused.

(c) If an investigation of the subject matter of an offense has been conducted before the accused is charged with the offense, and if the accused was present at the investigation and afforded the opportunities for representation, cross-examination, and presentation prescribed in subsection (b), no further investigation of that charge is necessary under this article unless it is demanded by the accused after he is informed of the charge. A demand for further investigation entitles the accused to recall witnesses for further cross-examination and to offer any new evidence in his own behalf.

(d) If evidence adduced in an investigation under this article indicates that the accused committed an uncharged offense, the investigating officer may investigate the subject matter of that offense without the accused having first been charged with the offense if the accused —

(1) is present at the investigation;

(2) is informed of the nature of each uncharged offense investigated; and

(3) is afforded the opportunities for representation, cross-examination, and presentation prescribed in subsection (b).

(e) The requirements of this article are binding on all persons administering this chapter but failure to follow them does not constitute jurisdictional error.

NOTES

1. Article 32(b)'s reference to Article 38 incorporates the right to a civilian defense counsel and a military counsel specifically requested by the accused if that counsel is determined to be reasonably available under regulations promulgated by the Service Secretary.

2. Article 32(c)'s reference to previous investigations includes courts of inquiry and similar proceedings. *See* Rule for Courts-Martial 405(b) discussion, MANUAL FOR COURTS-MARTIAL, UNITED STATES (2005 ed.).

Rule for Courts-Martial 405

Manual for Courts-Martial, United States (2005 ed.)

(a) *In general.* Except as provided in subsection (k) of this rule [addressing waiver by the accused], no charge or specification may be referred to a general court-martial for trial until a thorough and impartial investigation of all the matters set forth therein has been made in substantial compliance with this rule. Failure to comply with this rule shall have no effect if the charges are not referred to a general court-martial.

(b) *Earlier investigation.* If an investigation of the subject matter of an offense has been conducted before the accused is charged with an offense, and the accused was present at the investigation and afforded the rights to counsel, cross-examination, and presentation of evidence required by this rule, no further investigation is required unless demanded by the accused to recall witnesses for further cross-examination and to offer new evidence.

(c) *Who may direct investigation.* Unless prohibited by regulations of the Secretary concerned, an investigation may be directed under this rule by any court-martial convening authority. That authority may also give procedural instructions not inconsistent with these rules.

(d) *Personnel.*

(1) *Investigating officer.* The commander directing an investigation under this rule shall detail a commissioned officer not the accuser, as investigating officer, who shall conduct the investigation and make a report of conclusions and recommendations. The investigating officer is disqualified to act later in the same case in any other capacity.

(2) *Defense counsel.*

(A) *Detailed counsel.* Except as provided in subsection (d)(2)(B) of this rule, military counsel certified in accordance with Article 27(b) shall be detailed to represent the accused.

(B) *Individual military counsel.* The accused may request to be represented by individual military counsel. Such requests shall be acted on in accordance with R.C.M. 506(b). When the accused is represented by individual military counsel, counsel detailed to represent the accused shall ordinarily be excused, unless the authority who detailed the defense counsel, as a matter of discretion, approves a request by the accused for retention of detailed counsel. The investigating officer shall forward any request by the accused for individual military counsel to the commander who directed the investigation. That commander shall follow the procedures in R.C.M. 506(b).

(C) *Civilian counsel.* The accused may be represented by civilian counsel at no expense to the United States. Upon request, the accused is entitled to a reasonable time to obtain civilian counsel and to have such counsel present for the investigation. However, the investigation shall not be unduly delayed for this purpose. Representation by civilian counsel shall not limit the rights to military counsel under subsections (d)(2)(A) and (B) of this rule.

(3) *Others.* The commander who directed the investigation may also, as a matter of discretion, detail or request an appropriate authority to detail:

(A) Counsel to represent the United States;

(B) A reporter; and

(C) An interpreter.

(e) *Scope of investigation.* The investigating officer shall inquire into the truth and form of the charges, and such other matters as may be necessary to make a recommendation as to the disposition of the charges. If evidence adduced during the investigation indicates that the accused committed an uncharged offense, the investigating officer may investigate the subject matter of such offense and make a recommendation as to its disposition, without the accused first having been charged with the offense. The accused's rights under subsection (f) are the same with regard to investigation of both charged and uncharged offenses.

(f) *Rights of the accused.* At any pretrial investigation under this rule the accused shall have the right to:

(1) Be informed of the charges under investigation;

(2) Be informed of the identity of the accuser;

(3) Except in circumstances described in R.C.M. 804(b)(2) [exclusion due to persisting in disruptive conduct following a warning], be present throughout the taking of evidence;

(4) Be represented by counsel;

(5) Be informed of the witnesses and other evidence then known to the investigating officer;

(6) Be informed of the purpose of the investigation;

(7) Be informed of the right against self-incrimination under Article 31;

(8) Cross-examine witnesses who are produced under subsection (g) of this rule;

(9) Have witnesses produced as provided for in subsection (g) of this rule;

(10) Have evidence, including documents or physical evidence, within the control of military authorities produced as provided under subsection (g) of this rule;

(11) Present anything in defense, extenuation, or mitigation for consideration by the investigating officer; and

(12) Make a statement in any form.

(g) *Production of witnesses and evidence; alternatives.*

(1) *In general.*

(A) *Witnesses.* Except as provided in subsection (g)(4)(A) of this rule, any witness whose testimony would be relevant to the investigation and not cumulative, shall be produced if reasonably available. This includes witnesses requested by the accused, if the request is timely. A witness is "reasonably available" when the witness is located within 100 miles of the situs of the investigation and the significance of the testimony and personal appearance of the witness outweighs the difficulty, expense, delay, and effect on military operations of obtaining the witness' appearance. A witness who is unavailable under Mil. R. Evid. 804(a)(1)-(6), is not "reasonably available."

(B) *Evidence*. Subject to Mil. R. Evid., Section V [privileges], evidence, including documents or physical evidence, which is under the control of the Government and which is relevant to the investigation and not cumulative, shall be produced if reasonably available. Such evidence includes evidence requested by the accused, if the request is timely. As soon as practicable after receipt of a request by the accused for information which may be protected under Mil. R. Evid. 505 or 506, the investigating officer shall notify the person who is authorized to issue a protective order under subsection (g)(6) of this rule, and the convening authority, if different. Evidence is reasonably available if its significance outweighs the difficulty, expense, delay, and effect on military operations of obtaining the evidence.

(2) *Determination of reasonable availability.*

(A) *Military witnesses*. The investigating officer shall make an initial determination whether a military witness is reasonably available. If the investigating officer decides that the witness is not reasonably available, the investigating officer shall inform the parties. Otherwise, the immediate commander of the witness shall be requested to make the witness available. A determination by the immediate commander that the witness is not reasonably available is not subject to appeal by the accused but may be reviewed by the military judge under R.C.M. 906(b)(3).

(B) *Civilian witnesses*. The investigating officer shall decide whether a civilian witness is reasonably available to appear as a witness.

(C) *Evidence*. The investigating officer shall make an initial determination whether evidence is reasonably available. If the investigating officer decides that it is not reasonably available, the investigating officer shall inform the parties. Otherwise, the custodian of the evidence shall be requested to provide the evidence. A determination by the custodian that the evidence is not reasonably available is not subject to appeal by the accused, but may be reviewed by the military judge under R.C.M. 906(b)(3).

(D) *Action when witness or evidence is not reasonably available*. If the defense objects to a determination that a witness or evidence is not reasonably available, the investigating officer shall include a statement of the reasons for the determination in the report of investigation.

(3) *Witness expenses*. Transportation expenses and a per diem allowance may be paid to civilians requested to testify in connection with an investigation under this rule according to regulations prescribed by the Secretary of a Department.

(4) *Alternatives to testimony.*

(A) Unless the defense objects, an investigating officer may consider, regardless of the availability of the witness:

(i) Sworn statements;

(ii) Statements under oath taken by telephone, radio, or similar means providing each party the opportunity to question the witness under circumstances by which the investigating officer may reasonably conclude that the witness' identity is as claimed;

(iii) Prior testimony under oath;

(iv) Depositions;

(v) Stipulations of fact or expected testimony;

(vi) Unsworn statements; and

(vii) Offers of proof of expected testimony of that witness.

(B) The investigating officer may consider, over objection of the defense, when the witness is not reasonably available:

(i) Sworn statements;

(ii) Statements under oath taken by telephone, radio, or similar means providing each party the opportunity to question the witness under circumstances by which the investigating officer may reasonably conclude that the witness' identity is as claimed;

(iii) Prior testimony under oath;

(iv) Deposition of that witness; and

(v) In time of war, unsworn statements.

(5) *Alternatives to evidence.*

(A) Unless the defense objects, an investigating officer may consider, regardless of the availability of the evidence:

(i) Testimony describing the evidence;

(ii) An authenticated copy, photograph, or reproduction of similar accuracy of the evidence;

(iii) An alternative to testimony, when permitted under subsection (g)(4)(B) of this rule, in which the evidence is described;

(iv) A stipulation of fact, document's contents, or expected testimony;

(v) An unsworn statement describing the evidence; or

(vi) An offer of proof concerning pertinent characteristics of the evidence.

(B) The investigating officer may consider, over objection of the defense, when the evidence is not reasonably available:

(i) Testimony describing the evidence;

(ii) An authenticated copy, photograph, or reproduction of similar accuracy of the evidence; or

(iii) An alternative to testimony, when permitted under subsection (g)(4)(B) of this rule, in which the evidence is described.

(6) *Protective order for release of privileged information.* If, prior to referral, the Government agrees to disclose to the accused information to which

the protections afforded by Mil. R. Evid. 505 or 506 may apply, the convening authority, or other person designated by regulation of the Secretary of the service concerned, may enter an appropriate protective order, in writing, to guard against the compromise of information disclosed to the accused. The terms of any such protective order may include prohibiting the disclosure of the information except as authorized by the authority issuing the protective order, as well as those terms specified by Mil. R. Evid. 505(g)(1)(B) through (F) or 506(g)(2) through (5).

(h) *Procedure.*

(1) *Presentation of evidence.*

(A) *Testimony.* All testimony shall be taken under oath, except that the accused may make an unsworn statement. The defense shall be given wide latitude in cross-examining witnesses.

(B) *Other evidence.* The investigating officer shall inform the parties what other evidence will be considered. The parties shall be permitted to examine all other evidence considered by the investigating officer.

(C) *Defense evidence.* The defense shall have full opportunity to present any matters in defense, extenuation, or mitigation.

(2) *Objections.* Any objection alleging failure to comply with this rule, except subsection (j), shall be made to the investigating officer promptly upon discovery of the alleged error. The investigating officer shall not be required to rule on any objection. An objection shall be noted in the report of investigation if a party so requests. The investigating officer may require a party to file any objection in writing.

(3) *Access by spectators.* Access by spectators to all or part of the proceeding may be restricted or foreclosed in the discretion of the commander who directed the investigation or the investigating officer.

(4) *Presence of accused.* The further progress of the taking of evidence shall not be prevented and the accused shall be considered to have waived the right to be present, whenever the accused:

(A) After being notified of the time and place of the proceeding is voluntarily absent (whether or not informed by the investigating officer of the obligation to be present); or

(B) After being warned by the investigating officer that disruptive conduct will cause removal from the proceeding, persists in conduct which is such as to justify exclusion from the proceeding.

(i) *Military Rules of Evidence.* The Military Rules of Evidence — other than Mil. R. Evid. 301, 302, 303, 305, 412 and Section V — shall not apply in pretrial investigations under this rule.

(j) *Report of investigation.*

(1) *In general.* The investigating officer shall make a timely written report of the investigation to the commander who directed the investigation.

(2) *Contents.* The report of investigation shall include:

(A) A statement of names and organizations or addresses of defense counsel and whether defense counsel was present throughout the taking of evidence, or if not present the reason why;

(B) The substance of the testimony taken on both sides, including any stipulated testimony;

(C) Any other statements, documents, or matters considered by the investigating officer, or recitals of the substance or nature of such evidence;

(D) A statement of any reasonable grounds for belief that the accused was not mentally responsible for the offense or was not competent to participate in the defense during the investigation;

(E) A statement whether the essential witnesses will be available at the time anticipated for trial and the reasons why any essential witness may not then be available;

(F) An explanation of any delays in the investigation;

(G) The investigating officer's conclusion whether the charges and specifications are in proper form;

(H) The investigating officer's conclusion whether reasonable grounds exist to believe that the accused committed the offenses alleged; and

(I) The recommendations of the investigating officer, including disposition.

(3) *Distribution of the report.* The investigating officer shall cause the report to be delivered to the commander who directed the investigation. That commander shall promptly cause a copy of the report to be delivered to each accused.

(4) *Objections.* Any objection to the report shall be made to the commander who directed the investigation within 5 days of its receipt by the accused. This subsection does not prohibit a convening authority from referring the charges or taking other action within the 5-day period.

(k) *Waiver.* The accused may waive an investigation under this rule. In addition, failure to make a timely objection under this rule, including an objection to the report, shall constitute waiver of the objection. Relief from the waiver may be granted by the investigating officer, the commander who directed the investigation, the convening authority, or the military judge, as appropriate, for good cause shown.

NOTES

1. The Army Court of Military Review once observed:

It is our view that the grand-jury indictment right pales in practical significance in comparison to a servicemember's pretrial investigation rights under Article 32, UCMJ. This is especially true when those latter rights are coupled with the statutory conditions under Article 34(a), UCMJ, which must be present before a convening authority can refer a case to trial by general court-martial.

United States v. Henderson, 23 M.J. 860, 861 (A.C.M.R. 1987). Article 34 requires a convening authority to obtain legal advice from a staff judge advocate before referring any case to a general court-martial.

2. A former Judge Advocate General of the Air Force similarly argued:

> In the military, an independent investigating officer is appointed to conduct the inquiry to determine if sufficient evidence exists to support a prosecution unlike the civilian sector in which a federal prosecutor controls the proceeding. And a military accused, unlike his civilian counterpart, is entitled to be present throughout the proceeding with legal representation, is entitled to present evidence on his own behalf, and may subject prosecution witnesses to cross-examination.

Maj. Gen. William A. Moorman, *Fifty Years of Military Justice: Does the Uniform Code of Military Justice Need to be Changed?*, 48 A.F. L. Rev. 185, 189 (2000) (footnotes omitted). *See generally* Major Larry A. Gaydos, *A Comprehensive Guide to the Military Pretrial Investigation*, 111 Mil. L. Rev. 49 (1986).

Col. Francis A. Gilligan, *The Bill of Rights and Service Members*
Army Law., Dec. 1987, at 3

By its express terms, the fifth amendment right to grand jury indictment is not applicable to service members. This has been one of the reasons that the military system has been criticized. One should question the extent of the protection provided by the grand jury, in comparison to military practice. Most prosecutors will tell you that the grand jury serves as a common sense yardstick as to whether charges should be brought against an individual. When the prosecutor does not have an unanimous vote from the jurors, it would indicate some weakness in the case. And when a true bill cannot be delivered, it certainly is the ultimate test that the individual should not be prosecuted. In place of the grand jury, the military provides that an individual may not be tried by general court-martial unless there has been an Article 32 investigation or its equivalent. The Article 32 investigation performs four primary purposes. First, it protects the accused from baseless charges; second, it provides a convening authority with information on which to determine whether to refer charges to trial by court-martial; third, it provides the convening authority with information with which to determine a specific disposition of a case; and fourth, it provides the defense with pretrial discovery of evidence that may be introduced by either side, the prosecution or the defense.

Insofar as the Article 32 investigation is an inquiry into the facts surrounding the charges against the accused and thus an important pretrial screening device, it is functionally similar to both the preliminary hearing and the grand jury. It is an unique hybrid, however, and dissimilar in large part to both civilian proceedings. At its core, the Article 32 investigation is composed of an open hearing at which the accused and counsel are present with the right to cross-examine adverse witnesses and to present a defense. As it also supplies the convening authority with information, it has far broader scope than the normal preliminary hearing. In addition, unlike the Article 32 investigation, the grand jury is a secret proceeding that deprives a testifying accused of the right to confrontation, to present evidence, and generally the right to counsel before the grand jury when the accused does testify. Consequently, the Article 32 investigation is far more protective than the analogous civilian proceeding. It is, however, also more limited in that the recommendation of the investigating officer is advisory only and may be ignored by the convening authority. In the civilian procedure a finding by a magistrate at a preliminary hearing that there is no probable cause to hold an accused has greater legal effect and refusal to indict on the part of the grand jury is final subject only to the possible indictment of the defendant by another grand jury.

MacDONALD v. HODSON
United States Court of Military Appeals
19 U.S.C.M.A. 582, 42 C.M.R. 184 (1970)

Charges alleging premeditated murder have been preferred against petitioner, and are presently under investigation by an officer appointed pursuant to Article 32, Uniform Code of Military Justice, 10 U.S.C. § 832. Petitioner avers that when the investigation commenced, the investigating officer granted his motion to hold open hearings. Shortly thereafter, the investigating officer revoked his ruling and announced that further proceedings would be closed to all persons. . . .

Petitioner now submits this Petition for Writ of Injunction and Temporary Restraining Order enjoining respondents "from denying or interfering with Petitioner's right to an open hearing before the Article 32 Investigating Officer."

The Article 32 investigation partakes of the nature both of a preliminary judicial hearing and of the proceedings of a grand jury. As in any judicial hearing, the accused is entitled to representation by qualified counsel. *United States v. Tomaszewski*, 8 U.S.C.M.A. 266, 24 C.M.R. 76 (1957). However, the investigating officer has no authority to appoint counsel, but must refer a request for such appointment to the appointing authority who then acts upon it. Paragraph 34c, Manual for Courts-Martial, United States, 1969 (Revised edition). Article 32, *supra*, requires "thorough and impartial investigation" which "shall include inquiry as to the truth of the matter set forth in the charges, consideration of the form of charges, and a recommendation as to the disposition which should be made of the case in the interest of justice and discipline." However, finality does not attach to the investigating officer's recommendation; it is advisory only. *Green v. Widdecke*, 19 U.S.C.M.A. 576, 42 C.M.R. 178 (1970); paragraph 34a, Manual for Courts-Martial, *supra*.

During the course of the investigation, the accused has the right to cross-examine witnesses against him, if they are available; all testimony, oral or written, must be under oath; in certain limited circumstances, such testimony may be admissible as previously reported testimony. *United States v. Samuels,* 10 U.S.C.M.A. 206, 27 C.M.R. 280 (1959); *United States v. Eggers,* 3 U.S.C.M.A. 191, 11 C.M.R. 191 (1953). While the investigation has many of the trappings of an adversarial proceeding, it is *ex parte* in fact, for the Government is not formally represented as a party. *United States v. Samuels, supra.*

As an investigation, the strict rules of evidence applicable at trial are not followed. Rather testimony and other evidence of all descriptions normally will come to the attention of the investigating officer, some germane to the charges before him, and others of no material significance whatever; some will implicate the accused, and some will fail to do so, while tending to implicate others not then under charges. In making his reports, it is the officer's responsibility to cull from his final product all extraneous matters and present only such evidence as in his opinion will be admissible at trial. Because so much untested material may come before him, Army Regulation No. 345-60 curtails the release of such information to the public in order to reduce the possibility of prejudice to the accused subject, and to others not charged.

In view of the foregoing, it cannot be said that the Article 32 investigation is a trial within the meaning of the Sixth Amendment to the Constitution of the United States. Hence, there is no requirement that its proceedings be "public." The action taken in the instant case appears to be well within the discretionary powers of the investigating officer, and no abuse appears. . . .

NOTES AND QUESTIONS

1. This Article 32 investigation concerned charges that Captain MacDonald had murdered his wife and two daughters.

> At the conclusion of the Article 32 hearing, it was recommended that the charges be dismissed and that recommendation was accepted and adopted by the commanding general, with the result that as of October 23, 1970, the military charges against [MacDonald] were dismissed. Subsequently, in December, 1970, [MacDonald] requested and received an honorable discharge from the Army.

United States v. MacDonald, 635 F.2d 1115, 1117 n.4 (4th Cir. 1980) (Russell, J., dissenting from denial of rehearing en banc). He was later tried in federal district court, where on "August 29, 1979, the jury convicted [him] of two counts of second-degree murder and one count of first-degree murder, and [the] court sentenced him to three consecutive terms of life imprisonment." *United States v. MacDonald,* 979 F. Supp. 1057, 1059 (D.N.C. 1997), *aff'd,* 161 F.3d 4 (4th Cir. 1998) (summary disposition).

2. In 1997, the Court of Appeals for the Armed Forces held that "absent cause shown that outweighs the value of openness, the military accused is . . . entitled to a public Article 32 investigative hearing." *ABC v. Powell,* 47 M.J.

363, 365 (C.A.A.F. 1997) (internal quotation marks omitted). The court also held that "when an accused is entitled to a public hearing, the press enjoys the same right and has standing to complain if access is denied." *Id.* This case dealt with a pretrial investigation of allegations against the Army's highest-ranking enlisted soldier. The decision, however, seemed to misrepresent *MacDonald*'s holding. In *ABC v. Powell*, the Court of Appeals wrote: "Although we have never addressed the direct question whether the Sixth Amendment to the Constitution affords a military accused the right to a public Article 32 hearing, we have consistently held that the Sixth Amendment right does apply to a court-martial." The court cited *MacDonald v. Hodson* as one of four cases supporting this proposition. But *MacDonald v. Hodson* did directly address whether the Sixth Amendment affords a military accused the right to a public Article 32 hearing and concluded that it did not. 19 U.S.C.M.A. at 583, 42 C.M.R. at 185 ("[I]t cannot be said that the Article 32 investigation is a trial within the meaning of the Sixth Amendment. . . . Hence, there is no requirement that its proceedings be 'public.'"). *See United States v. Davis*, 64 M.J. 445, 450 (C.A.A.F. 2007) (Ryan, J., concurring). *See also* Chapter 14, § II.

Chapter 4

SUMMARY DISCIPLINE

"Good order and discipline" are familiar watchwords of military law. Discipline can be achieved both formally and informally. For example, military instruction, drills or simply "a word to the wise" can help instill discipline in military personnel. At times, informal — indeed, illegal — practices such as hazing can be thought of as a means of achieving discipline. The legal process for doing so can take a variety of forms, some of which are properly referred to as "summary" or "nonjudicial," while others, typically reserved for graver forms of misconduct, involve a process that more or less resembles civilian criminal justice. Summary disciplinary cases vastly outnumber courts-martial.

I. INTERNATIONAL HUMAN RIGHTS

ENGEL v. THE NETHERLANDS
European Court of Human Rights
[1976] Eur. Ct. Hum. Rts. 3, [1976] EHRR 647

12. All applicants were, when submitting their applications to the Commission, conscript soldiers serving in different non-commissioned ranks in the Netherlands armed forces. On separate occasions, various penalties had been passed on them by their respective commanding officers for offences against military discipline. The applicants had appealed to the complaints officer (*beklagmeerdere*) and finally to the Supreme Military Court (*Hoog Militair Gerechtshof*) which in substance confirmed the decisions challenged but, in two cases, reduced the punishment imposed. . . .

25. Articles 39 to 43 of the [Military Discipline Act of 1903] state who may impose disciplinary punishments. This is normally the commanding officer of the individual's unit. He investigates the case and hears the serviceman accused (Article 46 of the 1903 Act) and questions witnesses and experts if that proves necessary. For each offence committed the officer chooses which of the various punishments available under the law should be applied. "When determining the nature and severity of disciplinary punishments," he shall be "both just and severe," shall have "regard to the circumstances in which the offence was committed as well as to the character and customary behaviour of the accused" and shall base his decision "on his own opinion and belief" (Article 37 of the 1903 Act).

26. Article 44 of the 1903 Act provides that any superior who has sufficient indication to suppose that a subordinate has committed a severe offence against military discipline is entitled, if necessary, to give notice of his provisional arrest (*voorlopig arrest*); the subordinate is obliged to comply immediately with that

notification. Provisional arrest is usually served in the same way as light arrest, but, if required either in the interest of the investigation or in order to prevent disorder, it is served in a similar way to aggravated or, as was the case prior to the 1974 Act [which amended or repealed parts of the 1903 Act], strict arrest. The serviceman concerned is as a rule excluded from performing his duty outside the place where he is confined. Article 45 stipulates that provisional arrest shall not last longer than 24 hours and Article 49 states that the hierarchical superior of the officer imposing provisional arrest may set it aside after hearing the latter. The period of such provisional arrest may be deducted in whole or in part from the punishment imposed.

27. Under Article 61 of the 1903 Act the serviceman on whom a disciplinary penalty has been imposed may challenge before the complaints officer his punishment or the grounds thereof unless it has been imposed by a military court. The complaints officer is the hierarchical superior of the officer giving the initial decision rather than a specialist, but he is usually assisted by a colleague who is a lawyer, especially in cases (before the 1974 Act) of committal to a disciplinary unit.

The complaint must be submitted within four days; if the complainant is under arrest he may on request consult other persons named by him (maximum of three), unless the commanding officer considers their presence to be inadvisable (Article 62).

The complaints officer must examine the case as soon as possible; he questions witnesses and experts to the extent he thinks necessary and hears the complainant and the punishing officer. He then gives a decision which must be accompanied by reasons and communicated to the complainant and the punishing officer (Article 65).

28. Appeal against the decision imposing a disciplinary punishment has no suspensive effect although the Minister of Defence may defer the execution of such punishment on account of special circumstances. Article 64 of the 1903 Act provided an exception in the case of committal to a disciplinary unit; the serviceman's appeal did not, however, entail the suspension or termination of any interim custody imposed under Article 20.

29. If the punishment has not been quashed by the complaints officer, the complainant may appeal within four days to the Supreme Military Court (Article 67 of the 1903 Act). . . .

33. In March 1971, Mr. Engel was serving as a sergeant in the Netherlands Army. He in fact lived at home during off-duty hours. The applicant was a member of the Conscript Servicemen's Association (*Vereniging van Dienstplichtige Militairen* — V.V.D.M.) which was created in 1966 and aims at safeguarding the interests of conscripts. It was recognised by the Government for taking part in negotiations in this field and its membership included about two-thirds of all conscripts.

Mr. Engel was a candidate for the vice-presidency of the V.V.D.M. and on 12 March he submitted a request to his company commander for leave of absence on 17 March in order to attend a general meeting in Utrecht at which the elections were to be held. He did not, however, mention his candidature.

Subsequently he became ill and stayed home under the orders of his doctor who gave him sick leave until 18 March and authorised him to leave the house on 17 March. On 16 March, the company commander had a talk with the battalion commander and it was agreed that no decision should be taken regarding the above-mentioned request pending further information from the applicant who had given no notice of his absence or return. However, on the following day a check was made at the applicant's home and it was discovered that he was not there. In fact, he had gone to the meeting of the V.V.D.M. where he had been elected vice-president.

34. On 18 March Mr. Engel returned to his unit and on the same day his company commander punished him with four days' light arrest for having been absent from his residence on the previous day.

The applicant considered this penalty a serious interference with his personal affairs in that it prevented him from properly preparing himself for his doctoral examination at the University of Utrecht which had been fixed for 24 March. According to the applicant, he had made several attempts on 18 March to speak to an officer on this point but without success. Believing that under the army regulations non-commissioned officers were allowed to serve their light arrest at home, he left the barracks in the evening and spent the night at home. However, the next day his company commander imposed a penalty of three days' aggravated arrest on him for having disregarded his first punishment.

The applicant, who had just been informed that, with effect from 1 April 1971, he had been demoted to the rank of private, again left the barracks in the evening and went home. He was arrested on Saturday 20 March by the military police and provisionally detained in strict arrest for about two days, by virtue of Article 44 of the 1903 Act (paragraph 26 above). On Monday 22 March his company commander imposed a penalty of three days' strict arrest for having disregarded his two previous punishments.

35. The execution of these punishments was suspended by ministerial decision in order to permit the applicant to take his doctoral examination which he passed on 24 March 1971. Moreover, on 21, 22 and 25 March Mr. Engel complained to the complaints officer about the penalties imposed on him by the company commander. On 5 April the complaints officer decided, after having heard the parties, that the first punishment of four days' light arrest should be reduced to a reprimand, the second punishment of three days' aggravated arrest to three days' light arrest, and the third punishment of three days' strict arrest to two days' strict arrest. In the last two cases the decision was based on the fact that the previous punishment(s) had been reduced and that the applicant had obviously been under considerable stress owing to his forthcoming examination. The complaints officer further decided that Mr. Engel's punishment of two days' strict arrest should be deemed to have been served from 20 to 22 March, during his provisional arrest.

36. On 7 April 1971 the applicant appealed to the Supreme Military Court against the decision of the complaints officer relying, inter alia, on the Convention in general terms. The Court heard the applicant and obtained the opinion of the State Advocate for the Armed Forces. On 23 June 1971, that is

about three months after the date of the disciplinary measures in dispute, the Court confirmed the contested decision. It referred to Article 5 para. 1(b) (art. 5-1-b) of the Convention and held that the applicant's detention had been lawful and had been imposed in order to secure the fulfilment of an obligation prescribed by law. The system under the 1903 Act and the applicable Regulations required in fact that every serviceman should submit to and co-operate in maintaining military discipline. This obligation could be enforced by imposing disciplinary punishments in accordance with the procedure prescribed by the above Act. In these circumstances, the applicant's punishment of two days' strict arrest had been justified in order to secure the fulfilment of that obligation.

The applicant had not received the assistance of a legally trained person at any stage in the proceedings against him; perusal of the file in the case does not reveal if he asked for such assistance. . . .

As to the Law

54. As the Government, Commission and applicants concurred in thinking, the Convention applies in principle to members of the armed forces and not only to civilians. It specifies in Articles 1 and 14 (art. 1, art. 14) that "everyone within [the] jurisdiction" of the Contracting States is to enjoy "without discrimination" the rights and freedoms set out in Section I. Article 4 para. 3(b) (art. 4-3-b), which exempts military service from the prohibition against forced or compulsory labour, further confirms that as a general rule the guarantees of the Convention extend to servicemen. The same is true of Article 11 para. 2 (art. 11-2) in fine, which permits the States to introduce special restrictions on the exercise of the freedoms of assembly and association by members of the armed forces.

Nevertheless, when interpreting and applying the rules of the Convention in the present case, the Court must bear in mind the particular characteristics of military life and its effects on the situation of individual members of the armed forces. . . .

I. On the Alleged Violation of Article 5

A. On the alleged violation of paragraph 1 of Article 5
(art. 5-1) taken alone

56. The applicants all submit that the disciplinary penalty or penalties, measure or measures pronounced against them contravened Article 5 para. 1 (art. 5-1), which provides:

> Everyone has the right to liberty and security of person. No one shall be deprived of his liberty save in the following cases and in accordance with a procedure prescribed by law:
>
> (a) the lawful detention of a person after conviction by a competent court;
>
> (b) the lawful arrest or detention of a person for non-compliance with the lawful order of a court or in order to secure the fulfilment of any obligation prescribed by law;

(c) the lawful arrest or detention of a person effected for the purpose of bringing him before the competent legal authority on reasonable suspicion of having committed an offence or when it is reasonably considered necessary to prevent his committing an offence or fleeing after having done so;

(d) the detention of a minor by lawful order for the purpose of educational supervision or his lawful detention for the purpose of bringing him before the competent legal authority;

(e) the lawful detention of persons for the prevention of the spreading of infectious diseases, of persons of unsound mind, alcoholics or drug addicts or vagrants;

(f) the lawful arrest or detention of a person to prevent his effecting an unauthorised entry into the country or of a person against whom action is being taken with a view to deportation or extradition.

1. *On the right to liberty in the context of military service*

57. During the preparation and subsequent conclusion of the Convention, the great majority of the Contracting States possessed defence forces and, in consequence, a system of military discipline that by its very nature implied the possibility of placing on certain of the rights and freedoms of the members of these forces limitations incapable of being imposed on civilians. The existence of such a system, which those States have retained since then, does not in itself run counter to their obligations.

Military discipline, nonetheless, does not fall outside the scope of Article 5 para. 1 (art. 5-1). Not only must this provision be read in the light of Articles 1 and 14 (art. 1, art. 14) (paragraph 54 above), but the list of deprivations of liberty set out therein is exhaustive, as is shown by the words "save in the following cases." A disciplinary penalty or measure may in consequence constitute a breach of Article 5 para. 1 (art. 5-1). The Government, moreover, acknowledge this.

58. In proclaiming the "right to liberty," paragraph 1 of Article 5 (art. 5-1) is contemplating individual liberty in its classic sense, that is to say the physical liberty of the person. Its aim is to ensure that no one should be dispossessed of this liberty in an arbitrary fashion. As pointed out by the Government and the Commission, it does not concern mere restrictions upon liberty of movement (Article 2 of Protocol no. 4) (P4-2). This is clear both from the use of the terms "deprived of his liberty," "arrest" and "detention," which appear also in paragraphs 2 to 5, and from a comparison between Article 5 (art. 5) and the other normative provisions of the Convention and its Protocols.

59. In order to determine whether someone has been "deprived of his liberty" within the meaning of Article 5 (art. 5), the starting point must be his concrete situation. Military service, as encountered in the Contracting States, does not on its own in any way constitute a deprivation of liberty under the Convention, since it is expressly sanctioned in Article 4 para. 3(b) (art. 4-3-b). In addition, rather wide limitations upon the freedom of movement of the members of the armed forces are entailed by reason of the specific demands of military service

so that the normal restrictions accompanying it do not come within the ambit of Article 5 (art. 5) either.

Each State is competent to organise its own system of military discipline and enjoys in the matter a certain margin of appreciation. The bounds that Article 5 (art. 5) requires the State not to exceed are not identical for servicemen and civilians. A disciplinary penalty or measure which on analysis would unquestionably be deemed a deprivation of liberty were it to be applied to a civilian may not possess this characteristic when imposed upon a serviceman. Nevertheless, such penalty or measure does not escape the terms of Article 5 (art. 5) when it takes the form of restrictions that clearly deviate from the normal conditions of life within the armed forces of the Contracting States. In order to establish whether this is so, account should be taken of a whole range of factors such as the nature, duration, effects and manner of execution of the penalty or measure in question.

2. *On the existence of deprivations of liberty in the present case*

61. No deprivation of liberty resulted from the three and four days' light arrest awarded respectively against Mr. Engel (paragraphs 34-36 above, second punishment) and Mr. van der Wiel (paragraphs 37-39 above). Although confined during off-duty hours to their dwellings or to military buildings or premises, as the case may be, servicemen subjected to such a penalty are not locked up and continue to perform their duties (Article 8 of the 1903 Act and paragraph 18 above). They remain, more or less, within the ordinary framework of their army life.

62. Aggravated arrest differs from light arrest on one point alone: in off-duty hours, soldiers serve the arrest in a specially designated place which they may not leave in order to visit the canteen, cinema or recreation rooms, but they are not kept under lock and key (Article 9-B of the 1903 Act and paragraph 19 above). Consequently, neither does the Court consider as a deprivation of liberty the twelve days' aggravated arrest complained of by Mr. de Wit (paragraph 41 above).

63. Strict arrest, abolished in 1974, differed from light arrest and aggravated arrest in that non-commissioned officers and ordinary servicemen served it by day and by night locked in a cell and were accordingly excluded from the performance of their normal duties (Article 10-B of the 1903 Act and paragraph 20 above). It thus involved deprivation of liberty. It follows that the provisional arrest inflicted on Mr. Engel in the form of strict arrest (Article 44 of the 1903 Act; paragraphs 26, 34 and 35 above) had the same character despite its short duration (20-22 March 1971).

64. Committal to a disciplinary unit, likewise abolished in 1974 but applied in 1971 to Mr. Dona and Mr. Schul, represented the most severe penalty under military disciplinary law in the Netherlands. Privates condemned to this penalty following disciplinary proceedings were not separated from those so sentenced by way of supplementary punishment under the criminal law, and during a month or more they were not entitled to leave the establishment. The committal lasted for a period of three to six months; this was considerably longer than the duration of the other penalties, including strict arrest which could be imposed for one to fourteen days. Furthermore, it appears that

Mr. Dona and Mr. Schul spent the night locked in a cell (Articles 5, 18 and 19 of the 1903 Act, Royal Decree of 14 June 1971 and paragraphs 21 and 50 above). For these various reasons, the Court considers that in the circumstances deprivation of liberty occurred.

65. The same is not true of the measure that, from 8 October until 3 November 1971, preceded the said committal, since Mr. Dona and Mr. Schul served their interim custody in the form of aggravated arrest (Article 20 of the 1903 Act; paragraphs 22, 46, 48 and 62 above).

66. The Court thus comes to the conclusion that neither the light arrest of Mr. Engel and Mr. van der Wiel, nor the aggravated arrest of Mr. de Wit, nor the interim custody of Mr. Dona and Mr. Schul call for a more thorough examination under paragraph 1 of Article 5 (art. 5-1).

The punishment of two days' strict arrest inflicted on Mr. Engel on 7 April 1971 and confirmed by the Supreme Military Court on 23 June 1971 coincided in practice with an earlier measure: it was deemed to have been served beforehand, that is from 20 to 22 March 1971, by the applicant's period of provisional arrest (paragraphs 34-36 above, third punishment).

On the other hand, the Court is required to determine whether the last-mentioned provisional arrest, as well as the committal of Mr. Dona and Mr. Schul to a disciplinary unit, complied with Article 5 para. 1 (art. 5-1).

3. *On the compatibility of the deprivations of liberty found in the present case with paragraph 1 of Article 5 (art. 5-1)*

67. The Government maintained, in the alternative, that the committal of Mr. Dona and Mr. Schul to a disciplinary unit and the provisional arrest of Mr. Engel satisfied, respectively, the requirements of sub-paragraph (a) and of sub-paragraph (b) of Article 5 para. 1 (art. 5-1-a, art. 5-1-b) (paragraphs 21-23 of the memorial); they did not invoke sub-paragraphs (c) to (f) (art. 5-1-c, art. 5-1-d, art. 5-1-e, art. 5-1-f).

68. Sub-paragraph (a) of Article 5 para. 1 (art. 5-1-a) permits the "lawful detention of a person after conviction by a competent court."

The Court, like the Government (hearing on 29 October 1975), notes that this provision makes no distinction based on the legal character of the offence of which a person has been found guilty. It applies to any "conviction" occasioning deprivation of liberty pronounced by a "court," whether the conviction is classified as criminal or disciplinary by the internal law of the State in question.

Mr. Dona and Mr. Schul were indeed deprived of their liberty "after" their conviction by the Supreme Military Court. Article 64 of the 1903 Act conferred a suspensive effect upon their appeals against the decisions of their commanding officer (8 October 1971) and the complaints officer (19 October 1971), a fact apparently overlooked by the Commission (paragraph 85 and Appendix IV of the report) but which the Government have rightly stressed (paragraph 21 of the memorial). Consequently, their transfer to the disciplinary barracks at Nieuwersluis occurred only by virtue of the final sentences imposed on 17 November 1971 (paragraphs 28, 48 and 50 above).

It remains to be ascertained that the said sentences were passed by a "competent court" within the meaning of Article 5 para. 1(a) (art. 5-1-a).

The Supreme Military Court, whose jurisdiction was not at all disputed, constitutes a court from the organisational point of view. Doubtless its four military members are not irremovable in law, but like the two civilian members they enjoy the independence inherent in the Convention's notion of a "court" (*De Wilde, Ooms and Versyp* judgment of 18 June 1971, Series A no. 12, p. 41, para. 78, and paragraph 30 above).

Furthermore, it does not appear from the file in the case (paragraphs 31-32 and 48-49 above) that Mr. Dona and Mr. Schul failed to receive before the Supreme Military Court the benefit of adequate judicial guarantees under Article 5 para. 1(a) (art. 5-1-a), an autonomous provision whose requirements are not always co-extensive with those of Article 6 (art. 6). The guarantees afforded to the two applicants show themselves to be "adequate" for the purposes of Article 5 para. 1(a) (art. 5-1-a) if account is taken of "the particular nature of the circumstances" under which the proceedings took place (above-cited judgment of 18 June 1971, Series A no. 12, pp. 41-42, para. 78). As for Article 6 (art. 6), the Court considers below whether it was applicable in this case and, if so, whether it has been respected.

Finally, the penalty inflicted was imposed and then executed "lawfully" and "in accordance with a procedure prescribed by law." In short, it did not contravene Article 5 para. 1 (art. 5-1). . . .

69. The provisional arrest of Mr. Engel for its part clearly does not come within the ambit of sub-paragraph (a) of Article 5 para. 1 (art. 5-1-a).

The Government have derived argument from sub-paragraph (b) (art. 5-1-b) insofar as the latter permits "lawful arrest or detention" intended to "secure the fulfilment of any obligation prescribed by law."

The Court considers that the words "secure the fulfilment of any obligation prescribed by law" concern only cases where the law permits the detention of a person to compel him to fulfil a specific and concrete obligation which he has until then failed to satisfy. A wide interpretation would entail consequences incompatible with the notion of the rule of law from which the whole Convention draws its inspiration (*Golder* judgment of 21 February 1975, Series A no. 18, pp. 16-17, para. 34). It would justify, for example, administrative internment meant to compel a citizen to discharge, in relation to any point whatever, his general duty of obedience to the law.

In fact, Mr. Engel's provisional arrest was in no way designed to secure the fulfilment in the future of such an obligation. Article 44 of the 1903 Act, applicable when an officer has "sufficient indication to suppose that a subordinate has committed a serious offence against military discipline," refers to past behaviour. The measure thereby authorised is a preparatory stage of military disciplinary proceedings and is thus situated in a punitive context. Perhaps this measure also has on occasions the incidental object or effect of inducing a member of the armed forces to comply henceforth with his obligations, but only with great contrivance can it be brought under sub-paragraph (b) (art. 5-1-b). If the latter were the case, this sub-paragraph could moreover be extended to punishments stricto sensu involving deprivation of liberty on the ground of their deterrent qualities. This would deprive such punishments of the fundamental guarantees of sub-paragraph (a) (art. 5-1-a).

The said measure really more resembles that spoken of in sub-paragraph (c) Article 5 para. 1 (art. 5-1-c) of the Convention. However in the present case it did not fulfil one of the requirements of that provision since the detention of Mr. Engel from 20 to 22 March 1971 had not been "effected for the purpose of bringing him before the competent legal authority" (paragraphs 86-88 of the report of the Commission).

Neither was Mr. Engel's provisional arrest "lawful" within the meaning of Article 5 para. 1 (art. 5-1) insofar as it exceeded — by twenty-two to thirty hours according to the information provided at the hearing on 28 October 1975 — the maximum period of twenty-four hours laid down by Article 45 of the 1903 Act.

According to the Government, the complaints officer redressed this irregularity after the event by deeming to have been served in advance, that is from 20 to 22 March 1971, the disciplinary penalty of two days' strict arrest imposed by him on the applicant on 5 April 1971 and confirmed by the Supreme Military Court on 23 June 1971. However, it is clear from the case-law of the European Court that the reckoning of a detention on remand (*Untersuchungshaft*) as part of a later sentence cannot eliminate a violation of paragraph 3 of Article 5 (art. 5-3), but may have repercussions only under Article 50 (art. 50) on the basis that it limited the loss occasioned (*Stögmüller* judgment of 10 November 1969, Series A no. 9, pp. 27, 36 and 39-45; *Ringeisen* judgments of 16 July 1971 and 22 June 1972, Series A no. 13, pp. 20 and 41-45, and no. 15, p. 8, para. 21; *Neumeister* judgment of 7 May 1974, Series A no. 17, pp. 18-19, paras. 40-41). The Court sees no reason to resort to a different solution when assessing the compatibility of Mr. Engel's provisional arrest with paragraph 1 of Article 5 (art. 5-1).

In conclusion, the applicant's deprivation of liberty from 20 to 22 March 1971 occurred in conditions at variance with this paragraph.

B. On the alleged violation of Articles 5 para. 1 and 14 (art. 14+5-1) taken together

70. In the submission of the applicants, the disputed penalties and measures also contravened Article 5 para. 1 read in conjunction with Article 14 (art. 14+5-1) which provides:

> The enjoyment of the rights and freedoms set forth in this Convention shall be secured without discrimination on any ground such as sex, race, colour, language, religion, political or other opinion, national or social origin, association with a national minority, property, birth or other status.

71. Since certain of the said penalties and measures did not involve any deprivation of liberty (paragraphs 61, 62 and 65 above), the discrimination alleged in their connection does not give rise to any problem with regard to Article 14 (art. 14), in that it did not affect the enjoyment of the right set forth in Article 5 para. 1 (art. 5-1). The same does not apply to Mr. Engel's

provisional arrest, nor to the committal of Mr. Dona and Mr. Schul to a disciplinary unit (paragraphs 63 and 64 above).

72. Mr. Engel, Mr. Dona and Mr. Schul complain in the first place of distinctions in treatment between servicemen. According to Articles 10 and 44 of the 1903 Act, provisional arrest imposed in the form of strict arrest was served by officers in their dwellings, tent or quarters whereas non-commissioned officers and ordinary servicemen were locked in a cell (paragraph 20 above). As for committal to a disciplinary unit, privates alone risked this punishment (Articles 3 to 5 of the 1903 Act and paragraphs 16 and 21 above).

A distinction based on rank may run counter to Article 14 (art. 14). The list set out in that provision is illustrative and not exhaustive, as is shown by the words "any ground such as" (in French "*notamment*"). Besides, the word "status" (in French "*situation*") is wide enough to include rank. Furthermore, a distinction that concerns the manner of execution of a penalty or measure occasioning deprivation of liberty does not on that account fall outside the ambit of Article 14 (art. 14), for such a distinction cannot but have repercussions upon the way in which the "enjoyment" of the right enshrined in Article 5 para. 1 (art. 5-1) is "secured." The Court, on these two points, does not subscribe to the submissions of the Government (paragraph 40, first sub-paragraph, of the Commission's report), but rather expresses its agreement with the Commission (*ibid.*, paragraphs 133-134).

The Court is not unaware that the respective legislation of a number of Contracting States seems to be evolving, albeit in various degrees, towards greater equality in the disciplinary sphere between officers, non-commissioned officers and ordinary servicemen. The Netherlands Act of 12 September 1974 offers a striking example of this tendency. In particular, by abolishing strict arrest and committal to a disciplinary unit, this Act has henceforth put an end to the distinctions criticised by Mr. Engel, Mr. Dona and Mr. Schul.

In order to establish whether the said distinctions constituted discrimination contrary to Articles 5 and 14 (art. 14+5) taken together, regard must nevertheless be had to the moment when they were in existence. . . .

The hierarchical structure inherent in armies entails differentiation according to rank. Corresponding to the various ranks are differing responsibilities which in their turn justify certain inequalities of treatment in the disciplinary sphere. Such inequalities are traditionally encountered in the Contracting States and are tolerated by international humanitarian law (paragraph 140 of the Commission's report: Article 88 of the Geneva Convention of 12 August 1949 relative to the Treatment of Prisoners of War). In this respect, the European Convention allows the competent national authorities a considerable margin of appreciation.

At the time in question, the distinctions attacked by the three applicants had their equivalent in the internal legal system of practically all the Contracting States. Based on an element objective in itself, that is rank, these distinctions could have been dictated by a legitimate aim, namely the preservation of discipline by methods suited to each category of servicemen. While only privates risked committal to a disciplinary unit, they clearly were not subject to a serious penalty threatening the other members of the armed forces, namely reduction in rank. As for confinement in a cell during strict arrest, the Netherlands legislator could have had sufficient reason for not applying this to officers. On the whole, the legislator does not seem in the circumstances to have abused the latitude left to him by the Convention. Furthermore, the Court does not consider that the principle of proportionality, as defined in its previously cited judgment of 23 July 1968 (Series A no. 6, p. 34, para. 10, second sub-paragraph in fine), has been offended in the present case.

73. Mr. Engel, Mr. Dona and Mr. Schul in the second place object to inequalities of treatment between servicemen and civilians. In point of fact, even civilians subject by reason of their occupation to a particular disciplinary system cannot in the Netherlands incur penalties analogous to the disputed deprivations of liberty. However, this does not result in any discrimination incompatible with the Convention, the conditions and demands of military life being by nature different from those of civil life (paragraphs 54 and 57 above).

74. The Court thus finds no breach of Articles 5 para. 1 and 14 (art. 14+5-1) taken together. . . .

II. On the Alleged Violations of Article 6

A. On the alleged violation of Article 6 (art. 6) taken alone

78. The five applicants allege violation of Article 6 (art. 6) which provides:

1. In the determination of his civil rights and obligations or of any criminal charge against him, everyone is entitled to a fair and public hearing within a reasonable time by an independent and impartial tribunal established by law. Judgment shall be pronounced publicly but the press and public may be excluded from all or part of the trial in the interests of morals, public order or national security in a democratic society, where the interests of juveniles or the protection of the private life of the parties so require, or to the extent strictly necessary in the opinion of the court in special circumstances where publicity would prejudice the interests of justice.

2. Everyone charged with a criminal offence shall be presumed innocent until proved guilty according to law.

3. Everyone charged with a criminal offence has the following minimum rights:

(a) to be informed promptly, in a language which he understands and in detail, of the nature and cause of the accusation against him;

(b) to have adequate time and facilities for the preparation of his defence;

(c) to defend himself in person or through legal assistance of his own choosing or, if he has not sufficient means to pay for legal assistance, to be given it free when the interests of justice so require;

(d) to examine or have examined witnesses against him and to obtain the attendance and examination of witnesses on his behalf under the same conditions as witnesses against him;

(e) to have the free assistance of an interpreter if he cannot understand or speak the language used in court.

79. For both the Government and the Commission, the proceedings brought against Mr. Engel, Mr. van der Wiel, Mr. de Wit, Mr. Dona and Mr. Schul involved the determination neither of "civil rights and obligations" nor of "any criminal charge."

Led thus to examine the applicability of Article 6 (art. 6) in the present case, the Court will first investigate whether the said proceedings concerned "any criminal charge" within the meaning of this text; for, although disciplinary according to Netherlands law, they had the aim of repressing through penalties offences alleged against the applicants, an objective analogous to the general goal of the criminal law. . . .

SEPARATE OPINION OF JUDGE VERDROSS

. . . If one compares disciplinary detention in a cell in the barracks with incarceration of a civilian or a serviceman in a prison (paragraph 1 (a) of Article 5) (art. 5-1-a), one is bound to see that there is a fundamental difference between the two. In the second case, the convicted person is completely cut off from his ordinary environment and occupation since he is removed from his home. On the other hand, the soldier detained for disciplinary reasons stays in the barracks and may, from one moment to the next, be ordered to carry out one of his military duties; he thus remains, even whilst so detained, potentially within the confines of military service. It seems to me from this that such detention does not in principle amount to a deprivation of liberty within the meaning of Article 5 para. 1 (art. 5-1). This does not mean that all disciplinary detention imposed by the competent military authority escapes the Court's supervision. It may contravene the Convention if it violates Article 3 (art. 3) or if its duration, or its severity, exceeds the norm generally admitted by the member States of the Council of Europe in the matter of disciplinary sanctions; I take the view that, in the final analysis, the nature of a punishment depends on this yardstick which can, of course, vary with the requirements of international military life.

SEPARATE OPINION OF JUDGE ZEKIA

. . . In my view, once, in the light of the criteria enunciated by this Court, a conscript or soldier is charged with an offence which entails deprivation of his liberty such as committal to a disciplinary unit, and proceedings are directed to that end, such conscript or soldier is fully entitled to avail himself of the provisions of the Articles under consideration. For all intents and purposes the proceedings levelled against him are criminal in character and as far as court proceedings are concerned there need not be any difference between him and a civilian. I am not suggesting that such proceedings should be referred to civil courts. On the contrary, I consider it very appropriate that military courts composed of one or more judges, assisted by assessors or lawyers if needed, might take cognisance of cases where army servicemen are to be tried. . . .

It is evident from the statement of facts made in the judgment and from the short reference I have given to certain facts that the superior commanding officer assumed the status of a judge who constituted a court of first instance and after hearing the case convicted the applicants and sentenced them for committal to a disciplinary unit. Likewise, the complaints officer assumed the status of a revisional court in dealing with complaints made by persons convicted and sentenced by a lower court, here by the superior commanding officer. The decision of the complaints officer is also subject to appeal to the Supreme Military Court which is empowered to confirm or reverse conviction and sentence or to alter them. The Supreme Military Court exercises an appellate jurisdiction over the decisions of the commanding and complaints officers. The conviction and sentence do not emanate from this Court. The sentence for committal to a disciplinary unit originated in the decision of the superior commanding officer who is neither a judge nor entitled to constitute a court. The proceedings before him are conducted partly in a quasi-judicial manner and not in full compliance with Articles 6 para. 1 and 6 para. 3(c) and (d) (art. 6-1, art. 6-3-c, art. 6-3-d) of the Convention. The same considerations more or less apply to the status of the complaints officer. The Supreme Military Court is correctly denominated as a court although the proceedings before the court are conducted in camera in contravention of Article 6 para. 1 (art. 6-1). This court is not supposed to take the place of a trial court but rather to correct decisions already taken and convictions and sentences already passed. Therefore I am of the opinion that the requirements of Article 5 para. 1(a) (art. 5-1-a) have not been met. It is a great advantage to persons facing charges to have a hearing, first before a trial court which affords equality of arms and observes the rules of fair trial. In case of conviction and receiving sentence, again it is a further advantage for a convicted man to have the chance to assert his innocence before a higher court. Usually a court of appeal considers itself as bound by the findings of fact of the lower court unless there is strong reason to upset such findings. The significance in the administration of justice of a trial court of first instance cannot be regarded as over-emphasised. On the other hand if I am right in my way of thinking that, once a soldier is sought to be deprived of his right to liberty to the extent inadmissible and impermissible with regard to his status as a soldier or conscript, he is entitled to be treated as a civilian, then the detention of the applicants either in the form of aggravated arrest or interim arrest before their cases were heard by the Supreme Military Court amounted to a detention before a conviction by a competent court had been passed. Furthermore, the detention of the applicants for the period indicated above before the Supreme Military Court heard the case was made on the strength of a conviction and sentence passed by a superior commanding officer who was not a competent court and such detention was not linked with the exigencies of service.

SEPARATE OPINION OF JUDGE CREMONA

. . . Having already excluded certain punitive measures (also described as arrests) from the purview of deprivation of liberty for the purposes of Article 5 para. 1 (art. 5-1) of the Convention solely on the accepted ground that "when interpreting and applying the rules of the Convention in the present case, the Court must bear in mind the particular characteristics of military life and its effects on the situation of individual members of the armed forces" (paragraph

54 of the judgment), then, in proceeding to identify as possible charges of a criminal nature (for the purposes of Article 6 para. 1 of the Convention) (art. 6-1) certain "disciplinary charges" which involve liability to punishments entailing unquestionable deprivation of liberty, I am unable to distinguish further, as the majority of my colleagues do (paragraph 82), particularly on the basis of the relative duration of such deprivation of liberty. . . .

JOINT SEPARATE OPINION OF JUDGES O'DONOGHUE AND PEDERSEN

We are in agreement with the view that no breach has been found in any of the cases before the Court under Articles 10, 11, 14, 17 and 18 (art. 10, art. 11, art. 14, art. 17, art. 18) of the Convention. It is clear from the judgment that the difficulties arise from the consideration of the applicability of two Articles 5 and 6 (art. 5, art. 6). These Articles (art. 5, art. 6) can be said to have a certain inter-relationship because if Article 5 (art. 5) is applicable in the sense that there has been a deprivation of liberty involving a criminal charge the full impact of the obligation to comply with Article 6 (art. 6) will follow.

We feel unable to adopt the conclusion of the majority of the Court that the clear obligation of members of the armed forces to observe the code of discipline applicable to such forces is an unspecified obligation and therefore outside the reach of Article 5 para. 1(b) (art. 5-1-b). There is a clear distinction in our opinion between the obligation of citizens at large to obey the law and the special position of military personnel to obey the disciplinary code which is a vital and integral constituent of the force of which they are members.

. . . There is an elementary factor which should be looked at in the structure and character of a military establishment in any country which is party to the Convention. This factor is the disciplinary code, the maintenance of which is vital to the very continued existence of an armed force, and quite different from any other body or association which purports to exercise a measure of discipline over its members.

The special importance of discipline in an armed force and the recognition of this by its members, lead us to take the view that you have here a clear case of a specific and concrete obligation prescribed by law and imposed on the members. In the light of these considerations we are satisfied that in none of the cases before the Court has there been a breach of Article 5 para. 1 (art. 5-1) of the Convention because of the exception stated in Article 5 para. 1(b) (art. 5-1-b). . . .

It is to be recognised that difficulty may be experienced by States in dealing with cases which are a breach of discipline and at the same time an offence under the criminal law. It seems to us that a test should be whether the complaint is predominantly a disciplinary breach or a criminal offence. If the latter, the provisions of Article 6 (art. 6) must be observed. The nature of the complaint and the punishment prescribed under the disciplinary code and under the criminal law would be helpful pointers as to the course to be followed in order to comply with the Convention. Any attempt to dilute the procedure in the case of a grave crime by treating it as a disciplinary infraction would in our opinion be such a serious abuse, and indeed quite powerless under the Convention to exclude the application of Article 6 (art. 6) and would oblige full compliance with the requirements of that Article (art. 6). . . .

SEPARATE OPINION OF JUDGE BINDSCHEDLER-ROBERT

The first part of the judgment ("as to the law") is based on the idea that Article 5 para. 1 (art. 5-1) is applicable *de plano* to disciplinary measures and penalties occasioning deprivation of liberty imposed in the context of military disciplinary law. It follows from this (i) that disciplinary penalties occasioning deprivation of liberty would comply with the Convention only if imposed by a court, in conformity with Article 5 para. 1(a) (art. 5-1-a); and (ii) that, in conformity with sub-paragraph (c) (art. 5-1-c), there may be provisional arrest or detention only for the purpose of bringing the person arrested before the competent legal authority, and not before the hierarchical superior even if he is impowered to impose a disciplinary penalty. Whilst, on the facts of the case, the first of these consequences does not result in the finding of a violation of the Convention, the second leads the Court to conclude that there has been a violation of Article 5 para. 1 (art. 5-1) as regards Mr. Engel's provisional arrest.

To my great regret, I cannot share this point of view; I think that, despite the apparently exhaustive nature of Article 5 para. 1 (art. 5-1), the measures and penalties of military disciplinary law should not be put on the scales of Article 5 para. 1 (art. 5-1). Here are my reasons:

(1) Account must be taken of the nature of military service and the role of disciplinary law in instilling and maintaining discipline which is a sine qua non for the proper functioning of that special institution, the army. It is not enough to adopt, as does the Court, a narrow concept of deprivation of liberty; what must be borne in mind is the whole system of disciplinary law. Military discipline calls in particular for speedy and effective measures and penalties, adapted to each situation, and which, therefore, the hierarchical superior must be able to impose.

(2) The Convention itself recognises in its Article 4 para. 3(b) (art. 4-3-b) the special characteristics of military service. This provision reflects a basic choice made by the Contracting States and establishes in a general way the compatibility with the Convention of military service. The derogations from and restrictions on the fundamental rights to which it may give rise — for example, the right to liberty of movement guaranteed by Article 2 of Protocol no. 4 (P4-2) — are thus not contrary to the Convention, even if there is no express reservation about them. Now the system of discipline peculiar to the army constitutes one of these derogations; Article 5 para. 1 (art. 5-1) does not concern military disciplinary law and its exhaustive nature relates only to situations in civil life. Judge Verdross is right to emphasise in his separate opinion that disciplinary penalties in the framework of military service are sui generis.

(3) The fact that disciplinary law does not fall under Article 5 para. 1 (art. 5-1) is the only explanation for the wording of this provision and its complete lack of adaptation to the situations which military disciplinary law concerns. These factors, as well as the place of Article 5 (art. 5) in the Convention and its logical link with Article 6 (art. 6), are an indication that the drafters of the Convention really had in mind situations belonging to criminal procedure.

(4) The above points are corroborated by the way in which the States party to the Convention have dealt with the question in their domestic law. Even

today, in their military disciplinary law, the hierarchical superior is generally the authority empowered to take measures or impose penalties whether occasioning deprivation of liberty or not. Some States certainly provide for judicial review but this does not always have a suspensive effect; furthermore, Article 5 para. 1(a) (art. 5-1-a) makes no distinction in its requirements between the different authorities. The governments do not seem to have envisaged the possibility that their military disciplinary law — as opposed to their military penal procedure — could be affected by the Convention. It appears difficult in these circumstances to countenance an interpretation that disregards so widespread a conception, namely, the "common denominator of the respective legislation of the various Contracting States," to adopt the Court's language in another context (paragraph 82 of the judgment).

I conclude from the above that Mr. Engel's provisional arrest, since it occurred in the framework of disciplinary procedure, was not subject to Article 5 para. 1(a) (art. 5-1-a) and that, as a result, it has not violated this provision on the ground that Mr. Engel was arrested and detained for the purpose of being brought before his hierarchical superior and not before a legal authority. . . .

[There were several other separate opinions.]

A.D. v. TURKEY
European Court of Human Rights
Application No. 29986/96 (2005)

8. At the time of filing the petition, petitioner was serving in the armed forces as a sergeant. On October 14, 1994, Lt. Col. Ö.Ç. accused him of military disobedience and asked that he present his defense.

9. On the same date, the lieutenant colonel punished petitioner with 21 days of simple arrest for military disobedience within the meaning of Article 171 of the Military Penal Code. Petitioner served his sentence in jail and the prison for officers and noncommissioned officers.

10. On October 31, 1994, petitioner objected to the battalion commander concerning this decision and disputed the authority of the lieutenant colonel to impose the penalty in question. On November 30, 1994, his request was dismissed by the commander, who pointed out to him that the penalty imposed in the case was in compliance with the terms of Article 171 of the Military Penal Code.

11. Petitioner's request to set aside the sentence to simple arrest was rejected on April 26, 1995 by the Military Administrative High Court on the ground that because of Article 129 of the Constitution and Article 21 of Law No. 1602 concerning the High Court, military disciplinary sanctions were withdrawn from judicial review.

12. Petitioner's request to correct the judgment was rejected by the High Court on October 4, 1995.

13. During 1995, petitioner was hit with numerous penalties of simple arrest by his military superiors for breaches of military discipline and the appeals he submitted were rejected.

II. Pertinent Domestic Law

14. During the pertinent period, the rules governing various punishments incurred by those guilty of breaches of discipline appeared in Article 171 of the Military Penal Code (Law No. 1632). The nature of the punishments depended on the grade of the offender and of the officer imposing discipline. According to this article, lieutenant colonels were entitled to impose on soldiers a sentence of 21 days of simple arrest in cases involving breaches of military discipline.

15. Article 129 of the Constitution provides:

> . . . Decisions in disciplinary matters cannot be withdrawn from judicial review. Decisions concerning members of the armed forces as well as judges and prosecutors are reserved.

16. By virtue of Article 21 of Law No. 1602 concerning the High Court, disciplinary sanctions imposed by superiors for breach of military discipline are reserved from judicial review.

Law

I. On the alleged violation of Article 5 § 1 of the Convention

17. Petitioner complains that the punishment of simple arrest was imposed on him by his military superior and not by a competent court within the meaning of Article 5 § 1 of the Convention, which reads as follows:

> 1. Every person has the right to liberty and safety. No one can be deprived of his liberty except in the following cases and by legal means:
>
> a) if he is regularly detained following conviction by a competent tribunal. . . .

B. On the merits

19. The government disputes the existence of a violation while deriving an argument from paragraph (b) of Article 5 § 1, as the latter permits detention for the purpose of ensuring the performance of a duty prescribed by law. According to the government, obedience to superior orders being an obligation prescribed by the Military Penal Code, petitioner's detention was necessary to ensure the performance of that inherent duty of military discipline.

20. The Court recalls that the phrase "ensure the performance of a duty prescribed by law" contained in paragraph (b) of Article 5 § 1 concerns cases where the law authorized detention for the purpose of ensuring the future performance of a specific duty. To be justified from the standpoint of paragraph (b) of Article 5 § 1, the detention need not have a repressive or punitive character. *See, e.g., Engel v. The Netherlands*, Judgment of June 8, 1976, ser. A No. 22, § 69. In this case, the punishment of simple arrest imposed on petitioner for having breached military discipline concerns past conduct. It falls within the category of punishment and is not saved by paragraph (b) of that Article.

21. The Court recalls that, to satisfy the terms of Article 5 § 1(a), a deprivation of liberty must result from a judicial decision. It must be imposed by a

competent court with power to adjudicate the matter, enjoying independence with respect to the executive and providing adequate judicial guarantees (*Engel, supra*). The Court does not underestimate the special circumstances of military life: a penalty or disciplinary measure that one would analyze as a deprivation of liberty if applied to a civilian may not have that character if imposed on a soldier. . . . [Article 5] applies to every "judgment" that deprives one of liberty, whether the internal law of the State treats it as penal or disciplinary.

22. In this case, the Court notes that petitioner served 21 days in jail and the prison reserved for officers and noncommissioned officers. He thus was deprived of his liberty within the meaning of Article 5 of the Convention. This detention was ordered by his military superior. The latter exercised his authority within the military hierarchy, responsible to other superior authorities, and therefore was not independent of them. In addition, the disciplinary proceeding conducted by the military superior also did not provide the judicial guarantees required by Article 5 § 1(a). As a result, petitioner's detention lacked the character of a detention "following conviction by a competent tribunal."

There was therefore a violation of Article 5 § 1(a) of the Convention.

[The Court found that Article 5 § 1 of the Convention had been violated, and awarded the petitioner, who had sought €400,000 in moral damages, €2000 in moral damages and €1500 in costs.]

ČANÁDY v. SLOVAKIA
European Court of Human Rights
[2004] Eur. Ct. Hum. Rgts. 626

8. On 22 May 1997 the applicant's neighbour damaged a fence and entered the applicant's land while fixing the connection of his house pipes to the gas supply in the street. The applicant requested that the neighbour and the workers stop the works as he had not been notified and the neighbour had not shown that he had been authorised to do so. As the neighbour and the workers refused to stop the works, the applicant attempted to prevent them from continuing. The neighbour called the police.

9. Later an employee of the municipal office in Turany asked the applicant to allow the neighbour to fix the connection. As the applicant still prevented the works from being carried out, the police took him, with his consent, to a police station where he was asked to explain his behaviour.

10. On 7 July 1997 the Martin Office of Investigation charged the applicant with an offence in that he had tried to prevent his neighbour from having a gas supply extension fixed. On 6 August 1997 the Banská Bystrica District Military Prosecutor quashed this decision as, in view of their character, the applicant's actions did not constitute a criminal offence. They could be qualified as minor offences falling under the Minor Offences Act of 1990. As a result, the case was transmitted to the rector of the Military Academy in Liptovský Mikuláš where the applicant was attached as a professional soldier.

11. On 27 October 1997 the rector of the Military Academy in Liptovský Mikuláš issued a decision by which he imposed a fine of 1,000 Slovakian korunas (SKK) on the applicant under the Minor Offences Act of 1990. The decision stated that the applicant had committed a disciplinary offence under the Military Order and that his actions constituted a minor offence under sections 49(1)(d) and 50(1) of the Minor Offences Act of 1990. According to the decision, the applicant had acted contrary to the rules of civic propriety in that he had cut through two electric wires belonging to a building company and had forcibly detached a steel pipe. He had thereby rendered difficult works which had been authorised by a public authority and had disregarded his civil obligations. Reference was made to the police case file.

12. The applicant appealed arguing that the neighbour and the authorities had acted contrary to the law.

13. On 10 December 1997 the Ministry of Defence dismissed the applicant's appeal. In March 1998 the Minister of Defence refused to review that decision.

14. On 9 January 1998 the applicant requested the Bratislava III District Court to examine the lawfulness of the decision delivered by the Ministry of Defence on 10 December 1997. On 29 May 1998 the District Court found, with reference to section 83(1) of the Minor Offences Act of 1990, that the decision in question could not be reviewed by courts. The proceedings were discontinued. The applicant appealed. On 26 November 1998 the Bratislava Regional Court discontinued the proceedings as an appeal was not available. On 29 June 1998 the Supreme Court refused to review the above decisions by which the applicant had been fined with reference to Article 248(2)(f) of the Code of Civil Procedure.

15. On 23 March 1999 the applicant complained to the Constitutional Court that, *inter alia*, his right to judicial protection had been violated in that he could not have the administrative decisions imposing a fine on him reviewed by a tribunal. The applicant qualified his submissions as both a petition under Article 130(3) of the Constitution and a constitutional complaint.

16. On 3 June 1999 the Constitutional Court dismissed both the petition and the constitutional complaint. In its decision the Constitutional Court recalled that it had declared unconstitutional section 83(1) of the Minor Offences Act of 1990 by a finding of 15 October 1998. As that finding had no retroactive effect and since the judicial decisions in question had been taken in accordance with the law in force at the relevant time, they did not interfere with the applicant's constitutional right to judicial protection. . . .

B. The Minor Offences Act of 1990

20. Section 49, as in force at the relevant time, governs minor offences against civic propriety. Its paragraph 1(d) provides that a minor offence is committed by a person who deliberately offends against civic propriety by threat of bodily harm, by causing minor bodily injury, by unjustifiably accusing another person of a minor offence, by annoyances or other rude behaviour. Under section 49(2) such a minor offence is punishable with a maximum fine of SKK 3000.

21. Section 50(1) provides that a person who deliberately damages other persons' property or attempts to do so commits a minor offence against property provided that the damage does not exceed twice the minimum monthly salary as defined in the relevant law. Paragraph 2 of section 50 provides that such a minor offence may be sanctioned by a maximum fine of SKK 10,000.

22. According to section 83(1), as operational until 14 October 1998, decisions on minor offences imposing a fine exceeding SKK 2000, prohibiting the exercise of a certain activity for a period exceeding six months or confiscating an object having a value exceeding SKK 2000 can be reviewed by the courts.

C. The Code of Civil Procedure

23. Article 248(2)(f), as in force until 31 December 2003, provides that courts shall not review administrative decisions imposing sanctions on members of the armed forces unless such sanctions restrain the latter's personal liberty or result in termination of their service.

D. Practice of the Constitutional Court

24. In a complaint lodged in 1994 a plaintiff alleged a violation of Article 6 of the Convention in that, in the context of proceedings leading to imposition of a fine under the Minor Offences Act of 1990, there had been no fair and public hearing before a tribunal in his case and that the administrative authorities dealing with it had not been impartial.

25. On 24 November 1994 the Constitutional Court dismissed the complaint as being manifestly ill-founded. It held, *inter alia*:

> A minor offence is characterised, in general, by a wrongful breach of law or legal obligations in different spheres of public administration which represents a minor danger to the society. Because of its character, a minor offence is not subject to examination by a court. . . . In accordance with the Minor Offences Act, the examination of minor offences falls within the competence of administrative authorities. Pursuant to section 83 of the Minor Offences Act, in conjunction with Articles 244 et seq. of the Code of Civil Procedure, the lawfulness of administrative organs' decisions on minor offences can be reviewed by courts only in cases where a fine exceeding SKK 2000 has been imposed, the exercise of a certain activity has been prohibited for a period exceeding six months or an object of a value exceeding SKK 2000 has been confiscated. The aforesaid provision of the special Act governing minor offences is fully binding also on the Constitutional Court of the Slovak Republic.

26. In a finding of 15 October 1998 the Constitutional Court held, in proceedings brought by the General Prosecutor, that section 83(1) of the Minor Offences Act of 1990 was unconstitutional and contrary to Article 6 § 1 of the Convention to the extent that it limited the judicial review of decisions on minor offences to, *inter alia*, fines exceeding SKK 2000. The Constitutional Court's finding was published in the Collection of Laws on 23 October 1998. As from that date, the relevant provisions of section 83(1) of the Minor Offences Act of 1990 became ineffective. . . .

II. Alleged Violation of Article 6 § 1 of the Convention

29. The applicant complained that his right of access to a court had been violated in that he could not have reviewed by a court the decisions relating to the imposition of a fine on him. He relied on Article 6 § 1 of the Convention the relevant part of which provides:

> In the determination of his civil rights and obligations . . . , everyone is entitled to a fair . . . hearing . . . by an independent and impartial tribunal established by law.

30. In their observations on the admissibility and merits of the case the Government admitted that the applicant's complaint was not unsubstantiated.

31. The Court has previously found that the general character of the legal provisions governing minor offences under the Minor Offences Act of 1990 together with the deterrent and punitive purpose of the penalty imposed for their infringement suffices to show that such offences are, in terms of Article 6 of the Convention, criminal in nature (see *Lauk v. Slovakia*, judgment of 2 September 1998, *Reports* 1998-VI, § 58). It recalls that, while entrusting the prosecution and punishment of similar minor offences to administrative authorities is not inconsistent with the Convention, the person concerned must have an opportunity to challenge any decision made against him or her before a tribunal that offers the guarantees of Article 6 (see *Kadubec v. Slovakia*, judgment of 2 September 1998, *Reports* 1998-VI, § 57).

32. In the present case the applicant was fined under the Minor Offences Act of 1990 by the rector of the Military Academy in Liptovský Mikuláš where he was employed. This decision was reviewed by the Ministry of Defence. Thus the decisions in question were taken by administrative authorities which — and this has not been disputed before the Court — did not meet the requirements of an independent and impartial tribunal within the meaning of Article 6 § 1 of the Convention. Since section 83(1) of the Minor Offences Act of 1990 and Article 248(2)(f) of the Code of Civil Procedure, as in force at the relevant time, precluded such decisions from being examined by ordinary courts, and given that the Constitutional Court failed to redress the situation complained of, the Court concludes that the applicant's right to a hearing by a tribunal has not been respected. The fact that the relevant legal provisions preventing the ordinary courts from reviewing administrative decisions on minor offences in similar cases were later repealed cannot affect the position in the present case.

33. Accordingly, there has been a violation of Article 6 § 1 of the Convention.

II. NONJUDICIAL PUNISHMENT AND SUMMARY COURTS-MARTIAL

Uniform Code of Military Justice
Article 15. Commanding officer's non-judicial punishment

(a) Under such regulations as the President may prescribe, and under such additional regulations as may be prescribed by the Secretary concerned, limitations may be placed on the powers granted by this article with respect to the kind and amount of punishment authorized, the categories of commanding officers and warrant officers exercising command authorized to exercise those powers, the applicability of this article to an accused who demands trial by court-martial, and the kinds of courts-martial to which the case may be referred upon such a demand. However, except in the case of a member attached to or embarked in a vessel, punishment may not be imposed upon any member of the armed forces under this article if the member has, before the imposition of such punishment, demanded trial by court-martial in lieu of such punishment. Under similar regulations, rules may be prescribed with respect to the suspension of punishments authorized hereunder. If authorized by regulations of the Secretary concerned, a commanding officer exercising general court-martial jurisdiction or an officer of general or flag rank in command may delegate his powers under this article to a principal assistant.

(b) Subject to subsection (a), any commanding officer may, in addition to or in lieu of admonition or reprimand, impose one or more of the following disciplinary punishments for minor offenses without the intervention of a court-martial —

(1) upon officers of his command —

(A) restriction to certain specified limits, with or without suspension from duty, for not more than 30 consecutive days;

(B) if imposed by an officer exercising general court-martial jurisdiction or an officer of general or flag rank in command —

(i) arrest in quarters for not more than 30 consecutive days;

(ii) forfeiture of not more than one-half of one month's pay per month for two months;

(iii) restriction to certain specified limits, with or without suspension from duty, for not more than 60 consecutive days;

(iv) detention of not more than one-half of one month's pay per month for three months;

(2) upon other personnel of his command —

(A) if imposed upon a person attached to or embarked in a vessel, confinement on bread and water or diminished rations for not more than three consecutive days;

(B) correctional custody for not more than seven consecutive days;

(C) forfeiture of not more than seven days' pay;

(D) reduction to the next inferior pay grade, if the grade from which demoted is within the promotion authority of the officer imposing the reduction or any officer subordinate to the one who imposes the reduction;

(E) extra duties, including fatigue or other duties, for not more than 14 consecutive days;

(F) restriction to certain specified limits, with or without suspension from duty, for not more than 14 consecutive days;

(G) detention of not more than 14 days' pay;

(H) if imposed by an officer of the grade of major or lieutenant commander, or above —

(i) the punishment authorized under clause (A);

(ii) correctional custody for not more than 30 consecutive days;

(iii) forfeiture of not more than one-half of one month's pay per month for two months;

(iv) reduction to the lowest or any intermediate pay grade, if the grade from which demoted is within the promotion authority of the officer imposing the reduction or any officer subordinate to the one who imposes the reduction, but an enlisted member in a pay grade above E-4 may not be reduced more than two pay grades;

(v) extra duties, including fatigue or other duties, for not more than 45 consecutive days;

(vi) restrictions to certain specified limits, with or without suspension from duty, for not more than 60 consecutive days;

(vii) detention of not more than one-half of one month's pay per month for three months.

Detention of pay shall be for a stated period of not more than one year but if the offender's term of service expires earlier, the detention shall terminate upon that expiration. No two or more of the punishments of arrest in quarters, confinement on bread and water or diminished rations, correctional custody, extra duties, and restriction may be combined to run consecutively in the maximum amount imposable for each. Whenever any of those punishments are combined to run consecutively, there must be an apportionment. In addition, forfeiture of pay may not be combined with detention of pay without an apportionment. For the purposes of this subsection, "correctional custody" is the physical restraint of a person during duty or nonduty hours and may include extra duties, fatigue duties, or hard labor. If practicable, correctional custody will not be served in immediate association with persons awaiting trial or held in confinement pursuant to trial by court-martial.

(c) An officer in charge may impose upon enlisted members assigned to the unit of which he is in charge such of the punishments authorized under subsection (b)(2)(A)-(G) as the Secretary concerned may specifically prescribe by regulation.

(d) The officer who imposes the punishment authorized in subsection (b), or his successor in command, may, at any time, suspend probationally any part or amount of the unexecuted punishment imposed and may suspend probationally a reduction in grade or a forfeiture imposed under subsection (b), whether or not executed. In addition, he may, at any time, remit or mitigate any part or amount of the unexecuted punishment imposed and may set aside in whole or in part the punishment, whether executed or unexecuted, and restore all rights, privileges, and property affected. He may also mitigate reduction in grade to forfeiture or detention of pay. When mitigating —

(1) arrest in quarters to restriction;

(2) confinement on bread and water or diminished rations to correctional custody;

(3) correctional custody or confinement on bread and water or diminished rations to extra duties or restriction, or both; or

(4) extra duties to restriction;

the mitigated punishment shall not be for a greater period than the punishment mitigated. When mitigating forfeiture of pay to detention of pay, the amount of the detention shall not be greater than the amount of the forfeiture. When mitigating reduction in grade to forfeiture or detention of pay, the amount of the forfeiture of detention shall not be greater than the amount that could have been imposed initially under this article by the officer who imposed the punishment mitigated.

(e) A person punished under this article who considers his punishment unjust or disproportionate to the offense may, through the proper channel, appeal to the next superior authority. The appeal shall be promptly forwarded and decided, but the person punished may in the meantime be required to undergo the punishment adjudged. The superior authority may exercise the same powers with respect to the punishment imposed as may be exercised under subsection (d) by the officer who imposed the punishment. Before acting on an appeal from a punishment of —

(1) arrest in quarters for more than seven days;

(2) correctional custody for more than seven days;

(3) forfeiture of more than seven days' pay;

(4) reduction of one or more pay grades from the fourth or a higher pay grade;

(5) extra duties for more than 14 days;

(6) restriction for more than 14 days; or

(7) detention of more than 14 days' pay;

the authority who is to act on the appeal shall refer the case to a judge advocate or a lawyer of the Department of Homeland Security for consideration and advice, and may so refer the case upon appeal from any punishment imposed under subsection (b).

(f) The imposition and enforcement of disciplinary punishment under this article for any act or omission is not a bar to trial by court-martial for a serious crime or offense growing out of the same act or omission, and not properly punishable under this article; but the fact that a disciplinary punishment has been enforced may be shown by the accused upon trial, and when so shown shall be considered in determining the measure of punishment to be adjudged in the event of a finding of guilty.

(g) The Secretary concerned may, by regulation, prescribe the form of records to be kept of proceedings under this article and may also prescribe that certain categories of those proceedings shall be in writing.

Article 20. Jurisdiction of summary courts-martial

Subject to section 817 of this title (article 17), summary courts-martial have jurisdiction to try persons subject to this chapter, except officers, cadets, aviation cadets, and midshipmen, for any noncapital offense made punishable by this chapter. No person with respect to whom summary courts-martial have jurisdiction may be brought to trial before a summary court-martial if he objects thereto. If objection to trial by summary court-martial is made by an accused, trial may be ordered by special or general court-martial as may be appropriate. Summary courts-martial may, under such limitations as the President may prescribe, adjudge any punishment not forbidden by this chapter except death, dismissal, dishonorable or bad-conduct discharge, confinement for more than one month, hard-labor without confinement for more than 45 days, restriction to specified limits for more than two months, or forfeiture of more than two-thirds of one month's pay.

MIDDENDORF v. HENRY
Supreme Court of the United States
425 U.S. 25 (1976)

Mr. Justice Rehnquist delivered the opinion of the Court.

In February 1973 plaintiffs — then enlisted members of the United States Marine Corps — brought this class action in the United States District Court for the Central District of California challenging the authority of the military to try them at summary courts-martial without providing them with counsel. Five plaintiffs had been charged with "unauthorized absences" in violation of Art. 86, UCMJ, 10 U.S.C. § 886, convicted at summary courts-martial, and sentenced, inter alia, to periods of confinement ranging from 20 to 30 days at hard labor. The other three plaintiffs, two of whom were charged, inter alia, with unauthorized absence and one with assault, Art. 128, UCMJ, 10 U.S.C. § 928, had been ordered to stand trial at summary courts-martial which had not been convened. Those who were convicted had not been provided counsel — those who were awaiting trial had been informed that counsel would not be provided. All convicted plaintiffs were informed prior to trial that they would not be afforded counsel and that they could refuse trial by summary court-martial if they so desired. In the event of such refusal their cases would be referred to special courts-martial at which counsel would be provided. . . .

In the District Court, plaintiffs brought a class action seeking habeas corpus (release from confinement), an injunction against future confinement resulting from uncounseled summary court-martial convictions, and an order vacating the convictions of those previously convicted. . . .

I

The UCMJ provides four methods for disposing of cases involving offenses committed by servicemen: the general, special, and summary courts-martial, and disciplinary punishment administered by the commanding officer pursuant to Art. 15, UCMJ, 10 U.S.C. § 815. General and special courts-martial resemble judicial proceedings, nearly always presided over by lawyer judges with lawyer counsel for both the prosecution and the defense. General courts-martial are authorized to award any lawful sentence, including death. Art. 18, UCMJ, 10 U.S.C. § 818. Special courts-martial may award a bad-conduct discharge, up to six months' confinement at hard labor, forfeiture of two-thirds pay per month for six months, and in the case of an enlisted member, reduction to the lowest pay grade, Art. 19, UCMJ, 10 U.S.C. § 819. Article 15 punishment, conducted personally by the accused's commanding officer, is an administrative method of dealing with the most minor offenses. *Parker v. Levy*, 417 U.S. 733, 750 (1974).

The summary court-martial occupies a position between informal nonjudicial disposition under Art. 15 and the courtroom-type procedure of the general and special courts-martial. Its purpose "is to exercise justice promptly for relatively minor offenses under a simple form of procedure." Manual for Courts-Martial ¶ 79a (1969) (MCM). It is an informal proceeding conducted by a single commissioned officer with jurisdiction only over noncommissioned officers and other enlisted personnel. Art. 20, UCMJ, 10 U.S.C. § 820. The presiding officer acts as judge, factfinder, prosecutor, and defense counsel. The presiding officer must inform the accused of the charges and the name of the accuser and call all witnesses whom he or the accused desires to call. MCM ¶ 79d(1). The accused must consent to trial by summary court-martial; if he does not do so, trial may be ordered by special or general court-martial.

The maximum sentence elements which may be imposed by summary courts-martial are: one month's confinement at hard labor; 45 days' hard labor without confinement; two months' restriction to specified limits; reduction to the lowest enlisted pay grade; and forfeiture of two-thirds pay for one month. Art. 20, UCMJ, 10 U.S.C. § 820.

II

The question of whether an accused in a court-martial has a constitutional right to counsel has been much debated and never squarely resolved. *See Reid v. Covert*, 354 U.S. 1, 37 (1957). Dicta in *Ex parte Milligan*, 4 Wall. 2, 123 (1866), said that "the framers of the Constitution, doubtless, meant to limit the right of trial by jury, in the sixth amendment, to those persons who were subject to indictment or presentment in the fifth." In *Ex parte Quirin*, 317 U.S. 1, 40 (1942), it was said that "'cases arising in the land or naval forces' . . . are expressly excepted from the Fifth Amendment, and are deemed excepted by implication from the Sixth."

We find it unnecessary in this case to finally resolve the broader aspects of this question, since we conclude that even were the Sixth Amendment to be held applicable to court-martial proceedings, the summary court-martial provided for in these cases was not a "criminal prosecution" within the meaning of that Amendment.

This conclusion, of course, does not answer the ultimate question of whether the plaintiffs are entitled to counsel at a summary court-martial proceeding, but it does shift the frame of reference from the Sixth Amendment's guarantee of counsel "[i]n all criminal prosecutions" to the Fifth Amendment's prohibition against the deprivation of "life, liberty, or property, without due process of law."

Argersinger v. Hamlin, 407 U.S. 25 (1972), held that the Sixth Amendment's provision for the assistance of counsel extended to misdemeanor prosecutions in civilian courts if conviction would result in imprisonment. A summary court-martial may impose 30 days' confinement at hard labor, which is doubtless the military equivalent of imprisonment. Yet the fact that the outcome of a proceeding may result in loss of liberty does not by itself, even in civilian life, mean that the Sixth Amendment's guarantee of counsel is applicable. . . .

The Court's distinction between various civilian proceedings, and its conclusion that, notwithstanding the potential loss of liberty, neither juvenile hearings nor probation revocation hearings are "criminal proceedings," are equally relevant in assessing the role of the summary court-martial in the military.

The summary court-martial is, as noted above, one of four types of proceedings by which the military imposes discipline or punishment. If we were to remove the holding of *Argersinger* from its civilian context and apply it to require counsel before a summary court-martial proceeding simply because loss of liberty may result from such a proceeding, it would seem all but inescapable that counsel would likewise be required for the lowest level of military proceeding for dealing with the most minor offenses. For even the so-called Art. 15 "nonjudicial punishment," which may be imposed administratively by the commanding officer, may result in the imposition upon an enlisted man of "correctional custody" with hard labor for not more than 30 consecutive days. 10 U.S.C. § 815(b). But we think that the analysis made in cases such as *Gagnon* and *Gault*, as well as considerations peculiar to the military, counsel against such a mechanical application of *Argersinger*. . . .

. . . Undoubtedly both *Gault* and *Gagnon* are factually distinguishable from the summary court-martial proceeding here. But together they surely stand for the proposition that even in the civilian community a proceeding which may result in deprivation of liberty is nonetheless not a "criminal proceeding" within the meaning of the Sixth Amendment if there are elements about it which sufficiently distinguish it from a traditional civilian criminal trial. The summary court-martial proceeding here is likewise different from a traditional trial in many respects, the most important of which is that it occurs within the military community. This latter factor, under a long line of decisions of this Court, is every bit as significant, and every bit as entitled to be given controlling weight, as the fact in *Gagnon* that the defendant had been previously sentenced, or the fact in *Gault* that the proceeding had a rehabilitative purpose.

We have only recently noted the difference between the diverse civilian community and the much more tightly regimented military community in *Parker v. Levy*, 417 U.S. 733, 749 (1974). We said there that the UCMJ "cannot be equated to a civilian criminal code. It, and the various versions of the Articles of War which have preceded it, regulate aspects of the conduct of members of the military which in the civilian sphere are left unregulated. While a civilian criminal code carves out a relatively small segment of potential conduct and declares it criminal, the Uniform Code of Military Justice essays more varied regulation of a much larger segment of the activities of the more tightly knit military community." *Ibid.* Much of the conduct proscribed by the military is not "criminal" conduct in the civilian sense of the word. *Id.,* at 749-751.

Here, for example, most of the plaintiffs were charged solely with "unauthorized absence," an offense which has no common-law counterpart and which carries little popular opprobrium. Conviction of such an offense would likely have no consequences for the accused beyond the immediate punishment meted out by the military, unlike conviction for such civilian misdemeanors as vagrancy or larceny which could carry a stamp of "bad character" with conviction.

By the same token, the penalties which may be meted out in summary courts-martial are limited to one month's confinement at hard labor, 45 days' hard labor without confinement, or two months' restriction to specified limits. Sanctions which may be imposed affecting a property interest are limited to reduction in grade with attendant loss of pay, or forfeiture or detention of a portion of one month's pay.

Finally, a summary court-martial is procedurally quite different from a criminal trial. In the first place, it is not an adversary proceeding. Yet the adversary nature of civilian criminal proceedings is one of the touchstones of the Sixth Amendment's right to counsel which we extended to petty offenses in *Argersinger v. Hamlin,* 407 U.S. 25 (1972).

Argersinger relied on *Gideon v. Wainwright,* 372 U.S. 335 (1963), where we held:

> "[I]n our adversary system of criminal justice, any person haled into court . . . cannot be assured a fair trial unless counsel is provided for him. This seems to us to be an obvious truth. Governments, both state and federal, quite properly spend vast sums of money to establish machinery to try defendants accused of crime. Lawyers to prosecute are everywhere deemed essential to protect the public's interest in an orderly society. . . ." *Id.,* at 344.

The function of the presiding officer is quite different from that of any participant in a civilian trial. He is guided by the admonition in ¶ 79a of the MCM: "The function of a summary court-martial is to exercise justice promptly for relatively minor offenses under a simple form of procedure. The summary court will thoroughly and impartially inquire into both sides of the matter and will assure that the interests of both the Government and the accused are safeguarded." The presiding officer is more specifically enjoined to attend to the interests of the accused by these provisions of the same paragraph:

> "The accused will be extended the right to cross-examine the witness. The summary court will aid the accused in the cross-examination, and, if the accused desires, will ask questions suggested by the accused. On behalf of the accused, the court will obtain the attendance of witnesses, administer the oath and examine them, and obtain such other evidence as may tend to disprove or negative guilt of the charges,

explain the acts or omissions charged, show extenuating circumstances, or establish grounds for mitigation. Before determining the findings, he will explain to the accused his right to testify on the merits or to remain silent and will give the accused full opportunity to exercise his election." MCM ¶ 79d(3).

We believe there are significant parallels between the Court's description of probation and parole revocation proceedings in *Gagnon* and the summary court-martial, which parallels tend to distinguish both of these proceedings from the civilian misdemeanor prosecution upon which *Argersinger* focused. When we consider in addition that the court-martial proceeding takes place not in civilian society, as does the parole revocation proceeding, but in the military community with all of its distinctive qualities, we conclude that a summary court-martial is not a "criminal prosecution" for purposes of the Sixth Amendment.[1]

III

The Court of Appeals likewise concluded that there was no Sixth Amendment right to counsel in summary court-martial proceedings such as this, but applying the due process standards of the Fifth Amendment adopted a standard from *Gagnon v. Scarpelli*, 411 U.S. 778 (1973), which would have made the right to counsel depend upon the nature of the serviceman's defense. We are unable to agree that the Court of Appeals properly applied *Gagnon* in this military context.

We recognize that plaintiffs, who have either been convicted or are due to appear before a summary court-martial, may be subjected to loss of liberty or property, and consequently are entitled to the due process of law guaranteed by the Fifth Amendment.

However, whether this process embodies a right to counsel depends upon an analysis of the interests of the individual and those of the regime to which he is subject. *Wolff v. McDonnell*, 418 U.S. 539, 556 (1974).

In making such an analysis we must give particular deference to the determination of Congress, made under its authority to regulate the land and naval forces, U.S. Const., Art. I, § 8, that counsel should not be provided in summary courts-martial. As we held in *Burns v. Wilson*, 346 U.S. 137, 140 (1953):

> "[T]he rights of men in the armed forces must perforce be conditioned to meet certain overriding demands of discipline and duty, and the civil courts are not the agencies which must determine the precise balance to be struck in this adjustment. The Framers especially entrusted that task to Congress." (Footnote omitted.)

The United States Court of Military Appeals has held that *Argersinger* is applicable to the military and requires counsel at summary courts-martial.

---

[1] [n.19] No one of the factors discussed above — the nature of the proceedings, of the offenses, and of the punishments — is necessarily dispositive. Rather, all three combine with the distinctive nature of military life and discipline to lead to our conclusion. The dissent, by discussing these factors independently and attempting to demonstrate that each factor cannot stand by its own force does not come to grips with this analysis.

United States v. Alderman, 22 U.S.C.M.A. 298, 46 C.M.R. 298 (1973). Dealing with areas of law peculiar to the military branches, the Court of Military Appeals' judgments are normally entitled to great deference. But the 2-to-1 decision, in which the majority itself was sharply divided in theory, does not reject the claim of military necessity. Judge Quinn was of the opinion that *Argersinger*'s expansion of the Sixth Amendment right to counsel was binding on military tribunals equally with civilian courts. *Alderman, supra*, at 300, 46 C.M.R., at 300. Judge Duncan, concurring in part, disagreed, reasoning that decisions such as *Argersinger* were not binding precedent if "there is demonstrated a military necessity demanding nonapplicability." *Id.*, at 303, 46 C.M.R., at 303. He found no convincing evidence of military necessity which would preclude application of *Argersinger*. Chief Judge Darden, dissenting, disagreed with Judge Quinn, and pointed to that court's decisions recognizing "the need for balancing the application of the constitutional protection against military needs." *Id.*, at 307, 46 C.M.R., at 307. Taking issue as well with Judge Duncan, he stated his belief that the Court of Military Appeals "possesses no special competence to evaluate the effect of a particular procedure on morale and discipline and to require its implementation over and above the balance struck by Congress." *Id.*, at 308, 46 C.M.R., at 308.

Given that only one member of the Court of Military Appeals took issue with the claim of military necessity, and taking the latter of Chief Judge Darden's statements as applying with at least equal force to the Members of this Court, we are left with Congress' previous determination that counsel is not required. We thus need only decide whether the factors militating in favor of counsel at summary courts-martial are so extraordinarily weighty as to overcome the balance struck by Congress.[2]

We first consider the effect of providing counsel at summary courts-martial. As we observed in *Gagnon v. Scarpelli, supra*, at 787:

> "The introduction of counsel into a . . . proceeding will alter significantly the nature of the proceeding. If counsel is provided for the [accused], the State in turn will normally provide its own counsel; lawyers, by training and disposition, are advocates and bound by professional duty to present all available evidence and arguments in support of their clients' positions and to contest with vigor all adverse evidence and views."

In short, presence of counsel will turn a brief, informal hearing which may be quickly convened and rapidly concluded into an attenuated proceeding which consumes the resources of the military to a degree which Congress

---

[2] [n.21] Prior to the enactment of the UCMJ into positive law in 1956 it was suggested that summary courts-martial be abolished. Congress rejected this suggestion and instead provided that no person could be tried by summary court-martial if he objected thereto (unless he had previously refused Art. 15 punishment). 70A Stat. 43. Prior to the 1968 amendments to the Code the elimination of summary courts-martial was again proposed and rejected. *E.g.,* Subcommittee on Constitutional Rights of Senate Committee on the Judiciary, 88th Cong., 1st Sess., Summary — Report of Hearings on Constitutional Rights of Military Personnel, 34-36 (1963). Instead, the Art. 15 exception to the right to refuse was eliminated as a compromise between those favoring retention of summary courts-martial and those who would abolish them. S. Rep. No. 1601, 90th Cong., 2d Sess., 6 (1968). It is thus apparent that Congress has considered the matter in some depth.

could properly have felt to be beyond what is warranted by the relative insignificance of the offenses being tried. Such a lengthy proceeding is a particular burden to the Armed Forces because virtually all the participants, including the defendant and his counsel, are members of the military whose time may be better spent than in possibly protracted disputes over the imposition of discipline.

As we observed in *United States ex rel. Toth v. Quarles*, 350 U.S. 11, 17 (1955):

> "[I]t is the primary business of armies and navies to fight or be ready to fight wars should the occasion arise. But trial of soldiers to maintain discipline is merely incidental to an army's primary fighting function. To the extent that those responsible for performance of this primary function are diverted from it by the necessity of trying cases, the basic fighting purpose of armies is not served. . . . [M]ilitary tribunals have not been and probably never can be constituted in such way that they can have the same kind of qualifications that the Constitution has deemed essential to fair trials of civilians in federal courts."

However, the Court of Appeals did not find counsel necessary in all proceedings but only, pursuant to *Daigle v. Warner*, where the accused makes

> "a timely and colorable claim (1) that he has a defense, or (2) that there are mitigating circumstances, and the assistance of counsel is necessary in order adequately to present the defense or mitigating circumstances." 490 F.2d, at 365.

But if the accused has such a claim, if he feels that in order to properly air his views and vindicate his rights, a formal, counseled proceeding is necessary he may simply refuse trial by summary court-martial and proceed to trial by special or general court-martial at which he may have counsel. Thus, he stands in a considerably more favorable position than the probationer in *Gagnon* who, though subject to the possibility of longer periods of incarceration, had no such absolute right to counsel.

It is true that by exercising this option the accused subjects himself to greater possible penalties imposed in the special court-martial proceeding. However, we do not find that possible detriment to be constitutionally decisive. We have frequently approved the much more difficult decision, daily faced by civilian criminal defendants, to plead guilty to a lesser included offense. *E.g., Brady v. United States*, 397 U.S. 742, 749-750 (1970). In such a case the defendant gives up not only his right to counsel but his right to any trial at all. Furthermore, if he elects to exercise his right to trial he stands to be convicted of a more serious offense which will likely bear increased penalties.

Such choices are a necessary part of the criminal justice system:

> "The criminal process, like the rest of the legal system, is replete with situations requiring 'the making of difficult judgments' as to which course to follow. *McMann v. Richardson*, 397 U.S., at 769. Although a defendant may have a right, even of constitutional dimensions, to fol-

low whichever course he chooses, the Constitution does not by that token always forbid requiring him to choose." *McGautha v. California*, 402 U.S. 183, 213 (1971).

We therefore agree with the defendants that neither the Sixth nor the Fifth Amendment to the United States Constitution empowers us to overturn the congressional determination that counsel is not required in summary courts-martial. The judgment of the Court of Appeals is therefore

Reversed.

MR. JUSTICE MARSHALL, with whom MR. JUSTICE BRENNAN joins, dissenting.

We only recently held that, absent a waiver, "no person may be imprisoned for any offense, whether classified as petty, misdemeanor, or felony, unless he was represented by counsel at his trial." *Argersinger v. Hamlin*, 407 U.S. 25, 37 (1972). Today the Court refuses to apply *Argersinger*'s holding to defendants in summary court-martial proceedings. Assuming for purposes of its opinion that the Sixth Amendment applies to courts-martial in general, the Court holds that, because of their special characteristics, summary courts-martial in particular are simply not "criminal prosecutions" within the meaning of the Sixth Amendment, and that the right to counsel is therefore inapplicable to them. I dissent.

I

Preliminarily, summary courts-martial aside, it is clear to me that a citizen does not surrender all right to appointed counsel when he enters the military. It is inconceivable, for example, that this Court could conclude that a defendant in a general court-martial proceeding, where sentences as severe as life imprisonment may be imposed, is not entitled to the same protection our Constitution affords a civilian defendant facing even a day's imprisonment. *See Argersinger v. Hamlin, supra.* Surely those sworn to risk their lives to defend the Constitution should derive some benefit from the right to counsel, a right that has become even more firmly entrenched in our jurisprudence over the past several generations. *See Gideon v. Wainwright*, 372 U.S. 335 (1963); *Powell v. Alabama*, 287 U.S. 45 (1932).

The only question that might arise is whether the general guarantee of counsel to court-martial defendants is to be placed under the Fifth Amendment or under the Sixth Amendment. It is my conviction that it is a Sixth Amendment guarantee. That Amendment provides an explicit guarantee of counsel "in all criminal prosecutions." Since, as we recently observed, courts-martial are "convened to adjudicate charges of criminal violations of military law," *Parisi v. Davidson*, 405 U.S. 34, 42 (1972), it would seem that courts-martial are criminal prosecutions and that the Sixth Amendment therefore applies on its face.

There is legitimate dispute among scholars, it is true, about whether the Framers expressly intended the Sixth Amendment right to counsel to apply to the military. *See ante*, at 33-34, and n.12. While the historical evidence is somewhat ambiguous, my reading of the sources suggests that the Sixth Amendment right to counsel was intended by the Framers to apply to courts-martial. But even if the historical evidence plainly showed to the contrary — and it certainly does not — that would not be determinative of the contemporary scope of the Sixth Amendment. As Mr. Chief Justice Hughes observed:

> "If by the statement that what the Constitution meant at the time of its adoption it means to-day, it is intended to say that the great clauses of the Constitution must be confined to the interpretation which the framers, with the conditions and outlook of their time, would have placed upon them, the statement carries its own refutation." *Home Bldg. & Loan Assn. v. Blaisdell*, 290 U.S. 398, 442-443 (1934).

Application of the Sixth Amendment right to counsel to the military follows logically and naturally from the modern right-to-counsel decisions, in which the right has been held fully applicable in every case in which a defendant faced conviction of a criminal offense and potential incarceration. *See, e.g., Argersinger v. Hamlin, supra; Gideon v. Wainwright, supra.* The due process right to counsel, usually applied on a case-by-case basis, extends a qualified right to counsel to persons not involved in criminal proceedings, *see Gagnon v. Scarpelli,* 411 U.S. 778 (1973), but has not been viewed as a replacement for the Sixth Amendment right to counsel in situations in which a defendant stands to be convicted of a criminal offense.

In short, it is my belief that the Sixth Amendment demands that court-martial defendants ordinarily be accorded counsel. Only if the special characteristics of summary courts-martial in particular deprive them of the status of "criminal prosecutions" is the Sixth Amendment inapplicable in the cases before us today. It is, of course, this proposition to which the major part of the Court's opinion is addressed and to which I now turn.

II

The Court's conclusion that summary courts-martial are not "criminal prosecutions" is, on its face, a surprising one. No less than in the case of other courts-martial, summary courts-martial are directed at adjudicating "charges of criminal violations of military law," and conviction at a summary court-martial can lead to confinement for one month. Nevertheless, the Court finds its conclusion mandated by a combination of four factors: the limitations on the punishment that can be meted out by a summary court-martial, the nature of the offenses for which a defendant can be tried, the nature of the summary court-martial proceeding itself, and "the distinctive nature of military life and discipline." *Ante,* at 42 n.19. I am totally unpersuaded that these considerations — or any others — whether taken singly or in combination, justify denying to summary court-martial defendants the right to the assistance of counsel, "one of the safeguards of the Sixth Amendment deemed necessary to insure fundamental human rights of life and liberty." *Johnson v. Zerbst,* 304 U.S. 458, 462 (1938).

A

It is of course true, as the Court states, that a summary court-martial may not adjudge confinement in excess of one month. Manual for Courts-Martial ¶ 16b (1969) (MCM). But *Argersinger* itself held the length of confinement to be wholly irrelevant in determining the applicability of the right to counsel. Aware that "the prospect of imprisonment for however short a time will seldom be viewed by the accused as a trivial or 'petty' matter," *Baldwin v. New York*, 399 U.S. 66, 73 (1970) (plurality opinion), we held in *Argersinger* that the fact of confinement, not its duration, is determinative of the right to counsel. Insofar as the Court today uses the 30-day ceiling on a summary court-martial defendant's sentence as support for its holding, it is not so much finding *Argersinger* "inapplicable" as rejecting the very basis of *Argersinger*'s holding.

B

In further support of its holding, the Court observes that "[m]uch of the conduct proscribed by the military is not 'criminal' conduct in the civilian sense of the word," *ante*, at 38, and intimates that conviction for many offenses normally tried at summary court-martial would have no consequences "beyond the immediate punishment meted out by the military." *Ante*, at 39. The Court's observations are both misleading and irrelevant.

While the summary court-martial is generally designed to deal with relatively minor offenses, *see* MCM ¶ 79, as a statutory matter the summary proceeding can be used to try any noncapital offense triable by general or special court-martial. Art. 20, UCMJ, 10 U.S.C. § 820.[3] *See United States v. Moore*, 5 U.S.C.M.A. 687, 697, 18 C.M.R. 311, 321 (1955). And while the offense for which most of the plaintiffs here were tried — unauthorized absence — has no common-law counterpart, a substantial proportion of the offenses actually tried by summary court-martial are offenses, such as larceny and assault, that would also constitute criminal offenses if committed by a civilian.[4] Indeed, one of the servicemen in these cases was charged with assault. It is therefore misleading to suggest, as the Court does, that there is a fundamental difference between the type of conduct chargeable at summary court-martial and the type of conduct deemed criminal in the civilian sector.

The Court's further implication that a summary court-martial conviction has no consequences beyond "the immediate punishment" *ante*, at 39, is also inaccurate. One of the central distinctions between Art. 15 nonjudicial punishment and a summary court-martial conviction is that the latter is regarded as a criminal conviction. And that criminal conviction has collateral consequences both in military and civilian life. As the Army itself has readily acknowledged:

> "Conviction by [any] court-martial creates a criminal record which will color consideration of any subsequent misconduct by the soldier. A noncommissioned officer may survive one summary court-martial

---

[3] [n.7] Of course the punishment ceilings imposed by 10 U.S.C. § 820 on summary courts-martial are applicable no matter what offense is being tried. But the "popular opprobrium" resulting from conviction of a serious crime — a factor in which the Court places considerable stock, *ante*, at 39 — is likely to be severe whatever the magnitude of the punishment; that "popular opprobrium" could, of course, have significant "practical effect," *ante*, at 40 n. 17, on a serviceman's future.

[4] [n.8] *See* 10 U.S.C. 921, 928. Figures supplied by the federal parties indicate that in 1973, 14% of the summary courts-martial conducted by the Navy were for "nonmilitary offenses." Brief for Federal Parties 33; *see also* Fidell, *The Summary Court-Martial: A Proposal*, 8 Harv. J. Legis, 571, 599 n.121 (1971). *See also* Joint Hearings on Military Justice before the Subcommittee on Constitutional Rights of the Senate Committee on the Judiciary and a Special Subcommittee of the Senate Committee on Armed Services, 89th Cong., 2d Sess., 1056 (1966) (hereinafter cited as 1966 Hearings).

without reduction being effected, but it is unlikely that, with one conviction on his record, he will survive a second trial and retain his status. A conviction of an officer by any court-martial could have a devastating aftereffect upon his career. It could be described in some cases as a sentence to a passover on a promotion list and may serve as a basis for initiation of administrative elimination action.

"For any man, the fact of a criminal conviction on his record is a handicap in civilian life. It may interfere with his job opportunities; it may be counted against him if he has difficulty with a civilian law enforcement agency; and in general he tends to be a marked man."

The MCM itself belies any claim that no significant consequences beyond immediate punishment attach to a summary court-martial conviction. Paragraph 127c of the MCM establishes a comprehensive scheme by which an offender is made subject to increased punishment if he has a record of previous convictions — even if all of those previous convictions were by summary court-martial.

It is therefore wholly unrealistic to suggest that the impact of a summary court-martial conviction lies exclusively in the immediate punishment that is meted out. Summary court-martial convictions carry with them a potential of stigma, injury to career, and increased punishment for future offenses in the same way as do convictions after civilian criminal trials and convictions after general and special courts-martial.

Quite apart from their flimsy factual basis, the Court's observations as to both the nature of the offenses tried at summary court-martial and the lack of collateral consequences of convictions have already been determined by *Argersinger* to be irrelevant to the applicability of the Sixth Amendment's right to counsel. *Argersinger* teaches that the right to counsel is triggered by the potential of confinement, regardless of how trivial or petty the offense may seem. *See* 407 U.S., at 37. Logic itself would therefore preclude the suggestion that the right to counsel, activated by the potential of confinement, is deactivated by the absence of collateral consequences of conviction.

C

The nature of the summary court-martial proceeding — the proceeding's nonadversary nature and, relatedly, the protective functions of its presiding officer — is a third factor which, according to the Court, helps to make unnecessary the provision of counsel to the accused. Again, the Court's reliance is without substantial foundation.

The Court characterizes summary courts-martial as "nonadversary," but offers little explanation as to how that characterization advances the contention that the right to counsel is inapplicable. If the Court's argument is simply that furnishing counsel will transform the proceeding into an adversary proceeding, it is no argument at all, but simply an observation. The argument must be either that there is something peculiar about the goal of the summary court-martial proceeding that makes the right to counsel inapplicable, or that there are elements in the conduct of the proceeding itself that render counsel unnecessary.

To the extent that the Court's characterization of summary courts-martial as "nonadversary" is meant to convey something about the goal or purpose of the proceeding, it is totally unpersuasive. In this sense the summary court-martial proceeding is far less "nonadversary" than the juvenile delinquency proceedings to which we held the right to counsel applicable in *In re Gault*, 387 U.S. 1 (1967). . . .

As distinguished from the situation in *Gault*, summary courts-martial have no special rehabilitative purpose; rather, their central immediate purpose is to discipline those who have violated the UCMJ. If the goals of juvenile delinquency proceedings are an insufficient justification for the denial of counsel, it follows a fortiori that the goals of the summary court-martial are similarly insufficient.

The second possible meaning conveyed by characterizing the summary court-martial as "nonadversary" — the presence of elements in the conduct of the proceeding itself which render independent counsel unnecessary — is reflected in the Court's observation that the "function of the presiding officer is quite different from that of any participant in a civilian trial." *Ante*, at 41. It is the responsibility of the presiding officer to act as judge, jury, prosecutor, and defense counsel combined. The Court intimates that the presiding officer's duty to advise the accused of his rights and his ability to help the accused assemble facts, examine witnesses, and cross-examine his accusers make defense counsel unnecessary, particularly in light of the absence of a formal prosecutor in the proceeding. I find this argument unpersuasive. In *Powell v. Alabama*, 287 U.S. 45 (1932), we rejected the notion that a judge could "effectively discharge the obligations of counsel for the accused," largely because a judge "cannot . . . participate in those necessary conferences between counsel and accused which sometimes partake of the inviolable character of the confessional." *Id.*, at 61. . . .

The irreconcilable conflict among the roles of the summary court-martial presiding officer inevitably prevents him from functioning effectively as a substitute for defense counsel. For instance, a defendant has a right to remain silent and not testify at his court-martial. *See* Art. 31, UCMJ, 10 U.S.C. § 831; MCM ¶ 53h. An intelligent decision whether to exercise that right requires consultation as to whether testifying would hurt or help his case and inevitably involves the sharing of confidences with counsel. Full consultation cannot possibly take place when "defense counsel" is also playing the role of judge and prosecutor. The defense counsel who also serves as prosecutor and judge is effectively unavailable for many of the "necessary conferences between counsel and accused," *Powell v. Alabama, supra*, at 61, as well as for the making and implementation of critical tactical and strategic trial decisions. As helpful as the presiding officer might be to the defendant, his inconsistent roles bar him from being an adequate substitute for independent defense counsel.

In sum, there is nothing about the assertedly "non-adversary" nature of the summary court-martial — either in terms of its goals or alternative safeguards — that renders unnecessary the assistance of counsel.

D

Finally, the Court draws on notions of military necessity to justify its conclusion that the right to counsel is inapplicable to summary court-martial proceedings. Concerns for discipline and obedience will on occasion, it is true, justify imposing restrictions on the military that would be unconstitutional in a civilian context. *See Parker v. Levy*, 417 U.S. 733, 758 (1974). But denials of traditional rights to any group should not be approved without examination, especially when the group comprises members of the military, who are engaged in an endeavor of national service, frequently fraught with both danger and sacrifice. After such examination, I am persuaded that the denial of the right to counsel at summary courts-martial cannot be justified by military necessity.

The substance of the asserted justification here is that discipline, efficiency, and morale demand the utilization of an expeditious disciplinary procedure for relatively minor offenses. It would seem, however, that Art. 15 nonjudicial punishment — which can be speedily imposed by a commander, but which does not carry with it the stigma of a criminal conviction — provides just such a procedure. Indeed, the 1962 amendments to Art. 15, 10 U.S.C. § 815, greatly expanded the availability of nonjudicial punishment and resulted in a sharp decrease in the utilization of the summary court-martial. There is, therefore, no pressing need to have a streamlined summary court-martial proceeding in order to supply an expeditious disciplinary procedure. Moreover, it is by no means clear that guaranteeing counsel to summary court-martial defendants would result in significantly longer time periods from preferral of charges to punishment than fairly conducted proceedings in the absence of counsel; any timesaving that is now enjoyed might well result from the presiding officer's being something less than an adequate substitute for independent defense counsel.

It is especially difficult to accept the federal parties' claim of "military necessity" in view of the fact that well before our decision in *Argersinger*, each of the services allowed summary court-martial defendants to retain counsel at their own expense. Given this fact, the federal parties' argument is reduced to a contention that only those defendants who cannot afford to retain counsel must, as a matter of "military necessity," be denied counsel at summary court-martial proceedings. Sustaining that contention means a defeat for those very principles of equality and justice that the military is sworn to defend; the most fundamental notions of fairness are subverted when the rights of the poor alone are sacrificed to the cause of "military necessity."

It is also significant that the United States Court of Military Appeals (USCMA), a body with recognized expertise in dealing with military problems, has applied *Argersinger* to summary courts-martial without giving any hint that military necessity posed a problem. *United States v. Alderman*, 22 U.S.C.M.A. 298, 46 C.M.R. 298 (1973).[5] Indeed, Judge Duncan of that court

---

[5] [n.19] The decisions of the USCMA are final. 10 U.S.C. § 876. It is indeed ironic that the federal parties — statutorily barred from appealing *Alderman* — have now secured its rejection through this lawsuit, originally brought in federal court by servicemen seeking the very protections later accorded them by *Alderman*.

explicitly noted that "the record contains no evidence which convinces me that application of the *Argersinger* rule should not be followed in our system because of military necessity." *Id.*, at 303, 46 C.M.R., at 303 (concurring in part and dissenting in part). And even before *Alderman* was decided, both the Air Force and the Army applied *Argersinger* to summary courts-martial rather than advancing the theoretically available "military necessity" argument. *See United States v. Priest*, 21 U.S.C.M.A. 564, 45 C.M.R. 338 (1972). That they did so leads me to doubt whether even the military was then of the opinion that military necessity dictated the denial of counsel.

Virtually ignoring all the factors that cast doubt on the military-necessity justification, the Court defers to an asserted congressional judgment that "counsel should not be provided in summary courts-martial." *Ante*, at 43. While Congress' evaluation of military necessity is clearly entitled to defer- ence, it would be a departure from our position in the past to suggest that the Court need not come to its own conclusion as to the validity of any argument based on military necessity. *See, e.g., United States v. Robel*, 389 U.S. 258, 264 (1967); *Parker v. Levy*, 417 U.S. 733 (1974); *cf. New York Times Co. v. United States*, 403 U.S. 713 (1971). But regardless of what weight is properly accorded a clear congressional determination of military necessity, there has been no such determination in this case.

The only congressional action referred to by the Court is Congress' refusal in 1956 and 1968 to abolish summary courts-martial altogether and its con- current extending of the serviceman's opportunity to reject trial by summary court-martial. The Court refers to that action as evidence that Congress has considered "in some depth" the matter whether counsel is required in sum- mary courts-martial. *Ante*, at 45 n. 21. But there is no evidence offered of any detailed congressional consideration of the specific question of the feasibility of providing counsel at summary courts-martial. And, more importantly, there is no indication that Congress made a judgment that military necessity requires the denial of the constitutional right to counsel to summary court- martial defendants.

If Congress' lack of discussion of military necessity is not enough to throw substantial doubt on the Court's inferences, the timing of the congressional action cited by the Court should certainly do so. All that action occurred sub- stantially before our decision in *Argersinger*. Thus, even if we assume that Congress' decision to retain the summary court-martial represents a consid- ered conclusion that "counsel should not be provided," that judgment was made at a time when even civilian defendants subject to prison terms of less than six months had no recognized constitutional right to counsel. There would, therefore, have been little reason for Congress in 1956 or 1968 to undertake the detailed consideration necessary to make a finding of "military necessity" before concluding that counsel need not be provided to summary court-martial defendants.

In sum, there is simply no indication that Congress ever made a clear determination that "military necessity" precludes applying the Sixth Amendment's right to counsel to summary court-martial proceedings. Indeed, the Court characterizes the congressional determination in the vaguest of terms, and never expressly claims that Congress made a determination of military necessity. Thus, I can only read the Court's opinion as a grant of almost total deference to any Act of Congress dealing with the military.

III

The Court rejects even the limited holding of the Court of Appeals that the provision of counsel in summary court-martial proceedings should be evaluated as a matter of due process on the basis of the accused's defense in any particular case. The Court explains that summary court-martial defendants can have counsel appointed by refusing trial by summary court-martial and then proceeding to trial by special court-martial — the acknowledged consequence of which is exposure to greater possible penalties. Given my conviction that a summary court-martial is a criminal prosecution under the Sixth Amendment, it is unnecessary for me to deal in detail with this due process question.[6] In the event, however, that the special court-martial option may be offered as additional support for the Court's treatment of the Sixth Amendment issue, I shall briefly assess its significance.

The Court analogizes the decision whether to expose oneself to special court-martial with counsel or to proceed by summary court-martial without counsel to the decision faced by a civilian defendant whether to proceed to trial or plead guilty to a lesser included offense. According to the Court, the right given up by such a civilian defendant is "not only his right to counsel but his right to any trial at all." . . . The analogy is a flawed one. The civilian defendant who pleads guilty necessarily gives up whatever rights he might thereafter have been accorded to enable him to protect a claim of innocence; the conditions on his pleading guilty are logically mandated ones. By contrast, the condition on the military defendant's opting to be tried by summary court-martial — *i.e.*, the denial of counsel — is an imposed one, and must therefore be viewed with suspicion.

Indeed, the force of the Court's analogy is entirely dissipated by the fact that a civilian defendant who pleads guilty forfeits only so much of his right to counsel as is a necessary consequence of his plea. He is fully entitled to counsel in the process leading up to the plea — including negotiations with the Government as to the possibility of a plea and the actual decision to plead. The defendant is also entitled to counsel in any sentencing proceeding that might follow the making of his plea. I have no doubt that a scheme in which the acceptance of guilty pleas was conditioned on a full abandonment of the right to counsel would be unconstitutional.

By contrast, the Court today approves the denial of counsel to the summary court-martial defendant at all stages and for all purposes — including, at least as regards sailors and marines, the very decision whether to reject trial by

---

[6] [n.22] It does seem to me, however, that the serviceman's "option" of subjecting himself to the possibility of a special court-martial lends little support to the Court's due process analysis. We held in *In re Gault*, 387 U.S. 1 (1967) — a decision left unmentioned in the Court's treatment of the Fifth Amendment question — that, as a matter of due process accused offenders have an absolute right to counsel at juvenile delinquency proceedings. Surely that holding would be no different in the case of a juvenile given the opportunity "voluntarily" to subject himself to adult criminal proceedings, in which he would have counsel, but at which he would be subject to harsher punishment.

summary court-martial. And if the accused opts for the summary court-martial — the Court's parallel to the accepted guilty plea — he has no right to counsel either at the adjudicative or sentencing phase of the proceeding.[7]

Conditioning the provision of counsel on a defendant's subjecting himself to the risk of additional punishment suffers from the same defect as the scheme disapproved by the Court in *United States v. Jackson*, 390 U.S. 570 (1968), in which the right to a trial by jury was conditioned on a defendant's subjecting himself to the possibility of capital punishment. If the Court's analysis is correct as applied to the Sixth Amendment, then *Argersinger's* guarantee of counsel for the trial of any offense carrying with it the potential of imprisonment could be reduced to a nullity; a State could constitutionally establish two levels of imprisonment for the same offense — a lower tier for defendants who are willing to proceed to trial without counsel, and a higher one for those who insist on having the assistance of counsel. It is inconceivable to me that the Sixth Amendment would tolerate such a result.

IV

The right to counsel has been termed "the most pervasive"[8] of all the rights accorded an accused. As a result of the Court's action today, of all accused persons protected by the United States Constitution — federal defendants and state defendants, juveniles and adults, civilians and soldiers — only those enlisted men[9] tried by summary court-martial can be imprisoned without having been accorded the right to counsel. I would have expected that such a result would have been based on justifications far more substantial than those relied on by the Court. I respectfully dissent.

NOTES AND QUESTIONS

1. Were you persuaded by Justice Rehnquist's opinion? Which arguments struck you as strong and which struck you as weak?

2. As Justice Marshall noted in footnote 19, there was an irony in the fact that the law would have been more favorable to military personnel had the *Middendorf* plaintiffs not sued. If you were the plaintiffs' counsel, would you have followed some other strategy?

---

[7] [n.24] Assuming the "option scheme" presents the serviceman with any sort of realistic choice, its availability also substantially undercuts the federal parties' military-necessity argument. . . . The federal parties argue that as a matter of "military necessity" minor offenses must be disposed of at summary court-martial proceedings without giving defendants the benefit of counsel. Yet, under the option scheme any serviceman can be assured of counsel simply by rejecting trial by summary court-martial. Thus the scheme itself could render unattainable a goal which is claimed to be a matter of military necessity.

[8] [n.26] Schaefer, *Federalism and State Criminal Procedure*, 70 HARV. L. REV. 1, 8 (1956).

[9] [n.27] Officers are not subject to summary courts-martial. 10 U.S.C. § 820.

TZUFAN v. JUDGE ADVOCATE GENERAL
Supreme Court of Israel, 1989
PD 43(4) 718

[At issue in this Israeli case was whether the court should order that charges against a senior officer that were previously handled summarily and by retirement be tried by court-martial.]

BAISKY, J.

1. This Court's Alternative Mandamus ordered Respondents to explain:

A. Why Respondent 1, the Judge Advocate General ("JAG"), did not order the Army Prosecutor to indict Respondent 4 [Colonel Judah Meir] in a court-martial on charges of first degree battery for the events that took place in the villages of Hawara and Beita in Samaria [in the West Bank] in January 1988.

B. Why Respondents 2 and 3 [the Army Chief of Staff and the Head of the Army Personnel Directorate] did not indict Respondent 4 in a court-martial, under Article 171(b) of the Military Justice Law ("MJL") on charges stemming from the same events that led to disciplinary charges against him.

Following a complaint from the International Red Cross, the investigative unit of the military police ("IMP") investigated the January 1988 events in Hawara and Beita. Under Article 279 of the MJL, the IMP submitted its findings to the JAG. The JAG reviewed the investigative findings and submitted a comprehensive and detailed report, dated May 5, 1989, to the Army Chief of Staff (Exhibit R/3). It is sufficient for factual background, to quote only some of the report's conclusions:

19. The evidence led to the following prima facie factual conclusions:

A. On January 19 and 21, 1988 officers and soldiers from Company D of Battalion 50 took part in operations in Hawara and Beita, during which 20 young villagers were brutally beaten.

B. The young men were picked according to a list prepared by the Israeli Security Service ("Shin Bet"). They were taken on a bus out of the village, divided into smaller groups and beaten. They were beaten with wooden clubs and kicked.

C. The soldiers directed the beatings to the men's legs and hands. During the beatings the men's hands and legs were tied and some had their eyes covered.

Officers present at the scene took part in the beatings and made sure the order was strictly followed. . . .

G. Captain Eldad Ben-Moshe delivered the order to the soldiers. However, it is clear from the evidence that the soldiers were told the order comes from higher ranking officers and that their Captain is only the "middle man." In a meeting with officials from the West Bank Civil Administration, the soldiers repeated their impression that the order originated from a high-ranking officer and was part of the "Iron

Fist" policy, which was published in the media and presented directly to them. The soldiers said that Colonel Judah Meir gave the list of local men to their Captain and it was clear he approved and directed the operation.

23. According to all of his subordinates, Colonel Judah Meir (Respondent 4) was the source of the order. Captain Eldad Ben-Moshe's testimony implicates Colonel Meir and shows he was directly responsible for the order to beat the villagers, as described above (*see supra* paragraphs 6 and 9). Ben-Moshe's testimony was corroborated by soldiers' testimonies, which indicate that Colonel Meir was in Beita on January 19, 1988 and monitored the gathering of the men. Once all the detainees were on the bus, Colonel Meir took off. Other soldiers (*see supra* paragraph 10) testified that Lieutenant Colonel (his rank at the time of the events) Judah Meir specifically ordered to beat the detainees and then to release them.

2. The JAG mentioned in his report that initially he found Meir's intolerable behavior to merit an indictment in a court-martial and added:

25. after much hesitation I decided not to prosecute the officer from the following reasons:

A. The events took place on January 19 and 22, 1988 — the beginning of the "Intifada" and only a few days after the use of force was approved for riot control in the West Bank.

B. The orders as to the use of force were not clear at that time, due to different announcements in the media and gaps in the Army chain of command. The Army Chief of Staff's approval of the use of force order was published on February 23, 1988, after the events of Hawara and Beita.

C. As a result of his conduct in the above-mentioned events, the Army Chief of Staff decided to relieve Judah Meir from duty.

26. The above reasons, especially the third, convinced me to charge Colonel Meir before a Senior Adjudicating Officer, the Deputy Chief of Staff, with the disciplinary offense of an unauthorized action that endangers life, under Article 72 of the MJL.

Colonel Meir was charged with a disciplinary offense and tried before Respondent 2. He was convicted of exceeding his authority and awarded a severe reprimand — the maximum disciplinary punishment for a Colonel under Article 153 of the MJL. The disciplinary proceedings involved an additional sanction: Colonel Meir was forced to resign from the Army. Such termination of a military career is a painful punishment, even if it is accompanied by retirement, as mentioned in Annex 5 to the Petition.

3. Petitioners 1-4 are residents of Hawara and victims of the above-mentioned events. Their petition describes the severe beating they took in their limbs and other body parts, while their hands and mouths were tied. As a result of the beatings, some of villagers needed medical attention and some were hospitalized.

All of the Petitioners attack the JAG's decision not to press charges against Respondent 4 in a court-martial and to use only the disciplinary route. Petitioners ague that the evidence against Colonel Meir are sufficient for a charge of first degree battery, under Article 329 of the Penal Code, 1977. The investigative findings are enough to convict Meir under Article 329, if found reliable by a court-martial. They further argue that the JAG never disputed the reliability of such findings. Under these circumstances and especially when the events and abuse of power were so severe, the JAG had a duty to indict Colonel Meir before a court-martial. The failure to indict, Petitioners argue, is extremely unreasonable, was taken with consideration of irrelevant factors, and lacks good faith. Moreover, Petitioners argue, the JAG's decision is contrary to the public interest, unjust, and discriminates in favor of Colonel Meir, whereas other soldiers and officers were indicted in a court-martial on lesser charges.

4. Petitioners do challenge the JAG's authority under Article 281 of the MJL to select the type of legal proceeding. Article 281 provides as follows: "When a Military Advocate receives a complaint, as set forth in Article 277, to which Article 279 does not apply, he may do one of the following: . . . (3) File charges under disciplinary law, as provided for in Article 157."

An offense that can be tried in a disciplinary proceeding is defined in Article 136(a) of the MJL as an "offense for which the punishment does not exceed three years of imprisonment." Colonel Meir was indicted on charges of unauthorized action that endangers life — an offense for which the punishment is three years imprisonment, and therefore, within the reach of the disciplinary law.

Petitioners argue that the JAG abused his discretion by failing to press criminal charges based on the evidence before him — evidence the JAG found to be reliable. Petitioners argue that the JAG should have charged Meir with offenses under Article 329 of the Penal Code, 1977, for which the penalty is 20 years imprisonment. Under the disciplinary law, Colonel Meir never faced imprisonment because Article 153(b) effectively prohibits imprisonment of a Colonel as punishment for a disciplinary offense. Therefore, according to Petitioners, the JAG effectively blocked indictment on the true charges against Colonel Meir.

Disciplinary proceedings were created for relatively minor disciplinary offenses, as demonstrated by Article 136(a) of the MJL and by Article 153(a), which stipulates the hierarchy of punishments available to a Senior Adjudicating Officer:

    (1) Warning;

    (2) Confinement to a military base or a vessel up to 35 days;

    (3) A fine equal to twice the basic salary of a private in compulsory service at the time of sentencing, and if the soldier is in compulsory service — one third of such salary;

    (4) Reprimand;

    (5) Severe reprimand;

    (6) Imprisonment for up to 35 days;

(7) Reduction in rank, provided the accused is a First Sergeant or below.

5. *The JAG's Authority to Indict*:

Like the Attorney General, the JAG has independent discretion as to indictments. Unlike the Attorney General, the JAG, although appointed by the Minister of Defense, is a subordinate of the Army Chief of Staff. The JAG operates within the military hierarchy and his decisions, as in the case before us, are influenced by and coordinated with the Army Central Command. The JAG's authority and discretion are directed, among other goals, at maintaining the Army's unique organizational features, its discipline, the need to follow orders, and executing a broad range of uniquely military tasks.

E. M. Byrne, a legal scholar and a soldier once wrote:

The purpose of law in civilian society is to produce satisfactory order. A civilian's conduct should be orderly and should interact with others as smoothly as possible. There should be no loss of freedom for any person unless such loss is of benefit to the community. Military justice has a similar but much more positive purpose in that it must not only promote good order but also high morale and discipline. Discipline is defined as instant obedience to lawful orders. In the military, the most essential form of discipline is self-discipline, i.e., an individual's willingness to carry out his duties regardless of danger to himself or lack of immediate supervision.

E. M. Byrne, Military Law (Naval Institute Press, Annapolis, Maryland, 1976, p.72); and on page 75:

A senior commander/commanding officer often has powers similar to those of a civilian district attorney regarding disposition of offenses (prosecutorial discretion). However, he has to consider much more carefully which avenue each case shall take than does the average civilian district attorney. The commanding officer is in a unique and delicate position. He is personally and legally responsible for the morale, good order, and discipline of a closely knit unit. Any arbitrariness, unfairness, or partiality can eventually be reflected in the performance of his personnel. Unlike the civilian district attorney, who often disposes of minor and even semi-serious cases in comparative obscurity, almost everyone in a military unit is aware of the day-to-day military justice decisions of the commander. With the "spotlight" of his unit's men on him, the commander has to administer military justice at the highest ethical and moral level. His decisions directly affect morale, good order, and discipline in his command.

6. Articles 280-282 of the MJL enumerate the JAG's options upon receiving a complaint. Under Article 281, the JAG is authorized, among other options, "to cancel the complaint, if he finds the file to provide no basis for indictment" (paragraph (2)); "to refer the complaint to a disciplinary proceeding, as provided for in Article 151" (paragraph (3)); "to order a Military Advocate to press criminal charges, based on the file" (paragraph (4)).

Unlike some of the powers of the Attorney General, the JAG's indictment decisions are subject to broad judicial review. The existing case law, though sparse, has never questioned this Court's authority to review the JAG's decisions and exercise of his discretion. In earlier cases this Court has found no basis for interfering.

In HCJ 372/88 PD 42(3) 154 Chief Justice Shamgar wrote:

> On the merits, we found no reason to interfere with the Army Prosecution's decision. The various prosecution bodies have the power to indict and to choose the appropriate tribunal. This Court will interfere with a prosecutorial decision only in extreme circumstances when there is a material mistake in the decision, or other material distortion. Such mistake was not shown in the case before us.

In HCJ 442/87 PD 42(2) 649, 753 this Court reviewed the JAG's discretion and ruled that:

> This Court has no reason to interfere with the conclusions of the JAG, Brigadier General Amnon Straschnov, regarding the question of the examiner or whether other legal steps are to be taken against the Adjudicating Officers who tried Petitioner. These decisions are the JAG's to make, and unless the decisions are materially unreasonable or lack good faith, this Court has no reason to interfere.

Therefore, subject to the necessary changes which stem from the unique character of the military and the special status of the JAG, who is responsible for the special needs of the military justice system, the same considerations for review of the Attorney General's decisions, must guide us when we review the JAG's exercise of discretion and decisions.

The similarity between the indictment powers of these two positions justifies similar standards of judicial review.

7. Lacking significant case law concerning judicial review of the JAG's decisions, we shall refer to some case law concerning the Attorney General, which should guide us as to the JAG.

According to the original approach of HCJ 156/56 PD 11, 285, judicial review of the Attorney General's decisions was narrow and limited to examining whether the Attorney General acted "in good faith, honesty and with proper motives" (pp. 300-01). This narrow approach was followed in HCJ 4/64 PD 18, 29 and in HCJ 853/78 PD 33 (1), 166, in which this Court said: "Incorrect judgment on behalf of the Attorney General is not enough to justify judicial interference. We are limited to the Attorney General's morality and purity of motives. As long as no claim of lack of good faith is raised, we must leave the discretion whether to press criminal charges in the hands of the Attorney General" (p. 168). Justice Vitkon took a similar approach in HCJ 665/79 PD 34 (2), 634. Justice Shamgar opened the judicial review door a little by mentioning that a substantially unjust decision merits judicial interference (p. 641). Ever since HCJ 665/79, this Court has repeatedly used "substantial injustice" as another reason to interfere. In HCJ 248/81 PD 37 (3), 533, 540-41, this Court extended the grounds for interference to "extreme and material unreasonableness."

Later, as administrative law has developed, interference has extended to the Attorney General's discriminatory acts (HCJ 317/76 PD 30 (3), 477, 479; HCJ 94/81 PD 35 (3), 417, 418), foul or void considerations (HCJ 746/80 PD 35 (2), 453, 455), or considerations that disserve the public interest (HCJ 650/82 PD 37 (4), 216). In HCJ 329/81 PD 37 (4), 326, Justice Barak wrote: "the approach that puts judicial review of the Attorney General's action on the same normative grounds as any other administrative agency is a welcome approach for the following reasons: first, it prevents distinctions between different levels of judicial review — distinctions that are often unfounded; second, it equally enforces the rule of law with no discrimination as among different government officials. The prestigious position of the Attorney General is not immune from the judicial scrutiny, like any other officer. . . ."

Justice Barak's view is not widely accepted, especially because this Court was reluctant to broaden the scope of judicial review of the Attorney General's actions. This Court was slow to broaden such scrutiny because it found the position of the Attorney General unique — a position that involves a broad spectrum of considerations, including interpretation of law, examination of evidence, and consideration of the public interest in its broadest context (*see* HCJ 223/88, Unpublished).

The case before us does not require us to decide whether an expansion of the scope of review of actions of the Attorney General or the JAG is merited. The agreed-upon scope of review, which includes substantial injustice, extreme and material unreasonableness, discrimination, and contradiction to the public interest, is sufficient. This approach is in accordance with Justice Bach's position in HCJ 292/86 PD 42 (4), 406, 411:

> . . . This Court's power to interfere with the Attorney General's decisions is not limited to decisions lacking good faith . . . we can interfere when we are convinced the decision was made based on wrong and unrelated considerations. A prima facie illogical decision may point toward such mistaken and irrelevant considerations, and such decision will not be "saved" by an inability to show lack of good faith.

8. The above principle will guide us when we examine the JAG's discretion in the case at bar: whether the JAG's decision is within the zone of reasonableness, or whether it is improper, as Petitioners argue. I must note that in his report, the JAG underlined the severe nature of Respondent 4's conduct. A few quotations from the report will suffice:

> . . . The order given to the soldiers was, in my view, inherently illegal order that raised a black warning flag and created a duty, not a mere option, to disobey . . . (paragraph 20).

> Beating people as a mere punishment method, even if they are suspected of some offense, is unacceptable and intolerable behavior. There was no room for such an extreme and illegal interpretation of the "Iron Fist" policy. Moreover, beating villagers as a punishment was specifically prohibited under Central Command's "Iron Fist" guidelines (paragraph 23C).

Similar language can be found in section 7(c) of the affidavit supporting the response to the Petition.

Among other factors, the JAG should have considered whether the evidence before him tends to prove the elements of the serious offense under Article 329 of the Penal Code, 1977, and whether the order to beat defenseless human beings in violation of Central Command's guidelines, was an inherently illegal order.

9. The JAG's decision not to prosecute Respondent 4 before a court-martial was justified by three arguments. These are described in paragraph 2 and can be summarized as follows:

First: the event and the decision to use force to control the riots took place in the past;

Second: the actual standards for the application and use of force were not clear at the time;

Third: the Army Chief of Staff decided to end Respondent 4's military career.

We will examine each of these arguments.

The first part of the first argument — the passage of time after the event — is unconvincing; 15 months elapsed between the event and the JAG's decision. Such a period of time is not rare for instituting criminal proceedings, as long as the statute of limitations has not expired. Moreover, Petitioners pointed to a similar incident that occurred within two weeks of the Hawara and Beita incident and resulted in criminal charges before a court-martial in 1989. The passage of time does not outweigh the need to bring criminals to justice. This argument is even more questionable in light of the decision to try Respondent 4 before the Army Chief of Staff.

10. The second part of the first argument is related to the second argument and we will examine them together. Both refer to the early days of the uprising and to confusion, at the time, regarding the use of force.

We can safely assume that officers and soldiers had difficulty controlling the uprising in its first days. However, we cannot accept the argument concerning "the lack of clarity as to the application and the use of force."

Lack of clarity is not an issue when there is an order to take people out of their homes, tie their hands and mouths, and beat them with clubs until their limbs break. Such an order, as the JAG himself said, raises a black warning flag of illegality and must not be followed.

Actions of this kind infuriate any civilized human being and cannot take shelter under the fog of battle or any lack of clarity, especially when the order to act this way comes from a senior officer who should have been aware that the Israel Defence Force's moral standards prohibit such conduct. The JAG's report tells us that soldiers found it difficult to execute the order and one of the officers told Colonel Meir that this kind of conduct is immoral and asked the soldiers to maintain their humanity in executing the order that "came from above." The soldiers, for their part, did show restraint in executing the order.

Chief Justice Shamgar commented on such conduct in HCJ 253/88 PD 42 (2), 823:

> An immoral and prohibited act humiliates and degrades both the detainee and the actor; hurting a tied and helpless human being is a shameless and cruel deed, which requires a harsh and swift response.

Therefore, the lack of clarity argument has no merit.

11. The third argument — the termination of Respondent 4's career — was critical to the JAG's decision to settle for a disciplinary charge of an unauthorized action that endangers life, under Article 72 of the MJL. In his letter to the Organization of Parents against Silence, the JAG wrote:

> In response to your above referenced telegram, it is my opinion that charging the senior officer with a disciplinary offence before the Army Chief of Staff, and the decision to terminate the officer's military career — a decision with significant implications on his future in our society — are sufficient to meet the public interest in this case.

The affidavit before us states:

> It is the JAG's opinion that by forcing him to retire from the military, Respondent 4 was severely sanctioned. This is not a mere replacement of a military position with a civil one. Respondent 4 is forced to end his military career and his way of life, which he purposely chose. Forced retirement is a severe punishment for a senior officer such as Respondent 4.

> Following the JAG's advice, the Army Chief of Staff ended Colonel Meir's military career, sending an immediate and clear message to commanders in the army that such misconduct will not be tolerated.

12. The consequences of the forced retirement of a senior officer like Respondent 4 cannot be underestimated. It is a hard event, even if the retirement arrangements and pension are reasonable. However, retirement is not required as a criminal sanction — it is needed for the military to keep its ranks pure of perpetrators of such misconduct.

Respondent 4 still owes a debt to society and to the rule of law for the criminal offense he allegedly committed. Can we say he paid this debt because he was forced to retire from the military? That argument can serve to reduce the criminal sanction, but the forced retirement does not eliminate the criminal offense allegedly committed.

Civilian law supports this conclusion. A lawyer who commits a criminal offense will face both disciplinary and criminal charges and if found guilty will be both disbarred and sanctioned by the criminal justice system. The same applies to a physician, whose license is suspended by the Health Minister for committing an offence specified in Article 41 of the Physicians Ordinance (New Version), 1976 — a sanction separate from the physician's criminal liability. In both of these examples the end of the professional career does not limit criminal liability. The same is true of state employees.

13. As we mentioned before, a disciplinary proceeding is appropriate for relatively minor offenses (Articles 136 and 153 of the MJL) and similar to nonjudicial punishment, which one scholar, James Snedeker, has described as follows:

> Nonjudicial punishment is designed to take care of the minor offenses, which are usually susceptible of a summary determination on facts not seriously open to contest. The system of nonjudicial punishment serves to prevent disruption of the military mission by allowing disciplinary matters of less serious import to be determined in a manner requiring less time and diversion from more important duties of the personnel involved. . . . The use of nonjudicial punishment is limited by law to minor offenses. Whether an offense is minor can be determined only be reference to the nature of the acts committed, the time and place of commission, the persons committing the offense, and the punishment authorized to be inflicted in the event of a conviction by court-martial. An offense is not minor if it involves moral turpitude or if the maximum limitation of punishment on conviction by court-martial is confinement for one year or more or is the death penalty. Offenses such as larceny, robbery, forgery, maiming, and similar offenses based upon misconduct which is wrong in itself involve moral turpitude. The nature and effect and punishment for desertion indicate that it is not to be treated as a minor offense.

See J. Snedeker, Military Justice (Little Brown and Company), 1965, 64, 53.

An offense is not minor when it involves moral turpitude; and moral turpitude, according to Snedeker, is an offense based upon misconduct which is wrong in itself (J. Snedeker, *Ibid.* at pp. 64-65).

From the reasons detailed in paragraphs 11-13 above, the JAG's third argument concerning the ending of Respondent 4's career, cannot prevail.

14. I could have ended my decision here; however Petitioners' counsel raised additional claims arguing that the JAG's decision is extremely unreasonable and substantially unjust.

It was argued that the JAG discriminated against other soldiers and officers who faced criminal charges by court-martial for lesser offenses, all related to and during the uprising. The Response Affidavit refers to these claims as follows:

> During that period, the JAG ordered that 70 soldiers and officers be prosecuted for offenses committed against the local population in the West Bank and Gaza and that the careers of senior officers who were criminally prosecuted be ended. The JAG also ordered the trial of tens of officers and soldiers by disciplinary proceedings (Paragraph 11(a) of the Affidavit).

A discrimination claim was raised against the Attorney General in several instances, but the issue was never decided because the Court was never provided with specific data.

In HCJ 665/79 PD 34 (4), 634, 638, this Court said:

> It was argued that other similar cases ended with indictment and that failing to indict in this case constitutes discrimination. However, this argument was general and mentioned no specific cases which can be examined by the Court.

In HCJ 329/81 PD 37 (4), 326, 332, this Court said similar things about a failure to substantiate a claim of discrimination.

In the case before us Petitioners specified 52 cases in which 86 soldiers were indicted before a court-martial for conduct during the uprising since 12/9/87 and for various offenses, such as negligent homicide, assault, improper conduct, beating, firing without permission, etc. — but mainly for torturing the local population. This list was published by the Army spokesperson and included details of the charges, the outcome, and the sentence. The list ended with the following words:

> The Army will not tolerate soldiers' illegal and inappropriate conduct, will prosecute such soldiers and request appropriate punishment.

Other than the JAG's report as to Respondent 4, we received no response concerning the disparate treatment of the 86 soldiers who faced criminal charges by court-martial. Moreover, the Response Affidavit clearly states that among those who faced criminal charges were senior officers who in addition were forced to retire from the military.

In the absent of a sufficient answer from respondents, we have a prima facie case of discrimination.

This conclusion is not to be interpreted as holding simply that whenever the JAG's treatment is different in similar cases, a finding of discrimination is warranted. The JAG must weigh the nature of the offense, special and personal circumstances, and every relevant consideration — as long as it is material and reasonable. Avoiding discrimination is just one of these considerations. . . .

Especially as a military force and even in turbulent times, the IDF has maintained its morality and strictly followed the rules of the international law, which impose a duty on the State of Israel to protect the local population in the Occupied Territories and to enforce the rule of law in these territories.

The difficult task facing the IDF in the Occupied Territories may require the use of force to secure law and order, which are often violated in these territories. However, we must condemn an order that is viewed by the JAG as inherently illegal — such as the order at issue in this case, and try the perpetrators according to the Penal Code.

Taking into account all the relevant considerations, as described above, the JAG's decision creates a substantial injustice that justifies this Court's intervention.

16. Counsel for Respondent 4 argued that his client cannot be tried by court-martial because he had already been convicted by a Senior Adjudicating Officer in a disciplinary proceeding and, under a quasi plea bargain, received

the maximum sentence available in disciplinary proceedings — a severe reprimand. Such a sentence, argues Respondent 4's counsel, constitutes a final decision of the court (res judicata) and must be seen as fully performed by his client. Moreover, the sentencing Senior Adjudicating Officer was the Army Chief of Staff and therefore no officer can legally cancel the sentence.

We need not discuss all the counter argument of Petitioners' counsel, among them a far-reaching argument that the whole disciplinary process was without authority and therefore void. Suffice it to say that the offense under Article 72 of the MJL, the subject of the disciplinary proceeding against Respondent 4, is different from the offense under Article 329 of the Penal Law in both elements and punishment. The first offense carries a three year prison term and the latter carries a sentence of twenty years imprisonment. This Court held in HCJ 69/85 PD 40 (2), 617, that in such case the defendant can stand trial in two different courts.

As to the res judicata argument, Article 171 (b) of the MJL states:

A disciplinary ruling will not be considered as a final decision by any other military tribunal or court, but a person will not face trial before a military tribunal for a transaction for which he was tried in a disciplinary proceeding, unless the head of the judicial county ordered it, after consulting with an Army Advocate . . . .

This raises no risk of double jeopardy because Article 172 of the MJL provides as follows:

Should a defendant stand trial in a military tribunal or any other court on a transaction for which he was disciplined, the disciplinary ruling is automatically vacated.

Therefore the res judicata argument should be rejected.

If my opinion is accepted, the temporary order (Alternative Mandamus) issued on July 20, 1989 should become final.

KEDMI, J.

1. *Opening Remarks*

A. I agree with my honorable colleague, Justice Baisky, as to this Court's power to review the JAG's discretion and like my colleague, I adopt the standards set forth in HCJ 372/88 and HCJ 442/97 for such review.

These standards are two: the first — an objective standard to examine the "reasonableness" of the JAG's decision, under which material unreasonableness that includes substantial discrimination, material mistake, and material injustice, renders the decision invalid; the second — a subjective standard to examine the JAG's "good faith" and under which a lack of good faith that includes decency, fairness and relevant considerations, renders the decision invalid.

It is easier to invalidate a decision under the second subjective standard because its variables and components are clear and generally accepted. The first objective has vague variables and components and can lead to borderline cases surrounded by doubt.

B. As a rule, when this Court is asked to interfere with a JAG decision — as with any other executive decision — it cannot put itself in the shoes of the JAG and ask what conclusion this Court should have came to in such shoes. This Court as the judicial arm of the government can only examine the legality of the decision, according to the above two standards.

I must add that this Court does not judge Respondent 4 on his behavior and has no position as to his guilt or the appropriate punishment for his misconduct.

In this proceeding we are limited to the examination of the legality of the JAG's decision. This Court cannot turn itself into an executive agency or into a trial court.

C. There can be no dispute that Respondent 4's conduct should be condemned and detested: such conduct stands against the fundamental values of the Jewish people and against the basic legal norms of the Israeli society.

There can be no dispute that the order given by Respondent 4 was inherently illegal — the illegality was apparent to every eye with no need for any "external" interpretation; even a simple enlisted man could point to its illegality, without hesitation and without a need for further explanation.

Under such circumstances it is intriguing how the detainees list was prepared and the order carried out without questions; this is also a factor to be considered when deciding whether Respondent 4 should have faced a court-martial.

2. "Good Faith"

No one argued before us, at least not directly, that the JAG's decision lacked good faith. To the contrary, the JAG's report and recommendations testify to his good faith: he did not hide the ugly facts and fully explained his reasoning, exposing Respondent 4's despicable behavior.

3. "Material Unreasonableness"

As mentioned by my honorable colleague in his decision, the JAG's decision is justified by three arguments: the passage of time since the event, the lack of clarity as to the application and scope of the use of force, and the termination of Respondent 4's military career.

I will examine each of these arguments:

A. "The Passage of Time"

I agree with my honorable colleague that the passage of time does not contribute to the reasonableness of the JAG's decision and has no effect on this Court's decision whether to interfere.

Time does not diminish the severity of Respondent 4's conduct, does not decrease the public interest in an appropriate response, and confers on Respondent no right to claim discrimination or unjust delay.

B. I reach the same conclusion as my honorable colleague on the lack of clarity as to the application of force. Lack of clarity cannot diminish the nature and the illegality of the order given by Respondent 4. The order's extreme illegality cannot be cured by any clarification that could have been given at the time.

Every part of the order was inherently void and any lack of clarity should have led to its cancellation and not to its execution.

C. As mentioned by my honorable colleague, the termination of Respondent 4's military career was the critical consideration that led the JAG to forgo a trial before a court-martial.

Keeping in mind that mere unreasonableness is not enough to invalidate the decision; we must find a material unreasonableness — an extreme unreasonableness that renders the decision so unjust that no court can approve it.

After much hesitation, I have concluded as my colleague does, for the following reasons:

(1) I agree that termination of a military career is a serious blow to a senior field officer who after many years of service had his future vested in the military. I find it difficult to compare such a termination to revoking an attorney's or a physician's license to practice or the termination of a career of a civil servant.

The phrases "career termination" or "ending his military service" are too antiseptic and fail to convey the true impact of such a termination. In the case of Respondent 4, termination means removal from a senior position in a hierarchical organization and expulsion from the military ranks.

Respondent 4 chose the military as a way of life and tied his destiny to the struggle for a secure society in a state that has been fighting for its independence, sovereignty and existence for 40 years. The removal and expulsion of a Colonel who was in the prime of his career have their own unique meaning and cannot be compared to a professional suspension, even if the profession became a "way of life."

To Respondent 4 the military service was not a "way of life" in its usual meaning — for him the military service was the essence of life. The service was his life; after his removal he has to start all over in a strange and hostile world and to face all the social consequences that follow such removal.

Therefore, the termination of Respondent 4's military career should have been given serious consideration and significant weight.

I must emphasize that such timely removal, as a response to an immoral act, can advance the educational and preventive goals of punishment. The educational goal is satisfied by setting a norm of behavior that the military uncompromisingly promotes. The preventive aspect benefits from clearly portraying the consequences of a breach of such a norm.

My words should not be misconstrued. I do not claim that that in every case, regardless of the circumstances, removal will suffice. All I am saying is that removal is not a meager response and should be given full consideration by the JAG.

Removal is not the only consideration, or a deciding one. Every case has its own circumstances and a response appropriate to the facts.

Under the circumstances of the case before us, the JAG could consider the removal of Respondent 4 from the military ranks.

In this case removal was the formal response. However, the response lost its effect due to the way it was brought: first — removal was not immediate and decisive and did not express disdain for Respondent 4's conduct, and; second — these steps were taken in agreement with the respondent, and accompanied by leave and retirement arrangements including securing a job for Respondent 4 as a civil servant. Under these circumstances, the removal lost its sanction-like character and became a forced retirement on mutually agreed terms.

Recognizing the pain felt by removed officer, we must not forget that the reaction must be a sanction that satisfies the pain of the public that suffered from the wrongful behavior of the removed.

A liberal approach toward the removed officer diminishes the reaction's strength and ability to meet the public interest in an appropriate response that promotes the normative interest and the preventive interest. The smoother the removal, the less the role it plays in deciding the appropriate response to the wrongful conduct.

In the case before us, the outcome might have been different if the removal and expulsion had been more of a punishment. Preserving Respondent 4's retirement rights did not diminish the sanction-like nature of the removal. However, taking a contractual approach toward the removal did.

(3) I have not overlooked the fact that in addition to his removal, Respondent 4 was disciplined before the Deputy Chief of Staff.

Trying a senior officer on a serious disciplinary offense is a trial; it would be wrong to consider disciplinary proceedings as a waiver of judicial proceedings, as if it was a quasi-judicial administrative process.

Originally, disciplinary proceedings were created to enforce discipline and used for offenses with a disciplinary nature. However, in the IDF, the disciplinary law has been used for criminal offenses as well and under certain circumstances became an appropriate alternative to a trial before a judicial panel.

It is correct, therefore, to view the disciplinary proceeding as a judicial process and not as a waiver of such process. In the context of the case before us, we must give the disciplinary proceeding its appropriate weight, as one of the legitimate responses to a soldier's wrongful conduct.

Nevertheless, each case has its unique circumstances and we should not pre-set rules for finding when the disciplinary proceeding alone will suffice.

(4) The wrongfulness of Respondent 4's conduct required a decisive and immediate response corresponding to the process of filing serious criminal charges in court. Filing criminal charges was the natural and appropriate response for the conduct attributed to Respondent 4. A judicial process is best suited to express the condemnation of such misconduct, to publicly acknowl-

edge its severity and to appropriately sentence Respondent 4. Any alternative response had to yield the same results; a response with different results misses its goals, diminishes the wrongfulness of the misconduct, and increases the chances of similar moral failures in the future.

Prima facie — in light of the execution of his illegal order, Respondent 4's misconduct demands pressing charges before a judicial panel; and although I am not disposed to exclude other responses — the JAG's reaction cannot substitute a judicial process, merely for the way it was taken.

Finally I reach the question before us: whether the JAG's decision, limiting the response to removal and disciplinary charges, is materially unreasonable. I conclude that considering the degree of Respondent 4's wrongful conduct and the consequences of the execution of his illegal order, the JAG's decision not to prosecute before a court-martial is materially unreasonable. The nature of the actual removal of Respondent 4 from military service and the way it was handled played a significant role in my decision.

Therefore, I join the conclusion of my honorable colleague, Justice Baisky.

LEVIN, J.

I agree with the result of my colleagues' detailed opinions. I would like to add, note and emphasize the following:

A. I agree that the conduct attributed to Respondent 4 is so grave that he should stand trial for such conduct.

B. The discretion given to the JAG as to trying soldiers before military tribunals is equal to the discretion the Attorney General has in bringing criminal charges.

This Court's review of the exercise of discretion by both the Attorney General and the JAG is narrow and limited.

We will only interfere on the grounds described by Chief Justice Shamgar in HCJ 442/87 PD 42 (2), 649, 753 and in HCJ 372/88 PD 42 (3), 154. According to these rulings, we will interfere with the JAG's decision only under extreme circumstances of clear and material error or substantial injustice.

Our intervention is limited to those cases where one can point to: (a) lack of good faith on behalf of the decision maker; (b) bad motives or irrelevant considerations as the basis for the decision; or (c) an extreme and material unreasonable decision.

I see no justification to further expand the grounds for interference. The above grounds cover those extreme cases in which it is impossible to ignore the erroneous and unjust nature of the decision.

C. It is clear from his decision that the JAG was reluctant to forgo criminal proceeding before a court-martial and that he felt that the alleged conduct was so wrong and repulsive that it could not be ignored.

The JAG's decision is sought to be justified on three grounds, each will be examined separately. Like my colleagues, I conclude that these three arguments, separately and combined, do no not reasonably justify the JAG's decision not to try Respondent 4 before a court-martial.

D. The first argument raised by the JAG is that the relevant events took place at the beginning of the uprising and only a few days after the use of force to quell the rioting was approved.

I do not find this argument convincing. If such events were few and the IDF has managed to prevent similar occurrences, then why did others face criminal charges for similar conduct? If there was a good reason to try others before a court-martial (and there was), there is no reason to treat Respondent 4 differently. Moreover, we now know that such events were not isolated or local; they repeated themselves over and over again. Therefore, the need for the judicial system to deter and prevent still exists. The time that passed while the investigators and the JAG deliberated cannot give rise to an argument of delay and injustice significant enough to waive trial proceedings.

E. The second argument raised by the JAG is the lack of clarity as to the use of force due to contradictory statements in the media and the lack of clear guidance coming down through the Army's chain of command.

In my view, raising this lack of clarity argument promotes a lack of clarity. What can be unclear? Could Central Command have possibly directed Respondent 4 to act illegally, as he allegedly did? If this were the case, we would have an issue of unreasonable orders, not vague ones. If this was the issue, Respondent 4, as a senior officer, had a duty to notify his superiors and not to pass the order to his subordinates. Respondent 4 cannot shift his duty to decide whether an order is inherently illegal to his subordinates. He had the ability, experience, status, authority and duty to make the decision.

If he thought the order was inherently illegal, Respondent 4 had a duty to confront his superiors. If he found the order appropriate, then clarity or the lack thereof was not at issue.

If, as Respondent 4 argues, the Army had not yet developed a clear policy as to the use of force, then he had a duty to clear it up with his superiors before giving his soldiers the orders he did.

It is clear to me that the higher the rank of a commander, the greater his duty to examine the justification for and legality of an order.

F. The third and main argument raised by the JAG is the Army Chief of Staff's decision to terminate the military career of Respondent 4.

This could have been a sufficient reason had the Army Chief of Staff decided to remove Respondent 4 immediately. Such a swift and extreme measure towards a senior officer, who had an impressive career and had the military as his goal in life, would have satisfied the need for a strong and decisive reaction to the relevant misconduct.

I will not measure this reaction against criminal proceedings. That task is reserved to the JAG. However, if, after a swift removal, the JAG had decided as he eventually did, I would not find his decision extremely unreasonable. Removing a senior officer from the service is a powerful and harsh sanction that has a deterrent effect on the removed officer and every serviceman. In this case an immediate and swift deterrent was of the essence. The deterrent effect could have been best achieved by the immediate removal of Respondent 4 from the ranks of the military.

However, the Army Chief of Staff decided differently. The friendly retirement arrangement made with Respondent 4 eliminated the deterrent effect and punitive nature of the removal.

I am not criticizing the idea of a retirement arrangement. It is appropriate for the IDF to help an officer who has served for many years to reenter civil life. However, once the Army chose to afford Respondent 4 this comfortable retirement arrangement, it could not substitute that arrangement for the judicial process.

G. For all of the above reasons, I conclude that the temporary order should become final.

NOTES AND QUESTIONS

1. United States law is increasingly alert to the interests of victims, but even so it does not empower a victim to compel the military to conduct a court-martial. Article 4(a), UCMJ, permits an officer who has been dismissed by order of the President to demand a court-martial, and Article 15, UCMJ, permits personnel to demand a court-martial in lieu of nonjudicial punishment. Neither one compels the convening of a court-martial. Are there any circumstances in which a third-party or a member of the military ought to be able to compel the government to conduct a court-martial? What standards should govern such demands?

2. The United States Code provides that "[n]o officer of the Navy or the Marine Corps may be retired because of misconduct for which trial by court-martial would be appropriate." 10 U.S.C. § 6329. What effect do you think this statute has had on personnel decision making? Is it enforceable?

3. Nonjudicial punishment is said to be intended for minor offenses. According to the *Manual for Courts-Martial*, "[w]hether an offense is minor depends on several factors: the nature of the offense and the circumstances surrounding its commission; the offender's age, rank, duty assignment, record and experience; and the maximum sentence imposable for the offense if tried by general court-martial. Ordinarily, a minor offense is an offense which the maximum sentence imposable would not include a dishonorable discharge or confinement for longer than 1 year if tried by general court-martial. The decision whether an offense is 'minor' is a matter of discretion for the commander imposing nonjudicial punishment, but nonjudicial punishment for an offense other than a minor offense (even though thought by the commander to be minor) is not a bar to trial by court-martial for the same offense." *Manual for Courts-Martial*, pt. V, ¶ 1e (2005 ed.). Should the standard be tighter? Under what circumstances should nonjudicial punishments for non-minor offenses be subject to invalidation? *See, e.g., Turner v. Department of the Navy*, 325 F.3d 310 (D.C. Cir. 2003).

4. Should summary discipline be limited to disciplinary offenses as opposed to common law crimes? *See* Chapter 7, § II. Should it ever be available with respect to offenses by civilians subject to military justice? *See* Chapter 6, § V.

III. JUSTICE AT SEA

Herman Melville, White-Jacket, or The World in a Man-of-War
(1850)

In the English Navy, it is said, they had a law which authorized the sailor to appeal, if he chose, from the decision of the Captain — even in a comparatively trivial case — to the higher tribunal of a court-martial. It was an English seaman who related this to me. When I said that such a law must be a fatal clog to the exercise of the penal power in the Captain, he, in substance, told me the following story.

A top-man guilty of drunkenness being sent to the gratings, and the scourge about to be inflicted, he turned round and demanded a court-martial. The Captain smiled, and ordered him to be taken down and put into the "brig." There he was kept in irons some weeks, when, despairing of being liberated, he offered to compromise at two dozen lashes. "Sick of your bargain, then, are you?" said the Captain. "No, no! a court-martial you demanded, and a court-martial you shall have." Being at last tried before the bar of quarter-deck officers, he was condemned to two hundred lashes. What for? For his having been drunk? No! for his having had the insolence to appeal from an authority, in maintaining which the men who tried and condemned him had so strong a sympathetic interest.

Whether this story be wholly true or not, or whether the particular law prevails, or ever did prevail, in the English Navy, the thing, nevertheless, illustrates the ideas that man-of-war's-men themselves have touching the tribunals in question. . . .

In final reference to all that has been said in previous chapters touching the severity and unusualness of the laws of the American Navy, and the large authority vested in its commanding officers, be it here observed, that White-Jacket is not unaware of the fact, that the responsibility of an officer commanding at sea — whether in the merchant service or the national marine — is unparalleled by that of any other relation in which man may stand to man. Nor is he unmindful that both wisdom and humanity dictate that, from the peculiarity of his position, a sea-officer in command should be clothed with a degree of authority and discretion inadmissible in any master ashore. But, at the same time, these principles — recognized by all writers on maritime law — have undoubtedly furnished warrant for clothing modern sea-commanders and naval courts-martial with powers which exceed the due limits of reason and necessity. Nor is this the only instance where right and salutary principles, in themselves almost self-evident and infallible, have been advanced in justification of things, which in themselves are just as self-evidently wrong and pernicious.

. . . [I]t can not admit of a reasonable doubt, in any unbiased mind conversant with the interior life of a man-of-war, that most of the sailor iniquities practiced therein are indirectly to be ascribed to the morally debasing effects of the unjust, despotic, and degrading laws under which the man-of-war's-man lives.

UNITED STATES v. EDWARDS
United States Court of Appeals for the Armed Forces
46 M.J. 41 (C.A.A.F. 1997)

GIERKE, JUDGE:

A special court-martial convened at Naval Station, Philadelphia, Pennsylvania, convicted appellant, pursuant to his pleas, of six unauthorized absences, in violation of Article 86, Uniform Code of Military Justice, 10 U.S.C. § 886. The adjudged and approved sentence, imposed by officer members, provides for a bad-conduct discharge, confinement for 60 days, partial forfeiture of pay for two months, and reduction to the lowest enlisted grade. The Court of Criminal Appeals affirmed the findings and sentence. 43 M.J. 619 (1995).

Our Court granted review of the following issue:

WHETHER THE LOWER COURT ERRED IN DETERMINING THAT THE OPERATIONAL STATUS OF A NAVAL VESSEL WAS IRRELEVANT FOR THE PURPOSE OF IMPOSING NONJUDICIAL PUNISHMENT UNDER ARTICLE 15.

Because the court below based its decision on an incorrect view of the law, we reverse. For the reasons set out below, we hold that the operational status of a naval vessel is relevant to admissibility of evidence that a member of the vessel's crew received nonjudicial punishment without being afforded the opportunity to demand trial by court-martial in lieu of nonjudicial punishment. Because neither the military judge nor the court below elicited the relevant facts concerning the nonjudicial punishment at issue in this case, we must remand for factfinding and reconsideration.

This case involves the so-called "vessel exception" to Article 15, UCMJ, 10 U.S.C. § 815. Article 15 empowers commanding officers to impose nonjudicial punishment on members of their commands. It also provides that "[E]xcept in the case of a member attached to or embarked in a vessel, punishment may not be imposed upon any member of the armed forces under this article if the member has, before the imposition of such punishment, demanded trial by court-martial in lieu of such punishment." Art. 15(a).

The granted issue arose during appellant's sentencing hearing, when the prosecution offered evidence that appellant had received nonjudicial punishment for a short unauthorized absence and for carrying concealed weapons. The evidence reflected that when the nonjudicial punishment was imposed, appellant's unit was "USS CONSTELLATION (CV 64) AT NAVSHPYD PHILA PA." Defense counsel objected, citing *United States v. Yatchak*, 35 M.J. 379 (C.M.A. 1992), and *United States v. Lorance*, 35 M.J. 382 (C.M.A. 1992).

Defense counsel asserted that the USS CONSTELLATION was not in an operational status when the punishment was imposed, but was undergoing overhaul at the Philadelphia Navy Yard. Defense counsel argued that because the ship was not in an operational status, appellant was not "attached to or embarked in a vessel" within the meaning of Article 15. Thus, at the time the Article 15 was administered, appellant had the right to demand trial by court-martial and to consult with a lawyer before deciding whether to demand trial.

The military judge admitted the evidence of nonjudicial punishment without commenting on the merits of the defense objection. Defense counsel then asked, "[I]s the court stating that they [*sic*] believe the CONSTELLATION is an operational vessel?" The military judge responded that "it's the court's interpretation that the cases cited by the defense counsel refer to the issue of whether an accused is attached to or embarked on a vessel for the purposes of awarding bread and water as a punishment at a court-martial," and that "the court interprets that holding to apply only to that punishment." Defense counsel asked that it be "noted on the record that we feel that because it's not an operational vessel for those purposes that we feel that at the very least *Booker* warnings should be given." *See United States v. Booker*, 5 M.J. 238 (C.M.A. 1977) (right to consult with counsel before deciding whether to demand trial). The military judge concluded the discussion by informing defense counsel that "Your objection is made for the record."

The Court of Criminal Appeals held "that the operational status of a naval vessel is not relevant for the purpose of imposing [nonjudicial punishment] under Article 15(a), UCMJ," and "that a naval ship undergoing overhaul is a vessel at all times without regard to its operational status until a determination is made to the contrary by competent authority." 43 M.J. at 624-25. The court below construed our decision in *Yatchak* to be limited to the question of whether confinement on bread and water in that case was imposed under circumstances that made it "cruel or unusual" and thus prohibited by Congress in Article 55, UCMJ, 10 U.S.C. § 855. 43 M.J. at 624.

In *United States v. Yatchak, supra*, we construed the term "attached to or embarked in a vessel" as it appears in Article 15(b)(2)(A). We held that confinement on bread and water was not an authorized punishment in that case because the accused was not "attached to or embarked in a vessel" within the meaning of Article 15(b)(2)(A). We relied on several factors: (1) the sentence was imposed by a court-martial conducted ashore; (2) the sentence was imposed on a sailor assigned to a vessel undergoing long-term overhaul that would not be completed until several months after the trial; (3) the Government and the defense agreed that the vessel "was never in an operational status throughout the period of appellant's naval service"; and (4) the sentence was served in a shore facility. 35 M.J. at 380.

The question raised by the military judge's ruling and the decision of the court below is whether the term "attached to or embarked in a vessel" has the same meaning in Article 15(a) as it does in Article 15(b)(2)(A). We hold that it does. It is a fundamental rule of statutory construction that "[u]nless the context indicates otherwise, words or phrases in a provision that were used in a prior act pertaining to the same subject matter will be construed in the same sense." N. Singer, 2B *Sutherland Statutory Construction* § 51.02 at 122 (5th ed. 1992). Both Article 15(a) and 15(b)(2)(A) use the exact same term pertaining to nonjudicial punishment. The context does not invite a different construction. Accordingly, we hold that the military judge and the court below erred by limiting the *Yatchak* definition of the "vessel exception" to cases involving confinement on bread and water.

Our review of the decision of the court below does not involve the legality of appellant's nonjudicial punishment, but only its admissibility in a subsequent court-martial. The jurisdiction of our Court does not extend to direct review of nonjudicial punishment proceedings. *See Jones v. Commander, Naval Air Force, U.S. Atlantic Fleet*, 18 M.J. 198 (C.M.A. 1984); *Dobzynski v. Green*, 16 M.J. 84 (C.M.A. 1983).

In *United States v. Booker, supra,* this Court held that evidence of previous nonjudicial punishment is not admissible unless the person being punished was advised of his or her right to confer with "independent counsel" before deciding whether to demand trial by court-martial. Of course, if the evidence relating to the nonjudicial punishment shows that the person being punished had no right to demand trial because he was "attached to or embarked in a vessel," then *Booker* is inapplicable. *See United States v. Mack*, 9 M.J. 300, 320 (C.M.A. 1980) (*Booker* not intended to apply to persons "attached to or embarked in a vessel").

In determining whether appellant was "attached to or embarked in a vessel," two issues must be resolved: (1) Was appellant's relationship to the ship sufficient to satisfy what Congress intended by the words "attached to or embarked in," and thus sufficient to trigger the exception to the statutory right to demand trial and the ancillary right to consult with counsel before deciding whether to demand trial? and (2) Was the ship a "vessel" within the meaning of Article 15? Both questions are preliminary questions of fact. *See* Mil. R. Evid. 104(b), Manual for Courts-Martial, United States (1995 ed.) (ruling on sufficiency of evidence to support a finding of fulfillment of a condition of fact is sole responsibility of military judge).

With respect to the first preliminary question, the legislative history of Article 15 is instructive in discerning what Congress meant by the words, "attached to or embarked in." When Congress first enacted Article 15 in 1950, the statute contained no right to demand trial by court-martial. Instead, Congress merely empowered the service secretaries to, "by regulation, place limitations on the powers granted by this article with respect to . . . the applicability of this article to an accused who demands trial by court-martial." Act of May 5, 1950, ch. 169, 64 Stat. 107, 113, *reprinted in* 1950 U.S. Code Cong. & Admin. News 115. Paragraph 132, Manual for Courts-Martial, United States, 1951, set out the service regulations as follows:

> Pursuant to the authority of Article 15b, the following departmental regulations with respect to the applicability of Article 15 to persons who demand trial by court-martial are announced by the several Secretaries:
>
> *Army and Air Force.* — No disciplinary punishment under the provisions of Article 15 may be imposed upon any member of the

Army or of the Air Force for an offense punishable thereunder if the accused has, prior to the imposition of such punishment, demanded trial by court-martial in lieu of such disciplinary punishment. . . .

Navy and Coast Guard. — No member of the Navy or the Coast Guard may demand trial by court-martial in lieu of punishment under the provisions of Article 15.

In 1962 Article 15 was amended in several respects, including the addition of a statutory right to demand trial by court-martial, "except in the case of a member attached to or embarked on a vessel." Act of September 7, 1962, Pub. L. No. 87-648, 76 Stat. 447, 448, *reprinted in* 1962 U.S. Code Cong. & Admin. News 523. This statutory amendment had the effect of extending to members of the Navy and Coast Guard the right to demand trial by court-martial in lieu of nonjudicial punishment, subject to the "vessel exception."

The legislative history of the 1962 amendment suggests that Congress intended the "vessel exception" to apply only to "military members aboard ship." *See* S. Rep. No. 1911, 87th Cong., 2d Sess. 1-2, *reprinted in* 1962 U.S. Code Cong. & Admin. News 2379-80. The Senate adopted the amendments to Article 15 on the representation of the Senate Armed Services Committee chairman that the amendment would give all military members a right to demand trial in lieu of nonjudicial punishment except "in some cases where a ship is at sea." 108 Cong Rec. 17,560 (1962), *cited in* Sullivan, *Overhauling the Vessel Exception*, 43 NAVAL LAW REVIEW 57, 71 n.62 [hereafter cited as Sullivan].

When the proposed executive order implementing the amendments to Article 15 was transmitted to the President, it was accompanied by a memorandum from Assistant Attorney General Norbert A. Schlei addressing the ambiguity of the vessel exception and the possibility that it might be applied to persons "considerably removed from the vessel involved, and without regard to whether actual boarding of the vessel is planned for the immediate future. . . ." Mr. Schlei opined that such an interpretation "would appear to be inconsistent with the congressional intent." Mr. Schlei assured the President that "[r]epresentatives of the Air Force [the executive agent for promulgating the changes], on behalf of all the services, state that the military services have no intention of denying an election to any member . . . unless he is either aboard [a] vessel or unless he is in the immediate vicinity of a vessel and is in the process of boarding." Appendix A to Sullivan, *supra* at 106-09. Mr. Schlei advised the President that the services also intended to apply the vessel exception "to members attached to vessels who are absent without authority in foreign ports." Mr. Schlei proposed to the President that the implementing rules be issued as drafted to avoid considerable delay required to redraft them. Finally, Mr. Schlei informed the President that "[i]n order to avoid any misunderstanding concerning this matter," a copy of his memorandum would be disseminated to the services for their guidance. *Id.* at 108. The President signed the proposed executive order as recommended by Mr. Schlei. *See* Exec. Order No. 11, 081, 28 Fed. Reg. 945 (1963), *reprinted in* 1963 U.S. Code Cong. & Admin. News 1680. We conclude from the foregoing that both Congress and the President intended the "vessel exception" to be limited to situations such as where service members were aboard a vessel, in the immediate vicinity and in the process of boarding, or attached to vessels and absent without authority in foreign ports.

Turning to the second preliminary question of fact, we note that the term "vessel" has been defined by Congress, and that the statutory definition has been incorporated into the Manual for Courts-Martial. R.C.M. 103(20), Manual, *supra*, expressly adopts "[t]he definitions and rules of construction in 1 U.S.C. §§ 1 through 5 and in 10 U.S.C. §§ 101 and 801." The term "vessel" is defined in 1 U.S.C. § 3 as follows: "The word 'vessel' includes every description of watercraft or other artificial contrivance used, or capable of being used, as a means of transportation on water." Nothing in the legislative history or legal context suggests that Congress intended a different definition of "vessel" in connection with nonjudicial punishment. Based on this definition, we reject the position taken by the court below that operational status is irrelevant. We hold that a ship's operational status is relevant to a factual determination whether it is "used or capable of being used, as a means of transportation on water." As in *Yatchak, supra*, it is one of several factors involved in determining whether withdrawing the right to demand trial is consistent with the congressional intent behind the vessel exception.

We are mindful of the concerns of the court below that "operational status" is "undefined," and that a ship might become nonoperational under circumstances for which the vessel exception should apply, such as a casualty at sea, accidental grounding or collision, or wartime damage. 43 M.J. at 624. We have little difficulty defining "operational." *See* Webster's Ninth Collegiate Dictionary 827 (1991) ("operational" defined as "ready for or in condition to undertake a destined function").

We have no difficulty imagining situations where a ship is not "operational" because it is disabled or destroyed, but where discipline "at sea" must be maintained. We note, however, that none of those circumstances are present in this case. We will resolve those situations, consistent with our reading of the intent of Congress, when they come before us on a properly developed record.

We also note that the Department of the Navy has issued no regulatory guidance to define the term "operational status" in the four years since this Court used that term in *Yatchak* to limit the phrase "attached to or embarked on a vessel" under Article 15. While we must necessarily reserve judgment on the application of any such guidance to a particular case, we have no reason to doubt that the Navy is capable of publishing guidance that would cover many reasonably foreseeable circumstances. Regardless of whether such guidance is published, we are confident that military judges and the courts of criminal appeals can apply their wisdom and experience in assessing whether the right to demand trial by court-martial was denied properly in a particular situation.

In appellant's case the record of nonjudicial punishment contains *prima facie* evidence that the vessel exception applied, because it reflects that appellant was assigned to the crew of the USS CONSTELLATION, a commissioned ship of the United States Navy and facially a "vessel" within the meaning of

Article 15. Defense counsel's objection at trial asserted matters not reflected on the document. Because the document appears regular on its face, defense counsel had the burden of raising the issues as to the applicability of the vessel exception and *Booker. See United States v. Moschella*, 20 U.S.C.M.A 543, 43 C.M.R. 383 (1971) (official document entitled to presumption of regularity).

Once the defense objection was timely made and the defense asserted that the CONSTELLATION was undergoing long-term overhaul and was not an operational vessel, the military judge should have given the parties an opportunity to present evidence. If the defense had produced sufficient evidence to raise the *Booker* issue, the Government would have had the burden, as proponent of the evidence, to show compliance with *Booker* or the applicability of the vessel exception.

Because the relevant facts were not elicited on the record and the military judge did not make the necessary predicate findings, we cannot determine whether the ship met the statutory definition of a "vessel," nor can we determine appellant's relationship to the ship: whether he lived aboard, performed duties aboard, was administered nonjudicial punishment aboard, or served his punishment aboard. *See United States v. Yatchak, supra.* Accordingly, we cannot determine whether the vessel exception operated to make *Booker* inapplicable to appellant's nonjudicial punishment. Therefore, we must remand this case for further proceedings in light of the legal principles set out above in this opinion. . . .

SULLIVAN, JUDGE (concurring in part and dissenting in part):

The record in this case shows that appellant received nonjudicial punishment on April 24, 1992, for unauthorized absence and carrying a concealed weapon (a 357 magnum revolver and a .22 caliber pistol). The record also shows the punishment of a reduction from Petty Officer Third Class to Airman, 30 days extra duty, 30 days restriction, and forfeiture of $350.00 pay per month for 2 months was administered by the commanding officer of the USS CONSTELLATION (CV 64) at the Naval Shipyard, Philadelphia, Pennsylvania. Finally, defense counsel represented to the Court, without Government contravention, that "the USS CONSTELLATION like the KITTY HAWK in those cases was not an operational vessel at the time it was in the yards here in Philadelphia. . . ."

I agree with the majority opinion that the military judge erred in holding that *United States v. Yatchak*, 35 M.J. 379 (C.M.A. 1992), and *United States v. Lorance*, 35 M.J. 382 (C.M.A. 1992), were not applicable in this case. Nevertheless, the record before me shows that appellant was attached to the USS CONSTELLATION (CV 64) at the time of his nonjudicial punishment, and that it was not a vessel for purposes of Article 15, Uniform Code of Military Justice, 10 U.S.C. § 815. *See* Mil. R. Evid. 104(a), Manual for Courts-Martial, United States, 1984 (in making admissibility determination, military judge not bound by rules of evidence). I would direct the Court of Criminal Appeals to reconsider appellant's sentence in light of the erroneous admission of this non-judicial punishment. *See* Art. 59(a), UCMJ, 10 U.S.C. § 859(a).

NOTES AND QUESTIONS

1. Melville was probably not very popular with the Navy after *White-Jacket* appeared. One admiral wrote:

> The author an unalloyed villain, has given us through his talents & lies, the worst stab yet — one that we will reel under, if it do not swamp us — . . . [Y]ou can conceive an educated, gifted, unprincipled man, brought by his vices to a whaler & a man of war, ascribing his condition to any thing and any body but his own worthless self, with his intellect keen and his sense of depredation complete — a precious fellow this to [word illegible] of a system or to speak for sailors — his lies are plausible difficult often to meet & yet more false, in the inference they produce, than if they were of the most barefaced description — the time was propitious for his making money too.

Letter from Rear Admiral Samuel F. Du Pont to Sen. Henry W. Davis, Apr. 17, 1850, *in* JAMES E. VALLE, ROCKS & SHOALS: ORDER AND DISCIPLINE IN THE OLD NAVY 1800-1861, 253-54 & n.17 (1980). Was Melville unfair to the Navy?

2. After *Edwards*, the Navy never issued a regulation defining operational status for purposes of the vessel exception and continued to resist efforts to confine the vessel exception to the limited circumstances identified in Assistant Attorney General Schlei, Memorandum to President Kennedy. *See, e.g., Piersall v. Winter*, 435 F.3d 319 (D.C. Cir. 2006).

Chapter 5

PROFESSIONAL RESPONSIBILITY

The Army, Navy, and Air Force have adopted their own rules of professional conduct for lawyers. These rules are based on the American Bar Association's Model Rules of Professional Conduct, but include some significant additions and departures. The Coast Guard has taken a different approach, adopting the ABA Model Rules to the extent that they do not conflict with Coast Guard regulations.

This chapter will first examine the rules that govern the licensing of military justice practitioners. We will focus on one recurring issue: may lawyers who maintain only inactive status in their licensing jurisdictions' bars practice in the military justice system? We will see that the answer to that question varies among the licensing jurisdictions.

This chapter will also explore differences between military and civilian ethical rules. The services have adopted rules specifying that the client of most military lawyers is the service itself, not any particular official who the lawyer advises. But the services have also adopted special rules recognizing a military defense counsel's duty of loyalty to the client and professional independence when representing a client. While these rules are unique to military practice, in one area, the military rules directly conflict with their ABA Model Rules of Professional Conduct counterpart. This chapter will explore the military services' rejection of the imputed disqualification rule that generally prohibits lawyers from representing a client if another lawyer working for the same firm would be disqualified from representing that client.

Professional responsibility rules sometimes become the source of law applied within the court-martial system, and not merely a code to regulate its participants. This chapter will conclude with an analysis of two such areas: conflicts of interest and prosecutorial misconduct.

I. LICENSING

Uniform Code of Military Justice

Article 26. Military judge of a general or special court-martial

(b) A military judge shall be a commissioned officer of the armed forces who is a member of the bar of a Federal court or a member of the bar of the highest court of a State and who is certified to be qualified for duty as a military judge by the Judge Advocate General of the armed forces of which such military judge is a member.

Article 27. Detail of trial counsel and defense counsel

(b) Trial counsel or defense counsel detailed for a general court-martial —

(1) must be a judge advocate who is a graduate of an accredited law school or is a member of the bar of a Federal court or of the highest court of a State; or must be a member of the bar of a Federal court or of the highest court of a State; and

(2) must be certified as competent to perform such duties by the Judge Advocate General of the armed force of which he is a member.

NOTE

Neither Article 26 nor Article 27 requires that court-martial judges or counsel be members of any bar. But service regulations require that a military judge or counsel practicing before a court-martial be a member of a U.S. bar in good standing. As the following Professional Responsibility Notes and case demonstrate, controversy has recently surrounded whether that requirement is satisfied by a military lawyer's inactive membership in his or her licensing jurisdiction's bar.

Professional Responsibility Notes, *Judge Advocate General of the Army, Standards of Conduct Office*
ARMY LAW., Dec. 1995, at 101

Army military and civilian lawyers who elect inactive bar status may find that they no longer qualify to practice law in the Army if their states do not recognize inactive members as being in good standing. Army lawyers always have been required to establish their good standing with a bar before being commissioned in the Judge Advocate General's Corps (JAG Corps) or being hired for a civilian position. Now, that requirement extends for the duration of lawyer's Army service.

Three regulations require Army military and civilian lawyers to maintain good standing. The first is *Army Regulation 27-1, Judge Advocate Legal Services*, revised effective 3 March 1995 (*AR 27-1*). Chapter 13, Voluntary Active Duty with the Judge Advocate General's Corps, now affirmatively requires that JAG Corps officers remain members in good standing of the bar of the highest court of a state of the United States, the District of Columbia, or the Commonwealth of Puerto Rico. The second is *Army Regulation 600-8-24, Officer Transfers and Discharges*, effective 1 November 1995 (*AR 600-8-24*), which permits elimination action for officers who lose their professional licenses. . . . In practical terms, Army attorneys must continuously maintain their ability to obtain a certificate of good standing.

The definition of good standing varies among the states. In some states, inactive members are members in good standing. In some states, inactive status members may not be considered in good standing where attorneys request inactive status to qualify for waived or reduced membership fees, disciplinary fees, or fees for mandatory continuing legal education (MCLE).

The clarifying additions to the regulations were promulgated to prevent recurrence of bar membership issues that first surfaced with the Pennsylvania Bar. In one case, the Standards of Conduct Office (SOCO) notified the state that The Judge Advocate General (TJAG) had disciplined an Army civilian attorney who, according to Army records, was a member of the Pennsylvania Bar. Pennsylvania Bar officials responded that the attorney had been registered as "involuntarily inactive," paying no fees for more than twenty years. In a second case, TJAG received an allegation that an officer's good standing had lapsed for nonpayment of mandatory fees. In two additional cases, Pennsylvania would not issue Army attorneys certificates of good standing because the attorneys had elected inactive status.

Indiana also provides an instructive example. Inactive status in Indiana is elected by filing an affidavit stating that the attorney is not practicing law in Indiana. Inactive status allows an attorney to remain on the Indiana Supreme Court's roll of attorneys, subject to reactivation at a later date. Attorneys who elect inactive status are not required to pay Indiana's annual disciplinary fee; however, they also are not considered in good standing under the state's admission and discipline rules. On the other hand, Utah and Kansas have recently certified Army lawyers as being in good standing even though they are presently in "inactive" status.

UNITED STATES v. STEELE
United States Court of Appeals for the Armed Forces
53 M.J. 274 (C.A.A.F. 2000)

JUDGE EFFRON delivered the opinion of the Court.

I. Background

Appellant was represented at trial by detailed military counsel, Captain T, and by a civilian defense counsel, Mr. C. Detailed defense counsel announced that he was "qualified and certified in accordance with Article 27(b) and sworn in accordance with Article 42(a) of the Uniform Code of Military Justice." Similarly, civilian defense counsel announced, "I am licensed to practice law by the highest courts of the States of Iowa, Hawaii, and Texas; and I am previously qualified and certified and sworn in accordance with Articles 27(b) and 42(a) of the Uniform Code of Military Justice." The military judge then advised appellant of his rights to counsel, and appellant stated that he wished to be represented by Captain T and Mr. C. . . .

Mr. C was a member of the bar in three states, Iowa, Hawaii, and Texas, as he had stated on the record. He was admitted to the bar of Iowa in 1982, but his status was later changed to "retired and inactive." According to a letter from the Board of Professional Ethics and Conduct of the Iowa Supreme Court, "[a] person who has been admitted to practice law in Iowa and has had their license to practice law suspended or is on inactive status, cannot practice law under the authority of the Iowa license outside of Iowa." Mr. C was admitted to bar membership in Hawaii in 1989, but he later entered inactive status. According to Hawaii Supreme Court Rule 17(d)(7), an attorney may "desire to assume inactive status and discontinue the practice of law in Hawaii." The rule notes that an attorney on inactive status "shall no longer be eligible to practice law." Mr. C became a member of the bar of the State of Texas in 1992. Shortly thereafter, at his request, he was placed on inactive status. The result of that action was that civilian counsel was "not authorized to practice as an attorney and counselor at law in the STATE of TEXAS."

II. Qualifications of Counsel

. . . The President has established basic qualifications for civilian counsel in RCM 502, Manual for Courts-Martial, United States (1995 ed.). Civilian counsel representing an accused before a court-martial must be "[a] member of the bar of a Federal court or of the bar of the highest court of a State." R.C.M. 502(d)(3)(A). If that civilian lawyer is "not a member of such a bar," then he or she must be "a lawyer who is authorized by a recognized licensing authority to practice law and is found by the military judge to be qualified to represent the accused upon a showing to the satisfaction of the military judge that the counsel has appropriate training and familiarity with the general principles of criminal law which apply in a court-martial." R.C.M. 502(d)(3)(B). Neither the Code nor the Manual expressly disqualifies a civilian attorney on the grounds that his or her bar status is designated as "inactive."

Federal courts in the civilian sector have dealt with the question of an attorney's bar status vis-à-vis an accused's Sixth Amendment right to counsel. In general, they hold that once an attorney is found competent and admitted to practice law in a licensing jurisdiction, subsequent changes to his or her bar membership status do not render that counsel incompetent or disqualified. "Though admission to practice before a federal court is derivative from membership in a state bar, disbarment by the State does not result in automatic disbarment by the federal court. Though that state action is entitled to respect, it is not conclusively binding on the federal courts." *In re Ruffalo*, 390 U.S. 544, 547 (1968), citing *Theard v. United States*, 354 U.S. 278, 281-82 (1957). . . .

Our Court has addressed the significance of a licensing authority's decision to admit a person to the bar. In *Soriano v. Hosken*, [9 M.J. 221 (C.M.A. 1980)], we noted that civilian counsel must be "qualified" in order to make the right to civilian counsel "meaningful as intended by the Code." 9 M.J. at 221. Civilian counsel must also be "authorized by some recognized licensing authority to engage in the practice of law." [*United States v.*] *Kraskouskas*, 9 U.S.C.M.A. [607, 609, 26 C.M.R. 387, 389 (1958)]. There are no other restrictions on an accused's right to counsel under Article 38(b). Once licensed, "such lawyers are presumed competent for the professional undertaking of the defense of a military accused at a court-martial." *Soriano*, 9 M.J. at 222.

The decisions of our Court and other federal courts reflect that admission to practice is the necessary indicia that a level of competence has been achieved and reviewed by a competent licensing authority. This determination of competence is not necessarily eviscerated when sanctions are imposed by a state bar or by changes in counsel's status where those matters do not demonstrate a negative determination of counsel's competence. As the Ninth Circuit concluded in [*United States v. Mouzin*, 785 F.2d 682 (9th Cir.), *cert. denied sub nom. Carvajal v. United States*, 479 U.S. 985 (1986)]:

Neither suspension nor disbarment invites a per se rule that continued representation in an ongoing trial is constitutionally ineffective.
Admission to the bar allows us to assume that counsel has the training, knowledge, and ability to represent a client who has chosen him.
Continued licensure normally gives a reliable signal to the public that
the licensee is what he purports to be — an attorney qualified to advise
and represent a client. But it is an undeniable fact of experience that
lawyers unhappily incur sanctions ranging from censure to disbarment; that sometimes that discipline flows from revealed incompe-
tence or untrustworthiness or turpitude such as to deserve no client's
confidence. All we need hold here is that a lawyer's services were
ineffective on a case, not a per se, basis.

785 F.2d at 698. . . .

III. Discussion

In light of the foregoing considerations, we hold that Mr. C was not disqualified by virtue of his status as an "inactive" member of the bars of Iowa,
Hawaii, and Texas. Contrary to appellant's assertions in his brief, there is no
evidence that Mr. C was suspended from practicing in any of the states in
which he held bar membership. Rather, Mr. C merely assumed an inactive status in each of those jurisdictions. This status does not reflect adversely upon
his competence; nor does it reflect any change in the determination of his competence to practice law by any of these state bar associations. It follows that
the mere fact that appellant's counsel did not maintain an active status in his
licensing states is not a *per se* disqualifying factor.

We also note that Rule 8-6e, Comment, Department of the Navy JAGINST
5803.1A (Ch. 3, 30 May 1996), states that "an individual may be considered
'inactive' as to the practice of law within a particular jurisdiction and still be
considered 'in good standing[.]'" Under this rule, therefore, inactive status
does not bar military counsel from being certified as competent under Article
27(b)(2) to practice before Navy and Marine Corps courts-martial. We decline
to adopt a more stringent rule for civilian counsel practicing before courts-
martial. Unless an accused can demonstrate that civilian counsel had never
attained any bar membership and could not be certified, we shall not deny or
limit a military accused's right under Article 38 to elect civilian representation
and pick his own civilian counsel. Once counsel is licensed to practice law by
a state or competent licensing authority, we shall presume that civilian counsel are competent to appear as defense counsel at courts-martial. . . .

We agree with the federal cases cited above that once a state licensing
authority has reviewed the qualifications and admitted an attorney to practice, a subsequent change in bar status alone does not necessarily result in a
determination that there has been a denial of the Sixth Amendment right to
counsel. We conclude that appellant's civilian counsel was not disqualified to
practice before courts-martial by virtue of the fact that he was "inactive" in the
three states within which he was licensed.

In any case, in at least one state, Texas, Mr. C's inactive status prohibited
practice of law only within the state. Texas bar membership was adequate,

therefore, to support counsel's appearance before a court-martial regardless of any limitations imposed by Hawaii or Iowa. . . .

Cox, Senior Judge (concurring):

I agree with the resolution of the granted and specified issues. However, I am disquieted by the idea that it is acceptable to allow counsel, military or civilian, to practice before courts-martial when they could not represent civilians in civilian courts. Intuitively, it is my belief that military defendants, as well as their family and friends, operate under the assumption that "JAGs" are lawyers who are duly authorized to practice law in one or more of the sovereign States of this country.

Furthermore, notwithstanding the cases relied upon in the majority opinion which have let convictions stand even though the lawyer was disqualified from active practice, I know of no federal or state judge who would willingly let a disbarred, suspended, or inactive lawyer practice in his or her court. We should accept no less for our military accused.

If I were writing the rules, I would require that counsel (military or civilian) be in an "officially" recognized status which makes clear that they may be appointed to represent parties in a criminal trial or that they may, for a fee from a client, go into a courtroom and represent that client. That status carries with it the simple recognition that the attorney is "legally competent" to represent clients. I would accept nothing less in order to meet the requirements of Article 27, United States Code of Military Justice, 10 U.S.C. § 827. To permit less seems to me to demean the noble profession of the law and to perpetrate a fraud upon the servicemembers, their families, and the public at large.

NOTES AND QUESTIONS

1. Challenges based on the inactive civilian bar status of the lone military defense counsel in a case and the military judge in a case have similarly failed. *United States v. Morris*, 54 M.J. 898, 903 (N-M. Ct. Crim. App. 2001); *United States v. Maher*, 54 M.J. 776 (A.F. Ct. Crim. App. 2001), *aff'd*, 55 M.J. 361 (C.A.A.F. 2001) (summary disposition).

2. An Australian appellate court was critical of the apparently common practice of Australian Defence Force lawyers serving as legal advisors without maintaining "practicing certificates" from their civilian licensing authorities. *Commonwealth of Australia v. Vance* [2005] 158 ACTR 47. The Australian Capital Territory Court of Appeal held that the absence of such a practicing certificate, while not dispositive, was a factor that could be considered in deciding whether the attorney-client privilege should apply to ADF officials' consultations with Defence Legal Officers.

3. Do you agree with Senior Judge Cox that, as a matter of policy, counsel at a court-martial should be authorized to practice law in a civilian jurisdiction? Is an active member of a bar likely to perform differently than an inactive member?

4. In a case in which the military defense counsel had never been a member of a civilian bar, the Navy-Marine Corps Court of Criminal Appeals nevertheless upheld the results at trial, because the accused was also represented by civilian defense counsel. *United States v. Harness*, 44 M.J. 593 (N-M. Ct. Crim. App. 1996). *See also United States v. Jackson*, 54 M.J. 527 (N-M. Ct. Crim. App. 2000) (affirming results at trial where accused was represented by a properly licensed military defense counsel and a civilian defense counsel whose license to practice law had been suspended).

5. The Court of Military Appeals has noted that foreign attorneys who are not members of any U.S. bar have sometimes appeared at courts-martial as civilian defense counsel. *Soriano v. Hosken*, 9 M.J. 221, 222 (C.M.A. 1980). The court held that while a military accused has no right to have a foreign attorney appear on his or her behalf, foreign attorneys who are not members of a U.S. bar are not *per se* precluded from representing the accused at courts-martial. *Id.* The military judge exercises discretion to decide whether such an attorney may appear, evaluating whether the foreign attorney "demonstrate[s] that he possesses a requisite degree of appropriate training or familiarity with the general principles of law in operation at courts-martial in order to undertake the defense of a military accused on trial for a crime." *Id.* Chief Judge Everett suggested that military judges ruling on whether a particular foreign attorney may represent the accused at a court-martial should consider:

> (a) the availability of the foreign attorney at times when court-martial sessions have been scheduled; (b) whether the accused proposes that the foreign civilian attorney appear in conjunction with military counsel; (c) familiarity of the attorney with English as spoken; (d) the practical alternatives for disciplining the attorney in the event of misconduct; (e) whether there would likely be foreign witnesses for the prosecution or the defense with whom the local attorney may be able to communicate more readily than could military defense counsel; and (f) similarity of ethnic or other background between the accused and the civilian attorney which might facilitate communication between the two, so that the accused feels more confident in the quality of the representation he will be receiving.

Id. at 223 (Everett, C.J., concurring). In *Soriano*, the court held that the military judge did not abuse his discretion by prohibiting the accused's father, who was a member of the bar of the Republic of the Philippines, from representing the accused.

II.   REGULATION

Professional Responsibility for Lawyers, *United States Army Regulation 27-26 (1992)*

Every Army lawyer subject to these Rules is also subject to rules promulgated by his or her licensing authority or authorities. In case of a conflict

between these Rules and the rules of the lawyer's licensing authority, the
lawyer should attempt to resolve the conflict with assistance of the lawyer
exercising technical supervision over him or her. If the conflict is not
resolved —

(1) these Rules will govern the conduct of the lawyer in the performance of
the lawyer's official responsibilities;

(2) the rules of the appropriate licensing authority will govern the conduct
of the lawyer in the private practice of law unrelated to the lawyer's official
responsibilities.

Comment

Almost all lawyers (as defined by these Rules) practice outside the territorial limits of the jurisdiction in which they are licensed. While lawyers remain
subject to the governing authority of the jurisdiction in which they are licensed
to practice, they are also subject to these Rules.

When Army lawyers are engaged in the conduct of Army legal functions,
whether servicing the Army as a client or serving an individual client as
authorized by the Army, these Rules are regarded as superseding any conflicting rules applicable in jurisdictions in which the lawyer may be licensed. As
for civilian lawyers practicing in tribunals conducted pursuant to the Manual
for Courts-Martial or the Uniform Code of Military Justice, violation of these
Rules may result in suspension from practice before such tribunals. However,
lawyers practicing in state or federal civilian court proceedings will abide by
the rules adopted by that state or federal civilian court during the proceedings.

Every lawyer subject to these Rules is also subject to rules promulgated by
his or her licensing authority or authorities. This raises the possibility of a
conflict in the governing rules, albeit a conflict likely more theoretical than
practical. If a conflict does arise, the lawyer is advised to attempt to resolve
the conflict with the assistance of the lawyer exercising technical supervision
over him or her. In most cases, the conflict can be resolved by a change of
assignment or withdrawal from the matter that gives rise to it. If such assistance is not effective in resolving the conflict, then the subparagraphs (1) and
(2) of Rule 8.5(f) provide clear guidance.

NOTES AND QUESTIONS

1. "The Army, Air Force, and Navy have each adopted the American Bar
Association Model Rules of Prof'l Conduct R. 1.6. (2003). *See* Dep't of the Army,
Regulation No. 27-26, Rules of Professional Conduct for Lawyers Rule 1.6, at
App. B (May 1, 1992); Dep't of the Navy, JAGINST 5803.1B, Professional
Conduct of Attorneys Practicing Under the Cognizance and Supervision of the
Judge Advocate General Rule 1.6, at encl. B (February 11, 2000); Dep't of the
Air Force, TJAG Policy No. 26, Rules of Professional Conduct Rule 1.6, at
Attachment 1 (February 4, 1998). The Coast Guard has indicated that '[a]s far
as practicable and when not inconsistent with law, the MCM, Coast Guard
Regulations, COMDTINST M5000.3 (series), and [sic] the American Bar
Association Model Rules of Professional Conduct . . . apply to Coast Guard

courts-martial.' Coast Guard Military Justice Manual, COMDTINST M5810.1D Art. 6.C.1 (August 17, 2000)." *United States v. Dorman*, 58 M.J. 295, 298 n.2 (C.A.A.F. 2003). As *Dorman* indicates, the Coast Guard uses a different approach to the rules of professional responsibility compared to the Army, Navy, and Air Force. While the latter three services have adopted their own complete free-standing codes of professional responsibility, the Coast Guard simply adopts the American Bar Association's ethical rules when not inconsistent with military rules. Which approach is better? Do Coast Guard lawyers have sufficient notice of which ABA rules are inapplicable under this standard?

2. Both the Army and Navy JAG Corps first adopted their Rules of Professional Conduct in October 1987. *See generally* Major Bernard P. Ingold, *An Overview and Analysis of the New Rules of Professional Conduct for Army Lawyers*, 124 MIL. L. REV. 1 (1989); Colonel Eileen M. Albertson, *Rules of Professional Conduct for the Naval Judge Advocate*, 35 FED. BAR NEWS & J. 334 (1988). "The Army Rules were drafted by an inter-service committee appointed in 1984 by the service Judge Advocate Generals." Ingold, 124 MIL. L. REV. at 1 n.3. The Air Force rules were first issued in December 1989. "Because they are based on the ABA Model Rules, the Air Force Rules are very similar to the Army's and Navy's. There are differences, however." Colonel Charles R. Myers, USAF, *Rules of Professional Responsibility for Air Force Lawyers*, 37 FED. BAR NEWS & J. 312 (1990). In addition to regulating military lawyers, the Army, Navy, and Air Force rules also govern civilian counsel practicing in courts-martial.

3. The three services with free-standing codes of professional responsibility risk that portions of their rules will become obsolete if they do not consider incorporating changes to any comparable ABA Model Rules. For example, an insightful 2000 *Military Law Review* article noted that all of the armed services' rules of professional conduct suffered from the constitutional defect identified in *Gentile v. State Bar of Nevada*, 501 U.S. 1030 (1991) (holding that a Nevada professional responsibility rule almost identical to ABA Model Rule of Professional Conduct 3.6 was unconstitutionally void for vagueness). While the ABA responded to *Gentile* by amending Model Rule 3.6 in 1994, the military services had not changed their versions of Rule 3.6. "Thus," the article concluded, "all of the armed services' ethics rules governing trial publicity are void for vagueness and may not be enforceable." Lt. Col. Denise R. Lind, *Media Rights of Access to Proceedings, Information, and Participants in Military Criminal Cases,* 163 MIL. L. REV. 1, 77 (2000) (footnotes omitted). Air Force Rule 3.6 has now been revised to correct that constitutional defect. *See* Air Force Rule of Professional Conduct 3.6, TJAG Policy Memorandum: TJAGC Standards — 2, attachment 1 (17 Aug 05). But the Army and Navy versions of Rule 3.6 remain constitutionally defective. *See also* Seth R. Deam, *Current Development 2005-2006: Does Labeling the System "Unfair" Threaten Fairness? Trial Publicity Rules for Defense Attorneys in Military Commissions,* 19 GEO. J. LEGAL ETHICS 663 (2006).

4. The Court of Appeals for the Armed Forces has adopted the ABA's Model Rules of Professional Conduct as the rules of conduct for practice before that court. C.A.A.F. R. 15(a).

5. The services and the Court of Appeals for the Armed Forces have been faulted for failing to agree to a uniform set of professional responsibility rules:

> In 1983, the American Bar Association's Code of Professional Responsibility was superseded by the Model Rules of Professional Conduct. In 1990, the Court [of Military Appeals] modified Rule 15 to recognize this change. In accordance with R.C.M. 109(a), the Model Rules had already been adopted by the Army and Navy in 1987, and by the Air Force in 1989, although the services were unable to agree as to certain provisions. . . . The power of the Judge Advocates General to make rules under R.C.M. 109(a) extends to "professional supervision and discipline of military trial and appellate judges, judge advocates, and other lawyers who practice in proceedings governed by" the UCMJ and Manual for Courts-Martial. The disciplinary reach of such rules, however, is confined to "practices in courts-martial and in the Courts of [Criminal Appeals]. R.C.M. 109(a). Hence, the drafters of R.C.M. 109(a) apparently chose not to intrude on the Court of [Appeals for the Armed Forces'] authority to govern practice before it. . . . The Court and the Judge Advocates General should clearly reach agreement on a single set of professional standards that would govern every lawyer in every phase of the military justice process in each armed force. The fact that this has not been achieved suggests a breakdown in the collegial process contemplated by the congressional provision for a Code Committee under Article 146. . . .

Eugene R. Fidell, Guide to the Rules of Practice and Procedure for the United States Court of Appeals for the Armed Forces 81-82 (12th ed. 2006) (citations omitted).

Air Force Colonel Charles R. Myers, on the other hand, points to potential advantages of separate rules for the various services:

> Whether it is desirable eventually to prescribe rules of professional conduct that are identical to all the armed services is not clear. It is a question of whether such rules are analogous more to rules of criminal procedure like those in the Manual for Court-Martial (where uniformity is desirable to ensure fundamental fairness in maintaining discipline) or to personnel standards for judge advocates (where diversity is desirable to serve the missions and practices unique to the each of the services). Regardless of how that question is answered, however, there are at least two reasons not to prescribe uniform rules at this time. The first is that, despite their differences, the Air Force, Army, and Navy Rules are similar enough to provide a high degree of uniformity. The second is that, in the face of this relative uniformity, the diversity among the services' rules provides an opportunity for each to learn from the others' experiences. For some issues of professional responsibility — such as jurisdiction over non-service lawyers, confidentiality, and the organization as client — there are no easy answers. The successes and failures of one of the services' approach can point out ways for the other services to improve their rules.

Charles R. Myers, *Rules of Professional Responsibility for Air Force Lawyers*, 37 FED. B. NEWS & J. 312 (1989) (footnote omitted). Colonel Myers' argument reflects the fact that, at the time, the Air Force Rules did not apply to civilian counsel practicing in courts-martial while the Army and Navy Rules did. The current version of Air Force Rule 8.5, however, follows the Army and Navy approach by applying the Air Force Rules to civilians "who practice in Air Force courts and other proceedings."

With which perspective on uniformity do you agree, Mr. Fidell's or Colonel Myers'?

6. The Army's Rules of Professional Conduct for Lawyers provide that in cases of conflict between the Army Rules and an Army lawyer's licensing authority's rules, the Army Rules "will govern the conduct of the lawyer in the performance of the lawyer's official responsibilities" while "the rules of the appropriate licensing authority will govern the conduct of the lawyer in the private practice of law unrelated to the lawyer's official responsibilities." Army Reg. 27-10, Rules of Professional Conduct for Lawyers, Rule 8.5(f) (1 May 1992). The Department of the Navy, whose regulations govern both Navy and Marine Corps lawyers, has a similar regulation. *See* JAGINST 5803.1C, Professional Conduct of Attorneys Practicing Under the Cognizance and Supervision of the Judge Advocate General, Rule 8.5 (comment 2) (9 November 2004) ("When covered USG attorneys are engaged in the conduct of Navy or Marine Corps legal functions, whether serving the Navy or Marine Corps as a client or serving an individual client as authorized by the Navy or Marine Corps, these Rules supersede any conflicting rules applicable in jurisdictions in which the covered attorney may be licensed."). The United States Air Force's regulation is somewhat more opaque, providing that the Air Force Rules of Professional Responsibility apply "to all military and civilian lawyers, paralegals and nonlawyer assistants in the Air Force Judge Advocate General's Department." Air Force Rule of Professional Conduct 8.5, TJAG Policy Memorandum: TJAGC Standards — 2, attachment 1 (17 Aug 05). As we have previously seen, Coast Guard judge advocates are directed to follow the American Bar Association Model Rules of Professional Conduct "when not inconsistent with law, the MCM, [and] Coast Guard Regulations." Coast Guard Military Justice Manual, COMDTINST M5810.1D Art. 6.C.1 (August 17, 2000).

7. While the U.S. Army and Navy regulations clearly compel judge advocates performing official duties in those services to obey the military's regulations in cases of conflict with the judge advocate's licensing jurisdiction's rules, a judge advocate who does so may nevertheless be vulnerable to disciplinary action by his or her licensing jurisdiction. One federal court has emphasized that federal civilian attorneys must follow the ethical rules of their licensing jurisdictions:

> [T]he general statutes cited by the DOJ do not authorize it to issue regulations which exempt its attorneys from the requirements of state ethical rules. The Department of Justice Appropriation Authorization Act requires all DOJ attorneys to be licensed to practice as an attorney under the laws of a state, territory, or the District of Columbia. To be licensed to practice, an attorney must comply with the state bar's

ethical standards. Accordingly, the Court concludes that Congress intended federal lawyers to be subject to regulation by the state bars of which they are members, and to comply with the appropriate ethical standards.

United States ex rel. O'Keefe v. McDonnell Douglas Corp., 961 F. Supp. 1288, 1294 (D. Mo.) (internal citations and quotation marks omitted), *aff'd*, 132 F.3d 1252 (8th Cir. 1997). One particularly prominent case presented the issue of whether a federal prosecutor could speak directly with a criminal defendant who was represented by counsel. The prosecutor was a member of the New Mexico bar, whose rules of professional conduct prohibit an attorney's contact with a represented party. A federal court in New Mexico rejected the argument that under the United States Constitution's Supremacy Clause, a federal prosecutor was not subject to professional discipline by a state bar for conduct in the execution of his federal duties. *In re Doe*, 801 F. Supp. 478 (D.N.M. 1992). Federal courts in Washington, D.C., where the federal prosecutor practiced, rejected a challenge to the New Mexico bar's disciplinary proceedings. *United States v. Ferrara*, 847 F. Supp. 966 (D.D.C. 1993), *aff'd*, 54 F.3d 825 (D.C. Cir. 1995). The New Mexico Supreme Court ultimately censured the federal prosecutor. *In the Matter of Howes*, 940 P.2d 159 (N.M. 1997). Should judge advocates be subject to discipline by their licensing jurisdictions for carrying out orders that may offend their state rules of professional conduct?

8. An Oregon State Bar Association informal ethics opinion concluded that Army judge advocates who "follow the Army Rules of Professional Conduct will not be subject to discipline in Oregon, even if the conduct is inconsistent with Oregon ethical standards." *See* Maj. Bernand Ingold, *Professional Responsibility Note: JAG Attorneys Following Military Ethics Rules Will Not be Subject to Discipline for Violating Oregon Rules*, ARMY LAW., Jan. 1990, at 42 (discussing Or. State Bar Ass'n Informal Ethics Opinion 88-19 (1988)).

9. One commentator has recommended amending the UCMJ to provide that military legal professional responsibility standards will preempt any inconsistent state bar standards. C. Peter Dungan, *Avoiding "Catch-22s": Approaches to Resolve Conflicts Between Military and State Bar Rules of Professional Responsibility*, 30 J. LEGAL PROF. 31 (2005/2006).

Army Rules of Professional Conduct for Lawyers

Rule 1.13. Army as Client

(a) Except when representing an individual client . . ., an Army lawyer represents the Department of the Army acting through its authorized officials. . . . When an Army lawyer is assigned to . . . an organizational element and designated to provide legal services to the head of the organization, the lawyer-client relationship exists between the lawyer and the Army as represented by the head of the organization as to matters within the scope of the official business of the organization. The head of the organization may not invoke the lawyer-client privilege or the rule of confidentiality for the head of the organization's own benefit but may invoke either for the benefit of the Army. In so invoking either the lawyer-client privilege or lawyer-client confidentiality on behalf of the Army,

the head of the organization is subject to being overruled by higher authority in the Army. . . .

(c) If a lawyer for the Army knows that an officer, employee, or other member associated with the Army is engaged in action, intends to act or refuses to act in a matter related to the representation that is either a violation of a legal obligation to the Army or a violation of law which reasonably might be imputed to the Army the lawyer shall proceed as is reasonably necessary in the best interest of the Army. In determining how to proceed, the lawyer shall give due consideration to the seriousness of the violation and its consequences, the scope and nature of the lawyer's representation, the responsibility in the Army and the apparent motivation of the person involved, the policies of the Army concerning such matters, and any other relevant considerations. Any measures taken shall be designed to minimize disruption of the Army and the risk of revealing information relating to the representation to persons outside the Army. Such measures may include among others:

> (1) advising the head of the organization that his or her personal legal interests are at risk and that he or she should consult counsel as there may exist a conflict of interest for the lawyer and the lawyer's responsibility is to the organization;

> (2) asking reconsideration of the matter;

> (3) advising that a separate legal opinion on the matter be sought for presentation to appropriate authority in the Army;

> (4) advising the person that the lawyer is ethically obligated to preserve the interests of the Army and, as a result, must consider discussing the matter with supervisory lawyers within the Army lawyer's office or at a higher level within the Army.

> (5) referring the matter to or seeking guidance from higher authority in the technical chain of supervision, including, if warranted by the seriousness of the matter, referral to the Army lawyer assigned to the staff of the acting official's next superior in the chain of command.

(d) If, despite the lawyer's efforts in accordance with paragraph (c), the highest authority that can act concerning the matter insists upon action, or refusal to act, that is clearly a violation of law, the lawyer may terminate representation with respect to the matter in question. In no event shall the lawyer participate or assist in the illegal activity.

(e) In dealing with the Army's officers, employees, or members, a lawyer shall explain the identity of The Army as the client when it is apparent that the Army's interests are adverse to those of the officers, employees, or members. . . .

Rule 5.4. Professional Independence of a Lawyer

(e) Notwithstanding a lawyer's status as a commissioned officer or Department of the Army civilian, a lawyer detailed or assigned to represent an individual soldier or employee of the Army is expected to exercise unfettered loyalty and professional independence during the representation consistent

with these Rules and to the same extent as required by a lawyer in private practice.

(f) The exercise of professional judgment in accordance with *(e)* above will not, standing alone, be a basis for an adverse evaluation or other prejudicial action.

Comment

Judge Advocates

Provisions (e) and (f) of this Rule recognize that judge advocates and Department of the Army civilian attorneys are required by law to obey the lawful orders of superior officers. Nevertheless, the practice of law requires the exercise of judgment solely for the benefit of the client and free of compromising influences and loyalties. Thus, when a judge advocate or other Army Lawyer is assigned to represent an individual client, neither the lawyer's personal interests, the interests of other clients, nor the interests of third persons should affect loyalty to the individual client.

Not all direction given to a subordinate lawyer is an attempt to improperly influence the lawyer's professional judgment. Each situation must be evaluated by the facts and circumstances, giving due consideration to the subordinate's training, experience and skill. A lawyer subjected to outside pressures should make full disclosure of them to the client. If the lawyer or the client believes that the effectiveness of the representation has been or will be impaired thereby, the lawyer should take proper steps to withdraw from representation of the client.

Additionally, the military lawyer has a responsibility to report any instances of unlawful command influence. *See* R.C.M. 104, MCM, 1984.

Rule 1.10. Imputed Disqualification: General Rule

(a) Army lawyers working in the same Army law office are not automatically disqualified from representing a client because any of them practicing alone would be prohibited from doing so by Rules 1.7, 1.8(c), 1.9 or 2.2. . . .

Comment

The circumstances of military service may require representation of opposing sides by Army lawyers working in the same law office. Such representation is permissible so long as conflicts of interest are avoided and independent judgment, zealous representation, and protection of confidences are not compromised. Thus, the principle of imputed disqualification is not automatically controlling for Army lawyers. The knowledge, actions, and conflicts of interest of one lawyer are not to be imputed to another simply because they operate from the same office. For example, the fact that a number of defense attorneys operate from one office and share clerical assistance, would not prohibit them from representing co-accused at trial by court-martial.

Army policy may address imputed disqualification in certain contexts. For example, Army policy discourages representation by one legal assistance office of both spouses involved in a domestic dispute.

Whether a lawyer is disqualified requires a functional analysis of the facts in a specific situation. The analysis should include consideration of whether the following will be compromised: preserving attorney-client confidentiality; maintaining independence of judgment; and avoiding positions adverse to a client.

Preserving confidentiality is a question of access to information. Access to information, in turn, is essentially a question of fact in a particular circumstance, aided by inferences, deductions or working presumptions that reasonably may be made about the way in which lawyers work together. A lawyer may have general access to files of all clients of a military law office and may regularly participate in discussions of their affairs; it may be inferred that such a lawyer in fact is privy to all information about all the office's clients. In contrast, another lawyer may have access to the files of only a limited number of clients and participate in discussion of the affairs of no other clients; in the absence of information to the contrary, it should be inferred that such a lawyer in fact is privy to information about the clients actually served but not to information of other clients. . . .

Maintaining independent judgment allows a lawyer to consider, recommend and carry out any appropriate course of action for a client without regard to the lawyer's personal interests or the interests of another. When such independence is lacking or unlikely, representation cannot be zealous.

Informal Opinion 1235, *American Bar Association Committee on Ethics and Professional Responsibility*
August 24, 1972

[A Coast Guard] legal office is staffed by four military law specialists. These men, who are lawyers, both prosecute and defend nearly all court martial cases convened within the command district. You note that in 1972, of a total of seventeen cases, lawyers from your office participated in the prosecution and defense of all of them. You note that the law specialists are responsible to a superior officer, who is also an attorney.

In addition, you relate that the law specialists all work out of the same office with partitioned desk spaces. All share the same library and clerical help. Copies of all motions and all correspondence are inserted into a "reading file" which, presumably, is circulated among all law specialists as well as the superior officer. You note specifically that this reading file includes matters of a privileged character.

On these facts, you have raised four questions: (1) whether there is a forbidden conflict of interest when "the same office" represents both the defendant and the government in a court martial; (2) whether the appointment of adversary attorneys from the same office contravenes Canon 7 of the [American Bar Association Code of Professional Responsibility, the ABA Model Rules of Professional Conduct's predecessor] in that it does not present the client with "the proper image" of his lawyer as a zealous defender of his rights; (3) whether the office practices detailed above conflict with Canon 4 of the Code which requires that a lawyer preserve the confidences and secrets of his client;

and (4) whether "[in] matters of professional ethics, [there are] grounds to distinguish attorneys in private practice from those who are not."

With regard to question 1, Conflict of Interest, Canon 5 of the Code of Professional Responsibility forbids a lawyer from accepting employment that will or is likely to affect adversely his independent professional judgment in behalf of a client. The Rules state an exception where it is obvious that the lawyer can adequately represent the interests apparently in conflict and where each client consents to the representation after full disclosure. Further, DR 5-105(D) states as follows:

> If a lawyer is required to decline employment or to withdraw from employment under DR 5-105 no partner or associate of his or his firm may accept or continue such employment. . . .

[R]ecently, this Committee approved the appointment of military lawyers by a military commander to represent military personnel in legal matters including court[s]-martial[] :

> There are, of course, many instances in which individuals are unable to bear the expense of employing counsel and in which they are furnished with legal assistance. Defense counsel are assigned by the Court in criminal cases when required, and public defenders are paid by the state in similar cases. Legal Aid and Lawyer Referral services normally assign counsel to those who seek their aid, in the first instance without any compensation and in the second with merely nominal compensation. In all of these instances, however, the individual has the right to be represented by counsel of his own selection would he elect to do so and should he be capable of bearing the expense involved.

> A similar situation would appear to exist in the military forces. It is our understanding that any member of those forces may be represented by individual counsel of his own selection, but at the same time has the right to avail himself of the services of the office of the Judge Advocate General.

> We see nothing in this situation which would transgress the Canons of Professional Ethics.

Informal Decision 567.

In dealing with your inquiry, we again state our understanding that a military "client" has the option to secure nonmilitary counsel of his choosing in lieu of a law specialist appointed to represent him. Also, though the public cannot consent ordinarily to an improper undertaking of private employment by a public prosecutor (*see, e.g.,* Formal Opinion 16), the case of a military law office may be different, as both prosecution and defense attorneys are public employees appointed to their tasks by the government. Thus, given the involuntary character of the employment in either case, and given our assumption that a defendant may secure outside counsel and the fact that both law specialists serve by authority of the state, we do not feel that representation of the government and the defendant by military lawyers from the same office necessarily offends DR 5-105 nor creates an impermissible conflict of interest.

However, we cannot approve the situation you relate without noting several important reservations. First, we note the provision of [Disciplinary Rule (DR)] 5-125(C) which requires, in addition to consent, that it be "obvious that [a lawyer] can represent the interest of each" of multiple clients before such representation may be sanctioned. Also, we note DR 5-105(D), quoted above, which makes it improper for a partner or associate of a lawyer to do that which it is improper for him to do. Of course, there is no partnership or association, strictly speaking, between military lawyers in a military legal office. The economic ties that bind the members of a private law firm are wholly absent. Yet, we feel that more than the prospect of direct or indirect pecuniary gain may deflect the independent professional judgment of a lawyer. Where opposing attorneys work together in close proximity, utilizing identical facilities, numerous influences might weigh against that unswerving fidelity to the client's interest that professional duty compels. We think that, wherever possible, opposing attorneys ought to be afforded separate facilities.

Second, the facts related to us make no mention of the detailing of individual lawyers either to prosecution or defense functions. We feel it is highly desirable that individual lawyers be assigned to performance of one of the other function for the duration of their service within the command, although we recognize that under the circumstances this may not always be practical. Performance of adverse roles in succeeding cases within the same jurisdiction, though the cases themselves may be entirely unrelated, will involve lawyers in potentially awkward situations. Depending on whether a lawyer is cast in a defense or prosecutorial role, he may be required to frame and advocate interpretations of established rules of law or procedure that are, or seem to be, poles apart. He may be required to criticize police actions in one case, then turn about to defend the same or similar actions in a subsequent case where the facts may be, or seem to be, the same. He will deal frequently with the same investigative or police personnel; he may appear before the same law officers. In the course of this, the temptations may be great to mute the force of advocacy, or adjust the handling of cases in subtle but serious ways.

Finally, your mention of the role of a superior officer, also an attorney, to whom the law specialists are responsible, invites attention to DR 5-107(B), which forbids the direction or regulation of professional judgment of a lawyer in the course of rendering legal services by any party, other than the client, who employs him. Since this superior officer is presumably charged with supervision of both prosecuting and defense law specialists, it is, of course, important that such supervision not extend to the exercise of professional judgment on behalf of a client, unless the superior confines such professional supervision to the separate functions of prosecution or defense. Most preferably, to the extent that military organization permits, prosecutors and defense counsel should answer to separate superior officers.

In regard to your inquiry 2, Zealous Representation, we do not believe that the appointment of adversary attorneys from the same office necessarily offends Canon 7, which provides that a lawyer should represent a client zealously within the bounds of law. Your adverting to the "image" which a client might have of his lawyer refers us to Canon 9 of the Code, which provides that a lawyer should avoid even the appearance of professional impropriety. We think that the reservations we noted in response to your first inquiry pertain to conditions that could easily generate the appearance of some impropriety, and that consideration of Canon 9 therefore supports those reservations. Insofar as zealous representation of a client is concerned, without regard to appearances, that responsibility falls squarely on the shoulders of the individual lawyer. If conditions do not favor this, the lawyer must nonetheless press forward in his client's interest, within the bounds of law.

Your question 3, Client Confidences and Secrets, pertains to the propriety of office procedures in light of Canon 4, which requires that a lawyer preserve the confidences and secrets of his client. In relevant part, DR 4-101 states as follows:

> (B) Except when permitted under DR 4-101(C), a lawyer shall not knowingly:
>
> > (1) Reveal a confidence or secret of his client.
> >
> > (2) Use a confidence or secret of his client for the advantage of himself or of a third person, unless the client consents after full disclosure.
>
> (C) A lawyer may reveal:
>
> > (1) Confidences or secrets with the consent of the client or clients affected, but only after full disclosure to them. . . .
>
> (D) A lawyer shall exercise reasonable care to prevent his employees, associates, and others whose services are utilized by him from disclosing or using confidences or secrets of a client, except that a lawyer may reveal the information allowed by DR 4-101(C) through an employee.

In our opinion, the office procedures you relate do not satisfy the requirements imposed by Canon 4 for protection of a client's confidences and secrets. If we correctly interpret your reference to an office "reading file" to indicate that this file is circulated among all law specialists, including adversary lawyers as well as the supervising attorney, then not only would it be improper to include therein matters that are privileged, but also a client's "secrets," or as defined in DR 4-101(A) "other information gained in the professional relationship that the client has requested be held inviolate or the disclosure of which would be embarrassing or would be likely to be detrimental to the client." A lawyer's responsibility extends beyond protection of the evidentiary privilege. Moreover, responsibility for determining what information might prove detrimental to the client's interest, if divulged, reposes in the lawyer, who must advise his client to this effect. Even then, if the client does not consent, disclosure cannot be made.

Aside from the reading file, use of common library and clerical facilities may impose a burden on individual lawyers, who must employ reasonable care to assure that disclosures are not made where the client has not consented thereto. Access to prosecution and defense files should be subject to strict controls. But where circumstances do not admit to these adjustments, the individual lawyer's responsibility under Canon 4 remains intact. He must adjust, as well as he can, without prejudice to his client.

... [W]hile the maintenance of a separate military justice system in our society may create novel and different circumstances within which the lawyer serves his client, we trust our responses to your specific inquiries make it clear that the lawyer's duty to observe the ethics of his profession remains intact. Certainly, combat situations may demand great flexibility. Yet, even then, adjustments wherever possible must be at the lawyer's expense and not his client's. No general distinction may be drawn which would permit practices otherwise frowned upon in the private context as acceptable in the military.

NOTES

1. One highly-regarded Army lawyer observed that this same analysis should govern cases of imputed disqualification within a defense offense, explaining:

> The significance of this problem is not limited to the matter of a single judge advocate office furnishing counsel for opposing sides. As to the Army, the recent establishment of the Trial Defense Service may have mooted that question in criminal matters. But the same considerations apply to the situation arising when a single Trial Defense Service office must furnish counsel for each of two or more accuseds whose defenses may be antagonistic. In my view, the practice is permissible under the same analysis.

Colonel William S. Fulton, Jr., *ABA Informal Opinion 1474 and the Proposed Rules of Professional Conduct: Some Ethical Aspects of Military Law Practice*, ARMY LAW., March 1982 at 1, 5.

2. The military is not alone in rejecting a *per se* imputed disqualification rule barring a single public defender's office from representing multiple defendants in related cases. In fact, courts have split on this issue. Many have adopted a functional, rather than *per se*, test for imputed disqualification. Under this approach, one public defender's office may be permitted to represent multiple co-conspirators with adverse interests. *See Asch v. State*, 62 P.3d 945, 952-53 (Wyo. 2003); *State v. Lentz*, 639 N.E.2d 784 (Ohio 1994); *State v. Pitt*, 884 P.2d 1150, 1156 (Haw. Ct. App. 1994); *Graves v. State*, 619 A.2d 123 (Md. Ct. Spec. App. 1993); *People v. Daniels*, 802 P.2d 906, 915 (Cal. 1991); *State v. Bell*, 447 A.2d 525, 528 (N.J. 1982); *People v. Miller*, 404 N.E.2d 199, 202 (Ill. 1980); *People v. Wilkins*, 268 N.E.2d 756 (N.Y. 1971); *see also Morales v. Bridgforth*, 136 N.M. 511, 512-14 (N.M. 2004). At least one state ethics opinion has also opined that "it is inappropriate to apply the per se conflict rule to public defender offices" that would apply to private law firms. *Ethics Opinion 960924: Is Office Sharing Arrangement an Ethical No-No?*, MONT. LAW., Dec. 1996 at 9. On the other hand, a number of other courts have applied the same *per se* imputed disqualification rule to public defenders' offices that applies to private law firms. *See, e.g., State v. Watson*, 620 N.W.2d 233, 241 (Iowa 2000); *Ward v. State*, 753 So. 2d 705, 708 (Fla. App. 2000); *Jackson v. State*, 495 S.E.2d 768, 773 (S.C. 1998); *Perkins v. State*, 487 S.E.2d 365, 368 (Ga. App. 1997); *Okeani v. Arizona*, 871 P.2d 727 (Ariz. App. 1994); *Williams v. Warden*, 586 A.2d 582 (Conn. 1991); *McCall v. District Court for Twenty-First Judicial*

Dist., 783 P.2d 1223, 1227 (Colo. 1989) (en banc); *State v. Hatfield*, 754 P.2d 126 (Wash. App. 1988); *State v. Smith*, 621 P.2d 697 (Utah 1980); *Hill v. State*, 566 S.W.2d 127 (Ark. 1978) (per curiam); *Commonwealth v. Via*, 316 A.2d 895 (Pa. 1974); *see also Selsor v. Kaiser*, 81 F.3d 1492, 1493-94 (10th Cir. 1996); *Espinoza v. Rogers*, 470 F.2d 1174, 1175 (10th Cir. 1972). While the authorities are split, these cases demonstrate that the military is not outside the mainstream in rejecting a *per se* imputed disqualification rule for appointed defense counsel who work in the same office.

UNITED STATES v. CAIN
United States Court of Appeals for the Armed Forces
59 M.J. 285 (C.A.A.F. 2004)

JUDGE EFFRON delivered the opinion of the Court.

I. Background

A. Court-Martial Proceedings

1. *Assignment of defense counsel to represent Appellant*

[A]ppellant was charged with three specifications of forcible sodomy under Article 125, UCMJ, 10 U.S.C. § 925 (2000). . . . Major S, the senior defense counsel at Fort Bragg[,] . . .assigned himself to represent Appellant during the Article 32 proceedings. The Article 32 proceedings and subsequent review by the chain of command resulted in referral of the charges . . . for trial by a general court-martial.

[A]ppellant was assigned temporarily to Fort Bragg for the duration of the trial. During pretrial sessions . . ., Appellant agreed to be represented at trial by Major S, adding that he was pursuing the possibility of representation by civilian counsel. He expressed concern with the large caseload facing defense counsel at Fort Bragg and the impact that it might have on his representation. He requested assignment of an additional counsel to assist Major S, noting that the prosecution already had two attorneys assigned to the case. In February, Major S detailed Captain L as assistant defense counsel and informed the military judge that Appellant would not be represented by civilian defense counsel. . . .

[T]he defense entered into negotiations with the Government, which resulted in a pretrial agreement. Appellant agreed to plead guilty to two specifications of indecent assault in lieu of two of the forcible sodomy specifications. The convening authority agreed to direct the trial counsel to dismiss the remaining forcible sodomy specification and to disapprove any sentence greater than a dishonorable discharge, 24 months' confinement, forfeiture of all pay and allowances, and reduction to Private E-1.

At a court-martial session on June 2, Appellant entered pleas consistent with the pretrial agreement. The military judge conducted a detailed inquiry into the providence of Appellant's pleas. After concluding that the pleas were provident, the military judge entered findings consistent with those pleas, and sentenced him to a dishonorable discharge, confinement for five years, forfeiture of all pay and allowances, and reduction to Private E-1.

B. Post-Trial Developments

1. *Defense counsel's suicide*

Two weeks after trial, a senior officer in the Army Trial Defense Service (TDS) visited Fort Bragg to investigate a professional conduct complaint that had been lodged against Major S. The complaint involved a matter distinct from his representation of Appellant. Major S, who was on leave in Chicago with his wife and son in preparation for an expected reassignment to Germany, returned to Fort Bragg alone to address the allegations. His reassignment had been tentatively placed on hold pending the results of the investigation.

Prior to meeting with Major S, the senior TDS officer visited the Staff Judge Advocate (SJA) of the XVIII Airborne Corps. The SJA showed the senior TDS officer a letter that had been sent to the convening authority by Appellant's parents. The letter, dated four days after the conclusion of trial, alleged that Major S had pressured the Appellant for sexual favors. . . . [T]he senior TDS officer informed Major S of the allegations made by Appellant's parents. Major S, who was upset, denied the allegations. He expressed concern that a long delay could cause the cancellation of his reassignment to Germany, but he appeared to be resigned to the fact that the matter could not be resolved on the spot by the senior TDS officer.

Early the next morning, Major S took his own life. In a package of materials prepared for his personal attorney, Major S left a tape recording made shortly before his death. Although the recording did not provide detailed information about his relationship with Appellant or his conduct as lead defense counsel, it contained the following statements:

> I fully deny that I ever forcibly had sex with [Appellant]. . . .

> My suicide is not an admission of guilt. . . .

> I want you to know that my death is not an admission of any of the charges against me . . . .

> Concerning [Appellant's] parents' allegation, that I forced their son to have sex with me, the allegation is preposterous. . . .

3. *The order for an evidentiary hearing*

[A]ppellant . . . challenge[d] the representation he had received at trial. . . . [T]he Army Court of Criminal Appeals ordered an evidentiary hearing pursuant to *United States v. DuBay*, 17 C.M.A. 147, 37 C.M.R. 411 (1967). . . .

C. The Personal and Professional Relationship Between
Major S and Appellant

1. *The sexual relationship*

Before he assigned himself to represent Appellant, Major S was aware of Appellant's homosexuality. According to Appellant, Major S had assisted him on another matter six years earlier. The assistant defense counsel at trial, Captain L, testified at the *DuBay* hearing that it was not unusual for Major S to involve himself in a case of this type because Major S was very interested in cases involving sexual misconduct or sex of any kind.

Major S initiated a sexual relationship with Appellant at the very outset of their attorney-client relationship in the present case. In the fall of 1998, Appellant traveled to Fort Bragg for their initial meeting. On the evening that Appellant arrived at Fort Bragg, Major S made sexual advances, which Appellant regarded as unwelcome and inappropriate. In December, when Major S came to Fort Devens for Appellant's Article 32 hearing, he made further sexual advances, which led to acts of oral and anal sodomy between Major S and Appellant.

Subsequent to referral of charges for trial by general court-martial, Appellant learned that he was being transferred temporarily to Fort Bragg in January 1998 at the behest of Major S. While at Fort Bragg, Appellant worked as an enlisted clerk-typist at the [Trial Defense Service] office under the supervision of Major S. He worked on the cases of other service members, as well as on his own, and also provided assistance to the ROTC program office.

In addition to his official duties, Appellant performed errands for Major S and frequently drove him to and from his home. On more than one occasion, they engaged in sexual activity during these drives. Another sexual encounter occurred in the TDS office. Although the military judge presiding at the *DuBay* hearing expressed skepticism as to some of Appellant's testimony, he nonetheless concluded that Major S engaged in six or seven acts of sodomy with Appellant during the period in which he served as counsel in the present case.

Major S did not manifest his homosexual activity to his colleagues. . . .

2. *The professional relationship*

. . . The information developed in the *DuBay* proceeding . . . indicates that Appellant had significant misgivings about Major S throughout the court-martial process. Early in December 1997, Appellant contacted Mr. C, who worked on the staff of an organization providing assistance to service members affected by military policies related to homosexuality. Because the organization did not directly represent persons before courts-martial, Mr. C referred Appellant to a civilian lawyer, Attorney W. Mr. C also contacted Attorney W directly and advised her that Appellant appeared to be "distraught about the nature of his relationship" with Major S. Mr. C also told Attorney W that when he suggested to Appellant that he report his concerns about Major S to the appropriate authorities, Appellant "expressed great fear of potential consequences should he expose Major [S's] misconduct."

Appellant contacted Attorney W per Mr. C's recommendation. Attorney W did not discuss the underlying court-martial charges with Appellant, confining the conversation to "the problem in his relationship with defense counsel, Major [S]." According to Attorney W, Appellant "was extremely tentative in tone, his voice quavered, and he rambled. He described himself as frightened and depressed."

Appellant told Attorney W that Major S had a reputation as "an extremely talented defense attorney." Appellant "believed that no one but Major [S] could help him be exonerated by the court." Appellant added that Major S had told him that he "would receive a very long prison sentence if he, Major [S], were not his defense counsel."

According to Attorney W, Appellant was torn by conflicting emotions. On the one hand, the sexual relationship initiated by Major S, who was married and had a son, "caused him a great deal of distress, anxiety, and fear." On the other hand, "he was fearful of discontinuing the sexual relationship or reporting it because of his entrenched belief that he would spend a lengthy time in prison without Major [S] as his defense attorney."

Attorney W informed Appellant that Major S's actions were "unethical and illegal" and that the sexual contact "was potentially criminal under Articles 125 or 134 . . . , whether related to sodomy or indecent acts." She expressed concern "that this improper relationship could impair [Major S's] objectivity with regard to his representation" of Appellant.

Appellant "continued to plead that he believed that he would be unable to 'survive' this court without the assistance of Major [S] and that he would simply find himself with inferior counsel were he to report Major [S]." Attorney W attempted to convince Appellant that he should seek new counsel, even if he did not report the misconduct of Major S to the authorities, but Appellant declined this advice. Appellant "reiterat[ed] his complete trust and dependence on [Major S's] legal skills, [and] he informed [Attorney W] that he did not believe he could take the risk of abandoning his [defense] counsel." According to Attorney W, "[i]t was apparent to me from my own experience as counsel and my conversation with him that he was incapable of rejecting [Major S's] professional services or his inappropriate advances because of the deep need of [Appellant] to believe his defense counsel could 'save' him."

Subsequent to his contact with Attorney W in December, Appellant expressed concern about his representation during the initial pretrial sessions of his court-martial. At the first pretrial session on January 15 — well after Major S initiated sexual activity with Appellant — the military judge provided Appellant with the standard advice as to his counsel rights, and inquired as to who would represent him. Appellant responded:

> I would like to retain Major [S]; but, due to the serious[ness] of the charges, I also — I am new to the area, like I said. I just — I just got here basically — here this morning; and, if I had the means — that I'd also like to pursue a civilian counsel and have that right to look for that civilian counsel. Like I said, I am not from here. I am not familiar with the area or the legal people who are out there. So, I would like to retain, at the time being, Major [S], but I want the election to seek out legal, civilian counsel. . . .

[Civilian Attorney] T met with Appellant on the evening of January 21 to discuss representation of Appellant at his court-martial. After obtaining assurances from Attorney T that any discussions preliminary to forming such an attorney-client relationship would be confidential, Appellant told the attorney that Major S had initiated a homosexual relationship with him shortly after Major S became his defense counsel. Attorney T told Appellant that the relationship was unethical, and that he would insist that the relationship cease if he became Appellant's counsel. Appellant responded that Major S was working hard and doing well with the case, and that although Major S was not his "type," the homosexual relationship had not become so burdensome that Appellant felt the need to terminate it.

Attorney T raised the possibility of disclosing the details of the illegal relationship to military officials with a view towards obtaining a dismissal of the case. Appellant responded that he did not want to anger Major S or affect his career, and emphasized the confidential nature of the information.

During further discussions the next day, Attorney T reiterated his view that the actions of Major S were unethical. He added that he could take the case only if Major S was removed from the defense team. According to the attorney, Appellant was anxious to ensure that he not tell anyone, including Major S, that Appellant had divulged the homosexual nature of the relationship. Attorney T maintained the confidence of their preliminary discussions, and did not represent Appellant at his court-martial. . . .

In May of 1998, Captain L told Major S and Appellant that he viewed the prosecution as having a strong case, and he recommended that the defense initiate discussions with a view towards obtaining a pretrial agreement. Major S by then had alienated the prosecution to the point that he was not in a position to conduct such negotiations, so he delegated the task to Captain L. After a week of negotiations, the parties reached an agreement, and Appellant entered his guilty pleas to two specifications of indecent assault. . . .

II. Discussion

A. Potential Criminal and Administrative Actions Resulting from the Conduct Between the Attorney and His Client

Major S, the attorney, engaged in a course of conduct with Appellant, his client, which exposed both of them to the possibility of prosecution, conviction, and substantial confinement for the military crimes of fraternization and sodomy. . . .

Fraternization and sodomy are not minor or obscure matters. The policies of the armed forces on both fraternization and homosexuality have been the subject of significant litigation and public controversy in recent years. . . . Less than five years before Appellant's trial — while both Major S and Appellant were members of the Army — the executive and legislative branches of government engaged in a highly publicized review of the policies pertaining to homosexuality in the armed forces. . . . This debate culminated in the passage of legislation, signed into law by the President, which declares that "[t]he presence in the armed forces of persons who demonstrate a propensity or intent to engage in homosexual acts would create an unacceptable risk to the high standards of morale, good order and discipline, and unit cohesion that are the essence of military capability." 10 U.S.C. § 654(a)(15). The legislation mandates discharge of any service member who has engaged in a homosexual act, subject to narrowly drawn exceptions. *Id.* at § 654(b). As a result, even if not prosecuted for sodomy in a court-martial, the conduct initiated by Major S exposed him and Appellant to administrative proceedings that could have resulted in involuntary termination for homosexuality. Moreover, Major S would have faced the possibility of a discharge for soliciting and committing homosexual acts "with a subordinate in circumstances that violate customary military superior-subordinate relationship." Dep't of the Army Regulation (AR) 600-8-24, Officer Transfers and Discharges (Feb. 3, 2003) para. 4-22h(3) (current version substantively identical to the version in effect at trial).

B. Ethical Considerations

In addition to potential criminal or administrative action for misconduct as an Army officer, Major S engaged in conduct that subjected him to the possibility of additional disciplinary action for violation of the ethical rules applicable to attorneys in the Army. Rule 1.7(b) of the Army Rules of Professional Conduct for Lawyers prohibits representational conflicts of interest, specifying that "[a] lawyer shall not represent a client if the representation of that client may be materially limited . . . by the lawyer's own interests. . . ." AR 27-26, Army Rules of Professional Conduct, Appendix B (May 1, 1992). Rule 1.2(d) states that "[a] lawyer shall not counsel a client to engage, or assist a client, in conduct that the lawyer knows is criminal or fraudulent." *Id.*

With respect to sexual activity between attorneys and clients, civilian jurisdictions have taken a variety of positions on whether there should be a complete prohibition during an ongoing attorney-client relationship, or whether sexual activity should be prohibited only in specified circumstances. *See, e.g.,* Abed Awad, *Attorney-Client Sexual Relations*, 22 J. Legal Prof. 131 (1998). The Army has endorsed the views of the American Bar Association Standing Committee on Ethics and Professional Responsibility, as expressed in Formal Opinion 92-364 (1992) [hereinafter ABA Formal Op. 92-364]. *See* Army Office of the Judge Advocate General Standards of Conduct Office, *Professional Responsibility Notes*, 1993 Army Law. 48 (August 1993) (quoting ABA Formal Op. 92-364 in full). The ABA opinion observed that sexual relations between an attorney and client —

> may involve unfair exploitation of the lawyer's fiduciary position and presents a significant danger that the lawyer's ability to represent the client adequately may be impaired. . . . The roles of lover and lawyer are potentially conflicting ones as the emotional involvement that is fostered by a sexual relationship has the potential to undercut the objective detachment that is often demanded for adequate representation.

Id. at 49. The ABA opinion also observed that

> the client may not feel free to rebuff unwanted sexual advances because of fear that such a rejection will either reduce the lawyer's ardor for the client's cause or, worse yet, require finding a new lawyer, causing the client to lose the time and money that has already been invested in the present representation and possibly damaging the client's legal position.

Id. at 51. *See Colorado v. Good*, 893 P.2d 101, 104 (Colo. 1995) (quoting ABA Formal Op. 92-364); *see also* Restatement (Third) of Law Governing Lawyers, § 16, Comment e (2000) ("A lawyer may not . . . enter a sexual relationship with a client when that would undermine the client's case, abuse the client's dependence on the lawyer, or create risk to the lawyer's independent judgment. . . .").

C. The Impact of Criminal Conduct and Ethical Violations on the Constitutional Right to Effective Assistance of Counsel

Members of the armed forces facing criminal charges, like their civilian counterparts, have a constitutional right to effective assistance of counsel. U.S. Const. amend VI. . . . An attorney's violation of the canons of legal ethics does not necessarily render the attorney's assistance ineffective. *Nix v. Whiteside*, 475 U.S. 157, 165 (1986). In some circumstances, the "high probability of prejudice" and the "difficulty of proving that prejudice" require the application of a rule that the conduct is inherently prejudicial. *See Mickens v. Taylor*, 535 U.S. 162, 175-76 (2002) (citing *Cuyler v. Sullivan*, 446 U.S. 335, 348-49 (1980); *Holloway v. Arkansas*, 435 U.S. 475, 490-91 (1978) (cases involving multiple concurrent representation)). The Court emphasized in *Mickens*, however, that "[n]ot all attorney conflicts present comparable difficulties," and that most cases will require specifically tailored analyses in which the appellant must demonstrate both the deficiency and prejudice under the standards set by *Strickland*. 535 U.S. at 175-76. . . .

In *United States v. Babbitt*, 26 M.J. 157 (C.M.A. 1988), our Court considered the impact on the effective assistance of counsel in a case where a male civilian defense attorney engaged in a consensual sexual act with his female military client during the evening before the final day of her trial. In those circumstances, our Court declined to hold that every sexual relationship between an attorney and client necessarily creates a conflict of interest that violates a client's Sixth Amendment right to the effective assistance of counsel. *Id.* at 158-59.

D. The Combination of Potential Criminal Liability and Ethical Misconduct

The appeal before us presents a case of first impression, with no direct counterpart in civilian law. The case involves a volatile mixture of sex and crime in the context of the military's treatment of fraternization and sodomy as criminal offenses.

Defense counsel's conduct with his client placed both the attorney and client at the risk of criminal prosecution for violating the very article of the UCMJ, Article 125, that was the subject of the present case. Well before the onset of trial, Major S repeatedly placed himself at risk of severe personal and professional consequences, including the possibility of confinement by court-martial, administrative termination of his military career, and professional discipline. The extraordinary pressure under which he labored during his representation of Appellant is underscored tragically by the fact that he took his own life less than a day after he was informed that his superiors had learned of his personal relationship with Appellant.

Because of counsel's suicide, we do not have the benefit of any testimony that he might have provided as to what consideration he gave potential defense strategies in this case. In the absence of such testimony, we consider the case from the perspective of a military defense counsel caught between the conflicting pressures generated by his own sexual misconduct and his professional responsibilities. By his actions, counsel placed himself and his client in a position where testimony by the client entailed significant risks. Any exploration into Appellant's conduct would have raised the possibility that the prosecution would have endeavored through cross-examination or rebuttal to elicit evidence of similar sexual misconduct. This would have created the potential for exposing counsel's sexual misconduct with Appellant.

In those circumstances, defense counsel faced a conflict between his personal interests and his responsibility to give thoughtful, dispassionate consideration and advice concerning the range of options facing the defense. We do not know whether the defense counsel in this case rejected any specific option on the grounds that it was not in his client's best interest, or because it was not in his own best interest. We do know that when confronted about the sexual misconduct with his client, it was only a matter of hours before he took his own life.

The uniquely proscribed relationship before us was inherently prejudicial and created a per se conflict of interest in counsel's representation of the Appellant. The facts of this case are distinguishable from the limited, consensual relationship between a civilian counsel and his client that we considered in *Babbitt*, where we declined to find such a per se conflict. 26 M.J. at 158-59. Here, we confront a course of conduct involving an attorney's abuse of a military office, a violation of the duty of loyalty, fraternization, and repeated commission of the same criminal offense for which the attorney's client was on trial. All of this is left unexplained due to the attorney's untimely death. As stated by the Second Circuit in *Cancilla*, the conflict created by this conduct was "real, not simply possible" and "so threatening as to justify a presumption that the adequacy of representation was affected." [*United States v. Cancilla*, 725 F.2d 867, 870 (2d Cir. 1984)].

The problems flowing from the conduct of Major S are not overcome in this case by actions of the assistant defense counsel, Captain L, who negotiated the pretrial agreement. Major S was the experienced, lead counsel in the case. Appellant relied on Major S and was entitled to the benefit of conflict-free advice from Major S about the range of alternatives before him. He did not receive that advice.

With respect to waiver, we note that the court below relied on Appellant's discussions with two civilian lawyers, Attorney W and Attorney T, in concluding that he waived any objection to Major S as his counsel. Both attorneys advised him to sever the relationship because the behavior of Major S was unethical. Neither attorney, however, provided him with a detailed explanation of the relationship between the merits of the case and the attorney's ethical obligations. Both focused on the matter from the attorney's perspective, not the client's perspective. Attorney W declined to discuss the substance of the charges with Appellant, and Attorney T focused primarily on the fact that he would not take the case if Major S remained on it. We do not fault either attorney for not engaging in a detailed discussion with Appellant of the impact of any unethical behavior by Appellant on the merits of his case. In both cases, the discussions between the apparently distraught Appellant and the cautious lawyers simply did not advance to the point of forming an attorney-client relationship with respect to the charged offenses. Appellant's conversations with the two civilian attorneys in this case did not involve the type of informed discussion of the specific pitfalls of retaining Major S that would demonstrate a knowing, intelligent waiver of the right to effective assistance of counsel. . . .

Decision

. . . The findings of guilty and sentence are set aside. . . . A rehearing may be ordered.

CRAWFORD, CHIEF JUDGE (dissenting):

I respectfully dissent from the majority's creation of a per se rule of ineffectiveness that is contrary to Supreme Court precedent. *Mickens v Taylor*, 535 U.S. 162, 172-73 (2002) (noting that because there is no rule of per se ineffectiveness, an appellant must demonstrate that "conflict significantly affected counsel's performance"). . . . This Court is, and should be, deeply concerned about an accused's right to effective assistance of counsel and a fair trial. Nevertheless, to determine whether counsel has rendered ineffective assistance to an accused, we are bound by our own and Supreme Court precedent. This precedent dictates that ineffective assistance requires *both* deficient performance *and* prejudice. Because Appellant has demonstrated no prejudice in this case, I respectfully dissent from the lead opinion. . . .

The type of conflict presented in this case is not unique to the military. In fact, there have been many federal cases addressing ineffectiveness where the client and attorney were allegedly involved in a related criminal endeavor. *See, e.g., United States v. Cancilla*, 725 F.2d 867 (2d Cir. 1984) (attorney participated with client's coconspirators in crime similar to client's); *United States v. Briguglio*, 675 F.2d 81 (3d Cir. 1982) (attorney under investigation by United States Attorney's Office prosecuting client). To assess ineffectiveness in these cases, the courts have rejected a per se rule and, instead, have examined the record to determine if there was prejudice. Unlike the instant case, in none of the federal cases was there the mitigating presence of an independent counsel, or a guilty plea tested through the extensive providence inquiry required in military practice.

Appellant in the case at bar has failed to demonstrate *any* prejudice. Despite his admission of guilt to the charge of indecent assault, Appellant availed himself of a pretrial agreement which reduced the charges and limited the duration of the adjudged confinement. Indeed, Major S's representation successfully gave Appellant the benefit of his bargain and, as the lower court noted, "it is difficult to imagine what more [the defense] could have done on [Appellant's] behalf to produce a more favorable result." *United States v. Cain*, 57 M.J. 733, 739 (A.C.C.A. 2002). In addition, the pretrial agreement which dictated the outcome of the case was negotiated by Captain L, who was unaffected by Appellant's relationship with Major S. The mitigating presence of an independent third party counsel who reviewed and endorsed the vehicle which secured Appellant's fate at trial renders prejudice simply untenable. In sum, given the absence of any prejudice in this case, there simply cannot have been ineffective assistance. . . .

Finally, even if Appellant had suffered prejudice, he affirmatively waived his right to conflict-free representation when he freely and deliberately entered into a relationship with his defense counsel. *See United States v. Mezzanatto*, 513 U.S. 196, 201 (1995) (establishing that an appellant may waive many of the most fundamental constitutional rights). "The determination of whether there has been an intelligent waiver . . . [depends] upon the particular facts and circumstances surrounding that case, including the background, experience, and conduct of the accused." *Johnson v. Zerbst*, 304 U.S. 458, 464 (1938). The lower court made extensive findings of fact regarding the consensual, informed, and deliberate nature of Appellant's relationship with Major S:

- Appellant was 33-years-old, a sergeant with more than 12 years of service, with a GT score of 112 and a two-year associate's degree.

- Appellant told several people that he continued the relationship only because *he* wanted defense counsel to continue to represent him. Appellant considered defense counsel to be an "excellent, dynamic, and aggressive" attorney, and believed that because counsel was gay, like Appellant, counsel would fight even harder on Appellant's behalf. Appellant believed Major S was the best military defense counsel available.

- Appellant never told defense counsel that he had any reservations about their relationship. Appellant testified at the [post-trial evidentiary hearing], "[N]ot once did I protest what he was doing to me or what he had me do to him."

Cain, 57 M.J. at 735. There was no doubt that Appellant *wanted* Major S to defend him, and did what he felt was necessary to secure Major S's "excellent, dynamic, and aggressive" representation. *Id.* Indeed, "Appellant knew what he was doing when he made his choice." *Id.* at 739. In short, through his calculated involvement with his defense counsel, Appellant waived his right to conflict-free representation.

NOTES

1. Professor William H. Simon of Columbia Law School endorsed the majority's resolution of the issue:

A recent American Bar Association ethics standard holds that lawyer-client sex is always improper unless the sexual relation began before the professional one, and in this instance it did not. The issue before the court here was not professional discipline, however. It was whether the client's guilty plea should be reopened. The soldier had to show that the lawyer's concededly improper conduct prejudiced his case.

As the panel reasoned, the lawyer had a conflict of interest that was likely to have biased his advice to the client. The lawyer was a military officer. He would have been professionally ruined if anyone discovered the relationship, which was both homosexual and adulterous on his part. His client's defense to the prosecution was that the incidents from which the charges arose were consensual. If the client had gone to trial and testified, the prosecution might well have sought to cross-examine him on his sexual relationships — and the defendant might have had to disclose his involvement with his lawyer.

The counterview is that consensual sex would not have been relevant in a rape trial. But as we learned from Paula Jones's suit against President Bill Clinton and the ensuing impeachment, when it comes to nonmarital sex, courts are often sympathetic to strained theories of relevance.

A rape defendant who alleges consent should be able to consider going to trial. Defense counsel had a strong conflict of interest in advising about that option. The consequences of the plea bargain were borne entirely by the defendant, but the trial threatened disaster for the lawyer. It is too much to expect the lawyer to give objective advice in this situation.

William H. Simon, *The Prudent Jurist*, LEGAL AFFAIRS, July/August 2004.

2. Major Robert Wm. Best of The Judge Advocate General's Legal Center and School (U.S. Army), on the other hand, was critical of the majority's decision. He reasoned that the majority's *per se* analysis for evaluating the ineffective assistance of counsel claim was unsupported by case law:

> This case created a new *per se* category of conflict on a very thin reed. With respect to the sexual nature of the conflict, the majority did cite a case with somewhat similar facts, *United States v. Babbit*[, 26 M.J. 157 (C.M.A. 1988),] and sought to distinguish it from the case at bar. The *Babbit* court refused to adopt a *per se* conflict rule in the context of a civilian attorney having a sexual relationship with his military client. Clearly distinguishable from *Babbit*, *Cain* did involve a commissioned officer who abused his military office, violated his duty of loyalty, fraternized, and committed a "same criminal offense" for which the appellant was on trial. The *Babbit* court's opinion, however, was not limited to its facts and the *Cain* majority's attempt to limit *Babbit* is unpersuasive. Also of some importance is that although there are no cases directly like this case, as observed by the majority, similar cases have required a showing of prejudice.

> What is more, even in the federal cases cited by Chief Judge Crawford's dissenting opinion, there was not "the mitigating presence of an independent counsel, or a guilty plea tested through the extensive providence inquiry required in military practice." [59 M.J. at 297 (Crawford, C.J., dissenting).] Importantly, CPT L did not labor under the conflict, and he *endorsed* the pretrial agreement — indeed he negotiated it. The CAAF majority did not fully explain how an unconflicted counsel's advice would not cure any conflict. Rather, they gave the dismissive comment that "[a]ppellant relied on Major S and was entitled to the benefit of conflict-free advice from Major S about the range of alternatives before him. He did not receive that advice." Also unexplained in the CAAF opinion is why the majority did not analyze the

performance under the "team concept," which the court recently reaffirmed. Is the CAAF saying that because one counsel was conflicted, the entire team was conflicted? If so, the majority cited no cases in support of that proposition. If the CAAF was not saying that, the majority should have looked at the defense team rather than looking only at MAJ S to reach its result.

Major Robert Wm. Best, *2003 Developments in the Sixth Amendment: Black Cats on Strolls*, ARMY LAW., July 2004, at 55, 71.

3. Despite the disagreement over whether the defense counsel's conduct should have led to the court-martial's outcome being reversed, no one seems to disagree with the proposition that Major S's actions were unethical.

4. Conflict issues sometimes arise from a lawyer's former government employment. For example, in *United States v. Nguyen*, 56 M.J. 252 (C.A.A.F. 2001), the Court of Appeals for the Armed Forces considered "an issue as to legality of a civilian counsel representing appellant during post-trial proceedings after said counsel represented appellant during the trial proceedings while serving as an active duty officer of the United States Armed Forces." The Judge Advocate General of the Navy had advised civilian counsel that continued representation would violate 18 U.S.C. § 207, the federal government's "revolving door statute," which places limitations on post-government employment. *Id.* The Court of Appeals granted a writ appeal and ordered that civilian counsel could continue to represent the appellant. *Id.* Regarding the same situation, the D.C. Bar later concluded:

> [W]here a government lawyer has, as part of his or her government employment, lawfully established an attorney-client relationship with an individual client, it does not constitute "other employment" for that lawyer to continue to represent the individual client in the same or in a substantially related matter once that lawyer is no longer a government employee. Under these unusual circumstances, Rule 1.11 would not prohibit the former government employee from representing the client in the same matter in which that employee participated personally and substantially while working for the government.

D.C. Bar Legal Ethics Opinion 313 (June 2002), *available at* http://www.dcbar.org/for_lawyers/ethics/legal_ethics/opinions/opinion313.cfm.

5. On the other hand, the Judge Advocate General of the Army concluded that a former trial counsel violated 18 U.S.C. § 207 and the Army Rules of Professional Conduct when he helped a soldier whom he had previously prosecuted attempt to obtain a certificate of innocence. The Army Standards of Conduct Office explained:

> In 1976, an Army trial counsel (TC) successfully prosecuted a soldier charged with premeditated murder. The soldier received a life sentence. In 1977, the Army Court of Military Review ordered a new trial because a key witness against the soldier had confessed to committing the murder. In 1978, the TC, thoroughly convinced of the soldier's innocence, devoted himself to coordinating deferment of the soldier's

confinement at Fort Leavenworth while the convening authority dismissed all charges against the soldier.

Both the innocent soldier and the TC left the Army. Years later, when the innocent veteran could find no one who could help him obtain a certificate of innocence, he turned to the former TC. The veteran informed the attorney that he wanted to clear his name, but did not intend to seek monetary damages from the government. The attorney agreed to represent the veteran pro bono.

The attorney appeared before the Army Court of Military Review to file a petition for a certificate of innocence. The Army court responded by ordering the attorney to show cause why he should not be required to withdraw his appearance. It noted pointedly that 18 U.S.C. § 207 (1988) forbids an individual who participated in a particular matter while employed by the government from switching sides and representing another party in the same matter.

Stating that he had not been aware of the statute's prohibitions, the attorney moved to withdraw the veteran's petition. . . . The Army court dismissed the petition, then asked the Executive, Office of The Judge Advocate General (OTJAG), to determine whether the attorney had violated 18 U.S.C. § 207 or any Army ethical rules. The attorney asked the Executive whether the attorney could let the veteran review his trial notes from the 1976 court-martial.

After studying the petition and allied papers, attorneys at OTJAG decided that the former TC had violated section 207. . . .

The investigating attorneys also found that the former TC had committed several ethical violations. In particular, they noted that the attorney (1) had used information relating to his representation of a client to the client's disadvantage without first obtaining the client's informed consent; (2) had failed to obtain a former client's consent before representing another client in a substantially related matter; (3) had used information relating to his representation of a former client to the disadvantage of the former client; and (4) had represented a private client in connection with a matter in which he previously had participated personally as a public officer. They also found that the former TC violated Army Regulation (AR) 600-50, which permanently prohibits a former officer from representing any party by "appearing before or . . . communicating with the government in connection with any matter involving specific parties" in which the officer participated personally and substantially on the government's behalf. The investigators, however, suggested that the attorney's obvious good intentions mitigated his ethical violations.

The investigators decided without hesitation that the former TC could share with the veteran the trial notes and other work product that the attorney compiled during the 1976 court-martial. They noted that a TC is not only an advocate, but also an officer of the court, charged with ensuring that justice is done. Significantly, Army Rule of Professional Conduct 3.8 requires a TC to disclose promptly to the defense any evidence or information of which he or she is aware that tends to negate the guilt of the accused. Moreover, 18 U.S.C. § 207(h) specifically authorizes a former government official to testify and make statements. In the instant case, the investigators concluded that the federal statute barred the attorney only from representing the innocent veteran.

OTJAG Standards of Conduct Office, *Professional Responsibility Notes*, ARMY LAW., Aug. 1992, at 45, 46-47.

UNITED STATES v. MEEK
United States Court of Appeals for the Armed Forces
44 M.J. 1 (C.A.A.F. 1996)

SULLIVAN, JUDGE:

The events in question unfolded at the Naval Legal Service Office Detachment, Kings Bay, Georgia, where witnesses had gathered for trial. The civilian defense counsel [Mr. Crudup] was interviewing the appellant and his wife when the DC [military defense counsel] entered the office and profanely declared that [Mr. Crudup] was ineffective, had not talked to the witnesses, and that he [the DC] would "have no part of it." The DC was quickly followed into the office by the TC [trial counsel], who, in agreeing with the DC and stating to the appellant that [Mr. Crudup] was "misrepresenting" him, rudely ordered the appellant's wife out of the office, and engaged the appellant in an unseemly verbal dispute. . . . During the tumultuous pretrial preparation period, the TC had also told most of the defense witnesses, who were gathered to be interviewed by the defense, that the appellant was "trying to worm out of the court-martial," or words to that effect. Furthermore, in an awkward arrangement, the TC forbade [Mr. Crudup] from using the appellant or his wife to summon the witnesses from the waiting area without her assistance or the assistance of a chief petty officer or secretary assigned to the Detachment. In addition, the TC provided legal counsel to one defense witness (F) — who had been punished under Article 15, UCMJ, 10 USC § 815, for aiding and abetting the appellant — regarding his concerns that he might face additional punishment. Finally, the TC contacted a defense-requested witness (B) and, in interviewing him, threatened and intimidated him by telling him he should be afraid to come to the trial site and talk with uniformed personnel because he would face a court-martial.

[*United States v. Meek*,] 40 M.J. [675,] 676 [N-M.C.M.R. 1994)].

. . . Prosecutorial misconduct can be generally defined as action or inaction by a prosecutor in violation of some legal norm or standard, e.g., a constitutional provision, a statute, a Manual rule, or an applicable professional ethics canon. *See Berger v. United States*, 295 U.S. 78, 88 (1935) (duty of a prosecutor "to refrain from improper methods calculated to produce a wrongful conviction"). . . . The characterization of certain action as "prosecutorial misconduct," however, does not in itself mandate dismissal of charges against an accused or ordering a rehearing in every case where it has occurred. *See Greer v. Miller*, 483 U.S. 756, 765 (1987). . . . Instead, an appellate court usually considers the legal norm violated by the prosecutor and determines if its violation actually impacted on a substantial right of an accused (i.e., resulted in prejudice). *See generally United States v. Hasting*, 461 U.S. 499 (1983). . . . If it did, then the reviewing court still considers the trial record as a whole to determine whether such a right's violation was harmless under all the facts of a particular case. *See generally United States v. Morrison*, [449 U.S. 361, 365 (1981)]. . . .

A. Trial Counsel's Interference with Defense Witness

. . . Several legal norms are violated when a trial counsel attempts to or unlawfully dissuades a defense witness from testifying at a court-martial. *See* Art. 38(a), UCMJ, 10 USC § 838(a) (trial counsel of a general or special court-martial "shall prosecute in the name of the United States. . . ."); *see generally Berger v. United States, supra*. Prosecutorial misconduct of this type can frustrate an accused's right to compulsory process under the Sixth Amendment even if done under the guise of advising the defense witness of his constitutional rights. *See* Art. 46, UCMJ, 10 USC § 846; *United States v. Morrison*, 535 F.2d 223, 226-27 (3d Cir. 1976). . . . We also note that such conduct towards a defense witness, if done with the requisite intent, can be both a military and civilian criminal offense. *See* Art. 134, UCMJ, 10 USC § 934, and para. 96, Part IV, Manual for Courts-Martial, United States, 1984 (Obstructing Justice); 18 USC § 1512; *cf.* Art. 37(a) (unlawful to influence the action of a court-martial or any other military tribunal or any member thereof). Finally, such conduct by a trial counsel clearly constitutes a gross ethical violation. *See* Rule 3.4, Rules of Professional Conduct, [Navy] Judge Advocate General Instruction (JAGINST) 5803.1 (26 Oct 1987); *see generally* Standard 3-3.2(b), ABA Standards for Criminal Justice: Prosecution Function and Defense Function (3d ed. 1993).

Of course, it is not the number of legal norms violated but the impact of those violations on the trial which determines the appropriate remedy for prosecutorial misconduct. In the constitutional context, a majority of the Supreme Court has generally held that a per se reversal rule is reserved only for "structural defects in the constitution of the trial mechanism" which render any trial unreliable and unfair. *See Arizona v. Fulminante*, 499 U.S. 279, 310-11 (1991). Moreover, the Supreme Court in *United States v. Hasting* and *United States v. Morrison*, both *supra*, has strongly suggested that prosecutorial misconduct is not per se reversible error but rather is error whose impact may vary in individual cases. In addition, the Supreme Court in a Fifth Amendment context has specifically held that a harmless-error rule is appropriate even where a prosecutor knowingly used perjured testimony. *See United States v. Bagley*, 473 U.S. 667, 679, and n.9 (1985). Finally, in the particular context of Article 37, this Court has applied a harmless-error rule where a defense witness was unlawfully influenced by a commander and his staff on the basis of their quasi-prosecutorial status. *See United States v. Thomas*, 22 M.J. at 393. Accordingly, we reject appellant's argument for a per se reversal rule in this case and hold that the prosecutorial misconduct towards the defense witness Boyer must be evaluated for prejudice to the accused's right to compel witnesses for his court-martial. *See United States v. Pepe*, 747 F.2d 632, 655-56 (11th Cir. 1984). . . .

B. Prosecutor's Invasion of Appellant's Right to Counsel

Appellant also contends that trial counsel unjustifiably, albeit temporarily, invaded or interfered with his constitutionally protected relationship with his civilian counsel, Mr. Crudup, under the Sixth Amendment. He asserts that trial counsel did not have "any legitimate state motivation" for such conduct and that it "chilled" his relationship with his defense attorney in terms of the trust and confidence which he thereafter placed in him. . . . Appellant urges this Court to adopt a per se reversal rule or a less demanding test for prejudice in this situation than used in those cases where a legitimate government reason exists for an invasion of the right to counsel. . . . *See* W. LaFave and J. Israel, 2 Criminal Procedures (hereafter LaFave and Israel) § 11.8(c) at 76 (1984). He then asks this Court to disregard the finding of the court below of no prejudice and order a rehearing in his case as a remedy per se tailored for this invasion of his Sixth Amendment rights. . . .

As a starting point, we note that it was detailed military defense counsel who first denigrated civilian defense counsel's effectiveness before his client. Trial counsel, however, openly joined in this denouncement of Mr. Crudup's legal service in appellant's presence. She told appellant, "Your lawyer hasn't interviewed witnesses. He's ineffective as your lawyer." Nevertheless, both the military judge and the appellate court below found that "TC's comments regarding civilian counsel's inadequate preparation were not intended to influence the appellant's decision as to employment of counsel and had no such effect." 40 M.J. at 677.

We are unsure on what basis either court below found that trial counsel's comments were not intended to influence appellant's civilian counsel decision. Lieutenant Simmons did not testify at this trial on this question, and the logical tenor of her comments and those of assigned military defense counsel suggest the opposite conclusion. In any event, for the reasons stated below, we are persuaded that her "inappropriate" comments did not prejudice appellant in any way with respect to his representation by this civilian counsel. *See generally Strickland v. Washington*, 466 U.S. 668, 687 (1984) (prejudice required to establish violation of an accused's Sixth Amendment right to effective assistance of counsel).

We initially note that Mr. Crudup continued to be civilian counsel in appellant's case despite trial counsel's comments. Moreover, once this incident came to light, the military judge particularly advised appellant that Lieutenant Simmons was "prohibited from advising you as to who you should and shouldn't have as a civilian attorney" and "you should not take her advice in that issue." Appellant was also asked by the military judge if he "rejected her advice on that issue" and he answered in the affirmative. Finally, before appellant's pleas were accepted, he openly declared that he was "satisfied" with his representation by his civilian attorney, Mr. Crudup. In these circumstances, we find no prejudice inured to appellant as a result of trial counsel's remarks and that appellant's right to effective assistance of counsel was not violated. . . .

NOTE

The Court of Appeals for the Armed Forces has also explained that when evaluating allegations of prosecutorial misconduct, "courts should gauge the overall effect of counsel's conduct on the trial, and not counsel's personal blameworthiness." *United States v. Thompkins*, 58 M.J. 43, 47 (C.A.A.F. 2003) (citing *Smith v. Phillips*, 455 U.S. 209, 220 (1982)). In *United States v. Rodriguez-Rivera*, 63 M.J. 372, 378 (C.A.A.F. 2006), the court adopted a three-part test for evaluating how to remedy prosecutorial misconduct:

> If prosecutorial misconduct is found, this court will examine the record as a whole to determine whether Appellant was prejudiced by the misconduct. *United States v. Fletcher*, 62 M.J. 175, 184 (C.A.A.F. 2005). This court weighs three factors in evaluating the impact of prosecutorial misconduct on a trial: (1) the severity of the misconduct; (2) the measures adopted to cure the misconduct; and (3) the weight of the evidence supporting the conviction. *Id.*

Chapter 6

JURISDICTION OVER THE PERSON

Not all countries maintain a separate system of military justice. In those that do, that system constitutes an exception to the normal arrangements for the administration of criminal justice. Where any particular country chooses to draw the boundary between the civilian and military justice systems reflects a fundamental judgment about the relationship between the armed forces and the larger society as well as the size, political power, and actual or contemplated operations of the country's military establishment. This line-drawing can be seen in the limits a country places on the subject-matter and personal jurisdiction of courts-martial: who is subject to trial in a military court, and for what offenses? Reliance on conscription or a history of domestic unrest, military coups, or terrorism may make these decisions politically sensitive. This chapter illustrates the range of national choices with respect to *in personam* jurisdiction of courts-martial. In Chapter 7 we will consider subject matter jurisdiction.

I. STATUTORY PROVISIONS

Uniform Code of Military Justice
Article 2. Persons subject to this chapter

(a) The following persons are subject to this chapter:

(1) Members of a regular component of the armed forces, including those awaiting discharge after expiration of their terms of enlistment; volunteers from the time of their muster or acceptance into the armed forces; inductees from the time of their actual induction into the armed forces; and other persons lawfully called or ordered into, or to duty in or for training in the armed forces, from the dates when they are required by the terms of the call or order to obey it.

(2) Cadets, aviation cadets, and midshipmen.

(3) Members of a reserve component while on inactive-duty training, but in the case of members of the Army National Guard of the United States or the Air National Guard of the United States only when in Federal Service.

(4) Retired members of a regular component of the armed forces who are entitled to pay.

(5) Retired members of a reserve component who are receiving hospitalization from an armed force.

(6) Members of the Fleet Reserve and Fleet Marine Corps Reserve.

(7) Persons in custody of the armed forces serving a sentence imposed by a court-martial.

(8) Members of the National Oceanic and Atmospheric Administration, Public Health Service, and other organizations, when assigned to and serving with the armed forces.

(9) Prisoners of war in custody of the armed forces.

(10) In time of declared war or a contingency operation, persons serving with or accompanying an armed force in the field.

(11) Subject to any treaty or agreement which the United States is or may be a party to any accepted rule of international law, persons serving with, employed by, or accompanying the armed forces outside the United States and outside the Canal Zone, the Commonwealth of Puerto Rico, Guam, and the Virgin Islands.

(12) Subject to any treaty or agreement which the United States is or may be a party to any accepted rule of international law, persons within an area leased by or otherwise reserved or acquired for use of the United States which is under the control of the Secretary concerned and which is outside the United States and outside the Canal Zone, the Commonwealth of Puerto Rico, Guam, and the Virgin Islands.

(13) Lawful enemy combatants (as that term is defined in section 948a(2) of this title) who violate the law of war.

(b) The voluntary enlistment of any person who has the capacity to understand the significance of enlisting in the armed forces shall be valid for purposes of jurisdiction under subsection (a) and change of status from civilian to member of the armed forces shall be effective upon the taking of the oath of enlistment.

(c) Notwithstanding any other provision of law, a person serving with an armed force who —

(1) Submitted voluntarily to military authority;

(2) met the mental competence and minimum age qualifications of sections 504 and 505 of this title at the time of voluntary submissions to military authority;

(3) received military pay or allowances; and

(4) performed military duties

is subject to this chapter until such person's active service has been terminated in accordance with law or regulations promulgated by the Secretary concerned.

(d)(1) A member of a reserve component who is not on active duty and who is made the subject of proceedings under section 815 (article 15) or section 830 (article 30) with respect to an offense against this chapter may be ordered to active duty involuntary for the purpose of —

(A) investigation under section 832 of this title (article 32);

(B) trial by court-martial; or

(C) non-judicial punishment under section 815 of this title (article 15).

(2) A member of a reserve component may not be ordered to active duty under paragraph (1) except with respect to an offense committed while the member was

(A) on active duty; or

(B) on inactive-duty training, but in the case of members of the Army National Guard of the United States or the Air National Guard of the United States only when in Federal service.

(3) Authority to order a member to active duty under paragraph (1) shall be exercised under regulations prescribed by the President.

(4) A member may be ordered to active duty under paragraph (1) only by a person empowered to convene general courts-martial in a regular component of the armed forces.

(5) A member ordered to active duty under paragraph (1), unless the order to active duty was approved by the Secretary concerned, may not —

(A) be sentenced to confinement; or

(B) be required to serve a punishment of any restriction on liberty during a period other than a period of inactive-duty training or active duty (other than active duty ordered under paragraph (1)).

Article 3. Jurisdiction to try certain personnel

(a) Subject to section 843 of this title (article 43), no person charged with having committed, while in a status in which he was subject to this chapter, an offense against this chapter, punishable by confinement for five years or more and for which the person cannot be tried in the courts of the United States or of a State, a Territory, or District of Columbia, may be relieved from amenability to trial by court-martial by reason of the termination of that status.

(b) Each person discharged from the armed forces who is later charged with having fraudulently obtained his discharge is, subject to section 843 of this title (article 43), subject to trial by court-martial on that charge and is after apprehension subject to trial by court-martial for all offenses under this chapter committed before the fraudulent discharge.

(c) No person who has deserted from the armed forces may be relieved form amenability to the jurisdiction of this chapter by virtue of separation from any later period of service.

(d) A member of a reserve component who is subject to this chapter is not, by virtue of the termination of a period of active duty or inactive-duty training, relieved from amenability to the jurisdiction of this chapter for an offense against this chapter committed during such period of active duty or inactive-duty training.

National Defence Act, Canada
§ 60. Persons subject to Code of Service Discipline

(1) The following persons are subject to the Code of Service Discipline:

(a) an officer or non-commissioned member of the regular force;

(b) an officer or non-commissioned member of the special force;

(c) an officer or non-commissioned member of the reserve force when the officer or non-commissioned member is

(i) undergoing drill or training, whether in uniform or not,

(ii) in uniform,

(iii) on duty,

(iv) [Repealed, 1998, c. 35, s. 19]

(v) called out under Part VI in aid of the civil power,

(vi) called out on service,

(vii) placed on active service,

(viii) in or on any vessel, vehicle or aircraft of the Canadian Forces or in or on any defence establishment or work for defence,

(ix) serving with any unit or other element of the regular force or the special force, or

(x) present, whether in uniform or not, at any drill or training of a unit or other element of the Canadian Forces;

(d) subject to such exceptions, adaptations and modifications as the Governor in Council may by regulations prescribe, a person who, pursuant to law or pursuant to an agreement between Canada and the state in whose armed forces the person is serving, is attached or seconded as an officer or non-commissioned member to the Canadian Forces;

(e) a person, not otherwise subject to the Code of Service Discipline, who is serving in the position of an officer or non-commissioned member of any force raised and maintained outside Canada by Her Majesty in right of Canada and commanded by an officer of the Canadian Forces;

(f) a person, not otherwise subject to the Code of Service Discipline, who accompanies any unit or other element of the Canadian Forces that is on service or active service in any place;

(g) subject to such exceptions, adaptations and modifications as the Governor in Council may by regulations prescribe, a person attending an institution established under section 47;

(h) an alleged spy for the enemy;

(i) a person, not otherwise subject to the Code of Service Discipline, who, in respect of any service offence committed or alleged to have been committed by the person, is in civil custody or in service custody; and

(j) a person, not otherwise subject to the Code of Service Discipline, while serving with the Canadian Forces under an engagement with the Minister whereby the person agreed to be subject to that Code.

Continuing liability

(2) Every person subject to the Code of Service Discipline under subsection (1) at the time of the alleged commission by the person of a service offence continues to be liable to be charged, dealt with and tried in respect of that offence under the Code of Service Discipline notwithstanding that the person may have, since the commission of that offence, ceased to be a person described in subsection (1).

Retention of status and rank

(3) Every person who, since allegedly committing a service offence, has ceased to be a person described in subsection (1), shall for the purposes of the Code of Service Discipline be deemed, for the period during which under that Code he is liable to be charged, dealt with and tried, to have the same status and rank that he held immediately before so ceasing to be a person described in subsection (1).

Armed Forces Act, Singapore

§ 5. Liability for offences under Emergency (Essential Powers) Act

(1) A person, who was subject to military law under section 3(*a*) or (*b*) and —

(a) who is liable to render operationally ready national service as a person subject to the Enlistment Act (Cap. 93); or

(b) who is exempted from liability to render operationally ready national service under section 28 of that Act, but comes within the definition of a person subject to the Enlistment Act in section 2 of that Act,

shall be regarded as continuing to be subject to military law and, where such person was a member of the Singapore Armed Forces, be regarded as continuing to be a member of the Singapore Armed Forces, for the purposes of proceedings for such offence under the Emergency (Essential Powers) Act (Cap. 90) as may be prescribed under subsection (5), notwithstanding that he has been discharged or released from the Singapore Armed Forces or has otherwise ceased to be subject to military law at the time of the commission of the offence.

(2) Subject to section 111(1), where such offence under the Emergency (Essential Powers) Act as may be prescribed under subsection (5) has been committed or is reasonably suspected of having been committed by a person who was, at the time of the commission of the offence, subject to military law under subsection (1), such person shall —

(a) be liable to be tried by a subordinate military court for the offence; and

(b) in relation to that offence, be treated for the purposes of the provisions of this Act relating to arrest, keeping in custody, investigation of offences, trial and punishment by a subordinate military court, and execution of sentences as continuing to be subject to military law, notwithstanding that he has been discharged or released from the Singapore Armed Forces or has otherwise ceased to be subject to military law at any time.

(3) Where a person, who is subject to military law by virtue of subsection (1), is sentenced by a subordinate military court to imprisonment, special detention or detention for such offence under the Emergency (Essential Powers) Act (Cap. 90) as may be prescribed under subsection (5), this Act shall apply to him during the term of his sentence, notwithstanding that he has been discharged or released from the Singapore Armed Forces, or has otherwise ceased to be subject to military law; and he may be kept, removed, imprisoned, made to undergo special detention or detention, and punished accordingly as if he continued to be subject to military law. . . .

§ 109. Trial and punishment of offences where offender ceases to be subject to military law

Subject to section 111, where an offence under this Act triable by a subordinate military court or by a disciplinary officer has been committed or is reasonably suspected of having been committed by any person while subject to military law then in relation to that offence he shall be treated for the provisions of this Act relating to arrest, keeping in custody, investigation of offences, trial and punishment by a subordinate military court or by a disciplinary officer (including review) and execution of sentences as continuing to be subject to military law notwithstanding his ceasing at any time to be subject thereto.

(1A) Without prejudice to the generality of subsection (1) but subject to section 111, where an offence under this Act triable by a subordinate military court or by a disciplinary officer has been committed or is reasonably suspected of having been committed by any person while subject to military law, the subordinate military court or disciplinary officer before which the offence is triable may order that person to report for trial for the offence as if that person continued to be subject to military law notwithstanding his ceasing at any time to be subject to military law.

(1B) Any person who fails to comply with any order under subsection (1A) —

   (a) shall be deemed to have failed to comply with a lawful order within the meaning of section 17(2); and

   (b) shall be liable to be arrested, proceeded against and punished for an offence under section 17(2) as if he continued to be subject to military law.

(2) Where a person subject to military law is sentenced by a subordinate military court to imprisonment, special detention or detention or by a disciplinary officer to detention, this Act shall apply to him during the term of his sentence, notwithstanding that he is discharged or dismissed from the Singapore Armed Forces, or has otherwise ceased to be subject to military law, and he may be kept, removed, imprisoned, made to undergo special detention or detention, and punished accordingly as if he continued to be subject to military law.

Code of Military Justice, Morocco
Article 3

[The following are subject to trial by military court:]

All persons, regardless of their occupation, who commit an act, designated as a crime, to the prejudice of members of the royal armed forces and the like;

All persons, regardless of their occupation, who commit an act, designated as a crime, when one or more members of the royal armed forces are co-actors or accomplices.

Article 4

All persons, regardless of their occupation, who have committed an infraction designated as an attack on the external security of the State, are subject to trial by military court.

Military Penal Code, Switzerland
Article 2(9)

[Persons subject to military penal law include:]

Civilians who, in the context of an armed conflict, commit crimes against the law of nations.

Code of Military Justice, France
as amended by Law No. 99-929 of Nov. 10, 1999

In peacetime

Art. 59. Without prejudice to international engagements, the armies tribunal adjudicates infractions of every kind committed outside the territory of the Republic by members of the armed forces or persons accompanying the army pursuant to authorization.

Art. 60. There shall be considered as members of the armed forces for purposes of the provisions of this chapter the persons referred to in articles 61 to 63, by whatever title, on foreign territory, civil service employees with statutory or contractual status with the armed forces, as well as those for whom they are responsible when they accompany the head of the family outside the territory of the Republic.

Art. 61. Soldiers referred to in this Code are:

Soldiers who have career military status;

Soldiers who serve under contract;

Soldiers who perform military service under the conditions provided for by the Code of National Service;

except for soldiers who are specially employed or retired, as well as deserters.

Art. 62. Persons who perform military service in the circumstances provided by the Code of National Service, as well as those who have enlisted, are subject to the provisions of this Code from the time of assembly of their detachment or, if they rejoin individually, from their arrival at their destination, until the day they return home. . . .

Art. 63. Also subject to the provisions of this Code are:

Those who are carried, by whatever title, on the personnel roster of a naval ship or the manifest of a military aircraft;

Those who, without being legally or contractually bound to the armed forces, are carried on the rolls and perform service;

Members of a prize crew;

Prisoners of war.

Art. 64. The armies tribunal is without jurisdiction over minors of the age of 18 unless they are members of the armed forces or when no French juvenile court has jurisdiction over them. The same tribunal is competent with regard to minors of the age of 18 unless they are members of the armed forces or when no French juvenile court has jurisdiction over them. The same tribunal is competent with regard to minors of the age of 18 when they are nationals of an occupied state or an enemy state at the time of the forbidden acts.

Art. 65. All perpetrators of and accomplices in a crime against the French armed forces or their installations or materiel are amenable to trial by the armies tribunal if the crime is proscribed by French penal law.

Art. 66. Without prejudice to the provisions of article 64, the competence of the armies tribunal extends to all perpetrators or accomplices when any one of them is subject to trial in that court.

In time of war

Art. 68. In time of war and without prejudice to article 322 and following [concerning crimes and offenses against the fundamental interests of the Nation] the court of the armed forces is regulated, in every place, by the jurisdictional rules defined by articles 59, 60, 65 and 66.

Art. 70. From the beginning of hostilities, the armed forces have jurisdiction over common crimes and offenses by enemy nationals or agents committed in the territory of the Republic or in territory subject to French authority or in any war zone. . . .

Revised Code of Military Procedure, Luxembourg

Art. 7. Councils of war will try, without exception, violations of the military penal code. The military court of appeal will hear appeals from judgments of councils of war. It will judge in the first and last instance:

all officers of the public force of a rank above captain;

all military members of councils of war for offenses committed in the exercise or in the course of exercising their functions.

Common law criminal courts will try all crimes not subject to the military penal code committed by persons subject to [the Code of Military Procedure].

Art. 8. When a person subject to military trial is prosecuted at the same time for a crime or offense within the competence of the military courts and for another crime or offense within the competence of the common law courts, he is tried first before the court with jurisdiction over the act carrying the heaviest penalty and only then for the other act before the competent tribunal.

Art. 9. When persons subject to the military penal code who are prosecuted for a crime or offense within the competence of the military courts have as co-actors or accomplices persons not subject to those courts, all of the accused are tried together before the common law courts.

Art. 10. In time of war, military courts will try offenses of all kinds committed by persons subject to the military penal code on duty as well as in barracks, quarters, military installations and in the field.

In the same way, co-actors or accomplices of military accuseds, whether or not subject to the military penal code, are subject to trial by military courts.

Offenses committed in the circumstances provided in article 8 of this code shall, in time of war, always be within the competence of military courts.

Interim Regulations of the People's Republic of China on Punishment of Servicemen who Commit Crimes Contrary to their Duties, 1982
Article 25

These regulations are applicable to staff members and workers on the regular payroll of military establishments, who commit crimes covered by these regulations.

Military Jurisdiction Act, Angola, Act No. 5 of 1994
Article 27 (Extension and Limitation of Competence)

Any offence committed by servicemen shall be tried by military courts even after the offender has ceased being a serviceman.

Any offence committed by servicemen before recruitment shall be tried by the judicial authorities having jurisdiction on the date of commission of said offense.

Uganda People's Defence Forces Act, No. 7 of 2005, § 119(1)(g)

The following persons shall be subject to military law —

(g) every person, not otherwise subject to military law, who aids or abets a person subject to military law in the commission of a service offence, and

(h) every person found in unlawful possession of —

(i) arms, ammunition or equipment ordinarily being the monopoly of the Defence Forces, or

(ii) other classified stores as prescribed.

Armed Forces Act 2006 (c. 52), United Kingdom, § 55

Time limit for charging former member of a regular or reserve force

(1) This section applies where a person ceases to be a member of a regular or reserve force.

(2) The person may not, after the end of six months beginning with the date he ceased to be a member of that force, be charged with a service offence committed while he was a member.

(3) Subsection (2) applies even if the person rejoins the force within those six months.

NOTE AND QUESTIONS

Professor Emmanuel Decaux has spearheaded the development of a broadly-applicable set of "Principles Governing the Administration of Justice Through Military Tribunals." UN Doc. E/CN.4/2006/58 (Jan. 13, 2006). His Principle No. 5, concerning jurisdiction of military courts to try civilians, states: "Military courts should, in principle, have no jurisdiction to try civilians. In all circumstances, the State shall ensure that civilians accused of a criminal offence of any nature are tried by civilian courts." Is this as straightforward as it sounds? Who is a civilian? Are there gray areas? For example, are Interior Ministry personnel, national constabularies, or conventional police forces covered? *E.g., Quilona v. General Court-Martial*, G.R. No. 96607 (Phil. 1992) (en banc) (ordering transfer of case against National Police officer to civilian court). Countries often rely on reserve forces as well as active duty or regular troops. Are reservists subject to military law when not on active duty? What of retired personnel? Is there a principled basis for subjecting them to military justice (and if so, for what kinds of offenses)? *See* Chapter 7, § II. Many countries, including the United Kingdom, attempt to subject to military justice former soldiers who have completely severed their ties to the armed forces. Some even claim military jurisdiction over dependents and others who have never worn the uniform. Not surprisingly, efforts to expand military jurisdiction beyond the core military forces has been a rich source of litigation.

II. FORMER SOLDIERS

LORD SACKVILLE'S CASE
Court of Chancery
28 ENG. REP. 940 (CH. 1760)

[In 1760 it was proposed to court-martial Lord George Sackville, a British Army officer, even though he was no longer serving on active duty, having been insubordinate in the Battle of Minden in 1759. In response to a request for their opinion, the judges reluctantly offered the following extrajudicial opinion. He was eventually tried and convicted, although it seems not to have done him too much harm, as he was later created a peer in his own right. *See* footnote 7 *infra*; *see also* FREDERICK BERNAYS WIENER, CIVILIANS UNDER MILITARY JUSTICE 159-60 & nn.127-28 (1967).]

In obedience to your Majesty's commands, signified to us by a letter from the Right Honourable the Lord Keeper, referring to us the following question, "Whether an officer of the army having been dismissed from his Majesty's service, and having no military employment, is triable by a Court-Martial for a military offence lately committed by him while in actual service and pay as an officer?"

We have taken the same into consideration, and see no ground to doubt of the legality of the jurisdiction of a Court-Martial in the case put by the above question.

But as the matter may several ways be brought, in due course of law, judicially before some of us by any party affected by that method of trial, if he thinks the court has no jurisdiction; or if the court should refuse to proceed, in case the party thinks they have jurisdiction; we shall be ready, without difficulty, to change our opinion, if we see cause, upon objections that may be then laid before us, though none have occurred to us at present which we think sufficient.

NEIMAN v. MILITARY GOVERNOR OF THE OCCUPIED AREA OF JERUSALEM AND CHIEF MILITARY PROSECUTOR
Supreme Court of Israel (1948)

The petitioner is forty-six years of age and therefore not liable to conscription. He has never sworn allegiance to the Defence Army of Israel. He was employed in the Engineers Corps of the Army during the months of June and July, 1948. As from August 1, 1948, he was no longer employed in the Army. On September 5, 1948, the petitioner was summoned — with others — to appear on an indictment before the District Court of the Defence Army of Israel in Jerusalem. The indictment, which is dated August 18, 1948, contains six charges against the petitioner. As is stated in the indictment, a copy of which is annexed to the petition, these are not offences of a military nature, being offences under various sections of the Criminal Code Ordinance, 1936, such as assault, threat of violence, unlawful arrest, malicious injury, and abuse of office.

According to the particulars of the first charge, the petitioner, on or about July 12, 1948, unlawfully assaulted Walter Yalski, who was then enlisted for part-time service in the Army. The remaining charges relate to acts which were done on the same day against the same person. The petitioner was charged before the Military Court pursuant to section 97 of the Army Code, 1948.

The questions which arise in the case before us are questions of law alone, and the submissions of the petitioner and of the respondents are shortly as follows:

The petitioner submits:

(1) He has never been a soldier according to the Army Code, 1948.

(2) Even if he had been a soldier, he ceased to be one on August 1, 1948, and he is not liable, therefore, to be tried by a Military Court.

[The Chief Military Prosecutor argued:]

(1) The petitioner must submit to the jurisdiction of the Military Court since, on the day of the commission of the offences, he was a soldier acting within the framework of or as an agent of the army.

(2) The High Court of Justice cannot intervene in this matter because:

a) No injustice has been caused to the petitioner;

b) The interests of the public and of good government demand that the petitioner be brought before a Military Court and not before a Civil Court;

c) The petitioner has an alternative remedy — to appear before a Military Court and argue before that court that it has no jurisdiction.

We have heard many general submissions from both parties as to the relationship between the Civil and Military Courts, the advantages to be gained from appearing before the Military Courts on the one hand and, on the other, the rights of the citizen to be tried by ordinary courts. We have no intention, however, of deciding the matter on first impression.

In our opinion the answer to the question raised by this petition is to be found in the basic provision contained in Article 38 of the Palestine Order in Council, 1922, as amended in 1935. We have no doubt that this provision, with which the Part on "Judiciary" in the Order in Council opens, is still in force today, by virtue of section 11 of the Law and Administration Ordinance, 1948. The text of Article 38 reads as follows:

> Subject to the provisions of this part of this Order or any Ordinance or rules, the Civil Courts hereinafter described and any other Courts or Tribunals constituted by or under any of the provisions of any Ordinance, shall exercise jurisdiction in all matters and over all persons in Palestine.

The principle which flows from this provision is that the Civil Courts exercise jurisdiction over all the inhabitants of the State, and according to Proclamation I of the Defence Army of Israel Command in Jerusalem — which is deemed to be in force as from May 15, 1948 — the Law of the State of Israel is made to apply to the occupied area of Jerusalem (section 2 of the Proclamation). In order to exclude a resident from the jurisdiction of the Civil Courts and render him subject to special Courts, special legislation is required. Such special legislation is to be found in the Emergency (Army Code 1948) Regulations, 1948 (Official Gazette No. 20 Supplement 2). These regulations were made by the Minister of Defence by virtue of the powers conferred upon him by section 9(a) of the Law and Administration Ordinance, 1948, and there is no appeal before us against the legality of these regulations. These regulations lay down, inter alia, the legal organisation of the army, its composition and its powers, the principles to be applied in regard to offences and punishment — of a special type for soldiers — and include, in section 97, a provision in regard to a soldier who commits an offence punishable by the general criminal law. It is under this provision that the petitioner is charged in the indictment before the Military Court.

And this is the text of section 97:

Any soldier who, within the framework of the army or by reason of his belonging to the army, has committed an offence punishable under the general criminal law which is in force or will be in force in the State from time to time, and whose belonging to the army, does not expressly relieve him from liability for such offence, may be tried for such offence by a Military Court and shall be liable to the same punishment as that to which he would be liable in the general courts.

The first question is whether the petitioner was a soldier at the time of the commission of the offences with which he is charged.

The definition of "soldier" is found in section 2 of the Army Code, 1948, and is as follows:

"Soldier" means any man or woman who has been accepted into the army under army regulations from time to time, and also includes any person who has acted from time to time in the framework of the army, or its agent, and also includes any person who is under a duty to enlist in the army or in the services associated with the army, even if such person has not been accepted into the army as aforesaid.

Mr. Haim Cohn, the State Attorney, who appeared on behalf of the second respondent, does not contend that the petitioner was accepted into the army under army regulations. Mr. Cohn also admitted before us that the petitioner is not subject to the duty of enlistment in the army or in the services associated with the army. His contention is that the petitioner acted on July 12, 1948, within the framework of the army and also as agent of the army. The words "from time to time" in the definition of the word "soldier" — Mr. Cohn argues — introduce an element of impermanence, and there is therefore no need for permanent service. The expression "framework of the army" is, says Mr. Cohn, an extremely wide one. The word "framework," he contends, must not be given an etymological but a colloquial interpretation. A person need not actually be in the army in order to be within its framework — any person who is in lawful association with the army is within its framework. The question is whether the association between the person and the army is one which introduces him or his activities into the framework of the army. The petitioner was a hired employee of the army, and his receipt of a salary does not exclude him from its framework, for the army is composed not only of active soldiers but also of other persons including those who work for a salary, such as army doctors and judges. The expression "agency of the army" is, so it is argued, even wider than "framework," since such agency does not even demand any lawful association between the person and the army. These are the submissions of counsel for the second respondent.

As against these arguments Dr. Frank, counsel for the petitioner, has made the following submissions:

> The petitioner did not act within the framework of the army or as its agent. In interpreting the expression "soldier" in section 2 of the Army Code, Dr. Frank directed our attention to section 176, subsections 9 and 10 of the English Army Act of 1881, in terms of which persons who are not soldiers but who are employed by the army are subject to Military law only if they are on active service, an expression defined in section 189 of that statute. Dr. Frank intended to prove the extent to which the English legislature has restricted the category of those who are subject to military law. The immediate answer to this argument is that proof of such a restricted interpretation cannot be furnished by the English statute since we are bound by the definition of a "soldier" in the Army Code, 1948, and that definition contains no such restriction.

> An act done by a soldier within the framework of the army, Dr. Frank submits, is one that results from an order given by the State or by the army. A person who performs some activity in the army as a contractor for a wage and as an official on a salary is one who works under a contract and not on the basis of an order given or compulsion exercised by the State or the army. A person falls within the framework of the army, Dr. Frank submits, only when the army gives him orders as one of its members, and not when he works under a special contract for a salary. In any event, says Dr. Frank, if the regulation defining the expression "soldier" is not clear, there is a presumption that the civil courts have jurisdiction, and in a case of doubt the decision will be in favour of such jurisdiction.

> The distinction referred to, which Dr. Frank wishes to introduce in interpreting the expression "soldier," is worthy of consideration. We are of the opinion, however, that, on the contrary, the legislature wished to widen the limits of the expression "soldier" as far as possible by introducing into that definition, as a category, any person "who has acted from time to time in the framework of the army, or as its agent." We think that the legislature, in framing the definition as it did, succeeded in extending the limits of the expression "soldier," and we do not agree with the submission that the receipt of a wage excludes a person from the framework of the army.

The definition of "soldier" in section 2 contains three categories:

> (a) the first category mentioned — "any man or woman who has been accepted into the army under army regulations from time to time" — refers to ordinary soldiers;

> (b) the third category — "any person who is under a duty to enlist in the army or in the services associated with the army, even if such person has not been accepted into the army as aforesaid" — refers to those

who in fact are not yet soldiers, but who are ordered to become and are about to become soldiers, and who are liable to be punished, for example, for offences such as feigning illness, or willful maiming, under section 90 of the Army Code, 1948;

(c) The second category includes just those people who have not been accepted into the army under army regulations and who are not about to be accepted into the army because of their duty to enlist, but those who work from time to time in the framework of the army or as agents of the army, such as the petitioner in the present case.

It is worthwhile pointing out, moreover, that in order that a person should be included in the first category, it is a condition precedent that he should be accepted into the army under army regulations. In order that a person should be included in the third category it is a condition precedent that he should be under a certain duty, namely, the duty of enlistment. In order that a person should be included within the second category there is no condition precedent at all. The very fact of his working within the framework of the army or as its agent brings him by definition into the category of "soldier," without any reference to the element of the desire or duty which led him to work within the framework of the army.

In regard to this point, therefore, we accept the submission of the State Attorney, counsel for the second respondent, that the petitioner was a "soldier" until the end of the month of July.

The second question which arises is whether a person who was a soldier at the time of the commission of the offence but who has ceased to be a soldier may still be charged before a Military Court. It is not disputed that on the date mentioned in the indictment, namely, August 18, 1948, the petitioner was no longer a soldier. Counsel for the second respondent submits, however, that the fact that the petitioner was a soldier at the time that he committed the offence on July 12th is sufficient to permit his being tried before a Military Court under section 97. . . .

The third ground relied upon by Mr. Cohn in regard to the interpretation of section 97 is based upon section 158 of the English Army Act of 1881. That section provides that if a person has committed an offence under military law at a time when he is subject to that law, and if he thereafter ceases to be subject to that law, he may still be tried before a Military Court within three months from the date that he ceased to be subject to military law — save in the case of a few serious felonies in regard to which this limitation of time does not apply. Mr. Cohn attempted to argue that this Law of 1881 limited the period in which it was still possible to try a person who had ceased to be a soldier in a military court, and that according to English common law there was no limitation of time whatsoever in regard to this possibility. The authorities cited to us by Mr. Cohn from English Law in regard to this question, such as *Dawkins v. Lord Paulet*, (1869) L.R. 5 Q.B. 94, in fact contain no solution of our problem, and Mr. Cohn stated frankly in the course of his argument before us that he found it necessary to abandon his submission based upon English common law. It is sufficient, in fact, to consult Dicey on Constitutional Law, which was referred to by Mr. Cohn, in order to realise that the principle of the supremacy of the ordinary Civil Courts is woven like a golden thread throughout the whole of the chapter in Dicey dealing with the army. At page 303 (eighth edition) he says: "The general principle on this subject is that the Courts of Law have jurisdiction to determine who are the persons subject to Military Law, and whether a given proceeding, alleged to depend upon Military Law, is really justified by the rules of law which govern the army. Hence flow the following (among other) consequences. The Civil Courts determine whether a given person is or is not 'a person subject to military law.'"

We are prepared to find some assistance in section 158 of the English Army Act, 1881, but in favour of the petitioner and not in favour of the respondent, for this section shows that the English legislature found it necessary to lay down by a specific provision that a person remains subject to military law for a certain period even after he has ceased to be a soldier. The Army Code, 1948, on the other hand, contains no parallel provision, and reading section 97 of that code literally, we are obliged to interpret it to mean that only a soldier — that is to say, a person who is still a soldier — may be tried before a military court for an offence which he committed within the framework of the army or by reason of his belonging to the army. In regard to this point, therefore, we accept the submission of the petitioner that since he ceased to be a soldier on August 1, 1948, he ceased from that date to be subject to the jurisdiction of the military court.

There remains the final argument of counsel for the second respondent that the High Court of Justice will not intervene in this matter since no injustice has been caused to the petitioner and the interests of the public and of good government demand that the petitioner be brought before a military court and not before a civil court, and that the petitioner has a legal remedy elsewhere. We cannot accept these submissions. The question before us is not whether an injustice will be done to the petitioner if he is arraigned before a military court. The rule is that every person is entitled to demand that he be tried before a competent court. In fact all the various constitutions of courts in different countries are extremely careful in defining the limits of jurisdiction. If, according to the rules laid down in the Code, an ordinary civil court is competent to try a person, and the authorities wish to arraign him before a special court, the accused is entitled to petition the High Court of Justice and to demand that it intervene in the matter.

We appreciate what has been said by counsel for the second respondent, that it is the duty of the army and its court to root out criminals, whose offences — even if they are also offences under the general criminal law — are in fact offences against the efficient and proper administration of the army; that the army is interested in imposing order in its ranks and beyond its ranks; and that this is particularly so in a case such as that of the petitioner who is charged with assuming authority which he did not possess. But the general consideration such as this cannot take the place of a specific legal provision as to the jurisdiction of the courts. This is one of the basic principles of every ordered regime.

We also cannot accept the submission that it was necessary for the petitioner to appear before the military court, present to that court a submission of want of jurisdiction, and attempt in that way to secure his remedy. . . .

UNITED STATES EX REL. TOTH v. QUARLES
Supreme Court of the United States
350 U.S. 11 (1955)

MR. JUSTICE BLACK delivered the opinion of the Court.

After serving with the United States Air Force in Korea, Robert W. Toth was honorably discharged. He returned to his home in Pittsburgh and went to work in a steel plant. Five months later he was arrested by military authorities on charges of murder and conspiracy to commit murder while an airman in Korea. At the time of arrest he had no relationship of any kind with the military. He was taken to Korea to stand trial before a court-martial under authority of a 1950 Act of Congress.[1] The Court of Appeals sustained the Act, rejecting the contention that civilian ex-servicemen like Toth could not constitutionally be subjected to trial by court-martial. 94 U.S. App. D.C. 28, 215 F.2d 22. We granted certiorari to pass upon this important constitutional question.

The 1950 Act cannot be sustained on the constitutional power of Congress "To raise and support Armies," "To declare War," or to punish "Offences against the Law of Nations."[2] And this assertion of military authority over civilians cannot rest on the President's power as commander-in-chief, or on any theory of martial law. *See Ex parte Milligan*, 4 Wall. 2, 124-127. The Government's contention is that the Act is a valid exercise of the power granted Congress in Article I of the Constitution "To make Rules for the Government and Regulation of the land and naval Forces," as supplemented by the Necessary and Proper Clause.

This Court has held that the Article I clause just quoted authorizes Congress to subject persons actually in the armed service to trial by court-martial for military and naval offenses. Later it was held that court-martial jurisdiction could be exerted over a dishonorably discharged soldier then a military prisoner serving a sentence imposed by a prior court-martial.[3] It has never been intimated by this Court, however, that Article I military jurisdiction could be extended to civilian ex-soldiers who had severed all relationship with the military and its institutions.[4] To allow this extension of military

---

[1] [n.2] Art. 3(a), Uniform Code of Military Justice, 64 Stat. 109, 50 U.S.C. §553, provides: "Subject to the provisions of article 43, any person charged with having committed, while in a status in which he was subject to this code, an offense against this code, punishable by confinement of five years or more and for which the person cannot be tried in the courts of the United States or any State or Territory thereof or of the District of Columbia, shall not be relieved from amenability to trial by courts-martial by reason of the termination of said status."

[2] [n.4] *See Ex parte Quirin*, 317 U.S. 1; *In re Yamashita*, 327 U.S. 1. [*see* Chapter 3, §I, *supra*.]

[3] [n.7] *Kahn v. Anderson*, 255 U.S. 1.

[4] [n.8] In 1863 Congress passed a statute authorizing trial of ex-soldiers for commission of fraud against the Government while in the service; this law also authorized court-martial trial of contractors not part of the military forces. 12 Stat. 696. The latter provision of the 1863 law appears never to have been sustained by any court. . . . A statute authorizing court-martial trial of inmates of the Soldiers' Home has been ruled unconstitutional by the Judge Advocate General of the Army. Dig. Op. J.A.G. (1912), pp. 1010, 1012. It was declared that "such inmates are not a part of the Army of the United States, but are civilians." *Id.*, at 1012. Col. Winthrop, concededly a leading authority on military law, expressed the view that "this class of statutes, which in terms or inferentially subject persons formerly in the army, but become finally and legally separated from it, to trial by court-martial, are all necessarily and alike unconstitutional. . . ." 1 Winthrop, Military Law and Precedents (2d ed. 1896), 146. . . .

authority would require an extremely broad construction of the language used in the constitutional provision relied on. For given its natural meaning, the power granted Congress "To make Rules" to regulate "the land and naval Forces" would seem to restrict court-martial jurisdiction to persons who are actually members or part of the armed forces. There is a compelling reason for construing the clause this way: any expansion of court-martial jurisdiction like that in the 1950 Act necessarily encroaches on the jurisdiction of federal courts set up under Article III of the Constitution where persons on trial are surrounded with more constitutional safeguards than in military tribunals.

Article III provides for the establishment of a court system as one of the separate but coordinate branches of the National Government. It is the primary, indeed the sole business of these courts to try cases and controversies between individuals and between individuals and the Government. This includes trial of criminal cases. These courts are presided over by judges appointed for life, subject only to removal by impeachment. Their compensation cannot be diminished during their continuance in office. The provisions of Article III were designed to give judges maximum freedom from possible coercion or influence by the executive or legislative branches of the Government. But the Constitution and the Amendments in the Bill of Rights show that the Founders were not satisfied with leaving determination of guilt or innocence to judges, even though wholly independent. They further provided that no person should be held to answer in those courts for capital or other infamous crimes unless on the presentment or indictment of a grand jury drawn from the body of the people. Other safeguards designed to protect defendants against oppressive governmental practices were included. One of these was considered so important to liberty of the individual that it appears in two parts of the Constitution. Article III, 2, commands that the "Trial of all Crimes, except in Cases of Impeachment, shall be by Jury; and such Trial shall be held in the State where the said Crimes shall have been committed; but when not committed within any State, the Trial shall be at such Place or Places as the Congress may by Law have directed." And the Sixth Amendment provides that "In all criminal prosecutions, the accused shall enjoy the right to a speedy and public trial, by an impartial jury of the state and district wherein the crime shall have been committed. . . ." This right of trial by jury ranks very high in our catalogue of constitutional safeguards.

We find nothing in the history or constitutional treatment of military tribunals which entitles them to rank along with Article III courts as adjudicators of the guilt or innocence of people charged with offenses for which they can be deprived of their life, liberty or property. Unlike courts, it is the primary business of armies and navies to fight or be ready to fight wars should the occasion arise. But trial of soldiers to maintain discipline is merely incidental to an army's primary fighting function. To the extent that those responsible for performance of this primary function are diverted from it by the necessity of trying cases, the basic fighting purpose of armies is not served. And conceding to military personnel that high degree of honesty and sense of justice which nearly all of them undoubtedly have, it still remains true that military tribunals have not been and probably never can be constituted in such way that they can have the same kind of qualifications that the Constitution has deemed essential to fair trials of civilians in federal courts.

For instance, the Constitution does not provide life tenure for those performing judicial functions in military trials. They are appointed by military commanders and may be removed at will. Nor does the Constitution protect their salaries as it does judicial salaries. Strides have been made toward making courts-martial less subject to the will of the executive department which appoints, supervises and ultimately controls them. But from the very nature of things, courts have more independence in passing on the life and liberty of people than do military tribunals.

Moreover, there is a great difference between trial by jury and trial by selected members of the military forces. It is true that military personnel because of their training and experience may be especially competent to try soldiers for infractions of military rules. Such training is no doubt particularly important where an offense charged against a soldier is purely military, such as disobedience of an order, leaving post, etc. But whether right or wrong, the premise underlying the constitutional method for determining guilt or innocence in federal courts is that laymen are better than specialists to perform this task. This idea is inherent in the institution of trial by jury.

Juries fairly chosen from different walks of life bring into the jury box a variety of different experiences, feelings, intuitions and habits. Such juries may reach completely different conclusions than would be reached by specialists in any single field, including specialists in the military field. On many occasions, fully known to the Founders of this country, jurors — plain people — have manfully stood up in defense of liberty against the importunities of judges and despite prevailing hysteria and prejudices. The acquittal of William Penn is an illustrious example. Unfortunately, instances could also be cited where jurors have themselves betrayed the cause of justice by verdicts based on prejudice or pressures. In such circumstances independent trial judges and independent appellate judges have a most important place under our constitutional plan since they have power to set aside convictions.

The 1950 Act here considered deprives of jury trial and sweeps under military jurisdiction over 3,000,000 persons who have become veterans since the Act became effective. That number is bound to grow from year to year; there are now more than 3,000,000 men and women in uniform. These figures point up what would be the enormous scope of a holding that Congress could subject every ex-serviceman and woman in the land to trial by court-martial for any alleged offense committed while he or she had been a member of the armed forces. Every veteran discharged since passage of the 1950 Act is subject to military trial for any offense punishable by as much as five years' imprisonment unless the offense is now punishable in a civilian court. And one need only glance at the Military Code to see what a vast number and variety of offenses are thus brought under military jurisdiction. Included within these are crimes such as murder, conspiracy, absence without leave, contempt toward officials, disrespect toward superior officers, willful or neglectful loss, damage, or destruction of government property, making false official statements, dueling, breach of the peace, forgery, fraud, assault, and many others. It is true that with reference to some of these offenses, very minor ones, veterans cannot now be tried because of a presidential order fixing the punishment for such offenses at less than five years. But that amelioration of the Military

Code may be temporary, since punishment can be raised or lowered at the will of the President. It is also true that under the present law courts-martial have jurisdiction only if no civilian court does. But that might also be changed by Congress. Thus there is no justification for treating the Act as a mere minor increase of congressional power to expand military jurisdiction. It is a great change, both actually and potentially.

Fear has been expressed that if this law is not sustained discharged soldiers may escape punishment altogether for crimes they commit while in the service. But that fear is not warranted and was not shared by the Judge Advocate General of the Army who made a strong statement against passage of the law. He asked Congress to "confer jurisdiction upon Federal courts to try any person for an offense denounced by the [military] code if he is no longer subject thereto. This would be consistent with the fifth amendment of the Constitution." The Judge Advocate General went on to tell Congress that "If you expressly confer jurisdiction on the Federal courts to try such cases, you preserve the constitutional separation of military and civil courts, you save the military from a lot of unmerited grief, and you provide for a clean, constitutional method for disposing of such cases." It is conceded that it was wholly within the constitutional power of Congress to follow this suggestion and provide for federal district court trials of discharged soldiers accused of offenses committed while in the armed services. This concession is justified. . . . There can be no valid argument, therefore, that civilian ex-servicemen must be tried by court-martial or not tried at all. If that is so it is only because Congress has not seen fit to subject them to trial in federal district courts.

None of the other reasons suggested by the Government are sufficient to justify a broad construction of the constitutional grant of power to Congress to regulate the armed forces. That provision itself does not empower Congress to deprive people of trials under Bill of Rights safeguards, and we are not willing to hold that power to circumvent those safeguards should be inferred through the Necessary and Proper Clause. It is impossible to think that the discipline of the Army is going to be disrupted, its morale impaired, or its orderly processes disturbed, by giving ex-servicemen the benefit of a civilian court trial when they are actually civilians. And we are not impressed by the fact that some other countries which do not have our Bill of Rights indulge in the practice of subjecting civilians who were once soldiers to trials by courts-martial instead of trials by civilian courts.

There are dangers lurking in military trials which were sought to be avoided by the Bill of Rights and Article III of our Constitution. Free countries of the world have tried to restrict military tribunals to the narrowest jurisdiction deemed absolutely essential to maintaining discipline among troops in active service. Even as late as the Seventeenth Century standing armies and courts-martial were not established institutions in England. Court-martial jurisdiction sprang from the belief that within the military ranks there is need for a prompt, ready-at-hand means of compelling obedience and order. But Army discipline will not be improved by court-martialing rather than trying by jury some civilian ex-soldier who has been wholly separated from the service for months, years or perhaps decades. Consequently considerations of discipline provide no excuse for new expansion of court-martial jurisdiction at the expense of the normal and constitutionally preferable system of trial by jury.

Determining the scope of the constitutional power of Congress to authorize trial by court-martial presents another instance calling for limitation to "the least possible power adequate to the end proposed."[5] We hold that Congress cannot subject civilians like Toth to trial by court-martial. They, like other civilians, are entitled to have the benefit of safeguards afforded those tried in the regular courts authorized by Article III of the Constitution.

Reversed.

Mr. Justice Reed, with whom Mr. Justice Burton and Mr. Justice Minton join, dissenting.

. . . The judgment just announced turns loose, without trial or possibility of trial, a man accused of murder. In future similar cases among the military, if Congress enacts the substitute law as the Court suggests, . . . the accused must face a jury far removed from the scene of the alleged crime and before jurors without the understanding of the quality and character of a military crime possessed by those accustomed to administer the Uniform Code of Military Justice. Or perhaps those accused will be extradited and tried by foreign law.

A dissent is justified, I think, if its argument may limit, in some degree, further interpreting limitations by the judiciary on the power granted by the Constitution to Congress: "To make Rules for the Government and Regulation of the land and naval Forces" without the jury and venue requirements of the Fifth and Sixth Amendments. These requirements are appropriate for civil trials but, by custom, our precedents and express language are inapplicable to "cases arising in the land or naval forces." . . .

The Code was enacted May 5, 1950, after careful military and congressional study to assure that the military justice of the unified services would be in accordance with the present-day standards of fairness. Article 3(a) was adopted in view of the decision of this Court in *Hirshberg v. Cooke*, 336 U.S. 210 (1949), holding the Articles for the Government of the Navy, then in force, did not allow trial on charges filed subsequent to honorable discharge "without a grant of congressional authority," *id.*, at 215, although the charges arose from acts committed while the defendant was in military service. The near escape from military justice of Army personnel accused of the theft in Germany of the Hesse crown jewels was also in mind. It was thought that a serviceman's discharge should not bar his prosecution in a military court for crimes committed when subject to military discipline.

The enactment of Article 3(a) was chosen instead of the alternative of federal district court jurisdiction, although thorough presentations of objections not only on constitutional but also on policy grounds appear in the committee report and the Congressional Record. The military were well aware, as was

---

[5] [n.23] *Anderson v. Dunn*, 6 Wheat. 204, 230-231.

Congress, of possible unfavorable public reaction to extension of the jurisdiction of military courts to discharged veterans for alleged misdeeds during service. The language of Article 3(a) was drawn to cover only the most serious offenses and restricted to those instances in which the guilty would otherwise escape trial or punishment in any American courts. Although Congress, under Art. I, 8, cl. 14, and the Necessary and Proper Clause, doubtless might have authorized the civil courts to try charges arising from violations of the Military Code during former service, even though committed on foreign soil,[6] it chose the method of Article 3(a).

No question of accommodating the liberty of the citizen to requirements of the military through the interpretation of an ambiguous Act arises. *Compare Ex parte Endo*, 323 U.S. 283, 300. It is not for courts to question the wisdom of the legislation. Its obvious purpose was to assure, insofar as discipline may do so, the proper conduct of our far-flung and numerous military personnel in foreign lands. One need not stress the necessity of orderly conduct by the military on foreign posts for the maintenance of good relations in friendly or vanquished countries. It also seems a reasonable choice that uniform treatment by courts-martial trial of all accused of crimes punishable by the Military Code is preferred for morale and disciplinary purposes to courts-martial trial only for those who remain in the service. This case itself would make a good example of the difficulty of a federal district court trial. We address ourselves to the constitutionality of Article 3(a).

(a)

The congressional power under Article I of the Constitution to regulate the armed forces is conceded by the Court to embrace the power to provide for trial by court-martial and military punishment for violations of the Military Code. But the Court holds that that power ceases when the serviceman becomes a civilian. Nothing, we think, in the words of Article I or in the history of that congressional power justifies limiting trial and punishment by the military, for crimes committed by members of the armed services, to the period of service. Certainly the power of Congress to provide for a military trial and punishment for a breach of the Military Code on charges brought before the end of enlistment or discharge may continue thereafter. The crime charged against Toth was one covered by the Code. The circumstance that he was discharged from the service prior to the detection of the alleged crime and prior to being charged with its commission should make no constitutional difference.

Courts-martial are deeply rooted in history. War is a grim business, requiring sacrifice of ease, opportunity, freedom from restraint, and liberty of action.

---

[6] [n.9] "The Trial of all Crimes, except in Cases of Impeachment, shall be by Jury; and such Trial shall be held in the State where the said Crimes shall have been committed; but when not committed within any State, the Trial shall be at such Place or Places as the Congress may by Law have directed." Art. III, 2, cl. 3. . . .

[7] [n.11] . . . At the time of our Constitutional Convention, there had already been held the well-known court-martial of Lord George Sackville for disobedience of orders of his Chief, Prince Ferdinand of Brunswick, at the battle of Minden. . . .

On conviction the King directed the sentence be recorded in the order book of every regiment, British and American. In view of the prominence of the parties and the subsequent distinguished

Experience has demonstrated that the law of the military must be capable of prompt punishment to maintain discipline. The power to regulate the armed forces must have been granted to Congress so that it would have the authority over its armed forces that other nations have long exercised, subject only to limitations of the Constitution. *Dynes v. Hoover*, 20 How. 65, 78-79; *Ex parte Reed*, 100 U.S. 13, 21. The Government calls our attention to the current provisions for military trial after discharge of other nations with legal background similar to ours. Each of them allows such trials under varying conditions.[7] Whether English courts-martial before 1789 exercised jurisdiction over charges preferred after separation from service cannot be categorically asserted in view of the paucity of cases. It would seem, however, that the language of Article I itself properly should be interpreted to empower Congress to authorize courts-martial after separation from the services. The crime charged was committed during service and violated the Military Code. Surely when read with the Necessary and Proper Clause, the conclusion must follow. Article 3(a) bears a reasonable relation to the "Government and Regulation" of the armed forces; it is appropriate and plainly adapted to that end. *McCulloch v. Maryland*, 4 Wheat. 316, 419 *et seq*. That has been the test of congressional power.

This is not an effort to make a civilian subject to military law, in distinction to martial law, as in *Ex parte Milligan*, 4 Wall. 2, 121, 123, 127. Such an effort would meet condemnation as an invasion of the liberty of the citizen. *See Duncan v. Kahanamoku*, 327 U.S. 304; *Ex parte Endo*, 323 U.S. 283. Congress was granted authority to regulate the armed forces in order to enforce obedience by members of the military establishment to military regulation during their service to the end that order may be ensured. Disobedience may occur in nationally critical times. What reason can there be for refusing courts-martial jurisdiction over crimes so committed by a serviceman merely because they passed undiscovered during the service period? Could there now be doubt as to the power of Congress under Art. I to make a draftee subject to courts-martial before actual induction into the armed forces? This Court had none in 1944. Then we said, when considering a habeas corpus for release from military imprisonment after trial by court-martial of a person claiming civilian status:

> "We have no doubt of the power of Congress to enlist the manpower of the nation for prosecution of the war and to subject to military jurisdiction those who are unwilling, as well as those who are eager, to come to the defense of their nation in its hour of peril." *Arver v. United States*, 245 U.S. 366 [Selective Draft Law Cases]. *Billings v. Truesdell*, 321 U.S. 542, 556.

Toth may be a civilian but his crime was a violation of military regulations.

Judicial history lends its weight to the conclusion that congressional power to institute criminal proceedings against a military person continues after the

---

career of Lord George Sackville, who died in 1785 after having been advanced in 1782 to the peerage as Viscount Sackville for his services in Parliament, the Irish administration, and as Secretary of State for the Colonies, the case could hardly have escaped the notice of the members of the Constitutional Convention. . . .

accused's discharge. In 1863, the Congress enacted an Act to prevent and punish frauds upon the Government of the United States. It provided that any person in the military forces shall be punished for fraud under military regulation "as the court-martial may adjudge, save the punishment of death." 12 Stat. 696-697, 1. Under 2, jurisdiction of the court-martial was extended to dischargees. The provision for charge and court-martial after discharge was ruled constitutional in 1866 by Attorney General Stanbery. The section was held constitutional in 1873. *In re Bogart*, 3 Fed. Cas. 796. It was apparently held unconstitutional in 1946 under Article I in the District Court for the Southern District of New York, although the problem under the Fifth Amendment was also considered. *United States ex rel. Flannery v. Commanding General*, 69 F. Supp. 661, 664. . . .

The Court finds a "compelling reason" for construing the clause for Army regulation more narrowly than has been done by the Congress and the Executive for many years. This is that trial by Article III judges and juries offers safeguards to military offenders superior to those offered by courts-martial. Under our judicial system the use of juries has been found satisfactory in civil life. The argument for the adoption of civil trials for the military might appeal to Congress, if presented there. But, with due respect to the premise of the majority, the assumed superiority of the civil courts in the trial of service crimes should have no force in the construction of the constitutional power of Congress to enact Article 3(a) of the Code. Belief that an accused has better opportunities to escape conviction in a civil court should not influence a conclusion as to constitutional power. As later appears in this opinion, the Fifth and Sixth Amendments except the land and naval forces from their commands. The advantages and disadvantages of indictment, venue and jury trial for the military have been weighed and determined adversely to the Court's conclusion by the Constitution and the Congress. Certainly the number of former members of the armed services now living is immaterial to the constitutional issue, as are the "dangers" suggested to be "lurking in military trials." The military is in position to give its personnel a fair trial. The only logical ground for declaring Article 3(a) unconstitutional is that military crimes cannot be so punished because such procedure is beyond the reach of the congressional authority to make rules for government of military personnel. Subsequent punishment by military procedures will help discipline during service. Such a conclusion by Congress is not strained or unreasonable but a natural use of its power to make regulations for the armed services. The choice is for Congress, not the Court.

(b)

Another constitutional problem arises, i.e., that Article 3(a) is unlawful by reason of the limitations on prosecutions of the Fifth and Sixth Amendments to the Constitution.

The argument upon the Sixth Amendment requires only summary treatment. The rights to a speedy and public trial, impartiality of the triers, information as to the charge, confrontation, compulsory process for witnesses and assistance of counsel are not in issue. This accused will not have for his trial a jury of the State and district of the crime, previously ascertained by our law. That is an impossibility in the circumstances of this case. Nor can it be that the Sixth Amendment requirements as to jury and place were intended to apply to the "cases arising in the land or naval forces" which were excepted from the protection of the grand jury by the Fifth. That would abrogate the authority of Congress to govern the military by courts-martial. It was so announced by this Court, unanimously, in *Ex parte Milligan*, 4 Wall. 2, 122. Defendants in cases arising in the armed forces, we think, are not entitled to demand trial by jury, whether the crime was committed on foreign soil or at a place within a State or previously ascertained district.

Turning to the Fifth Amendment, the critical words are obviously "cases arising in the land or naval forces." The events leading to the taking of Toth into custody occurred while he was enlisted. They constituted then and now a violation of the Uniform Code. Relator would limit the quoted words to cases where charges had been filed during service. She stresses the phrase "when in actual service," but this Court has held and all the history of our courts-martial shows that such phrase has reference only to "cases arising . . . in the Militia." *Johnson v. Sayre*, 158 U.S. 109, 114.

The Fifth, like the other early amendments, arose from the determination to protect the rights of citizens. As the Articles of Confederation, Article 9, granted authority to the central government to make rules for the government and regulation of the armed forces, the Nation was conversant with the problem. In the state conventions for ratification of the Constitution, Massachusetts, New Hampshire, New York and Rhode Island suggested words for regulation of the armed forces quite similar to the ones adopted by Congress. It will be observed that two employ "arise." Three speak of "cases." Since the state suggestions were made as the result of consideration of the proposed Constitution, it is quite natural that the language of Article III concerning the judicial power would find an echo in the suggestions. Article III, § 2, reads, "The judicial Power shall extend to all Cases, in Law and Equity, arising under this Constitution, the Laws of the United States, and Treaties made, or which shall be made, under their Authority. . . ." When the Congress considered the Act against military fraud in 1863, no one suggested that a "case," the prosecution for which under the Act did not begin until after discharge of a serviceman, would not be a "case arising in the land or naval forces." The concern of Congress was with the liability of contractors, as part of military personnel, under § 1 of the Act, when they had no true military service status. Because not service-connected, the contractors' clause has been held unconstitutional. *Ex parte Henderson*, 11 Fed. Cas. 1067, 1071. . . .

One of the purposes of the Fifth Amendment by this exception was to preserve the separation of military law from the requirements of civil law. The regulation of the armed forces by Congress under cl. 14 of § 8, Art. I, was to be left for legislative judgment that discipline might be maintained by speedy trial and punishment in accordance with military law. The reasons, set out in our discussion of Article I power to regulate the armed forces, need not be repeated here. We ask ourselves, "What law is the basis of this prosecution?" The answer is the Military Code. If so, the case arises "in the land or naval forces." . . .

(c)

The Court, of course, does not gainsay the constitutional authority of Congress to adopt a military code for regulation of members of the armed forces without regard to the generally applicable requirements of the Fifth and Sixth Amendments. It holds that where the constitutional safeguards of the Fifth and Sixth Amendments for a citizen's freedom from tyranny are at stake, they should not be withdrawn except through absolute necessity. There is no such necessity here for it would have been possible to have provided a proper civil trial with the full protection of the applicable clauses of the Amendments. But here we are considering an exception to the safeguards offered by the Fifth and Sixth Amendments. That exception has been written into the Constitution from the experience of history to protect the discipline of the armed forces. Of course, that exception from the protections of these Amendments should be strictly construed to hold those excluded to the minimum as was done in *Ex parte Henderson, supra*, ... Construction of the Constitution, however, should not be allowed to emasculate the natural meaning of language designed to protect the Nation in the regulation of its armed forces.

What we have argued in the foregoing pages of this opinion supports our conclusion on this tendered rule of construction. Granting that there are possible means of affording civil trials to persons discharged from the Army for military crimes committed during their service, we think that Congress has power to provide for punishment of these military crimes under the constitutional exceptions discussed. Such punishment, if our analysis of Article I and the Fifth and Sixth Amendments is correct, will be for military crimes of servicemen, not of civilians, and for the maintenance of discipline in the armed forces.

The relator phrases strongly her argument against Toth's prosecution by courts-martial. To her the issue is "military dictatorship." Though she concedes that Congress may have merely desired to bar absolution from crime by discharge from service, such purpose, she argues, should not override the Constitution or be allowed to foreshadow a "military dictatorship." She forebodes that every petty crime may be included and limitation of prosecution be extended until all discharged servicemen shall live their lives under fear of the Military. The law still has degrees of harshness and courts and legislatures must act in reason. The possibility of individual abuse of power is ever present even under our Constitution but the probability of obliteration of any such tendency through judicial, executive or legislative action is the citizen's protection under the Constitution. A fear that punishment by courts-martial of servicemen after discharge may bear a threat to the rights and security of citizens is extravagant. It is true today, as it was in the time of the Founding Fathers, that the methods for maintenance of Army discipline should be subject to public opinion as expressed through Congress. If trial of discharged servicemen by courts-martial under the carefully defined provisions of Article 3(a) seems harsh or hurtful to liberty, the door of Congress remains open for amelioration. This decision that a veteran, let out of the military forces before charges, must, by the Constitution, be tried by the civil courts for his military crimes impairs congressional power. Now only another Constitutional Amendment or a reversal of today's judgment will enable Congress to deal consistently with those violating the Uniform Code of Military Justice. We cannot agree that those who adopted the constitutional provisions for the protection of military discipline intended such a result. Toth's alleged accomplices have been convicted by military courts and we see no reason why he should not be tried as proposed.

The decision below should be affirmed.

MR. JUSTICE MINTON, whom MR. JUSTICE BURTON joins, dissenting.

I agree with the opinion of MR. JUSTICE REED, and I would add another reason why I think the judgment should be affirmed.

A civilian not under the jurisdiction of the Military Code has a right to be tried in a civil court for an alleged crime as a civilian. My trouble is that I don't think Toth was a full-fledged civilian. By 50 U.S.C. § 553, Congress had retained jurisdiction to try Toth for a crime he had committed while a soldier and for which admittedly he could have been tried by court-martial if the United States had discovered his crime one minute before discharge.

He was not a full-fledged civilian under his discharge. He was still a soldier to answer in court-martial for the crime he had committed while a soldier. He had a conditional discharge only. The United States clearly reserved the right to charge and try him by court-martial for a crime committed while in the status of a soldier. This is the way Congress had provided for his trial. No other way was provided. That it may have provided another way is not to say the way provided is invalid.

I know of no reason why Congress could not pass this statute, 50 U.S.C. § 553, retaining court-martial jurisdiction over Toth to answer for a crime he allegedly committed when he was clearly subject to court-martial. *Kahn v. Anderson*, 255 U.S. 1, holds that, even though discharged from service, one convicted and serving sentence for a military offense could still be tried by court-martial for murder and conspiracy to commit murder, even though the crime was alleged to have been committed within the limits of a state. Congress had made no provision for retention of status in that case as it had in this case, yet the Court implied the continuing military status to warrant the jurisdiction. No implied status is necessary here. It is expressly reserved by statute. Toth remained in that status by virtue of the statute.

NOTES AND QUESTIONS

1. Why should challenges to military jurisdiction be heard by civilian courts before the military court has decided the case? *See Hamdan v. Rumsfeld*, 126 S. Ct. 2749 (2006) (challenge to military commission by Guantánamo detainee), Chapter 19, § II.

2. Article 2(a)(13), as added by the Military Commissions Act of 2006, extended court-martial jurisdiction to lawful enemy combatants, while alien unlawful enemy combatants were subjected to trial by military commissions. *See* Military Commissions Act of 2006, Pub. L. No. 109-366, § 3(a), 120 Stat. 2600, 2062 (adding 10 U.S.C. § 948c). Why subject these two categories of accused to different forums and rules?

3. Under what circumstances should military jurisdiction continue even after a defendant has returned to civilian life? In *Martin v. Ver*, G.R. No. L-62810 (Phil. 1983) (en banc), the Supreme Court of the Philippines dismissed a habeas corpus petition filed by a former soldier who was held for trial by court-martial for stealing grenades before his discharge. One of the grenades had exploded at a picnic, killing three persons and wounding three others, before his discharge. Article 95 of the Philippine Articles of War provided that "if any person, being guilty of [a variety of frauds against the government] while in the service of the Armed Forces of the Philippines or of the Philippine Constabulary receives his discharge or is dismissed from the service, he shall continue to be liable to be arrested and held for trial and sentence by a court-martial in the same manner and to the same extent as if he had not received such discharge nor been dismissed."

4. What if a soldier is discharged while his case is pending on appeal? Execution of a punitive discharge "does not deprive the court of jurisdiction to grant a petition for review." *United States v. Engle*, 28 M.J. 299 (1989) (per curiam); *see also United States v. Woods*, 26 M.J. 372 (1988) (appellate jurisdiction unaffected by release from active duty); *State v. Sulaiman*, No. 4 of 1984 (Sing. Mil. App. 1984) (government appeal of sentence as manifestly inadequate; *held*, appellate jurisdiction unaffected by intervening discharge), *application dismissed, Sulaiman v. Commandant, Tanglin Detention Barracks*, 1984-85 Sing. L. Rep. 555 (High Ct. 1985).

III. DEPENDENTS

REID v. COVERT
Supreme Court of the United States
354 U.S. 1 (1957)

[Two women, one in England and one in Japan, murdered their active duty husbands. Neither wife was a member of the armed forces. One couple lived on base; the other lived off base.]

MR. JUSTICE BLACK announced the judgment of the Court and delivered an opinion, in which THE CHIEF JUSTICE, MR. JUSTICE DOUGLAS, and MR. JUSTICE BRENNAN join.

These cases raise basic constitutional issues of the utmost concern. They call into question the role of the military under our system of government. They involve the power of Congress to expose civilians to trial by military tribunals, under military regulations and procedures, for offenses against the United States thereby depriving them of trial in civilian courts, under civilian laws and procedures and with all the safeguards of the Bill of Rights. These cases are particularly significant because for the first time since the adoption of the Constitution wives of soldiers have been denied trial by jury in a court of law and forced to trial before courts-martial. . . .

The court-martial asserted jurisdiction over Mrs. Covert under Article 2(11) of the UCMJ, which provides:

"The following persons are subject to this code:

"(11) Subject to the provisions of any treaty or agreement to which the United States is or may be a party or to any accepted rule of international law, all persons serving with, employed by, or accompanying the armed forces without the continental limits of the United States. . . ."

The two cases were consolidated and argued last Term and a majority of the Court, with three Justices dissenting and one reserving opinion, held that military trial of Mrs. Smith and Mrs. Covert for their alleged offenses was constitutional. 351 U.S. 470, 487. The majority held that the provisions of Article III and the Fifth and Sixth Amendments which require that crimes be tried by a jury after indictment by a grand jury did not protect an American citizen when he was tried by the American Government in foreign lands for offenses committed there and that Congress could provide for the trial of such offenses in any manner it saw fit so long as the procedures established were reasonable and consonant with due process. The opinion then went on to express the view that military trials, as now practiced, were not unreasonable or arbitrary when applied to dependents accompanying members of the armed forces overseas. In reaching their conclusion the majority found it unnecessary to consider the power of Congress "To make Rules for the Government and Regulation of the land and naval Forces" under Article I of the Constitution.

Subsequently, the Court granted a petition for rehearing, 352 U.S. 901. Now, after further argument and consideration, we conclude that the previous decisions cannot be permitted to stand. We hold that Mrs. Smith and Mrs. Covert could not constitutionally be tried by military authorities.

[In the first two parts of the decision, the Court "reject[ed] the idea that when the United States acts against citizens abroad it can do so free of the Bill of Rights" and held that "no agreement with a foreign nation can confer power on the Congress, or on any other branch of Government, which is free from the restraints of the Constitution." As a result, "the constitution in its entirety applied to the trials of Mrs. Smith and Mrs. Covert. Since their court-martial did not meet the requirements of Art. III, §2 or the Fifth and Sixth Amendments we are compelled to determine if there is anything within the Constitution which authorizes the military trial of dependents accompanying the armed forces overseas."]

Article I, §8, cl. 14 empowers Congress "To make Rules for the Government and Regulation of the land and naval Forces." It has been held that this creates an exception to the normal method of trial in civilian courts as provided by the Constitution and permits Congress to authorize military trial of members of the armed services without all the safeguards given an accused by Article III and the Bill of Rights. But if the language of Clause 14 is given its natural meaning, the power granted does not extend to civilians — even though they may be dependents living with servicemen on a military base. The term "land and naval Forces" refers to persons who are members of the armed services and not to their civilian wives, children and other dependents. It seems inconceivable that Mrs. Covert or Mrs. Smith could have been tried by military authorities as members of the "land and naval Forces" had they been living on a military post in this country. Yet this constitutional term surely has the same meaning everywhere. The wives of servicemen are no more members of the "land and naval Forces" when living at a military post in England or Japan than when living at a base in this country or in Hawaii or Alaska.

The Government argues that the Necessary and Proper Clause when taken in conjunction with Clause 14 allows Congress to authorize the trial of Mrs. Smith and Mrs. Covert by military tribunals and under military law. The Government claims that the two clauses together constitute a broad grant of power "without limitation" authorizing Congress to subject all persons, civilians and soldiers alike, to military trial if "necessary and proper" to govern and regulate the land and naval forces. It was on a similar theory that Congress once went to the extreme of subjecting persons who made contracts with the military to court-martial jurisdiction with respect to frauds related to such contracts. . . .

It is true that the Constitution expressly grants Congress power to make all rules necessary and proper to govern and regulate those persons who are serving in the "land and naval Forces." But the Necessary and Proper Clause cannot operate to extend military jurisdiction to any group of persons beyond that class described in Clause 14 — "the land and naval Forces." Under the grand design of the Constitution civilian courts are the normal repositories of power to try persons charged with crimes against the United States. And to protect persons brought before these courts, Article III and the Fifth, Sixth, and Eighth Amendments establish the right to trial by jury, to indictment by a grand jury and a number of other specific safeguards. By way of contrast the jurisdiction of military tribunals is a very limited and extraordinary jurisdiction derived from the cryptic language in Art. I, § 8, and, at most, was intended to be only a narrow exception to the normal and preferred method of trial in courts of law. Every extension of military jurisdiction is an encroachment on the jurisdiction of the civil courts, and, more important, acts as a deprivation of the right to jury trial and of other treasured constitutional protections. Having run up against the steadfast bulwark of the Bill of Rights, the Necessary and Proper Clause cannot extend the scope of Clause 14.

Nothing said here contravenes the rule laid down in *McCulloch v. Maryland*, 4 Wheat. 316, at 421, that:

> "Let the end be legitimate, let it be within the scope of the constitution, and all means which are appropriate, which are plainly adapted to that end, which are not prohibited, but consist with the letter and spirit of the constitution, are constitutional."

In *McCulloch* this Court was confronted with the problem of determining the scope of the Necessary and Proper Clause in a situation where no specific restraints on governmental power stood in the way. Here the problem is different. Not only does Clause 14, by its terms, limit military jurisdiction to members of the "land and naval Forces," but Art. III, § 2 and the Fifth and Sixth Amendments require that certain express safeguards, which were designed to protect persons from oppressive governmental practices, shall be given in criminal prosecutions — safe-guards which cannot be given in a military trial. In the light of these as well as other constitutional provisions, and the historical background in which they were formed, military trial of civilians is inconsistent with both the "letter and spirit of the constitution."

Further light is reflected on the scope of Clause 14 by the Fifth Amendment. That Amendment which was adopted shortly after the Constitution reads:

> "No person shall be held to answer for a capital, or otherwise infamous crime, unless on a presentment or indictment of a Grand Jury, *except in cases arising in the land or naval forces*, or in the Militia, when in actual service in time of War or public danger; . . ." (Emphasis added.)

Since the exception in this Amendment for "cases arising in the land or naval forces" was undoubtedly designed to correlate with the power granted Congress to provide for the "Government and Regulation" of the armed services, it is a persuasive and reliable indication that the authority conferred by Clause 14 does not encompass persons who cannot fairly be said to be "in" the military service.

Even if it were possible, we need not attempt here to precisely define the boundary between "civilians" and members of the "land and naval Forces." We recognize that there might be circumstances where a person could be "in" the armed services for purposes of Clause 14 even though he had not formally been inducted into the military or did not wear a uniform. But the wives, children and other dependents of servicemen cannot be placed in that category, even though they may be accompanying a serviceman abroad at Government expense and receiving other benefits from the Government. We have no difficulty in saying that such persons do not lose their civilian status and their right to a civilian trial because the Government helps them live as members of a soldier's family.

The tradition of keeping the military subordinate to civilian authority may not be so strong in the minds of this generation as it was in the minds of those who wrote the Constitution. The idea that the relatives of soldiers could be denied a jury trial in a court of law and instead be tried by court-martial under the guise of regulating the armed forces would have seemed incredible to those men, in whose lifetime the right of the military to try soldiers for any offenses in time of peace had only been grudgingly conceded. The Founders envisioned the army as a necessary institution, but one dangerous to liberty if not confined within its essential bounds. Their fears were rooted in history. They knew that ancient republics had been overthrown by their military leaders. They were familiar with the history of Seventeenth Century England, where Charles I tried to govern through the army and without Parliament. During this attempt, contrary to the Common Law, he used courts-martial to try soldiers for certain non-military offenses. This court-martialing of soldiers in peacetime evoked strong protests from Parliament. The reign of Charles I was followed by the rigorous military rule of Oliver Cromwell. Later, James II used the Army in his fight against Parliament and the people. He promulgated Articles of War (strangely enough relied on in the Government's brief) authorizing the trial of soldiers for non-military crimes by courts-martial. This action hastened the revolution that brought William and Mary to the throne upon their agreement to abide by a Bill of Rights which, among other things, protected the right of trial by jury. It was against this general background that two of the greatest English jurists, Lord Chief Justice Hale and Sir William Blackstone — men who exerted considerable influence on the Founders — expressed sharp hostility to any expansion of the jurisdiction of military courts. For instance, Blackstone went so far as to assert:

> "For martial law, which is built upon no settled principles, but is entirely arbitrary in its decisions, is, as Sir Matthew Hale observes, in truth and reality no law, but something indulged rather than allowed as a law. The necessity of order and discipline in an army is the only thing which can give it countenance; and therefore it ought not to be permitted in time of peace, when the king's courts are open for all persons to receive justice according to the laws of the land."

The generation that adopted the Constitution did not distrust the military because of past history alone. Within their own lives they had seen royal governors sometimes resort to military rule. British troops were quartered in Boston at various times from 1768 until the outbreak of the Revolutionary War to support unpopular royal governors and to intimidate the local populace. The trial of soldiers by courts-martial and the interference of the military with the civil courts aroused great anxiety and antagonism not only in Massachusetts but throughout the colonies. For example, Samuel Adams in 1768 wrote:

> ". . . [I]s it not enough for us to have seen soldiers and mariners fore-judged of life, and executed within the body of the county by martial law? Are citizens to be called upon, threatened, ill-used at the will of the soldiery, and put under arrest, by pretext of the law military, in breach of the fundamental rights of subjects, and contrary to the law and franchise of the land? . . . Will the spirits of people as yet unsubdued by tyranny, unawed by the menaces of arbitrary power, submit to be governed by military force? No! Let us rouse our attention to the common law, — which is our birthright, our great security against all kinds of insult and oppression. . . ."

Colonials had also seen the right to trial by jury subverted by acts of Parliament which authorized courts of admiralty to try alleged violations of the unpopular "Molasses" and "Navigation" Acts. This gave the admiralty courts jurisdiction over offenses historically triable only by a jury in a court of law and aroused great resentment throughout the colonies. As early as 1765 delegates from nine colonies meeting in New York asserted in a "Declaration of Rights" that trial by jury was the "inherent and invaluable" right of every citizen in the colonies.

With this background it is not surprising that the Declaration of Independence protested that George III had "affected to render the Military independent of and superior to the Civil Power" and that Americans had been deprived in many cases of "the benefits of Trial by Jury." And those who adopted the Constitution embodied their profound fear and distrust of military power, as well as their determination to protect trial by jury, in the Constitution and its Amendments.

Perhaps they were aware that memories fade and hoped that in this way they could keep the people of this Nation from having to fight again and again the same old battles for individual freedom.

In light of this history, it seems clear that the Founders had no intention to permit the trial of civilians in military courts, where they would be denied jury trials and other constitutional protections, merely by giving Congress the power to make rules which were "necessary and proper" for the regulation of the "land and naval Forces." Such a latitudinarian interpretation of these clauses would be at war with the well-established purpose of the Founders to keep the military strictly within its proper sphere, subordinate to civil authority. The Constitution does not say that Congress can regulate "the land and naval Forces and all other persons whose regulation might have some relationship to maintenance of the land and naval Forces." There is no indication that the Founders contemplated setting up a rival system of military courts to compete with civilian courts for jurisdiction over civilians who might have some contact or relationship with the armed forces. Courts-martial were not to have concurrent jurisdiction with courts of law over non-military America.

On several occasions this Court has been faced with an attempted expansion of the jurisdiction of military courts. *Ex parte Milligan*, 4 Wall. 2, one of the great landmarks in this Court's history, held that military authorities were without power to try civilians not in the military or naval service by declaring martial law in an area where the civil administration was not deposed and the courts were not closed. In a stirring passage the Court proclaimed:

> "Another guarantee of freedom was broken when Milligan was denied a trial by jury. The great minds of the country have differed on the correct interpretation to be given to various provisions of the Federal Constitution; and judicial decision has been often invoked to settle their true meaning; but until recently no one ever doubted that the right of trial by jury was fortified in the organic law against the power of attack. It is now assailed; but if ideas can be expressed in words, and language has any meaning, this right — one of the most valuable in a free country — is preserved to everyone accused of crime who is not attached to the army, or navy, or militia in actual service."

In *Duncan v. Kahanamoku*, 327 U.S. 304, the Court reasserted the principles enunciated in *Ex parte Milligan* and reaffirmed the tradition of military subordination to civil authorities and institutions. It refused to sanction the military trial of civilians in Hawaii during wartime despite government claims that the needs of defense made martial law imperative.

Just last Term, this Court held in *United States ex rel. Toth v. Quarles*, 350 U.S. 11, that military courts could not constitutionally try a discharged serviceman for an offense which he had allegedly committed while in the armed forces. It was decided (1) that since Toth was a civilian he could not be tried by military court-martial, and (2) that since he was charged with murder, a "crime" in the constitutional sense, he was entitled to indictment by a grand jury, jury trial, and the other protections contained in Art. III, §2 and the Fifth, Sixth, and Eighth Amendments. The Court pointed out that trial by civilian courts was the rule for persons who were not members of the armed forces.

There are no supportable grounds upon which to distinguish the *Toth* case from the present cases. Toth, Mrs. Covert, and Mrs. Smith were all civilians. All three were American citizens. All three were tried for murder. All three alleged crimes were committed in a foreign country. The only differences were: (1) Toth was an ex-serviceman while they were wives of soldiers; (2) Toth was arrested in the United States while they were seized in foreign countries. If anything, Toth had closer connection with the military than the two women for his crime was committed while he was actually serving in the Air Force. Mrs. Covert and Mrs. Smith had never been members of the army, had never been employed by the army, had never served in the army in any capacity. The Government appropriately argued in *Toth* that the constitutional basis for court-martialing him was clearer than for court-martialing wives who are accompanying their husbands abroad. Certainly Toth's conduct as a soldier bears a closer relation to the maintenance of order and discipline in the armed forces than the conduct of these wives. The fact that Toth was arrested here while the wives were arrested in foreign countries is material only if constitutional safeguards do not shield a citizen abroad when the Government exercises its power over him. As we have said before, such a view of the Constitution is erroneous. The mere fact that these women had gone overseas with their husbands should not reduce the protection the Constitution gives them.

The *Milligan, Duncan* and *Toth* cases recognized and manifested the deeply rooted and ancient opposition in this country to the extension of military control over civilians. In each instance an effort to expand the jurisdiction of military courts to civilians was repulsed.

There have been a number of decisions in the lower federal courts which have upheld military trial of civilians performing services for the armed forces "in the field" during time of war. To the extent that these cases can be justified, insofar as they involved trial of persons who were not "members" of the armed forces, they must rest on the Government's "war powers." In the face of an actively hostile enemy, military commanders necessarily have broad power over persons on the battlefront. From a time prior to the adoption of the Constitution the extraordinary circumstances present in an area of actual fighting have been considered sufficient to permit punishment of some civilians in that area by military courts under military rules. But neither Japan nor Great Britain could properly be said to be an area where active hostilities were under way at the time Mrs. Smith and Mrs. Covert committed their offenses or at the time they were tried.

The Government urges that the concept "in the field" should be broadened to reach dependents accompanying the military forces overseas under the conditions of world tension which exist at the present time. It points out how the "war powers" include authority to prepare defenses and to establish our military forces in defensive posture about the world. While we recognize that the "war powers" of the Congress and the Executive are broad, we reject the Government's argument that present threats to peace permit military trial of civilians accompanying the armed forces overseas in an area where no actual hostilities are under way. The exigencies which have required military rule on the battlefront are not present in areas where no conflict exists. Military trial of civilians "in the field" is an extraordinary jurisdiction and it should not be expanded at the expense of the Bill of Rights. We agree with Colonel Winthrop, an expert on military jurisdiction, who declared: "*a statute cannot be framed by which a civilian can lawfully be made amenable to the military jurisdiction in time of peace.*" (Emphasis not supplied.)

As this Court stated in *United States ex rel. Toth v. Quarles*, 350 U.S. 11, the business of soldiers is to fight and prepare to fight wars, not to try civilians for their alleged crimes. Traditionally, military justice has been a rough form of justice emphasizing summary procedures, speedy convictions and stern penalties with a view to maintaining obedience and fighting fitness in the ranks. Because of its very nature and purpose the military must place great emphasis on discipline and efficiency. Correspondingly, there has always been less emphasis in the military on protecting the rights of the individual than in civilian society and in civilian courts.

Courts-martial are typically ad hoc bodies appointed by a military officer from among his subordinates. They have always been subject to varying degrees of "command influence." In essence, these tribunals are simply executive tribunals whose personnel are in the executive chain of command. Frequently, the members of the court-martial must look to the appointing officer for promotions, advantageous assignments and efficiency ratings — in short, for their future progress in the service. Conceding to military personnel that high degree of honesty and sense of justice which nearly all of them undoubtedly have, the members of a court-martial, in the nature of things, do not and cannot have the independence of jurors drawn from the general public or of civilian judges.

We recognize that a number of improvements have been made in military justice recently by engrafting more and more of the methods of civilian courts on courts-martial. In large part these ameliorations stem from the reaction of civilians, who were inducted during the two World Wars, to their experience with military justice. Notwithstanding the recent reforms, military trial does not give an accused the same protection which exists in the civil courts. Looming far above all other deficiencies of the military trial, of course, is the absence of trial by jury before an independent judge after an indictment by a grand jury. Moreover the reforms are merely statutory; Congress — and perhaps the President — can reinstate former practices, subject to any limitations imposed by the Constitution, whenever it desires. As yet it has not been clearly settled to what extent the Bill of Rights and other protective parts of the Constitution apply to military trials.

It must be emphasized that every person who comes within the jurisdiction of courts-martial is subject to military law — law that is substantially different from the law which governs civilian society. Military law is, in many respects, harsh law which is frequently cast in very sweeping and vague terms. It emphasizes the iron hand of discipline more that it does the even scales of justice. Moreover, it has not yet been definitely established to what extent the President, as Commander-in-Chief of the armed forces, or his delegates, can promulgate, supplement or change substantive military law as well as the procedures of military courts in time of peace, or in time of war. In any event, Congress has given the President broad discretion to provide the rules governing military trials. For example, in these very cases a technical manual issued under the President's name with regard to the defense of insanity in military trials was of critical importance in the convictions of Mrs. Covert and Mrs. Smith. If the President can provide rules of substantive law as well as procedure, then he and his military subordinates exercise legislative, executive and judicial powers with respect to those subject to military trials. Such blending of functions in one branch of the Government is the objectionable thing which the draftsmen of the Constitution endeavored to prevent by providing for the separation of governmental powers.

In summary, "it still remains true that military tribunals have not been and probably never can be constituted in such way that they can have the same kind of qualifications that the Constitution has deemed essential to fair trials of civilians in federal courts." In part this is attributable to the inherent differences in values and attitudes that separate the military establishment from civilian society. In the military, by necessity, emphasis must be placed on the security and order of the group rather than on the value and integrity of the individual.

It is urged that the expansion of military jurisdiction over civilians claimed here is only slight, and that the practical necessity for it is very great. The attitude appears to be that a slight encroachment on the Bill of Rights and other safeguards in the Constitution need cause little concern. But to hold that these wives could be tried by the military would be a tempting precedent. Slight encroachments create new boundaries from which legions of power can seek new territory to capture. "It may be that it is the obnoxious thing in its mildest and least repulsive form; but illegitimate and unconstitutional practices get their first footing in that way, namely, by silent approaches and slight deviations from legal modes of procedure. This can only be obviated by adhering to the rule that constitutional provisions for the security of person and property should be liberally construed. A close and literal construction deprives them of half their efficacy, and leads to gradual depreciation of the right, as if it consisted more in sound than in substance. It is the duty of courts to be watchful for the constitutional rights of the citizen, and against any stealthy encroachments thereon." Moreover we cannot consider this encroachment a slight one. Throughout history many transgressions by the military have been called "slight" and have been justified as "reasonable" in light of the "uniqueness" of the times. We cannot close our eyes to the fact that today the peoples of many nations are ruled by the military.

We should not break faith with this Nation's tradition of keeping military power subservient to civilian authority, a tradition which we believe is firmly embodied in the Constitution. The country has remained true to that faith for almost one hundred seventy years. Perhaps no group in the Nation has been truer than military men themselves. Unlike the soldiers of many other nations, they have been content to perform their military duties in defense of the Nation in every period of need and to perform those duties well without attempting to usurp power which is not theirs under our system of constitutional government.

Ours is a government of divided authority on the assumption that in division there is not only strength but freedom from tyranny. And under our Constitution courts of law alone are given power to try civilians for their offenses against the United States. The philosophy expressed by Lord Coke, speaking long ago from a wealth of experience, is still timely:

> "God send me never to live under the Law of Conveniency or Discretion. Shall the Souldier and Justice Sit on one Bench, the Trumpet will not let the Cryer speak in Westminster-Hall."

[Mrs. Covert and Mrs. Smith were ordered released from custody.]

THE QUEEN v. MARTIN
House of Lords
[1997] UKHL 56, [1998] A.C. 917

[The minor son of a British soldier stationed in Germany was convicted of murder by a court-martial. He argued that he should not have been tried by court-martial. The Court-Martial Appeal Court found that the proceedings complied with the procedure laid down by Parliament and were not abusive.]

LORD LLOYD OF BERWICK

. . . On Corporal Martin's return to England, the appellant would ordinarily have ceased to be subject to military law. But section 131 of the Act provides an exception. The appellant remained subject to military law in respect of offences committed while in Germany, provided his trial started within six months. Since it seemed unlikely that the trial could start by 24 October (six months after his father returned to England) it was necessary to obtain the consent of the Attorney-General under section 132(3A).

On 14 June 1994 the Attorney-General was asked for his consent. It was explained that the trial was to take place in Germany, since many of the witnesses were German and they could not be subpoenaed to attend a trial in England. It was also explained that this was a case in which the British military authorities had jurisdiction by reason of the German Government having waived its primary right to exercise jurisdiction under the NATO Status of Forces Agreement (Cmnd. 9363). On 10 December the Attorney-General gave his consent to the prosecution of the appellant by court-martial.

In due course the court-martial was convened, and the appellant was returned to Germany to stand trial. He had been in receipt of legal aid since 10 February 1994. The trial commenced on 21 April 1995. On the first day of the trial Lord Thomas made a submission under rule 36 of the Rules of Procedure that the court-martial had no jurisdiction. One of the grounds for this submission was that the Attorney-General's consent had been given too late. Another ground was that it was an abuse of process to bring the appellant from England, where he was eligible for trial by jury, to stand trial by court-martial in Germany. On 24 April 1995 the Judge Advocate ruled against the appellant, whereupon Lord Thomas asked for an adjournment. He said that he wished to apply for judicial review of the Judge Advocate's ruling, as well as the Attorney-General's consent. The application for an adjournment was refused. Thereafter a number of witnesses were called, including expert evidence from four German witnesses, one of whom had carried out D.N.A. testing of the appellant and the victim. The trial was concluded on 3 May 1995, when the appellant was convicted.

What is the basis for Lord Thomas's submission that there was an abuse of process? In the end it came down to this: that the trial of a young civilian by court-martial was inherently unfair and oppressive. Instead of being tried by a jury of his peers, the court-martial would consist of five senior officers and two civilians. It was said that the atmosphere in such a court would be very different from that of an English court, and for that reason, presumably, there was a risk that the appellant might not do himself justice. In particular it was unfair and oppressive that he should be returned to stand trial in Germany after spending many months in England, and after his father had ceased to be subject to military law. Lastly, the appellant could only be convicted in England by a majority of at least 10 to 2, whereas a simple majority suffices in a trial by court-martial.

. . . In ruling that there had been no abuse of process, the Judge Advocate said:

> I am satisfied that the prosecution have neither manipulated nor misused the process of the Court so as to deprive the defendant of a protection provided by the law or take unfair advantage of a technicality. I am also satisfied that the defendant has not been and will not be prejudiced in the preparation or conduct of his defence by delay on the part of the prosecution. Accordingly, I rule that there has been no abuse of process. . . .

. . . The decisive factor in the present case is that Parliament has itself approved trial by court-martial as a mode of trial which is appropriate for civilians in certain circumstances, and for juveniles who, like the appellant, have been charged with murder: see section 71A of the Act. Since the procedure has been approved by Parliament, it would seem obvious that the carrying out of the procedure cannot of itself be categorised as an abuse of process. In so far as the certified question is capable of a generalised answer, I would hold that the answer must be no.

But Lord Thomas does not leave the matter there. He draws attention to section 77A of the Act which provides:

> Where, in the course of investigating a charge, it appears to the accused's commanding officer that proceedings in respect of the matters to which the charge relates could be, and in the interests of the better administration of justice ought to be, taken against the accused otherwise than under this Act he may stay further proceedings on the charge.

Lord Thomas submits that the commanding officer ought to have exercised his power under section 77A to stay proceedings "in the interests of the better administration of justice" so as to allow the appellant to be tried in England. It appears that the power conferred by section 77A has seldom, if ever, been exercised since the section was first enacted in 1981. But the power is there, and the question is whether the failure to exercise the power in this case was an abuse of process.

There are a number of difficulties in the way of Lord Thomas's submission. In the first place it is not clear to me that the German waiver of jurisdiction under the Status of Forces Agreement (Cmnd. 9363) extended as far as to allow the appellant to be tried in England. It may be that the German authorities would have sought to reclaim jurisdiction if they had been told that the trial was not to take place by court-martial in Germany. We do not know.

Secondly, we know almost nothing of what took place during the commanding officer's investigation. Lord Thomas relies on this absence of information as itself pointing to an abuse of process. But this goes much too far. If there was to be an attack on the proceedings before the commanding officer, it was surely for the appellant to lay the evidential foundation for that attack. There is no presumption of irregularity.

Assuming the commanding officer directed his mind at all to the possibility of a trial in England instead of Germany, the question that then arises is whether he can be criticised for choosing Germany. Lord Bingham of Cornhill C.J. in giving judgment in the Courts-Martial Appeal Court pointed to the greater availability of factual witnesses in Germany. This was, he said, a legitimate reason for favouring a trial there. I respectfully agree. But it was not just the large number of factual witnesses who were to be found in Germany. The most important of the expert witnesses were also German, including Professor Weber who carried out the post mortem and Dr. Meyer who carried out D.N.A. testing on the appellant and the victim. The latter was a crucial witness for the prosecution. There was reason to suppose that he would not be willing to give evidence in England. In a criminal trial fairness to the accused has to be balanced against fairness to the prosecution. On the exiguous facts before us it is by no means clear that the balance of fairness came down in favour of trial in England.

But even if it did, that would not be an end of the matter. It is not enough that the commanding officer ought to have stayed the proceedings under section 77A "in the interests of the better administration of justice." It must be shown that his failure to do so was an abuse of process. . . . It could not possibly be said that the decision not to stay proceedings by court-martial in Germany, where the crime was committed, was contrary to the rule of law, or that it deprived the appellant of any of his basic human rights. Nor could it be said to be "something so unfair and wrong" (see *per* Lord Lowry in *Hui Chi-Ming v. The Queen* [1992] 1 A.C. 34, 57) that the courts ought to intervene. In my view the decision of the commanding officer not to stay the proceedings under section 77A, but to refer the case to higher authority, was one which was fully open to him under a procedure prescribed by Parliament. It may have been the wrong decision. We do not know enough to say. But it was not an abuse of process, or anything like it. . . .

Lord Slynn of Hadley

As a matter of first impression it seemed to me disturbing and indeed wrong in principle that a nineteen year old civilian, albeit the son of a serving soldier at the time of the murder he was alleged to have committed in Germany, who had with his father returned to England more than a year before trial, should be sent back to Germany for trial by court-martial and thereby be deprived of the right, or at the least of the opportunity, of trial by jury. That impression was only underlined by (a) my doubts as to whether the commanding officer had ever really considered whether pursuant to section 77A of the Army Act 1955 proceedings should, in the interests of the better administration of justice, be taken against the accused otherwise than under the Act, namely by proceedings before the ordinary courts in England; and (b) the fact that it was not shown that there was an opportunity for representations to be made by or on behalf of the accused before decisions were made by the commanding officer and by higher authority that the case should proceed before a court-martial.

It is, however, clear that Parliament has provided for a court martial to be held in the circumstances of this case and, after full argument on both sides, I do not consider that it has been shown that there was any breach of the rules required to be followed or that there has been any abuse of process entitling the Courts-Martial Appeal Court or your Lordships' House to interfere. In addition weight must be given to the fact that it seems that there would have been great difficulty in having the evidence of at any rate some of the crucial German witnesses before the English civilian court; trial somewhere there clearly had to be.

Accordingly, and despite my anxiety about the case, I agree that for the reasons given by my noble and learned friend Lord Lloyd of Berwick, whose speech in draft I have had the advantage of reading, the appeal should be dismissed.

I add, however, that whilst trial by court-martial abroad of a serving member of the armed forces, who has returned to England, may perhaps readily be justified, I hope that if circumstances analogous to the present where a civilian is involved arise again it will be shown clearly that the commanding officer has considered the exercise of his discretion under section 77A of the Army Act 1955 and what are the reasons for his decision.

LORD HOPE OF CRAIGHEAD

My Lords, at first sight the decision to prosecute the appellant at a general court-martial on a charge of murder was quite inappropriate. He was a civilian and was aged only 17 at the time of the alleged murder. He had been detained for a year in England while awaiting his trial, and he was no longer subject to military law. Although the crime was committed in Germany, his trial could have been held in the Crown Court under section 9 of the Offences against the Person Act 1861. Instead he was taken back to Germany so that he could be court-martialed there. As Lord Bingham of Cornhill C.J. said when delivering the judgment of the Courts-Martial Appeal Court, it seems plain with the benefit of hindsight that a trial could have been conducted in England without undue difficulty.

 But the question for us is not whether trial by jury in an English court would have been more appropriate. The question is whether the proceedings by way of general court-martial in this case were an abuse of process. I believe that when this question is examined with a proper regard to the statutory context and after a careful examination of the facts which are known to us — recognising that on some important matters we do not have the facts — there can be only one answer to it. This is that it must be answered in the negative. . . .

. . . [Section 133 of the Army Act] provides that, where a person subject to military law has been tried for an offence by court-martial, a civil court shall be debarred from trying him subsequently for an offence substantially the same as that offence. So it is clear that the effect of allowing the appeal in this case would be not only to quash the conviction by the court-martial but also to bring to an end all proceedings against this appellant for this offence in any court.

The effect of such a decision on the course of justice in this case would be profound. . . .

. . . But it is impossible to say that it would be an abuse of process for a civilian to be prosecuted for these offences by means of a court-martial if they were committed abroad. Parliament has provided by necessary implication to the contrary.

The question whether Parliament intended that juveniles should be capable of being prosecuted for murder committed abroad by means of a court martial was put beyond all doubt by section 10 of the Armed Forces Act 1976. This section inserted a new section 71A in both the Army Act 1955 and the Air Force Act 1955 dealing particularly with the powers of a court-martial under those Acts in relation to juvenile offenders. Subsection (3) of that section deals with the case of a person convicted of murder who was under the age of 18 years when the offence was committed. It applies directly to the circumstances of the present case. It provides that such a person shall not be sentenced to life imprisonment or to the imposition of the death penalty but that he shall be sentenced to be detained during Her Majesty's pleasure. In my opinion this subsection, when taken in the context of the other provisions to which I have referred, amounts to an acknowledgement by Parliament that it was open to the military authorities to proceed by way of court-martial on a charge of murder against a civilian who was under the age of 18 when the crime was committed. Here again it seems to me to be impossible to say that it would be an abuse of the process of court-martial for a juvenile to be prosecuted in this way. Such a proceeding is entirely in accordance with the procedures laid down by Parliament. . . .

. . . One obvious factor, I should have thought, was the availability of witnesses. In his letter of 14 June 1994 to the Attorney-General the Director of Army Legal Services had stated that many of the witnesses were German and that they could not be forced to attend a trial in England. Further details were provided at the request of the Attorney-General in a letter by the Director of Army Legal Services dated 25 November 1994. In this letter it is stated that there were 13 German witnesses who would be divided into three categories — those who saw the appellant in the woods near the scene of the murder, those concerned with the finding of the body and police and forensic experts. The defence had not yet indicated what evidence would be agreed. The Director thought that, while some of their evidence might be agreed, it was unlikely that this would include the police and forensic experts. He believed that they were the witnesses who would be most unlikely to cause difficulties if asked to travel to England to give evidence. He added that that one of the forensic scientists who was responsible for examining secretions and blood-stains — a matter which was of crucial importance in this case as there were no eyewitnesses — was being difficult to deal with and would only attend meetings if they were arranged through the German public prosecutor in the nearest large town. He explained that these witnesses were German because the police investigation was commenced by the German civil police as it was initially assumed that a German civilian had perpetrated the crime. . . .

. . . The proceedings were conducted within the rules laid down by Parliament. There is no sound basis for thinking that, at the time when a decision about this would have had to have been taken, a prosecution in the English courts within a reasonable time would have been seen to be practicable. The alternatives lay between taking proceedings by way of court-martial in Germany, leaving the matter in the hands of the German public prosecutor or taking no proceedings at all.

In the interests of justice proceedings clearly had to be taken in this case. The only way to secure the ends of justice other than returning the case to the German prosecutor was to proceed by way of a court-martial. There is no ground for saying that the appellant did not receive a fair trial. I would therefore dismiss this appeal.

Lord Clyde

. . . The gravamen of [Martin's] complaint is that he should have been tried by the ordinary criminal process of a jury trial in England and not by a military court in Germany. In this connection he points out that he was a civilian of eighteen years of age at the time of the trial, not under military discipline, facing a charge of murdering a woman who was evidently a member of an officers' mess before a court consisting of five senior officers and two civilians who could properly return a verdict by a simple majority. He had come under the military regime by no choice of his own but by virtue of the statutory provisions to which I have already referred. Had the case proceeded to England he would have had the advantage of a jury selected at random from his peers and their verdict would have required to be unanimous or at least by a majority of ten to two. His counsel touched on the intimidating nature of the military court for a youth of the appellant's age, although it does appear that some of the more rigorous formalities which may attend the trial of servicemen are relaxed in the case of civilians. In addition the appellant did not have the benefit of the provisions regulating bail nor of the possibility of varying the place of his remand which might have been afforded by the civilian procedures. Instead he was held in the Military Corrective Training Centre at Colchester which was primarily designed for service personnel. The essence of the appellant's complaint is that in the whole circumstances it was an abuse of process for him to have been removed from England, where he could have been tried before a judge and jury, and taken to Germany to stand trial before a court-martial. It was not the trial itself which was attacked. Indeed it is accepted that it was conducted fairly and in accordance with the proper procedures. The attack is directed against the pre-trial procedures and the proposition is advanced that they were unfair and oppressive. It is claimed that in that respect there was an abuse of process and the verdict should be quashed.

Counsel for the appellant identified three stages at each of which he argued that the fairness of the proceedings could and should have been considered. The first of these is contained in section 77A of the Act which provides that:

> Where, in the course of investigating a charge, it appears to the accused's commanding officer that proceedings in respect of the matters to which the charge relates could be, and in the interests of the better administration of justice ought to be, taken against the accused otherwise than under this Act he may stay further proceedings on the charge.

Counsel for the respondent pointed to the words "where it appears" and submitted that there was no obligation imposed on the commanding officer to ask and answer the question of a stay. I am not persuaded that that is correct. The words "where it appears" seem to me to be doing no more than making the decision whether or not to stay the proceedings a matter for the subjective decision of the commanding officer. They should not be construed as allowing the matter to be left to the chance that something might emerge in the course of the investigation which triggers the thought in the commanding officer's mind. In my view the section, by providing in effect that where he considers that there ought to be a stay he may grant one, imposes on him an obligation to apply his mind to the question in the course of his investigation. Parliament has made this express provision for the possibility of a stay in the interests of the better administration of justice and has given the commanding officer a discretion to be exercised in that regard. . . .

Two other questions arise. The first is whether if the question of stay for a trial in England was considered a decision to prefer a court-martial in Germany was irrational. Looking to the factors which I have already noted in comparing the two processes, and bearing in mind particularly the serious nature of the charge which the appellant was facing, there seem to me to be powerful arguments in favour of such a conclusion. The strongest argument for the contrary view to my mind is the consideration that there were several potential witnesses in Germany, and more particularly certain expert witnesses, whose evidence was of very considerable importance for the prosecution. It may of course be the case that all the witnesses would have been prepared to attend a trial in England, or that alternative means could have been arranged for having their evidence made available without their attendance. But it is at that point that I find it impossible to form a sufficiently confident view on the matter of irrationality. Some of the witnesses may have in fact been unwilling and the recognition of the difficulties then involved might well support the reasonableness of the decision. There is not sufficient detail available to lead me to a condemnation of such decision as there may have been to prefer a trial in Germany.

The other question is whether account should have been taken of any views which the appellant himself might have on the choice of venue. The procedure certainly makes no provision for him to be consulted, but that is not necessarily determinative. In the circumstances of the present case fairness might be thought to require that his views should be sought on a matter which so closely and significantly concerned him. I have however reached the conclusion that there is no sound basis for predicting an expectation on the part of the accused that he would contribute his views on the choice of venue for his trial. Matters relating to the preparation of criminal proceedings are matters for the prosecuting authority to determine. While consultation with the defence may help in resolving practical problems in the preparation or presentation of a case I see no room for an obligation to seek the views of the appellant in the present case on the issue of the venue for his trial. That kind of decision must be left to the prosecuting authority. . . .

But the question which remains is whether in the circumstances of the present case there was an abuse of process. The complaint resolves itself into a preference for trial by judge and jury over trial by court-martial. No issue arises as to any oppression, irregularity or impropriety so far as the latter alternative was concerned. No attack is made on the composition of the tribunal as having been other than in accordance with the law. No attack is made on the conduct of the trial as having been otherwise than fair.

My Lords, the process of the trial of criminal cases by judge and jury is one of the most valuable features of the legal systems of Britain. The instinctive sense of justice of ordinary people, and their ability to reflect and express the current values of the community, provide a healthy contribution to the assessment of guilt and innocence. It is in any event proper that the public should actively participate in what is essentially a matter of public interest and concern. But valuable as the institution may be I am not prepared to assert that the provision of the alternative which was followed in the present case amounted to so grave an invasion of human rights or was so grossly unfair or oppressive as to threaten the stability of the verdict of the court-martial. The decision of the European Court of Human Rights in *Findlay v. United Kingdom* (1997) 24 E.H.R.R. 221 related to the particular circumstances which were encountered in the court-martial and do not in my view assist the appellant here. In the terminology of section 12(1) of the Courts-Martial (Appeals) Act amended by section 29 and Schedule 2 of the Criminal Appeal Act 1995, the ground on which the Appeal Court is to allow an appeal is that they think that the conviction is unsafe. I am not persuaded that the fact that the appellant did not enjoy the traditional system of trial by judge and jury in England was so serious a factor in the whole process as to render his eventual conviction unsafe. Indeed, from a consideration of the brief record of the evidence which is in the papers before us and taking full account of the fact that the whole details have not been canvassed before us it is not immediately evident to me that any miscarriage of justice has occurred here.

I would dismiss the appeal.

MARTIN v. UNITED KINGDOM
European Court of Human Rights (2006)

[In 2006, the European Court of Human Rights, applying its decision in *Findlay v. United Kingdom*, 24 EHRR 221 (1997), unanimously found that the "composition, structure and procedure" of the proceedings denied Martin his right under Article 6 § 1 of the European Convention for the Protection of Human Rights and Fundamental Freedoms to "a fair . . . hearing . . . by an independent and impartial tribunal." In the process, the Court commented on the fact that Martin, a civilian, had been tried by court-martial.]

1. [The Court] recalls, by way of preliminary remark, that there is nothing in the provisions of Article 6 to exclude the determination by service tribunals of criminal charges against service personnel. The question to be answered in each case is whether the individual's doubts about the independence and impartiality of a particular court-martial can be considered to be objectively justified and, in particular, whether there were sufficient guarantees to exclude any such legitimate doubts (see *Cooper* [*v. United Kingdom*, 39 EHRR 8 (2004)], § 110).

2. It is, however, a different matter where the national legislation empowers a military court to try civilians on criminal charges (*Ergin v. Turkey (No. 6)*, no. 47533/99, § 41, 5 May 2006) [[2006] ECHR 529]. While it cannot be contended that the Convention absolutely excludes the jurisdiction of military courts to try cases in which civilians are implicated, the existence of such jurisdiction should be subjected to particularly careful scrutiny, since only in very exceptional circumstances could the determination of criminal charges against civilians in such courts be held to be compatible with Article 6 (*op. cit.*, §§ 42 and 44). The power of military criminal justice should not extend to civilians unless there are compelling reasons justifying such a situation, and if so only on a clear and foreseeable legal basis. The existence of such reasons must be substantiated in each specific case. It is not sufficient for the national legislation to allocate certain categories of offence to military courts *in abstracto* (*op. cit.*, § 47).

3. In the present case, the power to try the applicant by court-martial had a clear and foreseeable legal basis, namely section 209(2) of the 1955 Act. . . . Together with the Judge Advocate at first instance and the Court Martial Appeal Court, the House of Lords examined in detail whether such proceedings would be fair and appropriate, and found, generally, that the law permitting for the civilian members of a military entourage stationed abroad to be tried by court-martial was of utility. Moreover, the House of Lords found that in the applicant's particular case there were sound practical reasons militating, at the time the Director of Public Prosecutions made his decision, in favour of his trial by court-martial in Germany. . . . While the Court has considerable doubts whether such considerations were sufficiently "compelling" to justify the trial of a civilian before a military tribunal, it is not necessary for it finally to decide the point since it considers, for the reasons set out below, that the composition, structure and procedure of the applicant's court-martial were in themselves sufficient to raise in him a legitimate fear as to its lack of independence and impartiality.

QUESTIONS

The European Court seems to be saying that (1) the statute must prescribe criteria that make court-martial jurisdiction over civilians readily predictable, and (2) facts showing that those criteria have been satisfied in any given case must be set forth with particularity on the record. Can you tell from *Martin* what reasons for subjecting a civilian to trial by court-martial the European Court would find "compelling"? If you had been on the Court, would you have reached the issue, and if you had, what would you have held? If you had not rested your decision on the issue, would you have addressed it in dicta, and if so, what would you have said?

IV. RESERVISTS

WILLENBRING v. NEURAUTER
United States Court of Appeals for the Armed Forces
48 M.J. 152 (C.A.A.F. 1998)

[Willenbring, an Army Reservist, was charged with rapes that occurred while he was still on active duty, that is, before he was became a Reservist. He was called back to active duty to stand trial, in accordance with Article 2(d), UCMJ. The court held that there was court-martial jurisdiction.]

EFFRON, JUDGE:

. . . The reserve components perform a critical role in the national defense policy of the United States. *See* 10 U.S.C. § 10102. During Operations Desert Shield and Desert Storm, over 245,000 reservists were called to active duty. Of the 541,000 troops actually deployed to the Persian Gulf during those operations in 1990 and 1991, approximately 106,000 were reservists. *See* Department of Defense, Conduct of the Persian Gulf War 471, 482 (April 1992); M. Clodfelter, Warfare and Armed Conflicts 1080 (1991). . . .

The increasing dependence of our armed forces upon the Reserves has been underscored by numerous congressional actions, including establishment of authority for the President to order up to 200,000 reservists to active duty for 270 days for any operational mission without requiring a declaration of war or national emergency, 10 U.S.C. § 12304, and amendments to the Uniform Code of Military Justice concerning court-martial jurisdiction over reservists for offenses committed while on active duty or during inactive-duty training. *See* Part II.C.3 of this opinion, *infra* (discussing Articles 2(d) and 3). These provisions reflect the vital importance of the morale, welfare, good order, and discipline of members of the reserve components to the national security of the United States.

Appellant was a member of the armed forces in 1987 and 1988 when he allegedly committed the three charged rapes, including the two involving the spouses of fellow service-members; he was a member of the armed forces in 1996 when he received the order to report to active duty for purposes of standing trial on those charges; and he is a member of the armed forces today.

Appellant does not contest the constitutional power of Congress to authorize court-martial jurisdiction over a servicemember in his position — i.e., a reservist charged with offenses committed during a prior period of military service in a regular component. Rather, his claim is that, because of his honorable discharge from active duty with the regular component of the Army, the statutes in place at the time of the alleged offenses and which are applicable to the charges he now faces preclude exercise of court-martial jurisdiction over offenses committed during his period of active service prior to the date of the discharge, March 31, 1992.

A. Constitutional Considerations

The jurisdiction of courts-martial is governed by statutes enacted under the constitutional power of Congress to establish "Rules for the Government and Regulation of the" armed forces. U.S. Const. art. I, § 8, cl. 14. Congress and the courts have ensured that military trials are similar in many respects to civilian proceedings, but it is well established that courts-martial — which are authorized by statutes enacted pursuant to Article I of the Constitution — need not provide a military accused with the same procedural rights available to a civilian defendant in a criminal trial conducted under Article III.

In view of these differences, both the Supreme Court of the United States and this Court have insisted that courts-martial not exercise jurisdiction beyond that granted by the applicable statutes. As a matter of constitutional law, the Supreme Court has held that Congress may not extend court-martial jurisdiction to cover civilians who have no military status in peacetime, even if they are accompanying United States forces overseas as employees or dependents. Likewise, a court-martial may not exercise jurisdiction over a former servicemember whose relationship with the armed forces has been severed completely as a result of a valid discharge and who is not otherwise in a status that is subject to court-martial jurisdiction. *See United States ex rel. Toth v. Quarles*, 350 U.S. 11, 14-15 (1955); *Smith v. Vanderbush*, 47 M.J. 56, 58-59 (1997).

A discharge or other separation from military service, however, does not preclude trial by court-martial, as a matter of constitutional law, if, at the time military jurisdiction is exercised, the individual is still a member of the armed forces or is otherwise in a status subject to military law. For example, a prisoner in the custody of the armed forces as a result of a court-martial sentence remains subject to court-martial jurisdiction regardless of a discharge from military service. *See* Art. 2(a)(7); *Kahn v. Anderson*, 255 U.S. 1, 7-8 (1921); *United States v. Nelson*, 14 U.S.C.M.A. 93, 94-95, 33 C.M.R. 305, 306-07 (1963). In addition, a servicemember who is discharged before his enlistment expires and immediately reenlists may be tried for pre-discharge offenses occurring during the prior enlistment. *See United States v. Clardy*, 13 M.J. 308, 316 (C.M.A. 1982). Likewise, certain statutorily designated categories of military retirees are subject to trial by court-martial, including trial for offenses committed during a prior enlistment, even though they no longer are performing military duties. *See* Arts. 2(a)(4)-(5) and 3(a); *United States v. Sloan*, 35 M.J. 4, 7-8 (C.M.A. 1992); *Pearson v. Bloss*, 28 M.J. 376 (C.M.A. 1989).

Furthermore, a person who deserts during one period of service and subsequently obtains a discharge for a different period of service is nonetheless subject to trial by court-martial for the pre-discharge, prior-service offense of desertion, even if the discharge was not obtained by fraud, and any other such offense. *See* Art. 3(c); *United States v. Huff*, 7 U.S.C.M.A. 247, 22 C.M.R. 37 (1956). Finally, when a person is charged with obtaining a discharge by fraud, a court-martial has jurisdiction over the offense of fraudulent separation in violation of Article 84, U.C.M.J., 10 U.S.C. § 884; if convicted of obtaining a fraudulent separation, the individual may be tried in a separate trial for all other offenses committed before the fraudulent discharge. *See* Art. 3(b); *United States v. Reid*, 46 M.J. 236, 238-39 (1997); *Wickham v. Hall*, 12 M.J. 145 (C.M.A. 1981); *accord Wickham v. Hall*, 706 F.2d 713 (5th Cir. 1983).

While appellant was subject to a different version of Article 3(a), *see* Part II.C., *infra*, we note that, under current law, if a person is subject to military jurisdiction at the time of the trial and was subject to military jurisdiction at the time of the offense, that person may be tried for offenses occurring during a prior period of military service. The current version of Article 3(a) provides that, subject to the statute of limitations in Article 43 —

> a person who is in a status in which the person is subject to this chapter and who committed an offense while formerly in a status in which the person was subject to this chapter is not relieved from amenability to the jurisdiction of this chapter for that offense by reason of a termination of that person's former status.

This provision makes clear that a servicemember who is discharged from and then reenters the armed forces after a break in service may be tried for offenses that occurred during a prior enlistment, regardless of the intervening discharge.

When Congress enacted the present version of Article 3(a), the statute was given prospective effect, applying only to offenses occurring on or after October 23, 1992. *See* National Defense Authorization Act for Fiscal Year 1993, Pub. L. No. 102-484, §§ 1063 and 1067, 102 Stat. 2315, 2505, 2506 (1992). All the offenses charged in this case are alleged to have occurred before October 23, 1992. In that context, the issue before us is not whether Congress has the power under the Constitution to provide for the exercise of court-martial jurisdiction over appellant, but whether the statutes and regulations applicable to charges alleging offenses committed prior to October 23, 1992, authorize the exercise of jurisdiction in this case.

B. Jurisdiction Under Article 2

Article 2(a) of the Uniform Code of Military Justice, 10 U.S.C. § 802(a) (enacted in 1950 and modified in 1986), lists the persons who are subject to the Code. The primary provision authorizing jurisdiction over reservists is Article 2(a)(1), which includes "other persons lawfully called or ordered into, or to duty in or for training in, the armed forces, from the dates when they are required by the terms of the call or order to obey it."

One of the provisions under which a reservist may be lawfully called to duty in the armed forces is Article 2(d) (enacted in 1986). Under Article 2(d)(1)(B), "[a] member of a reserve component who is not on active duty and who is made the subject of proceedings under . . . section 830 (article 30) with respect to an offense against this chapter may be ordered to active duty involuntarily for the purpose of . . . trial by court-martial[.]" Congress limited this authority to circumstances where the offenses are alleged to have been committed during a period when the reservist is clearly performing military duties. *See* Art. 2(d)(2)(A) & (B) (authority to activate a reservist under Article 2(d) applies only with respect to offenses committed while the member was "on active duty" or "on inactive-duty training").

The authority to activate a reservist for disciplinary proceedings is further circumscribed by Article 2(d)(4), which provides that it may be exercised only by a general court-martial convening authority in a regular component.

Appellant does not contest the military judge's findings that: (1) he was on active duty as a member of a regular component on the dates of the alleged offenses, as set forth in the Charge and its specifications; (2) he was a member of a reserve component at the time he received his orders to active duty under Article 2(d); and (3) the orders were issued by a regular component general court-martial convening authority. Rather, appellant argues that the court-martial did not have jurisdiction to try him for the charged offenses because Article 2(d) authorizes jurisdiction only over offenses committed while he was on active duty in the reserves, not over offenses that occurred while he was on active duty in a regular component. The Government, on the other hand, argues that Article 2(d) confers unqualified jurisdiction over reservists for any offenses committed while on any active duty, notwithstanding any breaks in military service. This case, therefore, concerns the limits, if any, on a court-martial's exercise of jurisdiction to try reservists for pre-discharge offenses under the statutes applicable to appellant's case.

C. The Jurisdictional Implications of the Relationship Between Article 2 and Article 3

The Government urges us to read the activation authority of Article 2(d) as providing an unqualified grant of jurisdiction over a reservist for any offense committed while on active duty, regardless of any intervening discharge or other break in service. Article 2, however, does not exist in isolation. Consideration also must be given to Article 3, which is entitled "Jurisdiction to try certain personnel." Although the current version of Article 3(a) is broadly worded and encompasses offenses committed by a member of the armed forces during an earlier period of service, the version of Article 3(a) applicable to appellant's case was more restrictive:

> Subject to section 843 of this title (article 43) [the statute of limitations], no person charged with having committed, while in a status in which he was subject to this chapter, an offense against this chapter, punishable by confinement for five years or more and for which the person cannot be tried in the courts of the United States or of a State, a Territory, or the District of Columbia, may be relieved from amenability to trial by court-martial by reason of the termination of that status.

(Version prior to amendment in 1992). Issues I and II raise the question whether Article 2(d) provides an unqualified grant of jurisdiction to order a reservist to active duty to stand trial by court-martial for all prior offenses committed while on active duty or whether Article 2(d) must be read in conjunction with Article 3(a).

1. Legislative Development and Implementation of Article 3(a)

The version of Article 3(a) applicable to appellant's case was included by Congress in the Uniform Code of Military Justice enacted in 1950 in response to the decision of the Supreme Court in *United States ex rel. Hirshberg v. Cooke*, 336 U.S. 210 (1949), a case which predated establishment of our Court. *Hirshberg*, which was decided on statutory rather than constitutional grounds, involved a sailor who was serving his third period of enlistment. After his second period of enlistment, which included service during World War II, he was discharged and then reenlisted the next day. *Id.* at 211.

During his third period of enlistment, Hirshberg was charged with having maltreated fellow servicemembers during his prior enlistment while a prisoner of war of Japan. Following his conviction by a general court-martial, he sought relief in the federal courts through a writ of habeas corpus. *Id.* at 211-12. The Supreme Court reviewed the then-existing statutes governing military jurisdiction and unanimously concluded that, as a matter of statutory law, discharged servicemembers — "whether reenlisted or not" — were not subject to court-martial jurisdiction for prior-service offenses. *Id.* at 218-19.

The impact of the *Hirshberg* decision was promptly considered in the contemporaneous hearings before the House Armed Services Committee on the proposed new Uniform Code of Military Justice. *See* Hearings on H.R. 2498 Before a Subcomm. of the House Armed Services Comm., 81st Cong., 1st Sess. 617, 1262 (1949) [hereinafter 1949 House Hearings], *reprinted in* Index and Legislative History, Uniform Code of Military Justice (1950). When the subcommittee charged with drafting the new Code considered and adopted Article 3(a), Subcommittee Chairman Brooks described the language as closing the "loophole" resulting from the *Hirshberg* case. *Id.* at 1262. The subcommittee drafted the provision governing prior-service offenses to provide for court-martial jurisdiction over reservists "for [serious] offenses committed while they were on active duty, even after they had returned to an inactive status," if civilian courts did not have jurisdiction over the case. *Id.* (remarks of Mr. Smart). The House provision was intended to cover not only servicemembers who reenlisted, but also civilians who previously had served but completely severed their connection with the armed forces. *Id.* ("that will get the Hirschberg [sic] case where he reenlisted [and] even [if] he had not reenlisted"). . . .

The restrictions that limited court-martial jurisdiction to serious offenses not triable in civilian courts reflected the dual concerns of the committee in proposing and adopting Article 3(a) — first, to close the loophole left by *Hirshberg* when there is a break in military service, and second, to exercise caution in view of the proposed use of Article 3(a) for military trials of civilian ex-servicemembers with no continuing military status. . . .

The initial version of the Manual for Courts-Martial which implemented the new Uniform Code of Military Justice reflected the statutory relationship between Articles 2 and 3. It set forth "[t]he general rule . . . that court-martial jurisdiction over" military personnel "and other persons subject to the code ceases on discharge from the service or other termination of such status and that jurisdiction as to an offense committed during a period of service or status thus terminated is not revived by re-entry into the military service or return into such status." Para. 11a, Manual for Courts-Martial, United States, 1951. The drafters of the Manual noted that this general rule was "consistent with the Army precedents of over 100 years" and with *Hirshberg. See* Legal and Legislative Basis, Manual for Courts-Martial, United States, 1951 at 11 [hereinafter Legal and Legislative Basis] (prepared by the drafters of the 1951 Manual).

The drafters also noted that "[t]o this general rule there are many exceptions." *Id.* The text of the Manual (¶ 11b) described various exceptions to this general rule under Article 3, including the provisions of Article 3(a) for jurisdiction over serious offenses which "cannot be tried" in the civilian courts. The drafters observed in the Legal and Legislative Basis, *supra* at 12:

> Perhaps the most difficult single jurisdictional fact to be established under Article 3a [*sic*] with respect to offenses committed overseas, is that the offense is not punishable by a civil court. If the offense can be punished by any civil court of the United States, any of its States, Territories, [or the] District of Columbia, a court-martial lacks jurisdiction.

Reflecting the anticipated use of Article 3(a) to prosecute civilian former servicemembers, the drafters stated that "jurisdiction under Article 3a [*sic*] will not be exercised without the consent of the Secretary of [the] Department" concerned. *Id.* at 11. This is contained in the first subparagraph of ¶ 11b.

In addition to the exceptions set forth in Article 3, the Manual provided (¶ 11b, subpara. 5) that the general rule concerning termination of jurisdiction upon discharge did not apply when there was a change in status that did not involve a break in amenability to court-martial jurisdiction:

> In those cases when the person's discharge or other separation does not interrupt his status as a person belonging to the general category of persons subject to the code, court-martial jurisdiction does not terminate.

The Manual then provided four examples of circumstances in which a discharge would not terminate jurisdiction: first, when an officer in a reserve component serving on active duty was discharged for purposes of accepting a regular commission, jurisdiction would not terminate in view of "there being no interval between the periods of service under the respective commissions;" second, "when an enlisted person" was "discharged . . . in order to re-enlist before the expiration of his prior period of service," jurisdiction would continue "provided there is no hiatus between the two enlistments;" third, a member of the armed forces discharged overseas who "immediately becomes" a person in a civilian status subject to the Code "remains amenable to trial by court-martial for offenses committed prior to his discharge because such discharge does not interrupt his status as a person subject to the code;" and fourth, a "dishonorably discharged prisoner" in military custody was subject to trial for offenses committed "while a member of the armed forces and prior to the execution of his dishonorable discharge."

In the Legal and Legislative Basis, *supra* at 12, the drafters emphasized that "uninterrupted status as a person subject to military law in one capacity or another does not terminate jurisdiction." The drafters noted that, in *Hirshberg*, "there was a definite, although brief, hiatus" in his status as a person subject to military law, and they cautioned that the case should not be read as applying to "cases where there is no hiatus but merely a change in particular status within the general status of being a person subject to military law." *Id.* at 12-13.

The Manual did not expressly address the jurisdictional consequences of continuing military status (e.g., either as a reservist or as a regular who enlists in the Reserves without a break in status) when there had been a break in actual active duty or inactive-duty service (e.g., when the person's performance of military service had been interrupted by one or more breaks between periods of active duty or inactive-duty service) but no hiatus in the person's military affiliation with the armed forces. It is noteworthy, however, that the circumstances described in the Manual did not constitute an exclusive list, but were set forth as examples of situations in which there was no break in service.

2. Developments Leading to the 1986 Amendments

In a series of cases that arose during the first decade under the Uniform Code of Military Justice, the Supreme Court held that portions of Articles 2 and 3 were unconstitutional to the extent that they attempted to extend court-martial jurisdiction in peacetime over civilians. These cases included *United States ex rel. Toth v. Quarles*, 350 U.S. 11 (1955), in which the Supreme Court held that Article 3(a) could not be used to subject a former service-member to trial by court-martial for prior service offenses. Justice Black stated:

> Court-martial jurisdiction sprang from the belief that within the military ranks there is need for a prompt, ready-at-hand means of compelling obedience and order. But Army discipline will not be improved by court-martialing rather than trying by jury some civilian ex-soldier who has been wholly separated from the service for months, years or perhaps decades. Consequently considerations of discipline provide no excuse for new expansion of court-martial jurisdiction at the expense of the normal and constitutionally preferable system of trial by jury.

Id. at 22-23. In reaching its decision, the Court relied on broad constitutional principles and did not consider the specific language of Article 3(a) or application of the statute to persons not "wholly separated" from the armed forces.

Over the next three decades, this Court considered the relationship between Articles 2 and 3 in light of *Toth* in a variety of circumstances, culminating in our consideration in *United States v. Caputo*, 18 M.J. 259 (1984). In *Caputo*, our Court addressed the issue of military jurisdiction over a reservist charged, while on inactive duty for training, with offenses committed during a prior period of active duty for training, *id.* at 260, when there had been a temporal rather than a status break in the reservist's amenability to court-martial jurisdiction during the time between the offense and the time of trial, *id.* at 261.

Caputo was charged with committing various offenses during a 2-week tour of active duty for training, which could have been tried in the state courts. Although a number of these offenses came to the attention of military authorities during his 2-week period of active duty, no action was taken at that time with a view towards a trial by court-martial. Caputo was allowed to complete his period of active duty and return to civilian life. *Id.* at 261. At that point, although he remained a member of the Reserves, he was not subject to court-martial jurisdiction under Article 2.

Subsequently, charges were prepared and sworn to by reserve authorities. When Caputo reported to his reserve unit for a period of inactive-duty training, he was advised of the charges against him and was placed temporarily in pretrial confinement, his period of inactive-duty training was extended for an indefinite period, and a special court-martial was convened. Caputo moved to dismiss the case for lack of personal jurisdiction. After this motion was twice denied, Caputo sought extraordinary relief from this Court. *Id.* at 261-62, 260.

Chief Judge Everett, in an opinion joined by Judge Fletcher, expressly declined to reach any of the statutory issues in the case and resolved it based upon language in Manual for Courts-Martial, United States, 1969 (Revised edition), which was then in effect. 18 M.J. at 266-67. Chief Judge Everett noted that Caputo was on active duty at the time he committed the offenses, which established jurisdiction over the offenses under Article 2(a)(1). *Id.* at 263, 268-69 n.9. He also noted that, as a matter of constitutional law, Article 2(a)(3) — covering reservists "while they are on inactive duty training authorized by written orders which are voluntarily accepted by them and which specify that they are subject to this chapter" — provided a statutory basis for establishing personal jurisdiction during a period of inactive-duty training. He observed:

> We perceive no constitutional problem with Article 2(a)(3). . . . Contrary to Caputo's position, a reservist is not in every respect a civilian. Instead, by joining the Reserve Forces, he assumes special obligations — such as to train himself and to be prepared for extended active duty.

Id. at 265. With regard to the constitutional power of Congress to authorize jurisdiction over reservists, Chief Judge Everett noted the increased reliance of the armed forces on reservists as part of the "total force" and cited the use of training assignments for reservists "integrated more closely with the assignments of active-duty personnel," the regular use of reservists in functions such as transport to render "valuable service to the armed forces," and the "continued vitality of the tradition of the citizen-soldier." *Id.* at 265-66.

The *Caputo* opinion specifically rejected the assertion that Article 2(a)(3) should be interpreted narrowly to implement comments in its legislative history, which suggested that such jurisdiction should be exercised only over those involved in the use of expensive or dangerous equipment:

> [E]ven if the Navy were seeking to invoke Article 2(a)(3) for purposes and under circumstances not contemplated during the 1949 hearings on the Code, we doubt that Congress intended for this Court — or an Article III Court — to decide whether various military duties

performed by inactive reservists for training were among those mentioned in the hearings.

Id. at 265. The opinion added that significant prudential considerations cautioned against using the legislative history to expand the express limitations
in the statute in a manner that would unnecessarily interject the courts into
military assignment policies: "[T]hat type of inquiry would lead us into the
sort of thicket which courts have traditionally sought to avoid." *Id.*, citing
Chappell v. Wallace, 462 U.S. 296 (1983), and *Orloff v. Willoughby*, 345 U.S.
83 (1953). The opinion concluded that, "if Caputo's situation falls within the
letter of [Article 2(a)(3)], we shall not seek to determine whether it conforms
to the spirit of this legislation." 18 M.J. at 265. . . .

3. Legislative Development and Implementation of the 1986 Amendments to Articles 2 and 3

Subsequent to *Caputo, Poole*, and *Duncan*, the state of the law was as follows: First, paragraph 11a, 1969 Manual, *supra,* set forth a "general rule" precluding exercise of court-martial jurisdiction during a period of active duty or
inactive-duty training for an offense committed during an earlier period of regular or reserve service, absent an exception to this "general rule;" second, the
issue of whether the applicable statutes required such an interpretation was
left open; third, there was no statutory authority to order a reservist to active
duty for disciplinary purposes; and fourth, Congress was vested with constitutional authority to provide for jurisdiction over offenses committed during a
prior period of service and to provide for a reservist to be ordered to active duty
solely for disciplinary purposes.

The President addressed the first matter — the restrictions imposed by the
provisions of paragraph 11a concerning termination of jurisdiction — through
issuance of Executive Order No. 12473, 49 Fed. Reg. 17152 (April 13, 1984),
which deleted from the Manual for Courts-Martial all of the language concerning termination of jurisdiction, including consideration of the effects of a discharge or other changes in status. *See* R.C.M. 201-203, Manual for
Courts-Martial, United States, 1984. These matters were addressed in the
non-binding "Discussion" sections, which are not part of the Manual and
which do not contain official rules or policy. *See* Part I, §4, Discussion. The
Discussion sections attempted to distill some general principles from the then-
existing case law and to use a non-binding format that would not preclude the
courts from adopting different interpretations of the law. *Id.*

With respect to the balance of the issues raised in *Caputo*, legislative action
appeared to be necessary. In the aftermath of *Caputo, Poole*, and *Duncan*,
Congress enacted legislation that, in three separate steps, revised the laws
governing court-martial jurisdiction over reservists. *See* National Defense
Authorization Act for Fiscal Year 1987, Pub. L. No. 99-661, §804, 100 Stat.
3906-07 (1986).

First, the amendments eliminated the language in subsection (a)(3) of
Article 2 that had precluded jurisdiction over persons on inactive-duty training absent "written orders which are voluntarily accepted by them and which
specify that they are subject to this chapter." They also revised Article 2 to pro-

vide for comprehensive jurisdiction over reservists on federal inactive-duty training as follows:

(a) The following persons are subject to this chapter: . . .

(3) Members of a reserve component while on inactive-duty training, but in the case of members of the Army National Guard of the United States or the Air National Guard of the United States only when in Federal service.

100 Stat. 3906.

Second, the 1986 amendments addressed the problem identified in *Caputo* concerning the lack of authority to "order[] a reservist to active duty when a primary purpose of the active duty would be to allow his court-martial for prior violations of the Uniform Code." 18 M.J. at 268 n.8 (citing *United States v. Schuering*, 16 U.S.C.M.A. 324, 36 C.M.R. 480 (1966), and *United States v. Wheeler*, 10 U.S.C.M.A. 646, 28 C.M.R. 212 (1959)). The amendments established subsection (d) of Article 2, which provides broad authority to involuntarily activate "[a] member of a reserve component who is not on active duty" for purposes of nonjudicial punishment proceedings under Article 15, U.C.M.J., 10 U.S.C. § 815, or disposition of court-martial charges concerning offenses committed while the member was "on active duty" or "on inactive-duty training." *See* Art. 2(d)(1) and (2).

The third element of the 1986 legislation was to make clear that termination of a period of reserve service did not constitute the type of break in service that would preclude court-martial jurisdiction. The amendments established subsection (d) under Article 3, which provides:

(d) A member of a reserve component who is subject to this chapter is not, by virtue of the termination of a period of active duty or inactive-duty training, relieved from amenability to the jurisdiction of this chapter for an offense against this chapter committed during such period of active duty or inactive-duty training.

100 Stat. 3907. As a result, termination of a period of amenability to the UCMJ would not preclude exercise of court-martial jurisdiction over a prior service offense during a subsequent period of service.

The purpose of these three provisions was not to simply address the specific facts of the *Caputo* case, but also to undertake a comprehensive revision of the statutes governing court-martial jurisdiction over reservists. The House Armed Services Committee, which initiated the amendments, stated in its report on the legislation that the provision "would conform the UCMJ to the total-force policy by subjecting members of the reserve components in Federal status to the same disciplinary standards as their regular component counterparts." H.R. Rep. No. 718, 99th Cong., 2d Sess. 225 (1986). The Report noted that, when the U.C.M.J. initially was enacted, the reserve components were "viewed as a separate force," but this was no longer the case since reserve training had become "closely integrated with the missions of active-component units," so "reservists provide valuable services to the armed forces," and "[r]eserve units routinely participate with regular units in realist[i]c arms training and field exercises at home and abroad" and "directly augment actual active-component missions." *Id.* at 226. . . .

The primary effect of the 1986 legislation was that a reservist would no longer be relieved of amenability to court-martial jurisdiction for offenses committed on active duty or during inactive-duty training by virtue of a return to civilian life at the end of a period of such duty. In other words, even though a return to civilian life would mean that a reservist could not be tried by court-martial for offenses committed while a civilian, that break in the status of being subject to military law would not constitute a break in service so long as the person continued his or her military status as a member of the reserve components. The new legislation also provided express authority to involuntarily activate such a reservist for the sole purpose of conducting disciplinary proceedings with respect to offenses committed during a prior period of service.

The President implemented these amendments effective March 12, 1987, by promulgating R.C.M. 204, entitled "Jurisdiction over reserve component personnel," which remains in effect. In addition to implementing Articles 2(d) and 3(d), R.C.M. 204 includes subsection (d), "Changes in type of service," which provides:

> A member of a reserve component at the time disciplinary action is initiated, who is alleged to have committed an offense while on active duty or inactive-duty training, is subject to court-martial jurisdiction without regard to any change between active and reserve service or within different categories of reserve service subsequent to commission of the offense. This subsection does not apply to a person whose military status was completely terminated after commission of an offense.

Exec. Order No. 12586, § 1b, 52 Fed. Reg. 7104. This Rule, like the statute, does not distinguish between past regular or past reserve service. *See also* R.C.M. 204(d), Discussion. However, consistent with both *Toth* and *Hirshberg*, the Rule notes that subsection (d), insofar as it provides that a change in status within categories of military service did not terminate jurisdiction, would "not apply to a person whose military status was completely terminated after commission of an offense." R.C.M. 204(d). The Discussion accompanying that Rule notes —

> A "complete termination" of military status refers to a discharge relieving the servicemember of any further military service. It does not include a discharge conditioned upon acceptance of further military service.

The Drafter's Analysis of the Rule, 1984 Manual, *supra* at A21-13, states that subsection (d) "reflects legislative intent 'not to disturb the jurisprudence of *United States ex rel. Hirshberg v. Cooke*, 336 U.S. 210 (1949)' (H.R. Rep. No. 718, 99th Cong., 2d Sess. at 227 (1986))."

In view of these developments, the state of the law with respect to reservists following the 1986 amendments to Articles 2 and 3 was as follows: If there was a complete termination of military status with no subsequent military service, then the former servicemember would not be subject to court-martial jurisdiction for prior-service offenses as a matter of constitutional law under *Toth*. If, however, there was a complete termination of military status followed by reentry into reserve service, then the reservist would be subject to court-martial jurisdiction for prior-service offenses, subject to the major offense and nontriability conditions of Article 3(a). Finally, if there was a change in status between regular and reserve service, or within various forms of reserve service, unaccompanied by a complete termination of military status, then the reservist would be subject to court-martial jurisdiction for all prior-service offenses to the same extent as a regular whose military status had changed in form without a complete termination of military status.

D. The Effect on the Present Case of Legislation Subjecting Reservists to the Same Disciplinary Standards as Their Regular Component Counterparts

In ruling on appellant's motion to dismiss for lack of jurisdiction, the military judge entered findings of fact and conclusions of law which focused on appellant's military status as a member of the Regular Army at the time of the alleged offenses and his military status as a member of the Army Reserve at the time he received the active-duty orders related to the present proceedings. The military judge did not specifically address the issue of whether appellant's military status was "completely terminated" for purposes of R.C.M. 204(d) after the dates on which the offenses allegedly were committed, although some of his findings and conclusions bear on this issue.

In reaching his decision, the military judge stated: "In this case, [appellant] has maintained a constant and active affiliation with the United States Army since his original enlistment began on 13 January 1982." This conclusion is supported by the factual findings that, while on active duty, appellant requested an early discharge for purposes of accepting civilian employment and signed a contract for enlistment in the Army Reserve for the 1-year period following his separation from active duty.

On the other hand, the military judge described appellant's discharge from the Regular Army and his enlistment in the Reserves in terms that would not necessarily preclude a determination that there was a complete termination of military status followed by a subsequent enlistment. *Cf. United States v. King*, 27 M.J. 327 (C.M.A. 1989); *United States v. Clardy*, 13 M.J. 308 (C.M.A. 1982). The judge, for example, noted that appellant "was honorably discharged from the Regular Army" on March 31, 1992, and that "[t]he next day, 1 April 1992, he began his enlistment in the Army Reserve." The military judge also stated, "His change in status from the Regular Army to the reserve component occurred the day following his discharge from active duty." These comments leave open the possibility that there was no direct relationship between the discharge and the reserve enlistment and that there was a complete termination on March 31, 1992, followed by a new period of service on April 1, 1992.

Each party in the present case, for separate reasons, contends that there was no need for the military judge to definitively rule on whether there was a break in appellant's military service.

The Government takes the position that Article 2(d) provides an unqualified grant of jurisdiction that subjects reservists to court-martial jurisdiction for all offenses committed during a prior period of service, regardless whether there was a break that completely terminated the person's military service. Under this view, enactment of Article 2(d) rendered Article 3(a) inapplicable to reservists. Under the Government's theory, there was no need for the court to consider whether there had been a complete termination of service and, if so, whether the crime involved an offense punishable by 5 years' confinement that could not be tried in U.S. civilian courts.

Appellant, on the other hand, contends that Article 2(d) grants court-martial jurisdiction over reservists only as to offenses committed while on active duty in a reserve component. If appellant is correct, Article 2(d) could be used to activate a person whose prior service offenses were committed while in a reserve component, but it could not be used to activate a person, such as appellant, whose alleged offenses were committed while in a regular component.

We reject both of these positions as inconsistent with the applicable statutes.

1. Article 2(d) Does Not Exclude Reservists from the Coverage of Article 3(a)

According to the Government, it was unnecessary for the military judge to determine whether there was a complete termination of appellant's military status, so long as there was court-martial jurisdiction over appellant at the time of the offense and at the time of trial. The Government suggests that our opinion in *Murphy v. Garrett,* 29 M.J. 469 (1990), stands for the proposition that the text of Article 2(d) — which authorizes activation of reservists for disciplinary purposes — provides an unqualified grant of jurisdiction over reservists with respect to both current and prior-service offenses. Under the Government's reading of that opinion, even when there has been a complete termination of an accused's military status followed by a separate unrelated period of service, the restrictions in Article 3(a) do not apply, so the Government need not demonstrate that the case involves a major offense not triable in civilian courts.

The Government reads too much into *Murphy v. Garrett.* In that case, we denied a request for extraordinary relief that would have enjoined the Marine Corps from ordering a reservist to "active duty to participate in" an investigation under Article 32, U.C.M.J., 10 U.S.C. § 832, and possibly to stand trial by court-martial. 29 M.J. at 470. Our opinion addressed the authority to order a reservist to active duty under Article 2(d). We did not find it necessary at the preliminary stage of the proceedings, however, to address the implications of Article 3(a), and our interlocutory ruling did not consider whether there had been a complete termination of the accused's service. *Id.* at 471. Accordingly, we do not regard *Murphy v. Garrett* as establishing a definitive precedent on the relationship between Articles 2(d) and 3(a).

The Government's theory is based upon the premise that Article 2(d) provides an independent grant of jurisdiction and that there is no relationship between Articles 2(d) and 3(a). The necessary implication of this theory is that the limitations in Article 3(a) — providing for court-martial jurisdiction only over serious offenses that cannot be tried in U.S. civilian courts — apply only to members of the regular components.

The Government's view would produce an anomalous distinction between reservists and regulars. For example, if a reservist had two periods of reserve service separated by a complete termination of military status, he could be called to active duty under Article 2(d) for any offense committed during the earlier period of service, no matter how minor, without regard to the limitations in the applicable version of Article 3(a). The Government, however, does not suggest that Article 2(d) somehow rendered Article 3(a) inapplicable to members of the regular components. Therefore, a regular component service-member who committed an offense during a prior period of active duty and subsequently had a complete termination of military service could not be tried by court-martial during a later enlistment, unless the offense met the then-applicable Article 3(a) criteria (i.e., it was a major offense not triable in the U.S. civilian courts).

The Government's reading of the statutes would provide for a degree of court-martial jurisdiction over reservists far more extensive than that provided over regulars. Nothing in the wording of Article 3(a) suggests that its restrictions apply only to regulars and not to reservists, and nothing in the legislative history of the 1986 amendments suggests that Congress intended to provide for a more extensive degree of court-martial jurisdiction over reservists than over regulars. On the contrary, the legislative history emphasizes that the intent of the legislation was to subject reservists "to the same disciplinary standards as their regular component counterparts." *See* 48 M.J. at 169. In this regard, we also note that interpreting the statutes in a manner that would subject Reserves to a greater amenability to court-martial jurisdiction than Regulars — absent a clear indication that Congress intended to do so — would be inconsistent with the general congressional policy that the "[l]aws applying to both Regulars and Reserves shall be administered without discrimination. . . ." 10 U.S.C. § 10209.

2. Articles 2(d) and 3(d) Do Not Shield Reservists from Accountability for Misconduct Committed During Prior Regular-Component Service

Appellant, taking a different perspective, suggests that Article 2(d) cannot be used to support jurisdiction in this case, even if the conditions of Article 3(a) are met. According to appellant, the phrase "active duty" in Article 2(d)(2) applies only to offenses that occurred while the individual was on active duty as a member of a reserve component, so Article 2(d) does not provide authority to order a reservist to active duty to stand trial for offenses committed while he was on active duty as a member of a regular component.

We do not agree with appellant's reading of the statute. Article 2(d)(2), which provides the authority to order reservists to active duty, states:

> A member of a reserve component may not be ordered to active duty . . . [for purposes of investigation, trial by court-martial, or non-judicial punishment] except with respect to an offense committed while the member was —
>
> (A) on active duty; or

(B) on inactive duty training[.]

Although Article 2(d)(2) limits jurisdiction to offenses committed while the reservist was "on active duty" or "on inactive-duty training," it does not distinguish between regular or reserve status with respect to the prior period of "active duty" service during which the offense allegedly was committed. . . .

We do not find, in either the express words of the applicable statutes, the purposes of the legislation, or the legislative history of Article 2(d), an intent to create a haven from accountability for those reservists whose prior service was in a regular rather than a reserve component. Such an arbitrary distinction would be inconsistent with one of the main purposes of the 1986 legislation, which was to "subject[] members of the reserve components in Federal status to the same disciplinary standards as their regular-component counterparts." H.R. Rep. No. 718, *supra* at 225. Moreover, such an interpretation would be inconsistent with the statutory policy that the "[l]aws applying to both Regulars and Reserves shall be administered without discrimination. . . ." 10 U.S.C. §10209. If Congress intended to leave such an enormous "jurisdictional gap" in Article 2, we are confident that a phrase other than "active duty" (which encompasses both regular and reserve components) would have been used, or it would have been expressly modified to designate any restrictions on eligibility for activation to stand trial for prior-service offenses.

We conclude that Articles 2(d), 3(a), and 3(d) should be read in harmony, in conjunction with R.C.M. 204(d), as follows: First, Article 2(d) authorizes a reservist to be ordered to active duty to face trial by court-martial for both current-service and prior-service offenses, including offenses committed while a member of a regular component; second, when there has been a complete termination of military status, the version of Article 3(a) applicable to offenses occurring before October 23, 1992, permits a reservist, like a regular component member, to be tried for prior-service offenses only if the offenses cannot be tried in a civilian court and if confinement for 5 years or more is authorized for the offense; and third, Article 3(d) makes clear that the mere movement of a reservist on and off active duty does not terminate jurisdiction whenever a period of active duty terminates.

3. Jurisdiction in the Present Case

Both the prosecution and the defense have introduced substantial evidence on the issue of whether appellant's discharge from regular component service represented a complete break in service or whether the discharge was conditioned upon appellant's enlistment in the Reserves and was effected without a complete termination in service. Although the current version of Article 3(a) clearly provides for jurisdiction over prior-service offenses without regard to a break in service, the question whether there was a complete termination of service is important under the statutes and Manual provisions applicable to appellant's trial.

During further proceedings in this case, it will be necessary for the military judge to make findings of fact and conclusions of law specifically directed to the issue of termination of service. If there was such a complete break, then it will be necessary to consider whether the criteria of the applicable version of Article 3(a) have been met. . . .

H.M. THE QUEEN v. BRADY
Court Martial Appeal Court of Canada
2004 CMAC 3

[A reserve warrant officer challenged court-martial jurisdiction when he was charged with misuse of his government credit card.]

[1] Warrant Officer Brady (WO Brady) was charged under the Code of Service Discipline (the Code) as a result of using a Canadian Forces credit card on two occasions to purchase computer software for his own use. When he appeared before the Standing Court Martial to answer to the charges, he objected to its jurisdiction on the ground that as a member of the Canadian Forces on Class A Reserve Service, the Code only applied to him if he was "on duty." While the purchases in question were made in the course of restocking office supplies for his unit, a secondary duty assigned to WO Brady, he did not ask for, nor did he receive, any pay from the Canadian Forces for the time spent obtaining supplies. The transaction occurred outside his regular parade hours and WO Brady was not in uniform at the time. As a result, WO Brady argued that he was not on duty at the material time and therefore not subject to the Code.

[2] The Military Judge hearing the case agreed with him and terminated proceedings against him for lack of jurisdiction. Her Majesty the Queen has appealed that decision to this Court. The issue raised by the appeal is the extent to which members on Class A Reserve Service are subject to the military justice system when they perform military functions on a voluntary unpaid basis. . . .

[12] The issue of jurisdiction arises because of section 60 of the NDA [reprinted in §I, *supra*] which specifies who is subject to the Code:

60. (1) The following persons are subject to the Code of Service Discipline: . . .

(c) an officer or non-commissioned member of the reserve force when the officer or non-commissioned member is

    (i) undergoing drill or training, whether in uniform or not,

    (ii) in uniform,

    (iii) on duty,

    (iv) [Repealed, 1998, c. 35, s. 19]

    (v) called out under Part VI in aid of the civil power,

    (vi) called out on service,

    (vii) placed on active service,

    (viii) in or on any vessel, vehicle or aircraft of the Canadian Forces or in or on any defence establishment or work for defence,

    (ix) serving with any unit or other element of the regular force or the special force, or

(x) present, whether in uniform or not, at any drill or training of a unit or other element of the Canadian Forces; . . . .

[13] It was common ground that the only disposition which could apply to WO Brady's situation was subparagraph 60(1)(c)(iii) "on duty." The Military Judge rejected the appellant's argument that a member on Class A Reserve Service performing a secondary duty on his own time, *i.e.*, during a period for which he was not being paid by the Canadian Forces, was on duty. . . .

In the case of a reservist on Class "A" Reserve Service, the rate and condition of pay is set out on the basis of the period of service or instruction being performed and as it is referred in the Compensation and Benefits Instruction, on the period of duty or training. By nature, Class "A" service is part-time and rigorously structured. There is no unpaid Class "A" service. Military service in Canada is always remunerated. Whether someone is fairly compensated for the work he or she performs is another issue. Whether someone is so dedicated that he performs tasks at home, on his own time, and for no remuneration or compensation is also another issue. However, when members of the reserve choose willfully and voluntarily to perform tasks that are in part one or more of their military secondary duties, on their own time, this initiative does not make them on duty for the purpose of being subject to the Code of Service Discipline. For a reservist, being on duty cannot be dissociated from the type of service, either Class "A," Class "B" or Class "C" reserve service he is performing at the time and compensated pursuant to Treasury Board Directives or in accordance with Treasury Board Directives. Everything else is volunteer work or dedication, unlike the member is of the Regular Force. . . .

The use of that [Unit Acquisition] card, on his own time, in order to perform at least in part one of his military duties, did not make him "on duty." . . .

[14] The Military Judge concluded that he had no jurisdiction over WO Brady and terminated the proceedings against him.

The Position of the Parties

[15] Counsel for the appellant argued that the issue before the Court was simply one of statutory interpretation. . . .

[16] Counsel for the appellant argued that the grammatical and ordinary sense of a word or phrase is the meaning actually understood by a reader upon reading the word or expression in its immediate context. The dictionary mandated for use in interpreting the *Queen's Regulations and Orders* (QR & O), for terms not specifically defined, is the *Concise Oxford Dictionary* in English and *Le Petit Robert* in French. The *Concise Oxford Dictionary* defines "on duty" as "engaged in one's regular work" while the *Merriam-Webster's Collegiate Dictionary* defines the same expression as "engaged in or responsible for an assigned task or duty." Counsel argued that WO Brady was engaged in his military duty, albeit a secondary duty, when he attended at the vendors in question and purchased supplies for his unit. Since he purchased items for his personal use in the course of discharging his military duty, he was "on duty" and therefore subject to the Code.

[17] Counsel also argued that when the issue was considered in the broader context of the Code, there was no reason to depart from the grammatical and ordinary meaning of the expression "on duty."

[18] Finally, counsel took the position that the Military Judge erred in concluding that there was no unpaid military service in Canada. . . .

[19] Taking all of this together, the appellant's position is that the Military Judge's conclusion that there is no unpaid Class A Reserve Service was clearly wrong and ought to be set aside. Since that conclusion was the foundation of the Military Judge's finding that WO Brady was not on duty, it must also be set aside.

[20] Counsel for the respondent argued that there was no basis in the NDA for the notion of secondary duty, at least as it relates to the Code or to the entitlements which flow from "on duty" status. He argued that the conditions of service of the members of the Reserve Force are highly structured. By way of example, he pointed to a number of Canadian Forces Administrative Orders (CFAO) and Defence Administrative Orders and Directives (DAOD) dealing with pay and various entitlements for members of the Reserve Force. In his view, the only exception to paid service was with respect to Cadet Instructors as set out in Appendix 2 to Annex A to NDHQ INSTRUCTION — ADM(PER) 2/93. For all of those reasons, counsel urged the Court to dismiss the appeal.

Analysis

[21] I take the reasoning behind the appellant's reliance on dictionary definitions to be the following:

"On duty" means "engaged in one's regular work."

WO Brady was engaged in his regular work.

Therefore WO Brady was "on duty."

[22] This reasoning redirects the inquiry from whether WO Brady was on duty to whether he was engaged in his regular work. But, in a military environment, the question as to whether one is on duty or not can be answered just as easily as the question as to whether one is engaged in one's regular work. Furthermore, the definition assumes that one is only on duty when engaged in one's regular work whereas the notion of "on duty" can extend to extraordinary or unusual assignments. Consequently, it is more appropriate to focus on the question of "on duty" directly rather than on a proxy for that question.

[23] While the expression "on duty" is not defined in the NDA, it is nonetheless used in other parts of the Act. . . .

[25] The expression "on duty" is also used in the QR & O. . . .

[26] As can be seen from this survey of the NDA and the QR & O, members of the Canadian Forces have many reasons to know whether they are on duty or not. It is a concept which must be current and meaningful to members since it requires them to govern themselves accordingly on a daily basis, i.e., whether one is required to wear a uniform or not. If "on duty" is not defined in the NDA or the QR & O, it must necessarily be defined at a lower level of authority, since it is inconceivable that members, or the chain of command,

would have no standard by which to determine whether a member was on duty. And since Parliament declined to define "on duty," it is not implausible to suggest that it was content to adopt, where the notion of "on duty" arose, the definition used by the Canadian Forces for operational purposes. That definition will necessarily be found in documents having a lesser legal status than the NDA or the QR & O, but so long as they define "on duty" status in a way which is consistent with the NDA, there is no reason why that definition of "on duty" cannot be incorporated into subparagraph 60(1)(c)(iii) of the NDA.

[27] In the case of WO Brady, the document which defines his status is NDHQ INSTRUCTION — ADM(PER) 2/93, a document put before the Court by counsel for the appellant who argued that it refuted the Military Judge's conclusion that there is no unpaid Class A Reserve Service. It is true that the document shows that there can be unpaid Class A Reserve Service. It sets out the conditions under which a member on Class A Reserve Service undertaking voluntary unpaid service will be considered to be on duty. While this refutes the Military Judge's thesis as to unpaid service, it also effectively disposes of this appeal. WO Brady did not meet the conditions stipulated in NDHQ INSTRUCTION — ADM(PER) 2/93 and, as a result, would not be considered to be on duty at the material time. . . .

[31] The appellant asserts that WO Brady was on duty because he was discharging a military duty, albeit on a voluntary unpaid basis. The subject of Voluntary Service Without Pay by a Member on Class A Reserve Service is dealt with in Annex D of the INSTRUCTION which stipulates that voluntary service without pay may be authorized by a Commanding Officer, subject to the admonition that this facility is not to be abused. The types of duty for which voluntary service without pay can be authorized are specified and include administrative and logistic duties. The INSTRUCTION sets out the procedure by which voluntary service without pay is to be recorded in the Reserve Force Basic Attendance Register. When all of these conditions are satisfied, the member is considered to be on duty for the period of the voluntary service and, as a result, is entitled to pay (if funding subsequently becomes available), transportation, rations, a disability benefit if injured, and a death benefit if death occurs while on duty. . . .

[33] There are very specific criteria to be satisfied in order for a member on Class A Reserve Service to be considered on voluntary unpaid service and therefore on duty. Those criteria were not met in the case of WO Brady. There was no specific authorization on the part of his Commanding Officer, Captain Van Slyke. While the type of duties undertaken was perhaps within the scope of the INSTRUCTION, it is clear that the Reserve Force Basic Attendance Register was not completed so as to reflect that voluntary unpaid service was being undertaken when the offences are alleged to have occurred. By the terms of the INSTRUCTION, WO Brady would not have been eligible for any of the incidents of "on duty" status such as pay, transportation and rations. I find that he was not on duty at the time of the commission of the offences with which he is charged.

[The appeal was dismissed.]

SOMMACAL v. CHIEF AUDITOR OF THE ARMY AND CONFEDERAL MILITARY DEPARTMENT
Swiss Federal Court, 1971 BGE 97 I 143

[Is a conscript who is not on active duty subject to trial by court-martial for a newspaper article critical of his commander where there is no evidence it was written while on active duty for refresher training?]

Facts

A. Infantry Regiment 29 is composed of troops from the canton of Schwyz, and was on a refresher course from 10 to 29 November 1969. During this period, the regiment was, for the first time, under the command of Colonel Carlo Baumann, Education Officer and School Commander in Losone. Due to the inclement weather and the high expectations of the commander, the exercises during the course were exceptionally strict. Towards the end of the course, and after the course, several regional newspapers published critical accounts of the course. An article in the newspaper *Bote der Urschweiz* appeared on 5 December 1969 with the headline "Unpleasant Memories of [Refresher Course] 69." The article was signed with the pseudonym "Gunner Bang" and reported several incidents, as well as the name of Colonel Baumann, whose behavior was criticized. The writer of the article was later determined to be Gunner Carlo Sommacal, who runs an insurance agency and who is also a part-time journalist. Sommacal was on Refresher Course 69 (RC69) as part of Battalion 86, which is part of Regiment 29. Upon becoming aware of this and other articles, a member of the Schwyz Cantonal Council submitted a question on 16 December 1969 in which he asked the council, i.e., the Military Department, to investigate the matter.

On 4 February 1970, the Directorate of the Confederal Military Administration instructed the investigating judge of the Divisional Court 9A to start a preliminary investigation in order to clarify the accusations in the newspaper article as well as the dishonorable character of the allegations. The investigating judge obtained reports from all unit commanders and from all professional officers of the regiment and also questioned a large number of officers, non-commissioned officers and soldiers as witnesses and submitted a detailed report on 31 March 1970. The report concluded that the allegations in the newspaper articles were either falsehoods or exaggerations and that no military leaders or soldiers committed punishable offences. The accusations made against Colonel Baumann were mostly insulting remarks, but the jurisdiction of such actions fall clearly under civil courts, since the requirements of Article 2, Para. 4 of the MCC are not fulfilled. The investigating judge therefore petitioned the council not to undertake any further action relating to the incidents during RC69 of Regiment 29. Furthermore, he indicated that it was up to Colonel Baumann to decide whether or not to press charges and request a further investigation [in the civil courts].

The Directorate of the Confederal Military Administration subsequently instructed the same investigating judge to initiate a preliminary investigation for legal proceedings against Sommacal for insult to honor on 17 June 1970. During this investigation Sommacal was interviewed several times. During the interview, Sommacal retracted some accusations (in whole or in part) as untrue, but insisted on the veracity of others based on his experience as well as information from fellow soldiers, and offered proof. The investigating judge heard several other witnesses and completed the investigation on 10 November 1970.

On 24 November 1970, the Auditor initiated proceedings against Sommacal for slander (Article 145 MCC) and breach of service regulations (Article 72 MCC). The bases of the indictment are seven excerpts of the newspaper article which "targeted the responsible commanders, especially Colonel Baumann" and which are, individually and collectively, geared towards harming their reputation. The statements include:

- expectations during the RC were too high and the program was too intensive

- some soldiers were only allowed one furlough

- some of the trainees had to go for four days without sleep or a warm meal

- in violation of regulations, some truck drivers were on duty for 22 hours

- during a supply exercise over the Kinzig Pass, during which horses collapsed, reality was abandoned with the ridiculous attempt to push all of the mail over the Kinzig, so that no mail was received during a full week and once packages did arrive, their contents were spoiled

- during an RC orientation in Hotel Adler in Arth, Colonel Baumann explained that if he issued an order, no matter how ridiculous, soldiers were to obey and that the opinion of the soldiers was unimportant

- under an order issued during RC 69, it was determined that there would be no free time or company evenings during RC70.

In his pronouncement of 15 December 1970, the Chief Judge of Divisional Court 9A determined that the full hearing would be held on 29 December 1970, appointed an official defense counsel, and transferred the relevant dossiers to him.

On 27 December 1970, Carlo Sommacal submitted a Conflict of Jurisdiction (Article 223 MCC) claim to the Federal Court with the request to reject the jurisdiction of the Divisional Court 9A for the slander allegation according to Article 145 MCC. He claims further that the jurisdiction of the MCC could only apply to Article 2, Para. 4 MCC, for which there is no basis. Sommacal claims that the comments he made did not violate any official duties. Furthermore, there is no link between his comments and his personal military position. He did not write the article due to his military position, but rather as a journalist in order to fulfill a legitimate need for information. What he did write could have been written by any Swiss man, whether or not he was in service, since the individual incidents were more or less well-known within the whole regiment. As in the case BGE 61 I 113 ff, the newspaper article described a general, both political and military situation.

The Chief Auditor of the Army applied to have Sommacal's complaint dismissed and stated: the alleged actions of Sommacal are closely related, in both time and content, to his military service which the law intended to regulate in 1927 with Article 2, Para. 4 of the MCC. Sommacal collected his material for the newspaper article during the refresher course. The article describes activities that were experienced or observed by a soldier, and thus, unlike case BGE 61 I 113 ff, are related solely to the military service of the soldier with respect to interaction with his superiors. The "military position" of the complainant is, in every sense, the occasion, origin and basis for the incriminating comments. Subjecting this case to a military court is thus also in the interest of an appropriate judgment since the military judges possess their own service-related experience. . . .

1. That there is no appropriate (positive or negative) jurisdictional conflict between military or civil jurisdiction. The conflicts of jurisdiction that are to be judged under Article 223 MCC by the Federal Court, also include, according to existing jurisprudence, so-called "virtual conflicts", also including cases such as the present, in which the accused claims that not the presently prosecuting authority, but another authority has competence (BGE 61 I 123/124, 63 I 183 E.1, 66 I 61/62, 163 E.4, 80 I 256 E.1). The complaint, with which the complainant presents this conflict to the Federal Court, does not fall under a statute of limitations, but is only available as a recourse until the military judge convenes the main hearing before the divisional court (BGE 66 I 62 E.2, 161 E.2, 71 I 30, 80 I 257 E.1). The present case, based on a complaint submitted before the hearing, is thus to be heard.

2. The Federal Court has jurisdiction over not only legal, but also factual questions concerning conflicts of jurisdiction according to Article 223 MCC, but only to the extent that they concern the determination of competence. . . . In the present case, the competence of military courts rests only on Article 2, Para 4 of the MCC, according to which the Military Code of Conduct and military jurisdiction is applied to "draftees and temporary draftees not on active duty with respect to their military position and service-related responsibilities." The complainant is subject to compulsory military service. It is accepted that he wrote the article, which contains comments that are claimed to be damaging to honor, while he was off-duty. Since the article appeared shortly after [Sommacal] was released, it cannot be ruled out that it was written while on duty. Nonetheless, this possibility has not been raised, nor do the documents contain any indication that this is the case, and therefore this possibility is not considered. A determination is to be made whether the complainant made the allegedly honor-damaging comments based on his military position or his service-related responsibilities.

3. With the entry into force of the MCC of 13 June 1927, decisions concerning appropriate jurisdiction, which were formerly included in Articles 1 to 8 of the Code of the Military Criminal Court (CMCC), were annulled (Article 233 Para 2 Number 2 MCC) and placed under the MCC. The remaining articles of the CMCC remain in force. Article 2 Number 4 MCC replaced Article 1 Number 5 CMCC. According to the former regulation, draftees not in active service were only subject to the Military Code of Conduct and the jurisdiction of military courts only "with respect to their service-related responsibilities." Article 2 Number 4 MCC enlarged the competence to include "with respect to their military position." With this addition, which has independent meaning

. . . , the legislature clearly intended to expand military jurisdiction, including damage to honor outside of active duty . . . . Naturally, the term "with respect to their military position" is, as determined by the previously cited case . . . , very vague. The difficulties which arise out of the application of this regulation to individual cases can also not be removed if consideration is given to the history of the allegation, as stated in the previously cited case. The fact that a preliminary expert commission proposed, but subsequently failed to endorse, a special regulation concerning competence in the case of damage to honor (Article 2 Number 6, BGE 61 I 126) since Number 4 was sufficient does not mean that the legislature intended to subject all cases to military justice. This is confirmed by the statement on the MCC (BB1 1918 V 349 ff) in which the history of this special regulation was mentioned during the discussion among the confederal counselors. The pertinent point is the range accorded to the regulation by its wording and its purpose and intention. . . . This confirms the basis that civil law takes precedence over military law in case of doubt. . . .

4. Despite the fact that Article 2 Number 4 MCC states that draftees are subject to military law with respect to "their military position," this does not mean that honor-damaging statements made by draftees can automatically be pursued under military law, even if these comments are based on official procedures or are made against a commander. It cannot be the intention of the regulation that a soldier, once no longer on active duty, remains subject to indictment for damage to honor in military courts and under military law for an indeterminate period for critical statements made on the basis of personal experience or hearsay at work, in private or in the press. An immediate link between the personal military position of the honor-damaging aggressor and that of the victim is required. Such a relationship is to be assumed when the attack, both in timeframe and content is in direct correlation to the military hierarchy, that is the attacker being militarily subordinate to the victim. . . . This requirement was absent in Federal Court case BGE 61 113 ff, where a subaltern severely criticized the political opinion of a commander he was subordinate to, since the criticism was not related to the subaltern's military position. The requirement was present in a series of cases submitted to the MCA where the honor-damaging (and in one case threatening) comments by soldiers either against a direct commanding officer, or an officer who had allegedly disciplined a soldier unjustly. In these cases, it was clear that the soldier was subject to treatment by his commanding officer within the context of military service. . . .

5. In the present case, the complainant is recognizable as a soldier who participated in the refresher course, since the newspaper article referred to "us Schwyzer," was signed "Gunner Bang" and appeared shortly after the course. The complainant was also under the direct command of the only named officer, Colonel Baumann. However, it cannot be confirmed that the attacks in the article on Colonel Baumann and other commanders were made in direct relation (whether on content or occasion) to the personal military position of the complainant, despite his status as a subordinate to the officers that were attacked. The report does not indicate whether the complainant was directly affected by the actions described, in which too great a demand was placed on certain soldiers. Furthermore, the report does not clarify, nor are there indications, that the complainant and Colonel Baumann ever met during the

refresher course. The complainant did not criticize actions aimed at him directly, but rather the general situation. The occasion was, as described in the newspaper article, that the refresher course was generally described in a positive manner in the media, and that the complainant wanted to report on the less-than-positive aspects. The content of the newspaper article, and references to Colonel Baumann, whether true, exaggerated or untrue, is of the type that soldiers tend to tell and spread. In such stories, as in this one, there is no direct and immediate relationship between the personal military position of the narrator and the officers named in the story — a requirement for the application of military criminal justice and competence of the MCC. The fact that the complainant's article appeared in the press and thereby was spread further than by simple gossip does not change the fact that military courts are not competent in this matter. The question of competence is not determined by whether military courts are better placed to ensure a proper judgment. Furthermore, a civil court is just as capable as a military court in judging whether, such as in the present case, a statement is damaging to honor, whether the accused should be permitted to give evidence and whether proof has been submitted. The complainant's case should thus be heard [in the Federal Court] and Divisional Court 9A is therefore not competent to judge the accusation of slander within the scope of Article 145 MCC.

[The Federal Court held that the Divisional Court lacked jurisdiction over Colonel Bauman's slander complaint but that the military could try Sommacal for refusing to comply with regulations.]

NOTES AND QUESTIONS

1. For further discussion of *Sommacal,* see Roberta Arnold, *Military Criminal Procedures and Judicial Guarantees: The Example of Switzerland,* 3 J. INT'L CRIM. JUST. 749, 764-65 (2005).

2. Should there be a presumption against court-martial jurisdiction over personnel who are not on full-time active duty? Is the answer to that question a function of the extent to which reservists are integrated with full-time personnel?

3. Article 2 of the UCMJ subjects certain retired military personnel to court-martial jurisdiction. *See, e.g., Hooper v. United States,* 9 U.S.C.M.A. 637, 26 C.M.R. 417 (1958); *Hooper v. United States,* 326 F.2d 982 (Ct. Cl. 1964). Is there a plausible basis for doing so? Assuming there is, should that jurisdiction extend to all offenses under the Code, or should there be some limitation? The Constitutional Tribunal of Peru, for example, has held that retired members of the armed forces are "excluded from the possibility of perpetrating service-related crimes" because "on recovering the full exercise of their civil rights . . . they no longer belong to the armed forces, and therefore the constitutional legal regime in force for civilian cases applies to them." *Carlos Alfredo Villalba Zapata,* No. 585-96-HC/TC (Peru Const. Trib. June 19, 1998), http://www.tc.gob.pe/jurisprudencia/1998/0585-1996-HC.html, *quoted in Cesti Hurtado* (Inter-Am. Ct. of Hum. Rgts. Sept. 29, 1999), ¶ 129. *See also* Chapter 7, § II.

V. CIVILIANS

DUNCAN v. KAHANAMOKU
Supreme Court of the United States
327 U.S. 304 (1946)

[Two civilians were prosecuted in military provost courts in Hawaii during the period of martial law that was declared following the December 7, 1941, attack on Pearl Harbor. One, a stockbroker, was charged eight months later with embezzling stock from a civilian, and was sentenced to five years in jail, later reduced to four years. The other, a civilian Navy employee, was sentenced to six months in jail for violating a military order by brawling with Marine sentries at the Pearl Harbor Navy Yard over two years after the Japanese attack.]

Mr. Justice Black delivered the opinion of the Court.

The petitioners in these cases were sentenced to prison by military tribunals in Hawaii. Both are civilians. The question before us is whether the military tribunals had power to do this. The United States District Court for Hawaii in habeas corpus proceedings held that the military tribunals had no such power and ordered that they be set free. The Circuit Court of Appeals reversed, and ordered that the petitioners be returned to prison. 9 Cir., 146 F.2d 576. Both cases thus involve the rights of individuals charged with crime and not connected with the armed forces to have their guilt or innocence determined in courts of law which provide established procedural safeguards, rather than by military tribunals which fail to afford many of these safeguards. Since these judicial safeguards are prized privileges of our system of government we granted certiorari. . . .

The following events led to the military tribunals' exercise of jurisdiction over the petitioners. On December 7, 1941, immediately following the surprise air attack by the Japanese on Pearl Harbor, the Governor of Hawaii by proclamation undertook to suspend the privilege of the writ of habeas corpus and to place the Territory under "martial law." Section 67 of the Hawaiian Organic Act, 31 Stat. 141, 48 U.S.C.A. § 532, authorizes the Territorial Governor to take this action "in case of rebellion or invasion, or imminent danger thereof, when the public safety requires it." His action was to remain in effect only "until communication can be had with the President and his decision thereon made known." The President approved the Governor's action on December 9th. The Governor's proclamation also authorized and requested the Commanding General, "during . . . the emergency and until danger of invasion is removed, to exercise all the powers normally exercised" by the Governor and by "the judicial officers and employees of the Territory."

Pursuant to this authorization the Commanding General immediately proclaimed himself Military Governor and undertook the defense of the Territory and the maintenance of order. On December 8th, both civil and criminal courts were forbidden to summon jurors and witnesses and to try cases. The Commanding General established military tribunals to take the place of the courts. These were to try civilians charged with violating the laws of the

United States and of the Territory, and rules, regulations, orders or policies of the Military Government. Rules of evidence and procedure of courts of law were not to control the military trials. In imposing penalties the military tribunals were to be "guided by, but not limited to the penalties authorized by the court martial manual, the laws of the United States, the Territory of Hawaii, the District of Columbia, and the customs of war in like cases." The rule announced was simply that punishment was "to be commensurate with the offense committed" and that the death penalty might be imposed "in appropriate cases." Thus the military authorities took over the government of Hawaii. They could and did, by simply promulgating orders, govern the day to day activities of civilians who lived, worked, or were merely passing through there. The military tribunals interpreted the very orders promulgated by the military authorities and proceeded to punish violators. The sentences imposed were not subject to direct appellate court review, since it had long been established that military tribunals are not part of our judicial system. *Ex parte Vallandigham*, 1 Wall. 243. The military undoubtedly assumed that its rule was not subject to any judicial control whatever, for by orders issued on August 25, 1943, it prohibited even accepting of a petition for writ of habeas corpus by a judge or judicial employee or the filing of such a petition by a prisoner or his attorney. Military tribunals could punish violators of these orders by fine, imprisonment or death. . . .

. . . By the time of [Duncan's (the shipyard employee)] arrest the military had to some extent eased the stringency of military rule. Schools, bars and motion picture theatres had been reopened. Courts had been authorized to "exercise their normal functions." They were once more summoning jurors and witnesses and conducting criminal trials. There were important exceptions, however. One of these was that only military tribunals were to try "Criminal Prosecutions for violations of military orders." As the record shows, these military orders still covered a wide range of day to day civilian conduct. Duncan was charged with violating one of these orders, paragraph 8.01, Title 8, of General Order No. 2, which prohibited assault on military or naval personnel with intent to resist or hinder them in the discharge of their duty. He was therefore, tried by a military tribunal rather than the Territorial Court, although the general laws of Hawaii made assault a crime. Revised L.H.1935, ch. 166. A conviction followed and Duncan was sentenced to six months imprisonment.

. . . The District Court, after separate trials found in each case, among other things, that the courts had always been able to function but for the military orders closing them, and that consequently there was no military necessity for the trial of petitioners by military tribunals rather than regular courts. It accordingly held the trials void and ordered the release of the petitioners. . . .

Since both the language of the Organic Act and its legislative history fail to indicate that the scope of "martial law" in Hawaii includes the supplanting of courts by military tribunals, we must look to other sources in order to interpret that term. We think the answer may be found in the birth, development and growth of our governmental institutions up to the time Congress passed the Organic Act. Have the principles and practices developed during the birth and growth of our political institutions been such as to persuade us that

Congress intended that loyal civilians in loyal territory should have their daily conduct governed by military orders substituted for criminal laws, and that such civilians should be tried and punished by military tribunals? Let us examine what those principles and practices have been, with respect to the position of civilian government and the courts and compare that with the standing of military tribunals throughout our history.

People of many ages and countries have feared and unflinchingly opposed the kind of subordination of executive, legislative and judicial authorities to complete military rule which according to the government Congress has authorized here. In this country that fear has become part of our cultural and political institutions. The story of that development is well known and we see no need to retell it all. But we might mention a few pertinent incidents. As early as the 17th Century our British ancestors took political action against aggressive military rule. When James I and Charles I authorized martial law for purposes of speedily punishing all types of crimes committed by civilians the protest led to the historic Petition of Right which in uncompromising terms objected to this arbitrary procedure and prayed that it be stopped and never repeated. When later the American colonies declared their independence one of the grievances listed by Jefferson was that the King had endeavored to render the military superior to the civil power. The executive and military officials who later found it necessary to utilize the armed forces to keep order in a young and turbulent nation, did not lose sight of the philosophy embodied in the Petition of Right and the Declaration of Independence, that existing civilian government and especially the courts were not to be interfered with by the exercise of military power. In 1787, the year in which the Constitution was formulated, the Governor of Massachusetts colony used the militia to cope with Shay's rebellion. In his instructions to the Commander of the troops the Governor listed the "great objects" of the mission. The troops were to "protect the judicial courts . . . ," "to assist the civil magistrates in executing the laws . . . ," and to "aid them in apprehending the disturbers of the public peace. . . ." The Commander was to consider himself "constantly as under the direction of the civil officer, saving where any armed force shall appear and oppose . . . [his] . . . marching to execute these orders." President Washington's instructions to the Commander of the troops sent into Pennsylvania to suppress the Whiskey Rebellion of 1794 were to the same effect. The troops were to see to it that the laws were enforced and were to deliver the leaders of armed insurgents to the regular courts for trial. The President admonished the Commanding General "that the judge can not be controlled in his functions." In the many instances of the use of troops to control the activities of civilians that followed, the troops were generally again employed merely to aid and not to supplant the civilian authorities. The last noteworthy incident before the enactment of the Organic Act was the rioting that occurred in the Summer of 1892 at the Coeur-d'Alene mines of Shoshone County, Idaho. The President ordered the regular troops to report to the Governor for instructions and to support the civil authorities in preserving the peace. Later the State Auditor as agent of the Governor, and not the Commanding General, ordered the troops to detain citizens without trial and to aid the Auditor in doing all he thought necessary to stop the riot. Once more, the military authorities did not undertake to supplant the courts and to establish military tribunals to try and punish ordinary civilian offenders.

Courts and their procedural safeguards are indispensable to our system of government. They were set up by our founders to protect the liberties they valued. *Ex parte Quirin, supra*, 317 U.S. at page 19. Our system of government clearly is the antithesis of total military rule and the founders of this country are not likely to have contemplated complete military dominance within the limits of a Territory made part of this country and not recently taken from an enemy. They were opposed to governments that placed in the hands of one man the power to make, interpret and enforce the laws. Their philosophy has been the people's throughout our history. For that reason we have maintained legislatures chosen by citizens or their representatives and courts and juries to try those who violate legislative enactments. We have always been especially concerned about the potential evils of summary criminal trials and have guarded against them by provisions embodied in the constitution itself. *See Ex parte Milligan*, 4 Wall. 2; *Chambers v. Florida*, 309 U.S. 227. Legislatures and courts are not merely cherished American institutions; they are indispensable to our government.

Military tribunals have no such standing. For as this Court has said before: ". . . the military should always be kept in subjection to the laws of the country to which it belongs, and that he is no friend to the Republic who advocates the contrary. The established principle of every free people is, that the law shall alone govern; and to it the military must always yield." *Dow v. Johnson*, 100 U.S. 158, 169. Congress prior to the time of the enactment of the Organic Act had only once authorized the supplanting of the courts by military tribunals. Legislation to that effect was enacted immediately after the South's unsuccessful attempt to secede from the Union. Insofar as that legislation applied to the Southern States after the war was at an end it was challenged by a series of Presidential vetoes as vigorous as any in the country's history. And in order to prevent this Court from passing on the constitutionality of this legislation Congress found it necessary to curtail our appellate jurisdiction. Indeed, prior to the Organic Act, the only time this Court had ever discussed the supplanting of courts by military tribunals in a situation other than that involving the establishment of a military government over recently occupied enemy territory, it had emphatically declared that "civil liberty and this kind of martial law cannot endure together; the antagonism is irreconcilable; and, in the conflict, one or the other must perish." *Ex parte Milligan*, 4 Wall. 2, 124, 125.

We believe that when Congress passed the Hawaiian Organic Act and authorized the establishment of "martial law" it had in mind and did not wish to exceed the boundaries between military and civilian power, in which our people have always believed, which responsible military and executive officers had heeded, and which had become part of our political philosophy and institutions prior to the time Congress passed the Organic Act. The phrase "martial law" as employed in that Act, therefore, while intended to authorize the military to act vigorously for the maintenance of an orderly civil government and for the defense of the island against actual or threatened rebellion or invasion, was not intended to authorize the supplanting of courts by military tribunals. Yet the government seeks to justify the punishment of both White and Duncan on the ground of such supposed Congressional authorization. We hold that both petitioners are now entitled to be released from custody.

Reversed.

Mr. Justice Murphy, concurring.

The Court's opinion, in which I join, makes clear that the military trials in these cases were unjustified by the martial law provisions of the Hawaiian Organic Act. Equally obvious, as I see it, is the fact that these trials were forbidden by the Bill of Rights of the Constitution of the United States, which applies in both spirit and letter to Hawaii. Indeed, the unconstitutionality of the usurpation of civil power by the military is so great in this instance as to warrant this Court's complete and out-right repudiation of the action.

Abhorrence of military rule is ingrained in our form of government. Those who founded this nation knew full well that the arbitrary power of conviction and punishment for pretended offenses is the hallmark of despotism. *See* The Federalist, No. 83. History had demonstrated that fact to them time and again. They shed their blood to win independence from a ruler who they alleged was attempting to render the "military independent of and superior to the civil power" and who was "depriving us of the benefits of trial by jury." In the earliest state constitutions they inserted definite provisions placing the military under "strict subordination" to the civil power at all times and in all cases. And in framing the Bill of Rights of the Federal Constitution they were careful to make sure that the power to punish would rest primarily with the civil authorities at all times. They believed that a trial by an established court, with an impartial jury, was the only certain way to protect an individual against oppression. The Bill of Rights translated that belief into reality by guaranteeing the observance of jury trials and other basic procedural rights foreign to military proceedings. This supremacy of the civil over the military is one of our great heritages. It has made possible the attainment of a high degree of liberty regulated by law rather than by caprice. Our duty is to give effect to that heritage at all times, that it may be handed down untarnished to future generations.

Such considerations led this Court in *Ex parte Milligan*, 4 Wall. 2, to lay down the rule that the military lacks any constitutional power in war or in peace to substitute its tribunals for civil courts that are open and operating in the proper and unobstructed exercise of their jurisdiction. Only when a foreign invasion or civil war actually closes the courts and renders it impossible for them to administer criminal justice can martial law validly be invoked to suspend their functions. Even the suspension of power under those conditions is of a most temporary character. "As necessity creates the rule, so it limits its duration; for, if this government is continued after the courts are reinstated, it is a gross usurpation of power." *Id.*, 4 Wall. at page 127.

Tested by the *Milligan* rule, the military proceedings in issue plainly lacked constitutional sanction. . . .

It is undenied that the territorial courts of Hawaii were open and functioning during the period when the foregoing events took place. Martial law was proclaimed on December 7, 1941, immediately after the attack on Pearl Harbor; provost courts and military commissions were immediately established for the trial of civilians accused of crime. General Orders No. 4. On the next day, December 8, the territorial courts were closed by military order. Thereafter criminal cases of all description, whether involving offenses against federal or territorial law or violations of military orders, were handled in the provost courts and military commissions. Eight days later, however, the military permitted the reopening of the courts for the trial of limited classes of cases not requiring juries or the subpoenaing of witnesses. General Orders No. 29. On January 27, 1942, further power was restored to the courts by designating them "as agents of the Military Governor" to dispose of civil cases except those involving jury trials, habeas corpus and other specified matters and to exercise criminal jurisdiction in limited types of already pending cases. General Orders No. 57. Protests led to the issuance of General Orders No. 133 on August 31, 1942, expanding the jurisdiction of civil courts to cover certain types of jury trials. But General Orders No. 135, issued on September 4, 1942, continued military jurisdiction over offenses directed against the Government or related to the war effort. Proclamations on February 8, 1943, provided that the jurisdiction of the courts was to be reestablished in full except in cases of criminal and civil suits against persons in the armed forces and except for "criminal prosecutions for violations of military orders." These proclamations became effective on March 10, together with a revised code of military orders. Martial law was finally lifted from Hawaii on October 24, 1944.

There can be no question but that when petitioners White and Duncan were subjected to military trials on August 25, 1942, and March 2, 1944, respectively, the territorial courts of Hawaii were perfectly capable of exercising their normal criminal jurisdiction had the military allowed them to do so. The Chief Justice of the Supreme Court of Hawaii stated that after the month of April, 1942, he knew of "no sound reason for denial of trial by jury to civilians charged with criminal offense under the laws of the Territory." The Governor of the Territory also testified that the trial of civilians before military courts for offenses against the laws of the Territory was unnecessary and unjustified by the conditions in the Territory when petitioner White was charged with embezzlement in August, 1942. In short, the Bill of Rights disappeared by military fiat rather than by military necessity. . . .

The so-called "open court" rule of the *Milligan* case, to be sure, has been the subject of severe criticism, especially by military commentators. That criticism is repeated by the Government in these cases. It is said that the fact that courts are open is but one of many factors relevant to determining the necessity and hence the constitutionality of military trials of civilians. The argument is made that however adequate the "open court" rule may have been in 1628 or 1864 it is distinctly unsuited to modern warfare conditions where all of the territories of a warring nation may be in combat zones or imminently threatened with long-range attack even while civil courts are operating. Hence if a military commander, on the basis of his conception of military necessity, requires all civilians accused of crime to be tried summarily before martial law tribunals, the Bill of Rights must bow humbly to his judgment despite the unquestioned ability of the civil courts to exercise their criminal jurisdiction.

The argument thus advanced is as untenable today as it was when cast in the language of the Plantagenets, the Tudors and the Stuarts. It is a rank appeal to abandon the fate of all our liberties to the reasonableness of the judgment of those who are trained primarily for war. It seeks to justify military usurpation of civilian authority to punish crime without regard to the potency of the Bill of Rights. It deserves repudiation.

The untenable basis of this proposed reversion back to unlimited military rule is revealed by the reasons advanced in support of the reasonableness of the military judgment that it was necessary, even though the civil courts were open and fully able to perform their functions, to impose military trials on all persons accused of crime in Hawaii at the time when the petitioners were tried and convicted:

First. According to the testimony of Admiral Nimitz and General Richardson, Hawaii was in the actual theatre of war from December 7, 1941 through the period in question. They stated that there was at all times a danger of invasion, at least in the nature of commando raids or submarine attacks, and that public safety required the imposition of martial law. For present purposes it is unnecessary to dispute any of such testimony. We may assume that the threat to Hawaii was a real one; we may also take it for granted that the general declaration of martial law was justified. But it does not follow from these assumptions that the military was free under the Constitution to close the civil courts or to strip them of their criminal jurisdiction, especially after the initial shock of the sudden Japanese attack had been dissipated.

From time immemorial despots have used real or imagined threats to the public welfare as an excuse for needlessly abrogating human rights. That excuse is no less unworthy of our traditions when used in this day of atomic warfare or at a future time when some other type of warfare may be devised. The right to jury trial and the other constitutional rights of an accused individual are too fundamental to be sacrificed merely through a reasonable fear of military assault. There must be some overpowering factor that makes a recognition of those rights incompatible with the public safety before we should consent to their temporary suspension. If those rights may safely be respected in the face of a threatened invasion no valid reason exists for disregarding them. In other words, the civil courts must be utterly incapable of trying criminals or of dispensing justice in their usual manner before the Bill of Rights may be temporarily suspended. "Martial law [in relation to closing the courts] cannot arise from a threatened invasion. The necessity must be actual and present; the invasion real, such as effectually closes the courts and deposes the civil administration." *Ex parte Milligan, supra,* 4 Wall. at page 127.

Second. Delays in the civil courts and slowness in their procedure are also cited as an excuse for shearing away their criminal jurisdiction, although lack of knowledge of any undue delays in the Hawaiian courts is admitted. It is said that the military "cannot brook a delay" and that "the punishment must be swift; there is an element of time in it, and we cannot afford to let the trial linger and be protracted." This military attitude toward constitutional processes is not novel. Civil liberties and military expediency are often irreconcilable. It does take time to secure a grand jury indictment, to allow the accused to procure and confer with counsel, to permit the preparation of a defense, to form a petit jury, to respect the elementary rules of procedure and evidence and to judge guilt or innocence according to accepted rules of law. But experience has demonstrated that such time is well spent. It is the only method we have of insuring the protection of constitutional rights and of guarding against oppression. The swift trial and punishment which the military desires is precisely what the Bill of Rights outlaws. We would be false to our trust if we allowed the time it takes to give effect to constitutional rights to be used as the very reason for taking away those rights. It is our duty, as well as that of the military, to make sure that such rights are respected whenever possible, even though time may be consumed.

Third. It is further said that the issuance of military orders relating to civilians required that the military have at its disposal some sort of tribunal to enforce those regulations. Any failure of civil courts to convict violators of such regulations would diminish the authority and ability to discharge military responsibilities. This is the ultimate and most vicious of the arguments used to justify military trials. It assumes without proof that civil courts are incompetent and are prone to free those who are plainly guilty. It assumes further that because the military may have the valid power to issue regulations there must be an accompanying power to punish the violations of those regulations; the implicit and final assumption is then made that the military must have power to punish violations of all other statutes and regulations. Nothing is more inconsistent with our form of government, with its distinction between the power to promulgate law and the power to punish violations of the law. Application of this doctrine could soon lead to the complete elimination of civil jurisdiction over crime.

Moreover, the mere fact that it may be more expedient and convenient for the military to try violators of its own orders before its own tribunals does not and should not furnish a constitutional basis for the jurisdiction of such tribunals when civil courts are in fact functioning or are capable of functioning. Constitutional rights are rooted deeper than the wishes and desires of the military.

Fourth. Much is made of the assertion that the civil courts in Hawaii had no jurisdiction over violations of military orders by civilians and the military courts were therefore necessary. Aside from the fact that the civil courts were ordered not to attempt to exercise such jurisdiction, it is sufficient to note that Congress on March 21, 1942, vested in the federal courts jurisdiction to enforce military orders with criminal penalties. 56 Stat. 173, 18 U.S.C.A. §97a. It is undisputed that the federal court in Hawaii was open at all times in issue and was capable of exercising criminal jurisdiction. That the military refrained from using the statutory framework which Congress erected affords no constitutional justification for the creation of military tribunals to try such violators.

Fifth. Objection is made to the enforcement in civil courts of military orders on the ground that it would subject the military to "all sorts of influences, political and otherwise, as happened in the cases on the east coast in both Philadelphia and Boston" and that "it is inconceivable that the military commander should be subjected for the enforcement of his orders to the control of other agents." This is merely a military criticism of the proposition that in this nation the military is subordinate to the civil authority. It does not qualify as a recognizable reason for closing the civil courts to criminal cases.

Sixth. Further objection is made that the holding of civil trials might interrupt vital work through the attendance as jurors of war workers. This also is too unmeritorious to warrant serious or lengthy discussion. War workers could easily have been excused from jury duty by military order if necessary.

Seventh. The final reason advanced relates to the testimony of military leaders that Hawaii is said to have a "heterogeneous population with all sorts of affinities and loyalties which are alien in many cases to the philosophy of life of the American Government," one-third of the civilian population being of Japanese descent. The Court below observed, 9 Cir., 146 F.2d 576, 580, that "Governmental and military problems alike were complicated by the presence in the Territory of tens of thousands of citizens of Japanese ancestry besides large numbers of aliens of the same race. Obviously the presence of so many inhabitants of doubtful loyalty posed a continuing threat to the public security. Among these people the personnel of clandestine landing parties might mingle freely, without detection. Thus was afforded ideal cover for the activities of the saboteur and the spy. . . . To function in criminal matters the civilian courts must assemble juries; and citizens of Japanese extraction could not lawfully be excluded from jury panels on the score of race — even in cases of offenses involving the military security of the Territory. Indeed the mere assembling of juries and the carrying on of protracted criminal trials might well constitute an invitation to disorder as well as interference with the vital business of the moment." The Government adds that many of the military personnel stationed in Hawaii were unaccustomed to living in such a community and that "potential problems" created in Hawaii by racially mixed juries in criminal cases have heretofore been recognized "although, on the whole, it has been found that members of such mixed juries have not acted on a racial basis." The implication apparently is that persons of Japanese descent, including those of American background and training, are of such doubtful loyalty as a group as to constitute a menace justifying the denial of the procedural rights of all accused persons in Hawaii. It is also implied that persons of Japanese descent are unfit for jury duty in Hawaii and that the problems arising when they serve on juries are so great as to warrant dispensing with the entire jury system in Hawaii if the military so desires. The lack of any factual or logical basis for such implications is clear. It is a known fact that there have been no recorded acts of sabotage, espionage or fifth column activities by persons of Japanese descent in Hawaii either on or subsequent to December 7, 1941. There was thus no security reason for excluding them from juries, even making the false assumption that it was impossible to separate the loyal from the disloyal. And if there were problems arising from the use of racially mixed juries, elimination of all jury trials was hardly a reasonable or sensible answer to those problems. Especially deplorable, however, is this use of the iniquitous doctrine of racism to justify the imposition of military trials. Racism has no place whatever in our civilization. The Constitution as well as the conscience of mankind disclaims its use for any purpose, military or otherwise. It can only result, as it does in this instance, in striking down individual rights and in aggravating rather than solving the problems toward which it is directed. It renders impotent the ideal of the dignity of the human personality, destroying something of what is noble in our way of life. We must therefore reject it completely whenever it arises in the course of a legal proceeding.

The reasons here advanced for abandoning the "open court" rule of the *Milligan* case are without substance. To retreat from that rule is to open the door to rampant militarism and the glorification of war, which have destroyed so many nations in history. There is a very necessary part in our national life for the military; it has defended this country well in its darkest hours of trial. But militarism is not our way of life. It is to be used only in the most extreme circumstances. Moreover, we must be on constant guard against an excessive use of any power, military or otherwise, that results in the needless destruction of our rights and liberties. There must be a careful balancing of interests. And we must ever keep in mind that "The Constitution of the United States is a law for rulers and people, equally in war and in peace, and covers with the shield of its protection all classes of men, at all times, and under all circumstances." *Ex parte Milligan, supra*, 4 Wall. at pages 120, 121.

Mr. Chief Justice Stone, concurring.

. . . The Executive has broad discretion in determining when the public emergency is such as to give rise to the necessity of martial law, and in adapting it to the need. *Cf. Hirabayashi v. United States*, 320 U.S. 81. But executive action is not proof of its own necessity, and the military's judgment here is not conclusive that every action taken pursuant to the declaration of martial law was justified by the exigency. In the substitution of martial law controls for the ordinary civil processes, "what are the allowable limits of military discretion, and whether or not they have been overstepped in a particular case, are judicial questions." *Sterling v. Constantin, supra*, 287 U.S. at page 401.

I take it that the Japanese attack on Hawaii on December 7, 1941, was an "invasion" within the meaning of §67. But it began and ended long before these petitioners were tried by military tribunals in August 1942 and February 1944. I assume that there was danger of further invasion of Hawaii at the times of those trials. I assume also that there could be circumstances in which the public safety requires, and the Constitution permits, substitution of trials by military tribunals for trials in the civil courts. But the record here discloses no such conditions in Hawaii, at least during the period after February, 1942, and the trial court so found. After closing places of amusement, and after closing the civil courts on December 8, 1941, the military authorities, on December 24, 1941, ordered places of amusement to be opened. On January 27, 1942, they permitted the courts to exercise their normal functions except as to jury trials and the issuance of writs of habeas corpus. On February 4, 1942, they authorized the sale of liquor at bars. The full record in this case shows the conditions prevailing in Hawaii throughout 1942 and 1943. It demonstrates that from February, 1942 on, the civil courts were capable of functioning, and that trials of petitioners in the civil courts no more endangered the public safety than the gathering of the populace in saloons and places of amusement, which was authorized by military order. I find nothing in the entire record which would fairly suggest that the civil courts were unable to function with their usual efficiency at the times these petitioners were tried, or that their trial by jury in a civil court would have endangered good order or the public safety. The Governor of Hawaii and the Chief Justice of the Hawaiian Supreme Court testified to the contrary. The military authorities themselves testified and advanced no reason which has any bearing on public safety or good order for closing the civil courts to the trial of these petitioners, or for trying them in military courts. I can only conclude that the trials and the convictions upon which petitioners are now detained, were unauthorized by the statute, and without lawful authority. . . .

MR. JUSTICE BURTON, with whom MR. JUSTICE FRANKFURTER concurs, dissenting.

. . . The controlling facts in the cases before us are the extraordinary conditions created by the surprise Japanese invasion by air of Pearl Harbor on December 7, 1941. Visualizing the devastating success of that attack and the desperate conditions resulting from it, the primary question is what discretionary action by the executive branch of our Government, including the Army and Navy, was permissible on that day and in the period following it. Pearl Harbor and the Hawaiian Islands were the key to America's defenses in the Pacific. The attack of December 7th destroyed more of America's naval forces than our Government felt it safe to announce. America's first line of defense was pierced. The attack demonstrated that it was part of a carefully planned major military operation against not only Hawaii but the United States. Presumably it would be pressed further. It might well be followed by a land invasion of the Islands and by aerial attacks upon their centers of population. Handicapped by major losses to air and sea power, the commander of this isolated outpost was faced with imminent danger of further invasions under conditions calling for a desperate defense of the Islands. The Islands suddenly had become the focal point of a major action which converted them into an outpost of critical military importance to the world in general and to the United States in particular. Their invasion and possible capture overshadowed every other consideration. The Islands were a white-hot center of war ready to burst into flames.

Military attack by air, sea and land was to be expected. The complete disregard of international law evidenced by the first attack and the possible presence on the Islands of many Japanese collaborators gave warning that the enemy's next move might take the form of disastrous sabotage and terrorism among civilians. The extraordinary breach of international law evidenced by the attack made it essential to take extraordinary steps to protect the Islands against subversive action that might spring from deeply laid plans as secret, well aimed, and destructive as the original attack.

On December 7 and in the period immediately following, every inch of the Territory of Hawaii was like a frontier stockade under savage attack with notice that such attack would not be restrained by the laws of civilized nations. Measures of defense had to be taken on the basis that anything could happen. The relation of the Constitution of the United States to such a situation is important. Of course, the Constitution is not put aside. It was written by a generation fresh from war. The people established a more perfect union, in part, so that they might the better defend themselves from military attack. In doing so they centralized far more military power and responsibility in the

Chief Executive than previously had been done. The Constitution was built for rough as well as smooth roads. In time of war the nation simply changes gears and takes the harder going under the same power.

The conduct of war under the Constitution is largely an executive function. Within the field of military action in time of war, the executive is allowed wide discretion. While, even in the conduct of war, there are many lines of jurisdiction to draw between the proper spheres of legislative, executive and judicial action, it seems clear that at least on an active battle field, the executive discretion to determine policy is there intended by the Constitution to be supreme. The question then arises: What is a battle field and how long does it remain one after the first barrage?

It is well that the outer limits of the jurisdiction of our military authorities is subject to review by our courts even under such extreme circumstances as those of the battle field. This, however, requires the courts to put themselves as nearly as possible in the place of those who had the constitutional responsibility for immediate executive action. For a court to recreate a complete picture of the emergency is impossible. That impossibility demonstrates the need for a zone of executive discretion within which courts must guard themselves with special care against judging past military action too closely by the inapplicable standards of judicial, or even military, hindsight. The nature of judicial authority is largely negative as contrasted with the generally positive nature of executive authority, and it is essential that the opportunity for well directed positive action be preserved and vigorously used if the Government is to serve the best interests of the people.

For this Court to intrude its judgment into spheres of constitutional discretion that are reserved either to the Congress or to the Chief Executive, is to invite disregard of that judgment by the Congress or by executive agencies under a claim of constitutional right to do so. On the other hand, this Court can contribute much to the orderly conduct of government, if it will outline reasonable boundaries for the discretion of the respective departments of the Government, with full regard for the limitations and also for the responsibilities imposed upon them by the Constitution. . . .

. . . [T]here is a period, bearing a reasonable relation to the original emergency, during which it must be within the discretion of the executive agencies of the Government to decide when and how to restore the battle field to its peacetime controls. In view of the responsibility placed upon the executive branch of the Government and especially upon its armed forces in time of invasion and threatened invasion, it is essential that that branch of the Government have freedom of action equal to its needs. At the center of invasion, military control is the proper control to be applied, subject to provisions of the Constitution, treaties and laws of the United States applicable to a battle field. On December 7, 1941, I believe that the facts of the invasion and threatened further invasion amply established such a condition and justified at the time the military control established on that basis throughout the Islands.

Whether or not from the vantage point of the present this Court may disagree with the judgment exercised by the military authorities in their schedule of relaxation of control is not material unless this Court finds that the schedule was so delayed as to exceed the range of discretion which such conditions properly vest in the military authorities.

It is all too easy in this postwar period to assume that the success which our forces attained was inevitable and that military control should have been relaxed on a schedule based upon such actual developments. In fact, however, even now our Chief of Staff in his report to the Secretary of War as of June 30, 1945, reminds us that in "the black days of 1942 when the Japanese conquered all of Malaysia, occupied Burma, and threatened India while the German armies approached the Volga and the Suez. . . . Germany and Japan came so close to complete domination of the world that we do not yet realize how thin the thread of Allied survival had been stretched." Biennial Report of the Chief of Staff of the United States Army (1945) 1. Those were critical days when the United States could afford no military mistakes and when the safety and control of the Hawaiian key to the Pacific was essential. It was the responsibility of our military commanders not only to do the right thing in the interests of safety but to take no chances of error or surprise. It was the obligation of our military commanders to insure safety rather than to risk it. Acting as they were in the "fog of war," they were entitled to a wide range of discretion if they were to meet the obligations imposed upon them. It is not justifiable to tear Hawaii out from the context of the war as a whole. Our military policy there, as elsewhere, had to be guided by its relation to the global war.

Under these circumstances it is conceivable that the military authorities might have tried to continue complete military control in effect for a substantial period with a view to later relaxation of all such control when conditions made it obvious that there was no longer a need for any control. Such a course was not attempted here. The Commanding General of the Hawaii Department followed from the beginning the policy foreshadowed in his original proclamation. He restored civilian control of civilian activities wherever and whenever he felt that a partial restoration of it was in the public interest. In the meantime he had the primary duty of maintaining law and order and of fostering civilian activities as much as possible. Perhaps he could have arrested and detained individuals charged with violation of laws or regulations and held them for later trial by civilian courts. However, in view of the size of the population and the necessarily limited facilities for large scale detentions, he owed an equal duty to dispose promptly of violations of the law. . . .

One way to test the soundness of a decision today that the trial of petitioner White on August 25, 1942, before a provost court on a charge of embezzlement and the trial of petitioner Duncan on March 2, 1944, before a similar court on a charge of maliciously assaulting marine sentries were unconstitutional procedures, is to ask ourselves whether or not on those dates, with the war against Japan in full swing, this Court would have, or should have, granted a writ of habeas corpus, an injunction or a writ of prohibition to release the petitioners or otherwise to oust the provost courts of their claimed jurisdiction. Such a test emphasizes the issue. I believe that this Court would not have been justified in granting the relief suggested at such times. Also I believe that this Court might well have found itself embarrassed had it ordered such relief and then had attempted to enforce its order in the theater of military operations, at a time when the area was under martial law and the writ of habeas corpus was still suspended, all in accordance with the orders of the President of the United States and the Governor of Hawaii issued under their interpretation of the discretion and responsibility vested in them by the Constitution of the United States and by the Organic Act of Hawaii enacted by Congress. In order to recognize the full strength of our Constitution, both in time of peace and in time of war, it is necessary to protect the authority of our legislative and executive officials, as well as that of our courts, in the performance of their respective obligations to help to "establish Justice, insure domestic Tranquility, provide for the common defence, promote the general Welfare, and secure the Blessings of Liberty to ourselves and our Posterity."

NOTE

Delbert E. Metzger, the district judge who granted habeas corpus in *Duncan*, was a territorial official who served for a fixed term of years. When his term expired, President Truman refused to reappoint him. *See* Delbert E. Metzger, *No Longer a Judge: An Ex-Jurist Tells Why*, THE NATION, July 18, 1953, at 52.

Military Extraterritorial Jurisdiction Act of 2000
18 U.S.C. §§ 3261 et seq.

§ 3261. Criminal offenses committed by certain members of the Armed Forces and by persons employed by or accompanying the Armed Forces outside the United States

(a) Whoever engages in conduct outside the United States that would constitute an offense punishable by imprisonment for more than 1 year if the conduct had been engaged in within the special maritime and territorial jurisdiction of the United States —

(1) while employed by or accompanying the Armed Forces outside the United States; or

(2) while a member of the Armed Forces subject to chapter 47 of title 10 (the Uniform Code of Military Justice), shall be punished as provided for that offense.

(b) No prosecution may be commenced against a person under this section if a foreign government, in accordance with jurisdiction recognized by the United States, has prosecuted or is prosecuting such person for the conduct constituting such offense, except upon the approval of the Attorney General or the Deputy Attorney General (or a person acting in either such capacity), which function of approval may not be delegated.

(c) Nothing in this chapter may be construed to deprive a court-martial, military commission, provost court, or other military tribunal of concurrent jurisdiction with respect to offenders or offenses that by statute or by the law of war may be tried by a court-martial, military commission, provost court, or other military tribunal.

(d) No prosecution may be commenced against a member of the Armed Forces subject to chapter 47 of title 10 (the Uniform Code of Military Justice) under this section unless —

(1) such member ceases to be subject to such chapter; or

(2) an indictment or information charges that the member committed the offense with one or more other defendants, at least one of whom is not subject to such chapter.

§ 3267. Definitions

As used in this chapter:

(1) The term "employed by the Armed Forces outside the United States" means —

(A) employed as a civilian employee of the Department of Defense (including a nonappropriated fund instrumentality of the Department), as a Department of Defense contractor (including a subcontractor at any tier), or as an employee of a Department of Defense contractor (including a subcontractor at any tier);

(B) present or residing outside the United States in connection with such employment; and

(C) not a national of or ordinarily resident in the host nation.

(2) The term "accompanying the Armed Forces outside the United States" means —

(A) a dependent of —

(i) a member of the Armed Forces;

(ii) a civilian employee of the Department of Defense (including a nonappropriated fund instrumentality of the Department); or

(iii) a Department of Defense contractor (including a subcontractor at any tier) or an employee of a Department of Defense contractor (including a subcontractor at any tier);

(B) residing with such member, civilian employee, contractor, or contractor employee outside the United States; and

(C) not a national of or ordinarily resident in the host nation. . . .

NOTES AND QUESTIONS

1. The gap created by *Reid v. Covert* and other U.S. Supreme Court cases from the 1950s and 1960s remained in existence for decades despite a steady drumbeat of academic criticism. It took a decision of the Second Circuit, *United States v. Gatlin*, 216 F.3d 207 (2d Cir. 2000), to break the logjam and drive Congress to act by passing the Military Extraterritorial Jurisdiction Act of 2000 ("MEJA"). What took so long? Was the resulting legislation well-crafted? Very few cases have been prosecuted under MEJA. Why?

2. In 2006, Congress amended Art. 2(a)(10), UCMJ, 10 U.S.C. § 802(a)(10), to subject civilians serving with or accompanying the armed forces in the field in time of declared war or a contingency operation to court-martial jurisdiction. The statute had long included such a provision but it applied only in "time of war," a phrase understood to mean war formally declared by Congress. *United States v. Averette*, 19 U.S.C.M.A. 363, 41 C.M.R. 363 (1970) (2-1 decision); *see generally* Lawrence J. Schwarz, *The Case for Court-Martial Jurisdiction Over Civilians Under Article 2(a)(10) of the Uniform Code of Military Justice*, ARMY LAW., Oct.-Nov. 2002, at 31 (urging reconsideration of "excessively strict construction of Article 2(a)(10) in light of today's circumstances and more recent changes in case law"). Was the 2006 amendment necessary? To whom does it apply: civilian government employees, government contractors, "embedded" journalists? Was it desirable? Is it constitutional? If you were general counsel to a private security company doing business in a combat area, what would you advise your client to do in light of the legislation?

VI.   INTERNATIONAL HUMAN RIGHTS

General Comment No. 13: Equality before the courts and the right to a fair and public hearing by an independent court established by law (Art. 14)
Office of the UN High Commissioner for Human Rights, 1984

4. The provisions of article 14 [of the International Covenant on Civil and Political Rights (ICCPR)[8]] apply to all courts and tribunals within the scope of that article whether ordinary or specialized. The Committee notes the exis-

---

[8] Article 14 provides:

   1. All persons shall be equal before the courts and tribunals. In the determination of any criminal charge against him, or of his rights and obligations in a suit at law, everyone shall be entitled to a fair and public hearing by a competent, independent and impartial tribunal established by law. The press and the public may be excluded from all or part of a trial for reasons of morals, public order (ordre public) or national security in a democratic society, or when the interest of the private lives of the parties so requires, or to the extent strictly necessary in the opinion of the court in special circumstances where publicity would prejudice the interests of justice; but any judgement rendered in a criminal case or in a suit at law shall be made public except where the interest of juvenile persons otherwise requires or the proceedings concern matrimonial disputes or the guardianship of children.

tence, in many countries, of military or special courts which try civilians. This could present serious problems as far as the equitable, impartial and independent administration of justice is concerned. Quite often the reason for the establishment of such courts it to enable exceptional procedures to be applied which do not comply with normal standards of justice. While the Covenant does not prohibit such categories of courts, nevertheless the conditions which it lays down clearly indicate that the trying of civilians by such courts should be very exceptional and take place under conditions which genuinely afford the full guarantees stipulated in article 14. . . .

Report on Terrorism and Human Rights
Inter-American Commission on Human Rights, 2002

230. In the context of these fundamental requirements, the jurisprudence of the Inter-American system has long denounced the creation of special courts or tribunals that displace the jurisdiction belonging to the ordinary courts or judicial tribunals and that do not use the duly established procedures of the legal process. This has included in particular the use of *ad hoc* or special

---

2. Everyone charged with a criminal offence shall have the right to be presumed innocent until proved guilty according to law.

3. In the determination of any criminal charge against him, everyone shall be entitled to the following minimum guarantees, in full equality:

    (a) To be informed promptly and in detail in a language which he understands of the nature and cause of the charge against him;

    (b) To have adequate time and facilities for the preparation of his defence and to communicate with counsel of his own choosing;

    (c) To be tried without undue delay;

    (d) To be tried in his presence, and to defend himself in person or through legal assistance of his own choosing; to be informed, if he does not have legal assistance, of this right; and to have legal assistance assigned to him, in any case where the interests of justice so require, and without payment by him in any such case if he does not have sufficient means to pay for it;

    (e) To examine, or have examined, the witnesses against him and to obtain the attendance and examination of witnesses on his behalf under the same conditions as witnesses against him;

    (f) To have the free assistance of an interpreter if he cannot understand or speak the language used in court;

    (g) Not to be compelled to testify against himself or to confess guilt.

4. In the case of juvenile persons, the procedure shall be such as will take account of their age and the desirability of promoting their rehabilitation.

5. Everyone convicted of a crime shall have the right to his conviction and sentence being reviewed by a higher tribunal according to law.

6. When a person has by a final decision been convicted of a criminal offence and when subsequently his conviction has been reversed or he has been pardoned on the ground that a new or newly discovered fact shows conclusively that there has been a miscarriage of justice, the person who has suffered punishment as a result of such conviction shall be compensated according to law, unless it is proved that the non-disclosure of the unknown fact in time is wholly or partly attributable to him.

7. No one shall be liable to be tried or punished again for an offence for which he has already been finally convicted or acquitted in accordance with the law and penal procedure of each country.

courts or military tribunals to prosecute civilians for security offenses in times of emergency, which practice has been condemned by this Commission, the Inter-American Court and other international authorities. The basis of this criticism has related in large part to the lack of independence of such tribunals from the Executive and the absence of minimal due process and fair trial guarantees in their processes.

231. It has been widely concluded in this regard that military tribunals by their very nature do not satisfy the requirements of independent and impartial courts applicable to the trial of civilians, because they are not a part of the independent civilian judiciary but rather are a part of the Executive branch, and because their fundamental purpose is to maintain order and discipline by punishing military offenses committed by members of the military establishment. In such instances, military officers assume the role of judges while at the same time remaining subordinate to their superiors in keeping with the established military hierarchy.

232. This is not to say that military tribunals have no place within the military justice systems of member states. The Inter-American Court and this Commission have recognized in this connection that military courts can in principle constitute an independent and impartial tribunal for the purposes of trying members of the military for certain crimes truly related to military service and discipline and that, by their nature, harm the juridical interests of the military, provided that they do so with full respect for judicial guarantees. Military tribunals may not, however, be used to try violations of human rights or other crimes that are not related to the functions that the law assigns to military forces and that should therefore be heard by the regular courts. Military tribunals are also precluded from prosecuting civilians, although certain human rights supervisory bodies have found that in exceptional circumstances military tribunals or special courts might be used to try civilians but only where the minimum requirements of due process are guaranteed.

NOTES AND QUESTIONS

1. Do you agree with General Comment 13's assertion that "the conditions which [article 14] lays down clearly indicate that the trying of civilians by [military] courts should be very exceptional"? The African Commission on Human and Peoples' Rights goes further: "Military courts should not in any circumstances whatsoever have jurisdiction over civilians." African Union, Principles and Guidelines on the Right to a Fair Trial and Legal Assistance in Africa § L(c), AU COC/OS(XXX)247, at 10.

2. Article 6 of the European Convention for the Protection of Human Rights and Fundamental Freedoms provides: "In the determination of . . . any criminal charge against him, everyone is entitled to a . . . hearing . . . by an independent and impartial tribunal. . . ." In *Öcalan v. Turkey*, No. 46221/99, May 12, 2005, the European Court of Human Rights was called upon to apply Article 6 to the prosecution of a Turkish national who was leader of the

Workers' Party of Kurdistan. Öcalan had been convicted by a State Security Court that included an Army colonel through most of the proceedings. That judge was replaced by a civilian a week before Öcalan was convicted, and two months after the trial began, as a result of legislation passed in response to *Incal v. Turkey*, No. 41/1997/825/1031 (Eur. Ct. Hum. Rts. 1998). (Incal had been "convicted of disseminating separatist [*i.e.*, Kurdish] propaganda capable of inciting people to resist the government and commit criminal offenses." *Id.* § 72.) The civilian judge had been following the proceedings from the outset, had attended all of the hearings, and could have asked for additional evidence or investigations. Declining to follow an earlier decision that midstream replacement of a military judge with a civilian solved the problem of judicial independence and impartiality, *Imrek v. Turkey*, No. 57175/00 (Eur. Ct. Hum. Rts. 2003), the European Court found a violation of Article 6, noting in § 116 that "[i]n its previous judgments, the Court attached importance to the fact that a civilian had to appear before a court composed, even if only in part, of members of the armed forces (see, among other authorities, *Incal*, cited above, § 72). Such a situation seriously affects the confidence which the courts must inspire in a democratic society (see, *mutatis mutandis, Piersack v. Belgium*, judgment of 1 October 1982, Series A no. 53, pp. 14-15, § 30)." Six judges found it "hard to agree with what is said in paragraph 116 of the judgment. The applicant is there described as a civilian (or equated to a civilian). However, he was accused of instigating serious terrorist crimes leading to thousands of deaths, charges which he admitted at least in part. He could equally well be described as a warlord, which goes a long way to putting into perspective the fact that at the start of his trial one of the three members of the court before which he appeared was himself from the military." Wildhaber, J., dissenting in part, *Öcalan, supra*, at 70, § 8. Is the objection to trying civilians before military (or partly military) courts a judicial independence issue, *see* Chapter 12 *infra*, or something more?

3. "While Egypt's military judges may have considerable experience in applying the Code of Military Justice to infractions by military personnel, they do not have such experience applying criminal laws to civilian defendants. Before President Mubarak began referring civilian cases to military courts in October 1992, military courts tried only military cases. One military judge explained to Amnesty International that in his 30 years experience as a military judge he had not tried civilian cases until his involvement in two cases referred to military courts by President Mubarak earlier in 1993 involving alleged 'terrorism.' Both cases resulted in death sentences. This lack of experience is particularly worrying given the complexity of the civilian cases now being tried by military judges in Egypt, and given the fact that so many of the defendants are charged with crimes which may carry the death penalty. The concern about lack of experience with criminal trials of civilians also applies to military prosecutors." Amnesty Int'l, Egypt: Military Trials of Civilians 3 (Oct. 1993). Amnesty International recommended that Egypt "stop referring civilians to be tried in military courts." *Id.* at 17. Under what circumstances should a civilian be subject to trial by a court-martial?

4. In 2002, the International Commission of Jurists protested the threatened trial of a lawyer and three other civilian defendants by a Syrian military court. Attorney Haythem Al-Maleh was charged with establishing a human rights association without the approval of the Military of Social Affairs and Labor; publishing a magazine in Lebanon and distributing it without permission in Syria; disseminating false information; joining a political association having an international character without government permission; and publishing printed material which advocates sectarian strife and stirs disorder among the people. Letter from Louise Doswald-Beck, Secretary-General, Int'l Comm'n of Jurists, to Pres. Bashar al-Assad, Sept. 27, 2002 (arguing, among other things, that "[t]he military judiciary, outside of its ordinary jurisdiction over infractions by military personnel, plainly does not constitute a competent, independent and impartial tribunal").

5. In 2001, the civilian director of a Lebanese human rights organization and the head of a gay-oriented Beirut-based internet service provider were convicted by a military tribunal under a statute that punishes insults to the army or flag:

> Still more serious, though, is the practice of trying civilians before military courts. Article 1567 of the Military Penal Code protects the Lebanese army and flag against defamation. It reportedly contains no mention of the *Police des Moeurs* [vice squad] — a non-military police force — nor of other non-military security forces. Why, then, did Mugraby and el Batal face military charges?

> Because the military itself decides on its own power to arrest and try civilians. The trial, which opened on September 25, was repeatedly postponed as defense attorneys questioned the military tribunal's jurisdiction. On January 5, however, Brigadier General Maher Safieddine, head of the tribunal, issued his own ruling in the matter. He held that the court could indeed try civilians who had defamed the Police des Moeurs. He based this on paragraph 4 of Article 157, which stated that in matters relating to the honor of the flag and army, internal security forces — although civilian in status — were covered by extension.

> Defense attorneys objected strongly. They noted that paragraph 4 had been deleted from Article 157, in an amendment dated July 8, 1971. The military, however, arrogated to itself the right to fix the limits of its own jurisdiction — and to resurrect legal provisions discarded thirty years before. The military does not abide by the law: it decides it. . . .

> Particularly ominous is the decision to try Mr. el Batal and Mr. Mugraby before a military court, on the pretense that they defamed the police. Military trials have become widespread in Lebanon, revealing an increasing and dangerous erosion of the administration of justice in the country. On the day of Mr. Mugraby and Mr. Batal's trial, the military tribunal heard a total of 93 cases. Of these, only 24 involved military defendants. The rest were civilians. A military court provides no neutral administration or investigation. Rather than preserving the ordinary judiciary's independence of executive authority, the military is an enforcing arm of the executive branch.

The unacceptability of such trials is also established in international law. Principle 5 of the United Nations' "Basic Principles on the Independence of the Judiciary" holds that "Everyone shall have the right to be tried by ordinary courts or tribunals using established legal procedures. Tribunals that do not use the duly established procedures of the legal process shall not be created to displace the jurisdiction belonging to the ordinary courts or judicial tribunals." Moreover, the United Nations Human Rights Committee has condemned the use of military tribunals against civilians — most notably in a number of communications against Uruguay, in which the Committee held that this practice could only be justified in the most exceptional circumstances, failing which it violated Article 14.1 of the ICCPR [footnote 8 *supra*]. The reliance on military charges and a military tribunal in this case is a blatant attempt not only to continue the harassment of Mr. el Batal and Mr. Mugraby, but to deny them equality before, and fair treatment by, the law. It is also a barely veiled attempt to threaten all the human rights activists in Lebanon who might dare to speak out against their government's abuses. IGLHRC demands an end to the practice of military trials in Lebanon, and an end to the harassment of Kamal el Batal and Ziad Mugraby.

International Gay and Lesbian Human Rights Commission, Lebanon: Injustice in Uniform: Military Court Convicts Civilian Human Rights Defenders (March 2001). The two defendants were sentenced to three months in prison, but this was later reduced to one month, and then to a fine of approximately $200. *Id.* On what basis can referral of the Syrian and Lebanese charges to a military court be defended?

6. Should different standards for the administration of justice apply when a military court tries a civilian rather than a soldier? Why? In what respects should the standards differ?

7. It sometimes happens that some co-defendants are military personnel and others are civilian. How much weight should be given to the fact that some are clearly subject to military jurisdiction? In a case arising in Nigeria, the African Commission on Human and Peoples' Rights commented: "The civilian accused is part of the common conspiracy and as such it is reasonable that he be charged with his military co-accused in the same judicial process. We are making this decision conscious of the fact that Africa continues to have military regimes who are inclined to suspend the constitution, govern by decree and seek to oust the application of international obligations. Such was the case in Nigeria under Military strongman Sani Abacha." *Civil Liberties Organisation, Legal Defence Center, Legal Defense and Assistance Project v. Nigeria*, Comm. No. 218/98 (Afr. Comm'n on Hum. & Peoples' Rgts.).

8. Turning the telescope the other way around, are there circumstances in which, out of concern for human rights and the danger of impunity, even active duty military personnel — widely acknowledged to be properly subject to military justice (for service-connected offenses, *see* Chapter 7, §II, and in some countries — including the United States — for any offense) — should be subject to trial *only* in the civilian courts? *See generally* Chapter 7, §III; PETER

Rowe, The Impact of Human Rights Law on Armed Forces 176-80 (2006). Can the question of *in personam* court-martial jurisdiction be considered in isolation from subject-matter jurisdiction?

Chapter 7

JURISDICTION OVER THE OFFENSE

Second in importance to who may be tried in a court-martial is what offenses such a court may try. If military courts are exceptional, presumably they would have jurisdiction only to the extent justified by their special role in the legal system. Is it inevitable that a nation that takes a broad view of the *in personam* jurisdiction of military courts will take an equally broad view of subject-matter jurisdiction?

I. STATUTORY AND REGULATORY PROVISIONS

Manual for Courts-Martial, United States (2005 ed.), Rules for Courts-Martial
Rule 203. Jurisdiction over the offense

To the extent permitted by the Constitution, courts-martial may try any offense under the code and, in the case of general courts-martial, the law of war.

Latin American Model Code of Military Justice
Article 4. Scope of application.

Military jurisdiction includes all personnel in the service of the Armed Forces, for their acts or omissions in the exercise of their military duties and those civilian personnel who, as a result of a legal provision, would be included within this jurisdiction. In time of War and in accordance with International Law, prisoners of war shall be subject to military jurisdiction.

Military Jurisdiction includes:

a. The offenses listed in Book Two of this Code and those infractions included under this jurisdiction by special law.

b. All other offenses when they affect the particular interests of the Armed Forces provided that any of the following circumstances are present:

(1) That it is committed in a military location or under its exclusive military authority, whether permanently or temporarily.

(2) That it is committed in the performance of, or in relation to, an act of service.

(3) That it is committed while in the conduct of authorized military operations ordered by competent authority.

c. In time of war, military jurisdiction will extend to the following:

(1) All offenses committed in a military location, or committed in the performance of, or in relation to an act of service.

(2) Offenses committed by members of the armed forces while in the performance of a duty ordered by their superiors at the request of civilian authorities or while responding to their request.

(3) All other cases of criminal infractions as expressly established in this Code.

Statement of Policy on Military Justice
Alaska Statutes § 26.05.300

An offense committed by a member of the militia, organized or unorganized, shall be tried in civil courts and prosecuted by civil authorities except offenses of a purely military nature. This policy shall be executed and carried into effect at all times and applies to all encampments, armory drill periods, and parade periods in addition to any duty performed by the militia under [Alaska Stat. §] 26.05.070. [*See also, e.g.,* 20 Vt. Stats. § 941.]

Philippines, Republic Act No. 7055, June 20, 1991[1]

Section 1. Members of the Armed Force of the Philippines and other persons subject to military law, including members of the Citizens Armed Forces Geographical Units, who commit crimes or offenses penalized under the Revised Penal Code, other special laws, or local government ordinances, regardless of whether or not civilians are co-accused, victims, or offended parties which may be natural or juridical persons, shall be tried by the proper civil court, except when the offense, as determined before arraignment by the civil court, is service-connected, in which case the offense shall be tried by court-martial.

Provided, That the President of the Philippines may, in the interest of justice, order or direct at any time before arraignment that any such crimes or offenses be tried by the proper civil courts.

As used in this Section, service-connected crimes or offenses shall be limited to those defined in Article 54 to 70, Article 70 to 92, and Article 95 to 97 of Commonwealth Act No. 408, as amended. . . .

Cambodia, Law of Feb. 8, 1993, on the Organization of Courts, art. 9, cl. 2

The military court is authorized to render judgments, subject to appeal, over military cases.

---

[1] The full title of Act No. 7055, passed under the post-Marcos government of President Corazon Aquino, is "An Act strengthening civilian supremacy over the military by returning to the civil courts the jurisdiction over certain offenses involving members of the Armed Forces of the Philippines, other persons subject to military law, and the members of the Philippine National Office, repealing for the purpose certain presidential decrees."

A military offense is an offense committed by a member of the army concerning the military field or property of the armed forces. In a case in which a soldier commits a common law offense, the provincial or municipal court has jurisdiction.

Code of Service Discipline, Canada
§ 70. Offences not triable by service tribunal

A service tribunal shall not try any person charged with any of the following offences committed in Canada:

(a) murder;

(b) manslaughter; or

(c) an offence under any of sections 280 to 283 of the *Criminal Code*.[2]

Offences Punishable by Ordinary Law
§ 130. (1) Service trial of civil offences.

An act or omission —

(a) that takes place in Canada and is punishable and would, if it had taken place in Canada, be punishable under Part VII, the *Criminal Code* or any other Act of Parliament, or

(b) that takes place outside Canada and would, if it had taken place in Canada, be punishable under Part VII, the *Criminal Code* or any other Act of Parliament,

is an offence under this Division and every person convicted thereof is liable to suffer punishment as provided in subsection (2).

Military Discipline Supplementary Measures Act
South Africa, 1999

§3(3). When a person who is subject to the Code is suspected of having committed murder, treason, rape or culpable homicide, the matter will be dealt with in accordance with section 27 of the National Prosecution Authority Act, 1998 (Act No. 32 of 1998), and any ensuing trial shall take place in a civilian court.

Military Justice Law, 1955, Israel

§ 14. A court-martial is competent to try a soldier, other than a person to whom this law applies by virtue of section 8(2) or (3),[3] who has committed, whether in the State or outside it, any offence whatsoever which is not a military offense:

> Provided that if the Attorney General is of the opinion that the offence was not committed within the framework of the Army or in consequence of the accused's belonging to the Army, he may at any time,

---

[2] Those sections refer to the abduction of children.

[3] Those sections refer to persons employed by the Army or in an undertaking that serves the Army or is employed on a mission on behalf of the Army.

until the decision as to conviction or acquittal . . . , order that the accused be tried in another court.

II. SERVICE CONNECTION

SOLORIO v. UNITED STATES
Supreme Court of the United States
483 U.S. 435 (1987)

[A Coast Guard petty officer was accused of misconduct involving dependents of other servicemembers. Some of his offenses occurred where there was no base. At the time of the offenses, the case law held that the offense had to be "service-connected" and that the victim's status as a military dependent was insufficient. Purporting to apply the "service-connection" test, the United States Court of Military Appeals affirmed, finding that the law had evolved to take more fully into account the interests of victims.]

CHIEF JUSTICE REHNQUIST delivered the opinion of the Court.

This case presents the question whether the jurisdiction of a court-martial convened pursuant to the Uniform Code of Military Justice (U.C.M.J.) to try a member of the Armed Forces depends on the "service connection" of the offense charged. We hold that it does not, and overrule our earlier decision in *O'Callahan v. Parker*, 395 U.S. 258 (1969).

While petitioner Richard Solorio was on active duty in the Seventeenth Coast Guard District in Juneau, Alaska, he sexually abused two young daughters of fellow coastguardsmen. Petitioner engaged in this abuse over a 2-year period until he was transferred by the Coast Guard to Governors Island, New York. Coast Guard authorities learned of the Alaska crimes only after petitioner's transfer, and investigation revealed that he had later committed similar sexual abuse offenses while stationed in New York. The Governors Island commander convened a general court-martial to try petitioner for crimes alleged to have occurred in Alaska and New York.

There is no "base" or "post" where Coast Guard personnel live and work in Juneau. Consequently, nearly all Coast Guard military personnel reside in the civilian community. Petitioner's Alaska offenses were committed in his privately owned home, and the fathers of the 10- to 12-year-old victims in Alaska were active duty members of the Coast Guard assigned to the same command as petitioner. Petitioner's New York offenses also involved daughters of fellow coast-guardsmen, but were committed in Government quarters on the Governors Island base.

After the general court-martial was convened in New York, petitioner moved to dismiss the charges for crimes committed in Alaska on the ground that the court lacked jurisdiction under this Court's decisions in *O'Callahan v. Parker*, supra, and *Relford v. Commandant*, U.S. Disciplinary Barracks, 401 U.S. 355 (1971). Ruling that the Alaska offenses were not sufficiently "service connected" to be tried in the military criminal justice system, the court-martial judge granted the motion to dismiss. The Government appealed the dismissal of the charges to the United States Coast Guard Court of Military Review, which reversed the trial judge's order and reinstated the charges. 21 M.J. 512 (1985).

The United States Court of Military Appeals affirmed the Court of Military Review, concluding that the Alaska offenses were service connected within the meaning of *O'Callahan* and *Relford*. 21 M.J. 251 (1986). Stating that "not every off-base offense against a servicemember's dependent is service-connected," the court reasoned that "sex offenses against young children . . . have a continuing effect on the victims and their families and ultimately on the morale of any military unit or organization to which the family member is assigned." *Id.*, at 256. In reaching its holding, the court also weighed a number of other factors, including: the interest of Alaska civilian officials in prosecuting petitioner; the hardship on the victims, who had moved from Alaska, that would result if they were called to testify both at a civilian trial in Alaska and at the military proceeding in New York; and the benefits to petitioner and the Coast Guard from trying the Alaska and New York offenses together. . . . We now affirm. . . .

In an unbroken line of decisions from 1866 to 1960, this Court interpreted the Constitution as conditioning the proper exercise of court-martial jurisdiction over an offense on one factor: the military status of the accused. *Gosa v. Mayden*, 413 U.S. 665, 673 (1973) (plurality opinion); *see Kinsella v. United States ex rel. Singleton*, 361 U.S. 234, 240-241, 243 (1960); *Reid v. Covert*, 354 U.S. 1, 22-23 (1957) (plurality opinion); *Grafton v. United States*, 206 U.S. 333, 348 (1907); *Johnson v. Sayre*, 158 U.S. 109, 114 (1895); *Smith v. Whitney*, 116 U.S. 167, 183-185 (1886); *Coleman v. Tennessee*, 97 U.S. 509, 513-514 (1879); *Ex parte Milligan*, 4 Wall. 2, 123 (1866); *cf. United States ex rel. Toth v. Quarles*, 350 U.S. 11, 15 (1955); *Kahn v. Anderson*, 255 U.S. 1, 6-9 (1921); *Givens v. Zerbst*, 255 U.S. 11, 20-21 (1921). This view was premised on what the Court described as the "natural meaning" of Art. I, § 8, cl. 14, as well as the Fifth Amendment's exception for "cases arising in the land or naval forces." *Reid v. Covert, supra,* at 19; *United States ex rel. Toth v. Quarles, supra,* at 15. As explained in *Kinsella v. Singleton, supra*:

> "The test for jurisdiction . . . is one of *status*, namely, whether the accused in the court-martial proceeding is a person who can be regarded as falling within the term 'land and naval Forces.' . . ." *Id.*, at 240-241 (emphasis in original).

> "Without contradiction, the materials . . . show that military jurisdiction has always been based on the 'status' of the accused, rather than on the nature of the offense. To say that military jurisdiction 'defies definition in terms of military "status"' is to defy the unambiguous language of Art. I, § 8, cl. 14, as well as the historical background thereof and the precedents with reference thereto." *Id.*, at 243.

Implicit in the military status test was the principle that determinations concerning the scope of court-martial jurisdiction over offenses committed by servicemen was a matter reserved for Congress. . . .

In 1969, the Court in *O'Callahan v. Parker* departed from the military status test and announced the "new constitutional principle" that a military tribunal may not try a serviceman charged with a crime that has no service connection. *See Gosa v. Mayden, supra*, at 673. Applying this principle, the *O'Callahan* Court held that a serviceman's off-base sexual assault on a civilian with no connection with the military could not be tried by court-martial. On reexamination of *O'Callahan*, we have decided that the service connection test announced in that decision should be abandoned.

The constitutional grant of power to Congress to regulate the Armed Forces, Art. I, §8, cl. 14, appears in the same section as do the provisions granting Congress authority, inter alia, to regulate commerce among the several States, to coin money, and to declare war. On its face there is no indication that the grant of power in Clause 14 was any less plenary than the grants of other authority to Congress in the same section. Whatever doubts there might be about the extent of Congress' power under Clause 14 to make rules for the "Government and Regulation of the land and naval Forces," that power surely embraces the authority to regulate the conduct of persons who are actually members of the Armed Services. As noted by Justice Harlan in his *O'Callahan* dissent, there is no evidence in the debates over the adoption of the Constitution that the Framers intended the language of Clause 14 to be accorded anything other than its plain meaning. Alexander Hamilton described these powers of Congress "essential to the common defense" as follows:

> "These powers ought to exist without limitation, because it is impossible to foresee or define the extent and variety of national exigencies, or the correspondent extent and variety of the means which may be necessary to satisfy them. . . .

> ". . . Are fleets and armies and revenues necessary for this purpose [common safety]? The government of the Union must be empowered to pass all laws, and to make all regulations which have relation to them." The Federalist No. 23, pp. 152-154 (E. Bourne ed. 1947).

The *O'Callahan* Court's historical foundation for its holding rests on the view that "[b]oth in England prior to the American Revolution and in our own national history military trial of soldiers committing civilian offenses has been viewed with suspicion." 395 U.S., at 268. According to the Court, the historical evidence demonstrates that, during the late 17th and 18th centuries in England as well as the early years of this country, courts-martial did not have authority to try soldiers for civilian offenses. The Court began with a review of the 17th-century struggle in England between Parliament and the Crown over control of the scope of court-martial jurisdiction. As stated by the Court, this conflict was resolved when William and Mary accepted the Bill of Rights in 1689, which granted Parliament exclusive authority to define the jurisdiction of military tribunals. *See ibid.* The Court correctly observed that Parliament, wary of abuses of military power, exercised its new authority sparingly. Indeed, a statute enacted by Parliament in 1689 provided for court-martial only for the crimes of sedition, mutiny, and desertion, and exempted members of militia from its scope. Mutiny Act of 1689, 1 Wm. & Mary, ch. 5.

The *O'Callahan* Court's representation of English history following the Mutiny Act of 1689, however, is less than accurate. In particular, the Court posited that "[i]t was . . . the rule in Britain at the time of the American Revolution that a soldier could not be tried for a civilian offense committed in

Britain; instead military officers were required to use their energies and office to insure that the accused soldier would be tried before a civil court." 395 U.S., at 269. In making this statement, the Court was apparently referring to Section XI, Article I, of the British Articles of War in effect at the time of the Revolution. This Article provided:

> "Whenever any Officer or Soldier shall be accused of a Capital Crime, or of having used Violence, or committed any Offence against the Persons or Property of Our Subjects, . . . the Commanding Officer, and Officers of every Regiment, Troop, or Party to which the . . . accused shall belong, are hereby required, upon Application duly made by, or in behalf of the Party or Parties injured, to use . . . utmost Endeavors to deliver over such accused . . . to the Civil Magistrate." British Articles of War of 1774, *reprinted in* G. Davis, Military Law of the United States 581, 589 (3d rev. ed. 1915).

This provision, however, is not the sole statement in the Articles bearing on court-martial jurisdiction over civilian offenses. Specifically, Section XIV, Article XVI, provided that all officers and soldiers who

> "shall maliciously destroy any Property whatsoever belonging to any of Our Subjects, unless by Order of the then Commander in Chief of Our Forces, to annoy Rebels or other Enemies in Arms against Us, he or they that shall be found guilty of offending herein shall (besides such Penalties as they are liable to by law) be punished according to the Nature and Degree of the Offence, by the Judgment of a Regimental or General Court Martial." *Id.*, at 593.

Under this provision, military tribunals had jurisdiction over offenses punishable under civil law. Nelson & Westbrook 11 [*Court-Martial Jurisdiction Over Servicemen for "Civilian" Offenses: An Analysis of* O'Callahan v. Parker, 54 MINN. L. REV. 1 (1969)]. Accordingly, the *O'Callahan* Court erred in suggesting that, at the time of the American Revolution, military tribunals in England were available "only where ordinary civil courts were unavailable." 395 U.S., at 269, and n.11.

The history of early American practice furnishes even less support to *O'Callahan*'s historical thesis. The American Articles of War of 1776, which were based on the British Articles, contained a provision similar to Section XI, Article I, of the British Articles, requiring commanding officers to deliver over to civil magistrates any officer or soldier accused of "a capital crime, . . . having used violence, or . . . any offence against the persons or property of the good people of any of the United American States" upon application by or on behalf of an injured party. American Articles of War of 1776, Section X, Article I, *reprinted in* 2 Winthrop [Military Law and Precedents] 1494. It has been postulated that American courts-martial had jurisdiction over the crimes described in this provision where no application for a civilian trial was made by or on behalf of the injured civilian. Indeed, American military records reflect trials by court-martial during the late 18th century for offenses against civilians and punishable under civil law, such as theft and assault.

The authority to try soldiers for civilian crimes may be found in the much-disputed "general article" of the 1776 Articles of War, which allowed court-martial jurisdiction over "[a]ll crimes not capital, and all disorders and neglects which officers and soldiers may be guilty of, to the prejudice of good order and military discipline." American Articles of War of 1776, Section XVIII, Article 5, *reprinted in* 2 Winthrop 1503. Some authorities, such as those cited by the *O'Callahan* Court, interpreted this language as limiting court-martial jurisdiction to crimes that had a direct impact on military discipline. Several others, however, have interpreted the language as encompassing all noncapital crimes proscribed by the civil law. Even W. Winthrop, the authority relied on most extensively by the majority in *O'Callahan*, recognized that military authorities read the general article to include crimes "committed upon or against civilians . . . at or near a military camp or post." 2 Winthrop 1124, 1126, n. 1.

We think the history of court-martial jurisdiction in England and in this country during the 17th and 18th centuries is far too ambiguous to justify the restriction on the plain language of Clause 14 which *O'Callahan* imported into it. There is no doubt that the English practice during this period shows a strong desire in that country to transfer from the Crown to Parliament the control of the scope of court-martial jurisdiction. And it is equally true that Parliament was chary in granting jurisdiction to courts-martial, although not as chary as the *O'Callahan* opinion suggests. But reading Clause 14 consistently with its plain language does not disserve that concern; Congress, and not the Executive, was given the authority to make rules for the regulation of the Armed Forces.

The *O'Callahan* Court cryptically stated: "The 17th century conflict over the proper role of courts-martial in the enforcement of the domestic criminal law was not, however, merely a dispute over what organ of government had jurisdiction. It also involved substantive disapproval of the general use of military courts for trial of ordinary crimes." 395 U.S., at 268. But such disapproval in England at the time of William and Mary hardly proves that the Framers of the Constitution, contrary to the plenary language in which they conferred the power on Congress, meant to freeze court-martial usage at a particular time in such a way that Congress might not change it. The unqualified language of Clause 14 suggests that whatever these concerns, they were met by vesting in Congress, rather than the Executive, authority to make rules for the government of the military.

Given the dearth of historical support for the *O'Callahan* holding, there is overwhelming force to Justice Harlan's reasoning that the plain language of the Constitution, as interpreted by numerous decisions of this Court preceding *O'Callahan*, should be controlling on the subject of court-martial jurisdiction. 395 U.S., at 275-278 (dissenting); *cf. Monell v. New York City Dept. of Social Services*, 436 U.S. 658, 696 (1978) ("[W]e ought not 'disregard the implications of an exercise of judicial authority assumed to be proper for 100 years'"), *quoting Brown Shoe Co. v. United States*, 370 U.S. 294, 307 (1962).

Decisions of this Court after *O'Callahan* have also emphasized that Congress has primary responsibility for the delicate task of balancing the rights of servicemen against the needs of the military. As we recently reiterated, "[j]udicial deference . . . is at its apogee when legislative action under the congressional authority to raise and support armies and make rules and regulations for their governance is challenged." *Goldman v. Weinberger*, 475 U.S. 503, 508 (1986), *quoting Rostker v. Goldberg*, 453 U.S. 57, 70 (1981). Since *O'Callahan*, we have adhered to this principle of deference in a variety of contexts where, as here, the constitutional rights of servicemen were implicated. *See, e.g., Goldman v. Weinberger, supra*, at 509-510 (free exercise of religion); *Chappell v. Wallace*, 462 U.S. 296, 300-305 (1983) (racial discrimination); *Rostker v. Goldberg, supra*, at 64-66, 70-71 (sex discrimination); *Brown v. Glines*, 444 U.S. 348, 357, 360 (1980) (free expression); *Middendorf v. Henry*, 425 U.S. 25, 43 (1976) (right to counsel in summary court-martial proceedings); *Schlesinger v. Councilman*, 420 U.S. 738, 753 (1975) (availability of injunctive relief from an impending court-martial); *Parker v. Levy*, 417 U.S. 733, 756 (1974) (due process rights and freedom of expression).

The notion that civil courts are "ill equipped" to establish policies regarding matters of military concern is substantiated by experience under the service connection approach. *Chappell v. Wallace, supra*, at 305. In his *O'Callahan* dissent, Justice Harlan forecasted that "the infinite permutations of possibly relevant factors are bound to create confusion and proliferate litigation over the [court-martial] jurisdiction issue." 395 U.S., at 284. In fact, within two years after *O'Callahan*, this Court found it necessary to expound on the meaning of the decision, enumerating a myriad of factors for courts to weigh in determining whether an offense is service connected. *Relford v. Commandant, U.S. Disciplinary Barracks*, 401 U.S. 355 (1971). Yet the service connection approach, even as elucidated in *Relford*, has proved confusing and difficult for military courts to apply.

Since *O'Callahan* and *Relford*, military courts have identified numerous categories of offenses requiring specialized analysis of the service connection requirement. For example, the courts have highlighted subtle distinctions among offenses committed on a military base, offenses committed off-base, offenses arising from events occurring both on and off a base, and offenses committed on or near the boundaries of a base. Much time and energy has also been expended in litigation over other jurisdictional factors, such as the status of the victim of the crime, and the results are difficult to reconcile. The confusion created by the complexity of the service connection requirement, however, is perhaps best illustrated in the area of off-base drug offenses. Soon after *O'Callahan*, the Court of Military Appeals held that drug offenses were of such "special military significance" that their trial by court-martial was unaffected by the decision. *United States v. Beeker*, 18 U.S.C.M.A. 563, 565, 40 C.M.R. 275, 277 (1969). Nevertheless, the court has changed its position on the issue no less than two times since *Beeker*, each time basing its decision on *O'Callahan* and *Relford*.

When considered together with the doubtful foundations of *O'Callahan*, the confusion wrought by the decision leads us to conclude that we should read Clause 14 in accord with the plain meaning of its language as we did in the many years before *O'Callahan* was decided. That case's novel approach to court-martial jurisdiction must bow "to the lessons of experience and the force of better reasoning." *Burnet v. Coronado Oil & Gas Co.*, 285 U.S. 393, 406-408 (1932) (Brandeis, J., dissenting). We therefore hold that the requirements of the Constitution are not violated where, as here, a court-martial is convened to try a serviceman who was a member of the Armed Services at the time of the offense charged. The judgment of the Court of Military Appeals is

Affirmed.

Justice Stevens, concurring in the judgment.

Today's unnecessary overruling of precedent is most unwise. The opinion of the United States Court of Military Appeals demonstrates that petitioner's offenses were sufficiently "service connected" to confer jurisdiction on the military tribunal. Unless this Court disagrees with that determination — and I would be most surprised to be told that it does — it has no business reaching out to reexamine the decisions in *O'Callahan v. Parker*, 395 U.S. 258 (1969), and *Relford v. Commandant, U.S. Disciplinary Barracks*, 401 U.S. 355 (1971). While there might be some dispute about the exact standard to be applied in deciding whether to overrule prior decisions, I had thought that we all could agree that such drastic action is only appropriate when essential to the disposition of a case or controversy before the Court. The fact that any five Members of the Court have the power to reconsider settled precedents at random, does not make that practice legitimate.

For the reasons stated by the Court of Military Appeals, I agree that its judgment should be affirmed.

Justice Marshall, with whom Justice Brennan joins, and with whom Justice Blackmun joins in all but the last paragraph, dissenting.

Less than 20 years ago, this Court held in *O'Callahan v. Parker*, 395 U.S. 258 (1969), that, to be subject to trial by court-martial, a criminal offense charged against a member of the Armed Forces had to be "service connected," lest the phrase "cases arising in the land or naval forces" in the Fifth Amendment "be expanded to deprive every member of the armed services of the benefits of an indictment by a grand jury and a trial by a jury of his peers." *Id.*, at 273. Today the Court overrules *O'Callahan*. In doing so, it disregards constitutional language and principles of stare decisis in its singleminded determination to subject members of our Armed Forces to the unrestrained control of the military in the area of criminal justice. I dissent.

I

The majority begins by assuming that the limitation on court-martial jurisdiction enunciated in *O'Callahan* was based on the power of Congress, contained in Art. I, §8, cl. 14, "[t]o make Rules for the Government and Regulation of the land and naval Forces." It then rejects this asserted limitation of congressional power on the ground that the Framers intended to give Congress plenary authority over the government of the military. But the Court in *O'Callahan* did not simply address whether Art. I, §8, cl. 14, granted Congress the authority to create court-martial jurisdiction over all crimes committed by members of the Armed Forces. Congress' Article I power to regulate the Armed Forces is limited by the Fifth Amendment right to indictment or presentment by a grand jury and the Sixth Amendment right to trial by jury. "[T]he constitutional grant of power to Congress to regulate the armed forces," this Court has previously stated, "itself does not empower Congress to deprive people of trials under Bill of Rights safeguards, and we are not willing to hold that power to circumvent those safeguards should be inferred through the Necessary and Proper Clause." *United States ex rel. Toth v. Quarles*, 350 U.S. 11, 21-22 (1955). The majority simply disregards the limitations the Bill of Rights imposes on the reach of Art. I, § 8, cl. 14.

The rights to grand jury process and to trial by jury are, of course, of restricted application in military cases. The Fifth Amendment excepts from the grand jury requirement "cases arising in the land or naval forces, or in the Militia, when in actual service in time of War or public danger," and the Court has held this exception applicable to the Sixth Amendment right to trial by jury as well. *Ex parte Milligan*, 4 Wall. 2, 123 (1867). But the text of the exception is inconsistent with the majority's conclusion that the only relevant factor in determining whether a court-martial has jurisdiction over a case is the status of the defendant as a member of the Armed Services.

The Fifth Amendment's exception covers only "cases *arising in* the land and naval forces" (emphasis added). It makes no reference to the status of the individual committing the crime. Had that been the Framers' intent, it would have been easy to have said so, given that the grand jury provision of the Amendment, which states that "[n]o Person shall be held to answer for a capital, or otherwise infamous crime, unless on a presentment or indictment of a Grand Jury," speaks not in terms of "crimes" or "cases," but of individual defendants. Nonetheless, the exception contained in the Fifth Amendment is expressed — and applies by its terms — only to cases arising in the Armed Forces. *O'Callahan* addressed not whether Art. I, § 8, cl. 14, empowered Congress to create court-martial jurisdiction over all crimes committed by service members, but rather whether Congress, in exercising that power, had encroached upon the rights of members of Armed Forces whose cases did not "arise in" the Armed Forces. This is clear from the Court's statement of its holding in *O'Callahan*:

> "We have concluded that the crime to be under military jurisdiction must be service connected, lest "cases arising in the land or naval forces, or in the Militia, when in actual service in time of War or public danger," as used in the Fifth Amendment, be expanded to deprive every member of the armed services of the benefits of an indictment by a grand jury and a trial by a jury of his peers." 395 U.S., at 272-273 (footnote omitted).

The protections afforded individuals by the Fifth and Sixth Amendments are central to our constitutional scheme of justice. The right to trial by jury, in particular, "ranks very high in our catalogue of constitutional safeguards." *United States ex rel. Toth v. Quarles*, 350 U.S., at 16. These protections should not be lightly abrogated. Consequently, the exception in the Fifth Amendment for cases arising in the Armed Forces must be strictly construed. This was the basis for the Court's conclusion, in *Toth*, that the power to authorize trial by court-martial should be limited to "'the least possible power adequate to the end proposed.'" *Id.*, at 23 (emphasis omitted), *quoting Anderson v. Dunn*, 6 Wheat. 204, 231 (1821).

The historical evidence considered by the Court in *O'Callahan* is therefore relevant, not to what the Framers intended to include in the scope of the congressional power to regulate the Armed Forces in Art. I, § 8, cl. 14, but to what the Framers, wary of military jurisdiction and familiar with strong restrictions on the scope of that jurisdiction, considered "cases arising in the armed forces." Even assuming that they intended to assign control over the scope of the Article I power to the Legislature, this does not imply that the meaning of the Fifth Amendment's "arising in" exception can be interpreted without reference to the practices of that time.

In that respect it is significant that the British political and legal writing of the 17th and 18th centuries demonstrates a longstanding suspicion of broad court-martial jurisdiction. This suspicion was well known in colonial America, and was based on familiar history. British writers and legislators took a narrow view of the appropriate scope of court-martial jurisdiction, which manifested itself in a very limited grant of authority to try offenses by court-martial during the period of which the Framers would have been most acutely aware. *See, e.g.*, M. Hale, The History of the Common Law of England 42-43 (6th ed. 1820). Not only was that jurisdiction narrow, it was expressly limited to cases having some connection with the military. The test was not one of status, but one of military relationship. See S. Adye, A Treatise on Courts Martial 60 (1786) ("The crimes that are cognizable by a court martial, as repugnant to military discipline, are pointed out by the mutiny act and articles of war . . . and as to other crimes which officers and soldiers being guilty of, are to be tried for by the ordinary course of law, in like manner with other subjects"; *see also* 1 C. Clode, Military Forces of the Crown; Their Administration and Government 158 (1869) ("it has been a subject of controversy to distinguish the offences that are purely Military (and therefore properly within the cognizance of a Court-martial), from others that are Civil or Political (and therefore properly within the cognizance of the civil tribunals of the community)"; *Grant v. Gould*, 2 H. Bl. 69, 99-100, 126 Eng. Rep. 434, 450 (C.P. 1792) ("in this country, all the delinquencies of soldiers are not triable, as in most countries in Europe, by martial law; but where they are ordinary offences against the civil peace they are tried by the common law courts. . . . The object of the mutiny act . . . is to create a court invested with authority to try those who are a part of the army . . . and the object of the trial is limited to breaches of military duty" (emphasis omitted)). The reach of military law in Britain at the time of the Revolution thus permitted courts-martial only for offenses committed by members of the Armed Forces that had some connection with their military service.

The majority disputes the *O'Callahan* Court's suggestion that the British Articles of War forbade the trial of civil offenses by court-martial. The Court points to Section XIV, Article XVI, of the British Articles of War of 1774, *reprinted in* G. Davis, Military Law of the United States 581, 593 (3d rev. ed. 1915), which provided:

> "All Officers and Soldiers are to behave themselves orderly in Quarters, and on their March; and whosoever shall commit any Waste or Spoil either in Walks of Trees, Parks, Warrens, Fish Ponds, Houses or Gardens, Corn Fields, Inclosures or Meadows, or shall maliciously

destroy any Property whatsoever belonging to any of Our Subjects, unless by order of the then Commander in Chief of Our Forces, to annoy Rebels or other Enemies in Arms against Us, he or they that shall be found guilty of offending herein shall (besides such Penalties as they are liable to by law) be punished according to the Nature and Degree of the Offence, by the Judgment of a Regimental or General Court Martial.

The majority contends that this provision counters any argument that court-martial jurisdiction in Britain at the time of the American Revolution was in any respect limited to offenses not punishable by civil law. *Ante,* at 443. The latter provision, however, appears in a section of the Articles of War captioned "Of Duties in Quarters, in Garrison, or in the Field," and its text suggests that the activities it forbade were considered derelictions of military duty, and were punishable by court-martial on that basis.

American colonists shared the British suspicion of broad military authority in courts-martial. One of the grievances stated in the Declaration of Independence was King George III's assent to "pretended Legislation: For quartering large bodies of armed troops among us: For protecting them, by a mock Trial, from punishment for any Murders which they should commit on the Inhabitants of these States." The Framers thus were concerned both with protecting the rights of those subjected to courts-martial, and with preventing courts-martial from permitting soldiers to get away with murder — literally — in the civilian community. This "known hostility of the American people to any interference by the military with the regular administration of justice in the civil courts," *Coleman v. Tennessee,* 97 U.S. 509, 514 (1879), makes it unlikely that the Framers considered any crime committed by a member of the Armed Forces, regardless of its lack of connection to military service, to give rise to a "case arising in" the Armed Forces of the new Nation.

This is borne out by provisions in the American Articles of 1776 that are comparable to those in the British Articles of War of 1774. *See* Section X, Article I, *reprinted in* 2 W. Winthrop, Military Law and Precedents 1494 (1896); Section XIII, Article 16, *reprinted in* 2 Winthrop, *supra,* at 1497; Section XVIII, Article 5, *reprinted in* 2 Winthrop, *supra,* at 1503. The provisions created military offenses where the crimes involved were service connected. This tradition continued after the adoption of the Constitution. With respect to the 1874 Articles of War, for example, Davis wrote:

"As to whether an act which is a civil crime is also a military offense no rule can be laid down which will cover all cases, for the reason that what may be a military offense under certain circumstances may lose that character under others. . . . But if the act be committed on a military reservation, or other ground occupied by the army, or in its neighborhood, so as to be in the constructive presence of the army; or if committed while on duty, particularly if the injury be to a member of the community whom it is the offender's duty to protect; or if committed in the presence of other soldiers, or while in uniform; or if the offender use his military position, or that of another, for the purpose of intimidation or other unlawful influence or object — such facts would be sufficient to make it prejudicial to military discipline . . . ." Davis, *supra*, at 476.

Viewed historically, then, *O'Callahan's* recognition of the service connection requirement did not signify a meaningful change in what could be tried in courts-martial. Quite the reverse: not until the enactment of the Uniform Code of Military Justice in 1950 did Congress attempt to give courts-martial the authority to try the crimes of murder and rape committed in peacetime within the United States. *See* Duke & Vogel, *The Constitution and the Standing Army: Another Problem of Court-Martial Jurisdiction*, 12 VAND. L. REV. 435, 452-453 (1960). Common-law felonies in peacetime were only brought within the court-martial jurisdiction in 1916. Wiener, *Courts-Martial and the Bill of Rights: The Original Practice I*, 72 HARV. L. REV. 1, 10-12 (1958). The Framers' conception of what could properly be tried in a court-martial must have informed their understanding of what cases arise in the Armed Forces, thus permitting what would otherwise be unconstitutional infringements of Fifth and Sixth Amendment rights. The relatively recent expansion of the authority of military tribunals appears to disregard the Framers' understanding.

Instead of acknowledging the Fifth Amendment limits on the crimes triable in a court-martial, the Court simply ignores them. But "[t]he concept that the Bill of Rights and other constitutional protections against arbitrary government are inoperative when they become inconvenient or when expediency dictates otherwise is a very dangerous doctrine and if allowed to flourish would destroy the benefit of a written Constitution and undermine the basis of our Government." *Reid v. Covert*, 354 U.S. 1, 14 (1957) (plurality opinion). The limitations may not, in the view of the majority, be desirable, but that does not mean they do not exist.

The requirement of service connection recognized in *O'Callahan* has a legitimate basis in constitutional language and a solid historical foundation. It should be applied in this case.

II

Application of the service connection requirement of *O'Callahan*, as further elaborated in *Relford v. Commandant, U.S. Disciplinary Barracks*, 401 U.S. 355 (1971), demonstrates that petitioner's Alaska crimes do not have an adequate service connection to support the exercise of court-martial jurisdiction. Petitioner's offenses did not detract from the performance of his military duties. He committed these crimes while properly absent from his unit, and there was no connection between his assigned duties and his crimes. Nor did petitioner's crimes threaten people or areas under military control. The crimes were committed in petitioner's private home in the civilian community in Juneau, where there is not even a base for Coast Guard personnel. Petitioner's acts were not likely to go unpunished; the court-martial judge determined that the offenses were of a type traditionally prosecuted by civilian courts, that such courts were available, and that, while the Alaska courts had deferred prosecution in light of the court-martial proceeding, the State had not declined to prosecute the offenses. Nor did the crimes implicate any authority stemming from the war power; they were committed within the territorial United States while the Nation was at peace.

Moreover, the crimes caused no measurable interference with military relationships. Though the victims were dependents of Coast Guard members, the court-martial judge found that there was only de minimis military interaction between petitioner and the fathers of the victims, and that the relationships between petitioner and the families of the victims "were founded primarily upon the ages and activities of the children and additionally upon common sporting interests, common spousal interest and employment and neighborly relationships," App. To Pet. for Cert. 58a, rather than the connection of petitioner and the families through the Coast Guard. Because the crimes did not take place in an area within military control or have any effect on petitioner's military duties, their commission posed no challenge to the maintenance of order in the local command. The military judge found that the Government had not demonstrated any impact of the offenses on "morale, discipline, [or] the reputation or the integrity of the Coast Guard in Juneau." The only connection between the military and the offenses at issue was the fact that the victims were military dependents. But the military judge found explicitly that the military association of petitioner and the victims' fathers did not facilitate petitioner's crimes, and that "[t]he impact apparent in this case, that is, on the parents and the victims themselves is no different than that which would be produced by [a] civilian perpetrator." *Id.*, at 57a.

The military judge, after properly reviewing the *Relford* factors, concluded correctly that they did not render petitioner's offenses service connected and dismissed the charges. Engaging in what can only be described as impermissible appellate factfinding, the Coast Guard Court of Military Review reversed the dismissal. 21 M.J. 512 (1985). It concluded that the military judge's finding that the offenses had had no impact on morale or discipline was erroneous because the judge should have considered the effect the offenses would have had on the community in Juneau had they come to light while the victims and their families were still in Alaska, and the impact of the offenses on morale and discipline at Governors Island. Without remanding for further factfinding, the court held that the Alaska offenses had a direct impact upon the good order, discipline, morale, and welfare of Coast Guard personnel at Governors Island. *Id.*, at 519. It further asserted, again without basis in the facts found by the military judge, that the Coast Guard's interest in deterring the offenses was greater than that of the civilian authorities, and that the concerns of the victims' parents would have been different had the offender been a civilian. *Id.*, at 519-520. On the basis of these newly found facts, the Court of Military Review held petitioner's crime sufficiently service connected to justify the exercise of court-martial jurisdiction. *Id.*, at 522.

The Court of Military Appeals affirmed. 21 M.J. 251 (1986). While conceding that its "precedents involving off-base sex offenses against civilian dependents of military personnel would point to a different conclusion," *id.*, at 254, it concluded that a "recent development in our society" — specifically, an increase in concern for the victims of crimes — meant that sex offenses committed against young children of members of the military, which would have "a continuing effect on the victims and their families," *id.*, at 256, sufficed to establish service connection.

The military judge's straightforward application of *O'Callahan* and *Relford* was plainly correct given the facts as he found them, facts that the reviewing courts have not demonstrated to have been clearly erroneous. The Court of Military Appeals' apparent conclusion that serious or disturbing crimes committed upon military dependents sufficed to create court-martial jurisdiction ignored this Court's prior decisions.

The majority asserts that "the service connection approach, even as elucidated in *Relford*, has proved confusing and difficult for military courts to apply." . . . It is true that the test requires a careful, case-specific factual inquiry. But this is not beyond the capacity of the military courts. Indeed, the military judge in this case engaged in a thorough and thoughtful application of the *Relford* factors. It should not be surprising that such determinations may at times be difficult or time consuming or require the drawing of narrow distinctions. The trial of any person before a court-martial encompasses a deliberate decision to withhold procedural protections guaranteed by the Constitution. Denial of these protections is a very serious matter. The Framers declined to draw an easy line, like that established by the Court today, which would sweep an entire class of Americans beyond the reach of the Bill of Rights. Instead, they required that the protections of the Fifth and Sixth Amendments be applied in any case not "arising in" the Armed Forces. This requirement must not be discarded simply because it may be less expeditious than the majority deems appropriate.

III

O'Callahan v. Parker remains correct and workable today. The Court nonetheless insists on reopening a question which was finally and properly resolved in 1969. In doing so, it shows a blatant disregard for principles of *stare decisis*, and makes more dubious the presumption "that bedrock principles are founded in the law rather than in the proclivities of individuals." *Vasquez v. Hillery*, 474 U.S. 254, 265 (1986). This in turn undermines "the integrity of our constitutional system of government, both in appearance and in fact." *Ibid.*; *see also Pollock v. Farmers' Loan & Trust Co.*, 158 U.S. 601, 663 (1895) (Harlan, J., dissenting).

The Court's willingness to overturn precedent may reflect in part its conviction, frequently expressed this Term, that members of the Armed Forces may be subjected virtually without limit to the vagaries of military control. *See United States v. Stanley*, post, p. 669; *United States v. Johnson*, 481 U.S. 681 (1987). But the Court's decision today has, potentially, the broadest reach of any of these cases. Unless Congress acts to avoid the consequences of this case, every member of our Armed Forces, whose active duty members number in the millions, can now be subjected to court-martial jurisdiction — without grand jury indictment or trial by jury — for any offense, from tax fraud to passing a bad check, regardless of its lack of relation to "military discipline, morale and fitness." *Schlesinger v. Councilman*, 420 U.S. 738, 761 n.34 (1975). Today's decision deprives our military personnel of procedural protections that are constitutionally mandated in trials for purely civilian offenses. The Court's action today reflects contempt, both for the members of our Armed Forces and for the constitutional safeguards intended to protect us all. I dissent.

NOTES AND QUESTIONS

1. The parties and *amici curiae* in *Solorio* framed the Questions Presented in a variety of ways:

BRIEF FOR THE PETITIONER

1. May a court find that an offense committed off-base at a place where there is no military post or enclave is service-connected simply because of the civilian dependent status of the victim?

2. May a court depart from its precedents setting out the constitutional limits of court-martial jurisdiction over offenses against civilian dependents and apply a more expansive interpretation in the very same case?

BRIEF OF THE UNITED STATES

1. Whether the offense charged against petitioner — sexual assault on the dependent children of fellow servicemen — is sufficiently "service connected" to authorize a prosecution in the military courts.

2. Whether petitioner's court-martial violated the Due Process Clause because petitioner was denied fair warning that he was subject to prosecution in the military system.

BRIEF OF THE AMERICAN CIVIL LIBERTIES UNION AS *AMICUS CURIAE* IN SUPPORT OF PETITIONER

1. Is the fact that the victim is a military dependent, without more, sufficient "service connection" to support the exercise of court-martial jurisdiction over an off-base civilian-type offense?

2. Was the decision below, which found court-martial jurisdiction in circumstances in which previous decisions had refused to do so, a plain violation of the rule of *Bouie v. City of Columbia*, 378 U.S. 347 (1964)?

BRIEF OF THE APPELLATE DEFENSE DIVISION, UNITED STATES NAVY-MARINE CORPS APPELLATE REVIEW ACTIVITY, AS *AMICUS CURIAE* IN SUPPORT OF THE PETITION FOR A WRIT OF CERTIORARI

1. Whether retroactive judicial expansion of court-martial jurisdiction violates due process of law?

2. Whether the victim's dependent status, without more, is sufficient service-connection to establish court-martial jurisdiction?

BRIEF OF DEFENSE APPELLATE DIVISION, UNITED STATES ARMY, AS *AMICUS CURIAE* IN SUPPORT OF PETITIONER

1. Whether it is constitutionally permissible for the military to exercise court-martial jurisdiction over an offense which, upon application of the detailed analysis mandated by this Court, is not "service connected."

2. Whether any cogent or compelling reasons exist for the Court of Military Appeals to depart from a detailed application of the "service connection" test set forth by this Court in *O'Callahan* and *Relford*.

BRIEF OF APPELLATE DEFENSE DIVISION, UNITED STATES NAVY-MARINE CORPS APPELLATE REVIEW ACTIVITY AS *AMICUS CURIAE* IN SUPPORT OF PETITIONER

1. Whether the United States Court of Military Appeals has slowly expanded court-martial jurisdiction thereby eroding the constitutional principle announced in *O'Callahan v. Parker?*

2. Whether in light of the changes in the military justice system, the constitutional principle announced in *O'Callahan v. Parker* is still valid?

Why were there so many variations? Which ones seem best and worst? How would you have framed the issues?

2. In *Relford v. Commandant, U.S. Disciplinary Barracks*, 401 U.S. 355, 365 (1971), the Court identified what the *O'Callahan* holding emphasized:

1. The serviceman's proper absence from the base.

2. The crime's commission away from the base.

3. Its commission at a place not under military control.

4. Its commission within our territorial limits and not in an occupied zone of a foreign country.

5. Its commission in peacetime and its being unrelated to authority stemming from the war power.

6. The absence of any connection between the defendant's military duties and the crime.

7. The victim's not being engaged in the performance of any duty relating to the military.

8. The presence and availability of a civilian court in which the case can be prosecuted.

9. The absence of any flouting of military authority.

10. The absence of any threat to a military post.

11. The absence of any violation of military property. . . .

12. The offense's being among those traditionally prosecuted in civilian courts.

The *Relford* Court went on to identify nine additional considerations:

(a) The essential and obvious interest of the military in the security of persons and of property on the military enclave. . . .

(b) The responsibility of the military commander for maintenance of order in his command and his authority to maintain that order. . . .

(c) The impact and adverse effect that a crime committed against a person or property on a military base, thus violating the base's very security, has upon morale, discipline, reputation and integrity of the base itself, upon its personnel and upon the military operation and the military mission.

(d) The conviction that [U.S. Const.] Art. I, § 8, cl. 14, vesting in the Congress the power "To make Rules for the Government and Regulation of the land and naval Forces," means, in appropriate areas beyond the purely military offense, more than the mere power to arrest a serviceman offender and turn him over to the civil authorities. . . .

(e) The distinct possibility that civil courts, particularly nonfederal courts, will have less than complete interest, concern, and capacity for all the cases that vindicate the military's disciplinary authority within its own community. . . .

(f) The very positive implication in *O'Callahan* itself, arising from its emphasis on the absence of service-connected elements there, that the presence of factors such as geographical and military relationships have important contrary significance. . . .

(g) The recognition in *O'Callahan* that, historically, a crime against the person of one associated with the post was subject even to the General Article. . . .

(h) The misreading and undue restriction of *O'Callahan* if it were interpreted as confining the court-martial to the purely military offenses that have no counterpart in nonmilitary criminal law.

(i) Our inability appropriately and meaningfully to draw any line between a post's strictly military areas and its nonmilitary areas, or between a serviceman-defendant's on-duty and off-duty activities and hours on the post.

401 U.S. at 367-69.

The official "Discussion" of R.C.M. 203 in the *Manual for Courts-Martial, 1984,* summarized the pre-*Solorio* criteria for determining service-connection in little more than one page of text. After reciting *Relford*'s 12 "factors" and 9 "considerations," the authors observed that military offenses "are always service-connected"; "[v]irtually all offenses which occur on a military base . . . are service-connected"; "[a]lmost every involvement of service personnel with the commerce in drugs, including use, possession, and distribution, is service-connected, regardless of location"; the victim's status as a servicemember or the use of a military identification card "may establish service-connection"; and "[d]uring a declared war, or a period of hostilities as a result of which Congress is unable to meet, virtually all offenses would be service-connected." They also noted exceptions for petty offenses and for offenses committed overseas and not triable in civilian United States courts. MCM, 1984, R.C.M. 203 (Discussion), pp. II-14 to -15.

Was the *Solorio* Court right to find the law of service-connection unworkable?

3. *O'Callahan* is no longer good law, but is "service connection" dead? In *Loving v. United States*, 517 U.S. 748 (1996), which recognized the President's power to prescribe aggravating factors in military capital cases, Justice Stevens (joined by Justices Souter, Ginsburg, and Breyer) concurred, but wrote separately:

> The question whether a "service connection" requirement should obtain in capital cases is an open one both because *Solorio* was not a capital case, and because *Solorio*'s review of the historical materials would seem to undermine any contention that a military tribunal's power to try capital offenses must be as broad as its power to try non-capital ones. . . . Moreover, the question is a substantial one because, when the punishment may be death, there are particular reasons to ensure that the men and women of the Armed Forces do not by reason of serving their country receive less protection than the Constitution provides for civilians.
>
> As a consequence of my conclusion that the "service connection" requirement has been satisfied here, I join not only the Court's analysis of the delegation issue, but also its disposition of the case. By joining in the Court's opinion, however, I do not thereby accept the proposition that our decision in *Solorio* must be understood to apply to capital offenses. Nor do I understand the Court's decision to do so. That question, as I have explained, remains to be decided.

517 U.S. at 774-75.

The current Discussion of R.C.M. 203 makes no reference to service connection, even in capital cases. Is there a principled basis for applying a "service connection" requirement only in capital cases? What if the accused is sentenced to life without parole for a non-service-connected offense? Does the Constitution require service connection for prosecution of military retirees or of civilians serving with or accompanying the armed forces in the field in time of declared war or a contingency operation?

4. In United States military justice, adultery remains an offense, but the *Manual for Courts-Martial* encourages commanders to "consider all relevant circumstances, including but not limited to the following factors, when determining whether adulterous acts are prejudicial to good order and discipline or are of a nature to bring discredit upon the armed forces:"

(b) the co-actor's marital status, military rank, grade, and position, or relationship to the armed forces;

(c) the military status of the accused's spouse or the spouse of co-actor, or their relationship to the armed forces;

(d) The impact, if any, of the adulterous relationship on the ability of the accused, the co-actor, or the spouse of either to perform their duties in support of the armed forces;

(e) The misuse, if any, of government time and resources to facilitate the commission of the conduct; . . .

(g) The negative impact of the conduct on the units or organizations of the accused, the co-actor or the spouse of either of them, such as detrimental effect on unit or organization morale, teamwork, and efficiency . . . .

MCM, 2002, Pt. IV, ¶ 62c(2). If *ad hoc* decision making is feasible with respect to the decision to prosecute, why not with respect to jurisdiction? *See also United States v. Hutchinson*, 55 M.J. 574, 581 (C.G. Ct. Crim. App. 2001) (Baum, C.J.) (suggesting reference to service connection tests when deciding whether to prosecute court-martial where there has already been a state civilian trial; "If two trials for the same offense continue to be authorized, without better justification than we have here, we fear a disposition towards restricting military jurisdiction by those with authority to do so could very well develop"), *set aside & remanded on other grounds*, 57 M.J. 231 (C.A.A.F. 2002). See further discussion of adultery in Chapter 8, §IV, *infra*.

5. After *Solorio*, Representative Patricia Schroeder (D.-Colo.) introduced a bill to reinstate the service connection test. Under it, courts-martial would have had jurisdiction only if the offense was committed in time of war; on a military installation, vessel or aircraft; outside the United States or any territory or possession and not punishable under any other U.S. law; or punishable without indictment by grand jury or trial by jury under another law of the U.S. or any state, the District of Columbia, or U.S. territory or possession. H.R. 4282, 100th Cong., 2d Sess. (1988). The bill died in committee. How would you have drafted such a measure?

RE COLONEL AIRD; EX PARTE ALPERT
High Court of Australia
[2004] HCA 44

[Is there court-martial jurisdiction over a rape committed overseas while the accused is on recreation leave? In *Alpert*, the High Court of Australia held there was, by a 4-3 vote.]

McHugh, J.

A Justice of the Court has stated a special case for the Full Court of this Court that asks:

> Insofar as s 9 of the *Defence Force Discipline Act* 1982 ("DFDA") purports to apply the provisions of that Act, including s 61 DFDA, so as to permit the trial by general court martial under that Act of the Prosecutor in respect of the alleged offence, described in par 28(a) below, is it beyond the legislative power of the Commonwealth and, to that extent, invalid?

The offence with which the prosecutor is charged is sexual intercourse without consent. The offence is alleged to have occurred in Thailand while the prosecutor, a soldier, was on recreation leave. In my opinion, the question should be answered, No.

The facts stated

The prosecutor is a soldier in the Regular Army and a member of D Company, 6th Battalion of The Royal Australian Regiment. In August 2001, along with other members of D Company, he was deployed to the Royal

Malaysian Air Force base at Butterworth in Malaysia. The deployment ended on 10 November 2001. The deployment enabled members of D Company to have infantry training in Malaysia and to train with the Malaysian Armed Forces and other regional military forces. The deployed soldiers also had responsibility for securing Australian Defence Force assets including Royal Australian Air Force aircraft at the Butterworth base. A staff instruction known as Land Command Staff Instruction 1/00 governed the deployment.

Upon arrival in Malaysia in August 2001, the prosecutor and other members of D Company were briefed in respect of the Land Command Staff Instruction. Paragraph 59 of that document stated that:

> Personnel serving in or with [Rifle Company Butterworth] are subject to the DFDA.

On 22 September 2001, the prosecutor was granted stand down leave for the period 22 September 2001 to 30 September 2001 inclusive. Stand down leave was governed by par 53 of the Land Command Staff Instruction. That paragraph declared that, in the absence of express prior approval of the Officer Commanding, leave was required to be taken in the peninsula area of Malaysia or Thailand or Singapore. The prosecutor took his leave in Thailand. To do so, he was required to lodge a leave application with the unit's orderly room of D Company at the Butterworth air base. The application contained his leave destination, accommodation address and telephone number. These details were given so as to facilitate the immediate recall to duty from leave of the prosecutor if circumstances so required. If those details were to change while he was on leave, he was required to notify the unit's orderly room by telephone of the change.

After the prosecutor was granted leave, he went to Phuket in Thailand in the company of fellow soldiers. They were driven to the Thai border by RAAF bus. From the border, they proceeded by private transport to Phuket. The prosecutor entered Thailand from Malaysia on his personal, civilian Australian passport without using any form of military identification and without acting under any arrangement between the Australian and Thai governments. At no relevant time has the Commonwealth of Australia had a Status of Forces Agreement with the Kingdom of Thailand maintaining Australian jurisdiction over visiting Australian service personnel in September 2001 or thereafter. The prosecutor's visit was purely recreational. It had no military content of any nature. He paid for his own accommodation, meals and incidental expenses. He wore civilian clothes when he entered and while he remained in Thailand.

During the evening of 28 September 2001, the prosecutor, while in the company of about 20 fellow soldiers, met a woman at the Shark Bar at Patong Beach, Phuket. His fellow soldiers were also on leave. None of them were in uniform. The soldiers included officers and other ranks.

The woman alleges that the prosecutor raped her in the early hours of 29 September 2001. On 2 October 2001, she asked an Army officer for the prosecutor's full name and contact details. She told the officer she was "going to try and have him charged with rape." Subsequently, by letter dated 26 November 2001, addressed to the Commanding Officer of 6th Royal Australian Regiment at that unit's headquarters in Brisbane, she alleged that the prosecutor had raped her. She sought details as to the steps that she would need to take to press a charge of rape against him. . . .

Section 3 of the DFDA defines "service tribunal" to mean "a court martial, a Defence Force magistrate or a summary authority." It defines "service offence" to mean, inter alia, "an offence against this Act or the regulations." It defines "defence member" to include a member of the Regular Army.

Section 115 of the DFDA confers jurisdiction on a court martial to try any charge against a defence member, subject to conditions which are not relevant in the present case.

The validity of s 61 of the DFDA

Section 51 of the Constitution authorised the making of the DFDA. It empowers the Parliament of the Commonwealth to make laws for the peace, order and good government of the Commonwealth with respect to: . . .

> (vi) the naval and military defence of the Commonwealth and of the several States, and the control of the forces to execute and maintain the laws of the Commonwealth; . . .
>
> (xxix) external affairs; . . .
>
> (xxxii)the control of railways with respect to transport for the naval and military purposes of the Commonwealth; . . .
>
> (xxxix) matters incidental to the execution of any power vested by this Constitution in the Parliament . . . or in the Government of the Commonwealth . . . or in any department or officer of the Commonwealth. . . .

Whatever the peace-time limits of the defence power may be, however, no one has ever doubted that it extends to recruiting and maintaining armed forces during peace-time. . . .

Moreover, the primary aspect of the defence power extends to the setting up of courts martial to deal with offences against the discipline. Because that is so, I would have thought that it was beyond argument that, independently of Ch III, the defence power extended to making it an offence for a serving member of the armed forces to commit the offence of rape while on leave in a foreign country.

A trilogy of cases in this Court has held that, although a court martial tribunal exercises judicial power, it does not exercise the judicial power of the Commonwealth. That is because the power to make laws with respect to the defence of the Commonwealth under s 51(vi) of the Constitution contains the power to enact a disciplinary code that stands outside Ch III of the Constitution.[4] In *Re Tracey; Ex parte Ryan*, a majority of the Court held that a Defence Force magistrate, not appointed in accordance with Ch III of the Constitution, had jurisdiction to hear a charge of making an entry in a service

---

[4] [n.22] *Re Tracey; Ex parte Ryan* (1989) 166 CLR 518; *Re Nolan; Ex parte Young* (1991) 172 CLR 460; *Re Tyler; Ex parte Foley* (1994) 181 CLR 18.

document with intent to deceive, as well as two charges of being absent with-out leave. Mason CJ, Wilson and Dawson JJ held that "it is not possible to draw a clear and satisfactory line between offences committed by defence members which are of a military character and those which are not." Their Honours said:

> It is open to Parliament to provide that any conduct which constitutes a civil offence shall constitute a service offence, if committed by a defence member. As already explained, the proscription of that con-duct is relevant to the maintenance of good order and discipline in the defence forces. The power to proscribe such conduct on the part of defence members is but an instance of Parliament's power to regulate the defence forces and the conduct of the members of those forces. In exercising that power it is for Parliament to decide what it considers necessary and appropriate for the maintenance of good order and dis-cipline in those forces.

Two other Justices in the majority in *Re Tracey* (Brennan and Toohey JJ) took a different view of the power of Parliament to invest service tribunals with jurisdiction to hear offences. Brennan and Toohey JJ said that two con-stitutional objectives had to be reconciled. The first was dictated by s 51(vi) which empowered the Parliament to give service authorities a broad authority to impose discipline on defence members and defence civilians. The second was dictated by Ch III and s 106 of the Constitution. It consisted in the recogni-tion of the pre-ordinate jurisdiction of the civil courts and the protection of civil rights which those courts afforded civilians and defence members includ-ing defence civilians who are charged with criminal offences. Their Honours said:

> To achieve these objectives, civil jurisdiction should be exercised when it can conveniently and appropriately be invoked and the jurisdiction of service tribunals should not be invoked, except for the purpose of maintaining or enforcing service discipline.

They went on to say that "proceedings may be brought against a defence member or a defence civilian for a service offence if, but only if, those proceed-ings can reasonably be regarded as substantially serving the purpose of main-taining or enforcing service discipline." Brennan and Toohey JJ said that the power conferred on service tribunals was "sui generis which is supported solely by s 51(vi) for the purpose of maintaining or enforcing service disci-pline." Deane and Gaudron JJ, the other Justices who heard *Re Tracey*, dis-sented.

The division of opinion that arose in *Re Tracey* continued in *Re Nolan; Ex parte Young*, a case decided after Wilson J had left the Court. In *Re Nolan*, a majority of the Court held that a Defence Force magistrate, not appointed in accordance with Ch III, had jurisdiction to hear charges concerning falsifying and using a service document — a pay list. Mason CJ and Dawson J said that they saw no reason to resile from the views that they had expressed in *Re Tracey* as to the scope of legislative power. They considered that it was open to the Parliament to provide that any conduct which constitutes a civil offence should constitute a service offence if committed by a defence member.

Brennan and Toohey JJ also maintained the views that they had expressed in *Re Tracey*. They said that "the relevant power conferred by s 51(vi) does not extend to the making of a law to punish defence members and defence civilians for their conduct unless the proceedings taken in order to punish them can reasonably be regarded as substantially serving the purpose of maintaining or enforcing service discipline." Later their Honours said:

> Service discipline is not merely punishment for wrongdoing. It embraces the maintenance of standards and morale in the service community of which the offender is a member, the preservation of respect for and the habit of obedience to lawful service authority and the enhancing of efficiency in the performance of service functions. Here, the charges are obviously "service connected" but that is not the ultimate criterion though it is an important element in determining whether proceedings on those charges could reasonably be regarded as serving the purpose of maintaining and enforcing service discipline.

Deane and Gaudron JJ again dissented, holding to the views that they had expressed in *Re Tracey*. I agreed with the judgment of Deane J.

As I explained in the third of the trilogy — *Re Tyler; Ex parte Foley* — the "divergent reasoning of the majority judges in *Re Tracey* and *Re Nolan* means that neither of those cases has a ratio decidendi." In *Re Tyler*, a majority of the Court held that a general court martial had jurisdiction to hear a charge against an Army officer that he had dishonestly appropriated property of the Commonwealth. *Re Tyler* also failed to obtain a majority of Justices in favour of any particular construction of the defence power in relation to offences by service personnel.

The difference between the views of Mason CJ, Wilson and Dawson JJ and on the other hand Brennan and Toohey JJ in these cases is the difference between the "service status" view of the jurisdiction and the "service connection" view of that jurisdiction. The "service status" view — which is now applied in the United States — gives a service tribunal jurisdiction over a person solely on the basis of the accused's status as a member of the armed forces. The "service connection" view of the jurisdiction requires a connection between the service and the offence. It was the view formerly accepted in the United States. However, *Solorio v United States* rejected the "service connection" view. . . .

The argument of the parties in the present case accepted, sometimes expressly but more often by assumption, that the general words of s 51(vi) of the Constitution must be read down to comply with Ch III of the Constitution, as interpreted in the trilogy of *Tracey*, *Nolan* and *Tyler*. Since those cases, it seems to have been generally accepted — indeed it was accepted by the Judge Advocate in the present case — that the proper test is the "service connection" test and not the "service status" test.

The question then in this case is whether the discipline of the Australian Defence Force may be enhanced by requiring service personnel to conduct themselves in accordance with the prohibitions in the legislation of the Australian Capital Territory in its application to the Jervis Bay Territory. More particularly, it is whether that discipline is enhanced by a rule that requires a soldier while overseas on recreation leave not to engage in non-consensual sexual intercourse with another person.

The prosecutor contends that, while he was in Thailand, he had no connection with the Army. He points out that, when the offence allegedly occurred, he was on leave in Thailand from his posting as a member of an infantry company. He was wearing civilian attire at all material times. He did not enter Thailand under any military arrangement or for any military purposes and his visit to Thailand was for recreational purposes only. He also points out that he paid for his own accommodation, meals and incidental expenses. The prosecutor concedes, however, that, if he had committed the alleged offence while he was in Malaysia, his offence would be within the jurisdiction of the service tribunal because his presence would be connected to his military service. But he contends his presence in Thailand was unconnected with his Army service. His argument was concerned with the scope of the defence power. He did not seek to re-open the question whether Ch III of the Constitution precluded a court martial from hearing an offence that would be a civil offence under the general law. In contrast, the Commonwealth contends that ss 9 and 61 of the DFDA impose minimum standards of conduct on defence members and that those standards are reasonably appropriate for maintaining discipline in the service.

In determining whether the standards of conduct imposed on Defence Force personnel by reference to the legislation of the Australian Capital Territory have the potential to maintain and enhance the discipline of the Defence Force, an important factor is that, when overseas, they are likely to be perceived by the government of the foreign country and members of the local population as representatives of the Australian government. In this respect, they are different from ordinary Australians who visit a foreign country as tourists. It is not to the point that, so far as dress and other matters are concerned, they cannot be distinguished from an ordinary Australian tourist. If a soldier on recreation leave is involved in conduct that is prohibited by the *Crimes Act* of the Australian Capital Territory, it is likely that that conduct will also be unlawful under the laws of the foreign country or at all events regarded as undesirable conduct. And it is not unlikely that the local citizenry will soon become aware that the person involved in that conduct was a member of the Australian Defence Force. It is a likely consequence of such conduct, therefore, that the local citizenry will be critical of its occurrence and may even become hostile to Australian Defence Force members.

Moreover, even if the local citizens do not become aware of the soldier's connection with the Australian Defence Force, it is likely that the government of the country will be aware of the identity of the soldier. If such conduct occurred regularly, it might have the consequence that the government of the foreign country would deny entry to Australian Defence Force members in so far as they seek to visit areas for rest and recreation. If that happened, it would have a direct impact on the morale and discipline of the Defence Force. It is possible that in extreme cases the unruly behaviour of personnel would cause a foreign country to refuse entry to Australian Defence Force members for Defence Force purposes such as training exercises. It may be that some conduct that is an offence under the law of the Australian Capital Territory in its relation to the Jervis Bay Territory has no relation to the defence power. If so, the operation of s 61 of the DFDA would have to be read down to exclude such conduct.

However, even if some of the standards of conduct required by the *Crimes Act* of the Australian Capital Territory go beyond the defence power — go beyond what is required for maintaining the discipline and morale of the Defence Force — the prohibition against rape goes to the heart of maintaining discipline and morale in the Defence Force. Rape and other kinds of sexual assault are acts of violence. It is central to a disciplined defence force that its members are not persons who engage in uncontrolled violence. And it need hardly be said that other members of the Defence Force will be reluctant to serve with personnel who are guilty of conduct that in the Australian Capital Territory amounts to rape or sexual assault. This may be out of fear for personal safety or rejection of such conduct or both. Such reluctance can only have a detrimental effect on the discipline and morale of the armed services.

Accordingly, the standard of conduct imposed by the legislation of the Australian Capital Territory in respect of the offence of sexual intercourse without consent "can reasonably be regarded as substantially serving the purpose of maintaining or enforcing service discipline". In so far as ss 9 and 61 of the DFDA make it an offence for a soldier, while on stand down leave in a foreign country, to commit non-consensual sexual intercourse, they are valid enactments of the federal Parliament.

The prosecutor made much of the fact that objectively his position could not be distinguished from that of an ordinary tourist. But this submission concentrates on the events of the recreation leave itself and leaves out the many factors that show that his presence at Phuket on the night in question was connected with his Army service. First, he was in Malaysia and thereafter Thailand as a result of his deployment by and service with the Australian Defence Force. Indeed, his presence in Thailand resulted from his military service because his recreation leave arose out of his military service and was no doubt designed to ensure that the prosecutor would be better able to carry out his military duties. Furthermore, he was not a free agent who could visit any country that he wished. There were only three countries in which he could spend his leave without the permission of his Commanding Officer. Thailand was one of them. Moreover, he was liable to immediate recall to his duties. It was for that reason that on his leave form he had to show his destination, his address and his telephone number.

It is true that the twelve factors referred to in *Relford* point strongly against there being a service connection. If that list was regarded as exhaustive, it would be impossible to say that there was a service connection. But the twelve factors listed in *Relford* cannot be regarded as an exhaustive indicia of what constitutes a "service connection." In any event, as Brennan and Toohey JJ pointed out in *Re Tracey*, a service connection is evidence of but not definitive of what is necessary to maintain discipline and morale in the armed forces. A soldier who rapes another person undermines the discipline and morale of his army. He does so whether he is on active service or recreation leave.

Accordingly, the prosecutor has failed to show that it is beyond the legislative power of the Commonwealth to enact s 9 of the DFDA in so far as it applies s 61 of that Act so as to permit the trial by general court martial of the prosecutor in respect of the offence of rape occurring while he was in Thailand. . . .

The question of law for the opinion of the Court should be answered, No.

KIRBY, J.

In *Re Tracey; Ex parte Ryan*, Mason CJ, Wilson and Dawson JJ acknowledged that s 61 of the *Defence Force Discipline Act* 1982 (Cth) ("the Act"), by applying to defence personnel "the one law whether [an] offence is committed anywhere within Australia or overseas," could produce "some curious results." So it has proved in this case, stated for the opinion of the Full Court.

If the provision permitting the result defended in this case is constitutionally valid, an Australian soldier, serving in Malaysia, is rendered liable before a military tribunal in Queensland (not a jury) for an alleged rape, which he denies, said to have happened not in Australia but on a beach in the Kingdom of Thailand during an interval of recreation leave. Moreover, he is liable not for the crime as provided by the law of Thailand, or even Queensland, but for an offence against the law of the Jervis Bay Territory of Australia, applying there the provisions of the *Crimes Act* 1900 of the Australian Capital Territory. By this triple fiction, a law made by the Federal Parliament purports to put the soldier on trial outside the judicature of Thailand and even outside any of the courts of the judicature of Australia, for acts allegedly done whilst a tourist. A curious result indeed. . . .

. . . I agree with Callinan and Heydon JJ that, in every past case before this Court, the offences, of their intrinsic nature, were immediately connected with aspects of the accused's *service* in the ADF.

Divisions in past authority: As McHugh J explains in his reasons, the earlier decisions of this Court failed to yield a majority for a settled principle to govern the constitutional connection necessary to render an offence cognisable in the service tribunal established for discipline under the Act, outside the ordinary courts of law.

The broadest view in the earlier decisions was close to the "service status" test now prevailing in the Supreme Court of the United States, as expressed in *Solorio v. United States*. According to that view, it was enough to render the offence cognisable before a service tribunal if the Parliament decided that this was "necessary and appropriate for the maintenance of good order and discipline" in the service. The intermediate view adopted a test that required that the offence "reasonably be regarded as substantially serving the purpose of maintaining or enforcing service discipline." That view was close to the "service connection" criterion followed by the Supreme Court of the United States in its earlier decision in *O'Callahan v. Parker*.

The third and narrowest view, which McHugh J twice pronounced convincing, imposed a still stricter test. To survive as an offence of "service discipline," prosecuted outside Ch III of the Constitution, the offence had to be "exclusively disciplinary in character." It followed that, if its "character" were essentially that of a civilian crime of general application, it would, at least normally, fall outside the ambit of service discipline. As a consequence, if it were to be prosecuted at all, that would normally have to occur in a civil court.

Common ground: I say "normally" because, in the present case, as in the trilogy that preceded it, this Court has not been concerned with four potentially important circumstances. The constitutional position might be different were those circumstances different:

(1) The prosecutor is a serving member of the ADF, so that the validity of the purported extension of the Act to civilian or "prescribed" employees of the ADF need not be considered;

(2) The issue of constitutional validity is also to be assessed upon the basis that Australia is presently at peace. The special needs of the ADF in respect of discipline in times of war (or other times when the services "stand in most urgent need" of disciplinary powers) were inapplicable at the time of the prosecutor's alleged offence;

(3) The offence did not occur in an actual theatre of combat or during military, policing or peacekeeping operations in which, whether at home or abroad, special needs for military discipline might be inherent in the functions of "defence"; and

(4) The case is not one where the accused was in a place outside Australia "beyond the reach of the ordinary criminal law" or where there is no effective law at all. It was accepted that Thailand is a place with a functioning legal system, applicable to visitors and with a law of rape which, whilst different in limited respects from that of the Australian territories named, is still recognisably similar in its essentials. It was legally applicable to the prosecutor's alleged offence.

The parties' confined submissions: The respective cases of the parties presented curious features. Doubtless discouraged by the three earlier challenges to the Act, the prosecutor did not mount an outright attack on the validity of the Act based on Ch III of the Constitution. However, he did invoke the requirements of that Chapter (and the exception to the normal rule that service tribunals constitute) as a reason for confining the reach of military discipline under the powers in the Constitution propounded to support the validity of the impugned section, especially s 51(vi). I disagree with Gummow J's statement that "no Ch III question was raised by the parties or now arises." True, it does not arise as a basis for an all-out attack on the separate system of military tribunals outside Ch III of the Constitution. The prosecutor disclaimed such an argument and in the present state of this Court's authority that was a correct position to adopt. But he did not — nor could he — ignore the implications of Ch III for the scope of the constitutional foundation of the contested law. The transcript of argument in this Court in the present case, including many interventions from the Court itself, demonstrates that this is so. In *Al-Kateb v. Godwin*, Gummow J correctly pointed to the necessity, in that case, to consider the constitutional context in approaching and deciding the question of construction. The same is true in this case.

For their part, the respondents did not seek to sustain the validity of the contested provision on the basis of the external affairs power. Presumably this was for the reason explained by McHugh J. Whatever the scope of military discipline included in the grant of legislative power with respect to the defence of the Commonwealth, no immunity from Ch III of the Constitution could operate with respect to a law sustained only by the legislative power with respect to "external affairs." Although s 61 of the Act in its application to the prosecutor is clearly a law with respect to matters external to Australia, that head of power would not avail the respondents given the mode of trial in a service tribunal which the respondents invoked and for which the Act provides. It is this consideration that makes it irrelevant to call in aid the Australian law rendering overseas sexual offences against children amenable to the jurisdiction of Australian courts. Indeed they are. However, such procedures occur not before military tribunals but in the ordinary (civilian) courts of the land with all of the protections that this entails.

This Court, including in constitutional matters, resolves the controversies brought to it by the parties. Where, by narrowing the focus of the matters in contest, or by addressing the interpretation of impugned legislation, the Court can properly avoid issues of constitutional invalidity, it does so. However, it is not competent for parties, by concession, argument or oversight, to oblige a court to give meaning and operation to a law in a way that conflicts with the Constitution. In Australia, courts are not merely arbitrators of the competing arguments of litigants. Ultimately, they owe a higher duty to the law. Most particularly is this so where the matter in contest is before this Court, which is created by the Constitution with the primary responsibility to uphold the federal compact in the exercise of the judicial power of the Commonwealth. Especially is this the case where a party comes before the Court (as the prosecutor does) specifically to challenge proceedings brought against him, presenting a contention that the federal law propounded to support those proceedings is invalid under the Constitution. Chapter III is not, and cannot be, disjoined from the Constitution. Donning judicial blinkers, for whatever reason, will not make Ch III go away.

No rule of practice, no judicial observations and no agreement of the parties may therefore deflect the Court's attention from the legal context, viewed as a whole. The constitutional validity of the offence charged against the prosecutor cannot be considered without postulating a test for the suggested link between the offence and the Constitution. This Court cannot ignore the fact, significant for validity, that the Parliament has purported to provide for the trial of the subject offence before a service tribunal, constituted by a convening order under s 119 of the Act. The contested offence is *only* triable before such a military tribunal. It is not triable in any Australian court, least of all before a jury.

Absence of a legally binding rule: The absence of a simple rule, established by decision of a majority of this Court in any of the three earlier decisions, has two immediate consequences. The first is factual; the second legal.

Since the earlier decisions, service prosecuting authorities have sensibly adopted a "conservative" approach in the charges that they have laid against

ADF members before service tribunals. This approach is described in the following terms:

> [F]or over a decade now, service tribunals in Australia have applied Brennan and Toohey JJ's test [in *Re Tracey*] in determining whether or not they have jurisdiction to try charges. This has not given rise to the type of problem which beset military law in the United States before *Solorio*. The main reason is that convening authorities have adopted a conservative approach when determining whether to refer charges to service tribunals. Where doubt exists, cases are referred to the appropriate Director of Public Prosecutions. Protocols have been developed under which consultation regularly occurs between military lawyers and DPP solicitors before any decisions are made about whether charges, which have civilian counterparts, should be dealt with in service tribunals or civil courts.

Such sensible arrangements within Australia will generally have little or no application where the competing law involved is that of a foreign country.[5] Yet, if the present prosecutor's trial is held valid, the precedent set for the trial in a service tribunal of a charge of rape happening *abroad* will necessarily apply *within* Australia, as well as overseas. Accordingly, the question in the stated case must be answered with due attention to that consequence.

The second result of the division of opinion in the earlier decisions is one of law. There is no legal principle that binds this Court to the application of a given rule in the present case. . . . The highest common denominator of agreement established by the earlier authority is that which the prosecuting military authorities accepted. It is found in the reluctant alternative application by Mason CJ and Dawson J in *Re Tyler; Ex parte Foley* of the principle expounded in the earlier cases by Brennan and Toohey JJ and the even more reluctant application of that principle by McHugh J in the same case, although his Honour remained "convinced that the reasoning of the majority . . . is erroneous." A flimsier foundation for a constitutional rule could scarcely be imagined.

Not for the first time, I find myself in agreement with the approach of Deane J to a fundamental constitutional question. Alike with his Honour (and with McHugh J in *Re Nolan; Ex parte Young*) it is my view that unless a service tribunal is established under Ch III of the Constitution, it has jurisdiction to deal with an "offence" by a member of the armed forces *only* if such an "offence" is exclusively disciplinary in character or is concerned with a distinct disciplinary aspect of conduct constituting an offence against the general law. The absence of a different binding rule, and the apparent departure of the service prosecutors in this case from the "conservative" approach hitherto adopted, suggests the need for this Court to reinstate this simple rule of principle derived from the constitutional language and structure. One day that

---

[5] [n.101] By the Act, s 144(3), where a person has been acquitted or convicted by an overseas court of an "overseas offence," the person "is not liable to be tried by a service tribunal for a service offence that is substantially the same offence." There is no attempted restriction upon subsequent trial in an overseas court of a person acquitted or convicted by a service tribunal in Australia.

will happen, unless the present decision puts the law on a mistaken track that proves irreversible.

In the absence of a wider argument on the part of the prosecutor, challenging the validity of the provisions of the Act under Ch III, and in order to refine the point upon which this Court now divides, I will assume in these reasons that the rule applicable to constitutional validity is that stated by Brennan and Toohey JJ in *Re Tracey*. This adopts, in effect, the "service connection" test. It has the merit of rejecting the "service status" test, which is overbroad, however attractive it may be to some service personnel. As Brennan and Toohey JJ pointed out in *Re Tracey* (and later repeated), the greater enlargement of the powers of service tribunals is incompatible with many considerations that need to be taken into account in resolving the question now presented for decision.

Where, as here, there is no earlier decision clearly applicable to the legal question before this Court, our duty is to answer the question in the special case by reference to the usual sources which judges call upon in such matters. These are the state of legal authority; any relevant legal principles; and any applicable considerations of legal policy. I turn to those considerations.

Considerations of legal authority

The scope of military discipline: The language of the Constitution, granting power to the Federal Parliament to make laws for the defence of the Commonwealth (and of the States), should be given a broad meaning, capable of varying with changing circumstances and different dangers for the security of the nation.

Thus, in times of war, federal law has been accorded a very large ambit to regulate activities that would "conduce to the more effectual prosecution of the War." In times of immediate danger, and preparation for possible combat, this Court has accepted the existence of substantial federal law-making authority. The position is the same in times of demobilisation and thereafter in respect of appropriate post-war arrangements. Nevertheless, this Court has never surrendered to the Parliament, or the Executive, the conclusive determination of the constitutional validity of a military regulation. The defence power, and the other heads of power relied upon in this case, are not disjoined from the Constitution. They are part of the "one coherent instrument" which is "intended to be construed and applied in the light of other provisions of the Constitution."

It is for this reason that the defence power is subject to s 51(xxxi) and s 116. Likewise, both by the structure of the Constitution and by the express statement that the grants of legislative power in s 51 are "subject to this Constitution," the defence power is also subject to the requirements of Ch III.

This last mentioned qualification has to be reconciled with the necessity for a measure of power over service discipline, inherent in the grant in s 51(vi). No one doubts the power to establish a non-judicial system of military discipline in time of war or civic danger. Before the Constitution was adopted, this was long a feature of British constitutional law, at least since the first *Mutiny Acts*. The issue in this case is one of reconciling the "two sets of constitutional objectives" just stated. It involves doing so in a time of peace, in respect of activity not specifically service-related, that happened in a place that was not lawless and whose laws provide for the punishment of an offence, if the alleged conduct could be proved.

Adopting the criteria accepted by Brennan and Toohey JJ in *Re Tracey* does not, it is true, provide a "bright line" that will distinguish every offence for which members of the ADF are subject to military discipline from those for which they are not. But if there is uncertainty of classification, this is inherent in many tasks of constitutional characterisation. The uncertainty can be reduced by the provision of criteria that will assist in classifying an offence, in effect, as "service related" (and thus subject to military discipline) or "non-service related" (and thus subject to civilian law). Such criteria were adopted in the past by the courts in the United States. In my view, the extension of service "offences" to include that of rape, happening in the circumstances of this case, pushes the boundary of service discipline beyond its constitutional limits. Effectively, it adopts the "service status" test although this is incompatible with Australia's constitutional history and text and with the highest measure of agreement to which past judicial concurrence in this Court has extended.

A list of criteria of service connection is set out in the reasons of McHugh J. As his Honour points out, this list is not exhaustive. However, it provides a useful guide, as illustrated by the application of the criteria to the present case in the reasons of Callinan and Heydon JJ. As additional support, the Commonwealth Director of Public Prosecutions and relevant military authorities have agreed upon a set of guidelines which incorporated some of these criteria for use in Australia. Their list reinforces the conclusion that the offence in the present case was not one that is "service connected." Clearly enough, it suggests that this case represents an attempt to move away from a "service connected" approach to one of "service status." That move should be rejected.

I agree with Callinan and Heydon JJ that, if an alleged act of rape whilst on leave as a tourist in a foreign beach resort far from military deployment can be classified as "service connected," virtually every serious criminal offence by service personnel must be so catalogued. This would effectively render the requirement of connection to some aspect of national "defence" meaningless. Yet that connection is imperative because of the text of the Constitution and the obligation, resting on the respondents, to demonstrate that the offence is a service offence, and thus, exceptionally, susceptible to trial outside the judicature referred to in Ch III of the Constitution.

It was this task of reconciliation of two constitutional imperatives that prevented Brennan and Toohey JJ from embracing the approach favoured by Mason CJ, Wilson and Dawson JJ in *Re Tracey*. Now, without saying so directly, this Court effectively endorses the "service status" approach. To the extent that the differentiation between service and non-service offences is glossed over, the anomaly to Ch III is enlarged. To the extent that *any* serious criminal offence is deemed a "service offence," because committed by a serving member of the ADF, this denies the obligation of the Commonwealth to justify the large exception that the system of service tribunals carves out of the obligations of Ch III.

None of the earlier cases decided by this Court has come even close to the present circumstances. Nor, for that matter, have any of the reported decisions concerning offences by ADF personnel whilst overseas. In virtually all such cases to this time the offences have occurred in the course of actual combat. In the pretended application of the middle road accepted by Brennan and Toohey JJ in *Re Tracey*, this Court is therefore, effectively, accepting the approach of Mason CJ, Wilson and Dawson JJ in that case. But that was an approach that has never, until now, commanded the assent of a majority of this Court.

Lessons of constitutional history: That this is so may be demonstrated by reference to the pains to which Brennan and Toohey JJ went, in *Re Tracey*, to explain why they could not agree in the view of service offences endorsed by Mason CJ, Wilson and Dawson JJ. They did so by reference to ancient and modern constitutional history concerning military law. The reasons of Brennan and Toohey JJ recall the long struggles in Britain before the adoption of the Australian Constitution. By those struggles, the Parliament in Great Britain ultimately prevailed over the assertion of the prerogatives of the Crown in the matter of martial law and military tribunals. It is a famous history. It illustrates repeatedly the jealousy with which the British Parliament viewed the growth of military law and its general unwillingness to accord such powers in the control of military and naval personnel until it became absolutely necessary to do so for the immediate defence of the realm.

Before the Australian Constitution was adopted, the English courts repeatedly insisted on the ultimate superiority of civil law; the distinction of the law of England, in this respect, from the laws of Europe; and the fundamentally non-military character of the British state. Thus in *Grant v Gould*,[6] cited by Brennan and Toohey JJ in *Re Tracey*, Lord Loughborough declared:

> In this country, all the delinquencies of soldiers are not triable, as in most countries in Europe, by martial law; but where they are ordinary offences against the civil peace, they are tried by the common law courts.

Moreover, in *Burdett v Abbot*,[7] also cited by their Honours, Lord Mansfield CJ said in lambent words:

> [S]ince much has been said about soldiers, I will correct a strange mistaken notion which has got abroad, that because men are soldiers they cease to be citizens; a soldier is gifted with all the rights of other citizens, and is bound to all the duties of other citizens. . . . It is therefore highly important that the mistake should be corrected which supposes that an Englishman, by taking upon him the additional character of a soldier, puts off any of the rights and duties of an Englishman.

Given the great care that Brennan and Toohey JJ took to expound these principles of basic constitutional doctrine, to explain the position they reached in *Re Tracey*, it is unthinkable that their Honours intended their test of "service connection" to be so debased as effectively to expand "disciplinary offences" so as to apply to circumstances such as those alleged in the present

---

[6] [n.128] (1792) 2 H Bl 69 at 99 [126 ER 434 at 450].

[7] [n.130] (1812) 4 Taunt 401 at 449-450 [128 ER 384 at 403].

case. Such an interpretation of the authority of *Re Tracey* would have rendered redundant the pains that Brennan and Toohey JJ took to demonstrate the special resistance of British constitutional law to the extension of martial law preceding the grant of legislative powers relating to matters of "defence" contained in the Australian Constitution.

It is true that the constitutional powers with respect to "defence" are not limited forever to those accepted in the United Kingdom and Australia in 1900. The needs of the armed services and the needs of the defence of the Commonwealth have changed significantly in the intervening century. The Constitution is a living document. It adapts and changes with the changing circumstances of Australia and the world to which it must apply.

Yet it remains the case that the Australian Commonwealth is the beneficiary of the resolution of the great constitutional struggles occurring in England in this connection. The grant of law-making power with respect to "defence" picks up, and carries with it into Australian constitutional law, the fundamental notions of national "defence" that derive from British constitutional history. The word expands and contracts in its potential application to the differing circumstances, as cases over the past century illustrate. But the word is not without a core or essential meaning. It does not connote anything that the Parliament decides to attribute to it. Ultimately, it is for this Court, not the Parliament, to say whether a propounded enactment is within the constitutional word. And the word must be understood in its context. In Australia, that context includes the provisions of Ch III and the important rights and obligations that it imports.

The strict containment of military law and the powers of service tribunals, together with the refusal to treat service personnel as mere servants of the Crown's prerogative but rather as citizens too, are basic features of Australian constitutional doctrine. This Court should do nothing to impair such fundamentals. As Brennan and Toohey JJ explained in *Re Tracey*:

> If the [contrary] view were adopted without qualification, service tribunals would be authorized to trespass upon the proper jurisdiction of the civil courts over defence members and defence civilians and their civil rights would be impaired. The protection of Magna Charta and the victory of Parliament over the Royal forces which resulted in the Bill of Rights would become the unintended casualties of the Australian Constitution.

It must not be so. This Court has a duty to preserve the predominance of the judicature and the civil power over matters of defence as inherent, and also expressly stated, in the Constitution.

Constitutional separation of powers: Whilst Australia does not have a general Bill of Rights or a charter of rights, the separation of the judicial power of the Commonwealth, under the Constitution, provides a bulwark against both federal and State attempts to confer incompatible functions on the judiciary or to deploy any part of the judicial power of the Commonwealth otherwise than in accordance with Ch III.

Although this case is not the occasion to reconsider the general validity of courts martial created by the Act, the consistently rigorous approach taken by this Court in recent years to the application of Ch III carries clear lessons for the ambit of the "pragmatic exception" permitted in the case of service tribunals. To the extent that this exception is expanded beyond clear *service* offences, into the very core of *general* criminal offences (and then in a non-military circumstance and context), this Court effectively condones invasions by service tribunals of the essential functions of courts of law.

In the present case, the Court does this in relation to the courts of a foreign state. But, in so far as this is permissible under the Constitution, this Court necessarily condones a like intrusion into the functions of the criminal courts within Australia. Even acknowledging a legitimate ambit for service justice, including in peacetime, comprising a form of "judicial power" outside Ch III, the dangers of depriving citizens, who are serving members of the ADF, of rights that, in practice, they would otherwise enjoy in courts of law, must inform the line of constitutional validity that this Court draws in a case such as the present.

The need for vigilance is especially clear where what is involved is an accusation by one arm of the Executive of criminal conduct on the part of a citizen serving another part of the Executive. That is what the present case involves. Consistency with this Court's recent decisions about Ch III obliges a stringent approach in limiting the expansion of the ambit of service discipline. This case, and those that may follow its holding, illustrate why that must be so.

Because of the provisions of the Act, and the narrow view that this Court has taken to the operation of the guarantee of jury trial in s 80 of the Constitution, it is fruitless to complain that the expansion of service prosecutions, absent an indictment, diminishes the availability under federal law of jury trial for federal offenders accused of serious offences against a law of the Commonwealth. If the prosecutor were tried in Thailand (the place of the alleged crime) he would not be entitled to jury trial. But if the principle urged by the respondents is established, that for the offence of rape anywhere in the world Australian service personnel are subject to prosecution before a service tribunal for that offence, the constitutional validity of the provision is acknowledged. Logically, it would also permit trial by service tribunals of such offences happening anywhere within Australia.

That conclusion could effectively exclude Australian criminal courts from their usual role in such trials. It could authorise a switch of the trials of defence personnel for crimes of rape to military tribunals, away from the ordinary courts, whose adjudications members of the public may more conveniently view, learn from and criticise. In practical terms, the election by a complainant could deprive service personnel in Australia of the ordinary right of jury trial in such matters. It could exclude citizens, as jurors, from participation in such trials. This Court may, as it pleases, ignore these consequences of expanding the ambit of service offences outside Ch III. But it is a step opposed to past legal authority. It is antagonistic to very long constitutional history. It is also inconsistent with the Court's recent doctrine on Ch III. And it is antithetical to the functions of citizen jurors and the rights of service personnel, enjoyed as Australian citizens, and long observed in the courts of our legal tradition. The foregoing represent very strong reasons of legal authority for holding back from the step which the respondents urged this Court to take. But there are also issues of legal principle and legal policy to consider.

Considerations of legal principle

Provisions of international law: Differing views have been expressed concerning the extent to which it is permissible, in the interpretation of the Constitution, to take into account universal principles of international law. Some members of this Court have objected to this notion, believing it to be inconsistent with the history and function of the Constitution as a charter for national government. My own view is that the Constitution, like all other law in Australia, now operates in a context profoundly affected by international law. Context is always a vital consideration in deriving legal rules.

In the twenty-first century, national final courts must accommodate the global context in which municipal law, including constitutional law, has its operation.[8] The proliferation of international law, especially in the last three decades, demands of this Court recognition that "[w]e cannot have trade and commerce in world markets and international waters exclusively on our terms, governed by our laws, and resolved in our courts."[9] In giving meaning to the Australian Constitution, this Court is therefore inevitably influenced by conceptions of the world in which the Constitution operates and the application of the constitutions and laws of other nation states that impinge upon it.

Ignoring international law will sometimes result not only in chaos and futility. It will reduce the enlargement of the international rule of law, to which municipal, regional and international law together contribute. In particular, to be unconcerned about any relevant universal principle of international law, when giving meaning to an uncertain or ambiguous provision of a national constitution, is to "act on [a] blinkered view [and] to wield power divorced from responsibility."[10]

The decisions of national courts, in so far as they affect the operation of universal principles of international law, contribute to the content of public international law, as the Statute of the International Court of Justice recognises. In making such decisions, including in respect of their national constitutions, municipal courts exercise a form of international jurisdiction. They should do so alert to any applicable rules of international law and so as to avoid, as far as they lawfully can, conflict with such rules. It makes little sense to acknowledge such obligations in connection with other municipal laws but to deny them when it comes to the national constitution. Even the Supreme Court of the United States, long resistant to the use of international law in its constitutional decisions, has lately taken that law into account in constitutional elaboration.[11] This Court should do likewise.

---

8 [n.145] Martinez, "Towards an International Judicial System," (2003) 56 STAN. L. REV. 429; Ginsburg and Merritt, "Affirmative Action: An International Human Rights Dialogue," (1999) 21 CARDOZO L. REV. 253 at 282.

9 [n.146] *The Bremen v. Zapata Off-Shore Co*, 407 U.S. 1 at 9 (1972).

10 [n.148] *Semanza v. Prosecutor,* International Criminal Tribunal for Rwanda, ICTR-97-20-A (Decision of 31 May 2000), Separate Opinion of Judge Shahabuddeen at [25].

11 [n.152] *Atkins v. Virginia* 536 U.S. 304 at 316 (2002); *Lawrence v Texas* 539 U.S. 558 at 572-573, 576-577 (2003) per Kennedy J. *See* Koh, "International Law as Part of Our Law," (2004) 98 AM. J. INT'L L. 43; Bodansky, "The Use of International Law Sources in Constitutional Opinion," (2004) 32 GA. J. INT'L & COMP. L. 421.

The language of the Charter of the United Nations, to which Australia is a founding signatory, appears mainly intended to provide that nation states, members of the Organisation, are juridically equal. Thus, each such state enjoys the rights inherent in full sovereignty. Each state has a duty to respect the legal personality of other states. The territorial integrity and political independence of each state are inviolable. Each state has a legal obligation to comply fully, and in good faith, with its international obligations and to live in peace with other states.

It is a fundamental principle of international law that the nation state ordinarily has the exclusive authority to govern its own territory and all events and persons there, except so far as this authority may have been modified by consent of the territorial sovereign. Certainly, where "public law" is involved, that is, the law involving sovereignty or governance, it is recognised that the nation state normally enjoys exclusive jurisdiction to prescribe any laws applicable to its territory.

Historically, criminal law is part of public law. Thus, by public international law, the enforcement and punishment of conduct constituting a *crime* are normally reserved to the sovereign in the territory where the crime occurred, except where it consents to the application of another nation's criminal law in its territory. The common law recognises the general principle that "crime is local." There is a good reason why this is so. It derives from the nature of crime as an offence against the peace of the community in which it occurs. Crime is thus an affront to the state, not simply a dispute between private individuals.

So, would it offend international law for Australia's Constitution to be construed so as to empower the Federal Parliament to render the criminal law of the Australian Capital Territory, as applicable in the Jervis Bay Territory, applicable in turn to conduct on a beach in Thailand? Would it be contrary to international law for this to be enacted by the Parliament of Australia, at least without the consent of Thailand? An affirmative answer might appear conformable to notions of jurisdiction and judicial power based on considerations of geography. It could provide a reason of legal principle to reinforce the prosecutor's objection to the application to the facts of his case of the provisions of the Australian Act. However, an analysis of the applicable international law discloses that the purported extension of jurisdiction involved in the Act would not violate such law.

An established basis upon which a state is entitled, at international law, to exercise jurisdiction in a particular case is personal jurisdiction (the nationality principle). This includes: (a) the active nationality principle — when the person against whom proceedings are taken is a national of the state taking proceedings; and (b) the passive nationality principle — jurisdiction may be assumed by the state of which the person suffering the injury is a national.

The active nationality principle appears to be settled in international law. Professor O'Connell wrote of it:[12]

---

12 [n.161] O'Connell, *International Law*, 2nd ed (1970), vol 2 at 824. *See also* Shearer, *Starke's International Law*, 11th ed (1994) at 210-211; Shaw, *International Law*, 5th ed (2003) at 588-589; *Restatement of the Foreign Relations Law of the United States* 3d, § 421(2)(d).

"There is no restriction on the competence in international law of a State to prosecute its own nationals for acts done on foreign territory."

The nationality principle so described sits alongside the territorial principle of jurisdiction. One does not "trump" the other. They are concurrent. Thus, in the present case, by international law, Thailand (under the territorial principle) and Australia (under the active nationality principle) and also the United Kingdom (under the passive nationality principle) could exercise jurisdiction over the prosecutor. To conform with international law, there is no need for any of the three states to obtain the permission of the others, or to have in place a relevant treaty agreeing to such a course. Any rule against infringement of state sovereignty would not apply in the present case because Australia is not seeking to exercise jurisdiction *in* the territory of Thailand. Accordingly, it is not interfering with Thailand's internal affairs. Thailand would not be prevented from launching a subsequent prosecution against the prosecutor.

It follows that Australia's application of its own criminal law (rape) to an Australian national (the prosecutor) while that national was overseas (in Thailand) would not contravene international law. Accordingly, whilst the design and application of the Australian legislation to events on a beach in Thailand seems at first to be an intrusion of Australian law into Thailand's sovereignty, that is not the way international law has responded to such a case. Thus, the prosecutor can derive no comfort from this aspect of international law.

Universal human rights law: But what of another part of international law, which concerns the principles of human rights and fundamental freedoms? Are these rules available to help resolve doubts and ambiguities affecting the reach of Australian constitutional law in the present case?

I leave aside for present purposes those provisions of the international law of human rights that concern the rights of an individual to equality before the law and to an independent and impartial tribunal established by law. The latter aspect of such entitlements is expressly restricted, relevantly, to "the determination of any *criminal* charge" against the accused. I will assume for the purposes of this case that the provision of the Act, impugned in this case, might be distinguished on the basis that the charge is of a *military-disciplinary* character, not, as such, *criminal*.

One of the most fundamental principles of the international law of human rights (known as *non bis in idem* or *ne bis in idem*) is that "[n]o one shall be liable to be tried or punished again for an offence for which he has already been finally convicted or acquitted in accordance with the law and penal procedure of each country."[13] This principle gives effect to the rule against double jeopardy in any punishment for offences alleged by the state. Effectively, this rule is reflected in Australian law by a number of substantive, procedural and possibly constitutional requirements.

The exposure of a person, accused of a serious criminal offence before a service tribunal, to the risk of double jeopardy, in a further accusation and trial

---

[13] [n.166] ICCPR [International Covenant on Civil and Political Rights], Art 14.7.

before an Australian court, is serious enough. In practice, in most cases, arrangements might be made to avoid this risk by cooperation of the kind that now exists in Australia between military and civilian prosecuting authorities. However unsatisfactory this solution might be for the dangers of double jeopardy *within* Australia, it might work out adequately in practice. However, no such practical arrangements could be assured in respect of the prosecuting authorities in a foreign state (such as Thailand), operating in a different language, with different procedures, distinct substantive offences, different prosecutorial traditions and separate constitutional requirements. The unresolved possibility of a form of double jeopardy, unaddressed by the provisions of the Act, appears to illustrate the dangers of the application of the Act, in its terms, to events occurring in any place in the world in peacetime, outside the circumstances of combat or service deployment.

In Europe, by the operation of regional human rights obligations, independent judicial scrutiny of service disciplinary decisions has been enlarged, rather than reduced, in recent years.[14] The trend, occurring in most developed countries, has been to diminish rather than enhance the ambit of service discipline.[15] Recent events (such as the destruction of the World Trade Center in New York in September 2001) illustrate the indispensable role played in modern crises by disciplined services (police and fire officers) who certainly operate under the general law administered by independent courts without the need of exceptional tribunals functioning separately from the judicature.

But does the international law of human rights, with its express and implied protections against repeated exposure to punishment arising out of the same alleged facts, apply to a case such as the present? If it does, may that fact be invoked in elaborating the requirements of the Australian Constitution?

International law upholds the principle that the rule against double jeopardy (*non bis in idem*) does not apply in the international context to forbid successive prosecutions by *different* sovereigns based on the same facts.[16] Thus, the current rules of international law give no support of legal authority to a suggestion that the risk of successive exposure of the prosecutor to Australian

---

14 [n.169] Rubin, "United Kingdom Military Law: Autonomy, Civilianisation, Juridification," (2002) 65 Modern L. Rev. 36 at 51.

15 [n.170] *See* Ives and Davidson, "Court-Martial Jurisdiction over Retirees Under Articles 2(4) and 2(6): Time to Lighten Up and Tighten Up?," (2003) 175 Mil. L. Rev. 1 at 84. The extent to which, by constitutional and legislative changes and constitutional decisions, the peacetime jurisdiction and powers of military tribunals changed to assimilate them to judicial bodies is well described in Andreu-Guzmán, *Military Jurisdiction and International Law: Military Courts and Gross Human Rights Violations*, (2004), vol 1 at 153-168.

16 [n.172] *AP v. Italy*, Human Rights Committee Communication No 204/1986 (1990) at [7.3] ("The Committee observes that [Art 14.7 of the ICCPR] prohibits double jeopardy only with regard to an offence adjudicated in a given State"); *ARJ v. Australia*, Human Rights Committee Communication No 692/1996 (1997); *Cardot v. France* (1991) 13 EHRR 853 at 870; *US v. Duarte-Acero* 208 F 3d 1282 at 1287-1288 (2000); *Principle of* ne bis in idem *under International Law* (1987) BVerfGE 75, 1, translated into English in *Decisions of the* Bundesverfassungsgericht — *Federal Constitutional Court — Federal Republic of Germany*, vol 1/II (1992) 644 at 650: "There is presently no general rule of public international law that states that a person who has been sentenced to imprisonment in a third state and has also served this sentence is unable to be retried or reconvicted for the same offence in another state."

and Thai prosecutions, arising out of exactly the same facts, is offensive to the principles of human rights and fundamental freedoms as currently expounded.

Conclusion: International law is unavailing: The time may come when this approach will be modified in response to a recognition of the practical burdens imposed by globalisation and jurisdictional overlap.[17] But, for the moment, international law is clear. Once again, it gives no comfort to the prosecutor. Whilst noting the point, therefore, I will pass on and assume that it does not assist the resolution of the legal issues in this case. The foregoing analysis shows that attention to the principles of international law is not always availing. It is a coherent legal system. It is sometimes relevant and helpful. But it does not mean all things to all people.

Considerations of legal policy

Restricting exceptions to Ch III: But are there reasons of Australian constitutional policy for resisting any unnecessary enlargement of the exceptional jurisdiction of service tribunals in Australia, beyond that convenient and appropriate for the purpose of maintaining or enforcing service discipline, properly so called? In my view, there are. Such reasons lie in the undesirability of increasing the ambit of the exercise of judicial power outside the independent courts of the nation.

If such expansion could succeed in respect of the trial of members of the ADF accused of well-established criminal offences, such as rape, it may also succeed in respect of the trial of crimes of the federal public service, of the police, of security services, intelligence services, anti-terrorist squads and the many others that may demand a similar "exceptional" status. It is the nature of executive government (like the Crown before it under its prerogatives) to press for the expansion of exceptions to judicial supervision. This Court has elsewhere resisted such pretended exceptions. This is not an occasion for the Court to weaken in its resolve. On the contrary, it is a case for particular vigilance against the risks inherent in setting a bad precedent.

The danger of the posited ground for expanding the jurisdiction of the service tribunal in this case is obvious. It has grave implications for future cases. In every instance, it will be said, as it was here, that fellow "defence members" would not want to serve with a person guilty of "such a crime" (as if such an assertion proves the fact or should be given decisive weight for legal and constitutional purposes). Just imagine what wrongs could be done to citizens in the name of the "will of the people." A contrary concern exists that, if defence personnel consider that a military justice system incorporating the full range of civil offences is "not as fair or just as the civil system," this will be counterproductive to the true discipline and morale of the defence forces. Invocations of such considerations are therefore ultimately without legal merit.

The independent courts exist not for the benefit of the judiciary. They uphold the Constitution and defend the people of the Commonwealth and those dependent on its protection. The exceptions for service discipline should

---

[17] [n.173] *See* Lopez, "Not Twice for the Same: How the Dual Sovereignty Doctrine is Used to Circumvent *non bis in idem*," (2000) 33 Vand. J. Transnat'l L. 1263.

not be expanded. The true independence and impartiality of service tribunals has long been questioned in Australia. "Typical criticisms of service tribunals . . . include: the tribunal may be concerned to adhere to the views of those higher in the chain of command; the tribunal members may be personally acquainted with or even in command over the accused; and the members' career aspirations may influence their conduct in the trial."[18] Chapter III of the Constitution provides protections for judicial independence through security of tenure and the maintenance of a long tradition of impartiality. Extending the meaning of "service offence" to the present case means that such protections are bypassed.

Concerns over the independence of service tribunals have been addressed in recommendations contained in recent reports including the Abadee report,[19] a report by the Commonwealth Ombudsman and a report by the Joint Standing Committee on Foreign Affairs, Defence and Trade. The very fact that there have been three major investigations into "military justice" or the "military judicial system" in Australia in quick succession speaks volumes about the seriousness of the problems that tend to be endemic in such a system. The culture of the military is not one in which independent and impartial resolution of charges comes naturally. These considerations reinforce the need for great caution in expanding the reach of the system of service tribunals, particularly in time of peace.

The original statutory extension of the jurisdiction of courts martial in the United Kingdom for a crime such as rape was expressly restricted in that country to apply to personnel on active service and where the crime occurred at a place "more than one hundred miles . . . from any city or town in which the offender can be tried for such offence by a competent civil court."[20] Clearly, the purpose of that provision was to defend the determination of the rights and duties of military personnel, as citizens, in the ordinary courts of the land having jurisdiction over them — not in special tribunals made up of special people applying special laws.

In the present case, application of the approach that I favour would mean that any trial of the prosecutor for rape would have to take place in a court of Thailand. It should not be for the complainant, in effect, to select the jurisdiction of an Australian service tribunal when the relevant civilian court, applicable to her complaint of the crime of rape, was the criminal court of Thailand having jurisdiction with respect to allegations of that crime occurring on Patong Beach. The proper response of the Australian service authorities to the complainant's accusation was not, therefore, to abandon their hitherto "conservative" application of the law, as defined by Brennan and Toohey JJ in this Court. It was not to try out what is effectively a "service status" criterion for military offences. It was to inform the complainant that she should take her

---

18 [n.176] Mitchell and Voon, "Defence of the Indefensible? Reassessing the Constitutional Validity of Military Service Tribunals in Australia," (1999) 27 FED. L. REV. 499 at 504.

19 [n.178] Abadee, *A Study into Judicial System under the Defence Force Discipline Act,* (1997), referred to in Australia, Parliament, Joint Standing Committee on Foreign Affairs, Defence and Trade, *Military Justice Procedures in the Australian Defence Force,* (1999) at 5.

20 [n.181] *Army Act* 1881 (UK) (44 and 45 Vict c 58), s 41(5)(a).

complaint to the Thai authorities (and possibly to facilitate that complaint in practical ways).

In the case of an equivalent complaint in Australia, the proper response would have been to send the complainant to enliven the jurisdiction of "a competent civil court." Unless there is a specific service purpose for maintaining or enforcing service discipline, this Court should not authorise an expansion of the jurisdiction of service tribunals that necessarily diminishes the jurisdiction of the courts of law.

Restricting military exceptionalism: Still further reasons of policy reinforce the conclusion not to expand the reach of military law in the circumstances arising in the present case. As Douglas J, writing for the majority of the Supreme Court of the United States in *O'Callahan v Parker*, observed:

> Free countries of the world have tried to restrict military tribunals to the narrowest jurisdiction deemed absolutely essential to maintaining discipline among troops in active service. . . .

> Determining the scope of the constitutional power of Congress to authorize trial by court-martial presents another instance calling for limitation to "the least possible power adequate to the end proposed."

Later in the same decision, Douglas J noted:

> The 17th century conflict over the proper role of courts-martial in the enforcement of the domestic criminal law was not . . . merely a dispute over what organ of government had jurisdiction. It also involved substantive disapproval of the general use of military courts for trial of ordinary crimes.

In their joint reasons in *Re Tracey*, Brennan and Toohey JJ cited these passages with approval. They pointed to the existence of protections in the Bill of Rights in the United States which are absent from Australian law. This consideration increases the importance of maintaining the Australian resistance to the "general use of military courts for trial of ordinary crimes" compatibly with our constitutional text, judicial authority and historical tradition.

In the past, in other contexts, this Court has been attentive to the foregoing tradition and respectful of it. The services have sometimes endeavoured to cut themselves off from ordinary law. In special and limited circumstances, where it is proportional and appropriate for national defence, it must be so, at least for a short time, as during actual conflict. But under the Australian Constitution, the armed services are not divorced from civil law. Indeed, they exist to uphold it. It is the duty of this Court to maintain the strong civilian principle of the Constitution. It is one of the most important of Australia's legacies from British constitutional law.

It is particularly important to adhere to this time-honoured approach at a time when increased demands are being made for greater executive and legislative power. At such a time, as in the past, we should maintain the function of the courts to ensure that military power is only deployed in accordance with the Constitution. This is not an occasion to enhance the operation of military tribunals. The directions in which the expansion of military law can sometimes lead may be seen in other countries.[21] They afford a warning that this Court should heed.

In support of their broader view concerning the ambit of the Act, Mason CJ, Wilson and Dawson JJ called in aid the unfortunate decision of the United States Supreme Court in *Ex parte Quirin*. A reflection upon the failure of judicial supervision evident in that decision affords strong grounds of policy for this Court to avoid travelling in the same direction.[22] Faithful adherence to our own constitutional tradition, which has been different from that of the United States, is a reason for avoiding the unnecessary enlargement of the jurisdiction of Australian service tribunals. History teaches that such enlargement is rarely reversed. It usually comes at the cost of individual liberty, of the rights of citizens and of the essential functions of the independent courts in upholding the rule of law.

Other considerations of policy: Different issues of policy were raised during argument. They included the ease of transport of service personnel today to distant parts of the world; the special needs of the ADF in peacekeeping, policing and United Nations service; and the necessity to have effective operational discipline in countries where there is little or no law.

As to transport, this renders it easier (as do modern means of telecommunications) to bring cases before civilian courts having jurisdiction outside the immediate needs for maintaining or enforcing separate service discipline in what are essentially ordinary criminal cases. As to peacekeeping and similar deployments, where these are operational, and especially in places of potential or actual combat, different rules will apply. In places beyond the reach of effective law, or where there is no law, the ambit of service discipline will expand, just as it does in times of war or equivalent necessity for national defence, compared with times of peace. None of these considerations applies to this case.

Rape is an abhorrent crime. It is possible that a belated complaint of rape to the Thai authorities would now produce no redress for the complainant. However, had she complained, or been directed or assisted to complain, to the Thai authorities when she first made contact with the ADF, it cannot be assumed that they would not have acted. A court must also consider the rights of the prosecutor, who denies the accusation and contests the validity of the charge.

Most especially, this Court must uphold the Constitution. It must do so where the consequence of failure is a serious departure from past authority and constitutional history; the enlargement of a limited exception to Ch III of the Constitution; and an expansion of military law that is undesirable and out of keeping with our constitutional tradition. No agreement of the parties or concessions or assumptions in the course of advancing their arguments can excuse this Court from its duty to maintain the Constitution and its own past decisional authority in such an important matter.

---

21 [n.189] Steyn, "Guantanamo Bay: The Legal Black Hole," (2004) 53 Int'l & Comp. L.Q. 1.

22 [n.191] White, "Felix Frankfurter's 'Soliloquy' in *Ex parte Quirin*," (2002) 5 Green Bag 2d 423.

The citation with approval of the dissenting opinion of the second Justice Harlan, quoting in turn the military injunction of General George Washington, can only be explained by an adoption of the "service status" approach to the application of service discipline. This is an approach that, until now, has been rejected by the majority in this Court out of respect for the express subjection of s 51(vi) of the Australian Constitution to the requirements of Ch III. There is no exact equivalent to this in the United States Constitution. Particularly in matters of constitutional interpretation, it is the text of the written law, not the opinions of previous judges, that should prevail. It is to that text that the Justices of this Court are bound in duty to the people of Australia.

Conclusion and orders

Applying the approach expressed in the successive reasons of Brennan and Toohey JJ in this Court, I would therefore reject the validity of the proceedings against the prosecutor. Civilian jurisdiction in Thailand could conveniently and appropriately have been invoked in this case. It is the jurisdiction that should have been exercised. The jurisdiction of the service tribunal was only available under the Constitution for the limited purpose of maintaining or enforcing service discipline, properly so called. In the context of the exceptional character of service tribunals, standing outside Ch III, the crime of rape allegedly committed by the prosecutor, whilst a tourist off duty, in the circumstances described in the special case, was not one to which service discipline applied.

The present is not a time to expand, beyond this Court's established authority, the jurisdiction and powers of military tribunals in Australia — any more than the power of indefinite punishment or detention at the will of the Parliament and Executive Government. It is at times like the present that this Court — as it has done in the past — must adhere steadfastly to the protection of basic civil rights in Australia's constitutional arrangements. Other final courts are doing so.[23] We should be no less vigilant.

These are the reasons why the question asked in the stated case should be answered: "Yes."

CALLINAN and HEYDON, JJ.

. . . We come then to the relevant [*Relford*] factors.

1. The prosecutor was in all respects properly and lawfully away from his base. He was not even in the country in which it was situated and in which he had been deployed. Nothing turns on the fact that he was subject to recall. He had not in fact been recalled. Soldiers are entitled to leave and leisure to live as civilians until that leave expires, or they are recalled.

2. The alleged crime was committed far away from the prosecutor's base.

3. He was in no way subject, at Patong Beach, to military control or command, beyond being subject to recall.

---

23 [n.198] *cf Rasul v. Bush* 72 USLW 4596 (2004); *Beit Sourik Village Council v. The Government of Israel* HCJ 2056/04 at [86].

4. Not only was the prosecutor outside Australian territorial limits but he was also beyond the limits of the country in which the unit of the Australian Defence Force in which he was serving, was a guest.

5, 6 & 7. Nothing that the prosecutor was alleged to have done was done under colour of any military authority, or was or could have been done because he was a member of the Defence Force, or was materially facilitated by reason of his membership of it. The alleged offence was totally unconnected with any military duty. In this respect the qualification clearly stated in the judgment of Brennan and Toohey JJ in *Re Tracey; Ex parte Ryan* is important: that the "authority to punish military personnel who transgress the ordinary law of the land" is for their transgressions *"while acting or purporting to act as military personnel."*

8. All crime has been said to be local. The act alleged against the prosecutor would appear likely to constitute a crime according to the law of Thailand and to be triable in the courts of that country; certainly no party submitted to the contrary.

9. No military authority was flouted. It is true that military service in both peace-keeping and war requires the application of disciplined force. But military service requires discipline in all of its activities. Discipline is the nature of military service. Any form of criminal conduct involves a departure from self-discipline and is abhorrent. Whether the requisite degree of connexion exists cannot depend upon the presence or absence, or degree of force, involved in the commission of the crime, or whether, in greater or lesser degree other service people will regard it as abhorrent.

10 & 11. No military post or property was threatened.

12. The alleged crime is among those that have traditionally been prosecuted in civilian courts.

Something should be said of the trilogy of cases referred to by McHugh J. None are determinative of this case. This follows from an examination of the facts which led to the decisions in those cases. In *Re Tracey; Ex parte Ryan* the prosecutor was charged with three offences, first, of making an entry in a *service* document relating to leave which was false in a material particular. The other two charges related to absence (from *service*) without leave. In *Re Nolan; Ex parte Young* the prosecutor was charged with the falsification of military pay lists in order to receive an amount of pay greater than his entitlement. In *Re Tyler; Ex parte Foley* the prosecutor was charged with dishonestly claiming a military temporary rental allowance ("TRA"). Under the TRA scheme, any entitlement a recipient otherwise had to an allowance ceased on the acquisition of a home suitable for his or her family. The prosecutor had purchased a suitable family home but elected to rent the purchased home, for his own gain, while still receiving TRA. In every case therefore, each of the offences had an intimate connexion with military service.

If the test of service connexion is to be applied on the basis that it will be satisfied if the acts alleged constitute an undisciplined application of force, or conduct that would be regarded as abhorrent by other soldiers, then it is difficult to see how any serious crime committed anywhere, including in Australia, under any circumstances would not be susceptible to the military jurisdiction exclusively. The further consequence would be the denial to the soldier and the prosecuting authority of trial by jury. It is sometimes overlooked that the prosecuting authority and the community which it represents have as great as and as real an interest in trial by jury as the person on trial.

We do not, with respect, therefore subscribe to the view that to ask the question whether the discipline of the military service will be enhanced by a certain measure or course, is to ask the same question as "Is there a service connexion?" Any measure for the proscription of any form of misconduct has as its end, discipline. If enhancement of discipline is to be effectively the only test, there will be very few offences of any kind, committed anywhere, in any countries, which will escape the all-enveloping net of "service connexion."

The respondent in argument sought to rely upon part of a paragraph stated by General Washington on 24 February 1779. That part was quoted with approval by Harlan J in *O'Callahan v. Parker*. It is important to set out the whole of the relevant paragraph to indicate the context in which the General was speaking, and by which he emphasized the delicacy of the situation which prompted its promulgation:

> All improper treatment of an inhabitant by an officer or soldier being destructive of good order and discipline as well as subversive of the rights of society is as much a breach of military, as civil law and as punishable by the one as the other. The General does not mean to decide in the present case nor to include Colo. Craige's conduct in that description; but he seriously recommends it to all officers to consider the delicacy of their situation with respect to the inhabitants and cautiously to refrain from every thing that may have even the appearance of an abuse of power. A real one so far as depends upon him will never escape the severest notice.

That statement cannot be given general application, and certainly has no application to this case. It was part of a general order given by the leader of an army in rebellion against the colonial power in circumstances in which the loyalties of the inhabitants were divided. It was given during the course of an insurrection taking place in the General's homeland in circumstances in which injury to the inhabitants had a great potential to affect the outcome of the rebellion. It was directed to conduct adverse to the inhabitants of the colonies in which the hostilities were taking place at the time, and not to the inhabitants of another country in which a soldier was present but not performing military duties of any kind.

The difference between a soldier on leave in a foreign country in which he is neither on active duty, serving nor based, and a civilian tourist is not to be overstated. Nor are we persuaded that criminal misconduct, unrelated to the performance of a soldier's military duties is likely to provoke greater protest or reluctance on the part of another country to admit and harbour Australians, including, relevantly Australian military units, than criminal misconduct by Australian tourists. Equally it might be asserted that misbehaviour by other Australian groups of visitors to foreign countries, whether organized formally or informally or not, such as sporting teams and their followers, would be

likely to provoke protest and resistance to the reception of Australians generally, including members of its defence forces. Strictly these are factual matters
and no fact material to them appears in the case stated or otherwise. But this
is clear, misbehaviour, criminal and otherwise, whether committed by soldiers
or civilians reflects badly on a nation and is capable of adversely affecting its
interests. It would be a form of chauvinism to regard another nation and its
people as being incapable of drawing a distinction between the behaviour of a
soldier on leave from a base in a third country in an entirely civilian setting,
and the behaviour of a soldier there actually under military orders or carrying
out military duties. It would be equally chauvinistic to regard the country in
which the criminal conduct has occurred as being incapable of detecting it and
trying and punishing an offender for it. All foreigners or nationals present in
a country must obey its local laws. Although both the prosecutor and the complainant here were foreigners, each was under that obligation. The complainant was entitled to invoke the protection of those laws, and the
prosecutor liable to suffer their application to him.

The majority also stress the importance of discipline and morale in the
defence forces and McHugh J makes factual assertions about the reluctance of
both male and female military personnel to serve with rapists. Again, these
are factual issues which neither the case stated nor any evidence touches on.
But it may be assumed that the importance of morale in a defence force is no
doubt very great. It is likely to be put at serious risk however if charges
against soldiers in respect of criminal misconduct committed on leave in a foreign country in circumstances totally unrelated to their military activities and
duties, are to be heard and determined by court martial in Australia without
a jury. Indeed, the knowledge that the military authorities have the right to
intrude into the private life of soldiers, and to discipline them in military proceedings for conduct far removed from their military service, and that in such
proceedings there is no right to a committal and a jury, is likely to prove a dis-
incentive to enlistment itself, let alone to morale.

The contrary view rests on a conception of military service to the Crown
which, while it has strong historical roots, has tended to fade in modern conditions. If the Commonwealth desires to try and punish soldiers in the position
of the prosecutor, then it would probably be possible for it to make all crimes
of any character committed abroad by Australian nationals, whether soldiers
or not, triable and punishable in Australia. From the point of view of public
international law, the "nationality" basis for jurisdiction over extraterritorial
acts is well recognized, at least for serious offences. It is likely that the external affairs power would support legislation of that kind, and there would then
be no Ch III problems if the legislation provided for the trials to be conducted
by Ch III courts.

The prosecutor made a concession at the hearing that had he been alleged
to have committed the crime the subject of the charge in Malaysia he would
have been unable to contend that it was not service related. There are some
obvious differences between the actual circumstances, and the circumstances
as they would have been had they occurred in Malaysia, in particular the existence of the arrangements between that country and Australia regarding the
prosecutor's presence there, but whether they should give rise to a different

consequence, and whether the concession was properly made it is unnecessary to say.

The submissions of the respondents failed to grapple with the practical and legal problems that would arise, if, for example the prosecutor had been taken into the custody of the Thai authorities and if he were tried in Thailand. The respondents' response, that there would then be a case for the exercise of a prosecutorial discretion not to prosecute, was not an entirely satisfactory or convincing one. In a sense the alleged victim has sought to choose a different, her own preferred forum, a military tribunal, for the trial of her alleged aggressor, from the "natural forum," the criminal courts of Thailand. In particular, no attempt was made to explore what would happen if Australia and Thailand were each to assert jurisdiction, and the consequential difficulties of extradition if that occurred. None of these matters of themselves can be decisive of the answer to the question but they are matters of relevance which help to fortify us in the conclusion that we have reached.

We would answer the question in the stated case: "Yes."

NAVALES v. ABAYA; IN RE REASO
Supreme Court of the Philippines
G.R. No. 162318 (2004)

[After an attempted *coup d'état*, court-martial proceedings were instituted against a number of the participants. Seeking to block the court-martial, they argued that they should be tried in civilian court, which by statute had exclusive jurisdiction over the offense of *coup d'état*. The civilian court found the court-martial charges subsumed within the coup charge and not service connected.]

CALLEJO, J.:

Before the Court are two petitions essentially assailing the jurisdiction of the General Court-Martial to conduct the court-martial proceedings involving several junior officers and enlisted men of the Armed Forces of the Philippines (AFP) charged with violations of the Articles of War (Commonwealth Act No. 408, as amended) in connection with their participation in the take-over of the Oakwood Premier Apartments in Ayala Center, Makati City on July 27, 2003. . . .

Background

At past 1:00 a.m. of July 27, 2003, more than three hundred junior officers and enlisted men, mostly from the elite units of the AFP — the Philippine Army's Scout Rangers and the Philippine Navy's Special Warfare Group (SWAG) — quietly entered the premises of the Ayala Center in Makati City. They disarmed the security guards and took over the Oakwood Premier Apartments (Oakwood). They planted explosives around the building and in its vicinity. Snipers were posted at the Oakwood roof deck.

The soldiers, mostly in full battle gear and wearing red armbands, were led by a small number of junior officers, widely known as the *Magdalo* Group. . . .

Between 4:00 to 5:00 a.m., the soldiers were able to issue a public statement through the ABS-CBN News (ANC) network. They claimed that they went to Oakwood to air their grievances against the administration of President Gloria Macapagal-Arroyo. Among those grievances were: the graft and corruption in the military, the sale of arms and ammunition to the "enemies" of the State, the bombings in Davao City which were allegedly ordered by Brig. Gen. Victor Corpus, Chief of the ISAFP, in order to obtain more military assistance from the United States government, and the "micro-management" in the AFP by then Department of National Defense (DND) Secretary Angelo Reyes. They declared their withdrawal of support from the chain of command and demanded the resignation of key civilian and military leaders of the Arroyo administration.

Around 9:00 a.m., Pres. Arroyo gave the soldiers until 5:00 p.m. to give up their positions peacefully and return to barracks. At about 1:00 p.m., she declared the existence of a "state of rebellion" and issued an order to use reasonable force in putting down the rebellion. A few hours later, the soldiers again went on television reiterating their grievances. The deadline was extended twice, initially to 7:00 p.m., and later, indefinitely.

In the meantime, a series of negotiations ensued between the soldiers and the Government team led by Ambassador Roy Cimatu. An agreement was forged between the two groups at 9:30 p.m. Shortly thereafter, Pres. Arroyo announced that the occupation of Oakwood was over. The soldiers agreed to return to barracks and were out of the Oakwood premises by 11:00 p.m.

The Filing of Charges

Under the Information dated August 1, 2003 filed with the Regional Trial Court (RTC) of Makati City, the Department of Justice (DOJ) charged 321 of those soldiers who took part in the "Oakwood Incident" with violation of Article 134-A (*coup d'état*) of the Revised Penal Code. . . . [Two hundred and forty-three of the accused moved] that the trial court:

1. [A]ssume jurisdiction over all the charges filed before the military tribunal in accordance with Republic Act No. 7055 [reprinted in § I, *supra*]; and

2. Order the prosecution to present evidence to establish probable cause against 316 of the 321 accused and, should the prosecution fail to do so, dismiss the case as against the 316 other accused.

While the said motion was pending resolution, the DOJ issued the Resolution dated October 20, 2003 finding probable cause for *coup d'état* against only 31 of the original 321 accused and dismissing the charges against the other 290 for insufficiency of evidence. . . .

Meanwhile, 1Lt. Navales, *et al.* and Capt. Reaso, *et al.*, who were earlier dropped as accused in Criminal Case No. 03-2784, were charged before the General Court-Martial with violations of the Articles of War (AW), particularly: AW 67 (*Mutiny*), AW 97 (*Conduct Prejudicial to Good Order and Military Discipline*), AW 96 (*Conduct Unbecoming an Officer and a Gentleman*), AW 63 (*Disrespect to the President, the Secretary of Defense, etc.*) and AW 64 (*Disrespect Towards Superior Officer*). On the other hand,

Capt. Maestrecampo and the 30 others who remained charged under the Amended Information were not included in the charge sheets for violations of the Articles of War. . . .

[The civilian court assumed jurisdiction over the court-martial charges and declared them not service-connected, but rather absorbed and in furtherance to the alleged crime of *coup d'état*.]

[I]nvoking Section 1 of Rep. Act No. 7055, the respondents vigorously assert that the charges against 1Lt. Navales, *et al.* and Capt. Reaso, *et al.* filed with the General Court-Martial, *i.e.,* violations of the Articles of War 63, 64, 67, 96 and 97, are, in fact, among those declared to be service-connected under the second paragraph of this provision. This means that the civil court cannot exercise jurisdiction over the said offenses, the same being properly cognizable by the General Court-Martial. . . .

We agree with the respondents that the sweeping declaration made by the RTC (Branch 148) in the dispositive portion of its Order dated February 11, 2004 that all charges before the court-martial against the accused were not service-connected, but absorbed and in furtherance of the crime of *coup d'état*, cannot be given effect. For reasons which shall be discussed shortly, such declaration was made without or in excess of jurisdiction; hence, a nullity. . . .

The second paragraph of [Act No. 7055] explicitly specifies what are considered service-connected crimes or offenses under Commonwealth Act No. 408 (CA 408), as amended, also known as the Articles of War [listing offenses]. . . .

In view of the clear mandate of Rep. Act No. 7055, the RTC (Branch 148) cannot divest the General Court-Martial of its jurisdiction over those charged with violations of Articles 63 (*Disrespect Toward the President etc.*), 64 (*Disrespect Toward Superior Officer*), 67 (*Mutiny or Sedition*), 96 (*Conduct Unbecoming an Officer and a Gentleman*) and 97 (*General Article*) of the Articles of War, as these are specifically included as service-connected offenses or crimes under Section 1 thereof. Pursuant to the same provision of law, the military courts have jurisdiction over these crimes or offenses.

There was no factual and legal basis for the RTC (Branch 148) to rule that violations of Articles 63, 64, 67, 96, and 97 of the Articles of War were committed in furtherance of *coup d'état* and, as such, absorbed by the latter crime. It bears stressing that, after a reinvestigation, the Panel of Prosecutors found no probable cause for *coup d'état* against the petitioners and recommended the dismissal of the case against them. The trial court approved the recommendation and dismissed the case as against the petitioners. There is, as yet, no evidence on record that the petitioners committed the violations of Articles 63, 64, 96, and 97 of the Articles of War in furtherance of *coup d'état*.

In fine, in making the sweeping declaration that these charges were not service-connected, but rather absorbed and in furtherance of the crime of *coup d'état*, the RTC (Branch 148) acted without or in excess of jurisdiction. Such declaration is, in legal contemplation, necessarily null and void and does not exist.

At this point, a review of its legislative history would put in better perspective the *raison d'être* of Rep. Act No. 7055. As early as 1938, jurisdiction over offenses punishable under CA 408, as amended, also known as the Articles of War, committed by persons subject to military law was vested on the military courts. Thereafter, then President Ferdinand E. Marcos promulgated Presidential Decree (PD) Nos. 1822 [Providing for the Trial by Courts-Martial of Members of the Armed Forces Charged with Offenses Related to the Performance of their Duties (January 16, 1981)], 1850 [Providing for the Trial by Courts-Martial of Members of the Integrated National Police and Further Defining the Jurisdiction of Courts-Martial over Members of the Armed Forces of the Philippines (October 4, 1982)] and 1852 [Amending Section 1 of P.D. No. 1850 (September 5, 1984)]. These presidential decrees transferred from the civil courts to the military courts jurisdiction over all offenses committed by members of the AFP, the former Philippine Constabulary, the former Integrated National Police, including firemen, jail guards and all persons subject to military law.

In 1991, after a series of failed *coup[s] d'état[]*, Rep. Act No. 7055 was enacted. In his sponsorship speech, Senator Tañada explained the intendment of the law, thus:

> Senator Tañada. The long and horrible nightmare of the past continues to haunt us to this present day. Its vestiges remain instituted in our legal and judicial system. Draconian decrees which served to prolong the past dictatorial regime subsist to rule our new-found lives. Two of these decrees, Presidential Decree No. 1822 and Presidential Decree No. 1850, as amended, remain intact as laws, in spite of the fact that four years have passed since we regained our democratic freedom.

> The late Mr. Chief Justice Claudio Teehankee enunciated in the case of *Olaguer v. Military Commission No. 34* that "the greatest threat to freedom is the shortness of human memory."

> PD No. 1822 and PD No. 1850 made all offenses committed by members of the Armed Forces of the Philippines, the Philippine Constabulary, the Integrated National Police, including firemen and jail guards, and all persons subject to military law exclusively triable by military courts though, clearly, jurisdiction over common crimes rightly belongs to civil courts.

> Article II, Section 3 of the 1987 Constitution provides that civilian authority is, at all times, supreme over the military. Likewise, Article VIII, Section 1 declares that the judicial power shall be vested in one Supreme Court and in such lower courts as may be established by law.

In the case of *Anima v. The Minister of National Defense* (146 *Supreme Court Reports Annotated*, page 406), the Supreme Court through Mr. Justice Gutierrez declared:

> The jurisdiction given to military tribunals over common crimes at a time when all civil courts were fully operational and freely functioning constitutes one of the saddest chapters in the history of the Philippine Judiciary.

> The downgrading of judicial prestige caused by the glorification of military tribunals . . . the many judicial problems spawned by extended authoritarian rule which effectively eroded judicial independence and self-respect will require plenty of time and determined efforts to cure.

> The immediate return to civil courts of all cases which properly belong to them is only a beginning. . . .

Thus, as long as the civil courts in the land remain open and are regularly functioning, military tribunals cannot try and exercise jurisdiction over military men for criminal offenses committed by them which are properly cognizable by the civil courts. . . .

Clearly, in enacting Rep. Act No. 7055, the lawmakers merely intended to return to the civilian courts the jurisdiction over those offenses that have been traditionally within their jurisdiction, but did not divest the military courts jurisdiction over cases mandated by the Articles of War. . . .

[T]he General Court-Martial has jurisdiction over the charges filed against petitioners 1Lt. Navales, *et al.* under Rep. Act No. 7055. A writ of prohibition cannot be issued to prevent it from exercising its jurisdiction. . . .

NOTES AND QUESTIONS

1. Immediately after World War I, the British "Darling Report" commented: "We understand that before the War offences of a civil nature were usually dealt with by the civil Courts, except when the complainant and witnesses were almost all officers or soldiers. We recommend that this practice should be resumed and continued." REPORT OF THE COMMITTEE CONSTITUTED BY THE ARMY COUNCIL TO ENQUIRE INTO THE LAW AND RULES OF PROCEDURE REGULATING MILITARY COURTS-MARTIAL A-3 (1919) (Cmd. 428). If the civilian courts are open, does the country's involvement in a war justify referring all criminal misconduct by uniformed personnel to military courts?

2. How hard is it to tell whether a case is service connected? In *MacKay v. Regina*, [1980] 2 S.C.R. 370, 54 C.C.C.2d 129, 161-62 (1980), Justice McIntyre wrote: "[H]ow is a line to be drawn separating the service-related or military offence from the offence which has no connection with the service? In my view, an offence which would be an offence at civil law, when committed by a civilian, is as well an offence falling within the jurisdiction of the courts martial and within the purview of military law when committed by a serviceman if such offence is so connected with the service in its nature, and in the circumstances of its commission, that it would tend to affect the general standard of discipline and efficiency of the service. I do not consider it wise or possible to catalogue the offences which could fall into this category or try to describe them in their precise nature and detail. The question of jurisdiction to deal with such offences would have to be determined in a case-by-case basis." In No. 98-084, Sentencia No. 2.256 (Venez. Sala de Casación Penal 1999), 26 Oscar R. Pierre Tapia, Jurisprudencia de la Corte Suprema de Justicia, No. 12, at 681, 683 (Dec. 1999), the court explained that the expression *acto de servicio* in Article 123(3) of the Code of Military Justice highlights the relationship that must exist between the accused and the function he is performing at the time of the offense. The soldier must be carrying out a professional duty in order to find that the crime was committed during the performance of an act of service. The court held that a soldier on security rounds who abandons his post without apparent reason is not performing an act of service. "The concept of military functions, acts of service and commissions must not be understood *in abstracto*, but in terms of the facts and circumstances presented in the actual case." The case was transferred to the civilian courts. In No. 136-95 (1995), 23 Oscar R. Pierre Tapia, Jurisprudencia de la Corte Suprema de Justicia, No. 1, at 245 (Jan. 1996), the same court upheld military jurisdiction in the case of a soldier who used a government firearm to shoot and kill another person in an argument while the soldier was driving a government vehicle back to base.

3. As is clear from *Re Colonel Aird; Ex parte Albert*, the High Court of Australia has struggled for decades with whether and how court-martial subject-matter jurisdiction is limited. One approach is to focus on whether the case falls within "the judicial power of the Commonwealth"; another is to look for a nexus to the military. In *White v. Director of Military Prosecutions*, [2007] HCA 29, the accused argued the former, and expressly did not assert a service connection theory, even though at least one of the justices seemed open to such an argument. *See generally id.*, [2007] HCATrans 26-27 (Feb. 6-7, 2007) (Kirby, J.). Why would an accused *not* advance a service connection claim?

4. Even where the legislature seeks by statute to exclude some civilian-type offenses from court-martial jurisdiction, may that intent be thwarted by charging the same conduct in other terms? *See Marsaw v. H.M. The Queen*, 151 D.L.R.4th 667, 119 C.C.C.3d 3, No. CMAC-395 (Can. Ct.-Martial App. Ct. 1997) (2-1 decision) (rejecting claim that disgraceful conduct involving cigar tube was disguised sexual assault as to which statute required civilian trial).

5. Issues of service connection are not unique to military criminal justice. The British Army applies the following "Service Test" for administrative sanctions: "Have the actions or behaviour of a serviceman adversely impacted or are they likely to impact on the efficiency or operational effectiveness of the Army?" The Service Test requires consideration of whether the conduct or performance —

a. Adversely affects the standards, effectiveness or reputation of the Army.

b. Undermines confidence in a serviceman or calls into question his integrity or his suitability for his rank or appointment.

c. Damages or compromises command or management relationships.

d. Damages or hazards the marriage or personal relationships of others within the immediate defence community that supports them.

e. Adversely affects the Army as a corporate body, although it has no direct bearing on the unit to which the serviceman belongs. An example of this might be where a serviceman's failings have resulted in adverse media coverage.

f. Undermines morale, good order, discipline, trust or unit cohesion and standards of conduct in the broadest sense.

British Army Gen. Admin. Inst. ch. 67 (2005). Similar questions of nexus between misconduct and agency efficiency arise in the civil service. *E.g., Brown v. Department of the Navy*, 229 F.3d 1356, 1358 (Fed. Cir. 2000); *see* 5 U.S.C. § 7513(a) (2000). Should the test for nexus differ depending on whether the individual is part of a uniformed force or whether the sanction is criminal rather than civil or administrative?

III. INTERNATIONAL HUMAN RIGHTS

Draft Principles Governing the Administration of Justice through Military Tribunals
UN Commission on Human Rights, 2006

Principle No. 8. Functional authority of military courts

The jurisdiction of military courts should be limited to offences of a strictly military nature committed by military personnel. Military courts may try persons treated as military personnel for infractions strictly related to their military status.

29. The jurisdiction of military tribunals to try military personnel or personnel treated as military personnel should not constitute a derogation in principle from ordinary law, corresponding to a jurisdictional privilege or a form of justice by one's peers. Such jurisdiction should remain exceptional and apply only to the requirements of military service. This concept constitutes the "nexus" of military justice, particularly as regards field operations, when the territorial court cannot exercise its jurisdiction. Only such a functional necessity can justify the limited but irreducible existence of military justice. The national court is prevented from exercising its active or passive jurisdiction for practical reasons arising from the remoteness of the action, while the local court that would be territorially competent is confronted with jurisdictional immunities.

Principle No. 9. Trial of persons accused of serious human rights violations

In all circumstances, the jurisdiction of military courts should be set aside in favour of the jurisdiction of the ordinary courts to conduct inquiries into serious human rights violations such as extrajudicial executions, enforced disappearances and torture, and to prosecute and try persons accused of such crimes.

32. Contrary to the functional concept of the jurisdiction of military tribunals, there is today a growing tendency to consider that persons accused of serious human rights violations cannot be tried by military tribunals insofar as such acts would, by their very nature, not fall within the scope of the duties

performed by such persons. Moreover, the military authorities might be tempted to cover up such cases by questioning the appropriateness of prosecutions, tending to file cases with no action taken or manipulating "guilty pleas" to victims' detriment. Civilian courts must therefore be able, from the outset, to conduct inquiries and prosecute and try those charged with such violations. The initiation by a civilian judge of a preliminary inquiry is a decisive step towards avoiding all forms of impunity. The authority of the civilian judge should also enable the rights of the victims to be taken fully into account at all stages of the proceedings.

33. This was the solution favoured by the General Assembly when it adopted the Declaration on the Protection of All Persons from Enforced Disappearances, which stipulates that persons presumed responsible for such crimes "shall be tried only by the competent ordinary courts in each State, and not by any other special tribunal, in particular military courts." The constituent parts of the crime of enforced disappearance cannot be considered to have been committed in the performance of military duties. The Working Group on Enforced or Involuntary Disappearances mentioned this principle in its most recent report, referring to the need to have recourse to a "competent civilian court." The 1994 Inter-American Convention on Forced Disappearance of Persons establishes the same principle in article IX. It is noteworthy, however, that the draft international convention on the protection of all persons from enforced disappearance avoids the question, stipulating only in article 11, paragraph 3, that "any person tried for an offence of enforced disappearance shall benefit from a fair trial before a competent, independent and impartial court or tribunal established by law."

34. The scope of the principle has been extended in the updated set of principles for the promotion and protection of human rights through action to combat impunity: "The jurisdiction of military tribunals must be restricted solely to specifically military offences committed by military personnel, to the exclusion of human rights violations, which shall come under the jurisdiction of the ordinary domestic courts or, where appropriate, in the case of serious crimes under international law, of an international or internationalized criminal Court."[24]

35. Above all, it must be observed that the doctrine and jurisprudence of the Human Rights Committee, the Committee against Torture, the Committee on the Rights of the Child, the African Commission on Human and Peoples' Rights, the Inter-American Court of Human Rights and the Inter-American Commission on Human Rights and the country-specific and thematic procedures of the United Nations Commission on Human Rights, are unanimous: military tribunals are not competent to try military personnel responsible for serious human rights violations against civilians.[25]

---

24 [n.15] E/CN.4/2005/102/Add.1, Principle 29: Restrictions on the jurisdiction of military courts. See also Resolution 2005/81, April 21, 2005.

25 [n.16] See the numerous examples cited by Federico Andreu-Guzman, *Military jurisdiction and international law, Military courts and gross human rights violations*, vol. I, Int'l Comm'n of Jurists, Geneva, 2004. See also African Commission on Human and Peoples' Rights, *Principles and guidelines on the right to a fair trial and legal assistance in Africa*, DOC/OS/(XXX)247, 2003.

SENTENCE NO. C-358/97
Constitutional Court of Colombia, 1997
(from Mora v. Colombia, Inter-American Court of
Human Rights, 1998)

1. In order for an offense to come under the jurisdiction of the military criminal courts, there must be a clear link of origin between it and a service-related activity, *i.e.*, the punishable act must arise as an abuse of right or abuse of authority that has occurred in the context of an activity directly related to a function that is particular to the armed forces. But what is more, the link between the offense and the activity particular to the service must be proximate and direct, and not purely hypothetical and abstract. This means that the excess or abuse of right must occur directly during the performance of a task that in itself constitutes a legitimate development of the missions of the Armed Forces and National Police. To the contrary, if from the outset the agent has criminal designs, and then uses his investiture to carry out a punishable act, the case corresponds to the regular courts, even in those cases in which there may be a certain abstract relationship between the purposes of the Armed Forces and National Police and the actor's punishable act. In effect, in those events there is no concrete relationship between the offense and the service, since at no time was the agent carrying out activities particular to the service, as his conduct was, *ab initio*, criminal. The link between the criminal act and the service-related activity is broken down when the offense is unusually grave, as in the case of what are called crimes against humanity. In these circumstances, the case should come before the regular courts, given the total contradiction between the offense and the constitutional missions of the Armed Forces and National Police. In this respect, it should be noted that this Court has already indicated that all conduct that constitutes crimes against humanity is manifestly contrary to human dignity and the rights of the person, and consequently bears no relationship to the constitutional function of the Armed Forces or National Police, to the point that no obedience is due to an order to commit such an act. . . . Consequently, a crime against humanity is so foreign to the constitutional function of the Armed Forces and National Police that it can never bear any relationship with any service-related act, since the mere commission of these criminal acts dissolves any link between the conduct of the agent and the military or police discipline and function, properly speaking; thus they should be heard in the regular courts. The Court has noted, "it is obvious that a service-related act could never be criminal, which is why service-related conduct is not deserving of punishment. This is why the military courts do not hear cases involving 'service-related acts,' but service-'related' crimes. In other words, what this Court affirms is not that crimes against humanity are not acts of service, for it is obvious that in a State under the rule of law a crime, whether a crime against humanity or of another type, can never constitute legitimate conduct on the part of the agent. What the Court is indicating is that there are punishable forms of conduct that are so flagrantly contrary to the constitutional function of Armed Forces and National Police that the mere commission of them breaks any functional nexus between the agent and the service. . . ."

3. The relationship to the service should arise clearly in the evidence brought into the process. As jurisdiction in the military criminal courts is the exception to the regular rule, they will have jurisdiction only in those cases in which it is clear that the exception to the principle should be applied according to which the judge whose position is created by law, with general jurisdiction, should have jurisdiction over a given matter. This means that in those situations in which there is doubt as to where jurisdiction should lie in a given proceeding, the decision should be in favor of the regular jurisdiction, considering that it was not possible to fully demonstrate that the exception was met.

Colombia Human Rights Certification II, 2004
Amnesty International, Human Rights Watch, and Washington Office on Latin America

[Section 3201 of Pub. L. No. 106-246 established human rights conditions for U.S. military assistance to Colombia. The following extract reflects the opposition of several nongovernmental organizations to U.S. government certification of Colombia's compliance with the conditions, one of which requires armed forces "personnel who are credibly alleged to have committed gross violations of human rights will be brought to justice in Colombia's civilian courts, in accordance with the 1997 ruling of Colombia's Constitutional Court regarding civilian court jurisdiction in human rights cases."]

Analogous to the U.S. Supreme Court, Colombia's Constitutional Court rules on matters that involve a dispute over fundamental constitutional questions. Under Article 243 of the Constitution, the rulings of the Constitutional Court are binding and obligatory.

In one of its most important decisions, the court ruled in 1997 that cases involving allegations of crimes against humanity (*lesa humanidad*) and crimes of unusual gravity (*una gravedad inusitada*) fall under the jurisdiction of the civilian courts. Sentence No. C-358/97, the decision which instituted this rule, clearly covers crimes such as torture, genocide and forced disappearance, as well as other gross violations of human rights such as extrajudicial killings and the aiding and abetting of paramilitary groups.

The court also held that when there is doubt about military vs. civilian jurisdiction, the legal system should always favor civilian courts. As stated in Sentence No. C-358/97: "In situations where there is doubt about the proper jurisdiction to review a certain case, the decision should favor civilian courts."

This is precisely the ruling that the Colombian government continues to defy. Although the court's language is clear, the government has yet to enforce the full scope of this ruling. Specifically, the government continues to allow the armed forces to adjudicate cases involving allegations of serious human rights violations, in defiance of the clear intent of the Constitutional Court to exclude these cases from the military tribunals that have established a virtually unbroken record of impunity.

The 60-day Human Rights Report states, "According to the Ministry of Defense, in 1999, 207 public force members were sanctioned by the military justice system for violations of human rights or fundamental rights." Far from an old problem, this continues to be the policy of the Armed Forces according to its commander-in-chief, Gen. Fernando Tapias. He emphasized it in October 2000, when at a public conference he stated, "Over the past two years, the Superior Military Tribunal prosecuted eighty-five cases for possible human rights violations that concluded with guilty sentences, twenty-five of them for murder, forty for battery and twelve for arbitrary arrest."

But this is not progress; this is clear evidence of lack of compliance with Condition (A)(iii): Compliance with Conditions by Armed Forces. The highest ranking officer in the armed forces clearly and succinctly says that his institution continues to prosecute human rights violations. These cases should never have come to conclusion in military tribunals. If the military had obeyed the law — and complied with Condition (A)(iii) — these cases would have been transferred to civilian courts for trial. To the extent that the Ministry of Defense is referring to gross violations such as extrajudicial executions, the aiding and abetting of paramilitary groups, and other serious human rights violations, it is acknowledging that military tribunals continue to wrongly assert jurisdiction over cases that should be adjudicated in the civilian court system.

Moreover, the reference in this statement to "fundamental rights" is revealing. This phrase has been used by the Colombian military to falsely classify military infractions as human rights violations, thus boosting the numbers of so-called "human rights violations" that they claim have been properly prosecuted and punished. This promotes a false image of compliance that does not reflect reality or obedience to the law. In another example of this tactic, Colombian Gen. Mario Roa contended in a Washington, D.C. event sponsored by the U.S. Defense Intelligence Agency in 2000 that certain acts, like slapping a subordinate, are "human rights crimes" and are classified as human rights violations in Defense Ministry tabulations.

As the 60-day Human Rights Report correctly notes, statistics like these provided by the Ministry of Defense to demonstrate compliance with Sentence No. C-358/97 are notoriously unreliable, occasionally contradictory and often misleading. In citing a Defense Ministry survey that lists 864 cases transferred from military to civilian jurisdiction, the 60-day Human Rights Report includes a crucial caveat: "It is unclear how many of those cases involve human rights violations."

When we were provided with similar documentation by the Ministry of Defense in 2000, we found that, in fact, very few cases could be construed as involving military personnel linked to human rights violations. As we noted in the August certification document, most cases involved police and allegations of crimes that could never be construed as human rights violations, among them brawling, theft and drug trafficking. In a review of cases investigated by Amnesty International and Human Rights Watch since 1997, we have not found a single instance where the military has transferred a human rights case involving an officer with the rank of colonel or higher from a military tribunal to a civilian court, in compliance with Sentence No. C-358/97.

Another judicial body that is not fully reviewed in the introduction to the 60-day Human Rights Report is the Superior Judicial Council (*Consejo Superior de la Judicatura,* CSJ), charged with resolving jurisdictional disputes, among other things. Traditionally, the CSJ has demonstrated an unmistakable bias in favor of the military justice system in defiance of the Constitutional Court.

In a welcome decision, on July 21, 2000, the CSJ returned a case involving the forced disappearance of Nydia Erika Bautista to civilian courts for trial. Bautista had been detained by members of the army's Twentieth Brigade in Santafé de Bogotá in August 1987. Although the Attorney General's Human Rights Unit brought charges against four army members in 1996, the military filed a jurisdictional dispute, which the CSJ decided in its favor that same year. However, after the Constitutional Court ruled in 1997, Bautista's family filed a challenge, which eventually resulted in the case being returned to the CSJ for review. In its July ruling, the CSJ, for the first time, fully embraced Sentence No. C-358/97 and established a crucial precedent.

Unfortunately, this precedent has yet to be acted upon by the armed forces. So far, military judges have refused to transfer key cases back to civilian courts for trial in accordance with the Bautista ruling. Cases that are under investigation by military tribunals or that have not reached the stage of final appeal and their resolution is subject to Sentence No. C-358/97, among them cases we consider benchmarks for measuring Colombia's compliance with Sec. 3201.

1. *General Rodrigo Quiñónes, Commander, Navy's 1st Brigade*: Colombian government investigators linked Quiñónes to at least fifty-seven murders of trade unionists, human rights workers, and community leaders in 1991 and 1992, when he was head of Navy Intelligence and ran Network 7, based in Barrancabermeja. A military tribunal decided that there was insufficient evidence against him, meaning that the case remains subject to judicial review and should be transferred back to civilian courts. The only people to be convicted for these crimes were two civilian employees of Naval Intelligence Network No. 7, one of whom was later murdered in prison. In his ruling on the case, the civilian judge who sentenced the two civilian employees of the network stated that he was "perplexed" by the military tribunal's acquittals of Quiñónes and others, since he considered the evidence against them to be "irrefutable." "With [this acquittal] all that [the military] does is justify crime, since the incidents and the people responsible for committing them are more than clear." This judge also discounted the military's contention that Quiñónes was the victim of a smear campaign by drug traffickers, concluding that there was no evidence to support this claim. To the contrary, he concluded that evidence linking Quiñónes to the Barrancabermeja atrocities was clear and compelling.

The only punishment meted out to Quiñónes has been a "severe reprimand" ordered by the *Procuraduría*, which concluded that he was responsible for setting up the networks of assassins responsible for dozens of the murders and forced disappearances. In a disputable interpretation of existing norms, the *Procuraduría* has determined that murder is not classified as an administrative infraction in the existing regulations. Therefore, the maximum punishment it can impose for murder is a "severe reprimand," essentially a letter in an employment file. It is important to note that the *Procuraduría* itself has termed this punishment "embarrassingly insignificant, both within the national sphere and before the international community." Quiñónes was also the officer in charge of the region at the time of the February 2000 massacre in El Salado (Bolívar). Military and police units stationed nearby failed to stop the killing and established roadblocks which prevented human rights and relief groups from entering the town. Quiñónes was promoted to general in June 2000.

2. *General (ret.) Fernando Millán, former Commander, Fifth Brigade*: The Attorney General opened an investigation against General Millán based on evidence that he set up the *Las Colonias* CONVIVIR in Lebrija, Santander, while he commanded the Fifth Brigade. The *Las Colonias* CONVIVIR operated throughout 1997 without the license required by law but with army support, according to the testimony of former members. According to residents and victims' families, the group committed at least fifteen targeted killings before the director, "Commander Cañón," a retired army officer, and the employees he hired were arrested and prosecuted by civilian authorities under Decree 1194, which prohibits the formation of paramilitary groups. Among the cases currently under investigation by the Attorney General's Office are those of two Protestants, brothers Oscar and Armando Beltrán Correa, who were taken captive by the Las Colonias CONVIVIR as they went to work on July 29, 1997 and killed on the road leading from Lebrija to the hamlet of La Puente. Apparently, the CONVIVIR accused them of passing information to guerrillas. On September 4, 1997, father and son Leonardo and José Manuel Cadena were forced out of their home by CONVIVIR members and killed, according to a family member's testimony to the Attorney General's Office. The CONVIVIR apparently accused the Cadenas of providing food to guerrillas. According to a former CONVIVIR member who was also an army informant, during its months of operation, the Las Colonias CONVIVIR frequently went on operations with army units, setting up roadblocks and detaining suspected guerrillas and criminals. When the Attorney General's Office investigated this case, the army high command prevented prosecutors from questioning Millán, then interposed a jurisdictional dispute, claiming that since Millán was on active service and carrying out his official duties, the case should be tried before a military tribunal. Following a decision by the CSJ, the case was transferred to the military justice system in October 1998. A prosecutor assigned to investigate the May 1998 massacre of eleven people in Barrancabermeja fled the country after receiving threats from General Millán, then-Commander of the Fifth Brigade. Nine members of the military and police were disciplined in connection with the massacre, but there have been no prosecutions under civilian jurisdiction. The case against General Millán has not been transferred back to civilian jurisdiction in accordance with Sentence No. 358/97.

3. *General Freddy Padilla León, Commander of the Second Division, and Colonel Gustavo Sánchez Gutiérrez, Army Personnel Director*: In July 2000, the press widely reported that the Procuraduría had formally charged (pliego de cargos) General Jaime Humberto Cortés Parada and these two officers with "omission" in connection with the massacre in Puerto Alvira in June 1997. Two other former generals who also face disciplinary charges, for "omission" — Generals Jaime Humberto Uscátegui and Agustín Ardila Uribe — are already retired. A review of the evidence conducted by Amnesty International and Human Rights Watch strongly suggests that these officers actively

supported and coordinated activities with the paramilitary groups that carried out this massacre. The Constitutional Court ruled that in cases where there is any doubt about whether a human rights violation has been committed, jurisdiction belongs to the civilian courts. Therefore, we believe all of these cases should be forwarded to civilian courts for trial in order to satisfy Condition (A)(iii). . . .

Directive 01, signed by President Pastrana on August 17, purported to meet the requirement laid out in Sec. 3201(1)(A)(i) requiring that the President of Colombia has directed in writing that Colombian Armed Forces personnel who are credibly alleged to have committed gross violations of human rights will be brought to justice in Colombia's civilian courts, in accordance with the 1997 ruling of Colombia's Constitutional Court regarding civilian court jurisdiction in human rights cases.

The directive is based on the entry into force in September of the new Military Penal Code. The State Department immediately certified that this directive meets the requirement.

We believe Directive 01 is not satisfactory and should not have been certified.

Directive 01 complies only partially with Sec. 3201(1)(A)(i). That condition did not call for *any* directive, but one which directly addressed one of the foundations of impunity in Colombia, continued military jurisdiction over gross human rights violations. Therefore, anything short of full compliance should have resulted in a *denial* of certification.

Instead of basing itself on the Constitutional Court, Directive 01 uses the new Military Penal Code, which specifically cites only three crimes as belonging before civilian courts: genocide, torture and forced disappearance. This reflects only part of the 1997 Constitutional Court ruling and falls short of the standard established in Sec. 3201(1)(A)(i), which is gross violations of human rights.

To comply with Sec. 3201(1)(A)(i), President Pastrana should have used Constitutional Court Sentence No. C-358/97 to frame the directive. As we have noted, that ruling stipulates that crimes against humanity and gross violations of human rights committed by armed forces personnel belong before civilian courts.

In fact, the crimes most often alleged to have been committed by members of Colombia's armed forces are not specifically excluded from military jurisdiction by the Military Penal Code, among them extrajudicial execution, rape and aiding and abetting the atrocities carried out by paramilitary groups. During prolonged debate over the Military Penal Code bill, Colombia's military lobbied aggressively and successfully against including the wording established by the Constitutional Court, as a way of maintaining a questionable legal foundation for their continued defiance of the law.

Given that Colombia's armed forces openly acknowledge that they continue to adjudicate these cases despite Directive 01, we call on the State Department to withdraw the certification on Sec. 3201(1)(A)(iii).

NINETEEN MERCHANTS v. COLOMBIA
Inter-American Court of Human Rights, 2004

[In 1987, a paramilitary force encountered and decided to kill a group of merchants and seize their merchandise and vehicles. The merchants were not paying taxes the paramilitary group was demanding in order to operate in the area and the paramilitary group believed the merchants were selling weapons, supposedly bought in Venezuela, to local guerrilla groups. Military officers were aware of and acquiesced in the plan. Seventeen of the merchants were stopped at an Army roadblock. Later the same day, they were stopped by the paramilitary group. Two or three days later they were killed and their bodies thrown into a river. Approximately 15 days later two other persons disappeared. The victims' merchandise and vehicles were taken and distributed among the paramilitary members and some farmers in the area. After a time, the vehicles were repainted and finally destroyed. After the second episode, relatives of the victims went to the authorities to denounce the disappearances. The government did not start an immediate search. At the time of the Inter-American Court's decision in 2004, the victims' bodies had still not been found.]

86. Relation between the paramilitary group and security forces

Several investigations by the judiciary and the "Procuraduría General de la Nación" (Attorney General's Office) have shown in numerous cases the active participation of security forces in so-called paramilitary groups. Some administrative and criminal sanctions have been applied.

The paramilitary group was receiving collaboration and support from local military authorities, who knew about and consented to the murders.

The local police knew the paramilitary group was in control of the region and was involved in criminal activities but did nothing to stop them.

88. Ordinary criminal courts

On February 10, 1995, the "Fiscalia Regional de Cúcuta" (Cúcuta Regional Prosecution Office) opened a formal investigation against several individuals on charges of murder and kidnapping.

On September 25, 1995, the case was sent to the "Fiscalía de la Unidad Nacional de Derechos Humanos" (Prosecution for the National Human Rights Unit), which in 1996 declared the criminal action extinct against some of the accused who were dead by that time. The same year, the "Fiscalía Regional de la Unidad Nacional de Derechos Humanos" (Regional Prosecution for the National Human Rights Unit) found that several military officers were involved with the murders and disappearance.

On May 28, 1997, three individuals were found guilty, but on appeal the decision was reversed in part by the National Tribunal. Later the "Sala de Casación Penal" (Court of Criminal Appeals) dismissed the case of a defendant who had died.

In 1999 and 2001, other individuals were found guilty.

Summary:

a. Three civilians were convicted as actors on a charge of first degree murder for the first seventeen victims. (One died before the decision was final and the judge dismissed the case.)

ii) Two civilians were convicted as accomplices to first degree murder for the first seventeen victims.

iii) One person was convicted of kidnapping the first seventeen victims.

iv) One person was convicted and six were acquitted of kidnapping the remaining two victims.

89. Conflict of jurisdiction between the ordinary criminal courts and military criminal courts

On October 31, 1996, the military criminal court declared itself competent to try the case against military officers involved in the murder and kidnapping of the merchants. The military judge based his decision on the fact that the accused were part of the XIV Brigade and the actions presumably committed by the military were indirect expressions of the specific functions of their positions. The Regional Prosecution for the National Human Rights Unit, which was handling the case, refused to send it to the military court on the ground that the acts had been committed outside the scope of military jurisdiction and belonged to the ordinary courts. On November 26, 1996, the "Sala Jurisdiccional Disciplinaria del Consejo Superior de la Judicatura" (Disciplinary Jurisdictional Chamber for the Higher Council of the Judiciary) held that the military court was the competent tribunal to judge the military officers in this case on the ground that they were acting within the scope of the military.

90. Military criminal courts

On November 29, 1996, the military judge received the case. On June 18, 1997, the case was closed because no merits were found to call for a "Consejo Verbal de Guerra" (Oral Council of War). The decision was appealed by the "Ministerio Público" based on the Constitutional Court's decision that crimes against humanity should be tried by the ordinary criminal courts.

On March 17, 1998, the "Tribunal Superior Militar" (Higher Military Court) affirmed the trial court decision and denied a request for review by the Court of Cassation.

91. Administrative processes

Several complaints for reparations were filled against the State, the Ministry of Defense, and the Army. As of May 3, 2004, no decision has been rendered.

92. Disciplinary Jurisdiction

In 1990, relatives of the victims presented several petitions to the Attorney General. A preliminary investigation was opened by the "Procuraduría Delegada para la Defensa de los Derechos Humanos" to determine if members of the police or the Army had been involved in misconduct. In 1992, the

Procuraduría, based on lack of evidence, decided that a formal investigation could not be opened.

In 1997, the "Consejería para los Derechos Humanos" (Human Rights Council) of the Presidency asked the Attorney General's Office to reopen the disciplinary investigation, but this was denied. . . .

VIII. Violation of Articles 8.1 and 25 in Relation with Article 1.1 (Judicial Guarantees and Judicial Protection)

157. Commission Arguments [Summary]:

a) The judicial remedies used by the State do not satisfy judicial standards established in the American Convention. Their provisions establish the obligation to provide access to justice with due guarantees of legality, independence and impartiality within a reasonable time, as well as the obligation to provide an effective judicial remedy. . . .

d) The serious situation of violence in the region where the acts have occurred does not justify the omission of the State to fulfill its basic obligation to render justice, such as the seven years delay to the formal opening of an investigation. The State did not take the necessary diligence to investigate the facts and to recuperate the remains of the victims.

e) The decision of military tribunals over military officers, presumed intellectual authors, holding the cease and desist order affected the guarantees provided in articles 8.1 and 25 of the American Convention.

f) The military criminal courts, by their nature and structure, do not satisfy the standards of independence and impartiality required by article 8.1 of the Convention.

g) On August 5, 1997, the Colombian Constitutional Court delivered decision C-358 regarding the jurisdiction of military courts. In that decision the Court held that the punishable act should be an excess or abuse of power within the scope of an activity directly linked to a proper function of the Armed Forces in order to confer jurisdiction on a military tribunal. The link between a criminal act and the military service's activity breaks when the crime is extremely grave, as in the case of crimes against mankind. Under those circumstances the case should be sent to the civil (ordinary) justice system. The acts attributed to members of the Army could not be considered legitimate and linked to the proper functions of the Armed Forces. This and the close relationship between members of the Armed Forces (who trained, provided weapons and condoned violent paramilitary activities) and the paramilitary groups in the region showed that the ordinary justice system should try the case. . . .

i) For more than a decade, the judicial activity of ordinary and military tribunals has not satisfied the standards established by the Convention. The situation described constitutes a violation of the State's obligation to investigate, judge, and punish those responsible for serious offenses, under the standards of reasonable time and effective judicial protection.

158. State Arguments [Summary]: . . .

b) Every investigative body and state sanction available has been committed in the fight against impunity in this case. . . .

e) Internal remedies for the protection of human rights and judicial guarantees have been effective.

f) Regarding the trial of those military officers involved on the facts of this case by the military courts, the State does not share the Commission's generic disqualification of the military criminal courts. The Commission has not presented evidence on the particular case, it just considered that jurisdiction as incompetent and partial. The conflict of jurisdiction between ordinary and military courts was resolved in favor of military tribunals since it was proven that the individuals involved were military officers on active duty and that the acts attributed to them could only be carried out in fulfillment or performance of the military positions they held at the time.

Nowadays, jurisprudence and legislation have evolved to the point that some serious crimes should not be judged by the military criminal courts. However, that was not the legal and jurisprudential concept at the time this case was analyzed by the courts of Colombia.

The military criminal process concluded with a cease and desist order because it was shown that the persons supposedly involved did not commit the acts imputed to them as principals or accomplices. The military judge found the acts carried out by the military officers proper and legitimate because they were within the proper legal framework and the scope of their profession. The military judge analyzed the supposedly intellectual responsibility of those military officers and found that they were not responsible.

g) Military criminal judges were characterized by their independence, autonomy and capacity to analyze the evidence, in accordance with conventional standards related with judicial guarantees.

h) Those who were responsible have been convicted. . . .

Decision of the Court [excerpts]

a) The competence of the military criminal courts to hear the present case.

164. First, the Court will address the competence of the military judges to conduct the investigation. Then it will address the liability of the public forces regarding the 19 merchants.

165. Regarding military criminal jurisdiction, the Court has established that within a democratic state, military jurisdiction should have a restricted and exceptional scope and be aimed at the protection of special legal interests related to the duties conferred by law on the armed forces. Hence, it should only judge military personnel for crimes and felonies that strike against military legal interests.

166. It is necessary to point out that military jurisdiction is established within several legal orders to provide for the order and discipline within the Armed Forces. In the case of the Colombian legal order, section 221 of the 1991 Political Constitution establishes that military courts shall have jurisdiction

over crimes committed by members of the "Fuerza Pública" on active duty and whenever the activity is related to that duty. This rule clearly indicates that military judges have an exceptional jurisdiction and it should be restricted to the conduct of members of the "Fuerza Pública" when directly related to a legitimate military or police duty.

167. In this regard, the Court has established that "when military justice assumes the jurisdiction empowered to ordinary justice, the right to a natural judge is affected and, a fortiori, the right to due process," which is directly related to the right of access to justice. As the Court has previously stated, the judge shall be competent, independent and impartial. . . .

169. During the investigation of the facts carried out by the Regional Prosecution for the National Human Rights Unit within the ordinary criminal courts between April and September 1996, four retired members of the Army were brought into the case, for the Prosecution had serious indications that they were the intellectual authors of the crimes, reason why they ordered their arrest and pretrial detention without bail for the crimes of kidnapping for ransom, murder, and compound larceny. On October 31 of the same year, the first instance military judge issued a decision in which he reserved jurisdiction over the criminal process against the soldiers for the death of the 19 merchants and consequently proposed the positive coalition of jurisdiction to the Regional Prosecution for the National Human Rights Unit which was in charge of the investigation within the ordinary criminal courts. The arguments of the first instance judge were that the events under investigation took place when the accused where still members of the military and the actions presumably carried out by the unit would come as indirect expressions of specific duties of the office they held. On November 26, 1996, the Disciplinary Jurisdictional Chamber for the Higher Council of the Judiciary issued an interlocutory judgment by which it decided the positive jurisdiction coalition in favor of the first instance judge on military criminal jurisdiction based on the fact that he considered "the existence of a cause and effect relationship with the military functions performed" to be obvious, and that "if said participation in the crimes is true accordingly with the modalities inferred by the coalition prosecution, it is related to the military activity, for, according to the legal documents reviewed, while on duty within the Magdalena Medio region they acknowledged the criminal activities of a group of outlaws, gave them support and covered the criminal actions that they have been charged for. . . ."

170. On June 18, 1997, the first instance judge with military criminal jurisdiction issued a cease and desist order in favor of the four accused. The official body in charge of protecting and defending the rights of the society and the State (the "Ministerio Público") appealed, arguing that according to a decision rendered by the Colombian Constitutional Court on August 5, 1997, the military criminal courts had no competence to hear cases on crimes of lese humanity. On March 17, 1998, the Higher Military Court rendered a decision giving effect to an order passed on December 4, 1997 by the Higher Council of the Judiciary that the judges have to obey an order resolving a conflict of jurisdiction unless new facts arise and modify the previously allocated jurisdiction.

171. The Court will not render judgment regarding the aforementioned internal dispute, for it is not a court of appeals or a cassation court for the national jurisdiction organisms. . . .

173. In the present case the right to due process shall be analyzed in accordance with the purpose and goal of the American Convention, which establishes the efficient protection of the human person, that is, a pro personae interpretation will be used. There is no doubt that the involvement that the military personnel under investigation may have had while "having knowledge of the criminal activities of the group of outlaws . . ., having supported them, and having being accessories after the illegal detention" (*supra* para. 169), the disappearance and the death of the 19 merchants, as well as the seizure of their vehicles and merchandise, is not directly related to any military service or duty. This Court considers that the previous attribution of competence to the military criminal courts to hear the alleged crimes committed against the 19 merchants by members of the Army who were already being investigated by the ordinary criminal courts, overruled the exceptionality and restrictive qualities that distinguish military courts, for those courts had no competence to try such matters, thus it violated the right to a natural judge that is part of the right to due process and the right to access justice, established by articles 8.1 and 25 of the American Convention.

174. The case against the military officers related to the investigation of crimes committed against the 19 merchants that was heard by criminal military judges who lacked jurisdiction, ending with a cease and desist order, constituted a violation of the principle of the natural judge and, consequently, to the right to due process and to access justice, and also led to the non-investigation and non-punishment of the members of the "Fuerza Pública" who were involved in the events by any competent tribunal.

175. The Court has repeatedly established that the state has a duty to prevent and fight impunity, which the Court defined as "the total lack of investigation, persecution, imprisonment, prosecution, and condemnation of those responsible for the violations of those rights protected by the American Convention." In this regard, the Court has warned that:

> [T]he state has the obligation to fight said situation by all legal means available since impunity propitiates the chronic repetition of human rights violations and the complete desertion of the victims and their relatives.

176. The Court has established that only with the full acknowledgement of the circumstances regarding the violation, would the State have granted an effective remedy for the victims and their relatives, and would have fulfilled its general duty to investigate and punish, providing the victim's families the possibility of access to the truth, not only regarding the location of the bodies, but also regarding the events that surrounded their deaths.

[The Court concluded that Colombia had violated articles 8.1 and 25 of the Inter-American Convention on Human Rights.]

Letter to Bolivian President Carlos Mesa Gisbert
Human Rights Watch, Dec. 22, 2003

[Human Rights Watch wrote to President Mesa after more than 50 Bolivians died in protests over plans to sell natural gas through Chile.]

In our view, to achieve justice, Bolivia's civilian courts must retain jurisdiction over the investigation and prosecution of members of the armed forces suspected of committing abuses when quelling protests and civil unrest. In addition, robust measures must be taken to strengthen the independence and effectiveness of the civilian justice system. . . .

The September and October deaths occurred in the context of anti-government protests sparked by plans to sell Bolivian natural gas through Chile. On September 20 three campesinos and an eight-year-old girl were killed by gunfire during a clash between armed protesters and army troops and police at Warisata, after the army intervened to ensure the safe passage of hundreds of tourists prevented by protesters from leaving Sorata. Two army conscripts also died in the exchange of fire. On October 12, at least twenty-six civilians were killed in El Alto. Many of them were shot when army troops armed with military combat rifles tried to break blockades preventing the passage of fuel tankers from El Alto to La Paz. At least fourteen civilians were shot and killed on the following day as the protests continued in La Paz. Given the high ratio of civilian to military and police casualties, Human Rights Watch is deeply concerned that the security forces may have failed to exercise proper care in responding to the protests. Under binding international standards, the intentional use of lethal force by law enforcement officials is permissible only when strictly unavoidable to protect life. Such standards require that impartial and independent investigations be carried out where there are indications that this principle was not followed or ignored.

In all, the Human Rights Ombudsman counted a total of fifty-nine deaths during street protests between September 20 and October 19, mainly in Warisata, El Alto, and La Paz. Other nongovernmental human rights groups, such as the Permanent Assembly of Human Rights, estimated the number of deaths at over eighty. Forty-nine civilians died from gunshot wounds, and more than 400 people were hospitalized with injuries. Three army conscripts also died. A prosecutor investigating the incidents told us that high caliber munitions used exclusively by the armed forces claimed the lives of most of the civilian victims.

Prosecutors attached to the district attorney's office for La Paz (Fiscalia del Distrito de La Paz) are conducting investigations into both the killings that took place in February 2003 and those of September and October. Unfortunately, several serious obstacles are hampering their work.

Military Jurisdiction and Lack of Military Cooperation with Civilian Justice Officials

We are deeply concerned that the armed forces have failed to cooperate fully with the attorney general's office. Officials of the office informed Human Rights Watch that the army had still not responded to requests for information made by the public prosecutor six weeks ago. In those requests, the prosecutor asked for information about the units dispatched to quell the October protests, including the names of their commanding officers. Nor has information been forthcoming about an army helicopter that flew over El Alto at the height of the October protests and from which soldiers are believed to have fired on the crowd. According to these sources, rather than provide the information requested by the prosecutor regarding the soldiers killed, the army is carrying out a separate investigation into the circumstances of their deaths.

Judging from past investigations into civilian deaths during protests, it is likely that if the civilian investigation advances and charges are brought against military personnel, the army will assert a competing claim for jurisdiction over the case. The president of the Supreme Tribunal of Military Justice, Gen. Jorge Rodríguez Bravo, stressed to Human Rights Watch that civilian courts lacked jurisdiction to prosecute a soldier for any crime committed while on active service. He also explained that military courts would normally dismiss charges against a soldier responsible for a civilian death who was obeying orders.

When the military courts obtain jurisdiction over a case involving members of the armed forces implicated in abuses against civilians, the case almost inevitably ends in an acquittal. The military's ruling of acquittal, moreover, blocks the civilian justice system from proceeding with its own prosecution.

The negative effects of military justice can be seen in several recent cases. In August 2003, for example, the Supreme Military Tribunal acquitted Cap. Robinson Iriarte Lafuente, an army marksman whom the public prosecutor had accused of the homicide of a seventeen-year-old during April 2000 protests in Cochabamba. After his acquittal, Iriarte was promoted to the rank of major. The Superior Court of Justice had ruled in February 2001 that the case fell under military jurisdiction because Iriarte was on active duty and under orders at the time, even though he was in civilian clothes. Another case in which a civilian prosecutor's investigation was preempted by a suspect's rapid acquittal by a military court was that of Col. Aurelio Burgos Blacutt, accused of killing a protestor in January 2002. After Burgos was acquitted in the military courts later in the year the attorney general's office had no choice but to drop the charges against him.

Most recently, the army has insisted on retaining jurisdiction over the case of four soldiers accused of killing a nurse and a porter in La Paz on February 13, 2003, during the unrest that followed the police riot. On October 4, the Superior District Court of La Paz transferred the case to a military tribunal. In doing so, it reversed an August court ruling that had confirmed the jurisdiction of the civilian courts.

By insisting on conducting criminal investigations in parallel with civilian prosecutors, the military justice authorities obstruct accountability. The pursuit of a single case within two separate jurisdictions violates article 45 of Bolivia's Code of Penal Procedures, which states: "different trials may not be held in respect of a single event, even if the accused are different." Most importantly, the defendant's acquittal in a military tribunal bars further proceedings in the civilian courts, in application of the principle of *non bis en idem*, or double jeopardy.

Human Rights Watch opposes the use of military tribunals try those responsible for human rights abuses committed in the course of military operations, or outside them. We do not believe that military courts enjoy sufficient independence to render impartial verdicts in such cases, and we fear that the predictable result is impunity. Moreover, we note that in Bolivia there is no civilian court review of the verdicts of the military courts.

International human rights bodies have consistently called on states to transfer jurisdiction over human rights cases from military to civilian authorities. The U.N. Human Rights Committee, which monitors states' compliance with the International Covenant on Civil and Political Rights, has repeatedly called on states parties to subject military personnel alleged to have committed human rights violations to civilian jurisdiction. The Inter-American Commission on Human Rights has found that "when the State permits investigations to be conducted by the entities with possible involvement, independence and impartiality are clearly compromised." The result is "de facto impunity," which has a corrosive effect on the rule of law and violates the principles of the American Convention on Human Rights, of which Bolivia is a State Party.

Given the large number of deaths at issue in the incidents mentioned, it is crucial that the civilian justice system be allowed to carry out a full and impartial investigation. I would therefore urge you to instruct military officials to cooperate fully with civilian prosecutors, and to order military prosecutors to desist from conducting a separate and competing investigation into the events. As a longer term measure, I would urge you to introduce legislation to limit the jurisdiction of military courts to military offenses in which civilians are not victims, thus ensuring that the civilian justice system retains jurisdiction in cases involving human rights abuses or the excessive use of lethal force. . . .

NOTES AND QUESTIONS

1. In 2001, a military court sentenced two Colombian officers to prison for 40 months for failing to prevent paramilitary organizations from massacring civilians. Applying Sentence No. C-358/97, the Constitutional Court held later that year that violations of human rights and international humanitarian law cannot be considered as "acts of duty," and ruled that the officers should have been tried in the civilian courts. Sentence No. SU.1184/01 (Colombia Const. Ct. Nov. 14, 2001), *discussed in* INT'L COMM'N OF JURISTS, ATTACKS ON JUSTICE: THE HARASSMENT AND PERSECUTION OF JUDGES AND LAWYERS 104 (11th ed. 2002).

2. In *Correa Belisle v. Argentina*, Rep. No. 2/04 (2004), the Inter-American Commission on Human Rights ("IACHR") held admissible a case in which an Army captain was prosecuted for disrespect after he gave damaging testimony about the Chief of Staff — and, according to the State, called him a liar — in a court-martial arising from the murder of a conscript. Argentina argued that "since the conduct in which Correa Belisle engaged constitutes an essentially military offense, he should be tried by the military justice system, which is intended for application in a special framework, and, therefore, has specific characteristics. Furthermore, the State adds that the motive that warrants a proceeding before the military courts and classifies the offense as a military one, is precisely the manner in which the testimony was presented to the ordinary courts, which constituted serious disrespect toward a superior. The State holds that the foregoing does not conflict with the duty to testify before the ordinary courts because Correa could have made statements that contradicted those of General Balza without the necessity to do so in discrediting terms. Therefore, the State considers that, rather than being in conflict, the civil obligation to testify and military discipline act together in harmony." The State also claimed that Correa Belisle "was not tried for the substance of his statements but for the form in which they were made. It maintains that the preservation of military discipline was the valid basis for his prosecution under the Code of Military Justice, and that the military proceedings were duly carried out in accordance with that purpose, as well as the prescribed law and procedure." He, on the other hand, argued that "his act of testifying was a duty, not a crime, and argued that any theoretical damages to the honor or reputation of another would be a matter for civilian jurisdiction," and invoked his right to trial by the *juez natural* pursuant to the Argentine Constitution and the American Convention on Human Rights. When the case settled in 2006, the Commission issued the following announcement:

> The IACHR expresses satisfaction with the signing of a friendly settlement agreement between the Government of Argentina and Captain Rodolfo Correa Belisle (Ret.), which includes a commitment to reform the Code of Military Justice so that it will provide the military with the same due process guarantees as for civilians. This reform would eliminate the special military jurisdiction and create a new system of sanctions that is respectful of the rights and guarantees of members of the Armed Forces.

> The IACHR highlights the importance of the agreement signed on September 18 in Argentina, not only for that country but for the region as a whole. The Commission has indicated on numerous occasions that various countries of the region should reform their military justice laws. Military case law requires that military jurisdiction be used solely and exclusively to prosecute the crimes of active-duty security forces and not other conduct. The Commission considers that the approval of the new Code of Military Justice would not only be a significant step forward in bringing Argentine laws into line with its commitments and duties under the American Convention on Human Rights, but would also serve as a benchmark for other countries of the region. As stated by the Commission during the hearing, once the Argentine Code of Military Justice has been reformed in accordance with that agreement, it will become an important benchmark for other countries, enabling them to bring their military justice systems into line with international standards and the requirements of justice in a democratic society.

The IACHR underscores the creativity of the petitioners, who, through an individual case, were able to have a positive influence, prompting Argentine legislation to meet international standards, as well as the political will of the Argentine State to meet its commitments under the inter-American human rights system. The Commission will continue to follow up on the process until its completion, including the adoption by the National Congress of the new Code of Military Justice. It calls upon the Argentine State to adopt the new Code quickly, expresses its support in that regard, and anticipates its adoption in order to approve the agreement and conclude the case.

3. Who should have the power to decide whether a particular case is tried by a civilian court or a military court? *See, e.g.*, Army Act § 125 (India) (conferring discretion on commanding officer to decide where criminal court and court-martial both have jurisdiction), *discussed in Union of India v. Sharma*, 2087 SOL Case No. 022 (India 1987). Are there workable standards for such decisions? Under what circumstances should civilian courts be denied concurrent jurisdiction over offenses by military personnel? For a disturbing summary of the military's exclusive jurisdiction over crimes by military police in Brazil see Inter-American Comm'n on Hum. Rgts., *Report on the Situation of Human Rights in Brazil*, ch. III, ¶¶ 59 *et seq.*, OEA/Ser.L/V/II.97, Doc. 29 rev. 1 (Sept. 29, 1997).

Chapter 8

MILITARY CRIMES

This chapter focuses on the law governing military offenses, acts that are deemed criminal only within the context of military service. Military criminal laws prohibit many of the same acts as civilian criminal laws; crimes against persons, such as assault, rape, and murder, and crimes against property, such as larceny, burglary, and arson, are prosecuted in both civilian and military courts. But military law also criminalizes offenses such as absence without leave, misbehavior before the enemy, and conduct prejudicial to good order and discipline. These crimes are purely military in nature and raise distinctive legal issues. Some military codes categorize offenses to lay out the military nature of these crimes. For example, the New Zealand Defence Force Discipline Act of 1982 specifies "offences relating to operations against the enemy"; "mutiny, desertion, and unauthorised absence"; "insubordination and violence"; "offences relating to performance of duty"; "offences relating to ships, vehicles, aircraft, and weapons"; "service property offences"; "fraudulent conduct"; and "looting." Most codes also include a provision to cover unspecified offenses; in the United States, such a provision appears in Article 134 of the UCMJ, the "general article." This chapter reviews three broad, sometimes overlapping categories of military-specific offenses: unauthorized absence; dereliction, disobedience, and negligence; and disorderly and discrediting acts. The chapter closes with a closer look at a hotly-contested arena of military justice: the criminalization of adultery. These peculiarly military offenses help to shed light on the special context of military justice by revealing the disciplinary challenges military commanders face and the standards of behavior to which service members are held.

I. UNAUTHORIZED ABSENCE: AWOL AND DESERTION

National Defence Act (Canada), Chapter 103.21 — Desertion

Section 88 of the National Defence Act provides:

(1) Every person who deserts or attempts to desert is guilty of an offence and on conviction, if the person committed the offence on active service or under orders for active service, is liable to imprisonment for life or to less punishment and, in any other case, is liable to imprisonment for a term not exceeding five years or to less punishment.

(2) A person deserts who —

(*a*) being on or having been warned for active service, duty during an emergency or other important service, is absent without authority with the intention of avoiding that service;

(b) having been warned that his vessel is under sailing orders, is absent without authority with the intention of missing that vessel;

(c) absents himself without authority from his place of duty with the intention of remaining absent from his place of duty;

(d) is absent without authority from his place of duty and at any time during such absence forms the intention of remaining absent from his place of duty; or

(e) while absent with authority from his place of duty, with the intention of remaining absent from his place of duty, does any act or omits to do anything the natural and probable consequence of which act or omission is to preclude the person from being at his place of duty at the time required.

(3) A person who has been absent without authority for a continuous period of six months or more shall, unless the contrary is proved, be presumed to have had the intention of remaining absent from his place of duty.

Excerpts from the Notes to §88

(A) It is an essential ingredient of the offence of desertion that the accused have had a wrongful intent. The question as to whether an accused intended not to return, or did any act which showed that the accused had an intention of not returning, is in each case a question of fact to be decided by the service tribunal upon the evidence submitted in the course of the trial. Prolonged absence which the accused fails to explain may be taken into account by the service tribunal as one of the factors relevant to the issue of whether the accused intended not to return. Where, however, the absence has lasted for six months or more, subsection 88(3) of the *National Defence Act* applies. Evidence relating to the following questions may assist the court in determining whether the accused intended to return:

(i) Did the accused make any remarks indicating that he did not intend to return?

(ii) Were the circumstances in which the accused was living during the absence inconsistent with an intention of returning?

(iii) Did the accused change his name during his absence?

(iv) Was the state of the accused's kit inconsistent with an intention of returning?

(B) In order to establish an offence of attempting to desert, the following two elements must be proven:

(i) an intent to commit the offence of desertion,

(ii) an act or omission towards the commission of the offence of desertion.

An intent to desert is not sufficient alone if nothing is done to carry it into effect. A distinction must, however, be drawn between acts or omissions toward the commission of an offence of desertion and those which are mere preparations. It is not possible to draw a clear line of distinction but, in general, preparation consists in devising or arranging the means for the commission of an offence while an act or omission sufficient to support a charge of attempting to desert must involve a direct movement towards the commission of the offence after the preparations have been made. For example, a person, having an intent to desert, might pack his kit. That fact would merely be a stage in his preparations and not such an act that would justify a charge of attempting to desert. An example of an act justifying a charge of attempting to desert would be the scaling of a fence surrounding the camp after preparations indicating an intent to desert.

National Defence Act (Canada), Chapter 103.23 — Absence Without Leave

Section 90 of the National Defence Act provides:

(1) Every person who absents himself without leave is guilty of an offence and on conviction is liable to imprisonment for less than two years or to less punishment.

(2) A person absents himself without leave who

(a) without authority leaves his place of duty;

(b) without authority is absent from his place of duty; or

(c) having been authorized to be absent from his place of duty, fails to return to his place of duty at the expiration of the period for which the absence of that person was authorized.

Excerpt from Notes to § 90

It is not necessary to establish that an absentee had a specific intent to commit the offence. As long as there are no circumstances amounting in law to a defence (and it may be so presumed until it is raised by the defence) the fact of the absence without authority together with the knowledge the absentee had or is presumed to have had as to his duty to be where required if wanted is sufficient to establish a guilty state of mind, whether the absence was deliberate or arose from forgetfulness, carelessness or negligence.

STATE v. LANCE CORPORAL (RES) POON CHEE SENG
Singapore Court of Military Appeals, 1995

The respondent is a reservist with the 150A PDF Battalion. He was, at all material times, liable to perform reserve service. This meant that he was obliged to perform reserve service from time to time and for such periods as may be required of him by a notice served on him by the proper authorities.

He was charged with desertion contrary to section 23(1) of the Singapore Armed Forces Act in that he had failed to attend at his place of duty, 1 SIR Guillemard Camp, from 7 December 1986 on or about 0730 hours to 25 March 1991 at or about 2325 hours with the intention, at the time, of so failing, or formed thereafter, of remaining permanently absent from duty without lawful authority. . . .

[After respondent received and acknowledged two requests to appear for physical fitness tests but did not appear, military personnel visited his flat four separate times between December 1987 and April 1990. Respondent was not present during any of those visits, but additional Singapore Armed Forces documents were left for him in the care of others, including letters entitled "Absence from Reserve Duty" and "Reporting to Reserve Unit." Respondent "explained that he had failed to attend the tests because he was too busy with his business affairs and had forgotten about them." He also said that he had moved from the flat, that he never received the additional letters about his absence, that he had no reason to suspect that his unit was searching for him, and that he had checked with the local police station and with passport authorities, neither of which had informed him that he was wanted by the Singapore Armed Forces.]

After hearing the defence, the General Court Martial acquitted the respondent. The General Court Martial found that there was reasonable doubt on the ingredient the prosecution had to prove as to whether the respondent had formed the necessary intention to permanently absent himself from duty without authority. . . .

[The Prosecution appealed.]

Now, it must be said that proof of this intention to remain permanently absent is not an easy task, for in most cases, it is not possible to obtain direct evidence of the intention of the deserter. In practical terms, a court has to consider all the relevant facts, and draw proper inferences from them to determine whether the person charged for desertion had this intention.

In the present appeal, on a careful consideration of the evidence found in the record of proceedings, we have to reluctantly disagree with the findings of fact made by the General Court Martial. . . . In our view, on these facts, the proper inference to be drawn from them [is] that the respondent was altogether unconcerned about his obligation to perform his duty required of him as a reservist. Despite having received [two notifications of his physical fitness test], the respondent had failed to turn up to take the tests. After that, he did not bother to respond to the letter left for him by the Singapore Armed Forces . . . [and] he did not think it necessary to check with his unit. . . .

We next turn to the evaluation of the evidence of the respondent. His stand before the General Court Martial was that he was too busy with his business affairs, and had forgotten about the [tests]. In our view, this cannot be a legitimate excuse. In fact, it is no excuse at all. Indeed, it shows an irresponsible attitude towards reserve service. As for his evidence that he did not know where and when to report . . . [it] simply cannot be believed. . . . In our view, the irresistible inference to be drawn from all the evidence in this case is that the respondent wanted to stay away from the Singapore Armed Forces permanently.

It remains for us to say a few words on the law relating to desertion concerning reservists. . . . [D]esertion is a continuing offence and, subject to proof of intention, begins to run from the date the reservist fails to perform his reserve service required of him by the notice that has been served on him. . . . Accordingly, we allow the appeal and convict the respondent on the charge against him. . . .

CONVENING AUTHORITY v. PRIVATE DOYLE
Court Martial Appeals Court of Ireland, 1996
2 ILRM 213 (1996)

Private William Doyle was convicted of the offence of deserting the defence forces, contrary to section 135 of the Defence Act 1954, before a limited court martial which was held on 17 August 1995, at Collins Barracks, Dublin. He was discharged from the defence forces.

He appeals to this court and has, by his counsel, advanced a single point concerning the judge advocate's summing up on the burden of proof.

The background facts to the case were not in dispute and are as follows. The appellant was absent from his unit from 5 March 1983 and remained absent until 27 June 1995 — over 12 years. He said that he always intended returning to his unit and never formed an intention of not returning. He said that he had drink problems and felt that he was being "persecuted" by his superior officers at the time that he left. He joined the French Foreign Legion where he had a stint of five years. He also detailed various jobs that he had worked at in England; his course of rehabilitation from his addiction to drink and the fact that on his return to the defence forces he was pronounced to be in good mental order.

Section 135 of the Defence Act 1954 provides:

> (1) Every person subject to military law who deserts or attempts to desert the defence forces is guilty of an offence against military law . . . .

Subsection (2) (iii) provides that for the purposes of the act the person deserts the defence forces if he absents himself without due authority from his unit or formation or from the place where his duty requires him to be, with the intention of not returning to that unit, formation, or place.

Paragraph (b) of subsection (2) provides [that] . . . a person who has been absent without authority for a continuous period of six months or more shall, unless the contrary is proved, be presumed to have had the intention of not returning to his unit or formation or the place where his duty requires him to be.

When the judge advocate came to sum up, he duly referred to the ingredients of the offence of desertion. He dealt with the presumption contained in paragraph (b), quoted above, as follows:

> A presumption — a statutory presumption — has been raised that the accused had the intention of not returning to the place where his duty required him to be. The accused may, however, rebut that presumption by evidence. Whereas the prosecution must establish the guilt of the accused beyond reasonable doubt, the same degree of proof is not required of the accused in rebutting such a presumption as has been raised. It is enough if the accused satisfies you of the probability that he had not the intention of remaining away from the place where his duty required him to be. If he does so you must find him not guilty of desertion . . . .

The judge advocate read all of the accused's evidence to the court. He then went on to say:

> If you believe his story and on the basis of what he has told you you are satisfied of the probability that he never formed the intention of remaining away you will acquit him of the charge — otherwise you may convict.

Before us it was submitted that this direction on the statutory presumption was incorrect and breached the presumption of innocence. However, the court is of the opinion that it is in accordance with the direction as definitively set out by the Court of Criminal Appeal in England . . . [that] "the jury should be directed that it is for them to decide whether the contrary is proved, that the burden of proof required is less than that required at the hands of the prosecution in proving the case beyond a reasonable doubt, and that the burden may be discharged by evidence satisfying the jury of the probability of that which the accused is called upon to establish."

We are satisfied that . . . the judge advocate's direction to the court was in accordance with [this decision]. . . .

Accordingly, the court holds that there was no misdirection in this case and we uphold the conviction and dismiss the appeal.

UNITED STATES v. TAYLOR
United States Air Force Court of Criminal Appeals, 2006[1]

The appellant is a 30-year-old second lieutenant assigned to the 4th Space Operations Squadron at Schriever Air Force Base, Colorado. At the time of his trial he had served approximately 30 months on active duty. While awaiting trial on charges of counterfeiting and passing approximately 160 $20 bills, the appellant, on 31 January 2002, mailed letters to his wife, his commander, his parents, and several congressmen to inform them that he was going to commit suicide. Included in the letter to his wife was information on how she could collect $250,000 from his Servicemember's Group Life Insurance policy after his death. Several days later a park ranger at Lake Powell, Utah, discovered an inflatable kayak that contained the appellant's wallet, some personal items, and a spent 9mm shell casing. There were blood smears on the inside wall of the kayak. The Air Force Office of Special Investigations investigated and quickly determined that the evidence found at the lake was consistent with someone faking suicide. After further investigation, the appellant was arrested approximately one month later in Las Vegas, Nevada. During the intervening month the appellant had created a new life for himself under a new identity. To support this new identity, the appellant created, among other things, a variety of forged identification cards, a college transcript, fake Air Force discharge documents, and death certificates for his wife, son, and parents. During a search of the appellant's new residence, investigators also found two informative articles the appellant had downloaded several months prior to his disappearance. One was entitled "How to Change Your Identity," and the other "How to Get Lost and Stay That Way." . . .

---

[1] This case was not reported.

On 26 and 27 March 2003, the appellant, through counsel, requested a deferment and waiver of automatic forfeitures pursuant to Articles 57(a)(2) and 58b(b), UCMJ, 10 U.S.C. §§ 857(a)(2), 858b(b), for the benefit of his dependents. On 2 April 2003, the convening authority granted both requests. A declaration submitted to this Court from the appellant's counsel indicates that the appellant actually continued to receive full pay and allowances for over a year after his trial concluded. Nonetheless, the appellant now alleges, and the government concedes, that the action failed to reflect the convening authority's approval of the deferment and waiver requests. We agree. . . .

We conclude the findings are correct in law and fact, and no error prejudicial to the substantial rights of the appellant occurred. . . .

NOTES AND QUESTIONS

1. Lest any service member misunderstand the imperative to appear as ordered, notes to The Queen's Regulations and Orders for the Canadian Forces, Vol. II, art. 103.23, set out circumstances that do *not* constitute a legitimate excuse to a charge of AWOL. These include "getting so drunk as to be unable to return in time"; "losing [one's] railway ticket and having insufficient money to get back in time"; "going to sleep when returning to duty, thereby being carried past [one's] station and unable to get back in time"; and "failing to obey an order of which [one] ought to have been aware." Do these interpretations seem unnecessarily harsh or appropriately severe?

2. A decision of the Constitutional Court of Azerbaijan (Oct. 26, 2001) held that citizens can be prosecuted for "failure to appear" as soon as they pass the medical examination required for military service. The criminal code specifies that the offense can be "voluntary leaving of a military unit" or "failure to appear without good reason." Based on the Queen's Regulations cited above, what might constitute "good reason" for failing to appear as ordered?

3. In many military justice systems, including the U.S., the critical distinction between the military crimes of desertion and AWOL is intent. In the *Poon Chee Seng* case above, the Singapore court reviews the finding of fact made at the court-martial and substitutes its own judgment. Could this happen in the U.S. military justice system? *See* Art. 66, UCMJ. In the case of Private Doyle, the Irish court reviews not the findings of fact, but the legality of the judge advocate's direction to the court. The court-martial that convicted Doyle imposed a discharge, which at first glance seems an inappropriate punishment for desertion. Does sentencing a deserter to be discharged serve the goals of military justice? Does it matter whether a nation adopts a policy of compulsory military service or maintains a volunteer armed force?

4. In the Canadian statute reproduced above, §88(3) shifts the burden of proving intent from the prosecution to the defense if the absence in question is six continuous months or more. Contrast Article 85 of the UCMJ, the United States' desertion statute, which includes no such presumption about the implications of an extended absence. Does this distinction matter?

II. DERELICTION, DISOBEDIENCE, AND NEGLIGENCE

Uniform Code of Military Justice

Article 90. Assaulting or willfully disobeying superior commissioned officer

Any person subject to this chapter who —

(1) strikes his superior commissioned officer or draws or lifts up any weapon or offers any violence against him while he is in the execution of his office; or

(2) willfully disobeys a lawful command of his superior commissioned officer;

shall be punished, if the offense is committed in time of war, by death or such other punishment as a court-martial may direct, and if the offense is committed at any other time, by such punishment, other than death, as a court-martial may direct.

Military Discipline Code, South Africa, 1999

Section 5: Any person in command of troops of the South African National Defence Force or of any vessel or aircraft who —

(a) when his duty requires him to engage with the enemy, fails to do so or to do so as expeditiously or effectively as circumstances permit;

(b) being in action without proper cause withdraws from the action or forsakes his post; or

(c) improperly fails to pursue an enemy or to consolidate any position gained,

shall be guilty of an offence and liable to conviction to imprisonment for a period not exceeding ten years.

Naval Discipline Act, Australia, § 19(a)

Every person subject to this Act who, either wilfully or by negligence, causes or allows to be lost, stranded or hazarded any of Her Majesty's ships or vessels; . . . shall be liable, if he acts wilfully or with wilful neglect, to imprisonment for any term or any less punishment authorised by this Act, and in any other case to imprisonment for a term not exceeding two years or any less punishment so authorised.

Defence Force Discipline Act, 1982, New Zealand, § 35

Negligence in performance of a duty

(1) A person who is a defence member is guilty of an offence if:

(a) the person is required, because of his or her office or appointment, to perform a duty; and

(b) the person engages in conduct; and

(c) that conduct results in a failure to perform the duty to the required standard.

Penalty: Imprisonment for 3 months.

(2) Negligence applies to paragraph (1)(c).

(3) In this section: *"required standard"*, in relation to performing a duty, means the standard to which a reasonably capable and careful defence member of the same training and experience would perform the duty.

NOTES AND QUESTIONS

1. Why do the sea services impose special burdens on commanders of ships and other vessels as compared to commanders of land-based forces? Are those burdens appropriate? The French Code of Military Justice, Article 472, requires that the captain be the last person to abandon ship. Is that an archaic rule? Consider the following description of an infamous World War II case, from Commander Roger D. Scott, *Kimmel, Short, McVay: Case Studies in Executive Authority, Law and the Individual Rights of Military Commanders*, 156 MIL. L. REV. 52, 53-54 (1998):

> Captain Charles B. McVay III was Commanding Officer of U.S.S. Indianapolis on 30 July 1945, when a Japanese submarine sank her, causing great loss of life. After delivering atomic bomb components from San Francisco to Tinian, Indianapolis sailed from Guam for Leyte, Philippines, on 28 July 1945. The intelligence provided to Indianapolis before her departure included reports of three possible submarine detections along her route. In transit, Indianapolis received a series of additional messages and monitored live radio traffic indicating real-time interdiction of a Japanese submarine along the route to Leyte. Fleet doctrine required ships to employ anti-submarine evasive maneuvering (zigzagging) in submarine waters during good visibility. On the evening of 29 July, at a time when visibility was poor, Captain McVay told the Officer of the Deck that he could cease zigzagging at twilight. The ship ceased zigzagging at approximately 2000, but visibility improved later that night and Indianapolis did not resume zigzagging. Struck by at least two torpedoes near midnight, Indianapolis sank within fifteen minutes. Approximately 400 men went down with the ship, and 800 escaped into the water. Over the next four days, adrift on the ocean, 480 of the survivors were preyed upon by sharks or succumbed to their wounds or the elements.

> The Commander in Chief, Pacific Fleet, Admiral Nimitz, convened a Court of Inquiry, which recommended the referral of charges against Captain McVay. The Chief of Naval Operations, Admiral King, concurred. After additional investigation and advice, the Secretary of the Navy referred charges for negligently hazarding a vessel (failure to zigzag) and dereliction of duty (delay in ordering abandon ship). A court-martial conducted at the Washington Navy Yard convicted Captain McVay of hazarding a vessel, and acquitted him of the dereliction charge. Consistent with the court-martial recommendation of clemency, Secretary Forrestal set aside all punishment. Captain McVay continued to serve on active duty until he retired as a Rear Admiral in 1949.

Was Captain McVay guilty of negligence under the standards of the New Zealand code reprinted above? Under the Australian code? What political, practical, and military factors present obstacle to the investigation of potentially criminal conduct in such a situation? *See* Cmdr. William Toti, *The Sinking of the Indy & Responsibility of Command,* NAV. INST. PROC. (Oct. 1999); U.S. Senate, Committee on Armed Services, *The Sinking of the USS Indianapolis and the Subsequent Court-martial of Rear Admiral Charles B. McVay III,* 1st session, 106th Congress, September 14, 1999; *see also* DOUG STANTON, IN HARM'S WAY: THE SINKING OF THE USS *INDIANAPOLIS* AND THE EXTRAORDINARY STORY OF ITS SURVIVORS (2003).

2. In *Captain Wong Chee Wai v. State* (Sing. Mil. App. 1985), an officer was convicted for violating a law that stated: "Every person subject to military law who, knowing that any other person has committed an offense . . . [who] fails to take any steps within his power to cause that person to be apprehended, shall be guilty of an offence and shall be liable on conviction by a subordinate military court to imprisonment for a term not exceeding two years or any lesser punishment authorised by this Act." Captain Wong had neglected to take any disciplinary action after a private "shouted at him in vulgar language." The private was upset about a pending AWOL charge and had brought his brother and two civilian friends to Captain Wong's office in an effort to convince him to drop the charges. When that effort failed, the private became angry. Captain Wong argued the private was not a danger to the camp, that there was no risk to government property, and that he realized the private's outburst was not the result of an intent to commit violence or cause further trouble. The court upheld Captain Wong's conviction, explaining that he had "no discretion in the matter" and he was obliged to have the private arrested. Is there a distinction between "willful disobedience" and a failure to act affirmatively? Is eliminating the discretion of superior officers to arrest and prosecute an effective way to counter allegations of arbitrariness in military justice?

QUINN v. CHIEF OF ARMY
Defence Force Discipline Appeal Tribunal, Australia
[2001] ADFDAT 4

The appellant was convicted by a Defence Force Magistrate (DFM) of one count of ill-treatment of an inferio r, contrary to s [section] 34 of the *Defence Force Discipline Act 1982* (The DFD Act) which provides:

> 34. A defence member who assaults, or ill-treats, a member of the Defence Force who is of inferior rank to the defence member is guilty of an offence for which the maximum punishment is imprisonment for 2 years.

The particulars of the charge were that at Kulim, Malaysia, on or about 4 March 1998, the appellant ill-treated Lieutenant David Steven Good, a member of the Defence Force who was inferior in rank to him. . . .

[The appellant was Lt Good's superior in A Company 3rd Battalion Royal Australian Regiment (3 RAR), a unit deployed to Malaysia for training in combat tactics in a jungle environment. In March 1998, Lt Good was a platoon commander whose platoon was undergoing an assessment exercise to test the effectiveness of its training in ambush and attack. In the course of the exercise, Lt Good was "captured."]

Lt Good was taken to the ground, a pillowcase was placed over his head and tape was placed over the pillowcase across his eyes to further minimise his ability to see. His hands were bound before him. He was then taken to company headquarters. The capture took place at between 0730 and 0930 hours. At some time shortly after his arrival, Lt Good was checked over by Cpl Gorman, a medic. The toggle rope used to bind his hands was removed. It appears that his hands were then rebound with tape. He complained that the binding was too tight, and the appellant, either personally or by direction to Cpl Gorman, removed the binding and replaced it with bandages binding his hands in front of him.

The DFM accepted the account given by Lt Good as to what happened to him next. First he was tied to a tree and required to stand for a number of hours against the tree during which time he was interrogated by the appellant. During breaks in the interrogation Lt Good sought to sit down, but he was lifted back by a person unknown and was not allowed to sit. This lasted for about three hours. . . . During this period he was moved and told by the appellant that there was an ants nest in the location to where to was being moved and he was going to be put on it. Something was then placed down his shirt and the appellant asked, "Are they biting?" After this, there was a lengthy gap in the interrogation. Lt Good was taken out into the sun in the hottest part of the day. The weather was hot and humid. . . .

Next, Lt Good was doused with water and placed on a stretcher in the shade. He was then given regular drinks of water although he had had none before this time. There was no finding that Lt Good became dehydrated. It is not clear if the interrogation continued after that time, but there was a finding that the interrogation overall lasted for a substantial number of hours . . . .

As to the elements of the offence, the DFM relied upon a passage from a report under s 154 of the DFD Act by Group Captain Kirkham in 994:

> In order to sustain a charge of ill-treatment under section 34 of the Defence Force Discipline Act I [] the prosecution must establish deliberate conduct on the part of the accused, whether by act or omission, that could reasonably be categorised as ill-treatment. Secondly, that at the time of such conduct the accused had knowledge or awareness that he was ill-treating the victim or was recklesss as to whether he was doing so.

The DFM said . . . [that ill-treatment may include] "the unlawful imposition of a punishment or the deliberate and improper withholding of benefits. The imposition of necessary or proper duties and the exaction of their performance will not constitute this offence even though the duties are arduous or hazardous or both." . . .

The DFM did not accept the submission of the appellant's counsel that the conduct was appropriate conduct for the purpose of conducting training and appropriate to increase Lt Good's officer qualities and toughen him up for the completing of his duties to the best abilities of a platoon commander. . . . The DFM concluded that the conduct amounted to ill-treatment, and that the necessary mental element had been proved. . . .

The term "ill-treats" is not defined in the DFD Act. It is an ordinary English word and not a technical term. Its dictionary meaning is "to treat badly or cruelly" (Macquarie). According to same dictionary "cruelly" means "indifferent to, or taking pleasure in, the pain or discomfort of another." . . . Mere causation of physical pain or mental suffering could not necessarily constitute ill-treatment. Physical pain is often inflicted for the benefit of the person upon whom it is inflicted. Dental treatment and surgical operations are examples.

For present purposes, the word takes its flavour from its context in a statue concerning military discipline. Of necessity, life in the armed forces can involve hardships and hazards not encountered in civilian life. Service personnel have to be trained to cope mentally and physically with the demands of wartime. Conduct which would be regarded as ill-treatment in civilian employment might be necessary and reasonable, indeed essential, as part of military training. Long route marches, unarmed combat training and survival course are some examples. But obviously there are limits. The armed forces, like all other sections of Australian society, are subject to the rule of law.

Whether conduct is ill-treatment within the meaning of s 34 of the DFD Act will depend on a careful assessment of all the circumstances, always bearing in mind the military environment in which the question arises. The conduct must be considered objectively. At least the following considerations would be relevant:

(i) Was the conduct likely to result in the person holding inferior rank suffering physical or mental ill-effects of more than a transient nature?

(ii) Did the conduct have a purpose related to the proper functioning of the armed forces?

(iii) Was the conduct cruel, vindictive, discriminatory or humiliating?

It follows from the foregoing that the fact that Lt Good underwent an experience that was exhausting and accompanied by some measure of pain and discomfort in itself did not necessarily establish that he was ill-treated by the appellant within the meaning of s 34. The evidence disclosed a number of uncontested facts and circumstances, some of which were the subject of express findings but others of which were not adverted to by the DFM in his reasons for decision:

(i) The appellant did not bear Lt Good any ill feeling;

(ii) No injury of any significant nature was suffered by Lt Good;

(iii) A Medical Corps NCO (Cpl Gorman) was present. The appellant told him to ensure that Lt Good was in no distress or had any problems;

(iv) Cpl Gorman saw Lt Good throughout the day and was satisfied he was not suffering ill effects;

(v) Lt Good was provided with water throughout the day;

(vi) There was a military purpose for the appellant's conduct.

To expand on the last point, it needs to be kept in mind that the events occurred in a jungle warfare training exercise involving infantrymen of the Regular Army. Subject to obvious limitations, such an exercise needs to be, as far as possible, a realistic approximation of conditions soldiers would encounter in warfare. . . .

[T]he purpose of toughening up is self-evidently a military purpose and the more so in the present case in that it related to all the appellant's platoon commanders and not just Lt Good. There is no suggestion in this case of the kind of malicious brutality commonly referred to as bastardisation. Toughening up, either for individuals or units, is an essential part of military training, as in route marches, physical training, and the like. We do not understand how characterising the appellant's purpose as the toughening up of Lt Good could lead to the conclusion that it was an improper purpose and one that made the appellant's conduct amount to ill-treatment. . . .

[I]t was not open on the evidence for the DFM to find that the conduct of the appellant amounted to ill-treatment of Lt Good within the meaning of s 34. . . .

UNITED STATES v. CARSON
United States Court of Appeals for the Armed Forces
57 M.J. 410 (C.A.A.F. 2002)

JUDGE EFFRON delivered the opinion of the Court.

A general court-martial composed of a military judge sitting alone convicted appellant, contrary to his pleas, of five specifications of maltreatment and three specifications of indecent exposure, in violation of Articles 93 and 134, Uniform Code of Military Justice (UCMJ), 10 U.S.C. §§ 893 and 934. He was sentenced to a bad-conduct discharge, confinement for forty-two months, and reduction to E-1. The convening authority approved the sentence as adjudged. . . . The Court of Criminal Appeals affirmed the findings and sentence. 55 M.J. 656 (2001).

On appellant's petition, we granted review of the following issue:

WHETHER THE ARMY COURT OF CRIMINAL APPEALS ERRED WHEN IT HELD SPECIFICATION 7 OF CHARGE III (MALTREATMENT) WAS LEGALLY SUFFICIENT WHEN THERE WAS NO EVIDENCE TO SHOW THAT APPELLANT'S ACTIONS CAUSED THE ALLEGED VICTIM ANY PHYSICAL OR MENTAL PAIN OR SUFFERING.

For the reasons discussed below, we affirm.

I. Facts

A. Trial

Appellant pleaded not guilty to a variety of charges and specifications alleging fraternization with junior enlisted personnel, dereliction of duty, maltreatment of subordinates, sodomy, indecent acts, and indecent exposure — all taking place over an 18-month period from late-1996 to mid-1998. He was acquitted of many of these specifications and was convicted of several others, including an allegation that he had maltreated Private (PVT) G, a person subject to his orders, by exposing his penis to her.

During the period at issue, appellant was the supervising desk sergeant in a military police (MP) station, and his victims were young enlisted female MPs. PVT G, who was 20 years old, had been in the Army for less than one year, and was serving in her first permanent duty assignment as an MP. Appellant was her duty supervisor during her shift. In her direct testimony, PVT G described an incident that occurred in the MP station on June 3, 1998, at 1:00 a.m., in which appellant twice exposed his penis to her while purporting to change clothes in the bathroom. In each instance, appellant — clothed only in black socks and a brown T-shirt that went "[m]aybe a little past his waist" — expressly drew PVT G's attention to himself while his penis was exposed. Appellant made no effort to cover himself on either occasion.

PVT G acknowledged on cross-examination that appellant did not touch her or make any sexual comments to her, and that she did not report appellant's conduct to anyone until 4:00 or 5:00 p.m., even though her shift ended at 6:00 a.m. In the interim, however, she told another young female MP what had transpired. She testified that she was "shocked" and "bother[ed]" by the exposure, and felt like "a victim."

At the conclusion of the prosecution's case, the defense moved for a finding of not guilty on the maltreatment and attempted fraternization charges. With respect to the maltreatment charges, defense counsel argued that even if the testimony of the prosecution witnesses was believable, "it certainly does not rise to the level of maltreatment, as defined and required by the elements within Article 93, UCMJ. . . ." After noting that "several of the witnesses . . . [testified that they were] not disturbed or distressed, and sometimes not even offended, by the behavior[,]" defense counsel argued that the alleged victims "have not experienced the anguish that the cases refer to. *Hanson* [*United States v. Hanson,* 30 M.J. 1198 (A.F.C.M.R. 1990)] talks about mental suffering, mental cruelty, physical cruelty or suffering, and looking at the maltreatment standard would be some level of pain, some suffering that's caused, that simply hasn't been satisfied by any testimony or any evidence that we've heard presented by the [G]overnment today. . . ."

In response, the trial counsel argued that under the definition of maltreatment in the Manual for Courts-Martial, the prosecution is not required to prove that the victims were harmed emotionally or physically. *See* Paragraph 17c(2), Part IV, Manual for Courts-Martial, United States (2000 ed.). The prosecution further argued that the Manual provides for "an objective standard[,] and the subjective belief of the . . . victim witness . . . has borderline relevance, at most. . . ." The military judge asked whether the prosecution was required to prove that there was "some perception of unwanted treatment by the actual victim in order for it to constitute maltreatment [.]" Trial counsel responded that although there was sufficient evidence to meet a subjective standard, the UCMJ and the Manual did not require proof of the subjective perception of the victim. *See id.* (the "maltreatment, although not necessarily physical, must be measured by an objective standard").

After dismissing one of the maltreatment specifications, the military judge, without further comment, denied the motion with respect to the remaining six maltreatment specifications and the fraternization charge. During closing arguments, the assistant defense counsel asserted that PVT G's view of appellant's exposed penis was unintended — an "accident" under the circumstances. The assistant defense counsel also contended that none of the alleged maltreatment victims, including PVT G, had been maltreated. He argued:

> They are not victims in the true sense of that word; they are not traumatized by this. There was no physical malady which has been put upon them; there is no mental anguish which they have really suffered from as a result of this. It does not rise to the level of maltreatment, as that is meant under the Uniform Code of Military Justice. . . . Being a little uncomfortable and being bothered a little bit, Your Honor, is not being maltreated by your senior non-commissioned officer. There needs to be more. Maltreatment is in the Uniform Code of Military Justice to make sure people like drill sergeants don't physically abuse their soldiers; not to make sure that soldiers who are made a little uncomfortable by NCOs can have recourse in a court of law against them.

The military judge was not persuaded, and found appellant guilty of five of the remaining six maltreatment specifications, with minor modifications. . . . .

II. Proof of Maltreatment Under Article 93

A. The Statute, the Manual, and the Military Judges' Benchbook

Article 93, UCMJ, proscribes "cruelty toward, or oppression or maltreatment of, any person subject to [the accused's] orders. . . ." The explanation of maltreatment in the Manual, states: "The cruelty, oppression, or maltreatment, although not necessarily physical, must be measured by an objective standard." Paragraph 17c(2), Part IV, Manual, *supra.* The current provision is based upon the guidance in prior editions of the Manual, which provided that the cruelty, oppression, or maltreatment "must be real, although not necessarily physical." Drafters' Analysis of Punitive Articles, Manual, *supra,* at A23-6; *see also* Paragraph 172, Manual for Courts-Martial, United States, 1969 (Rev. ed.); Paragraph 172, Manual for Courts-Martial, United States, 1951. The current Manual also states that "sexual harassment may constitute this offense," defining "sexual harassment" as including "influencing, offering to influence, or threatening the career, pay, or job of another person in exchange for sexual favors, and deliberate or repeated offensive comments or gestures of a sexual nature." Paragraph 17c(2), Part IV, Manual, *supra.* The Drafters' Analysis of Punitive Articles notes that "[t]he example of sexual harassment was added [in 1984] because some forms of such conduct are nonphysical maltreatment." Manual, *supra* at A23-6. The Military Judges' Benchbook contains a nonbinding model instruction describing maltreatment as "unwarranted, harmful, abusive, rough, or other unjustifiable treatment which, under all the circumstances . . .

results in mental or physical pain or suffering." Military Judges' Benchbook, Dept. of the Army Pamphlet 27-9 (Apr. 1, 2001) ("Benchbook").

B. Judicial Consideration

The question of whether actual victim harm is required under Article 93, UCMJ, has been discussed in a number of judicial opinions. In *United States v. Finch,* 22 C.M.R. 698, 700 (N.B.R. 1956), the appellant, who was in charge of prisoner detail, ordered the prisoners to kick and strike each other with their fists. The court upheld the conviction, observing that even if some of the witnesses regarded the treatment as "horseplay" and no one was physically harmed, the conduct amounted to maltreatment because it was improper for the accused to subject persons under his control to such "ill befitting treatment." *Id.* at 701.

United States v. Hanson, 30 M.J. 1198, 1200 (A.F.C.M.R. 1990), concerned a maltreatment conviction of an officer who made repeated sexual remarks and gestures to his subordinates in the duty environment over an extended period of time. At trial, the accused said that he was simply joking, and that his words and actions were designed to establish informal and effective office relationships. *See id.* at 1200-01. On appeal, he stressed that the testimony of his subordinates demonstrated that they did not take his words and actions literally as an invitation to engage in sexual activity. *Id.* The court rejected his argument, describing maltreatment as a general intent offense that may be proved by an objective view of the language or gestures without regard to the subjective intent of the accused. *Id.* In the course of providing a general description of the offense, the court noted the Benchbook's instruction that the "offense occurs when the treatment, viewed objectively, results in physical or mental pain or suffering. . . ." *Id.* at 1201. The court emphasized the need to consider the "totality" of the circumstances, noting:

> Appropriate conduct can only be discerned by examination of the relevant surrounding circumstances. For example, what is condoned in a professional athletes' locker room may well be highly offensive in a house of worship. A certain amount of banter and even profanity in a military office is normally acceptable and, even when done in "poor taste," will only rarely rise to the level of criminal misconduct.

Id. The court concluded that it was "clear from the totality of . . . [Captain Hanson's] actions that his conduct was so abusive and unwarranted as to support his conviction for maltreatment." *Id.*

In *United States v. Rutko,* 36 M.J. 798, 798 (A.C.M.R. 1993), a noncommissioned officer was convicted of a number of offenses, including consensual and nonconsensual sexual acts, and maltreatment of military subordinates. On appeal, one of the issues concerned the legal and factual sufficiency of the evidence with respect to the maltreatment specifications. *Id.* at 801. In the course of providing an overview of the offense, the Army court noted that the elements of the offense, under Para. 17b, Part IV, Manual for Courts-Martial, United States, 1984, as well as the explanation in Para. 17c(2), indicate that the maltreatment need not be physical, and that it includes sexual harassment. *Id.* at 801. Citing *Hanson, supra,* the court further stated that maltreatment "is a general intent crime," and noted that "the offense occurs when the treatment, viewed objectively, results in physical or mental pain or suffering and is abusive or otherwise unwarranted, unjustified and unnecessary for any lawful purpose." *Id.* Without discussing whether there was any physical or mental pain or suffering in the case, the court concluded that the appellant's actions constituted maltreatment:

> [He] used his position and prestige as the first sergeant to target soldiers in his unit to lure to his room to take advantage of them for unwarranted and unlawful sexual acts. We find that using a superior military position to induce soldiers to commit unwanted sexual acts is maltreatment.

Id.

In *United States v. Harris,* 41 M.J. 890, 891 (Army Ct. Crim. App.1995), the Army court considered the conviction of a noncommissioned officer for rape and maltreatment of a subordinate. The court reversed the appellant's conviction on the ground that exclusion of evidence relevant to consent constituted prejudicial error. *Id.* at 894. In the context of describing the offense of maltreatment, the court noted the reference in *Rutko* to physical or mental pain or suffering. *Id.* The court focused its decision, however, on the issue of consent and did not rely on the presence or absence of evidence regarding pain or suffering. *Id.*

In a subsequent case, the Navy-Marine Corps Court of Criminal Appeals held that proof of actual pain or suffering is not required in a maltreatment prosecution. *United States v. Goddard,* 47 M.J. 581, 584 (N-M. Ct. Crim. App. 1997) [hereinafter *Goddard I*], *vacated on other grounds upon reconsideration,* 54 M.J. 763 (N-M. Ct. Crim. App. 2000) [hereinafter *Goddard II*]. *Goddard I* sustained the conviction of a noncommissioned officer who engaged in "adulterous, indecent sexual activity with a subordinate, on duty, at least partially in uniform, on the floor of his unit's administrative office. . . ." *Id.* at 586. After stating that "in the naval service, specific findings of actual physical or mental pain or suffering on the part of any particular victim have never been required." *Id.* at 584 (citations omitted). The court added: "We recognize that the Military Judge's Benchbook can be read to require that the ill treatment subjectively result in 'physical or mental pain or suffering,' presumably on the part of the victim. . . . We find no legal or historical basis for this requirement. . . ." *Id.* at 584 n. 4. The court held that "[the] appellant objectively maltreated Private S, subjecting her to physical and mental oppression by encouraging her to engage in unlawful acts, which were . . . unnecessary for any lawful purpose." *Id.* at 584.

Following a rehearing on sentence and further review, the Navy-Marine Corps court reconsidered and vacated its prior decision, and affirmed only a lesser included conviction for a simple disorder under Article 134, 10 U.S.C. § 834. *See United States v. Goddard,* 54 M.J. 763, 767 (2000) (*Goddard II*). In *Goddard II,* the court did not discuss physical or mental pain or suffering, or otherwise revisit the legal framework employed in *Goddard I*. The court concluded, however, that the evidence was legally and factually insufficient to prove maltreatment, holding that a consensual sexual relationship between a superior and a subordinate, in the absence of other factors, did not meet the objective standard for a maltreatment conviction. *Id.* at 767.

Our Court has not addressed the issue of whether actual mental or physical pain and suffering on the part of the victim is a necessary component of the prosecution's case under Article 93, UCMJ. . . .

III. Discussion

Although the words used by Congress to describe the proscribed conduct — "cruelty," "oppression," and "maltreatment" — depict situations that frequently involve physical or mental suffering on the part of the victim, the legislative history does not indicate that Congress sought to exclude cases meeting an objective standard.

We do not interpret the statute as precluding a conviction when, as an objective matter, the accused has engaged in behavior that amounts to cruelty, oppression, or maltreatment, even though the proof of harm or injury to the victim might fall short of demonstrating actual physical and mental pain or suffering. The essence of the offense is abuse of authority. Whether conduct constitutes "maltreatment" within the meaning of Article 93, UCMJ, in a particular case requires consideration of the specific facts and circumstances of that case. The decisions in *Finch, Hanson, Rutko,* and *Goddard I,* which employed an objective evaluation of the record, reflect this approach. We conclude that an objective evaluation of the totality of the circumstances represents the appropriate mode of analysis under Article 93, UCMJ.

In the present case, the Army court appropriately reviewed appellant's conviction for legal and factual sufficiency under an objective standard. Although not necessary to our decision, we note that in other instances in which Congress intended actual harm to be an element of an offense under the UCMJ, the statute clearly expressed such a requirement. *See, e.g.,* Article 128(b)(2), UCMJ, 10 U.S.C. §928(b)(2) (aggravated assault where grievous bodily harm is inflicted). *Cf.* Article 90(1), UCMJ, 10 U.S.C. §890(1) (assaulting a superior commissioned officer by "strik[ing]" that officer); Article 91(1), UCMJ, 10 U.S.C. §891(1) (insubordinate conduct toward warrant, noncommissioned, or petty officer by "strik[ing] or assault[ing]" the victim); Articles 118 and 119, UCMJ, 10 U.S.C. §§918 and 919 (murder and manslaughter, respectively, by "kill[ing]" the victim); Article 122, UCMJ, 10 U.S.C. §922 (robbery "by means of force or violence or fear of immediate or future injury"); Article 128, UCMJ (assault by "attempt[ing] or offer[ing] with unlawful force or violence to do bodily harm to another person").

We conclude that in a prosecution for maltreatment under Article 93, UCMJ, it is not necessary to prove physical or mental harm or suffering on the part of the victim, although proof of such harm or suffering may be an important aspect of proving that the conduct meets the objective standard. It is only necessary to show, as measured from an objective viewpoint in light of the totality of the circumstances, that the accused's actions reasonably could have caused physical or mental harm or suffering.

IV. Decision

The decision of the United States Army Court of Criminal Appeals is affirmed.

NOTES AND QUESTIONS

1. Compare *Quinn* and *Carson*, both of which involve maltreatment of subordinates. These cases involve distinctive types of maltreatment, both triggered by the potential for abuse of the power that military superiors wield over subordinates. The first involves excessively harsh training methods, the second involves sexual exploitation. Would *Carson* have been decided differently under the Australian standard? Would *Quinn* have met a different fate in the U.S. Court of Appeals for the Armed Forces?

2. In *Ainsworth v. United Kingdom*, No. 35095/97 (Eur. Comm'n on Hum. Rts. 1998), a lieutenant in the Royal Marines appealed his court-martial conviction to the European Commission on Human Rights. He was convicted of "conduct prejudicial to good order and discipline" for failing to supervise his troops adequately at a Troop Party. At the party, some underage recruits consumed excessive amounts of alcohol, and one died as a result. He was sentenced to dismissal from the service and he appealed on the grounds that his court-martial was not impartial and independent and that the charges against him were unforeseeable; the court agreed on the former and rejected the latter. Does the harm caused by the excessive drinking of subordinates constitute a foreseeable military crime? Does it constitute "maltreatment" of subordinates? Why or why not? Did the lieutenant act negligently under the New Zealand Defence Force Discipline Act section quoted above?

III.　DISORDERLY AND DISCREDITING ACTS

Defence Force Discipline Act, 1982, New Zealand

§ 60. Prejudicial conduct

(1) A defence member is guilty of an offence if the member engages in conduct that is likely to prejudice the discipline of, or bring discredit on, the Defence Force. Maximum punishment: Imprisonment for 3 months.

(2) An offence under this section is an offence of strict liability. . . .

(3) It is a defence if the member proves that he or she had a reasonable excuse for the relevant conduct.

Uniform Code of Military Justice

Article 134. General article

Though not specifically mentioned in this chapter, all disorders and neglects to the prejudice of good order and discipline in the armed forces, all conduct of a nature to bring discredit upon the armed forces, and crimes and offenses not capital, of which persons subject to this chapter may be guilty, shall be taken cognizance of by a general, special, or summary court-martial, according to the nature and degree of the offense, and shall be punished at the discretion of that court.

PARKER v. LEVY
Supreme Court of the United States
417 U.S. 733 (1974)

MR. JUSTICE REHNQUIST delivered the opinion of the Court.

Appellee Howard Levy, a physician, was a captain in the Army stationed at Fort Jackson, South Carolina. He had entered the Army under the so-called "Berry Plan," under which he agreed to serve for two years in the Armed Forces if permitted first to complete his medical training. From the time he entered on active duty in July 1965 until his trial by court-martial, he was assigned as Chief of the Dermatological Service of the United States Army Hospital at Fort Jackson. On June 2, 1967, appellee was convicted by a general court-martial of violations of Arts. 90, 133, and 134 of the Uniform Code of Military Justice, and sentenced to dismissal from the service, forfeiture of all pay and allowances, and confinement for three years at hard labor.

The facts upon which his conviction rests are virtually undisputed. The evidence admitted at his court-martial trial showed that one of the functions of the hospital to which appellee was assigned was that of training Special Forces aide men. As Chief of the Dermatological Service, appellee was to conduct a clinic for those aide men. In the late summer of 1966, it came to the attention of the hospital commander that the dermatology training of the students was unsatisfactory. After investigating the program and determining that appellee had totally neglected his duties, the commander called appellee to his office and personally handed him a written order to conduct the training. Appellee read the order, said that he understood it, but declared that he would not obey it because of his medical ethics. Appellee persisted in his refusal to obey the order, and later reviews of the program established that the training was still not being carried out.

During the same period of time, appellee made several public statements to enlisted personnel at the post, of which the following is representative:

> The United States is wrong in being involved in the Viet Nam War. I would refuse to go to Viet Nam if ordered to do so. I don't see why any colored soldier would go to Viet Nam: they should refuse to go to Viet Nam and if sent should refuse to fight because they are discriminated against and denied their freedom in the United States, and they are sacrificed and discriminated against in Viet Nam by being given all the hazardous duty and they are suffering the majority of casualties. If I were a colored soldier I would refuse to go to Viet Nam and if I were a colored soldier and were sent I would refuse to fight. Special Forces personnel are liars and thieves and killers of peasants and murderers of women and children.

Appellee's military superiors originally contemplated nonjudicial proceedings against him under Art. 15 of the Uniform Code of Military Justice, 10 U.S.C. § 815, but later determined that court-martial proceedings were appropriate. The specification under Art. 90 alleged that appellee willfully disobeyed the hospital commandant's order to establish the training program, in violation of that article, which punishes anyone subject to the Uniform Code of Military Justice who "willfully disobeys a lawful command of his superior commissioned officer." Statements to enlisted personnel were listed as specifications under the charges of violating Arts. 133 and 134 of the Code. Article 133 provides for the punishment of "conduct unbecoming an officer and a gentleman," while Art. 134 proscribes, inter alia, "all disorders and neglects to the prejudice of good order and discipline in the armed forces."

The specification under Art. 134 alleged that appellee "did, at Fort Jackson, South Carolina, . . . with design to promote disloyalty and disaffection among the troops, publicly utter [certain] statements to divers enlisted personnel at divers times . . . ." The specification under Art. 133 alleged that appellee did "while in the performance of his duties at the United States Army Hospital . . . wrongfully and dishonorably" make statements variously described as intemperate, defamatory, provoking, disloyal, contemptuous, and disrespectful to Special Forces personnel and to enlisted personnel who were patients or under his supervision.

Appellee was convicted by the courtmartial, and his conviction was sustained on his appeals within the military. After he had exhausted this avenue of relief, he sought federal habeas corpus in the United States District Court for the Middle District of Pennsylvania, challenging his court-martial conviction on a number of grounds. The District Court, on the basis of the voluminous record of the military proceedings and the argument of counsel, denied relief. It held that the "various articles of the Uniform Code of Military Justice are not unconstitutional for vagueness," citing several decisions of the United States Court of Military Appeals. The court rejected the balance of appellee's claims without addressing them individually, noting that the military tribunals had given fair consideration to them and that the role of the federal courts in reviewing court-martial proceedings was a limited one.

The Court of Appeals reversed, holding in a lengthy opinion that Arts. 133 and 134 are void for vagueness. 478 F.2d 772 (3d Cir. 1973). The court found little difficulty in concluding that "as measured by contemporary standards of vagueness applicable to statutes and ordinances governing civilians," the general articles "do not pass constitutional muster." It relied on such cases as *Grayned v. City of Rockford*, 408 U.S. 104 (1972); *Papachristou v. City of Jacksonville*, 405 U.S. 156 (1972); *Giaccio v. Pennsylvania*, 382 U.S. 399 (1966); *Coates v. City of Cincinnati*, 402 U.S. 611 (1971), and *Gelling v. Texas*, 343 U.S. 960 (1952). The Court of Appeals did not rule that appellee was punished for doing things he could not reasonably have known constituted conduct proscribed by Art. 133 or 134. Indeed, it recognized that his conduct fell within one of the examples of Art. 134 violations contained in the Manual for Courts-Martial, promulgated by the President by Executive Order. Nonetheless, relying chiefly on *Gooding v. Wilson*, 405 U.S. 518 (1972), the Court found the possibility that Arts. 133 and 134 would be applied to future conduct of others as to which there was insufficient warning, or which was within the area of protected First Amendment expression, was enough to give appellee standing to challenge both articles on their face. While it acknowledged that different standards might in some circumstances be applicable in considering vagueness challenges to provisions which govern the conduct of members of the Armed Forces, the Court saw in the case of Arts. 133 and 134 no "countervailing military considerations which justify the twisting of established standards of due process in order to hold inviolate these articles, so clearly repugnant under current constitutional values." Turning finally to appellee's conviction under Art. 90, the Court held that the joint consideration of Art. 90 charges with the charges under Arts. 133 and 134 gave rise to a "reasonable possibility" that appellee's right to a fair trial was prejudiced, so that a new trial was required. . . .

This Court has long recognized that the military is, by necessity, a specialized society separate from civilian society. We have also recognized that the military has, again by necessity, developed laws and traditions of its own during its long history. The differences between the military and civilian communities result from the fact that "it is the primary business of armies and navies to fight or ready to fight wars should the occasion arise." *United States ex rel. Toth v. Quarles*, 350 U.S. 11, 17 (1955). In *In re Grimley*, 137 U.S. 147, 153 (1890), the Court observed: "An army is not a deliberative body. It is the executive arm. Its law is that of obedience. No question can be left open as to the right to command in the officer, or the duty of obedience in the soldier." More recently we noted that "[t]he military constitutes a specialized community governed by a separate discipline from that of the civilian," *Orloff v. Willoughby*, 345 U.S. 83, 94 (1953), and that "the rights of men in the armed forces must perforce be conditioned to meet certain overriding demands of discipline and duty . . . ." *Burns v. Wilson*, 346 U.S. 137, 140 (1953) (plurality opinion). We have also recognized that a military officer holds a particular position of responsibility and command in the Armed Forces:

> The President's commission . . . recites that "reposing special trust and confidence in the patriotism, valor, fidelity and abilities" of the appointee he is named to the specified rank during the pleasure of the President.

Orloff v. Willoughby, supra, at 91.

Just as military society has been a society apart from civilian society, so "[m]ilitary law . . . is a jurisprudence which exists separate and apart from the law which governs in our federal judicial establishment." *Burns v. Wilson*, *supra*, at 140. And to maintain the discipline essential to perform its mission effectively, the military has developed what "may not unfitly be called the customary military law" or "general usage of the military service." *Martin v. Mott*, 12 Wheat. 19, 35 (1827). . . . An examination of the British antecedents of our military law shows that the military law of Britian had long contained the forebears of Arts. 133 and 134 in remarkably similar language. The Articles of the Earl of Essex (1642) provided that "[a]ll other faults, disorders and offenses, not mentioned in these Articles, shall be punished according to the general customs and laws of war." One of the British Articles of War of 1765 made punishable "all Disorders or Neglects . . . to the Prejudice of good Order and Military Discipline . . ." that were not mentioned in the other articles.

In 1775 the Continental Congress adopted this last article, along with 68 others for the governance of its army. The following year it was resolved by the Congress that "the committee on spies be directed to revise the rules and articles of war; this being a committee of five, consisting of John Adams, Thomas Jefferson, John Rutledge, James Wilson and R.R. Livingston . . . ." The article was included in the new set of articles prepared by the Committee, which Congress adopted on September 20, 1776. After being once more re-enacted without change in text in 1786, it was revised and expanded in 1806, omitting the terms "scandalous" and "infamous" . . . .

From 1806, it remained basically unchanged through numerous congressional re-enactments until it was enacted as Art. 133 of the Uniform Code of Military Justice in 1951. The British article punishing "all Disorders and Neglects . . ." was also adopted by the Continental Congress in 1775 and re-enacted in 1776. Except for a revision in 1916, which added the clause punishing "all conduct of a nature to bring discredit upon the military service," substantially the same language was preserved throughout the various re-enactments of this article too, until in 1951 it was enacted as Art. 134 of the Uniform Code of Military Justice.

Decisions of this Court during the last century have recognized that the longstanding customs and usages of the services impart accepted meaning to the seemingly imprecise standards of Arts. 133 and 134. In *Dynes v. Hoover*, 20 How. 65 (1857), this Court upheld the Navy's general article, which provided that "[a]ll crimes committed by persons belonging to the navy, which are not specified in the foregoing articles, shall be punished according to the laws and customs in such cases at sea." The Court reasoned:

> [W]hen offences and crimes are not given in terms or by definition, the want of it may be supplied by a comprehensive enactment, such as the 32d article of the rules for the government of the navy, which means that courts martial have jurisdiction of such crimes as are not specified, but which have been recognised to be crimes and offences by the usages in the navy of all nations, and that they shall be punished according to the laws and customs of the sea. Notwithstanding the apparent indeterminateness of such a provision, it is not liable to abuse; for what those crimes are, and how they are to be punished, is well known by practical men in the navy and army, and by those who have studied the law of courts martial, and the offences of which the different courts martial have cognizance.

Id., at 82.

. . . In *United States v. Fletcher*, 148 U.S. 84 (1893), the Court considered a court-martial conviction under what is now Art. 133, rejecting Captain Fletcher's claim that the court-marital could not properly have held that his refusal to pay a just debt was "conduct unbecoming an officer and a gentleman." The Court of Claims decision which the Court affirmed in *Fletcher* stressed the military's "higher code termed honor, which holds its society to stricter accountability" and with which those trained only in civilian law are unfamiliar. In *Swaim v. United States*, 165 U.S. 553 (1897), the Court affirmed another Court of Claims decision, this time refusing to disturb a court-martial conviction for conduct "to the prejudice of good order and military discipline" in violation of the Articles of War. The Court recognized the role of "unwritten law or usage" in giving meaning to the language of what is now Art. 134. . . .

II

The differences noted by this settled line of authority, first between the military community and the civilian community, and second between military law and civilian law, continue in the present day under the Uniform Code of Military Justice. That Code cannot be equated to a civilian criminal code. It, and the various versions of the Articles of War which have preceded it, regulate aspects of the conduct of members of the military which in the civilian sphere are left unregulated. While a civilian criminal code carves out a relatively small segment of potential conduct and declares it criminal, the Uniform Code of Military Justice essays more varied regulation of a much larger segment of the activities of the more tightly knit military community. In civilian life there is no legal sanction — civil or criminal — for failure to behave as an officer and a gentleman; in the military world, Art. 133 imposes such a sanction on a commissioned officer. The Code likewise imposes other sanctions for conduct that in civilian life is not subject to criminal penalties: disrespect toward superior commissioned officers, Art. 89, 10 U.S.C. § 889; cruelty toward, or oppression or maltreatment of subordinates, Art. 93, 10 U.S.C. § 893; negligent damaging, destruction, or wrongful disposition of military property of the United States, Art. 108, 10 U.S.C. § 908; improper hazarding of a vessel, Art. 110, 10 U.S.C. § 910; drunkenness on duty, Art. 112, 10 U.S.C. § 912; and malingering, Art. 115, 10 U.S.C. § 915.

But the other side of the coin is that the penalties provided in the Code vary from death and substantial penal confinement at one extreme to forms of administrative discipline which are below the threshold of what would normally be considered a criminal sanction at the other. . . .

In short, the Uniform Code of Military Justice regulates a far broader range of the conduct of military personnel than a typical state criminal code regulates of the conduct of civilians; but at the same time the enforcement of that Code in the area of minor offenses is often by sanctions which are more akin to administrative or civil sanctions than to civilian criminal ones.

The availability of these lesser sanctions is not surprising in view of the different relationship of the Government to members of the military. It is not only that of lawgiver to citizen, but also that of employer to employee. Indeed, unlike the civilian situation, the Government is often employer, landlord, provisioner, and lawgiver rolled into one. That relationship also reflects the different purposes of the two communities. As we observed in *In re Grimley*, 137 U.S., at 153, the military "is the executive arm" whose "law is that of obedience." While members of the military community enjoy many of the same rights and bear many of the same burdens as do members of the civilian community, within the military community there is simply not the same autonomy as there is in the larger civilian community. The military establishment is subject to the control of the civilian Commander in Chief and the civilian departmental heads under him, and its function is to carry out the policies made by those civilian superiors. . . .

III

Appellee urges that both Art. 133 and Art. 134 (the general article) are "void for vagueness" under the Due Process Clause of the Fifth Amendment and overbroad in violation of the First Amendment. We have recently said of the vagueness doctrine:

> The doctrine incorporates notions of fair notice or warning. Moreover, it requires legislatures to set reasonably clear guidelines for law enforcement officials and triers of fact in order to prevent "arbitrary and discriminatory enforcement." Where a statute's literal scope, unaided by a narrowing state court interpretation, is capable of reaching expression sheltered by the First Amendment, the doctrine demands a greater degree of specificity than in other contexts.

Smith v. Goguen, 415 U.S. 566, 572-573 (1974).

Each of these articles has been construed by the United States Court of Military Appeals or by other military authorities in such a manner as to at least partially narrow its otherwise broad scope.

The United States Court of Military Appeals has stated that Art. 134 must be judged "not in vacuo, but in the context in which the years have placed it." *United States v. Frantz*, 2 U.S.C.M.A. 161, 163, 7 C.M.R. 37, 39 (1953). Article 134 does not make "every irregular, mischievous, or improper act a court-martial offense," *United States v. Sadinsky*, 14 U.S.C.M.A. 563, 565, 34 C.M.R. 343, 345 (1964), but its reach is limited to conduct that is "directly and palpably — as distinguished from indirectly and remotely — prejudicial to good order and discipline." *Ibid*; *United States v. Holiday*, 4 U.S.C.M.A. 454, 456, 16 C.M.R. 28, 30 (1954). It applies only to calls for active opposition to the military policy of the United States, *United States v. Priest*, 21 U.S.C.M.A. 564, 45 C.M.R. 338 (1972), and does not reach all "[d]isagreement with, or objection to, a policy of the Government." *United States v. Harvey*, 19 U.S.C.M.A. 539, 544, 42 C.M.R. 141, 146 (1971).

The Manual for Courts-Martial restates these limitations on the scope of Art. 134. It goes on to say that "[c]ertain disloyal statements by military personnel" may be punishable under Art. 134. "Examples are utterances designed to promote disloyalty or disaffection among troops, as praising the enemy, attacking the war aims of the United States, or denouncing our form of government." Extensive additional interpretative materials are contained in the portions of the Manual devoted to Art. 134, which describe more than sixty illustrative offenses.

The Court of Military Appeals has likewise limited the scope of Art. 133. Quoting from W. Winthrop, Military Law and Precedents (2d ed. 1920), 711-712, that court has stated:

> . . . To constitute therefore the conduct here denounced, the act which forms the basis of the charge must have a double significance and effect. Though it need not amount to a crime, it must offend so seriously against law, justice, morality or decorum as to expose to disgrace, socially or as a man, the offender, and at the same time must be of such a nature or committed under such circumstances as to bring dishonor or disrepute upon the military profession which he represents.

United States v. Howe, 17 U.S.C.M.A. 165, 177-178, 37 C.M.R. 429, 441-442 (1967).

The effect of these constructions of Arts. 133 and 134 by the Court of Military Appeals and by other military authorities has been twofold: It has narrowed the very broad reach of the literal language of the articles, and at the same time has supplied considerable specificity by way of examples of the conduct which they cover. It would be idle to pretend that there are not areas within the general confines of the articles' language which have been left vague despite these narrowing constructions. But even though sizable areas of uncertainty as to the coverage of the articles may remain after their official interpretation by authoritative military sources, further content may be supplied even in these areas by less formalized custom and usage. *Dynes v. Hoover*, 20 How. 65 (1857). And there also cannot be the slightest doubt under the military precedents that there is a substantial range of conduct to which both articles clearly apply without vagueness or imprecision. . . . It is within that range that appellee's conduct squarely falls, as the Court of Appeals recognized: "Neither are we unmindful that the Manual for Courts-Martial offers as an example of an offense under Article 134, 'praising the enemy, attacking the war aims of the United States, or denouncing our form of government.' With the possible exception of the statement that 'Special Forces personnel are liars and thieves and killers of peasants and murderers of women and children,' it would appear that each statement for which [Levy] was court-martialed could fall within the example given in the Manual." 478 F.2d, at 794. . . .

For the reasons which differentiate military society from civilian society, we think Congress is permitted to legislate both with greater breadth and with greater flexibility when prescribing the rules by which the former shall be governed than it is when prescribing rules for the latter. But each of these differentiations relates to how strict a test of vagueness shall be applied in judging a particular criminal statute. None of them suggests that one who has received fair warning of the criminality of his own conduct from the statute in question is nonetheless entitled to attack it because the language would not give similar fair warning with respect to other conduct which might be within its broad and literal ambit. One to whose conduct a statute clearly applies may not successfully challenge it for vagueness.

Because of the factors differentiating military society from civilian society, we hold that the proper standard of review for a vagueness challenge to the articles of the Code is the standard which applies to criminal statutes regulating economic affairs. Clearly, that standard is met here. . . . "Void for vagueness" simply means that criminal responsibility should not attach where one could not reasonably understand that his contemplated conduct is proscribed. *United States v. Harriss*, 347 U.S. 612, 617 (1954). In determining the sufficiency of the notice a statute must of necessity be examined in the light of the conduct with which a defendant is charged. *Robinson v. United States*, 324 U.S. 282 (1945).

Since appellee could have had no reasonable doubt that his public statements urging Negro enlisted men not to go to Vietnam if ordered to do so were both "unbecoming an officer and a gentleman," and "to the prejudice of good order and discipline in the armed forces," in violation of the provisions of Art. 133 and Art. 134, respectively, his challenge to them as unconstitutionally vague under the Due Process Clause of the Fifth Amendment must fail.

We likewise reject appellee's contention that Arts. 133 and 134 are facially invalid because of their "over-breadth." ... While the members of the military are not excluded from the protection granted by the First Amendment, the different character of the military community and of the military mission requires a different application of those protections. ...

Reversed.

MR. JUSTICE BLACKMUN, with whom THE CHIEF JUSTICE joins, concurring.

I wholly concur in the Court's opinion. ... In actuality, what is at issue here are concepts of "right" and "wrong" and whether the civil law can accommodate, in special circumstances, a system of law which expects more of the individual in the context of a broader variety of relationships than one finds in civilian life. ... The subtle airs that govern the command relationship are not always capable of specification. The general articles are essential not only to punish patently criminal conduct, but also to foster an orderly and dutiful fighting force. One need only read the history of the permissive — and shortlived — regime of the Soviet Army in the early days of the Russian Revolution to know that command indulgence of an undisciplined rank and file can decimate a fighting force. Moreover, the fearful specter of arbitrary enforcement of the articles, the engine of the dissent, is disabled, in my view, by the elaborate system of military justice that Congress has provided to servicemen, and by the self-evident, and self-selective, factor that commanders who are arbitrary with their charges will not produce the efficient and effective military organization this county needs and demands for its defense. ...

MR. JUSTICE STEWART, with whom MR. JUSTICE DOUGLAS and MR. JUSTICE BRENNAN join, dissenting.

Article 133 of the Uniform Code of Military Justice, 10 U.S.C. § 933, makes it a criminal offense to engage in "conduct unbecoming an officer and a gentleman." Article 134, 10 U.S.C. § 934 makes criminal "all disorders and neglects to the prejudice of good order and discipline in the armed forces" and "all conduct of a nature to bring discredit upon the armed forces." The Court today, reversing a unanimous judgment of the Court of Appeals, upholds the constitutionality of these statutes. I find it hard to imagine criminal statutes more patently unconstitutional than these vague and uncertain general articles, and I would, accordingly, affirm the judgment before us. ...

The clause in Art. 134 prohibiting all "crimes and offenses not capital" applies only to crimes and offenses proscribed by Congress. *See* Manual for Courts-Martial ¶ 213(e) (1969) (hereinafter sometimes referred to as Manual). *Cf. Grafton v. United States*, 206 U.S. 333. As such, this clause is simply assimilative, like 18 U.S.C. § 13, and is not the subject of the vagueness attack mounted by appellee on the balance of Art. 134. *See generally* Wiener, *Are the General Military Articles Unconstitutionally Vague?*, 54 A.B.A.J. 357, 358; Note, *Taps for the Real Catch-22*, 81 Yale L.J. 1518 n.3.

While only Art. 134 is expressly termed the "general article," Arts. 133 and 134 are commonly known as the "general articles" and will be so referred to herein.

I

As many decisions of this Court make clear, vague statutes suffer from at least two fatal constitutional defects. First, by failing to provide fair notice of precisely what acts are forbidden, a vague statute "violates the first essential of due process of law." *Connally v. General Construction Co.*, 269 U.S. 385, 391. As the Court put the matter in *Lanzetta v. New Jersey*, 306 U.S. 451, 453: "No one may be required at peril of life, liberty or property to speculate as to the meaning of penal statutes. All are entitled to be informed as to what the State commands or forbids." "Words which are vague and fluid . . . may be as much of a trap for the innocent as the ancient laws of Caligula." *United States v. Cardiff*, 344 U.S. 174, 176.

"The constitutional requirement of definiteness is violated by a criminal statute that fails to give a person of ordinary intelligence fair notice that his contemplated conduct is forbidden by the statute. The underlying principle is that no man shall be held criminally responsible for conduct which he could not reasonably understand to be proscribed."

Secondly, vague statutes offend due process by failing to provide explicit standards for those who enforce them thus allowing discriminatory and arbitrary enforcement. *Papachristou v. City of Jacksonville*, 405 U.S. 156, 165-171. "A vague law impermissibly delegates basic policy matters to policemen, judges, and juries for resolution on an ad hoc and subjective basis . . . ." *Grayned v. City of Rockford*, 408 U.S. 104, 108-109. The absence of specificity in a criminal statute invites abuse on the part of prosecuting officials, who are left free to harass any individuals or groups who may be the object of official displeasure.

It is plain that Arts. 133 and 134 are vague on their face; indeed, the opinion of the Court does not seriously contend to the contrary. Men of common intelligence — including judges of both military and civilian courts — must necessarily speculate as to what such terms as "conduct unbecoming an officer and a gentleman" and "conduct of a nature to bring discredit upon the armed forces" really mean. In the past, this Court has held unconstitutional statutes penalizing "misconduct," conduct that was "annoying," "reprehensible," or "prejudicial to the best interests" of a city, and it is significant that military courts have resorted to several of these very terms in describing the sort of acts proscribed by Arts. 133 and 134.

Facially vague statutes may, of course, be saved from unconstitutionality by narrowing judicial construction. But I cannot conclude, as does the Court, . . . that the facial vagueness of the general articles has been cured by the relevant opinions of either the Court of Military Appeals or any other military tribunal. In attempting to give meaning to the amorphous words of the statutes, the Court of Military Appeals has repeatedly turned to Winthrop's Military Law and Precedents, an 1886 treatise. That work describes "conduct unbecoming an officer and a gentleman" in the following manner:

> To constitute therefore the conduct here denounced, the act which forms the basis of the charge must have a double significance and effect. Though it need not amount to a crime, it must offend so seriously against law, justice, morality or decorum as to expose of disgrace,

socially or as a man, the offender, and at the same time must be of such a nature or committed under such circumstances as to bring dishonor or disrepute upon the military profession which he represents.

Such authoritative publications as The Officer's Guide do little better in defining "conduct unbecoming an officer and a gentleman":

> There are certain moral attributes which belong to the ideal officer and the gentleman, a lack of which is indicated by acts of dishonesty or unfair dealing, of indecency or indecorum, or of lawlessness, injustice, or cruelty. Not every one can be expected to meet ideal standards or to possess the attributes in the exact degree demanded by the standards of his own time; but there is a limit of tolerance below which the individual standards in these respects of an officer or cadet cannot fall without his being morally unfit to be an officer or cadet or to be considered a gentleman. This article contemplates such conduct by an officer or cadet which, taking all the circumstances into consideration, satisfactorily shows such moral unfitness.

R. Reynolds, The Officer's Guide 435-436 (1969 rev.).

This language is substantially repeated in Manual ¶ 212.

. . . At best, the limiting constructions referred to by the Court represent a valiant but unavailing effort to read some specificity into hopelessly vague laws. Winthrop's definitions may be slightly different in wording from Arts. 133 and 134, but they are not different in kind, for they suffer from the same vagueness as the statutes to which they refer.

If there be any doubt as to the absence of truly limiting constructions of the general articles, it is swiftly dispelled by even the most cursory review of convictions under them in the military courts. Article 133 has been recently employed to punish such widely disparate conduct as dishonorable failure to repay debts, selling whiskey at an unconscionable price to an enlisted man, cheating at cards, and having an extramarital affair. Article 134 has been given an even wider sweep, having been applied to sexual acts with a chicken, window peeping in a trailer park, and cheating while calling bingo numbers. Convictions such as these leave little doubt that "[a]n infinite variety of other conduct, limited only by the scope of a commander's creativity or spleen, can be made the subject of court-martial under these articles." Sherman, *The Civilianization of Military Law*, 22 Maine L.Rev. 3, 80.

In short, the general articles are in practice as well as theory "catch-alls," designed to allow prosecutions for practically any conduct that may offend the sensibilities of a military commander. Not every prosecution of course, results in a conviction, and the military courts have sometimes overturned convictions when the conduct involved was so marginally related to military discipline as to offend even the loosest interpretations of the General Articles. But these circumstances can hardly be thought to validate the otherwise vague statutes. As the Court said in *United States v. Reese*, 92 U.S. 214, 221: "It would certainly be dangerous if the legislature could set a net large enough to catch all possible offenders, and leave it to the courts to step inside and say who could be rightfully detained, and who should be set at large." At best, the General

Articles are just such a net, and suffer from all the vices that our previous decisions condemn. . . .

Perhaps in recognition of the essential vagueness of the general articles, the Court today adopts several rather periphrastic approaches to the problem before us. Whatever the apparent vagueness of these statutes to us civilians, we are told, they are models of clarity to "practical men in the navy and army." . . .

It might well have been true in 1858 or even 1902 that those in the Armed Services knew, through a combination of military custom and instinct, what sorts of acts fell within the purview of the general articles. But times have surely changed. Throughout much of this country's early history, the standing army and navy numbered in the hundreds. The cadre was small, professional, and voluntary. The military was a unique society, isolated from the mainstream of civilian life, and it is at least plausible to suppose that the volunteer in that era understood what conduct was prohibited by the general articles.

It is obvious that the Army into which Dr. Levy entered was far different. It was part of a military establishment whose members numbered in the millions, a large percentage of whom were conscripts or draft-induced volunteers, with no prior military experience and little expectation of remaining beyond their initial period of obligation. Levy was precisely such an individual, a draft-induced volunteer whose military indoctrination was minimal, at best. To presume that he and others like him who served during the Vietnam era were so imbued with the ancient traditions of the military as to comprehend the arcane meaning of the general articles is to engage in an act of judicial fantasy. In my view, we do a grave disservice to citizen soldiers in subjecting them to the uncertain regime of Arts. 133 and 134 simply because these provisions did not offend the sensibilities of the federal judiciary in a wholly different period of our history. In today's vastly "altered historic environment," the *Dynes* case and its progeny have become constitutional anachronisms, and I would retire them from active service. . . .

It is perhaps appropriate to add a final word. I do not for one moment denigrate the importance of our inherited tradition that the commissioned officers of our military forces are expected to be men of honor, nor do I doubt the necessity that servicemen generally must be orderly and dutiful. An efficient and effective military organization depends in large part upon the character and quality of its personnel, particularly its leadership. The internal loyalty and mutual reliance indispensable to the ultimate effectiveness of any military organization can exist only among people who can be counted on to do their duty.

It is, therefore, not only legitimate but essential that in matters of promotion, retention, duty assignment, and internal discipline, evaluations must repeatedly be made of a serviceman's basic character as reflected in his deportment, whether he be an enlisted man or a commissioned officer. But we deal here with criminal statutes. And I cannot believe that such meaningless statutes as these can be used to send men to prison under a Constitution that guarantees due process of law.

STUART v. CHIEF OF GENERAL STAFF
Defence Force Discipline Appeal Tribunal, Australia
133 A.L.R. 513 (1995)

[In considering the conviction of a lieutenant colonel prosecuted for both losing service property and for a violation of section 60 of the Defence Force Discipline Act 1982 by behaving "in a manner likely to prejudice the discipline of, or bring discredit upon, the Defence Force," the Defence Force Discipline Appeal Tribunal explained the nature and history of crimes under the "general article":]

The offence created by section 60 is an old one. Although expressed in different language to its precursors, it is the successor to the old charge of engaging in conduct to the prejudice of good order and military discipline. For instance, the provision of the Army Act (44 and 45 Victoria c.58) comparable to section 60 of the Act was section 40 which provided:

Conduct to the Prejudice of Military Discipline:

> Every person subject to military law who commits any of the following offences: that is to say: is guilty of any act, conduct, disorder or neglect to the prejudice of good order and military discipline, shall be [guilty of an offence and] liable to suffer a term of imprisonment or other less punishment.

The current legislation in the United Kingdom is the Army Act 1955, section 69, as amended by the Armed Forces Act 1971 and the Armed Forces Act 1986. Section 69 reads:

> Any person subject to military law who is guilty, whether by any act or omission or otherwise, of conduct to the prejudice of good order and military discipline shall, on conviction by court-martial, be liable to imprisonment for a term not exceeding two years or any less punishment provided by this Act.

Charges of this same kind have been present in the military codes of Australia and other countries for many years: see, for example, Article 134 (General Article) of the United States Uniform Code of Military Justice. . . .

Conduct likely to prejudice the good order and the discipline of the Defence Force may take many forms. It is impossible, indeed unwise, to attempt any exhaustive definition of the words employed in section 60. The Manual of Military Law 1941 (Aust 2d) at 427 contains a list of instances of offences said to be not uncommonly the subject of charges under the equivalent section of the Army Act. . . . The type of conduct which has been included in the phrase has been considered by courts and military tribunals not infrequently. . . .

Historically, the offence has been cast always in wide terms, as it is with section 60. The words of the section are clear. It is for the courts and military disciplinary tribunals when hearing charges under section 60 or appeals from convictions under that section to determine the application of the section in particular contexts. In my view it is unnecessary and unwise to substitute other words for those that appear in the section itself in an attempt to guide military personnel and Appeals Tribunals in construing and applying the section.

It was said in argument that, if interpreted literally, the terms of the section would make punishable all conduct which had a prejudicial effect on discipline however slight that effect and however indirect. I doubt the correctness of this proposition. For behaviour to be of such a kind as to be likely to prejudice the discipline of the Defence Force or likely to bring discredit upon it, would not embrace trivial behaviour, nor behaviour that could only remotely be said to be prejudicial to that discipline. . . .

NOTES AND QUESTIONS

1. How does a military service provide notice of the conduct prohibited by a crime like "conduct unbecoming an officer and a gentleman" or "conduct prejudicial to good order and discipline"? In *Parker v. Levy*, the dissenters do not share the majority's certainty that service members are aware of the boundaries of acceptable behavior. Is this a factual or a legal question? Do the changing demographics of military service play a role in answering the question?

2. Robert N. Strassfeld, *The Vietnam War on Trial: The Court-Martial of Dr. Howard B. Levy*, 1994 WIS. L. REV. 839, analyzes the case of Dr. Levy and places his court-martial into historical context. Professor Strassfeld points out that while the Supreme Court's opinion focused on the issue of vagueness, at court-martial the case was about far more than that relatively narrow legal question. At trial, Dr. Levy put the war itself on trial, an act of rebellion triggered by his background and experience in the Army:

> Dr. Howard Levy staunchly opposed U.S. involvement in the Vietnam War when he arrived at Fort Jackson, South Carolina, on July 13, 1965, to begin two years of active military duty. Subject to an expansive doctors' draft, Levy chose in 1962 to avail himself of the "Berry Plan." Under the Berry Plan, the Army deferred induction until a doctor had completed his medical specialty training and guaranteed him assignment within his medical specialty. Consequently, Levy was able to delay inevitable military service. His commitment, made without thought to Vietnam, did not come due until he completed his residency in 1965, during the escalation of U.S. involvement in Vietnam. Like many other draftees, Levy confronted what he saw as three dreary choices: flight to Canada, prison for refusing induction, or military service. Levy would subsequently say that he never considered going to Canada to be a palatable option and feared prison too much to refuse induction. Instead, he entered the Army hoping that the time would pass as painlessly as possible, but recognizing that his beliefs might eventually come into conflict with Army command.

> In the years between medical school and active duty, Levy's political views had evolved significantly. Once very much a part of the generation of the 1950s, Levy had come to describe himself politically as "liberal left." In interviews Levy has suggested various cultural influences from the fifties and early sixties that may have played a role in this

evolution, most notably the writings of C. Wright Mills, the beats, new wave cinema, and absurdist or avant-garde theater. More important were the images and ideas of the civil rights movement, coupled with the reality of poor people's medicine encountered by Levy during his residency. At Bellevue Hospital in particular, Levy saw the medical treatment available to the poor. He noted that his patient population was largely black or Puerto Rican and drew connections between what was occurring in the South and the experiences of poor nonwhites in the North.

As Levy's politics gravitated leftward, the U.S. widened its involvement in Vietnam. In August 1964, Congress provided President Johnson with what would prove to be a blank check for escalation, in the Tonkin Gulf Resolutions. As the time for Levy's military service approached, U.S. troop levels in Vietnam increased dramatically. By May 1965, U.S. combat strength in South Vietnam was more than 46,500. On July 28 of that year, Johnson publicly announced that he would immediately increase troop strength from 75,000 to 125,000, and secretly agreed to deploy an additional 50,000 troops.

In the meantime, stirrings of opposition to U.S. policy in Southeast Asia were beginning to occur. The first nationwide demonstration against the war, organized by Students for a Democratic Society, drew 25,000 protesters to Washington, D.C., on April 17, 1965. Antiwar teach-ins, beginning at the University of Michigan and spreading to other campuses, also marked that spring. By late 1964, Levy, having read sporadically but apparently widely about the war, concluded that the U.S. should immediately withdraw.

Opposition to U.S. Vietnam policy was but one reason that the match of Howard Levy and the Army was unpromising from the start. Levy was in important ways an atypical soldier, often to the Army's irritation.

Nonetheless, some of the tension between Levy and the Army was unexceptional within the medical corps. Levy was by his own admission lacking in matters of military dress and deportment. Among military doctors, however, Levy's failings in these areas were hardly remarkable, if slightly more pronounced than average. The military, in desperate need of doctors, and perhaps regarding them as different, tolerated in its doctors a high degree of deviation from accepted standards of military dress and manner. Yet a separate standard in these matters, along with such benefits as conferral of rank and more rapid promotion, did little to offset the resentment felt by drafted physicians. At Levy's court-martial, Lieutenant Colonel Richard Coppedge, Center Surgeon of the John F. Kennedy Center for Special Warfare from 1962 to 1966, testified that drafted physicians often resented the military. He noted that those doctors he spoke to at Fort Jackson about training Special Forces aidmen were apathetic, and he characterized their apathy as a "passive-aggressive reaction." The military retained few doctors once they fulfilled their obligated tour of duty. In addition to the usual inconveniences of military service and the reduced earnings endured by drafted physicians, the low morale of military doctors undoubtedly stemmed from the military medical bureaucracy's cramping of physician autonomy. The conflict between military medicine's stated goals of "preserv[ing] the fighting strength," and providing "the greatest good for the greatest number," and the doctors' allegiance to individual patients also contributed to morale problems. Yet another cause of low morale must have been the doctors' awareness that others of similar social and educational background had successfully avoided military service.

However typical Levy's casual approach to such military formalities as saluting and proper display of his insignia was among military doctors, his situation was distinctive in other important ways. At his trial, defense counsel offered evidence in mitigation to show that the Army sent Levy to Fort Jackson without his having undergone the normal course of basic training for doctors at Fort Sam Houston in Texas. Levy thus missed the normal socialization process that would have alerted him to military customs and helped him to internalize military norms. This gap in his training may have contributed to Levy's tin ear for military customs and practices.

Whether because of a tin ear, or simply indifference, Levy was not a typical officer. Soon after his arrival at Fort Jackson, Levy refused to join the Officers' Club, an apparently unprecedented act that caused considerable upset before the matter was resolved in Levy's favor. He seemed indifferent to rank and did not differentiate between what he said to enlisted men and what he said to officers. His willingness to cross the boundaries of rank was remarked upon too many times in the court-martial testimony to have produced mere indifference among many of his fellow officers.

Levy also crossed racial boundaries. On a Saturday morning in July shortly after Levy had arrived at Fort Jackson, he noticed a newspaper article that mentioned a campaign to register black voters in nearby Newberry County, South Carolina. Levy drove to Newberry, found the offices of the Summer Community Organization and Political Education ("SCOPE") project of the Southern Christian Leadership Conference ("SCLC"), and volunteered. That summer Levy spent his off-duty hours working in the Newberry County voter registration drive. After that project ended, Levy continued his civil rights activity as a volunteer with the South Carolina Voter Education Project ("VEP"). He also wrote for and assisted in the publication of Carolina Contrast, a newspaper published by the Voter Education Project. Moreover, in his day-to-day dealings with black soldiers at Fort Jackson, Levy paid no heed to racial boundaries. A point of controversy in his court-martial was Levy's assertion that the court-martial was set in motion to punish him for his civil rights activities. . . .

Finally, Levy was not reticent about his opposition to the Vietnam War. Having discovered that Army regulations, which would sometimes have required medical discharges if strictly adhered to, were being overlooked or deliberately ignored, he took advantage of such regulations to provide discharges for soldiers seeking a way out of the war. He also shared his views about the war with those willing (or perhaps, at times, obliged) to listen, without regard for the listeners' rank.

Strassfeld, 1994 WIS. L. REV. 839, 845-53. Should the military standards of discipline for doctors be different than those for other military officers? What conflicts does the practice of medicine create when combined the practice of war? For this issue in a more recent armed conflict, *see, e.g.*, Steven Miles, *Abu Ghraib: Its Legacy for Military Medicine*, 364 THE LANCET 725 (2004) (detailing complicity of U.S. military medical personnel in abuse of detainees in Iraq, Afghanistan, and Guantánamo Bay); M. Gregg Bloche & Jonathan H. Marks, *Doctors and Interrogators at Guantánamo Bay*, NEW ENG. J. MED. (June 22, 2005) (revealing that clinical confidentiality was violated in use of medical information in U.S. interrogations at Guantánamo Bay).

UNITED STATES v. ROGERS
United States Court of Appeals for the Armed Forces
54 M.J. 244 (C.A.A.F. 2000)

[The commander of the 90th Fighter Squadron, Lt. Col. Shelley E. Rogers, was convicted of conduct unbecoming an officer for "wrongfully and willfully develop[ing] an unprofessional relationship of inappropriate familiarity" with a female first lieutenant under his command. He challenged his conviction on the ground that the charges of conduct unbecoming an officer was too vague because it "failed to identify a relevant custom or regulation which prohibits relationships between officers." Excerpts below from the opinion of the Court of Appeals for the Armed Forces, which denied the appeal, review the history and legality of the military offense of "conduct unbecoming an officer and a gentleman."]

SENIOR JUDGE COX delivered the opinion of the Court.

. . . In its entirety, Article 133, UCMJ, 10 U.S.C sec. 933, provides:

Any commissioned officer, cadet, or midshipman who is convicted of conduct unbecoming an officer and a gentleman shall be punished as a court-martial may direct.

Thus, by its terms, Article 133 contains no requirement of proof of violation of a service regulation or custom. . . . Indeed, in the instant case, the specification . . . did not allege that appellant had violated a service regulation or custom. . . .

In *Parker v. Levy,* 417 U.S. 733 (1974), Article 133 survived a claim that it was "'void for vagueness' under the Due Process Clause of the Fifth Amendment and overbroad in violation of the First Amendment." The Supreme Court noted that our Court and other military courts had "narrowed the very broad reach of the literal language of the articles [Arts. 133 and 134], and at the same time ha[d] supplied considerable specificity by way of examples of the conduct which they cover." The Court cited approvingly our invocation of Colonel Winthrop's venerable observation on conduct unbecoming an officer:

> To constitute therefore the conduct here denounced, the act which forms the basis of the charge must have a double significance and effect. Though it need not amount to a crime, it must offend so seriously against law, justice, morality or decorum as to expose to disgrace, socially or as a man, the offender, and at the same time must be of such a nature or committed under such circumstances as to bring dishonor or disrepute upon the military profession which he represents.

William Winthrop, *Military Law and Precedents* 711-12 (2d ed.1920 Reprint); *see* 417 U.S. at 753-54.

The Supreme Court acknowledged, however, that "[i]t would be idle to pretend that there are not areas within the general confines of the articles' language which have been left vague despite these narrowing constructions." Where "areas of uncertainty as to the coverage of the articles . . . remain[ed]," the Court added that *"further content may be supplied . . . by less formalized custom and usage"* (emphasis added). Nothing in the opinion intimated that proof of a custom or usage was a requirement.

On the other hand, the Supreme Court noted "there is a substantial range of conduct to which both articles clearly apply without vagueness or imprecision." And the Court made it clear that an officer charged with an Article 133 offense must have fair notice that his or her conduct was punishable. . . .

In the instant case, there is no question that appellant was on notice of what sorts of relationships were impermissible. Albeit it was an apparently nonpunitive regulation, an Air Force Instruction in effect at the time of the charged conduct proscribed, and gave examples of, unprofessional relationships. It stated:

> *Relationships in the Same Chain of Command, the Same Unit, or a Closely Related Unit.* Personal relationships between members of different grades or positions within an organization or chain of command can easily become unprofessional. *Dating* and indebtedness commonly get out of hand because they appear to create favoritism or partiality. Consequently, *senior members should not date* or become personally obligated or indebted to *junior members.* This is also because seniors have, or are perceived to have, authority to influence the junior member's career.

Paragraph A1.3.1., AFI 36-2909 (20 Feb. 1995) (emphasis added).[2]

Further, as commander, appellant had occasion to both discuss and apply the standards relating to personal relationships. Cpt Lovrak [the officer assigned as a sponsor, or mentor, to the 1Lt Clemm, the female officer with whom the appellant was involved] testified that she and appellant had had "several" professional discussions on the subject, even before the deployment to Italy, particularly concerning a relationship that involved a senior noncommissioned officer. Appellant acknowledged in his testimony having "many discussions of professionalism" with Cpt Lovrak, "each one may have been

---

[2] [n.25] We decline to attempt to walk a line between "dating" and the evidence adduced at appellant's court-martial.

related to another act or incident." Appellant also had to deal with at least one relationship matter in Italy, involving enlisted members within 1Lt Clemm's intelligence section.

In sum, [this Court is asked to decide] whether the specification was unconstitutionally vague in failing to allege violation of a regulation or custom of the service which forbade a relationship such as his and 1Lt Clemm's. The Constitution, however, does not require that a regulation or custom of the service be established.

Obviously, there will be many gradations of relationships and associations between servicemembers that will not put the parties fairly on notice that the conduct might be inappropriate. However, as the Supreme Court suggested in *Parker v. Levy, supra,* there is certain conduct to which Article 133 "clearly appl[ies] without vagueness or imprecision." 417 U.S. at 754. Under the circumstances of this case, we are satisfied that appellant's conduct falls into this latter category. *See United States v. Frazier,* 34 M.J. 194 (C.M.A. 1992). Any officer would be on notice that this type of behavior was punishable.

RE ANNING
Defence Force Discipline Appeal Tribunal, Australia, 1990
DFDAT No. 5 of 1989

[In considering the appeal of a petty officer convicted for sexual harassment, the Australian Defence Force Discipline Appeal Tribunal remarked on the difficulty of prosecuting such cases and which charges under the military disciplinary code were most appropriate in cases of sexual misconduct:]

Before leaving this case, we should say that we are conscious of the problems facing the Services in dealing with cases of sexual harassment, particularly where rank differences are involved. The Services would not wish to lag behind general community standards in such matters. . . .

Although we have found that the words complained of in the first two charges in the present case were not, in law, provocative within the meaning of sub-section 33(d) of the Act [this statute defines the offence of using "insulting or provocative words to another person"], one can easily imagine language which, in given circumstances, would be provocative to anger and could provoke a disturbance. The type of derogatory personal remark which invites a retaliatory slap, even if that slap is unlikely to be delivered by a subordinate in all the circumstances, could be sufficient. A remark to another person about that person's low moral standards could well constitute insulting words.

However it may well be that section 60 [the Australian general article] would provide the more appropriate basis for a charge in most cases of sexual harassment. This Tribunal, differently constituted, has today given judgment rejecting an appeal in just such a case. In that matter, a male warrant officer on several occasions privately importuned a female member, working under his direction, to have sex with him. His defending counsel did not dispute that, if the alleged conduct was established, it amounted to a breach of section 60. It would certainly be difficult to maintain proper discipline between two people of different rank in such circumstances. It would also be difficult to maintain discipline generally if such conduct became widely known and the offender lost the respect of his subordinates.

When behaviour is sexist and objectionable but not such as to threaten discipline, and words used are not insulting or provocative in law, the case may well be one for counselling or reprimand rather than the laying of formal charges.

Service establishments must continue to be places where language can be robust without giving rise to disciplinary proceedings. For example, drill sergeants must be given some latitude in the way in which they speak to other ranks on parade who are clumsy or lazy or inattentive. This may even involve a degree of personal abuse which could prove embarrassing or annoying to the victim.

The line between what must be endured in the interests of discipline, and what goes so far that it actually imperils discipline, is one which those in authority may often have to draw. . . .

NOTES AND QUESTIONS

1. Does the general article, or the "conduct unbecoming" article, impose different constraints on a male soldier's conduct as opposed to a female officer's conduct? Is "prejudicial" conduct under the New Zealand code likely to be defined in the same way as violations of the U.S. code? Is this sort of military crime culture-specific?

2. In *United States v. Sadinsky*, 14 U.S.C.M.A. 563, 34 C.M.R. 343 (1964), the Court of Military Appeals addressed the issue of whether a specification alleging that a sailor "did, wrongfully and unlawfully, . . . through design jump from U.S.S. INTREPID (CVS-11) into the sea" stated an offense. The court held that this was in fact a recognized offense because it was easily distinguished from merely jumping overboard, which could be a lawful act in some circumstances. The court wrote:

> It was shown that the incident occurred in the early evening, as it was beginning to get dark. The ship was underway, in a rough sea, proceeding at the rate of approximately ten to fifteen knots. The accused and other members of the crew were standing on an elevator positioned at the flight deck, waiting for aircraft to come down. Accused had wagered a substantial amount with shipmates who did not believe he would jump, one of whom offered an additional sum if accused would do a backflip. He distributed his wallet and watch, along with other items, to his companions, so that they would not get wet. It would have been impossible to swim ashore and, prior to jumping, accused discussed the length of time it would take to rescue him. Further, he asked witnesses to say at any resulting inquiry that he slipped. Accused then jumped from the ship, and in fact did a backflip as he went over the side into the sea. The aircraft carrier did not stop to pick him up, but accused was subsequently recovered from the sea by a destroyer. . . .

As early as *United States v Snyder*, 1 U.S.C.M.A. 423, 4 C.M.R. 15, we indicated that the critical inquiry, with regard to the first category of offenses covered by Article 134, was whether the act was palpably and directly prejudicial to the good order and discipline of the service — this notwithstanding that the act was not otherwise denounced. That reasoning is equally applicable here and, as we have seen, it is clear the act committed by accused meets that test.

Sadinsky, 34 C.M.R. at 345-46. Sadinsky, a Navy airman recruit, was convicted of AWOL, missing movement, and breach of restriction in addition to an offense under the general article, and sentenced to a bad-conduct discharge, confinement for five months at hard labor, and partial forfeiture of pay. Given the circumstances, was this punishment appropriate to the crime? Did the Navy need the general article in order to punish Airman Recruit Sadinsky? Does his offense — an athletic feat of bravado as well as a reckless act (an intrepid leap from USS *Intrepid*?) — indicate his unfitness for military duty?

3. In many instances, offenses charged under a "general article" are part of a course of conduct that can also be charged as a specified crime. *Sadinsky* involved whether an act is "prejudicial to good order and discipline"; other cases address whether an act is "conduct of a nature to bring discredit upon the armed forces," which is a separate clause of the UCMJ's general article. Consider *United States v. Vaughan*, 58 M.J. 29 (C.A.A.F. 2003), which involved the question of whether child neglect, charged under the "service-discrediting" clause of the general article, that does not result in harm to the child is an offense under the UCMJ. The appellant pleaded guilty "to child neglect for leaving her 47-days-old daughter, SK, alone in her crib for six hours from 11:00 p.m. to 5:00 a.m. while she went to a club that was a 90-minute drive away." She was stationed at Spangdahlem Air Base, Germany, and lived nearby. Judge Baker writes for the court:

> Appellant challenges her conviction on three bases. First, she argues that she did not have notice that her conduct was subject to criminal sanction under Article 134 and that the specific charge and military judge's subsequent guidance, did not provide proper notice as to the specific elements of the offense. Second, she argues that her conduct falls outside the definition of child neglect because SK was not harmed by being left alone. Third, she argues that her actions were not service discrediting. We address each argument in turn. . . .

> Due process requires "fair notice" that an act is forbidden and subject to criminal sanction. . . . It also requires fair notice as to the standard applicable to the forbidden conduct. *Parker v. Levy*, 417 U.S. 733, 755 (1974). . . .

> . . . The question is whether Appellant had fair notice that leaving her child alone for six hours under the conditions presented, and without apparent harm, was subject to sanction under Article 134.

> Both sides agree that child neglect is not specifically listed in the *MCM* as an Article 134 offense. Therefore, we must look elsewhere to determine whether Appellant should have reasonably contemplated that her conduct was subject to criminal sanction, and not simply the moral condemnation that accompanies bad parenting. . . .

[Through reference to case law, state law, and custom and regulations, the court concludes that "appellant should reasonably have understood that her contemplated conduct was subject to military criminal sanction." The court also concludes that the military judge's definition of the elements of child neglect adhered to "military custom and regulation as well as a majority of state statutes," which require culpable neglect and not harm to the child."]

[W]e now look to Appellant's final contention that her conduct was not, in any event, service-discrediting and, therefore, not an offense under *MCM* Part IV, at para. 60.b. An unlawful act can serve to establish service discredit. As a result, the Government urges adoption of a per se rule of service discredit in the case of child neglect. However, given the range of conduct that might reasonably be charged under the specified elements above, inter alia, raising questions of fact regarding time, risk, and location, we decline to do so. . . .

We are satisfied, based on the facts of the case that Appellant's plea was provident regarding the service-discrediting element of the offense. Not only did Appellant violate service custom and the norms of many states, her actions while living abroad would not reflect well on the United States military. . . . The behavior of U.S. service members abroad is the face of the armed forces in many countries, and the reputation of the military is equally at stake worldwide.

Rogers, 58 M.J. at 30-36. Who must decide whether an act is "discrediting" to the service? Are some acts discrediting only if committed while "living abroad"? Chief Judge Crawford's concurring opinion asserts that all "generally recognized illegal conduct" should be deemed "per se service-discrediting." *Rogers*, 58 M.J. at 42. Consider the section below on adultery as you contemplate the ramifications of a rule that relies on such a category. Is adultery "generally recognized illegal conduct"?

4. The "service-discrediting" clause is a favorite of U.S. military prosecutors and its malleability is frequently challenged before the military's highest court. *See, e.g., United States v. Saunders*, 59 M.J. 1 (C.A.A.F. 2003) ("stalking" constitutes service-discrediting behavior); *United States v. Bivins*, 49 M.J. 328 (C.A.A.F. 1998) (permitting a bigamy prosecution even when elements of specified Article 134 bigamy not met); *United States v. Sullivan*, 42 M.J. 360 (C.A.A.F. 1995) (asserting that "any reasonable officer would know that asking strangers of the opposite sex intimate questions about their sexual activities, using a false name and a bogus publishing company as a cover, is service-discrediting conduct under Article 134"); *see generally United States v. Choate*, 32 M.J. 423, 425 (C.M.A. 1991) (explaining that "the specific elements of the crime" are "not particularly relevant" when the discrediting clause is at issue); *United States v. Davis*, 26 M.J. 445, 447 (C.M.A. 1988); *United States v. Padgett*, 48 M.J. 273 (C.A.A.F. 1998).

5. What function do unspecified crimes perform in military disciplinary systems? Is there an alternative to this sort of criminal regime, or is charging flexibility essential to the operation of a military justice system? Does the existence of a "general article" make it easier or more difficult for a military service to adapt to changing norms of social behavior?

IV. A CASE STUDY: ADULTERY

Manual for Courts-Martial, United States, Part IV, ¶ 62(c) (2002)

[Describing the offense of adultery under the general article, Article 134, UCMJ:]

(1) Nature of offense. Adultery is clearly unacceptable conduct, and it reflects adversely on the service record of the military member.

(2) Conduct prejudicial to good order and discipline or of a nature to bring discredit upon the armed forces. To constitute an offense under the UCMJ, the adulterous conduct must either be directly prejudicial to good order and discipline or service discrediting. Adulterous conduct that is directly prejudicial includes conduct that has an obvious, and measurably divisive effect on unit or organization discipline, morale, or cohesion, or is clearly detrimental to the authority or stature of or respect toward a servicemember. Adultery may also be service discrediting, even though the conduct is only indirectly or remotely prejudicial to good order and discipline. Discredit means to injure the reputation of the armed forces and includes adulterous conduct that has a tendency, because of its open or notorious nature, to bring the service into disrepute, make it subject to public ridicule, or lower it in public esteem. While adulterous conduct that is private and discreet in nature may not be service discrediting by this standard, under the circumstances, it may be determined to be conduct prejudicial to good order and discipline. Commanders should consider all relevant circumstances, including but not limited to the following factors, when determining whether adulterous acts are prejudicial to good order and discipline or are of a nature to bring discredit upon the armed forces:

(a) The accused's marital status, military rank, grade, or position;

(b) The co-actor's marital status, military rank, grade, and position, or relationship to the armed forces;

(c) The military status of the accused's spouse or the spouse of co-actor, or their relationship to the armed forces;

(d) The impact, if any, of the adulterous relationship on the ability of the accused, the co-actor, or the spouse of either to perform their duties in support of the armed forces;

(e) The misuse, if any, of government time and resources to facilitate the commission of the conduct;

(f) Whether the conduct persisted despite counseling or orders to desist; the flagrancy of the conduct, such as whether any notoriety ensued; and whether the adulterous act was accompanied by other violations of the UCMJ;

(g) The negative impact of the conduct on the units or organizations of the accused, the co-actor or the spouse of either of them, such as a detrimental effect on unit or organization morale, teamwork, and efficiency;

(h) Whether the accused or co-actor was legally separated; and

(i) Whether the adulterous misconduct involves an ongoing or recent relationship or is remote in time.

(3) Marriage. A marriage exists until it is dissolved in accordance with the laws of a competent state or foreign jurisdiction.

(4) Mistake of fact. A defense of mistake of fact exists if the accused had an honest and reasonable belief either that the accused and the co-actor were both unmarried, or that they were lawfully married to each other. If this defense is raised by the evidence, then the burden of proof is upon the United States to establish that the accused's belief was unreasonable or not honest.

Comments to Department of Defense on Adultery Policy
National Institute of Military Justice, Aug. 4, 1997

Should adultery be an offense under the Uniform Code of Military Justice? . . . Adultery is not prohibited *eo nomine* by any of the punitive articles, but rather has long been viewed as an offense under the general articles, and of course it is listed by the President in the *Manual for Courts-Martial.* . . .

[The decision about whether to criminalize adultery] should not only reflect a moral judgment, the traditional functions of the criminal law, and the special purposes of military criminal justice, but should also rest on empirical data, the overall approach of American criminal law to adultery as we approach the next century, and potential effect of decriminalization on other aspects of the social/legal structure of the Armed Forces of the United States. For example, given the special stresses which military service places on military families (especially in times of high tempo military operations), does it make sense to have a crime of adultery under military law even if it were not felt necessary to have such an offense in civilian criminal law? Conversely, is concern for the family truly served by criminalization, or does criminalization merely foster more lies and make healing of family structure even harder? . . .

Are there ways to channel the exercise of discretion in dealing with adultery, especially given the broad public and congressional sense that discretion has seemed to have been essentially unfettered in the past? . . .

Should there be a requirement that an individual be warned in writing to terminate an apparent adulterous relationship as a prerequisite to military criminal or administrative proceedings? . . . Should adultery be subject to military prosecution . . . only if it would be service-connected under the factors that were identified in *Relford v. Commandant*, 401 U.S. 355 (1971)? . . . Should adultery be an offense only in the case of commissioned officers? . . .

UNITED STATES v. JOHANNS
United States Court of Military Appeals
20 M.J. 155 (C.M.A. 1985)

EVERETT, CHIEF JUDGE:

I

Contrary to his pleas, Captain Michael A. Johanns was found guilty by general court-martial of four specifications of conduct unbecoming an officer, in violation of Article 133 of the Uniform Code of Military Justice, 10 U.S.C. § 933, and one specification of conduct prejudicial to good order and discipline or of a nature to bring discredit on the armed forces, in violation of Article 134, UCMJ, 10 U.S.C. § 934. The court members sentenced him to dismissal from the armed forces on July 2, 1982. The convening authority approved these findings of guilty and the sentence. The United States Air Force Court of Military Review on October 26, 1983, set aside three of the findings of guilty under Article 133 and ordered a rehearing on sentence on the remaining findings of guilty. 17 M.J. 862. A government motion for reconsideration of this decision was denied by that Court on December 7, 1983.

On December 16, 1983, the Judge Advocate General of the Air Force, pursuant to Article 67(b)(2), UCMJ, 10 U.S.C. § 867(b)(2), certified the following questions for review by this Court:

I

UNDER THE CIRCUMSTANCES OF THIS CASE, WAS THE COURT OF [MILITARY] REVIEW CORRECT IN NOT SUSTAINING CONVICTION OF CONDUCT UNBECOMING AN OFFICER IN VIOLATION OF ARTICLE 133 AS TO SPECIFICATIONS 2, 3, AND 4 OF CHARGE I?

II

IF THE FOREGOING IS ANSWERED IN THE AFFIRMATIVE, WAS THE COURT OF MILITARY REVIEW CORRECT IN NOT SUSTAINING A CONVICTION OF CONDUCT TO THE PREJUDICE OF GOOD ORDER IN VIOLATION OF ARTICLE 134 AS TO SPECIFICATIONS 2, 3 AND 4 OF CHARGE I?

Thereafter, on July 6, 1984, this Court granted the accused's cross-petition for review of the following question raised by appellate defense counsel:

III

WHETHER SPECIFICATION OF CHARGE I AND CHARGE II SHOULD HAVE BEEN DISMISSED AS THAT SPECIFICATION WAS MULTIPLICIOUS FOR FINDINGS PURPOSES WITH SPECIFICATION 1 OF CHARGE I.

The above questions were raised with respect to the findings of guilty entered at the accused's trial on the following charges and specifications:

CHARGE I: Violation of the Uniform Code of Military Justice, Article 133.

Specification 1: In that CAPTAIN MICHAEL A. JOHANNS, United States Air Force, 91st Strategic Missile Wing, did, at Minot Air Force Base, North Dakota, on or about 5 October 1981, wrongfully, dishonorably, and disgracefully have sexual intercourse with Donna R., Sergeant, United States Air Force, the said Sergeant Donna R. being, at that time, the lawful wife of an active duty enlisted member of the United States Air Force, contrary to the customs and traditions of the armed forces of the United States.

Specification 2: In that CAPTAIN MICHAEL A. JOHANNS, United States Air Force, 91st Strategic Missile Wing, did, at Minot Air Force Base, North Dakota, on or about 8 October 1981, wrongfully, dishonorably, and disgracefully fraternize and associate on terms of military equality with enlisted members of the United States Air Force, to wit: Sergeant Donna R., by going into the military quarters of the said Sergeant Donna R. at Minot Air Force Base, North Dakota and sharing the same bed with the said Sergeant Donna R. while the said Sergeant Donna R. was intoxicated and at a time when the said Sergeant Donna R. was the lawful wife of an enlisted member of the United States Air Force, contrary to the customs and traditions of the armed forces of the United States.

Specification 3: In that CAPTAIN MICHAEL A. JOHANNS, United States Air Force, 91st Strategic Missile Wing, did, at Minot, North Dakota, on three or four separate occasions during September, 1981, wrongfully, dishonorably, and disgracefully fraternize and associate on terms of military equality with Staff Sergeant, then Sergeant, Sheryl K., a female active duty enlisted member of the United States Air Force, by engaging in acts of sexual intercourse with the said Staff Sergeant, then Sergeant, Sheryl K., contrary to the customs and traditions of the armed forces of the United States.

Specification 4: In that CAPTAIN MICHAEL A. JOHANNS, United States Air Force, 91st Strategic Missile Wing, did, at Minot Air Force Base, North Dakota, on two or three occasions, during November, 1981, wrongfully, dishonorably, and disgracefully fraternize and associate on terms of military equality with Senior Airman Michelle P., then known as Senior Airman Michelle S., a female active duty enlisted member of the United States Air Force, by engaging in acts of sexual intercourse with the said Senior Airman Michelle P., then known as Senior Airman Michelle S., contrary to the customs and traditions of the armed forces of the United States.

CHARGE II: Violation of the Uniform Code of Military Justice, Article 134.

Specification: In that CAPTAIN MICHAEL A. JOHANNS, United States Air Force, 91st Strategic Missile Wing, did, at Minot Air Force Base, North Dakota, on or about 5 October 1981, wrongfully have sexual intercourse with Donna R., a married woman, not his wife.

The Court of Military Review in its decision below delineated the facts surrounding these offenses as follows:

. . . The accused was a single, 28 year old missile combat crew commander who had been stationed at Minot Air Force Base, North Dakota, since completion of training in 1978. The Officers' Open Mess at Minot was being redecorated; as a result, officers had been authorized to utilize the facilities of the Noncommissioned Officers' Open Mess. The accused availed himself of the opportunity and socialized at the NCO Club. There he met Sgt R. (who was married), SrA P. and SSgt K. He dated each and ultimately had sexual relations with them all. On one occasion, the accused and Sgt R. went on a date downtown, and thereafter returned to her house on base. Sgt. R. was intoxicated and therefore remembers nothing other than the next morning the accused was asleep next to her in her bed.

All this interaction was completely consensual, private, nondeviate, and sometimes instigated by the women involved. The accused was neither the commander nor supervisor of any of these enlisted members, and their respective relationships were not publicized. In the opinion of the enlisted women, the accused's activities were neither dishonorable nor service discrediting. The charges resulted from the apparently private, voluntary liaisons.

17 M.J. 864.

The Government had contended before the Court of Military Review that there was a custom in the Air Force which prohibited fraternization and made criminal "the association of officers with enlisted personnel on terms of military equality." However, the court below found "that at the time of the offenses in issue, there did not exist a clearcut standard for gauging so called 'fraternization' in the Air Force." *Id.* at 865. "Furthermore, the court specifically [found] that as a matter of fact and law the custom in the Air Force against fraternization has been so eroded as to make *criminal prosecution* against an officer for engaging in mutually voluntary, private, non-deviate sexual intercourse with an enlisted member, neither under his command nor supervision, unavailable." *Id.* at 869 (footnote omitted).

II

[Omitted is the court's discussion of *Parker v. Levy*.]

. . . A breach of a custom of the service may result in a violation of this clause of Article 134. In its legal sense the word "custom" imports something more than a method of procedure or a mode of conduct or behavior which is merely of frequent or usual occurrence. *Custom arises out of long established practices which by common consent have attained the force of law in the military or other community affected by them.* There can be no such thing as a custom that is contrary to existing law or regulation. *A custom which has not been adopted by existing statute or regulation ceases to exist when its observance has been long abandoned.* Many customs of the service are now set forth in regulations of the various armed forces. Violations of those customs should be charged under Article 92 as violations of the regulations in which they appear.

Para. 213b, Manual, *supra* (emphasis added). The language of the 1951 Manual for Courts-Martial is almost identical. *See* paras. 213 and 213b,

Manual for Courts-Martial, United States, 1951; *see also* paras. 182 and 183, Manual for Courts-Martial, United States Army, 1949 (discussing Articles of War 95 and 96). Interestingly, none of these three Manuals contains a form specification for "fraternization." *See* App. 6, 1969 Manual; App. 6c, 1951 Manual; App. 4, 1949 Manual, all *supra.*

Consistent with these Manual provisions, this Court has "indicated that Article 134, 10 U.S.C. § 934, is not intended 'to regulate the wholly private moral conduct of an individual.'" *See United States v. Berry*, 6 U.S.C.M.A. 609, 614, 20 C.M.R. 325, 330 (1956); *United States v. Snyder*, 1 U.S.C.M.A. 423, 427, 4 C.M.R. 15, 19 (1952). These pronouncements have been interpreted to mean that "[f]ornication in the absence of aggravating circumstances is recognized as not an offense under military law." *United States v. Wilson*, 32 C.M.R. 517, 518 (A.B.R. 1962). Certainly officers hold a special status, whereunder a higher standard of conduct is required of them by law and custom. *United States v. Means*, 10 M.J. 162 (C.M.A. 1981). Nonetheless, even for an officer, private fornication in the absence of some other aggravating circumstance would not seem subject to prosecution under Articles 133 and 134 — regardless of the moral censure to which this activity might be subject.

If the officer's sexual partner is an enlisted person, does this constitute sufficient aggravation to make private fornication subject to prosecution? For two reasons, the answer to this question depends on whether there was a custom proscribing this type of relationship. In the first place, if such a custom exists, violation of that custom would tend to have a much more direct and palpable effect on good order and discipline and would more seriously compromise the officer's standing. He would be perceived as flouting military authority — which, of course, no officer may do.

Second — and constitutionally more important — the existence of such a custom would provide notice to officers, so that they would have no reasonable doubt as to the legal requirements to which they are subject. Obviously, "not every social contact between an officer and enlisted man is or even can reasonably be prohibited. To do so would be inconsistent with our democratic concept of social relations and, probably, unavailing." *United States v. Pitasi*, 20 U.S.C.M.A. 601, 608, 44 C.M.R. 31, 38 (1971). Custom can help define which relationships between officers and enlisted persons are improper.

Customs differ among the armed services. Coast Guard customs and regulations still allow the wearing of a beard, as did the Navy until recently; but the other services require their members to be clean-shaven. In the Army, an officer still may not protect himself from rain with an umbrella; but in the Air Force this custom has been abandoned. Indeed, the Air Force — the most recently created of the armed services — has never honored some of the customs recognized in the senior services; and perhaps because both officers and airmen at one time served together in small flight crews, the barriers placed by custom between officers and enlisted persons have probably always been lower in that service than in the others.

Undoubtedly, the entry into the armed services of large numbers of "citizen soldiers" during World War II, the Korean War, and the Vietnam War led to abandonment of the observance of many military customs. *Cf.* para. 213a of the 1969 and 1951 Manuals, both *supra*. Moreover, since few women other than nurses served in uniform before World War II, there was little opportunity for custom to develop concerning officer-enlisted relationships where different sexes were involved. Indeed, as officer-enlisted marriages have been increasingly condoned by service directives, it has become increasingly difficult for servicepersons to infer that officer-enlisted dating and social contact — an inevitable prelude to wedlock — are forbidden by custom. The uncertainty as to the proper parameters of social contacts between officers and enlisted persons — especially when they are of different sexes — led this Court to comment fourteen years ago concerning fraternization: "While the drafting of an appropriate regulation might be difficult, we recommend it to the responsible military authorities." *United States v. Pitasi, supra* at 608, 44 C.M.R. at 38. Apparently, this suggestion was not heeded by the Air Force, for we have been cited to no directive of that service which specifically deals with fraternization or with the type of relationship in which Captain Johanns was involved. Moreover, as already noted, previous Manuals for Courts-Martial did not treat this topic — although a form specification for fraternization is now included in the 1984 Manual. *See* para. 83f, Part IV, Manual for Courts-Martial, United States, 1984.

The court below apparently determined that no custom of that service prohibited Captain Johanns' private sexual relationships with several enlisted women. In the face of this determination by a tribunal which has factfinding powers, it must be assumed that Johanns did not receive notice from an Air Force custom or long-established practice that his amorous activities might transgress Articles 133 and 134. Significantly, Captain Johanns made an effort to determine whether Air Force policy forbade sexual involvements with enlisted women. In response to his inquiry, his supervisor gave him a copy of an article in an Air Force publication which had been written by a highly regarded judge advocate. *See* Flatten, *Fraternization*, 10 Air Force Reporter 109 (1981). According to the Court of Military Review, "Our reading of this article reveals that the author believes there is no longer a violation of custom for an officer to 'fraternize' with an enlisted member, so long as they have no command or supervisory relationship." 17 M.J. at 869 n. 20.

Although the barriers separating officers and enlisted persons in the Air Force may be lower than in the other services, the problem of fraternization is not limited to the Air Force. In *United States v. Stocken*, 17 M.J. 826 (A.C.M.R. 1984), the United States Army Court of Military Review held defective two specifications under Article 134 alleging "fraternization" between a male staff sergeant and two female privates. In an opinion by Judge Yawn, the court observed:

> The conduct proscribed by the general article has always been confined to cases where the prejudice is direct and palpable. *Such conduct must be easily recognizable as criminal*; must have a direct and immediate adverse impact on discipline; and must be judged in the context in which the years have placed it . . . . The allegations against appellant fail to meet this test.

Id. at 829 (emphasis added).

Subsequently, on November 29, 1984, the Army issued new guidelines with examples in order to clarify the limitations on social contacts between officers and enlisted persons. *See* HQDA LTR 600- 84-2 (Letter from MG Robert M. Joyce, USA, The Adjutant General, November 23, 1984).

Obviously, clear directives as to permissible contacts between officers and enlisted persons will obviate the issues present in this case. Under the first amendment and also in light of the Supreme Court's interpretation of Article I, Section 8, Clause 14 of the Constitution in *O'Callahan v. Parker,* 395 U.S. 258 (1969), some social contacts may be constitutionally protected. For example, officers could not be prohibited from attending bona fide religious services with enlisted persons. *Cf. United States v. Nation,* 9 U.S.C.M.A. 724, 26 C.M.R. 504 (1958); *United States v. Wysong,* 9 U.S.C.M.A. 249, 26 C.M.R. 29 (1958); *United States v. Milldebrandt,* 8 U.S.C.M.A. 635, 25 C.M.R. 139 (1958). On the other hand, restrictions on contacts — male/female or otherwise — where there is a direct supervisory relationship, can be imposed. However, we need not speculate further about the legality of hypothetical directives that may be issued at some future time.

III

With respect to the case at bar, it appears that Captain Johanns lacked the notice from custom or otherwise which, even under the relaxed standard of review established by *Parker v. Levy, supra,* is constitutionally necessary to meet the due-process requirements of the fifth amendment. Therefore, the Court of Military Review properly dismissed specifications 2, 3, and 4 of Charge I; and the two certified questions must be answered in the affirmative. Because of multiplicity, Charge II and its specification must also be dismissed. *United States v. Rodriquez,* 18 M.J. 363 (C.M.A. 1984).

Accordingly, the decision of the United States Air Force Court of Military Review as Charge II and its specification is reversed; the findings of guilty theron are set aside and that Charge and its specification are dismissed. In all other respects, the decision below is affirmed.

UNITED STATES v. GREEN
United States Court of Appeals for the Armed Forces
64 M.J. 289 (C.A.A.F. 2007)

CHIEF JUDGE EFFRON delivered the opinion of the Court.

A general court-martial composed of a military judge sitting alone convicted Appellant, pursuant to mixed pleas, of cruelty and maltreatment (seven specifications), false official statement, assault consummated by a battery, indecent assault (two specifications), solicitation to commit adultery (two specifications), and adultery (three specifications), in violation of Articles 93, 107, 128, and 134, Uniform Code of Military Justice (UCMJ), 10 U.S.C. §§ 893, 907, 928, 934 (2000). The sentence adjudged by the court-martial included a bad-conduct discharge, confinement for thirteen months, forfeiture of all pay and allowances, and reduction to the lowest enlisted grade. The convening authority approved the findings and approved that portion of the sentence that provided for a bad-conduct discharge, confinement for thirteen months, and reduction to the lowest enlisted grade. The United States Army Court of Criminal Appeals affirmed in an unpublished opinion. *United States v. Green,* No. ARMY 20021126 (A. Ct. Crim. App. Mar. 20, 2006).

On Appellant's petition, we granted review of the following issue:

WHETHER THE MILITARY JUDGE VIOLATED APPELLANT'S DUE PROCESS RIGHTS WHEN HE SENTENCED HIM BASED UPON HIS PERSONAL RELIGIOUS BELIEFS RATHER THAN LEGITIMATE SENTENCING PRINCIPLES.

For the reasons set forth below, we affirm.

I. Judicial Comments During Sentencing

A court-martial has broad discretion to adjudicate the sentence, subject to the punishment limitations set forth in the UCMJ and the *Manual for Courts-Martial,* United States (*MCM*). Article 56, UCMJ, 10 U.S.C. § 856 (2000); Rule for Courts-Martial (R.C.M.) 1002. Sentencing information is developed in an adversarial proceeding, subject to evidentiary rules designed for the sentencing process. *See* R.C.M. 1001; *United States v. Mack,* 9 M.J. 300, 319 (C.M.A.1980); *MCM,* Analysis of the Rules for Courts-Martial app. 21 at A21-70 (2005 ed.) [hereinafter Drafters' Analysis]. As part of the sentencing process, the accused may make a sworn or unsworn statement. R.C.M. 1001(c)(2). Although an unsworn statement is not subject to cross-examination by trial counsel or examination by the court-martial, the prosecution may present facts in rebuttal. R.C.M. 1001(c)(2)(C). If a military judge erroneously permits consideration of inadmissible evidence during sentencing, the error is tested for prejudice. *See United States v. Hysong,* 47 M.J. 126, 126 (C.A.A.F. 1997); Article 59(a), UCMJ, 10 U.S.C. § 859(a) (2000). The court-martial must announce the terms of the sentence on the record. R.C.M. 1007. When the sentence is adjudicated by a court-martial panel, the president of the court-martial reads the sentence. *See* Dep't of the Army, Pamphlet 27-9, Legal Services, *Military Judges' Benchbook* ch. 2, § IV, para. 2-5-25 (2002) [hereinafter *Benchbook*]. When the court-martial is composed of a military judge sitting alone, the military judge reads the sentence. *Id.* at para. 2-4-1.

Although the 1951 *MCM* authorized the court-martial to include in the record "a brief statement of the reasons for the sentence," that provision was eliminated in 1969. *Compare MCM* para. 76.b.(4) (1951 ed.), *with MCM* para. 76.b.(4) (1969 rev. ed.). According to the Drafters' Analysis to the 1969 *MCM,* the provision was deleted to remove the potential for improper command influence that might flow if court-martial panel members felt obligated to justify the panel's decision to a convening authority. *See* Dep't of the Army, Pamphlet 27-2, *Analysis of Contents, Manual for Courts-Martial, United States, 1969, Revised Edition* ch. 13, para. 76.b.(4), at 13-9 (1970) (citing ch. 13, para. 74.f.(3), at 13-4). The Drafters' Analysis also noted that the 1969 change was not intended to preclude the military judge, in a bench trial, from setting forth reasons for the judge's decision. *See id.* at ch. 13, para. 74.f.(4), at 13-14. If the military judge comments on the sentence, the remarks may be reviewed on appeal to determine whether the military judge relied on inadmissible matter in determining the sentence. *See United States v. Hill*, 62 M.J. 271, 275 (C.A.A.F. 2006).

II. Appellant's Sentencing Proceeding

The prosecution's sentencing case focused on testimony from Appellant's victims concerning the details of the offenses and the harm caused by his conduct. The defense sentencing case sought to emphasize the positive aspects of Appellant's character. During the sentencing proceeding, defense counsel provided the military judge with a number of defense exhibits for identification, including a letter signed by Appellant's supervisors at a fast food establishment where Appellant held a part-time job. The letter, which described Appellant in very positive terms, observed that Appellant "always talks a great deal about his wife and four children and about his beliefs in God."

Prior to formally introducing the letter into evidence, defense counsel presented the testimony of a noncommissioned officer to demonstrate that several of the complainants had chosen not to make formal statements. The witness also testified that Appellant was a "good worker" and that he never personally observed Appellant engage in inappropriate sexual conduct. On cross-examination, the witness acknowledged that Appellant had talked "about being a Christian." When the trial counsel asked the witness to describe his "feelings on that," the defense counsel objected on the grounds of relevance. The trial counsel responded that the line of questioning was relevant because the witness would "talk about" Appellant "not being a Christian." The defense counsel countered that the questioning was "highly prejudicial" and that he did not "want any court to consider the religious aspects of what is going on in —."

Although the trial counsel attempted to interject that he was not addressing "the religious aspect," the military judge cut him off and directed his comments to defense counsel. The military judge observed that defense counsel had provided him with a document — the letter marked as a defense exhibit for identification — that "sort of indicates that the accused is a good Christian, God believing person." After observing that defense counsel did not disagree with his characterization of the letter, the military judge said "but I'll tell you what, even good Christians can make mistakes, okay, that's what the church is for, so I am not going to consider that aspect of it. Whether he's a good Christian or he's not a good Christian, okay." The trial counsel apparently viewed this exchange as a caution against pursuing the subject of religion, and revised his cross-examination to focus on the witness's opinion of Appellant's ethics and integrity. Subsequently, defense counsel introduced into evidence the letter from the supervisors at Appellant's part-time civilian job which included the comment that Appellant "always talks a great deal about his wife and four children and about his beliefs in God." Appellant made an unsworn statement in which he apologized to his victims and his family. He noted the high cost of his conduct, in terms of the cost to his career, his freedom, and his family. He also interjected matters of religion at several points:

Instead of giving my matters to God and seeking comfort with my wife I went [sic] the people that I was close to, they were the people I worked with daily. . . .

God has always been the center of my life but in my moment of distress I fell short of his glory. I pray for his forgiveness as I have repented and claimed my rightful place as his servant. . . .

[T]here is no excuse for what I have done and I sincerely apologize but I pray to God that I can have the opportunity to take care of my family and make it up to them.

Appellant faced a maximum sentence to confinement of twenty-five years and three months. *MCM* pt. IV, paras. 17.e., 31.e., 54.e.(1)(A), 62.e., 63.e., 105.e. (2005 ed.). In the quantum portion of the pretrial agreement, which the military judge did not review prior to announcing the sentence, the convening authority had agreed to a confinement cap of forty months if Appellant otherwise fulfilled the terms of the agreement. The prosecution argued for a sentence that would include confinement for five years. Defense counsel argued for a sentence limited to a punitive discharge and reduction to the lowest enlisted grade, with no confinement in light of Appellant's acceptance of guilt and his otherwise "credible and honorable service." The sentence announced by the military judge included thirteen months confinement.

Immediately prior to announcing the sentence, the military judge addressed Appellant to explain "why I think the sentence is appropriate for you." The military judge began with a description of basic sentencing principles, including rehabilitation, punishment, protection of society, preservation of good order and discipline in the military, and deterrence. *See Benchbook* ch. 2, § V, para. 2-5-21, § VI, para. 2-6-10. The military judge noted that the "weight I give any or all of these along with the other sentencing matters in this case, rest[s] solely within my discretion."

The military judge then turned to the harm Appellant's actions caused his victims, his family, and the Army. In particular, the military judge noted that Appellant abused his leadership role as a noncommissioned officer, caused his victims mental duress, damaged the Army's reputation, and caused the Army financial detriment because several of Appellant's victims testified that they would not reenlist.

In the course of addressing Appellant, the military judge made the comments which are the subject of the present appeal. After describing Appellant as "a predator" who operated "in secret," the military judge said: "Some of the documents I've seen describe you as God fearing, strong in your belief in God. The last time I looked there were 10 commandments. Apparently one of those, which addresses your actions, you must have missed in the reading."

The military judge characterized Appellant's crimes as betraying his family and the Army:

Trust and confidence was placed in you. You abused it. This Army's not high school, it is not a place for maltreating others. You do unto others as you would expect to be treated. That's the golden rule. My job is now to set the matter straight. Whatever I do cannot make up for what the soldiers experienced, to include having you as a leader.

In his concluding remarks, the military judge told Appellant that his actions "weren't mistakes, these were choices." He added:

> Every choice in life has a repercussion. It kind of reminds me of an old Charlie Daniels saying from a country music song. "You know what the problem [sic] in the world today is? People done gone and put their Bibles away. They're living by the law of the jungle, not the law of the land."

III. Discussion

Appellant contends that the military judge's comments: (1) reflected improper consideration of factors not relevant to sentencing; and (2) interjected the personal religious views of the military judge into the sentencing process, establishing an impermissible bias.

We review a military judge's consideration of sentencing factors under an abuse of discretion standard. *See United States v. McDonald*, 55 M.J. 173, 178 (C.A.A.F. 2001). We evaluate a claim of judicial bias by considering, in view of the sentencing proceeding as a whole, whether a reasonable person would doubt the court-martial's legality, fairness, and impartiality. *United States v. Burton*, 52 M.J. 223, 226 (C.A.A.F. 2000).

At the outset, we note that the military judge's comments during the prosecution's cross-examination of a defense witness do not demonstrate improper consideration of religion or bias. The military judge stated that he would not consider Appellant's fealty to religious principles, and the prosecution did not pursue the subject of religion.

A number of remarks made by the military judge during his explanation of the sentence directly addressed the subject of religion. The military judge observed that Appellant had "[a]pparently . . . missed" one of the "10 commandments" and that Appellant's conduct reminded him of the lament in a country music song that the "problem in the world today" is that people have "put their bibles away."

Even if we view his references to the "golden rule" as invoking a nonsectarian ethical concept, *see* Jeffrey Wattles, *The Golden Rule* 172-74 (1996), the other remarks have a specific religious connotation. The suggestion that Appellant had apparently overlooked one of the "10 commandments" represented a thinly veiled reference to Appellant's conviction for adultery, an offense specifically denounced in the Decalogue. *Exodus* 20:14; *Deuteronomy* 5:18. The quotations from the country music song expressly invoked a religious text.

A military judge may not interject his or her personal beliefs into the sentencing process. *See United States v. Bakker*, 925 F.2d 728, 740-41 (4th Cir. 1991). An accused, however, has a broad right during allocution to bring aspects of his or her personal life for consideration in extenuation or mitigation. *See* Drafters' Analysis app. 21 at A21-69 to A21-71; *United States v. Tschip*, 58 M.J. 275, 276 (C.A.A.F. 2003). An accused, for example, may attempt to demonstrate "repentance and readiness for rehabilitation." *See United States v. Warren*, 13 M.J. 278, 284 (C.M.A. 1982).

Just as an accused during sentencing may seek to depict a positive image by describing adherence to the tenets of a civic organization, an accused, such as the Appellant in this case, may attempt to convince the military judge that his or her religious practices and beliefs demonstrate repentance and readiness for rehabilitation. When the accused does so, the military judge may properly take into account the credibility and context of the accused's statement. *See Warren*, 13 M.J. at 284. The military judge must ensure that the evidence is considered for the appropriate purpose, and that the military judge does not interject his or her personal religious beliefs into the sentencing process. *See Bakker*, 925 F.2d at 740-41. In assessing the allegations of error in the present case, we take the following considerations into account. First, Appellant, who was convicted of numerous offenses, received a sentence which included confinement for only thirteen months. The adjudged confinement was far less than the authorized maximum of twenty-five years, the prosecution's request of five years, or the pretrial agreement cap of forty months. In that context, the sentence does not reflect prejudicial consideration of extraneous factors. Second, the subject of religion was not first interjected into the proceedings by the military judge. The defense initially raised the subject when counsel provided the military judge with a document indicating that Appellant would rely on matters of religion in the sentencing case. The defense subsequently interjected the subject of religion repeatedly into the proceedings through the introduction of a document that addressed Appellant's religion and through Appellant's unsworn statement. Third, when the prosecution sought to pursue the question of whether Appellant thought of himself as a "good Christian," the military judge expressly stated that he would not consider the Appellant's fealty to his religious tenets as a sentencing factor. Fourth, defense counsel did not object to the military judge's remarks. While a defense counsel might be reluctant to object to judicial remarks immediately prior to the announcement of the sentence, defense counsel had no reason to be reticent in challenging the impartiality of the military judge immediately thereafter if counsel perceived the remarks as reflecting consideration of improper factors or bias. *See Burton*, 52 M.J. at 226. Finally, we note that the military judge's sentencing remarks primarily discussed appropriate sentencing considerations, with incidental references to religion. The first two references involved matters of common knowledge, and the third referred to the lyrics of a popular song.

In context, and in the absence of defense objection, the military judge's remarks in the present case reflect a judge attempting to address Appellant's sentencing case, and do not reflect an effort to interject religion as either a sentencing factor or a matter of bias. *Compare Bakker*, 925 F.2d at 740-41 (trial judge impermissibly interjected his religious beliefs into the proceedings). The military judge's comments in their entirety evoked established sentencing principles and tied those principles to Appellant's actions and the effect of those actions on his victims, his family, and the Army. Appellant's unsworn statement provides a relevant context in which to view the military judge's comments, most of which were made in response to the unsworn statement. In light of the military judge's sentencing statement as a whole and the context of his references to religion, we conclude that if the military judge erred, any error was harmless.

IV. Decision

The decision of the United States Army Court of Criminal Appeals is affirmed.

NOTES AND QUESTIONS

1. Fraternization, adultery, sexual harassment, and sexual assault are often linked in allegations of sexual misconduct among military forces. Consider C. Quince Hopkins, *Rank Matters But Should Marriage?: Adultery, Fraternization, and Honor in the Military*, 9 UCLA WOMEN'S L.J. 177, 203-05 (1999):

> Numerous sex-related scandals have rocked the United States military. They include the Tailhook fiasco when, among other incidents, female members of the Air Force were forced to run a gauntlet where they were grabbed and harassed by male members of the Air Force, allegations of widespread sexual harassment of new recruits in military training facilities including military academies, and the possible disparate handling of the adultery charges against Lieutenant Kelly Flinn and General Joseph Ralston. In the wake of these scandals, the United States Secretary of Defense and the Joint Services Committee began reviewing military policies and practices related to various forms of sexual activity in the military.

> The Task Force's mission was to address policies and practices around "gender integrated training" (read: sexual harassment and rape), and "related morale and discipline issues" (read: fraternization and adultery). The Task Force presented its report on the first issue, gender integrated training, in early 1998. Secretary of Defense William Cohen issued orders on fraternization and adultery in July 1998. President Clinton's sexual escapades in the Oval Office subsequently brought into greater relief the disjuncture between civilian moral standards and the military's continuing sanctions, not to mention the double standard that applies thereby to soldiers in contrast to their Commander-in-Chief.

> Prosecutions of adultery in the military, whether through disciplinary action, discharge, or court-martial, are definitely on the rise. As one author has reported,

>> In the past five years, the Air Force, Army, Navy, and Marine Corps have court-martialed 900 men and women for charges that include adultery. In addition, the numbers of such prosecutions are growing within some branches of the service. . . . [A]dultery-related prosecutions in the Air Force grew from 36 in 1990 to 67 in 1996.

At the same time, civilian prosecutions for adultery are becoming obsolete. Why is the military increasingly prosecuting, discharging, or disciplining service members for adultery at the very time when adultery prosecutions in civilian courts have all but disappeared? Is this increased level of emphasis merely the result of integrating women into the armed forces, or does it reflect a slow-bubbling but increasing moral backlash in American society such that we can anticipate a similar wave of increasing civilian prosecutions in the future? Is prosecution of adultery generally consistent with the typical underlying rationales for military criminal prosecutions? We should grapple with how and why the military has come to this place of criminalizing conduct that is essentially no longer seen as criminal in the community it is sworn to protect.

2. In *United States v. Hickson*, 22 M.J. 146, 147 (C.M.A. 1986), Chief Judge Everett discussed the military's criminalization of adultery:

> In military law, the history of adultery and fornication is comparatively recent. Colonel Winthrop does not discuss these offenses in his treatise, *Military Laws and Precedents*. The Manuals for Courts-Martial contain no reference to these offenses prior to 1949. Section 127, Naval Courts and Boards (1937), notes that unlawful cohabitation, adultery, and fornication "are provided for under the 22d" Article for the Government of the Navy "and by 18 U.S. Code . . . 514, 516, 518," as those provisions read at that time. . . .
>
> In its discussion of these offenses, Naval Courts and Boards states that "[a]dultery comprises voluntary sexual intercourse" and that "[f]ornication is unlawful carnal knowledge by an unmarried person of other." Two form specifications are provided for adultery; the first alleging that the accused committed the offense "by having voluntary sexual intercourse with" a married woman; and the second alleging that the accused, "being then a married man, did . . . commit adultery by having voluntary sexual intercourse with a woman not his wife." A form specification for fornication alleged that the accused, "being then an unmarried man, did . . . commit fornication by having carnal knowledge of a woman." The same section refers to a lesser-included offense of "[s]candalous conduct tending to the destruction of good morals." Sec. 127.
>
> The Manual for Courts-Martial, U.S. Army, 1949, recognized adultery in the Table of Maximum Punishments and authorized a dishonorable discharge and confinement for 1 year for the offense. (Page 138.) Also, in Appendix 4, that Manual provided the following form specification for alleging adultery under Article of War 96:
>
> > 117. In that _____ (a married man) did, at _____, on or about _____ 19__, wrongfully have sexual intercourse with _____, (a married woman) (a woman) not his wife. *See United States v. Butler*, 5 C.M.R. 213, 215 (A.B.R.1952).
>
> The 1951 and the 1969 Manuals for Courts-Martial gave the same treatment to adultery in the Table of Maximum Punishments, and the

form specifications use language identical with the 1949 Manual for alleging violations of Article 134 of the Uniform Code. *See* para. 127c and App. 6(c), form specification 119, Manual for Courts-Martial, United States, 1951; para. 127c and App. 6(c), form specification 127, Manual for Courts-Martial, United States, 1969 (Revised edition). This specification contemplates that the crime of adultery has been committed if the accused has sexual intercourse with someone not his spouse when either of the parties is married to a third person.

In the 1984 Manual, adultery receives a slightly more extensive treatment. The elements of the offense are set out as well as acknowledgment of attempted adultery as a lesser-included offense. The maximum punishment is established, and a sample specification is provided. The Manual also contains an *"Explanation"* to the effect that "[a]dultery is not a lesser included offense of rape." *See* Part IV, para. 62, Manual for Courts-Martial, United States, 1984. In support of this proposition, the drafters' analysis cites *United States v. Ambalada,* 1 M.J. 1132 (N.C.M.R.), *pet. denied,* 3 M.J. 164 (1977). *See* App. 21, para. 62, 1984 Manual, *supra.* Again, the conduct proscribed is sexual intercourse between the accused and another person at a time when one of them was married to someone else.

The fact that adultery remains a viable offense against military law is clear from recent judicial action. In *United States v. Johanns,* 20 M.J. 155 (C.M.A.1985), the accused, an Air Force Captain, had been convicted of various offenses of adultery and fraternization. . . .

In summary, the treatment of adultery and fornication in military law seems to be this: (a) two persons are guilty of adultery whenever they engage in illicit sexual intercourse if either of them is married to a third person; (b) if unmarried, they are guilty of fornication whenever they engage in illicit sexual intercourse under circumstances in which the conduct is not strictly private; and (c) private sexual intercourse between unmarried persons is not punishable. This treatment is the same as that in some, but not most, states; but it differs from that in the Federal courts where, apart from trials under 18 U.S.C. § 13, these offenses no longer can be prosecuted.

How does Chief Judge Everett determine whether adultery is "a viable offense" against military law? Does the military significance of adultery rise to a level that makes it a military crime even when it is no longer a crime in — at least some — civil societies?

3. Does the retention of adultery as a separate criminal charge inject religion into military justice? The issue of religion in military service is a complex one. *See, e.g.,* Kenneth J. Schweiker, *Military Chaplains: Federally Funded Fanaticism and the United States Air Force Academy,* 8 RUTGERS J.L. & RELIGION 5 (2006) (assessing concerns over the legality of military chaplains' action at the U.S. Air Force Academy). *See also* Chapter 10, § II.

Chapter 9

MILITARY DEFENSES

This chapter explores military-specific defenses. Although the defenses used before courts-martial are similar to those used in civilian criminal trials, the special context of military service creates defenses not available to civilian defendants. Because the most notable of special military defenses, the defense of superior orders, is rooted in the military imperative for obedience, the first section below presents material on courts-martial for disobedience to orders, building on Chapter 7's study of military-only crimes. The second section turns to the defense of superior orders, a defense available only to service members accused of criminal acts, which exonerates some crimes committed at the order of a superior officer. The final section canvasses other defenses that operate distinctively in military courts, including condonation, necessity, duress, and the "good soldier" defense.

I. CRIMES OF DISOBEDIENCE

THAKUR v. UNION OF INDIA
Supreme Court of India
AIR 1987 S.C. 2386

Appellant, Ranjit Thakur, joined the Armed Services on September 7, 1972, and was, at the relevant time, a Signal Man in "4 Corps Operating Signal Regiment." Apparently, appellant had not commended himself well to respondent No. 4, who was the commanding officer of the regiment. On March 29, 1985, appellant was already serving out a sentence of 28 days' rigorous imprisonment for a punishment imposed on him for violating the norms for presenting representations to higher officers. Appellant is stated to have sent representation complaining of ill-treatment at the hands of respondent 4 directly to the higher officers. Appellant was punished for that by respondent 4. Appellant was held in the Quarterguard Cell in handcuffs to serve that sentence of rigorous imprisonment.

While so serving the sentence appellant is stated to have committed another offence on March 29, 1985, for which the punishment now impugned was handed down by respondent 4. The nature of this offence had better be excerpted from the charge-sheet itself: ". . . Disobeying a lawful command given by his superior officer in that he, at 15.30 hrs. on 29-5-1985 when ordered by [Ram Singh], the Orderly Officer of [his Regiment] to eat his food did not do so."

To try this offence a Summary Court-Martial was assembled the very next day. . . . A sentence of rigorous imprisonment for one year was imposed in pursuance of which appellant was immediately removed to the civil prison at

457

Tejpur to serve out the sentence. Appellant has served out the sentence. He was also dismissed from the service, with the added disqualification of being declared unfit for any future civil employment. . . .

[The appeal is upheld on grounds that basic "procedural safeguards" were not followed during the trial, since, contrary to specified rules, appellant was not asked whether he objected to being tried by the officer who presided at his Summary Court-Martial. But another of the asserted grounds for appeal was that appellant's refusal to accept food "did not amount to disobedience" of a lawful command of a superior. The court rejected that argument in a discussion that included the following explanation:]

The submission that a disregard of an order to eat food does not by itself amount to a disobedience to a lawful command . . . has to be examined in the context of the imperatives of the high and rigorous discipline to be maintained in the Armed Forces. Every aspect of the life of a soldier is regulated by discipline. Rejection of food might, under circumstances, amount to an indirect expression of remonstrance and resentment against the higher authority. To say that a mere refusal to eat food is an innocent, neutral act might be an oversimplification of the matter. Mere inaction need not always necessarily be neutral. Serious acts of calumny could be done in silence. A disregard of a direction to accept food might assume the complexion of disrespect to, and even defiance of, authority. But an unduly harsh and cruel reaction to the expression of the injured feelings may be counter-productive and even by itself be subversive of discipline. Appellant was perhaps expressing his anguish at what he considered an unjust and disproportionate punishment for airing his grievances before his superior officers. . . .

IN RE HLONGWANE
Council of Review, South Africa, 1999

On 5 March 1998 the applicant was convicted on a charge of contravening . . . Section 19(1) of the Military Discipline Code (MDC) in that he wrongfully and intentionally in wilful defiance of military authority disobeyed a lawful order given personally by his superior officer [Lt Col Peacock] in the execution of his duties, namely to remove an amulet ("isiphandla") he was wearing and which order he refused to obey. . . .

The evidence indicated that there was and apparently still is, an Army Order which stipulated that no bracelets, except a medic alert bracelet, may be worn. Copper bracelets may be worn only by virtue of a medical certificate supporting this. The bracelet which the applicant wore, was not one of those exceptions. His bracelet was a so-called "isiphandla" and related to his cultural beliefs.

The evidence also revealed that the OC [officer in command] of the Unit concerned, however, allowed the wearing of a "isiphandla," albeit in such a way that it should not be visible. There was, thus, some flexibility in the application of the Army Order concerned. Furthermore, the defence contended that the applicant had worn his "isiphandla" for a period of two months without ever being challenged on it and had all this time worn a short-sleeved shirt without his wearing it ever being challenged and it being covered.

The question arises whether Lt Col Peacock's instruction can be regarded as a *command* as contemplated in section 19(1) and (2) of the MDC. Section 19(1) MDC provides that *"[a]ny person who in wilful defiance of authority disobeys any lawful command . . . shall be guilty of an offence. . . ."* The dictionaries indicate that there is a correlation between a command and an order. Both amount to instructions being given by a superior to his/her subordinate. However, a command is seemingly treated in military context as something more direct and compelling than an order. The Military Dictionary of the SA National Defence Force explains the distinction as follows: *"Order: Communication, written or oral or by signal, which conveys instructions from a superior to a subordinate. An order implies discretion as to the details of execution, whereas a command does not."* It is evident that a command must be direct and specific. No ambiguity must exist regarding its execution.

In casu, Lt Col Peacock gave an order which conflicted with the orders/instructions given by the OC regarding the wearing of "isiphandla" by members of the Unit concerned. The Council is of the view that Lt Col Peacock's instruction cannot be construed as a command if it is in conflict with the OC's direction in this regard. Neither can Lt Col Peacock's instruction be regarded as a direct and specific command if the OC allowed a deviation from the original Army Order which was the foundation on which Lt Col Peacock had based his instruction/order.

The prosecution argued that Lt Col Peacock's instruction/order was in accordance with the Army Order and should, thus, be viewed as a command in conformity with that Order. This might be so, but the fact of the matter is that a reasonable doubt exists as to whether or not the said instruction can be regarded as a *specific and direct command* if it did not conform with his OC's accommodating and deviating instruction/order in this regard.

The Council has come to the conclusion that a reasonable doubt exists whether the instruction to remove the "isiphandla" can be regarded as a command as contemplated in section 19(1) of the MDC. . . . The Council condemns the conduct of Lt Col Peacock and the other members of the group who removed applicant's "isiphandla" by force. They should have called the Military Police. They did not behave as the officers and gentlemen they should be and which is required of them. Their actions toward the applicant are deplorable. The convictions and sentence should be set aside.

R. v. KIPLING
Court Martial Appeal Court, Canada, 2002
CMAC-437, 2002 CMAC 1

This appeal raises questions as to whether a member of the Canadian Armed Forces may be prosecuted under section 126 of the *National Defence Act* (RSC 1985, c. N-5) for refusing to submit to a vaccination when ordered to do so if, in the opinion of a military court, the vaccine was "unsafe and hazardous." . . .

The salient facts as to the respondent's conduct are not in dispute.

The respondent had been in the Armed Forces since 1973. At the time relevant to this proceeding he was a flight engineer with 435 Squadron. In early 1998 a detachment from the Squadron was ordered to go to the Middle East as part of a multi-national force deployed to put pressure on Iraq to comply with UN Security Council resolutions in respect of submitting to weapons inspections. The deployment of the respondent's unit was originally to Bahrain but while it was en route the destination was changed to Kuwait City, some 61 kilometres from the Iraq border. There was evidence that Canadian authorities had an intelligence assessment indicating that Iraq might use weaponised anthrax against the multinational forces if armed conflict ensued. On March 12, 1998 the Commander of the respondent's detachment ordered all personnel to undergo vaccination with an anthrax vaccine. The respondent refused to undergo such vaccination and on March 14, 1998, he was charged under section 126 of the *National Defence Act*. Section 126 provides as follows:

> Every person who, on receiving an order to submit to inoculation, re-inoculation, vaccination, re-vaccination, other immunization procedures, immunity tests, blood examination or treatment against any infectious disease, wilfully and without reasonable excuse disobeys that order is guilty of an offence and on conviction is liable to imprisonment for less than two years or to less punishment.

> Shortly thereafter he was deployed back to Canada because of his refusal. . . .

[Sergeant Kipling's counsel sought to bar his trial based on the *Charter of Rights and Freedoms*, arguing that the inoculation required "informed consent from the members of the Canadian Forces." He also argued that the vaccination violated Kipling's "rights to life, liberty, and security of the person, the right not to be subjected to cruel and unusual treatment, and the right to equal protection and equal benefit of the law." The military judge agreed and stayed the charge, ruling that:]

> There was no requirement [that Kipling] show that the vaccine was deadly or would have caused irreparable or incurable physical or psychological damages to our soldiers. It was sufficient and the court is satisfied on the balance of probabilities that the defence has successfully demonstrated that the anthrax vaccine contained in lot 020 [from which Sergeant Kipling would have been vaccinated] was unsafe and hazardous and could be responsible for the important symptoms reported by so many persons who received that vaccine.

> In those circumstances, the court concludes that the accused's right to life, liberty, and security of the person in section 7 of the *Charter of Rights and Freedoms* were infringed. And as the court stated earlier, the government, through its Department of National Defence and the Canadian Forces, could never be justified to impose inoculation of soldiers with an unsafe and dangerous vaccine as a limit of their rights under section 7.

[The Crown appealed the decision of the trial court to the Court Martial Appeal Court, which ordered a new trial before a new judge.]

I have concluded that this appeal must be allowed, the stay of prosecution set aside, and a new trial ordered. . . .

Section 126 does three things. First, it makes clear by implication that an order to submit to vaccination is an order authorized by Parliament under the *National Defence Act*. Secondly, it exposes to prosecution anyone who refuses to obey such an order. Thirdly, it allows that person, if tried under section 126, to raise the defence of "reasonable excuse". . . .

[The court points out that by preventing the trial from going forward, the trial court failed to build an adequate record for deciding whether or not the vaccine was safe. There were no briefs submitted and no conclusive evidence presented about the vaccine in the hearing on the defence's motion to bar trial because of the hazards of inoculation.]

The decision under section 7 of the Charter as taken by the trial judge was of extreme importance not only for its implication as to the use of a vaccine which, for example, had been licensed for use in the United States for 28 years prior to 1998, but also for the constitutional implications with respect to other laws in various Canadian jurisdictions which require immunization, quarantine, etc. The unwisdom of dealing with such grave matters in the kind of loose procedure employed here is obvious. As noted above, there was no proper written notice or clear oral definition of the issue which was in fact decided. It appears from the record as demonstrated that counsel for the respondent framed his issue orally in terms of the need for consent as a constitutional principle. This was the issue which the appellant thought it had to meet, and this was the issue upon which both parties presented evidence and cross-examined adverse witnesses. . . .

The learned military judge found that to order, in good faith and with reasonable care, the administration of a vaccine that in future some court might hold on the balance of probabilities to be unsafe, is *per se* a violation of section 7 as an invasion of a right to personal security. I think the parties would agree that forcible vaccination of an individual would *per se* be an infringement of the right to security, but that is not what was involved here. Sergeant Kipling was never vaccinated but sent home instead to face the consequences of a possible trial where it might be demonstrated that he had a "reasonable excuse" for refusing vaccination. . . .

A cursory review of the evidence reveals many other questions which should have been considered in determining whether the alleged invasion of "security" interests was nevertheless in accordance with the principles of fundamental justice. For example, were there balancing societal interests such as the defence of Canada and of Canadian interests abroad or the effectiveness and efficiency of the Canadian Forces? . . . The evidence in this case demonstrated some conflicting views of experts. All agreed that there are some short-term side effects from the vaccine for some people, and that there have been no studies of its long-term effects or indeed of many vaccines which continue to be used because the benefits outweigh any known risks. . . .

NOTES AND QUESTIONS

1. In 2003, a federal district court enjoined the military from administering the anthrax vaccine to military personnel and civilian contract employees of the Department of Defense who did not consent to the vaccination. *Doe v. Rumsfeld*, 297 F. Supp. 2d 119 (D.D.C. 2003); 341 F. Supp. 2d 1 (D.D.C. 2004), *remanded as moot*, 172 Fed. Appx. 327 (D.C. Cir. 2006). Should a civilian court be able to stop the military from vaccinating servicemembers? What public health and safety concerns justify invasive public health measures or judicial intervention in cases of potential biological weapons? What should be the limits of the military's authority to order mandatory vaccinations? *See also United States v. Washington*, 57 M.J. 394 (2002).

2. In *United States v. Robinson*, 20 C.M.R. 63 (1955), an enlistee who refused orders to work as a cook's helper relied on a federal statute that prohibits officers from using enlisted men as servants. That statute, derived from an 1870 act, established a rule that "[n]o officer shall use an enlisted man as a servant in any case whatever." The court explained that "the real purpose of the enactment was to prevent the use of enlisted men in assignments which contributed only to the convenience and personal benefit of individual officers and which had no reasonable connection with the efficient employment of the armed services as a fighting force." 20 C.M.R. at 68. Is this distinction between orders designed to provide "personal benefit" to an officer and orders intended to further "efficient employment" a useful one? Is the difference between what the South African court terms a "command" and an "order" similarly useful? What recourse does a soldier have if she or he does not want to obey an order or command? What are limits of what a commanding officer can order a subordinate to do?

3. In *R. v. Wisely* (2001) (unreported), a Summary Appeal Court at Bulford quashed a sentence of seven days of confinement imposed by a court-martial that convicted Signaller Bobby Lee Wisely for wilfully or through neglect disobeying an order to appear, sober, for a parade at 20.00 hours. The appeals court explained that the order "had been given at a time when the appellant was under the influence of intoxicating liquor, and in civilian clothes, and there was no evidence that the court could be satisfied that the appellant would have been sober by 20.00 hours, and therefore could not lawfully be required to parade in uniform and sober." If inability to comply with an order is a defense, should ignorance of an order also be a defense?

4. Consider *United States v. Tolkach*, 14 M.J. 239 (C.M.A. 1982), reviewing a conviction for driving while intoxicated and violating an Eighth Air Force regulation that banned consumption of alcohol by alert force and flying personnel while on duty. The convicted soldier claimed that the order was not properly "published," and therefore his knowledge of it should not be presumed. The court refers to the "old custom of publishing orders 'by sound of drum and trumpet, that no man may pretend ignorance,'" 14 M.J. at 242, and quotes Judge Latimer's opinion (concurring in part and dissenting in part) in *United States v. Curtin*, 26 C.M.R. 207, 215 (1958), on the necessity of relying on constructive, rather than personal knowledge, because "[t]he turnover of personnel is rapid, and the giving of personal orders to every individual is virtually impossible." In this case, the court helds that the order was not properly published, and the conviction for violating a lawful general order could not stand. Should the standard for knowledge be actual or constructive in these cases? What constitutes constructive notice?

II. THE DEFENSE OF SUPERIOR ORDERS

Military Penal Code
Austria

Art. 17 Lawfulness of not following orders

An act is not punishable [as disobeying an order] if the order:

1. violates human dignity,

2. was given by a person or position lacking the authority to do so,

3. became ineffective consequently to another order,

4. is overtaken by a change of circumstances and its observance would entail a risk of substantial disadvantage,

5. bears no relation to the military service, or

6. entails the commission of an act punishable by court.

Military Criminal Code
Denmark, 1973

Chapter 3, § 9

Any person who commits a punishable offence by obeying a superior officer's official order shall not be liable to punishment unless he knew that the order was aimed at such an act or this was self-evident.

NWAOGA v. STATE
Supreme Court of Nigeria
1972 A.N.L.R. 149, 52 Int'l L. Rep. 494 (1972)

[The appellant was charged, convicted, and sentenced to death for the murder of Robert Ngwu on July 20, 1969, at Ibagwa Nike. The incident took place during a civil war. Both the appellant and the victim were soldiers in the rebel forces. The appellant was in command of a rebel company near Ibagwa Nike when he was instructed by a superior officer to "identify the deceased to the two lieutenants who would eliminate him." Apparently, Ngwu was to be killed because he had profited illegally from money intended for the repair of an airfield. Disguised in civilian clothes, the appellant and the lieutenants went to Ngwu's house, where the appellant identified him, a lieutenant killed Ngwu, and then all three ran away. The appellant's defense at trial was that he was obliged to obey the orders of his superior officers.]

It is argued before us that the learned trial judge was wrong to have adopted the attitude that the order in this case was an order by an officer of an illegal regime. It was submitted that in a civil war, the status of an illegal regime or rebels cannot be considered differently, and officers in that regime are entitled to give orders to junior officers in the same way as officers do in a legal recognised regime, and that such orders must be carried out by the junior officers; that in carrying out such orders, junior officers in the one case are protected in the same way as the other case. In other words, superior orders *qua* the forces to which the soldier carrying it out applies.

. . . The learned trial judge, in the present case, considered in his judgment the case of *R. v. Smith* (1900) 17 S.C.R. 561, and said: "It was held that a soldier is responsible by military and civil law and it is monstrous to suppose that a soldier could be protected when the order is grossly and manifestly illegal. Of course, there is the other proposition that a soldier is only bound to obey lawful orders and is responsible if he obeys an order not strictly lawful."

He went on, "In the case before me that order to eliminate the deceased was given by an officer of an illegal regime, his orders therefore are necessarily unlawful and obedience to them involves a violation of the law and the defence of superior orders is untenable."

We would not necessarily disagree with the conclusions reached by the learned trial judge in this matter. We however prefer to view the case from another standpoint; and viewing the facts before him, we direct our minds to the following facts:

1. That the appellant and those with him were rebel officers.

2. That they were operating inside the Federal Territory as the evidence shows that the area was in the hands of the Federal Government and Federal Army.

3. That the appellant and those with him were operating in disguise in the Federal Territory, as saboteurs.

4. That the appellant and those with him were not in the rebel army uniform but were in plain clothes, appearing to be members of the peaceful private population.

On these facts, if any of the rebel officers, as indeed the appellant did, commits an act which is an offence under the Criminal Code, he is liable for punishment, just like any civilian would be, whether or not he is acting under orders.

We are fortified in this view by a passage from Oppenheim's *International Law*, 7th Edition, Volume II, at page 575, dealing with War Treason, which says: —

> Enemy soldiers — in contradistinction to private enemy individuals — may only be punished for such acts when they have committed them during their stay within a belligerent's lines under disguise. If, for instance, two soldiers in uniform are sent to the rear of the enemy to destroy a bridge, they may not, when caught, be punished for "war treason," because their act was one of legitimate warfare. But if they

exchanged their uniforms for plain clothes, and thereby appear to be members of the peaceful private population, they are liable to punishment.

In the footnote under this paragraph, Oppenheim refers to a remarkable case during the Russo-Japanese War in 1904, where two Japanese officers disguised in Chinese clothes were caught attempting to destroy with dynamite a railway bridge in Manchuria. They were tried, found guilty, and shot.

We apply the above case to the matter before us. To our mind, deliberate and intentional killing of an unarmed person living peacefully inside the Federal Territory as in this case is a crime against humanity, and even if committed during a civil war is in violation of the domestic law of the country, and must be punished. In the event, the conviction of the appellant is upheld and this appeal is dismissed.

UNITED STATES v. CALLEY
United States Court of Military Appeals
22 U.S.C.M.A. 534, 48 C.M.R. 19 (1973)

[Atrocity has been a feature of virtually every war. During the Vietnam War, however, atrocities committed by U.S. troops received unprecedented media coverage. Most infamously, because of its severity and the cover-up that followed its disclosure, was the My Lai massacre on March 16, 1968. In the course of a combat assault on a Vietnamese village, U.S. Army troops killed several hundred unarmed Vietnamese, raped dozens of women and girls, and destroyed villagers' homes and other property.[1] Army prosecutors faced enormous political, legal, and practical obstacles, but eventually brought criminal charges against eighteen officers. All but one were acquitted or had the charges against them dismissed prior to trial. The one officer convicted was Lieutenant William Laws Calley, Jr., found guilty for killing twenty-two civilians, sentenced to life imprisonment, and paroled after three and a half years of house arrest.[2] When this hotly contested and highly publicized case reached the Court of Military Appeals, a key legal issue was the defense of superior orders.]

QUINN, J.

. . . We turn to the contention that the judge erred in his submission of the defense of superior orders to the court. After fairly summarizing the evidence, the judge gave the following instructions pertinent to the issue:

> The killing of resisting or fleeing enemy forces is generally recognized as a justifiable act of war, and you may consider any such killings justifiable in this case. The law attempts to protect those persons not actually engaged in warfare, however; and limits the circumstances under which their lives may be taken.

---

[1] *See, e.g.*, MICHAEL BILTON & KEVIN SIM, FOUR HOURS IN MY LAI (1992).

[2] *See, e.g.*, MICHAL R. BELKNAP, THE VIETNAM WAR ON TRIAL: THE MY LAI MASSACRE AND THE COURT-MARTIAL OF LIEUTENANT CALLEY (2002).

Both combatants captured by and noncombatants detained by the opposing force, regardless of their loyalties, political views, or prior acts, have the right to be treated as prisoners until released, confined, or executed, in accordance with law and established procedures, by competent authority sitting in judgment of such detained or captured individuals. Summary execution of detainees or prisoners is forbidden by law. Further, it's clear under the evidence presented in this case, that hostile acts or support of the enemy North Vietnamese or Viet Cong forces by inhabitants of My Lai (4) at some time prior to 16 March 1968, would not justify the summary execution of all or a part of the occupants of My Lai (4) on 16 March, nor would hostile acts committed that day, if, following the hostility, the belligerents surrendered or were captured by our forces. I therefore instruct you, as a matter of law, that if unresisting human beings were killed at My Lai (4) while within the effective custody and control of our military forces, their deaths cannot be considered justified, and any order to kill such people would be, as a matter of law, an illegal order. Thus, if you find that Lieutenant Calley received an order directing him to kill unresisting Vietnamese within his control or within the control of his troops, *that order would be an illegal order.*

A determination that an order is illegal does not, of itself, assign criminal responsibility to the person following the order for acts done in compliance with it. Soldiers are taught to follow orders, and special attention is given to obedience of orders on the battlefield. Military effectiveness depends upon obedience to orders. On the other hand, the obedience of a soldier is not the obedience of an automaton. A soldier is a reasoning agent, obliged to respond, not as a machine, but as a person. The law takes these factors into account in assessing criminal responsibility for acts done in compliance with illegal orders.

The acts of a subordinate done in compliance with an unlawful order given him by his superior are excused and impose no criminal liability upon him unless the superior's order is one which a man of *ordinary sense and understanding* would, under the circumstances, know to be unlawful, or if the order in question is actually known to the accused to be unlawful. . . .

. . . In determining what orders, if any, Lieutenant Calley acted under, if you find him to have acted, you should consider all of the matters which he has testified reached him and which you can infer from other evidence that he saw and heard. Then, unless you find beyond a reasonable doubt that he was not acting under orders directing him in substance and effect to kill unresisting occupants of My Lai (4), you must determine whether Lieutenant Calley actually knew those orders to be unlawful.

. . . In determining whether or not Lieutenant Calley had knowledge of the unlawfulness of any order found by you to have been given, you may consider all relevant facts and circumstances, including Lieutenant Calley's rank; educational background; OCS schooling;

other training while in the Army, including basic training, and his training in Hawaii and Vietnam; his experience on prior operations involving contact with hostile and friendly Vietnamese; his age; and any other evidence tending to prove or disprove that on 16 March 1968, Lieutenant Calley knew the order was unlawful. If you find beyond a reasonable doubt, on the basis of all the evidence, that *Lieutenant Calley actually knew* the order under which he asserts he operated was unlawful, the fact that the order was given operates as no defense.

Unless you find beyond reasonable doubt that the accused acted with actual knowledge that the order was unlawful, you must proceed to determine whether, under the circumstances, *a man of ordinary sense and understanding would have known the order was unlawful. Your deliberations on this question do not focus on Lieutenant Calley and the manner in which he perceived the legality of the order found to have been given him. The standard is that of a man of ordinary sense and understanding under the circumstances.*

Think back to the events of 15 and 16 March 1968. . . . Then determine, in light of all the surrounding circumstances, whether the order, which to reach this point you will have found him to be operating in accordance with, is one which a man of ordinary sense and understanding would know to be unlawful. Apply this to each charged act which you have found Lieutenant Calley to have committed. Unless you are satisfied from the evidence, beyond a reasonable doubt, that a man of ordinary sense and understanding would have known the order to be unlawful, you must acquit Lieutenant Calley for committing acts done in accordance with the order. (Emphasis added.)

Appellate defense counsel contend that these instructions are prejudicially erroneous in that they require the court members to determine that Lieutenant Calley knew that an order to kill human beings in the circumstances under which he killed was illegal by the standard of whether "a man of ordinary sense and understanding" would know the order was illegal. They urge us to adopt as the governing test whether the order is so palpably or manifestly illegal that a person of "the commonest understanding" would be aware of its illegality. They maintain the standard stated by the judge is too strict and unjust; that it confronts members of the armed forces who are not persons of ordinary sense and understanding with the dilemma of choosing between the penalty of death for disobedience of an order in time of war on the one hand and the equally serious punishment for obedience on the other. Some thoughtful commentators on military law have presented much the same argument.

The "ordinary sense and understanding" standard is set forth in the present Manual for Courts-Martial, United States, 1969 (Rev) and was the standard accepted by this Court in *United States v. Schultz*, 18 U.S.C.M.A. 133, 39 C.M.R. 133 (1969), and *United States v. Keenan*, 18 U.S.C.M.A. 108, 39 C.M.R. 108 (1969). It appeared as early as 1917. Manual for Courts-Martial, U.S. Army, 1917, paragraph 442. Apparently, it originated in a quotation from F.

Wharton, Homicide § 485 (3d ed. 1907). Wharton's authority is *Riggs v State*, 3 Coldwell 85, 91 American Decisions 272, 273 (Tenn 1866), in which the court approved a charge to the jury as follows:

> [I]n its substance being clearly illegal, so that a man of ordinary sense and understanding would know as soon as he heard the order read or given that such order was illegal, would afford a private no protection for a crime committed under such order.

Other courts have used other language to define the substance of the defense. Typical is *McCall v. McDowell*, 15 F. Cas. 1235, 1240 (C.C.D. Cal. 1867), in which the court said:

> But I am not satisfied that Douglas ought to be held liable to the plaintiff at all. He acted not as a volunteer, but as a subordinate in obedience to the order of his superior. Except in a plain case of excess of authority, where at first blush it is apparent and palpable to the commonest understanding that the order is illegal, I cannot but think that the law should excuse the military subordinate when acting in obedience to the orders of his commander. Otherwise he is placed in the dangerous dilemma of being liable in damages to third persons for obedience to an order, or to the loss of his commission and disgrace for disobedience thereto. . . . The first duty of a soldier is obedience, and without this there can be neither discipline nor efficiency in an army. If every subordinate officer and soldier were at liberty to question the legality of the orders of the commander, and obey them or not as they may consider them valid or invalid, the camp would be turned into a debating school, where the precious moment for action would be wasted in wordy conflicts between the advocates of conflicting opinions.

Colonel William Winthrop, the leading American commentator on military law, notes:

> But for the inferior to assume to determine the question of the lawfulness of an order given him by a superior would of itself, as a general rule, amount to insubordination, and such an assumption carried into practice would subvert military discipline. Where the order is apparently regular and *lawful on its face*, he is not to go behind it to satisfy himself that his superior has proceeded with authority, but is to obey it according to its terms, *the only exceptions recognized to the rule of obedience being cases of orders so manifestly beyond the legal power or discretion of the commander as to admit of no rational doubt of their unlawfulness.* . . .

> Except in such instances of palpable illegality, which must be of rare occurrence, the inferior should presume that the order was lawful and authorized and obey it accordingly, and in obeying it can scarcely fail to be held justified by a military court.

Winthrop's Military Law and Precedents, 2d ed., 1920 Reprint, at 296-297 (footnotes omitted) (emphasis added).

In the stress of combat, a member of the armed forces cannot reasonably be expected to make a refined legal judgment and be held criminally responsible if he guesses wrong on a question as to which there may be considerable disagreement. But there is no disagreement as to the illegality of the order to kill in this case. For 100 years, it has been a settled rule of American law that even in war the summary killing of an enemy, who has submitted to, and is under, effective physical control, is murder. Appellate defense counsel acknowledge that rule of law and its continued viability, but they say that Lieutenant Calley should not be held accountable for the men, women and children he killed because the court-martial could have found that he was a person of "commonest understanding" and such a person might not know what our law provides; that his captain had ordered him to kill these unarmed and submissive people and he only carried out that order as a good disciplined soldier should.

Whether Lieutenant Calley was the most ignorant person in the United States Army in Vietnam, or the most intelligent, he must be presumed to know that he could not kill the people involved here. The United States Supreme Court has pointed out that "[t]he rule that 'ignorance of the law will not excuse' [a positive act that constitutes a crime] . . . is deep in our law." *Lambert v. California*, 355 U.S. 225, 228 (1957). An order to kill infants and unarmed civilians who were so demonstrably incapable of resistance to the armed might of a military force as were those killed by Lieutenant Calley is, in my opinion, so palpably illegal that whatever conceptional difference there may be between a person of "commonest understanding" and a person of "common understanding," that difference could not have had any "impact on a court of lay members receiving the respective wordings in instructions," as appellate defense counsel contend. In my judgment, there is no possibility of prejudice to Lieutenant Calley in the trial judge's reliance upon the established standard of excuse of criminal conduct, rather than the standard of "commonest understanding" presented by the defense, or by the new variable test postulated in the dissent, which, with the inclusion of such factors for consideration as grade and experience, would appear to exact a higher standard of understanding from Lieutenant Calley than that of the person of ordinary understanding.

In summary, as reflected in the record, the judge was capable and fair, and dedicated to assuring the accused a trial on the merits as provided by law; his instructions on all issues were comprehensive and correct. Lieutenant Calley was given every consideration to which he was entitled, and perhaps more. We are impressed with the absence of bias or prejudice on the part of the court members. They were instructed to determine the truth according to the law and this they did with due deliberation and full consideration of the evidence. Their findings of guilty represent the truth of the facts as they determined them to be and there is substantial evidence to support those findings. No mistakes of procedure cast doubt upon them.

Consequently, the decision of the Court of Military Review is affirmed.

DARDEN, CHIEF JUDGE (dissenting):

Although the charge the military judge gave on the defense of superior orders was not inconsistent with the Manual treatment of this subject, I believe the Manual provision is too strict in a combat environment. Among other things, this standard permits serious punishment of persons whose training and attitude incline them either to be enthusiastic about compliance with orders or not to challenge the authority of their superiors. The standard also permits conviction of members who are not persons of ordinary sense and understanding.

The principal opinion has accurately traced the history of the current standard. Since this Manual provision is one of substantive law rather than one relating to procedure or modes of proof, the Manual rule is not binding on this Court, which has the responsibility for determining the principles that govern justification in the law of homicide. *United States v. Smith*, 13 U.S.C.M.A. 105, 32 C.M.R. 105 (1962). My impression is that the weight of authority, including the commentators whose articles are mentioned in the principal opinion, supports a more liberal approach to the defense of superior orders. Under this approach, superior orders should constitute a defense except "in a plain case of excess of authority, where at first blush it is apparent and palpable to the commonest understanding that the order is illegal." *McCall v. McDowell*, 15 F. Cas. 1235, 1240 (No. 8,673) (C.C.D. Cal. 1867); *In re Fair*, 100 F. 149, 155 (C.C.D. Neb. 1900); Winthrop's Military Law and Precedents, 2d ed, 1920 Reprint, at 296-97.

While this test is phrased in language that now seems "somewhat archaic and ungrammatical," the test recognizes that the essential ingredient of discipline in any armed force is obedience to orders and that this obedience is so important it should not be penalized unless the order would be recognized as illegal, not by what some hypothetical reasonable soldier would have known, but also by "those persons at the lowest end of the scale of intelligence and experience in the services." This is the real purpose in permitting superior orders to be a defense, and it ought not to be restricted by the concept of a fictional reasonable man so that, regardless of his personal characteristics, an accused judged after the fact may find himself punished for either obedience or disobedience, depending on whether the evidence will support the finding of simple negligence on his part.

It is true that the standard of a "reasonable man" is used in other areas of military criminal law, e.g., in connection with the provocation necessary to reduce murder to voluntary manslaughter; what constitutes an honest and reasonable mistake; and, indirectly, in connection with involuntary manslaughter. But in none of these instances do we have the countervailing consideration of avoiding the subversion of obedience to discipline in combat by encouraging a member to weigh the legality of an order or whether the superior had the authority to issue it. *See Martin v. Mott*, 25 U.S. 19, 30 (1827).

The preservation of human life is, of course, of surpassing importance. To accomplish such preservation, members of the armed forces must be held to standards of conduct that will permit punishment of atrocities and enable this nation to follow civilized concepts of warfare. In defending the current standard, the Army Court of Military Review expressed the view that:

Heed must be given not only to the subjective innocence-through-ignorance in the soldier, but to the consequences for his victims. Also, barbarism tends to invite reprisal to the detriment of our own force or disrepute which interferes with the achievement of war aims, even though the barbaric acts were preceded by orders for their commission. Casting the defense of obedience to orders solely in subjective terms of mens rea would operate practically to abrogate those objective restraints which are essential to functioning rules of war.

United States v. Calley, 46 C.M.R. 1131, 1184 (A.C.M.R. 1973).

I do not disagree with these comments. But while humanitarian considerations compel us to consider the impact of actions by members of our armed forces on citizens of other nations, I am also convinced that the phrasing of the defense of superior orders should have as its principal objective fairness to the unsophisticated soldier and those of somewhat limited intellect who nonetheless are doing their best to perform their duty.

The test of palpable illegality to the commonest understanding properly balances punishment for the obedience of an obviously illegal order against protection to an accused for following his elementary duty of obeying his superiors. Such a test reinforces the need for obedience as an essential element of military discipline by broadly protecting the soldier who has been effectively trained to look to his superiors for direction. It also promotes fairness by permitting the military jury to consider the particular accused's intelligence, grade, training, and other elements directly related to the issue of whether he should have known an order was illegal. Finally, that test imputes such knowledge to an accused not as a result of simple negligence but on the much stronger circumstantial concept that almost anyone in the armed forces would have immediately recognized that the order was palpably illegal.

I would adopt this standard as the correct instruction for the jury when the defense of superior orders is in issue. Because the original case language is archaic and somewhat ungrammatical, I would rephrase it to require that the military jury be instructed that, despite his asserted defense of superior orders, an accused may be held criminally accountable for his acts, allegedly committed pursuant to such orders, if the court members are convinced beyond a reasonable doubt (1) that almost every member of the armed forces would have immediately recognized that the order was unlawful, and (2) that the accused should have recognized the order's illegality as a consequence of his age, grade, intelligence, experience, and training.

The temptation is to say that even under this new formulation Lieutenant Calley would have been found guilty. No matter how such a position is phrased, essentially it means that the appellate judge rather than the military jury is functioning as a fact finder. . . .

In the instant case, Lieutenant Calley's testimony placed the defense of superior orders in issue, even though he conceded that he knew prisoners were normally to be treated with respect and that the unit's normal practice was to interrogate Vietnamese villagers, release those who could account for themselves, and evacuate those suspected of being a part of the enemy forces.

Although crucial parts of his testimony were sharply contested, according to Lieutenant Calley, (1) he had received a briefing before the assault in which he was instructed that every living thing in the village was to be killed, including women and children; (2) he was informed that speed was important in securing the village and moving forward; (3) he was ordered that under no circumstances were any Vietnamese to be allowed to stay behind the lines of his forces; (4) the residents of the village who were taken into custody were hindering the progress of his platoon in taking up the position it was to occupy; and (5) when he informed Captain Medina of this hindrance, he was ordered to kill the villagers and to move his platoon to a proper position.

In addition to the briefing, Lieutenant Calley's experience in the Pinkville area caused him to know that, in the past, when villagers had been left behind his unit, the unit had immediately received sniper fire from the rear as it pressed forward. Faulty intelligence apparently led him also to believe that those persons in the village were not innocent civilians but were either enemies or enemy sympathizers. For a participant in the My Lai operation, the circumstances that could have obtained there may have caused the illegality of alleged orders to kill civilians to be much less clear than they are in a hindsight review.

Since the defense of superior orders was not submitted to the military jury under what I consider to be the proper standard, I would grant Lieutenant Calley a rehearing.

NOTES AND DISCUSSION

1. Do the instructions in *Calley* accord with the superior orders defense adopted in the Austrian military code that appears above? the Danish version? Do you prefer the standard adopted by the majority or the standard advanced by Chief Judge Darden in dissent?

2. Does the context of civil war alter the applicability of the superior orders defense? The Nigerian case of *Nwaoga v. State* involves crimes committed less than a year later than the *Calley* case but in a very different legal and political environment.[3] Should military justice give way to civilian criminal law when assessing culpability during or after a civil war? Or should the superior orders defense be narrowly circumscribed to encourage soldiers to act on their own moral instincts? The defense of superior orders is sometimes called the "Nuremberg defense" because it was raised by Nazi officers during their post-World War II trials for crimes against humanity. *See, e.g.*, Richard Falk, *Telford Taylor and the Legacy of Nuremberg*, 37 COLUM. J. TRANSNAT'L L. 693 (1999). As Dean Koh explains:

> Nuremberg changed the valence of personal responsibility. Before the Nuremberg trials, lax rules of responsibility had created conditions under which gross atrocities could be committed and yet nobody would

---

[3] *See also Nigerian Army v. Abdullahi* (Nigeria 2002), reported in Rabiu Ibrahim, *Echoes of Kaduna Crisis: How Army Captain Regained Freedom*, WEEKLY TRUST (Nigeria), July 19, 2002 (describing prosecution of officer for attempting to rescue his mother from religious riot).

be held responsible. Street-level officials who had committed torture and genocide could claim that they were "just following orders." Yet at the same time, their commanders could claim that they were so high in the chain of command that they did not know what was going on, and therefore should not bear command responsibility for illegal acts committed by their subordinates. After Nuremberg, the law recognized that commanders bore command responsibility to know what atrocities were being committed in their names, and that street-level officials could not escape accountability by saying that they were "just following orders." These principles are now embodied in the basic instruments of international criminal law.

Harold Hongju Koh, *Can the President be Torturer-in-Chief?*, 81 IND. L.J. 1145, 1152-53 (2006).

In denying the appeal of a Japanese general convicted and sentenced to death by an international tribunal, the U.S. Supreme Court endorsed the principle of "command responsibility," a doctrine that holds military commanders liable for the war crimes of subordinates if those commanders knew or should have known of the unlawful conduct and failed to take steps to prevent it. *See In re Yamashita*, 327 U.S. 1, 14-16 (1946). Professor Kennedy comments:

> Where the military may seek to isolate responsibility, humanitarians may seek to trace the chain of command, insisting that the buck stops with the broadest level of political or military responsibility. Law marks the links in the chain that lead to the president, or the secretary of defense, just as it separates the military professional from responsibility for the war's overall legitimacy.

DAVID KENNEDY, OF WAR AND LAW 153 (2006).

3. Is the existence of a "superior orders" defense a matter of law or fact? Consider *United States v. New*, 55 M.J. 95 (C.A.A.F. 2001). New, a U.S. medic, was to deploy with a United Nations Protective Force to the former Yugoslavia in 1995. He was court-martialed for refusing to wear modifications — such as a UN blue beret, blue shoulder patch, blue scarf, and badge — to his military uniform required for this assignment. New considered U.S. participation in the UN protective force illegal, a position for which he attracted considerable support and publicity. He appealed his conviction for "failure to obey an order," prompting the Court of Appeals for the Armed Forces to consider at length the legality of the order that he disobeyed. The court quoted from the discussion accompanying R.C.M. 801(e)(5) in the *Manual for Courts-Martial*:

> Questions of the applicability of a rule of law to an undisputed set of facts are normally questions of law. *Similarly, the legality of an act is normally a question of law. For example, the legality of an order when disobedience of an order is charged*, the legality of restraint when there is a prosecution for breach of arrest, or the sufficiency of warnings before interrogation are normally questions of law. It is possible, however, for such questions to be decided solely upon some factual issue, in which case they would be questions of fact. . . .

55 M.J. at 101 (emphasis added by the court). The court continued:

> The test for assessing the lawfulness of an order under Article 92 comes from paragraph 14c(2)(a)(iii), Part IV, Manual for Courts-Martial, United States (1995 ed.) which states in pertinent part:
>
> > The order must relate to military duty, which includes all activities reasonably necessary to accomplish a military mission, or safeguard or promote the morale, discipline, and usefulness of members of a command and directly connected with the maintenance of good order in the service. The order may not, without such a valid military purpose, interfere with private rights or personal affairs. However, the dictates of a person's conscience, religion, or personal philosophy cannot justify or excuse the disobedience of an otherwise lawful order.
>
> Orders are clothed with an inference of lawfulness. "An order requiring the performance of a military duty or act may be inferred to be lawful and it is disobeyed at the peril of the subordinate. This inference does not apply to a patently illegal order, such as one that directs the commission of a crime." Para. 14c(2)(a)(i), Part IV, Manual, *supra* (1995 ed.). Appellant has the burden to establish that the order is not lawful. . . .
>
> We hold that the military judge did not err in determining that the order given to appellant to wear his uniform with UN accoutrements was lawful. The military judge correctly determined that the evidence presented by appellant did not overcome the presumption of lawfulness given to military orders and that the order related to military duty.
>
> Appellant argues that (1) the UN insignia violates Army uniform regulations (AR 670-1) by transferring his allegiance to the United Nations, 50 M.J. at 734, and (2) the order stems from an illegal deployment of the Armed Forces because President Clinton misrepresented the nature of the deployment to Congress and failed to comply with the United Nations Participation Act [UNPA]. 50 M.J. at 736. These arguments fail because they would unacceptably substitute appellant's personal judgment of the legality of an order for that of his superiors and the Federal Government. . . .

See also United States v. Jeffers, 57 M.J. 13 (2002) (involving a married captain and a private who violated a "no contact" order that their company commander issued after he became aware of the soldiers' adulterous relationship). For further discussion of *New*, see Chapter 18, § III(B), *infra*.

4. In *United States v. Huet-Vaughn*, 43 M.J. 105 (C.A.A.F. 1995), the Court of Appeals held that Captain Huet-Vaughn, who was convicted of desertion with intent to avoid hazardous duty and shirk important service, did not have a valid superior orders defense. Captain Huet-Vaughn, an anti-war activist and a medical doctor, disobeyed orders to deploy to the Persian Gulf. Her conviction had been set aside by the Court of Military Review, which ruled that the trial judge had improperly prohibited evidence of her motive in disobeying the order. The Court of Appeals reinstated her conviction and supported the decision of the military judge to exclude some evidence of the accused's intent.

The court wrote: "The so-called 'Nuremberg defense' applies only to individual acts committed in wartime; it does not apply to the Government's decision to wage war. . . . The duty to disobey an unlawful order applies only to 'a positive act that constitutes a crime' that is 'so manifestly beyond the legal power or discretion of the commander as to admit of no rational doubt of their unlawfulness.'" Because Captain Huet-Vaughn was not ordered to commit a war crime, and because the legality of war is a non-justiciable political question, she could not raise a superior orders defense. Should soldiers be required to obey all orders except orders to commit crimes of war? For further discussion, see Michael J. Davidson, *War and the Doubtful Soldier*, 19 NOTRE DAME J.L. ETHICS & PUB. POL'Y 91 (2005); Michal R. Belknap, *The Warren Court and the Vietnam War: The Limits of Legal Liberalism*, 33 GA. L. REV. 65 (1999).

5. *United States v. Pacheco*, 56 M.J. 1 (C.A.A.F. 2001), involved a private who tried to use a "superior orders" defense against a charge of stealing a weapon, which he intended to take home as a "war trophy," during U.S. military operations in Haiti. He argued that he had been ordered to take a Desert Eagle pistol by a non-commissioned officer (NCO). The court, however, considered the NCO a co-conspirator rather than a military superior issuing him an order. When a superior is engaged in wrongdoing, how can the court tell whether subordinates are also culpable?

III. OTHER SPECIAL DEFENSES

A. Condonation

Armed Forces Act, 1975 *Malaysia*
§ 146(1)(c)

Where a person subject to service law under this Act has had an offence condoned by his commanding officer, he shall not be liable in respect of that offence to be tried by court-martial or to have the case dealt with summarily by his commanding officer or an appropriate superior authority.

Queen's Regulations and Orders for the Canadian Forces
Article 103.03. Civil Defenses Available to Accused

(1) Section 151 of the *National Defence Act* provides: All rules and principles from time to time followed in the civil courts that would render any circumstance a justification or excuse for any act or omission or a defence to any charge are applicable in any proceedings under the Code of Service Discipline.

(2) The condonation of an act or omission on any ground whatsoever, whether by superior authority or otherwise, shall not be a justification, excuse or defence for the act or omission.

Notes to § 151

(A) The grounds of justification, excuse or defence most likely to be relied on under this section are: drunkenness, compulsion, self-defence, defence of property and use of force to prevent the commission of an offence. Other grounds of justification, excuse or defence, exist in the *Criminal Code*, other statutes and the common law.

(B) Drunkenness is no defence unless, in cases where a specific intent forms part of the offence, it can be shown that the accused was so drunk at the time of the commission of the offence that he was incapable of forming the necessary intent. Evidence of drunkenness which renders the accused incapable of forming the specific intent essential to constitute the crime should be taken into consideration with the other facts proved in order to determine whether or not he had this intent.

(C) Evidence of drunkenness which does not prove that the accused was incapable of forming the necessary intent, and which merely established that his mind was so affected by drink, that he more readily gave way to some violent passion does not negate specific intent.

(D) A person charged with having committed an offence may raise compulsion as justification, excuse or defence if all of the following conditions were present:

(i) he received threats of immediate death or grievous bodily harm from a person actually present at the commission of the offence,

(ii) he believed that such threats would be executed,

(iii) he was not a party to any association or conspiracy which rendered him subject to compulsion in the commission of the offence.

(E) Compulsion may not be raised as justification, excuse or defence in respect of offences of high treason or treason, murder, piracy, attempted murder, sexual assault with a weapon, threats to a third party or causing bodily harm, aggravated sexual assault, forcible abduction, robbery, assault with a weapon or causing bodily harm, aggravated assault, unlawfully causing bodily harm, arson or abduction or detention of young persons.

ATTORNEY GENERAL *EX REL*. ROYAL N.Z. NAVY v. LAWRENCE
Court of Appeals of New Zealand
[1999] NZCA 261

This appeal concerns the concept of condonation in military law. The Attorney General, representing the Royal New Zealand Navy, appeals from an order made by Gendall, J. in the High Court at Wellington declaring that an alleged offence of rape said to have been committed by the Respondent, Lieutenant Commander Lawrence (Mr Lawrence), had been condoned in terms of section 22 of the Armed Forces Discipline Act 1971 (the Act). The effect of the Judge's decision was that the appropriate Naval authorities could not try Mr Lawrence on a charge of rape as was their intention. . . .

In October 1996 Mr Lawrence was a lieutenant based in Bahrain. Following a social function he had sexual intercourse with a female rating. She claimed it was rape; he said it was consensual. In early 1998 the matter ultimately came before Mr Lawrence's then commanding officer, Commander McLennan, who came to the view that the allegation of rape was not well founded. . . .

[Shortly thereafter, Mr Lawrence was tried by a new commanding officer.] The essential issue is whether the conduct of Commander McLennan amounted to a condonation of the alleged offence of rape making it unlawful for a charge of rape to be subsequently tried. . . .

There is no dispute between the parties that condonation as ordinarily understood in military law occurs when a commanding officer indicates to the person concerned that he will not be charged with an offence which the commanding officer considers he has or at least may have committed. You cannot be said to have condoned an offence unless you think the person concerned has or at least may have committed it. This is indeed the ordinary dictionary meaning of the word condone in the sense of forgiveness, and such meaning is supported by authorities in the field of law. . . .

In the present case Mr Lawrence contends that his commanding officer condoned the offence of rape alleged against him in spite of the fact that the commanding officer came to the view . . . that the allegation of rape was not well founded. . . . To take the view that a not well founded conclusion amounts to a condonation of the alleged offence involves turning on its head the ordinary concept of condonation, as understood in military law. . . .

Commander McLennan did not condone [Mr Lawrence's] offence when he indicated to Mr Lawrence that he considered the allegation was not well founded. The appeal by the Attorney General is allowed. . . .

NOTES AND DISCUSSION

1. In *Lawrence*, would the Malaysian or Canadian definition of condonation provide a cognizable defense? How is the defense of "condonation" distinct from that of "superior orders"?

2. What kinds of crimes are most apt to be excused by a defense of condonation? What types of servicemembers are most likely to benefit from this defense?

3. Should the concept of condonation apply to unlawful acts committed by soldiers who are encouraged to commit such acts by military superiors? Consider the following comment by law professor Diane Marie Amann, referring to a key Army investigation and February 2004 report, on the scandal surrounding the U.S. military abuse of detainees at Abu Ghraib during the U.S. war in Iraq:

> Disclosed less than a week after the CBS program [that, in April 2004, ran photographs of graphic detainee abuse] was an internal Army report which found that "numerous incidents of sadistic, blatant, and wanton criminal abuses were inflicted on several detainees" at Abu Ghraib; among these were incidents of kicking, punching, and other physical abuse, coerced masturbation and other sexual humiliation, forced nudity, and the use of unmuzzled dogs as weapons of intimidation. The report by Major General Antonio M. Taguba attributed the "systemic and illegal abuse of detainees" to "several members of the military police guard force." . . . The report found . . . that the Army's

and "Other US Government Agency's (OGA) interrogators" — the latter typically a reference to the CIA — "actively requested that MP guards set physical and mental conditions for favorable interrogation of witnesses." . . . In Taguba's view, the mistreatment violated two pertinent bodies of law; specifically, the Army's own regulations and the Third Geneva Convention. Taguba drew a link, moreover, between those activities and Guantánamo: he noted that the abuses he documented had occurred right after the visit to Abu Ghraib of Major General Geoffrey D. Miller, commander of the Joint Task Force at Guantánamo. After stating that Miller's team deemed it "essential" that prison guards "be actively engaged in setting the conditions for successful exploitation of the internees," Taguba voiced his own disagreement with any adoption in Iraq of techniques used at Guantánamo.

Diane Marie Amann, *Abu Ghraib*, 153 U. PA. L. REV. 2085, 2092-93 (2005). As of March 2007, 11 soldiers had been convicted at court-martial for the abuse at Abu Ghraib.

B. Necessity and Duress

UNITED STATES v. WASHINGTON
United States Court of Appeals for the Armed Forces
57 M.J. 394 (2002)

JUDGE EFFRON delivered the opinion of the Court.

A special court-martial composed of officer and enlisted members convicted appellant, contrary to his pleas, of willfully disobeying a lawful order given by a superior commissioned officer, in violation of Article 90, Uniform Code of Military Justice (UCMJ), 10 U.S.C. § 890. He was sentenced to a bad-conduct discharge and confinement for two months. . . .

Anthrax is an infectious animal disease that can be employed as a deadly biological weapon. Over the last decade, the Department of Defense (DoD) has focused attention on the possibility that such weapons might be used against deployed U.S. forces. As a countermeasure, DoD, for a period of time, implemented a program involving widespread vaccination of U.S. military personnel. The program subjected numerous members of the armed forces to a series of six vaccinations designed to counter the effects of any exposure to anthrax.

Appellant, who was stationed in the United States, received five of the six vaccinations without objection. In 1999, he was deployed to Saudi Arabia, where he declined to receive the sixth vaccination. On December 21, his squadron commander ordered him to receive the required vaccination. Appellant refused to obey the order, and he received nonjudicial punishment under Article 15, UCMJ, 10 USC § 815, for disobedience of the order. The nonjudicial punishment consisted of reduction from pay grade E-4 to E-1 and a suspended forfeiture of $483.00 per month for two months.

Appellant's commander issued appellant a new order on January 7, 2000, directing that he receive the anthrax vaccination within 24 hours. On January

8, appellant informed his commander that he would not obey the order. Appellant's refusal occurred after he had considered articles in the media and testimony in congressional proceedings raising questions about the safety and effectiveness of the anthrax vaccine.

Appellant was charged with a violation of Article 90, UCMJ, which prohibits willful disobedience of a lawful order from a superior commissioned officer. The charge was referred to a special court-martial. During pretrial proceedings, the prosecution asked the military judge to rule that the order was lawful. The defense expressly stated that it would not contest the lawfulness of the order. The military judge ruled that the order was lawful, and he advised the parties that he would so instruct the members of the court-martial.

The prosecution then moved to preclude the defense from introducing evidence challenging the safety and effectiveness of the vaccination program. The defense objected, contending that such evidence was central to the defense case, which would be based upon the defenses of duress and necessity. The military judge granted the prosecution's motion. The military judge indicated that the defense of duress was unavailable because it requires an unlawful threat from a human being, and that the defense of necessity was unavailable because it requires a threat from a natural physical force — neither of which was present in this case. The military judge reasoned, in effect, that any threat to appellant's health came from human implementation of a lawful policy decision, not from an unlawful threat or a natural physical force. On appeal, appellant contends that the military judge committed prejudicial error by not permitting him to present pertinent evidence regarding the defenses of duress and necessity. . . .

In *United States v. Rockwood,* 52 M.J. 98 (1999), we considered the nature of the duress defense in the military justice system, as well as the question of whether the defense of necessity is available in courts-martial. With respect to duress, we observed: (1) "[c]lassically, duress was seen as a defense to crime if the defendant was compelled or coerced to commit the crime by some human agency, under a threat of serious imminent harm to the defendant or others"; (2) "[f]or the defense of duress to apply, the crime committed must have been of lesser magnitude than the harm threatened"; (3) "the duress must [have] consist[ed] of threatening conduct which produced in the defendant . . . a reasonable fear of . . . immediate (or imminent) . . . death or serious bodily harm"; and (4) "[a]n obviously safe avenue of escape before committing the prohibited act nullifies the defense." *Id.* at 112 (citing 1 Wayne R. LaFave & Austin W. Scott, Jr., *Substantive Criminal Law* 614-27 (1986); Rollin M. Perkins & Ronald N. Boyce, *Criminal Law* 1959-65 (3d ed.1982); *United States v. Vasquez,* 48 M.J. 426, 429-30 (1998) (internal quotations and emphasis omitted)).

With respect to the defense of necessity, we noted: (1) necessity "was traditionally seen as a choice of evils defense" in which "the pressure of circumstances was not brought by human agency, but by the situation itself"; and (2) "[t]he defendant's belief that his actions were necessary must have been reasonable, and there must have been no alternative that would have caused lesser harm." *Id.* at 112 (citing 1 LaFave & Scott, *supra,* at 627-31, 635, 638;

Perkins & Boyce, *supra,* at 1069; *United States v. Bailey,* 444 U.S. 394, 410 (1980) (footnote and internal quotations omitted)).

In our discussion of applicable military law, we took note of R.C.M. 916(h), Manual for Courts-Martial, United States (2000 ed.) which provides for the defense of duress. We also observed that the defense of necessity was not specifically provided for in the Manual for Courts-Martial, and that under the circumstances of the case it was unnecessary to decide whether, as a matter of law, it should be available in the military justice system. *Id.* at 113-14.

Appellant places primary reliance on R.C.M. 916(h), which states:

> It is a defense to any offense except killing an innocent person that the accused's participation in the offense was caused by a reasonable apprehension that the accused or another innocent person would be immediately killed or would immediately suffer serious bodily injury if the accused did not commit the act. The apprehension must reasonably continue throughout the commission of the act. If the accused has any reasonable opportunity to avoid committing the act without subjecting the accused or another innocent person to the harm threatened, this defense shall not apply.

Appellant contends that a plain reading of the text provides a defense to a charge of disobeying a lawful order if the accused had a reasonable belief that compliance with the order would result in death or serious bodily injury to the accused or another person. According to appellant, the military judge erred in two respects: first, by grafting onto the rule a requirement that the duress result from the unlawful threat of a human being; and second, by declining to consider the necessity defense in the absence of a threat imposed by a natural physical force.

Appellant's narrow reading of R.C.M. 916(h) would permit a member of the armed forces to disobey a lawful order if the servicemember had a reasonable apprehension that he or she, or another innocent person, would immediately be killed or suffer serious bodily injury if he or she complied with the order. Such an interpretation suggests that the President designed the rule to alter one of the core values of military service — the willingness of the individual to sacrifice his or her life or well-being for the sake of the nation. As the Supreme Court has emphasized, "[t]he essence of military service 'is the subordination of the desires and interests of the individual to the needs of the service.'" *Goldman v. Weinberger,* 475 U.S. 503, 507 (1986) (quoting *Orloff v. Willoughby,* 345 U.S. 83, 92 (1953)).

The requirement to place the needs of the nation above a servicemember's personal welfare applies in peacetime as well as in war. "[I]t is the primary business of armies and navies to fight or be ready to fight should the occasion arise." *United States ex rel. Toth v. Quarles,* 350 U.S. 11, 17 (1955). Every day, members of the armed forces engage in operational missions or training activities in which there is a risk of death or serious bodily injury to themselves or others. Although the armed forces rely on unit cohesion and leadership to foster a willingness to undertake such risks, legal sanctions are available to promote obedience should positive measures prove insufficient. Congress has expressly provided criminal sanctions in Article 90, UCMJ, as well as Articles

91 and 92, UCMJ, 10 U.S.C. §§ 891 and 892, for failure to obey a lawful order, including authority in Article 90(2) for capital punishment in time of war for disobedience of the lawful order of a superior commissioned officer.

The President's guidance with respect to the disobedience offenses embodies longstanding military law. "An order requiring the performance of a military duty or act may be inferred to be lawful and it is disobeyed at the peril of the subordinate." Paragraph 14c(2)(a)(1), Part IV, Manual, *supra.* "The order must relate to military duty, which includes all activities reasonably necessary to accomplish a military mission, or safeguard or promote the morale, discipline, and usefulness of members of a command and directly connected with the maintenance of good order in the service." *Id.* at para. 14c(2)(a)(iii). When a commander gives an order that is reasonably necessary to accomplish the mission — including an order involving protective measures, such as defensive positioning, wearing protective armor, or taking a vaccine to counter a biological weapon — the servicemember is obligated to obey or face punishment under Articles 90, 91, or 92, UCMJ. If servicemembers could disobey lawful orders to participate in military training or operations out of a reasonable apprehension that they or others might suffer death or serious bodily injury, the President's guidance in paragraph 14c(2)(a) Part IV, Manual, *supra,* would be rendered meaningless.

In light of the foregoing, it would be inappropriate to read the President's guidance on the duress defense in R.C.M. 916(h), Manual, *supra,* in isolation. Instead, it must be read in conjunction with the guidance on disobedience of lawful orders and the essential purposes of military law. In that context, the military judge correctly ruled that the duress defense in R.C.M. 916(h) should be viewed in a manner consistent with the requirement in prevailing civilian law that the threat emanate from the unlawful act of another person. Likewise, if the defense of necessity applies in the military justice system — a question which we need not resolve at this time — similar considerations would call for an application of the prevailing civilian doctrine regarding the requirement for the necessity to arise from a natural force, as opposed to a human action.

As we noted in *Rockwood, supra,* "[t]here may indeed be unusual situations in which an assigned military duty is so mundane, and the threat of death or grievous bodily harm . . . is so clearly defined and immediate, that consideration might be given to a duress or necessity defense." 52 M.J. at 114. This is not such a case. The evidence offered at trial demonstrated that the vaccination program was designed and implemented as a defensive measure in the face of a significant military threat. Assuming the validity of the data provided by appellant concerning the risk of adverse effects from the vaccination, such information does not demonstrate that the purpose of the vaccination program was "mundane" or that such risks were so immediate and widespread as to undermine its purpose.

The foregoing discussion is based on the premise — not challenged by appellant in this case — that the order was lawful. A servicemember charged with a disobedience offense may challenge the lawfulness of the order on a variety of grounds, *e.g.,* that the order directed the commission of a crime; that the issuing officer lacked authority; that the order did not relate to a military duty; that it interfered with private rights or personal affairs without a valid military purpose; that it was solely designed to achieve a private purpose; that it conflicted with a person's statutory or constitutional rights. *See* para. 14c(2)(a)(i)-(iv), Part IV, Manual, *supra; United States v. New,* 55 M.J. 95 (2001). In the present case, however, appellant chose not to challenge the lawfulness of the order he received to participate in the anthrax vaccination program. Accordingly, we have no occasion in this case to determine whether the program is based upon lawful authority or whether there are other legal grounds for questioning the program. Based on the foregoing, we resolve this issue against appellant.

NOTES AND QUESTIONS

1. In *United States v. Rockwood,* 52 M.J. 98 (C.A.A.F. 1999), the Court of Appeals considered the case of an Army officer who took it upon himself to investigate alleged abuses at a prison facility. During a United Nations-sanctioned military action in Haiti in 1994, Captain Lawrence P. Rockwood, II served as a counter intelligence officer with the 10th Mountain Division. He was "personally concerned about intelligence reports which reflected deplorable conditions at the National Penitentiary in Port au Prince," and he tried to get his superiors to inspect the penitentiary in order to identify human rights violations. Without authorization, Captain Rockwood inspected the prison for himself, returned to his post and was ordered to undergo psychiatric evaluation, which he resisted. He was then evacuated from Haiti, refused nonjudicial punishment under Article 15 of the UCMJ, was charged with and convicted of a series of charges by a general court-martial. One of the issues on appeal was whether the military judge had properly instructed the court-martial on the special defenses presented by the appellant. The court upheld the military judge's instructions, noting that:

> Under the formulation of the Manual for Courts-Martial, "justification" is denominated a defense for a "death, injury, or other act caused or done in the proper performance of a legal duty." RCM 916(c) . . . Appellant cites us to no legal authority — international or domestic, military or civil — that suggests he had a "duty" to abandon his post in counterintelligence and strike out on his own to "inspect" the penitentiary. Neither does he suggest any provision of any treaty, charter, or resolution as authority for the proposition. Further, he does not here claim that he received personal orders via television from the Commander-in-Chief. . . .

> Classically, duress was seen as a defense to crime if the defendant was compelled or coerced to commit the crime by some human agency, under a threat of serious imminent harm to the defendant or others. . . . There is no Manual provision specifically denominated "necessity," nor is there a standard military instruction under that heading. . . . Be that as it may, the military judge decided to provide what was functionally a necessity instruction. The judge recognized that the standard duress

instruction did not fit the circumstances, in that there was no coercion by human agency in the classic sense. That is, no one put a gun to appellant's head and said, "Inspect the prisons or somebody dies." So the judge tried to "blend" the duress instruction to fit the circumstances, including the elements of necessity. Thus, he instructed the members:

> Now I'd like to talk to you about what we're going to call "duress." It's a defense. And the evidence has raised the issue of duress in relation to all of the charges that have been charged against Captain Rockwood.
>
> Duress is a complete defense to each offense to which it applies, which is all of them. In evaluating this defense, keep in mind that you must apply the defense to each offense separately. To be a defense, Captain Rockwood's participation in the offense must have been caused by *a well-grounded apprehension that a prisoner in, or prisoners in, the National Penitentiary would immediately die or would immediately suffer serious bodily harm* if Captain Rockwood did not commit the charged act.
>
> *The amount of compulsion, coercion or force must have been sufficient to have caused an officer who was faced with the same situation and who was of normal strength and courage, to act. The fear which caused Captain Rockwood to commit the offense must have been fear of death or serious bodily injury* and not simply fear of injury to reputation or property, or to bodily injury less severe than serious bodily harm. The threat and resulting fear must have continued throughout the commission of the offense.

(Emphasis added.)

> Specifically absent from this instruction was any limitation that the coercion or reasonable apprehension be caused by human agency.
>
> At trial, appellant objected to the officer "of normal strength and courage" phrase. On appeal, he contends he was entitled to a duress instruction *sans* this language. We agree with the military judge that classic duress was not raised, and thus this point is moot. Even if duress were raised, the complained-of language merely expresses an objective standard, which is unquestionably a component of both duress and necessity. . . .

52 M.J. at 112-13. Is the objective standard used by the military judge, and endorsed by the CAAF, appropriate? Why would defense counsel for Captain Rockwood want a subjective standard instead?

2. What are the differences between the military defense of necessity and the civil version of the same? In *Huet-Vaughn*, the Court of Appeals rejected a necessity defense because "[t]he defense is not available where the accused's purpose is to cause a change in government policy." *United States v. Huet-Vaughn*, 43 M.J. 105, 114 (C.A.A.F. 1995).

3. Judge Andrew S. Effron, author of the *Washington* opinion above, also wrote for the court in *United States v. Olinger*, 50 M.J. 365 (C.A.A.F. 1999). In that case, a sailor convicted of AWOL and missing movement claimed that his absence had been motivated by concern for his wife's health and asserted on appeal that the military judge should have instructed the court-martial on the defense of necessity. In rejecting the appeal, the court held:

> As noted by the court below, these questions address some of the most fundamental principles in the military justice system:
>
>> [T]he ramifications of an individual choosing to commit an illegal act, in order to avoid what they perceive to be a greater harm, are drastically different in the military than they are in civilian life. In civilian life, innocent individuals may be adversely affected by the commission of the illegal act. In the military, however, the consequences may be much greater. Such a decision affects an individual's shipmates, the safety and efficiency of the ship, as well as the effectiveness of the mission. Ultimately, the consequences may extend to the severity of the action.
>
> 47 M.J. at 551; *accord United States v. Banks,* 37 M.J. 700, 702 (A.C.M.R. 1993) ("[R]ejecting the necessity defense goes to the core of discipline within a military organization. In no other segment of our society is it more important to have a single enforceable set of standards."). . . .
>
> In the present case, appellant's unsworn statement during the sentencing proceeding contained a brief speculative comment that at the time he absented himself, he felt that his wife's "depression might kill her from the stress if [he] went on the UNITAS deployment." Appellant did not provide any further details indicating an immediate threat of death or serious bodily harm or that there were no alternative sources of assistance for his wife other than his unauthorized absence and missing movement; nor did appellant provide other facts that would establish either the defense of duress under R.C.M. 916(h) or the common-law defense of necessity. *See Rankins,* 34 M.J. at 328-29. Even if we were to hold that the defense of duress could be established through a threat emanating from physical or natural sources, or that the broader common-law defense of necessity should be applicable to courts-martial, appellant's remarks would be insufficient to render his plea improvident. . . .
>
> While the issues raised by appellant are important, we conclude that it would be inappropriate to resolve these questions on the basis of the record before us. These matters could have been raised at trial had appellant contested his guilt on the grounds of necessity. Alternatively, these matters could have been raised through testimony during the providence inquiry or at sentencing, had such testimony included facts providing a substantial basis for addressing the applicability of the necessity defense in the military justice system. Appellant's vague speculation as to what might have happened had he remained with his shipmates provides an insufficient basis for considering whether the law should be interpreted or extended as he has urged.

50 M.J. 366-67. The court avoids the question of whether necessity ought to be defense at court-martial. What do you think?

C.   The Good Soldier Defense

UNITED STATES v. CLEMONS
United States Court of Military Appeals
16 M.J. 44 (1983)

[An Army sergeant convicted of wrongful appropriation, larceny, and unlawful entry argued that the military judge at his court-martial had unlawfully prevented evidence of "good military character" from being admitted at trial. The Court of Military Appeals agreed.]

FLETCHER, JUDGE:

The findings in this case included conviction of unlawfully entering a barracks room, wrongfully appropriating a television set found therein, and stealing a cassette player. Appellant did not deny entering the unlocked barracks room or taking the television and the cassette player. Rather he asserted that, in order to secure the television and teach the room's occupants a lesson about securing property, it was taken from the room and placed in his office. Also to secure property the cassette player found in a latrine was placed in his office, and later inadvertently placed in his duffle bag following the termination of his duty. During all of these events appellant was on duty as Charge of Quarters the night of February 6 and 7, 1981.

Before defense counsel proceeded to his case-in-chief, trial counsel moved, *in limine,* to prevent introduction of evidence of appellant's general good character. Acknowledging that he intended to introduce evidence of appellant's good military character and character for lawfulness, defense counsel cited as authority for its production Mil.R.Evid. 404(a)(1), which states:

> Rule 404. *Character Evidence Not Admissible to Prove Conduct; Exceptions; Other Crimes*
>
> (a) *Character evidence generally.* Evidence of a person's character or a trait of a person's character is not admissible for the purpose of proving that the person acted in conformity therewith on a particular occasion, except:
>
> (1) *Character of the accused. Evidence of a pertinent trait of the character of the accused offered by an accused, or by the prosecution to rebut the same.*

(Emphasis in last sentence added.)

Nevertheless, the military judge, granting the Government's motion, forbade testimony regarding appellant's good military character and his character for lawfulness, and permitted only evidence of his character for trustworthiness. The military judge stated:

> All right. Before I get to that, as to the case you cited [*United States v. Hewitt,* 634 F.2d 277 (5th Cir.1981), discussed herein], I have read it, and I find that although they say — state in there that "the character for lawfulness is admissible under the Rule 404," I do not find that

> that case is binding upon me, and I find that the finding of that appel-
> late court is contrary to what I have been taught and my interpreta-
> tion of the current rule, Military Rule 404, and in fact contrary to what
> the law should even be under the Federal Rules of Evidence. And since
> that is not an appellate court that is senior to this court, I find that
> although it is interesting and I found it enlightening to read the arti-
> cle, I do not find it binding in any way upon this court, and in fact I
> find it contrary to what our law is.

The military judge erred both in his misguided view of the applicability of federal precedent, *and* in his substantive rulings regarding Mil. R. Evid. 404(a)(1). . . .

[The court points out that the Military Rules of Evidence, specifically M.R.E. 101, expressly adopts federal precedent "insofar as practicable and not incon-sistent with or contrary to the Uniform Code of Military Justice or [the Manual for Courts-Martial."]

It is entirely clear that had this military judge applied Federal precedent, he would have acknowledged clear legal precedent for admission in this case of evidence of appellant's character for lawfulness. *United States v. Hewitt, supra.* The common law made a distinction between general good character and particular traits of character. *See McCormick's Handbook of the Law of Evidence* § 191 at 455 (E. Cleary 2d ed. 1972); J. Wigmore, *A Treatise on the Anglo-American System of Evidence in Trials at Common Law* §§ 59 and 458 (3d ed. 1940); Wright and Graham, *Federal Practice and Procedure: Evidence* § 5236 at 382 (1978) (hereafter cited as Wright). At common law, "the prevail-ing and more practical view" excludes proof of "general good character." *McCormick's, supra* at 453. *United States v. Angelini,* 678 F.2d 380 (1st Cir.1982), published subsequent to trial of the instant case, addresses admis-sibility of evidence of law-abidingness in light of Fed. R. Evid. 404. It con-cluded that "Rule 404 permits evidence of traits only" and "that evidence of a defendant's character as a law-abiding person is admissible." *Id.* at 382. As *Angelini* states: "Thus, the basic issue is whether the character trait in ques-tion would make any fact 'of consequence to the determination' of the case more or less probable than it would be without evidence of the trait. *See* Fed. R. Evid. 401; *United States v. Staggs,* 553 F.2d 1073" (7th Cir.1977). *Id.* at 381.

In the instant case, it is clear that the traits of good military character and character for lawfulness each evidenced "a pertinent trait of the character of the accused" in light of the principal theory of the defense case. Mil. R. Evid. 404(a)(1). "The word 'pertinent' is read as synonymous with 'relevant'. *United States v. Staggs,* . . . [*supra* at] 1075; 22 Wright & Graham, *Federal Practice and Procedure: Evidence* §5236, at 383 (1978)." *United States v. Angelini, supra* at 381. The "Drafters' Analysis" to Mil. R. Evid. 404(a)(1) indicates that "[i]t is the intention of the Committee, however, to allow the defense to introduce evidence of good military character when that specific trait is pertinent." Analysis, *supra,* Mil. R. Evid. 404(a)(1). *United States v. Angelini* and *United States v. Hewitt,* both *supra,* make clear the admissibility of the specific trait of law-abidingness.

In not denying entry into the barracks room or taking the television and cas-sette player, defense counsel posited the theory that appellant, functioning as

Charge of Quarters, was teaching his subordinates a lesson in security and personally securing the property in accordance with military responsibilities. We conclude that, to this end, the excluded evidence was entirely relevant and should have been admitted. Mil. R. Evid. 404(a)(1); *compare United States v. Angelini* with *United States v. Hewitt,* both *supra.* In line with *United States v. Hewitt, supra,* we are unable to say that appellant was not prejudiced. Article 59(a), 10 U.S.C. § 859(a). Accordingly, the decision of the United States Army Court of Military Review is reversed. The findings and sentence are set aside. The record of trial is returned to the Judge Advocate General of the Army. A rehearing may be ordered.

EVERETT, CHIEF JUDGE (concurring):

. . . The willingness of courts-martial to receive evidence of an accused's good character is quite understandable. As we noted in *United States v. Browning,* 1 U.S.C.M.A. 599, 601, 5 C.M.R. 27, 29 (1952), "Wigmore goes so far as to say that evidence of good soldierly character is even stronger than the customary evidence of good general character. Wigmore, Evidence, 3d ed., § 59." Dean Wigmore's rationale was that:

> The soldier is in an environment where all weaknesses or excesses have an opportunity to betray themselves. He is carefully observed by his superiors, — more carefully than falls to the lot of any member of the ordinary civil community; and all his delinquencies and merits are recorded systematically from time to time on his "service record," which follows him throughout his army career and serves as the basis for the terms of his final discharge.

Courts-martial were not unique in admitting evidence of general good character. As Dean Wigmore observed: "Doubtless in practice Courts often are liberal in permitting the defendant to offer his general character." J. Wigmore, *A Treatise on the Anglo-American System of Evidence in Trials at Common Law* § 59 (3d ed. 1940). A court of appeals recently noted:

> Our own survey convinces us that the actual practice in the states has generally been to permit defendants to establish their character for lawfulness, and that the federal courts have unanimously assumed that to be the practice.

In *Michelson v. United States,* 335 U.S. 469, 476 (1948), Justice Jackson pointed out in the majority opinion that the prosecution is not allowed to offer evidence of a defendant's bad general reputation unless he has put his character in issue; but he also explained that

> this line of inquiry firmly denied to the State is opened to the defendant because character is relevant in resolving probabilities of guilt. *He may introduce affirmative testimony that the general estimate of his character is so favorable that the jury may infer that he would not be likely to commit the offense charged.* This privilege is sometimes valuable to a defendant for this Court has held that such testimony alone, in some circumstances, may be enough to raise a reasonable doubt of guilt and that in the federal courts a jury in a proper case should be so instructed.

Edgington v. United States, 164 U.S. 361 [1896]. (Footnote omitted; emphasis supplied.) In *Michelson,* Justice Jackson also quoted "[a] typical examination in chief" of the character witnesses who had been offered by the defendant; and this examination illustrates how character evidence was handled in federal criminal trials before the Federal Rules of Evidence took effect. . . .

To support the exclusion of the evidence offered by appellant to show that he was a person of law-abiding character, the Government now relies on Mil.R.Evid. 404(a), which prescribes when character evidence is admissible. According to the "Drafters' Analysis, Mil. R. Evid. 404(a)(1), which "allows only evidence of a pertinent trait of character of the accused to be offered in evidence by the defense," makes

> a significant change from paragraph 138*f* of the [1969] Manual which also allows evidence of "general good character" of the accused to be received in order to demonstrate that the accused is less likely to have committed a criminal act. Under the new rule, evidence of general good character is inadmissible because only evidence of a specific trait is acceptable.

Analysis of the Military Rules of Evidence, Appendix 18, 1969 Manual, *supra,* Mil. R. Evid. 404(a)(1). The Government also insists that the reference in Mil. R. Evid. 404(a)(1) to "a pertinent trait of the character of the accused" was intended to impose a more rigorous requirement for reception of character evidence than would have existed if the rule had referred to a "relevant" trait. Otherwise, according to the Government, the Rule would have used the adjective "relevant," which has a meaning explained in Mil. R. Evid. 401.

In *Michelson,* the Supreme Court referred to its holdings that testimony as to a defendant's good character "alone, in some circumstances, may be enough to raise a reasonable doubt of guilt and that in the federal courts a jury in a proper case should be so instructed." 355 U.S. at 476. Many years before, in *Edgington v. United States, supra* 164 U.S. at 367, the Court quoted approvingly the observation of a state supreme court that "[p]roof of . . . [good character] may sometimes be the only mode by which an innocent man can repel the presumption arising from the possession of stolen goods. It is not proof of innocence, although it may be sufficient to raise a doubt of guilt." Our Court has adhered scrupulously to the same view that evidence of an accused's good character may raise a reasonable doubt as to his guilt. *See, e.g., United States v. Browning, supra.* In light of such precedents, it is hard to understand how evidence of a defendant's character as a law-abiding person — or, indeed, his general good character — would not be pertinent in the present case or, indeed, in almost any case that can be imagined. This seems especially true in light of the great weight which for decades has been attributed to character evidence in trials by courts-martial.

In construing Fed. R. Evid. 404(a), from which the corresponding Military Rule was derived, the Court of Appeals held in *United States v. Hewitt,* 634 F.2d 277, 280 (5th Cir.1981), that evidence of a defendant's "law-abiding" character should not have been excluded. Another Court of Appeals reached a similar conclusion in *United States v. Angelini,* 678 F.2d 380 (1st Cir.1982). Thus, Federal precedents — which, while not binding, clearly are highly instructive — indicate that in the present case the military judge erred in ruling that appellant could not introduce evidence of his law-abiding character.

Furthermore, if Mil. R. Evid. 404(a) were applied as the Government would urge, a substantial constitutional issue would be raised. Under the guarantees of due process and the sixth amendment, a technical rule of evidence cannot be used to exclude highly material evidence. *Cf. Washington v. Texas,* 388 U.S. 14 (1967) (co-indictee incompetent as defense witness); *Chambers v. Mississippi,* 410 U.S. 284 (1973) (voucher rule and hearsay rule applied to prevent cross-examination of defense witness as to prior statements); *Davis v. Alaska,* 415 U.S. 308 (1974) (cross-examination of prosecution witness prohibited as to his probation for juvenile offense). Since character evidence can itself generate reasonable doubt, its importance cannot be denied. As has already been noted, this is especially true in trials by courts-martial because of the reliability of character evidence under the conditions that prevail in the military community. . . .

In candor, I also must confess that I see very little difference between a person's being of "law-abiding" character and being of "good" character; and I suspect that over the years many witnesses who have testified about a defendant's "good" character really meant to say that he was "law-abiding." To say that the "goodness" of someone's character is a "trait" of his character may involve an unusual construction of the latter term. However, just as the Courts of Appeal in *Hewitt* and *Angelini* stretched "trait" to include "law-abiding" character in order to avoid an unjust — and possibly unconstitutional — result, I would take the same approach with respect to evidence of "general good character." Of course, under my view the scope of the Government's right to present rebuttal evidence would be co-extensive with the scope of the character evidence offered by the accused. . . .

NOTES AND QUESTIONS

1. Do soldiers with long and distinguished service records deserve the extra boost at trial that the good soldier defense provides? What is the purpose of prosecuting a person held in high esteem within the military community? Is such a person less likely to get a fair trial than someone less well-known or less privileged? Consider the assessment of one of the authors of this casebook:

> The good soldier defense is broadly available and frequently used at courts-martial. Although official guidance on Rule 404(a)(1) limits the introduction of "evidence of good military character" to those instances "when that specific trait is pertinent," military courts have deemed military character pertinent to every category of criminal offense. For an accused servicemember, the good soldier defense has many advantages. It is simple, easy to mount, and almost universally applicable. Nearly every servicemember can introduce good military character evidence, as officers and enlisted personnel receive periodic performance evaluations as a matter of routine, providing extensive documentary evidence of good character to supplement the affidavits and live testimony of military colleagues and commanders. . . .

The broad availability of the good soldier defense is supported by many legal doctrines and policy arguments, but none withstand close analysis. Cloaked in the mantle of longstanding court-martial tradition, justified by doctrines of questionable salience, and preserved by judges resistant to the Military Rules of Evidence's limitations on character evidence, the good soldier defense advances the perception that one of the privileges of high rank and long service is immunity from conviction at court-martial. The defense privileges a certain type of accused servicemember — a person of high rank and reputation in the military community — at the expense of the overall fairness of the court-martial system. By permitting the introduction of good military character evidence during the guilt phase of a court-martial, the good soldier defense encourages factfinders to focus on the reputation of accused individuals rather than on their alleged criminal acts. In a system already marked by extraordinary discretion, from a commander's decision about whether and how to bring criminal charges to the separate sentencing phase of trial, the good soldier defense undercuts the military justice system's commitment to an objective trial process by adding an element of subjectivity to the merits phase of a court-martial.

Elizabeth Lutes Hillman, *The "Good Soldier" Defense: Character Evidence and Military Rank at Courts-Martial*, 108 YALE L.J. 879 (1999). Professor Hillman's arguments provoked a response defending this evidentiary doctrine from students of Duke law professor (and former Chief Judge — see his concurrence above) Robinson O. Everett; *see* Randall D. Katz & Lawrence D. Sloan, *In Defense of the Good Soldier Defense*, 170 MIL. L. REV. 117 (2001).

2. Professor Chris Chambers Goodman argues in *The Color of Our Character: Confronting the Racial Character of Rule 404(B) Evidence*, 25 LAW & INEQ. 1 (2007), that character evidence permits prejudice and stereotypes to infiltrate the courtroom. Professor, and former U.S. Army judge advocate, Edward J. Imwinkelried writes in *The Dubiety of Social Engineering through Evidence: A Reply to Professor Sanchirico's Recent Article on Character Evidence*, 51 DRAKE L. REV. 283, 284 (2003), that:

> The United States Supreme Court has bemoaned the fact that the character evidence doctrine is a "grotesque structure." In Justice Jackson's words, the doctrine is "paradoxical and full of compromises and compensations by which an irrational advantage to one side is offset by a poorly reasoned counterprivilege to the other." The doctrine contains a number of troubling asymmetries. For example, although litigants ordinarily may not use a person's character as circumstantial evidence of the person's conduct on the historical merits of the case, the same litigants may employ a witness's character of untruthfulness as evidence that the witness lied during his or her testimony.

Are the rules governing the admission of character evidence irrational? Are the reasons for excluding character evidence from civilian criminal trials applicable at court-martial? Why is this area of law so confused and contested?

Chapter 10

FREEDOM OF SPEECH AND CONSCIENCE

I. FREEDOM OF SPEECH

One of the Supreme Court's most significant military justice decisions was its 1974 opinion in *Parker v. Levy*. That decision, which concerned an Army Captain making comments to enlisted soldiers that were critical of the United States' involvement in Vietnam during the height of that conflict, endorsed substantial limitations on servicemembers' First Amendment right to free speech. The Court reasoned:

> While the members of the military are not excluded from the protection granted by the First Amendment, the different character of the military community and of the military mission requires a different application of those protections. The fundamental necessity for obedience, and the consequent necessity for imposition of discipline, may render permissible within the military that which would be constitutionally impermissible outside it.

Parker v. Levy, 417 U.S. 733, 758 (1974). Applying this principle, military courts have repeatedly upheld convictions for political speech and communicative acts that would be constitutionally protected in a civilian setting. The Court of Appeals for the Armed Forces has also upheld child pornography convictions as service discrediting conduct or conduct prejudicial to good order and discipline even where conviction in a civilian setting would have been constitutionally prohibited.

Military courts have also rejected attempts to use the First Amendment's Free Exercise of Religion Clause as a defense to violation of orders and other military requirements. Finally, the U.S. military justice system has been hostile to attempts to use conscientious objection as a defense to charges arising from failure to deploy to a combat zone. The leitmotif of the military jurisprudence of freedom of speech and conscience is that virtually any asserted military rationale will prevail over an individual servicemember's First Amendment rights.

In the final part of this chapter, we will examine a foreign court decision and a United Nations Human Rights Committee decision thoughtfully addressing two important questions of freedom of conscience: (1) should a state accord conscientious objector status to citizens who object to a particular military operation rather than to military service in general; and (2) may a state that is a signatory to the Optional Protocol to the International Covenant on Civil and Political Rights decline to recognize any right to conscientious objection? On these issues, the United States appears to be in the international mainstream: Congress has established a system for conscientious objectors to be exempted from performing combatant duties, but the Supreme Court has refused to recognize an objection to a particular military operation, rather than participating in war in general, as falling within that congressionally established protection.

PARKER v. LEVY
Supreme Court of the United States
417 U.S. 733 (1974)

MR. JUSTICE REHNQUIST delivered the opinion of the Court.

Appellee Howard Levy, a physician, was a captain in the Army stationed at Fort Jackson, South Carolina. He . . . agreed to serve for two years in the Armed Forces if permitted first to complete his medical training. From the time he entered on active duty in July 1965 until his trial by court-martial, he was assigned as Chief of the Dermatological Service of the United States Army Hospital at Fort Jackson. On June 2, 1967, appellee was convicted by a general court-martial of violations of Arts. 90, 133, and 134 of the Uniform Code of Military Justice, and sentenced to dismissal from the service, forfeiture of all pay and allowances, and confinement for three years at hard labor.

The facts upon which his conviction rests are virtually undisputed. The evidence admitted at his court-martial trial showed that one of the functions of the hospital to which appellee was assigned was that of training Special Forces aide men. As Chief of the Dermatological Service, appellee was to conduct a clinic for those aide men. In the late summer of 1966, it came to the attention of the hospital commander that the dermatology training of the students was unsatisfactory. After investigating the program and determining that appellee had totally neglected his duties, the commander called appellee to his office and personally handed him a written order to conduct the training. Appellee read the order, said that he understood it, but declared that he would not obey it because of his medical ethics. Appellee persisted in his refusal to obey the order, and later reviews of the program established that the training was still not being carried out.

During the same period of time, appellee made several public statements to enlisted personnel at the post, of which the following is representative:

> "The United States is wrong in being involved in the Viet Nam War. I would refuse to go to Viet Nam if ordered to do so. I don't see why any colored soldier would go to Viet Nam: they should refuse to go to Viet Nam and if sent should refuse to fight because they are discriminated against and denied their freedom in the United States, and they are sacrificed and discriminated against in Viet Nam by being given all the hazardous duty and they are suffering the majority of casualties. If I were a colored soldier I would refuse to go to Viet Nam and if I were a colored soldier and were sent I would refuse to fight. Special Forces personnel are liars and thieves and killers of peasants and murderers of women and children."

Appellee's military superiors originally contemplated nonjudicial proceedings against him under Art. 15 of the Uniform Code of Military Justice, 10

U.S.C. §815, but later determined that court-martial proceedings were appropriate. The specification under Art. 90 alleged that appellee willfully disobeyed the hospital commandant's order to establish the training program, in violation of that article, which punishes anyone subject to the Uniform Code of Military Justice who "willfully disobeys a lawful command of his superior commissioned officer." Statements to enlisted personnel were listed as specifications under the charges of violating Arts. 133 and 134 of the Code. Article 133 provides for the punishment of "conduct unbecoming an officer and a gentleman," while Art. 134 proscribes, *inter alia*, "all disorders and neglects to the prejudice of good order and discipline in the armed forces."

The specification under Art. 134 alleged that appellee "did, at Fort Jackson, South Carolina, . . . with design to promote disloyalty and disaffection among the troops, publicly utter [certain] statements to divers enlisted personnel at divers times. . . ." The specification under Art. 133 alleged that appellee did "while in the performance of his duties at the United States Army Hospital . . . wrongfully and dishonorably" make statements variously described as intemperate, defamatory, provoking, disloyal, contemptuous, and disrespectful to Special Forces personnel and to enlisted personnel who were patients or under his supervision.

Appellee was convicted by the court-martial, and his conviction was sustained on his appeals within the military. [*United States v. Levy*, 39 C.M.R. 672 (1968), *petition for review denied*, 18 U.S.C.M.A. 627 (1969).] After he had exhausted this avenue of relief, he sought federal habeas corpus in the United States District Court for the Middle District of Pennsylvania, challenging his court-martial conviction on a number of grounds. The District Court, on the basis of the voluminous record of the military proceedings and the argument of counsel, denied relief. . . .

This Court has long recognized that the military is, by necessity, a specialized society separate from civilian society. We have also recognized that the military has, again by necessity, developed laws and traditions of its own during its long history. The differences between the military and civilian communities result from the fact that "it is the primary business of armies and navies to fight or be ready to fight wars should the occasion arise." *United States ex rel. Toth v. Quarles*, 350 U.S. 11, 17 (1955). In *In re Grimley*, 137 U.S. 147, 153 (1890), the Court observed: "An army is not a deliberative body. It is the executive arm. Its law is that of obedience. No question can be left open as to the right to command in the officer, or the duty of obedience in the soldier." More recently we noted that "the military constitutes a specialized community governed by a separate discipline from that of the civilian," *Orloff v. Willoughby*, 345 U.S. 83, 94 (1953), and that "the rights of men in the armed forces must perforce be conditioned to meet certain overriding demands of discipline and duty. . . ." *Burns v. Wilson*, 346 U.S. 137, 140 (1953) (plurality opinion). We have also recognized that a military officer holds a particular position of responsibility and command in the Armed Forces:

> "The President's commission . . . recites that 'reposing special trust and confidence in the patriotism, valor, fidelity and abilities' of the appointee he is named to the specified rank during the pleasure of the President." *Orloff v. Willoughby, supra*, at 91. . . .

III

Appellee urges that both Art. 133 and Art. 134 (the general article) are . . . overbroad in violation of the First Amendment. . . .

We . . . reject appellee's contention that Arts. 133 and 134 are facially invalid because of their "overbreadth." In *Gooding v. Wilson*, 405 U.S., at 520-521, the Court said:

> "It matters not that the words appellee used might have been constitutionally prohibited under a narrowly and precisely drawn statute. At least when statutes regulate or proscribe speech and when 'no readily apparent construction suggests itself as a vehicle for rehabilitating the statutes in a single prosecution,' *Dombrowski v. Pfister*, 380 U.S. 479, 491 (1965), the transcendent value to all society of constitutionally protected expression is deemed to justify allowing 'attacks on overly broad statutes with no requirement that the person making the attack demonstrate that his own conduct could not be regulated by a statute drawn with the requisite narrow specificity'. . . ."

While the members of the military are not excluded from the protection granted by the First Amendment, the different character of the military community and of the military mission requires a different application of those protections. The fundamental necessity for obedience, and the consequent necessity for imposition of discipline, may render permissible within the military that which would be constitutionally impermissible outside it. Doctrines of First Amendment overbreadth asserted in support of challenges to imprecise language like that contained in Arts. 133 and 134 are not exempt from the operation of these principles. The United States Court of Military Appeals has sensibly expounded the reason for this different application of First Amendment doctrines in its opinion in *United States v. Priest*, 21 U.S.C.M.A., at 570, 45 C.M.R., at 344:

> "In the armed forces some restrictions exist for reasons that have no counterpart in the civilian community. Disrespectful and contemptuous speech, even advocacy of violent change, is tolerable in the civilian community, for it does not directly affect the capacity of the Government to discharge its responsibilities unless it both is directed to inciting imminent lawless action and is likely to produce such action. *Brandenburg v. Ohio*, [395 U.S. 444 (1969)]. In military life, however, other considerations must be weighed. The armed forces depend on a command structure that at times must commit men to combat, not only hazarding their lives but ultimately involving the security of the Nation itself. Speech that is protected in the civil population may nonetheless undermine the effectiveness of response to command. If it does, it is constitutionally unprotected." *United States v. Gray*, [20 U.S.C.M.A. 63, 42 C.M.R. 255 (1970)].

In *Broadrick v. Oklahoma*, 413 U.S. 601, 610 (1973), we said that "embedded in the traditional rules governing constitutional adjudication is the principle that a person to whom a statute may constitutionally be applied will not be heard to challenge that statute on the ground that it may conceivably be applied unconstitutionally to others, in other situations not before the Court."

We further commented in that case that "in the past, the Court has recognized some limited exceptions to these principles, but only because of the most 'weighty countervailing policies.'" *Id.*, at 611. One of those exceptions "has been carved out in the area of the First Amendment." *Ibid.* In the First Amendment context attacks have been permitted "on overly broad statutes with no requirement that the person making the attack demonstrate that his own conduct could not be regulated by a statute drawn with the requisite narrow specificity." *Dombrowski v. Pfister*, 380 U.S. 479, 486 (1965).

This Court has, however, repeatedly expressed its reluctance to strike down a statute on its face where there were a substantial number of situations to which it might be validly applied. Thus, even if there are marginal applications in which a statute would infringe on First Amendment values, facial invalidation is inappropriate if the "remainder of the statute . . . covers a whole range of easily identifiable and constitutionally proscribable . . . conduct. . . ." *CSC v. Letter Carriers*, 413 U.S. 548, 580-581 (1973). And the Court recognized in *Broadrick, supra,* that "where conduct and not merely speech is involved" the overbreadth must "not only be real, but substantial as well, judged in relation to the statute's plainly legitimate sweep." 413 U.S., at 615. Here, as the Manual makes clear, both Art. 133 and Art. 134 do prohibit a "whole range of easily identifiable and constitutionally proscribable . . . conduct."

Both *Broadrick* and *Letter Carriers* involved basically noncriminal sanctions imposed on federal and state employees who were otherwise civilians. The Uniform Code of Military Justice applies a series of sanctions, varying from severe criminal penalties to administratively imposed minor sanctions, upon members of the military. However, for the reasons dictating a different application of First Amendment principles in the military context described above, we think that the "'weighty countervailing policies,'" *Broadrick, supra,* at 611, which permit the extension of standing in First Amendment cases involving civilian society, must be accorded a good deal less weight in the military context.

There is a wide range of the conduct of military personnel to which Arts. 133 and 134 may be applied without infringement of the First Amendment. While there may lurk at the fringes of the articles, even in the light of their narrowing construction by the United States Court of Military Appeals, some possibility that conduct which would be ultimately held to be protected by the First Amendment could be included within their prohibition, we deem this insufficient to invalidate either of them at the behest of appellee. His conduct, that of a commissioned officer publicly urging enlisted personnel to refuse to obey orders which might send them into combat, was unprotected under the most expansive notions of the First Amendment. Articles 133 and 134 may constitutionally prohibit that conduct, and a sufficiently large number of similar or related types of conduct so as to preclude their invalidation for overbreadth. . . .

MR. JUSTICE DOUGLAS, dissenting.

Congress by Art. I, § 8, cl. 14, has power "To make Rules for the Government and Regulation of the land and naval Forces."

Articles 133 and 134 of the Uniform Code of Military Justice, 10 U.S.C. §§ 933 and 934, at issue in this case, trace their legitimacy to that power.

So far as I can discover the only express exemption of a person in the Armed Services from the protection of the Bill of Rights is that contained in the Fifth Amendment which dispenses with the need for "a presentment or indictment" of a grand jury "in cases arising in the land or naval forces, or in the Militia, when in actual service in time of War or public danger."

By practice and by construction the words "all criminal prosecutions" in the Sixth Amendment do not necessarily cover all military trials. One result is that the guarantee of the Sixth Amendment of trial "by an impartial jury" is not applicable to military trials. But Judge Ferguson in *United States v. Tempia*, 16 U.S.C.M.A. 629, 37 C.M.R. 249, properly said:

> "[B]oth the Supreme Court and this Court itself are satisfied as to the applicability of constitutional safeguards to military trials, except insofar as they are made inapplicable either expressly or by necessary implication. The Government, therefore, is correct in conceding the point, and the Judge Advocate General, United States Navy, as *amicus curiae*, is incorrect in his contrary conclusion. Indeed, as to the latter, it would appear from the authorities on which he relies that the military courts applied what we now know as the constitutional protection against self-incrimination in trials prior to and contemporaneous with the adoption of the Constitution. Hence, we find Major Andre being extended the privilege at his court-martial in 1780. Wigmore, Evidence, 3d ed, § 2251. The same reference was made in the trial of Commodore James Barron in 1808. Proceedings of the General Court Martial Convened for the Trial of Commodore James Barron (1822), page 98. And, the Articles of War of 1776, as amended May 31, 1786, provided for objection by the judge advocate to any question put to the accused, the answer to which might tend to incriminate him. See Winthrop's Military Law and Precedents, 2d ed, 1920 Reprint, pages 196, 972. 16 U.S.C.M.A., at 634, 37 C.M.R., at 254."

But the cases we have had so far have concerned only the nature of the tribunal which may try a person and/or the procedure to be followed. This is the first case that presents to us a question of what protection, if any, the First Amendment gives people in the Armed Services:

Congress shall make no law . . . abridging the freedom of speech, or of the press.

On its face there are no exceptions — no preferred classes for whose benefit the First Amendment extends, no exempt classes.

The military by tradition and by necessity demands discipline; and those necessities require obedience in training and in action. A command is speech brigaded with action, and permissible commands may not be disobeyed. There may be a borderland or penumbra that in time can be established by litigated cases.

I cannot imagine, however, that Congress would think it had the power to authorize the military to curtail the reading list of books, plays, poems, periodicals, papers, and the like which a person in the Armed Services may read. Nor can I believe Congress would assume authority to empower the military to suppress conversations at a bar, ban discussions of public affairs, prevent enlisted men or women or draftees from meeting in discussion groups at times and places and for such periods of time that do not interfere with the performance of military duties.

Congress has taken no such step here. By Art. 133 it has allowed punishment for "conduct unbecoming an officer and a gentleman." In our society where diversities are supposed to flourish it never could be "unbecoming" to express one's views, even on the most controversial public issue.

Article 134 covers only "all disorders and neglects to the prejudice of good order and discipline in the armed forces, all conduct of a nature to bring discredit upon the armed forces."

Captain Levy, the appellee in the present case, was not convicted under Arts. 133 and 134 for failure to give the required medical instructions. But as he walked through the facilities and did his work, or met with students, he spoke of his views of the "war" in Vietnam. Thus he said:

> "The United States is wrong in being involved in the Viet Nam War. I would refuse to go to Viet Nam if ordered to do so. I don't see why any colored soldier would go to Viet Nam; they should refuse to go to Viet Nam and if sent should refuse to fight because they are discriminated against and denied their freedom in the United States, and they are sacrificed and discriminated against in Viet Nam by being given all the hazardous duty and they are suffering the majority of casualties. If I were a colored soldier I would refuse to go to Viet Nam and if I were a colored soldier and were sent I would refuse to fight. Special Forces personnel are liars and thieves and killers of peasants and murderers of women and children."

Those ideas affronted some of his superiors. The military, of course, tends to produce homogenized individuals who think — as well as march — in unison. In *United States v. Blevens*, 5 U.S.C.M.A. 480, 18 C.M.R. 104, the Court of Military Appeals upheld the court-martial conviction of a serviceman who had "affiliated" himself with a Communist organization in Germany. The serviceman argued that there was no allegation that he possessed any intent to overthrow the Government by force, so that the Smith Act, 18 U.S.C. § 2385, would not reach his conduct. The Court of Military Appeals affirmed on the theory that his affiliation, nonetheless, brought "discredit" on the Armed Forces within the meaning of Art. 134:

> "Most important to the case is the Government's contention that regardless of any deficiencies under the Smith Act, the specification properly alleges, and the evidence adequately establishes, conduct to the discredit of the armed forces, in violation of Article 134. . . .

Membership by a school teacher in an organization advocating the violent disestablishment of the United States Government has been regarded as conduct requiring dismissal. *Adler v. Board of Education*, 342 U.S. 485. It seems to us that such membership is even more profoundly evil in the case of a person in the military establishment. True, affiliation implies something less than membership (*Bridges v. Wixon*, 326 U.S. 135, 143), but the supreme duty of the military is the protection and security of the government and of the people. Hence, aside from a specific intent on the part of the accused to overthrow the government by violence, the conduct alleged is definitely discrediting to the armed forces." 5 U.S.C.M.A., at 483-484, 18 C.M.R., at 107-108.

The limitations on expressions of opinion by members of the military continue to date. During the Vietnam war, a second lieutenant in the reserves, off duty, out of uniform, and off base near a local university, carried a placard in an antiwar demonstration which said "END JOHNSON'S FACIST [*sic*] AGGRESSION IN VIET NAM." He was convicted by a court-martial under Art. 88 for using "contemptuous words" against the President and under Art. 133 for "conduct unbecoming an officer." The Court of Military Appeals affirmed, theorizing that suppression of such speech was essential to prevent a military "man on a white horse" from challenging "civilian control of the military." *United States v. Howe*, 17 U.S.C.M.A. 165, 175, 37 C.M.R. 429, 439. The Court did not attempt to weigh the likelihood that Howe, a reserve second lieutenant engaging in a single off-base expression of opinion on the most burning political issue of the day, could ever be such a "man on a white horse." Indeed, such considerations were irrelevant:

> "True, petitioner is a reserve officer, rather than a professional officer, but during the time he serves on active duty he is, and must be, controlled by the provisions of military law. In this instance, military restrictions fall upon a reluctant 'summer soldier'; but at another time, and differing circumstances, the ancient and wise provisions insuring civilian control of the military will restrict the 'man on a white horse.'" *Ibid.* See generally Sherman, *The Military Courts and Servicemen's First Amendment Rights*, 22 Hastings L.J. 325 (1971.)

The power to draft an army includes, of course, the power to curtail considerably the "liberty" of the people who make it up. But Congress in these articles has not undertaken to cross the forbidden First Amendment line. Making a speech or comment on one of the most important and controversial public issues of the past two decades cannot by any stretch of dictionary meaning be included in "disorders and neglects to the prejudice of good order and discipline in the armed forces." Nor can what Captain Levy said possibly be "conduct of a nature to bring discredit upon the armed forces." He was uttering his own belief — an article of faith that he sincerely held. This was no mere ploy to perform a "subversive" act. Many others who loved their country shared his views. They were not saboteurs. Uttering one's beliefs is sacrosanct under the First Amendment. Punishing the utterances is an "abridgment" of speech in the constitutional sense.

NOTES AND QUESTIONS

1. The tone of Justice Douglas' dissent is similar to his opinion for the Court in *O'Callahan v. Parker*, 395 U.S. 258 (1969), where a 5-3 majority had sharply curtained the military justice system's subject-matter jurisdiction. But the Supreme Court of 1974 was markedly different than that of 1969. Four of the five justices in the *Parker v. Levy* majority had not been on the Court when it decided *O'Callahan* five years before.

2. Should the outcome in *Parker v. Levy* have been affected by the existence of the military draft when Captain Levy committed his offenses? Are restrictions on servicemembers' constitutional rights more defensible for an all-volunteer military than for a force that includes a substantial percentage of conscripts?

UNITED STATES v. WILSON
United States Army Court of Military Review
33 M.J. 797 (A.C.M.R. 1991)

GRAVELLE, J.

. . . The issue presented is whether the appellant's act of blowing his nose on the American flag, while he was a member of a flag-raising detail, was conduct protected by the free speech provisions of the First Amendment. We hold that it was not protected speech.

I

The appellant, a military policeman (MP), while preparing for a flag-raising detail, complained to his fellow MPs that the Army and the United States "sucked." Another MP told him that he should move to a communist country if he didn't like it. The appellant replied, "[this] is what I think," and blew his nose on the American flag, leaving on the flag "a small wet circle." After another brief exchange of words, the appellant participated without further incident in the flag-raising detail. For his action the appellant was charged with dereliction of duty in that he "willfully failed to ensure that the United States flag was treated with proper respect by blowing his nose on the flag when it was his duty as a military policeman on flag call to safeguard and protect the flag." . . .

II

Members of the armed forces enjoy the First Amendment's protections of freedom of speech. This includes not only the right to verbally express ideas but also to utilize non-verbal means of communication. However, members of the armed forces may be subject to restraints on the exercise of their freedom of speech not faced by civilians. This is so because the needs of the armed forces may warrant regulation of conduct that would not justified in the civilian community. *United States v. Womack*, 29 M.J. 88 (C.M.A. 1989), citing *Parker v. Levy*, 417 U.S. 733 (1974), and *United States v. Hoard*, 12 M.J. 563 (A.C.M.R. 1981), *pet. denied*, 13 M.J. 31 (C.M.A. 1982). The Supreme Court has said:

> Our review of military regulations challenged on First Amendment grounds is far more deferential than constitutional review of similar laws or regulations designed for civilian society. The military need not encourage debate or tolerate protest to the extent that such tolerance

is required of the civilian state by the First Amendment; to accomplish its mission the military must foster instinctive obedience, unity, commitment and esprit de corps. . . . The essence of military service "is the subordination of the desires and interests of the individual to the needs of the service."

Goldman v. Weinberger, 475 U.S. 503, 507 (1986*)*, citing *Orloff v. Willoughby*, 345 U.S. 83, 92, (1953). Military necessity, including the fundamental necessity for discipline, can be a compelling government interest warranting the limitation of the right of freedom of speech. *See e.g., United States v. McFarlin*, 19 M.J. 790 (A.C.M.R. 1985), *pet. denied*, 20 M.J. 314 (C.M.A. 1985) (governmental interest in preventing sexual liaisons between noncommissioned officers and subordinates is sufficiently compelling to justify governmental regulation of privacy right). "[The] right of free speech in the armed services is not unlimited and must be brought into balance with the paramount consideration of providing an effective fighting force for the defense of our Country." *United States v. Priest*, 45 C.M.R. 338, 344 (C.M.A. 1972).

The First Amendment protects not only words but "expressive conduct." *Texas v. Johnson*, [491 U.S. 397, 403-04 (1989)]. Desecration of the American flag can amount to expressive conduct protected by the First Amendment. *Id.* Such conduct cannot be prohibited simply because society may find the idea embodied in the symbolic act offensive or disagreeable. *Id.* at 2544. The government has a freer hand in limiting expressive conduct than it has in restricting the written or spoken word. *Id.* at 2540.

In addressing the First Amendment issue, two questions need to be answered. First, was the conduct expressive in nature? Second, if the conduct was expressive, was the government's regulation only incidentally related to the suppression of free speech? *Johnson*, 491 U.S. 397. If both questions are answered in the affirmative, we apply a four-part test established by the Supreme Court in *United States v. O'Brien*, 391 U.S. 367, *reh'g denied*, 393 U.S. 900 (1968). *Johnson*, 491 U.S. 397; *Barnes v. Glen Theatre, Inc.*, 501 U.S. 560 (1991). The four-part test in *O'Brien*, to determine if a government regulation is sufficiently justified, is as follows:

> [If the regulation] is within the constitutional power of the Government; if it furthers an important or substantial governmental interest; if the governmental interest is unrelated to the suppression of free expression; and if the incidental restriction on alleged First Amendment freedoms is no greater than is essential to the furtherance of that interest.

391 U.S. at 377.

III

In addressing the First Amendment issue, the military judge specifically found that the appellant's conduct was expressive and that the government's regulation of the conduct was related only incidentally to the appellant's free speech, therefore, the *O'Brien* four-part test applied. We agree with the military judge's conclusions.

The government regulation in the case at bar is Article 92(3), UCMJ, which proscribes derelictions in the performance of duty. We find that Article 92(3), UCMJ, meets the four-part test of *O'Brien*. First, Article 92, UCMJ, is a legitimate regulatory measure because the government may regulate the conduct of soldiers. United States Constitution, article I, section 8. The military judge correctly concluded that the government may regulate a soldier's conduct while on duty and in uniform. *See, e.g., Weinberger*, 475 U.S. 503. Second, Article 92, UCMJ, furthers an important and substantial government interest in promoting an effective military force. "To prepare for and perform its vital role, the military must insist upon a respect for duty and a discipline without counterpart in civilian life." *United States v. Heyward*, 22 M.J. 35, 37 (C.M.A.), *aff'd*, 23 M.J. 49 (C.M.A.), *cert. denied*, 479 U.S. 1011 (1986), quoting *Schlesinger v. Councilman*, 420 U.S. 738, 757 (1975). Third, the purpose of Article 92, UCMJ, in proscribing failures to perform military duty is, on its face, unrelated to the suppression of free speech. Finally, the incidental restriction of alleged First Amendment freedoms is no greater than is essential to further the government interest in promoting the disciplined performance of military duties.

The military judge properly considered several factors in determining that the appellant had violated a legitimate military duty. He properly took into account the unique needs of the military community, the appellant's flag-raising duty as a military policeman at the time of the incident, and the fact that the prosecution was for dereliction of a duty to safeguard the government-owned flag. Furthermore, the military judge correctly balanced the needs of the government in promoting a disciplined military force with the rights of the appellant under the First Amendment.[1] Under the facts of this case, the appellant's claim that his First Amendment rights were violated is without merit. . . .

NOTES

1. *United States v. Brown*, 45 M.J. 389 (C.A.A.F. 1996), involved a Louisiana National Guardsman who was convicted of several offenses arising from his attempt to organize a strike among soldiers in his unit, which had mobilized and deployed to Fort Hood in support of Operation Desert Shield/Desert Storm. The Court of Appeals for the Armed Forces observed, "The interest in maintaining good order and discipline has few counterparts in the civilian community. Thus, courts will 'not overturn a conviction unless it is clearly apparent that, in the face of a First Amendment claim, the military lacks a legitimate interest in proscribing the defendant's conduct.'" 45 M.J. at 396 (quoting *Avrech v. Secretary of the Navy*, 520 F.2d 100, 103 (D.C. Cir. 1975)). The court found that the military had such a legitimate interest in preventing a soldier from attempting to organize a labor action, particularly in the context of mobilization for Operation Desert Shield/Desert Storm. *See* 45 M.J. at 397-98.

---

[1] [n.6] The military judge, immediately following announcement of sentence, said, "[for] the record I did not punish the accused for the content of his message expressed on the morning of 31 December."

2. Cases like *Parker v. Levy, United States v. Brown,* and the pre-*Parker v. Levy* decision in *United States v. Howe,* 17 U.S.C.M.A. 165, 37 C.M.R. 429 (1967) (rejecting First Amendment challenge to Article 88 conviction of Army second lieutenant who carried sign at public demonstration referring to President Johnson as a "facist" [*sic*]), involved political speech. Most recent military appellate decisions dealing with the Free Speech Clause have concerned child pornography. Clause 3 of Article 134 of the UCMJ provides that a court-martial can convict a servicemember for violating "crimes and offenses not capital," which generally allows a court-martial to enforce federal criminal statutes. In 2001, the Court of Appeals for the Armed Forces initially affirmed a conviction for violating the Child Pornography Prevention Act of 1996, 18 U.S.C. § 2252A (CPPA). *United States v. O'Connor,* 56 M.J. 141 (C.A.A.F. 2001) (summary disposition). Shortly after deciding *Ashcroft v. Free Speech Coalition,* 535 U.S. 234 (2002), however, the Supreme Court granted O'Connor's petition for a writ of certiorari, vacated the Court of Appeals' judgment, and remanded for further consideration in light of *Free Speech Coalition. O'Connor v. United States,* 535 U.S. 1014 (2002) (mem.). *Free Speech Coalition* held that portions of the CPPA criminalizing visual depictions that "appear to be" minors engaging in sexually explicit conduct and material that "conveys the impression" that it depicts minors engaging in sexually explicit conduct were unconstitutionally overbroad. But the Supreme Court upheld other provisions of the CPPA dealing with child pornography depicting actual children. On remand, the Court of Appeals applied *Free Speech Coalition* and set aside O'Connor's conviction under the CPPA. *United States v. O'Connor,* 58 M.J. 450 (C.A.A.F. 2003). But the court expressly held open the possibility that a child pornography offense that could not be constitutionally upheld under the CPPA might nevertheless be the basis for a finding of guilty under Clause 2 of Article 134, which prohibits "all conduct of a nature to bring discredit upon the armed forces." *Id.* at 454-55. The next case directly addressed that issue, as well as whether conduct that could not be constitutionally proscribed by the CPPA might nevertheless violate Clause 1 of Article 134, which prohibits "all disorders and neglects to the prejudice of good order and discipline in the armed forces."

UNITED STATES v. MASON
United States Court of Appeals for the Armed Forces
60 M.J. 15 (C.A.A.F. 2004)

JUDGE ERDMANN delivered the opinion of the Court.

Major Robert L. Mason, Jr., entered guilty pleas and was convicted by a general court-martial of violating a lawful general order, engaging in conduct unbecoming an officer and a gentleman and knowingly receiving child pornography in violation of Articles 92, 133 and 134, Uniform Code of Military Justice [UCMJ], 10 U.S.C. §§ 892, 933 and 934 (2000), respectively. . . .

Background

Mason served as a contracting officer assigned to the Defense Supply Center Columbus (DSCC), an arm of the Defense Logistics Agency. The DSCC routinely handles highly sensitive and classified procurement matters, including multi-million dollar contracts. It is primarily staffed with over 2500 civilian employees, but is also staffed by a small contingent of military members, of which Mason was a part.

The DSCC monitored its employees' access to the Internet and during the course of that general monitoring process, Mason was identified as having accessed inappropriate websites. Subsequent monitoring and investigation disclosed that Mason had utilized two different DSCC computers to (1) view and/or download from the Internet various items with pornographic and obscene images or language; (2) participate in teen "chat rooms" and engage in discussions of a sexual nature; and (3) receive images of child pornography.

Mason was ultimately charged under Article 92 with three specifications of violating a general regulation pertaining to use of government computers, under Article 133 with one specification for conduct unbecoming an officer and a gentleman based on certain activities that he engaged in on the computers and under clause 3 of Article 134 with one specification of violating the Child Pornography Prevention Act of 1996 (CPPA), 18 U.S.C. § 2252A (2000).

The present appeal concerns the providence of Mason's guilty plea to the Article 134 charge. For this Court to reject a guilty plea on appellate review, the record of trial must show a substantial basis in law and fact for questioning the plea. *United States v. Jordan*, 57 M.J. 236, 238 (C.A.A.F. 2002) (citing *United States v. Prater*, 32 M.J. 433, 436 (C.M.A. 1991)).

Discussion

A. The Providence Inquiry and Record of Trial

Under the clause 3 Article 134 specification, Mason was charged with a violation of the CPPA. The military judge explained that the statutory offense involved the knowing receipt of child pornography that had been transported in interstate or foreign commerce and was "assimilated into the [UCMJ] as another crime or offense not capital" under Article 134. The military judge advised Mason that the definitions for the CPPA offense were found in 18 U.S.C. § 2256 (2000) and went on to define numerous terms, specifically including the alternative definitions of "child pornography" under §§ 2256(8)(A)-(D):

> Child pornography means any visual depiction, including any photograph, film, video picture, or computer, or computer generated image or picture, whether made or produced by electronic, mechanical or other means for [sic] sexually explicit conduct where: a) the production of such visual depiction involves the use of a minor engaging in sexually explicit conduct; b) such visual depiction is or appears to be of a minor engaging in sexually explicit conduct; c) such visual depiction has been created, adapted or modified to appear that an identifiable minor is engaging in sexually explicit conduct; or, d) such visual depiction is advertised, promoted, presented, described, or distributed in such a manner that conveys the impression that the material is or contains a visual depiction of a minor engaging in sexually explicit conduct.

In addition to advising Mason of the definitional elements of the CPPA offense, the military judge included what he termed a "fourth element":

> Fourth — and I instruct on this only in this case if it is determined that your plea is improvident on the charged offense, since the crime has been charged as an other crime or offense not capital — such conduct was of a nature to bring discredit upon the armed forces or was to the conduct [*sic*] of good order and discipline in the armed forces.

He went on to specifically ask Mason if he understood that "fourth element" and why it had been included. After consulting with his defense counsel, Mason answered in the affirmative and indicated that he understood the element required that "his conduct must also be such to bring discredit upon the Air Force." The military judge then further explained to Mason why it had been included:

> Now, it's my position with the charged offense as it is charged in Charge III, that is not an element of the charged offense. However, in the abundance of caution, I add that as an element in case for some reason the appellate courts, if this case goes to the appeals system, determines your plea to the . . . [CPPA] charge is improvident, it would find that it was service discrediting or armed forces discrediting. That is why I have added that element.

Mason indicated his understanding as to why that element had been added, indicated that he had no questions about any of the elements and acknowledged that he believed and admitted that the elements and definitions he had been given, taken together, correctly described what he had done. He explained to the military judge that he had viewed several pictures of "minors doing lascivious poses" on his government computers and that he understood the movement of those images over the Internet was considered movement through interstate commerce. He admitted during his discussion with the military judge and in his stipulation of fact that the images were "child pornography." He also admitted during his discussion with the military judge that his conduct was of a nature to bring discredit upon the armed forces or was to the prejudice of good order and discipline.

B. The Impact of *Free Speech Coalition* and *O'Connor*

The granted issue asks whether Mason's plea to the charged offense under clause 3 of Article 134 is provident in light of the Supreme Court's decision in *Free Speech Coalition* and our subsequent decision in *O'Connor*. The specified issue asks whether, in the event of a negative answer to the granted issue, Mason's guilty plea can nonetheless be upheld as provident to a lesser-included offense under clauses 1 or 2 of Article 134. We turn first to the granted issue.

1. The Providence of the Plea under Clause 3

As explained to him by the military judge, Mason's conduct in receiving "child pornography" was charged as a "clause 3" offense under Article 134, with the "crime or offense not capital" being a violation of the CPPA. Thus, the criminal nature of Mason's conduct, as charged, derived from violating an independent federal criminal statute proscribing the receipt of "child pornography." *O'Connor*, 58 M.J. at 452.

The military judge defined the elemental term "child pornography" to Mason by using portions of its statutory definition that were later struck down by the Supreme Court in *Free Speech Coalition*. As occurred in *O'Connor*, the military judge's explanation to Mason of the elements of the CPPA offense utilized terms that were constitutionally overbroad. The judge's explanation made specific reference to visual depictions that "appear to be" of a minor engaging in sexually explicit conduct and materials that were pandered in a manner that "conveys the impression" that they include images of minors engaging in sexually explicit conduct. Finally, as was also the case in *O'Connor*, the record here contains no clear focus or discussion on those aspects of the CPPA not affected by the Supreme Court's ruling, i.e., "actual" child pornography under 18 U.S.C. §§ 2256(8)(A)-(B) or "computer morphed" images of an identifiable minor under § 2256(8)(C). *O'Connor*, 58 M.J. at 452.

Under our decision in *O'Connor*, a provident guilty plea to a violation of the CPPA must reflect that the accused violated those portions of the statute not affected by the Supreme Court's ruling in *Free Speech Coalition*. 58 M.J. at 454. The absence of any focus on or discussion concerning those aspects of the statute in the present record coupled with the use of the unconstitutionally overbroad definition during Mason's plea colloquy render this case indistinguishable from *O'Connor*. Accordingly, we cannot view Mason's plea of guilty to violating the CPPA, and thus to violating clause 3 of Article 134, as provident.

2. The Providence of the Plea under Clauses 1 and 2

That conclusion leads us to the specified issue — can Mason's guilty plea nonetheless be viewed as provident to a lesser-included offense under clauses 1 and/or 2 of Article 134? As noted in *O'Connor*, we have recognized in the past that an improvident plea to a clause 3 offense based on a federal child pornography statute may be upheld as a provident plea to a lesser-included offense under clause 2 of Article 134. 58 M.J. at 454 (citing *United States v. Augustine*, 53 M.J. 95 (C.A.A.F. 2000); *United States v. Sapp*, 53 M.J. 90 (C.A.A.F. 2000)).

In *O'Connor*, we ultimately concluded that the guilty plea could not be viewed as provident to a lesser-included offense under the approach embodied in *Sapp* and *Augustine*. While O'Connor had stipulated to the service-discrediting character of his conduct, there was no discussion of that element by the military judge during the plea inquiry. Both *Sapp* and *Augustine* involved admissions by the accused during the plea inquiry as to the service-discrediting character of their conduct and we characterized those discussions as demonstrating that the accused "clearly understood the nature of the prohibited conduct." 58 M.J. at 454 (quoting *Sapp*, 53 M.J. at 92).

The plea colloquy in *O'Connor* was focused solely on "the nature of the prohibited conduct" under the CPPA, without any discussion or acknowledgement of the criminal nature of the conduct deriving alternatively (and independently) from its character as service-discrediting or prejudicial to good order and discipline. 58 M.J. at 455. Absent any discussion with the military judge as to how his conduct might be criminal under clause 1 or 2 as distinct from criminal under clause 3, we could not view O'Connor's guilty plea as provident to a lesser-included offense under clause 2.

The record here is clearly distinguishable from *O'Connor* in terms of the discussion between Mason and the military judge concerning the character of his conduct as service-discrediting and prejudicial to good order and discipline. The military judge openly explained that those were not elements of the "crime or offense not capital" that Mason was charged with under clause 3 and explained why he was including the additional element. Mason indicated his understanding as to why the element had been added. In the context of his explanations that he had viewed pictures of "minors doing lascivious poses" and the images of "child pornography" on his government computer, Mason then went on to affirmatively admit to the military judge that his conduct in doing so was both service-discrediting and to the prejudice of good order and discipline in the armed forces.

The record here thus contains what was missing in *O'Connor* and was present in both *Sapp* and *Augustine*. The plea colloquy between the military judge and Mason demonstrates that he "clearly understood the nature of the prohibited conduct" in terms of that conduct being service-discrediting and prejudicial to good order and discipline. *O'Connor*, 58 M.J. at 455. Those clause 1 and clause 2 elements were explained to him as a basis for finding his conduct criminal apart from clause 3 and his discussions with and admissions to the military judge were made in that context.

Absent some other distinguishing factor, we could deem Mason's guilty plea provident as to a lesser-included offense under clause 1 and clause 2 under the principles embodied in *Sapp* and *Augustine*. We recognized in *O'Connor*, however, that there is a distinguishing factor at play here: the impact of *Free Speech Coalition* and its creation of "a constitutional dimension that was not at issue in *Sapp* or *Augustine*." 58 M.J. at 454.

That constitutional dimension flows from the Supreme Court's extension of First Amendment protection to certain depictions of minors engaging in sexually explicit conduct, i.e., "virtual" as opposed to "actual" images. *Id.* at 454-55. We expressly acknowledged in *O'Connor*, but did not answer, the question as to whether, in the wake of *Free Speech Coalition*, the possession, receipt or distribution of images of minors engaging in sexually explicit conduct (regardless of their status as "actual" or "virtual") could constitute service-discrediting conduct for purposes of Article 134. *Id.* at 455. Such inquiry must necessarily be undertaken on a case-by-case basis.

In analyzing this constitutional dimension, the ultimate question is whether the status of the images in the present case as "virtual" or "actual" is of consequence in the context of assessing the providence of Mason's guilty plea under clauses 1 and 2. We conclude that it is not. The receipt or possession of "virtual" child pornography can, like "actual" child pornography, be service-discrediting or prejudicial to good order and discipline. Even if we were to assume that the specific images that serve as the basis for Mason's "child pornography" charge are "virtual" in nature, this still involves a commissioned officer of the United States Air Force receiving and viewing such images on a government computer in his workplace. Under those circumstances, the distinction between "actual" child pornography and "virtual" child pornography does not alter the character of Mason's conduct as service-discrediting or prejudicial to good order and discipline.

Mason stipulated to a sexual maturity assessment of the images at issue here as depicting children between the ages of 12 and 16. He acknowledged to the military judge that the images depicted "minors doing lascivious poses" and constituted "child pornography." While the issue as to whether the images are "virtual" or "actual" may have a potentially dispositive effect in prosecutions under the CPPA in both civilian and military settings, it is not inherently dispositive of their impact on the esteem of the armed forces or good order and discipline. Those are the yardsticks by which the criminality of conduct under clauses 1 and 2 are measured. As the Supreme Court recognized:

> While the members of the military are not excluded from the protections granted by the First Amendment, the different character of the military community and of the military mission requires a different application of those protections. The fundamental necessity for obedience, and the consequent necessity for imposition of discipline, may render permissible within the military that which would be constitutionally impermissible outside it.

Parker v. Levy, 417 U.S. 733, 758 (1974). Even assuming the images at issue here are "virtual," Mason's conduct in receiving those images on his government computer can constitutionally be subjected to criminal sanction under the uniquely military offenses embodied in clauses 1 and 2 of Article 134. . . .

QUESTIONS

Is the case for departing from civilian Free Speech Clause jurisprudence stronger in a political context such as *Parker v. Levy* or a child pornography context such as *Mason*? Do you disagree with any of the appellate decisions declining to recognize servicemembers' free speech rights where a civilian would enjoy First Amendment protection?

II.   FREE EXERCISE OF RELIGION
Manual for Courts-Martial
Pt. IV, ¶ 14.c.(2)(a)(iii)

[T]he dictates of a person's conscience, religion, or personal philosophy cannot justify or excuse the disobedience of an otherwise lawful order.

UNITED STATES v. BURRY
United States Coast Guard Board of Review
36 C.M.R. 829 (C.G.B.R. 1966)

Aboard the CGC [Coast Guard Cutter] TAMARACK on Saturday the second day of April 1966, the Commanding Officer gave a commissaryman the direct order "Cook the day's meals."

The commissaryman was the only qualified cook aboard the TAMARACK on that day. He refused to obey the order.

He told the commanding officer that he would not cook because it was against his religious beliefs to work on Saturdays; that the fear of God's punishment kept him from obeying the order; that he realized it was his military duty, and that military law required him to perform his duty, but "I would be punished more by God by breaking His laws than by man by breaking his laws."

Thereafter on 5 May 1966 the commissaryman faced a special court-martial. Represented by both civilian and military lawyers, he was found guilty of willfully disobeying the lawful command of his superior officer in violation of Article 90 UCMJ. He was sentenced to be reduced to the grade of seaman recruit, to be confined at hard labor for three months and to be discharged from the service with a bad conduct discharge. The convening authority approved the findings and sentence.

The first words of the First Amendment to the Constitution and of the Bill of Rights are:

> Congress shall make no law respecting an establishment of religion or prohibiting the free exercise thereof; . . .

This right to freedom of worship applies to persons in the armed forces just as do the great companion rights of due process of law, to the assistance of counsel, to a speedy trial, and to be protected against unreasonable searches and seizures and compulsory self-incrimination. Our Board must therefore decide whether the order which the accused was convicted of disobeying was an order given in violation of his right to free exercise of his religion. If it was, the order was unlawful.

The accused, Clayton R. Burry, enlisted in the Coast Guard in 1963. He served six years with the Air Force before that. In February 1965, while stationed at St Paul Island Loran Station in Alaska, he joined the Radio Church of God, a religious organization. This church commands its members to abstain from any and all types of work on the Sabbath from sunset Friday to sunset Saturday.

Burry was able to observe this tenet of his church while at the Loran Station. But in October 1965 he was transferred to Huron Lightship and immediately had difficulty in keeping the Sabbath. Twice he breached the command not to work on Saturdays. Then in January he was assigned to the TAMARACK as its mess cook.

He asked for and at first was granted the privilege of Saturday liberty. Another man aboard the ship, a nonrated enlisted man, was able to cook the Saturday meals. The TAMARACK was icebound during January, February, and part of March, and the other man was always available. Then, in mid-March, the other man was transferred off the ship. Burry, as the only competent cook left, was told that the Saturday liberty would have to be terminated, and that he would have to perform the duties of his rating and prepare the meals.

On Friday, 25 March 1966, he went ashore on regular evening liberty. Although required to be aboard on Saturday morning, he stayed ashore without leave, and did not return until Sunday morning. The commanding officer brought him to mast and imposed Article 15 nonjudicial punishment — seven days restriction to the limits of the ship — for the AWOL offense.

The following Saturday, April second, the commanding officer learned that Burry had neglected to prepare breakfast for the crew. Burry was brought to him, and the officer gave him the order which led to this court-martial. It appears as a fact that when the order was given, the commanding officer did not expect that it would be obeyed.

Some days prior to trial the accused was interviewed by an Air Force Base chaplain. The chaplain's statement, accepted in evidence pursuant to stipulation, certifies:

> a. The serviceman is a member of the Radio Church of God, world headquarters, Pasadena, California, which he joined in February 1965.
>
> b. The tenets of the church are clearly and uncompromisingly pacifistic.
>
> c. The observance of the seventh day of the week as the Sabbath is required unqualifiedly.
>
> d. The serviceman is very well indoctrinated in his faith and has an amazingly acute ability to defend the position of his church, which I question that he could do without wholeheartedly accepting and practicing it.
>
> e. As evidence of his conviction he does not make an excuse or wish to have errors of judgment overlooked simply because of his faith.

Before the court retired to deliberate on the findings, the president included in his instructions the following:

> That obedience to a command involving a violation of the religious scruples of the accused is not a defense.

He also instructed:

> A factual issue concerning the intent behind the order having been raised, which it is your duty to resolve, you are further instructed that you cannot convict the accused unless you are convinced beyond a reasonable doubt that the order was not given for the sole purpose of increasing the punishment for an offense which it was expected the accused would commit. . . .

The Preamble to the Constitution tells us that, among the purposes for which the people of the United States ordained and established the Constitution were: to "provide for the common defence" and to "secure the Blessings of Liberty to ourselves and our Posterity."

Among the "Blessings of Liberty" is the right to freedom of religion. The First Amendment's statement of this freedom is a statement of one of the attributes of liberty. *Douglas v. City of Jeannette*, 130 F.2d 652, *aff'd*, 319 U.S. 157; *Cantwell v. Connecticut*, 310 U.S. 296.

Freedom to believe in one's chosen religion is absolute. *Zorach v. Clausen*, 343 U.S. 306; *United States v. Mohammed*, 288 F.2d 236. No person can be punished for professing religious beliefs. *People ex rel. McCollum v. Board of Ed.* 333 U.S. 203.

To "provide for the common defence" the United States has organized its armed forces: The Army, Navy, Air Force, Marine Corps and Coast Guard; and Congress prescribed rules for their government.

The United States may compel citizens to give military service. *Selective Draft Law Cases*, 245 U.S. 366. The freedom of religion does not exempt from the duty to participate in the common defense. *Van Bibber v. United States*, 151 F.2d 444.

> [T]hose subject to military discipline are under many duties and may not claim many freedoms that we hold inviolable as to those in civilian life.

West Va. Bd. of Ed. v. Barnette, 319 U.S. 624 at 642.

Like liberty itself, of which it is only one part, the free exercise of religion is not an absolute freedom. It is a qualified freedom. *United States v. MacIntosh*, 283 U.S. 605.

The Supreme Court recognizes that:

> We are a religious people whose institutions presuppose a Supreme Being. We guarantee the freedom to worship as one chooses. We make room for as wide a variety of beliefs and creeds as the spiritual needs of man deem necessary.

Zorach v. Clausen, 343 U.S. 306 at p. 313.

At the same time it is established beyond any doubt that:

> Government has a right to survive. . . . It may make war and raise armies. To that end it may compel citizens to give military service . . . and subject them to military training despite their religious objections.

Mr. Justice Stone in *Minersville School District v. Gobitis*, 310 U.S. 586 at 602.

A volunteer is in no better position than one compelled to serve to be exempted from lawful requirements. *Cf. Hamilton v. Regents of the University of California*, 293 U.S. 245; *McCord v. Page*, 124 F.2d 68. Religious freedom is not a license to freedom of conduct. *West Va. Bd. of Ed. v. Barnette, supra; Cantwell v. Connecticut, supra; United States v. Kissinger*, 250 F.2d 940; *Warren v. United States*, 177 F.2d 596; *Davis v. Beason*, 133 U.S. 333. To the extent that a military man's freedom of conduct in practicing his religion is curtailed by the demand that he obey proper orders, that curtailment is a permissible result of the operation of a government under law. We hold that the accused had no legal right or privilege under the First Amendment to refuse obedience to the order, and that the order was not given for an illegal purpose. The finding of guilty is affirmed. *United States v. Cupp*, 24 C.M.R. 565; *United*

States v. Morgan, 17 C.M.R. 584; *United States v. Minnix*, NCM 66-0804, 6/9/66. . . .

NOTES

1. Free Exercise Clause challenges to prosecution for failure to salute an officer and failure to submit to an inoculation were similarly unsuccessful. *United States v. Cupp*, 24 C.M.R. 565 (A.F.B.R. 1957); *United States v. Chadwell*, 36 C.M.R. 741 (N.B.R. 1965).

2. This military case law is consistent with the Supreme Court's later holding in *Goldman v. Weinberger*, 475 U.S. 503 (1986), that the Free Exercise Clause did not exempt an Orthodox Jewish officer who wore a yarmulke indoors for religious reasons from an Air Force uniform policy prohibiting covering the head indoors while in uniform.

3. Congress responded to *Goldman* by promptly adopting a statute providing "a member of the armed forces may wear an item of religious apparel while wearing the uniform of the member's armed force." 10 U.S.C. § 774(a) (2006); *see generally* First Lieutenant Dwight H. Sullivan, *The Congressional Response to Goldman v. Weinberger*, 121 MIL. L. REV. 125 (1988). The statute however, recognizes exceptions allowing the Secretary of a military department to adopt regulations prohibiting religious apparel that "would interfere with the performance of the member's military duties" or religious apparel that "is not neat and conservative." 10 U.S.C. § 774(b).

LIEUTENANT (N) G.D. SCOTT v. HER MAJESTY THE QUEEN
Court Martial Appeal Court of Canada, 2004

[1] The appellant appeals his conviction by a military judge (Standing Court Martial) of refusing to obey a lawful order, an offence under s. 83 of the *National Defence Act*, R.S.C. 1985, c. N-5. . . .

[2] The essential facts are not in dispute. The appellant was ordered to attend a Divisions parade at Canadian Forces Base Esquimalt on November 28, 2002. As part of the routine usually followed on such occasions, the chaplain of the unit was on hand and at one point pronounced a short prayer which was followed by the playing of the naval hymn. Prior to the prayer, the parade commander had sought from the reviewing officer "permission to carry on with prayers" and had duly received such permission. The order was given for the parade to "remove headdress," but the appellant, who says that he has no religious belief, did not do so. That is the act for which he was charged and convicted.

[3] At his trial the appellant said that his *Charter* right to freedom of religion had been violated by his enforced participation in a religious ceremony with which he did not agree and in which he did not believe. [*See* Canadian Charter of Rights and Freedoms § 2 ("Everyone has the following fundamental freedoms: a) freedom of conscience and religion. . . .").] Some one to two months

prior to the parade in question, he had expressed his concerns in this regard to a superior officer and had received the reply that he must nevertheless attend the parade and remove his headdress when ordered to do so.

[4] The military judge's finding of guilt was predicated on his finding of fact that the order to remove headdress did not have a religious connotation. The judge purported to base that finding on his acceptance of the opinions given by the parade commander and a senior non-commissioned officer who had been present at the parade. He also seems to have attached some importance to his finding that the prayer was "non-denominational."

[5] With respect, we think that the judge's finding was unreasonable and is not supportable on the whole of the evidence. The "non-denominational" character of the prayer was wholly irrelevant except, of course, to the extent that it served to undermine the judge's view that the order to remove headdress did not have a religious connotation. The order was only given once that day and immediately preceded the saying of the prayer. A prayer is always and by definition religious. That character does not change depending upon the organized religion with which it may or may not be associated. In finding that the order to remove headdress did not have a religious connotation, the judge relied on the opinions of lay witnesses who had no particular qualifications on the question. However, the judge does not appear to have taken into account the opinion of another prosecution witness, the chaplain himself, who clearly was qualified, and who said that what he had conducted was a "short" service "of a religious nature." The judge's disregard of that evidence is not explained.

[6] Even more significantly the judge had before him a full account of the circumstances surrounding the occasion: the asking and receiving of "permission to carry on with prayers"; the fact that what was pronounced was in fact a prayer; the further fact that the chaplain was dressed in ecclesiastical garb, and that the prayer was followed by the playing of what is generally recognized as a hymn; and finally, the evidence of both the witnesses on whom the judge relied to the effect that the order to remove headdress would not have been given had the prayers not been the next order of business. Indeed, paragraph 13 of the *Canadian Forces Dress Instructions*, A-AD-265-000/AG-001 itself seems to recognize the religious nature of the order to remove headdress for prayers in that it provides specific exemptions for persons whose religious beliefs require that their heads remain covered, notably adherents of the Jewish and Sikh religions.

[7] It is simply impossible in these circumstances not to see both the order itself and the prayer that followed as having a religious connotation that required all those present at least to appear to participate in the sentiments expressed. There was no room for dissent, reservation, or abstention.

[8] The fact that the appellant kept his hat on not because of religious convictions, but because of a lack of them, seems to us to be quite irrelevant. The order that was given and that he knowingly disobeyed was one with the acknowledged purpose, according to both prosecution witnesses and section 3 of the *Canadian Forces Dress Instructions* was to show "respect" for what was being done and not mere passive toleration. That is to say, it was designed to constrain him to make a public gesture of approval for a religious ceremony in

which he did not believe. Since that is a purpose which is clearly inimical to the freedom of religion guaranteed by paragraph 2(a) of the *Charter*, the order given fails the first branch of the test laid down in *R. v. Big M Drug Mart*, [1985] 1 S.C.R. 295.

[9] In these circumstances, it is not necessary to consider the further questions of the effect of the order or the possible availability to the Crown of a section 1 plea. We note parenthetically, however, that such a plea would almost certainly founder on the proportionality test, the military having already demonstrated the ease with which it can accommodate those whose religious scruples forbid them from removing their headdress.

[10] We also note that the appellant's action in speaking to his superior officer well ahead of time and in revealing his concerns about being made to participate in a prayer service in which he did not believe — in his words, a "heads up" to his superiors — far from being, as the judge viewed it, an aggravating circumstance, clearly put the authorities on notice that an effort must be made to accommodate non-believers. It should not be difficult to craft an order that would make provision for non-participation in prayers by such persons or to accommodate them by Regulation, as had already been done for some members of other religious beliefs. The provision of paragraph 13 of section 3 of the Canadian Forces Dress Instruction respecting adherents of the Jewish religion is particularly apposite: such a member who wishes to wear a yarmulke ". . . may be authorized to retain normal headdress on parade when others remove theirs . . .". There is no explanation as to why such an accommodation was not extended to the appellant. The fact that the practice of pronouncing prayers at parades and requiring some form of public assent thereto has been hallowed by a tradition of many years in the military as well as other circles cannot justify a breach of the appellant's *Charter* rights. We emphasize that what was required of the appellant was active participation in the religious ceremony with which he disagreed. The question of enforced passive participation by mere presence is an entirely different issue and one that we do not reach today.

[11] While we recognize that military exigency may serve to justify the giving of many orders that might otherwise result in *Charter* breaches (an order to advance under fire is an obvious example), the present is not such a case. Orders placing troops in harm's way will generally have a clear military purpose that will take them past the first branch of the *Big M. Drug Mart, supra*, test and their legality will stand or fall (more generally, one would expect, the former) on a section 1 justification. We also recognize that such orders may not necessarily be limited to circumstances where troops are engaged in combat. Obedience to lawful orders is essential to maintaining necessary discipline in the military. Here, however, there was no clearly military purpose, but simply the impermissible one of having the entire parade show some level of participation in and assent to the prayers that followed. The order was not lawful and the appellant's disobedience of it was justified.

[12] The conviction will be set aside and a finding of not guilty will be entered. . . .

QUESTIONS

How would the *Scott* case have been resolved in the United States? Would the order to remove headgear for a prayer have been considered a lawful order? In *Anderson v. Laird*, 466 F.2d 283 (D.C. Cir. 1972), the United States Court of Appeals for the District of Columbia Circuit invalidated the compulsory chapel attendance policies of the United States Military Academy, United States Naval Academy, and United States Air Force Academy on Establishment Clause grounds.

III.   CONSCIENTIOUS OBJECTION

UNITED STATES v. WALKER
United States Court of Appeals for the Armed Forces
41 M.J. 462 (C.A.A.F. 1995)

SULLIVAN, CHIEF JUDGE:

The facts pertinent to resolving the certified issues were found by the Court of Military Review as follows:

> The appellant's offenses occurred following the alert of his unit for deployment to Operation Desert Shield. On 8 November 1990, after his unit was notified of its deployment to Saudi Arabia, the appellant applied for conscientious objector status. He maintained that his Islamic beliefs forbad him from engaging in offensive action against fellow Muslims. Following an interview with his company commander, the appellant was reassigned to the Military Affiliated Radio Systems (MARS) station. His reassignment was ordered so that the appellant would have duties which did not conflict with his religious beliefs and because elements of the MARS station would remain in the United States after the majority of units departed to Operation Desert Shield. In compliance with the conscientious objection regulation, the appellant discussed his request with the division chaplain on 16 November. On 14 December, a mental status evaluation was conducted.

> In late November or early December 1990, the appellant's unit commander, while attending a 2d Armored Division staff meeting, became aware of [Desert Shield Personnel Message Number 31 (DSPM 31)], dated 19 October 1990. The gist of the message provided that soldiers assigned to units alerted for deployment to Operation Desert Shield would deploy, and once in their new location, would then be eligible to apply for conscientious objector status. Following this briefing, processing of appellant's application ceased. Appellant's unit commander testified that sometime between 5 and 12 December, he notified the appellant that he could submit an application for conscientious objector status upon his arrival in Saudi Arabia.

> On 2 January 1991, the Department of the Army revised DSPM 31. The modification permitted soldiers assigned to units deploying to

Operation Desert Shield to submit a conscientious objector application as operational and mission requirements permitted. The decision whether a conscientious objector applicant would deploy was reserved to the commanding officer exercising general court-martial authority. Under the revised message, applicants could now apply for conscientious objector status at their present duty location instead of waiting until arrival at their new location. It further provided that soldiers were not precluded from deployment and, unless an application has been approved by the appropriate authority, the soldier would prepare for deployment.

In the instant case, appellant's chain of command was not aware of the 2 January modification of DSPM 31, nor was he advised of its content. Additionally, his record is void of any matter indicating whether the appellant's application was presented to the commanding officer exercising general court-martial authority or whether that officer weighed operational and mission requirements with appellant's request for conscientious objector status.

On 6 January 1991, the Deputy Staff Judge Advocate of the 2d Armored Division, spoke to appellant encouraging him to deploy with his unit to Saudi Arabia. Appellant declined to participate based on his conscientious objection and missed the movement of his unit to Operation Desert Shield. Later, the deputy and staff judge advocate met with the appellant's company commander to discuss appellant's refusal to deploy with his unit. On 8 January 1991, the appellant was ordered "to process through the deployment site and board the bus to Hamburg." The appellant again declined to obey the order.

Id. at 893-94 (footnote omitted).

I. Introduction

Law of Conscientious Objection

As a starting point, we note that it is well established that a soldier has no constitutional right to be discharged from the service or to disobey military orders because he is a conscientious objector. Moreover, there is no express statutory right to a discharge or to disobey orders based on such a belief. *See Parisi v. Davidson*, 405 U.S. 34, 38 n.2 (1972). A soldier, however, may request a discharge on this basis, and in accordance with military regulations, it may be granted as a matter of administrative grace. *See Cole v. Spear*, 747 F.2d 217, 221 n.6 (4th Cir. 1984). *See generally* Department of Defense Directive No. 1300.6 — Conscientious Objectors (August 20, 1971), 32 CFR Part 75.

In this regard, Section I of the above-noted DoD Directive generally states that it "updates uniform Department of Defense procedures governing conscientious objectors and processing requests for discharge based on conscientious objection." Moreover, the above regulation further states in Section IV:

Policy

A. Administrative discharge prior to the completion of an obligated term of service is discretionary with the Military Service concerned, based on a judgment of the facts and circumstances in the case. However, insofar as may be consistent with the effectiveness and efficiency of the Military Services, a request for classification as a conscientious objector and relief from or restriction of military duties in consequence thereof will be approved to the extent practicable and equitable. . . .

In addition, we note that this regulation clearly creates no right in the soldier to disobey military orders while his application for discharge is pending. Section VI specifically states:

H. To the extent practicable under the circumstances, during the period applications are being processed and until a decision is made by the Headquarters of the Service concerned, every effort will be made to assign applicants to duties within the command to which they are assigned which will conflict as little as possible with their asserted beliefs. However, members desiring to file application who are on orders for reassignment may be required by the military service concerned to submit applications at their next permanent duty station. During the period applications are being processed, applicants will be expected to conform to the normal requirements of military service and to perform satisfactorily such duties to which they are assigned. Applicants may be disciplined for violations of the Uniform Code of Military Justice while awaiting action on their applications. . . .

Finally, under this regulation, the soldier has no right to disobey orders during an appeal of an adverse decision on his request for discharge. Section VIIC states:

C. Persons who are assigned to non-combatant duties, and persons who are assigned to normal military duties by reason of disapproval of their applications, will be expected to conform to the normal requirements of military service and to perform satisfactorily such duties to which they are assigned. Violations of the Uniform Code of Military Justice by these members will be treated as in any other situation. . . .

The Department of the Army has also issued specific regulations concerning the processing of conscientious objector applications. *See* AR 600-43 — Personnel-General: Conscientious Objection (1 Aug 83). Moreover, it has issued other regulations which may apply in certain circumstances to soldiers who have submitted such applications. *E.g.*, Rule 29, Table 2-1; Rule 8, Table 3-1, AR 614-30 — Assignments, Details, and Transfers, Oversea Service (1 April 1988); para. 3-7g(2)(h), AR 600-83 — Personnel-General: The New Manning System-COHORT Unit Replacement System (26 Nov 1986).

II. Decision of the Court of Military Review

The [Army Court of Military Review] reversed the convictions for missing movement and disobedience of orders. It initially said in pertinent part:

[We] . . . hold that the order given the appellant to prepare for deployment and board the bus to Hamburg, under the unique facts of this case, was illegal.

Under the facts of this case, we are satisfied that the appellant attempted to submit a formal conscientious objector application. Since DSPM 31 had no legal effect, [as the court had earlier held, 37 M.J. at 894] the parent Army Regulation 600-43 controls. *See generally Wiley*, 37 M.J. 885 (A.C.M.R. 1993). Accordingly, the appellant could submit an application for conscientious objector status any time up until deployed. When the appellant missed the movement of his unit on 6 January and disobeyed the order to deploy on 8 January 1991, he was in that protected class that the Secretary of the Army had designated as not eligible for deployment. *See* Army Reg. 614-30, Assignments, Details, and Transfers: Overseas Service, Table 2-1, Rule 29 (1 Apr 88). Because he was not eligible for deployment to Operation Desert Shield, the appellant's missed movement and disobedience of the order to deploy were not violations of the UCMJ.

37 M.J. at 894 . . . . We disagree with this legal conclusion. . . .

III. Legal Basis of Court of Military Review Decision

Our initial problem with the Court of Military Review's decision is that it did not articulate its legal basis for concluding that Rule 29 of Table 2-1, AR 614-30, applied to the accused's unit deployment orders. That regulation is entitled, "Assignment, Details and Transfers, Oversea Service," and Rule 29 of Table 2-1 states, "If a soldier claims conscientious objection (See AR 600-43), then the soldier is ineligible [for overseas service] unless the soldier is rejected by a decision made by HQDA." Moreover, paragraph 2-5 of Section III of that regulation states:

Section III. Overseas Assignment Restrictions

2-5. Soldiers who may not be moved overseas

Soldiers may be temporarily or permanently ineligible for overseas movement for the reasons shown in tables 2-1 and 3-1. . . .

Nevertheless, paragraph 2-5 of AR 614-30 applies to the overseas movement of an individual soldier through assignment or reassignment orders. *See* para. 1-5b (selecting a soldier for service overseas); para. 2-1a (eligibility of a soldier). Paragraph 2-1h of the same regulation recognizes this distinction in movement method. It states:

> h. Eligibility for soldiers assigned to companies or battalions (or their equivalent) of the COHORT [Cohesion, Operational Readiness Training] unit manning system is predicated on unit life cycles and deployment schedules. OCONUS [outside Continental U.S.] assignment patterns for these soldiers may differ from soldiers selected for overseas assignment by individual assignment methods.

As noted above, the accused's unit — Headquarters and Headquarters Company, 2d Armored Division (Forward) — was already overseas (stationed in Germany) when it was ordered to deploy to South West Asia as part of Operation Desert Shield/Storm. Accordingly, we conclude that the Court of Military Review legally erred in holding that Rule 29, Table 2-1, AR 614-30 rendered his movement orders illegal.

IV. Related Legal Bases for Court of Military Review Decision

In any event, paragraph 3-2 of AR 614-30 does provide:

3-2. Contingency operations

For contingency operations that do not require mobilization or in the event of the two hundred thousand call up, the assignment restrictions in Table 3-1 apply. HQDA will modify or rescind those restrictions as appropriate, depending on the circumstances.

. . . Other panels of the Army Court of Military Review have relied on Rule 8, Table 3-1, AR 614-30 to deal with unit deployment cases arising from Operation Desert Shield/Storm. *See United States v. Johnson*, 37 M.J. 982, 985 (A.C.M.R. 1993); *United States v. Wiley*, 37 M.J. 885, 887 (A.C.M.R. 1993). Table 3-1 is entitled, "Eligibility for Oversea Service-Contingency Operations and M-Day." Similar to Rule 29 of Table 2-1, relied on by the Court of Military Review, Rule 8 of Table 3-1 provides, "If a soldier has submitted a formal claim for conscientious objector status under AR 600-43 . . . , then the soldier is ineligible until HQDA takes final action." We agree that the accused's movement as part of Operation Desert Shield/Storm was a contingency operation. *See United States v. Wiley*, 37 M.J. at 887 n.4.

The critical question we must decide is whether the accused's unit deployment to Operation Desert Shield/Storm was a contingency operation within the meaning of paragraph 3-2, AR 614-30. Initially, we note that on both January 6 and 8, 1991, he was a member of Headquarters and Headquarters Company, 2d Armored Division (Forward). Moreover, his unit was located at Garlstedt, Germany, and in the process of deploying to Saudi Arabia as part of Operation Desert Shield/Storm.

Paragraph 4-1 of AR 614-30, however, provides:

Chapter 4. Unit Deployments

4-1. General

Unit deployments, for purpose of this regulation, are movements of units from CONUS to an overseas location as directed in an Office of Deputy Chief of Staff for Operations (ODCSOPS) unit movement directive. Unless otherwise indicated, these are PCS moves. Deployment of units under the Unit Manning System are covered in AR 600-83.

On the basis of this paragraph of AR 614-30, we can reasonably conclude that the ineligibility standard of Rule 8 did not apply to the accused's particular unit deployment. As noted above, his unit was deployed from Germany (OCONUS) to the Persian Gulf (OCONUS). This conclusion of inapplicability is buttressed by review of other sections of AR 614-30, which do not note this ineligibility in different situations involving the movement of soldiers who are already overseas. *E.g.*, Chapter 7, Section II: Consecutive Overseas Tours; Chapter 8: Curtailment of Overseas Tours, AR 614-30.

V. Alternative Holding of the Court of Military Review

The Court of Military Review alternatively held that the accused's deployment orders were illegal because they were issued in violation of the Army Message of January 2, 1991. *See generally Dodson v U.S. Government, Department of the Army*, 988 F.2d 1199, 1204 (Fed. Cir. 1993). The court below said:

> Additionally, when the appellant missed the movement of his unit and disobeyed the order to deploy, the 2 January 1991 modification of DSPM 31 was applicable. There is, however, no showing that the procedures outlined in that change were ever followed in appellant's case. While we acknowledge that during this period of time events were moving very quickly, that does not excuse a failure to follow procedural mandates.

Id. at 894. We disagree. *See also United States v. Lenox*, 21 U.S.C.M.A. 314, 319, 45 C.M.R. 88, 93 (1972) (where conscientious objector regulation creates no right to refuse military duties, its violation creates no defense to missing movement or disobedience of orders).

Turning first to the content of the January 2, 1991, Army Message, we note that it does create an expanded right to submit a conscientious-objector application for a soldier alerted for unit deployment beyond that provided in paragraph 2-10c, AR 600-43 (1 Aug. 83) and DSPM 31 (Oct. 14, 1990).[2] The accused in this case, however, had previously submitted his application to appropriate command authorities around November 13, 1990, and its processing was

---

[2] [n.8] Desert Shield Personnel Message Number 31 (19 Oct. 1990) provided:

UNCLAS ALARACT 089/90

SUBJECT: DESERT SHIELD PERSONNEL MESSAGE NUMBER 31

PERSONNEL APPLYING FOR CONSCIENTIOUS OBJECTOR STATUS A. AR 600-43, CHAPTER 2.

B. AR 614-30, CHAPTER 4, TABLE 3-1.

1. FOR THE PURPOSES OF AR 600-43, PARAGRAPH 2-10C, THE TERM "REASSIGNMENT" INCLUDES THE DEPLOYMENT OF PERSONNEL AWAY FROM THEIR PRESENT DUTY LOCATION.

2. NOTICE OF "REASSIGNMENT," TO INCLUDE AN ALERT FOR DEPLOYMENT, TEMPORARILY PRECLUDES SOLDIERS FROM SUBMITTING APPLICATIONS FOR CONSCIENTIOUS OBJECTOR STATUS UNTIL AFTER THEY HAVE ARRIVED AT THEIR NEW DUTY LOCATION.

3. AR 614-30, TABLE 3-1, RULE 8 APPLIES ONLY TO THOSE SOLDIERS WHO HAVE SUBMITTED A FORMAL APPLICATION FOR CONSCIENTIOUS OBJECTOR STATUS PURSUANT TO AR 600-43, PRIOR TO RECEIVING NOTICE OF "REASSIGNMENT." A FORMAL APPLICATION CONSIST OF DA FORM 4187 AND ALL OF THE PERSONAL INFORMATION REQUIRED BY APPENDIX B, AR 600-43.

4. SOLDIERS SUBMITTING APPLICATIONS FROM UNITS THAT ARE DEPLOYED OVERSEAS WILL BE RETAINED IN THEIR UNIT AND ASSIGNED DUTIES PROVIDING MINIMUM PRACTICABLE CONFLICT WITH THEIR ASSERTED BELIEFS PENDING FINAL DECISION OF THEIR APPLICATION.

This message applies to a soldier deploying with his unit, but it provides a soldier no right to apply for conscientious objector status after he is notified of impending deployment until he has arrived at the new duty station.

discontinued some 30 days later. The January 2 message simply does not further require that previously submitted and denied or discontinued applications be revived or that soldiers in general be notified of this expanded right. (Message calls for attention of Personnel Processing Conscientious Objector Applications).

In any event, this message also provides that such an application will be processed by his unit "as operational and mission requirements permit." We recognize that the processing of his earlier application was discontinued by his unit in late November or early December by reason of a briefing on an earlier Army Message of October 19, 1990. However, it is pure speculation that resubmission of this same application on or after January 2, 1991, could or would be completed by the time of his movement orders on January 6, 1991. *See* para. 2-1b, AR 600-43 (90-day processing time). A putative violation of this message is not sufficient to invalidate military movement orders. *See United States v. Lenox*, 21 U.S.C.M.A. 314, 45 C.M.R. 88 (1972).

Finally, and most importantly, the message provides that "the soldier will prepare for deployment and deploy with the unit unless the application for conscientious objector status has been approved by the approving authority designated in paragraph 2-8a." Such a processing condition was permissible to the extent that the revised message expanded his right to file a conscientious objector application beyond that provided in AR 600-43. *See generally Cole v. Spear, supra.* Clearly, the accused's application was not approved on the dates of January 6 and 8, 1991, and, therefore, he was required to deploy by this message. Moreover, prior to January 6 and 8, 1991, he did not request the General Court-Martial Convening Authority over him to forward his earlier discontinued application to the Department of the Army Conscientious Objector Review Board (paragraph 2-8d) and to excuse him from deployment. Accordingly, no right created by the Army Message of January 2 was violated by the orders to deploy in this case.

VI. Conclusion

We conclude that the Court of Military Review erred in holding that the accused's deployment orders on January 6 and 8, 1991, violated AR 614-30 (1 Apr 88) and the Army Message of January 2, 1991. Moreover, even assuming that the accused was erroneously denied his expanded right to file a conscientious objector application as provided in the Army Message of January 2, 1991, that same message expressly required him to deploy with his unit unless his application had been approved by appropriate authorities. In sum, the service regulation and message relied on by the Court of Military Review did not, as a matter of administrative grace, preclude the accused's deployment with his unit on January 6 and 8, 1991, to Saudi Arabia as part of Operation Desert Shield/Storm. *United States v. Lenox, supra. See also Jones v. Mundy*, 792 F. Supp. 1009, 1012 (E.D.N.C. 1992). . . .

JUDGE WISS concurs.

COX, JUDGE, with whom CRAWFORD and GIERKE, JUDGES, join (concurring in part and in the result):

I agree with much of the lead opinion, but perhaps from a different perspective.

Army Regulation 614-30 (1 Apr 88)

Insofar as I can determine, Army Regulation (AR) 614-30 ("Overseas Service") has nothing whatever to do with this accused. That regulation deals primarily with the question whether an individual soldier meets the criteria for selection for overseas service in the first place. Para. 1-1. The regulation addresses the basic question of whether a given soldier has the qualifications, training, and personal circumstances such that the United States of America is prepared to loose him or her on foreign soil. The accused, of course, was already overseas. Obviously, he had met those criteria sometime earlier. The regulation does not pertain to the matter of overseas redeployment of individuals or units already abroad.

Had AR 614-30 anything to do with the accused's situation, one would have expected it to appear in Chapter 8, which deals with "Curtailment of Overseas Tours." Reasons listed for curtailment run the gamut from security and safety risks, to unusual pregnancy circumstances, to emergency and compassionate reassignments. *See* Table 1-1. There is no mention, however, of a conscientious-objection curtailment or of any rights triggered by the filing of such an application by an overseas soldier.

Even the chapter in the regulation dealing with unit deployments clearly reiterates the following:

> Unit deployments, for purpose of this regulation, are movements of units from CONUS [continental United States] to an overseas location as directed in an Office of Deputy Chief of Staff for Operations (ODC-SOPS) unit movement directive.

Para. 4-1.

The Court of Military Review erred, therefore, in holding that the various tables attached to AR 614-30 — tables that might preclude sending CONUS soldiers overseas — provided this accused a right to refuse to obey the order to deploy with his unit.

Army Regulation 600-43 (1 Aug 83)

AR 600-43 ("Conscientious Objection") is the regulation pertaining to this accused's circumstances. One sentence only of the regulation (here quoted in pertinent part) in effect at the time of his refusal to deploy applies particularly to this situation:

> Persons who have submitted applications . . . will be retained in their unit and assigned duties providing minimum practicable conflict with their asserted beliefs, pending a final decision on their applications. . . .

Para. 2-10a ("Use, assignment, and training"), AR 600-43.

The Court of Military Review's conclusion, following *United States v. Wiley*, 37 M.J. 885 (ACMR 1993), and *United States v. Johnson*, 37 M.J. 982 (ACMR 1993), that this sentence conferred a right on this accused to remain in Germany with the unit's rear detachment and a right to refuse to obey the order to deploy is irrational. This accused's rights were to remain with his unit

— wherever it was — and, to the extent "practicable," to be assigned duties involving minimal conflict with his asserted beliefs. Whether the accused was assigned such duties in Germany, Saudi Arabia, Kuwait, Iraq, or elsewhere was a unit call, not his. Since he refused to deploy as ordered, he cannot possibly argue that his command violated his right to minimum practicable conflict with his asserted beliefs. Needless to say, in a theater of operation such as southwest Asia, the opportunities for service not involving compromise of the accused's asserted religious beliefs may have been substantial. Other portions of AR 600-43 (pertaining to persons who have "received orders for reassignment") plainly do not, on their face, apply to him. This accused was not being reassigned; he had merely been ordered to deploy with his unit.

Desert Shield Personnel Message (DSPM Number 31)

The Court of Military Review concluded that DSPM 31, dated 19 October 1990, was invalid, as it involved a sub-Secretarial modification of AR 600-43. The accused agrees. Clearly, DSPM 31 provided him no relief, however, as it sought to preclude soldiers (such as the accused) who had received notice that their unit was to deploy from filing conscientious objector applications until after arriving at their new duty stations. As no relief from the message is conceivable, it is unnecessary for us, for the purpose of resolving these certified issues, to revisit the Court of Military Review's determination that the message was invalid.

January Change to AR 600-43

The change to paragraph 2-10c, AR 600-43, dated 2 January 1991 (a few days before the accused refused to deploy), also provides him no possible relief. This Secretarial (i.e., lawful) change specifies that applications for conscientious objector status under AR 600-43 could be filed prior to deployment, but that the command might determine that an applicant would not deploy. Clearly, no right to refuse to deploy was granted. As no relief from this revised message is conceivable, it is unnecessary even to determine whether the revision was received in time by the command to become effective and binding on the parties. *See United States v. Tolkach*, 14 M.J. 239 (CMA 1982).

Conclusions

No other regulations or provisions having apparent bearing on the accused's circumstances have been identified. I conclude, therefore, that he was within his right to submit his conscientious objector application to his commander in Germany — albeit it was invalid on its face.[3] Arguably, his commander erred, however unwittingly, in informing the accused that the application would have to be resubmitted after deployment. Nevertheless, the command was

---

[3] [n.*] Para. 1-7a, AR 600-43, states:

Requests by personnel for qualification as a conscientious objector after entering military service will not be favorably considered when these requests are —

(4) Based on objection to a certain war.

The accused's asserted religious beliefs, on the other hand, only forbade him from killing other Muslims, not from war in general. Also not lost is the irony that the United States' basis for military intervention in southwest Asia at the time was the invasion of one Muslim nation by another.

clearly within its rights in ordering him to deploy. At the point when he refused to deploy, the command had certainly done nothing to compromise his espoused religious principles.

Admittedly, AR 600-43 provides certain timeliness standards for review of conscientious objector applications. The regulation also provides, however, that "extraordinary circumstances . . . may lengthen this period." Para. 2-1b. Given the circumstances then in place in his unit, we assume the conditions for processing personnel applications (such as for conscientious objection) were far from maximal. In any event, his proper recourse for protesting delay in processing was administrative, not self-help. The Court of Military Review was mistaken in concluding that AR 600-43 and AR 614-30 conferred a right on this accused to refuse an order to deploy with his unit. Therefore, that court's action in setting aside the findings of guilty of missing movement and disobeying an order was error.

To the extent my reasoning conforms with the lead opinion, I concur outright. In any event, I concur in the result.

NOTE

During Operation Desert Shield/Desert Storm, attempts to use application for conscientious objector status as a defense to charges of failing to report for duty were similarly unsuccessful. *See, e.g., United States v. Walker*, 41 M.J. 462 (C.A.A.F. 1995); *United States v. Lwin*, 42 M.J. 279 (C.A.A.F. 1995).

ZONSCHEIN v. JUDGE ADVOCATE GENERAL
Supreme Court of Israel, 2002

JUSTICE A. BARAK

Facts and Proceedings

1. The eight petitioners before us serve in the IDF reserves. They were called to reserve duty, and all reported to duty except petitioner number six. When they discovered that their service would be in the [Administered Territories] they informed their commanding officers of their objection to serving in that region. Petitioner number six, who was aware that his service would be in the area, informed the authorities, at the outset, that he would not be reporting to duty. The petitioners were consequently brought to disciplinary trial before military judicial officers for refusing to comply with an order, an offence under section 12 of the Military Justice Law — 1955, and for not complying with an order, an offence under section 123 of the law. They were sentenced to periods of detention ranging from 28 to 35 days.

2. Following his conviction, petitioner number one approached this court with a petition directed against the decision to subject him to a disciplinary hearing before a military judicial officer, as opposed to a Military Court. *See* HCJ 5026/02. On July 16, 2002 a judgment was given approving the parties' agreement that the petitioner would withdraw his petition and instead approach the Judge Advocate General [hereinafter the respondent], with a

request to rescind the disciplinary judgment, under section 186 of the law. The petitioner, along with six of the other petitioners before us (save petitioner number eight), then approached the respondent with that request. They based their request that the disciplinary judgments be rescinded on the argument that the actions attributed to the petitioners do not constitute offences. They offered two reasons for this. First, petitioners asserted the defense found in section 125 of the law — that service in the area inherently involves illegal activity, and refusing to carry out illegal orders constitutes a recognized legal defense. Second, petitioners asserted that the orders they were given violated their right to freedom of conscience and were thus unreasonable and invalid.

3. On August 3, 2002, respondent denied the requests of petitioners 1-7 to rescind the disciplinary judgments handed down against them. The respondent's decision stated that the petitioner's actions were offences, that the petitioners have no available defense, and that the orders themselves were reasonable. The decision emphasized that the army's activities in the area are legal and accord with the standards of international and humanitarian law — the goals of the activities in the area are to preserve peace and security and protect Israeli civilians from terrorist activities. As to the existence of a defense of conscientious objection, the decision added that such a defense only applies where there is a general conscientious objection to serving in the military altogether, and not in a case where one has selective objections which stem from ideological and/or political perspectives. The decision also stated that the procedure employed by petitioners was unlawful. The applicants should have refused the call to duty itself (a "direct attack"), and not acted as they did by reporting to duty, then refusing to comply with a specific order, and only then raising an argument of defense (an "indirect attack"). Petitioners' application was denied for these reasons, which brought about the petition before us. . . .

The Normative Framework

7. The Defense Service Law (Consolidated Version) — 1986, § 39(c) exempts from military service "a female person of military age who has proved . . . that reasons of conscience . . . prevent her from serving in defense service." What is the law regarding a male of military age who requests an exemption from military service? This issue is governed by section 36 of the law:

> The Minister of Defense may, by order, if he sees fit to do so for reasons connected with the size of the regular forces or reserve forces in the Israeli Defense Forces or for reasons connected with the requirements of education, security, settlement or the national economy or for family or other reasons —
>
> (1) exempt a person of military age from the duty of regular service or reduce the period of his service;
>
> (2) exempt a person of military age from the duty of reserve service for a specific period or absolutely

All agree that exemptions for conscientious reasons are included in those "other reasons" which allow the Minister of Defense to exempt a person from regular or reserve service. *See* HCJ 4062/95 *Epstien v. Minister of Defense* (unreported decision); HCJ 2700/02 *Barnowski v. Minister of Defense* (unreported decision). Justice M. Cheshin noted as much:

> The Minister of Defense and those acting on his behalf agree that those "other reasons" include conscientious reasons for objection, in other words, a person of military age may be exempt from regular service if he is a conscientious objector and objects to the framework of military service as a matter of principle

HCJ 1380/02 *Ben Artzi v. Minister of Defense.* A special military committee for exercising the Minister of Defense's authority was established, which would investigate issues of conscientious objection. *See Baronowski.*

8. The possibility of granting exemptions from military service for conscientious reasons is not unique to our situation or to Israel. Justice M. Elon correctly stated that "the issue of conscientious objection has been much debated by jurists and philosophers, and has experienced many developments and various stages." HCJ 734/83 *Shane v. Minister of Defense*, at 401. Indeed, the question of granting exemptions for conscientious reasons has often been raised over the course of human history. Originally, these reasons were principally religious. In time, they expanded to include reasons of conscience which were not necessarily religious. These non-religious reasons are founded on serious moral considerations — an individual's perspective regarding right and wrong, which that individual considers himself bound to act in accordance with, and which acting against would severely injure that individual's conscience. *See* BVerfGE 12, 45, 55. Different countries have reacted to this problem in various ways. Many of the modern, democratic countries have established explicit statutory provisions which grant an exemption from military service for conscientious objectors. *See* L. Shlef, *The Voice of Dignity: Consciencious Objection Due to Civic Loyalty* (1989); *Conscientious Objection in the EC Countries* (1992); N. Keijzer *Military Obedience* 265 (1978); C. Evans, *Freedom of Religion Under the European Convention on Human Rights* 170 (2001) [hereinafter Evans].

9. The justification for granting exemptions from military service for reasons of conscience is not simple. In *Artzi,* Justice M. Cheshin correctly noted "the question of exempting persons of military age from the duty of regular service due to conscientious objection is not at all an easy question." Ultimately, we are dealing with a delicate balance between conflicting considerations. *See* K. Greenwalt, *All or Nothing at All: The Defeat of Selective Conscientious Objection*, 1971 SUP. CT. REV. 31, 47. On one side stands the important principle of freedom of conscience. "Every person in Israel is entitled to freedom of conscience . . . as it is one of the basic principles upon which the State of Israel is founded." *See* HCJ 292/83 *Temple Mount Faithful Movement v. Police Commander of the Jerusalem Region*, at 454. Freedom of conscience originates in the Proclamation of Independence, and is derived from the democratic nature of the State. It is evident in the central status of human dignity and liberty in our legal system. *See* HCJ 3261/93 *Manning v. Minister of Justice*, at 286. The need to take the objector's conscience into account stems from our respect for individual dignity and for the need to allow its development. It is derived from a humanist position and from the value of tolerance. "Democratic government is founded on tolerance. . . . This is

tolerance of the actions and opinions of others. . . . In a pluralistic society such as ours, tolerance is a unifying force which allows us to live together." HCJ 399/85 *Kahane v. The Managing Committee of the Broadcasting*, at 278. *See also* CA 294/91 *Jerusalem Burial Society v. Kestenbaum*, at 481; CA 105/92 *Re'em Engineer Contractors v. Nazareth-Illit Municipality*, at 210; HCJ 257/89 *Hoffman v. Trustee of the Western Wall*, at 355.

10. On the other hand stands another consideration — it is neither proper nor just to exempt part of the public from a general duty imposed on all others. This is especially true when fulfilling the duty subjects a person to the ultimate trial — sacrificing his life. This is certainly true when granting exemptions may harm security and lead to administrative unfairness and discrimination in specific cases.

11. In balancing these conflicting considerations, many of the modern democracies have, as we have seen, concluded that it would be proper, in all things related to exemption from military service, to attribute greater weight to considerations of conscience, as well as those of personal development, humanism and tolerance, over opposing considerations. Consequently, many modern legal systems grant military service exemptions to pacifists, who conscientiously object to bearing arms and participating in war. This balance presumes that national security may be preserved without drafting those who request exemptions. However, it seems that all agree that, where security needs are extreme, not even pacifists should be exempted. *See* M. Walzer, *Obligations: Essay on Disobedience, War and Citizenship* 138 (1970) [hereinafter Walzer]. "Civil rights are not a national suicide pact . . . . Civil rights derived from the existence of the State, and they should not be used as a weapon for its annihilation." *See also* EA 2/84 *Neiman v. Chairman of the Central Elections Committee for the Eleventh Knesset*, at 310. Moreover, although many democratic countries recognize pacifism as a cause for military service exemption, many of them require that the pacifists perform national service and impose various sanctions if they refuse to do so. *See* Evans, at 170.

12. The question at hand arises against this normative background. This question involves striking the proper balance between these aforementioned interests, where the request for exemption from service does not involve a general objection to bearing arms and fighting in war, whatever its cause — but an objection to a *specific* war or military operation. The question concerns the law regarding *selective* objection. We presume that the selective objector acts, as does his colleague the "full" objector, out of conscientious motives. Our fundamental point of departure is that the selective objector's refusal to serve in a particular war is based on true conscientious reasons, just as is the case with the "full" objector. Of course, this factual presumption raises evidential difficulties. However, in those situations where these problems may be overcome, and there is no reason to presume that they are impossible to overcome, we come face to face with the fundamental issue of the status of the selective conscientious objector.

13. This issue is not unique to us. It has arisen in modern democratic states, and has been resolved in various ways. Most of the democratic states that recognize military service exemptions due to "full" conscientious objection do not acknowledge selective conscientious objection as a cause for exemption. For

example, United States federal law recognizes exemption for those who object to participating "in war in any form." *See* the Military Selective Service Act of 1967, § 456(j), *codified at* 50 U.S.C. App. § 456(j) (2002). The United States Supreme Court has held that this provision, which denies selective objectors military exemptions, is constitutional. *Gillette v. United States*, 401 U.S. 437 (1971). Germany and France have also adopted this position. Nevertheless, there are some democratic states which do grant exemptions to selective objectors. This is the case in Holland. *See* Ben. P. Vermeulen, *Conscientious Objection in Dutch Law, in* Conscientious Objection in the EC Countries, at 276. A similar approach has been taken by Australia, where section 61A(i) of the Defense Act of 1903, after its 1992 amendment, specifies that military service exemptions are granted to "persons whose conscientious beliefs do not allow them to participate in a particular war or particular warlike operations." Aside from these two positions are other states, such as Spain, which have not yet come to a decision in this matter. What is the law in Israel?

14. This question arose in HCJ 470/80 *Algazi v. Minister of Defense* (unreported case). The petitioner was in the army and requested not to serve in the area. The petition was denied. Justices M. Bejski and S. Levin noted in their judgment:

> No military system can accept the existence of a general principle which allows any soldiers to dictate where they will serve, whether for economic, social, or conscientious reasons.

This problem also arose in the case of *Shane*. There, a soldier had refused to fulfill a reserve order which required him to serve in South Lebanon. He claimed that according to his "conscientious outlook, the IDF's presence in Lebanon is illegal and is not in accord with any fundamental justification of military activity." The court held that this argument was invalid. Justice M. Elon wrote:

> This is a case of a draft objection, which is based on ideological-political reasons not to fight in a *particular location*. Recognizing such an objection damages the operation of Israel's democratic system of decision-making, and leads to discrimination in military drafting. Such selective objection is not even recognized in those states which acknowledge the right to general objection as a cause for exemption from military service. *A fortiori*, the right to selective objection should not be recognized in the Israeli legal system, which does not see draft objection as excusing a male of military age from military service. It would be proper to add an additional comment. This important, complicated issue of balancing the law against the freedom of conscience — of balancing, on the one hand, the need to maintain military service to protect the sovereignty of the State and the safety of its residents against, on the other hand, the objection to participate in war for personal conscientious reasons — must take the particular circumstances of time and location into account. The severe state of security in Israel should not be compared to the state of security in other countries, which dwell within secure borders. This essential difference is a substantial and significant factor.

at 402-03. This position was adopted in yet another case. *See* HCJ 630/89 *Machnes v. The Chief of Staff* (unreported case). In the petition here we have been asked, for two reasons, to depart from this ruling — it having been mistaken when it was originally handed down and, furthermore, because it does not comply with the Basic Law: Human Dignity and Liberty, which was passed since that decision was handed down, and which establishes the constitutional status of the freedom of conscience.

15. We do not think that there is room to deviate from the decisions of the Court regarding selective conscientious objection. As we have seen, granting an exemption from military service due to conscientious objection is in the discretion of the Minister of Defense. This discretion is based on a delicate balance between conflicting considerations. In striking this balance, the Minister of Defense came to the conclusion that there is room to grant exemptions from military service in cases of "full" objection. This balance does not necessarily require that a similar exemption should be granted in the case of selective conscientious objection. We are willing to presume — without ruling in the matter — that considerations of freedom of conscience, personal development and tolerance, which are taken into account regarding the exemption for military service in the case of "full" conscientious objection, should similarly be taken into account regarding exemptions due to selective conscientious objection. This presumption is not self-evident. Yet, we are willing to accept this presumption for the purpose of this petition. There is a certain power to the argument that, from the point of view of the individual himself who claims conscientious objection — and assuming that we believe his objection is conscientious and not political or social — there is no essential difference between "full" conscientious objection and selective conscientious objection.

Petitioner number one expressed this well when responding to the charges against him for refusing to fulfill his reserve service in the area:

In my opinion it is comparable to giving a religious person non-kosher food.

If we believe this — and it was not argued before us that the petitioner's argument is a cover for considerations which are not conscientious — then apparently there is no essential difference, from the perspective of the conscience of the objector, between "full" objection and selective objection. Hence, we are willing to presume — again, without ruling on the matter — that, on our metaphorical scales, the side bearing conscience, personal development and tolerance justifies granting exemptions from military service not only to the "full" conscientious objector, but also to the selective conscientious objector. How shall we regard the other side of those metaphoric scales? What is the proper balance between the conflicting considerations? Is there a difference between the "full" conscientious objector and the selective conscientious objector regarding this "other hand"? We think there is a difference.

16. In our opinion, refusal to serve in the army for "full" conscientious reasons is not similar to refusal to serve in army for selective conscientious reasons. Indeed, the weight of the side which leans towards recognizing conscientious objection is much heavier in the case of selective conscientious objection than in "full" conscientious objection. However, the severe problem of granting an exemption from fulfilling a duty, a duty that is imposed on all, is

apparent. The phenomenon of selective conscientious objection would be broader than "full" objection, and would evoke an intense feeling of discrimination "between blood and blood." Moreover, it would affect security considerations themselves, since a group of selective objectors would tend to increase in size. Additionally, in a pluralistic society such as ours, recognizing selective conscientious objection may loosen the ties which hold us together as a nation. Yesterday, the objection was against serving in South Lebanon. Today, the objection is against serving in Judea and Samaria. Tomorrow, the objection will against vacating this or that settlement. The army of the nation may turn into an army of different groups comprised of various units, to each of which it would be conscientiously acceptable to serve in certain areas, whereas it would be conscientiously unacceptable to serve in others. In a polarized society such as ours, this consideration weighs heavily. Furthermore, it becomes difficult to distinguish between one who claims conscientious objection in good faith and one who, in actuality, objects to the policy of the government or the Knesset. It is a fine distinction — occasionally an exceedingly fine distinction — between objecting to a state policy and between conscientious objection to carrying out that policy. The ability to manage an administrative system which will act impartially is especially complicated in selective conscientious objection. *See* Walzer, at 143. Justice Marshall correctly noted in *Gillette*, at 456:

> [T]here is considerable force in the Government's contention that a program of excusing objectors to particular wars may be impossible to conduct with any hope of reaching fair and consistent results.

17. As such, selective conscientious objection requires striking a separate balance. This balance can not be derived from the balance struck in the case of "full" conscientious objection. What is the necessary balance in the case of selective objection? We need not analyze all aspects of this issue. We are willing to presume — again, without ruling in the matter — that the State may cause harm to the conscience of the conscientious objector (whether selective or "full") only where substantial harm would otherwise almost certainly be caused to the public interest. *Compare Temple Mount Faithful Movement*, at 454; HCJ 87, 73/53 *Kol Ha'am v. Minister of Interior*, at 882; HCJ 953/89 *Indor v. Mayor of Jerusalem*, at 689-91. The Minister of Defense decided that in contemporary Israel, both in light of its inner conflicts and in light of current events, exemptions from military service will not be granted to selective conscientious objectors. It is our opinion that, even by the strict standard enunciated above, the balance struck by the Minister of Defense is a balance which a reasonable defense minister, acting reasonably, would have been permitted to strike.

For these reasons, the petition is denied.

JUSTICE D. BEINISCH

I agree with the judgment and reasoning of my colleague, the President. I find it necessary to emphasize that I too am of the opinion that, in the current situation — where Israeli society is split and polarized, and includes groups and persons who, due to their strong moral conscience and belief in the truth of their ways — it becomes difficult to identify legitimate selective conscientious objection.

Many among us desire to set the limits of obedience according to their own beliefs and consciences, and even according to their own political perspectives. The distinction between selective conscientious objection and one's political worldview is in fact, as the President has stated, "fine — and occasionally exceedingly fine." Political conflicts in Israeli society agitate its most sensitive nerves. Israeli society is characterized by its intense ideological conflicts, including conflicts based on reasons of conscience and reasons of religious faith. These conflicts are generally legitimate in an open and pluralistic society. Society can withstand such conflicts when they are played out in a democratic arena.

Even if they are sincere, conscientious and faith-based considerations do not stand alone. Against them stand considerations of preserving the security and peace of Israeli society. Since its establishment, the State of Israel has been in a situation that requires military action. This has always been the position of the Israeli government regarding national security. Petitioners themselves served in fighter units and participated in military activities. Their current objection is to serving in the area, which is held by the IDF. This is in objection to the steps being taken there during the military actions against terrorism. The questions which arose as a result of the war against terrorism are at the heart of an intense political conflict. If this conflict is conducted within the army it may substantially harm the army.

According to the Basic Law: The Military, the army is under the authority of the government. The Minister of Defense is the government official responsible for the army. The government is responsible for national security, and the minister acts on its behalf. According to the Defense Service Law, the Minister of Defense has broad discretion in granting exemptions from military service, including those granted for conscientious reasons. Therefore, I concur with the President's opinion that the decision to attribute the decisive weight to security needs — due to the tangible fear that recognizing selective objection will damage the framework of the military — stands up to judicial review and does not establish a cause for our intervention.

YOON v. REPUBLIC OF KOREA
Human Rights Committee, 2006

The Human Rights Committee, established under article 28 of the International Covenant on Civil and Political Rights, . . . [m]eeting on 3 November 2006, . . . [a]dopts the following:

The facts as presented by the authors

Mr. Yoon's case

2.1 Mr. Yoon is a Jehovah's Witness. On 11 February 2001, the State party's Military Power Administration sent Mr. Yoon a notice of draft for military service. On account of his religious belief and conscience, Mr. Yoon refused to be drafted within the prescribed period of time, whereupon he was arrested and charged under article 88 (section 1) of the Military Service Act.[4] In February 2002, Mr. Yoon was bailed.

2.2 On 13 February 2004, the Eastern Seoul District Court convicted Mr. Yoon as charged and sentenced him to one and a half years of imprisonment. On 28 April 2004, the First Criminal Division of the Eastern Seoul District Court upheld the conviction and sentence, reasoning *inter alia*:

> . . . it cannot be said that an internal duty of acting according to one's conscience motivated by an individual belief is greater in value than the duty of national defence, which is essential to protect the nation's political independence and its territories, the people's life, body, freedom and property. Furthermore, since whether there is an expectancy for compliance or not must be determined based on specific actors but on the average person in society, so-called "conscientious decisions", where one objects to the duty of military service set by the law on grounds of religious doctrine, cannot justify acts of objection to military service in violation of established law.

2.3 On 22 July 2004, a majority of the Supreme Court in turn upheld both the conviction and sentence, reasoning, *inter alia*:

> [If [Mr. Yoon's] freedom of conscience is restricted when necessary for national security, the maintenance of law and order or for public welfare, it would be a constitutionally permitted restriction. . . . Article 18 of the [Covenant] appears to provide essentially the same laws and protection as Article 19 (freedom of conscience) and Article 20 (freedom of religion) of the Korean Constitution. Thus, a right to receive an exemption from the concerned clause of the Military Service Act does not arise from Article 18 of the [Covenant].

2.4 The dissenting opinion, basing itself on resolutions of the (then) UN Commission on Human Rights calling for institution of alternative measures to military service as well as on broader State practice, would have held that genuinely-held conscientious objection amounted to "justifiable reasons", within the meaning of Article 88(1) of the Military Services Act, allowing for exemption from military service.

Mr. Choi's case

2.5 Mr. Choi is also a Jehovah's Witness. On 15 November 2001, the State party's Military Power Administration sent Mr. Choi a notice of draft. On account of his religious belief and conscience, Mr. Choi refused to be drafted within the prescribed period of time, whereupon he was arrested and charged under article 88 (section 1) of the Military Service Act.

---

[4] [n.1] Article 88 of the Military Service Act provides as follows:

Evasion of Enlistment

(1) Persons who have received a notice of enlistment or a notice of call (including a notice of enlistment through recruitment) in the active service, and who fails to enlist in the army or to comply with the call, even after the expiration of the following report period from the date of enlistment or call, without any justifiable reason, shall be punished by imprisonment for not more than three years: 1. Five days in cases of enlistment in active service [. . . .]

2.6 On 13 February 2002, the Eastern Seoul District Court convicted Mr. Choi as charged and sentenced him to one and a half years of imprisonment. On 28 February 2002, Mr. Yoon was bailed. On 28 April 2004 and on 15 July 2004, the First Criminal Division of the Eastern Seoul District Court and the Supreme Court, respectively, upheld the conviction and sentence, on the basis of the same reasoning described above with respect to Mr. Yoon.

Subsequent events

2.7 On 26 August 2004, in a case unrelated to Messrs. Yoon or Choi, the Constitutional Court rejected, by a majority, a constitutional challenge to article 88 of the Military Service Act on the grounds of incompatibility with the protection of freedom of conscience protected under the Korean Constitution. The Court reasoned, *inter alia*:

> The freedom of conscience as expressed in Article 19 of the Constitution does not grant an individual the right to refuse military service. Freedom of conscience is merely a right to make a request to the State to consider and protect, if possible, an individual's conscience, and therefore is not a right that allows for the refusal of one's military service duties for reasons of conscience nor does it allow one to demand an alternative service arrangement to replace the performance of a legal duty. Therefore the right to request alternative service arrangement cannot be deduced from the freedom of conscience. The Constitution makes no normative expression that grants freedom of expression a position of absolute superiority in relation to military service duty. Conscientious objection to the performance of military service can be recognised as a valid right if and only if the Constitution itself expressly provides for such a right.

2.8 While accordingly upholding the constitutionality of the contested provisions, the majority directed the legislature to study means by which the conflict between freedom of conscience and the public interest of national security could be eased. The dissent, basing itself on the Committee's General Comment No. 22, the absence of a reservation by the State party to article 18 of the Covenant, resolutions of the (then) UN Commission on Human Rights and State practice, would have found the relevant provisions of the Military Services Act unconstitutional, in the absence of legislative effort to properly accommodate conscientious objection.

2.9 Following the decision, the authors state that some 300 conscientious objectors whose trials had been stayed were being rapidly processed. Accordingly, it was anticipated that by the end of 2004, over 1,100 conscientious objectors would be imprisoned.

The complaint

3. The authors complain that the absence in the State party of an alternative to compulsory military service, under pain of criminal prosecution and imprisonment, breaches their rights under article 18, paragraph 1, of the Covenant.

The State party's submissions on admissibility and merits

4.1 By submission of 2 April 2005, the State party submits that neither communication has any merit. It notes that article 18 provides for specified limitations, where necessary, on the right to manifest conscience. Although article 19 of the State party's Constitution protects freedom of conscience, article 37(2) provides that: "The freedoms and rights of citizens may be restricted by Act only when necessary for national security, the maintenance of law and order or for public welfare . . . . Even when such restriction is imposed, no essential aspect of the freedom or right shall be violated." Accordingly, the Constitutional Court ruled that "the freedom of conscience prescribed in Article 19 of the Constitution does not grant one the right to object to fulfilling one's military service duty" based on limitations of principle that all basic rights must be exercised within the boundary of enabling pursuit of civic engagement and keeping the nation's "law order" intact. Hence, the freedom to manifest one's conscience may be restricted by law when it is harmful to public safety and order in pursuing civic engagement or when it threatens a nation's "law order."

4.2 The State party argues that in view of its specific circumstances, conscientious objection to military service needs to be restricted as it may incur harm to national security. Unlike the freedom to form or determine inner conscience, the freedom to object to fulfilling military service duty for reasons of religion may be restricted, as recognised in article 18 of the Covenant, for public causes in that it manifests or realizes one's conscience through passive non-performance.

4.3 Under the specific security circumstances facing a hostile Democratic People's Republic of Korea (DPRK), the State party, as the world's sole divided nation, adopted the Universal Conscription System, which recognises all citizens' obligation to military service. Thus, the equality principle of military service duty and responsibility carries more meaning in the State party than in any other country. Considering the strong social demand and anticipation for the equality of the performance of military service duty, allowing exceptions to military service duty may prevent social unification, greatly harming national security by eroding the basis of the national military service system — the Universal Conscription System — especially considering the social tendency of attempting to evade military service duty by using any and every means.

4.4 The State party argues that a nation's military service system is directly linked to issues of national security, and is a matter of legislative discretion vested in the lawmakers for the creation of the national army with the maximum capabilities for national defence, after considering a nation's geopolitical stance, internal and external security conditions, economic and social state and national sentiment, along with several other factors.

4.5 The State party contends that given its security conditions, the demand for equality in military service and various concomitant restricting elements in adopting an alternative service system, it is difficult to argue that it has reached the stage of improved security conditions that would allow for limitations to military service, as well as the formation of national consensus.

4.6 The State party concludes that the prohibition of conscientious objection to military service is justified by its specific security and social conditions, which makes it difficult to conclude that the decision violates the essential meaning of the freedom of conscience set out in paragraph 3 of article 18 of the Covenant. Considering the State party's security conditions, the demand for equality in military service duty, and the absence of any national consensus, along with various other factors, the introduction of any system of alternative service is unlikely.

The authors' comments on the State party's submission

5.1 By letter of 8 August 2005, the authors responded to the State party's submissions. They note that the State party does not identify which of the permissible restrictions in section 3 of article 18 is invoked, though accept that the general import of argument is on "public safety or order." Here, however, the State party has not identified why conscientious objectors can be considered to harm public safety or order. Strictly speaking, as conscientious objection has never been allowed, the State party cannot determine whether or not any such danger in fact exists.

5.2 The authors note a vague fear on the State party's part that allowing conscientious objection would threaten universal conscription. But such a fear cannot justify the severe punishments meted out under the Military Service Act to thousands of objectors and the discrimination faced by objectors after their release from prison. In any event, the authors question the real value of conscience, if it must be kept internal to oneself and not expressed outwardly. The authors note the long history, dating from the Roman Republic, of conscientious objection and the pacifist rejection of violence of objectors. Referring to the Committee's General Comment No. 22, the authors argue that conscientious objectors, far from threatening public safety or order or others' rights, in fact strengthens the same, being a noble value based on deep and moral reflection.

5.3 On the aspect of the threat posed by the DPRK, the authors note that the State party's population is almost twice as large, its economy thirty times as large and its annual military spending over the last decade nearly ten times as large as that of its northern neighbour. That country is under constant satellite surveillance, and is suffering a humanitarian crisis. By contrast, the State party fields almost 700,000 soldiers, and 350,000 young people perform military service each year. The number of 1,053 imprisoned objectors, as of 11 July 2005, is a very small number incapable of adversely affecting such military power. Against this background, it is unreasonable to argue that the threat posed by the DPRK is sufficient justification for the punishment of conscientious objectors.

5.4 On the issue of equitability, the authors argue that the institution of alternative service arrangements would preserve this, if necessary by extending the term of the latter kind of service. The authors note the positive experience gained from the recent institution of alternative service in Taiwan, facing at least equivalent external threat to its existence as the State party, and in Germany. Such an institution would contribute to social integration and development and respect for human rights in society. The social tendency to avoid military service, for its part, is unrelated to the objection issue and stems from the poor conditions faced by soldiers. Were these improved, the tendency to avoid service would lessen.

5.5 The authors reject the argument that the introduction of alternative service is at the discretion of the legislative branch, noting that such discretion cannot excuse a breach of the Covenant and in any event little if any work in this direction has been done. Moreover, the State party has not observed its duty as a member of the UN Commission on Human Rights, and, whether deliberately or not, has failed to report to the Committee in its periodic reports on the situation of conscientious objectors.

Supplementary submissions of the State party

6.1 By submission of 6 September 2006, the State party responded to the authors' submissions with supplementary observations on the merits of the communications. The State party notes that under article 5 of its Constitution, the National Armed Forces are charged with the sacred mission of national security and defence of the land, while article 39 acknowledges that the obligation of military service is an important, indeed one of the key, means of guaranteeing national security, itself a benefit and protection of law. The State party notes that national security is an indispensable precondition for national existence, maintaining territorial integrity and protecting the lives and safety of citizens, while constituting a basic requirement for citizen's exercise of freedom.

6.2 The State party notes the freedom to object to compulsory military service is subject to express permission of limitations set out in article 18, paragraph 3, of the Covenant. Allowing exceptions to compulsory service, one of the basic obligations imposed on all citizens at the expense of a number of basic rights to protect life and public property, may damage the basis of the national military service which serves as the main force of national defence, escalate social conflict, threaten public safety and national security and, in turn, infringe on the basic rights and freedoms of citizens. Hence, a restriction on the basis of harm to public safety and order or threat to a nation's legal order when undertaken in a communal setting is permissible.

6.3 The State party argues that while it is true that the situation on the Korean peninsula has changed since the appearance of a new concept of national defence and modern warfare, as well as a military power gap due to the disparities in economic power between North and South, military manpower remains the main form of defence. The prospect of manpower shortages caused by falling birth rates must also be taken into account. Punishing conscientious objectors, despite their small overall number, discourages evasion of military service. The current system may easily crumble if alternative service systems were adopted. In light of past experiences of irregularities and social tendencies to evade military service, it is difficult to assume alternatives would prevent attempts to evade military service. Further, accepting conscientious objection while military manpower remains the main force of national defence may lead to the misuse of conscientious objection as a legal device to evade military service, greatly harming national security by demolishing the conscription basis of the system.

6.4 On the authors' arguments on equality, the State party argues that exempting conscientious objectors or imposing less stringent obligations on them risks violating the principle of equality enshrined in article 11 of the Constitution, breach the general duty of national defence imposed by article 39 of the Constitution and amount to an impermissible awarding of decorations or distinctions to a particular group. Considering the strong social demand and anticipation of equality in performance of military service, allowing exceptions may hinder social unification and greatly harm national capabilities by raising inequalities. If an alternative system is adopted, all must be given a choice between military service and alternative service as a matter of equity, inevitably threatening public safety and order and the protection of basic rights and freedoms. The State party accepts that human rights problems are a major reason for evasion of service and substantially improved barracks conditions. That notwithstanding, the two year length of service — significantly longer than that in other countries — continues to be a reason for evasion unlikely to fade even with improved conditions and the adoption of alternative service.

6.5 On the authors' arguments as to international practice, the State party notes that Germany, Switzerland and Taiwan accept conscientious objection and provide alternative forms of service. It had contacted system administrators in each country and gathered information on the respective practices through research and seminars, keeping itself updated on an ongoing basis on progress made and reviewing the possibility of its own adoption. The State party notes however that the introduction of alternative arrangements in these countries was adopted under their own particular circumstances. In Europe, for example, alternative service was introduced in a general shift from compulsory to volunteer military service post-Cold War, given a drastic reduction in the direct and grave security threat. Taiwan also approved conscientious objection in 2000 when over-conscription became a problem with the implementation in 1997 of a manpower reduction policy. The State party also points out that in January 2006, its National Human Rights Commission devised a national action plan for conscientious objection, and the Government intends to act on the issue.

Issues and proceedings before the Committee

Consideration of admissibility

7.1 Before considering any claims contained in a communication, the Human Rights Committee must, in accordance with article 93 of its rules of procedure, decide whether or not it is admissible under the Optional Protocol to the Covenant.

7.2 In the absence of objection by the State party to the admissibility to the communication, as well as any reasons suggesting that the Committee should *proprio motu*, declare the communication inadmissible in whole or in part, the Committee declares the claim under article 18 of the Covenant admissible.

Consideration of the merits

8.1 The Human Rights Committee has considered the present communication in the light of all the information made available to it by the parties, as provided in article 5, paragraph 1, of the Optional Protocol.

8.2 The Committee notes the authors' claim that article 18 of the Covenant guaranteeing the right to freedom of conscience and the right to manifest one's religion or belief requires recognition of their religious belief, genuinely held, that submission to compulsory military service is morally and ethically impermissible for them as individuals. It also notes that article 8, paragraph 3, of the Covenant excludes from the scope of "forced or compulsory labour," which is proscribed, "any service of a military character and, in countries where conscientious objection is recognized, any national service required by law of conscientious objectors." It follows that the article 8 of the Covenant itself neither recognizes nor excludes a right of conscientious objection. Thus, the present claim is to be assessed solely in the light of article 18 of the Covenant, the understanding of which evolves as that of any other guarantee of the Covenant over time in view of its text and purpose.

8.3 The Committee recalls its previous jurisprudence on the assessment of a claim of conscientious objection to military service as a protected form of manifestation of religious belief under article 18, paragraph 1.[5] It observes that while the right to manifest one's religion or belief does not as such imply the right to refuse all obligations imposed by law, it provides certain protection, consistent with article 18, paragraph 3, against being forced to act against genuinely-held religious belief. The Committee also recalls its general view expressed in [General Comment No. 22 (1993), para. 11] that to compel a person to use lethal force, although such use would seriously conflict with the requirements of his conscience or religious beliefs, falls within the ambit of article 18. The Committee notes, in the instant case, that the authors' refusal to be drafted for compulsory service was a direct expression of their religious beliefs, which it is uncontested were genuinely held. The authors' conviction and sentence, accordingly, amounts to a restriction on their ability to manifest their religion or belief. Such restriction must be justified by the permissible limits described in paragraph 3 of article 18, that is, that any restriction must be prescribed by law and be necessary to protect public safety, order, health or morals or the fundamental rights and freedoms of others. However, such restriction must not impair the very essence of the right in question.

8.4 The Committee notes that under the laws of the State party there is no procedure for recognition of conscientious objections against military service. The State party argues that this restriction is necessary for public safety, in order to maintain its national defensive capacities and to preserve social cohesion. The Committee takes note of the State party's argument on the

---

[5] [n.3] In *Muhonen v. Finland* (Case No. 89/1981), for example, the Committee declined to decide whether article 18 guaranteed a right of conscientious objection. In *L.T.K. v. Finland* (Case No. 185/1984), the Committee declined to address the issue fully on the merits, deciding as a preliminary matter of admissibility on the basis of the argument before it that the question fell outside the scope of article 18. *Brinkhof v. The Netherlands* (Case No. 402/1990) addressed differentiation between total objectors and Jehovah's Witnesses, while *Westerman v. The Netherlands* (Case No. 682/1996) involved a procedure for recognition of conscientious objection under domestic law itself, rather than the existence of underlying rights as such. Although the statement was not necessary for its final decision, in *J.P. v. Canada* (Case No. 446/1991) the Committee noted, without further explanation, that article 18 "certainly protects the right to hold, express and disseminate opinions and convictions, including conscientious objection to military activities and expenditures."

particular context of its national security, as well as of its intention to act on the national action plan for conscientious objection devised by the National Human Rights Commission (see paragraph 6.5, *supra*). The Committee also notes, in relation to relevant State practice, that an increasing number of those States parties to the Covenant which have retained compulsory military service have introduced alternatives to compulsory military service, and considers that the State party has failed to show what special disadvantage would be involved for it if the rights of the authors' under article 18 would be fully respected. As to the issue of social cohesion and equitability, the Committee considers that respect on the part of the State for conscientious beliefs and manifestations thereof is itself an important factor in ensuring cohesive and stable pluralism in society. It likewise observes that it is in principle possible, and in practice common, to conceive alternatives to compulsory military service that do not erode the basis of the principle of universal conscription but render equivalent social good and make equivalent demands on the individual, eliminating unfair disparities between those engaged in compulsory military service and those in alternative service. The Committee, therefore, considers that the State party has not demonstrated that in the present case the restriction in question is necessary, within the meaning of article 18, paragraph 3, of the Covenant.

9. The Human Rights Committee, acting under article 5, paragraph 4, of the Optional Protocol to the International Covenant on Civil and Political Rights, concludes that the facts as found by the Committee reveal, in respect of each author violations by the Republic of Korea of article 18, paragraph 1, of the Covenant. . . .

Dissenting opinion by Committee member MR. HIPÓLITO SOLARI-YRIGOYEN

While I agree with the majority's conclusion in paragraph 9 that the facts before the Committee reveal a violation of article 18, paragraph 1, I disagree with the reasoning of the majority, as will be apparent from the following observations:

Consideration of the merits

8.2 The Committee notes the authors' claim that the State party breached article 18, paragraph 1, of the Covenant by prosecuting and sentencing the authors for their refusal to perform compulsory military service on account of their religious beliefs as Jehovah's Witnesses.

The Committee also notes the comment by the State party that article 19 of its Constitution does not grant one the right to object to fulfilling one's military service duty. The State party also argues that conscientious objection may be "restricted" as it may harm national security. The State party concludes that the prohibition of conscientious objection to military service is justified and that, given the wording of article 18, paragraph 3, it does not violate the Covenant. The Constitutional Court (see paragraph 2.7, *supra*) would limit the right to freedom of conscience to a mere right to request the State to consider and protect the objector's right "if possible."

The fundamental human right to conscientious objection entitles any individual to an exemption from compulsory military service if this cannot be reconciled with that individual's religion or beliefs. The right must not be impaired by coercion. Given that the State party does not recognize this right, the present communication should be considered under paragraph 1 of article 18, not paragraph 3.

8.3 The right to conscientious objection to military service derives from the right to freedom of thought, conscience and religion. As stated in article 4, paragraph 2, of the Covenant, this right cannot be derogated from even in exceptional circumstances which threaten the life of the nation and justify the declaration of a public emergency. When a right to conscientious objection is recognized, a State may, if it wishes, compel the objector to undertake a civilian alternative to military service, outside the military sphere and not under military command. The alternative service must not be of a punitive nature. It must be a real service to the community and compatible with respect for human rights.

In General Comment No. 22, the Committee recognized this right "inasmuch as the obligation to use lethal force may seriously conflict with the freedom of conscience and the right to manifest one's religion or belief." The same General Comment states that the right to freedom of thought, conscience and religion "is far-reaching and profound," and that "the freedom of thought and the freedom of conscience are protected equally with the freedom of religion and belief."

Because of their religious beliefs, the authors invoked this right, established in article 18, paragraph 1, to avoid compulsory military service. The prosecution, conviction and prison term imposed on the authors directly violated this right.

The mention of freedom to manifest one's religion or belief in article 18, paragraph 3, is a reference to the freedom to manifest that religion or belief in public, not to recognition of the right itself, which is protected by paragraph 1. Even if it were wrongly supposed that the present communication does not concern recognition of the objector's right, but merely its public manifestation, the statement that public manifestations may be subject only "to such limitations as are prescribed by law" in no way implies that the existence of the right itself is a matter for the discretion of States parties.

The State party's intention to act on the national plan for conscientious objection devised by the National Human Rights Commission (see paragraph 6.5, *supra*), which the Committee notes in paragraph 8.4, must be considered alongside the statement in paragraph 4.6 that the introduction of any system of alternative service is unlikely. Moreover, intentions must be acted upon, and the mere intention to "act on the issue" does not establish whether, at some point in the future, the right to conscientious objection will be recognized or denied.

9. The Human Rights Committee, acting under article 5, paragraph 4, of the Optional Protocol to the International Covenant on Civil and Political Rights, concludes that the Republic of Korea has, in respect of each author, violated the authors' rights under article 18, paragraph 1, of the Covenant.

Dissenting opinion by Committee member Ms. RUTH WEDGWOOD

I concur with the Committee that a State party wishing to apply the principles of the International Covenant on Civil and Political Rights with a generous spirit should respect the claims of individuals who object to national military service on grounds of religious belief or other consistent and conscientious beliefs. The sanctity of religious belief, including teachings about a duty of non-violence, is something that a democratic and liberal state should wish to protect.

However, regrettably, I am unable to conclude that the right to refrain from mandatory military service is strictly required by the terms of the Covenant, as a matter of law. Article 18 paragraph 1, of the Covenant states that "Everyone shall have the right to freedom of thought, conscience and religion. This right shall include freedom to have or to adopt a religion or belief of his choice, and freedom, either individually or in community with others and in public or private, to manifest his religion or belief in worship, observance, practice and teaching."

Article 18 thus importantly protects the right to worship in public or private, to gather with others for worship, to organize religious schools, and to display outward symbols of religious belief. The proviso of article 18 paragraph 3 — that the "Freedom to manifest one's religion or beliefs may be subject only to such limitations as are prescribed by law and are necessary to protect public safety, order, health, or morals or the fundamental rights and freedoms of others" — cannot be used by a state party as a backdoor method of burdening religious practice. The Human Rights Committee has appropriately rejected any attempt to limit the protections of article 18 to "traditional" religions or to use forms of administrative regulation to impede or deny practical implementation of the right to worship.

But article 18 does not suggest that a person motivated by religious belief has a protected right to withdraw from the otherwise legitimate requirements of a shared society. For example, citizens cannot refrain from paying taxes, even where they have conscientious objections to state activities. In its present interpretation of article 18, seemingly differentiating military service from other state obligations, the Committee cites no evidence from the Covenant's negotiating history to suggest that this was contemplated. The practice of States parties may also be relevant, whether at the time the Covenant was concluded or even now. But we do not have any record information before us, most particularly, in regard to the number of parties to the Covenant that still rely upon military conscription without providing de jure for a right to conscientious objection.

To be sure, in the "concluding observations" framed upon the examination of country reports, the Human Rights Committee has frequently encouraged states to recognize a right of conscientious objection to military practice. But these concluding observations permissibly may contain suggestions of "best practices" and do not, of themselves, change the terms of the Covenant. It is also true that in 1993, the Committee stated in "General Comment 22", at paragraph 11, that a right to conscientious objection "can be derived" from article 18. But in the interval of more than a decade since, the Committee has never suggested in its jurisprudence under the Optional Protocol that such a "derivation" is in fact required by the Covenant.[6] The language of article 8, paragraph 3(c)(ii), of the Covenant also presents an obstacle to the Committee's conclusion.

This does not change the fact that the practice of the state party in this case has apparently tended to be harsh. The "stacking" of criminal sentences for conscientious objection, through repeated re-issuance of notices for military service, can lead to draconian results. The prohibition of employment by public organizations after a refusal to serve also is a severe result.

In a recent decision of the Constitutional Court of Korea, the national defence minister suggested that "present conditions for life as a serviceman within the military [are] poor" and therefore that "the number of objectors to military service will increase rapidly" if "alternative service is allowed in a country like ours." [See 2002 HeonGal, Alleging Unconstitutionality of Article 88, Section 1, Clause 1 of Military Service Act, Constitutional Court of Korea, in the case of Kyung-Soo Lee.] This may suggest the wisdom of seeking to ameliorate the living conditions of service personnel. In any event, many other countries have felt able to discern which applications for conscientious objection are based upon a bona fide moral or religious belief, without impairing the operation of a national service system. Thus, a state party's democratic legislature would surely wish to examine whether the religious conscience of a minority of its citizens can be accommodated without a prohibitive burden on its ability to organize a national defence.

QUESTIONS

Do you find the Committee's position or Professor Wedgwood's position more convincing? Why?

---

[6] [n.5] In the case of *J.P. v. Canada*, Communication No. 446/1991, 7 November 1991, the Committee rejected the claim of a petitioner that she had a right to withhold taxes to protest Canada's military expenditures. The Committee stated that "Although article 18 of the Covenant certainly protects the right to hold, express and disseminate opinions and convictions, including conscientious objection to military activities and expenditures, the refusal to pay taxes on grounds of conscientious objection clearly falls outside the scope of protection of this article." In other words, an individual's conscientious objection to taxes for military activities did not require the state to refrain from collecting those taxes.

Chapter 11

RIGHTS OF ASSOCIATION AND IDENTITY

While serving in the military, individuals gain the authority and shoulder the burden of using force to pursue governmental objectives. That authority and responsibility exacts a toll, however, in the reduced autonomy that soldiers enjoy as compared to civilians. The extent to which servicemembers must relinquish basic rights is much debated in military jurisprudence. This chapter explores the balance the law must strike between protecting human rights and enforcing military discipline. It focuses on three related areas of human rights — freedom of association, privacy, and sexual orientation — to explore the law and limits of human rights within military institutions.

I. FREEDOM OF ASSOCIATION

Membership in military unions, organizing of military unions, and recognition of military unions prohibited
10 U.S.C. § 976

(a) In this section:

(1) The term "member of the armed forces" means (A) a member of the armed forces who is serving on active duty, (B) a member of the National Guard who is serving on full-time National Guard duty, or (C) a member of a Reserve component while performing inactive-duty training.

(2) The term "military labor organization" means any organization that engages in or attempts to engage in —

(A) negotiating or bargaining with any civilian officer or employee, or with any member of the armed forces, on behalf of members of the armed forces, concerning the terms or conditions of military service of such members in the armed forces;

(B) representing individual members of the armed forces before any civilian officer or employee, or any member of the armed forces, in connection with any grievance or complaint of any such member arising out of the terms or conditions of military service of such member in the armed forces; or

(C) striking, picketing, marching, demonstrating, or any other similar form of concerted action which is directed against the Government of the United States and which is intended to induce any civilian officer or employee, or any member of the armed forces, to —

(i) negotiate or bargain with any person concerning the terms or conditions of military service of any member of the armed forces,

(ii) recognize any organization as a representative of individual members of the armed forces in connection with complaints and grievances of such members arising out of the terms or conditions of military service of such members in the armed forces, or

(iii) make any change with respect to the terms or conditions of military service of individual members of the armed forces.

(3) The term "civilian officer or employee" means an employee, as such term is defined in section 2105 of title 5.

(b) It shall be unlawful for a member of the armed forces, knowing of the activities or objectives of a particular military labor organization —

(1) to join or maintain membership in such organization; or

(2) to attempt to enroll any other member of the armed forces as a member of such organization.

(c) It shall be unlawful for any person —

(1) to enroll in a military labor organization any member of the armed forces or to solicit or accept dues or fees for such an organization from any member of the armed forces; or

(2) to negotiate or bargain, or attempt through any coercive act to negotiate or bargain, with any civilian officer or employee, or any member of the armed forces, on behalf of members of the armed forces, concerning the terms or conditions of service of such members;

(3) to organize or attempt to organize, or participate in, any strike, picketing, march, demonstration, or other similar form of concerted action involving members of the armed forces that is directed against the Government of the United States and that is intended to induce any civilian officer or employee, or any member of the armed forces, to —

(A) negotiate or bargain with any person concerning the terms or conditions of service of any member of the armed forces,

(B) recognize any military labor organization as a representative of individual members of the armed forces in connection with any complaint or grievance of any such member arising out of the terms or conditions of service of such member in the armed forces, or

(C) make any change with respect to the terms or conditions of service in the armed forces of individual members of the armed forces; or

(4) to use any military installation, facility, reservation, vessel, or other property of the United States for any meeting, march, picketing, demonstration, or other similar activity for the purpose of engaging in any activity prohibited by this subsection or by subsection (b) or (d).

(d) It shall be unlawful for any military labor organization to represent, or attempt to represent, any member of the armed forces before any civilian officer or employee, or any member of the armed forces, in connection with any grievance or complaint of any such member arising out of the terms or conditions of service of such member in the armed forces.

(e) No member of the armed forces, and no civilian officer or employee, may —

(1) negotiate or bargain on behalf of the United States concerning the terms or conditions of military service of members of the armed forces with any person who represents or purports to represent members of the armed forces, or

(2) permit or authorize the use of any military installation, facility, reservation, vessel, or other property of the United States for any meeting, march, picketing, demonstration, or other similar activity which is for the purpose of engaging in any activity prohibited by subsection (b), (c), or (d).

Nothing in this subsection shall prevent commanders or supervisors from giving consideration to the views of any member of the armed forces presented individually or as a result of participation on command-sponsored or authorized advisory councils, committees, or organizations.

(f) Whoever violates subsection (b), (c), or (d) shall be fined under title 18 or imprisoned not more than 5 years, or both, except that, in the case of an organization (as defined in section 18 of such title), the fine shall not be less than $25,000.

(g) Nothing in this section shall limit the right of any member of the armed forces —

(1) to join or maintain membership in any organization or association not constituting a "military labor organization" as defined in subsection (a)(2) of this section;

(2) to present complaints or grievances concerning the terms or conditions of the service of such member in the armed forces in accordance with established military procedures;

(3) to seek or receive information or counseling from any source;

(4) to be represented by counsel in any legal or quasi-legal proceeding, in accordance with applicable laws and regulations;

(5) to petition the Congress for redress of grievances; or

(6) to take such other administrative action to seek such administrative or judicial relief, as is authorized by applicable laws and regulations.

Right to Association for Members of the Professional Staff of the Armed Forces
Council of Europe, Committee on Legal Affairs and Human Rights, 2002

Summary

Although Article 11 of the European Convention on Human Rights guarantees freedom of association and Article 5 of the European Social Charter (Revised) sets out the right to form, join and actively participate in associations designed to protect their members' professional interests, military personnel in many Council of Europe member states are still denied this right. The committee calls for the right to be recognised in member states' military regulations and codes and for the possible setting up of national ombudsmen's offices for military personnel, while also proposing an amendment to Article 5 of the European Social Charter (Revised) that would bring the freedom of association of members of the armed forces into line with that of the police.

I. Draft recommendation

1. The Assembly recalls its Resolution 903 (1988) on the right to association for the members of the professional staff of the armed forces, in which it called on all member states of the Council of Europe to grant professional members of the armed forces, under normal circumstances, the right to association, with an interdiction of the right to strike. It also recalls its Order No. 539 (1998) calling on the member states to implement the European Social Charter.

2. The freedom of association is guaranteed by Article 11 of the European Convention on Human Rights and Fundamental Freedoms and the right to organise is a right foreseen in Article 5 of the European Social Charter (revised). However, these articles are of limited scope in relation to violations of the recognition of the right of members of the armed forces to form trade unions.

3. The Assembly observes that, notwithstanding efforts to promote the civic right to association of certain professional groups, the right to organise is still not recognised for members of the professional staff of the armed forces in all member states of the Council of Europe. Furthermore, several member states who recognised the right to organise to this category put severe limitations on the conditions governing it.

4. In the past years, armies from certain member states converted from a conscription system to a purely professional system. As a consequence, military personnel are becoming increasingly "regular" employees whose employer is the Ministry of Defence and should be fully eligible for the employees' rights established in the European Convention on Human Rights and Fundamental Freedoms and the European Social Charter.

5. Members of the armed forces, as "citizens in uniform," should enjoy the full right, under normal circumstances, to establish, join and actively participate in specific associations formed to protect their professional interests within the framework of democratic institutions, while performing their service duties.

6. The military personnel should be entitled to the exercise of the same rights, including the right to join legal political parties.

7. Therefore, the Assembly recommends that the Committee of Ministers calls on the governments of the member states:

i. to allow members of the armed forces and military personnel to organise in representative associations with the right to negotiate on matters concerning salaries and conditions of employment;

ii. to lift the current unnecessary restrictions on the right to association for members of the armed forces;

iii. to allow members of the armed forces and military personnel to be members of legal political parties;

iv. to establish these rights in the military regulations and codes of member states;

v. to examine the possibility of setting up an office of an Ombudsman to whom military personnel can apply in case of labour and other service-related disputes.

8. The Assembly also calls on the Committee of Ministers to examine the possibility to revise the text of the European Social Charter (Revised), by introducing a new article 5, which would read: "With a view to ensuring or promoting the freedom of workers and employers to form local, national or international organisations for the protection of their economic and social interests and to join those organisations, the Parties undertake that national law shall not be such as to impair, nor shall it be so applied as to impair, this freedom. The extent to which the guarantees provided for in this article shall apply to the police and the members of the armed forces shall be determined by national laws or regulations."

II. Explanatory memorandum by Mrs. van Ardenne-van der Hoeven, Rapporteur

A. Introduction

1. Western democratic societies hold a high degree of respect for the protection of human rights. The many different forms of European co-operation thus all find their basis in the preservation of the universal human rights. Although many rights are established in the European Convention of Human Rights and Fundamental Freedoms, a substantial part of society is excluded from a large part of their inalienable human rights. The basic rights of military personnel in many member states of the Council of Europe are seriously limited.

2. First of all it is important to realise that Article 11 (Freedom of assembly and association) of the European Convention on Human Rights and Fundamental Freedoms reads as follows:

1. Everyone has the right to freedom of peaceful assembly and to freedom of association with others, including the right to form and to join trade unions for the protection of his interests

2. No restrictions shall be placed on the exercise of these rights other than such as are prescribed by law and are necessary in a democratic society in the interests of national security or public safety, for the prevention of disorder or crime, for the protection of health or morals or for the protection of the rights and freedoms of others. This article shall not prevent the imposition of lawful restrictions on the exercise of these rights by members of the armed forces, of the police or of the administration of the State.

3. It is well known that the right of assembly and association to protect the interests of professional groups is in the interest of mature democracies. It is important that employees have the opportunity to unite in some form of

federation to represent their professional interests in the sphere of working conditions, conditions of employment and pay. This right has been established on several occasions, in the European Convention on Human Rights and fundamental Freedoms and by the Parliamentary Assembly of the Council of Europe. Your Rapporteur holds the opinion that it is unsatisfactory that still in many member states an entire professional group is denied this right.

4. Also the exercise of this basic right is included in Article 5 of the European Social Charter which is considered by the Committee of Ministers to be one of the benchmarks for all the Council of Europe's activities in the social field. In this Article remains the possibility to make an exception for members of the police force and military personnel: "The principle governing the application to the members of the armed forces of these guarantees and the extent to which they shall apply to persons in this category shall equally be determined by national laws or regulations."

5. In 1988 the Assembly adopted Resolution 903 on the right to association for members of the professional staff of the armed forces. Paragraph 8 specifically calls on all member states of the Council of Europe — insofar as they have not yet done so — to grant professional members of the armed forces of all ranks the right, under normal circumstances, to establish, join and actively participate in specific associations formed to protect their professional interests within the framework of democratic institutions. . . .

7. Since the adoption of Resolution 903 however, no significant progress has been made in this matter. Still less than half of the 43 member states of the Council of Europe recognise the right of professional staff of the armed forces to freedom of peaceful assembly and to freedom of association with others, although this right is guaranteed in the European Convention on Human Rights and Fundamental Freedoms and the European Social Charter. Also the fact that many member states impose rigorous restrictions on the freedom of assembly and association for professional military personnel is considered alarming by your Rapporteur. . . .

B. Developments

10. The last years have seen continuous motion towards military co-operation and integration between European countries and the establishment of a common European Defence and Security Identity with a European Rapid Reaction Force. Also the Partnership for Peace has resulted in military co-operation in both exercises and missions. The enlargement of NATO and the European Union will result in even more and further-reaching co-operation and integration. In the case of combined action by armed forces, for example in peace keeping missions, the differences in human rights and fundamental freedoms for military personnel between member states become all the more visible. The encouragement of equality, security, and stability in European armed forces is of vital importance. The granting of democratic rights to professional members of the armed forces makes up an important part of this.

11. A second development that has taken place in the member states in the past years is the conversion from military systems with conscription to armed forces that rely entirely on professional soldiers. As a consequence of this military personnel become increasingly "regular" employees whose employer is

the Ministry of Defence. Therefore they should, in the opinion of your Rapporteur, be fully eligible for the social — employees' — rights established in the European Convention on Human Rights and Fundamental Freedoms and the European Social Charter.

12. In the third place, with the declining share of conscripts in military personnel, the Departments of Defence will have to rely more heavily on volunteers to fill their vacancies. Eventually this not only means that the working conditions in the armed forces will have to become more competitive towards the working conditions elsewhere at the labour market, but also that the armed forces may not exclude themselves from society by denying human rights and fundamental freedoms to their members. This could be achieved to a large extent by allowing military personnel to make full use of their social rights.

13. Paragraph 2 of Article 11 of the European Convention on Human Rights and Fundamental Freedoms leaves open the possibility for governments to impose restrictions on the right to freedom of assembly and association for certain groups in society. However, this far-reaching right must be treated with care and should only be used in case of a serious threat to national security. Improper uses of this paragraph, by taking away every right of assembly for military personnel should be prevented. Accordingly, in a normal situation freedom of association for members of the armed forces must be allowed and should be regulated by law.

14. According to contemporary conceptions, employees may not be restricted in their fundamental freedoms any more than is strictly necessary in the industrial relation, whereby it must be reviewed that such restriction is not disproportionate in proportion to the goal. Moreover, respecting fundamental freedoms is a general interest. Governments have to ensure that employers respect these fundamental freedoms, if need be with legislation.

15. In the opinion of your Rapporteur, all member states should allow professional military personnel to form, establish and join professional associations aimed at improving working conditions in the armed forces. Such organisations would provide a much-needed independent and professional support network. The form of these associations — trade unions, trade associations or at least representative associations — is a national prerogative and may be lead by social, cultural, historical and legal considerations. The right to association however is fully applicable to professional military personnel and should therefore be embedded in the laws and regulations of the member states.

16. What's more, the ILO states that the ILO-Treaty 87, on the right to association to look after the professional interests of a certain professional group cannot be treated separately from Treaty 98 on the right of that professional group to negotiate. This should also apply to military personnel.

C. Present situation

17. The questionnaire sent to the national parliamentary delegations inquired about the present restrictions imposed to military personnel on the right of association which go beyond the general restrictions on the right to

association in the member state concerned. A total of 22 replies to the questionnaire of the Rapporteur were received (Azerbaijan, Cyprus, Croatia, the Czech Republic, Denmark, Estonia, Finland, France, Germany, Hungary, Italy, Luxembourg, "the former Yugoslav Republic of Macedonia," the Netherlands, Norway, Poland, Slovenia, Sweden, Switzerland, Ukraine, United Kingdom, Yugoslavia).

18. The restrictions put by the Council of Europe member states on the right to freedom of association vary. Many countries have not implemented Article 11 of the ECHR in national legislation at all. Others have done so, but military regulations impose severe restrictions. The European Committee of Social Rights concluded to the non-violation of article 5 of the European Social Charter in three different cases brought to it by EUROFEDOP (European Federation of Employees in Public Services) and recalled its constant case-law in which it says that the member states are entitled to bring any kind of limitation and even the full suppression of trade unions' freedom of members of staff of armed forces. A modification of article 5 could be envisaged, so as to permit a more dynamic interpretation of the article, such as the one the Committee gives for the trade union's freedom of police.

19. There are however some exemplary member states. In Austria, Denmark, Finland, Norway, Sweden and Switzerland for example, no restrictions whatsoever are placed on the freedom of assembly and association of military personnel. They are allowed to participate actively in a political party or association to protect their professional interests, just as other citizens. The Netherlands and Belgium — that country did not respond to the questionnaire — allow members of the armed forces the same rights. In Norway professional military personnel are entitled to unpaid leave for a maximum of 3 years to work for such an association, more than 30 independent associations exist and almost 95% of personnel in the Norwegian armed forces are members of one or more associations. Sweden has known no restrictions for military personnel on the right to association since 1974. Switzerland only limits the right to strike for members of the armed forces when matters of national security are involved. Although Ireland, Portugal and Bulgaria did not respond to the questionnaire, the governments of these member states have allowed members of the armed forces the right to association. Ireland has done so in 1991, Portugal in 2001 and Bulgaria very recently, in April 2002. These member states provide an example worth following.

20. Other member states such as Germany, Hungary, The Netherlands and Luxembourg choose intermediate forms by allowing members of the armed forces to be members of and actively participate in associations protecting their professional interests, but regulating in some form their membership of political parties. In the Netherlands consultative structures of military personnel have existed since the late 1920's; in the late 1980's negotiations were introduced in the primary working conditions. All political activities are allowed with the exception of being a Member of Parliament. In Germany military personnel can be active members of political parties, however they must comply with their service duties. In Luxembourg professional associations and political activities of military personnel are allowed, but they can not be members of representative bodies on the national or local level. Hungarian military

personnel have the possibility to be candidate in parliamentary or municipal elections; but their military status is in intermission until after the termination of their mandate. After that their status can be set back if they wish so.

21. In many member states however taking part in political activities and membership of political parties is not allowed. Members of the armed forces are seen to maintain a position of political neutrality. Azerbaijan, the Czech Republic, Estonia, Finland, Romania, Slovenia and Ukraine forbid membership of political parties, but allow (in restricted forms) the right to association to protect the professional interests of military personnel. The right to strike is withheld from military personnel in these countries.

22. Azerbaijan imposes no restrictions on military personnel on the right of association. In the Czech Republic military personnel is allowed to associate in "professional associations", but the activities of such an association are to be guaranteed by a co-operation arrangement with the Ministry of Defence. Romania — a country that did not respond to the questionnaire — imposes the restriction that members of the armed forces are not allowed to *join trade unions or associations, which contravene the unique command.* Apart from that, participation in an association protecting the professional interests of members of the armed forces is allowed. The Slovenian Ministry of Defence assists and finances the Association of Slovene Officers and other organisations whose activities are of particular importance for defence. Ukraine allows setting up voluntary associations to protect the professional interests of military personnel, with the exception of organisations having *"statutory provisions that contradict the precepts of the activities of the armed forces of Ukraine."*

23. In conclusion a number of replies to the questionnaire revealed that in several member states association of members of the professional staff of the armed forces is still forbidden, in defiance to Article 11 of the European Convention on Human Rights and Fundamental Freedoms. Croatia, France, Italy, Poland and Yugoslavia specifically prohibit military personnel to organise trade unions and political parties in the armed forces. All of these member states except for Croatia also prohibit members of the armed forces to set up any professional association. In Italy organising any non-duty related gathering of military personnel is illegal. However the Italian Parliament is currently considering measures reforming military representation. Members of the French armed forces are allowed to be candidate in elections for representative bodies at the local and national level. Several restricting sections of the law on military personnel are in that case suspended for the duration of the political campaign.

D. Concluding remarks

24. Your Rapporteur concludes that despite the existence of Article 11 of the European Convention on Human Rights and Fundamental Freedoms and despite Article 5 of the ESC, Assembly Resolution 903 and Recommendation 1415, at this moment the right to establish, join and actively participate in associations formed to protect their professional interests is still withheld from military personnel in many member states of the Council of Europe.

25. The replies to the questionnaire revealed that many different forms of association for members of the armed forces are established in the laws and military regulations in the member states. In some states military personnel are granted full freedom of assembly and association, something worth striving for in all member states. Many other countries however know limiting conditions, place professional associations under government supervision or downright prohibit members of the armed forces to associate.

26. Although lawful restrictions on the freedom of assembly and association for certain professional groups are permissible by Article 11 of the European Convention on Human Rights and Fundamental Freedoms — for reasons of the protection of national security and public order — these measures should not apply to military personnel under *normal circumstances*, as is also established in Resolution 903 (1988). These restrictions for exceptional situations are however in many cases made standard for military personnel by the governments of member states. These member states are in that way going past the basic principle of the freedom of assembly and association for all citizens. The principle that military personnel are considered as "citizens in uniform" implies that they should also have basic social rights. It should be recalled that according to the case-law of the European Court of Human Rights, the trade union's right is a minor right which modalities are not fixed, and the specificity of the trade union's right is not recognised. Many cases concerning the trade union's right were declared inadmissible by the Commission or the Court.

27. In the opinion of your Rapporteur, taking into account the original intention of the second paragraph of Article 11, in all member states at least *representative associations* of military personnel should be allowed. With that members of the professional staff of the armed forces should have the full opportunity of negotiation on working conditions, conditions of employment and pay.

28. Other, already existing forms of freedom of association should however not be excluded or abolished. Some member states already grant military personnel the same rights as regular citizens with regard to the right of assembly or association, but even in most of these countries an exception is made with respect to the right of members of the armed forces to go on strike. This is a comprehensible restriction, but only when matters of national security or stability are involved. According to your Rapporteur the situation in these countries must remain the eventual aim for all member states of the Council of Europe.

29. There is no reason why military personnel, as "citizens in uniform," should not be allowed to be members of political parties. The political neutrality of the armed forces can be guaranteed by restricting overt political activities of military personnel in uniform or identifying themselves as military personnel. Also their military status can be suspended while being a candidate or a member of a representative body.

30. Apart from allowing professional staff of the armed forces to associate and be members of political parties, some member states have appointed an independent ombudsman for the armed forces (inspector general). In case of a

labour dispute an individual or groups of military personnel can apply to this impartial mediator. The reports and advice of this ombudsman are subsequently reckoned with in outlining the labour policy of the Ministry of Defence. Your Rapporteur is of the opinion that in addition to the removal of restrictions to the right to association member states should also seriously consider appointing an ombudsman.

Guidelines for Handling Dissident and Protest Activities among Members of the Armed Forces
United States Department of Defense Directive 1325.6 (October 1, 1996)

1. Reissuance and Purpose

This Directive reissues reference (a) to update DoD policy and responsibilities governing the handling of dissident activities by members of the Army, Navy, Air Force, and Marine Corps. Specific problems should be resolved only on the basis of the particular facts of the situation and in accordance with the provisions of applicable DoD regulations and reference (b).

2. Applicability

This Directive applies to the Office of the Secretary of Defense, the Military Departments (including the Coast Guard when it is operating as a Military Service in the Navy), the Chairman of the Joint Chiefs of Staff, the Combatant Commands, the Defense Agencies, and the DoD Field Activities (hereafter referred to collectively as "the DoD Components"). The term "Military Services," as used herein, refers to the Army, the Navy, the Air Force, and the Marine Corps.

3. Policy

It is DoD policy that:

3.1. The Department of Defense shall safeguard the security of the United States.

3.2. The Service members' right of expression should be preserved to the maximum extent possible, consistent with good order and discipline and the national security.

3.3. No commander should be indifferent to conduct that, if allowed to proceed unchecked, would destroy the effectiveness of his or her unit.

3.4. The proper balancing of these interests will depend largely upon the calm and prudent judgment of the responsible commander.

3.5. The following guidelines be applied to principal activities that the Armed Forces have encountered:

3.5.1. *Possession and Distribution of Printed Materials*

3.5.1.1. A commander is not authorized to prohibit the distribution of a specific issue of a publication distributed through official outlets such as post exchanges and military libraries. In the case of distribution of publications through other than official outlets, commanders may require that prior approval be obtained for any distribution on a military installation to determine whether there is a clear danger to the loyalty, discipline, or morale of military personnel, or if the distribution of the publication would materially interfere with the accomplishment of a military mission. Distribution of any publication determined to be a danger in any of these areas shall be prohibited.

3.5.1.2. While the mere possession of unauthorized printed material may not be prohibited, printed material that is prohibited from distribution shall be impounded if the commander determines that an attempt will be made to distribute.

3.5.1.3. The fact that a publication is critical of government policies or officials is not, in itself, a ground on which distribution may be prohibited.

3.5.2. *Off-Post Gathering Places.* Commanders have the authority to place establishments "off-limits" in accordance with established procedures when, for example, the activities taking place there include counseling members to refuse to perform duty or to desert; pose a significant adverse effect on Service members' health, morale, or welfare; or otherwise present a clear danger to the loyalty, discipline, or morale of a member or military unit.

3.5.3. *Servicemen Organizations.* Commanders are not authorized to recognize or to bargain with any union representing or seeking recognition to represent Service members.

3.5.4. *Publication of "Underground Newspapers."* Personal writing for publication may not be pursued during duty hours, or accomplished by the use of Government or non-appropriated fund property on- or off-duty. While publication of "underground newspapers" by military personnel off-post, on their own time, and with their own money and equipment, is not prohibited, if such a publication contains language the utterance of which is punishable under Federal law, those involved in the printing, publication, or distribution may be disciplined for such infractions.

3.5.5. *On-Post Demonstrations and Similar Activities.* The commander of a military installation or other military controlled facility under the jurisdiction of the United States shall prohibit any demonstration or activity on the installation or facility that could result in interference with or prevention of orderly accomplishment of the mission of the installation or facility, or present a clear danger to loyalty, discipline, or morale of the troops. It is a crime for any person to enter a military reservation for any purpose prohibited by law or lawful regulations, or for any person to enter or re-enter an installation after having been barred by order of the commander under 18 U.S.C. 1382 (reference (c)).

3.5.6. *Off-Post Demonstrations by Members.* Members of the Armed Forces are prohibited from participating in off-post demonstrations when they are on-duty, in a foreign country, when their activities constitute a breach of law and order, when violence is likely to result, or when they are in uniform in violation of DoD Directive 1334.1 (reference (d)).

3.5.7. *Grievances.* The right of members to complain and request redress of grievances against actions of their commanders is protected by Article 138 of the Uniform Code of Military Justice (reference (b)). In addition, a member may petition or present any grievance to any Member of Congress or an Inspector General under 10 U.S.C. 1034 (reference (e)). An open door policy for complaints is a basic principle of good leadership, and commanders should personally ensure that adequate procedures exist for identifying valid complaints and taking corrective action.

3.5.8. *Prohibited Activities.* Military personnel must reject participation in organizations that espouse supremacist causes; attempt to create illegal discrimination based on race, creed, color, sex, religion, or national origin; advocate the use of force or violence; or otherwise engage in efforts to deprive individuals of their civil rights. Active participation, such as publicly demonstrating or rallying, fund raising, recruiting and training members, organizing or leading such organizations, or otherwise engaging in activities in relation to such organizations or in furtherance of the objectives of such organizations that are viewed by command to be detrimental to the good order, discipline, or mission accomplishment of the unit, is incompatible with Military Service, and is, therefore, prohibited. Commanders have authority to employ the full range of administrative procedures, including separation or appropriate disciplinary action, against military personnel who actively participate in such groups. Functions of command include vigilance about the existence of such activities; active use of investigative authority to include a prompt and fair complaint process; and use of administrative powers, such as counseling, reprimands, orders, and performance evaluations to deter such activities. Military Departments shall ensure that this policy on prohibited activities is included in initial active duty training, precommissioning training, professional military education, commander training, and other appropriate Service training programs. . . .

NOTES AND QUESTIONS

1. Does the U.S. approach to military labor unions follow the recommendations of the Council of Europe's Committee on Legal Affairs and Human Rights? Should the shift from conscription to a professionalized, "all-volunteer force" affect the rights of servicemembers to organize? See the November 15, 2006 report, *The Right to Organise and to Bargain Collectively in the Perspective of the Council of Europe: The Case Law of the European Social Charter* (available at http://www.epsu.org/IMG/pdf/Draft_long_version_ november_06.pdf) and the 2007 judgment of the Constitutional Court of South Africa regarding military trade unions, *South African National Defence Union* *v. Minister of Defence*, (CCT 65/06), ZACC 10 (30 May 2007), (RSA), as well as an earlier judgment, *South African National Defence Union v. Minister of Defence* No. CCT 27/98 (S. Afr. Const. Ct. 1999).

2. Are human rights a misplaced concern in military service? Consider the motto of the Indian Military Academy:

> The safety, honour, and welfare of your country come first, always and every time.

> The honor, welfare, and comfort of the men you command come next.

> Your own ease, comfort, and safety come last, always and every time.

Where do the individual rights of military officers fit into this framework of service?

3. What sorts of activities or beliefs could be censured by commanding officers under DoD Directive 1325.6? Does it adequately protect servicemembers' rights to associate freely under the First Amendment of the U.S. Constitution? A history of the Army's policy toward political dissidence among servicemembers helps to place this directive into context:

Maj. Walter M. Hudson, *Racial Extremism in the Army*
159 MIL. L. REV. 1, 30-40 (1999)

[In December 1995, two African American men were murdered in Fayetteville, North Carolina by U.S. Army soldiers. A police investigation revealed an unsettling motive for the murders: the neo-Nazi "skinhead" philosophy embraced by some of the Army troops in Fort Bragg's 82d Airborne Division. The soldiers were white supremacists and the murders were an act of race war. While violence is a part of the culture of the 82d Airborne (whose informal motto is "Kill them all and let God sort them out"), this episode triggered media outrage and an immediate response by military leaders. The Army's policy on extremism was revised as a result. The following excerpt explores the history of the policy.]

At the time of the 7 December 1995 shootings, the Army policy on extremism . . . stated that "[t]he activities of extremist organizations are inconsistent with the responsibilities of military service." It then defined "extremist organizations" as organizations that: (a) espouse supremacist causes; (b) attempt to create illegal discrimination based on race, creed, color, gender, religion, or national origin; or (c) advocate the use of force or violence, or otherwise engage in efforts to deprive individuals of their civil rights.

The regulation distinguished so-called "passive" participation, such as "mere membership, receiving literature in the mail, or presence at an event" from "active" participation, which included recruiting others to join and participating in public rallies or demonstrations. The policy did not prohibit passive participation in extremist organizations, though it did not condone it. It prohibited active participation, though did not indicate whether those prohibitions were punitive.

Much of [this policy] came almost verbatim from *Department of Defense Directive 1325.6, Guidelines for Handling Dissent and Protest Activities*

Among Members of the Armed Forces (change 2). At the time the directive was initially promulgated in 1969, the Defense Department was concerned with the infiltration of anti-war and anti-military organizations within the services. The directive focused on dissident and protest activities within the military, and especially on activities such as underground newspapers, on-post demonstrations, and serviceman organizations.

In 1986, following the discovery that military personnel in North Carolina were involved with the White Patriot Party, the Secretary of Defense updated the directive. The directive's new language prohibited "active" participation in "extremist organizations." It was silent, however, on whether "passive" participation could also be prohibited, or why it only prohibited active participation in extremist organizations/groups, rather than extremist activity itself.

This use of "active" participation in "extremist organizations" comes from language in Executive Order (EO) 11,785. President Eisenhower had issued its predecessor, EO 10,450 in 1953, during the height of the Cold War, when the government feared Communist infiltration. Executive Order 10,450 stated that the government had wide authority to investigate its employees to determine "whether the employment in the federal service of the person being investigated is clearly consistent with the interests of the national security." The government could investigate the following:

> Membership in, or affiliation or sympathetic association with, any foreign or domestic organization, association, movement, group, or combination of persons which is totalitarian, Fascist, Communist, or subversive, or which has adopted, or shows, a policy of advocating or approving the commission of acts of force or violence to deny other persons their rights under the Constitution of the United States, or which seeks to alter the form of government of the United States by unconstitutional means.

By 1974, the national mood had dramatically changed. Executive Order 11,785 amended EO 10,450. It forbade designating *any* groups as "totalitarian, fascist, Communist, or subversive" and forbade any circulation or publication of a list of such groups. Furthermore, action against federal employees now required "knowing membership with the specific intent of furthering the aims of, or adherence to and *active participation* in" a group which "unlawfully advocates or practices the commission of acts of force or violence to prevent others" from exercising constitutional rights.

Both the term *"active participation"* and the focus on organizations carried over into *DOD Directive 1325.6* and the subsequent Army policy on extremism. In doing so, the directive and regulation adopted language not intended for extremism, but for subversion. In the 1950s, the executive branch decided to attempt to investigate infiltration (especially by Communists) into the government. Years later, that seemed an overreaction, and in 1974, the President severely limited what could be investigated.

Extremism, particularly white supremacist extremism, posed different challenges and required its own definitions. This need became apparent following the Fayetteville murders. The Army policy caused confusion among commanders and judge advocates; questions arose. What was an "organization"? Did it mean a formal organization with membership, recruiting drives, and dues? Was it something far less formal? Where did someone like Burmeister [the ringleader of the Fayetteville murder co-conspirators] fit in? He apparently was not a formal member of any hate group or white supremacist organization like the American Nazi Party or the Ku Klux Klan. He seemed to be involved with an informal network of neo-Nazi skinheads in and around Fort Bragg.

"Active" and "passive" participation caused confusion also. If a soldier were a "passive" participant, presumably the command could not punish or tell him to stop his "passive" activity. How could the command punish him if the Army said passive activities were "not prohibited"? There were also questions over whether anything in the policy was punitive or could be made punitive. It listed six prohibitions, but did not state that they were punitive, though the regulation stated that commanders could initiate "UCMJ action against soldiers whose activities violate military law."

At the 82d Airborne Division, these problems became real. According to reports, twenty-two soldiers had alleged skinhead connections. Fayetteville police charged and arrested three — Burmeister, Wright, and Meadows [the three men involved in the 1995 murders] — for murder or conspiracy to commit murder. Other soldiers either were charged with violent crimes or had committed other acts of separate misconduct. This left twelve identified as possible neo-Nazi skinheads or associates. Further investigation revealed that three of these twelve had no ties to racist skinheads, leaving nine soldiers in a gray area. These nine were involved to varying degrees with racist skinhead activities but had not committed any offenses.

Thus, in several cases, the command took no disciplinary action against avowed skinheads, even racist ones. This frustrated commanders, as indicated in the task force's report. The language of the regulation contributed to this frustration. The regulation focused exclusively on organizations. It gave commanders unclear direction on what was active and passive extremist participation. It appeared to be non-punitive.

For these reasons, the task force recommended several changes to the regulation. It recognized that "[t]he current policy on participation in extremist organizations is confusing and complicates the commander's interpretation of extremist activity." The task force recommended the following: "[E]liminate the confusion created by the distinctions between active and passive participation in organizations and activities[,] . . . specify more clearly when commanders will counsel and/or take adverse action against soldiers who are displaying extremist behavior, and . . . make the regulation punitive." . . .

The task force findings and recommendations caused the Army to change its extremist policy. The new policy speaks directly to, and is a mandate for, commanders. . . .

The new policy does more than provide a broad mandate for commanders. It clarifies the commander's role. It defines extremism more broadly, as "participation in extremist organizations *or activities.*" Commanders and legal advisors no longer have to engage in legal hair-splitting as to what is an "organization." Furthermore, the old policy included the definition that an organization must "espouse[s] supremacist causes." The new policy is more specific: "Extremist organizations or activities are ones that advocate racial, gender, or ethnic hatred or intolerance; [or] advocate, create, or engage in illegal discrimination based on race, color, sex, religion, or national origin. . . ." The policy resolves defining "supremacist causes" by labeling them as hatred or intolerance regarding gender and minorities. . . .

Finally, the new regulation no longer uses "active" and "passive" participation to distinguish prohibited from non-prohibited conduct. Eliminating this distinction apparently gives commanders much greater discretion. The new policy eliminates the language that "[p]assive activities, such as mere membership, receiving literature in the mail, or presence at an event . . . are not prohibited by Army policy." . . .

Ironically, the abolition of the active/passive participation dichotomy is the new policy's only real source of ambiguity. While it eliminated the distinction, the policy does not clearly state when commanders can act against activities once considered "passive," such as mere membership. While testifying before the House Subcommittee on National Security, the Secretary of the Army indicated that he did not think that the Army policy prohibited membership alone. One may conclude that formerly "passive" activities are still only administratively actionable and that the old active/passive distinction perhaps comes in through the back door.

Yet, the regulation also states that a unit commander may "order soldiers not to participate in those activities that are contrary to good order and discipline of the unit or pose a threat to health, safety, and security of military personnel or a military installation." This appears to give the commander great authority. One can reconcile the two by focusing on what a soldier *does*, not what he believes. The regulation focuses on prohibiting participation in organizations and *activities*, not mere beliefs. Read this way, the boundary for what a commander can prohibit is at "mere" membership or association. A soldier who is a "mere" member, but does not act, distributes no literature, or propagates no views, cannot be prohibited from being a member. His conduct, however, is another matter. Once he engages in activity beyond merely being a member or merely having extremist beliefs, the commander can act to prohibit that activity.

In contrast to the language in the old policy, the new policy directs commanders to "lean forward" to aggressively combat extremism in their units. This makes the role of the judge advocate more demanding, and fortunately, more explicit. Subparagraph F states that "commanders should seek the advice and counsel of their legal advisor when taking actions pursuant to this policy." The new policy, thus, specifically tasks the judge advocate, not the equal opportunity officer, the chaplain, or anyone else, with advising the commander.

NOTES AND QUESTIONS

1. Does Maj. Hudson's review of the policy assuage any concerns about the wisdom of giving commanding officers the authority to punish soldiers' affiliation with various groups? Should the policy give commanders more latitude to censure servicemembers' off-duty activities?

2. *United States v. Zimmerman*, 43 M.J. 782 (A.C.C.A. 1996), upheld the conviction of an Army private for larceny and other offenses related to his appropriation of military property. At issue was a First Amendment challenge to the military judge's instruction about Private Zimmerman's affiliation with a white supremacist organization. Zimmerman "discussed selling stolen military C-4 plastic explosives and agreed to sell a half pound of military TNT, hand grenade simulators, flares and numerous rounds of 5.56mm ammunition" to the organization, and his off-post storage locker contained "34 stolen M-16 barrels; eight stolen U.S. military smoke canisters; three stolen U.S. military CS tear gas grenades; one stolen M-16 military magazine containing 30 stolen 5.56mm rounds of ammunition; one stolen military ammunition pouch containing 122 stolen 5.56mm military ammunition; two stolen 5.56mm military Squad Automatic Weapon (SAW) pouches containing 200 stolen rounds each; one plastic garbage bag containing 305 rounds of stolen 5.56mm military ammunition; one stolen U.S. Army ammunition box containing 414 rounds of stolen 5.56mm military ammunition; twenty rounds of stolen 7.62mm military ammunition; one stolen U.S. military signal flare; one stolen one pound block of military TNT high explosive; one stolen one quarter pound of military TNT high explosive; one stolen medic bag containing two M-16 military magazines; three boxes of 10 safety lights, one box of 50 small safety lights, two D rings, and one stolen M-16 cleaning kit; and various stolen parts for an M-16 rifle." 43 M.J. at 784 n.2. After hearing from counsel, the military judge issued the following instruction:

> Now there's been some specific information that has been provided to you during sentencing that I need to review with you. You have had testimony that the accused might have entertained certain views that society as a whole does not approve of . . . views of being a white supremacist. You've also heard testimony that the accused might have been associating, drinking, having a party with members of a white supremacist group. As the trial counsel and defense counsel have pointed out, it is America [—] not constitutionally prohibited, certainly, and we do not punish individuals for entertaining particular social or political views. So therefore, *whatever his political or social views were, and whatever his friendships were is not to be considered by you except to prove knowledge of who he was giving the items to.* Secondly, *I advise you that if you believe the accused's knowledge of the nature of the group was a factor in relinquishing the items to that group, or members of that group, you may consider the nature of the intended recipient group only for the purposes of its tendency, if any, to put potentially dangerous materials into the stream of the civilian community, and as it bears on the accused's sense of responsibility.* Now we do not know the name of the group. I'm sure that no one approves of a white supremacist group, but I suppose there are groups that are . . . dangerous, or there are groups that are benign. We don't know, and you can't speculate on them. So in other words, you don't go back and say, "Well, this must have been group XYZ, therefore, they would have done something so and so." But *you may consider the nature of the group if you first believe it was a factor in who he relinquished it to and*

*you may consider the nature of the intended recipient for the purposes
of its tendency, if any, to put potentially dangerous materials into the
stream of the civilian community and as it bears on the accused's sense
of responsibility.*

46 M.J. at 784-85 (emphasis added by court). The court resolved the issue as
follows:

> Evidence that appellant was motivated by white supremacist views
> when he wrongfully disposed of stolen military munitions to what he
> believed was a white supremacist group constitutes aggravating cir-
> cumstances that directly relate to the offense. R.C.M. 1001(b)(4). This
> is especially true because racist attitudes and activities are perni-
> ciously destructive of good order and discipline in the armed services.
> The right to abstract racist beliefs and freedom of association must
> yield to the overriding military interest in good order and discipline
> when a soldier acts on those beliefs and associations in a manner that
> violates the law or is likely to result in violence. We conclude, there-
> fore, that these stipulated facts were relevant on the issue of appel-
> lant's motive, were properly admitted for consideration by the
> sentencing authority, and did not violate appellant's First Amendment
> rights. *Wisconsin v. Mitchell,* 508 U.S. at 487-88; *Dawson v. Delaware,*
> 503 U.S. at 165-67; *Barclay v. Florida,* 463 U.S. at 949; *United States
> v. Frazier,* 33 M.J. at 262.

> Contrary to the implication in the appellant's assignment of error,
> the military judge did not *introduce* the appellant's affiliation with
> white supremacists to the members. What the military judge did was
> *limit* how the members used the stipulated white supremacist evi-
> dence in arriving at an appropriate sentence. We believe the military
> judge could have instructed the members that the appellant's
> supremacist motive was a matter in aggravation because his active
> participation in furtherance of the white supremacist cause was inim-
> ical to good order and discipline. R.C.M. 1001(b)(4). Instead, he chose
> a more conservative approach by limiting the members' use of the evi-
> dence more severely than required.

> The military judge instructed the members that appellant was not to
> be punished for his friendships or political/social views, but that they
> could consider appellant's views to prove his knowledge of the nature
> of the group to whom he gave stolen military explosives. Further, if the
> members believed appellant's knowledge was a factor in deciding to
> give the munitions/explosives to a particular group, they could con-
> sider the nature of the group: (1) for "its tendency, if any, to put poten-
> tially dangerous materials into the stream of the civilian community,"
> and (2) "as it bears on the appellant's sense of responsibility."

> We believe the military judge did not err by giving these instruc-
> tions. While not pattern instructions, they articulated a viable theory
> of relevance and, within that context, appropriately limited the mem-
> bers' use of the white supremacist evidence during sentencing. Even
> under this constrained approach, the members could reasonably infer

that these white supremacists, who sought to receive stolen military munitions and other dangerous equipment, might bring them to bear in illegal or destructive ways.

46 M.J. at 786-87. Did the court rule correctly? Why or why not?

II. THE RIGHT TO PRIVACY

REPP v. UNITED STATES
United States Claims Court
23 Cl. Ct. 628 (1991)

[The United States Claims Court addressed the issue of privacy in a military context in hearing an action for back pay by a former Air Force pilot who had been court-martialed for heroin use. The former officer, Harold Repp, challenged the legality of the search, described below, that led to his conviction.]

On March 1, 1985, William Bethke, a detective with the San Bernadino County sheriff's office, was watching the home of Steve Collins, a known heroin user and suspected heroin dealer, in Hisperia, California. During his surveillance, Bethke saw several individuals, many of whom Bethke knew to be heroin users, approach Collins' residence. Each caller followed the same pattern in contacting Collins: the caller would approach the house trailer located behind Collins' house, knock on the door, and call out "Steve, Steve." Collins would then open the door, and exchange something with the visitor. The visitor would leave. Bethke concluded that Collins was making heroin sales.

Sometime between noon and 1 p.m., that day, Bethke noticed a red, late-model Corvette with an Oregon license plate pull into Collins' driveway. Bethke described the car's driver and only occupant as a male, six feet two inches in height, with sandy-colored hair. He was wearing a green, one-piece jump-suit covered with patches. Bethke believed that the man was wearing a military uniform. The man got out of the car and walked up to Collins' trailer. He knocked on the door, calling out "Steve, Steve." There was apparently no answer. The man returned to his car and drove off very quickly. Bethke did not notice a license plate on the front of the car. Shortly thereafter, Bethke obtained a warrant to search Collins' residence. The search turned up 27 balloons of heroin, $6,000 in cash, several syringes and a quantity of methamphetamine.

The following Monday, March 4, 1985, Bethke called Technical Sergeant Weinstock of nearby George Air Force base's Air Police. Bethke described the events of the past week concerning the red Corvette and its driver. Weinstock initiated a search on base for a new model, red Corvette with an Oregon plate. He found a car matching that description in a parking lot adjacent to the flight simulator building. The car was registered to then Captain Harold U. Repp.

The following day, March 5, 1985, security police investigators contacted Repp. They escorted him to the Office of Special Investigations (OSI). There he was informed that he was suspected of drug-related offenses. He was advised of his Article 31, Uniform Code of Military Justice (UCMJ), 10 U.S.C. § 831 (1982), rights and his right to counsel, which he asserted. Sergeant Timothy Peters then asked Repp to remove his flight jacket and the top portion of his flight suit so that his forearms could be viewed for evidence of puncture marks. Repp unwillingly complied. Peters noticed 10 to 15 puncture marks on each arm. Peters and Repp were alone during the viewing, and the door to the room was closed. Repp was wearing a tee-shirt; he was not required to remove the flight suit below the waist. Peters, who had experience and training in narcotics methods, noted intravenous marks on the forearms. He concluded that the marks appeared to be needle marks. Some marks appeared fresh.

After Peters' initial visual inspection, Repp was required to totally disrobe for a complete inspection. Standard procedures called for spreading apart the buttocks to check for needle marks. There was conflicting testimony that Repp's body cavities were searched. Repp alleges that Peters checked under his tongue. Peters denies looking in Repp's mouth. Following these inspections at the OSI, Repp was transported to the hospital for a physical examination. OSI investigators then obtained a search authorization [the military equivalent to a search warrant] for bodily fluids. Analysis of these samples disclosed the presence of the metabolite of heroin and morphine in the body.

At trial, Repp attempted to suppress the test results, claiming that they were the fruits of an unlawful search. Specifically, Repp alleged that the inspection of his arms for needle marks and the subsequent full body examinations constituted "body views" without prior authorization, in violation of Mil.R.Evid. 312. The military judge, after hearing testimony and argument, denied the motion and admitted the evidence. He held that Repp had no reasonable expectation of privacy in his forearms. On August 29, 1985, the court convicted Repp of use of heroin. The court sentenced Repp to be dismissed from the Air Force, confined for three years, and to forfeit $2300 per month for three years. On February 24, 1986, the general courts-martial convening authority approved the findings and sentence, though the forfeitures were reduced to $1583 per month for three years. . . .

[Repp's appeals through the Air Force Court of Military Review and the Court of Military Appeals failed, and the Supreme Court of the United States denied his petition for a writ of certiorari.]

The "narrow window" for challenging decisions of courts-martial in this court is open only for the purpose of addressing issues of "fundamental fairness in military proceedings and constitutional guarantees of due process." *Matias,* at 826 (quoting lower court opinion). To succeed in this court the plaintiff must demonstrate a fundamental deprivation of due process. A fundamental deprivation of due process is defined as a situation in which "the barriers and safeguards are so relaxed or forgotten . . . that the proceeding is more a spectacle . . . or trial by ordeal . . . than a disciplined contest." *Matias* [*v. United States,* 923 F.2d 821] at 826 [(Fed. Cir. 1990)] (citing *United States v. Augenblick,* 393 U.S. 348, 356 (1969)). In addressing these issues, the court is aware that an individual's constitutional rights are not totally surrendered once he puts on a uniform. *Chappell v. Wallace,* 462 U.S. 296, 304 (1983). However, the fourth amendment does not always apply in the military setting. *United States v. Grisby,* 335 F.2d 652 (4th Cir.1964). Servicemembers' rights must be conditioned to meet the demands of military duty. *Parker v. Levy,* 417 U.S. 733 (1974). . . .

[The court addressed several issues, the first being whether the search that incriminated Repp was lawful.]

It is undisputed that Repp was forced to remove the top portion of his flight suit to expose his forearms and elbows to the OSI. This action has been characterized as both an inspection (not a search) and a search. If this action is not a search as the Air Force Court of Military Review held in *United States v. Repp,* 23 M.J. 589 (A.F.C.M.R.1986), then the court must deny Repp's request for back-pay. Even if it were a search, it would have had to have been an unreasonable one for plaintiff to prevail here. Therefore, the court must decide first whether a search occurred, and if so, whether it was reasonable.

A search is looking for or seeking out something which is not in public view. It is an infringement on a person's reasonable expectation of privacy. Whether something is a violation of a person's expectation of privacy is determined by a two-part test: First, the person must have shown a subjective expectation of privacy; second, the expectation must be one which society is prepared to recognize as reasonable. *Katz v. United States,* 389 U.S. 347 (1967). The asserted expectation of privacy here fails to meet the second prong of the privacy expectation test because any expectation of privacy was not reasonable in these circumstances.

The fourth amendment, while applicable to the military, must be applied in light of the special demands of the military mission. As a member of the armed forces, Repp had no say over the clothes he was to wear. His commander could have easily changed the mode of dress. The uniform of the day could have been short-sleeved shirts. Repp, and indeed all service personnel, are expected, when the need arises, to work for long periods of time without proper rest or nourishment. Repp was an Air Force pilot. As such he operated some of the most sophisticated machinery known to man, which would require his peak mental and physical abilities. Had Repp's commander probable cause to believe that Repp had been sleepy or ill or drinking there can be no doubt that he would have been able to inspect Repp's eyes, breath, and general steadiness to determine if he was fit to fly. That situation is analogous to the instant case.

The court finds that when Repp's forearms were inspected, he was not searched within the meaning of the fourth amendment. . . .

UNITED STATES v. STEVENSON
United States Court of Appeals for the Armed Forces
53 M.J. 257 (C.A.A.F. 2000)

EFFRON, JUDGE:

I. Background

In November 1997, Naval Criminal Investigative Service (NCIS) investigators determined that appellee was a possible suspect in a November 1992 rape of a military dependent in Hawaii, where appellee had been stationed. At that time, appellee was assigned to the temporary disability retired list (TDRL), *see* Part II, *infra,* and was being treated for diabetes at the Veterans Administration (VA) hospital in Memphis, Tennessee.

During the investigation, the NCIS sought to obtain a sample of appellee's blood for purposes of making a DNA comparison between his blood and the samples of blood and semen gathered at the time of the crime. The NCIS asked the VA hospital to obtain a blood sample from appellee the next time he presented himself for a physical examination in which a blood sample would be taken during the normal course of his treatment.

According to the stipulation of fact agreed to by both parties at trial:

> On 3 June 1998, blood was drawn from Stevenson by staff of the VA Hospital in Memphis, TN. This was accomplished by inserting one vacuum needle (with an open end) into Stevenson's arm. While this needle was in his arm, one tube of blood was drawn for treatment and diagnosis of his diabetes. Within five or six seconds after the first tube was withdrawn from the needle, hospital staff inserted a second tube in order to obtain a separate blood sample for NCIS. When the second tube was filled and withdrawn, hospital staff withdrew the needle out of Stevenson's arm. The needle was in Stevenson's arm during the entire time both tubes were filled.

The findings of fact by the military judge added:

> The initial tube of blood drawn on 3 June 1998 occurred during a normally scheduled medical visit and was drawn for medical purposes to monitor the accused's diabetes.

> The second tube of blood drawn on 3 June 1998 was drawn *solely* for law enforcement purposes at the request of NCIS and was not drawn for any medical purpose. . . .

> The VA hospital staff obtained the accused's consent to draw blood for medical purposes. The VA hospital staff did not, however, tell the accused that a second tube of blood would be drawn solely for forensic purposes for use in the [rape] investigation, nor did he give consent for a second tube of blood to be drawn for that purpose.

II. The Temporary Disability Retired List

If a servicemember while on active duty becomes disabled, the Service Secretary may retire the member with pay, subject to detailed statutory and regulatory procedures. These procedures provide two basic types of disability retirement — permanent and temporary. When there is a determination that a disability is "permanent . . . and stable," the Service Secretary may retire the member with pay. 10 U.S.C. § 1201. If, however, the disability "may be of a permanent nature," but the circumstances do not permit a final determination that the condition is, in fact, "permanent . . . and stable," the Secretary is required to place the member on the "temporary disability retired list, with retired pay." 10 U.S.C. § 1202.

While on the TDRL, a member is required to submit to periodic physical examinations "to determine whether there has been a change in the disability for which he was temporarily retired." Failure to submit to such a periodic examination may lead to termination of retired pay. 10 U.S.C. § 1210(a).

When a periodic examination leads to a determination that the member is "physically fit" to perform his or her duties, there are a number of options. The member may be returned to active duty with his or her consent, retired if otherwise eligible for retirement, discharged, or transferred to the inactive reserves. If the member does not consent to a proposed return to active duty, "his status on the temporary disability retired list and his disability retired pay shall be terminated as soon as practicable and the member shall be discharged." 10 U.S.C. § 1211(c).

If a member remains on the TDRL for 5 years, the Secretary is required to make a final determination. If there is a determination that the disability "still exists," it is considered at that point to be "permanent . . . and stable," and the member is retired. 10 U.S.C. § 1210. If the member is determined to be fit for duty, the service has the same options as when such a determination is the result of a periodic examination: return to active duty with consent, retirement if otherwise eligible, discharge, or transfer to the inactive reserves.

In *United States v. Bowie,* 14 U.S.C.M.A. 631, 34 C.M.R. 411 (1964), our Court held that members on the TDRL are subject to court-martial jurisdiction under Article 2, which includes jurisdiction over retired members who are entitled to pay. *See* Art. 2(a)(4), UCMJ, 10 U.S.C. § 802(a)(4). We specifically noted the potential for recalling persons on the TDRL to active duty, particularly in times of national need. 14 U.S.C.M.A. at 632, 34 C.M.R. at 412.

III. Discussion

A. Applicability of Mil. R. Evid. 312(f) to Members on the TDRL

At trial and on appeal, the Government has relied on Mil. R. Evid. 312(f), Manual for Courts-Martial, United States (1998 ed.), which provides:

> Nothing in this rule [dealing with admissibility of evidence obtained from "body views and intrusions"] shall be deemed to interfere with the lawful authority of the armed forces to take whatever action may be necessary to preserve the health of a servicemember. Evidence or contraband obtained from an examination or intrusion conducted for a valid medical purpose may be seized and is not evidence obtained from an unlawful search or seizure within the meaning of Mil. R. Evid. 311.

As noted by the Court below, "[t]he sole basis offered by the Government for the admissibility of the . . . [evidence] is that it was obtained as a result of an intrusion conducted for a valid medical purpose, as authorized by Mil. R. Evid. 312(f)." 52 M.J. at 508. The Government has not contended that the evidence in question was obtained as a result of any of the other rules governing probable cause and non-probable cause searches and seizures. *See id.*

There is no exclusion under the Military Rules of Evidence for members on the TDRL. Mil. R. Evid. 1101(a), entitled "Rules applicable," provides: "Except as otherwise provided in this Manual, these rules apply generally to all courts-martial. . . ." Subsection (d) of that rule, entitled "Rules inapplicable," contains no indication that the Rules are not applicable to persons on the TDRL, nor is there anything elsewhere in the Manual for Courts-Martial that would exempt members on the TDRL from Mil. R. Evid. 312(f).

The court below asserted, however, that the military services do not rely on members on the TDRL to perform military missions. In its view, application of Mil. R. Evid. 312(f) to persons on the TDRL would violate the Fourth Amendment because the rule is not a "needed exception to the Fourth Amendment protections applicable to the general populace based upon military exigencies." 52 M.J. at 510.

We do not agree with the lower court's assessment of the TDRL. The exercise of court-martial jurisdiction over members on the TDRL, as affirmed in *Bowie,* underscores the continuing military status of a member on the TDRL, even if the member is not then performing regular duties. Court-martial jurisdiction reflects the statutory concept that the TDRL is a "temporary" assignment, not a permanent separation from active duty. Congress expressly denominated status on the TDRL as "temporary" and specifically required members on the TDRL to undergo periodic physical examinations to determine whether each member is "physically fit to perform" military duties. 10 U.S.C. § 1210(f).

The statutory requirement that a member consent to return to active duty does not diminish the interest of the military in the member's fitness for duty while on the TDRL. The detailed statutory provisions for return to duty reflect a congressional expectation that servicemembers who are determined to be fit for duty, and who thereby lose entitlement to retirement pay, may well seek to return to duty after receiving a fitness determination — whether motivated by patriotism, financial interest, or other considerations. *See, e.g., Craft v. United States,* 544 F.2d 468, 210 Ct. Cl. 170 (1976) (holding that the service erred in finding unfit for duty a servicemember who sought to return to active duty).

Moreover, even if a member on the TDRL is finally determined to be unfit for duty and is retired for physical disability, the member retains military status and may be recalled to active duty under certain circumstances. *See, e.g., Akol v. United States,* 167 Ct. Cl. 99 (1964) (wartime needs required recall to active duty of servicemembers who had been retired for physical disability); *cf. McCarty v. McCarty,* 453 U.S. 210, 222 (1981) (discussing amenability of non-disability retirees to UCMJ jurisdiction and recall to active duty).

Under the lower court's view of the law, a person on the TDRL observed using an illegal drug could be tried and convicted by court-martial, so long as the prosecution did not rely on evidence obtained under Mil. R. Evid. 312(f). If, however, bodily fluids extracted during a routine medical examination of a person on the TDRL reflected the same or a greater level of drug abuse, the lower court's ruling would preclude prosecution if the only evidence was obtained through a medical examination covered by Mil. R. Evid. 312(f). We do not agree that the Constitution requires such an anomaly. The constitutional considerations that support the exercise of court-martial jurisdiction over a military member on the TDRL — the receipt of military pay and continuing military status — are no less significant when it comes to the use of evidence obtained during a valid medical procedure concerning the member's continued fitness for military duty.

In view of the receipt of military pay and the potential for further active duty service by members who are temporarily removed from active duty by reason of disability, we conclude that evidence obtained in compliance with Mil. R. Evid. 312(f) may be used in a court-martial of a person on the TDRL.

B. Application of Mil. R. Evid. 312(f) to Appellee

The parties appear to agree that insertion of the needle into appellee's arm and extraction of the first vial of blood was undertaken for a "valid medical purpose" and was "necessary to preserve the health of a servicemember." Under the plain language of Mil. R. Evid. 312(f), if some of the blood in the first vial was made available to the NCIS for its investigative purposes, any evidence relating thereto would be admissible.

The prolonged insertion of the needle to extract a second vial of blood, solely for law enforcement purposes, raises a separate question under Mil. R. Evid. 312(f). In *United States v. Fitten,* 42 M.J. 179 (C.M.A. 1995), our Court unanimously upheld under Rule 312(f) the taking of a second bottle of urine for command investigation purposes when the catheterization and taking of the first bottle of urine was for a medical purpose. We noted that taking the second bottle of urine had only "a *de minimis* impact by prolonging the flow of urine only long enough to fill the second bottle." *Id.* at 182. Under the circumstances of a *de minimis* intrusion, we concluded that the intrusion did not violate the Fourth Amendment or the Military Rules of Evidence.

In any further proceedings in the present case concerning admissibility of the evidence at issue, the military judge will need to determine — in light of *Fitten* — whether the prolonged intrusion of the needle in appellee's arm while a second vial was placed on the vacuum needle, and then for some additional period while the blood was extracted into the vial, was a *de minimis* intrusion with respect to the Fourth Amendment and Mil. R. Evid. 312(f). In determining whether *Fitten* permits admission of the evidence at issue, the military judge should include in his consideration the effects of the type of intrusion, the length of the prolonged insertion, the quantity of fluid extracted, the nature of the fluid extracted, and whether there is a legally significant difference between the nature of the fluid extracted in this case as compared to *Fitten* (*e.g.,* blood versus urine).

IV. Decision

The first certified question is answered in the affirmative. Accordingly, the decision of the United States Navy-Marine Corps Court of Criminal Appeals is reversed, and the case is returned to the Judge Advocate General of the Navy for remand to the court-martial for trial on the merits. Upon appropriate motion at such trial, the military judge shall consider the issues raised by the second certified question in light of this opinion.

UNITED STATES v. ROBERTS
United States Court of Military Appeals
2 M.J. 31 (C.M.A. 1976)

PERRY, JUDGE:

The appellant [an Air Force sergeant] was convicted by general court-martial of possession of 438 grams of marihuana, in violation of Article 92, Uniform Code of Military Justice, 10 U.S.C. § 892, and was sentenced to a bad-conduct discharge and confinement at hard labor for 4 months. The findings and sentence have been approved at all review levels below. The appellant complains to this Court that his conviction is fatally tainted by the improper admission into evidence at trial, over his objection, of marihuana seized during an unlawful search of his quarters. We agree.

Shortly after assuming command of the 449th Supply Squadron at Kincheloe Air Force Base, about 2 months before the incident in question, Lieutenant Colonel English was advised by his fuels branch chief [the "fuels branch" worked with explosive substances such as aviation gas on the flightline] and that some 21 of the 60 men in that branch were "suspected" of being involved with drugs. In fact, some time after that, two men from that branch were apprehended by the Office of Special Investigations (OSI) with drugs at their duty stations, the last of which occurred about a week prior to the incident of concern.

Sometime during the week of December 13, 1974, the commander decided to conduct a "shakedown inspection" of the squadron for the sole purpose of discovering marihuana. It was decided to hold this search on Saturday, December 14, at 4:30 a.m. The reason for selecting the early Saturday morning hour according to Colonel English was to insure as many airmen present as possible during the activity.

At the designated predawn hour, Colonel English, his first sergeant, several senior noncommissioned officers, a security policeman, a qualified marihuana dog named Butch, and the dog's handler all gathered outside the barracks. Prior to the search party entering the building, a number of the noncommissioned officers were stationed outside to prevent marihuana from being discarded successfully out the windows during the activity inside. The remainder of the group then entered the barracks and the search began.

The procedure was simple. The first sergeant opened the barracks door with his passkey, turned on the lights, and announced the beginning of the "inspection." The dog handler then entered with his dog who sniffed around for marihuana. If Butch did not alert, the door to the particular room was closed and the party moved on to the next room. If he did alert, as in the case of the appellant's room, the security policeman entered the room and advised all occupants of their *Miranda-Tempia* [see *United States v. Tempia*, 37 C.M.R. 249 (1967)] rights. Also, a noncommissioned officer was stationed at the doorway to prevent any tampering with the marihuana.

At the appellant's room, the security policeman apparently detected the odor of marihuana when the door was opened. Once inside the room, Butch alerted on a cabinet, his handler opened the door thereto which already was about 3 inches ajar, and Butch seized a bag of marihuana. Thereafter, the OSI was called and told of the discovery, and an OSI agent obtained permission of the base commander for a search of the room. During this search, and after being advised of his rights, the appellant admitted ownership of the marihuana in question.

As both parties to this case argue, the Fourth Amendment does not prohibit all searches and seizures, but only those which are "unreasonable." *Terry v. Ohio*, 392 U.S. 1, 9 (1968); *United States v. Kazmierczak*, 16 U.S.C.M.A. 594, 37 C.M.R. 214 (1967). It would be calming judicially to search and seizure law if a satisfactory pervasive definition of that adjective could be conjured, but the reality is that reasonableness cannot be stated in rigid and absolute terms. *Harris v. United States*, 331 U.S. 145 (1947). An appraisal of reasonableness necessarily is a variable of the factors brought to bear in a given situation.

However, even with this degree of amorphism, certain conclusions may be stated with a comforting degree of confidence. The most obvious, of course, is that a search founded upon requisite probable cause and properly authorized by a valid warrant, *Spinelli v. United States*, 393 U.S. 410 (1969); *Aguilar v. Texas*, 378 U.S. 108 (1964), when conducted within the scope of that warrant, *Marron v. United States*, 275 U.S. 192 (1927), is reasonable. Contrariwise, general exploratory searches, with or without a warrant, are forbidden as unreasonable. *United States v. Rabinowitz*, 339 U.S. 56 (1950); *Go-Bart Importing Co. v. United States*, 282 U.S. 344 (1931); *see Berger v. New York*, 388 U.S. 41 (1967); *Chimel v. California*, 395 U.S. 752 (1969). It is my opinion that this case falls within the latter and that this is an instance of a dragnet-type of search operation which, even in its military context, is constitutionally intolerable. . . .

[The court compares this case with *United States v. Thomas*, 1 M.J. 397 (1976), in which Judge Cook's opinion for the court "resolved the question of the legality of the search on the dual grounds of (1) the insufficiency of the information provided the commander to constitute probable cause and (2) the extent of the information either not conveyed or misrepresented to the commander which bore on the issue of probable cause." Chief Judge Fletcher and Senior Judge Ferguson concurred in the result with separate opinions.]

[In this case], [i]nitially, the Government contends that there was no intrusion at all into the appellant's reasonable expectation of privacy, as a serviceperson's barracks quarters traditionally have been subject to both announced and unannounced visits by commanders inspecting same. *See United States v. King*, 2 M.J. 4 (1976). This argument, whether the activity in question was a traditional military inspection or a search, we believe correctly was determined adversely to the Government by the Air Force Court of Military Review. *United States v. Roberts*, 50 C.M.R. 699, 703 n. 4 (A.F.C.M.R.1975); *see United States v. Grace*, 19 U.S.C.M.A. 409, 42 C.M.R. 11 (1970); *United States v. Lange*, 15 U.S.C.M.A. 486, 35 C.M.R. 458 (1965). . . .

Counsel for the Government also argue that the intrusion may be sustained on the ground utilized by the intermediate appellate court: that it was a lawful "shakedown inspection." The so-called "shakedown inspection" is not a new phenomenon to this Court. *E.g., United States v. Drew*, 15 U.S.C.M.A. 449, 35 C.M.R. 421 (1965); *United States v. Harman*, 12 U.S.C.M.A. 180, 30 C.M.R.

180 (1961); *United States v. Gebhart*, 10 U.S.C.M.A. 606, 28 C.M.R. 172 (1959). Apparently, the event is contemplated as a thorough search of a general area, such as a barracks or a group of buildings (as opposed to a particular living area or room) of all persons and things in that area (as opposed to a particular, suspected person) for specific fruits or evidence of a crime, based upon "probable cause" to believe that such material will be found somewhere in that general area. This Court is unable to discern the constitutional basis for such a fishing expedition, nor is one apparent in this Court's precedents which seem merely to accept such a procedure as one "which has long been recognized." *United States v. Harman, supra* at 183, 30 C.M.R. at 183.

In their effort to justify this operation constitutionally, Government counsel liken the "shakedown inspection" to an "administrative regulatory inspection." Chief Judge Fletcher commented on this theory briefly in his separate opinion in *Thomas*:

> The Supreme Court has been careful to limit such statutorily authorized inspections to instances in which a regulated business impliedly consented to the intrusions thereby justifying the searches on a well-recognized exception to the usual probable cause and warrant requirements of the Fourth Amendment. *See Almeida Sanchez v. United States*, 413 U.S. 266, 270-72, (1973), *comparing United States v. Biswell*, 406 U.S. 311 (1972), *and Colonnade Catering Corp. v. United States*, 397 U.S. 72 (1970), *with See v. Seattle*, 387 U.S. 541 (1967), *and Camara v. Municipal Court*, 387 U.S. 523 (1967).

Aside from the fact that the Congress has not chosen to enact legislation permitting specific-object oriented regulatory inspections in the military and defining the permissible ambit of such intrusions, as it did in the instances discussed in the cases cited by the Chief Judge — a matter which we deem of no little import — we do not believe that the young American citizen who enters the nation's armed forces, whether by enlistment or by conscription, can truly be said to have "impliedly consented" to a search of his or her personal living quarters, lockers, and belongings for evidence of a crime in the same sense that a gun merchant or a liquor dealer impliedly consents to an inspection of his or her records and certain areas of the business establishment. It may well be, as the United States Court of Appeals for the District of Columbia suggested in *Committee for G.I. Rights v. Callaway*, 171 U.S. App. D.C. 73, 518 F.2d 466, 477 (1975), that the "soldier cannot reasonably expect the Army barracks to be a sanctuary like his civilian home," but military quarters have some aspects of a dwelling or a home and in those respects the military member may reasonably expect privacy protected by the Fourth Amendment.

While the traditional military inspection which looks at the overall fitness of a unit to perform its military mission is a permissible deviation from what may be tolerated in civilian society, generally recognizing that such procedure is a reasonable intrusion which a serviceperson must expect in a military society, the "shakedown inspection" as earlier defined in search specifically of criminal goods or evidence is not such a permissible intrusion into a person's reasonable expectation of privacy, even in the military setting. We hold, therefore, that the opening of the door to the appellant's room by the first sergeant and the entry by the marihuana dog and his handler into the room in search of marihuana without probable cause to believe that the appellant was in possession of that contraband violated the appellant's right to be free from unreasonable searches and seizures. Fourth Amendment, United States Constitution.

The decision of the United States Air Force Court of Military Review is reversed. The charge is dismissed.

COOK, JUDGE (dissenting):

I disagree with the majority's conclusion that there is no constitutional support for what was done here. In my opinion the "shakedown inspection," as it has been applied by this Court in earlier cases, has the force of tradition and reason behind it. Adherence to its tenets fully justifies the action taken by the commander in this case, but even if all the Court's previous decisions are disregarded, I believe that the essential nature of the shakedown inspection is analogous to the sort of "area code-enforcement inspection" that has been explicitly approved by the Supreme Court for the prevention, as well as the abatement, of conditions dangerous to the community. *Camara v. Municipal Court*, 387 U.S. 523 (1967).

It is my conviction that, if informed that approximately half of the members of the unit were suspected of drug possession and two were very recently apprehended, while on duty, with prohibited substances in their possession, an ordinary prudent person considering the nature of the volatile and high explosive material and equipment routinely handled by the personnel of the unit would fear for the safety of the men and the quality of the performance of their mission. Confronted with this information, the unit commander, who has the power of a magistrate in the civilian community to authorize an area code-enforcement search, could, I believe, properly determine that a search of the area to ferret out the instruments of danger to his community was reasonable.

The general impact of drug abuse in the military community has been documented elsewhere. *See Committee for G.I. Rights v. Callaway*, 171 U.S. App. D.C. 73, 518 F.2d 466, 477 (1975). In my judgment, all the reasons that led the Supreme Court to sustain the area code-enforcement inspection as a reasonable balance of "the need to search against the invasion which the search entails" are present in this case. *Camara v. Municipal Court, supra*, 387 U.S. at 537.

Superficially, the hour approved by the commander for the search appears to be unacceptable, but the time is not unusual for military activity. Aside from the hour, the conditions of the search were, in my opinion, as unintrusive as the circumstances allowed. Only the dog and his handler entered the non-public rooms of the barracks; and only when the dog's conduct evidenced the probable presence of marihuana were further steps taken to discover the contraband. Recently, I noted my opinion that utilization of a dog "trained to use his natural sense of smell to detect special odors does not transform otherwise lawful Government conduct into an illegal search." *United States v. Thomas*,

1 M.J. 397, 401 (1976). I am confirmed in that opinion by the decision of the United States Court of Appeals for the Ninth Circuit in *United States v. Solis*, 536 F.2d 880 (1976). There, as here, a trained dog was used to obtain evidence of the probable presence of marihuana to justify further intrusion into private areas.

For the foregoing reasons, I would affirm the decision of the Court of Military Review.

NOTES AND DISCUSSION

1. Do you agree with the Claims Court that there was no search in *Repp*? If there had been a search, did the police have probable cause to execute it? The court asserts that they did in a part of the opinion not reproduced here. What are the parameters of a servicemembers' right to bodily privacy, integrity, and dignity as compared to a civilian's right to the same? For further discussion of military search and seizure, see Chapter 15, § III, *infra*.

2. In *Roberts*, do you find Judge Perry's opinion for the court more convincing than Judge Cook's dissent? Given that servicemembers are already subject to bodily inspection and inspection of their dwellings, how should the court determine the legality of a "shakedown" search? Is military tradition dispositive? *See United States v. Middleton*, 10 M.J. 123, 127-28 (C.M.A. 1981):

> In considering what expectations of privacy a service member may reasonably entertain concerning military inspections, we must recognize that such inspections are time-honored and go back to the earliest days of the organized militia. They have been experienced by generations of Americans serving in the armed forces. Thus, the image is familiar of a soldier standing rigidly at attention at the foot of his bunk while his commander sternly inspects him, his uniform, his locker, and all his personal and professional belongings. . . .

> This Court has dealt on many occasions with various types of military inspections. Indeed, we have long acknowledged that the inspection has traditionally been a "tool" for a commander to use in insuring "the overall fitness of [his] unit to perform its military mission." . . .

> While the living conditions of the modern serviceperson may be more comfortable — and, indeed, more private than those known by their fathers, still the basic purpose for existence of the military has not altered; and neither has the need for the tool of inspection to insure the readiness of the individual serviceperson and of his unit to respond to an emergency.

> Upon this analysis, then, we may safely conclude that during a traditional military inspection, no serviceperson whose area is subject to the inspection may reasonably expect any privacy which will be protected from the inspection. The service member would not normally expect it; and if he did, the parent society would not be willing to honor that expectation. *Cf. Smith v. Maryland, supra.* . . .

Accordingly, during a legitimate health and welfare inspection, the area of the inspection becomes "public" as to the commander, for no privacy from the commander may be expected within the range of the inspection. Furthermore, if the commander sees what he can readily identify as a prohibited item — whether it be alcohol, a weapon, or controlled drugs — he may seize it. *Coolidge v. New Hampshire*, 403 U.S. 443 (1971).

Consider, too, the definition of an inspection in *United States v. Hay*, 3 M.J. 654, 655-56 (A.C.M.R. 1977):

A military inspection is an examination or review of the person, property, and equipment of a soldier, the barracks in which he lives, the place where he works, and the material for which he is responsible. An inspection may relate to readiness, security, living conditions, personal appearance, or a combination of these and other categories. Its purpose may be to examine the clothing and appearance of individuals, the presence and condition of equipment, the state of repair and cleanliness of barracks and work areas, and the security of an area or unit. Except for the ceremonial aspect, its basis is military necessity.

Among the attributes of an inspection are: that it is regularly performed; often announced in advance; usually conducted during normal duty hours; personnel of the unit are treated evenhandedly; and there is no underlying law enforcement purpose. An inspection is distinguished from a generalized search of a unit or geographic area based upon probable cause in that the latter usually arises from some known or suspected criminal conduct and usually has a law enforcement as well as a possible legitimate inspection purpose.

3. In *Ferguson v. City of Charleston*, 532 U.S. 67 (2001), the Supreme Court held that a state hospital's diagnostic test — in this case, the testing of urine samples during women's prenatal care to screen for cocaine use — constitutes an unreasonable search if the patient has not consented and the test is intended to obtain evidence of a patient's criminal conduct for law enforcement purposes. Does the military context differ enough from the civilian situation to justify a different result? Drug abuse is not a problem only in the U.S. military; *see CPL Cornelius Colin Cuthbert v. The State*, [1977] SGMCA 4 (upholding non-random urinalysis conducted on orders of officer-in-charge); *PTE Tee Lian Seng v. State*, Sing. Mil. App. 1978 (upholding drug-use conviction in which chain of custody was at issue).

4. Consider Maj. Keven Jay Kercher, *Time for Another Haircut: A Re-Look at the Use of Hair Sample Testing for Drug Use in the Military*, 188 MIL. L. REV. 38, 38-39 (2006):

The Army's urinalysis program has made great strides in reducing drug use in the military ranks. However, the current military operational tempo and the prevalence of illegal drugs in local communities warrant a more comprehensive approach to eliminating drug use in the service. An annual national drug survey by the U.S. Department of Health and Human Services' Substance Abuse and Mental Health Services Administration reflects the gravity of the drug problem in

America. According to the 2004 survey, 19.1 million Americans, age twelve and over, currently use illegal drugs. Seventy-five percent of the 16.4 million drug users, aged eighteen and older, had current employment. Since those serving in our armed forces are a cross-section of society as a whole, commanders can expect servicemembers to have easy access to people who use drugs and to people who sell drugs.

Also, increased servicemember usage of popular "club drugs," especially ecstasy, has left commanders wondering whether current urinalysis programs sufficiently ensure good order and discipline in their units. Several dilution products, cleansing products, chemical adulterants, and prosthetic devices (e.g., an artificial penis) currently exist to assist servicemembers in avoiding a positive urinalysis test result. An Internet Google search using the words "beat a drug test" provided over 1,200,000 hits. Many of these sites offer to provide pills or chemical solutions that counter urinalysis tests. These products claim to help avoid a positive drug test result by flushing drugs out of a person's urine prior to a test.

This article argues that a commander should be able to order the seizure of a servicemember's hair so long as the manner of collection and search do not violate established norms. Do servicemembers have a reasonable expectation of privacy in their hair?

III. SEXUAL ORIENTATION

UNITED STATES v. JAMESON
United States Navy-Marine Corps Court of Military Review
33 M.J. 669 (N.M.C.M.R. 1991)

Accused, a sergeant in the United States Marine Corps, was convicted by general court-martial convened by Commander, Marine Corps Recruit Depot, Parris Island, South Carolina, H.R. Sims, J., of failure to obey a lawful order and four specifications of committing indecent acts with another and she appealed. The United States Navy-Marine Corps Court of Military Review, Freyer, J., held that record demonstrated unlawful command influence on the convening authority's action.

Action set aside.

FREYER, JUDGE:

This appellant was convicted by a general court-martial, in accordance with her pleas, of one specification of failure to obey a lawful general order and four specifications of committing indecent acts with another, for which she was sentenced to dishonorable discharge, forfeiture of all pay and allowances, confinement for one year, and reduction to pay grade E-1. Her case was the second of three tried at the U.S. Marine Corps Recruit Depot, Parris Island, South Carolina (hereinafter, "the Depot"), resulting from an investigation into alleged lesbian activity in the Recruit Training Regiment there. The essence of the appellant's misconduct is that, while a drill instructor, she met privately with a recruit who was a member of her platoon, and who she had determined would be interested in engaging in lesbian activity, and arranged for them to get together for that purpose after the recruit graduated from recruit training. The first three specifications of indecent acts refer to the consummation of that arrangement, occurring over a three-day period immediately after the former recruit's graduation, in hotels in Savannah, Georgia, and Knoxville, Tennessee. The fourth specification of indecent acts refers to acts committed both on board and in the vicinity of the Depot in the course of a seven-month lesbian relationship which she maintained with a staff sergeant stationed in a recruit training battalion there.

At the appellant's trial, two women Marine character witnesses testified in her behalf on sentencing.

Sergeant Hilinski, a member of the Depot Inspector's staff, testified that the appellant had performed very competently and that she would be willing to work with the appellant in the future, notwithstanding her conviction. She expressed her disapproval of a homosexual relationship between a drill instructor and a recruit, but, when asked specifically about a recruit that had already graduated, she replied: "Well, since the homosexual affair didn't happen while she was training the recruit, then I have no bad opinion of that. If it didn't happen right there, then the recruit was no longer a recruit."

Staff Sergeant Gurule, a senior drill instructor attached to the Fourth Recruit Training Battalion, which included the appellant's platoon, testified that she had investigated a complaint against the appellant of favoritism towards the recruit involved in the first three specifications of indecent acts; that she had found the complaint to be inaccurate in a material respect, although not totally without foundation, and so had counselled the appellant; that the appellant was a very good drill instructor whom she would rate a 7 or 8 on a scale of 10; and that she would want the appellant working for her again. When asked specifically if the appellant's pleas of guilty to committing indecent acts with a recruit from her platoon would affect her willingness to work with the appellant in the future, she responded: "It would not effect [sic] the willingness to work with her, sir. I may have doubts in the beginning and watch her more closely; but I would work with Sergeant Jameson again."

At the conclusion of the appellant's trial, then-Major (now Lieutenant Colonel) D.L. Beck, the trial counsel, reported the substance of Sergeant Hilinski's and Staff Sergeant Gurule's testimony to Lieutenant Colonel W.E. Bubsey, Acting Staff Judge Advocate of the Depot (the Staff Judge Advocate being then on terminal leave incident to his prospective retirement). Lieutenant Colonel Bubsey directed Major Beck to have transcripts of the Hilinski and Gurule testimony prepared and delivered to him forthwith. Upon receipt of the transcripts, Lieutenant Colonel Bubsey promptly distributed them to the Chief of Staff of the Depot, the Depot Inspector, and the Commanding Officers of the Recruit Training Regiment and the Fourth Recruit Training Battalion.

Shortly thereafter a meeting was convened, attended by the Chief of Staff, the Depot Inspector, the Regimental and Fourth Battalion Commanding Officers, and the Staff Judge Advocate. At this meeting it was decided summarily to relieve Sergeant Hilinski and Staff Sergeant Gurule from their recruit training positions and to revoke their recruit training military occupational specialty (MOS). Mention was made at the meeting of the potential effect that adverse actions taken against defense witnesses based on their testimony alone might have on the third pending court-martial and on the several pending administrative discharge boards; it appears that no thought was given to any potential effect that such actions might have on the review process in the appellant's case.

Shortly after that meeting, actions were taken in accordance with the decisions reached thereat, and, as part of the process, adverse fitness reports were submitted on both individuals, each of whom has since obtained relief by decision of the Board for Correction of Naval Records.

On 12 February 1990, a panel of this Court ordered a post-trial hearing in accordance with Article 39(a) and *United States v. DuBay,* 17 U.S.C.M.A. 147, 37 C.M.R. 411 (1967):

> concerning whether anyone exercised illegal command influence over those witnesses at appellant's court-martial who gave testimony on her behalf and those persons who may have been willing to make recommendations of clemency on her behalf, but who declined to do so because of command influence.

United States v. Jameson, No. 89 1154 (N.M.C.M.R. 12 February 1990) (unpublished order).

The court-ordered hearing was convened by the original convening authority, as permitted by the order, was conducted between 22 and 27 March 1990 at the Depot, and was presided over by Colonel Richard G. Walls, U.S. Marine Corps, Circuit Military Judge of the Mid-South Judicial Circuit. The appellant was voluntarily absent from the hearing. At the conclusion of the hearing, the military judge found for the Government in all material respects. . . .

[The court discussed the definition and law regarding command influence, explaining: "In the instant case, there are intimations that the Marine Corps was faced with a serious situation which was having adverse consequences not only on good order and discipline and morale within the Recruit Training Regiment but also on external relations with the families of current and prospective recruits and potentially with the media." The court then addressed the adverse actions taken after Hilinski and Gurule testified on behalf of the appellant, Sergeant Jameson.]

One who holds a particular attitude or belief which is, or may be, relevant to a litigation, if approached by counsel or a party seeking testimony which would reveal that attitude or belief, has two choices: to disclose the attitude or belief, or to conceal it by refusing to be interviewed or by lying about it so as to avoid being called as a witness. If called to testify nonetheless, and if there is no applicable testimonial privilege, the witness has three choices: to admit the attitude or belief, to commit perjury by falsely denying it, or to refuse to testify. Of course, the very statement of these supposed choices reveals that there is, in the first instance, only one choice that is consistent with the obligation of each citizen to aid the administration of justice, and, in the second instance, only one choice that is consistent with the duty of the witness to obey the law. Consequently, however willing the witness may otherwise have been, there can be no doubt that, once placed in the witness box and sworn, the witness, in testifying to his or her true attitude or belief, is clearly acting under testimonial compulsion in accordance with the demands of military law. Thus, while it is undoubtedly true that military personnel may, under certain circumstances, be sanctioned, and severely so, for gratuitously making public statements contrary to official policy, *see Parker v. Levy,* 417 U.S. 733 (1974); *see also United States v. Priest,* 21 U.S.C.M.A. 564, 45 C.M.R. 338 (1972), we simply cannot equate the testimony of a witness, even if contrary to official policy and given in open court, to extrajudicial statements gratuitously made in public. The distinction is that, in the former case, while the substance of the testimony may be contrary to official policy, the giving of it not only is not contrary to official policy but is actually required by military law; and it admits of no serious argument that that which is required by military law cannot, at the same time, be contrary to official policy, unless, of course, the policy, itself, is illegal (which the policy in this case is not). We see nothing radical or even controversial about any of the propositions set forth in this paragraph, and we doubt that, when stated as abstract propositions, as they are here, anyone would seriously think to question them.

Likewise, if the testimony of a witness discloses a basis for adverse action against the witness, neither the government nor a private party is precluded from taking such adverse action as the circumstances may warrant merely because the basis therefor was disclosed during testimony, even under testimonial compulsion. *See Ullmann v. United States,* 350 U.S. 422 (1956). Thus, if the testimony of either Sergeant Hilinski or Staff Sergeant Gurule had been (which it was not) to the effect that she, herself, was a lesbian; or that she, herself, had committed or solicited homosexual acts; or that she had failed to deter or report such acts, or would do so in the future, after learning that they had occurred, were occurring, or were about to occur among drill instructors, recruits, or both, then the actions taken against her would be unassailable, because her propensities or conduct, as revealed by her testimony, would be disqualifying for her billet and her MOS, and perhaps even her retention in the Marine Corps. The distinction here is that, while the testimony would have been the vehicle by which the basis for the adverse action was disclosed, the adverse action is predicated upon the basis disclosed by the testimony, not upon the mere giving of the testimony. This is the analog of the situation discussed in the preceding paragraph, because, in each case, the problem resides, not in the giving of the testimony, nor even in the content of the testimony, but in some extrinsic matter (in this case, the attitudes and beliefs of Sergeant Hilinski and Staff Sergeant Gurule) which, under the circumstances, necessarily determines — and, thus, is exposed by — the content of the testimony. As noted elsewhere in this opinion, however, neither the testimony of Sergeant Hilinski or Staff Sergeant Gurule nor the testimony of any other witness exposed any of the disqualifications enumerated above; to the contrary, both individuals had excellent performance records, and the commanding officer of Staff Sergeant Gurule expressly denied any doubts about the latter's willingness or ability to uphold Marine Corps standards in the future. . . .

[A]ny attempt to justify the adverse actions against Sergeant Hilinski and Staff Sergeant Gurule on the ground that they made statements contrary to Marine Corps policy in a public forum, or that they showed poor judgment in doing so, must fail. Since, as we have shown, their testimony was the unavoidable product of their attitudes and beliefs, the true and actual ground for the adverse actions taken against them could not have been the *legally compelled expression* of those attitudes and beliefs; it could only have been the attitudes and beliefs, themselves; and we find that it was so.

The armed forces would likely be immobilized if they confined themselves to relying for the accomplishment of their diverse missions exclusively upon those who subjectively agreed with all their policies. The success of great military campaigns depends upon the willingness of subordinates at all levels to carry out everything from minute tasks to broad aims and strategies with which they do not necessarily agree, and it may also require them actively to suppress the disagreement of others, or even to feign their own agreement, therewith in the interest of fostering unity of purpose and action. It must, nevertheless, be acknowledged that, human nature being what it is, the ultimate degree of confidence may rationally be withheld from anyone whose support is not based on personal belief in the correctness and desirability of the policies to be implemented, and who may, therefore, prove to be less than "hard-core" in the face of determined opposition or, worse yet, become involved in acts of subversion and intrigue.

Consequently, it appears that the courts have upheld, as not inconsistent with the Constitution of the United States, the power of the President to employ an attitude test for at least commissioned military service, *Orloff v. Willoughby,* 345 U.S. 83, 92 (1953), and the power of the government in general to prescribe a private belief and opinion test for other public employment, at least where the government can demonstrate an overriding interest of vital importance requiring that a person's private beliefs conform to those of the hiring authority. *Branti v. Finkel,* 445 U.S. 507, 515-16 (1980). Tests of this kind are probably most familiar in the area of national security, where little, if any, justification is demanded for denying the high levels of security clearances required for many sensitive positions. But, while attitude and belief tests may be constitutional, they distinctly implicate First Amendment values and will, therefore, not be lightly implied in the absence of manifest necessity or, at least, a very clear prescription by competent authority.

To be sure, no one has a right to a position as a drill intructor or to a recruit training MOS. *Orloff v. Willoughby.* The vulnerability of recruits is well-understood by us and is well-documented in this record. Had the Marine Corps validly prescribed as a formal qualification for all drill instructors and holders of a recruit training MOS that they entertain a negative and intolerant attitude towards homosexuality and those who practice or condone it, such prescription would almost certainly override whatever First Amendment values would be implicated, and the neutral attitudes of Sergeant Hilinski and Staff Sergeant Gurule, albeit evidenced solely by their testimony, would then be disqualifying, *per Ullmann v. United States.* We have carefully examined the criteria in Marine Corps Order 1326.6A (which we have procured to be made a part of the record on appeal) for selecting recruit training personnel and those in Parris Island Marine Corps Recruit Depot Order 1300.3N (Appellate Exhibit V) for relieving them, and we find in the materials of record not a single criterion whereby the adverse actions taken against either Sergeant Hilinski or Staff Sergeant Gurule may fairly be justified. It should be emphasized that nothing in this opinion purports in any way to restrict what is otherwise the prerogative of commanders to transfer or reassign personnel on the basis of such commanders' evaluation of individual suitability for, or performance of, duty, or simply optimum utilization of assigned personnel. The actions under review, however, are not of that character; they are, in all respects, adverse personnel actions. Even though Sergeant Hilinski and Staff Sergeant Gurule had no right to drill instructor positions or a recruit training MOS, they had the right, grounded in substantive due process — *see Perry v. Sindermann,* 408 U.S. 593 (1972); *see also United States v. Anderson,* 12 M.J. 539 (A.F.C.M.R.1981) — not to be stripped of their positions or MOS illegally and in such a manner as to stigmatize them without just cause in the process of destroying their Marine Corps careers — *cf. Harmon v. Brucker,* 355 U.S. 579 (1958), citing *Joint Anti-Fascist Refugee Committee v. McGrath,* 341 U.S. 123 (1951). Thus, although the record does not reveal the specific grounds for the remedial actions taken by the Board for Correction of Naval Records, such actions certainly come as no surprise to us.

That Sergeant Hilinski and Staff Sergeant Gurule were subjected to unlawful administrative actions obviously does not, by itself, establish that the appellant's case was affected by unlawful command influence. . . .

In addition to the summary reliefs of Sergeant Hilinski and Staff Sergeant Gurule following their testimony, while the post-trial review in *Jameson,* the trial in *Jones,* and several administrative discharge boards were pending, the Commanding Officer of the Fourth Recruit Training Battalion addressed the members of her battalion in response to a seemingly widespread conception, directly attributable to the adverse actions taken against Sergeant Hilinski and Staff Sergeant Gurule, that testifying for the defense could be hazardous to one's Marine Corps career. The substance of her remarks was that persons with relevant information were encouraged to testify for the defense, but that, if their testimony deviated from Marine Corps policy, they would be held accountable for it. Although her remarks were ostensibly intended as a remedy for the foregoing conception, we think that they could only have had just the opposite effect of tending to induce her listeners, if they got involved at all, to engage in fear-based self-censorship calculated to tailor the content of their testimony to Marine Corps policy. . . .

To summarize the key points, this record includes evidence that severely adverse and ill-timed command actions, for which we can find no legal basis, were summarily taken against two apparently truthful defense witnesses immediately after they gave testimony deemed contrary to Marine Corps policy; that such actions were soon followed by an official admonition to other potential defense witnesses that they would be held accountable for testimony which deviated from Marine Corps policy; and that the foregoing produced a command environment containing clearly identifiable elements of consternation, disillusionment, and, above all, reticence — telltale after-effects of unlawful command influence. . . .

We set aside the action of the convening authority and return the record to the Judge Advocate General in order that a new staff judge advocate's review may be prepared and a new action taken, these to be done outside the Piedmont and Mid-South Judicial Circuits by officers not in any way previously involved in this or any companion case. . . .

LUSTIG-PREAN & BECKETT v. UNITED KINGDOM
European Court of Human Rights, 1999
[1999] ECHR 71, [1999] 29 E.H.R.R. 548

[In *Lustig-Prean & Beckett v. United Kingdom*, the European Court of Human Rights considered the appeals of two British nationals who alleged that "investigations into their homosexuality and their discharge from the Royal Navy on the sole ground that they are homosexual constituted violations" of the Convention on Human Rights. Both Lustig-Prean and Beckett were exemplary members of the Royal Navy who were discharged solely because of their homosexuality. The court held that their rights were violated by the policy and issued a lengthy opinion. Below are a few paragraphs from both the majority opinion and a dissent.]

42. . . . [The] Armed Forces' Policy and Guidelines on Homosexuality ("the Guidelines") were distributed to the respective service directorates of personnel in December 1994. The Guidelines provided, *inter alia*, as follows:

> Homosexuality, whether male or female, is considered incompatible with service in the armed forces. This is not only because of the close physical conditions in which personnel often have to live and work, but also because homosexual behaviour can cause offence, polarise relationships, induce ill-discipline and, as a consequence, damage morale and unit effectiveness. If individuals admit to being homosexual whilst serving and their Commanding Officer judges that this admission is well-founded they will be required to leave the services. . . .

> The armed forces' policy on homosexuality is made clear to all those considering enlistment. If a potential recruit admits to being homosexual, he/she will not be enlisted. Even if a potential recruit admits to being homosexual but states that he/she does not at present nor in the future intend to engage in homosexual activity, he/she will not be enlisted. . . .

> In dealing with cases of suspected homosexuality, a Commanding Officer must make a balanced judgment taking into account all the relevant factors. . . . In most circumstances, however, the interests of the individual and the armed forces will be best served by formal investigation of the allegations or suspicion. Depending on the circumstances, the Commanding Officer will either conduct an internal inquiry, using his own staff, or he will seek assistance from the Service Police. When conducting an internal inquiry he will normally discuss the matter with his welfare support staff. Homosexuality is not a medical matter, but there may be circumstances in which the Commanding Officer should seek the advice of the Unit Medical

Officer on the individual concerned and may then, if the individual agrees, refer him/her to the Unit Medical Officer. . . .

A written warning in respect of an individual's conduct or behaviour may be given in circumstances where there is some evidence of homosexuality but insufficient . . . to apply for administrative discharge. . . . If the Commanding Officer is satisfied on a high standard of proof of an individual's homosexuality, administrative action to terminate service . . . is to be initiated. . . .

One of the purposes of the Guidelines was the reduction of the involvement of the service police whose investigatory methods, based on criminal procedures, had been strongly resented and widely publicised in the past. . . .

43. The affidavit of Air Chief Marshal Sir John Frederick Willis KCB, CBE, Vice Chief of the Defence Staff, Ministry of Defence dated 4 September 1996, which was submitted to the High Court in the case of *R. v. Secretary of State for Defence, ex parte Perkins* (13 July 1998), read, in so far as relevant, as follows:

The policy of the Ministry of Defence is that the special nature of homosexual life precludes the acceptance of homosexuals and homosexuality in the armed forces. The primary concern of the armed forces is the maintenance of an operationally effective and efficient force and the consequent need for strict maintenance of discipline. [The Ministry of Defence] believes that the presence of homosexual personnel has the potential to undermine this.

The conditions of military life, both on operations and within the service environment, are very different from those experienced in civilian life. . . . The [Ministry of Defence] believes that these conditions, and the need for absolute trust and confidence between personnel of all ranks, must dictate its policy towards homosexuality in the armed forces. It is not a question of a moral judgement, nor is there any suggestion that homosexuals are any less courageous than heterosexual personnel; the policy derives from a practical assessment of the implications of homosexuality for fighting power. . . .

46. The HPAT [Homosexuality Policy Assessment Team, convened in February 1996 to undertake an intensive review of the military policy] report defined "fighting power" (often used interchangeably with combat effectiveness, operational efficiency or operational effectiveness) as the "ability to fight" which is in turn made up of three components. These are the "conceptual" and "physical" components together with the "moral component," the latter being defined as "the ability to get people to fight including morale, comradeship, motivation, leadership and management."

47. The focus throughout the assessment was upon the anticipated effects on fighting power and this was found to be the "key problem" in integrating homosexuals into the armed forces. It was considered well established that the presence of known or strongly suspected homosexuals in the armed forces would produce certain behavioural and emotional responses and problems

which would affect morale and, in turn, significantly and negatively affect the fighting power of the armed forces.

These anticipated problems included controlling homosexual behaviour and heterosexual animosity, assaults on homosexuals, bullying and harassment of homosexuals, ostracism and avoidance, "cliquishness" and pairing, leadership and decision-making problems including allegations of favouritism, discrimination and ineffectiveness (but excluding the question of homosexual officers taking tactical decisions swayed by sexual preference), sub-cultural friction, privacy/decency issues, increased dislike and suspicions (polarised relationships), and resentment over imposed change especially if controls on heterosexual expression also had to be tightened (see Section F.II of the report). . . .

51. The HPAT observed that there were a wide variety of official positions and legal arrangements evolving from local legal and political circumstances and ranging from a formal prohibition of all homosexual activity (the United States), to administrative arrangements falling short of real equality (France and Germany), to a deliberate policy to create an armed force friendly to homosexuals (the Netherlands). According to the HPAT, those countries which had no legal ban on homosexuals were more tolerant, had written constitutions and therefore a greater tradition of respect for human rights. The report continued:

> But nowhere did HPAT learn that there were significant numbers of open homosexuals serving in the Forces. . . . Whatever the degree of official toleration or encouragement, informal pressures or threats within the military social system appeared to prevent the vast majority of homosexuals from choosing to exercise their varying legal rights to open expression of their active sexual identity in a professional setting. . . . It goes without saying that the continuing reticence of military homosexuals in these armed forces means that there has been little practical experience of protecting them against ostracism, harassment or physical attack.
>
> Since this common pattern of a near absence of openly homosexual personnel occurs irrespective of the formal legal frameworks, it is reasonable to assume that it is the informal functioning of actual military systems which is largely incompatible with homosexual self-expression. This is entirely consistent with the pattern of British service personnel's attitudes confirmed by the HPAT. . . .

54. Alternative options were considered by the HPAT including a code of conduct applicable to all, a policy based on the individual qualities of homosexual personnel, lifting the ban and relying on service personnel reticence, the "don't ask, don't tell" solution offered by the USA and a "no open homosexuality" code. It concluded that no policy alternative could be identified which avoided risks for fighting power with the same certainty as the present policy and which, in consequence, would not be strongly opposed by the service population (paragraphs 153-75).

55. The HPAT found that:

the key problem remains and its intractability has indeed been re-con-firmed. The evidence for an anticipated loss in fighting power has been set out in section F and forms the centrepiece of this assessment. The various steps in the argument and the overall conclusion have been shown not only by the Service authorities but by the great majority of Service personnel in all ranks.

Current service attitudes were considered unlikely to change in the near future. While clearly hardship and invasion of privacy were involved, the risk to fighting power demonstrated why the policy was, nevertheless, justified. It considered that it was not possible to draw any meaningful comparison between the integration of homosexuals and of women and ethnic minorities into the armed forces since homosexuality raised problems of a type and inten-sity that gender and race did not.

The HPAT considered that, in the longer term, evolving social attitudes towards homosexuality might reduce the risks to fighting power inherent in change but that their assessment could "only deal with present attitudes and risks." It went on:

> . . . certainly, if service people believed that they could work and live alongside homosexuals without loss of cohesion, far fewer of the antic-ipated problems would emerge. But the Ministry must deal with the world as it is. Service attitudes, in as far as they differ from those of the general population, emerge from the unique conditions of military life, and represent the current social and psychological realities. They indicate military risk from a policy change. . . .

> . . . after collecting the most exhaustive evidence available, it is also evident that in the UK homosexuality remains in practice incompati-ble with service life if the armed services, in their present form, are to be maintained at their full potential fighting power. . . . Furthermore, the justification for the present policy has been overwhelmingly endorsed by a demonstrated consensus of the profession best able to judge it. It must follow that a major change to the Ministry's current Tri-service Guidelines on homosexuality should be contemplated only for clearly stated non-defence reasons, and with a full acknowledge-ment of the impact on Service effectiveness and service people's feel-ings. . . .

[The court next turns to assessing the applicability of the law to the policy.]

87. . . . [T]he Court must consider whether, taking account of the margin of appreciation open to the State in matters of national security, particularly convincing and weighty reasons exist by way of justification for the interfer-ences with the applicants' right to respect for their private lives.

88. The core argument of the Government in support of the policy is that the presence of open or suspected homosexuals in the armed forces would have a substantial and negative effect on morale and, consequently, on the fighting power and operational effectiveness of the armed forces. The Government rely in this respect on the report of the HPAT. . . .

Although the Court acknowledges the complexity of the study undertaken by the HPAT, it entertains certain doubts as to the value of the HPAT report for present purposes. The independence of the assessment contained in the report is open to question given that it was completed by Ministry of Defence civil servants and service personnel. . . . [O]nly a very small proportion of the armed forces' personnel participated in the assessment. Moreover, many of the methods of assessment (including the consultation with policy-makers in the Ministry of Defence, one-to-one interviews and the focus group discussions) were not anonymous. It also appears that many of the questions in the attitude survey suggested answers in support of the policy.

89. Even accepting that the views on the matter which were expressed to the HPAT may be considered representative, the Court finds that the perceived problems which were identified in the HPAT report as a threat to the fighting power and operational effectiveness of the armed forces were founded solely upon the negative attitudes of heterosexual personnel towards those of homosexual orientation. The Court observes, in this respect, that no moral judgment is made on homosexuality by the policy. . . . It is also accepted by the Government that neither the records nor conduct of the applicants nor the physical capability, courage, dependability and skills of homosexuals in general are in any way called into question by the policy.

90. The question for the Court is whether the above-noted negative attitudes constitute sufficient justification for the interferences at issue.

The Court observes from the HPAT report that these attitudes, even if sincerely felt by those who expressed them, ranged from stereotypical expressions of hostility to those of homosexual orientation, to vague expressions of unease about the presence of homosexual colleagues. To the extent that they represent a predisposed bias on the part of a heterosexual majority against a homosexual minority, these negative attitudes cannot, of themselves, be considered by the Court to amount to sufficient justification for the interferences with the applicants' rights outlined above, any more than similar negative attitudes towards those of a different race, origin or colour.

91. The Government emphasised that the views expressed in the HPAT report served to show that any change in the policy would entail substantial damage to morale and operational effectiveness. The applicants considered these submissions to be unsubstantiated.

92. The Court notes the lack of concrete evidence to substantiate the alleged damage to morale and fighting power that any change in the policy would entail. . . . [T]he Court further considers that the subsequent HPAT assessment did not, whatever its value, provide evidence of such damage in the event of the policy changing. Given the number of homosexuals dismissed between 1991 and 1996, the number of homosexuals who were in the armed forces at the relevant time cannot be said to be insignificant. . . .

93. However, in the light of the strength of feeling expressed in certain submissions to the HPAT and the special, interdependent and closely knit nature of the armed forces' environment, the Court considers it reasonable to assume that some difficulties could be anticipated as a result of any change in what is

now a long-standing policy. Indeed, it would appear that the presence of women and racial minorities in the armed forces led to relational difficulties of the kind which the Government suggest admission of homosexuals would entail.

94. The applicants submitted that a strict code of conduct applicable to all personnel would address any potential difficulties caused by negative attitudes of heterosexuals. The Government, while not rejecting the possibility out of hand, emphasised the need for caution given the subject matter and the armed forces context of the policy and pointed out that this was one of the options to be considered by the next Parliamentary Select Committee in 2001.

95. The Court considers it important to note, in the first place, the approach already adopted by the armed forces to deal with racial discrimination and with racial and sexual harassment and bullying. The January 1996 Directive, for example, imposed both a strict code of conduct on every soldier together with disciplinary rules to deal with any inappropriate behaviour and conduct. This dual approach was supplemented with information leaflets and training programmes, the army emphasising the need for high standards of personal conduct and for respect for others.

The Government, nevertheless, underlined that it is "the knowledge or suspicion of homosexuality" which would cause the morale problems and not conduct, so that a conduct code would not solve the anticipated difficulties. However, in so far as negative attitudes to homosexuality are insufficient, of themselves, to justify the policy, they are equally insufficient to justify the rejection of a proposed alternative. In any event, the Government themselves recognised during the hearing that the choice between a conduct code and the maintenance of the policy lay at the heart of the judgment to be made in this case. This is also consistent with the Government's direct reliance . . . on the HPAT's report, where the anticipated problems identified as posing a risk to morale were almost exclusively problems relating to behaviour and conduct.

The Government maintained that homosexuality raised problems of a type and intensity that race and gender did not. However, even if it can be assumed that the integration of homosexuals would give rise to problems not encountered with the integration of women or racial minorities, the Court is not satisfied that the codes and rules which have been found to be effective in the latter case would not equally prove effective in the former. The "robust indifference" reported by the HPAT of the large number of British armed forces' personnel serving abroad with allied forces to homosexuals serving in those foreign forces, serves to confirm that the perceived problems of integration are not insuperable.

96. The Government highlighted particular problems which might be posed by the communal accommodation arrangements in the armed forces. Detailed submissions were made during the hearing, the parties disagreeing as to the potential consequences of shared single-sex accommodation and associated facilities.

The Court notes that the HPAT itself concluded that separate accommodation for homosexuals would not be warranted or wise and that substantial expenditure would not, therefore, have to be incurred in this respect. Nevertheless, the Court remains of the view that it has not been shown that the conduct codes and disciplinary rules referred to above could not adequately deal with any behavioural issues arising on the part either of homosexuals or of heterosexuals.

97. The Government, referring to the relevant analysis in the HPAT report, further argued that no worthwhile lessons could be gleaned from the relatively recent legal changes in those foreign armed forces which now admitted homosexuals. The Court disagrees. It notes the evidence before the domestic courts to the effect that the European countries operating a blanket legal ban on homosexuals in their armed forces are now in a small minority. It considers that, even if relatively recent, the Court cannot overlook the widespread and consistently developing views and associated legal changes to the domestic laws of Contracting States on this issue.

98. Accordingly, the Court concludes that convincing and weighty reasons have not been offered by the Government to justify the policy against homosexuals in the armed forces or, therefore, the consequent discharge of the applicants from those forces.

99. While the applicants' administrative discharges were a direct consequence of their homosexuality, the Court considers that the justification for the investigations into the applicants' homosexuality requires separate consideration in so far as those investigations continued after the applicants' early and clear admissions of homosexuality.

100. The Government maintained that investigations, including the interviews and searches, were necessary in order to detect false claims of homosexuality by those seeking administrative discharges from the armed forces. The Government cited five examples of individuals in the armed forces who had relatively recently made such false claims. However, since it was and is clear, in the Court's opinion, that at the relevant time both Mr Lustig-Prean and Mr Beckett wished to remain in the navy, the Court does not find that the risk of false claims of homosexuality could, in the case of the present applicants, provide any justification for their continued questioning.

101. The Government further submitted that the medical, security and disciplinary concerns outlined by the HPAT justified certain lines of questioning of the applicants. However, the Court observes that, in the HPAT report, security issues relating to those suspected of being homosexual were found not to stand up to close examination as a ground for maintaining the policy. The Court is, for this reason, not persuaded that the risk of blackmail, being the main security ground canvassed by the Government, justified the continuation of the questioning of either of the present applicants. Similarly, the Court does not find that the clinical risks (which were, in any event, substantially discounted by the HPAT as a ground for maintaining the policy) justified the extent of the applicants' questioning. Moreover, no disciplinary issue existed in the case of either applicant. . . .

103. In such circumstances, the Court considers that the Government have not offered convincing and weighty reasons justifying the continued investigation of the applicants' sexual orientation once they had confirmed their homosexuality to the naval authorities.

104. In sum, the Court finds that neither the investigations conducted into the applicants' sexual orientation, nor their discharge on the grounds of their homosexuality in pursuance of the Ministry of Defence policy, were justified under Article 8 § 2 of the Convention.

105. Accordingly, there has been a violation of Article 8 of the Convention. . . .

Partly concurring, partly dissenting, opinion of JUDGE LOUCAIDES:

I agree with the majority on all points except as regards the finding that there has been a violation of Article 8 of the Convention by reason of the applicants' discharge from the armed forces on account of their homosexuality.

In this respect I have been convinced by the argument of the Government that particular problems might be posed by the communal accommodation arrangements in the armed forces. The applicants would have to share single-sex accommodation and associated facilities (showers, toilets, etc.) with their heterosexual colleagues. To my mind, the problems in question are in substance analogous to those which would result from the communal accommodation of male members of the armed forces with female members. What makes it necessary for males not to share accommodation and other associated facilities with females is the difference in their sexual orientation. It is precisely this difference between homosexuals and heterosexuals which makes the position of the Government convincing.

I find the answer given by the majority regarding this aspect of the case unsatisfactory. The Court noted (at paragraph 96 of the judgment) that the HPAT considered that "separate accommodation for homosexuals would not be warranted or wise" and the Court found that, in any case, "it ha[d] not been shown that the conduct codes and disciplinary rules . . . could not adequately deal with any behavioural issues arising on the part either of homosexuals or of heterosexuals." The fact that separate accommodation is not "warranted or wise" does not justify communal accommodation if such accommodation is really problematic. On the other hand, "conduct codes and disciplinary rules" cannot change the sexual orientation of people and the relevant problems which — for the purposes of the issue under consideration — in the analogous case of women makes it incumbent to accommodate them separately from male soldiers. It is the compulsory living together of groups of people of different sexual orientation which creates the problem. I should add here that if homosexuals had a right to be members of the armed forces their sexual orientation could become known either through them disclosing it or manifesting it in some way.

The aim of not allowing homosexuals in the armed forces was to ensure the operational effectiveness of the armed forces and to this extent the resulting interferences pursued the legitimate aims of "the interests of national security" and "the prevention of disorder." This was accepted by the Court. My disagreement with the majority relates to the question of whether the interference in the present case can be considered "necessary in a democratic society" for the aim in question. The majority underlined the principle that when the relevant restrictions to a Convention right concern a most intimate part of an individual's private life there must exist particularly serious reasons before the interferences can satisfy the requirements of Article 8 of the Convention. However, I agree with the Government that the narrow margin of appreciation which is applied to cases involving intimate private-life matters is widened in cases like the present, in which the legitimate aim of the relevant restriction relates to the operational effectiveness of the armed forces and, therefore, to the interests of national security. . . .

I do not think that the facts of the present case justify our Court's interference. As I have already stated above, the sexual orientation of homosexuals does create the problems highlighted by the Government as a result of the communal accommodation with heterosexuals. There is nothing patently disproportionate in the approach of the Government. On the contrary, it was in the circumstances reasonably open to them to adopt the policy of not allowing homosexuals in the armed forces. . . .

In the circumstances, I find that the applicants' discharge on account of their homosexuality in pursuance of the Ministry of Defence policy was justified under Article 8 § 2 of the Convention, as being necessary in a democratic society in the interests of national security and the prevention of disorder.

Homosexuality in the Armed Forces
United Kingdom Ministry of Defence, 2000

The issue of homosexuality in the Armed Forces was last debated in Parliament in 1996 and a vote to retain the ban was carried in the House of Commons on 9 May. Much of the evidence for the debate was based on the findings of the Homosexual Policy Assessment Team (HPAT) report, commissioned in September 1995, to undertake and report on an internal assessment of attitudes within the Services towards homosexuality.

When the present administration assumed office in May 1997, it made clear that the policy would be reviewed in the lifetime of that first Parliament. At that time it was anticipated that the Armed Forces Bill in 2000/01 would be a convenient framework for Parliamentary debate [and free vote on the issue]. However, following the announcement on 27 September 1999 of the judgement by the European Court of Human Rights (ECHR) against the MOD in the cases brought by four homosexual ex-Service personnel (Lustig-Prean, Beckett, Smith and Grady), there was an urgent need to review existing policy on the employment of homosexuals in the UK Armed Forces. The Court ruled that all four applicants had their rights violated in respect of Article 8, the right to respect for private life, and further ruled in the case of two of them that their rights had also been violated under Article 13, the right to an effective domestic remedy.

In response to the ECHR ruling on 27 Sep 99, the then Secretary of State stated that, "The UK Government, like all governments, has to accept the ruling of the European Court of Human Rights. The details of this complex judgement and its practical implications are being studied carefully. After consulting the Service Chiefs, Ministers will be making their recommendations in a timely manner. In the meantime, cases in the system will be put on hold." Despite previous Service concerns, the ECHR judgement made it clear that the bar against homosexuals serving in the Armed Forces was unsustainable and illegal under the Articles of the ECHR. Following advice from leading counsel, Ministers decided that there should be no appeal against the ECHR judgement.

As a result, the Chief of Defence Staff announced 30 September 1999, that a review of the current policy was to be commissioned, with a view to making recommendations to Ministers as soon as possible. It was emphasised that the review needed to identify a ". . . long term policy and sustainable code of conduct that retains our operational effectiveness and is within the law."

In considering the options for change it was paramount to ensure that whatever the final decision, the revised policy complies with the legal aspects of the ECHR ruling, is non-discriminatory (i.e., takes no account of sexual orientation), so far as is possible preserves operational effectiveness, meets Service needs while, at the same time, protecting the rights of the individual under the HRA. A number of options were examined with the clear recommendation for a policy underpinned by a code of social conduct based on sexual behaviour which applies equally to heterosexuals and homosexuals without the need to refer to sexual orientation. The policy is founded on the need to maintain combat effectiveness, based on the principles of group cohesion and discipline, which are, in turn, underpinned by factors such as mutual trust and respect, and a requirement to avoid conduct which offends others.

The Code of Social Conduct firmly recognises the right to privacy, including sexual orientation. Accordingly the new policy lifting the ban on homosexuals, and firmly underpinned by the Code of Social Conduct, was considered the most appropriate solution for the UK Armed Forces.

The "Armed Forces Code of Social Conduct" sets out a policy based on behaviour and whether an individual's conduct may impact adversely on the cohesion, efficiency or operational effectiveness of the Service. In setting out this policy, no account or distinction is made on the basis of the individual's gender or sexual orientation, which is taken to be a private matter for the individual. The Code of Social Conduct is based on an assessment of the potential or actual impact of social conduct on operational effectiveness and, as a start point, operates on the principle that the Services will only interfere in an individual's private life where the actions or behaviour of an individual have adversely impacted, or are they likely to impact, on the efficiency or operational effectiveness of the Service. It therefore recognises an individual's right to a private life in line with the intent of Article 8 of the HRA.

To summarise, the policy to bar homosexuals from the Armed Forces was not legally sustainable and has now been replaced with a new policy which recognises sexual orientation as a private matter. It was formulated with the full consultation and support of the three Service Chiefs and is firmly underpinned by a code of social conduct that applies to all regardless of their sexual orientation.

Armed Forces Code of Social Conduct: Policy Statement
United Kingdom Ministry of Defence, 2000

1. This Code of Social Conduct explains the Armed Forces' revised policy on personal relationships involving Service personnel. It applies to all members of the Armed Forces regardless of their gender, sexual orientation, rank or status. The provisions apply equally to members of the Regular and the Reserve Forces.

2. In the area of personal relationships, the overriding operational imperative to sustain team cohesion and to maintain trust and loyalty between commanders and those they command imposes a need for standards of social behaviour which are more demanding than those required by society at large. Such demands are equally necessary during peacetime and on operations. Examples of behaviour which can undermine such trust and cohesion, and therefore damage the morale or discipline of a unit (and hence its operational effectiveness) include: unwelcome sexual attention in the form of physical or verbal conduct; over-familiarity with the spouses or partners of other Service personnel; displays of affection which might cause offence to others; behaviour which damages or hazards the marriage or personal relationships of Service personnel or civilian colleagues within the wider defence community; and taking sexual advantage of subordinates. It is important to acknowledge in the tightly knit military community a need for mutual respect and a requirement to avoid conduct which offends others. Each case will be judged on its merits.

3. It is not practicable to list every type of conduct that may constitute social misbehaviour. The seriousness with which misconduct will be regarded will depend on the individual circumstances and the potential for adversely affecting operational effectiveness. Nevertheless, misconduct involving abuse of position, trust or rank, or taking advantage of an individual's separation, will be viewed as being particularly serious.

4. Unacceptable social conduct requires prompt and positive action to prevent damage. Timely advice and informal action can often prevent a situation developing to the point where it could impair the effectiveness of a Service unit. However, if the misconduct is particularly serious, it may be appropriate to proceed directly to formal administrative or to disciplinary action. Such action is always to be proportionate to the seriousness of the misconduct. It may constitute a formal warning, official censure, the posting of one or more of the parties involved or disciplinary action. In particularly serious cases, or where an individual persists with, or has a history of acts of social misconduct, formal disciplinary or administrative action may be taken, which might lead to termination of service.

5. The Service Test. When considering possible cases of social misconduct, and in determining whether the Service has a duty to intervene in the personal lives of its personnel, Commanding Officers at every level must consider each case against the following Service Test:

> Have the actions or behaviour of an individual adversely impacted or are they likely to impact on the efficiency or operational effectiveness of the Service?

In assessing whether to take action, Commanding Officers will consider a series of key criteria. This will establish the seriousness of the misconduct and its impact on operational effectiveness and thus the appropriate and proportionate level of sanction.

Policy concerning homosexuality in the armed forces
10 U.S.C. § 654 (enacted in 1993)

(a) Findings. — Congress makes the following findings:

(1) Section 8 of article I of the Constitution of the United States commits exclusively to the Congress the powers to raise and support armies, provide and maintain a Navy, and make rules for the government and regulation of the land and naval forces.

(2) There is no constitutional right to serve in the armed forces.

(3) Pursuant to the powers conferred by section 8 of article I of the Constitution of the United States, it lies within the discretion of the Congress to establish qualifications for and conditions of service in the armed forces.

(4) The primary purpose of the armed forces is to prepare for and to prevail in combat should the need arise.

(5) The conduct of military operations requires members of the armed forces to make extraordinary sacrifices, including the ultimate sacrifice, in order to provide for the common defense.

(6) Success in combat requires military units that are characterized by high morale, good order and discipline, and unit cohesion.

(7) One of the most critical elements in combat capability is unit cohesion, that is, the bonds of trust among individual service members that make the combat effectiveness of a military unit greater than the sum of the combat effectiveness of the individual unit members.

(8) Military life is fundamentally different from civilian life in that —

(A) the extraordinary responsibilities of the armed forces, the unique conditions of military service, and the critical role of unit cohesion, require that the military community, while subject to civilian control, exist as a specialized society; and

(B) the military society is characterized by its own laws, rules, customs, and traditions, including numerous restrictions on personal behavior, that would not be acceptable in civilian society.

(9) The standards of conduct for members of the armed forces regulate a member's life for 24 hours each day beginning at the moment the member enters military status and not ending until that person is discharged or otherwise separated from the armed forces.

(10) Those standards of conduct, including the Uniform Code of Military Justice, apply to a member of the armed forces at all times that the member

has a military status, whether the member is on base or off base, and whether the member is on duty or off duty.

(11) The pervasive application of the standards of conduct is necessary because members of the armed forces must be ready at all times for world-wide deployment to a combat environment.

(12) The worldwide deployment of United States military forces, the international responsibilities of the United States, and the potential for involvement of the armed forces in actual combat routinely make it necessary for members of the armed forces involuntarily to accept living conditions and working conditions that are often spartan, primitive, and characterized by forced intimacy with little or no privacy.

(13) The prohibition against homosexual conduct is a longstanding element of military law that continues to be necessary in the unique circumstances of military service.

(14) The armed forces must maintain personnel policies that exclude persons whose presence in the armed forces would create an unacceptable risk to the armed forces' high standards of morale, good order and discipline, and unit cohesion that are the essence of military capability.

(15) The presence in the armed forces of persons who demonstrate a propensity or intent to engage in homosexual acts would create an unacceptable risk to the high standards of morale, good order and discipline, and unit cohesion that are the essence of military capability.

(b) Policy. — A member of the armed forces shall be separated from the armed forces under regulations prescribed by the Secretary of Defense if one or more of the following findings is made and approved in accordance with procedures set forth in such regulations:

(1) That the member has engaged in, attempted to engage in, or solicited another to engage in a homosexual act or acts unless there are further findings, made and approved in accordance with procedures set forth in such regulations, that the member has demonstrated that —

(A) such conduct is a departure from the member's usual and customary behavior;

(B) such conduct, under all the circumstances, is unlikely to recur;

(C) such conduct was not accomplished by use of force, coercion, or intimidation;

(D) under the particular circumstances of the case, the member's continued presence in the armed forces is consistent with the interests of the armed forces in proper discipline, good order, and morale; and

(E) the member does not have a propensity or intent to engage in homosexual acts.

(2) That the member has stated that he or she is a homosexual or bisexual, or words to that effect, unless there is a further finding, made and approved in accordance with procedures set forth in the regulations, that the member has demonstrated that he or she is not a person who engages

in, attempts to engage in, has a propensity to engage in, or intends to engage in homosexual acts.

(3) That the member has married or attempted to marry a person known to be of the same biological sex.

(c) Entry standards and documents. —

(1) The Secretary of Defense shall ensure that the standards for enlistment and appointment of members of the armed forces reflect the policies set forth in subsection (b).

(2) The documents used to effectuate the enlistment or appointment of a person as a member of the armed forces shall set forth the provisions of subsection (b).

(d) Required briefings. — The briefings that members of the armed forces receive upon entry into the armed forces and periodically thereafter under section 937 of this title (article 137 of the Uniform Code of Military Justice) shall include a detailed explanation of the applicable laws and regulations governing sexual conduct by members of the armed forces, including the policies prescribed under subsection (b).

(e) Rule of construction. — Nothing in subsection (b) shall be construed to require that a member of the armed forces be processed for separation from the armed forces when a determination is made in accordance with regulations prescribed by the Secretary of Defense that —

(1) the member engaged in conduct or made statements for the purpose of avoiding or terminating military service; and

(2) separation of the member would not be in the best interest of the armed forces.

(f) Definitions. — In this section:

(1) The term "homosexual" means a person, regardless of sex, who engages in, attempts to engage in, has a propensity to engage in, or intends to engage in homosexual acts, and includes the terms "gay" and "lesbian."

(2) The term "bisexual" means a person who engages in, attempts to engage in, has a propensity to engage in, or intends to engage in homosexual and heterosexual acts.

(3) The term "homosexual act" means —

(A) any bodily contact, actively undertaken or passively permitted, between members of the same sex for the purpose of satisfying sexual desires; and

(B) any bodily contact which a reasonable person would understand to demonstrate a propensity or intent to engage in an act described in subparagraph (A).

Brief of *Amici Curiae* Constitutional Law Professors in Support of Appellants

Cook v. Gates, U.S. Court of Appeals for the First Circuit (pending)

Interest of the *Amici Curiae*

Amici Curiae are scholars who write, research and teach in the field of Constitutional Law, with particular interests in free speech and the First Amendment, equality, and sexual identity. . . . [Professors Akhil Reed Amar, C. Edwin Baker, Erwin Chemerinsky, Owen M. Fiss, Pamela S. Karlan, Andrew Koppelman, Kathleen M. Sullivan, Laurence H. Tribe, and Tobias Barrington Wolff; Professor Wolff is attorney for *amici*.]

Amici represent a wide range of views on the proper interpretation of the principle of free speech embodied in the First Amendment to the U.S. Constitution. Nonetheless, *Amici* are united in their conclusion that the U.S. military's "Don't Ask, Don't Tell" policy is offensive to the Free Speech Clause of the First Amendment.

Introduction

As its name suggests, the "Don't Ask, Don't Tell" policy is a speech restriction. . . . "Don't Ask, Don't Tell" discriminates on the basis of viewpoint and requires a false affirmation of identity as a condition of military service. It sweeps far more broadly than a mere restriction of on-duty speech. It does not simply use speech as evidence. Nor is it a mere evidentiary presumption, and even if it were, it unconstitutionally shifts the burden of proof to the servicemember in a manner that chills protected expression. These First Amendment principles apply even in the military context.

By its terms, the statute under consideration, 10 U.S.C. § 654, subjects gay, lesbian and bisexual servicemembers — and only them — to immediate sanction if they speak about their sexual identities. That prohibition applies "24 hours each day beginning at the moment the member enters military status and not ending until that person is discharged or otherwise separated from the armed forces," "whether the member is on base or off base, and whether the member is on duty or off duty." *Id.* §§ 654(a)(9)–(11) & (b)(2). The speech restriction is "pervasive" (in the statute's own words), applying both to public discourse and to private conversations with friends and family. *Id.* In this, the "Don't Ask, Don't Tell" policy lives up to its name: Gay servicemembers are regularly discharged solely because they "tell" by speaking honestly about their sexual identities. The policy thus imposes a more serious, pervasive and one-sided restriction on speech than any the Supreme Court has upheld in the military, prohibiting gay servicemembers from contributing their perspectives to ongoing public debates, including the debate over the policy itself. The resulting distortion of the political process exemplifies the central harm that the First Amendment was designed to prevent. Moreover, the policy necessarily compels gay servicemembers to affirm a false identity by forcing them to pretend that they are straight. It thereby offends a fundamental right of personal autonomy that the Supreme Court has found the First Amendment to protect.

As a first step in illustrating these principles, we ask this Court to imagine its reaction if the government were to impose "Don't Ask, Don't Tell" upon the entire American population, subjecting all gay, lesbian and bisexual civilians to the threat of severe sanction whenever they speak about their sexual identities. Even when the now-discredited *Bowers v. Hardwick* was the law of the land and same-sex intimacy could be criminalized, we submit that no court would have failed to recognize that such a policy could not have been reconciled with the First Amendment. The only question for this Court is whether the particular context of this restriction — a prohibition on speech by members of the military, on pain of discharge — renders the First Amendment inapplicable. The answer is no. That fact alone demonstrates the need for a remand here, since the district court dismissed this case on the pleadings, preventing any inquiry into the facts surrounding the policy's enforcement and the cogency of the justifications the government offers in its defense. For these reasons, we respectfully submit that this Court should reinstate the complaint and allow Plaintiffs to conduct discovery on these important First Amendment issues so that they may be fully briefed and analyzed in a judgment on the merits.

"Don't Ask, Don't Tell" is a Viewpoint Based Prohibition on Protected Speech that is Categorical in Nature and Sweeping in Scope

Speech about sexual identity is protected expression under the First Amendment. As the Supreme Court found in the St. Patrick's Day parade case, speech about gay identity "bear[s] witness" to a gay person's existence and "suggest[s] the view that [gay] people . . . have as much claim to unqualified social acceptance as heterosexuals." *Hurley v. Irish-American Gay, Lesbian and Bisexual Group of Boston*, 515 U.S. 557, 574–75 (1995). *See also Gay Students Organization v. Bonner*, 502 F.2d 652, 660–61 (1st Cir. 1974) (holding that self-identification is of vital importance in seeking social acceptance). Of course, "Don't Ask, Don't Tell" does not prohibit *all* speech about sexual identity among members of the military, nor does it prohibit all speech about gay identity. The statute targets only speech by gay, lesbian and bisexual servicemembers about their own identities — their thoughts, experiences and views as gay people. 10 U.S.C. § 654(b)(2). Straight servicemembers remain free to discuss their sexual identities. They also remain free to discuss their views about gay people. Homosexuality is a frequent topic of discussion among members of the armed forces, but that topic may be discussed only from the perspective of *they* and *them*, never *we* or *us*. This is viewpoint discrimination, illustrating why "[t]he *Hurley* Court recognized that the statement 'I am homosexual' expresses a viewpoint." *Elzie v. Aspin*, 897 F. Supp. 1, 5 (D.D.C. 1995).

In order to appreciate the impact of this viewpoint-based restriction, it is necessary to understand the sweep of "Don't Ask, Don't Tell." The policy does not merely prohibit gay, lesbian and bisexual servicemembers from discussing their identities on base, or during active duty. The policy prohibits them from *ever* discussing their identities with *anyone* — "24 hours each day . . . on base or off base . . . on duty or off duty." *Id.* §§ 654(a)(9)–(11). A gay sailor is prohibited from writing about his identity in a private diary. A bisexual sailor is prohibited from discussing her identity at home with her husband. Gay servicemembers are forbidden from participating in the political process by identifying themselves as the targets of antigay policies and urging their representatives to change the law. The thirteen-year enforcement history of the policy, most of which post-dates the early challenges brought in other Circuits, reads like a textbook account of viewpoint-based speech restrictions at their worst. Each of the servicemembers in these examples is allowed to be in the military — they are not "admitting" to anything wrong by identifying themselves as gay. As the military insists, "sexual orientation is considered a personal and private matter, and is not a bar to continued service." Dep't of Def., Directive No. 1332.14, Enlisted Administrative Separations § E3.A1.1.8.1.1, at 26 (1993). But the policy categorically prohibits gay servicemembers from speaking about their identities. In order to serve, they must remain silent.

The effects of these restrictions reach far beyond their impact upon gay servicemembers themselves. "Don't Ask, Don't Tell" deprives the entire electorate of an essential voice in debates over issues of public importance: the voice of active-duty gay soldiers, sailors, airmen and Marines, all of whom are forced into invisibility.

As the Supreme Court has recognized, the meaning and credibility of a message often depend upon the identity of the speaker. The Court emphasized this principle when it struck down an ordinance prohibiting individuals from displaying political signs on their lawns. Explaining the impact of the ordinance on public debate, the Court wrote:

> [T]he identity of the speaker is an important component of many attempts to persuade. A sign advocating "Peace in the Gulf" in the front lawn of a retired general or decorated war veteran may provoke a different reaction than the same sign in a 10-year-old child's bedroom window or the same message on a bumper sticker of a passing automobile. An espousal of socialism may carry different implications when displayed on the grounds of a stately mansion than when pasted on a factory wall or an ambulatory sandwich board.

City of Ladue v. Gilleo, 512 U.S. 43, 56–57 (1994). Prohibiting a distinct class of citizens from ever identifying themselves skews public debate, for it silences a perspective that cannot be communicated effectively by others.

Consider the impact of "Don't Ask, Don't Tell" in this light. The military subjects gay and bisexual servicemembers to broad restrictions on conduct that their straight peers need never satisfy. *See* 10 U.S.C. § 654(b)(1). Whether these special restrictions are necessary and workable, or whether instead they are counter-productive and harmful to military readiness, is a question of great public concern. Yet the very gay and bisexual servicemembers who are subject to these restrictions are also prohibited from identifying themselves as the targets of the regulation. We are aware of no other law in America today that regulates a group of citizens and then prohibits those very citizens from identifying themselves as the regulated population and speaking up on their own behalf.

The impact upon public debate is obvious. No one else can describe what it is like to serve under "Don't Ask, Don't Tell" in America's ongoing military deployments. No one else can put a human face on the continuing cost to the tens of thousands of gay, lesbian and bisexual servicemembers who must live under the policy every day. Even now, as Members of Congress seek support for a bill to repeal "Don't Ask, Don't Tell," *see* H.R. 1059, The Military Readiness Enhancement Act of 2005 (introduced 03/02/2005), gay servicemembers are prohibited from identifying themselves to the electorate to speak on the bill's behalf. Of course, heterosexual servicemembers are free to speak about whether gay people should be allowed to serve openly in the military. The policy silences only one point of view: the viewpoint of active-duty gay, lesbian and bisexual servicemembers. There is no greater threat to First Amendment values than a law that skews political debate in this manner. As Justice Scalia has written, government may not "license one side of a debate to fight freestyle, while requiring the other to follow Marquis of Queensberry rules." *R.A.V. v. City of St. Paul*, 505 U.S. 377, 391 (1992).

And the censorial impact of "Don't Ask, Don't Tell" does not stop at debates about the policy itself. The statute reaches out to distort every political debate that might involve gay servicemembers. Consider the case of Representative Steve May.

From 1999 to 2002, May, a gay man, was a member of the Arizona State House of Representatives and a first lieutenant in the Army Reserves. In February 1999, while on inactive reserve status, Representative May gave a speech on the floor of the Arizona House, urging his fellow lawmakers to reject a bill that would have prohibited Arizona state agencies from extending domestic partner benefits to gay and lesbian employees. May's remarks were prompted by an antigay speech given by another legislator, and he couched his opposition to the bill in personal terms, offering himself as a counterexample to the picture of "homosexual promiscuity" painted by his opponent and describing the impact that the proposed law would have upon him personally.

Two months later, May was called back to active status and scheduled for overseas deployment. Shortly thereafter, May's speech on the floor of the Arizona House came to the Army's attention through an anonymous complaint. The military conducted an investigation, read the transcript of May's remarks, and initiated discharge proceedings against him for speaking about being gay to his legislative colleagues. May ultimately negotiated a voluntary separation from the Army.

When a federal law reaches onto the floor of a state assembly to penalize an elected official for expressing a disfavored viewpoint in a legislative debate, the First Amendment is placed in serious jeopardy. "Don't Ask, Don't Tell" does not just restrict speech within military spaces or among military personnel. It silences gay servicemembers in every walk of civilian and political life. Steve May's case is remarkable only in that he refused to be silenced when his voice was needed. For that and that alone, he was discharged.

The Policy Compels Gay Servicemembers to Affirm a False Identity and Live a Lie

In addition to its burdens upon public debate, "Don't Ask, Don't Tell" offends a fundamental right of private autonomy under the First Amendment: the freedom of mind that protects the individual from being compelled to affirm an identity, idea or belief that is not his own. As the Supreme Court held in its foundational opinion of *West Virginia v. Barnette*, government violates a central tenet of the Speech Clause when it seeks to "prescribe what shall be orthodox in politics, nationalism, religion, or other matters of opinion [and] force citizens to confess by word or act their faith therein." 319 U.S. 624, 642 (1943). In requiring gay servicemembers to remain silent about their identities, always and everywhere, the "Don't Ask, Don't Tell" policy "require[s] those self-identifying as homosexuals to hide their orientation and to pretend to be heterosexuals." *Able v. United States*, 968 F. Supp. 850, 861 (E.D.N.Y. 1997), *rev'd on other grounds*, 155 F.3d 628 (2d Cir. 1998). Simply put, they must live a lie.

It is impossible to be "agnostic" about one's sexual identity in the course of normal interactions. Rather, a presumption of heterosexuality pervades most settings. In all but the most unusual circumstances, people assume that an individual is straight unless they have reason to believe otherwise. That assumption informs every conversation, question and statement. When a friend asks a soldier what kind of man she hopes to marry, or when a buddy asks a Marine whether he has a girlfriend, "Don't Ask, Don't Tell" requires that they allow themselves to be labeled with the straight identity that is implicit in the question. As Judges Pregerson, Kozinski, Reinhardt, Hawkins and Tashima wrote in their dissent from denial of *en banc* review, "as a practical matter the silence that this policy imposes on gay and lesbian military personnel can lead others to presume that they assent to a view about their own sexuality that they do not espouse." *Holmes v. California Nat'l Army Guard*, 155 F.3d 1049 (9th Cir. 1998) (Pregerson, J., dissenting from denial of *en banc*). For a gay person, being in the closet does not mean having no public sexual identity at all. To be in the closet, one must pretend to be straight. As any gay servicemember could explain if given the opportunity through discovery, this coerced affirmation of straight identity is pervasive under the military policy.

The Supreme Court has repeatedly recognized that coerced silence can force an individual into a false affirmation of belief, and it has "invalidated laws that forced tacit speech on other groups." *Holmes*, 155 F.3d at 1049 (Pregerson, J. dissenting from denial of *en banc*). In *Hurley*, for example, the Court unanimously found that a law requiring a parade organizer to accept an unwanted unit marching under its own banner impermissibly forced the organizer to propound an involuntary message — that gay people of Irish descent exist and are entitled to "unqualified social acceptance." *Hurley*, 515 U.S. at 574–75. Because the organizer had no opportunity to distance himself from that message, his silence would communicate endorsement and approval to most audiences. *See also Lee v. Weisman*, 505 U.S. 577, 592–93 (1992) (requirement that public school students sit silently while sectarian prayer is read at commencement ceremony violates Establishment Clause because "standing or remaining silent can signify adherence to a view" and enforced silence "may appear to the nonbeliever or dissenter to be an attempt to employ the machinery of the State to enforce a religious orthodoxy"). In contrast, when there is an effective opportunity to offer a corrective and make clear one's identity or views in response to such an attribution, the compelled speech problem can be avoided. *See, e.g., Rumsfeld v. FAIR*, 126 S. Ct. 1297, 1307 (2006) (Solomon Amendment's requirement that law schools provide equal access to military recruiters poses no compelled speech problem because "[l]aw schools remain free . . . to express whatever views they may have on the military's congressionally mandated employment policy"); *Pruneyard Shopping Ctr. v. Robins*, 447 U.S. 74, 87 (1980) (requirement that shopping center provide access to protestors poses no compelled speech problem where proprietors could "expressly disavow any connection with the message").

Under "Don't Ask, Don't Tell," gay soldiers are expressly *forbidden* from issuing any such corrective. When a lesbian soldier is asked when she plans to settle down with a husband, or a gay Marine is asked whether he has a girl-friend, the policy prohibits them from saying, "You're assuming that I'm straight, but I'm not." *See* 10 U.S.C. §654(b)(2) (requiring discharge for any statement of gay identity "or words to that effect"). A gay soldier who remains silent when confronted with the constant assumption that he is straight is affirming that false identity as surely as if he framed the lie in words. "Silence," the Court has said, "gains more probative weight where it persists in the face of accusation, since it is assumed in such circumstances that the accused would be more likely than not to dispute an untrue accusation." *United States v. Hale*, 422 U.S. 171, 176 (1975).

Finally, it is important to recall that nothing in the policy prohibits members of the military from *asking* fellow servicemembers whether they are gay, much less does it prohibit civilians from doing so. How is a gay servicemember to answer that question when the policy "pervasive[ly]" forbids him from identifying himself truthfully, "24 hours each day," "on base or off base," "on duty or off duty." 10 U.S.C. §§654(a)(9)–(11). There is no realistic alternative: He must lie about the core of his being. As Judge Nickerson concluded following discovery: "It is unlikely in the extreme that any enlisted member fit to serve would believe that closeted homosexuals are not serving or would long retain that belief after asking another enlisted member his or her sexual orientation and receiving the reply 'no comment.'" *Able*, 968 F. Supp. at 859.

Labeling "Don't Ask, Don't Tell" a Rule of "Evidence" Cannot Evade the First Amendment

The district court followed the Fourth, Eighth and Ninth Circuits in evading all these First Amendment problems, relying upon the same reasoning that led those courts into error: It concluded that no First Amendment scrutiny is necessary when government restricts protected speech through a rule of "evidence." The Supreme Court has long since rejected this proposition.

"Don't Ask, Don't Tell" restricts speech about gay identity by requiring the military to initiate immediate discharge proceedings whenever a servicemember says "I am gay" (or "words to that effect"). The policy then raises a "presumption" that the speaker stands in violation of the prohibitions on same-sex conduct, and it shifts the burden onto him to "rebut the presumption" raised by his statement and prove that he is entitled to serve. 10 U.S.C. §654(b)(1)–(2). If the servicemember cannot "rebut the presumption" — an effectively impossible task unless he recants his statement, as Plaintiffs allege and discovery will prove — then he is discharged. Thus, this suit presents a simple question: When government uses protected speech as the sole basis for shifting the burden to the speaker to prove that he has *not* violated a law or policy, does that statutory presumption require careful scrutiny under the First Amendment?

The Supreme Court answered that question with a resounding "Yes" in the landmark case of *Speiser v. Randall*, 357 U.S. 513 (1958). *Speiser* made it crystal clear that chilling protected speech through an evidentiary presumption offends the First Amendment, just as chilling speech through a direct regulation would. "The power to create presumptions," the Court said, "is not a means of escape from constitutional restrictions." *Id.* at 526.

Speiser involved a California law that provided a tax exemption to discharged veterans but withheld that benefit from anyone who advocated "the overthrow of the Government . . . by force or violence or . . . the support of a foreign Government against the United States in event of hostilities." *Id.* at 514–15. California required veterans to sign an oath disavowing this "illegal advocacy," and any who refused were presumed to be engaged in the forbidden activity and hence ineligible for the exemption. The burden then shifted to them to rebut that presumption, if they could. *Id.* at 522–23 & n.7.

For purposes of argument, the Supreme Court assumed that California had the power to prohibit the advocacy specified in the oath. Nonetheless, the Court found that the method California chose to enforce that prohibition — requiring veterans to prove that they were *not* engaged in illegal advocacy — "create[d] the danger that . . . legitimate utterance will be penalized." *Id.* at 526. "The man who knows that he must bring forth proof and persuade another of the lawfulness of his conduct," the Court explained, "necessarily must steer far wider of the unlawful zone than if the State must bear these burdens." *Id.* Because the burden that California imposed on those who refused to sign the oath would "necessarily produce a result which the State could not command directly" — chilling legal speech and advocacy — its law violated the Constitution's guarantees of free speech and due process. *Id.* at 526, 528–29.

These principles apply with even more force in the present case. The California tax law in *Speiser* shifted the burden of proof to veterans because of their refusal to *disavow* speech that was concededly *illegal*. Nonetheless, the Court found that the method California chose for separating "legitimate from illegitimate speech" was constitutionally infirm. *Id.* at 525. In contrast, "Don't Ask, Don't Tell" shifts the burden to gay servicemembers because of their *protected speech* about sexual identity, *see Hurley*, 515 U.S. at 574–75; *Gay Students Organization*, 502 F.2d at 660–61, penalizing them for that speech by forcing them to prove that they have not violated the policy's restrictions on conduct and propensity. Even assuming *arguendo* that the underlying conduct restrictions are valid — a proposition that is contested in this litigation and is doubtful following *Lawrence v. Texas* — the method that the statute employs to enforce those restrictions silences gay servicemembers altogether. They "necessarily must steer [wide]" of discussing their sexual identities to avoid the burden that the statute imposes when they speak. *Speiser*, 357 U.S. at 526. For nearly fifty years, *Speiser* has confirmed what common sense dictates: "It is apparent that a constitutional prohibition cannot be transgressed indirectly by the creation of a statutory presumption any more than it can be violated by direct enactment." *Id.* at 526. This proposition applies with equal force in the U.S. military. *See, e.g., Frontiero v. Richardson*, 411 U.S. 677 (1973) (invalidating statutory presumption that used gender to determine spousal "dependence" in military benefits policy). . . .

The Supreme Court's Precedents on Speech in the Military Provide No Constitutional Sanctuary for "Don't Ask, Don't Tell"

It should be clear that "Don't Ask, Don't Tell" would violate the First Amendment if it were applied to the general civilian population. The same would be true if the policy were applied to public employees. The *Pickering* line of cases, which gives government employers additional leeway in setting rules for the speech of public workers, always requires that such restrictions not prohibit comment on matters of public concern, particularly if they operate to silence minority views. *Pickering* reaffirmed that "free and open debate is vital" on "matter[s] of legitimate public concern," and it "unequivocally reject[ed]" the assertion that comments on public matters "may furnish grounds for dismissal if they are sufficiently critical in tone." *Pickering v. Board of Education*, 391 U.S. 563, 570–72 (1968). If government employers were to prohibit all their gay workers from truthfully discussing their sexual identities — at work, at home, or in the political process — that would obviously intrude broadly upon "matter[s] of political, social, or other concern to the community" and overstep any deference government can claim when acting as an employer. *Connick v. Myers*, 461 U.S. 138, 146 (1983). Thus, the only question in this case is whether the fact that it is *military* personnel who are singled out and prohibited from ever speaking about their gay identities serves to exempt the "Don't Ask, Don't Tell" policy from constitutional scrutiny.

The answer is no. While the Supreme Court has afforded the government additional deference in matters of military policy, the Court has never upheld a prohibition on the speech of military personnel as restrictive as "Don't Ask, Don't Tell." Even in those First Amendment cases where it has emphasized "military deference" most strongly, the Court has taken pains to explain how carefully the government has circumscribed military speech restrictions, thereby enabling the restrictions to avoid the most serious free speech problems. The "Don't Ask, Don't Tell" policy is circumscribed in none of these ways and goes further in restricting the speech of servicemembers than the Court has ever permitted.

The case of *Brown v. Glines*, 444 U.S. 348 (1980), provides a sharp point of contrast with the present dispute. In *Glines*, the Court upheld an Air Force regulation that required airmen to obtain the permission of base commanders before soliciting support for petitions on military property, authorizing commanders to deny permission where circulation of the petition on base would present "a clear danger to the loyalty, discipline, or morale of members of the Armed Forces, or material interference with accomplishment of a military mission." *Id.* at 350. Glines, a Captain in the Air Force reserves, objected to Air Force standards relating to hair length, and he organized a petition addressed to Congress and the Secretary of Defense to have the grooming regulations changed. He initially limited himself to circulating the petition among civilians, but he later decided to distribute the document to servicemembers on a military base, and he did so without first obtaining permission.

Glines was disciplined for his failure to have the petition approved before circulating it, and he brought a facial First Amendment challenge to this prior restraint on speech.

The Supreme Court gave the Air Force the limited right of censorship that it sought. In doing so, however, it offered a detailed map of the avenues for expression and dissent that members of the armed forces retain, even during active duty. Glines was disciplined only when he sought to circulate his petition on base without first obtaining approval — he was entirely free to collect support for his disapproval of military grooming policies in civilian settings, as he in fact did. Indeed, he had a statutory right to do so. Federal law provides that "[n]o person may restrict a member of the armed forces in communicating with a Member of Congress or an Inspector General," and it specifically protects the right of servicemembers to bring evidence of "unlawful discrimination" to the attention of such officials without reprisal or penalty. 10 U.S.C. § 1034(a); *Glines*, 444 U.S. at 359–61. One of the disputed issues in *Glines* was whether the prior restraint on circulating petitions within a military base violated this very statute. The Court found that the challenged regulation was consistent with the statute precisely because it preserved the right of servicemembers to collect civilian support for petitions and send those petitions directly to their elected representatives. Moreover, the regulation specified that commanders could not refuse permission for the circulation of petitions solely because they were "critical of Government policies or officials." *Glines*, 444 U.S. at 350 n.2; Air Force Reg. 35-15(3)(a)(4) (1970).

As *Glines* illustrates, members of the armed forces retain broad rights to dissent and protest — rights that are qualified only by limitations specific to controlled military spaces, such as bases, foreign theaters of war, and activities undertaken while in uniform. The Court's opinion presumes the ability of servicemembers to criticize government policies, complain about working conditions, even question the actions of military commanders, and Congress guarantees the right to communicate such grievances directly to elected officials.

A comparison of this holding with the present policy is telling. "Don't Ask, Don't Tell" lopsidedly targets expression by one group within the armed forces on one specific but vital topic — truthful speech by gay, lesbian, or bisexual servicemembers about their own identities — and it prohibits those soldiers from disclosing or discussing those identities "24 hours each day . . . whether the member is on base or off base, and whether the member is on duty or off duty." The restraint that the Air Force showed in *Glines* when it preserved civilian spaces and the political process as avenues of expression for servicemembers — a restraint about which the Court spoke at length in sustaining the Air Force regulation — is entirely absent under "Don't Ask, Don't Tell."

Parker v. Levy, 417 U.S. 733 (1974), offers a similar point of contrast. In *Parker*, the Court rejected a facial First Amendment challenge to a prosecution under the provisions of the Uniform Code of Military Justice regarding "conduct unbecoming an officer." The defendant, Levy, was an Army Captain who had refused to obey an order to train special-forces personnel and had actively urged enlisted men on his base to refuse to fight in Vietnam. There was no question that Levy's actions and speech could be punished. He argued, however, that the "conduct unbecoming" provision under which he was prosecuted was vague and overbroad, and hence that it threatened to chill the protected speech of other soldiers and should accordingly be struck down on its face on First Amendment grounds.

The Court disagreed, finding that the vagueness and overbreadth doctrines did not apply with equal force in the military. In so holding, the Court used some of its broadest language to describe the "military deference" doctrine. Even so, in explaining why the "conduct unbecoming" statute did not violate the First Amendment, the Court emphasized the limits of that law. The statute, the Court explained, "does not make every irregular, mischievous, or improper act a court-martial offense." Rather, "its reach is limited to conduct that is directly and palpably — as distinguished from indirectly and remotely — prejudicial to good order and discipline." "It applies only to calls for active opposition to the military policy of the United States," the Court continued, "and does not reach all disagreement with, or objection to, a policy of the Government." Canvassing the law of war and the military's manuals for prosecution in courts martial, the Court concluded that the military "has narrowed the very broad reach of the literal language of [the provisions], and at the same time has supplied considerable specificity by way of examples of the conduct which they cover," alleviating the concern that they would excessively chill protected speech. *Id.* at 752–53. Thus, even when it has articulated the doctrine of "military deference" in its broadest terms, the Court has not given the military a free hand to prohibit the speech of soldiers. Instead, the Court has emphasized the restraint of military regulations in explaining why they have passed muster.

Such restraint could hardly be more absent in the case of "Don't Ask, Don't Tell." Under the express terms of the policy, the most "indirect" and "remote" statements of gay identity with no demonstrable impact upon "good order and discipline" — indeed, even those statements that demonstrably have *no* such impact, such as thoughts written in a diary or private statements by a bisexual soldier to his wife — result in immediate separation and discharge. There is no limit upon the time (the policy applies "24 hours each day"), the place ("whether the member is on base or off base") or the activity ("whether the member is on duty or off duty") in which the speech of gay soldiers may be selectively punished.

Equally important, the Court has only deployed its "military deference" doctrine in cases where serious impacts upon protected speech were confined to specifically *military* settings: petitions or protests on a military base, *see Glines, supra; Greer v. Spock*, 424 U.S. 828 (1976); speech at a military workplace, *see Goldman v. Weinberger*, 475 U.S. 503 (1986); or speech between officers and subordinates, *see Parker, supra*. In cases where a military law or regulation has restricted speech in *civilian* spaces, the Court has invoked no military deference at all. For example, in *Schacht v. United States*, 398 U.S. 58 (1970), the Court struck down a law that prohibited the wearing of military uniforms in civilian theatrical productions when they would "tend to discredit" the military. Although the law was ostensibly justified by military priorities (such as concern over public regard for the armed forces), the law's impact upon speech was felt in the civilian realm, and the Court unanimously invalidated the statute's prohibition without any hint of military deference.

Similarly, in *O'Brien v. United States*, 391 U.S. 367 (1968), the Court analyzed the constitutionality of a congressional measure that criminalized the deliberate defacing, mutilating, or burning of draft cards, a species of military property. In its opinion, the Court recognized that the law would affect expressive conduct in the civilian sphere in many of its typical applications, assumed *arguendo* that the conduct in the case before it deserved to be viewed as expressive, and proceeded with a First Amendment analysis that did not display any deference by virtue of the law's military context. Rather, in upholding the ability of government to prosecute a public draft-card burning that was intended and understood as a political protest, the Court rested its holding on the conclusion that the law did not intentionally single out instances of the prohibited behavior that were expressive in nature. Again, therefore, when a law had impacts upon speech in the civilian realm, the military character of the law's restrictions did not trigger more deferential review than a similarly situated law with no military dimension would have drawn. *See, e.g., Clark v. Community for Creative Non-Violence*, 468 U.S. 288 (1984) (applying *O'Brien* standard to purely civilian regulation).

As the case of Steve May makes clear, although the "Don't Ask, Don't Tell" policy targets the speech of servicemembers (even those who, like May, were on inactive status at the time), it regulates speech with and to civilians, and its unrestrained scope has profound impacts upon speech in the civilian world. By removing the voice of openly gay active-duty servicemembers from every facet of American life, the policy distorts public debate and the political process on matters of national importance. The Supreme Court has never applied the "military deference" doctrine to such a case.

Finally, in keeping with its continuing insistence that the Constitution is not silent on the speech of men and women in uniform, the Court has repeatedly emphasized the importance of applying military speech regulations in an evenhanded and objective fashion. In *Glines*, the Court explained that "[c]ommanders may apply [such] regulations irrationally, invidiously, or arbitrarily, thus giving rise to legitimate claims under the First Amendment." 444 U.S. at 358 n.15. In *Greer v. Spock*, 424 U.S. 828, 838 (1976), the Court upheld limits on the ability of the public to demonstrate on military bases, but only after explaining that those limits were "objectively and evenhandedly applied." And in *Goldman v. Weinberger*, 475 U.S. 503 (1986), in which the Court upheld the application of a dress regulation to an orthodox Jew who was forbidden from wearing a yarmulke, Justices Stevens, Powell and White explained that their votes in that 5-4 decision rested in part on the fact that the restriction was "based on a neutral, completely objective standard." *Id.* at 513 (Stevens, J., concurring).

Taken together, these cases make it clear that facts and context are of central importance in a military First Amendment dispute. Even when it has used its broadest language to describe the "military deference" doctrine, the Court has never given the military a free hand in prohibiting speech that is protected by the First Amendment. Instead, it has inquired carefully into the scope and enforcement history of military policies and has upheld speech restrictions only after concluding that they were limited in nature and tailored to important military purposes. It has indicated that the irrational or arbitrary enforcement of a speech restriction gives rise to legitimate First Amendment claims, finding that military speech restrictions pass muster only after concluding that the policy was objectively and evenhandedly applied. And it has relied upon its "military deference" doctrine only in cases that restricted speech in military spaces or among military personnel.

The "Don't Ask, Don't Tell" policy exhibits none of these saving characteristics. As Plaintiffs allege, and as the nature of the prohibition makes inevitable, "Don't Ask, Don't Tell" is regularly applied in an irrational, invidious and arbitrary fashion that lacks any objective relationship to good order and discipline. The policy prohibits only speech affirming a gay identity, leaving speech denying gay identity or affirming straight identity unrestricted — a prohibition that is not only content-based but viewpoint-based, the very antithesis of "evenhanded." *Goldman*, 475 U.S. at 513 (Stevens, J., concurring). And it prohibits that speech always and everywhere, eliminating the voice of gay soldiers from public debate on this topic of manifest public interest, thereby distorting the political process. "Don't Ask, Don't Tell" is a broader, more invasive and more uncompromising restriction on military speech than any that the Supreme Court has ever upheld. The Court's precedents offer the policy no constitutional sanctuary. To the contrary, those precedents demonstrate the need for careful inquiry into the circumstances surrounding the policy's enforcement and the factual cogency of the justifications that the military has offered in seeking to defend it.

Conclusion

The signatories to this brief have views about the principle of free speech embodied in the Constitution that differ in many ways. In this, however, we speak with one voice: If the "Don't Ask, Don't Tell" policy does not require careful and searching constitutional scrutiny, then the First Amendment is a dead letter in the U.S. military. The Supreme Court has repeatedly insisted that the same military that safeguards our Constitution must also be constrained by our Constitution. We urge this Court to rise above the landscape of error created by the early rulings on "Don't Ask, Don't Tell" and to instruct the district court to analyze this policy in a manner that is consistent with the best traditions and the highest aspirations of the Free Speech Clause.

NOTES AND QUESTIONS

1. *United States v. Free*, 14 C.M.R. 466 (N.B.R. 1953), upheld the conviction of a captain in the U.S. Marine Corps Reserve for fraternizing with a male enlistee. The Navy Board of Review discussed the class distinctions between officers and enlisted persons:

> The problem presented to us is to draw a line as to where acts of fraternization or association with enlisted men by officers cease to be the innocent acts of comradeship and normal social intercourse between members of a democratic military force and become a violation of

Article 134 of the Code, prejudicial to good order and discipline in the armed forces of the United States.

This subject is one of which a great deal has been said in the public press and especially in various novels and dramas presented to the public. It has become popular to deride as a fiction any distinction between officers, as a class, and enlisted men. It is the contention of some writers that any such distinction should be abolished, citing as an example of reasons therefor the fact that there are officers who are of the same social background as enlisted personnel and that situations such as the case here arise with a not un-alarming frequency. There has been a popular tendency, during a period of our history when a large citizen soldiery has become a necessity, to deprecate the traditional obligations of an officer to conduct himself as a gentleman. This attitude even went so far as to receive official sanction of a sort shortly after World War II when a board headed by a well-known Army Air Force General made an official report having to do with the so-called "caste system" in the services. The attitude is reflected in the almost universal use by the public press of the word "brass" as applied to senior officers with the unfortunate connotation that the metal thereof is somewhat more dross than precious. However this may be, it still remains as a fact that there is a custom in the military service, one of long standing and well recognized as such, and fulfilling all of the requirements set forth in the Manual for Courts-Martial, United States, 1951, for its breach to be an offense under Article 134, that officers shall not fraternize or associate with enlisted men under circumstances which prejudice the good order and discipline of the armed forces of the United States.

Counsel for the accused argues that if the facts of this case are such as to warrant a conviction, it would similarly be a violation of the law for an officer to offer an enlisted man a ride in an automobile, to play on the same athletic team, eat at the same table, or sleep in the same barracks at any time with an enlisted man. With this we cannot agree.

During war, the armed forces of our nation comprise, in large measure, people only recently from civilian life. As befits a military organization, these various people occupy different military positions, and it is not uncommon that in the same immediate family are both officers and enlisted men of one or more of the services. (Today it is even possible for an officer to be married to an enlisted person.) It is equally true that former close associates in business and society find themselves in different ranks and rates of their service. To say that these people by reason of their military positions should not associate with the other is inconsistent with our democratic concepts of social relations. (CMO 2, 1941, 271.) There is nothing reprehensible about officers and enlisted men playing on the same athletic team, riding in the same vehicle, or occupying the same billet under conditions usually acceptable. At a service dance, for instance, it would not be a violation of the custom of the service for a male commissioned officer to dance with a female enlisted person or vice versa.

On the other hand there are acts which, acceptable as between civilians and between officers themselves and enlisted men themselves, are recognized as being prejudicial to good order and discipline. Lending money and bestowing gifts are the subject of regulation as well as a custom. So, too, are other acts which under some circumstances are acceptable social practices but are prejudicial, by their nature, between officers and enlisted persons. While an officer might take an enlisted relative to dinner at a civilian restaurant, it might be an offense to take the same relative in uniform to dinner at an officer's mess. It is traditional for officers to take meals in an enlisted mess, while it is a violation of the same tradition for enlisted persons to take meals in an officer's mess. It would not be an offense for officers and enlisted men to sleep alongside each other on the topside decks of a destroyer at anchor in Guantánamo Bay, whereas it would be an offense on the same ship for enlisted men to sleep in officers' rooms. It is not the fact of eating together or sleeping in the same place which is the offense against discipline, but the appropriateness of the time and place and the circumstances which dictate the proprieties.

The military services demand a regard for authority by juniors towards their seniors which experience has shown is enhanced by the observance of decorum, tradition, custom, usage, and conventions which are peculiar to the services alone. The regard and respect for authority upon which rests the unquestioned obedience of the serviceman which is mandatory in time of battle or stress is lessened by the failure to observe niceties of military courtesy and other traditions and customs.

Because of the many situations which might arise, it would be a practical impossibility to lay down a measuring rod of particularities to determine in advance what acts are prejudicial to good order and discipline and what are not. As we have said, the surrounding circumstances have more to do with making the act prejudicial than the act itself in many cases. Suffice it to say, then, that each case must be determined on its own merits. Where it is shown that the acts and circumstances are such as to lead a reasonably prudent person, experienced in the problems of military leadership, to conclude that the good order and discipline of the armed forces has been prejudiced by the compromising of an enlisted person's respect for the integrity and gentlemanly obligations of an officer, there has been an offense under Article 134.

14 C.M.R. at 468-70. Are military distinctions between officers and enlistees (that is, distinctions of social class) related to limits on sexual relations? *See* Elizabeth L. Hillman, *Gentlemen Under Fire: The U.S. Military and "Conduct Unbecoming,"* 26 LAW & INEQUALITY ___ (2007).

2. The government's brief in *Cook v. Gates* emphasizes, *inter alia*, that the policy concerning homosexuality does not bar homosexuals from serving so long as they do not manifest any homosexual conduct. It casts the policy as a "carefully-crafted" compromise that respects the military's own assessment of its personnel and disciplinary needs and argues that all of the judicial decisions upholding the policy have appropriately deferred to the considered judgment of the legislature and executive as well as the armed forces. Do these arguments respond to the First Amendment questions posed by the *amicus* brief that appears above?

3. The military law concerning sexual harassment has been a contentious issue in recent years. In *United States v. Brown*, 55 M.J. 375 (C.A.A.F. 2001), the Court of Appeals for the Armed Forces considered whether a series of inappropriate comments among officers of similar rank constituted "conduct unbecoming an officer and a gentleman." In his opinion for the court, Judge Effron discussed social and professional relationships within the officer corps:

> As a general matter, personal interactions among military officers are not prohibited by law, regulation, policy, or custom. On the contrary, the unique conditions of military service — frequently involving long working hours, lengthy deployments for training and operations, harsh working and living conditions, and dangerous assignments — tend to break down the distinctions between personal and professional associations prevalent in civilian society. . . . As a general matter, military officers are not precluded from engaging in conversations with a fellow officer of the opposite sex involving the type of comments made in the present case with respect to physical appearance, social contacts, or sexual matters absent a pertinent custom or policy placed in evidence. This is not particularly remarkable, given the variety of comments that are likely to be made in conversations between officers of the opposite sex who may have relationships ranging from casual acquaintance through dating, courtship, and marriage. . . . Given the wide variety of personalities and relationships that may exist among officers, there is likely to be an equally wide variety of reactions to comments of a personal or sexual nature.

55 M.J. at 384-85. Concurring in part and dissenting in part, Judge Baker offered a different assessment:

> Rightly wary of criminalizing the day-to-day fabric of life, the majority describes the wide range of comments that are likely to be made between officers in the Air Force. The opinion illustrates this point with reference to a wide range of contexts involving interaction between officers. But the contexts are all social (casual acquaintance through dating, courtship, and marriage), where one might reasonably expect some discussion of sex or sexual innuendo. . . .
>
> Moreover, while the majority opinion cites to Air Force restrictions on *dating* between officers to illustrate the depth of relationships tolerated and accepted between officers of different grades, those same regulations also address more broadly unprofessional relationships between officers. The *per se* rule with respect to dating is limited to the same chain of command; however, the prohibition on unprofessional relationships extends to all personnel. AFI 36-2909 (1 May 1999), the successor to the Instruction cited in *United States v. Rogers,* 54 M.J. 244 (2000), states in paragraph 3.3:

Dating and Close Friendships. Dating, courtship, and close friendships between men and women are subject to the same policy considerations as are other relationships. *Like any personal relationship, they become matters of official concern when they adversely affect morale, discipline, unit cohesion, respect for authority, or mission accomplishment. Members must recognize that these relationships can adversely affect morale and discipline, even when the members are not in the same chain of command or unit.* The formation of such relationships between superiors and subordinates within the same chain of command or supervision is prohibited[.]

Like foxhole whispers, office banter is good for morale and unit cohesion. Likewise, humor can serve to promote mission accomplishment in the field, as well as in the operating room. However, sexual harassment is not a component of esprit de corps or unit morale. Officers should not confuse the two, particularly in the duty setting and particularly where the officer is on notice both as to expected behavior and that his remarks are unwelcome.

55 M.J. at 394. Does the special environment of military service, one of "foxhole whispers" as well as "office banter," in which danger and intimacy "break down the distinctions between personal and professional associations," require more or less rigorous enforcement of sexual norms, language, and behavior? How has the integration of women altered the situation? What sort of impact would the integration of lesbians and gay men have?

4. In *Chief Military Prosecutor v. 3SG (RES) Then Chee Keong*, [1993] SGMCA 2 (Sing. Mil. App. 1993), the military prosecutor appealed the punishment — one day of detention — to which a corporal in the Singapore military was sentenced for participating in a consensual homosexual act with another servicemember. The court declined to increase the sentence, holding that while "homosexual conduct in the Singapore Armed Forces is clearly detrimental to good conduct and discipline and offenders must be dealt with severally when detected," the "strong mitigating circumstances" in this case justified a relatively mild sentence. Does this sort of outcome — lenient punishment (at least for the often harsh Singapore military justice system) but confirmation of an offense — reconcile official condemnation of homosexuality with recognition of its inevitable presence within the armed forces?

Chapter 12

JUDICIAL INDEPENDENCE

Democratic countries take as a given that persons performing judicial functions will be independent and impartial. This can be assured by such means as terms of office, protection against arbitrary removal, financial disclosure, and criminal prohibitions on bribery. The United States and numerous other countries established military judiciaries in the years since World War II, and issues relating to the independence of those judges have arisen repeatedly. Because judicial independence is one of the key factors that contributes to (or, if compromised, can detract from) public confidence in the administration of justice, few aspects of contemporary military justice are as critical. Judicial independence is, of course, related to the struggle against unlawful command influence, a subject we address in Chapter 3, §III, *supra*.

I. STATUTORY AND REGULATORY PROVISIONS

Uniform Code of Military Justice

Article 6a. Investigation and disposition of matters pertaining to the fitness of military judges

The President shall prescribe procedures for the investigation and disposition of charges, allegations, or information pertaining to the fitness of a military judge or military appellate judge to perform the duties of the judge's position. To the extent practicable, the procedures shall be uniform for all armed forces.

Article 37. Unlawfully influencing action of court

(a) No authority convening a general, special, or summary court-martial, nor any other commanding officer, may censure, reprimand, or admonish the court or any member, military judge, or counsel thereof, with respect to the findings or sentence adjudged by the court, or with respect to any other exercises of its or his functions in the conduct of the proceedings. No person subject to this chapter may attempt to coerce or, by any unauthorized means, influence the action of a court-martial or any other military tribunal or any member thereof, in reaching the findings or sentence in any case, or the action of any convening, approving, or reviewing authority with respect to his judicial acts. The foregoing provisions of the subsection shall not apply with respect to (1) general instructional or informational courses in military justice if such courses are designed solely for the purpose of instructing members of a command in the substantive and procedural aspects of courts-martial, or (2) to statements and instructions given in open court by the military judge, president of a special court-martial, or counsel.

(b) In the preparation of an effectiveness, fitness, or efficiency report on any other report or document used in whole or in part for the purpose of determining whether a member of the armed forces is qualified to be advanced, in grade, or in determining the assignment or transfer of a member of the armed forces or in determining whether a member of the armed forces should be retained on active duty, no person subject to this chapter may, in preparing any such report (1) consider or evaluate the performance of duty of any such member as a member of a court-martial, or (2) give a less favorable rating or evaluation of any member of the armed forces because of the zeal with which such member, as counsel, represented any accused before a court-martial.

Manual for Courts-Martial, United States (2005 ed.), Rules for Courts-Martial

Rule 109. Professional supervision of military judges and counsel

(a) In general. Each Judge Advocate General is responsible for the professional supervision and discipline of military trial and appellate military judges, judge advocates, and other lawyers who practice in proceedings governed by the code and this Manual. To discharge this responsibility each Judge Advocate General may prescribe rules of professional conduct not inconsistent with this rule or this Manual. Rules of professional conduct promulgated pursuant to this rule may include sanctions for violations of such rules. Sanctions may include but are not limited to indefinite suspension from practice in courts-martial and in the Courts of Criminal Appeals. Such suspensions may only be imposed by the Judge Advocate General of the armed service of such courts. Prior to imposing any discipline under this rule, the subject of the proposed action must be provided notice and an opportunity to be heard. The Judge Advocate General concerned may upon good cause shown modify or revoke suspension. Procedures to investigate complaints against military trial judges and appellate military judges are contained in subsection (c) of this rule.

(b) Action after suspension or disbarment. When a Judge Advocate General suspends a person from practice or the Court of Appeals for the Armed Forces disbars a person, any Judge Advocate General may suspend that person from practice upon written notice and opportunity to be heard in writing.

(c) Investigation of judges.

(1) In general. These rules and procedures promulgated pursuant to Article 6a are established to investigate and dispose of charges, allegations, or information pertaining to the fitness of a military trial judge or appellate military judge to perform the duties of the judge's office.

(2) Policy. Allegations of judicial misconduct or unfitness shall be investigated pursuant to the procedures of this rule and appropriate action shall be taken. Judicial misconduct includes any act or omission that may serve to demonstrate unfitness for further duty as a judge, including, but not limited to violations of applicable ethical standards.

Model Code of Military Justice

Article 2. Independence.

Magistrates and Military Judges are independent in the exercise of their functions and bound only by the Law.

II.   MILITARY JUDGES

Eugene R. Fidell, *Military Judges and Military Justice: The Path to Judicial Independence*
74 JUDICATURE 14, 14-20 (June-July 1990)

While many of the institutional issues surrounding the military justice system have been resolved or ameliorated, one feature of the system that has proven to be change-resistant is the failure to afford military trial and appellate judges the basic protection of a fixed term of office.[1] The issue has been commented on repeatedly and remains a matter of concern because a judge who does not know with precision when his or her term will expire is a sitting duck for improper influence.[2] At the very least, the arrangement conveys an appearance of a lack of judicial independence. The purposes of this article are to summarize the results of a study conducted by the Department of Defense regarding, among other things, the concept of judicial terms of office, to reexamine the justifications that have been offered for the current arrangements, and to outline legislation that would remedy the problem while giving appropriate recognition to the needs of the military.

On November 18, 1616, it fell to Lord Chancellor Ellesmere to install Sir Henry Montagu as Lord Chief Justice of the Court of Common Pleas after James I fired Sir Edward Coke. Ellesmere's remarks have been preserved:

> [H]is Majesty is now graciously pleased to address unto you his Writ, under the Great Seal, calling you thereby to be his Chief Justice in this place, for Pleas to be holden before himself. A case rare, for you are called to a place vacant, not by death or cession, but by amotion and deposing of him that held the place before you, and that not as Sir William Thorpe in the time of the absence of King Ed[ward III) when

---

[1] [n.1] The judges in question are those who preside over general and special courts-martial or sit on the four service Courts of Military Review. There is no judge in a summary courts-martial, and the civilian judges of the Court of Military Appeals enjoy the protection of fixed 15-year terms.

[2] [n.2] *E.g.,* Note, *Service-Connection and Drug Related Offenses: The Military Courts' Ever Expanding Jurisdiction,* 54 GEO. WASH. L. REV. 118, 123, 125 & nn.56-58 (1985); Fidell, *Judicial Tenure Under the Uniform Code of Military Justice,* 31 FED. B. NEWS & J. 327 (1984); Pitkin, *The Military Justice System: An Analysis from the Defendant's Perspective,* 29 JAG J. 251, 257-58 (1977); Bruton, *Book Review,* 123 U. PA. L. REV. 1482, 1496-97, 1506 (1975); Sherman, *Book Review,* 84 YALE L.J. 356, 374 (1974); Bishop, JUSTICE UNDER FIRE: A STUDY OF MILITARY LAW, 44, 300-01 (1974); Hodson, *Military Justice: Abolish or Change?,* 11 U. KANSAS L. REV. 31, 33 (1973); Sherman, *The Civilianization of Military Law,* 22 ME. L. REV. 3, 48, 57, 103 (1970); Moyer, *Procedural Rights of the Military Accused: Advantages over a Civilian Defendant,* 22 ME. L. REV. 105, 139-40 n. 259 (1970).

there was a Custos Regni; nor as Sir Robert Tresilian in the disordered and unruly time of King R[ichard II], But in the peaceable and happy Reign of Great King James the great King of Great Brittain, wherein you see the Prophet David[']s word true, He putteth down one, and setteth up another; a Lesson to be learned of all, and to be remembered and feared of all that sit in Judicial places.[3]

Whether or not the ability to dispense summarily with a sitting judge was shocking in Jacobean England, surely a system of justice that today leaves judges insecure in their judicial office is a remarkable anachronism.

In each branch of the armed forces of the United States, trial and Court of Military Review judges serve without the protection of a fixed term of office. While they may not be summarily deprived of their judicial certification, they serve according to order — i.e., at the pleasure of the service. They may be transferred from judicial functions for any reason and at any time. Such an arrangement is subversive of the independence expected of those exercising judicial functions. It contrasts not only with the tenure of other judges in our society,[4] but also with the protected tenure of federal administrative law judges who by definition can never deprive a person of life or liberty, and even with the five-year terms of office of military judges in the Soviet Union.

Concern over the independence of the military judiciary was heightened by a recent, highly-publicized attempt by the Department of Defense Inspector General to probe the inner workings of the Navy-Marine Corps Court of Military Review on the basis of an anonymous "tip" — ultimately determined to be unfounded — that the reversal of the conviction of Navy surgeon Donal Billig was obtained through bribery.[5] That concern was not new.

The desirability of the current arrangements has been questioned repeatedly. Protected tenure was suggested in a 1976 decision of the United States Court of Military Appeals, the facts of which are still deeply disturbing. After

---

[3] [n.3] John P. Dawson, THE DEVELOPMENT OF LAW AND LEGAL INSTITUTIONS 439-40 (1965) (quoting Ps. 75:7).

[4] [n.4] With only the rarest of exceptions, significant trials are presided over in the United States by judges who have protected tenure of one kind or another. Judges who serve at the pleasure of an appointing authority represent a tiny minority and typically sit only in minor courts. Only in the most peculiar circumstances do judges of federal courts lack fixed or life terms. One such tribunal is the United States Court for Berlin, which figured in Judge Herbert J. Stern's highly critical book, Judgment in Berlin (1983). At one time, President Eisenhower appointed a Panama Canal Zone magistrate to act as a special judge of the zonal district court to preside over a single criminal trial. 23 Fed. Reg. 83 (1958) (Gov't v. Zapata, D.C.Z. Crim. No. 4794). According to the Council of State Court Administrators' State Court Organization (1987) (Table 20), the only state judges who serve at pleasure rather than for fixed terms are magistrates in Alaska, some justices of the peace and municipal judges, and special judges in Oklahoma. See also, e.g., Ark. Code Ann. § 16-17-107(a) (1987) (municipal court magistrates); 19 La. Rev. Stat. Ann. §§ 3:441.B, 33:441-27, 443-46 (West 1988) (mayor's court magistrates); see, e.g., State v. Fontenot, 424 So.2d 433 (La. App. 1988); Broussard v. Town of Delcambre, 458 So.2d 1003 (La. App. 1984).

[5] [n.7] See generally U.S. Navy-Marine Corps Court of Military Review v. Carlucci, 26 M.J. 328 (C.M.A. 1988). The implications of the NMCMR case are perceptively explored in Baum and Barry, United States Navy-Marine Corps Courts of Military Review v. Carlucci: A Question of Judicial Independence, 36 FED. B. NEWS & J. 242 (1989).

trial, the military judge received inquiries from higher authority as to why he had given sentences in that and two other cases that were believed to be excessively lenient.[6] By divided vote, the court barred such inquiries "outside the adversary process which question or seek justification for a judge's decision unless such inquiries are made by an independent judicial commission established in strict accordance with guidelines contained in section 9.1(a) of the ABA Standards, The Function of the Trial Judge. . . ." Finding that all of the inquiries occurred after the sentence was handed down, the court found no error. It did, however, evince a recognition that the problem was not an isolated one by observing, in a footnote, that "[t]he appearance of judicial tampering could be eliminated by congressional action to provide some form of tenure for all judges in the military justice system."[7]

Since then, the Court of Military Appeals has declined to grant review of the precise issue of whether due process requires a term of office. Other courts have dismissed constitutional objections to the current arrangements, deeming the matter one of policy for the executive branch or Congress to decide. Still, the Court of Military Appeals has remained alert to the dangers of undue influence on military judges. In one recent case, it had to examine (and decided to block) the Department of Defense Inspector General's investigation of the post-Billig allegation of bribery on the Navy-Marine Corps Court of Military Review. In another, it refused to sweep under the rug evidence of pressure on a Navy trial judge by that service's chief trial judge.[8] And in a third, *United States v. Beckermann*, it held that the command of Article 26 that a general court-martial judge having judging as his primary duty was not met where, as a practical matter, such a judge was specially assigned to hear a single case.[9] The judge — whose full-time assignment was as legal advisor to a large Coast Guard command — was given orders assigning him to duty as a judge, but he was reassigned to his regular job immediately after completion of a single trial. *Beckerman* was nearly a carbon copy of *United States v. Moorehead*, which also came up from the Coast Guard.[10] As a practical matter, both involved ad hoc military judges — i.e., judge advocates certified as military judges but not permanently assigned to judicial billets. . . .

The commission study

The fact that the current statutory arrangement may withstand constitutional scrutiny does not mean it is sound public policy. The Military Justice Act of 1983 directed the secretary of defense to convene an advisory commission to address this and other issues. The nine-member commission, which was dominated by uniformed officers, conducted a survey of commanders, trial and appellate military judges, staff judge advocates and military prosecutors and defense counsel. Tables 1-12 [*infra*] summarize the pertinent results.

---

[6] [n.8] *United States v. Ledbetter*, 2 M.J. 37 (C.M.A. 1976).

[7] [n.9] *Id.* at 43 n.12.

[8] [n.12] *United States v. Mabe*, 28 M.J. 326 (C.M.A. 1989) (per curiam) (directing submission of letter alleged to have stimulated increased sentences).

[9] [n.13] 27 M.J. 334 (C.M.A. 1989) (2-1).

[10] [n.14] 20 U.S.C.M.A. 374, 44 C.M.R. 4 (1971).

These results merit closer scrutiny than they have received. Without suggesting that the basic public policy question is one that should be decided merely by a show of hands among military lawyers and commanders, surely their views are entitled to careful consideration in the decisionmaking process. The responses to the "bottom-line" questions (Tables 1-2) show that there is broad support for the idea of guaranteed terms of office. That support was strongest among prosecutors and defense counsel, but most sitting judges also favored fixed terms.

The most disturbing result of the survey is its confirmation that substantial numbers of judge advocates and military judges were aware of instances in which judges had either been threatened with transfer from judicial functions or actually transferred as a result of their rulings. A quarter of the military trial and appellate benches were aware of instances of improper pressure. The chilling effect of this kind of widespread awareness is incalculable, but it seems fair to view the responses summarized in Table 1 and 2 as evidence of the felt concerns of the military legal and command communities.

Table 10 indicates that the instances of threatened or actual transfer usually did not affect subsequent decisions by the targeted judge. Nonetheless, it is interesting to note that the lowest percentages of officers who believed that were convening authorities and defense counsel. In other words, both the commanders who would have included the sources of such pressure and the lawyers with professional responsibility for the defense of accused personnel were the most likely to consider it efficacious. It is also worth noting that the percentage of trial and defense counsel who believed that command criticism had affected a judge's subsequent decisions was identical. One might be willing to discount the statistic that about three-quarters of defense counsel favor terms of office for trial appellate judges, but the fact that prosecutors are also overwhelmingly favorably disposed to terms of office is strong evidence indeed. Were conditions such as those disclosed in Table 6 found in a civilian court system, the threat to constitutional standards of due process would be self-evident and would not be tolerated.

In its report, the Commission majority recommended against action to provide terms of office for military judges. Three civilian members (Professor Kenneth F. Ripple, who was subsequently named to the United States Court of Appeals for the Seventh Circuit; Steven S. Honigman, formerly a Navy judge advocate, now in private practice in New York; and Christopher Sterritt, of the staff of the Court of Military Appeals) suggested a "middle ground" between rigid terms of office and the current absence of terms of office:

> Congress could, by statute, require that the secretary of every military department: 1 — provide by regulation for a fixed period of assignment of a military judge; 2 — specify the circumstances under which a military judge could be prematurely removed; 3 — require that any such "short tour" be approved by the Secretary or his designate. Such a system would permit the Armed Forces to reassign military judges to other duties for the good of the service. However, the requirement of a written explanation and approval at the secretarial level would also assure that the decision was based on permissible grounds and subject to scrutiny at a level above the parochialism of command influence.

The Code Committee (which consists of the judges of the Court of Military Appeals, the judge advocates general, the chief counsel of the Coast Guard, the staff judge advocate to the Commandant of the Marine Corps, and two members of the public) offered the following comments on the portion of the report that dealt with the terms-of-office issue:

> The Commission rejected a proposal that military judges at the trial and appellate level be granted fixed terms of office. There is no evidence[11] to suggest that judges are removed after a short time in office in order to punish them for unpopular rulings. Adequate administrative procedures presently exist to remove a military judge for misconduct or disability.
>
> Unlike most civilian judges, military judges currently enjoy many of the practical benefits of tenure because, as senior military officers, they usually are entitled to serve on active military duty for 20 years, after which they may retire and draw retirement pay. To impose a formal system of tenure at this time would be overkill.
>
> The Commission's consideration of tenure for military judges appears to have heightened the attention being given to the position of a military judge. Certainly, it is important that this position be viewed as career-enhancing. However, the grant of formalized tenure to military judges with consequent reduction in the present flexibility of military personnel assignments is not considered necessary to achieve this objective.

Argument against fixed terms

Three basic arguments have been advanced against legislation to require terms of office for military judges: first, that there is no evidence of a lack of independence that has prejudiced any defendant's right to a fair trial or appeal; second, that it would inject an element of rigidity into a system that requires flexibility both for operational reasons and to optimize long-range judge advocate career development; and third, "that it creates a situation where commands would be subject to the whim and caprice of a military judge whose actions are contrary to command authority, good order and discipline, but whose actions may be within permissible judicial discretion."

These arguments are unpersuasive. In the nature of things, it will rarely be the case that the kind of institutional flaw involved in untenured judges will produce the kind of "smoking gun" evidence of unfairness that is required to show actual prejudice. The judges themselves are hardly likely to admit to it, and it is improbably it could ever be demonstrated by extrinsic evidence. But beyond the search for specific prejudice to defendants, the system certainly pays a penalty because of the appearance of a lack of independence. This is reason enough to change the statute.

Nor is it sufficient to cite the fact that the Uniform Code of Military Justice (UCMJ) requires general court-martial judges to be "assigned and directly

---

[11] [n.20] *But see* Table 6.

responsible to" the judge advocate general or his designee[12] as proof that the code "ensures the independence of the military judge from local pressure or command influence."[13] Those arrangements have long been in place, but failed to prevent the kinds of abuses disclosed in *Ledbetter* and *U.S. Navy-Marine Corps Court of Military Review v. Carlucci* or in the results of the advisory commission's survey. Such an argument disregards the danger of undue influence emanating from within the military judicial structure itself. As Chief Judge Baum and Judge Barry of the Coast Guard Court of Military Review have cautioned. "[c]ommand influence can take many forms."[14]

Had there been no NMCMR case, one might be tempted to argue that the statutory terms of office of the judge advocate's general gives those officers sufficient independence that they would stand as a bulwark against undue influence on the military trial and appellate judges. This argument, too, does not persuade because only one of the four has, even on paper, the protection of a fixed term. The public policy that makes it advisable to have even the semblance of a term of office for those most senior of judge advocates — the need for independence — also applies to subordinates who serve in judicial billets. But the fact that a judge advocate general will already have achieved the highest rank attainable by an attorney suggests that, if anything, they are less in need of the protection Congress has afforded them than are their subordinates, whose independence might be affected by concern over retaliation affecting promotional opportunities. Thus, trial and appellate military judges present an a fortiori case for statutorily-protected terms.

As for the notion that military judges already have the practical equivalent of tenure since they can normally serve out a career leading to retirement by reason of longevity, that is like saying a civilian judge would be sufficiently protected if he or she were assured of a nonjudicial civil service job until eligible for retirement. Banishing a judge to a billet that pays the same but does not involve judging is no way to protect either the substance or the appearance of judicial independence.

The objection based on flexibility in personnel management is equally unpersuasive. Terms of office of only a few years' duration are as short [as] or shorter than the usual military tour of duty. As a result, they would have no detrimental effect on career development objectives. Such terms of office would, however, go beyond a mere tour of duty by guaranteeing that the individual will not be transferred prematurely — something no service has been willing to do to date. To the extent that exceptions might have to be made because of specific, unanticipated developments (e.g., if a particular officer were the only one with a narrow specialty and a need for that specialty arose in circumstances that could not have been anticipated), a safety valve provision would afford the services whatever flexibility they need.

A related concern is that terms of office might make the military bench unattractive, since it might thwart further advancement of officers who would

---

[12] [n.24] UCMJ art. 26(c), 10 U.S.C. § 826(c) (1988).

[13] [n.25] *The Practice of Criminal Law in the Military,* 30 FED. B. NEWS & J. 133, 134 (1984).

[14] [n.27] Baum and Barry, *supra* n.7, at 248 n.76.

otherwise be viable candidates for promotion to flag or general officer rank. This fear is unfounded, and probably is a result of the same concerns that gave rise to the demonstrably false impression among judge advocates that judicial assignments were non-career enhancing. Thus, in a 1985 report to the House Armed Services Committee, the Department of Defense reported that it had "reviewed recent promotion data and found no significant evidence that service on the military bench inhibited the career advancement of judge advocates. On the contrary, [the department] found that judge advocates with judicial experience generally fared better than their counterparts with respect to promotions."

Inadvisable as it plainly is to populate a bench with unwilling or disgruntled judges, moreover, the career-implications objection drops out of the equation if the terms of office correspond even roughly to current normal tours of duty. In addition, the objection can be effectively addressed as military value systems come to place a higher premium on service as a trial or appellate judge. Positive leadership from the highest levels of the armed services nonlegal communities can go far in this direction.

Other incentives such as ensuring at least one flag or general officer billet in the judicial structure of each service have been considered and rejected. A variant that one office with long experience in military justice has mentioned would be to retire as a brigadier general or rear admiral (lower half) any military judge retiring in the grade of colonel or naval captain, as is currently done for those with "long and distinguished" service as professors at the United States Military Academy.

The third argument against terms of office, quoted above, seems to rest on the internally inconsistent premise that a judge could render decisions which were infected with "whim and caprice" but which nonetheless were sustainable as the sound exercise of judicial discretion. If it proves to be the case that actions taken in the exercise of sound judicial discretion nonetheless subvert good order and discipline, then some adjustment should presumably be made in the pertinent rules of decision, rather than seeking to get rid of the judge in question. More likely, this argument is simply another way of complaining about improvident judicial appointments in the first place, and indeed it has been suggested that fixed terms of office are undesirable because they would only make it more cumbersome to remove judges who had been improvidently elevated to the bench.

Passing over the fact that the Department of Defense has stated its satisfaction with the quality of the military judiciary, this objection is reminiscent of the justification offered by the English Board of Trade in its fight to reduce the independence of judges in the American colonies by denying them tenure during good behavior. The board though it "necessary to preserve freedom of removal to improve the quality of judicial personnel in the colonies."[15] The

---

[15] [n.33] Smith, *An Independent Judiciary: The Colonial Background*, 124 U. PA. L. REV. 1104, 1137 (1976). Perhaps the basis for "the hostility [the Crown] displayed in 1759 and 1768 to colonial legislation which secured judicial salaries in return for tenure on good behavior . . . was, as imperial officials often said, the desire to keep a way open to displace incompetent colonial judges (whose numbers were said to be legion) with abler men, should any appear." Black, *Massachusetts and the Judges: Judicial Independence in Perspective*, 3 L. & HIST. Rev. at 109 n.27 (1985), citing Labaree, Royal Government 393-94.

simple answer to this objection would seem to be — assuming that a basis exists for dissatisfaction with the performance of significant numbers of military trial and appellate judges — to take greater pains in selecting them in the first place.

The practical consequences of a move to fixed terms of office of three and four years for military judges were explored in discovery in *Bozin v. Secretary of the Navy*. Although Judge Gasch concluded that the question of judicial tenure was for Congress to decide, the evidence showed that there would be no downside operational implications to such a change, and indeed, that it would save the taxpayers' money.[16] In short, the penalty the military justice system pays by continuing to rely on judges without tenure is all the more regrettable because it is unnecessary.

Suggested legislation

Congress should enact terms-of-office legislation generally along the lines recommended by the Advisory Commission dissenters. The legislation could be as simple as this:

> SECTION __. TERM OF OFFICE FOR MILITARY JUDGES. Section 826 of chapter 47 of Title 10, United States Code (article 26 of the Uniform Code of Military Justice), is amended by adding the following after subsection (e):

> (f) The regulations prescribed under subsection (a) shall provide a term of office of fixed duration for military judges of general courts-martial of not less than three years and a term of office of fixed duration for military judges of special courts-marital of not less than two years. Unless retired, released from active duty or decertified for cause and after notice and opportunity for hearing, no military judge shall, except in time of war, be transferred from duty as a military judge prior to the expiration of the term of office so prescribed except upon a detailed written finding by the judge advocate general setting forth specific and unanticipated military exigencies necessitating such transfer. The power to make such a finding shall be nondelegable, and a copy of any such finding shall be made available to any person upon request in accordance with section 552 of Title 5, United States Code.

> SECTION __. TERM OF OFFICE FOR APPELLATE MILITARY JUDGES. Section 866 of chapter 47 of Title 10, United States Code (article 66 of the Uniform Code of Military Justice), is amended by adding the following after subsection (h):

> (i) Each Judge Advocate General shall prescribe regulations providing a term of office of fixed duration of not less than three years for appellate military judges. Unless retired, released from active duty or decertified for cause and after notice and opportunity for hearing, no appellate military judge shall, except in time of war, be transferred from such duty prior to the expiration of the term of office so prescribed except upon a detailed written finding by the Judge Advocate

---

[16] [n.34] 657 F. Supp. 1463, 1467-68 (D.D.C. 1987).

General setting forth specific and unanticipated military exigencies necessitating such transfer. The power to make such a finding shall be nondelegable, and a copy of any such finding shall be made available to any person upon request in accordance with section 552 of Title 5, United States Code.

Such a bill would not supplant the authority of the judge advocates general with respect to the assignment of trial and appellate military judges, like other judge advocates. Thus, it would vest the safety-valve power in the judge advocate general, rather than the secretary concerned, as had been recommended by the dissenters. In keeping with their recommendation, however, Congress should provide that when the safety-valve power is employed (which should be extremely rare), the reasons must be stated with particularly. The standard of "specific and unanticipated military exigencies" would be intentionally narrower than "the good of the service" or "the needs of the service." As an added protection, Congress should require that any such findings be made a matter of record. Such a requirement would not be a novelty in military law, since detailed written findings are already required under the UCMJ where physical conditions or military exigencies prevent the assignment of a military judge or legally-trained defense counsel.

Second, Congress should not preclude reappointment of judges, although reappointments should be subject to the unusual minimum term of office provisions. Nor should terms-of-office legislation apply to lateral transfers from one general court-martial military judge billet to another or from one special court-martial military judge billet to another. It should, however, apply to transfers from a trial-level military judge billet, or vice versa.

Third, the legislation should acknowledge the armed forces' interest in flexibility in a number of respects. It should recognize that wartime conditions may require a different approach, although it is to be hoped that the armed services would — even in wartime — not wholly abandon fixed terms of office unless dictated by operational requirements or the demands of large-scale mobilization.

The judge advocates general should be afforded a suitable period in which to prepare transitional regulations and bring permanent regulations into effect. They should certainly have power to create staggered terms for incumbent judges. Because the personnel policies and needs of the armed services may differ from one branch to another, terms-of-office legislation should not require that the regulations be uniform, although one would expect that the judge advocates general would coordinate their efforts with a view of achieving regulations that are as uniform as practicable.

Fourth, given the importance of judicial independence, the implementing regulations should be made available to the Senate and House Committees on Armed Services prior to promulgation, and should be published for comment in the Federal Register, in keeping with Department of Defense policy on circulation of proposed changes to the *Manual for Courts-Martial.*

Fifth, terms-of-office legislation should make no exception for voluntary transfers from judicial duty prior to the end of a term of office. It would be difficult to protect against arm-twisting by personnel detailers or others that might in fact animate what purported to be "voluntary" transfers. Some requests for transfer may qualify for findings by the judge advocate general under this proposal, but the mere fact that a judge has requested a transfer should not be a sufficient basis for a finding.

Finally, the legislation should recognize that the services currently have disciplinary mechanisms applicable to trial and appellate military judges. No one may even be assigned to judicial functions without having first been "certified" as a military judge; actual assignment to judicial duties is a separate step. Protection in the form of a term of office of fixed duration is intended to be in addition to the procedural protections against arbitrary decertification. Of course, if a judge retires or is discharged or released from active duty or extended active duty, the judge's term of office should expire automatically. . . .

Table 1 Percent favoring some provision for guaranteed terms of office for Court of Military Review judges

Convening authorities	46
Staff judge advocates	46
Military judges	56
Court of Military Review judges	50
Trial counsel	68
Defense counsel	78

Table 2 Percent favoring some provision for guaranteed terms of office for military trial judges

Convening authorities	37
Staff judge advocates	42
Military judges	58
Court of Military Review judges	43
Trial counsel	61
Defense counsel	74

Table 3 Percent favoring *normal tour Length / 3-5 year term* of service for Court of Military Review judges

Convening authorities	59/32
Staff judge advocates	35/48
Military judges	34/41
Court of Military Review judges	50/23
Trial counsel	24/51
Defense counsel	20/51

Table 4 Percent favoring *normal tour Length / 3-5 year term* of service for general court-martial judges

Convening authorities	65/30
Staff judge advocates	43/44
Military judges	42/34
Court of Military Review judges	53/40
Trial counsel	34/45
Defense counsel	45/43

Table 5 Percent favoring *normal tour length / 3-5 year term* of service for special court-martial judges

Convening authorities	72/25
Staff judge advocates	56/39
Military judges	69/27
Court of Military Review judges	87/13
Trial counsel	54/38
Defense counsel	45/43

Table 6 Percent aware of instances in which a military judge was threatened with reassignment or actually reassigned because of his decisions

Convening authorities	-
Staff judge advocates	12
Military judges	25
Court of Military Review judges	24
Trial counsel	6
Defense counsel	7

Table 7 Percent answering yes to question in Table 6 who responded that it happened only *once/seldom*

Convening authorities	-
Staff judge advocates	54/42
Military judges	65/29
Court of Military Review judges	57/43
Trial counsel	71/25
Defense counsel	50/39

Table 8 Percent aware of a convening authority or subordinate acting for the commander criticizing a military judge directly or indirectly or through the military judge's superior for court-related decisions

Convening authorities	26
Staff judge advocates	46
Military judges	74
Court of Military Review judges	53
Trial counsel	36
Defense counsel	46

Table 9   Percent answering yes to question in Table 8 who responded that it happened only *once/seldom*

Convening authorities	20/51
Staff judge advocates	25/46
Military judges	26/43
Court of Military Review judges	24/24
Trial counsel	32/37
Defense counsel	25/34

Table 10   Percent of cases in which a convening authority criticized a judge that *affected/did not affect* the military judge's subsequent decisions

Convening authorities	4/44
Staff judge advocates	6/58
Military judges	4/62
Court of Military Review judges	0/59
Trial counsel	8/68
Defense counsel	8/41

Table 11   Percent believing a guaranteed term of office would *not at all/slightly* create the appearance of a more independent and fair military judiciary

Convening authorities	38/30
Staff judge advocates	28/31
Military judges	14/35
Court of Military Review judges	20/37
Trial counsel	19/29
Defense counsel	13/25

Table 12   Percent believing a guaranteed term of office would *not at all/slightly* actually create a more independent and fair military judiciary

Convening authorities	55/26
Staff judge advocates	50/33
Military judges	44/28
Court of Military Review judges	53/17
Trial counsel	40/30
Defense counsel	22/33

R. v. GÉNÉREUX
Supreme Court of Canada
[1992] 1 S.C.R. 259, 88 D.L.R.4th 100, 70 C.C.C.3d 1

[A corporal was convicted of possession of narcotics and absence without leave. The chief question presented on appeal was whether the court-martial was an independent and impartial tribunal as required by section 11(d) of the Canadian Charter of Rights and Freedoms.]

LAMER, C.J.

. . . Section 11(*d*) of the *Charter* guarantees a person who is charged with an offence the right

> to be presumed innocent until proven guilty according to law in a fair and public hearing by an independent and impartial tribunal;

I emphasize that the principles of independence and impartiality embraced by s. 11(*d*) seek to achieve a twofold objective: first, to ensure that a person is tried by a tribunal that is not biased in any way and is in a position to render a decision which is based solely on the merits of the case before it, according to law. The decision-maker should not be influenced by the parties to a case or by outside forces except to the extent that he or she is persuaded by submissions and arguments pertaining to the legal issues in dispute. Secondly, however, irrespective of any actual bias on the part of the tribunal, s. 11(*d*) seeks to maintain the integrity of the judicial system by preventing any reasonable apprehensions of such bias.

This Court has had the opportunity, recently, to define more precisely the content of the right to be tried by an independent and impartial tribunal. In particular, the Court has drawn a firm line between the concepts of independence and impartiality. In *Valente* [*v. The Queen*, [1985] 2 S.C.R. 673], Le Dain J. described the fundamental difference between these concepts. He noted that although the basic concerns of independence and impartiality are the same, the focus of each concept is different (at p. 685):

> Although there is obviously a close relationship between independence and impartiality, they are nevertheless separate and distinct

values or requirements. Impartiality refers to a state of mind or attitude of the tribunal in relation to the issues and the parties in a particular case. The word "impartial" . . . connotes absence of bias, actual or perceived. The word "independent" in s. 11(*d*) reflects or embodies the traditional constitutional value of judicial independence. As such, it connotes not merely a state of mind or attitude in the actual exercise of judicial functions, but a status or relationship to others, particularly to the executive branch of government, that rests on objective conditions or guarantees.

To assess the impartiality of a tribunal, the appropriate frame of reference is the "state of mind" of the decision-maker. The circumstances of an individual case must be examined to determine whether there is a reasonable apprehension that the decision-maker, perhaps by having a personal interest in the case, will be subjectively biased in the particular situation. The question of independence, in contrast, extends beyond the subjective attitude of the decision-maker. The independence of a tribunal is a matter of its status. The status of a tribunal must guarantee not only its freedom from interference by the executive and legislative branches of government but also by any other external force, such as business or corporate interests or other pressure groups. (See, for example, the recent judgment of this Court in *R. v. Lippé*, [1991] 2 S.C.R. 114). Dickson C.J. aptly summarized the essence of independence in *Beauregard, supra*, at p. 69:

> Historically, the generally accepted core of the principle of judicial independence has been the complete liberty of individual judges to hear and decide the cases that come before them; no outsider — be it government, pressure group, individual or even another judge — should interfere in fact, or attempt to interfere, with the way in which a judge conducts his or her case and makes his or her decision. This core continues to be central to the principle of judicial independence.
>
> . . . The ability of individual judges to make decisions in discrete cases free from external interference or influence continues . . . to be an important and necessary component of the principle.

Dickson C.J. noted that an additional purpose of judicial independence, over and above the principle that a tribunal have complete decision-making liberty in individual cases, is to allow the courts to fulfil their historical role as protector of constitutional law and values (p. 70).

It is important to note, at this stage, that the appellant does not question the impartiality of the General Court Martial by which he was tried. He does not suggest that the court martial was actually biased against him. Instead, his challenge is focused exclusively on the independence of the tribunal, in that under the structure of the court martial system as it existed at the time of his trial, a reasonable person would not have been satisfied that the General Court Martial was independent. . . .

The first essential condition of judicial independence, as defined in *Valente*, is security of tenure. This condition, like the other two, can be satisfied in a number of ways. What is essential is that the decision-maker be removable only for cause. In other words, at p. 698,

[t]he essence of security of tenure for purposes of s. 11(*d*) is a tenure, whether until an age of retirement, for a fixed term, or for a specific adjudicative task, that is secure against interference by the Executive or other appointing authority in a discretionary or arbitrary manner.

Similarly, s. 11(*d*) of the *Charter* requires that a decision-maker have a basic degree of financial security. The substance of this condition is as follows (at p. 704):

The essence of such security is that the right to salary and pension should be established by law and not be subject to arbitrary interference by the Executive in a manner that could affect judicial independence.

Within the limits of this requirement, however, the federal and provincial governments must retain the authority to design specific plans of remuneration that are appropriate to different types of tribunals. Consequently, a variety of schemes may equally satisfy the requirement of financial security, provided that the essence of the condition is protected.

The third essential condition of judicial independence is institutional independence with respect to matters of administration that relate directly to the exercise of the tribunal's judicial function. It is unacceptable that an external force be in a position to interfere in matters that are directly and immediately relevant to the adjudicative function, for example, assignment of judges, sittings of the court and court lists. Although there must of necessity be some institutional relations between the judiciary and the executive, such relations must not interfere with the judiciary's liberty in adjudicating individual disputes and in upholding the law and values of the Constitution. (See *MacKeigan v. Hickman, supra, per* McLachlin J.)

A tribunal will not satisfy the requirements of s. 11(*d*) of the *Charter* if it fails to respect these essential conditions of judicial independence. Although the conditions are susceptible to flexible application in order to suit the needs of different tribunals, the essence of each condition must be protected in every case.

I emphasize that an individual who wishes to challenge the independence of a tribunal for the purposes of s. 11(*d*) need not prove an actual lack of independence. Instead, the test for this purpose is the same as the test for determining whether a decision-maker is biased. The question is whether an informed and reasonable person would perceive the tribunal as independent. This approach was justified by this Court in *Valente* (at p. 689):

Although judicial independence is a status or relationship resting on objective conditions or guarantees, as well as a state of mind or attitude in the actual exercise of judicial functions, it is sound, I think, that the test for independence for purposes of s. 11(*d*) of the *Charter* should be, as for impartiality, whether the tribunal may be reasonably perceived as independent. Both independence and impartiality are fundamental not only to the capacity to do justice in a particular case but also to individual and public confidence in the administration of justice. Without that confidence the system cannot command the respect and acceptance that are essential to its effective operation. It is, therefore, important that a tribunal should be perceived as independent, as well as impartial, and that the test for independence should include that perception. The perception must, however, as I have suggested, be a perception of whether the tribunal enjoys the essential objective conditions or guarantees of judicial independence, and not a perception of how it will in fact act, regardless of whether it enjoys such conditions or guarantees.

With respect to the case at bar, therefore, the question is not whether the General Court Martial actually acted in a manner that may be characterized as independent and impartial. The appropriate question is whether the tribunal, from the objective standpoint of a reasonable and informed person, will be perceived as enjoying the essential conditions of independence.

I will now consider the General Court Martial system as it existed at the time of the appellant's trial in order to assess its consistency with s. 11(*d*) of the *Charter*. I should add, however, that since the appellant's trial took place various amendments have been made to the *Queen's Regulations and Orders for the Canadian Forces* ("Q.R. & O.") concerning the constitution of the General Court Martial. These have gone a considerable way towards addressing the concerns I express below.

3. Were the Appellant's Rights under Section 11(d) of the Charter Infringed in the Proceedings of the General Court Martial in this Case?

(a) Introduction

The appellant concedes that a separate system of military law, along with a distinct regime of service tribunals to apply this law, is consistent with s. 11(*d*) of the *Charter*. He agrees it is necessary that military discipline be enforced effectively and speedily by tribunals whose members are associated with the military and therefore sensitive to its basic concerns. At the same time, he submits that, within the inherent limits of an institution having the power to discipline its own members, the adjudicative or disciplinary body must meet the standards of independence and impartiality required by s. 11(*d*). The General Court Martial, in his view, fails this test.

I agree that this issue gives rise to two distinct questions. First, is a parallel system of military tribunals, staffed by members of the military who are aware of and sensitive to military concerns, *by its very nature* inconsistent with s. 11(*d*) of the *Charter*? Secondly, if the first question is answered in the negative, is the General Court Martial, as constituted at the time of the trial under the *National Defence Act* and regulations, an independent tribunal for the purposes of s. 11(*d*)? The appellant correctly, in my opinion, concedes that the answer to the first question is no. Nonetheless, I believe that it is useful to consider the extent to which, and the reasons why, the *Charter* permits a parallel system of justice, such as that found under the *National Defence Act*, to exist alongside the ordinary criminal courts. Indeed, the reasons for the existence of such a parallel system of courts provide guides as to the system's proper limits. It is appropriate to commence this inquiry with a brief examination of the reasons of this Court in *MacKay v. The Queen, supra.*

(b) The General Position of Military Law and Tribunals
Under Section 11(d) of the Charter

In *MacKay v. The Queen, supra*, a majority of this Court found that the trial of a member of the Canadian Armed Forces by a Standing Court Martial does not violate his or her rights under ss. 1(*b*) and 2(*f*) of the *Canadian Bill of Rights*. Sections 1(*b*) and 2(*f*) guarantee an individual the right to equality before the law and to be tried by an independent and impartial tribunal. . . .

MacKay v. The Queen assists us by revealing various concerns with the independence and impartiality of the court martial system. The question raised in this appeal, however, is not resolved by this earlier case. First, the majority of this Court in *MacKay* seems to have applied a subjective test. It asked whether the Standing Court Martial actually acted in an independent and impartial manner. This is not, in light of *Valente*, the appropriate test. Secondly, we must, in this appeal, apply the jurisprudence of this Court with respect to s. 11(*d*) of the *Charter*. We must now therefore undertake an analysis that was not undertaken in *MacKay*.

(b) The Purpose of a System of Military Tribunals

The purpose of a separate system of military tribunals is to allow the Armed Forces to deal with matters that pertain directly to the discipline, efficiency and morale of the military. The safety and well-being of Canadians depends considerably on the willingness and readiness of a force of men and women to defend against threats to the nation's security. To maintain the Armed Forces in a state of readiness, the military must be in a position to enforce internal discipline effectively and efficiently. Breaches of military discipline must be dealt with speedily and, frequently, punished more severely than would be the case if a civilian engaged in such conduct. As a result, the military has its own Code of Service Discipline to allow it to meet its particular disciplinary needs. In addition, special service tribunals, rather than the ordinary courts, have been given jurisdiction to punish breaches of the Code of Service Discipline. Recourse to the ordinary criminal courts would, as a general rule, be inadequate to serve the particular disciplinary needs of the military. There is thus a need for separate tribunals to enforce special disciplinary standards in the military. I agree, in this regard, with the comments of Cattanach J. in *MacKay v. Rippon*, [1978] 1 F.C. 233 (T.D.), at pp. 235-36:

> Without a code of service discipline the armed forces could not discharge the function for which they were created. In all likelihood those who join the armed forces do so in time of war from motives of patriotism and in time of peace against the eventuality of war. To function efficiently as a force there must be prompt obedience to all lawful orders of superiors, concern, support for and concerted action with their comrades and a reverence for and a pride in the traditions of the service. All members embark upon rigorous training to fit themselves physically and mentally for the fulfilment of the role they have chosen and paramount in that there must be rigid adherence to discipline.

> Many offences which are punishable under civil law take on a much more serious connotation as a service offence and as such warrant more severe punishment. Examples of such are manifold such as theft

from a comrade. In the service that is more reprehensible since it detracts from the essential *esprit de corps*, mutual respect and trust in comrades and the exigencies of the barrack room life style. Again for a citizen to strike another a blow is assault punishable as such but for a soldier to strike a superior officer is much more serious detracting from discipline and in some circumstances may amount to mutiny. The converse, that is for an officer to strike a soldier is also a serious service offence. In civilian life it is the right of the citizen to refuse to work but for a soldier to do so is mutiny, a most serious offence, in some instances punishable by death. Similarly a citizen may leave his employment at any time and the only liability he may incur is for breach of contract but for a soldier to do so is the serious offence of absence without leave and if he does not intend to return the offence is desertion.

Such a disciplinary code would be less effective if the military did not have its own courts to enforce the code's terms. However, I share the concerns expressed by Laskin C.J. and McIntyre J. in *MacKay v. The Queen* with the problems of independence and impartiality which are inherent in the very nature of military tribunals. In my opinion, the necessary association between the military hierarchy and military tribunals — the fact that members of the military serve on the tribunals — detracts from the absolute independence and impartiality of such tribunals. As I shall elaborate in greater detail below, the members of a court martial, who are the triers of fact, and the judge advocate, who presides over the proceedings much like a judge, are chosen from the ranks of the military. The members of the court martial will also be at or higher in rank than captain. Their training is designed to insure that they are sensitive to the need for discipline, obedience and duty on the part of the members of the military and also to the requirement for military efficiency. Inevitably, the court martial represents to an extent the concerns of those persons who are responsible for the discipline and morale of the military. In my opinion, a reasonable person might well consider that the military status of a court martial's members would affect its approach to the matters that come before it for decision.

This, in itself, is not sufficient to constitute a violation of s. 11(*d*) of the *Charter*. In my opinion the *Charter* was not intended to undermine the existence of self-disciplinary organizations such as, for example, the Canadian Armed Forces and the Royal Canadian Mounted Police. The existence of a parallel system of military law and tribunals, for the purpose of enforcing discipline in the military, is deeply entrenched in our history and is supported by the compelling principles discussed above. An accused's right to be tried by an independent and impartial tribunal, guaranteed by s. 11(*d*) of the *Charter*, must be interpreted in this context.

In this regard, I agree with the conclusion reached by James B. Fay in Part IV of his considered study of Canadian military law ("Canadian Military Criminal Law: An Examination of Military Justice" (1975), 23 *Chitty's L.J.* 228, at p. 248):

In a military organization, such as the Canadian Forces, there cannot ever be a truly independent military judiciary; the reason is that the

military officer must be involved in the administration of discipline at
all levels. A major strength of the present military judicial system
rests in the use of trained military officers, who are also legal officers,
to sit on courts martial in judicial roles. If this connection were to be
severed, (and true independence could only be achieved by such sever-
ance), the advantage of independence of the judge that might thereby
be achieved would be more than offset by the disadvantage of the eventual loss by the judge of the military knowledge and experience which
today helps him to meet his responsibilities effectively. Neither the
Forces nor the accused would benefit from such a separation.

In my view, any interpretation of s. 11(*d*) must take place in the context of
other *Charter* provisions. In this connection, I regard it as relevant that s. 11(*f*)
of the *Charter* points to a different content to certain legal rights in different
institutional settings:

11. Any person charged with an offence has the right . . .

(*f*) except in the case of an offence under military law tried before a
military tribunal, to the benefit of trial by jury where the maximum
punishment for the offence is imprisonment for five years or a more
severe punishment.

Section 11(*f*) reveals, in my opinion, that the *Charter* does contemplate the
existence of a system of military tribunals with jurisdiction over cases governed by military law. The s. 11(*d*) guarantees must therefore be construed
with this in mind. The content of the constitutional guarantee of an independent and impartial tribunal may well be different in the military context than
it would be in the context of a regular criminal trial. However, any such parallel system is itself subject to *Charter* scrutiny, and if its structure violates
the basic principles of s. 11(*d*) it cannot survive unless the infringements can
be justified under s. 1.

The first step in our inquiry, therefore, must be to consider whether the proceedings of the General Court Martial infringed the appellant's rights under
s. 11(*d*) of the *Charter*. The status of a General Court Martial, in an objective
sense, as revealed by the statutory and regulatory provisions which governed
its constitution and proceedings at the time of the appellant's trial, must be
examined to determine whether the institution has the essential characteristics of an independent and impartial tribunal. In the course of this examination the appropriate test to be applied under s. 11(*d*) should be borne in mind:
would a reasonable person, familiar with the constitution and structure of the
General Court Martial, conclude that the tribunal enjoys the protections necessary for judicial independence? . . .

(iii) Judge Advocate

Members of the Legal Branch of the Forces who have undergone special
training to qualify as military judges may be appointed by the Judge Advocate
General to positions in the Chief Judge Advocate's Division within the Office
of the Judge Advocate General. There, they perform legal duties related to the
judicial function, and may be called upon to preside at courts martial. When it
is proposed to convene a General Court Martial, the appointment of the judge

advocate is made by the Judge Advocate General from officers serving in the Chief Judge Advocate's Division. The length of postings to the Chief Judge Advocate's Division is controlled by the Judge Advocate General. Officers serving in that Division may be re-posted to other legal duties within the Judge Advocate General's Office, or elsewhere within the Legal Branch of the Forces.

The judge advocate officiates at a General Court Martial much as a judge presides over a hearing in an ordinary court of law. He is not, however, the trier of fact. The judge advocate is called upon to determine questions of law or mixed law and fact whether they arise before or after the commencement of the trial (s. 192(4) of the Act). If the permission of the president is obtained, he may address the members of the court martial on such matters as he deems necessary or desirable (art. 112.05(4a) Q.R. & O.). In certain circumstances, the president may direct the judge advocate to rule on a question of law or mixed law and fact (art. 112.06 Q.R. & O.). The court may only disregard the opinion of the judge advocate on questions of law and procedure "for very weighty reasons" (art. 112.54 Q.R. & O.).

Section 188 of the Act requires an oath to be taken by each of the members of the court martial and by the judge advocate before the commencement of proceedings. These persons must swear, in the relevant oath, to carry out their responsibilities "without partiality, favour or affection" (arts. 112.15 and 112.16 Q.R. & O.).

(c) The Independence of the General Court Martial

I will now examine the status of the General Court Martial in terms of the three conditions of judicial independence described in *Valente*. As noted above, these criteria are security of tenure, financial independence, and institutional independence. The first two criteria are personal to the adjudicator in terms of his or her direct relationship with the executive, while the third criterion relates to the independence of the tribunal considered as an institution.

(i) Security of Tenure

At the time of the appellant's trial, the Judge Advocate General had the authority to appoint the judge advocate at a General Court Martial (s. 169 of the Act and art. 111.22 Q.R. & O.). The Judge Advocate General is a barrister or advocate of not less than 10 years standing who is appointed by the Governor in Council (s. 9 of the Act). The Act does not require the Judge Advocate General to be a member of the Armed Forces, but, in practice, he has always been chosen from the ranks of the military. Captain Charles F. Blair, in an affidavit that was filed in this Court by the respondent, describes an important component of the Judge Advocate General's role as follows:

> 34. By historical custom of the service, and by written terms of reference, the Judge Advocate General is responsible for the provision of a military judiciary to take the judicial role in the military justice system provided for in the *National Defence Act*. To that end, he has established and maintains the Chief Judge Advocate's division of the Office of the Judge Advocate General. . . . [T]hat division consists of the Chief Judge Advocate (a military officer in the rank of Colonel or its naval equivalent Captain), a Deputy Chief Judge Advocate

(Lieutenant-Colonel or Commander), and two Assistant Chief Judge Advocates (also Lieutenant-Colonels or Commanders). All of these officers have been formally qualified as military judges, through the process of qualification, training, and experience described below.

Captain Blair also indicates that the Office of the Judge Advocate General maintains a reserve of legal officers who are similarly qualified as military judges. Judge advocates at General Courts Martial are appointed from this pool of military judges. Captain Blair notes that although the Judge Advocate General formally appoints a judge advocate, this appointment is made on the recommendation of the Chief Judge Advocate. Lastly, I note that officers holding a position with the Office of the Judge Advocate General are directly responsible to the Office for the performance of their responsibilities. They are, at the same time, subject to the orders of senior commanders in their region. No order by a senior commander, however, should interfere substantially with the primary functions of the officer. Furthermore, no such officer shall intermingle judicial and non-judicial functions; if an officer is consulted on a pre-trial matter, that officer shall not participate in the trial on that matter (*Canadian Forces Administrative Orders* 4-1).

Unlike the situation of the ordinary courts, a judge advocate is appointed to sit on a General Court Martial on an *ad hoc* basis. This temporary appointment reflects the nature of the General Court Martial, which is convened when necessary to deal with a breach of the Code of Service Discipline. At the conclusion of this type of court martial, the judge advocate and members return to their usual roles within the military. For the members of the General Court Martial, this means a return to their regular duties as officers. For the judge advocate, it means a return to legal duties within the Office of the Judge Advocate General.

It is my conclusion that this arrangement does not guarantee a judge advocate sufficient security of tenure to satisfy the requirements of s. 11(*d*) of the *Charter*. The *National Defence Act* and regulations fail to protect a judge advocate against the discretionary or arbitrary interference of the executive. The Judge Advocate General, who had the legal authority to appoint a judge advocate at a General Court Martial, is not independent of but is rather a part of the executive. Indeed, the Judge Advocate General serves as the agent of the executive in supervising prosecutions.

Furthermore, under the regulations in force at the time of the appellant's trial, the judge advocate was appointed solely on a case by case basis. As a result, there was no objective guarantee that his or her career as military judge would not be affected by decisions tending in favour of an accused rather than the prosecution. A reasonable person might well have entertained an apprehension that a legal officer's occupation as a military judge would be affected by his or her performance in earlier cases. Nothing in what I have said here should be taken to impugn the integrity of the judge advocate who presided at the appellant's trial, nor to suggest that judge advocates in fact are influenced by career concerns in the discharge of their adjudicative duties. The point is, however, that a reasonable person could well have entertained the apprehension that the person chosen as judge advocate had been selected because he or she had satisfied the interests of the executive, or at least has not seriously disappointed the executive's expectations, in previous proceedings. Any system of military tribunals which does not banish such apprehensions will be defective in terms of s. 11(*d*). At the very least, therefore, the essential condition of security of tenure, in this context, requires security from interference by the executive for a fixed period of time. An officer's position as military judge should not, during a certain period of time, depend on the discretion of the executive.

It was stated in *Valente* that according a decision-maker tenure for a "specific adjudicative task" may be a sufficient guarantee of security of tenure. I do not believe that this statement is applicable in this context. Although a General Court Martial is convened on an *ad hoc* basis, it is not a "specific adjudicative task." The General Court Martial is a recurring affair. Military judges who act periodically as judge advocates must therefore have a tenure that is beyond the interference of the executive for a fixed period of time. Consequently, security of tenure during the period of a specific General Court Martial, achieved by the fact that no provision of the statute or regulations allows for the removal of a judge advocate during a trial (except if the judge advocate is unable to attend: art. 112.64(2) Q.R. & O.), is not adequate protection for the purposes of s. 11(*d*) of the *Charter*.

I do not, however, consider that s. 11(*d*) requires that military judges be accorded tenure until retirement during good behaviour equivalent to that enjoyed by judges of the regular criminal courts. Officers who serve as military judges are members of the military establishment, and will probably not wish to be cut off from promotional opportunities within that career system. It would not therefore be reasonable to require a system in which military judges are appointed until the age of retirement. (See, in this regard, the judgment of the Court Martial Appeal Court in *R. v. Ingebrigtson*, (1990), 61 C.C.C. (3d) 541, at p. 555.) The requirements of s. 11(*d*) are sensitive to the context in which an adjudicative task is performed. The *Charter* does not require, nor would it be appropriate to impose, uniform institutional standards on all tribunals subject to s. 11(*d*).

It may very well be true (and I am quite prepared to believe this) that, in practice, under the rules that were in effect at the time of the appellant's trial, the Judge Advocate General appointed a judge advocate for a General Court Martial only on the recommendation of the Chief Judge Advocate. The judge advocate would therefore be appointed on the basis of merit and not by the arbitrary decision of the executive, that is, the Judge Advocate General. I emphasize, however, that the independence of a tribunal is to be determined on the basis of the *objective* status of that tribunal. This objective status is revealed by an examination of the legislative provisions governing the tribunal's constitution and proceedings, irrespective of the actual good faith of the adjudicator. Practice or tradition, as mentioned by this Court in *Valente* (p. 702), is not sufficient to support a finding of independence where the status of the tribunal itself does not support such a finding.

I would therefore conclude that, at the time the appellant was tried, the judge advocate at the General Court Martial did not enjoy sufficient security of tenure to satisfy s. 11(*d*) of the *Charter*.

However, I would note that recent amendments to the Q.R. & O., which came into force on January 22, 1991, subsequent to the trial in this case, appear to correct the primary deficiencies of the judge advocate's security of tenure. Under new art. 4.09 Q.R. & O., any officer who may act as judge advocate at a General Court Martial is first appointed to the position of a military trial judge for a period of two to four years. In addition, art. 111.22 Q.R. & O. now provides that the Chief Military Trial Judge, and not the Judge Advocate General, has formal authority to appoint a judge advocate at a General Court Martial. These are not before us and I refer to them solely for the purpose of completeness.

(ii) Financial Security

The promotions and pay rates of Canadian Armed Forces personnel are determined in accordance with regulations adopted under the *National Defence Act*. Regulations governing promotions are made by the Governor in Council (s. 28 of the Act). Regulations governing pay and allowances are made by the Treasury Board (s. 35 of the Act).

The president and other members of a General Court Martial are not compensated, above their usual salary as officers in the Armed Forces, for serving at the court martial. It therefore appears that the criteria of financial security, as described in *Valente*, cannot be applied easily to the General Court Martial. This condition is, nonetheless, relevant in these circumstances. The requirement of financial security will not be satisfied if the executive is in a position to reward or punish the conduct of the members and judge advocate at a General Court Martial by granting or withholding benefits in the form of promotions and salary increases or bonuses.

There were no formal prohibitions, at the time that the appellant was tried by the General Court Martial, against evaluating an officer on the basis of his or her performance at a General Court Martial. An officer's performance evaluation could potentially reflect his superior's satisfaction or dissatisfaction with his conduct at a court martial. Consequently, by granting or denying a salary increase or bonus on the basis of a performance evaluation, the executive might effectively reward or punish an officer for his or her performance as a member of a General Court Martial. This interference with the independence of the members of a General Court Martial would be an infringement of s. 11(*d*) of the *Charter*. Once again, this is not to suggest that the executive *in fact* sought to influence the outcomes of court martial proceedings by the granting or withholding of salary increases, but rather, that a reasonable person might have entertained such an apprehension under the system as constituted at the time of the appellant's trial.

Similar considerations apply in the case of the judge advocate. The executive's evaluation of a legal officer's performance as judge advocate directly affects his or her salary. The remuneration plan for legal officers is described in Captain Blair's affidavit:

> 45. Military judges, like all other legal officers in the Canadian Forces, are paid pursuant to regulations made by the Treasury Board and contained in Article 204.218 of Queen's Regulations and Orders for the Canadian Forces. . . . That pay plan contemplates the establish-

ment by Treasury Board of ranges of pay for legal officers in certain ranks, and for the movement of individual officers within those ranges, in accordance with both their time in rank, and their merit as assessed by a merit board. The pay of legal officers is reviewed annually, or sometimes less often, with the pay ranges and annual increase based on time in rank being set exclusively by the Treasury Board, without reference to any individual's performance.

A military legal officer's salary is thus determined in part, within the range established by the Treasury Board, according to a performance evaluation. The executive's opinion of an officer's performance as a military judge may therefore be a factor in the final determination of his or her salary. Again, this possibility of executive interference is inconsistent with s. 11(d).

I note that the recent amendments to the Q.R. & O. now prohibit an officer's performance as a member of a General Court Martial or as a military trial judge from being used to determine his qualification for a promotion or rate of pay (arts. 26.10 and 26.11 Q.R. & O.) In my view, this is sufficient to correct this aspect of the deficiencies of the system under which the appellant was tried.

I therefore conclude that the judge advocate and members of the General Court Martial did not enjoy sufficient financial security, for the purposes of s. 11(d), at the time of the appellant's trial. The executive clearly had the ability to interfere with the salaries and promotional opportunities of officers serving as judge advocates and members at a court martial. Although the practice of the executive may very well have been to respect the independence of the participants at the court martial in this respect, this was not sufficient to correct the weaknesses in the tribunal's status. A reasonable person would perceive that financial security, an essential condition of judicial independence, was not present in this case.

(iii) Institutional Independence

. . . An examination of the legislation governing the General Court Martial reveals that military officers, who are responsible to their superiors in the Department of Defence, are intimately involved in the proceedings of the tribunal. This close involvement is, in my opinion, inconsistent with s. 11(d) of the *Charter*. It undermines the notion of institutional independence that was articulated by this Court in *Valente*. The idea of a separate system of military tribunals obviously requires substantial relations between the military hierarchy and the military judicial system. The principle of institutional independence, however, requires that the General Court Martial be free from external interference with respect to matters that relate directly to the tribunal's judicial function. It is important that military tribunals be as free as possible from the interference of the members of the military hierarchy, that is, the persons who are responsible for maintaining the discipline, efficiency and morale of the Armed Forces.

In my opinion, certain characteristics of the General Court Martial system would be very likely to cast into doubt the institutional independence of the tribunal in the mind of a reasonable and informed person. First, the authority that convenes the court martial (the "convening authority") may be the

Minister, the Chief of the Defence Staff, an officer commanding a command, upon receipt of an application from a commanding officer, or another service authority appointed by the Minister (art. 111.05 Q.R. & O.). The convening authority, an integral part of the military hierarchy and therefore of the executive, decides when a General Court Martial shall take place. The convening authority appoints the president and other members of the General Court Martial and decides how many members there shall be in a particular case. The convening authority, or an officer designated by the convening authority, also appoints, with the concurrence of the Judge Advocate General, the prosecutor (art. 111.23 Q.R. & O.). This fact further undermines the institutional independence of the General Court Martial. It is not acceptable, in my opinion, that the convening authority, i.e., the executive, who is responsible for appointing the prosecutor, also have the authority to appoint members of the court martial, who serve as the triers of fact. At a minimum, I consider that where the same representative of the executive, the "convening authority," appoints both the prosecutor and the triers of fact, the requirements of s. 11(d) will not be met.

Secondly, the appointment of the judge advocate by the Judge Advocate General (art. 111.22 Q.R. & O.), undermines the institutional independence of the General Court Martial. The close ties between the Judge Advocate General, who is appointed by the Governor in Council, and the executive, are obvious. To comply with s. 11(d) of the *Charter*, the appointment of a military judge to sit as judge advocate at a particular General Court Martial should be in the hands of an independent and impartial judicial officer. The effective appointment of the judge advocate by the executive could, in objective terms, raise a reasonable apprehension as to the independence and impartiality of the tribunal. However, as I have concluded above, I consider that the new arts. 4.09 and 111.22 of the amended Q.R. & O. have largely remedied this defect to the extent required in the context of military tribunals.

I conclude, therefore, that the constitution and structure of the General Court Martial at the time of the appellant's trial did not meet the minimum requirements of s. 11(d) of the *Charter*. Unless this infringement of s. 11(d) can be justified under s. 1 the appeal must be allowed. However, before proceeding to s. 1, it will be convenient to deal with certain other submissions made by the appellant, which, while not strictly necessary to the outcome of this appeal, I feel should be dealt with in the interests of clarity. . . .

8. Section 1 of the Charter

The appellant's alternative grounds of appeal having been dealt with, we are left with the s. 11(d) violation flowing from the institutional setting in which he was tried. Unless this infringement can be justified under s. 1 of the *Charter*, this appeal must be allowed.

It is now settled that on an inquiry under s. 1 the appropriate starting point is the analysis of Dickson C.J. in *R. v. Oakes*, [1986] 1 S.C.R. 103. As I have already indicated in these reasons, the goal of maintaining order and discipline within the special regime constituted by the Armed Forces of this country is an important one. Indeed, the existence of a separate system of military tribunals with jurisdiction over matters governed by military law is contemplated in the wording of s. 11(*f*) of the *Charter*. In my view, the necessity of maintaining a high level of discipline in the special conditions of military life is a sufficiently substantial societal concern to satisfy the first arm of the proportionality test in *Oakes*.

However, I am equally convinced that the scheme of the General Court Martial as it existed at the time of the appellant's trial cannot pass the second stage of the test. I am prepared to admit that there may well exist a rational connection between the challenged structure of the General Court Martial and the goal of the maintenance of military discipline in the Armed Forces. However, it is not necessary for me to address this issue in any detail, because I am of the opinion that a trial before a tribunal which does not meet the requirements of s. 11(*d*) of the *Charter* will only pass the second arm of the proportionality test in *Oakes* in the most extraordinary of circumstances. A period of war or insurrection might constitute such circumstances. However, during periods of normality, the scheme of the General Court Martial, as it was at the time of the appellant's trial, went far beyond what was necessary to accomplish the goals for which it was established. Indeed, the amendments to the Q.R. & O. of January, 1991, which I have indicated constituted significant improvements over the regime under which the appellant was tried, attest to this fact.

It is not necessary, under normal circumstances, to try alleged military offenders before a tribunal in which the judge, the prosecutor, and the triers of fact, are all chosen by the executive to serve at that particular trial. Nor can it be said to be necessary that promotional opportunities, and hence the financial prospects within the military establishment, for officers serving on such tribunals should be capable of being affected by senior officers' assessments of their performance in the course of the trial. I note again that the amendments to the Q.R. & O. which came into affect after the appellant's trial have alleviated this latter problem. However, this appeal falls to be decided on the constitutionality of the structure of the General Court Martial in place at the time of trial.

In short, the structure of the General Court Martial with which we are here concerned incorporated features which, in the eyes of a reasonable person, could call the independence and impartiality of the tribunal into question, and are not necessary to attain either military discipline or military justice. This structure, therefore cannot be said to have impaired the appellant's s. 11(*d*) rights "as little as possible." The proportionality test prescribed in *Oakes* is thus not satisfied.

It follows that the General Court Martial before which the appellant was tried infringed the appellant's s. 11(*d*) right to a trial before an independent and impartial tribunal in a manner that cannot be justified under s. 1 of the *Charter*. The appeal must therefore be allowed. . . .

Stevenson, J.

I have read the judgments of Lamer C.J. and while I agree with his conclusion, I do not share his reasoning. . . .

Institutional Independence Within the Court Martial System

Given an *ad hoc* military tribunal, composed of military personnel, operating within a military hierarchy, what institutional independence should the *Charter* ensure?

The tribunal must be free to make its decisions on the merits.

Given that the members of the tribunal are necessarily operating within the military service, that means to me that no one who has an interest in seeing that the prosecution succeeds or fails should be in a position of influence.

Clearly, the accused and the "complainants" have that interest. That interest would, in my view, extend to the prosecutor and military personnel engaged in the investigation or in formulating or approving the charges.

I suggest that there must be found some point within the military hierarchy where the officer or official has no real or apparent concern about the outcome. There is, at that point, sufficient independence. I leave aside cases in which it can be shown to the contrary because the *Charter* provisions would clearly apply in such a case. In my view, the convening authority is sufficiently far removed from the investigative and complaint stages to convene the court martial and appoint its members.

I am concerned that the convening authority also appoints the prosecutor. This is done with the concurrence of the Judge Advocate General. With the scheme in force when this matter was tried, the judge advocate also was appointed by the Judge Advocate General.

I agree with the Chief Justice that the convergence of responsibilities in appointing the prosecutor and judge advocate is objectionable as it fails to meet the requirement that those appointing the tribunal have no apparent concern in the outcome.

In saying this, I do not do so on the basis that the Judge Advocate General and the convening authority are all part of the executive, but that there is at least an appearance that those responsible for choosing the tribunal, namely the convening authority and the Judge Advocate General, have an interest in the nomination of the prosecutor and, in effect, in a successful prosecution.

Financial Security

Again, I view this issue not from the point of view of "executive independence," but from the point of view of sufficient independence in the setting of military tribunals. Under the scheme in force when these proceedings took place there was nothing to prevent those who made decisions in relation to salaries and promotions from taking into consideration the outcome of a court martial. This could well include persons with an interest in that outcome. In my view, those who could be seen as having some interest in the outcome could be excluded from the salary or promotion processes, or the performance of court martial duties could be readily excluded from consideration thus obviating any apparent infringement.

I would, with these modifications, concur in the Chief Justice's disposition of the appeal.

L'HEUREUX-DUBE, J., dissenting.

. . . The position of the Chief Justice, as I understand it, is two-fold. First, given that the judge advocate for a particular case was, at the time of trial, chosen by the Judge Advocate General who was in turn appointed by the Governor in Council, there is insufficient protection from arbitrary interference from the executive because the Judge Advocate General is part of the executive. Second, there are no guarantees that a judge's career will not be affected by his or her performance on tribunals. Hence, there exists a reasonable apprehension that the judge advocate was chosen because of an expectation that he or she would satisfy the interests of the executive. To be free from this apprehension, according to the Chief Justice, there would have to be security from this potential interference for a fixed period of time. He continues that the caveat contained in Le Dain J.'s formulation pertaining to a "specific adjudicative task" is inapplicable because the General Court Martial is "a recurring affair."

I respectfully disagree with this reasoning. With respect to the first concern, it seems to me that the Chief Justice is arguing that, by definition, the performance of a judge advocate cannot be free from arbitrary interference from the executive because he or she is appointed by the executive. I cannot bring myself to believe that this is sufficient to constitute a violation of s. 11(*d*). The framers of the *Charter* could not have intended that provision to prevent the executive from appointing members of the judiciary when other sections of the Constitution explicitly give the executive authority to do so. Turning then to the second argument, while in some respects career aspirations might somehow relate to the requirement of security of tenure, to my mind they are more properly dealt with under the notion of financial security and I will discuss them in due course.

My own view is that the General Court Martial is a "specific adjudicative task" as contemplated by Le Dain J. in *Valente*. The *National Defence Act* and its accompanying regulations clearly call for the *ad hoc* convening of a General Court Martial, its functioning, and then its dissolution. While there may be various General Courts Martial sitting all over this country and even overseas, the legislation contemplates each as an entirely distinct entity. It simply does not reflect the Act and regulations to assert that each and every one of those General Courts Martial is part of a "recurring affair" as opposed to constituting a "specific adjudicative task" in its own right.

Furthermore, while the General Court Martial is taking place there are sufficient guarantees of the tenure of the persons involved from the executive. Article 112.64(2) of the *Queen's Regulations and Orders for the Canadian Forces* ("Q.R. & O.") provides, *inter alia*:

> (2) If a judge advocate has been appointed and is for any cause unable to attend, the president shall adjourn the court and report the circumstances to the convening authority. The convening authority may authorize the court to stand adjourned until the judge advocate is able to attend. If the judge advocate is unable to attend or if the convening authority considers delay to be inexpedient, the convening authority may:

(a) if the court is a General Court Martial,

> (i) request the Judge Advocate General to appoint another judge advocate and, after the Judge Advocate General has appointed the other judge advocate, direct the trial to proceed, or

> (ii) dissolve the court;

While of course conferring a certain amount of discretion on the convening authority, this article also acts as something of a limitation. Only if the judge advocate is, for some reason, unable to attend the General Court Martial, may the convening authority appoint a replacement judge advocate. Otherwise, once appointed, the judge advocate is at complete liberty to proceed with the undertaking with which he or she has been entrusted. No other provision in the Q.R. & O. allows for the removal of the judge advocate once he or she has been appointed. This provides sufficient insulation to the judge advocate to perform his or her duty because it means that, to interfere, the convening authority or other member of the executive would have to act unlawfully. Similar views were expressed by Cavanagh J. in *Schick v. The Queen* (1987), 4 C.M.A.R. 540, at p. 548. I would conclude, therefore, that a reasonable person would not be given cause to question the independence of the General Court Martial based on a purported lack of security of tenure.

Financial Security

In *Valente, supra*, at p. 704, Le Dain J. enunciated this criterion in the following manner:

> The essence of such security is that the right to salary and pension should be established by law and not be subject to arbitrary interference by the Executive in a manner that could affect judicial independence.

The Chief Justice is of the view that the provisions in place at the time of trial give rise to a reasonable apprehension that this essential condition was not met. He points out that promotions and pay rates are established according to regulations promulgated either by the Governor in Council or by the Treasury Board. Furthermore, since the President and the other members of the tribunal were not compensated above and beyond their usual salary, which depends upon their rank and therefore upon merit, the lack of formal prohibitions on taking performance on a military tribunal into account in assessing merit results in a reasonable apprehension that career concerns might motivate decisions favourable to the prosecution. The same difficulty, in his view, applied to judge advocates. Again I respectfully disagree. In my view, this is not problematic in the least having already been contemplated in *Valente*.

In *Valente* the same type of issue was raised when the appellant argued that a provision which enabled Provincial Court (Criminal Division) judges to be reappointed at the pleasure of the Lieutenant Governor in Council upon attaining the age of retirement violated the constitutional requirement of judicial independence because, *inter alia*, the need in some cases of such a reappointment to complete entitlement to a pension could give rise to a reasonable perception of dependence for one's financial well-being upon the executive (*Valente, supra,* at p. 698).

Le Dain J. took the position, and I agree with him, that the effect of the executive having control over certain discretionary benefits or advantages did not go to the heart of s. 11(*d*). At page 714 he states:

> While it may well be desirable that such discretionary benefits or advantages, to the extent that they should exist at all, should be under the control of the judiciary rather than the Executive, as recommended by the Deschênes report and others, I do not think that their control by the Executive touches what must be considered to be one of the essential conditions of judicial independence for purposes of s. 11(*d*) of the *Charter*.

I read this statement as recognizing that, at a certain point, there will be elements of judicial remuneration which are in the hands of another party — possibly the executive. While in the best of all possible worlds this might not be the case, such potential discretion is not sufficient to constitute "arbitrary interference by the Executive in a manner that could affect judicial independence" and hence to give rise to a reasonable apprehension that the essential condition of financial security was not met at the time the appellant was tried.

Institutional Independence

The final essential condition as articulated by Le Dain J. is "institutional independence" which he defines as "the institutional independence of the tribunal with respect to matters of administration bearing directly on the exercise of its judicial function" (*Valente, supra,* at p. 708).

Unless I misapprehend his position, Lamer C.J. finds numerous provisions in the *National Defence Act* and its regulations problematic and tending to show that this final criterion was not being fulfilled by the structure as it existed. Particularly offensive, in his view, was the dual role played by the convening authority who, as a member of the executive, decided when a General Court Martial would take place, the number of members who would take part in it, and appointed the prosecutor with the concurrence of the Judge Advocate General (arts. 111.05 and 111.23 Q.R. & O.). It is also repugnant to s. 11(*d*), he argues, that the Judge Advocate General (another member of the executive) appointed the judge advocate. Such institutional links, in his opinion, undermined the scheme to a point where a reasonable person would question the independence of the court.

As was the case with the conditions of security of tenure and financial security, I regret to say that I am unable to accede to his conclusion. I would begin by pointing out that this Court has recently recognized, in so far as the s. 11(*d*) guarantee to be tried by an independent and impartial tribunal is concerned, that it is unrealistic to demand the utter separation of the judiciary from the other branches of government. I recognize that some pronouncements of this Court may appear to go in the opposite direction, most notably perhaps those contained in *Beauregard v. Canada*, [1986] 2 S.C.R. 56, where, at p. 69, Dickson C.J. remarks:

Historically, the generally accepted core of the principle of judicial independence has been the complete liberty of individual judges to hear and decide the cases that come before them: no outsider — be it government, pressure group, individual or even another judge — should interfere in fact, or attempt to interfere, with the way in which a judge conducts his or her case and makes his or her decision. This core continues to be central to the principle of judicial independence.

However, when the issue was once again before this Court in *MacKeigan v. Hickman*, [1989] 2 S.C.R. 796, McLachlin J. took care to clarify the position. At page 827 she states:

> It is important to note that what is proposed in *Beauregard v. Canada* is not the absolute separation of the judiciary, in the sense of total absence of relations from the other branches of government, but separation of its *authority* and *function*. It is impossible to conceive of a judiciary devoid of any relationship to the legislative and executive branches of government. Statutes govern the appointment and retirement of judges; laws dictate the terms upon which they sit and are remunerated. Parliament retains the power to impeach federally-appointed judges for cause, and enactments such as the *Supreme Court Act*, R.S.C. 1970, c. S-19, stipulate on such matters as the number of judges required for a quorum. It is inevitable and necessary that relations of this sort exist between the judicial and legislative branches of government. [Emphasis in original.]

Similar sentiments are expressed by Lamer C.J. in *R. v. Lippé*, [1991] 2 S.C.R. 114. In assessing the constitutional validity of a Quebec statute which permitted part-time municipal court judges to continue to practice as lawyers, he notes at p. 142:

> I admit that a system which allows for part-time judges is not the *ideal* system. However, the Constitution does not always guarantee the "ideal." Perhaps the ideal system would be to have a panel of three or five judges hearing every case; that may be the ideal, but it certainly cannot be said to be constitutionally guaranteed. [Emphasis in original.]

On the basis of these remarks, it is apparent to me that absolute separation of a given tribunal from the executive is not to be expected. The question then becomes: what degree of connection between the executive and those who exercise a judicial role is permitted by the *Charter*?

It is at this point that the context in which this appeal arises becomes extremely significant. One must not lose sight of the fact that the judicial role being exercised in the case at bar is being exercised under the purview of the Canadian Armed Forces and at issue is the independence of a military tribunal. This means, as I have established earlier in these reasons, that it is essential both that discipline be maintained and that alleged instances of non-adherence to rules be tried by other members of the military. Section 11(*d*) might not condone a civilian system of justice where the same body which appointed the prosecutor also appoints the triers of fact, or where the executive and the presiding judge maintain close ties. However, in the context of the

Armed Forces, these characteristics may well be a necessary part of the chain of command which, when followed link by link, ultimately leads to the same destination no matter where one begins. Hence, in my opinion, the *Charter* permits a sufficient degree of connection between the executive and the participants of a General Court Martial such that the third criterion of institutional independence was satisfied at the time of the appellant's trial.

By way of addendum, I wish to respond to the reasons of Stevenson J. which I have lately had the opportunity to read. I understand his position to be more functional in approach, demanding, in the framework of the criterion of institutional independence, that anyone with an interest in seeing the prosecution fail or succeed not be in a position to influence the proceedings. Consequently, in his view, the appointment of the prosecutor by the convening authority resulted in a violation of the appellant's rights under s. 11(*d*) of the *Charter*. In the framework of the criterion of financial security his view is that persons with an interest in the outcome of a particular case may have been in a position to reward or punish decisions favourable or unfavourable to them. Presumably this also amounted to a *Charter* violation. I respectfully disagree with his reasoning on both these points.

With respect to financial security, I am of the view that, as was the case with the deficiencies perceived by the Chief Justice, the difficulties expressed by Stevenson J. were contemplated and dismissed by Le Dain J. in *Valente*. I have already quoted an extract from that case to the effect that while ideally no elements of judicial remuneration would ever be in the hands of another party, such discretion is not necessarily sufficient to constitute a violation of s. 11(*d*). There is no need for me to recite that passage again here. Suffice it to say that I am of the view that it is also applicable to the concerns expressed by Stevenson J.

Turning then to institutional independence, I would reiterate my view relating to the importance of context. It must be remembered that the appellant's trial was taking place within the military and that the problems identified by my colleague are, to my mind, part and parcel of that context. While I might entertain doubts as to the constitutionality of a civilian system of justice where the entity who convenes the court also appoints the prosecutor, I feel that the constitutional standard applicable in the civilian world is wholly inapplicable to measuring a trial by General Court Martial. In short, I remain unpersuaded that the rights of the appellant were violated by the scheme under which he was tried. . . .

Appeal allowed and new trial ordered.

DUNPHY v. HER MAJESTY THE QUEEN
Court Martial Appeal Court of Canada
CMAC-491-92 (2007)

1. These appeals are not factually related but they raise a common issue under paragraph 11(*d*) of the *Canadian Charter of Rights and Freedoms,* Part 1 of the *Constitution Act, 1982,* being Schedule B, to the *Canada Act 1982* (U.K.), 1982 c. 11 (the Charter): the independence of the tribunal that tried them. The same military judge decided both cases and incorporated his

reasons on the paragraph 11(*d*) motion from the *Parsons* case in his *Dunphy* decision. Although the military judge declared that the appointment renewal provisions of military judges violated paragraph 11(*d*) of the Charter he declined to grant an individual remedy pursuant to subsection 24(1) of the Charter. Both Parsons and Dunphy were found guilty of one count of conduct to the prejudice of good order and discipline contrary to section 129 of the *National Defence Act,* R.S., c. N-4. They are appealing their convictions. By way of cross-appeal the Crown appeals the declaration that paragraph 11(*d*) was violated and the declaration of invalidity pursuant to section 52 of the Charter. For the reasons that follow we are in substantial agreement with the military judge's conclusion that the articles in question violate the Charter and his conclusion that no individual remedy should be afforded. . . .

13. We now propose to deal with the cross-appeals by the Crown. The military judge declared that certain sections pertaining to the reappointment of military judges pursuant to the QR&O were of no force and effect. He held that articles 101.15(2), 101.15(3) and 101.17(2) of the QR&O, which provide for the composition of the Renewal Committee and the factors that it must and must not consider in making its recommendation as to whether or not a military judge should be reappointed, gave rise to a reasonable apprehension that the military judge would be unable to decide the case before him without interference from external actors. For ease of reference, the articles in issue are reproduced below.

101.15 — ESTABLISHMENT OF RENEWAL COMMITTEE

(1) A committee to be known as the Renewal Committee is hereby established for the purpose of subsection 165.21(3) of the *National Defence Act.*

(2) The Committee consists of three members appointed by the Governor in Council as follows:

    (*a*) a judge of the Court Martial Appeal Court nominated by the Chief Justice of the Court;

    (*b*) a barrister or advocate with standing at the bar of a province, other than an officer or non-commissioned member, nominated by the Minister of Justice; and

    (*c*) a person other than a legal officer or an officer or a non-commissioned member referred to in section 156 of the *National Defence Act,* nominated by the Minister of National Defence.

(3) The Chairperson of the Committee shall be the person nominated under subparagraph 2(*a*).

(4) Each member holds office for a period not exceeding four years.

101.17 — RECOMMENDATION BY RENEWAL COMMITTEE

1. The Renewal Committee shall deal with all matters before it as informally and expeditiously as the circumstances and the considerations of fairness permit.

2. In making a recommendation, the Renewal Committee shall consider as a minimum the following:

(*a*) the requirements of the Office of the Chief Military Judge, including:

(i) any planned change in strength which will increase or reduce the establishment within the unit of the Chief Military Judge,

(ii) the official language requirements within the unit of the Chief Military Judge, and

(iii) the need to maintain a minimum level of continuity within the unit of the Chief Military Judge having regard to the fixed term appointments and projected retirements of other currently serving military judges;

(*b*) any compelling military requirement to employ the military judge after the completion of the current term of appointment in a non-judicial capacity elsewhere in the Canadian Forces; and

(c) the military judge's physical and medical fitness to perform military duties as an officer of the legal classification.

3. The Committee shall not consider the record of judicial decisions of the military judge.

4. The Committee shall submit its recommendation to the Governor in Council no later than two months before the expiration of the appointment of the military judge. . . .

15. In determining whether or not a military judge has security of tenure, the test to be applied is an objective one. Would a reasonable and right-minded person, informed of the relevant legislative provisions, their historical background and the traditions surrounding them, after viewing the matter realistically and practically — and having thought the matter through — conclude that a military judge presiding at a court martial is at liberty to decide the case that comes before him on its merits without interference by any outsider with the way in which he conducts his case and makes his decision. See *R. v. Valente,* [1985] 2 S.C.R. 673 at paras. 12-13 and 22; *R. v. Lippé,* [1991] 2 S.C.R. 114 at para. 57.

16. In *R. v. Généreux,* [1992] 1 S.C.R. 259 at para. 86 Lamer C.J. said:

Officers who serve as military judges are members of the military establishment and will probably not wish to be cut off from promotional opportunities within that career system. It would therefore not seem reasonable to require a system in which military judges are appointed until the age of retirement.

17. Subsequently, in *R. v. Lauzon,* [1998] C.M.A.J. No.5, para. 27 this Court held:

In our view the fact that the posting of an officer to a military trial judge position is renewable does not necessarily lead to the conclusion that institutional independence is lacking if the reposting process is accompanied by substantial and sufficient guarantees to ensure that the Court and the military judge in question are free from pressure on the part of the Executive that could influence the outcome of future decisions.

18. The time has come to reconsider this decision.

19. The evidence filed before the military judge indicates that the rationale behind *Généreux*, above, and *Lauzon,* above, no longer exists. It is no longer true that a posting to a military judge's position is merely a step in a legal officer's career and that military judges would necessarily want to maintain their connections with the Canadian Forces to preserve their chances of promotion. A military judge doesn't receive a Performance Evaluation Report which is necessary for career advancement. Further the military judge could come back into the chain of command and find him/herself subject to a person he or she had tried. In addition, a return to regular military service would entail a significant financial loss.

20. With the evolution of time court martial courts have become quite different from the way they were. At General Courts Martial the military judge is no longer an adviser but now performs a role akin to a judge in the civilian courts; that is even more so at Standing Courts Martial such as the ones from which these appeals are brought.

21. Although the legislation sets out certain factors that the Renewal Committee must and must not consider, it is clear that the Committee's decision is not limited to those factors. Quite apart from the lack of transparency that results, the articles in question cannot act as a sufficient legislative restraint to remove concerns respecting security of tenure. As former Chief Justice Lamer observed in his last report . . . "institutional safeguards are currently not in place to protect a military judge from a reasonable apprehension of bias should it be determined that the military judge's term not be renewed."

22. He concluded by recommending that military judges be awarded security of tenure until retirement subject only to removal for cause on the recommendation of an Inquiry Committee.

23. We agree with his recommendation that military judges be awarded security of tenure until retirement subject to removal for cause. The deficiencies noted by the military judge in the judgments appealed from would cease to have any relevance if those recommendations were followed. We also note that the current provisions will become a dead letter if Bill C-7 is passed.

24. Accordingly, we are in substantial agreement with the conclusion of the military judge and would order that the cross-appeal be dismissed.

WEISS v. UNITED STATES
Supreme Court of the United States
510 U.S. 163 (1994)

[The Appointments Clause of the United States Constitution, Art. II, § 2, cl. 2, confers on the President power to "appoint Ambassadors, other public

Ministers and Consults, Judges of the supreme Court, and all other Officers of the United States, whose Appointments are not herein otherwise provided for, and which shall be established by Law. But the Congress may by law vest the Appointment of such inferior Officers, as they think proper, in the President alone, in the Courts of Law, or in the Heads of Departments." The extracts from *Weiss* reproduced below are confined to the second issue the Supreme Court addressed: "whether the lack of a fixed term of office for military judges violates the Fifth Amendment's Due Process Clause." Justice Souter's concurring opinion is omitted.]

CHIEF JUSTICE REHNQUIST delivered the opinion of the Court.

. . . The Court of Military Appeals granted plenary review in petitioner Weiss' case to address his contention that the judges in his case had no authority to convict him because their appointments violated the Appointments Clause, and their lack of a fixed term of office violated the Due Process Clause. Relying on its recent decision in *United States v. Graf*, 35 M.J. 450 (1992), *cert. pending*, No. 92-1102, in which the Court unanimously held that due process does not require military judges to have a fixed term of office, the Court rejected Weiss' due process argument. 36 M.J. 224, 235, n. 1 (1992). . . .

It will help in understanding the issues involved to review briefly the contours of the military justice system and the role of military judges within that system. Pursuant to Article I of the Constitution, Congress has established three tiers of military courts. *See* U. S. Const., Art. I, § 8, cl. 14. At the trial level are the courts-martial, of which there are three types: summary, special, and general. The summary court-martial adjudicates only minor offenses, has jurisdiction only over servicemembers, and can be conducted only with their consent. It is presided over by a single commissioned officer who can impose up to one month of confinement and other relatively modest punishments. Arts. 16(3), 20, UCMJ, 10 U.S.C. §§ 816(3), 820.

The special court-martial usually consists of a military judge and three court-martial members, although the Code allows the members to sit without a judge, or the accused to elect to be tried by the judge alone. Art. 16(2), UCMJ, 10 U.S.C. § 816(2). A special court-martial has jurisdiction over most offenses under the UCMJ, but it may impose punishment no greater than six months of confinement, three months of hard labor without confinement, a bad conduct discharge, partial and temporary forfeiture of pay, and a reduction in rank. Art. 19, UCMJ, 10 U.S.C. § 819. The general court-martial consists of either a military judge and at least five members, or the judge alone if the defendant so requests. Art. 16(1), UCMJ, 10 U.S.C. § 816(1). A general court-martial has jurisdiction over all offenses under the UCMJ and may impose any lawful sentence, including death. Art. 18, UCMJ, 10 U.S.C. § 818.

The military judge, a position that has officially existed only since passage of the Military Justice Act of 1968, acts as presiding officer at a special or general court-martial. Art. 26, UCMJ, 10 U.S.C. § 826. The judge rules on all legal questions, and instructs court-martial members regarding the law and procedures to be followed. Art. 51, UCMJ, 10 U.S.C. § 851. The members decide guilt or innocence and impose sentence unless, of course, the trial is before the judge alone. *Ibid.* No sentence imposed becomes final until it is approved by the officer who convened the court-martial. Art. 60, UCMJ, 10 U.S.C. § 860.

Military trial judges must be commissioned officers of the armed forces[17] and members of the bar of a federal court or a State's highest court. Art. 26, UCMJ, 10 U.S.C. § 826. The judges are selected and certified as qualified by the Judge Advocate General of their branch of the armed forces. They do not serve for fixed terms and may perform judicial duties only when assigned to do so by the appropriate Judge Advocate General. While serving as judges, officers may also, with the approval of the Judge Advocate General, perform other tasks unrelated to their judicial duties. *Ibid.* There are approximately 74 judges currently certified to preside at general and special courts-martial. An additional 25 are certified to preside only over special courts-martial.

At the next tier are the four Courts of Military Review, one each for the Army, Air Force, Coast Guard, and Navy-Marine Corps. These courts, which usually sit in three-judge panels, review all cases in which the sentence imposed exceeds one year of confinement, involves the dismissal of a commissioned officer, or involves the punitive discharge of an enlisted servicemember. Art. 66, UCMJ, 10 U.S.C. § 866. The courts may review *de novo* both factual and legal findings, and they may overturn convictions and sentences. *Ibid.*

Appellate judges may be commissioned officers or civilians, but each must be a member of a bar of a Federal court or of a State's highest court. *Ibid.* The judges are selected and assigned to serve by the appropriate Judge Advocate General. *Ibid.* Like military trial judges, appellate judges do not serve for a fixed term. There are presently 31 appellate military judges.

Atop the system is the Court of Military Appeals, which consists of five civilian judges who are appointed by the President, with the advice and consent of the Senate, for fixed terms of 15 years. Arts. 67, 142, UCMJ, 10 U.S.C. §§ 867, 942 (1988 ed., Supp. IV). The appointment and tenure of these judges are not at issue here. . . .

Petitioners next contend that the Due Process Clause requires that military judges must have a fixed term of office. Petitioners recognize, as they must, that the Constitution does not require life tenure for Article I judges, including military judges. *See United States ex rel. Toth v. Quarles*, 350 U.S. 11, 17 (1955). Nor does the trial by an Article I judge lacking life tenure violate a defendant's due process rights. *See Palmore v. United States*, 411 U.S. 389, 410 (1973). Petitioners thus confine their argument to the assertion that due process requires military judges to serve for some fixed length of time — however short.

Congress, of course, is subject to the requirements of the Due Process Clause when legislating in the area of military affairs, and that Clause provides some measure of protection to defendants in military proceedings. *See Rostker v. Goldberg*, 453 U.S. 57, 67 (1981); *Middendorf v. Henry*, 425 U.S. 25, 43 (1976).

---

[17] [n2] All commissioned officers are appointed by the President, with the advice and consent of the Senate. 10 U.S.C. § 531.

But in determining what process is due, courts "must give particular deference to the determination of Congress, made under its authority to regulate the land and naval forces, U. S. Const., Art. I, § 8," *Middendorf v. Henry*, 425 U.S. 25, 43 (1976). Petitioners urge that we apply the due process analysis established in *Mathews* v. *Eldridge*, 424 U.S. 319, 334-335 (1976). The Government contends that *Medina v. California*, 505 U. S. 437 (1992), supplies the appropriate analytical framework.

Neither *Mathews* nor *Medina*, however, arose in the military context, and we have recognized in past cases that "the tests and limitations [of due process] may differ because of the military context." *Rostker, supra*, at 67. The difference arises from the fact that the Constitution contemplates that Congress has "plenary control over rights, duties, and responsibilities in the framework of the Military Establishment, including regulations, procedures, and remedies related to military discipline." *Chappell v. Wallace*, 462 U.S. 296, 301 (1983). Judicial deference thus "is at its apogee" when reviewing congressional decisionmaking in this area. *Rostker, supra*, at 70. Our deference extends to rules relating to the rights of servicemembers: "Congress has primary responsibility for the delicate task of balancing the rights of servicemen against the needs of the military. . . . [W]e have adhered to this principle of deference in a variety of contexts where, as here, the constitutional rights of servicemen were implicated." *Solorio v. United States*, 483 U.S. 435, 447-448 (1987).

We therefore believe that the appropriate standard to apply in these cases is found in *Middendorf, supra*, where we also faced a due process challenge to a facet of the military justice system. In determining whether the Due Process Clause requires that servicemembers appearing before a summary court-martial be assisted by counsel, we asked "whether the factors militating in favor of counsel at summary courts-martial are so extraordinarily weighty as to overcome the balance struck by Congress." *Middendorf*, 425 U.S., at 44. We ask the same question here with respect to fixed terms of office for military judges.

It is elementary that "a fair trial in a fair tribunal is a basic requirement of due process." *In re Murchison*, 349 U.S. 133, 136 (1955). A necessary component of a fair trial is an impartial judge. *See ibid.*; *Tumey v. Ohio*, 273 U.S. 510, 532 (1927). Petitioners, however, do not allege that the judges in their cases were or appeared to be biased. Instead, they ask us to assume that a military judge who does not have a fixed term of office lacks the independence necessary to ensure impartiality. Neither history nor current practice, however, supports such an assumption.

a

Although a fixed term of office is a traditional component of the Anglo-American civilian judicial system, it has never been a part of the military justice tradition. The early English military tribunals, which served as the model for our own military justice system, were historically convened and presided over by a military general. No tenured military judge presided. *See* Schlueter, *The Court-Martial: An Historical Survey*, 87 MIL. L. REV. 129, 135, 136-144 (1980).

In the United States, although Congress has on numerous occasions during our history revised the procedures governing courts-martial, it has never required tenured judges to preside over courts-martial or to hear immediate appeals therefrom.[18] *See* W. Winthrop, Military Law and Precedents, 21-24, 953-1000 (2d ed. 1920) (describing and reprinting the Articles of War, which governed court-martial proceedings during the 17th and 18th centuries); F. Gilligan & F. Lederer, 1 Court-Martial Procedure 11-24 (1991) (describing 20th century revisions to Articles of War, and enactment of and amendments to UCMJ). Indeed, as already mentioned, Congress did not even create the position of military judge until 1968. Courts-martial thus have been conducted in this country for over 200 years without the presence of a tenured judge, and for over 150 years without the presence of any judge at all.

b

As the Court of Military Appeals observed in *Graf*, 35 M.J., at 462, the historical maintenance of the military justice system without tenured judges "suggests the absence of a fundamental fairness problem." Petitioners in effect urge us to disregard this history, but we are unwilling to do so. We do not mean to say that any practice in military courts which might have been accepted at some time in history automatically satisfies due process of law today. But as Congress has taken affirmative steps to make the system of military justice more like the American system of civilian justice, it has nonetheless chosen not to give tenure to military judges. The question under the Due Process Clause is whether the existence of such tenure is such an extraordinarily weighty factor as to overcome the balance struck by Congress. And the historical fact that military judges have never had tenure is a factor that must be weighed in this calculation.

A fixed term of office, as petitioners recognize, is not an end in itself. It is a means of promoting judicial independence, which in turn helps to ensure judicial impartiality. We believe the applicable provisions of the UCMJ, and corresponding regulations, by insulating military judges from the effects of command influence, sufficiently preserve judicial impartiality so as to satisfy the Due Process Clause.

Article 26 places military judges under the authority of the appropriate Judge Advocate General rather than under the authority of the convening officer. 10 U.S.C. § 826. Rather than exacerbating the alleged problems relating to judicial independence, as petitioners suggest, we believe this structure helps protect that independence. Like all military officers, Congress made military judges accountable to a superior officer for the performance of their duties. By placing judges under the control of Judge Advocates General, who have no interest in the outcome of a particular court-martial, we believe

---

18 [n.6] Congress did create a nine-member commission in 1983 to examine, *inter alia*, the possibility of providing tenure for military judges. Military Justice Act of 1983, Pub. L. 98-209, § 9(b), 97 Stat. 1393, 1404-1405 (1983). The commission published its report a year later, in which it recommended against providing a guaranteed term of office for military trial and appellate judges. *See* D. Schlueter, Military Criminal Justice: Practice and Procedure 33-34, and nn.86, 87 (3d ed. 1992) (listing members of commission and describing report). Congress has taken no further action on the subject.

Congress has achieved an acceptable balance between independence and accountability.

Article 26 also protects against command influence by precluding a convening officer or any commanding officer from preparing or reviewing any report concerning the effectiveness, fitness, or efficiency of a military judge relating to his judicial duties. *Ibid.* Article 37 prohibits convening officers from censuring, reprimanding, or admonishing a military judge "with respect to the findings or sentence adjudged by the court, or with respect to any other exercise of its or his functions in the conduct of the proceeding." 10 U.S.C. § 837. Any officer who "knowingly and intentionally fails to enforce or comply" with Article 37 "shall be punished as a court-martial may direct." Art. 98, UCMJ, 10 U.S.C. § 898. The Code also provides that a military judge, either trial or appellate, must refrain from adjudicating a case in which he has previously participated, Arts. 26(c), 66(h), UCMJ, 10 U.S.C. §§ 826(c), 866(h), and the Code allows a defendant to challenge both a court-martial member and a court-martial judge for cause, Art. 41, UCMJ, 10 U.S.C. § 841. The Code also allows a defendant to learn the identity of the military judge before choosing whether to be tried by the judge alone, or by the judge and court-martial members. Art. 16, UCMJ, 10 U.S.C. § 816.

The entire system, finally, is overseen by the Court of Military Appeals, which is composed entirely of civilian judges who serve for fixed terms of 15 years. That Court has demonstrated its vigilance in checking any attempts to exert improper influence over military judges. In *United States v. Mabe*, 33 M.J. 200 (1991), for example, the Court considered whether the Judge Advocate General of the Navy, or his designee, could rate a military judge based on the appropriateness of the judge's sentences at courts-martial. As the Court later described: "We held [in *Mabe*] that the existence of such a power in these military officers was inconsistent with Congress' establishment of the military 'judge' in Article 26 and its exercise violated Article 37 of the Code." *Graf*, 35 M.J., at 465. And in *Graf*, the Court held that it would also violate Articles 26 and 37 if a Judge Advocate General decertified or transferred a military judge based on the General's opinion of the appropriateness of the judge's findings and sentences. *Ibid.*[19]

The absence of tenure as a historical matter in the system of military justice, and the number of safeguards in place to ensure impartiality, lead us to reject petitioners' due process challenge. Petitioners have fallen far short of demonstrating that the factors favoring fixed terms of office are so extraordinarily weighty as to overcome the balance achieved by Congress. *See Middendorf*, 425 U.S., at 44.

For the reasons stated, we reject the petitioners' Appointments Clause and Due Process Clause attacks on the judges who convicted them and those who heard their appeals. The judgments of the Court of Military Appeals are accordingly

Affirmed.

---

[19] [n.7] This added limitation on the power of the Judge Advocates General to remove military judges refutes petitioners' contention that Judge Advocates General have unfettered discretion both to appoint and remove military judges.

JUSTICE GINSBURG, concurring.

The care the Court has taken to analyze petitioners' claims demonstrates once again that men and women in the Armed Forces do not leave constitutional safeguards and judicial protection behind when they enter military service. Today's decision upholds a system of military justice notably more sensitive to due process concerns than the one prevailing through most of our country's history, when military justice was done without any requirement that legally-trained officers preside or even participate as judges. Nevertheless, there has been no peremptory rejection of petitioners' pleas. Instead, the close inspection reflected in the Court's opinion confirms:

> "[I]t is the function of the courts to make sure, in cases properly coming before them, that the men and women constituting our Armed Forces are treated as honored members of society whose rights do not turn on the charity of a military commander. . . . A member of the Armed Forces is entitled to equal justice under law not as conceived by the generosity of a commander but as written in the Constitution. . . ." *Winters v. United States*, 89 S. Ct. 57, 59-60 (1968) (Douglas, J., opinion in chambers). *See also Frontiero v. Richardson*, 411 U.S. 677 (1973); *Harmon v. Brucker*, 355 U.S. 579 (1958); *Crawford v. Cushman*, 531 F.2d 1114 (2d Cir. 1976).

JUSTICE SCALIA, with whom JUSTICE THOMAS joins, concurring in part and concurring in the judgment.

. . . With respect to the Due Process Clause challenge, I think it neither necessary nor appropriate for this Court to pronounce whether "Congress has achieved an acceptable balance between independence and accountability". . . . As today's opinion explains, a fixed term of office for a military judge "never has been a part of the military justice tradition." "Courts-martial . . . have been conducted in this country for over 200 years without the presence of a tenured judge." Thus, in the Military Justice Act of 1968 the people's elected representatives achieved a "balance between independence and accountability" which, whether or not "acceptable" to five Justices of this Court, gave members of the military at least as much procedural protection, in the respects at issue here, as they enjoyed when the Fifth Amendment was adopted and have enjoyed ever since. That is enough, and to suggest otherwise arrogates to this Court a power it does not possess.

> "[A] process of law, which is not otherwise forbidden, must be taken to be due process of law, if it can show the sanction of settled usage both in England and in this country. . . . [That which], in substance, has been immemorially the actual law of the land . . . is due process of law." *Hurtado v. California*, 110 U.S. 516, 528 (1884).

As sometimes ironically happens when judges seek to deny the power of historical practice to restrain their decrees, *see, e.g., Burnham v. Superior Court of Cal., County of Marin*, 495 U.S. 604, 637-639 (1990) (Brennan, J., concurring in judgment), the present judgment makes no sense except as a consequence of historical practice. Today's opinion finds "an acceptable balance between independence and accountability" because the Uniform Code of

Military Justice "protects against command influence by precluding a convening officer or any commanding officer from preparing or reviewing any report concerning the effectiveness, fitness, or efficiency of a military judge relating to his judicial duties"; because it "prohibits convening officers from censuring, reprimanding, or admonishing a military judge '. . . with respect to any . . . exercise of . . . his functions in the conduct of the proceeding'"; and because a Judge Advocate General cannot decertify or transfer a military judge "based on the General's opinion of the appropriateness of the judge's findings and sentences." . . . But no one can suppose that similar protections against improper influence would suffice to validate a state criminal-law system in which felonies were tried by judges serving at the pleasure of the Executive. I am confident that we would not be satisfied with mere formal prohibitions in the civilian context, but would hold that due process demands the *structural* protection of tenure in office, which has been provided in England since 1700, *see* J.H. Baker, An Introduction to English Legal History 145-146 (2d ed. 1979), was provided in almost all the former English colonies from the time of the Revolution, *see* Ziskind, *Judicial Tenure in the American Constitution: English and American Precedents*, 1969 S. Ct. Rev. 135, 138-147 (1969), and is provided in all the States today, *see* National Center for State Courts, Conference of State Court Administrators, State Court Organization 1987, pp. 271-302 (1988). (It is noteworthy that one of the grievances recited against King George III in the Declaration of Independence was that "[h]e has made Judges dependent on his Will alone, for the tenure of their offices.").

Thus, while the Court's opinion says that historical practice is merely "a factor that must be weighed in [the] calculation," . . ., it seems to me that the Court's judgment today makes the fact of a differing military tradition utterly conclusive. That is as it should be: "[N]o procedure firmly rooted in the practices of our people can be so 'fundamentally unfair' as to deny due process of law." *Pacific Mut. Life Ins. Co. v. Haslip*, 499 U.S. 1, 38 (1991) (Scalia, J., concurring).

For these reasons, I concur in Parts I and II-a and concur in the judgment.

Army Regulation 27-10
Legal Services: Military Justice (2005)

8-1(g). *Tenure for military trial judges.* Judges Advocates are certified as military judges by TJAG [The Judge Advocate General] and assigned to the Trial Judiciary for a minimum of three years, except under any of the following circumstances:

(1) The military judge is assigned to the Sixth Judicial Circuit (Republic of Korea), or such other area where officers are normally assigned for a short tour of one or two years; in such cases the military judge will be appointed for a one or two year term;

(2) The military judge voluntarily requests to be reassigned to other duties, and TJAG approves such assignment;

(3) The military judge retires or otherwise separates from military service;

(4) The military judge is reassigned to other duties by TJAG based on the needs of the service in a time of war or national emergency;

(5) The officer's certification as a military judge is withdrawn by TJAG for good cause. . . .

13-13. *Tenure for military appellate judges*

Judge Advocates are certified as military judges by TJAG and assigned to the United States Army Court of Criminal Appeals for a minimum of three years, except under any of the following circumstances:

(1) The military judge voluntarily requests to be reassigned to other duties, and TJAG approves such assignment;

(2) The military judge retires or otherwise separates from military service;

(3) The military judge is reassigned to other duties by TJAG based on the needs of the service in a time or war or national emergency;

(4) The officer's certification as a military judge is withdrawn by TJAG for good cause. . . .

NOTES AND QUESTIONS

1. In *Weiss*, the Supreme Court was aware of *Généreux*. Should the Court have discussed it? In *Sekoati v. President of the Court Martial*, [2000] 4 LRC 511, [1999] ICHRL 158, 2001(7) BCLR 750, 761-62 (Lesotho 1999), the Lesotho Court of Appeal, citing Justice L'Heureux-Dubé's dissent, declined to follow *Généreux*, and suggested it was "far-fetched" to complain about the lack of financial security of court-martial members. The court also observed that the provisions said to deny security of tenure to the members were "all inherent in a system whereby a court-martial consisting of military personnel is constituted on an ad hoc basis and which is dissolved upon completion of the proceedings for which it has been appointed. These provisions do not, in our judgment, constitute an inroad into the judicial independence required in terms of the Constitution." Does the fact that the court-martial's judgments are subject to review by a court-martial appeal court whose members include a judge and a retired army officer with legal experience and in the civilian courts resolve any issue as to the court-martial's independence? *See id.* at 762. For another example of a "contextual" analysis that declines to follow *Généreux*, see *Naduaniwai v. Commander, Republic of Fiji Military Forces*, [2004] FJHC 10 (Fiji High Ct. 2004) ("In the context of the armed forces [security of tenure, financial security and institutional independence] are subordinate to the chain of command and the responsibility for discipline within a standing army"). In a later case, however, the Fiji Court of Appeal followed *Findlay* and *Généreux* and remanded for a new mutiny trial before a differently constituted court-martial. At the same time it noted that "a wholesale adoption of whatever may be appropriate in the current UK context can cause problems for a small military force such as Fiji's, given that Fiji can have no input into what the UK Parliament enacts." *Mills v. State*, [2005] FJCA 6; AAUU0035.2004S (Fiji Ct. App. 2005) (¶¶ 85, 88).

2. Is the lack of terms of office for military judges a matter of substance, or simply of appearance? Does it matter which? Would it be wise or rational to distinguish between trial and appellate judges when framing measures to ensure judicial independence? Consider the following remarks by Justice Kirby of the High Court of Australia:

> *Beware of military tribunals*: Dreyfus was twice convicted by a military tribunal. The first conviction was reached on the flimsiest evidence. The second occurred in the face of demonstrable proof of his innocence. Loyalty to the army swamped the evidence. One member of the first court martial admitted that he had scarcely looked at the handwriting tendered to secure the conviction. Accusation by the most senior officials of the nation was enough to prove the accusation.
>
> Loyalty, love of nation and belief in its institutions are marvelous things. In the modern world, patriotism has its place, at least in sporting contests. But there is a danger of tribunals that operate outside the independent courts deciding questions of liberty. It is why the independence of the courts, and the tenure of the judges, is so important for our freedoms.
>
> An examination of outcomes in the Australian Refugee Review Tribunal, after members were not regularly reappointed, shows a fall-off in decisions favourable to applicants for refugee status. This is what can happen where decision-makers do not enjoy guaranteed tenure. It is true that such guarantees sometimes entail disadvantages and cloak individual inadequacies. But over the centuries, judicial tenure has been a great protection for our liberties. It did not exist in the first or second tribunals that tried and convicted Dreyfus. Those military tribunals were not really independent. They evinced loyalty for their conception of the nation and for their military superiors. An affirmation of civilian rule is crucial to the just trial of serious accusations. It is ironic to read the American comments on the Dreyfus trials in the 1890s and the asserted superiority of American civil courts, contrasting them with the defence of military commissions today.

Hon. Michael Kirby, The Dreyfus Case A Century On — Ten Lessons for Australia, Remarks presented at the Jewish Museum of Australia, Melbourne, Mar. 26, 2006.

3. Does the Army's terms-of-office regulation, issued after the government prevailed in *Weiss*, solve the problem? Would you recommend changes in the regulation, or some other solution instead? *See, e.g.,* Fredric I. Lederer & Barbara Hundley Zeliff, *Needed: An Independent Military Judiciary. A Proposal to Amend the Uniform Code of Military Justice,* 3 WM. & MARY BILL OF RIGHTS J. 629 (1994), *reprinted in* EVOLVING MILITARY JUSTICE 27, 56-57 (Eugene R. Fidell & Dwight H. Sullivan eds. 2002) (initial probationary appointment for term of years, followed by permanent judicial status as naval captain/colonel until 30-year retirement).

4. The Army and the Coast Guard are the only branches of the United States armed forces that have established terms of office for military judges; the Air Force, Navy and Marine Corps have not done so. Does the resulting disparity violate Fifth Amendment equal protection? *See Bolling v. Sharpe*, 347 U.S. 497 (1954); *United States v. Gaines*, 61 M.J. 689, 692 (N-M. Ct. Crim. App. 2005), *aff'd mem.*, 64 M.J. 176 (C.A.A.F. 2006) (mem.); *Oppermann v. United States*, 2007 U.S. Dist. LEXIS 43270 (June 15, 2007).

5. Action to suspend or revoke the certification of Army judges may be initiated if the judge "[i]s, or has been found guilty of professional, personal, or judicial misconduct or of unfitness of such a serious nature as to show that the individual is lacking in integrity or judicial demeanor, or . . . [i]s otherwise unworthy or unqualified to perform the duties of a military judge." An Army judge may be censured, suspended from acting as such, or removed from the judicial role by revocation of his or her certification for acts that "[c]onstitute misconduct, or constitute judicial misconduct or unfitness, or . . . [v]iolate the Code of Judicial Conduct for Army Trial and Appellate Judges, the Army Rules of Professional Conduct for Lawyers, or other applicable standards." Are these standards too vague? What due process protections should a sitting judge have?

III. INTERNATIONAL HUMAN RIGHTS

Draft Principles Governing the Administration of Justice through Military Tribunals
UN Commission on Human Rights, 2006

Principle No. 13

Right to a competent, independent and impartial tribunal

The organization and operation of military courts should fully ensure the right of everyone to a competent, independent and impartial tribunal at every stage of legal proceedings from initial investigation to trial. The persons selected to perform the functions of judges in military courts must display integrity and competence and show proof of the necessary legal training and qualifications. Military judges should have a status guaranteeing their independence and impartiality, in particular vis-à-vis the military hierarchy. In no circumstances should military courts be allowed to resort to procedures involving anonymous or "faceless" judges and prosecutors.

45. This fundamental right is set out in article 10 of the Universal Declaration of Human Rights: "Everyone is entitled in full equality to a fair and public hearing by an independent and impartial tribunal, in the determination of his rights and obligations and of any criminal charge against him." Article 14 of the International Covenant on Civil and Political Rights, like the regional conventions, provides details of its practical scope. Regarding the concept of an independent and impartial tribunal, a large body of case law has spelled out the subjective as well as the objective content of independence and impartiality. Particular emphasis has been placed on the English adage that "justice should not only be done but should be seen to be done." It is also important to emphasize that the Human Rights Committee has stated that "the right to be tried by an independent and impartial tribunal is an absolute right that may suffer no exception."

46. The statutory independence of judges vis-à-vis the military hierarchy must be strictly protected, avoiding any direct or indirect subordination, whether in the organization and operation of the system of justice itself or in terms of career development for military judges. The concept of impartiality is still more complex in the light of the above-mentioned English adage, as the parties have good reason to view the military judge as an officer who is capable of being "judge in his own cause" in any case involving the armed forces as an institution, rather than a specialist judge on the same footing as any other. The presence of civilian judges in the composition of military tribunals can only reinforce the impartiality of such tribunals.

47. Emphasis should also be placed on the requirement that judges called on to sit in military courts should be competent, having undergone the same legal training as that required of professional judges. The legal competence and ethical standards of military judges, as judges who are fully aware of their duties and responsibilities, form an intrinsic part of their independence and impartiality.

48. The system of anonymous or "faceless" military judges and prosecutors has been heavily criticized by the Human Rights Committee, the Committee against Torture, the Special Rapporteur on the independence of judges and lawyers, and others. The Human Rights Committee has ruled that in a system of trial by "faceless judges," neither the independence nor the impartiality of the judges is guaranteed, and such a system also fails to safeguard the presumption of innocence.

FINDLAY v. UNITED KINGDOM
European Court of Human Rights
[1997] ECHR 8, 24 EHRR 221

[While drunk, a lance sergeant in the Scots Guards who suffered from post-traumatic stress disorder ("PTSD") as a result of prior combat service held two members of his unit at gunpoint, threatened to kill himself and fired two shots, hitting a television.]

2. The composition of the court martial

14. The position of "convening officer" (see paragraphs 36-41 below) for the applicant's court martial was assumed by the General Officer Commanding London District, Major General Corbett. He remanded Mr Findlay for trial on eight charges arising out of the incident of 29 July 1990 and decided that he should be tried by general court martial.

15. By an order dated 31 October 1991, the convening officer convened the general court martial and appointed the military personnel who were to act as prosecuting officer, assistant prosecuting officer and assistant defending officer (to represent Mr Findlay in addition to his solicitor) and the members of the court martial (see paragraph 37 below).

16. The court martial consisted of a president and four other members:

(1) the president, Colonel Godbold, was a member of London District staff (under the command of the convening officer: see paragraph 14

above). He was appointed by name by the latter and was not a permanent president;

(2) Lieutenant-Colonel Swallow was a permanent president of courts martial, sitting in the capacity of an ordinary member. He had his office in the London District Headquarters. He was appointed by name by the convening officer;

(3) Captain Tubbs was from the Coldstream Guards, a unit stationed in London District. His reporting chain was to his officer commanding, his commanding officer and the Brigade Commander, after which his report could, in exceptional circumstances, go to the convening officer; he was a member of a footguard unit and the convening officer, as General Officer Commanding, was responsible for all footguard units. He was appointed to the court martial by his commanding officer;

(4) Major Bolitho was from the Grenadier Guards, also a footguard unit stationed in London District. The convening officer was his second superior reporting officer. He was appointed to the court martial by his commanding officer;

(5) Captain O'Connor was from the Postal and Courier Department, Royal Engineers (Women's Royal Army Corps), which is under the direct command of the Ministry of Defence and is administered by the London District. She was appointed by her commanding officer.

In summary, all of the members of the court martial were subordinate in rank to the convening officer and served in units stationed within London District. None of them had legal training.

17. The assistant prosecuting and defending officers were both officers from the Second Scots Guards stationed in the London District and had the same reporting chain as Captain Tubbs (see paragraph 16(3) above).

18. The judge advocate for the general court martial was appointed by the Judge Advocate General (see paragraphs 42-45 below). He was a barrister and assistant judge advocate with the Judge Advocate General's Office.

3. The court martial hearing

19. On 11 November 1991, Mr Findlay appeared before the general court martial, at Regent's Park Barracks in London. He was represented by a solicitor.

He pleaded guilty to three charges of common assault (a civilian offence), two charges of conduct to the prejudice of good order and military discipline (a military offence) and two charges of threatening to kill (a civilian offence).

20. On 2 November 1991, his solicitor had made a written request to the prosecuting authorities to ensure the appearance of Dr Blunden at the court martial and on 5 November 1991 the prosecuting officer had issued a witness summons requiring her attendance. However, the defence was informed on the morning of the hearing that Dr Blunden would not be attending. Mr Findlay claims that her absence persuaded him to plead guilty to the above charges. However, his solicitor did not request an adjournment or object to the hearing proceeding.

21. The defence put before the court martial the medical reports referred to above . . . and called Dr Reid to give evidence. The latter confirmed his view that the applicant suffered from PTSD, that this had been the principal cause of his behaviour, that he had not been responsible for his actions and that he was in need of counselling. During cross-examination, Dr Reid stated that this was the first time he had dealt with battle-related PTSD.

The prosecution did not call any medical evidence in rebuttal or adopt any of the evidence prepared by the army-instructed psychiatrists, Drs McKinnon and Blunden. . . .

22. In the course of his speech in mitigation, Mr Findlay's solicitor urged the court martial that, in view of the fact that his client had been suffering from PTSD at the time of the incident and was extremely unlikely to reoffend, he should be allowed to complete the few remaining months of his service and leave the army with his pension intact and a minimal endorsement on his record.

23. Having heard the evidence and speeches, the court martial retired to consider their decision on sentence, accompanied by the judge advocate. On their return they sentenced the applicant to two years' imprisonment, reduction to the rank of guardsman and dismissal from the army (which caused him to suffer a reduction in his pension entitlement). No reasons were given for the sentence (see paragraph 46 below).

4. The confirmation of sentence and review process

24. Under the Army Act 1955, the decision of the court martial had no effect until it was confirmed by the "confirming officer" (see paragraph 48 below). In Mr Findlay's case, as was usual practice, the confirming officer was the same person as the convening officer. Mr Findlay petitioned him for a reduction in sentence.

Having received advice from the Judge Advocate General's Office, the confirming officer informed the applicant on 16 December 1991 that the sentence had been upheld.

25. The applicant, who had been under close arrest since the morning before the court martial hearing, was removed on 18 November 1991 to a military prison and thereafter to a civilian prison on 21 December 1991.

26. He appealed by way of petition to the first of the "reviewing authorities" (see paragraph 49 below), the Deputy Director General of Personal Services, as delegate of the Army Board, a non-legally qualified officer who obtained advice from the Judge Advocate General's Office. By a letter dated 22 January 1992, Mr Findlay was informed that this petition had been rejected.

27. He then petitioned the second of the reviewing authorities, a member of the Defence Council who also was not legally qualified and who also received advice from the Judge Advocate General's Office. This petition was rejected on 10 March 1992.

28. The advice given by the Judge Advocate General's Office at each of these three stages of review was not disclosed to the applicant, nor was he given reasons for the decisions confirming his sentence and rejecting his petitions.

29. On 10 March 1992, the applicant applied to the Divisional Court for leave to challenge by judicial review the validity of the findings of the court martial. He claimed that the sentence imposed was excessive, the proceedings were contrary to the rules of natural justice and that the judge advocate had been hostile to him on two occasions during the hearing.

On 14 December 1992 the Divisional Court refused leave on the basis that the court martial had been conducted fully in accordance with the Army Act 1955 and there was no evidence of improper conduct or hostility on the part of the judge advocate (R. v. General Court Martial (Regent's Park Barracks), ex parte Alexander Findlay, CO/1092/92, unreported).

5. Civil proceedings

30. Mr Findlay commenced a civil claim in negligence against the military authorities, claiming damages in respect of his back injury and PTSD. In a report dated 16 January 1994 prepared for these purposes, Dr Blunden confirmed her previous opinion (see paragraph 12 above) and clearly diagnosed PTSD.

31. In March 1994 the civil action was settled by the Secretary of State for Defence, who paid the applicant £100,000 and legal costs, without any admission of liability. The settlement did not differentiate between the claims in respect of PTSD and the back injury.

II. Relevant domestic law and practice

1. The law in force at the time of Mr Findlay's court martial

(a) General

32. The law and procedures which applied to the applicant's court martial were contained in the Army Act 1955 ("the 1955 Act"), the Rules of Procedure (Army) 1972 ("the 1972 Rules") and the Queen's Regulations (1975). Since the Commission's consideration of the case, certain provisions in the 1955 Act have been amended by the Armed Forces Act 1996 ("the 1996 Act"), which comes into force on 1 April 1997 (see paragraphs 52-57 below).

33. Many civilian offences are also offences under the 1955 Act (section 70(1)). Although the final decision on jurisdiction lies with the civilian authorities, army personnel who are accused of such offences are usually tried by the military authorities unless, for example, civilians are involved in some way.

Depending on their gravity, charges against army law can be tried by district, field or general court martial. A court martial is not a standing court: it comes into existence in order to try a single offence or group of offences.

34. At the time of the events in question, a general court martial consisted of a president (normally a brigadier or colonel in the army), appointed by name by the convening officer (see paragraphs 36-41 below), and at least four other army officers, either appointed by name by the convening officer or, at the latter's request, by their commanding officer.

35. Each member of the court martial had to swear the following oath:

I swear by almighty God that I will well and truly try the accused before the court according to the evidence, and that I will duly administer justice according to the Army Act 1955, without partiality, favour or affection, and I do further swear that I will not on any account at any time whatsoever disclose or discover the vote or opinion of the president or any member of this court martial, unless thereunto required in the due course of law.

(b) The convening officer

36. Before the coming into force of the 1996 Act, a convening officer (who had to be a field officer or of corresponding or superior rank, in command of a body of the regular forces or of the command within which the person to be tried was serving) assumed responsibility for every case to be tried by court martial. He or she would decide upon the nature and detail of the charges to be brought and the type of court martial required, and was responsible for convening the court martial.

37. The convening officer would draw up a convening order, which would specify, inter alia, the date, place and time of the trial, the name of the president and the details of the other members, all of whom he could appoint (see paragraph 15 above). He ensured that a judge advocate (see paragraph 43 below) was appointed by the Judge Advocate General's Office and, failing such appointment, could appoint one. He also appointed, or directed a commanding officer to appoint, the prosecuting officer.

38. Prior to the hearing, the convening officer was responsible for sending an abstract of the evidence to the prosecuting officer and to the judge advocate, and could indicate the passages which might be inadmissible. He procured the attendance at trial of all witnesses to be called for the prosecution. When charges were withdrawn, the convening officer's consent was normally obtained, although it was not necessary in all cases, and a plea to a lesser charge could not be accepted from the accused without it.

39. He had also to ensure that the accused had a proper opportunity to prepare his defence, legal representation if required and the opportunity to contact the defence witnesses, and was responsible for ordering the attendance at the hearing of all witnesses "reasonably requested" by the defence.

40. The convening officer could dissolve the court martial either before or during the trial, when required in the interests of the administration of justice (section 95 of the 1955 Act). In addition, he could comment on the "proceedings of a court martial which require confirmation." Those remarks would not form part of the record of the proceedings and would normally be communicated in a separate minute to the members of the court, although in an exceptional case "where a more public instruction [was] required in the interests of discipline," they could be made known in the orders of the command (Queen's Regulations, paragraph 6.129).

41. The convening officer usually acted as confirming officer also (see paragraph 48 below).

(c) Judge Advocate General and judge advocates

42. The current Judge Advocate General was appointed by the Queen in February 1991 for five years. He is answerable to the Queen and is removable from office by her for inability or misbehaviour.

At the time of the events in question, the Judge Advocate General had the role of adviser to the Secretary of State for Defence on all matters touching and concerning the office of Judge Advocate General, including advice on military law and the procedures and conduct of the court-martial system. He was also responsible for advising the confirming and reviewing authorities following a court martial (see paragraph 49 below).

43. Judge advocates are appointed to the Judge Advocate General's Office by the Lord Chancellor. They must have at least seven and five years experience respectively as an advocate or barrister.

44. At the time of the events in question, a judge advocate was appointed to each court martial, either by the Judge Advocate General's Office or by the convening officer. He or she was responsible for advising the court martial on all questions of law and procedure arising during the hearing and the court had to accept this advice unless there were weighty reasons for not doing so. In addition, in conjunction with the president, he was under a duty to ensure that the accused did not suffer any disadvantage during the hearing. For example, if the latter pleaded guilty, the judge advocate had to ensure that he or she fully understood the implications of the plea and admitted all the elements of the charge. At the close of the hearing, the judge advocate would sum up the relevant law and evidence.

45. Prior to the coming into force of the 1996 Act, the judge advocate did not take part in the court martial's deliberations on conviction or acquittal, although he could advise it in private on general principles in relation to sentencing. He was not a member of the court martial and had no vote in the decision on conviction or sentence.

(d) Procedure on a guilty plea

46. At the time of the events in question, on a plea of guilty, the prosecuting officer outlined the facts and put in evidence any circumstance which might have made the accused more susceptible to the commission of the offence. The defence made a plea in mitigation and could call witnesses (rules 71(3)(a) and 71(5)(a) of the 1972 Rules). The members of the court martial then retired with the judge advocate to consider the sentence, which was pronounced in open court. There was no provision for the giving of reasons by the court martial for its decision.

47. Certain types of sentence were not available to courts martial at the time of the applicant's trial, even in respect of civilian offences. For example, a court martial could not suspend a prison sentence, issue a probation order or sentence to community service.

(e) Confirmation and post-hearing reviews

48. Until the amendments introduced by the 1996 Act, a court martial's findings were not effective until confirmed by a "confirming officer." Prior to confirmation, the confirming officer used to seek the advice of the Judge

Advocate General's Office, where a judge advocate different to the one who acted at the hearing would be appointed. The confirming officer could withhold confirmation or substitute, postpone or remit in whole or in part any sentence.

49. Once the sentence had been confirmed, the defendant could petition the "reviewing authorities." These were the Queen, the Defence Council (who could delegate to the Army Board), or any officer superior in command to the confirming officer (section 113 of the 1955 Act). The reviewing authorities could seek the advice of the Judge Advocate General's Office. They had the power to quash a finding and to exercise the same powers as the confirming officer in relation to substituting, remitting or commuting the sentence.

50. A petitioner was not informed of the identity of the confirming officer or of the reviewing authorities. No statutory or formalized procedures were laid down for the conduct of the post-hearing reviews and no reasons were given for decisions delivered subsequent to them. Neither the fact that advice had been received from the Judge Advocate General's Office nor the nature of that advice was disclosed.

51. A courts martial appeal court (made up of civilian judges) could hear appeals against conviction from a court martial, but there was no provision for such an appeal against sentence when the accused pleaded guilty.

2. The Armed Forces Act 1996

52. Under the 1996 Act, the role of the convening officer will cease to exist and his functions will be split among three different bodies: the "higher authorities," the prosecuting authority and court administration officers (see 1996 Act, Schedule I).

53. The higher authority, who will be a senior officer, will decide whether any case referred to him by the accused's commanding officer should be dealt with summarily, referred to the new prosecuting authority, or dropped. Once the higher authority has taken this decision, he or she will have no further involvement in the case.

54. The prosecuting authority will be the Services' legal branches. Following the higher authority's decision to refer a case to them, the prosecuting authority will have absolute discretion, applying similar criteria as those applied in civilian cases by the Crown Prosecution Service to decide whether or not to prosecute, what type of court martial would be appropriate and precisely what charges should be brought. They will then conduct the prosecution (1996 Act, Schedule I, Part II).

55. Court administration officers will be appointed in each Service and will be independent of both the higher and the prosecuting authorities. They will be responsible for making the arrangements for courts martial, including arranging venue and timing, ensuring that a judge advocate and any court officials required will be available, securing the attendance of witnesses and selection of members. Officers under the command of the higher authority will not be selected as members of the court martial (1996 Act, Schedule I, Part III, section 19).

56. Each court martial will in future include a judge advocate as a member. His advice on points of law will become rulings binding on the court and he will have a vote on sentence (but not on conviction). The casting vote, if needed, will rest with the president of the court martial, who will also give reasons for the sentence in open court. The Judge Advocate General will no longer provide general legal advice to the Secretary of State for Defence (1996 Act, Schedule I, Part III, sections 19, 25 and 27).

57. Findings by a court martial will no longer be subject to confirmation or revision by a confirming officer (whose role is to be abolished). A reviewing authority will be established in each Service to conduct a single review of each case. Reasons will be given for the decision of the reviewing authority. As part of this process, post-trial advice received by the reviewing authority from a judge advocate (who will be different from the one who officiated at the court-martial) will be disclosed to the accused. A right of appeal against sentence to the (civilian) courts martial appeal court will be added to the existing right of appeal against conviction (1996 Act, section 17 and Schedule V). . . .

61. In his written and oral pleadings before the Court, Mr Findlay complained that the court martial was not an "independent and impartial tribunal," that it did not give him a "public hearing" and that it was not a tribunal "established by law."

62. The Government and the Commission's Delegate both observed at the hearing that since the latter two complaints had not been expressly raised before the Commission, the Court should decline to entertain them.

63. The Court recalls that the scope of its jurisdiction is determined by the Commission's decision on admissibility and that it has no power to entertain new and separate complaints which were not raised before the Commission (see, inter alia, the *Singh v. the United Kingdom* judgment of 21 February 1996, Reports of Judgments and Decisions 1996-I, p. 293, para. 44). However, while Mr Findlay in his application to the Commission may not expressly have invoked his rights under Article 6 para. 1 of the Convention (art. 6-1) to a "public hearing" and a "tribunal established by law," he does appear to have raised in substance most of the matters which form the basis of his complaints in relation to these two provisions. Thus, in the Commission's decision on admissibility, he is reported as referring in particular to the facts that the members of the court martial were appointed ad hoc, that the judge advocate's advice on sentencing was not disclosed, that no reasons were given for the decisions taken by the court-martial board and the confirming and reviewing officers, and that the post-hearing reviews were essentially administrative in nature and conducted in private (see the Commission's decision on admissibility, application no. 22107/93, pp. 32-35). It follows that these are not new and separate complaints, and that the Court has jurisdiction to consider these matters (see, inter alia and mutatis mutandis, the *James and Others v. the United Kingdom* judgment of 21 February 1986, Series A no. 98, p. 46, para. 80). . . .

C. The new legislation

66. In their written and oral pleadings, the Government asked the Court to take note in its judgment of the changes to be effected in the court-martial system by the Armed Forces Act 1996 (see paragraphs 52-57 above).

67. The Court recalls that this new statute does not come into force until April 1997, and thus did not apply at the time of Mr Findlay's court martial. It is not the Court's task to rule on legislation in abstracto and it cannot therefore express a view as to the compatibility of the provisions of the new legislation with the Convention (see, mutatis mutandis, the *Silver and Others v. the United Kingdom* judgment of 25 March 1983, Series A no. 61, p. 31, para. 79). Nonetheless, it notes with satisfaction that the United Kingdom authorities have made changes to the court-martial system with a view to ensuring the observance of their Convention commitments.

II. Alleged Violation of Article 6 Para 1 of the Convention (art. 6-1)

68. The applicant claimed that his trial by court martial failed to meet the requirements of Article 6 para. 1 of the Convention (art. 6-1), which provides (so far as is relevant):

> "In the determination of . . . any criminal charge against him, everyone is entitled to a fair and public hearing . . . by an independent and impartial tribunal established by law. . . ."

The Commission found that there had been a violation, in that the applicant was not given a fair hearing by an independent and impartial tribunal, and the Government did not contest this conclusion.

A. Applicability

69. In the view of the Court, Article 6 para. 1 (art. 6-1) is clearly applicable to the court-martial proceedings, since they involved the determination of Mr Findlay's sentence following his plea of guilty to criminal charges; indeed, this point was not disputed before it (see the *Engel and Others v. the Netherlands* judgment of 18 June 1976, Series A no. 22, pp. 33-36, paras. 80-85, and the *Eckle v. Germany* judgment of 15 July 1982, Series A no. 51, pp. 34-35, paras. 76-77).

B. Compliance

70. The applicant complained that the court martial was not an "independent and impartial tribunal" as required by Article 6 para. 1 (art. 6-1), because, inter alia, all the officers appointed to it were directly subordinate to the convening officer who also performed the role of prosecuting authority (see paragraphs 14-17 and 36-41 above). The lack of legal qualification or experience in the officers making the decisions either at the court martial or review stages made it impossible for them to act in an independent or impartial manner.

In addition, he asserted that he was not afforded a "public hearing" within the meaning of Article 6 para. 1 (art. 6-1), in that the judge advocate's advice to the court-martial board, the confirming officer and the reviewing authorities was confidential; no reasons were given for the decisions made at any of these stages in the proceedings; and the process of confirming and reviewing the verdict and sentence by the confirming officer and reviewing authorities was carried out administratively, in private, with no apparent rules of procedure (see paragraphs 42-46 and 48-51 above).

Finally, he claimed that his court martial was not a tribunal "established by law," because the statutory framework according to which it proceeded was too vague and imprecise; for example, it was silent on the question of how the convening officer, confirming officer and reviewing authorities were to be appointed.

71. The Government had no observations to make upon the Commission's conclusion that there had been a violation of Article 6 para. 1 of the Convention (art. 6-1) by reason of the width of the role of the convening officer and his command links with members of the tribunal. They asked the Court to take note of the changes to the court-martial system to be effected by the Armed Forces Act 1996 which, in their submission, more than satisfactorily met the Commission's concerns.

72. The Commission found that although the convening officer played a central role in the prosecution of the case, all of the members of the court-martial board were subordinate in rank to him and under his overall command. He also acted as confirming officer, and the court martial's findings had no effect until confirmed by him. These circumstances gave serious cause to doubt the independence of the tribunal from the prosecuting authority. The judge advocate's involvement was not sufficient to dispel this doubt, since he was not a member of the court martial, did not take part in its deliberations and gave his advice on sentencing in private.

In addition, it noted that Mr Findlay's court-martial board contained no judicial members, no legally qualified members and no civilians, that it was set up on an ad hoc basis and that the convening officer had the power to dissolve it either before or during the trial. The requirement to take an oath was not a sufficient guarantee of independence.

Accordingly, it considered that the applicant's fears about the independence of the court martial could be regarded as objectively justified, particularly in view of the nature and extent of the convening officer's roles, the composition of the court martial and its ad hoc nature. This defect was not, moreover, remedied by any subsequent review by a judicial body affording all the guarantees required by Article 6 para. 1 (art. 6-1), since the confirming officer was the same person as the convening officer, and the reviewing authorities were army officers, the second of whom was superior in rank to the first. The ineffectiveness of the post-hearing reviews was further underlined by the secrecy surrounding them and the lack of opportunity for Mr Findlay to participate in a meaningful way.

73. The Court recalls that in order to establish whether a tribunal can be considered as "independent," regard must be had, inter alia, to the manner of appointment of its members and their term of office, the existence of guarantees against outside pressures and the question whether the body presents an appearance of independence (see the *Bryan v. the United Kingdom* judgment of 22 November 1995, Series A no. 335-A, p. 15, para. 37).

As to the question of "impartiality," there are two aspects to this require-ment. First, the tribunal must be subjectively free of personal prejudice or bias. Secondly, it must also be impartial from an objective viewpoint, that is, it must offer sufficient guarantees to exclude any legitimate doubt in this respect (see the *Pullar v. the United Kingdom* judgment of 10 June 1996, Reports 1996-III, p. 792, para. 30).

The concepts of independence and objective impartiality are closely linked and the Court will consider them together as they relate to the present case.

74. The Court observes that the convening officer, as was his responsibility under the rules applicable at the time, played a significant role before the hearing of Mr Findlay's case. He decided which charges should be brought and which type of court martial was most appropriate. He convened the court mar-tial and appointed its members and the prosecuting and defending officers (see paragraphs 14-15 and 36-37 above).

Under the rules then in force, he had the task of sending an abstract of the evidence to the prosecuting officer and the judge advocate and could indicate passages which might be inadmissible. He procured the attendance at trial of the witnesses for the prosecution and those "reasonably requested" by the defence. His agreement was necessary before the prosecuting officer could accept a plea to a lesser charge from an accused and was usually sought before charges were withdrawn (see paragraphs 38 and 39 above).

For these reasons the Court, like the Commission, considers that the con-vening officer was central to Mr Findlay's prosecution and closely linked to the prosecuting authorities.

75. The question therefore arises whether the members of the court martial were sufficiently independent of the convening officer and whether the organ-isation of the trial offered adequate guarantees of impartiality.

In this respect also the Court shares the concerns of the Commission. It is noteworthy that all the members of the court martial, appointed by the con-vening officer, were subordinate in rank to him. Many of them, including the president, were directly or ultimately under his command (see paragraph 16 above). Furthermore, the convening officer had the power, albeit in prescribed circumstances, to dissolve the court martial either before or during the trial (see paragraph 40 above).

76. In order to maintain confidence in the independence and impartiality of the court, appearances may be of importance. Since all the members of the court martial which decided Mr Findlay's case were subordinate in rank to the convening officer and fell within his chain of command, Mr Findlay's doubts about the tribunal's independence and impartiality could be objectively justi-fied (see, mutatis mutandis, the *Sramek v. Austria* judgment of 22 October 1984, Series A no. 84, p. 20, para. 42).

77. In addition, the Court finds it significant that the convening officer also acted as "confirming officer." Thus, the decision of the court martial was not effective until ratified by him, and he had the power to vary the sentence imposed as he saw fit (see paragraph 48 above). This is contrary to the well-established principle that the power to give a binding decision which may not

be altered by a non-judicial authority is inherent in the very notion of "tribunal" and can also be seen as a component of the "independence" required by Article 6 para. 1 (art. 6-1) (see, mutatis mutandis, the *Van de Hurk v. the Netherlands* judgment of 19 April 1994, Series A no. 288, p. 16, para. 45).

78. The Court further agrees with the Commission that these fundamental flaws in the court-martial system were not remedied by the presence of safeguards, such as the involvement of the judge advocate, who was not himself a member of the tribunal and whose advice to it was not made public (see paragraphs 45-46 above), or the oath taken by the members of the court-martial board (see paragraph 35 above).

79. Nor could the defects referred to above (in paragraphs 75 and 77) be corrected by any subsequent review proceedings. Since the applicant's hearing was concerned with serious charges classified as "criminal" under both domestic and Convention law, he was entitled to a first-instance tribunal which fully met the requirements of Article 6 para. 1 (art. 6-1) (see the *De Cubber v. Belgium* judgment of 26 October 1984, Series A no. 86, pp. 16-18, paras. 31-32).

80. For all these reasons, and in particular the central role played by the convening officer in the organisation of the court martial, the Court considers that Mr Findlay's misgivings about the independence and impartiality of the tribunal which dealt with his case were objectively justified.

In view of the above, it is not necessary for it to consider the applicant's other complaints under Article 6 para. 1 (art. 6-1), namely that he was not afforded a "public hearing" by a tribunal "established by law."

In conclusion, there has been a violation of Article 6 para. 1 of the Convention (art. 6-1).

III. Application of Article 50 of the Convention (art. 50)

81. The applicant claimed just satisfaction pursuant to Article 50 of the Convention (art. 50), which states:

> If the Court finds that a decision or a measure taken by a legal authority or any other authority of a High Contracting Party is completely or partially in conflict with the obligations arising from the . . . Convention, and if the internal law of the said Party allows only partial reparation to be made for the consequences of this decision or measure, the decision of the Court shall, if necessary, afford just satisfaction to the injured party.

A. Pecuniary damage

82. The applicant claimed compensation for loss of income totaling 440,200 pounds sterling (GBP), on the basis that, had he not been convicted and sentenced as he was, he would have completed a twenty-two year engagement in the army, eventually attaining the rank of Colour Sergeant, with entitlement to a pension from the age of forty.

83. The Government submitted that a finding of a violation would constitute sufficient satisfaction, or, in the alternative, that only a very modest amount

should be awarded. First, there were no grounds for believing that the applicant would not have been convicted, sentenced to a term of imprisonment and dismissed from the army following his trial (at which he pleaded guilty), even if the court martial had been differently organised. Secondly, it was in any case unlikely that he would have enjoyed a long career in the army, in view of the post traumatic stress disorder and back injury from which he suffered . . . ; he had already received GBP 100,000 in settlement of his civil claim against the Ministry of Defence, a large part of which related to loss of earning capacity.

84. At the hearing, the Commission's Delegate observed that no causal link had been established between the breach of the Convention complained of by the applicant and the alleged pecuniary damage, and submitted that it was not possible to speculate as to whether the proceedings would have led to a different outcome had they fulfilled the requirements of Article 6 para. 1 (art. 6-1).

85. The Court agrees; it cannot speculate as to what the outcome of the court-martial proceedings might have been had the violation of the Convention not occurred (see, for example, the *Schmautzer v. Austria* judgment of 23 October 1995, Series A no. 328-A, p. 16, para. 44). It is therefore inappropriate to award Mr Findlay compensation for pecuniary damage.

B. Non-pecuniary damage

86. The applicant claimed compensation of GBP 50,000 for the distress and suffering caused by the court-martial proceedings and for the eight months he spent in prison. He also asked that his conviction be quashed.

87. The Government pointed out that it was beyond the power of the Court to quash the applicant's conviction.

88. The Court reiterates that it is impossible to speculate as to what might have occurred had there been no breach of the Convention. Furthermore, it has no jurisdiction to quash convictions pronounced by national courts (see the above-mentioned *Schmautzer* judgment, loc. cit.).

In conclusion, the Court considers that a finding of violation in itself affords the applicant sufficient reparation for the alleged non-pecuniary damage. . . .

CONCURRING OPINION OF JUDGE DE MEYER

To this judgment, the result of which I fully approve, I would add a brief remark.

Once again reference is made in its reasoning to "appearances" (paragraphs 73 and 76).

First of all, I would observe that the Court did not need to rely on "appearances," since there were enough convincing elements to enable it to conclude that the court-martial system, under which Lance-Sergeant Findlay was convicted and sentenced in the present case, was not acceptable.

Moreover, I would like to stress that, as a matter of principle, we should never decide anything on the basis of "appearances," and that we should, in particular, not allow ourselves to be impressed by them in determining whether or not a court is independent and impartial. We have been wrong to do so in the past, and we should not do so in the future.

COOPER v. UNITED KINGDOM
European Court of Human Rights, 2003
[2003] ECHR 686

. . .

(a) Service tribunals and Article 6 of the Convention

108. The first point to be considered is whether a service tribunal can try criminal charges against service personnel consistently with the independence and impartiality requirements of Article 6 § 1 of the Convention.

109. The Court recalls that the independence and impartiality of service tribunals was examined in the above-cited *Engel* and *Findlay* judgments and in certain subsequent judgments (including *Coyne v. the United Kingdom*, judgment of 24 September 1997, *Reports* 1997-V, *Hood v. the United Kingdom* [GC], no. 27267/95, ECHR 1999-I, and *Cable and Others v. the United Kingdom* [GC], nos. 24436/94 etc., 18 February 1999). In those cases, the Court examined in detail the structure and functioning of the relevant court-martial process but neither the parties to those cases nor the Court raised the more fundamental question of whether service tribunals could ever determine criminal charges against service personnel consistently with the independence or impartiality requirements of Article 6 § 1 of the Convention.

110. The Grand Chamber would agree with the Chamber's finding in the *Morris* case (at § 59 of that judgment) that there is nothing in the provisions of Article 6 which would, in principle, exclude the determination by service tribunals of criminal charges against service personnel. The question to be answered in each case is whether the individual's doubts about the independence and impartiality of a particular court-martial can be considered to be objectively justified and, in particular, whether there were sufficient guarantees to exclude any such legitimate doubts (see paragraph 104 above).

(b) The Higher Authority, the Prosecuting Authority and the CAO

111. The Court has, in the first instance, assessed the independence and impartiality of those bodies involved in the proceedings prior to the court-martial hearing itself namely, the Higher Authority, the Prosecuting Authority and the CAO.

112. While the Higher Authority decides on the basis of service considerations whether a charge should be brought before the Prosecuting Authority, it is the Prosecuting Authority which decides whether a prosecution by court-martial should be pursued or not. The 1996 Act has not conferred on the Higher Authority, and there is no evidence that the Higher Authority fulfils, any other role in the pursuit of charges by court-martial. Since the decision to prosecute by court-martial is one exclusively for the Prosecuting Authority, it is not relevant to the independence of the court-martial process whether the Higher Authority is legally qualified or not or whether there is a chain of command connection between that Authority and the CO. The applicant's sugges-

tion that the Higher Authority is the equivalent of the former Convening Officer is clearly incorrect.

113. The Prosecuting Authority is appointed by the Queen and is legally qualified. Members of his staff are legally qualified and are employed exclusively on prosecution duties. The decision to prosecute is made on the basis of legal criteria similar to those applied by the Crown Prosecution Service and in accordance with the Codes of Conduct of the respective branches of the legal profession. While the Prosecuting Authority is also the RAF Director of Legal Services, he is answerable to the Attorney General only, and is not reported upon within the service, on his prosecution duties. There being no chain of command or service connection between the Higher and Prosecuting Authorities either claimed or apparent, any seniority in rank of the Higher Authority over the Prosecuting Authority would not be sufficient to conclude, as the applicant suggests, that the latter is "likely to" be influenced by the former.

114. It is true that the CAOs are RAF officers appointed by the Defence Council. However, the applicant did not dispute that a CAO operates independently of the Higher and Prosecuting Authority, a conclusion also reached in the *Morris* judgment (at §§61 and 66). Moreover, the CAO's duties are largely administrative in nature, requiring the CAO to take steps which have been regulated in some detail in the 1955 Act, the 1997 Rules and the Queen's Regulations to ensure that a court-martial hearing takes place with the necessary persons in attendance and with the required facilities in place. As to the more significant and sensitive task of selecting members of a court-martial, the detailed criteria and procedures to be followed by a CAO (see paragraphs 34-35 above) allow that officer little discretion in that selection and rebut the applicant's claim that the selection process lacks transparency. In addition, these criteria expressly exclude from a court-martial any officer from the accused's RAF station and any of his COs as well as any officer who has been involved with the investigation and prosecution of the charges or with the convening of a court-martial. Furthermore, all officers selected to sit are reminded in the CMAU (RAF) Briefing Notes received by them (see paragraphs 45-62 above) of these and any other factors that could render them ineligible and members are encouraged to inform the CAO prior to the trial (or the Judge Advocate once the trial has commenced) if they are concerned that they may be ineligible.

115. For these reasons, the Grand Chamber finds that the applicant's submissions concerning these three bodies do not cast any doubt on the Chamber's findings in the *Morris* case (at §61 and 62 of that judgment) as to the genuineness of the separation of the prosecuting, convening and adjudicating roles in the court-martial process under the 1996 Act. The Grand Chamber further considers that there is no reason to doubt the independence of the decision-making of those bodies from chain of command, rank or other service influence.

(c) The members of the court-martial

116. The Court has also examined the position of the members of the court-martial having regard to the manner of their appointment, their terms of office, the existence of guarantees against outside pressures and whether the court-martial presents an appearance of independence (see paragraph 104 above).

(i) The Judge Advocate

117. The Judge Advocate is a legally qualified civilian appointed to the staff of the JAG (also a civilian) by the Lord Chancellor and from there to each court-martial by the JAG. The independence of air-force Judge Advocates is not questioned by the applicant and the Court considers that there is no ground upon which to do so.

Moreover, a Judge Advocate has a central role in the court-martial proceedings which, as Lord Rodger in the case of *R. v. Boyd and Others*, the Grand Chamber would compare to that of a Crown Court trial judge. The Judge Advocate is responsible for the fair and lawful conduct of the court-martial and his rulings on the course of the evidence and on all questions of law are binding and must be given in open court. The Judge Advocate has no vote on verdict and does not therefore retire with the other court-martial members to deliberate on verdict. However, he sums up the evidence and delivers further directions to the other members of the court-martial beforehand and he can refuse to accept a verdict if he considers it "contrary to law" in which case he gives the President and ordinary members further directions in open court, following which those members retire again to consider verdict. The Judge Advocate retires with the other members in order to provide advice, deliberate and vote on sentence. Moreover, and as Lord Rodger also noted (see paragraph 72 above), there is no evidence to suggest that members (the PPCM and the ordinary members) of a court-martial would be less diligent than civilian jurors in complying with binding rulings and directions on points of law given to them.

In such circumstances, the Court finds that the presence in a court-martial of a civilian with such qualifications and with such a pivotal role in the proceedings constitutes not only an important safeguard but one of the most significant guarantees of the independence of the court-martial proceedings.

(ii) The PPCM [Permanent President of the Court-Martial]

118. The Grand Chamber, like the Chamber in the *Morris* case (see §§ 68-69 of that judgment), considers certain factors illustrative of both the PPCM's independence and the important contribution of the post of PPCM to the independence of an otherwise *ad hoc* tribunal.

Most importantly, the Court observes that, while the PPCM is a serving officer, the post was a full-time one filled by a high ranking officer (Wing Commander) for a number of years prior to his retirement, at a time when that officer had "no effective hope of promotion" (Lord Bingham at paragraph 66 above). Such factors were considered demonstrative of the independence of the military members of the court-martial in the above-cited *Engel* case (at §§ 30 and 89 of that judgment).

The Court does not accept the applicant's suggestion that the full-time nature of the post of PPCM would undermine the objectivity of that officer's judgment (see paragraph 88 above). Since the PPCM was bound by the legal rulings and directions of the Judge Advocate, the PPCM's lack of legal qualifications did not undermine his independence or the guarantee of independence provided by that post. While he may have been more senior in rank to the ordinary members, he could not brief them in the absence of the Judge Advocate and, although he deliberated on verdict alone with the ordinary members, the Judge Advocate exercised firm control over those deliberations both before and after they took place (see paragraphs 29 and 117 above).

It is true that, in contrast to the army, appraisal reports were raised on PPCMs in the RAF and the Court would echo the concerns expressed by Lords Bingham and Rodger in this regard. However, the essential point for present purposes is that no appraisal report had been raised on the present PPCM since August 1997 and, crucially, such reports could not have referred to that officer's judicial decision-making. As Lord Bingham pointed out (see paragraph 66 above), PPCMs were answerable to no-one in the discharge of their court-martial functions.

It is also true that there was no express provision for their irremovability and that express security of tenure would be preferable as such a domestic provision is generally considered to be a corollary of judges' independence. However, its absence can be cured if irremovability is recognised in fact and if other necessary guarantees are present (*Campbell and Fell v. the United Kingdom* judgment of 28 June 1984, Series A no. 80, § 80, and the *Morris* judgment, at § 68). In this respect, the Court notes the finding of Lord Bingham (see paragraph 66 above) that a PPCM had "no effective fear of removal" and it is not disputed that a PPCM has never been removed from office.

(iii) The ordinary members

119. The Court considers it clear that, having regard to the matters outlined at paragraph 114 above, there was no reason to doubt the independence of the ordinary members by reason of the position and role of the CAO [Court Administration Officer] or because of the manner in which the CAO appointed them.

120. The Grand Chamber has noted the *ad hoc* nature of their appointment (they return to ordinary service immediately after the court-martial) and their relatively junior rank (they were junior in rank to the PPCM and may have been junior in rank to other participants in the court-martial process including the Prosecuting Authority). While such tenure and rank may not of themselves undermine their independence, it is considered, as it was in the *Morris* case (at § 70 of that judgment), that such factors emphasise the need for the existence of particularly convincing safeguards against outside pressure being brought to bear on those officers.

121. In its judgment in the *Morris* case, the Chamber went on to find important the protection offered by the Judge Advocate, by the PPCM and by the rules concerning eligibility for selection to a court-martial and the oath taken by its members. Other safeguards were also referred to in the *Morris* judgment including the right of the accused to object to any member sitting in the court-martial (paragraph 38 above); the confidentiality of the deliberations, a point repeated in the members' oath (also at paragraph 38 above); and the rule whereby the most junior ranking member expresses his or her view and votes first during deliberations on verdict and sentence (paragraphs 39, 58 and 60 above). Moreover, the Grand Chamber considers that the possibility of a prosecution for perverting the course of justice under the common law or under

section 69 of the 1955 Act (see paragraph 36 above) was implicit in the Chamber's assessment in the *Morris* case.

The Grand Chamber agrees that these safeguards constitute important safeguards of the independence of the ordinary members.

122. Nevertheless, the Chamber concluded in the *Morris* case that these safeguards were not sufficient to exclude the risk of outside pressure being brought to bear on the ordinary members because of three factors: those officers had no legal training, there were no statutory or other bars to their being made subject to external service influence and they remained subject to army discipline and reports (the *Morris* judgment, at §§ 71 and 72).

The Grand Chamber is of the view that the submissions and material before it in the present case are such as to justify it in departing from this latter conclusion in the *Morris* judgment.

123. As to the lack of legal qualification of the ordinary members, the Court recalls that the participation of lay judges on tribunals is not, as such, contrary to Article 6: the principles established in the case-law concerning independence and impartiality are to be applied to lay judges as to professional judges (*Langborger v. Sweden*, judgment of 22 June 1989, Series A no. 155, § 32, *Fey v. Austria* judgment of 24 February 1993, Series A no. 255-A, §§ 27, 28 and 30, and *Holm v. Sweden*, judgment of 25 November 1993, Series A no. 279-A, § 30).

The Court does not find particularly relevant the fact that the ordinary members in the applicant's court-martial attended brief legal courses. However, it notes the instruction provided to the ordinary members by the CMAU (RAF) Briefing Notes (paragraphs 45-62 above and 124 below). The Court also recalls the key role of the legally qualified and experienced Judge Advocate, whose directions the ordinary members would be careful to respect (see paragraph 117 above). In such circumstances, the Court considers that that the independence of the ordinary members is not undermined by their lack of legal qualifications.

124. Secondly, the submissions to the Court in the present case disclosed an additional safeguard of the independence of the ordinary members.

The Government relied on the CMAU (RAF) Briefing Notes distributed to all members of the applicant's court-martial. True it is that the actual notes applicable on that date could not be located by the Government, it being merely asserted that the Notes outlined at paragraphs 45-62 above were similar in all substantive respects to those actually distributed to members of the applicant's court-martial. However, in the absence of any precise and substantiated challenge to this assertion of the Government, the Court does not see any reason to doubt that the Notes submitted to it in the present case were similar in all material respects to those actually distributed to members of the applicant's court-martial in February 1998. Moreover, the Court considers these Notes to be genuine instructions to the members of courts-martial by which they were expected to abide.

The Notes provided a detailed step-by-step guide to the ordinary members of the procedures before a court-martial. They also constituted a comprehensive manual of the nature and limits of their role in those proceedings and, importantly, of the precise functions of the Judge Advocate and PPCM. The Court considers that the Briefing Notes thereby provided essential information and important orientation to officers who were appointed on an *ad hoc* basis to a court-martial and who had no legal qualifications and relatively little court-martial experience.

Further, the provisions of the Briefing Notes fully instructed ordinary members of the need to function independently of outside or inappropriate influence or instruction and of the importance of this being seen to be done, providing practical and precise indications of how this could be achieved or undermined in a particular situation. The Court considers that those instructions served not only to bring home to the members the vital importance of independence but also to provide a significant impediment to any inappropriate pressure being brought to bear.

Accordingly, the Grand Chamber is of the opinion that the distribution and content of these Briefing Notes constituted a further safeguard of the independence of the ordinary members, a safeguard of which the Chamber was not informed when it examined the *Morris* case.

125. Thirdly, the Court finds most important the Government's clarification in the present case that ordinary members of a court-martial could not be reported upon in relation to their judicial decision-making. As Lord Bingham pointed out in *R. v. Boyd and Others*, the prohibition on the members disclosing any opinion expressed or vote cast during the court-martial proceedings presents a practical obstacle to such reporting. The Court also notes that the evidence submitted by the appellants and the Ministry of Defence to the House of Lords produced no example of any reporting on the decision-making of the members of a court-martial (see paragraph 75 above).

126. For these reasons, the Court finds that there were sufficient safeguards of the independence of the ordinary members of the applicant's court-martial.

(d) The Reviewing Authority

127. The Government contested the finding in the *Morris* case on the role of the Reviewing Authority: they emphasised that such a review could only operate to the benefit of the convicted person and that that person would retain full access to the CMAC thereafter. The applicant relied on the above-cited *Brumărescu v. Romania* judgment, on the *Findlay* judgment (§§ 77 and 79) and on the *Morris* judgment (at §§ 73-77). He pointed out that, in any event, such reviews did not always operate in favour of the individual.

128. In the Court's opinion, the *Van de Hurk v. the Netherlands* judgment (of 19 April 1994, Series A no. 288, §§ 45 and 50) and the *Findlay* judgment (§ 77 and § 52, respectively) make it clear that it is the power of a non-judicial authority to interfere with the findings of a court-martial for which the 1996 Act provides which is to be examined by this Court, irrespective of whether that power was in fact used and of whether that power could only have been exercised in the applicant's favour.

129. In the post-1996 system under review in the present case, a court-martial reached a verdict and decided on sentence. Whether or not an individual

applied to the Reviewing Authority, the latter would automatically review both the verdict and sentence. Subsequently, the individual could appeal against the verdict and sentence to the CMAC. Consequently, the Reviewing Authority formed part of a process at the end of which the verdict and sentence became final. The Court would therefore agree with the Government that this can be contrasted with the position in the above-cited *Brumǎrescu* case, where the applicant had been deprived of the benefit of the legal certainty of a judicial decision which had already become final, irreversible and thus *res judicata*.

130. The Court further considers, as did Lords Bingham and Rodger in the House of Lords, that the Reviewing Authority is an anomalous feature of the present court-martial system and it would express its concern about a criminal procedure which empowers a non-judicial authority to interfere with judicial findings.

131. Nevertheless, the Court notes that the final decision in court-martial proceedings will always lie with a judicial authority, namely the CMAC. This is the case even if a Reviewing Authority quashes a verdict and authorises a re-trial: even if the Prosecuting Authority were to decide to bring a fresh prosecution and even if a court-martial were to refuse to stay those further proceedings as an abuse of process, the final review of any new conviction and sentence would remain with the CMAC.

In the above-cited *Van de Hurk* case, the Court did not exclude that the Crown's power partially or completely to deprive a court's judgment of its effect could have been remedied by a subsequent review by a judicial body that afforded all the guarantees required by Article 6, although no such review was found to exist in that case. The appeal to the CMAC was not considered sufficient in the *Findlay* case since he had pleaded guilty at first instance and no appeal lay against sentence only to the CMAC.

132. The Court regards as unsubstantiated the applicant's assertion that courts-martial adjust sentences upwards in anticipation of the Reviewing Authority assessment. Moreover, it does not consider persuasive his submission that the CMAC would be unduly influenced by the decision of the Reviewing Authority: the essential fact is that the CMAC is not in any way bound by the advice to, or the decision of, the Reviewing Authority. Indeed, one of the domestic cases on which the applicant relied (*R. v. Ball* and *R. v. Rugg*, cited above) resulted in the CMAC overturning the finding on sentence of the Reviewing Authority.

133. Accordingly, the Court finds that the role of the Reviewing Authority did not, in the circumstances of the present case, breach the principle outlined at paragraph 106 above and, in particular, did not undermine the independence or impartiality of the applicant's court-martial.

(e) Conclusion

134. In all of the above circumstances, the Court concludes that the applicant's misgivings about the independence and impartiality of his court-mar-

tial, convened under the 1996 Act, were not objectively justified and that the court-martial proceedings cannot consequently be said to have been unfair.

There has therefore not been a violation of Article 6 § 1 of the Convention.

NOTES AND QUESTIONS

1. What are the minimum protections needed to ensure military judicial independence? How would you prioritize them? What are the arguments for and against relying on civilian judges to adjudicate military cases?

2. Would the United States military justice system pass muster under *Findlay* or *Cooper*? If not, should we care?

3. Why couldn't the European Court set aside Findlay's conviction?

4. Is Judge De Meyer's objection to ruling on the basis of appearances well-founded?

Chapter 13

THE MILITARY JURY

The rules governing the qualifications, selection, and functions of United States court-martial panels vary markedly from those for civilian juries. A court-martial panel is rarely a jury of the accused's peers. Rather, by statute, court-martial members should be senior to the accused. Congress has also specified that court-martial members should be selected based on their qualifications as reflected by their "age, education, training, experience, length of service, and judicial temperament." But military appellate courts have placed restrictions on ruling out entire classes of servicemembers, such as junior ranking enlisted members, from consideration for service on a court-martial panel.

Court-martial member selection is one of the most controversial aspects of the military justice system. The convening authority, the same official who chooses to have a case prosecuted at a court-martial, selects the members who will hear that case. This power has, in some instances, been abused to stack the court with members perceived as favorable to the prosecution. Concerns over commanding officers' power to select court-martial members led the European Court of Human Rights to declare that the British military justice system violated the European Convention on Human Rights. The convening authority's selection of members was also one factor that led the Supreme Court of Canada to hold that the Canadian military justice system violated the Canadian Charter of Rights and Freedoms.

In the United States, proposals periodically arise to reform the court-martial system to eliminate the potential for abuse that arises when the convening authority selects the members. But the current system has defenders as well as critics and Congress has declined to change the system.

Under a series of Supreme Court opinions from the late 1970s, a five-member civilian jury would be unconstitutional, as would a system that allows non-unanimous convictions adjudged by a six-member jury. Yet a non-capital general court-martial can have as few as five members, and the vote of four of those five would be sufficient to convict the accused. The courts have thus far been hostile to legal challenges attempting to apply the civilian case law governing jury size and voting requirements to the military justice system.

The military justice system's court-martial panel remains far different than its civilian counterpart. As you review the materials in this chapter, consider whether the military court-martial panel is better, worse, or merely different than the civilian jury.

I. THE COURT-MARTIAL PANEL

Uniform Code of Military Justice
Article 25. Who may serve on courts-martial

(a) Any commissioned officer on active duty is eligible to serve on all courts-martial for the trial of any person who may lawfully be brought before such courts for trial.

(b) Any warrant officer on active duty is eligible to serve on general and special courts-martial for the trial of any person, other than a commissioned officer, who may lawfully be brought before such courts for trial.

(c)(1) Any enlisted member of an armed force on active duty who is not a member of the same unit as the accused is eligible to serve on general and special courts-martial for the trial of any enlisted member of an armed force who may lawfully be brought before such courts for trial, but he shall serve as a member of a court only if, before the conclusion of a session called by the military judge under section 839(a) of this title (article 39(a)) prior to trial or, in the absence of such a session, before the court is assembled for the trial of the accused, the accused personally has requested orally on the record or in writing that enlisted members serve on it. After such a request, the accused may not be tried by a general or special court-martial the membership of which does not include enlisted members in a number comprising at least one-third of the total membership of the court, unless eligible enlisted members cannot be obtained on account of physical conditions or military exigencies. If such members cannot be obtained, the court may be assembled and the trial held without them, but the convening authority shall make a detailed written statement, to be appended to the record, stating why they could not be obtained.

(2) In this article, "unit" means any regularly organized body as defined by the Secretary concerned, but in no case may it be a body larger than a company, squadron, ship's crew, or body corresponding to one of them.

(d)(1) When it can be avoided, no member of an armed force may be tried by a court-martial any member of which is junior to him in rank or grade.

(2) When convening a court-martial, the convening authority shall detail as members thereof such members of the armed forces as, in his opinion, are best qualified for the duty by reason of age, education, training, experience, length of service, and judicial temperament. No member of an armed force is eligible to serve as a member of a general or special court-martial when he is the accuser or a witness for the prosecution or has acted as investigating officer or as counsel in the same case. . . .

UNITED STATES v. KIRKLAND
United States Court of Appeals for the Armed Forces
53 M.J. 22 (C.A.A.F. 2000)

CRAWFORD, C.J.:

Facts

Prior to his court-martial, appellant submitted a request for the appointment of enlisted members. In response to that request, the General Court-Martial Convening Authority (GCMCA) selected senior enlisted servicemembers as members of appellant's court-martial panel. These enlisted members were selected from a nomination list of nine noncommissioned officers provided to the GCMCA by the Special Court-Martial Convening Authority (SPCMCA) and his servicing Staff Judge Advocate (SJA). At trial, appellant's defense counsel brought a motion to dismiss for lack of jurisdiction based on improper jury selection.

Two paralegal noncommissioned officers from the Base Legal Office testified at trial as to the process for nominating and recommending prospective enlisted court members for appellant's court-martial. Senior Airman G testified that the Legal Office sent out a quarterly letter to the group commanders, signed by the Base Commander, the SPCMCA, asking for nominees for a court member selection pool. The letter requested each commander nominate a specific number of qualified personnel from a variety of ranks. Each nominee was required to submit an updated court member data sheet to the Legal Office. Attached to the letter was a chart evidencing the specific number of personnel of each military rank a particular commander was asked to nominate. This chart was based on a "unit management document" utilized by the Base Legal Office military justice section. The number and rank of the personnel that each commander was asked to nominate for court member selection was derived from the unit management document in order to avoid overtasking the individual units. The chart had a column for E-7, E-8, and E-9, but no place to list a nominee in a lower grade. To nominate an E-6 or below, the nominating official would have to modify the form.

Staff Sergeant F, the other paralegal noncommissioned officer, stated that she supplied the names of enlisted personnel for court-martial duty by looking through a Legal Office notebook filled with the data sheets of the enlisted personnel nominated by their units as potential court-martial panel members. She then called the units to determine each potential member's availability, and compiled a list of the available members, which was provided to the SPCMCA with the court member data sheets.

Colonel C, the SPCMCA, testified he nominated prospective court members from the list provided by the Legal Office and then transmitted the list to the GCMCA, Major General H, who made the final selections. He also testified that he understood that he could recommend whomever he wanted for the court-martial, provided they met the requirements of Article 25, UCMJ, 10 U.S.C. § 825.

Lieutenant Colonel W, the acting SJA, testified that the Legal Office transmitted the list to the GCMCA. He also testified that he briefed Major General

H on his duties and his ability to select other military members, assuming they met Article 25 criteria.

In finding a lack of intent by the convening authority to systematically exclude enlisted members below the grade of E-7, the military judge made the following pertinent findings of fact and conclusions of law:

> Over the last three months, three enlisted members had requested enlisted members on their court. These requests required them to duplicate this process for enlisted members, and in order to save time, the military justice section NCOs requested the squadrons and groups to also nominate NCOs. The worksheet only had room for E-9s, E-8s, and E-7s. When the accused in this case requested enlisted members, the NCOs only contacted enlisted members for whom they had data sheets, specifically E-7s, E-8s and E-9s.

> The legal office then submitted Appellate Exhibit IV to the special court-martial convening authority to use to recommend names of enlisted members who were available for court duty. The special court-martial convening authority testified he knows he can pick any-one under his command as a court member. He has filled in names of persons not in the suggested list before, but chose not to do so in this case. . . .

> In this case, the original court panel contained a broad spectrum of ranks. The special court-martial convening authority has no recollec-tion as to why he chose to delete the junior officer members from this court when the accused requested enlisted members, other than he had appointed a lieutenant colonel to be an investigating officer and needed to excuse him. . . .

> In this case, the testimony of the special court-martial convening authority and the general court-martial convening authority['s] legal advisor is that rank was not a criterion for member selection, and both convening authorities know about their authority to appoint any mem-ber of their command as a court member.

> The likelihood is that subconsciously enlisted members below E-7 were not selected because they did not appear on the list which is Appellate Exhibit IV. The likelihood that someone not on the list will be selected is less than the likelihood someone on the list will be selected. However, does this equate to a violation of Article 25? In light of the explicit testimony, the answer is no.

Discussion

Whether a court-martial panel was selected free from systematic exclusion is a question of law which we review de novo. *United States v. McClain*, 22 M.J. 124 (C.M.A. 1986). The defense shoulders the burden of establishing the improper exclusion of qualified personnel from the selection process. *United States v. Roland*, 50 M.J. 66, 69 (1999). Once the defense establishes such exclusion, the Government must show by competent evidence that no impro-priety occurred when selecting appellant's court-martial members. *Cf.*

Castaneda v. Partida, 430 U.S. 482, 501 (1977) (state failed to rebut the presumption of purposeful discrimination by competent testimony).

While the military defendant does not enjoy a Sixth Amendment right to a trial by "impartial jury," he or she does have a right to "members who are fair and impartial." *Roland*, 50 M.J. at 68. In *Roland*, we stated that "members may not be selected solely on the basis of their rank." We also said:

> Presenting nominations to a convening authority is a reasonable means of assisting the convening authority, provided it does not improperly exclude eligible servicemembers. . . . This nomination process may not systematically exclude or include a certain category of servicemembers. When the request for nominations does improperly include or exclude certain members, this court will ensure that those actions do not taint the selection by the convening authority.

Id. at 68-69 (citation omitted).

Here, the Legal Office sent out a quarterly letter with an attached chart to the group commanders, signed by the Base Commander, asking for nominees for a court member selection pool. The letter from the SJA told the group commanders to nominate officers and senior enlisted persons using the attached chart. The chart did not provide any place to nominate court members below the grade of E-7.

Additionally, when suggested nominations were forwarded, there were no enlisted nominees below the grade of E-7. Finally, the GCMCA did not appoint any enlisted member not on the list.

Although this case does not involve the clear institutional bias found in *McClain*, the exclusion of potentially qualified members below the grade of E-7 in this case was improper. *See generally United States v. Daigle*, 1 M.J. 139 (C.M.A. 1975). Under these facts, we hold that the military judge erred in denying the defense request for a new court-martial panel.

Even though the military judge found that neither the SPCMCA nor the GCMCA used rank as a criterion in the selection process, where an unresolved appearance that potentially qualified court members below the grade of E-7 were excluded, "reversal of the sentence is appropriate to uphold the essential fairness and integrity of the military justice system." *McClain*, 22 M.J. at 133 (Cox, J., concurring in the result). . . .

SULLIVAN, J. (dissenting):

I fail to understand why the majority is departing from *United States v. Roland*, 50 M.J. 66 (1999), which was decided only a year ago. I concurred in the result of that case which affirmed the decision of the court below that the military judge did not err in failing to find that the jury had been improperly selected. I stated:

> The staff judge advocate (SJA)'s letter sought court nominations from every grade from E-5 to O-6 to be included in the recommended jury pool. The implicit exclusion of certain ranks (E-4 and below) in appellant's case troubles me. However, the SJA's letter, on its face, was designated as mere guidance, and the convening authority was informed

of his opportunity to select anyone from his command. Moreover, the military judge found that no bad intent to influence the court-martial and no deliberate stacking of the pool existed, as in *United States v. Hilow*, 32 M.J. 439 (C.M.A. 1991). I would hold there was no violation of Articles 25 and 37, Uniform Code of Military Justice, 10 USC §§ 825 and 837, in these circumstances. Perhaps, if a random jury selection system now being studied by the Department of Defense is adopted, challenges like the one in this case will occur less. *See United States v. Upshaw*, 49 M.J. 111, 114 (1998) (Sullivan, J., concurring).

50 M.J. at 70.

I am troubled by the implicit exclusion of certain ranks in appellant's case as well, but I reach the same conclusion here as I did in my separate opinion in *Roland*. The majority places too much emphasis on the "form" of the chart attached to the letter asking for court-martial member nominees in the instant case. As in *Roland*, the instant record shows no policy to exclude portions of the enlisted ranks. Specifically, the form of the chart demonstrates nothing but a mistake of the legal office and the command in putting together the composition of this court-martial. The majority truly elevates "form" over substance to reverse a case without adequate legal reason. I would affirm this felony drug conviction and the approved sentence.

NOTES

1. As the *Kirkland* majority opinion suggests, the Supreme Court has repeatedly indicated that the Sixth Amendment right to a jury trial does not apply at courts-martial. *See, e.g.*, *Whelchel v. McDonald*, 340 U.S. 122 (1950) ("the right to trial by jury guaranteed by the Sixth Amendment is not applicable to trials by courts-martial or military commissions"). Different commentators have offered competing explanations for why the Sixth Amendment jury right does not apply at courts-martial. *Compare* Gordon D. Henderson, *Courts-Martial and the Constitution: The Original Understanding*, 71 HARV. L. REV. 293, 305 (1957) (arguing that the Framers' "failure specifically to write" an intended court-martial exception into the Sixth Amendment's jury right "was the result of oversight or poor draftsmanship"), *with* Frederick Bernays Wiener, *Courts-Martial and the Bill of Rights: The Original Practice II*, 72 HARV. L. REV. 266, 280-84 (1958) (reviewing historical practice and concluding that the Sixth Amendment's phrase "all criminal prosecutions" did not include courts-martial).

2. The Defense Department study that Judge Sullivan mentioned in his *Kirkland* dissent advised against adopting a random selection method. Joint Service Committee on Military Justice, Report on the Methods of Selection of Members of the Armed Forces to Serve on Courts-Martial (1999). One Army Corps recently experimented with a random court-martial member selection system. *See generally* Lt. Col. Bradley J. Huestis, *Anatomy of a Random Court-Martial Panel*, ARMY LAW., Oct. 2006, at 22.

II. DIFFERENCES BETWEEN THE COURT-MARTIAL PANEL AND THE CIVILIAN JURY

LOVING v. HART
United States Court of Appeals for the Armed Forces
47 M.J. 438 (C.A.A.F. 1998)

EFFRON, J. (concurring in part and dissenting in part)

I. The Unique Purposes and Procedures of a Court-Martial Panel

. . . .

B. Selection of a Court-Martial Panel

[The rules of procedure governing court-martial panels] reflect the fundamental distinctions between a civilian jury and a court-martial panel. In a civilian proceeding, an accused person has a constitutional right to trial by a jury of peers selected at random from a representative cross-section of the community. U.S. Const. amend. VI; Jury Selection and Service Act of 1968, 28 U.S.C. §§ 1861-69; *Duren v. Missouri*, 439 U.S. 357 (1979). A person's status or stature in the community is not a permissible basis for selection to serve on a jury, although certain circumstances, such as a felony conviction, may disqualify an individual from serving. A civilian jury is concerned primarily with adjudication of guilt, although juries in some jurisdictions have a role in the sentencing process, particularly in capital cases.

A court-martial panel has a much broader function than a civilian jury. Unless the accused requests a bench trial, the court-martial panel determines guilt and adjudges the sentence. A court-martial panel is empowered not only to impose the typical criminal law punishments of confinement and fines, but also to adjudge a sentence that affects an individual's military status. Permissible punishments include reductions in rank, forfeiture of pay and allowances, and separation from military service. The court-martial panel is not simply an element of a criminal law system; it also plays a key role in management of military personnel and maintenance of good order and discipline in the armed forces. *See* R. Everett, Military Justice in the Armed Forces of the United States 4-7 (1956).

Given the unique functions of a court-martial, it has long been held that a military accused does not have a constitutional right to a panel randomly selected from a cross-section of the military community. Art. 25, UCMJ, 10 U.S.C. § 825; *Ex parte Quirin*, 317 U.S. 1, 39-41 (1942); *United States v. Smith*, 27 M.J. 242, 248 (C.M.A. 1988); *see also United States ex rel. Toth v. Quarles*, 350 U.S. 11, 17-18 (1955). Selection of panel members is a function of command, and the manner of selection reflects the disciplinary role of the proceedings.

The convening authority who refers a case to trial selects the panel that will adjudicate the issue of guilt and, in the event of a finding of guilty, adjudge the sentence. Stature and status are permissible considerations in selecting a court-martial panel. The persons chosen by the convening authority are those "best qualified for the duty by reason of age, education, training, experience, length of service, and judicial temperament." Art. 25(d)(2); *see also* R.C.M. 502(a)(1). All panel members are officers, unless an enlisted accused requests inclusion of enlisted members; and, if possible, members of a court-martial panel normally must be equal to or senior in rank and grade to the accused. Art. 25(c)(1) and (d)(1). As a result of these criteria, the military personnel detailed to sit on courts-martial are likely to be relatively senior and are likely to have command or supervisory experience.

Consistent with standard military practice, the officer senior in rank serves as the leader of the court-martial panel and is designated as the president. R.C.M. 502(b)(1). In addition to the duties assigned to other members, the president presides over the closed sessions of the court-martial during deliberations of the members. R.C.M. 502(b)(2)(A). We have recognized that the authority to preside includes "the discretion to call for a vote when, in their judgment, discussion of the issues is complete or further debate would be pointless." *United States v. Accordino*, 20 M.J. 102, 105 (1985). The president also speaks for the members in announcing decisions or when "requesting instructions from the military judge." R.C.M. 502(b)(2)(B).

Within the court-martial proceeding, specific attention is given to the rank structure of the panel. For example, the Discussion accompanying R.C.M. 911 notes: "The members are seated with the president, who is the senior member, in the center, and the other members alternately to the president's right and left according to rank. If the rank of a member is changed, or if the membership of the court-martial changes, the members should be reseated accordingly." Each member is in uniform, which contains a visible display of the insignia of rank.

The customs, traditions, and rules that govern military life reinforce the authority of the president of a court-martial and the willingness of members to respect that authority. Obedience to superiors is one of the fundamental norms of military life, emphasized from the very inception of military status in the oath of enlistment, 10 U.S.C. § 502, and reinforced by the criminal sanctions that may be imposed for disobedience, Arts. 90, 91, and 92, UCMJ, 10 U.S.C. §§ 890, 891, and 892, respectively. The Supreme Court has observed that "to accomplish its mission the military must foster instinctive obedience, unity, commitment, and esprit de corps." *Goldman v. Weinberger*, 475 U.S. 503, 507 (1986).

Congress and the President have determined that our national security requires a military justice system that involves the express recognition of rank in selection of court-martial members and in the role of the presiding officer. Although these characteristics find no parallel in the attributes of civilian juries, the Supreme Court has recognized that the differences are permissible because "the military constitutes a specialized community governed by a separate discipline from that of the civilian." *Orloff v. Willoughby*, 345 U.S. 83, 94 (1953).

Congress and the President have recognized that the maintenance of good order and discipline requires more than an unfettered role for command in the court-martial process. Military law, from the time of the first Articles of War through the establishment of the Uniform Code of Military Justice, has reflected an understanding that members of the armed forces are more likely to obey orders under a disciplinary system which is fair and which they perceive to operate without the unlawful influence of rank. This understanding is implemented through provisions such as the general prohibition against unlawful command influence, Art. 37, UCMJ, 10 U.S.C. § 837, as well as specific provisions designed to minimize the influence of rank within a court-martial panel. The general admonitions against use of rank to control the exercise of judgment, *e.g.*, R.C.M. 502(a)(2), 921(a), and 1006(a), are reinforced by the specific procedural rules . . ., such as the requirements for secret written ballots and written sentence proposals, reliance on the junior member to count the votes, and limitations on reconsideration.

III. SELECTION OF THE MEMBERS BY THE CONVENING AUTHORITY

UNITED STATES v. SMITH
United States Court of Military Appeals
27 M.J. 242 (C.M.A. 1988)

EVERETT, C.J.:

I

A

During March 1982, appellant, Lieutenant Engiles, and their company went to Fort Irwin, California, to support the Gallant Eagle Exercise. The entire platoon was bivouacked in two large tents, one of which Engiles shared with appellant and several enlisted men. One end of the tent had been cordoned off to insure Lieutenant Engiles some measure of privacy. On April 8, 1982, Smith, Engiles, and some other officers attended an awards dinner at a nearby officers' club. Lieutenant Engiles testified that, after returning to the tent later that evening, Smith had entered her portion of the tent in the dark, placed one or both hands on her right arm, and pulled it back. As he did so, her finger tips felt pubic hair, and the palm of her hand touched an erect penis. She jerked her arm away and told appellant: "Get out of here, get away. Get out of here, leave me alone." However, appellant did not leave immediately and made a salacious comment to her. After she had told him to leave several more times, he left her end of the tent.

Lieutenant Smith testified in his own defense and denied that this incident had ever occurred. The court members, however, found him guilty as charged.

B

Several weeks after Smith had been tried, his civilian defense counsel, Mr. Thomas L. Frazier, was speaking with a student whom he taught in a course at Monterey Peninsula College. This student, Specialist Five Kathryn Libra, was a legal clerk in the office of the staff judge advocate at Fort Ord and was responsible for contacting prospective court-martial members, monitoring their availability, receiving their requests for excusals, and locating replacement members. In the course of her conversation with the lawyer, Libra informed him that she had been directed by her superiors to place female members on appellant's court-martial. Mr. Frazier reported this information to appellant and to his military defense counsel. Thereafter, further information was obtained for submission to the Court of Military Review.

From the evidence obtained after trial, it appears that at Ford Ord court-martial panels sat for 4-month terms. About a month before the end of a term, the criminal law division of the staff judge advocate's office would request each of seven special court-martial convening authorities at the post to nominate potential court members in each rank and grade.

On April 19, 1982, Colonel Jack P. Hug, the staff judge advocate, wrote a memorandum to Major General Ayers, who was then the general court-martial convening authority, and requested that he select one general court-martial panel and two special court-martial panels to sit for a period of 4 months. The next day, Colonel Hug sent another memorandum to General Ayers and requested selection of additional enlisted members, especially from the grades of E-4 through E-7, "to obviate the appearance of any systematic exclusion of enlisted personnel." Both memoranda advised General Ayers to indicate his selections by placing a letter — A, B, C, and so on — in front of the name of the designated members. Neither memorandum intimated that race or gender should be considered as a selection factor. . . .

Under the procedure that prevailed at Fort Ord, Specialist Libra would telephone the members of a court panel to which a case had been referred for trial. If a member asked to be excused, he usually would submit a written request to Libra. She compiled these requests, together with the original court-martial convening orders, any requests for enlisted members, and the list of alternate members. Then, by telephone, she would determine which alternate members were available to act as replacements. Typically, if a member was excused, the replacement would be of the same rank. For example, if a major was excused, another major would be appointed as the replacement.

When an alternate court member was available for duty, Specialist Libra would place a check mark next to his name on the list of alternate members. Almost without exception, the general court-martial convening authority selected as replacements the alternate members who had the marks before their names.

According to her affidavit SP-5 Libra was convinced that a policy existed at Fort Ord to select certain members for particular cases. For example, in one case, where the accused was a black soldier named Anthony Bass, who was charged with aggravated assault on a white soldier, she had been "instructed by a member of the prosecution to ensure that black solders were on the panel because there had been allegations that the charges were based on a racial incident." She complied and typed a list of alternate members, including two blacks; and they were ultimately selected by the convening authority.

She also stated:

> By the time of *United States v. 2LT Rickie D. Smith,* the selection of court members had become a "game" for the trial counsel. Court-mar-

tial panels were tailored according to the needs of the case. Rape and sexual assault cases and cases where the accused was black were the two most specific types of cases where the panel composition was tainted. The Criminal Law Division attempted to insure that at least two women would sit on sex cases so at least one would survive a peremptory challenge and join the panel in deliberations. The Criminal Law Division also insured that blacks would sit on cases with a black accused. When I was informed that a court panel was needed, I would inform the trial counsel and/or Major Goo [Chief of the Criminal Law Division] regarding the members on the original orders and the possible replacements. Several "hard core" officers were in high demand. One panel member, a lieutenant colonel, had a reputation for being an easy peremptory challenge by the defense. The situation got to the point where the lieutenant colonel would have his driver stand by so he could return to his duties as a battalion commander after the peremptory challenge. Only 10% of the time that the lieutenant colonel was on court-martial duty did he actually sit on a case. The remaining time he was excused as a peremptory challenge. . . .

When I was informed of the need for a court panel in *United States v. Smith*, I screened all the court members on the basic convening order. Only two were available. The others (8 out of 10) either had knowledge of the case, knew the victim, or were unavailable due to duty commitments during the time of the trial. The one female officer on the court panel (2LT Gloria Dodd) was excused because, as the DISCOM Brigade Adjutant, she had knowledge of the case. Also, she was a member of the same unit as the accused. Following the traditional procedures for replacements in sex cases, I called the other two female court members; however, neither was available. I spoke with SFC Garnett [her supervisor] and MAJ Goo concerning the composition of the *Smith* panel. They did not tell me to find any lieutenant to replace 2LT Dodd; rather, I was informed to try contacting the females on the previous court panels. I did; however, none were available. I again informed SFC Garnett of the lack of any available female court members. He instructed me to utilize the female nominations of court members that were being compiled for a future panel change. After calling all the female officers senior in rank to the accused, only one was found to be available (CPT Belz). Due to the possibility of peremptory challenges from the defense, I was instructed to have at least two female officers on the court panel. I spoke with CPT Dennis P. Casey, Headquarters Command trial counsel, about the situation with the female court members. He suggested the names of several females from his command who would be "hardcore" and possibly would make good court members. I made several phone calls. In one of these phone calls, I talked to the female company commander of the 54th Military Police Company. She was not available. MAJ Goo told me to recontact her and tell her that she would be on the court though the GCMCA had not made any decision on this matter. I finally found 1LT Melanie J. Smith (now married and named Twomey), another military policewoman, to be available. Her name was inserted into the alternate court member master list along with CPT Belz's name for selection by the Commanding General. According to our practice, I placed pencil "X" marks next to the name of each replacement, including the female officers. The paperwork was sent to the Commanding General for "selection" and he chose each alternate according to the pencilled checkmarks.

None of Specialist Libra's superiors acknowledged existence of the policy which she described; but they could not explain why she had the belief that it existed. Captain Wayne E. Anderson, the senior trial counsel at Fort Ord, stated:

> Although there was no established policy, *we thought it was a good idea to have females on sex cases in order to avoid any idea of exclusion.* I never set this policy. However, if there was a policy, I thought it made for a broad cross section of the community. *Female members made for a better representative sample especially in sex cases due to the sexual issues.*

(Emphasis added.)

Some circumstantial evidence tends to indicate that in some cases members were selected in conformity with the alleged policy. For example, appellate defense counsel indicate in their final brief in this Court — without contradiction by the Government — that a review of all Fort Ord appointing orders located in the files of the Clerk of the Army Court of Military Review for calendar years 1982 and 1983 indicated that, out of ten cases involving sex offenses, there were female court members in at least six.

In Smith's case, the charges were referred to a court-martial that had the ten panel members who had been chosen by General Ayers in April 1982. One of these was a woman — Second Lieutenant Dodd. However, she had had some prior contact with the case, since she had administered the oath to Smith's commander when he preferred the charges. Indeed, for a variety of reasons, nine of the original ten members had to be excused from court duty. Consequently, Specialist Libra discussed this problem with her supervisor, Sergeant First Class Garnett, who was the noncommissioned officer in charge of the criminal law division in the office of the staff judge advocate. Although Garnett denies that he instructed Libra to find female members, she set out to follow what she believed to be the office policy of including female court members in cases which involved a sex offense.

At this time, Specialist Libra was teaching her job to another legal clerk, Specialist Five Lisa Lattimore. She instructed Lattimore that women officers would sit on Smith's case because it involved a sex crime with a female victim. Specialist Lattimore observed Libra as she contacted alternate court members in an effort to find two female members.

Libra had encountered problems in obtaining the female court members. She contacted two — presumably Lieutenant Lynch and Lieutenant Mason, who were on the list of alternate court members originally selected by General Ayers — but neither was available. She also attempted without success to contact female officers who had sat on previous court-martial panels or who had been nominated for a future court-martial panel. After calling all the female officers senior in rank to appellant, Libra could locate only one — Captain Cheryl L. Belz — who was available.

During this time, Captain Toni D. Allen, a female defense counsel, visited the office of the staff judge advocate to drop off some papers and to talk with the trial counsel. While there, she "heard a female clerk, probably Specialist . . . Libra, say" jokingly: "We're looking for women for Ricky Smith's jury. Hey, Captain Allen, you want to be on the jury?" However, Captain Allen did not mention this off-hand remark to Captain Richard Pocker, Smith's counsel, prior to the court-martial.

Specialist Libra was not satisfied to have only one female court member, because — as mentioned in her affidavit — the defense might use its one peremptory challenge to excuse that person and have an all-male panel. Therefore, Libra went to discuss female members with Captain Dennis P. Casey, the Headquarters Command trial counsel; and she asked him for some suggestions of female officers to sit on a case. Captain Casey did not know whether she was acting independently or pursuant to someone's instructions; but he did not think it was unusual that she asked him for female nominees. He was aware that Smith's case involved a sex crime; and he thought female members would be "a nice touch." He gave three names to Specialist Libra; and according to his affidavit:

> All three of these women were military police and I referred to them as "hardcore." As a trial counsel, you want court members who are "hardcore." However, I thought that any of these women would be intelligent and fair members who could acquit the defendant if the evidence was not there.

As a result of Captain Casey's nominations, Libra found Lieutenant Melanie J. Smith was available. In order to make room for this addition, Specialist Libra deleted from the alternate court member master list the name of Colonel Fargason, who was the provost marshal at Fort Ord. She also typed a memorandum for signature by the staff judge advocate, Colonel Hug, requesting the convening authority to excuse nine members from the court-martial panel and to select replacement members. The memorandum contained no reference to race or sex as a selection factor; and it did not suggest that the court-martial panel should constitute a cross-section of the military community.

To this memorandum, Specialist Libra attached a list of alternate court-martial members derived from the alternates selected by General Ayers in April 1982, court members who sat on other panels, and the two new female nominees — namely, Captain Belz and First Lieutenant Melanie Smith. In accord with office practice, she designated the replacement alternate members with a check mark.

Specialist Libra forwarded the memorandum and alternate list to her supervisor, Sergeant First Class Garnett. From his examination of the documents, he did not realize that she had deleted Colonel Fargason's name from the alternate list or that she had added the names of Captain Belz and First Lieutenant Melanie Smith. Major Goo, Chief of the criminal law division, also reviewed the documents but did not notice Libra's revision. Ultimately, the memorandum and alternate list, including the two new female members, were forwarded by Colonel Hug to Major General James E. Moore, Jr., who had become the convening authority less than 2 months before.

For "reasons ranging from retirement, to PCS, to prior knowledge of the case," General Moore excused nine of the ten officers who had originally been appointed to the court-martial panel. He observed that the list of alternate court members which had been presented to him "bore check marks before the names of those members who were available." According to General Moore:

> My philosophy regarding selection of court panels involves striking several balances. I look at age because I believe that it is associated with rank and experience. I look for a spread of units on the panel to include division units, non-division units, and tenant activities. I look at the types of jobs and positions of individuals in an effort to have a mix of court members with command or staff experience. I also look for some female representation on the panel. At no time have I had a concern for minority representation based upon race. *In sex cases, however, I have a predilection toward insuring that females sit on the court.* I did not generally articulate nor did I state this preference to Colonel Jack Hug regarding the *Smith* case.

(Emphasis added.) Although he did not know why two available females were included on the alternate list, Major General Moore decided to select them as court members because Smith's case involved a sex crime. Accordingly, he noted these and six other selections by writing his initials before each of the selected alternates. With two exceptions, General Moore selected all the alternate members who had check marks before their names.

When General Moore sent back these documents to the staff judge advocate's office, the criminal law division began to prepare amending court-martial convening orders. Specialist Libra erased all of the penciled check marks from the original alternate list; so the xerox copy of the list in the allied papers does not reflect these marks.

Because of some problems with the availability of Colonel Pellicci and Lieutenant Colonel Wylie, Colonel Hug sent another memorandum to General Moore to excuse and replace these officers. Using his initials, General Moore selected two other male members.

As finally convened, the court-martial panel consisted of one person — Major Savage — from the original court-martial panel; three persons — Lieutenant Colonel King, Lieutenant Colonel Dailey, and Major Giron — from the alternate list; and five persons — Colonel Graham, Colonel Harris, Captain Belz, Captain Rice, and First Lieutenant Melanie Smith — who had not been on either list. Belz and Smith were female.

When appellant's court-martial was finally convened, no challenge was made to the court-selection procedure. Later, after *voir dire* of the nine members, trial counsel peremptorily challenged Captain Rice and the defense peremptorily challenged Lieutenant Colonel Dailey. Thus, appellant, who is black, was tried before a panel of seven officers, two of whom — like his alleged victim — were white females.

II

The Sixth Amendment grants defendants in criminal cases the right to a jury trial. *See also* U.S. Const. art. III, § 2, 3d para. This right includes a requirement that the jury be drawn from a representative cross-section of the community. *Duren v. Missouri*, 439 U.S. 357 (1979); *Taylor v. Louisiana*, 419 U.S. 522 (1975). However, the right to trial by jury has no application to the appointment of members of courts-martial. *Ex Parte Quirin*, 317 U.S. 1, 40 (1942); *Ex parte Milligan*, 71 U.S. (4 Wall.) 2, 123 (maj. op.), 137-38 (sep. op.) (1866); *United States v. Kemp*, 22 U.S.C.M.A. 152, 154, 46 C.M.R. 152, 154 (1973).

"[I]ndeed, Article 25 of the Uniform Code, 10 U.S.C. § 825, contemplates that a court-martial panel will not be a representative cross-section of the military population." *United States v. Santiago-Davila*, 26 M.J. 380, 389 (C.M.A. 1988). That article prescribes that, "[w]hen convening a court-martial, the convening authority shall detail as members thereof such members of the armed forces as, in his opinion, are best qualified for the duty by reason of age, education, training, experience, length of service, and judicial temperament." Art. 25(d)(2), 10 U.S.C. § 825(d)(2).

Although Congress authorized military commanders to depart from the norm of representativeness in selecting the members of a court-martial, this Court, by divided vote, has held on one occasion that a convening authority might use a criterion not specified by Article 25 in order to have a more representative panel. *United States v. Crawford*, 15 U.S.C.M.A. 31, 35 C.M.R. 3 (1964). There, the convening authority intentionally selected a black to serve as a court member where the accused was black. In upholding this selection, Chief Judge Quinn emphasized that, "[i]f deliberately to include qualified persons is discrimination, it is discrimination in favor of, not against, an accused. Equal protection of the laws is not denied, but assured." *Id.* at 41, 35 C.M.R. at 13. Judge Kilday "concur[red] with the Chief Judge in his conclusion and the reasoning by which he reached the same." *Id.* at 49, 35 C.M.R. at 21.

Judge Ferguson, on the other hand, asserted in *Crawford* that a convening authority is not free to "ever select a member of a court-martial of the same race as the accused solely on the grounds of that race," *id.* at 57, 35 C.M.R. at 29. He observed that

> [w]hile, because of the nature of our national development, most cases have involved *exclusion* of Negroes from juries, the whole point of the discussion in this area is that race is an impermissible criterion for selection of jurors. In the administration of justice, we are to all be considered, not as Negroes, Whites, Chinese, Jews, or Christians, but as Americans.

Id. at 58, 35 C.M.R. at 30.

Appellant is black; and if the convening authority had intentionally selected black officers as members of the court-martial panel, *Crawford*'s holding would apply. Moreover, if appellant were a female whose case had been referred for trial and the convening authority had appointed female members, the rationale of *Crawford* would apply. In short, we infer from *Crawford* that a convening authority is not precluded by Article 25 from appointing court-martial members in a way that will best assure that the court-martial panel constitutes a representative cross-section of the military community.

As we interpret Article 25 in light of *Crawford*, Congress has not required that court-martial panels be unrepresentative of the military population. Instead, Congress has authorized deviations from the principle of representativeness, if the criteria of Article 25 are complied with. Thus, a commander is free to require representativeness in his court-martial panels and to insist that no important segment of the military community — such as blacks, Hispanics, or women — be excluded from service on court-martial panels.

We are aware that at times there have been experiments in the armed services with some form of random selection of court-martial members. In view of *Crawford*, it would appear that even this method of selection is permissible, if the convening authority decides to employ it in order to obtain representativeness in his court-martial panels and if he personally appoints the court members who have been randomly selected.

The defense complains that Article 25 implicitly prohibits use of gender in the selection of court members and also that such use is a violation of the equal-protection guarantees implicit in Fifth Amendment due process. As we already have indicated, to some extent *Crawford* undermines these contentions. In our view, a convening authority may take gender into account in selecting court members, if he is seeking in good faith to assure that the court-martial panel is representative of the military population.

Government appellate counsel also have suggested that Article 25 itself supports use of gender in the selection criteria. Their argument is that a female, as such, has unique "experience" within the meaning of Article 25(d)(2). While in some ways their "experience" may provide females a unique perspective, we do not believe that this was the sort of "experience" which the drafters of Article 25 of the Uniform Code had in mind. Instead, military experience was what they contemplated. We note, too, that the majority in *Crawford* never claimed that a black member was properly appointed to that court-martial because he had unique "experience;" and yet if the Government's interpretation of Article 25(d)(2) is correct, it would seem that the "experience" of a black, Hispanic, or a member of some other racial or ethnic group could also be viewed as satisfying this criterion. The Government's argument does, however, point to our major concern in this case. For whatever reason, the unique "experience" of females apparently was viewed at Fort Ord as being relevant *only* in cases involving sex offenses. Thus, as appellant complains, the policy applied in selecting court members was not designed to provide him or other males accused of sex crimes with a more representative court-martial panel. Instead, it seems to have been intended to "achieve a particular result as to findings or sentence;" this is prohibited. *United States v. McClain*, 22 M.J. 124, 132 (C.M.A. 1986).

The premise underlying selection of two female members for appellant's trial was that these members would have a unique ability to understand the testimony of the victim. From General Moore's statement, it would appear that he, too, shared that premise. Of course, no one can predict actually how jurors or court members will decide a case; and it may be true that in some sex cases female jurors are more skeptical about the claims of a female victim than male jurors would be. However, some take a different view as to the likely behavior of female jurors or court members — as is reflected in this exchange in the statement of Lisa Lattimore:

Q: Do [you] think women members sitting on a sex case would be more sympathetic to the accused or to the victim?

A: *To the victim.*

(Emphasis added.)

This Court constantly has endeavored to assure that "court packing" does not occur in courts-martial — or even seem to occur. The developments in this case, as revealed after trial, indicated that the female members were named to help assure a particular outcome. The circumstances are too akin to those in *McClain* for us to allow the findings and sentence to stand.

III

A convening authority is entitled to assistance from his staff members in appointing the members of a court-martial. *Cf. United States v. Kemp, supra.* However, a trial counsel who is engaged in prosecuting the accused should not participate in nominating or selecting the members of a court-martial he is involved in. As we observed in *United States v. Marsh*, 21 M.J. 445, 447 (C.M.A.), *cert. denied*, 479 U.S. 1016 (1986): "We believe it is well-established in military law that the trial counsel, being a partisan advocate, can play no part in the selection of court members."

Similarly, in *United States v. Crumb*, 10 M.J. 520 (A.C.M.R. 1980) — which involved the practice at Fort Lewis, Washington, of trial counsel nominating a replacement for a court member excused by the convening authority — Senior Judge Jones in a concurring opinion observed:

By involving the Chief Trial Counsel in the "culling" process and the Trial Counsel in the replacement scheme, . . . the authorities need-lessly injected an appearance of evil into the procedure that should have been avoided. There is no place for the use of partisan govern-ment advocates in the sensitive area of selection of court members.

Id. at 527-28. We agree.

Here, it seems clear from the affidavit of Specialist Libra and from other appellate exhibits that trial counsel at Fort Ord were not adequately insulated from the process of selecting court-martial members. For example, Captain Casey, who was a trial counsel at Fort Ord — although not involved directly in Smith's trial — should not have been suggesting female members to Specialist Libra. We do not know what he meant when he referred to his three female nominees as "hardcore" — a term which appears in several of the appellate exhibits. According to the Court of Military Review, his "use of the term 'hardcore,' although appearing to be sinister, apparently meant only that the recommended officers were dedicated and would perform their duty com-petently." 18 M.J. at 707. In the particular context of this case and especially since the female nominees were all military police officers and were being recommended by a prosecutor, we consider this interpretation by the court below to be implausible.

In his sworn statement, Captain Casey admits that he referred to his three nominees as "hardcore;" but he added: "*However,* I thought that any of these women would be intelligent and fair members who could acquit the defendant if the evidence was not there." Casey's use of the word "[h]owever" is an implicit recognition that most court members described as "hardcore" would be considered more prone to convict an accused and adjudge a heavier sentence.

In situations like this, we have always been especially concerned about the appearance of evil. Trial counsel in a court-martial is an advocate, who in his representation of the Government is usually seeking a conviction. The members of a court-martial — like the members of a civilian jury — are supposed to be fair and impartial. If a prosecutor is involved in selecting the members, it seems likely that, due to his institutional bias, he will want to have a certain type of member. Moreover, to the extent that the prosecutor participates in this selection process, it is inevitable that the public will suspect that the membership mirrors his preference.

Perhaps in this case, Captain Casey's participation in selecting one of the court members ultimately had no impact on the fairness of the court. Perhaps, too, the female member he recommended was as fair to appellant as any other officer would have been. Indeed, neither she nor the other female was peremptorily challenged by the defense. However, we need not indulge in speculation in this regard, because we are convinced that the selection of the entire court-martial panel was tainted here by the application of the Fort Ord policy of selecting female court members for sex cases. . . .

Cox, J. (concurring):

As I read Chief Judge Everett's opinion, it stands for two basic propositions of law regarding appointment of court members. Proposition one is that members may be selected on the basis of sex, race, religion, or rank if the convening authority "is seeking in good faith to assure that the court-martial panel is representative of the military population." 27 M.J. 242, 249. This rule is consistent with the view that I expressed in *United States v. McClain,* 22 M.J. 124 (C.M.A. 1986). "The deliberate selection . . . of a certain class of servicepersons for the purpose of increasing the severity of the sentence is wrong." *Id.* at 133. The same rationale applies to the selection of members who may be more likely to convict.

In any event, anyone who believes that women are more likely to empathize with the victim of a sex crime is purely speculating. My experience as a trial judge with jury members who are women has led me to the realization that they are no more biased for or against the victims or the accused than are men. The sex of the juror is an irrelevant factor, as is the sex of the victim. It is the quality of the Government's evidence and the defenses in response which are important. Women should be selected for the same reasons that men are, because of their "age, education, training, experience, length of service, and judicial temperament," and for no other reasons. Art. 25(d)(2), Uniform Code of Military Justice, 10 U.S.C. § 825(d)(2).

The second proposition of law is "that the trial counsel, being a partisan advocate, can play no part in the selection of court members." *United States v. Marsh*, 21 M.J. 445, 447 (C.M.A.), *cert. denied*, 479 U.S. 1016 (1986). That rule was violated here.

Judge Sullivan has criticized Chief Judge Everett and me for our "tortuous interpretations of Article 41(b)," *United States v. Carter*, 25 M.J. 471, 479 (C.M.A. 1988), and perhaps he is right. But if this case does not prove one of my basic premises, that "[t]he Government has the functional equivalent of an unlimited number of peremptory challenges," *id.* at 478, nothing ever will.

The irony of the case is that this issue would never have been uncovered if the legal clerk had not been taking a college course from the civilian defense counsel. I hope and I believe that this staff judge advocate and this convening authority would have been mortified if they had been aware of the cavalier and disrespectful manner by which the court members were being nominated. I know that young judge advocate officers love witty exchanges, practical jokes, and a sense of the macabre in their humor; and normally little if any significance should be given use of terms like "hardcore" to categorize a potential court member. However, the selection process is not a "game" and is no place to use pejorative terms to describe potential members.

Those responsible for nominating court members should reflect upon the importance of this task. It is a solemn and awesome responsibility and not one to be taken lightly or frivolously. It is a responsibility that Congress has entrusted to convening authorities and has not required some other method of selection, such as random choice. Even so, it is the most vulnerable aspect of the court-martial system; the easiest for critics to attack. A fair and impartial court-martial is the most fundamental protection that an accused servicemember has from unfounded or unprovable charges. There is a duty to nominate only fair and impartial members. . . .

FINDLAY v. UNITED KINGDOM
European Court of Human Rights
[1997] ECHR 8, 24 EHRR 221
See Chapter 12, § III

NOTES AND QUESTIONS

1. In 1992, the Supreme Court of Canada had similarly pointed to the convening authority's selection of court-martial members as one reason why Canadian general courts-martial violated the Canadian Charter of Rights and Freedoms' guarantee of "an independent and impartial tribunal." *Regina v. Généreux*, 70 C.C.C. (3d) 1 (1992), discussed in Chapter 12, § II. Writing for the majority, Chief Justice Lamer reasoned:

> In my opinion, certain characteristics of the General Court Martial system would be very likely to cast into doubt the institutional independence of the tribunal in the mind of a reasonable and informed person. First, the authority that convenes the court martial (the

"convening authority") may be the Minister, the Chief of the Defence Staff, an officer commanding a command, upon receipt of an application from a commanding officer, or another service authority appointed by the Minister (s. 111.05, Q.R. & O.). The convening authority, an integral part of the military hierarchy and therefore of the executive, decides when a General Court Martial shall take place. The convening authority appoints the president and other members of the General Court Martial and decides how many members there shall be in a particular case. The convening authority, or an officer designated by the convening authority, also appoints, with the concurrence of the Judge Advocate General, the prosecutor (s. 111.23, Q.R. & O.). This fact further undermines the institutional independence of the General Court Martial. It is not acceptable, in my opinion, that the convening authority, i.e., the executive, who is responsible for appointing the prosecutor, also have the authority to appoint members of the court martial, who serve as the triers of fact. At a minimum, I consider that where the same representative of the executive, the "convening authority," appoints both the prosecutor and the triers of fact, the requirements of s. 11(d) [of the Canadian Charter of Rights and Freedoms, requiring an "independent and impartial tribunal"] will not be met.

The majority declined to authorize a departure from Section 11(d) on the basis of Section 1 of the Charter, which provides: "The Canadian Charter of Rights and Freedoms guarantees the rights and freedoms set out in it subject only to such reasonable limits prescribed by law as can be demonstrably justified in a free and democratic society." The majority reasoned:

[A] trial before a tribunal which does not meet the requirements of s. 11(d) of the Charter will only [be permissible under Section 1 of the Charter] in the most extraordinary of circumstances. A period of war or insurrection might constitute such circumstances. However, during periods of normality, the scheme of the General Court Martial, as it was at the time of the appellant's trial, went far beyond what was necessary to accomplish the goals for which it was established. Indeed, the amendments to the Q.R. & O. of January, 1991, which I have indicated constituted significant improvements over the regime under which the appellant was tried, attest to this fact.

It is not necessary, under normal circumstances, to try alleged military offenders before a tribunal in which the judge, the prosecutor, and the triers of fact, are all chosen by the executive to serve at that particular trial. . . .

In short, the structure of the General Court Martial with which we are here concerned incorporated features which, in the eyes of a reasonable person, could call the independence and impartiality of the tribunal into question, and are not necessary to attain either military discipline or military justice. . . .

Justice L'Heureux-Dubé dissented, reasoning in part:

Section 11(d) might not condone a civilian system of justice where the same body which appointed the prosecutor also appoints the triers of fact, or where the executive and the presiding judge maintain close ties. However, in the context of the armed forces, these characteristics may well be a necessary part of the chain of command which, when followed link by link, ultimately leads to the same destination no matter where one begins. Hence, in my opinion, the Charter permits a sufficient degree of connection between the executive and the participants of a General Court Martial such that the third criterion of institutional independence was satisfied at the time of the appellant's trial.

2. As the European Court of Human Rights noted in *Findlay*, the United Kingdom adopted legislation requiring that court-martial members be appointed by a neutral official rather than by an officer who also performed prosecutorial functions. In the United States, however, the convening authority continues both to decide whether an accused should be prosecuted at a court-martial and, if so, to appoint the members of that court-martial. A debate has raged over whether the U.S. military justice system should remove convening authorities' power to appoint the members. The privately-sponsored Commission on the Fiftieth Anniversary of the Uniform Code of Military Justice ("the Cox Commission") — chaired by Senior Judge Walter T. Cox III of the Court of Appeals for the Armed Forces — concluded:

> Convening authorities must not be permitted to select the members of courts-martial.

> There is no aspect of military criminal procedures that diverges further from civilian practice, or creates a greater impression of improper influence, than the antiquated process of panel selection. The current practice is an invitation to mischief. It permits — indeed, requires — a convening authority to choose the persons responsible for determining the guilt or innocence of a servicemember who has been investigated and prosecuted at the order of that same authority. The Commission trusts the judgment of convening authorities as well as the officers and enlisted members who are appointed to serve on courts-martial. But there is no reason to preserve a practice that creates such a strong impression of, and opportunity for, corruption of the trial process by commanders and staff judge advocates. Members of courts-martial should be chosen at random from a list of eligible servicemembers prepared by the convening authority, taking into account operational needs as well as the limitations on rank, enlisted or officer status, and same-unit considerations currently followed in the selection of members. Article 25 of the UCMJ should be amended to require this improvement in the fundamental fairness of court-martial procedure.

WALTER T. COX III, ET AL., REPORT OF THE COMMISSION ON THE 50TH ANNIVERSARY OF THE UNIFORM CODE OF MILITARY JUSTICE 7 (2001), *available at* http://www.nimj.com/documents/cox_comm_report.pdf, *reprinted with commentary and without Appendices at* Kevin J. Barry, *A Face Lift (And Much More) for an Aging Beauty: The Cox Commission Recommendations to Rejuvenate the Uniform Code of Military Justice,* 2002 L. REV. MICH. ST. U-DETROIT C.L 57.

A rebuttal to the Cox Commission's report by two Air Force lawyers appears in Lt. Col. Theodore Essex & Maj. Leslea Tate Pickle, *A Reply to the Report of the Commission on the 50th Anniversary of the Uniform Code of Military Justice (May 2001): "The Cox Commission,"* 52 A.F. L. Rev. 233 (2002). The authors argued that *Findlay* and *Généreux* did not provide sound precedent for the U.S. military justice system and that convening authorities should retain the power to selection members:

A. Contrast with *Findlay*

In *Findlay*, the court was concerned about two issues. The first issue was the central role played by the convening officer in the organization of the court-martial. The second issue involved a review process that did not address Mr. Findlay's concerns about a fair and impartial trial. The *Findlay* court was concerned about the following facts: the convening officer decided the nature and detail of the charges and recommended the type of court-martial on his own; the convening officer could comment on the evidence and its admissibility; there was no independent review of the charges; no legal officer sat on the court-martial (the court did not state whether the accused had a right to examine the court members or challenge them for cause); the only safeguard to ensure court members were unbiased was the oath they took (there was no mention of any judicial review of the court member selection process); the convening officer could comment on the proceedings of a court-martial which required confirmation — these remarks would not form part of the record and could be communicated to the court members; the convening officer appointed the prosecuting officer and the defense counsel; the convening officer ruled on applications by the defense during the trial; the sentence had no effect until confirmed by the convening officer, who could withhold confirmation, substitute or postpone or remit in whole or in part, any sentence; and finally, there were no statutory or formalized procedures set out for post-trial reviews and hearings. The situation in *Findlay* stands in marked contrast to the procedures under the UCMJ.

Under the UCMJ, the convening authority determines the charges to refer and the type of court-martial to be convened. However, he or she does so only after reviewing the evidence (usually in the form of a report of investigation) and receiving advice on the charges from the base Staff Judge Advocate (SJA). The charges are drafted, not by the convening authority, but by lawyers in the base legal office. For a case to be referred to a general court-martial, an independent review of the charges must be held at an Article 32 investigation. The Article 32 investigation provides more procedural protections for the accused than a grand jury hearing. Furthermore, once a case is referred to a court-martial, the military judge has the responsibility and authority to review the charges. The judge can dismiss one or all of the charges for multiplicity or simply based on equity. Finally, even if court members are hearing the case, if the military judge believes a charge was not proven beyond a reasonable doubt, he may enter a finding of not guilty.

The procedures for choosing court members are also very different than those questioned under *Findlay*. Under the UCMJ, the convening authority does appoint the court members, but the convening authority also has an obligation to pick the best-qualified members. The court members are also required to take an oath. In addition to the court members, a military judge is required at all special and general courts-martial. The military judge is an independent member of the court and has a separate chain of command from the convening authority. It is the military judge that overseas the actual seating of the panel that will serve on the court-martial.

Additionally, the court member selection process is documented, and a copy of this documentation must be given to the defense during the discovery process. This enables the accused, through defense counsel, to better prepare questions for individual court members. The accused has the right to examine prospective court members and challenge them for cause. The accused also has the right to challenge one member peremptorily, that is, for no reason at all. Both trial and defense counsel may question the court members and may challenge them as stated above.

Members who are found to be "biased," whether the bias is actual or implied, may not sit on a court-martial, and case law provides that military judges are to grant challenges for "implied" bias very liberally. Military judges may also disqualify a court member for bias *sua sponte*.

Another possible area of concern with the convening authority appointing members is unlawful command influence. Under the UCMJ, the defense can raise a motion with the military judge at trial concerning unlawful command influence or improper court member selection. There are provisions in place to preserve such an objection for appellate review. Furthermore, if either unlawful command influence or improper court member selection is found, the case cannot proceed until the problem is corrected. The military judge may also rule on the bias of the convening authority and disqualify the convening authority from any participation in the case.

In addition to protecting the accused, the UCMJ also protects court members from unfair treatment based on their service in a court-martial. Article 37 of the UCMJ makes it unlawful for the convening authority to base an Officer Performance Report (OPR), promotion recommendation or assignment decision on a military member's performance as a court member. Military members who believe they are victims of reprisal based on their service as a court member can complain through Inspector General (IG) channels.

To further protect the neutrality of the members, once a court is convened, the convening authority may not speak to the court members about the pending court-martial. In fact, once a court-martial has been convened, neither the military judge, prosecution, nor defense may speak with the members off the record. None of the parties may communicate with the members about the case, and the court members are instructed as to these rules. Once convened, the court-martial proceedings are open to the public and any conversations between the military judge and the court members must take place in the presence of the counsel and the accused and be recorded verbatim. Any conversations between the military judge and the counsel, other than 802 conferences, must be on the record as well.

In *Findlay*, the convening officer appointed both the prosecuting officer and the defense counsel. Under the UCMJ, the SJA appoints the trial counsel. The defense counsel is appointed by, and falls under the supervision of, a separate chain of command. In *Findlay* the convening officer also controlled the trial and defense witnesses, with no review process of his decisions. Under the UCMJ, while the convening authority controls the production of trial and defense witnesses, her decisions are subject to judicial review.

Finally, unlike the situation in *Findlay*, there are statutory, formalized procedures set out for post-trial reviews and hearings. Under the UCMJ, the convening authority has the discretion to approve or disapprove the findings and sentence of the court and can lessen the degree of guilt to a lesser-included offense, set aside a finding of guilty, dismiss charges or direct a rehearing. The convening authority also has the power to lessen the severity of the punishment but cannot increase the severity of the sentence. Convening authorities are required to review certain matters before taking final action on the case. This review and the action are documented and a copy is provided to the defense. Finally, there is appellate review of all cases, unless waived by the accused.

B. Contrast with *Généreux*

In *Généreux*, the main issue was the independence and impartiality of the military judge. In this case, certain members of the legal branch of the Armed Forces could be appointed to the Judge Advocate General's office. There they performed legal duties, but could also be detailed by the convening authority to serve as military judges on an ad hoc basis. The court also focused on military judges' lack of financial security, as the legal officer's salary was determined, in part, according to his or her performance evaluation. There were no formal prohibitions against evaluating an officer on the basis of his or her performance as a military judge at a court-martial. Additionally, the convening authority appointed the prosecutor, defense counsel and the military judge. In effect, the convening authority had complete control over each court-martial.

These concerns are not present in the United States' system. Under the UCMJ, the military judges are ultimately under the authority of The Judge Advocate General (TJAG) of each service. They are not in the same chain of command as the convening authority and are not detailed to the case by him. Also, Article 37 of the UCMJ prevents the TJAG of each service, or anyone else, from censuring, reprimanding or admonishing a military judge for his functions at a court-martial. Finally, in contrast to a major concern in *Généreux*, a military judge's salary is not determined by his performance evaluation. He is paid the same as any other military member of the same rank and time in grade.

Findlay and *Généreux* highlighted the need for reform in the English and Canadian military justice systems. However, those systems are quite distinguishable from the United States' under the UCMJ. The procedures that gave too much power to the convening authority in the British system, and did not ensure an independent judiciary in the Canadian system, do not exist under the UCMJ. Additionally, *Findlay* and *Généreux* do not apply to the UCMJ as the United States is not a party to the European Convention on Human Rights, nor is the military subject to the European Court of Human Rights. To recommend that we change our military justice system because other countries have done so, without producing evidence that our system has the same flaws, stands logic on its head.

Regarding the Cox Commission's recommendation that convening authorities no longer select court-martial members, these commentators reply:

The Commission's proposal to stop convening authority selection of court members falls short of an actual remedy to the problem they concede does not exist:

> The Commission trusts the judgment of convening authorities as well as the officers and enlisted members who are appointed to serve on courts-martial. But there is no reason to preserve a practice that creates such a strong impression of, and opportunity for, corruption of the trial process by commanders and staff judge advocates. Members of courts-martial should be chosen at random from a list of eligible service members prepared by the convening authority, taking into account operational needs as well as the limitations on rank, enlisted or officer status, and same-unit considerations currently followed in the selection of members. Article 25 of the UCMJ should be amended to require this improvement in the fundamental fairness of court-martial procedure.

> The [Cox Commission Report] states, "Members of courts-martial should be chosen at random from a list of eligible service members prepared by the convening authority." If the convening authority prepares the list, the convening authority is still selecting the members. It is difficult to see how this step would prevent the appearance of injustice problem sited by the [Cox Commission]. The only difference is that the convening authority is building the pool from which members will be chosen for a particular case, rather than hand picking members on a case-by-case basis. Nevertheless, if he chose to do so, a convening authority could put only the toughest officers and enlisted members in the pool or those he knew would follow his slightest suggestion.

If this suggestion were implemented, it would not change the perception on which it is based. If the convening authority truly wanted to improperly influence the members under his command, he could do so prior to random selection. He can already influence the officer performance ratings, assignments, and disciplinary records of the potential members. Convening authorities today are ever mindful of their role in the military justice system and the potential impact of their remarks. If they are moved to the periphery, they may, in good faith, feel less restricted in their public statements. The convening authority can still make speeches and generate publicity, the source of many of the cases of unlawful command influence in the past. Those other than the convening authority, who, in the past have engaged in unlawful command influence, such as first sergeants speaking to potential witnesses or attorneys speaking to members, could continue such conduct.

Implementing random member selection would not in any way prevent these examples of unlawful command influence. In fact, it might make the potential problem worse. Removing the convening authority from the process also removes him from the advice and counsel of the SJA that went with the panel selection role. There would no longer be a legal requirement that the most qualified members serve. Consequently, the convening authority might feel less restrained to comment on the selected panel and its results. As the convening authority is removed from the process, courts and judges may feel his ability to influence a panel is lessened. Therefore, they may permit the convening authority more latitude when they determine the impact of remarks he may make or actions he may take. As a result, there may be more, rather than fewer, problems to address.

Giving the commander the authority to choose members also allows him the flexibility to minimize impact on mission accomplishment. First, the commander can remove from a list, or fail to nominate, select officers in key positions that are needed to accomplish the mission. For example, while preparing to deploy in support of combat operations, a commander can exclude the Operations Group Squadron Commanders and Operations Officers (and others specifically needed to prepare for the deployment). This flexibility does not deprive an accused of a fair trial yet it greatly enhances a commander's ability to accomplish his mission. Secondly, commanders are in a unique position to know of information regarding their officers that would render them unfit for a particular trial. This is especially true for disciplinary information that might impact their ability to perform their duty and that is otherwise protected by the Privacy Act. Rather than expose these officers to public inquiries, he can simply fail to nominate them.

Finally, giving the convening authority the responsibility for putting members on a court serves to protect the members from other influences. Were the members randomly chosen, others on base might feel more free to tell them what is expected of them on the court or to give them free advice or opinions as to how to deal with a certain case. They might be more likely to "brief" the members selected on what is expected of them, or the "military view" of their duty. Knowing that the commander has ownership of the process limits this kind of improper mentoring before trial. With random selection, rather than watch one commander, the system would be placed in the untenable situation of having to hunt for unlawful command influence under every bush.

Why should the commander's selection of those deemed most qualified to serve as court members be considered an invitation to corruption? The explanation appears to be simple mistrust of military leaders. Why? The commander makes similar choices every day, recommending promotions, command assignments, and school billets that impact careers. In wartime, the commander makes life and death decisions.

The commander's integrity is the very foundation of the military. If it is accepted that the system cannot trust its commanders, then the military as an institution cannot be trusted. The UCMJ incorporated the principle that service members benefit by having a commander involved in the military justice process. The commander reviews the information then decides whether to prosecute and, if so, what level of action to bring. The UCMJ drafters believed that the commander was the best individual to balance the interests of justice in each individual case. The Commission produces nothing that suggests the convening authority has failed in this function. They do not show that due process would be better served by placing an accused member in the hands of the lawyers or randomly selected court members. Absent a showing of actual, systemic improper influence, bias or unfairness, the principle of the convening authority selecting those best suited as court members should not be lightly abandoned.

Lt. Col. Theodore Essex & Maj. Leslea Tate Pickle, *A Reply to the Report of the Commission on the 50th Anniversary of the Uniform Code of Military Justice (May 2001): "The Cox Commission,"* 52 A.F. L. Rev. 233, 236-40, 248-50 (2002).

3. As a matter of policy, should convening authorities retain the power to appoint court-martial members? What is the best alternative system? Is reference to European and Canadian judicial opinions helpful in evaluating the United States' military justice system?

UNITED STATES v. WIESEN
United States Court of Appeals for the Armed Forces
56 M.J. 172 (C.A.A.F. 2001)

BAKER, J., delivered the opinion of the Court.

. . . .

Background

At trial, appellant elected to be tried by a panel of both officer and enlisted members. Ten members reported to the court-martial. COL Williams, a brigade commander, was the senior member.

During the military judge's preliminary voir dire of the members, the following information was revealed:

> MJ: Is any panel member in the rating chain, supervisory chain, or chain of command of any other panel member? If so, raise your hand.
>
> Colonel Williams, who's under your command or rating chain?
>
> MEM [COL WILLIAMS]: [Lieutenant] Colonel Mereness is a battalion commander for me, [Lieutenant] Colonel Rogers is a battalion commander for me, Major Gonsalves is a battalion XO [executive officer] for me. [Lieutenant] Colonel Hough is my forward support battalion commander and the first sergeant down there at the end is also in my chain.
>
> MJ: First Sergeant Waters. Who else?
>
> MEM [COL WILLIAMS]: Command Sergeant Major Arroyo also is in my BCT [Brigade].

Civilian defense counsel attempted to exercise a challenge for cause to remove COL Williams, based on implied bias, because of his supervisory position over six of the panel members. After questioning the members, the military judge denied the challenge for cause, stating:

> MJ: Well, if this were some sort of military offense that occurred in the 2nd Brigade [COL Williams's Brigade], I might look at it differently. But for a case of this type, I think the panel members can each approach this with an individual voice and consideration. They've all indicated that they could express their opinions' [sic] freely and openly and that they would not be inhibited or unduly influenced by any superior.
>
> Your challenge for cause is denied.

Defense counsel subsequently exercised his peremptory challenge against COL Williams and stated that, but for the military judge's denial of his challenge for cause against COL Williams, he would have peremptorily challenged Major Gonsalves.

Discussion

Testing Impartiality

As a matter of due process, an accused has a constitutional right, as well as a regulatory right, to a fair and impartial panel. *United States v. Mack*, 41 M.J. 51, 54 (C.M.A. 1994); *see* R.C.M. 912(f)(1)(N), Manual for Courts-Martial,

United States (2000 ed.). Indeed, "impartial court-members are a sine qua non for a fair court-martial." *United States v. Modesto*, 43 M.J. 315, 318 (1995). That is not to say that an accused has a right to the panel of his choice, just to a fair and impartial panel. *Id*. The UCMJ and common law incorporate a number of methods to validate this right, including voir dire, the challenge for cause, and the peremptory challenge.

In this case, appellant takes issue with the judge's application of, or to be more precise, his failure to apply his authority to remove a potential member for cause. R.C.M. 912(f)(1)(N) provides that "[a] member shall be excused for cause whenever it appears that the member . . . should not sit as a member in the interest of having the court-martial free from substantial doubt as to legality, fairness, and impartiality." In furtherance of this principle, this Court has determined that a member shall be excused in cases of actual bias or implied bias. . . . Further, "we have urged a 'liberal' view on granting challenges for cause." *United States v. Dale*, 42 M.J. 384, 386 (1995). Thus, "military judges must follow the liberal-grant mandate in ruling on challenges for cause. . . ." [*United States v. Daulton*, 45 M.J. 212, 217 (C.A.A.F. 1996),] quoting *United States v. White*, 36 M.J. 284, 287 (C.M.A. 1993).

"The test for actual bias is whether any bias 'is such that it will not yield to the evidence presented and the judge's instructions.'" [*United States v. Napoleon*, 46 M.J. 279, 283 (C.A.A.F. 1997),] quoting *United States v. Reynolds*, 23 M.J. 292, 294 (C.M.A. 1987). "While actual bias is reviewed through the eyes of the military judge or the court members, implied bias is reviewed under an objective standard, viewed through the eyes of the public." *Id*., quoting *Daulton, supra*. The focus "is on the perception or appearance of fairness of the military justice system." *Dale*, 42 M.J. at 386. At the same time, this Court has suggested that the test for implied bias also carries with it an element of actual bias. Thus, there is implied bias when "most people in the same position would be prejudiced." *United States v. Armstrong*, 54 M.J. 51, 53-54 (2000), quoting *United States v. Warden*, 51 M.J. 78, 81 (1999); *United States v. Smart*, 21 M.J. 15, 20 (C.M.A. 1985). This Court has also determined that when there is no actual bias, "implied bias should be invoked rarely." *United States v. Rome*, 47 M.J. 467, 469 (1998).

Given the factual underpinning for testing actual bias, we review a military judge's findings regarding actual bias for an abuse of discretion. *Napoleon*, 46 M.J. at 283. On the other hand, issues of implied bias, which entail both factual inquiry and objective application of legal principle, are reviewed under a less deferential standard. *Armstrong*, 54 M.J. at 54, quoting *Warden, supra*.

Implied Bias

In the case at hand, appellant did not, and does not, challenge the composition of his panel on the grounds of actual bias. These officers and senior enlisted personnel, who swore to defend the Constitution, stated to a federal judge that they would not be swayed by the Brigade Commander because he was their commanding, rating, or supervising officer. COL Williams stated that he would not expect any jury room deference given his position. Appellant does not challenge the veracity of these voir dire responses. Rather, defense counsel challenged on the grounds of implied bias, citing to this Court's decision in *Rome*. Thus, in accord with this Court's precedent on R.C.M. 912 and implied bias, including *Rome*, *Daulton*, and *Dale*, the issue here is one of public perception and the appearance of fairness in the military justice system.

It is well settled that a senior-subordinate/rating relationship does not per se require disqualification of a panel member. *Rome*, 47 M.J. at 469. . . . However, beyond that principle, this Court has struggled to define the scope of implied bias, or perhaps just disagreed on what that scope should be. The dissent in *Rome* argued that this Court had adopted a Justice Potter Stewart — "I know it when I see it" — standard when it comes to implied bias. 47 M.J. at 472. However, while this Court's application of implied bias may evolve with case law, at its core remains a concern with public perception and the appearance of fairness in the military justice system. . . .

Where a panel member has a supervisory position over six of the other members, and the resulting seven members make up the two-thirds majority sufficient to convict, we are placing an intolerable strain on public perception of the military justice system. This is a contextual judgment. The President anticipated in the preamble to the *Manual for Courts-Martial* that judges would need to carefully balance national security with individual rights in applying the UCMJ. That preamble states: "The purpose of military law is to promote justice, to assist in maintaining good order and discipline in the armed forces, to promote efficiency and effectiveness in the military establishment, and thereby to strengthen the national security of the United States."

What is reasonable and fair from the public's perception, as well as this Court's judgment as to what is reasonable and fair, would be different in the case of national security exigency or operational necessity. In a particular case, operational needs may impact the availability of members of a command, thereby significantly limiting the pool from which potential members might be selected. Here, deployed units may have diminished the potential pool of members, but the Government failed to demonstrate that it was necessary for the Brigade Commander to serve on this panel. The record shows that there were at least two combat brigades at Fort Stewart at the time of trial, in addition to support elements, from which to select a qualified member in lieu of COL Williams.

In short, in this case, the Government has failed to demonstrate that operational deployments or needs precluded other suitable officers from reasonably serving on this panel, thus necessitating the Brigade Commander's participation.

To address this issue from the standpoint of performance reports misses the point. With or without the prohibition against unlawful command influence under Article 37, UCMJ, 10 U.S.C. § 837, we reject the notion that officers and non-commissioned officers, who swear to uphold the Constitution, might breach that oath willfully in the deliberation room in an effort to influence a performance report. The American public should and does have great confidence in the integrity of the men and women who serve in uniform, including their integrity in the jury room.

However, public perception of the military justice system may nonetheless be affected by more subtle aspects of military life. An objective public might ask to what extent, if any, does deference (a.k.a. respect) for senior officers come into play? The public perceives accurately that military commissioned and noncommissioned officers are expected to lead, not just manage; to command, not just direct; and to follow, not just get out of the way. For lack of a more precise term, appellant's trial defense counsel described this concern as creating "the wrong atmosphere." In this context, there is simply too high a risk that the public will perceive that the accused received something less than a jury of ten equal members, although something more than a jury of one. . . .

Whether one agrees with appellant that the panel would constitute a "brigade staff meeting" or not, we have no doubt that "viewed through the eyes of the public," serious doubts about the fairness of the military justice system are raised when the senior member of the panel and those he commanded or supervised commanded a two-thirds majority of members that alone could convict the accused. This is not "knowing it when you see it," or appellate judges attempting to extrapolate "public perceptions" from the bench. This is a clear application of law to fact, and illustrates well why this court recognizes a doctrine of implied bias, as well as one of actual bias, in interpreting R.C.M. 912.

For these reasons, the military judge abused his discretion when he failed to grant appellant's challenge for cause against COL Williams. Having found error, we must now test for prejudice.

Prejudice

Appellant preserved this issue for appeal by peremptorily challenging COL Williams and indicating that, but for the military judge's denial of his challenge for cause, he would have used the peremptory challenge against another officer.

There is no constitutional right to a peremptory challenge. *Ross v. Oklahoma*, 487 U.S. 81, 88 (1988); *Armstrong*, 54 M.J. at 54. Therefore, if there is prejudice, its existence derives from the statutory and regulatory right to one peremptory challenge provided for in Article 41, UCMJ, 10 U.S.C. § 841, and R.C.M. 912(g). This Court recently addressed the question of prejudice in *Armstrong*, where the appellant also removed an issue of implied bias through exercise of his one peremptory challenge. In *Armstrong*, this Court held that the availability of a peremptory challenge does not remove the prejudice arising from an erroneous ruling on a challenge for cause. *Id.* at 55.

Armstrong remains the law in the military. When a statute or rule confers a right greater than the Constitution, an accused is entitled to the benefit of that greater right, unless it conflicts with a higher source of law. *Armstrong*, 54 M.J. at 55; *United States v. Davis*, 47 M.J. 484, 485-86 (1998). Accordingly, even though COL Williams was excused from the panel by a peremptory challenge, the military judge's denial of the challenge for cause against COL Williams prejudiced appellant's right to exercise a peremptory challenge against another member of his choice. To say that appellant cured any error by exercising his one peremptory challenge against the offending member is reasoning that, if accepted, would reduce the right to a peremptory challenge from one of substance to one of illusion only. . . .

CRAWFORD, C.J. (dissenting):

After the seven-game 1960 World Series victory by my hometown Pittsburgh Pirates over the heavily favored New York Yankees, that ended when Bill Mazeroski hit a dramatic ninth inning home run over Yogi Berra's head and the left center field wall of Forbes Field, Yogi explained the loss by saying, "We made too many wrong mistakes." Unfortunately, our performance in the arena of implied bias is filled with inconsistency, if not "wrong mistakes," and today's decision only compounds the confusion.

It is unclear whether the doctrine of implied bias even exists as a matter of law. See *Smith v. Phillips*, 455 U.S. 209 (1982); *United States v. Dinatale*, 44 M.J. 325, 329 (1996) (*Cox*, C.J., concurring). The Supreme Court has neither embraced nor rejected the doctrine. *See, e.g., Andrews v. Collins*, 21 F.3d 612, 620 (5th Cir. 1994); *Tinsley v. Borg*, 895 F.2d 520, 527 (9th Cir. 1990); *Person v. Miller*, 854 F.2d 656, 664 (4th Cir. 1988). If it does exist, a conflict exists among the federal Courts of Appeals concerning the standard of review and application of the doctrine.

The majority tests the military judge's denial of a causal challenge against Colonel (COL) Williams for abuse of discretion. . . . We have previously held, on numerous occasions, that the proper standard of review is "clear abuse of discretion." *See, e.g., United States v. White*, 36 M.J. 284, 287 (C.M.A. 1993), *cert. denied*, 510 U.S. 1090 (1994); *United States v. Dinatale, supra* at 328; *but see United States v. Warden*, 51 M.J. 78, 82 (1999) (abuse of discretion); *compare United States v. Cerrato-Reyes*, 176 F.3d 1253, 1260 (10th Cir. 1999) (a trial court's finding as to actual bias is reviewed for clear error, but the court's finding as to implied bias is reviewed de novo), *with United States v. Ai*, 49 M.J. 1, 5 n.4 (1998) (declining to decide a "precise" standard for appellate review of implied bias challenges).

All military accused, like their counterparts in civilian criminal courts, have a right to a trial before an impartial factfinder. *See Weiss v. United States*, 510 U.S. 163, 179 (1994); *Ai, supra,* 49 M.J. at 4; R.C.M. 912(f)(1), Manual for Courts-Martial, United States (2000 ed.). Assuming that the doctrine of implied bias does exist, other Courts of Appeals have limited its application to those exceptional and extraordinary circumstances where a juror's emotional attachment to an issue or participant in the court proceeding was such that it was very unlikely, by any objective measurement, that an average person could remain impartial in deciding the merits of the case. . . .

Unlike other courts, the majority finds that implied bias is an issue "of public perception and the appearance of fairness in the military justice system," . . . not one of individual court member disqualification based on that member's bias. The majority finds reversible error in the composition of the court-martial panel because COL Williams's presence erodes public confidence in the "legality, fairness, and impartiality" of the military justice system. *See* R.C.M. 912(f)(1)(N). Since I have a bit more confidence in the judgment of the American public than does the majority, I find no clear abuse of discretion in the military judge's denial of the causal challenge.

The American public with which I am familiar is both perceptive and informed. When presented with all the facts, it is most capable of making a fair and reasoned judgment. It is not limited to a handful of individuals dedicated either to vilifying or lionizing the role of a convening authority in the selection of court-martial members. The informed public understands the differences between courts-martial with members and trials in the civilian sector with civilian jurors. American citizens are also capable of understanding the differences between the military justice system and the various civilian criminal law systems, and knowing that in the military justice system, a convening authority selects court-martial members "by reason of age, education, training, experience, length of service, and judicial temperament." Art. 25(d)(2), UCMJ, 10 U.S.C. § 825(d)(2). The public can also understand why court-martial members have been referred to as blue ribbon panels due to the quality of their membership. *See United States v. Youngblood*, 47 M.J. 338, 346 (1997) (Crawford, J., dissenting); *United States v. Rome*, 47 M.J. 467, 471 (1998) (Crawford, J., dissenting).

The thoughtful, conscientious public with which I am familiar would first want to know the facts before jumping to a conclusion. The record of trial establishes the following facts:

(1) COL Williams, the 2d Brigade Commander, was a permanent member of Court-Martial Convening Order Number 4. Lieutenant Colonel (LTC) Rogers, one of COL Williams's battalion commanders, as well as LTC Rogers's executive officer (XO), Major (MAJ) Gonsalves, were also permanent members of Court-Martial Convening Order Number 4. Command Sergeant Major (CSM) Arroyo was also designated as a member by this Court-Martial Order whenever an accused requested enlisted membership on the court.

(2) LTC Mereness and LTC Hough were detailed to appellant's court-martial only by Court-Martial Convening Order Number 6.

(3) LTC Hough was a Forward Support Battalion (FSB) commander assigned to the Division Support Command. He had a command supervisory relationship with COL Williams only when LTC Hough's battalion was in direct support of the 2d Brigade, such as during deployment situations.

(4) COL Williams only had rating responsibility for three members — his two battalion commanders, LTC Rogers and LTC Mereness, and LTC Rogers's XO, MAJ Gonsalves. The record discloses that COL Williams was the reviewer of First Sergeant Waters's enlisted efficiency report, but not a rater.

(5) Appellant challenged three individuals based on implied bias at trial — COL Williams, MAJ Gonsalves, and CSM Arroyo. There is no stated rationale why trial defense counsel challenged the most senior member of the panel (COL Williams), but then challenged two subordinates (MAJ Gonsalves and CSM Arroyo) instead of those members' superior officers, LTC Rogers and LTC Hough, respectively.

(6) The military judge found that there were two combat brigades with the 3d Infantry Division stationed at Fort Stewart, one of which was deployed to Kuwait. The military judge also correctly found that the FSB (LTC Hough and CSM Arroyo) was not a part of the 2d Brigade.

Of course, an astute and inquisitive general public would not be limited to the record of trial when gathering facts to test the fairness and impartiality of appellant's court martial. Inquiring minds would also discover that one of Fort Stewart's brigades was deployed, shrinking the potential pool from which the General Court-Martial Convening Authority could select members.

Since the informed and reasonable American public understands the structure of the United States armed forces, to include the necessity for superior-subordinate relationships, the public would disagree with the majority when it finds that COL Williams had a superior-subordinate relationship with six of the other nine members. Actually, COL Williams was superior to all of the other members of the court-martial panel. Furthermore, the public would understand that the president of every court-martial is superior in rank to all other members of the panel. Since the public will accept the majority recognizing that the members were, in fact, impartial, and will know that appellant has not challenged the veracity of any individual member's responses to voir dire questions, the inquiring public could be perplexed by the majority's logic.

Finally, I believe that the American public, after reading the Supreme Court's views in *Weiss v. United States*, 510 U.S. 163 (1994), and looking at the legislative history of Article 37, UCMJ, 10 U.S.C. § 837, would have no difficulty with the various working relationships among the court members who adjudicated appellant's court-martial. However, the American public might be skeptical of this Court, which accords military judges "great deference" on questions of actual bias (because the trial judge has observed the demeanor of the participants), but gives less deference on questions of implied bias, presumably because we can gauge the perception of the American public better than a trial judge. Perhaps the informed American public, cognizant of the purpose of military justice, the history of the Uniform Code of Military Justice, and the creation of this Court, might ask why we have such limited confidence in a military judge's ability to understand and make reasoned, informed decisions about the impartiality of court-martial members.

In sum, the average American would find that since the first combat brigade at Fort Stewart was deployed to Kuwait at the time of trial, appellant's court-martial members were selected out of elements of the 3d Infantry Division remaining at Fort Stewart. After examining all of the underlying evidence associated with appellant's court-martial and knowing all the facts, I believe a reasonable member of the public would find no unfairness, bias, or other illegality in the selection of those members who heard appellant's court-martial, or in the denial of the challenge for cause against COL Williams.

> The fundamental goal of a military court-martial member selection system, as in civilian society, is to identify and select a panel of court-martial members that is competent, fair, and impartial. A military system, however, must also produce panel members who are available without unduly restricting the conduct of the military mission or national security.

Department of Defense Joint Service Committee on Military Justice, Report on the Method of Selection of Members of the Armed Forces to Serve on Courts-Martial 8 (1999). This goal was achieved in this case. Accordingly, I would affirm the decision of the Court of Criminal Appeals.

SULLIVAN, SENIOR JUDGE (dissenting):

The Majority's Holding

The majority effectively holds today that where one officer commands a significant number of the members of a panel, he may not sit as a member of that panel if challenged by the defense. The Congress and the President are the lawmakers for the military justice system, and they have not made such a rule. Based on all the circumstances of this case, I conclude that the military judge did not abuse his discretion when he refused to grant the defense challenge to Colonel (COL) Williams. *See United States v. Ai*, 49 M.J. 1, 5 (1998).

In my view, the majority's holding in this case creates new law, and it is law which Congress or the President should make, not the judiciary. *See* U.S. Const. Art. I, § 8, cl. 16; Article 36, UCMJ, 10 U.S.C. § 836. Congress could have provided that a member shall be disqualified if he or she is the military commander of a significant number of the members of the panel. . . . Congress has been aware that, for years, commanders have sat on panels with their subordinates. Congress could have prohibited this situation by law but failed to do so. A court should not judicially legislate when Congress, in its wisdom, does not.

With respect to judicial rulemaking (the clone of judicial legislation), the President, acting pursuant to Article 36, UCMJ, could also have provided that a challenge must be granted where a member is a brigade commander of a significant number of the members of a court-martial panel. . . .

The President could have made a new rule barring commanders of a significant number of other members of a panel from sitting on a court-martial, but he did not. Like judicial legislation, courts should refrain from judicial rulemaking. . . .

Congress has provided that a military accused may make challenges for cause, and the military judge is to decide these challenges. Article 41(a)(1), UCMJ, 10 U.S.C. § 841(a)(1). The President, pursuant to Article 36, UCMJ, has specifically delineated circumstances where a challenged member shall be excused. As noted above, nowhere is it said that a member shall be excused because he is the military commander of a significant number of the members of the panel. *See* R.C.M. 912(f)(1)(A)-(N). Congress passed the UCMJ legislation knowing that this law was intended to apply to remote bases and posts, as well as to ships at sea. Congress did not see fit to disqualify commanders from sitting on military juries in these circumstances. Accordingly, I must reject this Court's attempt to fashion such a rule to the contrary. *See generally United States v. Scheffer*, 523 U.S. 303 (1998) (the President, not the Court of Appeals for the Armed Forces, makes the rules for courts-martial).

To the extent that the majority relies on R.C.M. 912(f)(1)(N) as the legal basis or authority for its holding in this case, I also must disagree. It generally says:

> A member shall be excused for cause whenever it appears that the member . . .

> (N) should not sit as a member in the interest of having the court-martial free from substantial doubt as to legality, fairness, and impartiality.

In my view, R.C.M. 912(f)(1)(N) does not contemplate mandatory exclusion rules such as that fashioned by the majority in this case. *See United States v. Greer*, 223 F.3d 41, 52 (2d Cir. 2000) (defining inferred bias in terms of facts which permit a judge to remove a member in the judge's discretion). Instead, it calls for discretionary judgement by the trial judge, based on all the circumstances of a particular case. *See United States v. Smart*, 21 M.J. 15, 20 (C.M.A. 1985); *see also* para. 58e, Manual for Courts-Martial, U.S. Army, 1928 ("appreciable risk of injury to the substantial rights of an accused, which risk will not be avoided by a reading of the record"); *see also United States v. Warden*, 51 M.J. 78, 82 (1999); *United States v. Ai*, 49 M.J. at 5; *United States v. Minyard*, 46 M.J. 229, 231-32 (1997).

My analysis shows that the trial judge did not abuse his discretion in this case. The judge exercised his discretion with no knowledge that this Court would expand the law as the majority does today. When the judge made his ruling that is overturned today by the majority, there was no case law suggesting this holding. Interestingly enough, the majority cites no case law as support for this new extension of the law.

Review for Abuse of Discretion by the Trial Judge

The assigned legal question before us is whether the military judge abused his discretion when he denied the defense's challenge for cause against COL Williams. Appellant asserts that the judge clearly did, especially in light of the military justice system's "liberal grant policy" for such challenges,[3] . . . and certain facts in this case showing "implied bias." . . . Appellant particularly argues that COL Williams's role as a brigade commander of a majority of the panel members created an appearance of unfairness as to these proceedings. . . .

Implied bias has been said to exist in military law when, "regardless of an individual member's disclaimer of bias, 'most people in the same position would be prejudiced [i.e., biased].'" *United States v. Napolitano*, 53 M.J. 162, 167 (2000) (quoting *United States v. Schlamer*, 52 M.J. 80, 93 (1999)); *cf. United States v. Greer*, 223 F.3d at 52-53 (in federal civilian system, challenges must be granted on basis of implied bias if court concludes "an average person in the position of the juror in controversy would be prejudiced"). It calls for a judgment by the military judge on the propriety of a challenged member or members sitting in a case, through the eyes of the public. Implied bias focuses on "the perception or appearance of fairness of the military justice system," rather than the actual existence of bias. *United States v. Napoleon*, 46 M.J. 279, 283 (1997).

Appellant complains that the presence of COL Williams on a panel where so many members were subject to his command supervision created an appearance of its unfairness. Appellant argues "even with the panel members' disclaimers, an outside observer would reasonably perceive the court-martial to be unfair when COL Williams, a brigade commander, held such an influential position over a majority of the panel members. . . . The perception of unfair-

---

[3] [n.1]Interestingly, this policy is in sharp contrast with current practice in the British criminal justice system. In Britain, attorneys are not allowed to *voir dire* or cross-examine the jurors to ferret out possible grounds for bias, as is common in American criminal trials. As a result, very little is known about individual jurors, and attorneys rarely have grounds to support a challenge for cause. *See* Sean Enright, *Reviving the Challenge for Cause*, 139 NEW LAW JOURNAL 9 (1989).

ness," appellant further argues, "increases exponentially considering the fact that, including himself, COL Williams held a commander, supervisor or rating position over enough panel members (seven of ten) to convict SGT Wiesen. . . ." . . .

The military judge, however, provided several reasons for his rejection of the defense challenge for cause against COL Williams. First, the judge stated that military case law did not require him to grant such a challenge simply because a challenged member had a military supervisory relationship over another panel member. Second, the judge asserted that such a relationship, even with a majority of the members, would not be a significant factor raising a suspicion of unfairness in a case where that command's organizational interests were not directly at issue. Third, the judge noted that the extensive voir dire of all the members of the court-martial panel established no other circumstances suggesting COL Williams should not sit in this case in the interest of the appearance of fairness.

In my view, the military judge did not abuse his discretion in denying the defense challenge for cause for these reasons. *See generally United States v. Napolitano*, 53 M.J. at 167. He correctly recognized that a military supervisory relationship over another member, including writing the subordinate's fitness report, does not per se disqualify the supervisor from sitting on a court-martial panel with his subordinate. *See United States v. Murphy*, 26 M.J. 454, 455 (C.M.A. 1988). On this matter, we have generally subscribed to Chief Judge Quinn's view, expressed long ago in *United States v. Deain*, 5 U.S.C.M.A. 44, 52, 17 C.M.R. 44, 52 (1954):

> The mere fact that the senior, or other member of the court, coincidentally has the duty to prepare and submit a fitness report on a junior member, in and of itself, does not affect the junior's "sense of responsibility and individual integrity by which men judge men." *Dennis v. United States*, 339 U.S. 162. So, if, as in the hypothetical case cited by the board of review, the convening authority designates two officers to serve on a court, one of whom is the normal reporting senior of the other, *no reasonable man would believe that the senior is put in a position to exert undue control over the deliberations of the other.* Their association as court members and the submission of a fitness report is not incompatible. We seriously doubt that either member would give thought to the fact that one is charged with the responsibility of reporting on the general fitness of the other.

(Emphasis added.)

Moreover, the military judge was also correct in suggesting that the fact a number of members of the panel were subject to the military supervision or evaluation of the president of the court-martial did not per se require disqualification of that officer. *See United States v. Harris*, 13 M.J. 288, 292 (C.M.A. 1982); *United States v. Blocker*, 32 M.J. 281, 286-87 (C.M.A. 1991). Appellant's counsel, however, argued at trial that the number in his case, a clear majority of the panel, created a particular appearance of unfairness:

> So, if a reporter from the newspaper came in and said, "You mean to tell me that five of these guys work for the President?" I think that a

reasonable number of the American public who read that newspaper would say, "Yeah, right," about the military justice system. And that's why I'm saying in this case, five's a lot. . . .

In my view, attributing such skepticism to the American people was unwarranted, and the military judge acted properly in rejecting it. *Cf. Weiss v. United States*, 510 U.S. 163, 194 (1994) (Ginsburg, J., concurring) ("Today's decision upholds a system of military justice notably more sensitive to due process concerns than the one prevailing through most of our country's history . . . ."). Moreover, the members of the panel in this case took an oath to "faithfully and impartially try, according to the evidence, [their] consciences, and the laws applicable to trials by court-martial, the case of the accused . . . ." Manual, *supra* at A8-11. There is no support in this record to show that there was any likelihood that the panel in this case would be intimidated by the Brigade Commander into violating this oath.

In this regard, I note that in 1968, Congress specifically amended Article 37, UCMJ, to expressly prohibit the rating or evaluation of court members on their court-martial duty performance. Article 37(b) now states:

> (b) In the preparation of an effectiveness, fitness, or efficiency report, or any other report or document used in whole or in part for the purpose of determining whether a member of the armed forces is qualified to be advanced, in grade, or in determining the assignment or transfer of a member of the armed forces or in determining whether a member of the armed forces should be retained on active duty, *no person subject to this chapter may, in preparing any such report (1) consider or evaluate the performance of duty of any such member as a member of a court-martial*[.]

(Emphasis added.) I believe the American public is well aware of this bedrock of modern military law and would consider its statutory protection when forming a judgment as to the appearance of fairness of appellant's court-martial panel. *See also Weiss v. United States, supra* 510 U.S. at 180-81 (due process evaluated by Supreme Court in view of Article 37, UCMJ); *see generally United States v. Schlamer*, 52 M.J. at 93-94 (entire context of record to be considered).

Finally, I note that the evidence in this case showed brigade relationships between COL Williams and the other members of the panel, but that it also showed appellant was not a member of that brigade. *See United States v. Ai*, 49 M.J. at 5. In addition, as noted by the military judge below, the record before us does not directly or indirectly implicate any particular interest of COL Williams or his brigade in the successful prosecution of this case. *Cf. United States v. Rome*, 47 M.J. 467 (1998) (military supervisor member previously accused of unlawful command influence at prior court-martial by defense counsel). Finally, the extensive inquiry of the members by the trial judge did not disclose any other factual circumstance from which the public would perceive that unreasonable demands were being placed on the challenged members in this case by asking them to sit with COL Williams. *See United States v. Youngblood*, 47 M.J. at 343 (Sullivan, J., concurring in part and dissenting in part).

In closing, today's holding by the majority effectively bars commanders from sitting on courts-martial where their subordinate officers constitute a significant number of the members of the panel. Thus, it may preclude courts-martial in small commands or on ships, where procuring members outside the local chain of command is not a realistic option. I do not believe this is the will of Congress. *See generally* Article 5, UCMJ, 10 U.S.C. § 805 (the UCMJ applies in territory worldwide).

Congress and the President, not this Court, should make these important decisions. *See United States v. Scheffer*, 523 U.S. at 303. Accordingly, I dissent.

NOTES AND QUESTIONS

1. Do you agree with Senior Judge Sullivan that "the American public is well aware" of Article 37(b)'s provision that service on a court-martial may not be considered during any military members' performance evaluation? The competing *Wiesen* opinions have a surreal quality to them, appearing to assume an unrealistically high level of public familiarity with and interest in the military justice system.

2. Within the military justice system, *Wiesen* proved controversial. The government moved for reconsideration, resulting in yet another divided published decision in the case. *United States v. Wiesen*, 57 M.J. 48 (C.A.A.F. 2002) (per curiam). One faculty member at The Judge Advocate General's School of the Army condemned *Wiesen* as "judicial activism." Major Christopher W. Behan, *Don't Tug on Superman's Cape: In Defense of Convening Authority Selection and Appointment of Court-Martial Panel Members*, 176 MIL. L. REV. 190, 269 (2003). Major Behan argued:

> [A]n activist majority of the CAAF has opened a new front in the war against discretionary convening authority selection of panel members. *United States v. Wiesen* demonstrates that the CAAF majority is willing to use the court's implied bias doctrine in a way that effectively rewrites UCMJ Article 25(d)(2), burdening convening authorities with a requirement to consider actual and potential command and supervisory relationships when appointing panel members. . . .
>
> The foundation for the majority's opinion was the CAAF's implied-bias doctrine, derived from Rule for Courts-Martial (R.C.M.) 912(f)(1)(N), which provides that a member shall be excused for cause "whenever it appears that the member . . . should not sit as a member in the interest of having the court-martial free from substantial doubt as to legality, fairness, and impartiality." [Rule for Courts-Martial 912(f)(1)(N), Manual for Courts-Martial, United States (2002 ed.) [hereinafter R.C.M.].] As developed by the CAAF's case law over the years, the doctrine seeks to "view the situation [as to whether a member should sit] through the eyes of the public, focusing on the appearance of fairness." [*United States v. Rome*, 47 M.J. 467, 469 (1998).] This is a nebulous standard at best, and one that in the *Wiesen* majority's own words, the CAAF has "struggled to define . . . or just disagreed on what that scope should be." [*Wiesen*, 56 M.J. at 175.] *Wiesen* demonstrates that the struggle continues.

The *Wiesen* majority opinion fails to provide an objective, coherent analytical framework for analyzing implied bias. Without providing any standards for determining how to view the case "through the eyes of the public," the majority simply strung together a series of speculative statements on its perceptions of public opinion. The majority believes that the public trusts the integrity of military officers to abide by their oaths, in and out of the deliberation room. The problem is that the public, which understands that military personnel lead, command, and follow each other, might wonder to what extent institutional military deference for senior officers would come into play in the deliberation room. When a senior officer supervises a high enough percentage of the panel, it establishes "the wrong atmosphere," creating "simply too high a risk that the public will perceive that the accused received something less than a jury of ten equal members, although something more than a jury of one." [*Id.* at 176.] Nothing in the opinion assists military justice practitioners in determining how to measure public perception of the justice system; there is not, for example, a "reasonable person" test of the kind so familiar in American appellate jurisprudence.

The majority further complicated matters for the practitioner by shifting the burden of proof for causal challenges of panel members based on implied bias from the accused to the government. The normal burden of proof for causal challenges is on the party making the challenge. [*See* R.C.M. 912(f)(3).] The majority in *Wiesen* adopted a standard requiring the government to demonstrate the necessity for the challenged member to serve on the panel because of "operational deployments or needs." [*Wiesen*, 56 M.J. at 176.]

2. Response: The Theoretical Shortcomings and Practical Drawbacks of Wiesen

The *Wiesen* majority opinion reveals the limitations of an appellate court in determining public opinion. Without fact-finding ability, investigative resources, or a constituency to provide input, an appellate court is left to its imagination in trying to determine how the public might view a particular practice in the military justice system. Most critically, an appellate court has no way to measure the impact of its decisions on the military; this is one of the primary reasons for the military deference doctrine in the Article III courts. When an appellate court ventures into the domain of the legislature, the consequences to the military can be particularly serious:

A mistaken judicial conclusion that servicemen's individual rights can be protected without impairing military efficiency has the court do inadvertently what it has no standard for doing deliberately. *Because the uses to which the armed forces are put cannot be judged by the principles of the legal system, mistaken balancing that impairs those uses is not offset by vindication of the hierarchy of values within the system.*

[James M. Hirshhorn, *The Separate Community: Military Uniqueness and Servicemen's Constitutional Rights*, 62 N.C. L. REV. 177, 238 (1984).]

Issues of court-martial panel composition fall squarely within the legislative purview of Congress and the rule-making authority of the President. [*See* UCMJ art. 36 (2002) (establishing presidential authority to make rules of procedure for courts-martial).] As Judge Crawford noted in her dissent to the CAAF's denial of reconsideration in *Wiesen*, Congress made all commissioned officers eligible to serve on court-martial panels, making no exclusion for officers rated by another member of the panel. [*See Wiesen II*, 57 M.J. at 53 (Crawford, C.J., dissenting).] In his dissent, Judge Sullivan was even more specific:

> Congress *could have provided* that a member shall be disqualified if he or she is a military commander of a significant number of the members of the panel. Congress has been aware that, for years, commanders have sat on panels with their subordinates. *Congress could have prohibited this situation by law but failed to do so.* A court should not judicially legislate when Congress, in its wisdom, does not.

[*Id.* at 182 (Sullivan, J., dissenting) (emphasis added) (citations omitted).]

What the CAAF majority accomplished in *Wiesen* was a judicial revision of UCMJ Article 25(d)(2). Article 25(d)(2) requires a convening authority to select best-qualified members by criteria of age, experience, education, training, length of service, and judicial temperament. In effect, *Wiesen* has rewritten Article 25(d)(2), adding a new clause that never existed before requiring convening authorities to consider, in addition to — or more likely in spite of — the statutory provisions of Article 25(d)(2), "all the potential command and supervisory relationships of panel members in conjunction with final panel size and numbers needed for conviction." Furthermore, *Wiesen* has significantly changed the rules regarding challenges in implied bias cases, imposing new requirements on the government to be prepared to justify panel selections in the light of operational needs.

Thus, *Wiesen* has a debilitating effect on the convening authority's discretion in panel selection. No longer may a convening authority select those whom he believes to be best qualified based on age, education, experience, training, length of service, and judicial temperament. Now he must consider the interrelationships among candidate panel members, particularly what potential command and supervisory arrangements may exist. This potentially destroys a commander's authority to convene courts-martial in smaller commands, isolated installations, aboard ships, or in a deployed environment.

There should be no doubt that the *Wiesen* majority intended to strike a blow at the convening authority's discretionary ability to appoint court-martial panel members. In the penultimate sentence of its per curiam denial of the government's petition for reconsideration, the majority wrote, "The issue is appropriately viewed in the context of public perceptions of a system in which the commander who exercises prosecutorial discretion is the official who selects and structures the panel that will hear the case." [*Wiesen II*, 57 M.J. at 50.] The *Wiesen* majority's true policy concern, then, hearkens back to the objections that Congress heard and considered when enacting the UCMJ over fifty years ago. Viewed in that context, *Wiesen* is a prime example of an activist appellate court arrogating to itself the power to change constitutionally sound legislation with which it does not agree.

Behan, 176 MIL L. REV. at 269-76. Major Behan went on to advocate that they military justice system "counterattack" against *Wiesen*. *Id*. at 276. He recommended amending Rule for Courts-Martial 912 to expressly provide: "The existence of a command or supervisory relationship between two or more members of a court-martial panel (even where such members constitute a majority sufficient to reach a finding of guilty) shall not constitute grounds for removal for cause." *Id*. at 287.

3. In 2005, the *Manual for Courts-Martial* was amended to address *Wiesen*, though it did not adopt the change that Major Behan recommended. Rather than amending Rule 912's grounds for challenges to address the holding in *Wiesen*, the change amended the rule governing preservation of challenge issues to address the prejudice portion of the *Wiesen* opinion. In Executive Order 13387, the President amended Rule for Courts-Martial 912(f)(4) by inserting the following provision: "the successful use of a peremptory challenge by either party, excusing the challenged member from further participation in the court-martial, shall preclude further consideration of the challenge of that excused member upon later review." 70 FED. REG. 60,697 (Oct. 18, 2005). The drafters' analysis explained:

> This rule change is intended to conform military practice to federal practice and limit appellate litigation when the challenged panel member could have been peremptorily challenged or actually did not participate in the trial due to a peremptory challenge by either party. This amendment is consistent with the President's lawful authority to promulgate a rule that would result in placing before the accused the hard choice faced by defendants in federal district courts — to let the challenged juror sit on the case and challenge the ruling on appeal or to use a peremptory challenge to remove the juror and ensure an impartial jury. *See United States v. Miles*, 58 M.J. 192 (C.A.A.F. 2003); *United States v. Wiesen*, 56 M.J. 172 (C.A.A.F. 2001), *petition for reconsideration denied*, 57 M.J. 48 (C.A.A.F. 2002); *United States v. Armstrong*, 54 M.J. 51 (C.A.A.F. 2001).

70 FED. REG. at 60,708. Contrary to the drafters' analysis, this change to the Rules for Courts-Martial does not "conform military practice to federal practice." In a federal non-capital felony case, the prosecution receives six peremptory challenges and the defense ten. Fed. R. Crim. P. 24(b)(2). In a capital case, each party receives twenty peremptory challenges. *Id*. at (b)(1). In a court-martial, each party generally receives only one peremptory challenge. *See* Art. 41(a)(1), UCMJ, 10 U.S.C. § 841(a)(1). Does a military judge's erroneous ruling requiring the defense to exercise its sole peremptory challenge against a

member who should have been removed for cause prejudice the defense in a way that erroneously requiring the defense to use one of ten peremptory challenges does not? In the military justice system, where the convening authority selects the members, is there greater cause to ensure that the defense's right to a peremptory challenge is protected than in the federal criminal justice system, where members of the venire are selected based on a random process? Because the 2005 amendment to R.C.M. 912 arguably interferes with the defense's statutory right to a peremptory challenge, is it susceptible to challenge that it conflicts with the Code, which would violate Article 36's requirement that procedural rules prescribed by the President "may not be contrary to or inconsistent with" the Code? *See* Art. 36(a), UCMJ, 10 U.S.C. § 836(a).

IV.   COURT-MARTIAL SIZE AND VOTING REQUIREMENTS

Uniform Code of Military Justice
Article 16. Courts-martial classified

The three kinds of courts-martial in each of the armed forces are —

(1) general courts-martial, consisting of —

    (A) a military judge and not less than five members; or

    (B) only a military judge, if before the court is assembled the accused, knowing the identity of the military judge and after consultation with defense counsel, requests orally on the record or in writing a court composed only of a military judge and the military judge approves;

(2) special courts-martial, consisting of —

    (A) not less than three members; or

    (B) a military judge and not less than three members; or

    (C) only a military judge, if one has been detailed to the court, and the accused under the same conditions as those prescribed in clause (1)(B) so requests; and

(3) summary courts-martial, consisting of one commissioned officer.

Article 25a. Number of members in capital cases

In a case in which the accused may be sentenced to a penalty of death, the number of members shall be not less than 12, unless 12 members are not reasonably available because of physical conditions or military exigencies, in which case the convening authority shall specify a lesser number of members not less than five, and the court may be assembled and the trial held with not less than the number of members so specified. In such a case, the convening authority shall make a detailed written statement, to be appended to the record, stating why a greater number of members were not reasonably available.

UNITED STATES v. GUILFORD
United States Army Court of Military Review
8 M.J. 598 (A.C.M.R. 1979)

FULTON, SENIOR JUDGE:

A general court-martial convicted appellant of rape and sentenced him to a dishonorable discharge and confinement at hard labor for five years, as well as reduction to the grade of Private E-1 and forfeiture of all pay and allowances. The convening authority approved the sentence. . . .

Ballew, Burch, and Military Due Process

Appellant's final assignment of error is stated as follows:

THE APPELLANT WAS DENIED HIS RIGHTS UNDER THE FIFTH AND SIXTH AMENDMENTS TO THE CONSTITUTION OF THE UNITED STATES TO A TRIAL BY AN IMPARTIAL JURY AND DUE PROCESS OF LAW, IN THAT THE COURT-MARTIAL WHICH CONVICTED HIM CONSISTED OF ONLY SEVEN MEMBERS, AND ONLY FIVE OF THOSE MEMBERS WERE REQUIRED TO CONCUR IN THE FINDINGS OF GUILTY.[4]

In *Ballew v. Georgia*, 435 U.S. 223 (1978), the Supreme Court held that trial to a jury of less than six persons deprives a defendant of the right to trial by a jury as contemplated by the Sixth Amendment. The decision is based on empirical studies showing that "the purpose and functioning of the jury in a criminal trial is seriously impaired, and to a constitutional degree, by a reduction in size to below six members." *Id.* at 239. Subsequently, in *Burch v. Louisiana*, 441 U.S. 130 (1979), the Court held that conviction by a nonunanimous six-member jury also fails to comply with the Sixth Amendment, saying —

> [M]uch the same reasons that led us in *Ballew* to decide that use of a five-member jury threatened the fairness of the proceeding and the proper role of the jury, lead us to conclude now that conviction for a nonpetty offense by only five members of a six-person jury presents a similar threat to preservation of the substance of the jury trial guarantee and justifies our requiring verdicts rendered by six-person juries to be unanimous.

The decisions in *Ballew* and *Burch,* although urged upon us by the appellant, do not apply to his case. *Ballew* does not apply because the court-martial to which appellant's case was tried consisted of more than six members (viz., seven). *Burch* does not govern because the Court expressly eschewed any intimation of its views as to the constitutionality of nonunanimous verdicts rendered by juries of more than six members. . . . We need not rest our decision wholly on such arithmetical observations, however. Courts-martial have proved constitutionally acceptable for the trial of members of the armed forces and data indicating that jurors supposed to represent a cross-section of a local

---

[4] [n.3] Of the ten officers detailed to the court-martial, three were excused from appellant's trial. None of the remaining seven was challenged. Since concurrence of only two-thirds of the members was required to convict, it is possible that only five members concurred in the findings of guilty. Article 52(a)(2), Uniform Code of Military Justice, 10 U.S.C. § 852(a)(2) (1976). . . .

civilian community do not adequately perform their function under certain conditions cannot be taken to mean that the purpose and function of courts-martial are similarly impaired.

By clear implication of the Fifth and Sixth Amendments, the right to a trial by jury as contemplated in the Sixth Amendment does not apply to military trials of members of the armed forces in active service. *See United States v. Ezell*, 6 M.J. 307, 327 n.4 (C.M.A. 1979) (Fletcher, C.J., concurring). Appellant recognizes that *Ballew* has, accordingly, uniformly been held inapplicable to military trials. The later-decided *Burch* rests squarely on *Ballew* and is likewise inapplicable.

Appellant contends, however, that the underlying reasoning of *Ballew* and *Burch* implicates military trials because Article 16 of the Uniform Code of Military Justice, 10 U.S.C. § 816 establishes a right to jury trial, which the due process clause of the Fifth Amendment also requires be fair and impartial.

It cannot be gainsaid that the military trial must be fair and impartial. . . . The trial is, however, by a unique, military tribunal that is essentially different from the jury envisioned by the Sixth Amendment. The composition of courts-martial is different, as the members are drawn exclusively from the accused's own profession based on specified qualifications (one of which is judicial temperament), with specialized knowledge of the profession, and subject to only one challenge other than for cause. Their functioning differs, too. For example, it includes the questioning of witnesses and the determining of sentences. In view of such compositional and functional differences, the studies relied upon in *Ballew* and *Burch* are inapposite. [*United States v. Wolff*, 5 M.J. 923, 925 (N.C.M.R. 1978).] The differences between the institution of courts-martial and the institution known as a jury have been recognized as necessary as well as constitutional. *O'Callahan v. Parker*, 395 U.S. 258 (1969). When the use of courts-martial has impinged on constitutional rights, the remedy has been to limit the exercise of their jurisdiction rather than to alter the nature of the tribunal, for courts-martial are not fundamentally unfair. *Gosa v. Mayden*, 413 U.S. 665 (1973). . . .

NOTES AND QUESTIONS

1. One commentary published after the Army Court of Military Review's *Guilford* decision argued that military defense counsel should continue to challenge the combination of small court-martial panel size and lack of a unanimity requirement for a conviction:

> Court-martial voting rules apply regardless of the number of members voting on findings, whether the statutory minimum of five, or some larger number. Because Supreme Court precedent upholds convictions based on the vote of nine out of twelve jurors, it is unlikely that a vote, for example, of eight of twelve court-martial members is unconstitutional. The holdings of *Ballew v. Georgia* and *Burch v. Louisiana* further demonstrate that cases of five and six member courts-martial best present the lack of unanimity issue.

Small Juries Require Unanimity to Produce Reliable Results. The military accused who is convicted by a nonunanimous five or six member general court-martial must rely on the Due Process Clause of the fifth amendment to present the issue. He or she must invoke the conclusions of empirical studies concerning small juries that were relied on in *Ballew* and *Burch* demonstrating that smaller deliberative bodies produce results that are less well-considered and less accurate. The Supreme Court reached the following conclusions en route to its holdings that five-member and nonunanimous six-member juries are unconstitutional: "progressively smaller juries are less likely to foster effective group deliberation"; [*Ballew*, 435 U.S. at 232,] "the risk of convicting an innocent person . . . rises as the size of the jury diminishes"; [*id.* at 234,] "the verdicts of jury deliberation in criminal cases will vary as juries become smaller, and . . . the variance amounts to an imbalance to the detriment of one side, the defense"; [*id.* at 236,] "the presence of minority viewpoints [diminishes] as juries decrease in size . . ."; [*id.*,] and "when the case is close, and the guilt or innocence of the defendant is not readily apparent [larger juries] will insure evaluation by the sense of the community and will also tend to insure accurate factfinding." [*Id.* at 238.] . . .

The Navy and Army Courts of Military Review . . . have rejected [these empirical studies] as inapposite in light of the differences between court-martial members and civilian juries. [*Wolff*, 5 M.J. at 925; *Guilford*, 8 M.J. at 601-02.] . . . Professor Saks[, the expert upon whose studies the Supreme Court relied in *Ballew* and *Burch*,] opined that "the same principles [of group decisionmaking] would apply to the military as to civilian decision makers," and "in other areas of research, only negligible or no differences have been found between civilian and military populations." [Letter from Michael J. Saks, Department of Psychology, Boston College to Appellate Defense Division, Navy-Marine Appellate Review Activity.] . . .

Capt. Richard J. Anderson & Keith E. Hunsucker, *Is the Military Nonunanimous Finding of Guilty Still an Issue?*, ARMY LAW, Oct. 1986, at 57, 58-59.

Surprisingly, the Court of Appeals for the Armed Forces has never discussed the applicability of the *Ballew/Burch* line of cases to courts-martial. But in addition to decisions by the Army and Navy-Marine Corps Courts of Military Review, the United States Court of Appeals for the Tenth Circuit has held that those cases do not apply to the military justice system. *Mendrano v. Smith*, 797 F.2d 1538 (10th Cir. 1986).

2. Is a court-martial panel sufficiently different from a civilian jury that the empirical research upon which the Supreme Court relied in *Ballew* and *Burch* is inapplicable? Regardless of whether a constitutional challenge would be successful, as a matter of policy should Congress alter the court-martial size and vote requirements to meet the constitutional minimums that the Court has established for civilian criminal trials?

Chapter 14

SPEEDY AND PUBLIC TRIAL

The need for speed in military justice comes from two sources: the desire of commanding officers for quick and decisive disciplinary action (see Chapter 4's discussion of summary discipline) and the due process rights of servicemembers, which weigh against indefinite detention and extended judicial proceedings. This chapter focuses on the latter, exploring the rules that have evolved to limit delay and encourage timely resolution. It also takes up the related topic of whether military courts should be open to the public, another due process concern that has special implications in a military criminal context.

I. POST-TRIAL DELAYS AND JUDICIAL REMEDIES

UNITED STATES v. TARDIF
United States Court of Appeals for the Armed Forces
57 M.J. 219 (C.A.A.F. 2002)

JUDGE GIERKE delivered the opinion of the Court.

A general court-martial composed of officer and enlisted members convicted appellant, contrary to his pleas, of a 12-day unauthorized absence and assault on a child under the age of sixteen years (two specifications), in violation of Articles 86 and 128, Uniform Code of Military Justice (UCMJ), 10 U.S.C. §§886 and 928, respectively. The adjudged sentence provides for a dishonorable discharge, confinement for three years, total forfeitures, and reduction to the lowest enlisted grade. The convening authority reduced the confinement to 24 months but otherwise approved the sentence.

The Court of Criminal Appeals set aside the conviction of unauthorized absence and reassessed and affirmed the sentence. 55 M.J. 666 (2001). On reconsideration, the court below granted appellant 12 days of confinement credit under *United States v. Allen,* 17 M.J. 126 (C.M.A. 1984). 54 M.J. 954 and 55 M.J. 670 (2001).

This Court granted review of the following issue:

WHETHER THE COAST GUARD COURT OF CRIMINAL APPEALS ERRED IN CONCLUDING THAT APPELLANT HAD NOT BEEN PREJUDICED BY EXCESSIVE POST-TRIAL DELAY WHERE THE COURT BELOW CONCLUDED THAT THE DELAY WAS BOTH "UNEXPLAINED AND UNREASONABLE" AND "CASTS A SHADOW OF UNFAIRNESS OVER OUR MILITARY JUSTICE SYSTEM."

For the reasons set out below, we hold that a Court of Criminal Appeals has authority under Article 66(c), UCMJ, 10 U.S.C. §866(c), to grant appropriate relief for unreasonable and unexplained post-trial delays. . . .

Appellate History

The chronology of post-trial events in appellant's case is as follows:

Date	Action	Days Elapsed
October 29, 1999	Appellant sentenced	0
October 29, 1999	Confinement deferred	0
November 5, 1999	Deferment ends	7 days
December 21, 1999	Military Judge receives record of trial	53 days
February 7, 2000	Record authenticated	101 days
March 23, 2000	Record served on Defense Counsel (DC)	145 days
April 10, 2000	Recommendation of Staff Judge Advocate (SJA) prepared	163 days
May 15, 2000	DC responds to SJA recommendation	198 days
June 9, 2000	Convening Authority's action	223 days
Oct 2, 2000	Record forwarded to Headquarters, U.S. Coast Guard	338 days
November 1, 2000	Record received at Coast Guard Headquarters	368 days
November 17, 2000	Record referred to Coast Guard Court of Criminal Appeals	384 days

The court below focused on the 115 days that elapsed after the convening authority's action and before the record was forwarded to Coast Guard Headquarters. Concluding that the delay was "unexplained and unreasonable," and that it "casts a shadow of unfairness over our military justice system," the court nevertheless held that it was without authority to grant relief. Citing this Court's decisions in *United States v. Hudson,* 46 M.J. 226 (1997), *United States v. Jenkins,* 38 M.J. 287 (C.M.A. 1993), and *United States v. Banks,* 7 M.J. 92 (C.M.A. 1979), the court below concluded that "an appellant must show that the delay, no matter how extensive or unreasonable, prejudiced his substantial rights." 55 M.J. at 668. Chief Judge Baum dissented from the decision to not grant relief for the excessive delay in forwarding the case to the Court of Criminal Appeals. In Chief Judge Baum's view, no more than 21 months of confinement should have been approved. *Id.* at 669.

Before this Court, appellant argued that the court below applied the wrong standard of review by focusing on Article 59(a) instead of Article 66(c). Appellant requested that his case be remanded to the court below for consideration under Article 66(c), with instructions that unexplained and unreasonable post-trial delay is an appropriate factor for that court to consider in determining what sentence "should be approved," regardless of whether appellant has established legal prejudice.

The Government asserted that appellant was not harmed by the delay, and that it would be a windfall for appellant if he were granted sentence relief without showing that he has been harmed. The Government conceded, however, that if an appellant has suffered "harm" falling short of "prejudice" within the meaning of Article 59(a), a Court of Criminal Appeals may grant appropriate relief through its review of sentence appropriateness under Article 66(c).

The U.S. Army Government Appellate Division, as *amicus curiae,* urged this Court to hold that a Court of Criminal Appeals must be convinced that there was material prejudice to a substantial right under Article 59(a) before it grants relief for unreasonable post-trial delay. It further urged this Court to hold that, if a Court of Criminal Appeals concludes there has been material prejudice to an appellant's substantial rights, it may fashion appropriate relief under Article 66(c), without setting aside the findings and sentence. . . .

Discussion

1. Legal Context

A brief legal history is necessary to place the granted issue in context. This Court has long recognized that an accused has a right to timely review of the findings and sentence. *See United States v. Tucker,* 9 U.S.C.M.A. 587, 589, 26 C.M.R. 367, 369 (1958) ("Unexplained delays . . . [in appellate processes] should not be tolerated by the services, and they will not be countenanced by this Court.").

In *United States v. Burton,* 21 U.S.C.M.A. 112, 44 C.M.R. 166 (1971), the appellant asked this Court to set aside his conviction and sentence and dismiss the charges, on the ground that he had been denied his right to a speedy trial, in violation of Article 10, UCMJ, 10 U.S.C. § 810. This Court established a presumption of an Article 10 violation whenever an accused is held in pretrial confinement for more than three months. Under the *Burton* rule, there was a "heavy burden on the Government to show diligence, and in the absence of such a showing the charges [would] be dismissed." *Id.* at 118, 44 C.M.R. at 172.

In *Dunlap v. Convening Authority,* 23 U.S.C.M.A. 135, 48 C.M.R. 751 (1974), this Court considered a petition for extraordinary relief filed by a petitioner who remained in confinement at the United States Disciplinary Barracks for 11 months after his conviction was set aside, awaiting a convening authority's decision whether to order a rehearing or dismiss the charges. This Court concluded that the same considerations underlying the *Burton* rule for pretrial delays should be applied to post-trial delays. Thus, this Court held that "a presumption of a denial of speedy disposition of the case will arise when the accused is continuously under restraint after trial and the convening authority does not promulgate his formal and final action within 90 days of the date of such restraint after completion of trial." *Id.* at 138, 48 C.M.R. at 754. Like the *Burton* rule, the *Dunlap* rule placed a "heavy burden on the Government to show diligence, and in the absence of such a showing the charges [would] be dismissed." *Id.* . . .

[The court discusses subsequent limitations placed on the *Dunlap* rule regarding post-trial delays and on the authority of military appellate courts to remedy excessive delays.]

Thus, we hold that, in addition to its determination that no legal error occurred within the meaning of Article 59(a), the court below was required to determine what findings and sentence "should be approved," based on all the facts and circumstances reflected in the record, including the unexplained and unreasonable post-trial delay. Accordingly, we conclude that a remand is necessary so that the court below can exercise its broad authority under Article 66(c) to determine whether relief is warranted and, if so, what relief should be granted.

3. Remedies for Excessive Post-Trial Delay

The argument of *amicus curiae* raises the additional issue whether a Court of Criminal Appeals has authority to grant relief short of dismissal of the charges if it finds excessive post-trial delay. This argument reflects the longstanding concern of our Court and the Courts of Criminal Appeals about the draconian remedy required by *Dunlap* and its progeny for excessive post-trial delay. *See Hudson,* 46 M.J. at 227 ("[W]e are loath to declare that valid trial proceedings are invalid solely because of delays in the criminal process after the trial."); *United States v. Clevidence,* 14 M.J. 17, 21 (C.M.A. 1982) (Cook, J., dissenting) (dismissing charges is "burning the barn to kill the rats"); *Banks,* 7 M.J. at 93 ("The certified question expresses the frustration of the services over the inflexibility of the *Dunlap* rule."); *Dunlap,* 23 U.S.C.M.A. at 141, 48 C.M.R. at 757 (Duncan, C.J., dissenting) ("What the Court does today is provide a means where a person found guilty beyond a reasonable doubt in an error-free hearing may escape any sanction."); *see also* Department of the Army Pamphlet 27-50-336, The Army Lawyer, Criminal Law Note: *United States v. Collazo: The Army Court of Criminal Appeals Puts Steel on the Target of Post-Trial Delay,* at 37-38 (November 2000) (Army Court of Criminal Appeals "left with the options of finding prejudice and letting a rapist go free, or finding no prejudice and ratifying the sloppy administration of justice.").

Before this Court decided *Dunlap,* denial of the right to speedy trial resulted in dismissal of the charges only if reversible trial errors occurred and it was impossible to cure those errors at a rehearing because of the excessive post-trial delay. *See United States v. Timmons,* 22 U.S.C.M.A. 226, 227, 46 C.M.R. 226, 227 (1973), and cases cited therein. In *Timmons,* this Court noted that the court below had purged the effect of a trial error by modifying the findings, making dismissal of the charges unwarranted. In *United States v. Gray,* 22 U.S.C.M.A. 443, 445, 47 C.M.R. 484, 486 (1973), this Court repeated this principle:

> [B]efore ordering a dismissal of the charges because of post-trial delay there must be some error in the proceedings which requires that a rehearing be held and that because of the delay appellant would be either prejudiced in the presentation of his case at a rehearing or that

no useful purpose would otherwise be served by continuing the proceedings.

Although *Dunlap* is regarded as a post-trial delay case, the delay in that case actually involved the decision whether to order a rehearing. *See* 23 U.S.C.M.A. at 136, 48 C.M.R. at 752. Assuming without deciding that Article 10 applies only to proceedings through trial, this Court stated, "[T]he failure of the Uniform Code or the Manual for Courts-Martial to condemn directly unreasonable delay by the convening authority in acting on the record of trial does not mean that relief against such delay is unobtainable." This Court then decided that it was "appropriate" that the presumption of prejudice adopted for pretrial delays in *Burton* be applied to post-trial delays, along with the sanction of dismissing the charges whenever the presumption of prejudice was not overcome. *Id.* at 138, 48 C.M.R. at 754.

In *United States v. Becker,* 53 M.J. 229, 232 (2000), this Court provided the following guidance concerning remedies for "speedy trial" violations in the context of sentence rehearings: "[T]he remedy should be tailored to the harm suffered, such as an appropriate sentence credit or, in a case where the delay has interfered with the defense's ability to receive a fair hearing, a sentence to no punishment at all."

We conclude that the *Dunlap* "all-or-nothing" remedy for post-trial delays was laid to rest in *Banks*. We further conclude that appellate courts are not limited to either tolerating the intolerable or giving an appellant a windfall. The Courts of Criminal Appeals have authority under Article 66(c) to apply the *Timmons* approach, recently repeated in *Becker,* to post-trial delays, and to tailor an appropriate remedy, if any is warranted, to the circumstances of the case.

Finally, we note that counsel at the trial level are particularly well-situated to protect the interests of their clients by addressing post-trial delay issues before action by the convening authority. Trial counsel can ensure that the record contains an explanation for what otherwise might appear to be an unreasonable delay. Defense counsel can protect the interests of the accused through complaints to the military judge before authentication or to the convening authority after authentication and before action. After the convening authority's action, extraordinary writs may be appropriate in some circumstances. Appellate relief under Article 66(c) should be viewed as the last recourse to vindicate, where appropriate, an appellant's right to timely post-trial processing and appellate review. . . .

CRAWFORD, CHIEF JUDGE (dissenting):

The majority interprets Articles 66(c) and 59(a) in a manner that is contrary to the principles of statutory construction and legislative intent, as well as inconsistent with 50 years of established practice and case law. In so doing, the majority offers an incomplete recitation of the legislative history of Articles 66(c) and 59(a) and ignores the practical effects of its decision. The majority's misreading of Article 59 should not be further exacerbated. Unless there has been a substantial violation of an appellant's rights, the Courts of Criminal Appeals may not use their supervisory authority to grant further relief to the appellant. *United States v. Hasting,* 461 U.S. 499, 505 (1983).

Instead, this Court should encourage corrective action by those responsible for post-trial delays. *Id.* at 506 n.5. Because the majority is engaging in broad judicial rulemaking by amending the Code to expand Article 66(c) and contract Article 59(a), and thereby essentially creating a power of equity in the court below, I must respectfully dissent. . . .

I wholeheartedly endorse the goal of preventing unexplained or unreasonable post-trial delays, but believe there is a better means of achieving this end without violating the doctrine of separation of powers and principles established for judicial bodies. . . .

Legislative Action or Inaction. If Congress wanted to establish the remedy which the majority sanctions, it would have done so at the time of the UCMJ's enactment, or at any subsequent time that it became dissatisfied with decisions from the courts concerning post-trial delays. Numerous changes to the UCMJ have been enacted by Congress over the last 50 years, many in response to various judicial decisions. No changes have been forthcoming regarding the impact of post-trial delays. The majority's interpretation simply does not relate to the statutory objectives sought by Congress.

Practical Effects. There are practical reasons for not giving this authority to the lower courts. Contrary to the majority's assertion, final authority will not rest with the Courts of Criminal Appeals. Final review by this Court will be required to determine whether the lower courts abused their discretion. Neither the courts below nor this Court should be placed in the position of determining what constitutes a request for a delay, what circumstances justify delay, what constitutes extraordinary circumstances, and so forth. We do not have the flexibility or ability to gather facts that the President and his advisors have in exercising their rulemaking authority. Article 36, UCMJ, 10 U.S.C. § 836, is a clear grant of authority to the President to formulate these procedural rules. We should not be flirting with amending a statute or the Manual. That role should be left for Congress and the Executive Branch.

We would be shortsighted in not allowing the President and the services to exercise their rulemaking authority within established processes. I agree with Senior Judge Sullivan that neither this Court nor the courts below ought to exercise supervisory authority when the error is harmless. Rulemaking by the Executive Branch or Congress allows for flexibility and advance planning and avoids the distortion that takes place through judicial rulemaking. Once the rules are enacted, they will be subject to judicial review. We will ensure that servicemembers are not prejudiced by post-trial delays. . . .

SULLIVAN, SENIOR JUDGE (dissenting):

I see no reason to reverse and remand this case. I would affirm. There was no prejudice to appellant from the post-trial delay in this case, and no appellate relief is otherwise required by law. *See* Article 59(a), UCMJ. The majority today creates a new equity-type supervisory power for the Courts of Criminal Appeals. This is judicial activism, and I dissent. . . .

DIAZ v. JUDGE ADVOCATE GENERAL OF THE NAVY
United States Court of Appeals for the Armed Forces
59 M.J. 34 (2003)

PER CURIAM:

The Petitioner, Navy Firecontrolman Chief Salvador Diaz, initiated this proceeding by filing a Motion for Appropriate Relief which raised issues concerning the timeliness of the appellate process being afforded him as well as potential issues of ineffective assistance of appellate defense counsel. In response, this Court ordered the Respondent Judge Advocate General of the Navy (Government) to show cause why appropriate relief should not be granted. The Government's Answer in response to these serious issues is not persuasive. We conclude that the Navy-Marine Corps Court of Criminal Appeals should have taken action to ensure the protection of Petitioner's rights when he sought relief from that court. We therefore remand this matter to the Court of Criminal Appeals to take appropriate action and issue such orders as are necessary to ensure the timely filing of an Assignment of Errors and Brief on behalf of Petitioner, and we order such further action as directed in this opinion.

Background

Petitioner was tried by a general court-martial on June 14, October 30, and November 27-December 1, 2000. Contrary to his pleas of not guilty, he was convicted of multiple charges of rape and indecent acts with his 12-year-old daughter. On December 1, 2000 (day zero), Petitioner was sentenced to a dishonorable discharge, confinement for nine years, total forfeiture of all pay and allowances, and reduction to E-1. The convening authority approved the sentence without modification on December 21, 2001 (day 385).

The Navy-Marine Corps Appellate Review Activity received Petitioner's case on February 25, 2002 (day 451), and it was docketed with the Navy-Marine Corps Court of Criminal Appeals on February 28, 2002 (day 454). Petitioner's first appellate defense counsel filed ten requests for enlargement of time to file an assignment of errors. On December 3, 2002 (day 732), Petitioner filed a pro se petition for a Writ of Habeas Corpus with the Court of Criminal Appeals requesting release from confinement pending appeal. This request was based on an assertion that Petitioner's appellate defense counsel had not even commenced an initial review of the record of trial because of an excessive caseload. The court denied the writ petition on December 4, 2002 (day 733), though it did note that Petitioner "expressed concern with post-trial and appellate delay in his case." Petitioner filed for reconsideration, which was denied on February 11, 2003 (day 802).

Petitioner then filed a Motion for Appropriate Relief with this Court. We construed his motion as a Petition for Extraordinary Relief, and on June 16, 2003 (day 927), we ordered the Government to show cause why relief should not be granted. The Government filed an Answer to the Show Cause Order on June 26, 2003 (day 937). Represented by a new appellate defense counsel, Petitioner filed his Reply to Respondent's Answer on July 3, 2003 (day 944).

The Government's Answer

Although the Government acknowledges that the Due Process and Equal Protection Clauses of the Constitution apply to review of a case before the service Courts of Criminal Appeals, and that "[d]elays caused by Government or State paid attorneys representing an accused on appeal have been held attributable to the Government[,]" the Government broadly asserts that "[t]he appellate delay in this case was neither excessive nor has it amounted to a prejudicial violation of Petitioner's due process rights."

Despite the fact that Petitioner's appellate defense counsel have had this case since late February 2002, the Government argues that Petitioner has failed to show that this delay, "in and of itself, is sufficient to characterize the delay as inordinate and excessive giving rise to a due process claim." The Government also notes that Petitioner "has not even served one-third of his nine year sentence," although this fact would seem to underscore rather than excuse the failure to initiate a legal and factual review that could conceivably alter Petitioner's conviction, sentence, or both.

The Government makes several specific arguments why the delay should not be considered excessive:

- Due to the unique rights accorded servicemembers in our court-martial system, this Court should acknowledge that a detailed appellate counsel's caseload can be an appropriate factor in deciding when the length of appellate delay becomes inordinate and excessive;

- This Court should not judge the length of time it takes a detailed military counsel to perfect an appeal in relation to the time it takes to perfect such an appeal when an appellant decides to hire his own private civilian counsel;

- This Court should not judge the length of time it takes a detailed military counsel to perfect an appeal in relation to civilian "public defenders" who are required to represent only indigent defendants, not all defendants, before the court;

- The military justice system requires the mandatory review of a vast number of court-martial cases regardless of whether the servicemember files a notice of appeal, and it is therefore reasonable and not a violation of due process when an appeal takes longer to perfect and decide in the military justice system than in the civilian justice system;

- This delay is not inordinate or excessive because of the size of the record of trial, the seriousness of the charges, the number of issues identified by Petitioner, and the "high volume of cases submitted to the lower Court."

The Government summarizes that "the advocacy of the parties, the institutional vigilance of both the lower Court and the Government, as well as the reasons for the delay all justify the delay in this case."

Even if this Court were to find a violation of due process, the Government argues that Petitioner is not entitled to relief, because he has not established substantial prejudice. The Government urges that the factors to be used in determining substantial prejudice in a case of speedy appellate review are similar to those used to determine prejudice for lack of a speedy trial[1] and that Petitioner has not met his burden.

Petitioner's Reply

Petitioner argues in his Reply that the delay has been inordinate and excessive. Petitioner focuses primarily on the root problem that caused the delay but also addresses the various rationalizations offered by the Government for the delay.

Petitioner notes that his case is currently on its eleventh period of enlargement. He points out that his case has yet to receive any substantive review by his appellate counsel, even though counsel has had his case since February 28, 2002. He has been confined post-trial for more than two and one-half years; he has asserted his right to speedy appellate review; and his case is now in the hands of a second detailed appellate defense counsel. In her tenth request for enlargement, Petitioner's first appellate defense counsel cited her "caseload commitments" as cause for the requested relief. That "commitment" included "sixty-six cases on her docket totaling more than 16,000 pages [of trial transcript,] eleven [cases] in thirteenth enlargement or higher."

Now on an eleventh enlargement, Petitioner's case is in the hands of a new appellate defense counsel. That new counsel notes that there is "little hope of [Petitioner's] case being exhaustively read and the appellate issues briefed anytime soon given the present workload of the current Appellate Defense Counsel."

Petitioner's counsel also informs us that there are 1,463 cases pending initial review and filing by Navy-Marine Corps appellate defense counsel, and the average caseload, per counsel, in the Navy-Marine Corps Appellate Defense Division is "70 cases comprising [an] average total of 18,100 pages of trial transcript." Petitioner asserts that the increasingly long period of "continuing" appellate delay, during which he has actively pursued his appeal, is grounds for extraordinary relief.

In contending that he is being denied speedy appellate review, Petitioner takes specific issue with several of the Government's arguments. Petitioner disputes the suggestion that he should seek civilian counsel. Petitioner asserts that he is indigent, was sentenced to total forfeitures, has gone through bankruptcy, has no property, and has only about $3,200 in various accounts. Additionally, Petitioner notes that the suggestion that he should protect his right to a speedy appellate review by hiring civilian counsel "is entirely spurious insofar as it amounts to an assertion that a timely appeal under Article 66, UCMJ, is available only to those who can pay for it."

---

[1] [n.3] "(1) preventing oppressive incarceration pending appeal; (2) minimizing anxiety and concern of those convicted awaiting the outcome of their appeal; and (3) limiting of the possibility that Petitioner's grounds for appeal or, in the event of reversal, his defense in the case on retrial might be impaired."

Petitioner next disputes the Government's claim that the issues Petitioner identified for review do not make a "colorable claim of any possibility or probability of relief on Appeal." Petitioner notes that he has identified 14 issues in pro se pleadings filed at the Court of Criminal Appeals. These issues include "ineffective assistance of counsel, unlawful command influence, and other procedural and evidentiary errors" which have yet to be reviewed or ruled upon by any appellate court. Petitioner questions the soundness of the Government's claim that, in order to be entitled to relief from this delay, he must show that his direct appeal has merit, when he "has not had the assistance of an appellate defense attorney in identifying, researching, and briefing the legal issues which he has identified."

Petitioner further asserts that he is anxiously languishing in prison, a fact evidenced by his detailed pro se pleadings and his efforts to prosecute his appeal even though his appellate defense counsel have been unable to provide him professional assistance.

Discussion

This Court has long recognized that an accused has the right to a timely review of his or her findings and sentence. *See United States v. Williams,* 55 M.J. 302, 305 (C.A.A.F.2001). That review spans a continuum of process from review by the convening authority under Article 60, Uniform Code of Military Justice [hereinafter UCMJ], 10 U.S.C. § 860 (2000), to review by a Court of Criminal Appeals under Article 66, UCMJ, 10 U.S.C. § 866 (2000), to review, in appropriate cases, by this Court under Article 67, UCMJ, 10 U.S.C. § 867 (2000). An accused has the right to effective representation by counsel through the entire period of review following trial, including representation before the Court of Criminal Appeals and our Court by appellate counsel appointed under Article 70, UCMJ, 10 U.S.C. § 870 (2000). *See United States v. Palenius,* 2 M.J. 86 (C.M.A.1977).

We have had repeated opportunities to address issues of delay in the various stages of that review process. *See, e.g., United States v. Tardif,* 57 M.J. 219, 220 (C.A.A.F.2002) (13-month delay between sentencing and referral to Court of Criminal Appeals); *United States v. Hock, et al.,* 31 M.J. 334 (C.M.A.1990) (delay of several years between service of lower court decisions and petitions for review at this Court); *United States v. Dunbar,* 31 M.J. 70 (C.M.A.1990) (three-year delay between trial date and docketing at the service court); *United States v. Clevidence,* 14 M.J. 17 (C.M.A.1982) (313-day delay between sentence and final action by supervisory authority); *United States v. Green,* 4 M.J. 203 (C.M.A.1978) (nine-month delay in transmission of appeal from service court to this Court); *United States v. Timmons,* 22 C.M.A. 226, 46 C.M.R. 226 (1973) (six-month delay between sentencing and action by convening authority). We are, for present purposes, concerned with the delay in the processing of Petitioner's case under Article 66. *See* 59 M.J. at 35 n.2.

Petitioner's right to a full and fair review of his findings and sentence under Article 66 embodies a concomitant right to have that review conducted in a timely fashion. Additionally, Petitioner has a constitutional right to a timely review guaranteed him under the Due Process Clause. *Harris et al. v. Champion et al.,* 15 F.3d 1538 (10th Cir.1994) (quoting *Evitts v. Lucey,* 469 U.S. 387, 393 (1985) (where state has created appellate process as integral part of criminal justice system, procedures used in deciding appeal must comport with demands of due process and equal protection)); *United States v. Antoine,* 906 F.2d 1379 (9th Cir.1990); *United States ex rel. Green v. Washington,* 917 F. Supp. 1238 (N.D. Ill.1996).

The Government has advanced several arguments as to why the period of delay should not be considered as excessive or inordinate and should, in fact, be condoned by this Court as a part of the normal appellate process. We will address the Government's major arguments:

1. The Government argues that due to the unique rights afforded servicemembers by Congress, this Court should take the caseload of a detailed appellate defense counsel into account when determining whether an appellate delay is excessive. The Government, however, has not identified support in the applicable legislation or legislative history for the proposition that Congress intended that the rights afforded servicemembers under the UCMJ should be used as a basis to diminish their right to timely appellate review. Appellate counsel caseloads are a result of management and administrative priorities and as such are subject to the administrative control of the Government. To allow caseloads to become a factor in determining whether appellate delay is excessive would allow administrative factors to trump the Article 66 and due process rights of appellants. To the contrary, the Government has a statutory responsibility to establish a system of appellate review under Article 66 that preserves rather than diminishes the rights of convicted servicemembers. In connection with that responsibility, the Government has a statutory duty under Article 70 to provide Petitioner with appellate defense counsel who is able to represent him in both a competent and timely manner before the Court of Criminal Appeals.

2. The Government suggests that Petitioner should retain private counsel, but also argues that this Court should not compare the length of time it takes a detailed military counsel to perfect an appeal to the length of time that it takes a privately retained civilian counsel. This argument first assumes that Petitioner has the resources to retain a civilian counsel, which he has asserted that he does not. It further assumes that there are two standards in military justice — a standard for detailed military counsel and a standard for privately retained civilian counsel — and that the standards for the military counsel are lower than what is expected of a civilian counsel. In fact, the standards for representation of servicemembers by military or civilian counsel in military appellate proceedings are identical.

3. The Government argues that the length of time it takes detailed military appellate defense counsel to perfect an appeal should not be compared to public defenders in the public sector. The duty of diligent representation owed by detailed military counsel to servicemembers is no less than the duty of public defenders to indigent civilians. Courts have not hesitated to take action when public defender programs fail to represent their clients in a timely manner. *See, e.g., Harris,* 15 F.3d at 1538; *Green,* 917 F. Supp. at 1238; *In re Order on Prosecution of Criminal Appeals by the Tenth Judicial Circuit Public Defender,* 561 So.2d 1130 (Fla.1990) (per curiam). The military appellate courts should be no less diligent in protecting the rights of convicted servicemembers.

4. The Government argues that the military justice system requires that a "vast number" of court-martial cases be reviewed regardless of whether the servicemember files a notice of appeal, and that as a result the appellate process in the military necessarily takes longer than in the civilian justice system. In making this argument, the Government does not give appropriate consideration to the "awesome, plenary, de novo" nature of the review by the Courts of Criminal Appeals under Article 66. *United States v. Cole,* 31 M.J. 270, 272 (C.M.A.1990). Unlike the civilian criminal justice system, the Courts of Criminal Appeals have unique fact finding authority, and that aspect of a servicemember's case is not concluded until that review is completed. The nature of this review calls for, if anything, even greater diligence and timeliness than is found in the civilian system.

5. The Government argues that the "institutional vigilance" present in this and other cases ensures that there can be no due process violations. In making this argument, the Government asserts that Petitioner's first appellate defense counsel worked diligently, prioritized her cases, was available to Petitioner and guaranteed his access to appellate courts. The fact remains, however, that after February 28, 2002, through ten enlargements of time, Petitioner's first appellate defense counsel did not look at the substance of Petitioner's case and did not know when she would be able to do so. The appointment of a new appellate defense counsel did not rectify this problem, because that attorney concedes that he will not be able to look at the case in the foreseeable future. We reject any suggestion that "institutional vigilance" is evident in this case or that vigilance has been applied to ensure that Petitioner receives the rights he is entitled to under Article 66 and Article 70.

6. The Government argues that Petitioner cannot establish "prejudice" from the delays, but its argument is circular. It is disingenuous for the Government to argue that Petitioner has not made a "colorable claim of any possibility of relief," when the system that the Government controls has to date deprived Petitioner of the timely assistance of counsel that would enable him to perfect and refine the legal issues he has asserted.

Given the current posture of Petitioner's case as outlined above, Petitioner is not being afforded an appellate review of his findings and sentence that comports with the requirements of Article 66 and Article 70. These rights must be recognized, enforced and protected by the Government, by the appellate attorneys, by the Court of Criminal Appeals, and by this Court.

We reject any suggestion that continued delay or less diligence in completing appellate review of a criminal conviction should be tolerated under the UCMJ. We are confident that the right to a timely appellate review in the military justice system is no less important and no less a protection than its counterpart in the civilian criminal justice system. As noted, we reject any suggestion that institutional vigilance is evident in Petitioner's case. The Government's general proposition that "so far" there is no showing of excessive or inordinate delay warranting remedial action by this Court is not accurate. Instead, Petitioner's case illustrates that nothing has been done "so far" to respect or ensure Petitioner's right to timely review of his findings and sentence.

We are therefore returning this case to the Navy-Marine Corps Court of Criminal Appeals, as it is that court which is directly responsible for exercising "institutional vigilance" over this and all other cases pending Article 66 review within the Navy-Marine Corps Appellate Review Activity.

Decision and Order

The Petition for Extraordinary Relief is granted as follows:

1. This case is remanded to the Navy-Marine Corps Court of Criminal Appeals. That court shall expeditiously review the processing and status of Petitioner's Article 66 appeal.

2. The Court of Criminal Appeals shall take appropriate action to ensure that Petitioner receives the rights he is entitled to under Article 66 and Article 70, and issue such orders as are necessary to ensure timely filing of an Assignment of Errors and Brief on behalf of Petitioner and the timely filing of an Answer to the Assignment of Errors on behalf of the Government.

3. It is further directed that within 60 days of the date of this opinion, the Navy-Marine Corps Court of Criminal Appeals shall submit a report to this Court which specifies the steps taken to comply with the provisions of this opinion in regard to Petitioner and other appellants awaiting appellate review under Article 66 before the Navy-Marine Corps Court of Criminal Appeals.

4. This order is entered without prejudice to Petitioner's right to assert a violation of his statutory and constitutional rights to speedy appellate review in the ordinary course of appeal.

TOOHEY v. UNITED STATES
United States Court of Appeals for the Armed Forces
60 M.J. 100 (C.A.A.F. 2004)

PER CURIAM:

This case involves a request for extraordinary relief because of lengthy appellate delay. Petitioner is confined as the result of a general court-martial conviction for rape and assault. His trial concluded on August 13, 1998. He has challenged his conviction and sentence in his direct appeal to the Navy-Marine Corps Court of Criminal Appeals. However, almost six years after his conviction, Petitioner's first-level appeal as of right remains unresolved.

A general court-martial found Petitioner guilty of one specification of rape and one specification of assault in violation of Articles 120 and 128 of the Uniform Code of Military Justice. The court-martial was first called to order on May 21, 1998, and adjourned on August 13, 1998. The members sentenced Petitioner to confinement for 12 years, reduction to pay-grade E-1, forfeiture of all pay and allowances, and a dishonorable discharge. The convening authority approved the sentence as adjudged and, with the exception of the dishonorable discharge, ordered it executed. . . .

As we noted last term, "[t]his Court has long recognized that an accused has the right to a timely review of his or her findings and sentence." This includes a right to a reasonably timely convening authority's action, the reasonably prompt forwarding of the record of trial to the service's appellate authorities, and reasonably timely consideration by the military appellate courts. In this case, lengthy delay occurred at each of those three stages, producing an on-going aggregate delay of almost six years.

The right to timely appellate review has both statutory and constitutional roots. A military appellant's "right to a full and fair review of his findings and sentence under Article 66 embodies a concomitant right to have that review conducted in a timely fashion." We have observed that the Courts of Criminal Appeals' unique powers and responsibilities "call[ ] for, if anything, even greater diligence and timeliness than is found in the civilian system." Additionally, the Due Process Clause guarantees "a constitutional right to a timely review."

Other federal appellate courts have similarly recognized a due process right to a reasonably timely appeal. The United States Court of Appeals for the Sixth Circuit has bluntly articulated the rationale for protecting against unreasonable appellate delay: "An appeal that needlessly takes ten years to adjudicate is undoubtedly of little use to a defendant who has been wrongly incarcerated on a ten-year sentence." In its brief, the Government expressly acknowledges that the "Due Process Clause guarantees the right to a timely appellate review of a court-martial."

Federal courts generally consider four factors to determine whether appellate delay violates an appellant's due process rights: (1) length of the delay; (2) reasons for the delay; (3) the appellant's assertion of his right to a timely appeal; and (4) prejudice to the appellant. These factors are derived from the Supreme Court's speedy trial analysis in *Barker v. Wingo* [407 U.S. 514 (1972)].

The first factor's "length of delay" calculation includes time caused by "failures of [ ]appointed counsel and delays by the court" itself. The "length of delay" factor plays two roles. "First, the 'length of the delay is to some extent a triggering mechanism,' and unless there is a period of delay that appears, on its face, to be unreasonable under the circumstances, 'there is no necessity for inquiry into the other factors that go into the balance.'" "Second, if the constitutional inquiry has been triggered, the length of delay is itself balanced with the other factors and may, in extreme circumstances, give rise to a strong 'presumption of evidentiary prejudice' affecting the fourth *Barker* factor."

The first step in evaluating appellate delay is to determine whether the "length of delay" triggering mechanism has been pulled. This, in turn, requires us to consider a threshold question: How much delay is too much? The Tenth Circuit has adopted "a presumption of inordinate delay" upon "a two-year delay in finally adjudicating a direct criminal appeal." "[M]ost courts evaluating such delay," however, "apply the first factor on a case-by-case basis." Many factors can affect the reasonableness of appellate delay. These include not only such universal concerns as length of the record and complexity of the issues, but also military-unique considerations such as operational commitments that may delay transmission of the record to the Court of Criminal Appeals. These variables convince us that "there is no talismanic number of years or months [of appellate delay] after which due process is automatically violated."

Whether appellate delay satisfies the first criterion is best determined on a case-by-case basis.

In this case, Petitioner has made a threshold showing of "a period of delay that appears, on its face, to be unreasonable under the circumstances." Without analyzing the timeliness of each step that has occurred since Petitioner's court-martial ended in August 1998, the aggregate delay facially appears to be unreasonable, even for this serious contested case. This conclusion is consistent with civilian cases holding that six years of appellate delay in non-capital felony cases satisfies the "length of delay" criterion, thereby requiring a full due process analysis. We are further convinced that this case presents a prima facie case regarding length of delay because the Government has not attempted to defend the pace of Petitioner's appeal. . . .

We grant in part and deny in part the petition for extraordinary relief. We conclude that Petitioner has made a threshold showing of an appearance of facially unreasonable delay since the conclusion of his court-martial. We expect the Navy-Marine Corps Court of Criminal Appeals to use its best efforts to render a decision on Petitioner's appeal without delay. In deciding Petitioner's case, the Navy-Marine Corps Court will determine whether the lengthy delay in this case violated Petitioner's Fifth Amendment right to due process. The court will also determine whether the lengthy delay in this case warrants some form of relief. . . .

NOTES AND QUESTIONS

1. In *United States v. Moreno*, 63 M.J. 129 (C.A.A.F. 2006), the Court of Appeals held that Marine Staff Sergeant Moreno's right to a speedy appellate review was violated under a four-part standard. Judge Erdmann wrote for the court:

> The 490 days between the end of trial and the convening authority's action is excessive for the post-trial processing of this case. The processing in this segment is completely within the control of the Government and no exceptional circumstances have been offered to explain this delay. . . . It is striking that this period is over five times longer than that deemed reasonable by this court when we established the ninety-day rule in *Dunlap v. Convening Authority*, 23 C.M.A. 135, 48 C.M.R. 751 (1974). The seventy-six days between action and docketing the case before the Court of Criminal Appeals is also unexplained. Delays involving this essentially clerical task have been categorized as "the least defensible of all" post-trial delays. . . . The longest delay in this case — 925 days — involves the period from which the case was docketed at the Court of Criminal Appeals until briefing was complete.

63 M.J. at 136-37. The government argued that the delays were caused by Moreno himself, since his counsel requested and received eighteen extensions of the deadlines for filing briefs, citing "other case load commitments." Because of these delays, Moreno's appealed was resolved — in his favor — only after he had served his full term of confinement (sentenced to six years, he was released after about four years). The court added:

Unfortunately, our confidence that procedural protections would suffice to ensure the speedy post-trial and appellate rights of servicemembers has been eroded. It is of some concern that the Government brief asserts that the 1,688 day delay in this case was reasonable. We reject that contention and note that Moreno's case is not an isolated case that involves excessive post-trial delay issues. . . . This increase in processing time stands in contrast to the lower number of cases tried in the military justice system in recent years. . . . [S]ome action is necessary to deter excessive delay in the appellate process and remedy those instances in which there is unreasonable delay and due process violations.

The court then set forth a set of time limits that will trigger a presumption of unreasonable delay: when the convening authority fails to act within 120 days after trial; when the record of trial is not docketed by the service Court of Criminal Appeals within thirty days of the convening authority's action; and when appellate review is not completed and a decision is not rendered within eighteen months of docketing the case before the Court of Criminal Appeals. 63 M.J. at 142. Chief Judge Crawford again dissented, objecting to the court's over-reaching into the realm of legislative and executive authority. Is a post-trial delay ever long enough to warrant corrective action by a court? Is it the court's duty to protect the due process rights of convicted criminals?

2. The cases above focus on the issue of post-trial delay, but pre-trial delay is also a due process and human rights concern. Article 17.2(b) of the Rome Statute of the International Criminal Court (ICC) establishes a speedy trial requirement for the assertion of national jurisdiction over crimes that might come under the jurisdiction of the ICC. It states that "an unjustified delay in the proceedings" should be considered when assessing a nation's unwillingness to investigate or prosecute. What might constitute an "unjustified delay" during times of war, political instability, or national emergency? Is that period of time longer or shorter than the period of time for which an "enemy non-combatant" (*see* Chapter 19 on Military Commissions) can be held before the pre-charging delay should be considered unjustified?

II. PUBLIC ACCESS

Defence Force Discipline Appeal Act, 1982
Australia

Section 140. Public hearings

(1) Subject to this section, the hearing of proceedings before a court martial or a Defence Force magistrate shall be in public.

(2) In proceedings before a court martial or a Defence Force magistrate, the President of the court martial or the Defence Force magistrate may, if the President considers it necessary in the interests of the security or defence of Australia, the proper administration of justice or public morals:

(a) order that some or all of the members of the public shall be excluded during the whole or a specified part of the proceedings; or

(b) order that no report of, or relating to, the whole or a specified part of the proceedings shall be published.

(3) The President of a court martial shall not make an order under subsection (2) unless the President has first consulted the judge advocate.

(4) Where proceedings before a court martial or a Defence Force magistrate are held in a secure place, the appropriate service chief shall cause such steps to be taken as will permit the public to have reasonable access, subject to an order (if any) in force under subsection (2), to the proceedings.

(5) In subsection (4), *secure place* means a place the entry to which is controlled by guards who are constables or members of the Defence Force.

BARRY v. CHIEF OF NAVAL STAFF
Defence Force Discipline Appeal Tribunal, Australia
DFDAT 1 of 1994

Cox, J.

The appellant was charged before a general court-martial on seven counts of which the first three were charges of committing an act of indecency upon three naval ratings without their consent, contrary to the Defence Force Discipline Act 1982, § 61 and the Crimes Act 1900 (NSW) in its application to the Jervis Bay Territory, § ZJ. The fourth count alleged an assault upon a superior officer (Defence Force Discipline Act 1982, § 25); the fifth disobedience of a lawful command (Defence Force Discipline Act 1982, § 27); and the last two prejudicial behaviour contrary to the Defence Force Discipline Act 1982, § 60, firstly, in that he attended a service function at HMAS Derwent in a dishevelled state and while intoxicated, and lastly in that he urinated from HMAS Derwent into Devonport Harbour. He was convicted on counts four, five and six and acquitted on count seven. His appeal is confined to his convictions on counts one and two. . . .

[The court resolves several unrelated issues and then turns to a challenge based on the publicity related to the trial.]

The last challenge to the appellant's convictions is based on alleged irregularities in the trial process, leading to a miscarriage of justice. First it is claimed that the judge-advocate wrongly declined to close the court and prevent the media from publishing reports of or incidental to the trial. Prima facie, trials ought to be conducted publicly, a failure to do so can undermine the public's confidence in the judicial process and I refer to *Russell v. Russell* (1976) 134 CLR 495 and *R v. Tait & Bartley* (1979) 24 ALR 473, particularly at 487 and 488. The Defence Force Discipline Appeal Act, § 140 recognises this principle and confines the President's power to conduct a trial in camera to situations where this is necessary in the interests of national security, public morals or the administration of justice. There was no warrant for an order of closure on the first two bases and as to the basis of the administration of justice, I am unpersuaded that closure of the court was required for that reason. The members of the court were officers of equal or senior rank to the appellant, who had sworn to render an impartial verdict in accordance with the evidence and there was no reason to suppose that the ability of the media to publish even lurid accounts of the court-martial would have influenced their decision. . . .

UNITED STATES v. LONETREE
United States Court of Military Appeals
35 M.J. 396 (C.M.A. 1992)

SENTELLE, CIRCUIT JUDGE:

Sergeant Clayton Lonetree was a Marine Corps embassy guard on duty in Moscow when he met Soviet agent Violetta Seina in a subway station. He began a romantic liaison with Seina and eventually passed confidential information to a Soviet agent named Yefimov (a.k.a. "Uncle Sasha"). Ignorant of his activities, the Marine Corps transferred Lonetree to guard duty at the U.S. Embassy in Vienna, where he continued his contact with the Soviets through an agent named Lyssov (a.k.a. "George"). His double life came to an end on December 14, 1986, when, in the first of a series of meetings with two Vienna-station U.S. intelligence agents known as "Big John" and "Little John" ("the Johns"), Lonetree disclosed his involvement with the Soviet agents.

The Naval Investigative Service (NIS) took over questioning Lonetree from the Johns on December 24, 1986, and obtained a more detailed account of the information Lonetree had passed to the Soviets. Based on Lonetree's confessions to the Johns and the NIS, as well as verification through a U.S. government agent known as "John Doe" of Lonetree's relationship with George, a general court-martial found Lonetree guilty of conspiracy to commit espionage, disobeying Navy security regulations, disclosing the identities of covert agents, willfully communicating information in violation of the Federal Espionage Act, and committing espionage. Though the general court-martial sentenced Lonetree to confinement for 30 years, the convening authority reduced the sentence to 25 years in exchange for Lonetree's cooperation in damage assessment.

On August 30, 1990, the Court of Military Review set aside some aspects of Lonetree's conviction but dismissed his other complaints of error and affirmed the 25-year sentence. 31 M.J. 849. We thereupon granted review. . . .

I. Closure to the Public

The military judge, pursuant to a motion by the Government sought under Military Rule of Evidence 505(j)(5),[2] excluded the public during the complete testimony of some witnesses and a portion of the testimony of other witnesses. Sergeant Lonetree contends that these repeated closures denied him his right to a public trial under the Sixth Amendment of the U.S. Constitution for several reasons: (A) the military judge failed to find specific overriding national security interests each time the court was closed; (B) the military judge failed to narrowly tailor the closure each time the court was closed; and (C) the mil-

---

[2] [n.2] *Closed Session:* If counsel for all parties, the military judge, and the members have received appropriate security clearances, the military judge may exclude the public during that portion of the testimony of a witness that discloses classified information."

itary judge failed to *sua sponte* instruct the members against giving undue weight to evidence admitted in closed sessions.

The Government presented two supporting affidavits to close portions of the trial: Appellate Exhibits II and III. The first affidavit's factual summary stated:

> Certain witnesses to be called by the government are professional intelligence officers. All of these officers will provide testimony on classified matters. A list of these officers, and the government's rationale for requesting that they testify in closed session, is set forth in an Affidavit, classified Secret, provided in support of this motion. All parties, members and the Military Judge, will have received appropriate security clearances.

The Government also sought to protect certain specified intelligence sources and methods. . . .

The practical effect of the judge's ruling was that some intelligence agents testified in closed sessions and that the testimony of a number of other witnesses was divided between closed sessions and open sessions which the general public could attend. Either party would ask for a closed session when they were going to question a witness about matters the military judge had ruled were classified. Consequently, it was not the Government that controlled public access to the trial, as appellant asserts, but the military judge.

A. Each Closure Does Not Require Findings

Appellate defense counsel, citing *United States v. Grunden,* 2 M.J. 116 (C.M.A.1977) and *United States v. Hershey,* 20 M.J. 433 (C.M.A.1985), contend that the military judge relinquished and delegated his responsibilities to the prosecution by refusing to make judicial findings justifying closure of the court-martial to the public *each time* such a closure occurred. Such judicial findings for each closed session are not required. Mil. R. Evid. 505 is directed towards the *information* sought to be exempted from disclosure at a public trial. *See* Mil. R. Evid. 505(i)(4)(A) and (C). As the information may be divulged by a number of witnesses or documents, or both, the focus of exclusion is upon that specific information. Consequently, the specificity required addresses the information to be protected, not through what method it is disclosed. In contrast, rights of privacy of individuals such as were involved in *Press-Enterprise Co. v. Superior Court,* 464 U.S. 501 (1984), focus upon individual rights requiring particularized rulings as to each individual situation. To require a military judge to make specific findings each time a series of questions is to be asked of a witness, after the judge had already determined the responses were classified, would be to create unnecessary and disruptive bifurcation of the trial and constitute an exercise in redundancy. The confusion would make a difficult trial an incomprehensible one and would be the antithesis of a fair and orderly proceeding within the context of the facts of this case.

We do not believe *Grunden* mandated judicial findings for each closed session when the Court of Military Appeals stated that "limited portions" of a court-martial may be partially closed despite defense objection but in "each instance the exclusion must be used sparingly with the emphasis always toward a public trial." *Id.* at 120. Rather, as we noted regarding Mil. R. Evid. 505, the Court was addressing *individualized decision-making* as to *specific information* which the Government asserts must be exempted from disclosure at a public trial whenever that information is presented during the course of the trial. Further, we find nothing in *Hershey* that delineates such a requirement. . . .

B. The Closures Were Adequately Tailored

Appellant contends that as the military judge "failed to make specific findings concerning the need for closed proceedings each time the Government so requested, the portions of the trial which he did close were not narrowly tailored to limit the intrusion upon appellant's Sixth Amendment right. The extent of the closed proceeding was simply left to the discretion of the trial counsel." Appellate Defense Brief, 41-42.

We believe the closure procedure utilized in this case was the fairest and most practical that could be devised. The extent of the closures was determined by *either* Government or defense. The military judge had already determined which information, because of its classified status, would be presented in closed sessions. The fact that certain unclassified information was disclosed by individuals whose duties and identities could not be publicly matched-up was necessary to protect classified information. Further bifurcation of other witnesses' testimony, other than as occurred, was impracticable and would have created unnecessary chaos. In fact, the apparent inadvertent disclosure of classified information by both parties in public sessions occurred rather frequently despite the efforts of the court to ensure nondisclosure. The procedure utilized allowed both parties a reasonably normal context within which to pursue their respective positions. . . .

[The court addresses the military judge's instructions and finds error but "no prejudice, because the weight of the evidence against Sergeant Lonetree was so overwhelming that the failure to give the instructions had no effect upon the findings." 35 M.J. at 855.]

II. Confrontation and Cross-Examination of the John Doe Witness

Appellant alleges that he was denied his Sixth Amendment right to confront and thoroughly cross-examine a Government witness. Before trial the Government moved under Mil. R. Evid. 505 to prevent disclosure to the defense of specified classified information concerning the "John Doe" witness and to preclude cross-examination as to that information. The Government offered a top secret affidavit to support invoking the classified information privilege. Appellant Exhibit VII. Another document, classified secret, that contained John Doe's report on the observation of a suspected KGB agent was also not disclosed to the defense. The military judge ruled as to this second document that a redacted version of the report was a sufficient substitute for disclosure to the defense.

In opposing the Government motion the defense requested that the information be disclosed and that normal cross-examination be permitted, albeit in a closed session. The Government countered by asserting that using the precautions of a pseudonym and a closed session were not adequate to protect the classified information concerning John Doe's deep-cover and that the civilian defense counsel did not possess the necessary top secret clearance to access the information.

After reviewing the affidavit and the secret report *in camera,* the military judge ruled that the defense was not entitled to discover the classified information and, further, that they would not be allowed to cross-examine John Doe concerning his true name, address, and other background information. Also excluded from defense discovery and cross-examination was information concerning whether John Doe had been aided or assisted by any other covert agents in observing a suspected KGB officer who was identified in a photograph by the appellant. The military judge's ruling in pertinent part is set forth:

> So, from a reading of the affidavit in camera, it is my determination that this information can be restricted, a pseudonym can be used, and the cross-examination can otherwise be limited without prejudicing the rights of the accused.
>
> The third issue would be, should the Court make that decision without showing the evidence to the defense and the reasons why that should be done. The defense said, we're not shown. The reasons are contained in the affidavit. For the record, I would note that the reasons are sufficient. Therefore, I will make the ruling without further ruling that the government needs to disclose the affidavit to the defense.
>
> So, the motion of the government in this respect is granted. A pseudonym may be used. The restrictions requested on the scope of cross-examination, that is to say questions which would tend to disclose the protected background and activities is granted as well. . . .

A. The Military Standard

The use of classified information in a court-martial is controlled by the procedures and standards set forth in Mil. R. Evid. 505. Germane to this appeal are the subdivisions that authorize a military judge to limit or prevent disclosure to an accused of classified information. Mil. R. Evid. 505(g)(2) is applicable when the Government needs to limit or prevent disclosure. . . .

In making a motion to prevent or limit disclosure of classified information, "the Government shall submit the classified information for examination only by the military judge and shall demonstrate by affidavit that disclosure of the information reasonably could be expected to cause damage to the national security in the degree required to warrant classification under the applicable executive order, statute, or regulation." Mil. R. Evid. 505(i)(3). Once the Government has met this standard, then the "military judge shall determine whether the information may be disclosed at the court-martial proceeding." Mil. R. Evid. 505(i)(4).

Mil. R. Evid. 505(i)(4)(B) contains the standard to be employed by a military judge to determine when classified information must be disclosed to the defense. The general rule contained in Mil. R. Evid. 505(a), that classified information is privileged, will control unless the information, as determined by the military judge, is "relevant and necessary" to an element of the offense or to a legally cognizable defense.

B. Background and Purpose of Mil. R. Evid. 505

The analysis to Mil. R. Evid. 505 states that the rule is based upon the proposed House version of the Classified Information Procedures Act (CIPA), 18 U.S.C. App. §§ 1-16 (1982), and the Supreme Court's discussion of the executive privilege in *United States v. Reynolds,* 345 U.S. 1 (1953), and *United States v. Nixon,* 418 U.S. 683 (1974). *See* Maher, *The Right To A Fair Trial In Criminal Cases Involving The Introduction Of Classified Information,* 120 Military Law Review 83, 101-102, Spring 1988. The rule was proposed by the Executive Branch to combat the problem of "graymail." Graymail occurs when an accused seeks discovery or disclosure of sensitive national security information for the purpose of forcing the Government to discontinue prosecution to safeguard the information. *See, e.g., United States v. Smith,* 780 F.2d 1102, 1105 (4th Cir.1985). Mil. R. Evid. 505 attempts to eliminate this problem by balancing the "interest of an accused who desires classified information for his or her defense and the interests of the Government in protecting that information." Analysis, Mil. R. Evid. 505, Manual for Courts-Martial, United States, 1984, A22-37. . . .

[The court reviews federal precedents and applies *United States v. Alston,* 460 F.2d 48, 52 (5th Cir. 1972), in holding that "The Sixth Amendment is violated when an accused has been prejudiced by not being able to place an adverse witness in his proper setting." 35 M.J. 859.]

Since the disclosure right is not absolute, it is necessary to determine when the Government may constitutionally invoke a privilege that withholds information from an accused during discovery and limits cross-examination of a Government witness. In *Roviaro v. United States,* 353 U.S. 53 (1957), the Supreme Court stated two requirements that must be satisfied before the Government will be allowed to invoke the informant privilege. First, the privilege must be applicable to the circumstances of the case and not be limited by its underlying purpose. Accordingly, if the information to be protected is already known to an accused and can no longer be protected, then the privilege cannot be invoked. Second, based on notions of fundamental fairness, when the information is "relevant and helpful to the defense of an accused, or is essential to a fair determination of a cause, the privilege must give way." *Roviaro,* 353 U.S. at 60-61. With respect to when the privilege must give way, the Court stated that no fixed rule is justifiable but instead it is necessary to balance "the public interest in protecting the flow of information against the individual's right to prepare his defense." *Id.,* 353 U.S. at 62. This balancing determination depends on the particular circumstances of each case, taking into consideration the crime charged, the possible defenses, the possible significance of the information, and any other relevant factors. . . .

D. Meaning of Mil. R. Evid. 505 Standard

The Federal precedents that have incorporated the *Roviaro* standard and the balancing of needs test into CIPA are legally sound and sufficiently persuasive for us to utilize their holdings in applying the "relevant and necessary" standard in Mil. R. Evid. 505. This incorporation of the balancing of needs test into Mil. R. Evid. 505 is consistent with the drafters' intent that the rule "attempts to balance the interests of an accused who desires classified information for his or her defense and the interests of the Government in protecting that information." Analysis, Mil. R. Evid. 505, MCM, A22-37. . . .

E. Holding

In applying the first step of the analysis found in Mil. R. Evid. 505(i)(4)(B), we hold that the background information concerning the John Doe witness and the information as to whether he was assisted by any other covert agents was properly withheld from the appellant because it was not relevant and material in the face of the Government's privilege. The appellant's Sixth Amendment rights were not violated when he was prevented from cross-examining John Doe concerning this classified information when it would not have been helpful to his cause. At trial, the appellant could only offer theoretical relevance for wanting to discover and then cross-examine John Doe on his true identity and whether he had been assisted by any other agents. We find that this information would not have negated the guilt of the appellant which was over-whelmingly proven at trial. . . . John Doe's background as contained in the top secret affidavit contained nothing concerning John Doe that could have led to a fertile area for cross-examination on which he could have been impeached. . . . In finding that it was not error for the trial judge to have withheld disclosure of the classified information to the defense and to have prevented cross-examination on that information, we have been mindful of the dangers inherent in ongoing undercover work in a foreign country that trigger a compelling governmental interest to protect the identity of the undercover agent and the intelligence resources and methodologies used by that agent which could lead to his exposure. . . .

In holding that the military judge did not err in his application of Mil. R. Evid. 505, we further find that the defense was in all other respects fully permitted to place John Doe in the setting in which he observed the Soviet KGB officer. The cross-examination of John Doe constituted numerous pages of the record of trial. The defense fully probed whether John Doe's testimony concerning his observations of the KGB officer may have been incorrect or fallible by inquiring into the lighting and weather conditions, the distance at which the observations were made, any possible distractions, and the age of the photo John Doe was given to identify the KGB agent. The appellant was not prejudiced by the restrictions placed on cross-examination. Accordingly, because we find that the classified information in question was not relevant and necessary to an element of the offense or to a legally cognizable defense, no violation of the appellant's Sixth Amendment rights occurred.

We note the following nonexclusive corroborating facts and the precedents that merits their consideration as corroboration. . . .

[The court points out, *inter alia*, that "The appellant's 'profile' was consistent with an individual who could be recruited by the KGB. . . . The manner by which appellant asserts he was recruited conformed to KGB recruitment practices. . . . Sergeant Lonetree admired the KGB. He loved Violetta, a

Russian citizen employed at the U.S. Embassy in Moscow. . . . The two Russians, one assigned to Moscow and one to Vienna, who Sergeant Lonetree believed were KGB agents, were confirmed to be KGB agents. . . . Sergeant Lonetree's activities in Vienna were consistent with those of a recruited Soviet agent . . . ." Lonetree also took private Russian language classes, possessed a book on spying, requested leave for a period of time in which the KGB wanted him to visit Moscow, and sought to join the U.S. Foreign Service and return to Moscow.]

Even excluding John Doe's testimony, the court-martial could "reasonably conclude from . . . [the independent evidence] that appellant had told the truth at the time he gave his confession." [*United States v. Melvin,* 26 M.J. 145, 147 (C.M.A. 1988).] . . .

NOTE

In 1989, General Alfred M. Gray Jr., the Commandant of the Marine Corps, recommended that Lonetree's sentence be reduced from 30 to 15 years because the consequences of his actions were "minimal." The U.S. may have initially misunderstood the breaches of security caused by Lonetree because it did not yet know the full extent of CIA agent Aldrich Ames' trangressions. Ames was convicted in 1994 for spying for the Soviet Union and Russia throughout the 1980s. *See* Tim Weiner, David Johnson & Neil A. Lewis, Betrayal: The Story of Aldrich Ames, an American Spy (1995). General Gray considered Lonetree's actions motivated not by "treason or greed, but rather the lovesick response of a naive, young, immature and lonely troop in a lonely and hostile environment." A book published by a member of Lonetree's defense team argued that Lonetree was the fall guy when senior officials realized the extent of intelligence leaks at the U.S. Embassy in Moscow. Lake Headley, William Hoffman & William Kunstler, The Court-Martial of Clayton Lonetree (1989). Lonetree was released in 1996 after serving nine years in confinement.

LE PETIT v. UNITED KINGDOM
European Court of Human Rights, 2000
Application No. 35574/97

[A British national who was convicted at court-martial for offenses related to fraudulent travel claims brought an appeal to the European Court of Human Rights. He alleged, along with several other claims, that his "court-martial was not 'public' given the obligation on those who attended the court-martial to record their names and addresses with the naval authorities."]

1. The applicant complains under Article 6 § 1 of the [European] Convention [on Human Rights] that he did not receive a fair and public hearing by an independent and impartial tribunal established by law. The Government argue that the applicant's claims are manifestly ill-founded or, in the alternative, do not constitute a violation of the Convention. Article 6 § 1 of the Convention, insofar as relevant, reads as follows:

In the determination . . . of any criminal charge against him, everyone is entitled to a fair and public hearing within a reasonable time by an independent and impartial tribunal established by law. . . .

. . . The Government maintains that the court-martial hearing was public, pointing out that notice of the trial was placed on the main gate of HMS DRAKE and that the hearing was held in a court-martial complex to which the public had full access. Non-military visitors were required to provide their names to the gate staff as a security and safety measure made necessary by the proximity of the court-martial complex to a nuclear submarine base. No one was prevented from entering the court-martial and a member of the press attended on each day. Relying on the Commission's report in the Hood case (*Hood v. the United Kingdom*, application no. 27267/95, Commission report of 28 May 1998, unpublished), they point out that there was nothing in the applicant's submissions which would show that he did not have a "public" hearing within the meaning of Article 6 § 1 of the Convention. The applicant did not comment on these observations of the Government.

The Court recalls that the object pursued by the publicity requirement in Article 6 § 1 is to ensure scrutiny of the judicial process by the public with a view to safeguarding the right to a fair trial and that security reasons can justify the exclusion of the public from proceedings (see the *Pretto v. Italy* judgment of 8 December 1983, Series A no. 71, p. 13, § 27; and the *Campbell and Fell v. the United Kingdom* judgment of 28 June 1984, Series A no. 80, p. 42, §§ 87-88).

The Court notes that, in principle, courts-martial are open, that members of the press and public are permitted to attend and that trial listings are required to be posted beforehand in a place accessible to the public. The Court observes that the applicant does not contest the Government's factual submissions as regards the posting of a notice of the applicant's court-martial, and the access to and attendance at the applicant's court-martial by civilians. The Court does not consider that the obligation on civilians to provide their names and addresses to the naval authorities would amount to a deterrent to the public and press from attending a court-martial. Even assuming that it did, the Court considers that, in any event, the reasonable security concerns of the Government constitute sufficient reasons justifying any such restriction on the publicity requirement of Article 6 § 1 of the Convention (see, for example, *Baragiola v. Switzerland*, application no. 17265/90, Commission decision of 21 October 1993, Decisions and Reports (DR) 75, p. 76, at p. 125; and *Hood v. the United Kingdom*, application no. 27267/95, Commission report of 28 May 1998, unpublished). It is further noted that the applicant was tried in a military court-martial complex and that it is not contended by the applicant that that complex was anything other than a normal place of trial by court-martial (see the *Riepan v. Austria* judgment of 14 November 2000, § 29).

This complaint of the applicant under Article 6 § 1 of the Convention is, accordingly, manifestly ill-founded and is to be rejected pursuant to Article 35 §§ 3 and 4 of the Convention. . . .

SUTTER v. SWITZERLAND
European Court of Human Rights
74 Eur. Ct. H. R. (Ser. A) at 26 (1984)

I. The particular circumstances of the case

10. At the time of the events giving rise to this case, Mr. Peter Sutter, a Swiss national born in 1949, was a student and resident in Basel.

11. During refresher courses (Wiederholungskurse) organised in 1974 and 1975 as part of ordinary military obligations, he was subjected to five and seven days' strict arrest for refusing to comply with Article 203 of the service regulations, relating to haircuts.

12. Shortly before the beginning of the 1976 refresher course, the applicant received a registered letter from his unit commander instructing him to report for the course with a regulation haircut. He nevertheless presented himself on 28 August 1976 with his hair longer than authorised and refused to obey the officer's verbal order to have it cut.

13. On 8 November 1976, the Military Prosecutor (auditeur militaire) drew up a "bill of indictment" (Anklageschrift) against Mr. Sutter, charging him with repeated insubordination and, subsidiarily, failure to observe service regulations (Articles 61 and 72 of the Military Criminal Code).

14. On 16 May 1977, at the close of a public hearing, Divisional Court no. 5 delivered in public a judgment sentencing the applicant to ten days' imprisonment for the two offences.

Mr. Sutter's defence counsel had unsuccessfully requested the Divisional Court to decline jurisdiction on the ground that it lacked the independence and impartiality required by Article 6 (art. 6) of the Convention; he had also applied, in vain, for a supplementary enquiry into the futility, or indeed abusive nature, of the regulations on haircuts.

A copy of the decision was sent to the applicant on 23 June 1977.

15. Having been duly informed by the grand juge (President of the Divisional Court) that he could appeal on points of law within twenty-four hours from delivery of the judgment, Mr. Sutter had immediately given notice of appeal to the Registrar (section 189 para. 2 of the Federal Army (Constitution of Courts and Criminal Procedure) Act of 28 June 1889 — "the 1889 Act").

On 2 July 1977, within the prescribed period of ten days from service of the judgment, the applicant filed a memorial containing a "final" statement (section 189 para. 3 of the 1889 Act) of his grounds of appeal. . . .

[Mr. Sutter asserted several unrelated grounds for appeal and then one related to the public nature of the tribunal: "Mr. Sutter also drew the attention of the Military Court of Cassation to the fact that it was not consonant with Article 6 (art. 6) to conduct proceedings entirely in writing; he therefore requested it to hold at least one hearing and to pronounce its judgment publicly."]

18. . . . . As regards the public character of the proceedings, this Act [of 1889, governing military criminal procedure] drew a distinction according to the level of the court concerned.

The Divisional Courts, which heard military-law cases at first instance, were required to give their decisions after holding public hearings and to pronounce their judgments in open court.

On the other hand, proceedings before the Military Court of Cassation were conducted entirely in writing and its judgments were not delivered in public. Concerning the latter point, section 197 of the Act laid down merely that "an extract" of the judgment had to be communicated to the Chief Military Prosecutor, the accused and the grand judge.

19. The 1889 Act was repealed by the Federal Military Criminal Procedure Act of 23 March 1979 ("the 1979 Act"), which entered into force on 1 January 1980.

The existing system was maintained for proceedings before the Divisional Courts, and was extended to the Courts of Appeal which were set up by the same statute.

As regards the Military Court of Cassation, the 1979 Act provides that "There shall be no oral hearings" (section 189 para. 1). The Act did, however, make two innovations: in future, the Court of Cassation was to deliver judgment in open court (sections 48 para. 3 and 194 para. 1) and could in no circumstances itself rule on the merits of the case. . . .

21. . . . [Mr. Sutter asserted] that the proceedings before the Military Court of Cassation were conducted in writing and not in public and, furthermore, that it did not deliver its judgments in open court but only served them on the parties. . . . Mr. Sutter also claimed to be the victim of a violation of Article 8 (art. 8): he asserted that the regulations on haircuts prevented a Swiss citizen, for a period of thirty years, from wearing his hair as he chose and constituted an unjustified interference with the right to respect for private life. . . .

24. The applicant complained of the fact that the Military Court of Cassation had dismissed his appeal without previously holding a public hearing and had not pronounced its judgment of 21 October 1977 publicly (see paragraph 17 above). He alleged that there had been a violation of Article 6 para. 1 (art. 6-1) of the Convention, which reads:

> In the determination of . . . any criminal charge against him, everyone is entitled to a fair and public hearing . . . by [a] . . . tribunal. . . . Judgment shall be pronounced publicly but the press and public may be excluded from all or part of the trial in the interests of morals, public order or national security in a democratic society, where the interests of juveniles or the protection of the private life of the parties so require, or to the extent strictly necessary in the opinion of the court in special circumstances where publicity would prejudice the interests of justice.

The Government contended, on the contrary, that this two-fold absence of publicity did not contravene the Convention. A majority of the Commission was of the same opinion, whereas a minority of eight of its members agreed with Mr. Sutter.

25. In the present case, only the cassation proceedings are in issue. Mr. Sutter's complaints, in so far as they were declared admissible by the

Commission, did not concern the earlier procedure, Divisional Court no. 5 having pronounced judgment publicly following hearings conducted in public (see paragraph 14 above).

I. Preliminary Observations

26. The public character of proceedings before the judicial bodies referred to in Article 6 para. 1 (art. 6-1) protects litigants against the administration of justice in secret with no public scrutiny; it is also one of the means whereby confidence in the courts, superior and inferior, can be maintained. By rendering the administration of justice visible, publicity contributes to the achievement of the aim of Article 6 para. 1 (art. 6-1), namely a fair trial, the guarantee of which is one of the fundamental principles of any democratic society, within the meaning of the Convention (see the *Pretto and others* judgment of 8 December 1983, Series A no. 71, p. 11, para. 21, and the *Axen* judgment of 8 December 1983, Series A no. 72, p. 12, para. 25).

27. Whilst the member States of the Council of Europe all subscribe to this principle of publicity, their legislative systems and judicial practice reveal some diversity as to its scope and manner of implementation, as regards both the holding of hearings and the "pronouncement" of judgments. The formal aspect of the matter is, however, of secondary importance as compared with the purpose underlying the publicity required by Article 6 para. 1 (art. 6-1). The prominent place held in a democratic society by the right to a fair trial impels the Court, for the purposes of the review which it has to undertake in this area, to examine the realities of the procedure in question (see notably the two above-mentioned judgments, Series A no. 71, p. 12, para. 23, and Series A no. 72, p. 12, para. 26).

28. The applicability of Article 6 (art. 6) to the present facts was not disputed and, moreover, is to be inferred from the established case-law of the Court (see notably the *Delcourt* judgment of 17 January 1970, Series A no. 11, pp. 13-15, paras. 25-26, and, as the most recent authorities, the two above-mentioned judgments of 8 December 1983, Series A no. 71, p. 12, para. 23, and Series A no. 72, p. 12, para. 27).

The manner of application of this text depends, however, on the particular circumstances of the case (*ibid.*). The Court, concurring with the Government and the Commission, considers that account must be taken of the entirety of the proceedings conducted in the domestic legal order; what has to be determined is whether in the present instance the proceedings before the Military Court of Cassation had, like those before the Divisional Court, to be accompanied by each of the guarantees laid down in Article 6 para. 1 (art. 6-1).

II. Absence of Public Hearings

29. In the applicant's submission, the holding of public hearings is required even before a court of cassation because, amongst other things, it allows an exchange of argument by the parties and enables the public to be aware of the pleadings being put forward.

30. Whilst Mr. Sutter's case had been heard in public by the Divisional Court, the proceedings before the Military Court of Cassation were conducted in writing, as was then and is still provided by the Swiss federal legislation.

The latter Court received only a memorial filed by the applicant, since the grand juge, the Military Prosecutor and the Chief Military Prosecutor had confined themselves, without giving reasons, to submitting that the appeal should be dismissed. The Court of Cassation did not rule on the merits of the case, as regards either the question of guilt or the sanction imposed by the Divisional Court. It dismissed Mr. Sutter's appeal in a judgment that was devoted solely to the interpretation of the legal provisions concerned. There is therefore nothing to suggest that his trial before the Military Court of Cassation was less fair than his trial before the Divisional Court, and it is not in dispute that the latter trial fulfilled the requirements of Article 6 (art. 6). In the particular circumstances of the case, oral argument during a public hearing before the Court of Cassation would not have provided any further guarantee of the fundamental principles underlying Article 6 (art. 6).

The Court accordingly finds that the absence of public hearings at the cassation stage did not infringe Article 6 para. 1 (art. 6-1).

III. Absence of Public Pronouncement

31. In accordance with section 197 of the 1889 Act, the judgment delivered on 21 October 1977 by the Military Court of Cassation was served on the parties but not pronounced in open court (see paragraph 17 above). For the applicant and the minority of the Commission, this state of affairs violated the Convention.

32. The terms used in the second sentence of Article 6 para. 1 (art. 6-1) — "judgment shall be pronounced publicly," "le jugement sera rendu publiquement" — might suggest that a reading out aloud of the judgment is required. Admittedly the French text employs the participle "rendu" (given), whereas the corresponding word in the English version is "pronounced" (prononcé), but this slight difference is not sufficient to dispel the impression left by the language of the provision in question: in French, "rendu publiquement" — as opposed to "rendu public" (made public) — can very well be regarded as the equivalent of "prononcé publiquement."

At first sight, Article 6 para. 1 (art. 6-1) of the European Convention would thus appear to be stricter in this respect than Article 14 para. 1 of the 1966 International Covenant on Civil and Political Rights, which provides that the judgment "shall be made public," "sera public."

33. However, many member States of the Council of Europe have a long-standing tradition of recourse to other means, besides reading out aloud, for making public the decisions of all or some of their courts, and especially of their courts of cassation, for example deposit in a registry accessible to the public. The authors of the Convention cannot have overlooked that fact, even if concern to take it into account is not so easily identifiable in their working documents as in the travaux préparatoires of the 1966 Covenant (see, for instance, document A/4299 of 3 December 1959, pp. 12, 15 and 19, paras. 38(b), 53 and 63(c) in fine).

The Court therefore does not feel bound to adopt a literal interpretation. It considers that in each case the form of publicity given to the "judgment" under the domestic law of the respondent State must be assessed in the light of the special features of the proceedings in question and by reference to the object and purpose of Article 6 para. 1 (art. 6-1) (see the two above-mentioned judgments of 8 December 1983, Series A no. 71, p. 12, paras. 25-26, and Series A no. 72, pp. 13-14, paras. 30-31).

34. As indicated in paragraph 20 above, anyone who can establish an interest may consult or obtain a copy of the full text of judgments of the Military Court of Cassation; besides, its most important judgments, like that in the Sutter case, are subsequently published in an official collection. Its jurisprudence is therefore to a certain extent open to public scrutiny.

Having regard to the issues dealt with by the Military Court of Cassation in the instant case and to its decision — which made the judgment of the Divisional Court final and changed nothing in respect of its consequences for Mr. Sutter —, a literal interpretation of the terms of Article 6 para. 1 (art. 6-1), concerning pronouncement of the judgment, seems to be too rigid and not necessary for achieving the aims of Article 6 (art. 6).

The Court thus concurs with the Government and the majority of the Commission in concluding that the Convention did not require the reading out aloud of the judgment delivered at the final stage of the proceedings.

FOR THESE REASONS, THE COURT

1. Holds unanimously that the absence of public hearings before the Military Court of Cassation did not contravene Article 6 para. 1 (art. 6-1);

2. Holds by eleven votes to four that the absence of public pronouncement of that Court's judgment did not contravene the said Article (art. 6-1).

TRUSKOSKI v. THE QUEEN
Court Martial Appeal Court of Canada
48 C.R.R.2d 140 (1997)

WEILER, J.A.

1. The appellant was found guilty by a Standing Court Martial of striking a superior officer and using insulting language to a superior officer contrary to §84 and §130 of the *National Defence Act* respectively. A third charge of assault contrary to §266 of the Criminal Code of Canada was stayed. The appellant was sentenced to detention for a period of 30 days but the carrying into effect of the period of detention was suspended. The appellant appeals both his conviction and sentence.

2. The argument on conviction is founded on a procedural argument concerning the failure to give proper notice of the appellant's trial. Canadian Forces Administrative Order 111-1 paragraph 17 requires that every court martial shall be publicized in Routine Orders together with a notification that the court is open to the public. Routine Orders are a communication from the base commander to each individual unit for promulgation to the unit as a whole. Routine Orders are usually posted on a notice board outside the orderly room which is the administrative office and at other locations on the base. There is no provision which states what the effect of non compliance with the

administrative orders is. The Queen's Rules and Orders and the *National Defence Act* are silent as to whether or not a court hearing has to be publicized.

3. When the Standing Court Martial convened on April 16, 1997 the procedure specified in Administrative Order 111-1 had not been followed. A notice of the Court Martial hearing had been given by electronic mail but it is conceded that no notice had been published in the Routine Orders. At the hearing on April 16, 1997 the appellant's military defence counsel indicated that he wished to withdraw and permission to do so was given by the court. The appellant then raised a "plea in bar of trial" due to noncompliance with Administrative Order 111-1 and submitted that the failure to publish the notice of the proceedings in Routine Orders barred his trial. At this point in the proceedings the appellant had not yet pleaded to the charges. The Standing Court Martial Judge dismissed the appellant's motion that the Standing Court Martial could not try him unless the entire procedure including the laying of the charges was recommenced. The Standing Court Martial was ordered to be reconvened on August 13, 1997 in order for the appellant to obtain new counsel. Canadian Forces Administrative Order 111-1 was complied with in respect of the August 13th date. The appellant's submissions in relation to this ground of appeal may be summarized as follows:

4. In the civilian system there is a fixed location for a court of which the public is aware. In the military system there is no fixed location. If a standing court martial is to be open to the public the fact of the trial and its location must be publicized. Even if some members of the military are aware of a court martial hearing they might not assume that they have a right to attend the hearing unless they are specifically told of it. The failure to follow Administrative Order 111-1 was a jurisdictional error which was not cured by the adjournment and notification of proceedings in Routine Orders prior to the August hearing. It would have been necessary to withdraw the charges and recommence the proceedings in their entirety. The failure to follow Administrative Order 111-1 was also a violation of the appellant's Charter right to a fair and open hearing under s. 11(d) because the trial was not an open one. In addition, individual members of the armed forces are subject to disciplinary proceedings for failing to follow administrative orders. It is not fair if there are no consequences when there is a breach of administrative orders by those running the system.

5. The conviction appeal must fail. While the right to trial in public is a substantive right, the method of notification of the hearing is an administrative matter. The appellant has failed to show that his trial was not open to the public. The hearing in April was held openly and one which the public were entitled to attend. Notice had been given by electronic mail and some members of the public were in attendance. The evidence also indicates that through word of mouth at least one member of the public was in attendance and testified when the motion brought by the appellant was heard. The failure to give notification of the proceedings in April in the manner specified did not mean that the hearing was closed. The appellant's Charter right to a fair and public hearing under § 11(d) has not been shown to have been infringed. . . . There is no evidence that the appellant suffered individual prejudice as a result of the fail-

ure to publicize the hearing in the manner specified in April. The appeal as to conviction is dismissed. . . .

Armed Forces Act, Singapore
§ 104(4) & (5)

(4) No person shall be present during any deliberation by a panel court martial or a field general court martial without permission from the president of the court.

(5) The president of any panel court martial or field general court martial may, on any deliberation amongst the members of the court, cause the courtroom to be cleared of all other persons.

ABC, INC. v. POWELL
United States Court of Appeals for the Armed Forces
47 M.J. 363 (1997)

Cox, Chief Judge:

Petitioners sought a Writ of Mandamus requesting that this Court order that the investigation under Article 32, Uniform Code of Military Justice, 10 U.S.C. § 832, into the allegations of misconduct made against the Sergeant Major of the Army (SMA), Gene C. McKinney, be opened to the press and public.[3] *See* 28 U.S.C. § 1651(a). On June 23, 1997, following oral argument, we granted the Petition for Extraordinary Relief and issued a Writ of Mandamus opening the Article 32 proceedings to the press and public, as requested by Petitioners, with an opinion to follow. 47 M.J. 80 (1997). This is that opinion.

This case presented two questions for our consideration: First, whether Petitioners had good cause to seek an exception from this Court's rule requiring that they first file their petition with the Court of Criminal Appeals. *See* Rules 4(b)(1) and 27(a)(1)(E), Rules of Practice and Procedure, United States Court of Appeals for the Armed Forces. Second, whether the Article 32 hearing was properly closed to the public and press.

SMA McKinney's Article 32 hearing was ordered closed by Colonel Owen C. Powell, the special court-martial convening authority (SPCMCA), who appointed the Article 32 investigating officer. Colonel Powell also preferred the charges against SMA McKinney. Colonel Powell gave the following reasons in support of ordering a closed hearing: (1) to maintain the integrity of the military justice system and ensure due process to SMA McKinney; (2) to prevent dissemination of evidence or testimony that would be admissible at an Article 32 investigation, but might not be admissible at trial, in order to prevent contamination of the "potential pool of panel members"; and (3) to protect the alleged victims who would be testifying as witnesses against SMA

---

[3] [n.1] The preferred charges pending investigation at the time of oral argument on this writ were maltreatment of a subordinate (4 specifications), assault (2 specifications), and 12 specifications of various offenses, including adultery, solicitation of adultery, communication of a threat, indecent assault, and obstruction of justice, in violation of Articles 93, 128, and 134, Uniform Code of Military Justice, 10 U.S.C. §§ 893, 928, and 934, respectively.

McKinney, specifically to shield the alleged victims from possible news reports about anticipated attempts to delve into each woman's sexual history.

After receiving the petition for this Court to order the hearing opened, we required the Government to show cause why the hearing should remain closed. The Government submitted no additional information and relied upon the reasons recited above. Additionally, we required Petitioners to show cause why they should not first petition the Court of Criminal Appeals for relief.

Upon consideration of the case and the responses of the Government and Petitioners, we agreed to hear the case without further delay for three reasons: First, public access to Article 32 investigations is a question of common concern to all services under the UCMJ and is not unique to the Army. *See San Antonio Express-News v. Morrow,* 44 M.J. 706 (A.F. Ct. Crim. App. 1996). Second, in this case the parties to the Article 32 investigation, as well as administrative support personnel and witnesses, were already duly assembled and ready to proceed at the time the Petition for Extraordinary Relief was filed. Third, neither justice nor judicial economy would be served by delaying the Article 32 investigation pending remand to the Court of Criminal Appeals, albeit we would have welcomed the opinion of that court in these proceedings.

The question, therefore, is whether this Article 32 investigation must be generally open or whether it may be closed to the public.

The procedural rule adopted by the President on this issue is found at R.C.M. 405(h)(3), Manual for Courts-Martial, United States (1995 ed.), which states:

> *Access by spectators.* Access by spectators to all or part of the proceeding may be restricted or foreclosed in the discretion of the commander who directed the investigation or the investigating officer.

The Discussion of the Rule provides: "Closure may encourage complete testimony by an embarrassed or timid witness. *Ordinarily the proceedings of a pretrial investigation should be open to spectators.*" (Emphasis added.)

Although we have never addressed the direct question whether the Sixth Amendment to the Constitution affords a military accused the right to a public Article 32 hearing, we have consistently held that the Sixth Amendment right does apply to a court-martial. *United States v. Hershey*, 20 M.J. 433, 435 (C.M.A. 1985); *United States v. Grunden*, 2 M.J. 116, 120 (C.M.A. 1977); *MacDonald v. Hodson*, 19 U.S.C.M.A. 582, 42 C.M.R. 184 (1970); *United States v. Brown*, 7 U.S.C.M.A. 251, 256, 22 C.M.R. 41, 46 (1956). Today we make it clear that, absent "cause shown that outweighs the value of openness," the military accused is likewise entitled to a public Article 32 investigative hearing. *Press-Enterprise Co. v. Superior Court of California, Riverside County*, 464 U.S. 501, 509 (1984); *see also Richmond Newspapers, Inc. v. Virginia*, 448 U.S. 555, 581 (1980) ("Absent an overriding interest articulated in findings, the trial of a criminal case must be open to the public."). Similarly, when an accused is entitled to a public hearing, the press enjoys the same right and has standing to complain if access is denied. *Globe Newspaper Co. v. Superior Court for the County of Norfolk*, 457 U.S. 596 (1982); *Hershey, supra* at 435-36.

But the right to a public hearing is not absolute. *United States v. Brown, United States v. Grunden,* and *United States v. Hershey,* all *supra.* Therefore, we decline to adopt the broadcasting companies' expansive position that requiring a witness to testify about personal sexual history "plainly does not qualify" as a basis to close a pretrial hearing or court-martial. . . . Rather, we have proceeded as did the Supreme Court in *Globe,* which held that the determination must be made on a case-by-case, witness-by-witness, and circumstance-by-circumstance basis whether closure in a case is necessary to protect the welfare of a victim or alleged victim of sexual assault. *Globe, supra* at 609; *Hershey, supra* at 436; *see also* Mil. R. Evid. 412, Manual, *supra.* In *Hershey,* we recognized that "[u]ndeniably there is a certain amount of mortification imposed on victim-witnesses in sex cases, but that is a condition which cannot be eliminated from our judicial system." 20 M.J. at 436, citing *Brown, supra* at 259, 22 C.M.R. at 49; *see also* Mil. R. Evid. 412.

Every case that involves limiting access to the public must be decided on its own merits. Furthermore, the scope of closure must be tailored to achieve the stated purposes and should also be "reasoned," not "reflexive." *See San Antonio Express-News,* 44 M.J. at 710; *United States v. Hershey, supra.*

Civilian jurisdictions have similarly protected the right of public access to criminal trials and have required articulated and compelling factors to justify closure. *See, e.g., Globe, supra* at 608-09 (state's mandatory rule to close access to testimony of minor, sexual-assault victims is unconstitutional because overly broad; case-by-case determination required); *Commonwealth v. Martin,* 417 Mass. 187, 629 N.E.2d 297, 302 (1994) (trial judge required to determine on a case-by-case basis whether closure necessary to prevent psychological harm or trauma to minor witness, considering factors such as age, maturity, desires of complainant, nature of alleged crime, and interests of complainant's parents and relatives); *Austin Daily Herald v. Mork,* 507 N.W.2d 854, 857 (Minn. App. 1993) (trial judge's restrictive order on media access to attend testimony by minors affirmed as furthering state's compelling interest to safeguard juvenile records and protect psychological well-being of juvenile witnesses; however, practice not encouraged for future cases); *Renkel v. State,* 807 P.2d 1087, 1093-1094 (Alaska App. 1991) (conviction reversed where only evidence supporting closure of trial was letter from youngest child-complainant's therapist and guardian ad litem's statement to court that minor witnesses were under "a great deal of emotional stress"); *United States v. Jacobson,* 785 F. Supp. 563 (E.D. Va. 1992) (closure of courtroom for parents' testimony regarding whether their children were fathered by artificial insemination by defendant-doctor's sperm not narrowly tailored to achieve Government's interest).

Here, the SPCMCA decided to close the entire proceeding for unsubstantiated reasons. There is every reason to believe that he acted in good faith in closing the proceedings to protect the alleged victims' privacy and guard court members against potential tainting by outside influences. Regardless, we hold that these reasons alone are insufficient. As Chief Judge Fletcher noted in

Grunden, "In excising the public from the trial, the [convening authority] employed an ax in place of the constitutionally required scalpel." 2 M.J. at 120.

It may well have been necessary during these proceedings to limit public access to the investigation for some immediate valid reason; however, when we issued our disposition order, there was no record before us justifying a sweeping closure of the entire proceeding to the public and press. Therefore, we ordered that the Article 32 investigation in this case be opened to the public and press, unless future compelling circumstances dictated a different result.

NOTES AND QUESTIONS

1. In *Sutter*, four dissenting judges argued that "If the basic underlying concept of public scrutability is to be a reality, a restricted access to judgments such as existed in the present case, i.e. restricted only to persons who could establish an interest to the satisfaction of a court official, falls short of what is required by that provision of the Convention. Public knowledge of court decisions cannot be secured by confining that knowledge to a limited class of persons." Why is public knowledge of decisions essential? What is the impact of electronic publication on the concerns of the *Sutter* majority and dissenters? Does making judicial decisions available on the internet implicate privacy or due process concerns?

2. The extent to which military judges enforce the right of public access under the First Amendment varies. Consider the following analysis, co-authored by one of this casebook's authors:

> This scalpel approach to closure, first announced in *Grunden* in the context of a court-martial trial, recently was applied to an Article 32 hearing investigating allegations of prisoner abuse and homicide during Operation Iraqi Freedom. In November 2004, the Army charged four soldiers at Fort Carson, Colorado, with torturing and murdering Abed Mowhoush, a major general of the Iraqi Air Force and one of the highest-ranking members of Saddam Hussein's military command. The Department of Defense (DoD) originally issued an official press release stating that Mowhoush had died of natural causes. According to the Army's Criminal Investigation Division report, however, General Mowhoush died during interrogation in Iraq. He had been placed headfirst into a sleeping bag by Army officers and repeatedly rolled on the ground from his back to his stomach while the officers employed chest compressions, *i.e.*, sitting on his back and chest, ultimately suffocating General Mowhoush. It was later disclosed that General Mowhoush had also been restrained with an electrical cord wrapped around the sleeping bag in which he suffocated.
>
> An Article 32 hearing for three of the four accused soldiers was scheduled for December 2, 2004, at Fort Carson. The morning of the hearing, the investigating officer announced that he intended to close

the entire proceeding because classified information would be discussed. Arguing against the proposed closure, The Denver Post urged the investigating officer to follow *Powell* and decide whether closure was justified on a witness-by-witness basis. The investigating officer found that it would be "difficult if not impossible to separate the classified information from the non-classified information" and ordered the Article 32 proceeding closed in its entirety.

The next day, The Denver Post filed an emergency petition with the Army Court of Criminal Appeals seeking a stay of the Article 32 proceedings and an order directing the investigating officer to open all portions of the hearing not concerning classified information. The Army court immediately stayed any further closed proceedings. After full briefing, the court granted The Denver Post's petition and ordered the investigating officer to release a redacted transcript of the closed hearing and to open to the public all portions of the resumed hearing not involving classified evidence:

> The rule of law requires that the [investigating officer] engage in the necessary analysis as to each witness' expected testimony and to understand in advance how and why it could touch on a classified matter before excluding the public. . . . [W]here, as here, the defense counsel have willingly gone along with the government's desire to close the proceedings, doubtless to facilitate the broadest possible discovery of matters, classified or not, to be used at any trial in defense of their clients, the [investigating officer] alone is left to act impartially to safeguard the integrity of the military justice system by only authorizing the most limited necessary degree of closure.

Although the military appellate courts consistently have issued rulings such as those above that provide strong protection for the rights of the public (and press) to attend courts-martial and pretrial proceedings, investigating officers continue to disregard or ignore these precedents. . . .

Steven D. Zansberg, Matthew S. Freedus & Eugene R. Fidell, *The First Amendment in the Military Courts: A Primer for the Civilian Attorney*, 23 COMM. LAW. 10, 13 (Fall 2005).

3. Zansberg, Freedus, and Fidell also assessed the reporter's privilege before military courts:

> Most civilian federal circuit courts recognize a qualified First Amendment privilege against compelled disclosure of unreported or confidential information and materials. However, a recent string of high-profile federal court rulings has cast some doubt on the very existence and scope of a First Amendment-based privilege, at least with respect to subpoenas seeking grand jury testimony from reporters in their capacity as eyewitnesses to crimes under investigation. . . .

> Perhaps ironically, at a time that the civilian courts appear to be backing away from their prior precedents recognizing a First

Amendment-based privilege for reporters, the military is moving toward extending greater protections to members of the press from subpoenas issued in the military justice system. There is little (if any) binding precedent for a media lawyer to cite to a military judge in responding to a subpoena in a court-martial. Unreported decisions from prior courts martial exist, however, and provide strong, persuasive authority for recognizing and applying a qualified privilege for the press.

At least two military judges at the trial level have recognized and applied a First Amendment-based privilege to shield a journalist's nonconfidential but unreported information (video interview outtakes) from compelled production. In both cases, the judges quashed subpoenas issued to television news organizations to produce nonbroadcast video footage, on the grounds that the party on whose behalf the subpoenas had been issued had failed to make the showing required to overcome the privilege.

In *United States v. Ashby*, the U.S. Marine Corps convened a court-martial against two Camp Lejeune pilots charged with causing a fatal ski gondola accident in the Italian Alps that killed twenty people. The prosecutors served subpoenas on the news program *60 Minutes* and on *Rolling Stone* magazine, both seeking outtakes and audiotapes of interviews given by the accused. Both news organizations offered to provide recordings of the published portions of the interview but resisted producing unpublished portions, asserting their rights under the First Amendment. The military judge rejected the government's position that *Branzburg* [*Branzburg v. Hayes*, 408 U.S. 665 (1972)] held no First Amendment privilege for journalists to refuse to provide evidence in aid of criminal prosecution and ruled "there is a First Amendment media privilege."

Applying the three-part test generally articulated by federal courts for confidential sources, the judge quashed both subpoenas seeking nonconfidential information on the grounds that the material sought was "not case dispositive." The court further reasoned that the evidence sought was "not a percipient witness' evidence of a crime being committed . . ." and that the interview outtakes had been sought solely for their potential impeachment value. The court stated, "[F]rankly, I do find the government is on a bit of a fishing expedition. [It] is nice to have information possible for impeachment. It's not something necessary for the prosecution of the case and I'm unwilling to find no First Amendment protections."

Similarly, in *United States v. Bennett*, subpoenas were served on the news program *Dateline NBC* for outtakes of interviews with Marine Corps Staff Sergeant Arthur G. Bennett and others. In 1994, the U.S. Marine Corps had charged Bennett with rape and molestation. While his court-martial was pending, his commanding officer approved a leave request for Bennett. A few days later, authorities found a body inside Bennett's trailer that, although burned beyond recognition, was identified by dental records as Bennett. State and military authorities concluded that he had committed suicide by fire and closed the case. A couple of years later, a man named Joe Benson was arrested in Utah on charges of molesting and raping his daughter. Benson's fingerprints revealed that he in fact was the supposedly deceased Bennett, who apparently had been living in Utah with his wife and two daughters.

The military charged Bennett with desertion and sex offenses. During Bennett's pretrial confinement, *Dateline* interviewed Bennett and others and broadcast portions of those interviews in its report, including a portion of Bennett's interview in which he claimed that he had not molested, raped, or killed anyone.

The prosecution sought the outtakes of Bennett's interviews. Bennett in turn sought outtakes of interviews with witnesses from Bennett's Article 32 proceeding who were expected to testify at trial (including two alleged victims and the parents of several of the alleged child victims). NBC challenged the subpoenas, arguing that both the prosecution and the defense had failed to demonstrate that the information sought was essential to their case and otherwise unavailable.

The military trial judge applied the familiar three-part test derived from Justice Powell's concurrence in *Branzburg* and ruled that the defense had shown only a speculative need for the outtakes for potential impeachment purposes. He also found that adequate impeachment information was available from other sources, including the witnesses' sworn testimony during the Article 32 proceeding. The trial judge further found that the government's subpoena did not satisfy the "highly material and relevant" prong of the three-part test because the government could not "specify what the statements may be. Absent this articulation, the court would couch these requests as being speculative at best." As a result, the court concluded "that neither the government nor the defense [had] established a sufficient basis to override *Dateline NBC*'s qualified privilege to withhold this videotape outtake[s] under the First Amendment." . . .

In December 2004, the Air Force served subpoenas on fourteen news organizations in connection with a rape case involving two cadets at the Air Force Academy in Colorado Springs. The case involved allegations leveled by Jessica Brakey, the Air Force cadet who first went public with allegations that the Air Force had ignored or not punished a series of sexual assaults against female cadets within the academy. Brakey had given on-camera interviews to the news program *20/20*, *Oprah Winfrey*, CNN, and others in which she described her alleged attack and the Air Force's response to her allegations. The subpoenas served at the request of one of the defendants called for the reporters to turn over their notes of interviews with Brakey, unaired outtakes, and all other unpublished material relating to the cases.

In addition, the defense requested discovery of Brakey's records of her post-rape counseling and treatment by a civilian social worker. Applying a provision of the MRE that permits constitutional rights of the accused to trump other claims of privilege, the military judge ordered the records produced, but the social worker refused to turn them over. Brakey also objected to disclosure of her psychological treatment records. When Brakey's therapist refused to comply with the trial court's subpoena for an in-camera inspection, the military judge issued an arrest warrant for the therapist.

The therapist unsuccessfully sought injunctive relief in the federal civilian courts but was never arrested. In the interim, the military judge abated the defendant's rape prosecution because the alleged victim's psychological treatment records (deemed to be necessary to the defense) were unavailable. Thus, the military court has not resolved whether the numerous subpoenas issued to news media outlets should be quashed or enforced. Nevertheless, the plight of the alleged rape victim's therapist is instructive: it demonstrates that it is difficult to predict when military courts will find that an accused's constitutional rights trump a particular (nonconstitutional) privilege.

It appears that fallout from the sexual assault cases discussed above has prompted the Air Force to rethink its policy concerning serving subpoenas on the news media. On February 2, 2005, the Judge Advocate General, Major General Jack Rives, issued a memorandum to the entire Air Force JAG Corps, asking them to consult with senior attorneys at the headquarters level and to negotiate with media outlets before issuing subpoenas to reporters. Rives's memorandum emphasized the importance of striving for "the proper balance between the public's interest in the free dissemination of ideas and information and the public's interest in effective law enforcement." Although the memorandum is not a binding order or regulation, it mirrors the Department of Justice's policy on issuing subpoenas to the news media and signals an effort to restrict the future use of Air Force subpoenas against reporters. It remains to be seen how much effect, if any, this memorandum will have on the practices of trial counsel and trial judges within the Air Force and other military branches.

Zansberg, Freedus & Fidell, *supra*, at 14-16.

Chapter 15

EVIDENCE

In 1980, President Carter issued an Executive Order promulgating the Military Rules of Evidence. With some limited exceptions, these rules mirrored the Federal Rules of Evidence used in criminal trials in United States District Courts. While the specific rules have been revised over the years, the Military Rules of Evidence remain largely identical to their Federal Rules of Evidence counterparts. Military Rule of Evidence 1102 keeps the two sets of evidentiary rules in step by providing that amendments to the Federal Rules are automatically incorporated into military practice 18 months after their effective date unless the President takes contrary action.

But in some areas the Military Rules of Evidence are unique. For example, the 300 series of the Federal Rules of Evidence, which deal exclusively with civil matters, are omitted from the Military Rules. In their place are rules providing detailed guidance about self-incrimination, search and seizure, and eye-witness identification that have no Federal Rules counterparts. The Military Rules also depart from the Federal Rules' common-law based evidentiary privilege system. Instead, the 500 series of the Military Rules of Evidence adopts detailed privilege rules governing such areas as attorney-client communications, communications to clergy, spousal communications, and psychotherapist-patient communications. Military Rule of Evidence 505, the classified information privilege, adopts rules similar to those included in the Classified Information Procedures Act, 18 U.S.C. App. §§ 1-16. The military's hearsay exceptions are somewhat broader than their federal civilian counterparts. And the military has a unique evidentiary rule prohibiting the admissibility of polygraph results. This rule became the subject of a Supreme Court case that rejected a Sixth Amendment challenge to the exclusion of exculpatory polygraph results.

This chapter will focus exclusively on those areas where military practice is different from practice in United States District Courts, concentrating on the rules governing self-incrimination, search and seizure, privileges, hearsay, and polygraph results.

I. INTRODUCTION

A. Adopting the Military Rules of Evidence

Maj. Thomas J. Feeney & Capt. Margaret L. Murphy,
The Army Judge Advocate General's Corps, 1982-1987
122 MIL. L. REV. 1, 27 (1988)

In 1975 Congress codified federal evidentiary practice when it approved the Federal Rules of Evidence. This provided the impetus for a similar restructuring of military practice. In 1978 the Evidence Working Group of the Joint Service Committee on Military Justice received a charter to rewrite the military rules, using the Federal Rules of Evidence as a model. In 1980, after a two-year effort, the President promulgated the Military Rules of Evidence as an amendment to the 1969 Manual.

Stephen A. Saltzburg, Lee D. Schinasi & David A. Schlueter, *Military Rules of Evidence Manual (4th ed. 1997)*
Executive Order 12198 of March 12, 1980, Editorial Comment

On 12 March 1980, the President of the United States prescribed a new evidentiary code for military practice. His action was only the final step in a two-year process aimed at totally rewriting Chapter XXVII of the Manual for Courts-Martial. This revision was a joint effort in every sense of the term. Members from all services, departments, courts and agencies served by the Rules contributed to their development.

As the Rules themselves clearly demonstrate, the drafters attempted to adopt federal practice to the greatest extent possible, while still allowing for the necessities of a world wide criminal practice.

In order to assist military and civilian attorneys, and the bench in using these Rules, the drafters have provided a detailed Analysis describing their intentions. This Drafters' Analysis is not binding, however, and it is not part of the Executive Order itself. It also does not constitute or represent any official position with respect to the Rules. The Drafters' Analysis should be of great assistance as it highlights what the drafters intended and often traces each Rule back to its federal and *Manual* foundations.

The Drafters' Analysis has limitations, however. Sometimes there is little detailed information addressing known uncertainties in the Rule. There are also apparent conflicts between some Rules and the Drafters' Analysis itself. . . .

The President's action in promulgating the new Rules and subsequent amendments should improve military practice. The Rules will be more easily understood and uniformly applied than those they replaced. And they represent a convenient reference source for virtually all military evidence law.

B.   Amending the Military Rules of Evidence

Military Rule of Evidence 1102
Manual for Courts-Martial, United States (2005 ed.)

Amendments

(a) Amendments to the Federal Rules of Evidence shall apply to the Military Rules of Evidence 18 months after the effective date of such amendments, unless action to the contrary is taken by the President.

Drafters' analysis

Rule 1102 has been substantially revised from the original Federal Rule which sets forth a procedure by which the Supreme Court promulgates amendments to the Federal Rules subject to Congressional objection. Although it is the Committee's intent that the Federal Rules of Evidence apply to the armed forces to the extent practicable, *see* Article 36(a), the Federal Rules are often in need of modification to adapt them to military criminal legal system. Further, some rules may be impracticable. As Congress may make changes during the initial period following Supreme Court publication, some period of time after an amendment's effective date was considered essential for the armed forces to review the final form of amendments and to propose any necessary modifications to the President. Six months was considered the minimally appropriate time period. Amendments to the Federal Rules are not applicable to the armed forces until 180 days after the effective date of such amendment, unless the President directs earlier application. In the absence of any Presidential action, however, an amendment to the Federal Rule of Evidence will be automatically applicable on the 180th day after its effective date. The President may, however, affirmatively direct that any such amendment may not apply, in whole or in part, to the armed forces and that direction shall be binding upon courts-martial.

NOTE

A 1998 *Manual for Courts-Martial* amendment changed the date on which a Federal Rule of Evidence amendment would be applied automatically to the Military Rules from 180 days after the amendment's effective date to 18 months after its effective date. Exec. Order No. 13,086, 63 FED. REG. 30065 (June 2, 1998).

UNITED STATES v. PARKER
United States Army Court of Criminal Appeals
54 M.J. 700 (A. C. C. A. 2001)

CAIRNS, SENIOR JUDGE. . . .

a. Background

In Specification 4 of Charge II, the government charged that . . . at or near Heidelberg, Germany, the appellant raped Ms. AL. . . . By exceptions and substitutions, the court-martial panel found the appellant guilty of rape [while revising the dates alleged in the specification].

At the time of the alleged offense, AL was an active duty soldier assigned to the same unit as the appellant. At the time of trial, however, AL had been released from active duty and was in the United States. Because she declined to travel to Germany to testify at the appellant's court-martial, AL was deposed on 22 April 1996, in the United States, by the trial counsel in the presence of the appellant. The appellant's trial defense counsel cross-examined her.

At the appellant's court-martial, AL's videotaped deposition was played for the court- martial as the primary and essential evidence that the appellant raped AL. In her videotaped deposition, AL testified that she dated the appellant for one to two months, and they had engaged in consensual sexual intercourse six to seven times before the alleged rape. She testified that their sexual relations occurred in the appellant's car.

AL testified that she hosted a party in her barracks room one evening and that the appellant and other members of the unit attended. After consuming about twelve German beers, she passed out. When she awoke at about 0300 in the morning, the appellant was on top of her and was engaged in vaginal sexual intercourse with her. She testified that when she told the appellant to "get off," he said, "You wanted it," or words to that effect. AL raised her voice above the noise of the television and repeatedly insisted that the appellant stop before he eventually complied with her wishes. . . .

[AL] declined to report the incident for several months before confiding in her squad leader that she had been raped. The squad leader told AL that it was her [AL's] decision whether to report the rape. AL decided not to report it because, as she explained in her testimony, even though she had not consented to the intercourse, she had been drinking at the time that the appellant raped her and she had previously consented to having sexual intercourse with him. AL testified that after her squad leader subsequently began to work for the criminal investigation command (CID), investigators sought her out to question her about the incident.

To bolster the government's proof of this rape charge, the trial counsel offered the testimony of KG, an acquaintance of the appellant. KG testified that at a party in February 1996, the appellant tried to have sexual intercourse with her after she had passed out from alcohol intoxication. KG's testimony was admitted, over defense objection based on lack of relevance and timely notice, under Military Rule of Evidence 413 [hereinafter Mil. R. Evid.], as "evidence of similar crimes in sexual assault cases." . . .

d. KG's Testimony under Military Rule of Evidence 413

The appellant asserts . . . that the military judge erred when he allowed KG to testify, over defense objection, to uncharged misconduct under the provisions of Mil. R. Evid. 413 [because] the government failed to provide adequate notice under the rule. . . .

[T]he defense was provided adequate notice under the rule of the government's intent to offer the testimony of KG under Mil. R. Evid. 413. KG was interviewed on 23 February 1996 by a military police investigator who prepared a sworn statement summarizing the substance of the interview and thus her prospective testimony. The trial counsel first provided the trial defense counsel a copy of the agent's statement in mid-March 1996. Further, the trial counsel listed KG on his witness list and provided it to the defense in compliance with the defense discovery request. One week prior to the 29 April 1996 trial date, the trial counsel served another copy of KG's prospective testimony on the trial defense counsel. Four days before trial, the trial counsel explicitly notified the trial defense counsel of his intent to offer KG's testimony under Mil. R. Evid. 413. The military judge ruled that the defense had adequate notice of the substance of KG's prospective testimony and the government's intent to offer KG's testimony under Mil. R. Evid. 413, but he required the government to delay putting her on the witness stand until five days following formal notice.

As pointed out by the appellate defense counsel, Mil. R. Evid. 413 was not in effect at the time of the appellant's trial. [In accordance with the executive order which promulgated Mil. R. Evid. 413, the rule was to become effective for courts-martial in which arraignment was completed on or after 26 June 1998. The appellant was arraigned on 25 March 1996.] However, Federal Rule of Evidence 413 [hereinafter Fed. R. Evid.], upon which Mil. R. Evid. 413 is based, became effective on 9 July 1995. Under the provisions of Mil. R. Evid. 1102 in effect at the time of the appellant's trial, "[a]mendments to the Federal Rules of Evidence shall apply to the Military Rules of Evidence 180 days after the effective date of such amendments unless action to the contrary is taken by the President." [A change to Mil. R. Evid. 1102, effective 27 May 1998, requires an eighteen month waiting period before such federal rules apply to courts-martial.] Therefore, because the President took no such contrary action, by our calculations, Fed. R. Evid. 413 was applicable in trials by courts-martial on or about 5 January 1996. As the appellant's trial commenced on 25 March 1996, Fed. R. Evid. 413 properly applied through the provisions of Mil. R. Evid. 1102.

In cases in which the government intends to offer evidence under Fed. R. Evid. 413, the rule requires the government to "disclose the evidence" to the defense at least fifteen days before the scheduled date of trial or "at such later time as the court may allow for good cause." In this case, the military judge and counsel litigated the disclosure requirement by mistakenly relying on the five-day time requirements provided in the draft of Mil. R. Evid. 413. However, even applying the more stringent fifteen-day disclosure requirement of Fed. R. Evid. 413, which we believe was the correct notice requirement, we are satisfied that the government complied. The evidence was provided to the defense in mid-March, well before the fifteen-day notice requirement under the rule. Under the plain language of the rule, the government must "disclose the evidence." The rule does not require the government to formally announce to the defense that they intended to offer the evidence under Fed. R. Evid. 413. Even if that were the rule, we conclude that the military judge reasonably extended the time for notification under the rule, based on good cause, providing the defense with more than adequate time to prepare for and meet the evidence.

II.   SELF-INCRIMINATION

Uniform Code of Military Justice
Article 31. Compulsory self-incrimination prohibited

(a) No person subject to this chapter may compel any person to incriminate himself or to answer any question the answer to which may tend to incriminate him.

(b) No person subject to this chapter may interrogate, or request any statement from an accused or a person suspected of an offense without first informing him of the nature of the accusation and advising him that he does not have to make any statement regarding the offense of which he is accused or suspected and that any statement made by him may be used as evidence against him in a trial by court-martial.

(c) No person subject to this chapter may compel any person to make a statement or produce evidence before any military tribunal if the statement or evidence is not material to the issue and may tend to degrade him.

(d) No statement obtained from any person in violation of this article, or through the use of coercion, unlawful influence, or unlawful inducement may be received in evidence against him in a trial by court-martial.

NOTES

1. In its landmark decision in *Miranda v. Arizona*, 384 U.S. 436 (1966), the Supreme Court observed that before beginning an interrogation, Federal Bureau of Investigation agents advised the suspect "that he is not required to make a statement, that any statement may be used against him in court, that the individual may obtain the services of an attorney of his own choice and . . . that he has a right to free counsel if he is unable to pay." The Court then observed that English law required cautionary warnings to criminal suspects while Scottish law generally barred the admissibility of statements made during an interrogation. Indian and Ceylon law allowed the admissibility of the results of an interrogation only if the statements were made in a magistrate's presence. Chief Justice Warren's opinion for the Court then observed:

> Similarly, in our country the Uniform Code of Military Justice has long provided that no suspect may be interrogated without first being warned of his right not to make a statement and that any statement he makes may be used against him. [10 U.S.C. § 831(d) (1964 ed.).] Denial of the right to consult counsel during interrogation has also been proscribed by military tribunals. [*United States v. Rose*, 24 C.M.R. 251 (1957); *United States v. Gunnels*, 23 C.M.R. 354 (1957).] There appears to have been no marked detrimental effect on criminal law enforcement in these jurisdictions as a result of these rules. Conditions of law enforcement in our country are sufficiently similar to permit reference to this experience as assurance that lawlessness will not result from warning an individual of his rights or allowing him to exercise them. Moreover, it is consistent with our legal system that we give at least as much protection to these rights as is given in the jurisdictions described. We deal in our country with rights grounded in a specific requirement of the Fifth Amendment of the Constitution, whereas other jurisdictions arrived at their conclusions on the basis of principles of justice not so specifically defined.

Id. at 489-90.

2. The Supreme Court has observed that while it has never held that the Fifth Amendment's Self-Incrimination Clause applies in courts-martial, both the Military Rules of Evidence and military appellate case law had subjected court-martial practice to *Miranda* and its progeny:

> We have never had occasion to consider whether the Fifth Amendment privilege against self-incrimination, or the attendant right to counsel during custodial interrogation, applies of its own force to the military, and we need not do so here. The President, exercising his authority to prescribe procedures for military criminal proceedings, *see* Art. 36(a), UCMJ, 10 U.S.C. § 836(a), has decreed that statements obtained in violation of the Self-Incrimination Clause are generally not admissible at trials by court-martial. Mil. Rules Evid. 304(a) and (c)(3). Because the Court of Military Appeals has held that our cases construing the Fifth Amendment right to counsel apply to military interrogations and control the admissibility of evidence at trials by court-martial, *see, e.g., United States v. McLaren*, 38 M.J. 112, 115 (1993); *United States v. Applewhite*, 23 M.J. 196, 198 (1987), and the parties do not contest this point, we proceed on the assumption that our precedents apply to courts-martial just as they apply to state and federal criminal prosecutions.

Davis v. United States, 512 U.S. 452, 457 n.* (1994).

3. Military Rules of Evidence 304 and 305 provide detailed requirements governing rights warnings, interrogations, and the admissibility of confessions and admissions.

4. The warning requirements in Article 31(b) are to some extent narrower than *Miranda*'s requirements and to some extent broader. Unlike the *Miranda* warnings, Article 31(b) does not require advising a suspect that he or she may consult with counsel before deciding whether to remain silent. The Court of Military Appeals, however, applied this requirement to military practice in *United States v. Tempia*, 16 C.M.A. 629, 37 C.M.R. 249 (1967). On the other hand, Article 31(b) is broader than *Miranda* in at least two ways. First, unlike *Miranda*, Article 31 requires the interrogator to inform the suspect of "the nature of the accusation." Second, *Miranda* applies only to interrogations of suspects in custody. Article 31(b) applies regardless of the suspect's custodial status. As the next case demonstrates, however, military case law has narrowed the contexts in which Article 31(b) warnings must be given.

UNITED STATES v. LOUKAS
United States Court of Military Appeals
29 M.J. 385 (C.M.A. 1990)

SULLIVAN, JUDGE. . . .

The evidence developed during the suppression hearing was that [Loukas] was on temporary duty from Pope Air Force Base, North Carolina, along with other crew members. [Loukas] was the load-master. Following an overnight stay at Panama City, Panama, [Loukas'] crew was scheduled to depart Howard Air Force Base for an early morning flight to Trinidad, Bolivia, where they were to receive a load of unspecified cargo. [Loukas] was not present at the scheduled crew show time. When he finally arrived at the aircraft he was two hours late. The record, surprisingly, does not reflect that he received a particularly unfriendly or otherwise negative greeting from his fellow crew members, all of whom were senior in grade to him. The co-pilot kidded him about the number of ladies he had been with the evening before. SSgt Dryer recalled in his testimony that he teased [Loukas] about his lateness. Apparently none of the crew members, at that point, noted anything in [Loukas'] appearance or demeanor that was alarming.

After the aircraft had been in flight for four or more hours the assistant crew chief, an Airman First Class Taranto, stepped into the cargo section. [Loukas] was the only other person present in that portion of the plane. There was no cargo or equipment on board at that time. *Airman Taranto testified that he observed that [Loukas] was acting in an irrational manner. He pointed in the direction of the flight deck and inquired of Airman Taranto, "Do you see them?" and, "Do you see her?" Airman Taranto did not see anyone. It was apparent to him that [Loukas] was experiencing a hallucination. [Loukas] handed Airman Taranto his survival vest and .38 calibre pistol and told him to take it (apparently referring to the firearm) and that he didn't want it.* The witness reported the incident to his immediate superior, SSgt Dryer, the crew chief.

SSgt Dryer went to the back of the aircraft and confronted [Loukas]. He testified during the hearing on the motion to suppress that he noted he *[Loukas] appeared to be nervous and that he was perspiring profusely even though it was cool in that portion of the plane. [Loukas] continued to hallucinate. Gesturing in the direction of the flight deck, he inquired why "those people" were there and wondered why "they" didn't just come down and get him. The witness stated that he asked [Loukas] if he had taken any drugs.* [Loukas] responded that he had not. SSgt Dryer leaned over close to where [Loukas] was sitting so that he could observe his eyes and asked in a more insistent manner, *"Come on, what have you taken?" or, "What are you on?" or words to that effect. [Loukas] replied that he had taken some cocaine the night before. SSgt Dryer asked, "Is that all?" He received an affirmative answer.* SSgt Dryer advised [Loukas] to secure his seatbelt and relax. According to his testimony he was somewhat concerned for the safety of the aircraft and its flight crew, particularly if [Loukas] started "freaking out."

SSgt Dryer reported his observations of [Loukas] to the flight engineer, a Technical Sergeant Drummond. The latter went to the back of the aircraft and observed [Loukas]. He retrieved bullets that [Loukas] had on his person. He returned to the flight deck area and consulted with SSgt Dryer. They concluded that the situation was under control and that it would not be necessary to alert the aircraft commander, Captain Cottam. It was agreed that someone would maintain direct observation of [Loukas] during the remainder of the flight.

27 M.J. at 790-91 (emphasis added).

The stated premise of the Court of Military Review majority opinions, both panel and en banc, (6-3), was that Sergeant Dryer was obligated by Article 31(b) to warn the accused of his rights before questioning him about possible drug use. This legal conclusion was drawn on the basis of the decision of this Court in *United States v. Duga*, 10 M.J. 206 (C.M.A. 1981), and a finding of fact that Sergeant Dryer was acting officially and not simply out of "idle curiosity." 27 M.J. at 792. We disagree as a matter of law because the crew chief's inquiry was not a *law-enforcement or disciplinary* investigation which is also required before Article 31(b) becomes applicable. *United States v. Gibson*, 3 U.S.C.M.A. 746, 752, 14 C.M.R. 164, 170 (1954); *see United States v. Duga, supra* at 211. . . .

This Court has long intimated that [Article 31] requires warnings only when questioning is done during an official law-enforcement investigation or disciplinary inquiry. *See generally* Manuel E. Supervielle, *Article 31(b): Who Should Be Required To Give Warnings?*, 123 Mil. L. Rev. 151, 199 n.181 (1989); J. Munster and M. Larkin, *Military Evidence* § 7.2b at 153 n.86 (2d ed.1978). Chief Judge Quinn has articulated the following rationale for our construction of this important codal provision:

> Article 31(b), *supra*, extends the provisions of its predecessor, Article of War 24, . . . to persons "suspected" as well as "accused," but no intention to extend the requirement to other than "official investigation" is found in the legislative history of the Uniform Code. . . .

> Taken literally, this Article is applicable to interrogation by all persons included within the term "persons subject to the code" as defined by Article 2 of the Code, *supra*, 50 U.S.C. § 552, or any other who is suspected or accused of an offense. However, this phrase was used in a limited sense. *In our opinion, in addition to the limitation referred to in the legislative history of the requirement, there is a definitely restrictive element of officiality in the choice of the language "interrogate or request any statement," wholly absent from the relatively loose phrase "person subject to this code," for military persons not assigned to investigate offenses, do not ordinarily interrogate nor do they request statements from others accused or suspected of crime. See United States v. Wilson and Harvey*, 2 U.S.C.M.A. 248, 8 C.M.R. 48. This is not the sole limitation upon the Article's applicability, however. Judicial discretion indicates a necessity for denying its application to a situation not considered by its framers, and wholly unrelated to the reasons for its creation.

United States v. Gibson, supra at 752, 14 C.M.R. at 170 (emphasis added).

Judge Latimer opined similarly in his opinion concurring in the result in the same case:

> I would affirm the conviction on the basis of the test laid down by me in my dissent in *United States v. Wilson and Harvey, supra*. In that case I stated:

>> ". . . Accordingly, I believe before the advice required by the Article need be given, three conditions should be fulfilled: *first,*

the party asking the question should occupy some official posi-
tion in connection with law enforcement or crime detection; second, that the inquiry be in furtherance of some official
investigation; and third, the facts be developed far enough that
the party conducting the investigation has reasonable grounds
to suspect the person interrogated has committed an offense."

Collectively, all three conditions suggest that the interrogation be
surrounded with an air of some officiality and I believe the Manual for
Courts-Martial, United States, 1951, . . ., and the hearings before the
Committees of Congress support that proposition (see Comments,
pages 990-991, Hearings Before the House Committee on Armed
Services, 81st Congress, 1st Session, on H.R. 2498, Uniform Code of
Military Justice). Moreover, a reading of the Article is convincing that
Congress could not have intended Article 31(b) to cover casual conversations, because the language used compels the conclusion that the
interrogator is pursuing some official inquiry as he must know that
the person to whom he is talking is suspected of a crime; he must
inform him of the nature of the accusation; and he must explain to him
that what he says may be used against him in a court-martial.

3 U.S.C.M.A. at 763, 14 C.M.R. at 181 (emphasis added).

Finally, Chief Judge Everett, speaking for the Court in *United States v.
Duga,* 10 M.J. at 211, more recently suggested the same criteria when he
stated:

In the case at hand, the evidence only permits the conclusion reached
by the Air Force Court of Military Review that the questioning of
appellant by Byers did not fall within the purview of Article 31(b). The
two prerequisites which determine whether Article 31(b) warnings
were required are not met in this case. As found by the Court of
Military Review, the record reveals that the questioning was not done
in an official capacity — *that is, Byers was not acting on behalf of the
Air Force* — *either as a security policeman or as an agent of the OSI.*
Since the appellant declined to present any evidence on the issue, *cf.
United States v. Beck,* [15 U.S.C.M.A. 333,] at 339, 35 C.M.R. at [305,]
311, Byers' testimony is completely uncontroverted as to their camaraderie and affiliation in the same security police squadron, and his
statement that when the appellant rode up to the gate on his bike, he
was only "speaking [to him] more or less like a friend to a friend," or,
as elsewhere described by him — it was "more or less like-buddy-to-
buddy talk you might say." No evidence contradicts the inference that
the questioning by Byers was solely motivated by his own personal
curiosity and was entirely unconnected with his previous contact with
the OSI. *In any case, in what the OSI told Byers, it neither directed nor
advised him to question the appellant.* In view of the uncontradicted
nature of the testimony, we have no choice but to uphold the lower
court's finding of a lack of the officiality which is essential to requiring
the Article 31(b) warning.

(Emphasis added.) Accordingly, we conclude that the Court of Military Review in both its panel and its en banc decisions too broadly construed and applied this codal provision. 10 MJ at 210 n.6, citing *United States v. Dohle*, 1 M.J. 223 (C.M.A. 1975).

An example of official, but not law-enforcement or disciplinary, questioning which is permitted without warnings under Article 31 is found in *United States v. Fisher*, 21 U.S.C.M.A. 223, 44 C.M.R. 277 (1972). . . . In that case, we held that a military doctor, not performing an investigative or disciplinary function or engaged in perfecting a criminal case, was not required to preface his medical diagnostic questions to a military subordinate with Article 31 warnings. *See United States v. Malumphy*, 13 U.S.C.M.A. 60, 61-62, 32 C.M.R. 60, 61-62 (1962); *United States v. Malumphy*, 12 U.S.C.M.A. 639, 640, 31 C.M.R. 225, 226 (1962); *United States v. Baker*, 11 U.S.C.M.A. 313, 29 C.M.R. 129 (1960).

In the case before us, Sergeant Dryer was the crew chief of an operational military aircraft who was similarly responsible for the plane's safety and that of its crew, including the accused, his military subordinate. In addition, his questioning of the accused was limited to that required to fulfill his operational responsibilities, and there was no evidence suggesting his inquiries were designed to evade constitutional or codal rights. *United States v. Cross*, 14 U.S.C.M.A. 660, 662-63, 34 C.M.R. 440, 442-43 (1964). *See United States v. Malumphy*, 13 U.S.C.M.A. at 62, 32 C.M.R. at 62. *Cf. United States v. Lee*, 25 M.J. 457 (C.M.A. 1988). Finally, the unquestionable urgency of the threat and the immediacy of the crew chief's response underscore the legitimate operational nature of his queries. *See United States v. Hessler*, 7 M.J. 9 (C.M.A. 1979). *See also United States v. Henry*, 21 U.S.C.M.A. 98, 44 C.M.R. 152 (1971). Under our precedents, the prosecution satisfactorily showed that Article 31 warnings were not required in this operational context. *United States v. Beck*, 15 U.S.C.M.A. 333, 35 C.M.R. 305 (1965); *see* Mil. R. Evid. 304(e), Manual for Courts-Martial, United States, 1984. *See generally United States v. Battles*, 25 M.J. 58, 60 (C.M.A. 1987). . . .

COX, JUDGE (concurring):

Like Judge Sullivan — with whose opinion I concur entirely — I start with the *language* of Article 31(b), Uniform Code of Military Justice, 10 U.S.C. § 831(b):

> No person subject to this chapter may *interrogate, or request any statement* from an accused or a person suspected of an offense without first informing him of the nature of the accusation and advising him that he does not have to make any statement. . . .

(Emphasis added.) I presume Congress meant something when it chose this language.

In particular, the statute does not say: No person who, "because of military rank, duty, or other similar relationship," might apply "subtle pressure on a suspect to respond" shall talk to a suspect without first informing him of his rights, etc. *See United States v. Duga*, 10 M.J. 206, 210 (C.M.A. 1981).

"Person" refers to any person who "interrogates," etc. Thus, contrary to the assertion of the dissent (based upon the gloss of case law and the "purpose of Article 31(b)"), the focus of the statute is *precisely* on the nature and purpose of the questioning, not the happenstance position of the questioner.

Also, like Judge Sullivan, I look to the circumstances of the case to determine if what occurred was an interrogation or a request for a statement. While I must concede that reasonable people may sometimes disagree as to the meaning of those terms, I would infer from the placement of the language in a military justice code that the interrogation or request for a statement would in some way be connected with a criminal-justice or disciplinary purpose. Therefore, a most pertinent area for inquiry would be the motivation of the person asking the questions.

Without attempting to apply these principles to all cases that may come before us, I totally agree with Judge Sullivan that, when military aircraft personnel discover an armed servicemember hallucinating in the belly of an aircraft in flight, and they ask him whether he has taken some drugs, it is obvious that the *last* thing in their minds is the possibility of a criminal prosecution somewhere down the line. Thus, I detect no inference of an interrogation or a request for a statement within the meaning of Article 31(b) from these circumstances.

Even though the accused had been relieved of his pistol at the time of his questioning, it was not until *after* the questioning that the aircraft personnel could decide if there was an imminent threat of serious aberrational behavior or the need for an immediate landing — for either the safety of the aircraft or the medical needs of the accused.

In my view, the noninterrogational purposes of these immediate actions are so clear that, as a matter of law, we can reverse the Court of Military Review. Accordingly, I concur with the principal opinion.

EVERETT, CHIEF JUDGE (dissenting). . . .

Article 31(b) of the Uniform Code, 10 U.S.C. 831(b), provides that

> [n]o person subject to this chapter may interrogate, or request any statement from an accused or a person suspected of an offense without first informing him of the nature of the accusation and advising him that he does not have to make by any statement regarding the offense of which he is accused or suspected and that any statement made by him may be used as evidence against him in a trial by court-martial.

Some of this language has been given a broad interpretation. For example, "'[i]nterrogation' includes any formal or informal questioning in which an incriminating response either is sought or is a reasonable consequence of such questioning." Mil. R. Evid. 305(b)(2), Manual for Courts-Martial, United States, 1984; *see also United States v. Seay*, 1 M.J. 201 (C.M.A. 1975). The term "statement" includes such testimonial conduct as identifying the clothing items which belong to the suspect. *See United States v. Williams*, 10 U.S.C.M.A. 578, 28 C.M.R. 144 (1959); *United States v. Bennett*, 7 U.S.C.M.A. 97, 21 C.M.R. 223 (1956); *United States v. Holmes*, 6 U.S.C.M.A. 151, 19 C.M.R. 277 (1955); *United States v. Taylor*, 5 U.S.C.M.A. 178, 17 C.M.R. 178

(1954). Any "language, or its equivalent" may be a "statement" for purposes of Article 31(b). *See United States v. Bennett, supra* at 100, 21 C.M.R. at 226. Furthermore, a warning must precede "*any* statement 'regarding the offense of which [the servicemember] is accused or suspected' quite apart from whether he feels that his truthful reply would serve to incriminate him." *United States v. Taylor, supra* at 181, 17 C.M.R. at 181.

In one respect, however, Article 31(b) has been construed more narrowly than its language might suggest. In *United v. Gibson*, 3 U.S.C.M.A. 746, 14 C.M.R. 164 (1954), this Court considered admissibility of certain answers given by the accused to questions asked him by a fellow prisoner, Private First Class Ferguson. When Gibson had been placed in pretrial confinement, the Criminal Investigation Division (CID) had asked the provost sergeant "to assign another prisoner to watch the accused . . . and recommended that 'a good reliable rat' be selected for the purpose." Subsequently, Gibson made "incriminating statements" to Ferguson "in the course of what on its face was an ordinary conversation between inmates of a stockade." 3 U.S.C.M.A. at 750, 14 C.M.R. at 168. Chief Judge Quinn concluded that the purposes of Article 31(b) required an "element of officiality" in the interrogation or request for a statement in order to trigger the warning requirement. *Id.* at 752, 14 C.M.R. at 170. Judge Brosman, concurring, observed:

> Each of my brothers has construed Article 31(b) to apply only if an element of officiality attaches to the interrogation of a person accused or suspected of a crime. In doing this, each — because of the purpose revealed in the legislative background of Article 31(b) — has chosen to read into that enactment something not clearly visible in its verbiage. Nowhere do I find an express statement in the Uniform Code that Article 31(b) deals only with persons subject to the Code who are engaged in an *official* investigation. Yet I have no sort of quarrel with the practice of examining legislative history to ascertain the purpose of Congress in enacting a statute. Nor is such a procedure alien to recognized canons of statutory construction.

Id. at 753, 14 C.M.R. at 171 (footnote omitted).

Judge Latimer, concurring in the result, accused his fellow judges of "concur[ring] in a principle which results in a classic example of judicial legislation." *Id.* at 757, 14 C.M.R. at 175. In his view PFC Ferguson, the undercover agent, was free to "listen, observe, and report," *id.* at 758, 14 C.M.R. at 176, but was subject to the warning provision if he sought to obtain a confession or admission by questioning the accused.

In *United States v. Souder*, 11 U.S.C.M.A. 59, 28 C.M.R. 283 (1959), two accordions had been stolen from a person in the naval service, who duly reported his loss to naval security personnel. They, in turn, advised local music stores to be on the lookout for the instruments. Souder and a fellow sailor entered a music store in the area which was owned and operated by Lieutenant (jg) Gallagher. They had possession of one of the stolen accordions. Gallagher, a naval officer on active duty, observed that the accordion fit the description he had received from naval security personnel of one of the stolen instruments. During a conversation with the two sailors, Gallagher obtained incriminating admissions from them.

Judge Ferguson's opinion for the Court concluded that Lieutenant Gallagher had been under a duty to advise both sailors of their rights under Article 31(b) before questioning them about the stolen musical instruments, since he was a person subject to the Code and suspected them of a crime. Chief Judge Quinn, concurring, stated:

> The mere fact that Lieutenant Gallagher is a person subject to the Uniform Code of Military Justice is not, as the principal opinion implies, the whole of the matter in determining whether there has been a violation of Article 31. There are some situations to which Article 31 does not apply, even though the participants are persons subject to the Uniform Code. *United States v. Gibson*, 3 U.S.C.M.A. 746, 14 C.M.R. 164; *United States v. Dandaneau*, 5 U.S.C.M.A. 462, 18 C.M.R. 86.

11 U.S.C.M.A. at 61, 28 C.M.R. at 285.

Judge Latimer, concurring in the result, concluded that Lieutenant Gallagher should have given a warning because an official criminal investigation had begun, and he was aiding military authorities in that investigation.

In *United States v. Beck*, 15 U.S.C.M.A. 333, 35 C.M.R. 305 (1965), the Court considered a statement made by the accused to a military policeman, Grimsley, a personal friend who had no investigative duties. Grimsley had picked Beck up at a local civilian jail and, accompanied by another guard, had started to drive him back to their place of duty. On the way the accused started a "conversation . . . between two friends." *Id.* at 336, 35 C.M.R. at 308.

Judge Ferguson, writing for a unanimous Court, pointed out:

> This Court has long held that the preliminary warning under Code, *supra,* Article 31, is not necessary when it appears that the accused's statement was either spontaneously made or was not "officially" obtained. Whether a warning under the Article is required, however, because of the "officiality" of the inquiry necessarily depends upon the facts of each case.

15 U.S.C.M.A. at 337, 35 C.M.R. at 309 (citations omitted).

Thereafter, Judge Ferguson reviewed the cases and concluded:

> From the foregoing, certain, if not always well-defined, principles regarding the need for the preliminary warning emerge. It is certain, for example, that a military investigator, or one acting as such, who suspects an accused of an offense and questions him in connection with such allegations, is expressly required to advise him of his rights. At the other end of the spectrum, it is equally clear that inquiries made by a close friend on a personal basis and without regard to any military relationship between him and the accused is not within the ambit of Article 31. Lying between these two poles are situations involving purported action only on behalf of the civil authorities, participation in interviews by persons not subject to the Code on a claimed

private basis, perfunctory inquiries in the ordinary discharge of a non-military type of responsibility, and the lack of any police responsibility on the part of the interrogator. The ultimate inquiry in every case is whether the individual, in line of duty, is acting on behalf of the service or is motivated solely by personal considerations when he seeks to question one whom he suspects of an offense. If the former is true, then the interrogation is clearly official and a preliminary warning is necessitated. If the latter situation is presented, then the warning is not required as a predicate for receipt of accused's responses. . . .

Id. at 338, 35 C.M.R. at 310 (citations omitted).

In other words, the Court in *Beck* recognized a continuum: At one extreme — where warnings clearly are required — is a situation in which a law-enforcement agent questions the accused as a suspect; at the other extreme — where warnings clearly are not required — is a situation in which a close friend is engaged in a personal conversation with the accused as a friend, without regard to any military relationship between the two of them. In the middle are all the other myriad situations in which, until now, the question to be answered has been, simply: Was a questioner acting in line of duty in an official capacity on behalf of the Service?

In accord with this analysis, the Court concluded in *Beck* that it could "not hold, as a matter of law, that the law officer should have excluded the accused's conversations with Grimsley while he was in the latter's custody." On the other hand, the evidence also left "open" the possibility that "Grimsley, in talking with the accused, was acting 'officially' and thus was under a duty to advise him of his rights under Code, *supra,* Article 31." *Id.* at 339, 35 C.M.R. at 311.

In *United States v. Seay*, 1 M.J. 201 (C.M.A. 1975), the Court ruled on a statement made by the accused during an "informal" session with his troop commander, who was counseling him with regard to his obligations "to take care of his bad checks." 1 M.J. at 202. Chief Judge Fletcher's lead opinion concluded that, "[i]rrespective of whether an Article 31 warning may have alarmed the appellant or obfuscated the purpose of the interview, a warning was still required since the commander acting in his official capacity sought to question the appellant whom he suspected of a criminal offense." 1 M.J. at 203 (footnote omitted). Judge Cook, concurring in the result, did not agree that an Article 31(b) warning was required but concluded that there had been an implied promise of confidentiality which rendered the statement inadmissible.

Senior Judge Ferguson, also concurring in the result, would have "appl[ied] the literal language of Article 31," 1 M.J. at 205, and would have "remov[ed] from consideration such irrelevant factors as whether the questioner did or did not ask his questions in an official capacity." 1 M.J. at 206. In his view,

the reason for th[e] broad liberal proscription imposed by Congress is illustrated by the case at bar. In the military, unlike civilian society, the exact relationship at any given moment between the ordinary soldier and other service personnel in authority (i.e., commissioned and noncommissioned officers) often is unclear. In the civilian experience, it is unlikely that anyone to whom *Miranda* [*v. Arizona,* 384 U.S. 436

(1966),] might apply would question someone else other than in the former's official capacity — that is, as a law enforcement officer. However, in the military a company commander may advise or question a member of his command for any of a number of different legitimate reasons, only one of which might relate to a criminal offense. Thus, to simplify matters, and in recognition of the superior/subordinate atmosphere inherent in the military [but] not present in the civilian structure, the requirement is broader in the former than in the latter.

1 M.J. at 206 (footnote omitted).

Finally, in *United States v. Duga*, 10 M.J. 206 (C.M.A. 1981), this Court, almost a decade ago, provided additional guidance as to the purposes and scope of Article 31(b). Quoting at some length from *United States v. Gibson*, 3 U.S.C.M.A. at 752, 14 C.M.R. at 170, we affirmed:

"Careful consideration of the history of the requirement of warning compels a conclusion that its purpose is to avoid impairment of the constitutional guarantee against compulsory self incrimination. *Because of the effect of superior rank or official position upon one subject to military law,* the mere asking of a question under some circumstances is the equivalent of a command. A person subjected to these pressures may rightly be regarded as deprived of his freedom to answer or to remain silent. . . ."

10 M.J. at 209 (emphasis added). Accordingly, we held:

Therefore, in light of Article 31(b)'s purpose and its legislative history, the Article applies only to *situations in which, because of military rank, duty, or other similar relationship,* there might be subtle pressure on a suspect to respond to an inquiry. *United States v. Gibson, supra.* Accordingly, in each case it is necessary to determine whether (1) a questioner subject to the Code was *acting in an official capacity in his inquiry or only had a personal motivation;* and (2) whether the person questioned perceived that the inquiry involved more than a casual conversation. *United States v. Gibson, supra.* . . .

10 M.J. at 210 (emphasis added).

Because Duga's statement to a security policeman had occurred during a perceived casual conversation, we concluded that it was admissible. However, the test employed in *Duga* and in its predecessors has been whether the person asking the question or requesting a statement was acting in an official capacity — acting for the benefit of the armed services — or was only acting in a personal capacity. This standard is much broader than that which the present majority now seeks to substitute, whereunder a warning is required *"only when questioning is done during an official law-enforcement investigation or disciplinary inquiry"* — whatever that phrase means. 29 M.J. 385, 387 (Sullivan, J.) (emphasis added).

This test, which departs still further from the language of Article 31(b), has not been used heretofore in any majority opinion of this Court, so far as I am aware. It fails to recognize that, under our precedents, someone who has "disciplinary authority" over an accused or suspect, or who performs a "disciplinary function" with respect to that person, is required by Article 31(b) to give a warning even though he may not be involved in a "law-enforcement investigation or disciplinary inquiry." Most importantly, it does not fully carry out the purpose of Article 31(b) as recognized in our earlier opinions — namely, to protect an accused against subtle pressures to answer resulting from the superior rank or official position of the questioner.

Professors Munster and Larkin, in their *Military Evidence* § 7.2b (2d ed.1978) — cited today by the majority for its proposed narrow standard — wrote:

> On the other hand, even though a person subject to the Code may conduct an interrogation of or request a statement from a suspect, he does not come within the operation of Article 31(b) *unless he is doing so officially and not in a purely private capacity.*

Id. at 152 (emphasis added; footnote omitted). In an excellent footnote in this section, the authors set out at length and discuss contrasting situations in which this Court has held that Article 31(b) warnings were or were not required. Many in the former category involved situations where commanders or others with disciplinary authority over the accused had asked the questions at issue. *Id.* at 153 n.86. The pivotal distinguishing fact in those cases has *not* been whether the questioner was conducting an "official law-enforcement investigation or disciplinary inquiry."

In enacting Article 31(b), Congress was sensitive to the fact that, in the military, some questions by some people under some circumstances are not so much requests, to be answered in the discretion of the person questioned, but *commands* to be answered without hesitation. Consistent with that sensitivity, this Court should not whittle away any further at the scope of Congress' Article 31(b) warning requirement. . . .

NOTES AND QUESTIONS

1. Do you agree with Judge Sullivan's majority opinion or Chief Judge Everett's dissent? Why?

2. Despite Chief Judge Everett's scholarly dissent, *Loukas* has become firmly established in military justice case law. It has been cited and followed in several unanimous Court of Appeals for the Armed Forces decisions. *See, e.g., United States v. Cohen*, 63 M.J. 45, 49-51 (C.A.A.F. 2006); *United States v. Moses*, 45 M.J. 132, 134-35 (C.A.A.F. 1996); *United States v. Sullivan*, 42 M.J. 360, 364 (C.A.A.F. 1995).

3. Military appellate case law has tempered *Loukas* somewhat by emphasizing that "[w]hen the questioning is done by a military supervisor in the suspect's chain of command, the Government must additionally rebut a strong presumption that such questioning was done for disciplinary purposes." *United States v. Good*, 32 M.J. 105, 108 (C.M.A. 1991) (per Sullivan, J., with Everett, C.J., concurring in the result); *followed by, e.g., United States v. Cohen*, 63 M.J. 45, 50 (C.A.A.F. 2006).

III. SEARCH AND SEIZURE

Military Rule of Evidence 315
Manual for Courts-Martial, United States (2005 ed.)

Probable cause searches

(a) *General rule.* Evidence obtained from searches requiring probable cause conducted in accordance with this rule is admissible at trial when relevant and not otherwise inadmissible under these rules. . . .

(d) *Power to authorize.* Authorization to search pursuant to this rule may be granted by an impartial individual in the following categories:

(1) *Commander.* A commander or other person serving in a position designated by the Secretary concerned as either a position analogous to an officer in charge or a position of command, who has control over the place where the property or person to be searched is situated or found, or, if that place is not under military control, having control over persons subject to military law or the law of war; or

(2) *Military judge.* A military judge or magistrate if authorized under regulations prescribed by the Secretary of Defense or the Secretary concerned. An otherwise impartial authorizing official does not lose the character merely because he or she is present at the scene of a search or is otherwise readily available to persons who may seek the issuance of a search authorization; nor does such an official lose impartial character merely because the official previously and impartially authorized investigative activities when such previous authorization is similar in intent or function to a pretrial authorization made by the United States district courts. . . .

(f) *Basis for Search authorizations.*

(1) *Probable cause requirement.* A search authorization issued under this rule must be based upon probable cause.

(2) *Probable cause determination.* Probable cause to search exists when there is a reasonable belief that the person, property, or evidence sought is located in the place or on the person to be searched. A search authorization may be based upon hearsay evidence in whole or in part. A determination of probable cause under this rule shall be based upon any or all of the following:

(A) Written statements communicated to the authorizing officer;

(B) Oral statements communicated to the authorizing official in person, via telephone, or by other appropriate means of communication; or

(C) Such information as may be known by the authorizing official that would not preclude the officer from acting in an impartial fashion. . . .

(g) *Exigencies.* A search warrant or search authorization is not required under this rule for a search based on probable cause when:

(1) *Insufficient time.* There is a reasonable belief that the delay necessary to obtain a search warrant or search authorization would result in the removal, destruction, or concealment of the property or evidence sought;

(2) *Lack of communications.* There is a reasonable military operational necessity that is reasonably believed to prohibit or prevent communication with a person empowered to grant a search warrant or authorization and there is a reasonable belief that the delay necessary to obtain a search warrant or search authorization would result in the removal, destruction, or concealment of the property or evidence sought;

(3) *Search of operable vehicle.* An operable vehicle is to be searched, except in the circumstances where a search warrant or authorization is required by the Constitution of the United States, this Manual, or these rules; or

(4) *Not required by the Constitution.* A search warrant or authorization is not otherwise required by the Constitution of the United States as applied to members of the armed forces. For purpose of this rule, a vehicle is "operable" unless a reasonable person would have known at the time of search that the vehicle was not functional for purposes of transportation. . . .

NOTE

Military appellate courts have expressly held that the good faith exception to the exclusionary rule applies to searches authorized by commanders. *United States v. Lopez*, 35 M.J. 35 (C.M.A. 1992). To properly authorize a search, a commanding officer must be neutral and detached. A commander who abandons his or her neutrality by, for example, personally engaging in a criminal investigation loses the power to authorize a search. *See, e.g., United States v. Murray*, 12 M.J. 139 (C.M.A. 1981).

Military Rule of Evidence 313
Manual for Courts-Martial, United States (2005 ed.)

Inspections and inventories in the armed forces

(a) *General rule.* Evidence obtained from inspections and inventories in the armed forces conducted in accordance with this rule is admissible at trial when relevant and not otherwise inadmissible under these rules.

(b) *Inspections.* An "inspection" is an examination of the whole or part of a unit, organization, installation, vessel, aircraft, or vehicle, including an examination conducted at entrance and exit points, conducted as an incident of command the primary purpose of which is to determine and to ensure the security, military fitness, or good order and discipline of the unit, organization, installation, vessel, aircraft, or vehicle. An inspection may include but is not limited to an examination to determine and to ensure that any or all of the following requirements are met: that the command is properly equipped, functioning properly, maintaining proper standards of readiness, sea or air worthiness, sanitation and cleanliness, and that personnel are present, fit, and ready for duty. An inspection also includes an examination to locate and confiscate unlawful weapons and other contraband. An order to produce body fluids, such as urine, is permissible in accordance with this rule. An examination made for the primary purpose of obtaining evidence for use in a trial by court-martial or in other disciplinary proceedings is not an inspection within the meaning of this rule. If a purpose of an examination is to locate weapons or contraband, and if: (1) the examination was directed immediately following a report of a specific offense in the unit, organization, installation, vessel, aircraft, or vehicle and was not previously scheduled; (2) specific individuals are selected for examination; or (3) persons examined are subjected to substantially different intrusions during the same examination, the prosecution must prove by clear and convincing evidence that the examination was an inspection within the meaning of this rule. Inspections shall be conducted in a reasonable fashion and shall comply with Mil. R. Evid. 312, if applicable. Inspections may utilize any reasonable natural or technological aid and may be conducted with or without notice to those inspected. Unlawful weapons, contraband, or other evidence of crime located during an inspection may be seized. . . .

UNITED STATES v. GARDNER
United States Court of Military Appeals
41 M.J. 189 (C.M.T. 1994)

WISS, J. . . .

We reaffirm that it is constitutionally permissible to require servicemembers to submit to urine samples as part of an inspection. *United States v. Bickel*, 30 M.J. 277, 285 (C.M.A. 1990). We hold that this urinalysis was a valid inspection and not an impermissible pretextual search.

On July 30, 1990, Captain (CPT) Westburg, Commander of Headquarters and Headquarter's Company, 21st Theater Army Area Command (TAACOM) in Kaiserslautern, Germany, ordered a random unit urinalysis test. As appellant was assigned to this unit, he participated in this test. However, appellant did not submit a urine specimen but instead submitted a fluid specimen containing only water but no human urine. Appellant's willful failure to provide the required urine specimen resulted in the charged offense of dereliction of duty.

At trial, the defense moved to suppress the urinalysis results as the fruit of an illegal search because the entire 21st TAACOM urinalysis program was unconstitutional. Appellant argued that the Army abused its once-valid urinalysis inspection scheme by converting it into a pretextual search without probable cause and a tool for uncovering criminal evidence — essentially that the Army drug urinalysis program "has gone awry." Appellant asserted that the intrusiveness of the urinalysis, both in its manner (i.e., lack of privacy) and scope (i.e., results used in criminal prosecutions), took the Army's procedure out of the narrow exemption from traditional Fourth Amendment restrictions that has been carved out for legitimate urinalysis inspections. Appellant claimed that this case presents the provocative situation mentioned in footnote 5 of *Skinner v. Railway Labor Executives' Association*, 489 U.S. 602, 621 (1989), that states: "We leave for another day the question whether routine use in criminal prosecutions of evidence obtained pursuant to the administrative scheme would give rise to an inference of pretext, or otherwise impugn the administrative nature of the FRA [Federal Railroad Administration]'s program." Appellant relied on three principal matters to support the argument: first, a regulation that requires positive urinalysis test results to be reported to military law enforcement agencies: para. 4d(1), U.S. Army Europe Reg. 190-2, Military Police — USAREUR Drug Suppression Plan (20 Sep. 1991); second, CPT Westburg's written unit policy of no toleration of use of illegal drugs and promise of harsh treatment for drug offenses; and third, voluminous statistics of disciplinary action taken by various commands in the 21st TAACOM regarding positive urinalysis test results. As explained below, a careful review of these and other relevant matters leads us to reject appellant's argument.

In *United States v. Bickel, supra,* this Court held that requiring servicemembers to submit urine samples as part of an inspection is constitutionally permissible. This Court expressly recognized the differences between drug-testing procedures in the armed services and those upheld in *National Treasury Employees Union v. Von Raab,* 489 U.S. 656 (1989), and *Skinner v. Railway Labor Executives' Association, supra,* yet stated several reasons for concluding that testing of servicemembers pursuant to a Mil. R. Evid. 313, Manual for Courts-Martial, United States, 1984, inspection is constitutionally valid. 30 M.J. at 282-86. We have reviewed our rationale and holding in *Bickel* and reaffirm that both remain valid. Chief Judge Everett's observation in an earlier case concisely states the position of the present unanimous Court on this issue:

> The experience of recent years makes clear that mandatory drug testing of servicemembers contributes substantially to reduction of drug use in the armed services and to making the military community drug free. In our view, compulsory urinalysis is appropriate and necessary to maintain the effectiveness of the military establishment.

Unger v. Ziemniak, 27 M.J. 349, 357 (C.M.A. 1989) (footnote omitted).

Although approving the urinalysis inspection in *Bickel,* this Court stated that it "might take a different view if the drug testing were designed solely to obtain evidence for criminal prosecution." 30 M.J. at 285. We still need not address that situation, for the Government has established that the present urinalysis was a valid inspection and not a pretext or subterfuge for an otherwise illegal search. . . .

Mil. R. Evid. 313(a) states that evidence obtained during an inspection is admissible. Mil. R. Evid. 313(b) defines an "inspection" as "an examination of the whole or part of a unit . . . conducted as an incident of command the primary purpose of which is to . . . ensure the security, military fitness, or good order and discipline of the unit. . . ." Mil. R. Evid. 313(b) states that "an order to produce . . . urine, is permissible" but "an examination made for the primary purpose of obtaining evidence for use in a trial . . . is not an inspection . . . ." The litmus test is whether the examination is made primarily for administrative purposes or instead for obtaining incriminating evidence. The former is admissible under the rule, while the latter is not. What the Court said in *United States v. Barnett,* 18 M.J. 166, 169 (C.M.A. 1984), regarding an inventory is equally true of an inspection: "The case law does not indicate that the results of an inventory will be inadmissible in evidence when the inventory has been performed by someone whose 'secondary purpose' was to seek evidence of crime." *See United States v. Williams*, 35 M.J. 323 (C.M.A. 1992). . . .

Although the military judge's finding regarding the "primary purpose" is a matter of fact, the issue of whether the examination is an inspection is a matter of law that this Court will review de novo. . . .

The administrative nature of the Army urinalysis program is unquestionable. Even trial defense counsel conceded that the Army urinalysis program is at least facially administrative in nature and that any criminal prosecution which results from urinalysis testing would appear to be merely ancillary to the inspection rationale of the urinalysis testing.

Moreover, we are not presented with the situation where appellant asserts that he was improperly targeted for urinalysis. . . . Appellant instead asserts that his unit commander's purpose was to obtain criminal evidence. The record does not support this contention.

In February 1990, prior to the urinalysis ordered and involved here, CPT Westburg published a command alcohol and drug abuse policy that included the following statements:

> 1. The abuse of alcohol and use of illegal drugs will not be tolerated by this command. . . .

> 5. Any member of this company who is involved in the use of illegal drugs will be dealt with harshly. The minimum punishment will be non-judicial under article 15 [10 U.S.C. § 815] and the maximum punishment could be separation for the service.

At trial CPT Westburg testified that the only purpose of the urinalysis program was "to deter the use of drugs." She explained that this deterrence was accomplished by each soldier's knowing that "if they come up positive on a urinalysis that some punitive action can be taken." She published her policy on drugs to make it clear to soldiers what can result from a positive urinalysis. Essentially, CPT Westburg established a command policy that each soldier would be accountable for drug abuse. This statement of command policy alone did not make the urinalysis program primarily a tool for criminal prosecution. CPT Westburg testified that she always ordered the urinalysis for the purpose of "unit discipline, health and welfare, and as a deterrent for the use of illegal drugs." She specifically stated that, in ordering this particular urinalysis, her concerns were "good order and discipline; health, welfare, morale of the unit." She stated it was not her purpose to develop evidence to be used in a punitive or criminal proceeding and denied that she had ever ordered a urinalysis test for the sole reason of gathering evidence to use against someone.

CPT Westburg revealed that she had ordered approximately 20 random unit urinalyses that resulted in approximately 2,200 specimens being provided. Of these, only three specimens tested positive for drugs — one servicemember tested positive twice and another servicemember tested positive only once. Each individual received one Article 15 punishment, and neither was court-martialed. The soldier who twice tested positive was not punished for the second drug offense but was administratively processed for discharge.

After viewing CPT Westburg's testimony and her record of handling positive urinalyses, we uphold the military judge's factual finding that the primary purpose of this urinalysis was to protect the health of soldiers and their welfare and the readiness of the unit to accomplish its assigned mission.

Appellant's reliance on the number of Article 15 punishments following urinalyses revealing drug abuse in various commands in the 21st TAACOM to establish a pattern of prosecution is unpersuasive. Appellant's data is general, vague, incomplete, and fails to present an accurate record of positive urinalyis testing and dispositions taken. We reject appellant's argument that the large number of Article 15 punishments for drug offenses establishes that this inspection became a subterfuge. More importantly, CPT Westburg's decision not to punish but to process administratively the soldier who failed a second urinalysis test belies any assertion that the purpose of this urinalysis was other than for discipline, health, and welfare purposes and to deter illegal drug use.

Finally, the record does establish that in Europe, positive urinalysis results are reported to military law enforcement agencies. Para. 4d(1), Army Europe Reg. 190-2, Military Police — USAREUR Drug Suppression Plan (20 Sep. 1991). However, we have stated that, even though positive results of drug tests are made available to prosecutors, this requirement alone does not render the inspection an unreasonable intrusion. *See United States v. Bickel*, 30 M.J. at 282 and 285.

Having scrutinized the urinalysis at issue, we conclude that appellant's prosecution was merely incidental punitive action ancillary to an otherwise justifiable inspection. Neither the command policy letter nor the routine provision of test results to law enforcement agencies destroyed the validity of the otherwise lawful urinalysis inspection. As this was a lawful command-ordered urinalysis and inspection, evidence of appellant's substitute specimen was admissible to prove appellant's dereliction-of-duty offense. . . .

NOTE AND QUESTIONS

Do you agree with the *Gardner* court's conclusion that the primary purpose of the urinalysis was non-criminal? As a matter of policy, should urinalysis results be admissible at courts-martial? *See generally* Cynthia D. Marino, *Is the Army's Urinalysis Program Constitutional Under the Fourth Amendment in Light of* von Raab *and* Skinner?: *The Defense Perspective*, ARMY LAW., Dec. 1990, at 12.

IV.   PRIVILEGES

UNITED STATES v. RODRIGUEZ
United States Court of Appeals for the Armed Forces
54 M.J. 156 (C.A.A.F. 2000)

CHIEF JUDGE CRAWFORD announced the judgment of the Court and delivered an opinion in which JUDGE EFFRON joined. . . .

The Proposed Federal Rules of Evidence were submitted to the Supreme Court in October 1971. The Rules as originally approved by the Supreme Court on November 20, 1972, set forth in Article V nine nonconstitutional privilege rules applicable to federal trials, including a proposed psychotherapist-patient privilege. After these proposed Rules were sent to Congress, the Subcommittee on Criminal Justice of the Committee on the Judiciary of the House of Reprentatives held open hearings on the Proposed Rules. As a result of these hearings and numerous conferences, Congress did not accept the proposed privilege rules because a consensus could not be achieved as to a number of privileges. S. Rep. No. 1277, 93d Cong. 2d Sess. (1974), *reprinted in* 1974 U.S. Code Congressional & Administrative News 7051, 7052, 7053, 7058; *see also* Title 28 USCA Federal Rules of Evidence (Rules 701 to End) 614, 615, 620. Instead, Congress adopted Fed. R. Evid. 501:

> Except as otherwise required by the Constitution of the United States or provided by Act of Congress or in rules prescribed by the Supreme Court pursuant to statutory authority, the privilege of a witness, person, government, State, or political subdivision thereof shall be governed by the principles of the common law as they may be interpreted by the courts of the United States in the light of reason and experience. However, in civil actions and proceedings, with respect to an element of a claim or defense as to which State law supplies the rule of decision, the privilege of a witness, person, government, State, or political subdivision thereof shall be determined in accordance with State law.

The Rules, as revised by Congress, were approved by President Ford on January 2, 1975. Pub. L. No. 93-595, 88 Stat. 1926.

In contrast to the Federal Rules of Evidence, Congress has delegated to the President the authority to issue rules of evidence for courts-martial. *See* Art. 36. Under this authority, the President promulgated the Military Rules of Evidence in 1980, which were based upon the Federal Rules of Evidence, subject to exceptions based upon practicability and conformance with the Uniform Code of Military Justice. *See* Drafter's Analysis of Mil. R. Evid. 501, [MANUAL FOR COURTS-MARTIAL, UNITED STATES] (1998 ed.) at A22-37.

The President, in the Military Rules of Evidence, did not follow the approach taken by the Federal Rules of Evidence. Instead of a general rule allowing the courts to develop privileges through a common-law approach, *see* Fed. R. Evid. 501, the rules promulgated by the President used a combination of specific rules and a limited authority to incorporate common-law privileges. As noted in the Drafter's Analysis:

> Unlike the Article III court system, which is conducted almost entirely by attorneys functioning in conjunction with permanent courts in fixed locations, the military criminal legal system is characterized by its dependence upon large numbers of laymen, temporary courts, and inherent geographical and personnel instability due to the worldwide deployment of military personnel. Consequently, military law requires far more stability than civilian law. This is particularly true because of the significant number of non-lawyers involved in the military criminal legal system. Commanders, convening authorities, non-lawyer

investigating officers, summary court-martial officers, or law enforce-ment personnel need specific guidance as to what material is privi-leged and what is not.

Drafter's Analysis of Mil. R. Evid. 501, Manual, *supra* (1998 ed.) at A22-37. The privileges set forth by the President "provide the certainty and stability necessary for military justice." *Id.*

In *United States v. Scheffer*, 523 U.S. 303 (1998), the Supreme Court recog-nized that the President may promulgate rules of evidence for the military, which

> do not abridge an accused's right to present a defense so long as they are not "arbitrary" or "disproportionate to the purposes they are designed to serve." Moreover, we have found the exclusion of evidence to be unconstitutionally arbitrary or disproportionate only where it has infringed upon a weighty interest of the accused.

523 U.S. at 308 (citations omitted); *see also id.* at 323 & n.4.

The purpose of the Military Rules was to provide predictability, clarity, and certainty through specific rules rather than a case-by-case adjudication of what the rules of evidence would be. The addition of Mil. R. Evid. 501 is con-stitutional and an appropriate exercise of the President's authority under Article 36. We hold that Mil. R. Evid. 501 "is a rational and proportional means of advancing the legitimate interests of the military." *See* 523 U.S. at 312.

Mil. R. Evid. 501 provides in part:

> (a) A person may not claim a privilege with respect to any matter except as required by or provided for in:
>
> > (1) The Constitution of the United States as applied to members of the armed forces;
> >
> > (2) An Act of Congress applicable to trials by courts-martial;
> >
> > (3) These rules or this Manual; or
> >
> > (4) The principles of common law generally recognized in the trial of criminal cases in the United States district courts pur-suant to *rule 501 of the Federal Rules of Evidence* insofar as the application of such principles in trials by courts-martial is prac-ticable and not contrary to or inconsistent with the code, these rules, or this Manual. . . .
>
> (d) Notwithstanding any other provision of these rules, information not otherwise privileged does not become privileged on the basis that it was acquired by a medical officer or civilian physician in a profes-sional capacity.

Although the originally enumerated privileges contained within Mil. R. Evid. 502-509 establish the stability necessary for military justice, the President, in promulgating Mil. R. Evid. 501, provided a modest degree of flex-ibility in the application of federal common-law privileges to courts-martial.

Drafter's Analysis of Mil. R. Evid. 501, Manual, *supra* (1998 ed.) at A22-37. Mil. R. Evid. 501(a)(4) adopts the privileges recognized at common law pursuant to Fed. R. Evid. 501, insofar as "practicable and not contrary to or inconsistent with" the Code, the Military Rules of Evidence, or the Manual for Courts-Martial. . . .

NOTE

In *United States v. Rodriguez*, the Court of Appeals for the Armed Forces declined to recognize the psychotherapist-patient privilege that the Supreme Court established in *Jaffee v. Redmond*, 518 U.S. 1 (1996). In 1999, the President established a psychotherapist-patient privilege in a new Military Rule of Evidence 513. *See* Exec. Order No. 13,140, 64 FED. REG. 55,115, 55, 116 (Oct. 12, 1999). *See generally* Lt. Col. R. Peter Masteron, *The Military's Psychotherapist-Patient Privilege: Benefit or Bane for Military Accused?*, ARMY LAW., Nov. 2001, at 18.

2 Stephen A. Saltzburg, Lee D. Schinasi & David A. Schlueter, *Military Rules of Evidence Manual* 5-6 (5th ed. 2003)
Rule 501 Editorial Comment

Introduction to Section V

Like Section III [of the Military Rules of Evidence], which adds criminal procedure rules to the basic model of the Federal Rules of Evidence, Section V adds substantial material not found in the Federal Rules of Evidence. Article V of the Federal Rules contains only one Rule, Rule 501, as a result of a sometimes bitter struggle over specific rules of privilege. Rather than delay the adoption of the rest of the evidence rules while it debated privilege rules, Congress opted to follow the common law approach previously mandated by Rule 26 of the Federal Rules of Criminal Procedure.

Section V of the Military Rules does follow the Federal Rule to the extent that it recognizes federal common law, but also it provides for nine specific privileges. Additional privileges are located in Rules 301, 302, and 303. Most of the privileges in Section V are "communications" privileges. That is, there is a privilege for any confidential communications between the persons designated in the particular rule. Other rules, however, create privileges for non-communicative information. Rule 504, for example, recognizes a testimonial (or capacity) privilege and Rule 507 recognizes a privilege for a person's identity.

The drafters chose to include specific privileges in order to provide concrete guidance to a world-wide criminal justice system which makes wide use of lay persons in disposing of criminal charges. The specific provisions drew heavily from both prior *Manual* provisions and the proposed Federal Rules on Privilege which were rejected by Congress.

The privileges in Section V apply in virtually all proceedings conducted pursuant to provisions of the Uniform Code of Military Justice. This includes pretrial investigations, hearings on vacations of suspended sentences, search authorizations, and pretrial confinement determinations. *See* Rule 1101.

Section V covers not only oral testimony, but also situations in which a person claims a privilege not to testify at all or a privilege to decline to produce real evidence. It governs claims by witnesses, potential witnesses, and non-witnesses who wish to prevent disclosure of material.

NOTES AND QUESTIONS

1. The privileges expressly recognized in Section V of the Military Rules of Evidence are: (1) the lawyer-client privilege, Mil. R. Evid. 502; (2) the communications to clergy privilege, Mil. R. Evid. 503; (3) the husband-wife privilege, which includes both a spousal incapacity rule and a privilege for marital communications, Mil. R. Evid. 504; (4) the classified information privilege, Mil. R. Evid. 505, which is discussed in the next section; (5) the government information privilege, Mil. R. Evid. 506; (6) the identity of informant privilege, Mil. R. Evid. 507, (7) the political vote privilege, Mil. R. Evid. 508; (8) the deliberative privilege, Mil. R. Evid. 509; *see also* Mil R. Evid. 606, 606; and (9) the psychotherapist-patient privilege, Mil. R. Evid. 513.

2. The military does not recognize a general doctor-patient privilege. The Military Rules of Evidence's drafters observed: "Rule 501(d) prevents the application of a doctor-patient privilege. Such a privilege was considered to be totally incompatible with the clear interest of the armed forces in ensuring the health and fitness for duty of personnel." Mil. R. Evid. 501 drafters' analysis, MANUAL FOR COURTS-MARTIAL, UNITED STATES, at A22-38 (2005 ed.). The authors of the highly respected *Military Rules of Evidence Manual* note that Rule 501(d) "continues pre-Rules practice by specifically declining to recognize a doctor-patient privilege." 2 STEPHEN A. SALTZBURG, ET AL., MILITARY RULES OF EVIDENCE MANUAL 5-10 (5th ed. 2003).

3. In 2004, in the wake of sexual assault scandals at the United States military academies, Congress convened an expert task force to study the problem and identify solutions. The task force concluded that a lack of confidentiality hindered reporting and investigation of sexual violence, and recommended that Congress create a statutory privilege protecting communications between victims and health care providers and victim advocates. *See* REPORT OF THE DEFENSE TASK FORCE ON SEXUAL HARASSMENT AND VIOLENCE AT THE MILITARY SERVICE ACADEMIES 26 (Jun. 2005). The task force also recommended that commanders be permitted to close Article 32 hearings (pre-trial investigations) in order to protect victim confidentiality. *Id.* at 33. Do you support either recommendation? Why or why not? *See* Major Paul M. Schimpf, *Talk the Talk, Now Walk the Walk: Giving an Absolute Privilege to Communications between a Victim and Victim Advocate in the Military*, 185 MIL. L. REV. 149 (2005).

V. CLASSIFIED EVIDENCE

UNITED STATES v. DUNCAN
United States Army Court of Criminal Appeals
34 M.J. 1232 (A.C.C.A. 1992)

NAUGHTON, SENIOR JUDGE. . . .

"'Greymail' occurs when a defendant seeks to disclose classified information as part of his or her defense, requiring the government either to permit disclosure or to dismiss the prosecution." *United States v. Smith*, 899 F.2d 564, 565 n.1 (6th Cir. 1990), *cert. denied*, 112 L. Ed. 2d 103, 111 S. Ct. 135 (1990). There is also a potential for "greymail" when a defendant seeks discovery of classified information, thus compelling the government to produce or to drop the prosecution. *See United States v. Sarkissian*, 841 F.2d 959, 965 (9th Cir. 1988). . . .

Well aware that potential disclosure of such matters in an open forum might frustrate the ends of criminal justice by deterring prosecution, Congress passed the Classified Information Procedures Act, 18 U.S.C. App. §§ 1-16 (1982). *See United States v. Sarkissian*, 841 F.2d at 965 (citing S. Rep. No. 823, 96th Cong., 2d Sess. 4 (1980), reprinted in U.S.C.C.A.N. 4294, 4297). . . . CIPA permits the government "to have the trial court examine classified information in camera and ex parte" prior to disclosure to the defendant and prior to admission into evidence for a determination "whether it is necessary for the defense, or if a proffered substitution would suffice to protect the defendant's constitutional rights and the secrecy of the information." *United States v. Smith*, 899 F.2d at 565 n.1. CIPA also requires the defendant to disclose all classified information in his possession which he intends to offer at trial; the government may also obtain a preliminary ruling as to the admissibility of these matters as well. *See generally United States v. Collins*, 720 F.2d 1195 (11th Cir. 1983). . . .

Military Rule of Evidence 505 mirrors CIPA.

NOTES AND QUESTIONS

1. The leading military justice case construing Military Rule of Evidence 505 is *United States v. Lonetree*, 35 M.J. 396 (C.M.A. 1992), *cert. denied*, 507 U.S. 1017 (1993), which is set out and discussed in Chapter 14, § 2. The Court of Appeals for the Armed Forces observed:

> Mil. R. Evid. 505 recognizes a classified-information privilege. Under that Rule, consistent with civilian law, the accused is entitled to pierce that privilege where the "classified information . . . apparently contains evidence that is relevant and necessary to an element of the offense or a legally cognizable defense and is otherwise admissible in evidence. . . ." Mil. R. Evid. 505(f). . . . [T]he possible remedies where the Government refuses to relinquish classified information include dismissal [of the charges]. Mil. R. Evid. 505(i)(4)(E)(iv).

The court provocatively questioned "whether a balancing can be conducted consistent with due process and Mil. R. Evid. 505 if the evidence is in fact essential to a fair determination of the cause," suggesting that, in practice, Military Rule of Evidence 505 must yield to the accused's right to present a full defense.

2. For a detailed analysis of Military Rule of Evidence 505 using *Lonetree* as a case study, see Major Joshua E. Kastenberg, *Analyzing the Constitutional Tensions and Applicability of Military Rule of Evidence 505 in Courts-Martial Over United States Service Members: Secrecy in the Shadow of* Lonetree, 55 A.F. L. REV. 233 (2004).

3. As Major Kastenberg observes, while cases involving classified information are hardly rare in the military justice system, Military Rule of Evidence 505 was used little before *Lonetree* and has been little analyzed since. *Id.* at 233-34.

VI.   POLYGRAPH RESULTS

Military Rule of Evidence 707
Manual for Courts-Martial, United States (2005 ed.)

Polygraph Examinations

(a) Notwithstanding any other provision of law, the results of a polygraph examination, the opinion of a polygraph examiner, or any reference to an offer to take, failure to take, or taking of a polygraph examination, shall not be admitted into evidence.

(b) Nothing in this section is intended to exclude from evidence statements made during a polygraph examination which are otherwise admissible.

Drafters' Analysis

Rule 707 is new and is similar to Cal. Evid. Code 351.1 (West 1988 Supp.). The Rule prohibits the use of polygraph evidence in courts-martial and is based on several policy grounds. There is a real danger that court members will be misled by polygraph evidence that "is likely to be shrouded with an aura of near infallibility." *United States v. Alexander*, 526 F.2d 161, 168-69 (8th Cir. 1975). To the extent that the members accept polygraph evidence as unimpeachable or conclusive, despite cautionary instructions from the military judge, the members' "traditional responsibility to collectively ascertain the facts and adjudge guilt or innocence is preempted." *Id.* There is also a danger of confusion of the issues, especially when conflicting polygraph evidence diverts the members' attention from a determination of guilt or innocence to a judgment of the validity and limitations of polygraphs. This could result in the court-martial degenerating into a trial of the polygraph machine. *State v. Grier*, 300 S.E.2d 351 (N.C. 1983). Polygraph evidence also can result in a substantial waste of time when the collateral issues regarding the reliability of the particular test and qualifications of the specific polygraph examiner must be litigated in every case. Polygraph evidence places a burden on the administration of justice that outweighs the probative value of the evidence. The reliability of polygraph evidence has not been sufficiently established and its use at trial impinges upon the integrity of the judicial system. *See People v. Kegler*, 242 Cal. Rptr. 897 (Cal. Ct. App. 1987). Thus, this amendment adopts a bright-line rule that polygraph evidence is not admissible by any party to a court-martial even if stipulated to by the parties. This amendment is not intended to accept or reject *United States v. Gipson*, 24 M.J. 343 (C.M.A. 1987), concerning the standard for admissibility of other scientific evidence under Mil. R. Evid. 702 or the continued vitality of *Frye v. United States*, 293 F. 1013 (D.C. Cir. 1923). Finally, subsection (b) of the rule ensures that any statements which are otherwise admissible are not rendered inadmissible solely because the statements were made during a polygraph examination.

NOTE

While Military Rule of Evidence 707's drafters' analysis indicates that the rule is similar to California Evidence Code §351.1, there is actually an enormous difference between the two rules. Military Rule of Evidence 707 adopts an absolute ban on the admissibility of polygraph results while section 351.1 of the California Evidence Code prohibits the admissibility of polygraph results "unless all parties stipulate to the admission of such results." CAL. EVID. CODE § 351.1 (2006). The stipulation exception was in the California statute at the time Military Rule of Evidence 707 was drafted. *See Arden v. State Bar*, 739 P.2d 1236, 1241 n.10 (Cal. 1987) (quoting CAL. EVID. CODE §351.1).

UNITED STATES v. SCHEFFER
Supreme Court of the United States
523 U.S. 303 (1998)

THOMAS, J., announced the judgment of the Court and delivered the opinion of the Court with respect to Parts I, II-A, and II-D, in which REHNQUIST, C.J., and O'CONNOR, SCALIA, KENNEDY, SOUTER, GINSBURG, and BREYER, JJ., joined, and an opinion with respect to Parts II-B and II-C, in which REHNQUIST, C.J., and SCALIA and SOUTER, JJ., joined. KENNEDY, J., filed an opinion concurring in part and concurring in the judgment, in which O'CONNOR, GINSBURG, and BREYER, JJ., joined. STEVENS, J., filed a dissenting opinion.

THOMAS, J.:

This case presents the question whether Military Rule of Evidence 707, which makes polygraph evidence inadmissible in court-martial proceedings, unconstitutionally abridges the right of accused members of the military to present a defense. We hold that it does not.

I

In March 1992, respondent Edward Scheffer, an airman stationed at March Air Force Base in California, volunteered to work as an informant on drug investigations for the Air Force Office of Special Investigations (OSI). His OSI supervisors advised him that, from time to time during the course of his undercover work, they would ask him to submit to drug testing and polygraph examinations. In early April, one of the OSI agents supervising respondent requested that he submit to a urine test. Shortly after providing the urine sample, but before the results of the test were known, respondent agreed to take a polygraph test administered by an OSI examiner. In the opinion of the examiner, the test "indicated no deception" when respondent denied using drugs since joining the Air Force.

On April 30, respondent unaccountably failed to appear for work and could not be found on the base. He was absent without leave until May 13, when an Iowa state patrolman arrested him following a routine traffic stop and held him for return to the base. OSI agents later learned that respondent's urinalysis revealed the presence of methamphetamine.

Respondent was tried by general court-martial on charges of using methamphetamine, failing to go to his appointed place of duty, wrongfully absenting himself from the base for 13 days, and, with respect to an unrelated matter, uttering 17 insufficient funds checks. He testified at trial on his own behalf, relying upon an "innocent ingestion" theory and denying that he had knowingly used drugs while working for OSI. On cross-examination, the prosecution attempted to impeach respondent with inconsistencies between his trial testimony and earlier statements he had made to OSI.

Respondent sought to introduce the polygraph evidence in support of his testimony that he did not knowingly use drugs. The military judge denied the motion, relying on Military Rule of Evidence 707, which provides, in relevant part:

> (a) Notwithstanding any other provision of law, the results of a polygraph examination, the opinion of a polygraph examiner, or any reference to an offer to take, failure to take, or taking of a polygraph examination, shall not be admitted into evidence.

The military judge determined that Rule 707 was constitutional because "the President may, through the Rules of Evidence, determine that credibility is not an area in which a fact finder needs help, and the polygraph is not a process that has sufficient scientific acceptability to be relevant." App. 28. He further reasoned that the factfinder might give undue weight to the polygraph examiner's testimony, and that collateral arguments about such evidence could consume "an inordinate amount of time and expense." *Ibid.*

Respondent was convicted on all counts and was sentenced to a bad-conduct discharge, confinement for 30 months, total forfeiture of all pay and allowances, and reduction to the lowest enlisted grade. The Air Force Court of Criminal Appeals affirmed in all material respects, explaining that Rule 707 "does not arbitrarily limit the accused's ability to present reliable evidence." 41 M.J. 683, 691 (1995) (en banc).

By a 3-to-2 vote, the United States Court of Appeals for the Armed Forces reversed. 44 M.J. 442 (1996). Without pointing to any particular language in the Sixth Amendment, the Court of Appeals held that "[a] *per se* exclusion of polygraph evidence offered by an accused to rebut an attack on his credibility . . . violates his Sixth Amendment right to present a defense." *Id.,* at 445. Judge Crawford, dissenting, stressed that a defendant's right to present relevant evidence is not absolute, that relevant evidence can be excluded for valid reasons, and that Rule 707 was supported by a number of valid justifications. *Id.,* at 449-451. We granted certiorari, 520 U.S. 1227 (1997), and we now reverse.

II

A defendant's right to present relevant evidence is not unlimited, but rather is subject to reasonable restrictions. *See Taylor v. Illinois,* 484 U.S. 400, 410 (1988); *Rock v. Arkansas,* 483 U.S. 44, 55 (1987); *Chambers v. Mississippi,* 410 U.S. 284, 295 (1973). A defendant's interest in presenting such evidence may thus "'bow to accommodate other legitimate interests in the criminal trial process.'" *Rock, supra,* at 55 (quoting *Chambers, supra,* at 295); *accord, Michigan v. Lucas,* 500 U.S. 145, 149 (1991). As a result, state and federal rulemakers have broad latitude under the Constitution to establish rules excluding evidence from criminal trials. Such rules do not abridge an accused's right to present a defense so long as they are not "arbitrary" or "disproportionate to the purposes they are designed to serve." *Rock, supra,* at 56; *accord, Lucas, supra,* at 151. Moreover, we have found the exclusion of evidence to be unconstitutionally arbitrary or disproportionate only where it has infringed upon a weighty interest of the accused. *See Rock, supra,* at 58; *Chambers, supra,* at 302; *Washington v. Texas,* 388 U.S. 14, 22-23 (1967).

Rule 707 serves several legitimate interests in the criminal trial process. These interests include ensuring that only reliable evidence is introduced at trial, preserving the court members' role in determining credibility, and avoiding litigation that is collateral to the primary purpose of the trial. The Rule is neither arbitrary nor disproportionate in promoting these ends. Nor does it implicate a sufficiently weighty interest of the defendant to raise a constitutional concern under our precedents.

A

State and Federal Governments unquestionably have a legitimate interest in ensuring that reliable evidence is presented to the trier of fact in a criminal trial. Indeed, the exclusion of unreliable evidence is a principal objective of many evidentiary rules. *See, e.g.,* Fed. Rules Evid. 702, 802, 901; *see also Daubert v. Merrell Dow Pharmaceuticals, Inc.,* 509 U.S. 579, 589 (1993).

The contentions of respondent and the dissent notwithstanding, there is simply no consensus that polygraph evidence is reliable. To this day, the scientific community remains extremely polarized about the reliability of polygraph techniques. 1 D. Faigman, D. Kaye, M. Saks, & J. Sanders, Modern Scientific Evidence 565, n.†, §14-2.0 to §14-7.0 (1997); *see also* 1 P. Giannelli & E. Imwinkelried, Scientific Evidence §8-2(C), pp. 225-227 (2d ed. 1993) (hereinafter Giannelli & Imwinkelried); 1 J. Strong, McCormick on Evidence §206, p. 909 (4th ed. 1992) (hereinafter McCormick). Some studies have concluded that polygraph tests overall are accurate and reliable. *See, e.g.,* S. Abrams, The Complete Polygraph Handbook 190-191 (1989) (reporting the overall accuracy rate from laboratory studies involving the common "control question technique" polygraph to be "in the range of 87 percent"). Others have found that polygraph tests assess truthfulness significantly less accurately — that scientific field studies suggest the accuracy rate of the "control question technique" polygraph is "little better than could be obtained by the toss of a coin," that is, 50 percent. *See* Iacono & Lykken, *The Scientific Status of Research on Polygraph Techniques: The Case Against Polygraph Tests, in* 1 Modern Scientific Evidence, *supra,* § 14-5.3, at 629 (hereinafter Iacono & Lykken).

This lack of scientific consensus is reflected in the disagreement among state and federal courts concerning both the admissibility and the reliability of polygraph evidence. Although some Federal Courts of Appeals have abandoned the *per se* rule excluding polygraph evidence, leaving its admission or exclusion to the discretion of district courts under *Daubert, see, e.g., United States v. Posado,* 57 F.3d 428, 434 (5th Cir. 1995); *United States v. Cordoba,* 104 F.3d 225, 228 (9th Cir. 1997), at least one Federal Circuit has recently reaffirmed its *per se* ban, *see United States v. Sanchez,* 118 F.3d 192, 197 (4th Cir. 1997), and another recently noted that it has "not decided whether polygraphy has reached a sufficient state of reliability to be admissible." *United States v. Messina,* 131 F.3d 36, 42 (2d Cir. 1997). Most States maintain *per se* rules excluding polygraph evidence. *See, e.g., State v. Porter,* 241 Conn. 57, 92-95, 698 A.2d 739, 758-759 (1997); *People v. Gard,* 158 Ill. 2d 191, 202-204, 632 N.E.2d 1026, 1032 (1994); *In re Odell,* 672 A.2d 457, 459 (R.I. 1996) *(per curiam); Perkins v. State,* 902 S.W.2d 88, 94-95 (Ct. App. Tex. 1995). New Mexico is unique in making polygraph evidence generally admissible without the prior stipulation of the parties and without significant restriction. *See* N.M. Rule Evid. §11-707. Whatever their approach, state and federal courts continue to express doubt about whether such evidence is reliable. *See, e.g., United States v. Messina, supra,* at 42; *United States v. Posado, supra,* at 434; *State v. Porter, supra,* at 126-127, 698 A.2d, at 774; *Perkins v. State, supra,* at 94; *People v. Gard, supra,* at 202-204, 632 N.E.2d, at 1032; *In re Odell, supra,* at 459.

The approach taken by the President in adopting Rule 707 — excluding polygraph evidence in all military trials — is a rational and proportional means of advancing the legitimate interest in barring unreliable evidence. Although the degree of reliability of polygraph evidence may depend upon a variety of identifiable factors, there is simply no way to know in a particular case whether a polygraph examiner's conclusion is accurate, because certain doubts and uncertainties plague even the best polygraph exams. Individual jurisdictions therefore may reasonably reach differing conclusions as to whether polygraph evidence should be admitted. We cannot say, then, that presented with such widespread uncertainty, the President acted arbitrarily or disproportionately in promulgating a *per se* rule excluding all polygraph evidence. . . .

D

The three of our precedents upon which the Court of Appeals principally relied, *Rock* v. *Arkansas, Washington* v. *Texas,* and *Chambers* v. *Mississippi,* do not support a right to introduce polygraph evidence, even in very narrow circumstances. The exclusions of evidence that we declared unconstitutional in those cases significantly undermined fundamental elements of the defendant's defense. Such is not the case here.

In *Rock,* the defendant, accused of a killing to which she was the only eyewitness, was allegedly able to remember the facts of the killing only after having her memory hypnotically refreshed. *See Rock v. Arkansas*, 483 U.S., at 46. Because Arkansas excluded all hypnotically refreshed testimony, the defendant was unable to testify about certain relevant facts, including whether the killing had been accidental. *See id.*, at 47-49. In holding that the exclusion of this evidence violated the defendant's "right to present a defense," we noted that the rule deprived the jury of the testimony of the only witness who was at the scene and had firsthand knowledge of the facts. *See id.*, at 57. Moreover, the rule infringed upon the defendant's interest in testifying in her own defense — an interest that we deemed particularly significant, as it is the defendant who is the target of any criminal prosecution. *See id.*, at 52. For this reason, we stated that a defendant ought to be allowed "to present his own version of events in his own words." *Ibid.*

In *Washington*, the statutes involved prevented codefendants or coparticipants in a crime from testifying for one another and thus precluded the defendant from introducing his accomplice's testimony that the accomplice had in fact committed the crime. *See Washington v. Texas*, 388 U.S., at 16-17. In reversing Washington's conviction, we held that the Sixth Amendment was violated because "the State arbitrarily denied [the defendant] the right to put on the stand a witness who was physically and mentally capable of testifying to events that he had personally observed." *Id.*, at 23.

In *Chambers*, we found a due process violation in the combined application of Mississippi's common-law "voucher rule," which prevented a party from impeaching his own witness, and its hearsay rule that excluded the testimony of three persons to whom that witness had confessed. *See Chambers v. Mississippi*, 410 U.S., at 302. *Chambers* specifically confined its holding to the "facts and circumstances" presented in that case; we thus stressed that the ruling did not "signal any diminution in the respect traditionally accorded to the States in the establishment and implementation of their own criminal trial rules and procedures." *Id.*, at 302-303. *Chambers* therefore does not stand for the proposition that the defendant is denied a fair opportunity to defend himself whenever a state or federal rule excludes favorable evidence.

Rock, Washington, and *Chambers* do not require that Rule 707 be invalidated, because, unlike the evidentiary rules at issue in those cases, Rule 707 does not implicate any significant interest of the accused. Here, the court members heard all the relevant details of the charged offense from the perspective of the accused, and the Rule did not preclude him from introducing any factual evidence. Rather, respondent was barred merely from introducing expert opinion testimony to bolster his own credibility. Moreover, in contrast to the rule at issue in *Rock*, Rule 707 did not prohibit respondent from testifying on his own behalf; he freely exercised his choice to convey his version of the facts to the court-martial members. We therefore cannot conclude that respondent's defense was significantly impaired by the exclusion of polygraph evidence. Rule 707 is thus constitutional under our precedents.

For the foregoing reasons, Military Rule of Evidence 707 does not unconstitutionally abridge the right to present a defense. The judgment of the Court of Appeals is reversed.

It is so ordered.

KENNEDY, J., with whom O'CONNOR, GINSBURG, and BREYER, JJ., join, concurring in part and concurring in the judgment.

I join Parts I, II-A, and II-D of the opinion of the Court.

In my view . . . [t]he continuing, good-faith disagreement among experts and courts on the subject of polygraph reliability counsels against our invalidating a *per se* exclusion of polygraph results or of the fact an accused has taken or refused to take a polygraph examination. If we were to accept respondent's position, of course, our holding would bind state courts, as well as military and federal courts. Given the ongoing debate about polygraphs, I agree the rule of exclusion is not so arbitrary or disproportionate that it is unconstitutional.

I doubt, though, that the rule of *per se* exclusion is wise, and some later case might present a more compelling case for introduction of the testimony than this one does. Though the considerable discretion given to the trial court in admitting or excluding scientific evidence is not a constitutional mandate, *see Daubert v. Merrell Dow Pharmaceuticals, Inc.*, 509 U.S. 579, 587 (1993), there is some tension between that rule and our holding today. And, as JUSTICE STEVENS points out, there is much inconsistency between the Government's extensive use of polygraphs to make vital security determinations and the argument it makes here, stressing the inaccuracy of these tests. . . .

STEVENS, J., dissenting.

The United States Court of Appeals for the Armed Forces held that the President violated the Constitution in June 1991, when he promulgated Rule 707 of the Military Rules of Evidence. Had I been a member of that court, I would not have decided that question without first requiring the parties to brief and argue the antecedent question whether Rule 707 violates Article 36(a) of the Uniform Code of Military Justice, 10 U.S.C. § 836(a). As presently advised, I am persuaded that the Rule does violate the statute and should be held invalid for that reason. I also agree with the Court of Appeals that the Rule is unconstitutional. This Court's contrary holding rests on a serious undervaluation of the importance of the citizen's constitutional right to present a defense to a criminal charge and an unrealistic appraisal of the importance of the governmental interests that undergird the Rule. Before discussing the constitutional issue, I shall comment briefly on the statutory question.

I

Rule 707 is a blanket rule of exclusion. No matter how reliable and how probative the results of a polygraph test may be, Rule 707 categorically denies the defendant any opportunity to persuade the court that the evidence should be received for any purpose. Indeed, even if the parties stipulate in advance that the results of a lie detector test may be admitted, the Rule requires exclusion.

The principal charge against the respondent in this case was that he had knowingly used methamphetamine. His principal defense was "innocent ingestion"; even if the urinalysis test conducted on April 7, 1992, correctly indicated that he did ingest the substance, he claims to have been unaware of that fact. The results of the lie detector test conducted three days later, if accurate, constitute factual evidence that his physical condition at that time was consistent with the theory of his defense and inconsistent with the theory of the prosecution. The results were also relevant because they tended to confirm the credibility of his testimony. Under Rule 707, even if the results of the polygraph test were more reliable than the results of the urinalysis, the weaker evidence is admissible and the stronger evidence is inadmissible.

Under the now discredited reasoning in a case decided 75 years ago, *Frye v. United States*, 54 App. D.C. 46, 293 F. 1013 (1923), that anomalous result would also have been reached in nonmilitary cases tried in the federal courts. In recent years, however, we have not only repudiated *Frye*'s general approach to scientific evidence, but the federal courts have also been engaged in the process of rejecting the once popular view that all lie detector evidence should be categorically inadmissible. Well reasoned opinions are concluding, consistently with this Court's decisions in *Daubert v. Merrell Dow Pharmaceuticals, Inc.*, 509 U.S. 579 (1993), and *General Electric Co. v. Joiner*, 522 U.S. 136 (1997), that the federal rules wisely allow district judges to exercise broad discretion when evaluating the admissibility of scientific evidence. Those opinions correctly observe that the rules of evidence generally recognized in the trial of civil and criminal cases in the federal courts do not contain any blanket prohibition against the admissibility of polygraph evidence.

In accord with the modern trend of decisions on this admissibility issue, in 1987 the Court of Military Appeals held that an accused was "entitled to attempt to lay" the foundation for admission of favorable polygraph evidence. *United States v. Gipson*, 24 M.J. 246, 253 (1987). The President responded to *Gipson* by adopting Rule 707. The governing statute authorized him to promulgate evidentiary rules "which shall, so far as he considers practicable, apply the principles of law and the rules of evidence generally recognized in the trial of criminal cases in the United States district courts." 10 U.S.C. § 836(a). Thus, if there are military concerns that warrant a special rule for military tribunals, the statute gives him ample authority to promulgate special rules that take such concerns into account.

Rule 707 has no counterpart in either the Federal Rules of Evidence or the Federal Rules of Criminal Procedure. Moreover, to the extent that the use of the lie detector plays a special role in the military establishment, military practices are more favorable to a rule of admissibility than is the less structured use of lie detectors in the civilian sector of our society. That is so because the military carefully regulates the administration of polygraph tests to ensure reliable results. The military maintains "very stringent standards for polygraph examiners" [Department of Defense Polygraph Program, Annual Polygraph Report to Congress, Fiscal Year 1996, pp. 14-15] and has established its own Polygraph Institute, which is "generally considered to be the best training facility for polygraph examiners in the United States." [Honts & Perry, *Polygraph Admissibility: Changes and Challenges*, 16 Law and Human Behavior 357, 359, n.1 (1992).] The military has administered hundreds of thousands of such tests and routinely uses their results for a wide variety of official decisions. [Between 1981 and 1997, the Department of Defense conducted over 400,000 polygraph examinations to resolve issues arising in counterintelligence, security, and criminal investigations.]

The stated reasons for the adoption of Rule 707 do not rely on any special military concern. They merely invoke three interests: (1) the interest in excluding unreliable evidence; (2) the interest in protecting the trier of fact from being misled by an unwarranted assumption that the polygraph evidence has "an aura of near infallibility"; and (3) the interest in avoiding collateral debates about the admissibility of particular test results.

It seems clear that those interests pose less serious concerns in the military than in the civilian context. Disputes about the qualifications of the examiners, the equipment, and the testing procedures should seldom arise with respect to the tests conducted by the military. Moreover, there surely is no reason to assume that military personnel who perform the factfinding function are less competent than ordinary jurors to assess the reliability of particular results, or their relevance to the issues. [When the members of the court-martial are officers, as was true in this case, they typically have at least a college degree as well as significant military service.] Thus, there is no identifiable military concern that justifies the President's promulgation of a special military rule that is more burdensome to the accused in military trials than the evidentiary rules applicable to the trial of civilians.

It, therefore, seems fairly clear that Rule 707 does not comply with the statute. I do not rest on this ground, however, because briefing might persuade me to change my views, and because the Court has decided only the constitutional question.

II

The Court's opinion barely acknowledges that a person accused of a crime has a constitutional right to present a defense. It is not necessary to point to "any particular language in the Sixth Amendment," *ante*, at 307, to support the conclusion that the right is firmly established. It is, however, appropriate to comment on the importance of that right before discussing the three interests that the Government relies upon to justify Rule 707.

The Sixth Amendment provides that "the accused shall enjoy the right . . . to have compulsory process for obtaining witnesses in his favor." Because this right "is an essential attribute of the adversary system itself," we have repeatedly stated that few rights "are more fundamental than that of an accused to present witnesses in his own defense." [*Taylor v. Illinois,* 484 U.S. 400, 408-09 (1988).] According to Joseph Story, that provision was included in the Bill of Rights in reaction to a notorious common-law rule categorically excluding defense evidence in treason and felony cases. [*Washington v. Texas,* 388 U.S. 14, 19-20 (1967).] Our holding in *Washington v. Texas,* 388 U.S. 14 (1967), that this right is applicable to the States, rested on the premises that it "is in plain terms the right to present a defense" and that it "is a fundamental element of due process of law." [*Id.* at 19.] Consistent with the history of the provision, the Court in that case held that a state rule of evidence that excluded "whole categories" of testimony on the basis of a presumption of unreliability was unconstitutional. [*Id.* at 22.] . . .

State evidentiary rules may so seriously impede the discovery of truth, "as well as the doing of justice," that they preclude the "meaningful opportunity to present a complete defense" that is guaranteed by the Constitution. *Crane v. Kentucky,* 476 U.S. 683, 690 (1986) (internal quotation marks omitted). In *Chambers v. Mississippi,* 410 U.S. 284, 302 (1973), we concluded that "where constitutional rights directly affecting the ascertainment of guilt are implicated, the hearsay rule may not be applied mechanistically to defeat the ends of justice." As the Court notes today, restrictions on the "defendant's right to present relevant evidence" must comply with the admonition in *Rock v. Arkansas,* 483 U.S. 44, 56 (1987), that they "may not be arbitrary or disproportionate to the purposes they are designed to serve." Applying that admonition to Arkansas' blanket rule prohibiting the admission of hypnotically refreshed testimony, we concluded that a "State's legitimate interest in barring unreliable evidence does not extend to *per se* exclusions that may be reliable in an individual case." *Id.,* at 61. That statement of constitutional law is directly relevant to this case. . . .

IV

The Government's concerns would unquestionably support the exclusion of polygraph evidence in particular cases, and may well be sufficient to support a narrower rule designed to respond to specific concerns. In my judgment, however, those concerns are plainly insufficient to support a categorical rule that prohibits the admission of polygraph evidence in all cases, no matter how reliable or probative the evidence may be. Accordingly, I respectfully dissent.

NOTES

1. Justice Stevens' opinion in *Hamdan v. Rumsfeld* suggests that his view of whether a provision like Military Rule of Evidence 707 could be invalid under Article 36(a) of the Uniform Code of Military Justice had changed. In a portion of his opinion joined by the majority in *Hamdan,* Justice Stevens "assume[d]" that the courts owe "complete deference" to a President's finding under Article 36(a) that application of the United States district courts' rules is impracticable. *Hamdan v. Rumsfeld,* 126 S. Ct. 2749, 2792 (2006).

2. One commentator writing after *Scheffer* has argued that Military Rule of Evidence 707 should be amended to allow the defense to show that the accused took a polygraph to challenge the reliability of the results of a post-polygraph interrogation. Maj. Scott E. Reid, *Military Rule of Evidence 707 and the Art of the Post-Polygraph Interrogation: A Proposed Amendment to the Blanket Exclusionary Rule,* ARMY LAW., Nov. 2001, at 1.

VII. HEARSAY

Military Rule of Evidence 803
MANUAL FOR COURTS-MARTIAL, UNITED STATES (2005 ed.)

Hearsay exceptions; availability of declarant immaterial

The following are not excluded by the hearsay rule, even though the declarant is available as a witness. . . .

(6) *Records of regularly conducted activity.* A memorandum, report, record, or data compilation, in any form, of acts, events, conditions, opinions, or diagnoses,

made at or near the time by, or from information transmitted by, a person with knowledge, if kept in the course of a regularly conducted business activity, and if it was the regular practice of that business activity to make the memorandum, report, record, or data compilation, all as shown by the testimony of the custodian or other qualified witness, or by certification that complies with Mil. R. Evid. 902(11) or any other statute permitting certification in a criminal proceeding in a court of the United States, unless the source of the information or the method or circumstances of preparation indicate a lack of trustworthiness. The term "business" as used in this paragraph includes the armed forces, a business, institution, association, profession, occupation, and calling of every kind, whether or not conducted for profit. Among those memoranda, reports, records, or data compilations normally admissible pursuant to this paragraph are enlistment papers, physical examination papers, outline-figure and fingerprint cards, forensic laboratory reports, chain of custody documents, morning reports and other personnel accountability documents, service records, officer and enlisted qualification records, logs, unit personnel diaries, individual equipment records, daily strength records of prisoners, and rosters of prisoners. . . .

(8) *Public records and reports.* Records, reports, statements, or data compilations, in any form, of public offices or agencies, setting forth (A) the activities of the office or agency, or (B) matters observed pursuant to duty imposed by law as to which matters there was a duty to report, excluding, however, matters observed by police officers and other personnel acting in a law enforcement capacity, or (C) against the government, factual findings resulting from an investigation made pursuant to authority granted by law, unless the sources of information or other circumstances indicate lack of trustworthiness. Notwithstanding (B), the following are admissible under this paragraph as a record of a fact or event if made by a person within the scope of the person's official duties and those duties included a duty to know or to ascertain through appropriate and trustworthy channels of information the truth of the fact or event and to record such fact or event: enlistment papers, physical examination papers, outline figure and fingerprint cards, forensic laboratory reports, chain of custody documents, morning reports and other personnel accountability documents, service records, officer and enlisted qualification records, records of court-martial convictions, logs, unit personnel diaries, individual equipment records, guard reports, daily strength records of prisoners, and rosters of prisoners.

Drafters' Analysis

(6) *Record of regularly conducted activity.* Rule 803(6) is taken generally from the Federal Rule. Two modifications have been made, however, to adapt the rule to military practice. The definition of "business" has been expanded to explicitly include the armed forces to ensure the continued application of this hearsay exception, and a descriptive list of documents, taken generally from 1969 Manual Para. 144 *d*, has been included. Although the activities of the armed forces do not constitute a profit making business, they do constitute a business within the meaning of the hearsay exception, *see* Para. 144 *c*, of the 1969 Manual, as well as a "regularly conducted activity."

The specific types of records included within the Rule are those which are normally records of regularly conducted activity within the armed forces. They are included because of their importance and because their omission from the Rule would be impracticable. The fact that a record is of a type described within the subdivision does not eliminate the need for its proponent to show that the *particular* record comes within the Rule when the record is challenged; the Rule does establish that the *types* of records listed are normally business records.

Chain of custody receipts or documents have been included to emphasize their administrative nature. Such documents perform the critical function of accounting for property obtained by the United States Government. Although they may be used as prosecution evidence, their primary purpose is simply one of property accountability. In view of the primary administrative purpose of these matters, it was necessary to provide expressly for their admissibility as an exception to the hearsay rule in order to clearly reject the interpretation of Para. 144*d* of the 1969 Manual with respect to chain of custody forms as set forth in *United States v. Porter*, 7 M.J. 32 (C.M.A. 1979) and *United States v. Nault*, 4 M.J. 318 (C.M.A. 1978) insofar as they concerned chain of custody forms.

Laboratory reports have been included in recognition of the function of forensic laboratories as impartial examining centers. The report is simply a record of "regularly conducted" activity of the laboratory. *See, e.g., United States v. Strangstalien*, 7 M.J. 225 (C.M.A. 1979); *United States v. Evans*, 21 U.S.C.M.A. 579, 45 C.M.R. 353 (1972).

Paragraph 144*d* prevented a record "made principally with a view to prosecution, or other disciplinary or legal action . . ." from being admitted as a business record. The limitation has been deleted, *but see* Rule 803(8)(B) and its Analysis. It should be noted that a record of "regularly conducted activity" is unlikely to have a prosecutorial intent in any event. The fact that a record may fit within another exception, *e.g.*, Rule 803(8), does not generally prevent it from being admissible under this subdivision although it would appear that the exclusion found in Rule 803(8)(B) for "matters observed by police officers and other personnel acting in a law enforcement capacity" prevent any such record from being admissible as a record of regularly conducted activity. Otherwise the limitation in subdivision (8) would serve no useful purpose. *See also* Analysis to Rule 803(8)(B).

Rule 803(6) is generally similar to the 1969 Manual rule but is potentially broader because of its use of the expression "regularly conducted" activity in addition to "business". It also permits records of opinion which were prohibited by Para. 144*d* of the 1969 Manual. Offsetting these factors is the fact that the Rule requires that the memorandum was "made at or near the time by, or from information transmitted by a person with knowledge . . .", but Para. 144*c* of the 1969 Manual rule expressly did not require such knowledge as a condition of admissibility. . . .

(8) *Public records and reports.* Rule 803(8) has been taken generally from the Federal Rule but has been slightly modified to adapt it to the military environment. Rule 803(8)(B) has been redrafted to apply to "police officers and

other personnel acting in a law enforcement capacity" rather the Federal Rule's "police officers and other law enforcement personnel." The change was necessitated by the fact that all military personnel may act in a disciplinary capacity. Any officer, for example, regardless of assignment, may potentially act as a military policeman. The capacity within which a member of the armed forces acts may be critical.

The Federal Rule was also modified to include a list of records that, when made pursuant to a duty required by law, will be admissible notwithstanding the fact that they may have been made as "matters observed by police officers and other personnel acting in a law enforcement capacity." Their inclusion is a direct result of the fact, discussed above, that military personnel may all function within a law enforcement capacity. The Committee determined it would be impracticable and contrary to the intent of the Rule to allow the admissibility of records which are truly administrative in nature and unrelated to the problems inherent in records prepared only for purposes of prosecution to depend upon whether the maker was at that given instant acting in a law enforcement capacity. . . .

UNITED STATES v. BROADNAX
United States Court of Military Appeals
23 M.J. 389 (C.M.A. 1987)

SULLIVAN, J. . . .

[P]rivate Robert Hubbard, the alleged victim of the forgery offense, testified that in May of 1984 he discovered that a $100.00 check had been written on his account. The check had appellant's name written on the payee line and purported to have Private Hubbard's signature as the payor. Private Hubbard testified that he did not write the check or "authorize anyone else to write" it.

Special Agent William Merrell of the Criminal Investigation Command (CID) testified that he obtained samples of appellant's handwriting and that of Private Hubbard. He forwarded these samples and the forged check to the United States Army Criminal Investigation Laboratory-Pacific. The resulting report, which was admitted at trial, stated that appellant made all entries on the check except for the date. . . . The samples used in this handwriting analysis were not introduced as evidence in this court-martial.

Defense counsel at trial objected to admission of this report without the live testimony of the documents examiner who made the report. She asserted that the prosecution had failed to show what documents were analyzed and that her client was being denied his Sixth-Amendment right of confrontation. On questioning by the military judge, she admitted that she made no pretrial request for production of the documents examiner. The military judge denied the motion and apparently admitted the report under the official-records exception to the hearsay rule. . . .

Admissibility of Laboratory Report on Handwriting Exemplars

The challenged evidence in this case is a forensic laboratory report containing an opinion from a government documents examiner that appellant authored a forged check. Trial counsel asserted that this evidence was admissible "under [Mil. R. Evid.] 803(a) [*sic*], Public Records and Reports," and the military judge admitted it "as an official exhibit kept in [the] normal course of business in the United States Government." Defense counsel did not expressly assert that this laboratory report was inadmissible under Mil. R. Evid. 803(8). However, her constitutional objection to admission of this evidence and her improper foundation objection essentially challenged the trustworthiness of this evidence. Such concerns are similarly embraced in this evidentiary rule, *see generally United States v. Hines*, 23 M.J. 125, 134 (C.M.A. 1986). Accordingly, we must first decide whether the military judge properly ruled that this evidence was admissible under Mil. R. Evid. 803(8).

Mil. R. Evid. 803(8) provides:

> (8) *Public records and reports.* Records, reports, statements, or data compilations, in any form, of public office[s] or agencies, setting forth (A) the activities of the office or agency, or (B) matters observed pursuant to duty imposed by law as to which matters there was a duty to report, excluding, however, matters observed by police officers and other personnel acting in a law enforcement capacity, or (C) against the government, factual findings resulting from an investigation made pursuant to authority granted by law, unless the sources of information or other circumstances indicate lack of trustworthiness. *Notwithstanding (B), the following are admissible under this paragraph as a record of a fact or event if made by a person within the scope of the person's official duties and those duties included a duty to know or to ascertain through appropriate and trustworthy channels of information the truth of the fact or event and to record such fact or event:* enlistment papers, physical examination papers, outline figure and fingerprint cards, *forensic laboratory reports,* chain of custody documents, morning reports and other personnel accountability documents, service records, officer and enlisted qualification records, records of court-martial convictions, logs, unit personnel diaries, individual equipment records, guard reports, daily strength records of prisoners, and rosters of prisoners.

(Emphasis added.) We note that the portion of the rule beginning with the phrase "Notwithstanding (B)" and which later refers to forensic laboratory reports is not in Fed. R. Evid. 803(8). Moreover, a federal court of appeals has held that evaluative reports by law-enforcement officials offered by the prosecution are not admissible under this rule. *See United States v. Oates*, 560 F.2d 45, 67 (2d Cir.1977). Accordingly, if admission of this evidence is to be held authorized by Mil. R. Evid. 803(8), it must meet the requirements of this additional language.

As a starting point we note that the drafters of this rule of evidence stated their purpose in expressly noting forensic laboratory reports in Mil. R. Evid. 803(8) as follows:

> The exclusion in the Federal Rule for "matters observed by police officers" was intended to prevent use of the exception for evaluative reports as the House Committee believed them to be unreliable.

Because of the explicit language of the exclusion, normal statutory construction leads to the conclusion that reports which would be within Federal or Military Rule 803(8) but for the exclusion in (8)(B) are not otherwise admissible under Rule 803(6). Otherwise the inclusion of the limitation would serve virtually no purpose whatsoever. *There is no contradiction between the exclusion in Rule 803(8)(B) and the specific documents made admissible in Rule 803(8) (and Rule 803(6)) because those documents are not matters "observed by police officers and other personnel acting in a law enforcement capacity." To the extent that they might be so considered, the specific language included by the Committee is expressly intended to reject the subdivision (8)(B) limitation.* Note, however, that all forms of evidence not within the specific item listing of the Rule but within the (8)(B) exclusion will be admissible insofar as Rule 803(8) is concerned, whether the evidence is military or civilian in origin.

See App. 22, Drafters' Analysis at A22-49, Manual, *supra.* Accordingly, this forensic laboratory report was not inadmissible under this rule simply because its maker was a person acting in a law-enforcement capacity. *See United States v. Miller,* 23 U.S.C.M.A. 247, 49 C.M.R. 380 (1974). *Cf.* para. 144*d,* Manual for Courts-Martial, United States, 1969 (Revised edition).

Nevertheless, neither the additional language in the military rule nor its analysis provides that such a report is per se admissible simply because it emanates from a forensic laboratory. The additional language also replaced the broad requirement in section (B) that "matters observed" be set forth in the official records or reports. In its place, a more particular requirement was established for the listed items, including the forensic laboratory report, namely that such report set forth "a fact or event . . . know[n] or . . . ascertain[ed]." Also, "the truth of the fact or event" and its recordation must be "know[n] or . . . ascertain[ed] through appropriate and trustworthy channels of information." This last requirement mirrors in an affirmative way the general provision of this rule that a public record should be admitted "unless the sources of information or other circumstances indicate lack of trustworthiness." In summary, the military judge was required to consider the type of information in the report, the method of its acquisition, and the manner in which it was presented before admitting this specific report. *See* Mil. R. Evid. 803(6). *Cf.* para. 144*c,* 1969 Manual, *supra.*

The forensic laboratory report in this case set forth the documents examiner's opinion that appellant "authored the comparable questioned entries on" the forged check. We cannot equate what substantially amounts to an opinion of guilt with the factual type of result concerning the identity of an unknown substance which is produced by chemical analysis. *See United States v. Evans,* 21 U.S.C.M.A. 579, 581-82, 45 C.M.R. 353, 355-56 (1972). Moreover, although scientific or professional methods may be employed to some degree in reaching such an opinion, the element of subjectivity involved is greater than that in chemical analysis. *See generally* P. Giannelli and E. Imwinkelried, *Scientific Evidence* § 21-2(B) at 806 (1986). *See also McCormick's Handbook of the Law of Evidence* § 205 at 500-02 (E. Cleary 2d Ed.1972); 17 Am.Jur. *Proof of Facts Questioned Documents* § 36 at 536-38 (1966). Finally, the exemplars involved in the above analysis and noted in the report were not produced at trial. Omission of these documents eliminated a critical basis for the military judge to assess the trustworthiness of the bare assertion of authorship contained in the laboratory report. *See United States v. McFerren*, 6 U.S.C.M.A. 486, 491, 20 C.M.R. 202, 207 (1955). *See generally* 4 *Weinstein's Evidence* § 803(8)[03] at 803-206 (1979).

Of course, it is possible that the drafters of Mil. R. Evid. 803(8) intended this exception to the hearsay rule to be broader than our prior case law allows. Such an exception to the hearsay rule would also exceed Fed. R. Evid. 803(8). *See United States v. Oates, supra.* Accordingly, this recent expansion of this traditional hearsay exception could not reasonably be considered "firmly rooted," and the absence of the above guarantees of trustworthiness could be properly considered on the Sixth-Amendment-Confrontation question. *See Ohio v. Roberts*, 448 U.S. 56, 66 (1980). In either event, the result is the same: The challenged report was inadmissible. . . .

We conclude that appellant was materially prejudiced by the judge's ruling and that the conviction for forgery cannot stand. . . .

CHIEF JUDGE EVERETT concurs.

COX, J. (concurring):

In order to reconcile this decision with other holdings of this Court dealing with admissibility of forensic-laboratory reports, it is necessary to discuss the interaction of the evidentiary rules with the right of an accused to confront the witnesses against him at his trial or to compel the attendance of witnesses. *See* S.Saltzburg, L.Schinasi, D.Schlueter, *Military Rules of Evidence Manual* 647, 648 (2d ed. 1986). The power to promulgate rules of evidence means, by definition, that the traditional rules may be modified. Whatever else may be said of the Military Rules of Evidence, it cannot be doubted that the drafters specifically intended to, and did, include "forensic laboratory reports" within the *"Records of regularly conducted activity"* and *"Public records and reports"* exceptions to the hearsay rule. Mil. R. Evid. 803(6) and (8), Manual for Courts-Martial, United States, 1984.

Notwithstanding evidentiary rules, an accused has a constitutional right to confront the witnesses against him at trial. U.S. Const. amend. VI. This right has not been interpreted as being absolute, however. Indeed, it is said that, "where the evidence falls within a firmly rooted hearsay exception," an inference of "[r]eliability . . . [may be drawn] without more," and "certain hearsay exceptions rest upon such solid foundations that admission of virtually any evidence within them comports with the 'substance of the constitutional protection.'" *Ohio v. Roberts*, 448 U.S. 56, 66 (1980). In the case of such "firmly rooted" exceptions, the availability of the declarant is immaterial. *United States v. Hines*, 23 M.J. 125, 128-29 n.6 (C.M.A.1986). However, to the extent that the traditional common-law hearsay exceptions have been altered, as here, there can be no claim that the new exception is "firmly rooted." *Cf. United States v. Groves*, 23 M.J. 374 (C.M.A.1987).

Out-of-court statements may also be constitutionally admitted against an accused when: (A) the declarant is unavailable; and (B) the evidence bears such "indicia of reliability" as to be a veritable substitute for the preferred face-to-face confrontation. *See United States v. Hines, supra* at 130, 136, 137. The laboratory results here fail the "indicia of reliability" prong since, as pointed out by Judge Sullivan, evaluating handwriting exemplars is more subjective than many other scientific tests. In addition, the Government did not establish that the expert was unavailable. *Cf. Barber v. Page*, 390 U.S. 719 (1968).

In the area of chemical analysis of drugs, however, we have admittedly taken a more pragmatic approach to the Government's initial duty to demonstrate the unavailability of the expert before being permitted to introduce laboratory results. In short, the fact that the witness may not be available is not a prerequisite. *See, e.g., United States v. Vietor*, 10 M.J. 69 (C.M.A.1980); *United States v. Strangstalien*, 7 M.J. 225 (C.M.A.1979). Unfortunately, the judges were not able to settle upon a common theory in these cases. I extract from them a variety of factors to explain the different approaches. First, unlike the expert's conclusion here, the chemical identification of an unknown substance is essentially neutral and nonaccusatory. The technician is simply seeking to identify a substance, rather than to implicate a particular person. Second, as indicated, the analytical process involves little room for subjectivity. Third, experience has shown that objections to admitting laboratory results based on the technician's absence at trial are as apt to be tactical ploys as they are to be serious efforts to confront the witness. Such tactics are designed to capitalize on the practical impediments to routinely providing chemist-witnesses throughout the worldwide court-martial jurisdiction, a logistical problem unique to the military. Fourth, the *quid pro quo* for the accused is that we have adopted — in the area of drug analysis — Professor Westen's thesis that the Compulsory-Process Clause subsumes the Confrontation Clause. *See* Westen, *The Compulsory Process* Clause, 73 Mich. L. Rev. 71, 183-84 (1974); *United States v. Vietor, supra* at 75-76 (Everett, C.J., concurring in the result). Thus, the accused who actually wants to confront the expert can — just as he can with any other witness — simply by making the minimal showing that the testimony is "relevant and necessary." R.C.M. 703(b)(1), Manual, *supra*.

Handwriting analyses do not warrant this special treatment; thus, appellant was entitled to confront his accuser and permit the factfinder to make his own judgment as to the validity of the analysis. Moreover, the rules of evidence applicable to courts-martial prior to September 1, 1980, specifically recognized that even laymen could be competent to opine on the genuineness or lack thereof in handwriting. Para. 143*b*(1), Manual for Courts-Martial, United States, 1969 (Revised edition). The current Military Rules of Evidence do not purport to extinguish that capability. *See* Mil. R. Evid. 701 and App. 22, Analysis of the Military Rules of Evidence, 1984 Manual, *supra* at A22-45. Therefore, I believe appellant was entitled to have the factfinder personally examine the exemplars used by the expert to form his opinion so that the factfinder would be better able to evaluate the weight that should be accorded the expert's conclusion. Receiving evidence in the form of a laboratory report that would otherwise be subject to the rigors of cross-examination, Mil. R. Evid. 701-05, risks lending it an aura of scientific infallibility. As the expert's opinion was by far the most significant item linking appellant to the charge, I agree that prejudice is apparent from the erroneous admission of the exhibit.

NOTE

The Navy-Marine Corps Court of Criminal Appeals has recently provided this synopsis of the rule governing admissibility of public records and reports under Military Rule of Evidence 803(8) over a confrontation objection:

> . . . Under MIL. R. EVID. 803(8), a standard personnel accountability document such as a morning report is admissible, even if the document records a matter observed by law enforcement personnel. [*United States v. Taylor*, 61 M.J. 157, 159 (C.A.A.F. 2005).] Matters of fact in reports may be admitted pursuant to this rule, but not matters of opinion. *United States v. Broadnax*, 23 M.J. 389, 393 (C.M.A. 1987).

United States v. Rankin, 63 M.J. 552, 556 (N-M. Ct. Crim. App. 2006).

The Navy-Marine Corps Court further explained:

> In *Taylor*, the CAAF held two exhibits in an unauthorized absence case to be inadmissible under MIL. R. EVID. 803(8). One exhibit was a declaration of deserter message; however, the exhibit included extraneous and indecipherable information. 61 M.J. at 159. Because the document was obviously not prepared in accordance with service regulations, the MIL. R. EVID. 803(8) exception to the hearsay prohibition was inapplicable. *Id.* at 160. In addition, the exhibit was not properly certified as a true copy. *Id.* The second exhibit was a return deserter message, but was based upon a DD Form 553 arrest warrant. The CAAF held that the foundation for the underlying document was insufficient to remove a layer of hearsay for the return deserter message. *Id.* at 161. Notably, the CAAF did not question the longstanding practice, or the corresponding legal precedent, allowing the admission of routine personnel documents with the proper foundation.

Rankin, 63 M.J. at 556.

Chapter 16

PUNISHMENT

In the U.S. military justice system, the same authority who decides guilt or innocence also decides the sentence. So, in contrast to most American civilian jurisdictions, if the accused is tried before members, then the members adjudge the sentence. Similarly, if the accused is tried before a military judge alone, then the military judge will impose the sentence. Unlike the federal criminal system, there is no presentence report. Rather, before a sentence is adjudged the parties present their competing cases at an adversarial sentencing hearing. But the military's sentencing system shares one significant trait with its civilian counterparts: most cases are resolved through plea bargains, though military plea bargain procedures are highly formalized and rigorous.

The military justice system includes some sentences that are similar to those found in civilian systems, such as death, confinement, and fines. But the military justice system also includes a number of unique punishments, such as a punitive discharge, forfeiture of pay, and reduction in grade. Some more exotic forms of punishment, such as confinement on bread and water and loss of numbers (moving an officer down in seniority), were recently eliminated, bringing the military justice system closer to its civilian counterparts.

The military justice system retains the death penalty, though capital trials are rare and adjudged death sentences rarer still. The Supreme Court's decision in *Loving v. United States*, 517 U.S. 748 (1996), upheld the military death penalty system, rejecting a separation of powers challenge.

Another Supreme Court decision, *Clinton v. Goldsmith*, 526 U.S. 529 (1999), dealt with collateral consequences of a court-martial conviction. While these collateral consequences can be severe, the Supreme Court held that military appellate courts have no jurisdiction to review them.

I. SENTENCING PROCEDURES

A. Sentencing Authority

Major Kevin Lovejoy, *Abolition of Court Member Sentencing*
142 MIL. L. REV. 1, 7-8 (1994)

Soldiers facing [non-capital] courts-martial may choose from four different options regarding their plea and the composition of their court-martial. They may elect to: (1) be tried by members on both the merits and sentencing; (2) be tried by a military judge on both the merits and sentencing; (3) plead guilty before a military judge and be sentenced by members; or (4) plead guilty and be sentenced by a military judge. The option soldiers do not have is to be tried by members on the merits but sentenced by a military judge. This often poses a significant problem for the accused, because the sentencing consequences of his or her choice between members or the military judge may prevent him or her from choosing the most favorable forum with respect to guilt. A common belief exists among many of those who practice military justice that, as a general rule, an accused stands a better chance of acquittal with members. However, it is also the general consensus that if convicted by members, an accused often stands a greater risk of being punished severely by the same members during sentencing. In light of this phenomenon, defense counsel are more likely to advise their clients to forfeit their right to trial by members to avoid the heightened risk of a more severe sentence.

NOTE

As one prominent military appellate judge has noted, "Debate over whether military judges should be the sole sentencing authority has been percolating since at least 1919, when Samuel Ansell proposed such a scheme." Col. James A. Young III, *Revising the Court Member Selection Process*, 163 MIL. L. REV. 91, 108 (2000). "The Military Justice Act of 1983, 10 U.S.C. Sec. 867(g) (1983), created an advisory committee to study whether all noncapital sentencing should be exercised by the military judge." Lt. Col. Craig S. Schwender, *Trial Judiciary Note: Sentencing Guidelines for Courts-Martial: Some Arguments Against Adoption*, ARMY LAW., Aug. 1988, at 33, 34 n.19. That advisory commission's majority report "strongly recommended against mandatory judge alone sentencing," concluding that court-martial members panels "clearly comprise a 'blue-ribbon' decision making body when compared to civilian juries." THE MILITARY JUSTICE ACT OF 1983 ADVISORY COMMISSION, ADVISORY COMMISSION REPORT, 6, 19, 27 (1984). A minority report, however, disagreed. *See id.* at Minority Report in Favor of Proposed Change to Judge-Alone Sentencing, at 28.

In 2001, the House of Representatives adopted a bill providing that in non-capital courts-martial where

> an accused [is] convicted of an offense by a court-martial composed of a military judge and members, the sentence shall be tried before and adjudged by the military judge rather than the members if, after the findings are announced and before evidence in the sentencing proceeding is introduced, the accused, knowing the identity of the military judge and after consultation with defense counsel, requests orally on the record or in writing that the sentence be tried before and adjudged by the military judge rather than the members.

National Defense Authorization Act for Fiscal Year 2002, H.R. 2586, § 572, 107th Cong. (1st Sess. 2001). The version of the bill that was enacted, however, did not contain this provision. *See* National Defense Authorization Act for Fiscal Year 2002, 107 P.L. 17, 115 Stat. 1012 (2001). Senior Judge Robinson O. Everett has endorsed such a reform. Maj. Walter M. Hudson, *Two Senior Judges Look Back and Look Ahead: An Interview with Senior Judge Robinson O. Everett and Senior Judge Walter T. Cox, III*, 165 MIL. L. REV. 42, 88 (2000). Some commentators have suggested going even further and eliminating sentencing by court members altogether. *See, e.g.*, Maj. Kevin Lovejoy, *Abolition of Court Member Sentencing*, 142 MIL. L. REV. 1 (1994); Brig. Gen. John S. Cooke, *The Twenty-Sixth Annual Kenneth J. Hodson Lecture: Manual for Courts-Martial 20X*, 156 MIL. L. REV. 1, 20 (1998).

B. Adversarial Sentencing

UNITED STATES v. GREEN
United States Court of Appeals for the Armed Forces
64 M.J. 289 (C.A.A.F. 2007)

CHIEF JUDGE EFFRON delivered the opinion of the Court. . . .

A court-martial has broad discretion to adjudicate the sentence, subject to the punishment limitations set forth in the UCMJ and the *Manual for Courts-Martial*, United States (*MCM*). Article 56, UCMJ, 10 U.S.C. § 856 (2000); Rule for Courts-Martial (R.C.M.) 1002. Sentencing information is developed in an adversarial proceeding, subject to evidentiary rules designed for the sentencing process. *See* R.C.M. 1001; *United States v. Mack*, 9 M.J. 300, 319 (C.M.A. 1980); *MCM*, Analysis of the Rules for Courts-Martial app. 21 at A21-70 (2005 ed.) . . . . As part of the sentencing process, the accused may make a sworn or unsworn statement. R.C.M. 1001(c)(2). Although an unsworn statement is not subject to cross-examination by trial counsel or examination by the court-martial, the prosecution may present facts in rebuttal. R.C.M. 1001(c)(2)(C). If a military judge erroneously permits consideration of inadmissible evidence during sentencing, the error is tested for prejudice. *See United States v. Hysong*, 47 M.J. 126, 126 (C.A.A.F. 1997); Article 59(a), UCMJ, 10 U.S.C. § 859(a) (2000). . . .

Rule for Courts-Martial 1001, Drafters' Analysis
Manual for Courts-Martial, United States,
App. 21, A21-70 (2005 ed.)

Sentencing procedures in Federal civilian courts can be followed in courts-martial only to a limited degree. Sentencing in courts-martial may be by the military judge or members. *See* Article 16 and 52(b). The military does not have — and it is not feasible to create — an independent, judicially supervised probation service to prepare presentence reports. *See* Fed. R. Crim. P. 32(c). [Rule for Courts-Martial 1001] allows the presentation of much of the same information to the court-martial as would be contained in a presentence report, but it does so within the protections of an adversarial proceeding, to which rules of evidence apply (*but cf. Williams v. New York*, 337 U.S. 241 (1949)), although they may be relaxed for some purposes. *See* [R.C.M. 1001] subsections (b)(4) and (5), (c)(3), (d), and (e) . . . . The presentation of matters in the accused's service records (*see* [R.C.M. 1001] subsection (b)(2) . . .) provides much of the information which would be in a presentence report. Such records are not prepared for purposes of prosecution (*cf. United States v. Boles*, 11 M.J. 195 (C.M.A. 1981)) and are therefore impartial, like presentence reports. In addition, the clarification of the types of cases in which aggravation evidence may be introduced (*see* [R.C.M. 1001] subsection (b)(4) . . .) and authorization for the trial counsel to present opinion evidence about the accused's rehabilitative potential (*see* [R.C.M. 1001] subsection (b)(5) . . .) provide additional avenues for presenting relevant information to the court-martial. The accused retains the right to present matters in extenuation and mitigation (*see* [R.C.M. 1001] subsection (c) . . .).

C.   Principles

UNITED STATES v. LANIA
United States Court of Military Appeals
9 M.J. 100 (C.M.A. 1980)

EVERETT, CHIEF JUDGE. . . .

[T]he trial counsel's sentencing argument . . . suggested that, among other things, the court members should consider general deterrence.

For example, the trial counsel argued:

> He has been anything but [sic] a disgrace to the United States Army and a disgrace to the uniform that he wears. So therefore, the rehabilitation process should be passed by the wayside. . . .

> Let the sentence here today be a sentence that is heard throughout this post so that other members of the United States Army know that if they're writing bad checks, if they're engaging in offenses of theft, that their punishment will be dealt with in a similar manner to Private Lania. That is very harshly and very severely, because that is what a theft [sic] surely deserves, and a thief 15 times over as we have in this particular case. . . .

> Now gentlemen, that's what we are asking for in this case, retribution; and the only way we can show retribution; and the only way we can deter him and to possibly deter other people and perhaps while he's incarcerated the only way to rehabilitate him is to give him a substantial period of confinement and that's what we are going to ask for in this particular case gentlemen.

At the conclusion of trial counsel's argument, the defense counsel objected on several grounds — among them, that the trial counsel had argued general deterrence. In the defense's view, a jury may consider general deterrence, but the trial counsel may not ask for such consideration.

In evaluating the trial counsel's argument, we start from the premise that general deterrence is a proper function of sentencing. As Mr. Justice Stewart noted in his opinion for the Court in *Pell v. Procunier*, 417 U.S. 817 (1974):

> An important function of the corrections system is the deterrence of crime. The premise is that by confining criminal offenders in a facility where they are isolated from the rest of society, a condition that most

people presumably find undesirable, they and others will be deterred from committing additional criminal offenses. . . .

The propriety of considering general deterrence in sentencing has been affirmed by a near unanimity of views among federal and state sentencing authorities in this country. In fact, as Justice Marshall (concurring) observed in *Furman v. Georgia*, 408 U.S. 238, 343 (1972) "Our jurisprudence has always accepted deterrence in general . . . [among other factors] as proper goals of punishment[,]" citing *Trop v. Dulles*, 356 U.S. at 111 (Brennan, J., concurring). While general deterrence is undoubtedly, then, a factor in setting maximum punishments, it is also relevant to the determination of a just sentence within the maximum limits prescribed.

If our premise that general deterrence is a permissible consideration in sentencing is correct, then it ineluctably follows that a military judge may instruct court members in this regard. In view of the precedents of this Court which impose duties on a military judge to enlighten court-martial members on matters as to which no instruction was ever requested by counsel or by members, *see, e.g., United States v. Jones*, 7 M.J. 441, 443 (C.M.A. 1979); *United States v. Jackson*, 6 M.J. 261, 263 (C.M.A. 1979); *United States v. Sawyer*, 4 M.J. 64, 65 (C.M.A. 1977), it would be incongruous to hold that it is error for the military judge to advise the members of a factor which, according to almost every authority, may properly be considered in sentencing.

Of course, if the military judge apprises the court members of general deterrence, he should also mention that there are other factors — such as rehabilitation of the accused — which the court-martial members may properly consider. It is simply a hallmark of our criminal justice system that court members be evenly and adequately guided in their deliberations. But to give one sentencing criterion and not mention others might be misconstrued as suggesting that the members ignore those other criteria. Likewise, if general deterrence is mentioned, it should be accompanied with an admonition to the court-martial members that, in any event, they must individualize their consideration of the sentence — that is, they should take into account the circumstances surrounding that case together with the character and propensities of the accused, as demonstrated by the evidence in the case. Indeed, a principal danger that has been recognized in the consideration of general deterrence is that it may foster a "mechanistic" imposition of sentence without proper attention to the situation of the particular accused. *See, e.g., United States v. Foss*, [501 F.2d 522, 527 (1st Cir. 1974)].

Since general deterrence is suitable for consideration in sentencing and for instructions to the court-martial members, there is no reason to insulate this factor from argument by trial counsel. If the Government is to be allowed an opportunity to present argument on sentence, *see United States v. Olson*, 7 U.S.C.M.A. 242, 22 C.M.R. 32 (1956), then we can find no basis to prevent trial counsel from reminding the court members that general deterrence should be borne in mind. *Cf.* 75 Am. Jur. 2d, Trial, § 229. Typically, when a judge is allowed to advise a jury that they may consider certain information, counsel may argue that they should consider it.

Of course, just as the judge may not give an instruction which neglects the need for an individualized sentence and so, by implication, authorizes a mechanistic imposition of sentence predicated only on general deterrence, trial counsel may not invite the court members to rely on deterrence to the exclusion of other factors. Such an invitation borders on inflammatory argument. . . .

In borderline situations cautionary instructions from the military judge will minimize the possibility that court members have been misled by the argument of trial counsel. Thus, defense counsel should be alert to object and to seek cautionary instructions if they perceive a risk that court members are being diverted by trial counsel's argument from their duty to fit the punishment not only to the crime but also to the particular offender. Moreover, upon request or otherwise, military judges should not be parsimonious in giving instructions which make clear that sentencing must be an individualized process, even though general deterrence may be taken into account.

When we examine the record of the appellant's trial in light of the foregoing principles, no prejudicial error is discernible. Considered as a whole, the trial counsel's argument did not, in our view, constitute an invitation for court members to rely primarily on general deterrence; nor did it tend to distract the court members from their task of imposing a sentence tailored to the accused who stood before them. Furthermore, if fault can be found with trial counsel's argument, the instructions given by the military judge were adequate to shield the appellant from prejudice. Indeed, our conclusion that the appellant was not prejudiced in any way is supported by a comparison of the sentence that was adjudged with the maximum punishment that the military judge instructed the court members was imposable for appellant's myriad offenses. . . .

COOK, JUDGE (concurring):

Under the Manual for Courts-Martial, the Government is limited as to the kinds of matter it can ask a court-martial to consider in deliberation on an "appropriate sentence." Not included is argument that the sentence in a particular case may serve to deter others from committing the same crime. I believe, therefore, that military practice is, and intentionally was made, different from civilian practice. . . .

D. Pretrial Agreements

Rule for Courts-Martial 901(f)
Manual for Courts-Martial, United States (2005 ed.)

(3) *Disclosure.* If a plea agreement exists, the military judge shall require disclosure of the entire agreement before the plea is accepted, provided that in trial before military judge alone the military judge ordinarily shall not examine any sentence limitation contained in the agreement until after the sentence of the court-martial has been announced.

(4) *Inquiry.* The military judge shall inquire to ensure:

(A) That the accused understands the agreement; and

(B) That the parties agree to the terms of the agreement. . . .

[(h)](3) *Pretrial agreement inquiry.* After sentence is announced the military judge shall inquire into any parts of a pretrial agreement which were not previously examined by the military judge. If the military judge determines that the accused does not understand the material terms of the agreement, or that the parties disagree as to such terms, the military judge shall conform, with the consent of the Government, the agreement to the accused's understanding or permit the accused to withdraw the plea.

UNITED STATES v. JOBSON
United States Air Force Court of Military Review
28 M.J. 844 (A.F.C.M.R. 1989)

KASTL, SENIOR JUDGE. . . .

Prior to 1984, neither the UCMJ nor the Manual for Courts-Martial mentioned pretrial agreements. The Army began to employ the device to encourage speedier disposition of cases in 1953. *See* Army Pamphlet 27-173, *Trial Procedure*, para. 11-1 (15 February 1987). Pretrial arrangements were sanctioned by the Court of Military Appeals in 1957 in *United States v. Allen*, 8 U.S.C.M.A. 504, 25 C.M.R. 8 (1957). In the Air Force, acceptance of such bargaining has been more grudging. *See* Moyer, *Justice and the Military* 445-446 (1972). Even today, caution is advised whenever considering Air Force pretrial offers. Routinely, for example, only officers exercising general court-martial authority are authorized to accept such defense proposals. *See* Air Force Regulation 111-1, *Military Justice Guide*, paras. 7-1 and 7-2 (30 September 1988).

UNITED STATES v. McCANTS
United States Army Court of Military Review
47 C.M.R. 381 (A.C.M.R. 1973)

GHENT, SENIOR JUDGE. . . .

The "pretrial agreement" in military law is a creature of practicality and expediency, being adopted from that prevailing in civilian jurisdictions where defense counsel negotiate with the prosecutors for favorable recommendations to the trial judges in exchange for a guilty plea. Its integration as a valuable tool in the military justice system was accomplished on 23 April 1953 through a letter from the Acting Assistant Judge Advocate General of the Army to all staff judge advocates. It states, in part:

> "The convening authority's responsibility for discipline within his command and for seeing that consideration of justice to the Government as well as to accused persons are given due weight cannot be ignored. He must lean heavily on his staff judge advocate in fixing his policy. Those who deal with the defense must carefully avoid making any comment or entering into any understanding inconsistent

with the policy of the commander. No accused can be expected to plead guilty, and competent counsel will not advise him to do so, unless some benefit to the accused is reasonably certain. *Any understanding reached must be carried out with the utmost good faith. Should counsel for the government blunderingly exceed his authority, the full power of the commander exercising general court-martial jurisdiction must be exercised to preclude any prejudice to the accused.* It would be better to free an offender completely, however guilty he might be, than to tolerate anything smacking of bad faith on the part of the Government." (Emphasis supplied).

Unfortunately the letter, *supra*, did not delineate with whom the accused would negotiate. Unlike its civilian counter-part, military law has a built-in protection which insures that an accused will not be required to pay the steep price of waiving his constitutional rights to "buy a pig in a poke." In short, prior to trial or sentence an accused can negotiate with the convening authority and, if an agreement is entered, the accused knows in advance of his plea that the convening authority will approve no sentence in excess of the agreed maximum. . . .

NOTES

1. Major General Franklin P. Shaw's 1953 letter encouraging pretrial agreements — described in Senior Judge Ghent's opinion above — "resulted in a remarkable change in courts-martial practice. From its one percent rate of guilty pleas prior to 1953, the Army reported that sixty percent of all convictions resulted from guilty pleas in Fiscal Year 1956." Maj. Michael E. Klein, United States v. Weasler *and the Bargained Waiver of Unlawful Command Influence Motions: Common Sense or Heresy?*, ARMY LAW., Feb. 1998, at 3, 9.

2. Today, "[m]ost accused soldiers plead guilty pursuant to a pretrial agreement." Capt. James L. Pohl, *Practical Considerations of* United States v. Holt: *Use of the Accused's Answers During the Providence Inquiry as Substantive Evidence*, ARMY LAW., Nov. 1988, at 20, 22. "[I]n fiscal year (FY) 1992, of the 1168 GCM trials, 1097 resulted in convictions (a conviction rate of 93.9%). Of these 1097 GCM convictions, however, 701 — or sixty-four percent — were guilty pleas." United States Army Legal Services Agency, *USALSA REPORT: The Advocate for Military Defense Counsel: Clerk of Court Note*, ARMY LAW., Mar. 1993, at 26, 26.

3. An accused in a capital case may not plead guilty. UCMJ article 45(b); R.C.M. 910(a)(1), MANUAL FOR COURTS-MARTIAL, UNITED STATES (2005 ed.). Military appellate courts have rejected constitutional challenges to this prohibition. *See, e.g., United States v. Matthews*, 15 M.J. at 362 (C.M.A. 1983). Only three civilian death penalty jurisdictions — Arkansas, Louisiana, and New York — have similar prohibitions. Barry J. Fisher, *Judicial Suicide or Constitutional Autonomy? A Capital Defendant's Right to Plead Guilty*, 65 ALB. L. REV. 181, 181 (2001).

4. Pretrial agreement practice is now regulated by Rule for Courts-Martial 705. The rule includes lists of matters that may and may not be included in pretrial agreements. R.C.M. 705(c).

5. *See generally* Col. Carlton L. Jackson, *Plea-Bargaining in the Military: An Unintended Consequence of the Uniform Code of Military Justice*, 179 MIL. L. REV. 1 (2004); Maj. Mary M. Foreman, *Let's Make a Deal! The Development of Pretrial Agreements in Military Criminal Justice Practice*, 170 MIL. L. REV. 53 (2001).

II. AUTHORIZED PUNISHMENTS

Uniform Code of Military Justice
Article 56. Maximum limits

The punishment which a court-martial may direct for an offense may not exceed such limits as the President may prescribe for that offense.

Rule for Courts-Martial 1003(b)
Manual for Courts-Martial, United States (2005 ed.)

(b) *Authorized punishments.* Subject to the limitations in this Manual, a court-martial may adjudge only the following punishments:

(1) *Reprimand.* A court-martial shall not specify the terms or wording of a reprimand. A reprimand, if approved, shall be issued, in writing, by the convening authority;

(2) *Forfeiture of pay and allowances.* Unless a total forfeiture is adjudged, a sentence to forfeiture shall state the exact amount in whole dollars to be forfeited each month and the number of months the forfeitures will last. Allowances shall be subject to forfeiture only when the sentence includes forfeiture of all pay and allowances. The maximum authorized amount of a partial forfeiture shall be determined by using the basic pay, retired pay, or retainer pay, as applicable, or, in the case of reserve component personnel on inactive-duty, compensation for periods of inactive duty training, authorized by the cumulative years of service of the accused, and, if no confinement is adjudged, any sea or foreign duty pay. If the sentence also includes reduction in grade, expressly or by operation of law, the maximum forfeiture shall be based on the grade to which the accused is reduced.

(3) *Fine.* Any court-martial may adjudge a fine in lieu of or in addition to forfeitures. Special and summary courts-martial may not adjudge any fine or combination of fine and forfeitures in excess of the total amount of forfeitures that may be adjudged in that case. In order to enforce collection, a fine may be accompanied by a provision in the sentence that, in the event the fine is not paid, the person fined shall, in addition to any period of confinement adjudged, be further confined until a fixed period considered an equivalent punishment to the fine has expired. The total period of confinement so adjudged shall not exceed the jurisdictional limitations of the court-martial;

(4) *Reduction in pay grade.* Except as provided in R.C.M. 1301(d), a court-martial may sentence an enlisted member to be reduced to the lowest or any intermediate pay grade;

(5) *Restriction to specified limits.* Restriction may be adjudged for no more than 2 months for each month of authorized confinement and in no case for more than 2 months. Confinement and restriction may be adjudged in the same case, but they may not together exceed the maximum authorized period of confinement, calculating the equivalency at the rate specified in this subsection;

(6) *Hard labor without confinement.* Hard labor without confinement may be adjudged for no more than 1-1/2 months for each month of authorized confinement and in no case for more than three months. Hard labor without confinement may be adjudged only in the cases of enlisted members. The court-martial shall not specify the hard labor to be performed. Confinement and hard labor without confinement may be adjudged in the same case, but they may not together exceed the maximum authorized period of confinement, calculating the equivalency at the rate specified in this subsection.

(7) *Confinement.* The place of confinement shall not be designated by the court-martial. When confinement for life is authorized, it may be with or without eligibility for parole. A court-martial shall not adjudge a sentence to solitary confinement or to confinement without hard labor;

(8) *Punitive separation.* A court-martial may not adjudge an administrative separation from the service. There are three types of punitive separation.

(A) *Dismissal.* Dismissal applies only to commissioned officers, commissioned warrant officers, cadets, and midshipmen and may be adjudged only by a general court-martial. Regardless of the maximum punishment specified for an offense in Part IV of this Manual, a dismissal may be adjudged for any offense of which a commissioned officer, commissioned warrant officer, cadet, or midshipman has been found guilty;

(B) *Dishonorable discharge.* A dishonorable discharge applies only to enlisted persons and warrant officers who are not commissioned and may be adjudged only by a general court-martial. Regardless of the maximum punishment specified for an offense in Part IV of this Manual, a dishonorable discharge may be adjudged for any offense of which a warrant officer who is not commissioned has been found guilty. A dishonorable discharge should be reserved for those who should be separated under conditions of dishonor, after having been convicted of offenses usually recognized in civilian jurisdictions as felonies, or of offenses of a military nature requiring severe punishment; and

(C) *Bad conduct discharge.* A bad-conduct discharge applies only to enlisted persons and may be adjudged by a general court-martial and by a special court-martial which has met the requirements of R.C.M. 201(f)(2)(B). A bad-conduct discharge is less severe than a dishonorable discharge and is designed as a punishment for bad-conduct rather than as a punishment for serious offenses of either a civilian or military nature. It is also appropriate for an accused who has been convicted repeatedly of minor offenses and whose punitive separation appears to be necessary;

(9) *Death*. Death may be adjudged only in accordance with R.C.M. 1004; and

(10) *Punishments under the law of war*. In cases tried under the law of war, a general court-martial may adjudge any punishment not prohibited by the law of war.

NOTE

In 1997, Congress authorized a court-martial to adjudge a sentence of confinement for life without eligibility for parole. National Defense Authorization Act for Fiscal Year 1998, Pub. L. No. 105-85, § 581, 111 Stat. 1629, 1759 (1997) (codified at 10 U.S.C. § 856a). The President, however, did not incorporate confinement for life without eligibility for parole in R.C.M. 1003(b) until April 2002. Exec. Order No. 13,262, 67 Fed. Reg. 18,773 (Apr. 17, 2002). In a series of decisions, the Court of Appeals for the Armed Forces has held that confinement for life without eligibility for parole was an authorized sentence upon the authorizing statute's effective date, even before the President incorporated it in the Manual. *United States v. Ronghi*, 60 M.J. 83 (C.A.A.F. 2004); *United States v. Stebbins*, 61 M.J. 366, 368 (C.A.A.F. 2005); *United States v. Christian*, 63 M.J. 205 (C.A.A.F. 2006).

III. UNIQUE MILITARY PUNISHMENTS

UNITED STATES v. RUSH
United States Court of Appeals for the Armed Forces
54 M.J. 313 (C.A.A.F. 2001)

JUDGE SULLIVAN delivered the opinion of the Court. . . .

We hold that the military judge erred in refusing to give a defense-requested standard instruction on the "ineradicable stigma" of a punitive discharge without explaining the basis of his decision on the record. *See* R.C.M. 1005(c), Manual for Courts-Martial, United States (1995 ed.). Such error, however, was harmless in this case. *See United States v. Soriano*, 20 M.J. 337 (C.M.A. 1985).

The facts in this case which pertain to the granted issue are not disputed. The appellate court below summarized them as follows:

> The appellant was convicted of incidents involving two fellow servicemembers. First, the appellant pointed a knife at a soldier and lunged at him after the soldier followed him outside a building to smooth over a previous brief, minor, contentious discussion. Later, he threatened to injure this same soldier in retaliation for the soldier's reporting the aggravated assault. Second, in an unrelated incident, the appellant attacked a United States Marine Corps trainee, first with his fists, then with a knife, apparently because the appellant was offended by the trainee's stare. That aggravated assault resulted in a knife wound to the trainee's temple.

> During two brief Article 39(a), UCMJ, sessions held prior to presentation of sentencing evidence, the military judge discussed sentencing

instructions, but only to inquire whether the defense counsel desired the instruction explaining unsworn statements. The record contains no other indication of any in-court or out-of-court session concerning sentencing instructions.

During his sentencing instructions, the military judge read the standard bad-conduct discharge instruction:

> A bad-conduct discharge. You are instructed that a bad-conduct discharge deprives a soldier of virtually all benefits administered by the Veterans' Administration and the Army establishment. A bad-conduct discharge is a severe punishment, and may be adjudged for one who, in the discretion of the court, warrants more severe punishment for bad conduct, even though the bad conduct may not constitute commission of serious offenses of a military or civil nature. In this case, if you determine to adjudge a punitive discharge, you may sentence Private Rush to a bad-conduct discharge; no other type of discharge may be ordered in this case.

See Dep't of Army, Pam. 27-9, Military Judges' Benchbook 70 (30 Sep. 1996) (currently unchanged at 70.1, Change 1, 30 Jan. 1998) [hereinafter Benchbook]. He did not read any portion of the standard ineradicable stigma instruction.[1] After instructions, the military judge asked whether either counsel wanted additional instructions or objected to those given. The defense counsel replied, "Defense would request the ineradicable stigma instruction, Your Honor." The military judge answered, "I'm not going to give that instruction, Captain []." He offered no explanation.

51 M.J. at 606-07.

The Court of Criminal Appeals, after a lengthy historical analysis of the ineradicable stigma instruction, held that under the circumstances of the particular case, the military judge's action was arbitrary, clearly unreasonable, and constituted an abuse of discretion because he inexplicably refused to give the standard sentencing instruction after a timely request without stating any reason for his decision to deviate from the Benchbook. *Id.* at 610. Nevertheless, it concluded that in light of certain factors delineated in *United States v. Soriano, supra,* the omission of the instruction did not prejudice appellant as to his sentence.

Our starting point in resolving the granted issue is the opinion of the Court of Criminal Appeals. It exhaustively explored the origins of the standard instruction provided in the Military Judges' Benchbook on the ineradicable stigma of a punitive discharge. It said in pertinent part:

---

[1] [n. 1] Benchbook at 69:

> You are advised that the ineradicable stigma of a punitive discharge is commonly recognized by our society. A punitive discharge will place limitations on employment opportunities and will deny the accused other advantages which are enjoyed by one whose discharge characterization indicates that (he)(she) has served honorably. A punitive discharge will affect an accused's future with regard to (his)(her) legal rights, economic opportunities, and social acceptability.

Because the standard Benchbook instructions are based on a careful analysis of current case law and statute, an individual military judge should not deviate significantly from these instructions without explaining his or her reasons on the record. It is possible that this military judge harbored the belief that a punitive discharge no longer carried a stigma, or that the economic consequences of a discharge were not relevant to the members' sentencing decision, or that the instruction was not appropriate in this appellant's case. We cannot divine his reasons from a blank record. Under the circumstances of this case, because the military judge inexplicably refused to give the standard sentencing instruction after a timely request without stating any reason for his decision to deviate from the Benchbook, we find his action to be arbitrary and clearly unreasonable, and thus an abuse of discretion.

51 M.J. at 609-10 (footnotes omitted).

We share the lower appellate court's concern that military members be properly instructed as to the severe nature of a punitive discharge. *See United States v. Soriano*, 20 M.J. at 337. We also agree with the lower appellate court that the military judge has a duty to explain why he is refusing to give a standard instruction requested by the defense. *See* R.C.M. 1005(c) ("The military judge shall inform the parties of the proposed action on such requests before their closing arguments on sentence."); *see also United States v. Neal*, 17 U.S.C.M.A. 363, 365, 38 C.M.R. 161, 163 (1968). In our view, meaningful appellate review of the trial judge's decision on this important sentencing matter requires that he articulate his reason for his decision. *See United States v. Smith*, 50 M.J. 451, 455 (1999).

The remaining question before us is whether the failure of the trial judge to give the defense requested standard instruction without explanation was harmless error. There was no constitutional error here, but rather a violation of a Manual provision promulgated by the President to ensure a military accused a fair trial. *See* R.C.M. 1005(c). In this context, we must decide whether this objected to error substantially influenced the sentence proceedings such that it led to a bad-conduct discharge being unfairly imposed in this case. *See* Art. 59(a), UCMJ, 10 U.S.C. § 859(a). We conclude that it did not.

As noted above, the instructions actually given in this case did expressly state to the members that "a bad-conduct discharge is a severe punishment." (R. 436). *See United States v. Soriano, supra* at 343. Second, three of the four offenses for which appellant was found guilty were aggravated in nature and individually authorized a punitive discharge. *See* paras. 110(e) and 54(e)(8), Part IV, Manual, *supra*. Third, defense counsel conceded to the members that appellant would be otherwise stigmatized, lose benefits, and have his military career terminated by reason of his felony convictions. (R. 431-32). Finally, this case was tried before experienced members (*e.g.*, two colonels, two lieutenant colonels, and three command sergeant majors) who could reasonably be expected to appreciate the severity of this punishment on their own. In these circumstances, as in *Soriano, supra*, we find no prejudice and affirm.

The decision of the United States Army Court of Criminal Appeals is affirmed.

EFFRON, JUDGE (concurring in part and dissenting in part):

I agree with the lead opinion's conclusion that the military judge erred by not giving the requested instruction on the ineradicable stigma of a bad-conduct discharge. The instruction echoes the special attention of Congress to the stigma of a bad-conduct discharge, which is reflected in those portions of the UCMJ providing that a bad-conduct discharge may be imposed only when the accused has been provided with detailed defense counsel, a verbatim record has been prepared, a military judge has presided at trial (unless precluded by physical conditions or military exigencies), and judicial review has been conducted (unless waived or withdrawn). *See* Arts. 19, 66(b)(1), and 71(c), UCMJ, 10 U.S.C. §§ 819, 866(b)(1), and 871(c), respectively. It is noteworthy that Congress, by contrast, has authorized the imposition of confinement for up to 6 months without any of these protections. *See id.* Special attention to the stigma of a bad-conduct discharge is not simply a vestigial item from an earlier era, but reflects recent congressional attention to these issues. *See* National Defense Authorization Act for Fiscal Year 2000, Pub. L. No. 106-65, § 577(a), 113 Stat. 512, 625 (1999).

I disagree with that portion of the lead opinion finding that appellant was not prejudiced by the military judge's refusal to give this required instruction — a standard instruction that was specifically requested by appellant. The lead opinion finds the error to be harmless based upon the nature of the offenses, the general references by the military judge and defense counsel to the seriousness of a bad-conduct discharge, and the likely knowledge of the panel members. Although these factors might have rendered the error non-prejudicial if the case involved a general court-martial involving a lengthy sentence, this was not such a case.

The best measure of the nature of this case comes from the decision of the convening authority to refer it to a special, rather than a general, court-martial. In that context — a case the command itself viewed as relatively minor — it was particularly important that the military judge use the standard instruction to direct the attention of the members beyond generalized concerns about a bad-conduct discharge. The standard instruction would have required them to focus on the permanent stigma — the ineradicable stain — of a bad-conduct discharge. Under the circumstances of this case, the refusal of the military judge to give the standard instruction was prejudicial to the substantial rights of appellant. *See* Art. 59(a), UCMJ, 10 U.S.C. § 859(a). I would reverse and remand for a new sentencing proceeding.

CRAWFORD, CHIEF JUDGE (concurring in the result):

R.C.M. 1005(e), Manual for Courts-Martial, United States (2000 ed.), requires certain instructions. Nowhere at the time of appellant's trial did that rule require an instruction to the effect that a punitive discharge creates "an ineradicable stigma." The same holds true today. In particular, R.C.M. 1005(e)(2) requires members to be instructed that any sentence involving a punitive discharge and confinement, or confinement in excess of 6 months, will have an effect on a servicemember's entitlement to pay and allowances. If the

President had intended that members be instructed that punitive discharges carried a stigma of some type, he would have added it in this section.

In my view, the Court of Criminal Appeals erred when it rejected the contention that the ineradicable stigma instruction was optional. A Department of the Army Pamphlet, albeit a widely respected, constantly used and up-to-date Military Judges' Benchbook, published by the Secretary of the Army, does not take precedence over a Rule for Court-Martial promulgated by the President.

United States v. Soriano, 20 M.J. 337 (C.M.A. 1985), held that a punitive discharge was a severe punishment and court members were to be instructed accordingly. I completely agree. The court members in this case were properly instructed.

The ineradicable stigma instruction found in the Military Judges' Benchbook addresses the effect of a punitive discharge on one individual (the accused at trial) vis-à-vis all of the servicemembers who do not receive a punitive discharge. It is one thing to instruct court members that a punitive discharge is severe punishment. It is quite another thing to tell court members that an adjudged punitive discharge may have an ineradicable stigma when such may not be the case at all.

This court has frequently emphasized the importance of giving members appropriate instructions. *See, e.g., United States v. Greaves*, 46 M.J. 133 (1997). Instructions that are appropriate must be tailored to the facts of each case and may reflect perceptions as well as developments in social and labor trends. *See United States v. Tualla*, 52 M.J. 228, 233 (2000) (Crawford, C.J., concurring).

Even today, the majority does not hold that the ineradicable stigma instruction is required. They find that the military judge erred by not explaining why he was refusing to give the instruction. While an explanation from the military judge may have been helpful to both the lower court and this Court in reviewing this case, an explanation was not required because the ineradicable stigma instruction, albeit a "standard one," was not required by R.C.M. 1005(e) or the law of this Court. The onus was on trial defense counsel to justify why such an instruction was appropriate under the facts of this case. As I have said previously, "The forum for initiating a new or different application of facts to existing law is the trial court. The bellwether to bring changed conditions to the forefront should be either the trial or defense counsel." *Id.* at 232. Reliance on a 1978 law review article to determine what, if any, stigma is attached to a punitive discharge is no longer justified. [*See* Charles E. Lance, *A Criminal Punitive Discharge — An Effective Punishment?*, 79 Mil. L. Rev. 1 (1978).]

NOTES

1. After its decision in *Rush*, the Court of Appeals for the Armed Forces has appeared to move closer to Judge Crawford's position in her *Rush* dissent. In *United States v. Rasnick*, 58 M.J. 9 (C.A.A.F. 2003) (per curiam), the military judge gave the members this instruction:

Now members, you are advised that the stigma of a punitive discharge is commonly recognized by our society. A punitive discharge will place limitations on employment opportunities and will deny the accused other advantages which are enjoyed by one whose discharge characterization indicates that he has served honorably. A punitive discharge will affect an accused's future with regard to his legal rights, economic opportunities, and social acceptability.

You may adjudge a bad conduct discharge. Such a discharge deprives one of substantially all benefits administered by the Department of Veterans Affairs and the Air Force establishment. A bad conduct discharge is severe punishment and may be adjudged for one who in the discretion of the court warrants severe punishment for bad conduct, even though such bad conduct may not include commission of serious offenses of a military or civil nature.

The Court of Appeals for the Armed Forces ruled that this instruction was sufficient, concluding that "[a]lthough the word 'ineradicable' provides an appropriate means of describing the future impact of a punitive discharge, *see United States v. Rush*, 54 M.J. 313 (C.A.A.F.), it is not the exclusive means of doing so."

2. One commentator's review of recent empirical data led him to conclude that a bad-conduct discharge has only limited impact on a veteran's earnings and employment opportunities. Major Jeffrey D. Lippert, *Automatic Appeal under UCMJ Article 66: Time for a Change*, 182 MIL. L. REV. 1, 22-25 (2004). What sort of evidence should be considered in revisiting the conclusion of the 1978 law review article that Judge Crawford so disdained?

3. A long line of military appellate cases deals with the evidence that the government may, and may not, present to seek a punitive discharge. The Coast Guard Court of Criminal Appeals explained that military case law prohibits a government witness from either directly or indirectly suggesting that the accused be punitively discharged:

As the Court of Military Appeals held in *United States v. Ohrt*, R.C.M. 1001(b)(5) permits a trial counsel to introduce evidence of an accused's rehabilitative potential. *United States v. Ohrt*, 28 M.J. 301, 303 (C.M.A. 1989). Such evidence may be in the form of an opinion if a proper foundation is laid to show that the witness has personal knowledge of an accused's character, performance, and other relevant factors. *Ohrt*, 28 M.J. at 304. The Court also held that, although rehabilitative potential is "inextricably related" to whether an accused should be retained in military service or awarded a punitive discharge, a witness should not be allowed to express an opinion as to whether an accused should be given a punitive discharge or returned to his or her unit. 28 M.J. at 304-05. Other euphemisms for a punitive discharge are also prohibited. *Id.* at 305.

United States v. Warner, 59 M.J. 590, 594 (C.G. Ct. Crim. App. 2003).

The Air Force Court provided this helpful summary of the law limiting government sentencing witnesses' testimony about the accused's rehabilitative potential:

(1) Improper command influence. Military case law reflects significant concern that prosecutors would "bring a commanding officer before a court-martial preemptively to *influence* the court members" through opinion testimony. *Ohrt*, 28 M.J. at 303 (emphasis in the original). The presumed weight that a commander's testimony might carry has been viewed as an unfair opportunity for a commander to influence the sentencing authority's decision on a punitive discharge.

(2) Confusion. Another common concern is that such testimony would confuse court members about the critical distinction between a punitive discharge (punishment) and retention in the military (the appropriateness of continued military service). *Id.* at 305.

(3) Usurping the role of the sentencing authority. A belief that opinion testimony would usurp the sentencing authority's role has been a prominent concern in this area of sentencing jurisprudence. Appellate courts have made it clear such testimony should not express a "personal opinion concerning what punishment would be appropriate for the offense." *United States v. Wilson*, 31 M.J. 91, 93 (C.M.A. 1990). Testimony that indirectly suggests a particular punishment is considered a "euphemism" and has similarly been held improper. *Ohrt*, 28 M.J. at 305.

(4) Proper foundation for opinion. Rehabilitation witnesses must have a rational basis for their opinion and cannot offer an opinion if it is based primarily on the severity of the offense itself. *Wilson*, 31 M.J. at 94; *Horner*, 22 M.J. at 296.

(5) Uncharged misconduct. Government witnesses must avoid any references to uncharged misconduct, unless the defense opens the door on cross-examination. *Ohrt*, 28 M.J. at 303-05.

United States v. Griggs, 59 M.J. 712, 714 (A.F. Ct. Crim. App. 2004), *aff'd in part & rev'd in part*, 61 M.J. 402 (C.A.A.F. 2005).

Uniform Code of Military Justice
Article 55. Cruel and unusual punishments prohibited

Punishment by flogging, or by branding, marking, or tattooing on the body, or any other cruel or unusual punishment, may not be adjudged by a court-martial or inflicted upon any person subject to this chapter. The use of irons, single or double, except for the purpose of safe custody, is prohibited.

UNITED STATES v. YATCHAK
United States Court of Military Appeals
35 M.J. 379 (C.M.A. 1992)

GIERKE, JUDGE:

A military judge sitting as a special court-martial convicted appellant, in accordance with his pleas, of unauthorized absence and two wrongful uses of cocaine, in violation of Articles 86 and 112a, Uniform Code of Military Justice,

10 U.S.C. §§ 886 and 912a, respectively. The adjudged sentence provides for a bad-conduct discharge, "three days bread and water, followed by 100 days of confinement," and forfeiture of $350.00 pay per month for 5 months. Appellant did not contest the legality of his sentence at the time it was announced, but in a post-trial clemency petition to the convening authority dated June 1, 1990, appellant cited *United States v. Valead*, 30 M.J. 634 (N.M.C.M.R. 1990), and requested that the convening authority disapprove his punishment of confinement on bread and water. Appellant was released from the brig and placed on appellate leave on June 7, 1990. On June 12 the convening authority approved the sentence as adjudged. At that time he had served 59 days in confinement, and no forfeitures had been collected. . . .

At the time of his court-martial, appellant was assigned to the crew of the USS KITTY HAWK, which was undergoing a long-term overhaul that would not be completed until several months after the trial. Prior to his court-martial, appellant was in pretrial confinement in a shore facility brig. His court-martial took place ashore, and he served his sentence in a shore facility brig. The Government and the defense agree that the USS KITTY HAWK "was never in an operational status throughout the period of appellant's naval service." . . .

As he did before the court below, appellant now contends that his sentence to confinement on bread and water violated the Eighth Amendment and Article 55. We agree that his sentence violated Article 55, and, therefore, we need not reach the Constitutional question.

At the outset we note that the only mention of confinement on bread and water in the UCMJ is in Article 15(b)(2)(A), 10 U.S.C. § 815(b)(2)(A), which lists it as an authorized nonjudicial punishment for persons "attached to or embarked in a vessel." Courts-martial are authorized by R.C.M. 1003(b)(9), Manual for Courts-Martial, United States, 1984, to impose confinement on bread and water on enlisted persons "attached to or embarked in a vessel."

The fundamental question in this case is whether appellant was "attached to or embarked in a vessel." In *United States v. Wappler*, 2 U.S.C.M.A. 393, 9 C.M.R. 23 (1953), this Court examined the legislative history of the phrase. The Court concluded that Congress reluctantly authorized confinement on bread and water for those "at sea," 2 U.S.C.M.A. 393 at 396, 9 C.M.R. 23 at 26, in response to the Navy's argument that it "was one of the few effective punishments available for imposition aboard ship," 2 U.S.C.M.A. 393 at 395, 9 C.M.R. 23 at 25, but that Congress refused to authorize it for "land-based personnel" because they considered it unjustified by military necessity. Based on its reading of the intent of Congress, this Court concluded that imposition of confinement on bread and water on anyone other than "those at sea" was "cruel and [sic] unusual" and therefore prohibited by Article 55. 2 U.S.C.M.A. 393 at 396, 9 C.M.R. 23 at 26. Although the Congressional discussion concerned confinement on bread and water as a nonjudicial punishment rather than as a court-martial sentence, this Court concluded that "Congressional concern over bread and water confinement was not at all directed against the source of the action but, rather, was aimed at the very nature of the punishment itself." 2 U.S.C.M.A. 393 at 395, 9 C.M.R. 23 at 25. Accordingly, this Court held: "No court-martial . . . may adjudge confinement on bread and

water for personnel other than those 'attached to or embarked in a vessel' . . . ."
2 U.S.C.M.A. 393 at 396, 9 C.M.R. 23 at 26.

This Court again considered the legality of confinement on bread and water
in *United States v. Valead*, 32 M.J. 122 (C.M.A. 1991), which coincidentally
involved the same long-term overhaul of appellant's ship, USS KITTY HAWK.
In *Valead* Chief Judge Sullivan, with Judge Cox concurring, found it unnecessary to reach the Constitutional or Article 55 question in light of the Court of
Military Review's decision setting aside the punishment as inappropriate.
Senior Judge Everett, concurring in the result, "tended to agree" with the
defense contention that "Valead was not 'attached to' the USS KITTY HAWK
within the meaning of . . . R.C.M. 1003(b)(9) — which contemplates vessels at
sea or about to go to sea." *Id*. at 127-28. The legislative history supports Senior
Judge Everett's tentative interpretation of the term, since it reflects that
Congress devised the term, "attached to or embarked in a vessel," to cover
those actually at sea as well as those in port when their ship is about to depart.
See Uniform Code of Military Justice: Hearings on H.R. 2498 Before a
Subcomm. of the House Armed Services Comm., 81st Cong., 1st Sess. 945-46
(1949), reprinted in Index and Legislative History, Uniform Code of Military
Justice (1949).

After reviewing our prior decisions in *Wappler* and *Valead* and examining
the legislative history of congressional concerns about the punishment of confinement on bread and water, we hold that appellant was not "attached to or
embarked in a vessel," as that phrase was used by Congress. Since the punishment was imposed and executed in circumstances where Congress intended
that it be prohibited as "cruel or unusual," we hold that confinement on bread
and water in this case was prohibited by Article 55. *United States v. Wappler*,
supra. . . .

NOTE

President Clinton's 1995 amendments to the *Manual for Courts-Martial*
eliminated both confinement on bread and water and confinement on diminished rations as authorized court-martial punishments. Exec. Order No.
12,960, § 2.d, 60 FED. REG. 26647, 26647 (May 12, 1995). The drafters' analysis explains, "Confinement on bread and water or diminished rations was originally intended as an immediate, remedial punishment. While this is still the
case with nonjudicial punishment (Article 15), it is not effective as a court-
martial punishment." R.C.M. 1003 drafters' analysis, MANUAL FOR COURTS-
MARTIAL, UNITED STATES, App. 21, at A21-73 (2005 ed.).

Eugene R. Fidell & Jay M. Fidell, *Loss of Numbers*
48 NAVAL L. REV. 194, 194-99 (2001)

Until 1999, when President Clinton abolished it, "loss of numbers" [moving
an officer down in seniority] was a permissible court-martial sentence in the
sea services. Although this historical footnote may appear at first glance to be
little more than some "inside baseball" for military lawyers, in fact it is highly
pertinent in the conversation now taking place in naval circles and elsewhere

about accountability. Abolition of loss of numbers is one of those events that seem inconsequential at the time but later prove either to be or to reflect trends of far greater significance. There is no shortage of these events in the military justice context. . . .

The most recent example of these obscure but important actions occurred in 1999. Tucked away in that year's changes to the *Manual for Courts-Martial* was an amendment deleting Rule for Courts-Martial 1003(b)(4), which had been the basis for the court-martial punishment of loss of numbers.[2] Although loss of numbers had once been a permissible punishment even in the Army, it was rarely used by that service, and from the beginning of the UCMJ era it was applicable only in the Navy, Marine Corps and Coast Guard. As a cultural matter it had become quintessentially a sea services punishment, like "bread and water." The cases bear this out: while occasionally adjudged in shoreside settings, loss of numbers had a distinctly nautical ring. Indeed, while its use was not so limited, it probably had come to be associated above all with crimes of command, such as hazarding a vessel or related derelictions.

Among those who suffered this punishment were Captain Edward L. Beach (father of the author of *Run Silent, Run Deep*), who was sentenced to a loss of 20 numbers while commanding USS MEMPHIS (CL-13) in 1916. (The Secretary of the Navy later reduced the sentence to loss of five numbers.) Commanding officers of USS INDIANAPOLIS (CA-35), USS MISSOURI (BB-63), USS BASILONE (DDE-824), USCGC WINNEBAGO (WPG-40), USCGC OWASCO (WHEC-39), USCGC CUYAHOGA (WIX-157) and USCGC MESQUITE (WLB-305) all lost numbers as well, although in the last cited incident the conviction was overturned on appeal and the captain wound up at admiral's mast. The executive officer of USS PRESTIGE (MSO-465) lost numbers after a 1958 grounding, but this was set aside because the commanding officer had been acquitted. Loss of numbers certainly had a lot of history behind it. That history reflected a set of expectations based not so much on selection boards painstakingly comparing fitness reports as on a more mechanical process by which senior officers would more or less inexorably advance upwards through the list as the grim reaper created vacancies around and — better yet — above them.

Despite the Navy's tradition of resistance to military justice reforms, abolition of loss of numbers is one it affirmatively sought. Why did it do so? The explanation included in the Joint Service Committee's 1997 notice of proposed rulemaking identified no pressing need for action. Rather, it treated the matter as simply clearing away a provision that was misunderstood and served little purpose:

---

[2] [n. 9] MANUAL FOR COURTS-MARTIAL, UNITED STATES, R.C.M. 1003(b)(4) (1998 ed.) [hereinafter MCM] had read: "*Loss of numbers, lineal position, or seniority.* These punishments are authorized only in cases of Navy, Marine Corps, and Coast Guard officers[.]" The accompanying official "Discussion" was equally terse: "All losses of numbers will be numbers in the appropriate lineal list." MCM *supra* (1998 ed.), at II-125. The 1999 Executive Order renumbered the balance of R.C.M. 1003(b), so there remains an R.C.M. 1003(b)(4), but the text is simply that previously found in R.C.M. 1003(b)(5). *See* MCM *supra* (2000 ed.) at II-126.

Although loss of numbers had the effect of lowering precedence for some purposes, e.g., quarters priority, board and court seniority, and actual date of promotion, loss of numbers did not affect the officer's original position for purposes of consideration for retention or promotion. Accordingly, this punishment was deleted because of its negligible consequences and the misconception that it was a meaningful punishment.[3]

Was this a valid reason? One of the leading treatises makes you wonder. It indicates that loss of numbers generally "adversely affected the officer in terms of obtaining quarters *and in actual promotion in rank.*"[4] The National Institute of Military Justice commented: "While NIMJ intuitively agrees that this traditional punishment can now be dispensed with, we would feel more confident on this score if data on the actual imposition of loss of numbers were made available." Subsequently released internal records show that the Bureau of Naval Personnel had already estimated that there were one or two loss of numbers cases per year, but that estimate was not made known to the public at the time, and the proposal continued to wend its way through the protracted Executive Branch approval process. In the ensuing few years no one has sought to reinstate loss of numbers as a court-martial punishment. Indeed, scarcely anyone has even noticed the change.

Were we all too casual? Is abolition of loss of numbers more important than we thought? For one thing, it brought the services a notch closer for military justice purposes, making the Uniform Code that much more uniform. For another, it put less daylight between the punishment powers of a court-martial and those of a flag officer in command. Since, especially for crimes of command, dismissal or brig time are highly unlikely to be adjudged in a court-martial, and since involuntary separation can be effected through a board of officers (unless the offender chooses to retire or otherwise "go quietly"), abolition of loss of numbers means that essentially the same sanctions — notably, letters of reprimand — can be imposed at admiral's mast as are likely to emerge from a court-martial.

The net effect of abolition, therefore, coupled with the rise of administrative measures such as removal from promotion lists, detachment for cause, retirement grade determinations, and the like, seems to be either to mark or to accelerate the demise of the general court-martial as the forum of choice for the administration of justice in cases involving crimes of command by naval officers.

This evolution may make sense, but it is worth pondering since it is not without cost. It entails a rejection of the court-martial apparatus with all of its highly-touted protections for the individual (proof beyond a reasonable doubt, cross-examination of witnesses, "blue ribbon" juries, resolution of legal issues by a trained judiciary, to name a few) that have been developed especially over

---

[3] [n. 17] Notice of Proposed Amendments to the MANUAL FOR COURTS-MARTIAL, 62 FED. REG. 24,640, 24,642 (May 6, 1997).

[4] [n. 18] DAVID A. SCHLUETER, MILITARY CRIMINAL JUSTICE: PRACTICE AND PROCEDURE § 16-3(F), at 727 (5th ed. 2000) (emphasis added). For example, even the loss of numbers Captain Beach, Sr. suffered made it unlikely he would ever attain flag rank.

the last 50 years, as well as loss of the incalculable benefit of increased public confidence that justice has been done. Shifting a category of cases from the trial forum to a command-focused forum of, if anything, even greater antiquity, seems anomalous. Moreover, shifting to what may seem a more lenient forum a category of cases in which the accused is always an officer can be expected to generate consternation among enlisted personnel, not to mention the public. A court-martial can still reduce an enlisted member's pay grade; it can no longer even reduce an officer's seniority *within* a pay grade. The separate disciplinary treatment of officers and enlisted personnel has become a little more separate, and crimes of command have seemingly been decriminalized, the UCMJ notwithstanding.

Beyond all these considerations lies the loss of something even more elusive. The Joint Service Committee's explanation for abolition was right on a certain level: loss of numbers had become virtually a museum piece. It was essentially a 19th or even an 18th century sanction struggling to survive in a 21st century Navy. It had a certain anachronistic quality that tied the naval present to the naval past. Indeed, it also had an unmistakably ritualistic ring to it, like the old requirement that holiday colors be displayed when a general court-martial was in session. Even today, precise seniority has consequences at every turn, not simply for deciding who gets to be president of a court or board or who gets which quarters, but also, which ship renders passing honors and who salutes whom. Issues of seniority continue to pervade naval life. At the risk of sounding like old fogies, given all this, were we too hasty in throwing loss of numbers over the side? Will we one-day regret having done so?

NOTE

One unusual military punishment that remains is hard labor without confinement. One commentator has written favorably about this punishment, advocating its increased use. Maj. Joseph B. Berger III, *Making Little Rocks Out of Big Rocks: Implementing Sentences to Hard Labor Without Confinement*, ARMY LAW., Dec. 2004, at 1.

IV. DEATH PENALTY

LOVING v. UNITED STATES
Supreme Court of the United States
517 U.S. 748 (1996)

KENNEDY, J., delivered the opinion of the Court, in which REHNQUIST, C.J., and STEVENS, SOUTER, GINSBURG, and BREYER, JJ., joined, and in which O'CONNOR and SCALIA, JJ., joined as to Parts I, II, III, IV-B, and IV-C. STEVENS, J., filed a concurring opinion, in which SOUTER, GINSBURG, and BREYER, JJ., joined. SCALIA, J., filed an opinion concurring in part and concurring in the judgment, in which O'CONNOR, J., joined. THOMAS, J., filed an opinion concurring in the judgment.

JUSTICE KENNEDY delivered the opinion of the Court.

The case before us concerns the authority of the President, in our system of separated powers, to prescribe aggravating factors that permit a court-martial to impose the death penalty upon a member of the Armed Forces convicted of murder.

I

On December 12, 1988, petitioner Dwight Loving, an Army private stationed at Fort Hood, Texas, murdered two taxicab drivers from the nearby town of Killeen. He attempted to murder a third, but the driver disarmed him and escaped. Civilian and Army authorities arrested Loving the next afternoon. He confessed.

After a trial, an eight-member general court-martial found Loving guilty of, among other offenses, premeditated murder and felony murder under Article 118 of the Uniform Code of Military Justice (UCMJ), 10 U.S.C. §§ 918(1), (4). In the sentencing phase of the trial, the court-martial found three aggravating factors: (1) that the premeditated murder of the second driver was committed during the course of a robbery, Rule for Courts-Martial (R.C.M.) 1004(c)(7)(B); (2) that Loving acted as the triggerman in the felony murder of the first driver, R.C.M. 1004(c)(8); and (3) that Loving, having been found guilty of the premeditated murder, had committed a second murder, also proved at the single trial, R.C.M. 1004(c)(7)(J). The court-martial sentenced Loving to death.

The commander who convened the court-martial approved the findings and sentence. Cf. 10 U.S.C. § 860. The United States Army Court of Military Review and the United States Court of Appeals for the Armed Forces (formerly the United States Court of Military Appeals (CMA)) affirmed, 41 M.J. 213 (1994). . . .

II

Although American courts-martial from their inception have had the power to decree capital punishment, they have not long had the authority to try and to sentence members of the Armed Forces for capital murder committed in the United States in peacetime. In the early days of the Republic the powers of courts-martial were fixed in the Articles of War. Congress enacted the first Articles in 1789 by adopting in full the Articles promulgated in 1775 (and revised in 1776) by the Continental Congress. Act of Sept. 29, 1789, ch. 25, § 4, 1 Stat. 96. (Congress reenacted the Articles in 1790 "as far as the same may be applicable to the constitution of the United States," Act of Apr. 30, 1790, ch. 10, § 13, 1 Stat. 121.) The Articles adopted by the First Congress placed significant restrictions on court-martial jurisdiction over capital offenses. Although the death penalty was authorized for 14 military offenses, American Articles of War of 1776, reprinted in W. Winthrop, Military Law and Precedents 961 (reprint 2d ed. 1920) (hereinafter Winthrop); Comment, *Rocks and Shoals in a Sea of Otherwise Deep Commitment: General Court-Martial Size and Voting Requirements*, 35 Nav. L. Rev. 153, 156-158 (1986), the Articles followed the British example of ensuring the supremacy of civil court jurisdiction over ordinary capital crimes that were punishable by the law of the land and were not special military offenses. 1776 Articles, § 10, Art. 1, reprinted in Winthrop 964 (requiring commanders, upon application, to exert utmost effort to turn offender over to civil authorities). *Cf.* British Articles of War of 1765, § 11, Art.

1, reprinted in Winthrop 937 (same). That provision was deemed protection enough for soldiers, and in 1806 Congress debated and rejected a proposal to remove the death penalty from court-martial jurisdiction. Wiener, *Courts-Martial and the Bill of Rights: The Original Practice I*, 72 Harv. L. Rev. 1, 20-21 (1958).

Over the next two centuries, Congress expanded court-martial jurisdiction. In 1863, concerned that civil courts could not function in all places during hostilities, Congress granted courts-martial jurisdiction of common-law capital crimes and the authority to impose the death penalty in wartime. Act of Mar. 3, 1863, § 30, 12 Stat. 736, Rev. Stat. § 1342, Art. 58 (1875); *Coleman v. Tennessee*, 97 U.S. 509, 514 (1879). In 1916, Congress granted to the military courts a general jurisdiction over common-law felonies committed by service members, except for murder and rape committed within the continental United States during peacetime. Articles of War of 1916, ch. 418, § 3, Arts. 92-93, 39 Stat. 664. Persons accused of the latter two crimes were to be turned over to the civilian authorities. Art. 74, 39 Stat. 662. In 1950, with the passage of the UCMJ, Congress lifted even this restriction. Article 118 of the UCMJ describes four types of murder subject to court-martial jurisdiction, two of which [premeditated murder and murder "in the perpetration or attempted perpetration of burglary, sodomy, rape, robbery, or aggravated arson"] are punishable by death. . . . 10 U.S.C. § 918.

So matters stood until 1983, when the CMA confronted a challenge to the constitutionality of the military capital punishment scheme in light of *Furman v. Georgia,* 408 U.S. 238 (1972), and our ensuing death penalty jurisprudence. Although it held valid most of the death penalty procedures followed in courts-martial, the court found one fundamental defect: the failure of either the UCMJ or the R.C.M. to require that court-martial members "specifically identify the aggravating factors upon which they have relied in choosing to impose the death penalty." *United States v. Matthews,* 16 M.J. 354, 379. The court reversed Matthews' death sentence, but ruled that either Congress or the President could remedy the defect and that the new procedures could be applied retroactively. *Id.,* at 380-382.

The President responded to *Matthews* in 1984 with an Executive Order promulgating R.C.M. 1004. In conformity with 10 U.S.C. § 852(a)(1), the Rule, as amended, requires a unanimous finding that the accused was guilty of a capital offense before a death sentence may be imposed, R.C.M. 1004(a)(2). The Rule also requires unanimous findings (1) that at least one aggravating factor is present and (2) that any extenuating or mitigating circumstances are substantially outweighed by any admissible aggravating circumstances, 1004(b).

R.C.M. 1004(c) enumerates 11 categories of aggravating factors sufficient for imposition of the death penalty. The Rule also provides that the accused is to have "broad latitude to present evidence in extenuation and mitigation," 1004(b)(3), and is entitled to have the members of the court-martial instructed to consider all such evidence before deciding upon a death sentence, 1004(b)(6). . . .

III

A preliminary question in this case is whether the Constitution requires the aggravating factors that Loving challenges. The Government does not contest the application of our death penalty jurisprudence to courts-martial, at least in the context of a conviction under Article 118 for murder committed in peace-time within the United States, and we shall assume that *Furman* and the case law resulting from it are applicable to the crime and sentence in question. *Cf. Trop v. Dulles,* 356 U.S. 86 (1958) (analyzing court-martial punishments under the Eighth Amendment).

The Eighth Amendment requires, among other things, that "a capital sentencing scheme must 'genuinely narrow the class of persons eligible for the death penalty and must reasonably justify the imposition of a more severe sentence on the defendant compared to others found guilty of murder.'" *Lowenfield v. Phelps,* 484 U.S. 231, 244 (1988) (quoting *Zant v. Stephens,* 462 U.S. 862, 877 (1983)). Some schemes accomplish that narrowing by requiring that the sentencer find at least one aggravating circumstance. 484 U.S., at 244. The narrowing may also be achieved, however, in the definition of the capital offense, in which circumstance the requirement that the sentencer "find the existence of an aggravating circumstance in addition is no part of the constitutionally required narrowing process." *Id.,* at 246.

Although the Government suggests the contrary, . . ., we agree with Loving, on the assumption that *Furman* applies to this case, that aggravating factors are necessary to the constitutional validity of the military capital punishment scheme as now enacted. Article 118 authorizes the death penalty for but two of the four types of murder specified: premeditated and felony murder are punishable by death, 10 U.S.C. §§ 918(1), (4), whereas intentional murder without premeditation and murder resulting from wanton and dangerous conduct are not, §§ 918(2), (3). The statute's selection of the two types of murder for the death penalty, however, does not narrow the death-eligible class in a way consistent with our cases.

Article 118(4) by its terms permits death to be imposed for felony murder even if the accused had no intent to kill and even if he did not do the killing himself. The Eighth Amendment does not permit the death penalty to be imposed in those circumstances. *Enmund v. Florida,* 458 U.S. 782, 801 (1982). As a result, additional aggravating factors establishing a higher culpability are necessary to save Article 118. We turn to the question whether it violated the principle of separation of powers for the President to prescribe the aggravating factors required by the Eighth Amendment. . . .

IV

[B]y allocating specific powers and responsibilities to a branch fitted to the task, the Framers created a National Government that is both effective and accountable. Article I's precise rules of representation, member qualifications, bicameralism, and voting procedure make Congress the branch most capable of responsive and deliberative lawmaking. *See Chadha, supra,* [*I.N.S. v. Chadha* 462 U.S. 919 (1983)] at 951. Ill suited to that task are the Presidency, designed for the prompt and faithful execution of the laws and its own legitimate powers, and the Judiciary, a branch with tenure and authority independent of direct electoral control. The clear assignment of power to a branch, furthermore, allows the citizen to know who may be called to answer for making, or not making, those delicate and necessary decisions essential to governance.

Another strand of our separation-of-powers jurisprudence, the delegation doctrine, has developed to prevent Congress from forsaking its duties. Loving invokes this doctrine to question the authority of the President to promulgate R.C.M. 1004. The fundamental precept of the delegation doctrine is that the lawmaking function belongs to Congress, U.S. Const., Art. I, § 1, and may not be conveyed to another branch or entity. *Field v. Clark,* 143 U.S. 649, 692 (1892).

This principle does not mean, however, that only Congress can make a rule of prospective force. To burden Congress with all federal rulemaking would divert that branch from more pressing issues, and defeat the Framers' design of a workable National Government. Thomas Jefferson observed: "Nothing is so embarrassing nor so mischievous in a great assembly as the details of execution." 5 Works of Thomas Jefferson 319 (P. Ford ed. 1904) (letter to E. Carrington, Aug. 4, 1787). *See also A.L.A. Schechter Poultry Corp. v. United States,* 295 U.S. 495, 529-530 (1935) (recognizing "the necessity of adapting legislation to complex conditions involving a host of details with which the national legislature cannot deal directly"). This Court established long ago that Congress must be permitted to delegate to others at least some authority that it could exercise itself. *Wayman v. Southard,* 10 Wheat. 1, 42 (1825). "'The true distinction . . . is between the delegation of power to make the law, which necessarily involves a discretion as to what it shall be, and conferring authority or discretion as to its execution, to be exercised under and in pursuance of the law. The first cannot be done; to the latter no valid objection can be made.'" *Field, supra,* at 693-694, quoting *Cincinnati, W. & Z.R. Co. v. Commissioners of Clinton County,* 1 Ohio St. 77, 88-89 (1852). . . .

A

Loving's first argument is that Congress lacks power to allow the President to prescribe aggravating factors in military capital cases because any delegation would be inconsistent with the Framers' decision to vest in Congress the power "To make Rules for the Government and Regulation of the land and naval Forces." U.S. Const., Art. I, § 8, cl. 14. . . .

In the words of Alexander Hamilton, the power to regulate the Armed Forces, like other powers related to the common defense, was given to Congress

> "without limitation: Because it is impossible to foresee or define the extent and variety of national exigencies, or the corresponding extent & variety of the means which may be necessary to satisfy them. The circumstances that endanger the safety of nations are infinite, and for this reason no constitutional shackles can wisely be imposed on the power to which the care of it is committed.

> "This power ought to be co-extensive with all the possible combinations of such circumstances; and ought to be under the direction of the same councils, which are appointed to preside over the common defence." The Federalist No. 23, at 147 (emphasis deleted).

The later-added Bill of Rights limited this power to some degree, *cf. Burns v. Wilson,* 346 U.S. 137, 140 (1953) (plurality opinion); *Chappell v. Wallace,* 462

U.S. 296, 300 (1983), but did not alter the allocation to Congress of the "primary responsibility for the delicate task of balancing the rights of servicemen against the needs of the military," *Solorio*, 483 U.S., at 447-448. Under Clause 14, Congress, like Parliament, exercises a power of precedence over, not exclusion of, Executive authority. *Cf. United States v. Eliason*, 16 Pet. 291, 301 (1842) ("The power of the executive to establish rules and regulations for the government of the army, is undoubted"). This power is no less plenary than other Article I powers, *Solorio, supra*, at 441, and we discern no reasons why Congress should have less capacity to make measured and appropriate delegations of this power than of any other, *see Skinner v. Mid-America Pipeline Co.*, 490 U.S. 212, 220-221 (1989) (Congress may delegate authority under the taxing power); *cf. Lichter v. United States*, 334 U.S. 742, 778 (1948) (general rule is that "[a] constitutional power implies a power of delegation of authority under it sufficient to effect its purposes") (emphasis deleted). Indeed, it would be contrary to precedent and tradition for us to impose a special limitation on this particular Article I power, for we give Congress the highest deference in ordering military affairs. *Rostker v. Goldberg*, 453 U.S. 57, 64-65 (1981). And it would be contrary to the respect owed the President as Commander in Chief to hold that he may not be given wide discretion and authority. We decline to import into Clause 14 a restrictive nondelegation principle that the Framers left out.

There is no absolute rule, furthermore, against Congress' delegation of authority to define criminal punishments. We have upheld delegations whereby the Executive or an independent agency defines by regulation what conduct will be criminal, so long as Congress makes the violation of regulations a criminal offense and fixes the punishment, and the regulations "confin[e] themselves within the field covered by the statute." *United States v. Grimaud*, 220 U.S. 506, 518 (1911). *See also Touby v. United States*, 500 U.S. 160 (1991).

The exercise of a delegated authority to define crimes may be sufficient in certain circumstances to supply the notice to defendants the Constitution requires. *See M. Kraus & Bros., Inc. v. United States*, 327 U.S. 614, 622 (1946). In the circumstances presented here, so too may Congress delegate authority to the President to define the aggravating factors that permit imposition of a statutory penalty, with the regulations providing the narrowing of the death-eligible class that the Eighth Amendment requires.

In 1950, Congress confronted the problem of what criminal jurisdiction would be appropriate for Armed Forces of colossal size, stationed on bases that in many instances were small societies unto themselves. Congress, confident in the procedural protections of the UCMJ, gave to courts-martial jurisdiction of the crime of murder. *Cf. Solorio, supra*, at 450-451 (Congress may extend court-martial jurisdiction to any criminal offense committed by a service member during his period of service). It further declared the law that service members who commit premeditated and felony murder may be sentenced to death by a court-martial. There is nothing in the constitutional scheme or our traditions to prohibit Congress from delegating the prudent and proper implementation of the capital murder statute to the President acting as Commander in Chief.

B

Having held that Congress has the power of delegation, we further hold that it exercised the power in Articles 18 and 56 of the UCMJ. Article 56 specifies that "[t]he punishment which a court-martial may direct for an offense may not exceed such limits as the President may prescribe for that offense." 10 U.S.C. § 856. Article 18 states that a court-martial "may, under such limitations as the President may prescribe, adjudge any punishment not forbidden by [the UCMJ], including the penalty of death when specifically authorized by" the Code. § 818. As the Court of Military Appeals pointed out in *Curtis* [*United States v. Curtis*, 32 M.J. 252 (C.M.A. 1991)], for some decades the President has used his authority under these Articles to increase the penalties for certain noncapital offenses if aggravating circumstances are present. For example, by regulation, deserters who are apprehended are punished more severely than those who surrender; drunken drivers suffer a harsher fate if they cause an accident resulting in the death of a victim; and the punishment of thieves is graded by the value of the stolen goods. *See Curtis*, 32 M.J., at 261. The President has thus provided more precision in sentencing than is provided by the statute, while remaining within statutory bounds. This past practice suggests that Articles 18 and 56 support as well an authority in the President to restrict the death sentence to murders in which certain aggravating circumstances have been established.

There is yet a third provision of the UCMJ indicative of congressional intent to delegate this authority to the President. Article 36 of the UCMJ, which gives the President the power to make procedural rules for courts-martial, provides:

> Pretrial, trial, and post-trial procedures, including modes of proof, for [courts martial] . . . may be prescribed by the President by regulations which shall, so far as he considers practicable, apply the principles of law and the rules of evidence generally recognized in the trial of criminal cases in the United States district courts, but which may not be contrary to or inconsistent with this chapter.

10 U.S.C. § 836(a).

Although the language of Article 36 seems further afield from capital aggravating factors than that of Article 18 or 56, it is the provision that a later Congress identified as the source of Presidential authority to prescribe these factors. In 1985, Congress enacted Article 106a of the UCMJ, 10 U.S.C. § 906a, which authorized the death penalty for espionage. The Article requires a finding of an aggravating factor if the accused is to be sentenced to death; it enumerates three such factors, but allows death to be decreed on "[a]ny other factor that may be prescribed by the President by regulations under section 836 of this title (article 36)." § 906a(c)(4). Article 106a itself, then, is premised on the President's having authority under Article 36 to prescribe capital aggravating factors, and "'[s]ubsequent legislation declaring the intent of an earlier statute is entitled to great weight in statutory construction.'" *Consumer Product Safety Comm'n v. GTE Sylvania, Inc.*, 447 U.S. 102, 118, n.13 (1980) (quoting *Red Lion Broadcasting Co. v. FCC*, 395 U.S. 367, 380-381 (1969)). Whether or not Article 36 would stand on its own as the source of the delegated power, we hold that Articles 18, 36, and 56 together give clear authority to the President for the promulgation of R.C.M. 1004.

Loving points out that the three Articles were enacted as part of the UCMJ in 1950, well before the need for eliminating absolute discretion in capital sentencing was established in *Furman v. Georgia*, 408 U.S. 238 (1972), and the cases that followed. (Slight amendments to the Articles have been made since but are not relevant here.) In 1950, he argues, Congress could not have understood that it was giving the President the authority to bring an otherwise invalid capital murder statute in line with Eighth Amendment strictures. Perhaps so, but *Furman* did not somehow undo the prior delegation. What would have been an act of leniency by the President prior to *Furman* may have become a constitutional necessity thereafter, *see supra,* at 755-756, but the fact remains the power to prescribe aggravating circumstances has resided with the President since 1950.

C

It does not suffice to say that Congress announced its will to delegate certain authority. Congress as a general rule must also "lay down by legislative act an intelligible principle to which the person or body authorized to [act] is directed to conform." *J.W. Hampton, Jr., & Co. v. United States*, 276 U.S. 394, 409 (1928); *Touby*, 500 U.S., at 165. The intelligible-principle rule seeks to enforce the understanding that Congress may not delegate the power to make laws and so may delegate no more than the authority to make policies and rules that implement its statutes. *Field*, 143 U.S., at 693-694. Though in 1935 we struck down two delegations for lack of an intelligible principle, *A.L.A. Schecter Poultry Corp. v. United States*, 295 U.S. 495 (1935), and *Panama Refining Co. v. Ryan*, 293 U.S. 388 (1935), we have since upheld, without exception, delegations under standards phrased in sweeping terms. *See, e.g., National Broadcasting Co. v. United States*, 319 U.S. 190, 216-217, 225-226 (1943) (upholding delegation to the Federal Communications Commission to regulate radio broadcasting according to "public interest, convenience, or necessity"). Had the delegations here called for the exercise of judgment or discretion that lies beyond the traditional authority of the President, Loving's last argument that Congress failed to provide guiding principles to the President might have more weight. We find no fault, however, with the delegation in this case.

In *United States v. Curtis*, the Court of Military Appeals discerned a principle limiting the President's discretion to define aggravating factors for capital crimes in Article 36: namely, the directive that regulations the President prescribes must "apply the principles of law . . . generally recognized in the trial of criminal cases in the United States district courts, but which may not be contrary to or inconsistent with this chapter," 10 U.S.C. § 836(a). We think, however, that the question to be asked is not whether there was any explicit principle telling the President how to select aggravating factors, but whether any such guidance was needed, given the nature of the delegation and the officer who is to exercise the delegated authority. First, the delegation is set within boundaries the President may not exceed. Second, the delegation here was to the President in his role as Commander in Chief. Perhaps more explicit guidance as to how to select aggravating factors would be necessary if delegation were made to a newly created entity without independent authority in the area. *Cf. Mistretta [v. United States]*, 488 U.S. [361] at 374-379 [(1989)] (upholding delegation to the United States Sentencing Commission because of detailed congressional directives channeling agency discretion). The President's duties as Commander in Chief, however, require him to take responsible and continuing action to superintend the military, including the courts-martial. The delegated duty, then, is interlinked with duties already assigned to the President by express terms of the Constitution, and the same limitations on delegation do not apply "where the entity exercising the delegated authority itself possesses independent authority over the subject matter," *United States v. Mazurie*, 419 U.S. 544, 556-557 (1975). *See also United States v. Curtiss-Wright Export Corp.*, 299 U.S. 304, 319-322 (1936). *Cf. Swaim v. United States*, 165 U.S. 553, 557-558 (1897) (President has inherent authority to convene courts-martial).

Like the Court of Military Appeals, *Curtis*, 32 M.J., at 263, n. 9, we need not decide whether the President would have inherent power as Commander in Chief to prescribe aggravating factors in capital cases. Once delegated that power by Congress, the President, acting in his constitutional office of Commander in Chief, had undoubted competency to prescribe those factors without further guidance. "The military constitutes a specialized community governed by a separate discipline from that of the civilian," *Orloff v. Willoughby*, 345 U.S. 83, 94 (1953), and the President can be entrusted to determine what limitations and conditions on punishments are best suited to preserve that special discipline.

It is hard to deem lawless a delegation giving the President broad discretion to prescribe rules on this subject. From the early days of the Republic, the President has had congressional authorization to intervene in cases where courts-martial decreed death. American Articles of War of 1806, Art. 65, reprinted in Winthrop 976, 982. It would be contradictory to say that Congress cannot further empower him to limit by prospective regulation the circumstances in which courts-martial can impose a death sentence. Specific authority to make rules for the limitation of capital punishment contributes more toward principled and uniform military sentencing regimes than does case-by-case intervention, and it provides greater opportunity for congressional oversight and revision.

Separation-of-powers principles are vindicated, not disserved, by measured cooperation between the two political branches of the Government, each contributing to a lawful objective through its own processes. The delegation to the President as Commander in Chief of the authority to prescribe aggravating factors was in all respects consistent with these precepts, and the promulgation of RCM 1004 was well within the delegated authority. Loving's sentence was lawful, and the judgment of the Court of Appeals for the Armed Forces is affirmed. . . .

JUSTICE THOMAS, concurring in the judgment.

It is not clear to me that the extensive rules we have developed under the Eighth Amendment for the prosecution of civilian capital cases, including the requirement of proof of aggravating factors, necessarily apply to capital prosecutions in the military, *cf. Chappell v. Wallace*, 462 U.S. 296, 300-302 (1983), and this Court has never so held, *see Schick v. Reed*, 419 U.S. 256, 260 (1974).[5] I am therefore not certain that this case even raises a delegation question, for if Loving can constitutionally be sentenced to death without proof of aggravating factors, he surely cannot claim that the President violated the Constitution by promulgating aggravating factors that afforded more protection than that to which Loving is constitutionally entitled.

Like the majority, I conclude that the Government prevails even if we assume, without deciding, that aggravating factors are required in this context. There is abundant authority for according Congress and the President sufficient deference in the regulation of military affairs to uphold the delegation here, and I see no need to resort to our nonmilitary separation-of-powers and "delegation doctrine" cases in reaching this conclusion. I write separately to explain that by concurring in the judgment in this case, I take no position with respect to Congress' power to delegate authority or otherwise alter the traditional separation of powers outside the military context.

In light of Congress' express constitutional authority to regulate the Armed Forces, *see* U.S. Const., Art. I, § 8, cl. 14, and the unique nature of the military's mission, we have afforded an unparalleled degree of deference to congressional action governing the military. *See Rostker v. Goldberg*, 453 U.S. 57, 64-65 (1981). "It is the primary business of armies and navies to fight or be ready to fight wars should the occasion arise," *United States ex rel. Toth v. Quarles*, 350 U.S. 11, 17 (1955), and this Court has recognized the limits on its own competence in advancing this core national interest, *see Gilligan v. Morgan*, 413 U.S. 1, 10 (1973). Mindful of the factors that "differentiate military society from civilian society," we have concluded that the Constitution permits Congress "to legislate both with greater breadth and with greater flexibility when prescribing the rules by which the former shall be governed than it is when prescribing rules for the latter." *Parker v. Levy*, 417 U.S. 733, 756 (1974). This heightened deference extends not only to congressional action but also to executive action by the President, who by virtue of his constitutional role as Commander in Chief, *see* U.S. Const., Art. II, § 2, cl. 1, possesses shared authority over military discipline. *See Schlesinger v. Ballard*, 419 U.S. 498, 510 (1975) ("The responsibility for determining how best our Armed Forces shall attend to th[e] business [of fighting or preparing to fight wars] rests with Congress and with the President") (citations omitted). *See also Brown v. Glines*, 444 U.S. 348, 360 (1980) ("Both Congress and this Court have found that the special character of the military requires civilian authorities to accord military commanders some flexibility in dealing with matters that affect internal discipline and morale. In construing a statute that touches on such matters, therefore, courts must be careful not to 'circumscribe the authority of military commanders to an extent never intended by Congress'") (citations omitted). Under these and many similar cases reviewing legislative and executive control of the military, the sentencing scheme at issue in this case, and the manner in which it was created, are constitutionally unassailable. . . .

---

[5] [5]Although the applicability of *Furman v. Georgia*, 408 U.S. 238 (1972), and its progeny to the military is an open question, the United States surprisingly makes no argument that the military is exempt from the byzantine rules that we have imposed upon the States in their administration of the death penalty.

NOTES

1. The majority opinion indicates that Loving was tried and sentenced to death by an eight-member court-martial panel. In 2001, Congress amended the Uniform Code of Military Justice to generally require that court-martial panels in capital cases have at least twelve members. National Defense Authorization Act for Fiscal Year 2002, Pub. L. No. 107-107, §582, 115 Stat. 1012 (2001) (codified at UCMJ art. 25a, 10 U.S.C.A. §825a). For discussion of this reform see Chapter 20, §III, *infra*.

2. The *Loving* majority assumes that the Supreme Court's Eighth Amendment jurisprudence applies to the military death penalty. Justice Thomas emphasizes that the Supreme Court has never held that its Eighth Amendment jurisprudence applies to the military. In its decision in *United States v. Matthews*, 16 M.J. 354 (C.M.A. 1983), the Court of Military Appeals held that absent some military justification for departing from civilian standards, the Eighth Amendment applies to the military justice system:

> The most successful constitutional attacks on capital punishment have invoked the Eighth Amendment, which prohibits "cruel and unusual punishments." Article 55 of the Uniform Code, 10 U.S.C. §855, provides a servicemember comparable protection against "[p]unishment by flogging, or by branding, marking, or tattooing on the body, or any other cruel or unusual punishment." Indeed, we have held that, in enacting Article 55, Congress "intended to grant protection covering even wider limits" than "that afforded by the Eighth Amendment." *United States v. Wappler*, 2 U.S.C.M.A. 393, 396, 9 C.M.R. 23, 26 (1953).

> Since a servicemember is entitled both by statute and under the Eighth Amendment to protection against "cruel and unusual punishments," we shall seek guidance from Supreme Court precedent as to the significance of this protection in capital cases. However, we recognize that, since in many ways the military community is unique, *Schlesinger v. Councilman*, [420 U.S. 738 (1975)]; *Parker v. Levy*, 417 U.S. 733 (1974), there may be circumstances under which the rules governing capital punishment of servicemembers will differ from those applicable to civilians. This possibility is especially great with respect to offenses committed under combat conditions when maintenance of discipline may require swift, severe punishment, or in violation of the law of war, e.g., spying. *Cf. United States v. Gay*, 16 M.J. 586, 605-06 (A.F.C.M.R. 1982) (Hodgson, C.J., concurring.)

> However, the murder and rape committed by Matthews have no characteristics which, for purposes of applying the prohibition against "cruel and unusual punishments," distinguish them from similar crimes tried regularly in State and Federal courts. Although appellant's offenses were service-connected and subject to trial by court-martial, we see no reason why Matthews should be executed for his murder and rape of Mrs. Villanueva if the sentencing procedures used by the court-martial failed to meet the standards established by the Supreme Court for sentencing in capital cases in civilian courts. There

is no military necessity for such a distinction; and we do not believe that applying lower standards in this case would conform to the intent of Article 55 or of the Eighth Amendment.

16 M.J. 368-69.

LOVING v. HART
United States Court of Appeals for the Armed Forces
47 M.J. 428 (C.A.A.F. 1998)

GIERKE, JUDGE. . . .

The military capital sentencing procedure set out in R.C.M. 1004 and 1006 establishes four "gates" to narrow the class of death-eligible offenders. The first two gates [require that] the members must convict by unanimous vote (R.C.M. 1004(a)(2)) and then find at least one aggravating factor by unanimous vote (R.C.M. 1004(b)(4)(A)). Only after these two gates are passed does the weighing process begin. The third gate is a "weighing" gate, where the members must all "concur" that extenuating and "mitigating circumstances are substantially outweighed by any aggravating circumstances," including the aggravating factors under R.C.M. 1004(c). *See* R.C.M. 1004(b)(4)(C). Only after these three gates are passed does an accused become "death eligible."

The fourth and final gate is the sentencing decision itself under R.C.M. 1006. Even if all members concur that extenuating and mitigating circumstances are substantially outweighed by aggravating circumstances, they must separately consider whether to impose the death sentence. A death sentence requires the unanimous vote of all members. R.C.M. 1006(d)(4)(A). . . .

Several general principles guide us in determining whether capital sentencing procedures pass constitutional muster. First, sentencing standards "must genuinely narrow the class of persons eligible for the death penalty." Second, the standards "must reasonably justify the imposition of a more severe sentence on the defendant compared to others found guilty of murder." *Zant* [*v. Stephens*, 462 U.S. 862, 877 (1983)]; *see also Tuilaepa v. California*, 512 U.S. 967, 972 (1994); *Arave v. Creech*, 507 U.S. 463, 474 (1993). Third, the standards must provide "reliability in the determination that death is the appropriate punishment." *Zant, supra* at 884-85. Finally, in order to ensure reliability, the process must "make rationally reviewable the process for imposing a sentence of death." *Tuilaepa*, 512 U.S. at 973, quoting *Arave*, 507 U.S. at 471. . . .

NOTES

1. The decision at each of the "four gates" in a military death penalty case is made by members. Under Article 18 and Rule for Courts-Martial 201(f)(1)(C), all capital courts-martial must be tried before members. In the federal civilian system, a judge can preside over a capital case if both the defendant and the United States consent and the judge approves the parties' request. *See* Fed. R. Crim. P. 23a. Military appellate courts have rejected constitutional challenges to the prohibition against judge-alone trials in capital cases. *See, e.g., United*

States v. Gray, 51 M.J. 1, 49 (C.A.A.F. 1999); *United States v. Curtis*, 44 M.J. 106, 130 (C.A.A.F. 1996), *rev'd on other grounds*, 46 M.J. 129 (C.A.A.F. 1997); *United States v. Loving*, 41 M.J. 213, 291 (C.A.A.F. 1994), *aff'd on other grounds*, 517 U.S. 748 (1996); *United States v. Matthews*, 16 M.J. 354, 363 (C.M.A. 1983).

2. The first of the four gates is the finding of guilty to a capital offense. The UCMJ establishes 15 offenses that carry the death penalty, though for many of these, the death penalty is authorized only in time of war: desertion (art. 85; time of war only); assaulting or willfully disobeying superior commissioned officer (art. 90; time of war only); mutiny (art. 94); misbehavior before the enemy (art. 99); subordinate compelling surrender (art. 100); improper use of countersign (art. 101); forcing a safeguard (art. 102); aiding the enemy (art. 104); spying (art. 106; time of war is element of the offense); espionage (art. 106a); willfully hazarding a vessel (art. 110); misbehavior of sentinel or lookout (art. 113; time of war only); premeditated murder (art. 118(1)); felony murder (art. 118(4)); and rape (art. 120). The "time of war" requirement can be satisfied by either a congressional declaration of war or a presidential finding that a state of hostilities warrants a finding that a state of war exists. R.C.M. 103(19). The UCMJ also authorizes general courts-martial to "try any person who by the law of war is subject to trial by a military tribunal" and to "adjudge any punishment permitted by the law of war." UCMJ art. 18, 10 U.S.C. § 818. Uncertainty persists concerning whether death can be, in some circumstances, a constitutionally permissible punishment for rape. *See* Corey Rayburn, *Better Dead than Raped? The Patriarchal Rhetoric Driving Capital Rape Statutes*, 78 ST. JOHN'S L. REV. 1119, 1135-40 (2004) (discussing, *inter alia*, UCMJ art. 120); Capt. Douglas L. Simon, *Making Sense of Cruel and Unusual Punishment: A New Approach to Reconciling Military and Civilian Eighth Amendment Law*, 184 MIL. L. REV. 66, 115-16 (2005); Lt. Col. Robert T. Jackson, Jr., *Death — An Excessive Penalty for Rape of a Child?*, ARMY LAW., Sept. 1986, at 37. Every servicemember sentenced to death since President Reagan implemented the current military death penalty system in 1984 was convicted of premeditated murder, felony murder, or both. *See generally* Col. Dwight H. Sullivan, *Killing Time: Two Decades of Military Capital Litigation*, 189 MIL. L. REV. 1 (2006).

3. The United States military has not carried out an execution since April 13, 1961, when PFC John A. Bennett was hanged at the United States Disciplinary Barracks for the rape and attempted murder of an eleven-year-old girl in Austria. *See generally* Capt. Dwight H. Sullivan, *The Last Line of Defense: Federal Habeas Review of Military Death Penalty Cases*, 144 MIL. L. REV. 1, 1-3 (1994).

4. A military execution cannot be carried out unless the President of the United States has approved the death sentence. UCMJ art. 71(a), 10 U.S.C. §871(a). *See generally* Dwight H. Sullivan, *Executive Branch Consideration of Military Death Sentences*, *in* EVOLVING MILITARY JUSTICE 137 (Eugene R. Fidell & Dwight H. Sullivan eds. 2002).

5. Canada eliminated its military death penalty in 1998. Act of Dec. 10, 1998, S.C. 1998, c. 35, §24 *et seq.* (Can.). "Until 2 October 2000, a [British] general court-martial had a power, in certain circumstances, to impose a death penalty. However, the Human Rights Act 1998 abolished the death penalty, and therefore the maximum sentence which may be imposed at a [British] general court-martial is life imprisonment." Wing Cdr. Simon P. Rowlinson, *The British System of Military Justice*, 52 A.F. L. REV. 17, 36 (2002).

V.   ADMINISTRATIVE SANCTIONS AND COLLATERAL CONSEQUENCES

CLINTON v. GOLDSMITH
Supreme Court of the United States
526 U.S. 529 (1999)

JUSTICE SOUTER delivered the opinion of the Court.

The challenge here is to the use of the All Writs Act, 28 U.S.C. § 1651(a), by the Court of Appeals for the Armed Forces, to enjoin the President and various military officials from dropping respondent from the rolls of the Air Force. Because that court's process was neither "in aid of" its strictly circumscribed jurisdiction to review court-martial findings and sentences under 10 U.S.C. § 867 nor "necessary or appropriate" in light of a servicemember's alternative opportunities to seek relief, we hold that the Court of Appeals for the Armed Forces lacked jurisdiction to issue the injunction.

I

Respondent James Goldsmith, a major in the United States Air Force, was ordered by a superior officer to inform his sex partners that he was HIV-positive and to take measures to block any transfer of bodily fluids during sexual relations. Contrary to this order, on two occasions Goldsmith had unprotected intercourse, once with a fellow officer and once with a civilian, without informing either that he was carrying HIV.

As a consequence of his defiance, Goldsmith was convicted by general court-martial of willful disobedience of an order from a superior commissioned officer, aggravated assault with means likely to produce death or grievous bodily harm, and assault consummated by battery, in violation of Articles 90 and 128 of the Uniform Code of Military Justice (UCMJ), 10 U.S.C. §§ 890, 928(b)(1), (a). In 1994, he was sentenced to six years' confinement and forfeiture of $2500 of his pay each month for six years. The Air Force Court of Criminal Appeals affirmed his conviction and sentence in 1995, and when he sought no review of that decision in the United States Court of Appeals for the Armed Forces (CAAF), his conviction became final, *see* § 871(c)(1)(A).

In 1996, Congress expanded the President's authority by empowering him to drop from the rolls of the Armed Forces any officer who had both been sentenced by a court-martial to more than six months' confinement and served at least six months. *See* National Defense Authorization Act for Fiscal Year 1996, 110 Stat. 325, 10 U.S.C. §§ 1161(b)(2), 1167 (1994 ed., Supp. III). In reliance on this statutory authorization, the Air Force notified Goldsmith in 1996 that it was taking action to drop him from the rolls. Goldsmith did not immediately contest the proposal to drop him, but rather petitioned the Air Force Court of Criminal Appeals for extraordinary relief under the All Writs Act, 28 U.S.C. § 1651(a), to redress the unrelated alleged interruption of his HIV medication during his incarceration. The Court of Criminal Appeals ruled that it lacked jurisdiction to act, and it was in Goldsmith's appeal from that determination that he took the first steps to raise the issue now before us, an entirely new claim that the Air Force's action to drop him from the rolls was unconstitutional. He did not challenge his underlying court-martial conviction (the appeal period for which had expired, *see* Rule 19(a)(1), CAAF Rules of Practice and Procedure). But he charged that the proposed action violated the *Ex Post Facto* Clause, U.S. Const., Art. I, § 9, cl. 3 (arguing that the statute authorizing it had been enacted after the date of his conviction), and the Double Jeopardy Clause, U.S. Const., Amdt. 5 (arguing that the action would inflict successive punishment based on the same conduct underlying his first conviction). 48 M.J. 84, 89-90 (CAAF 1998). The CAAF, on a division of 3 to 2, granted the petition for extraordinary relief and relied on the All Writs Act, 28 U.S.C. § 1651(a), in enjoining the President and various other Executive Branch officials from dropping respondent from the rolls of the Air Force. We granted certiorari, 525 U.S. 961 (1998), and now reverse. . . .

II

When Congress exercised its power to govern and regulate the Armed Forces by establishing the CAAF, *see* U.S. Const., Art. I, § 8, cl. 14; 10 U.S.C. § 941; *see generally Weiss v. United States*, 510 U.S. 163, 166-169 (1994), it confined the court's jurisdiction to the review of specified sentences imposed by courts-martial: the CAAF has the power to act "only with respect to the findings and sentence as approved by the [court-martial's] convening authority and as affirmed or set aside as incorrect in law by the Court of Criminal Appeals." 10 U.S.C. § 867(c). *Cf. Parisi v. Davidson*, 405 U.S. 34, 44 (1972) (Court of Military Appeals lacked express authority over claim for discharge based on conscientious objector status). Despite these limitations, the CAAF asserted jurisdiction and purported to justify reliance on the All Writs Act in this case on the view that "Congress intended [it] to have broad responsibility with respect to administration of military justice," 48 M.J., at 86-87, a position that Goldsmith urges us to adopt. This we cannot do.

While the All Writs Act authorizes employment of extraordinary writs, it confines the authority to the issuance of process "in aid of" the issuing court's jurisdiction. . . .

We have already seen that the CAAF's independent statutory jurisdiction is narrowly circumscribed. To be more specific, the CAAF is accorded jurisdiction by statute (so far as it concerns us here) to "review the record in [specified] cases reviewed by" the service courts of criminal appeals, 10 U.S.C. §§ 867(a)(2), (3), which in turn have jurisdiction to "revie[w] court-martial cases," § 866(a). Since the Air Force's action to drop respondent from the rolls was an executive action, not a "findin[g]" or "sentence," § 867(c), that was (or could have been) imposed in a court-martial proceeding,[6] the elimination of

---

6 [n. 7] A court-martial is specifically barred from dismissing or discharging an officer except as in accordance with the UCMJ, which gives it no authority to drop a servicemember from the rolls.

Goldsmith from the rolls appears straightforwardly to have been beyond the CAAF's jurisdiction to review and hence beyond the "aid" of the All Writs Act in reviewing it.

Goldsmith nonetheless claims that the CAAF has satisfied the "aid" requirement of the Act because it protected and effectuated the sentence meted out by the court-martial. Goldsmith emphasizes that the court-martial could have dismissed him from service, but instead chose to impose only confinement and forfeitures. Hence, he says the CAAF merely preserved that sentence as the court-martial imposed it, by precluding additional punishment, which would incidentally violate the *Ex Post Facto* and Double Jeopardy Clauses. But this is beside the point, for two related reasons. First, Goldsmith's court-martial sentence has not been changed; another military agency has simply taken independent action. It would presumably be an entirely different matter if a military authority attempted to alter a judgment by revising a court-martial finding and sentence to increase the punishment, contrary to the specific provisions of the UCMJ, and it certainly would be a different matter when such a judgment had been affirmed by an appellate court. In such a case, as the Government concedes, *see* Tr. of Oral Arg. 15, 19, 52, the All Writs power would allow the appellate court to compel adherence to its own judgment. *See, e.g., United States v. United States Dist. Court for Southern Dist. of N.Y.*, 334 U.S. 258, 263-264 (1948). Second, the CAAF is not given authority, by the All Writs Act or otherwise, to oversee all matters arguably related to military justice, or to act as a plenary administrator even of criminal judgments it has affirmed. Simply stated, there is no source of continuing jurisdiction for the CAAF over all actions administering sentences that the CAAF at one time had the power to review. Thus the CAAF spoke too expansively when it held itself to be "empowered by the All Writs Act to grant extraordinary relief in a case in which the court-martial rendered a sentence that constituted an adequate basis for direct review in [the CAAF] after review in the intermediate court," 48 M.J., at 87.

III

Even if the CAAF had some seriously arguable basis for jurisdiction in these circumstances, resort to the All Writs Act would still be out of bounds, being unjustifiable either as "necessary" or as "appropriate" in light of alternative remedies available to a servicemember demanding to be kept on the rolls. The All Writs Act invests a court with a power essentially equitable and, as such, not generally available to provide alternatives to other, adequate remedies at law. . . . This limitation operates here, since other administrative bodies in the military, and the federal courts have authority to provide administrative or judicial review of the action challenged by respondent.

In response to the notice Goldsmith received that action was being considered to drop him from the rolls, he presented his claim to the Secretary of the Air Force. *See* Tr. of Oral Arg. 4-5. If the Secretary takes final action to drop him from the rolls (as he has not yet done), Goldsmith will (as the Government concedes) be entitled to present his claim to the Air Force Board for Correction

---

See Rules for Courts-Martial 1003(b)(9)(A)-(C); Rule 1003(b)(9) ("A court-martial may not adjudge an administrative separation from the service"). . . .

of Military Records (BCMR). This is a civilian body within the military service, with broad-ranging authority to review a servicemember's "discharge or dismissal (other than a discharge or dismissal by sentence of a general court-martial)," 10 U.S.C. § 1553(a), or "to correct an error or remove an injustice" in a military record, § 1552(a)(1).

Respondent may also have recourse to the federal trial courts. . . .

In sum, executive action to drop respondent from the rolls falls outside of the CAAF's express statutory jurisdiction, and alternative statutory avenues of relief are available. The CAAF's injunction against dropping respondent from the rolls of the Air Force was neither "in aid of [its] jurisdictio[n]" nor "necessary or appropriate." Accordingly, we reverse the court's judgment. . . .

NOTES

1. The Court of Appeals for the Armed Forces has held that it can be reversible error to fail to inform members sentencing an accused of the collateral consequences of a court-martial conviction. In *United States v. Greaves*, 46 M.J. 133 (C.A.A.F. 1998), for example, the accused was just two months from being eligible for military retirement when he was tried. Receiving a punitive discharge would prevent him from receiving any retirement pay. The Court of Appeals held "that the military judge erred by failing to correctly answer two relevant and proper questions asked by the members concerning the impact of a bad-conduct discharge on appellant's impending eligibility to retire." Three years later, the court announced a requirement that "military judges in all cases tried after the date of this opinion . . . instruct on the impact of a punitive discharge on retirement benefits, if there is an evidentiary predicate for the instruction and a party requests it." *United States v. Boyd*, 55 M.J. 217, 221 (C.A.A.F. 2001). The court favorably noted the instruction from the *Military Judges' Benchbook* informing the members that "a punitive discharge terminates the accused's military status and the benefits that flow from that status, including the possibility of becoming a military retiree and receiving retired pay and benefits." *Id.* (quoting *Military Judges' Benchbook* at 97 (Department of the Army Pamphlet 27-9 (April 1, 2001)). For further discussion of collateral review, see Chapter 17, § IV, *infra*.

2. In *United States v. Luster*, 55 M.J. 67 (C.A.A.F. 2001), the Court of Appeals held that a military judge erred by excluding defense evidence of the estimated retired pay of an accused who was one year and nine months away from retirement eligibility. The court noted that the probability of retirement was not remote and the estimated retired pay was substantial.

Chapter 17

REVIEW AND APPEAL

Perhaps because military justice was originally intended as a means of dispensing justice in the field where time may be of the essence and the finer points of the law may receive short shrift, it typically makes extensive provision for post-trial review. That process often includes review by the convening authority even before a case enters the available appellate court system. Appellate review will include legal issues but may also include sentencing review. In addition to direct appellate review, there may also be opportunities for collateral review through such mechanisms as writs of habeas corpus or other extraordinary writs. National practice varies considerably as to appellate review of courts-martial, but a common feature is reliance on a separate, specialized appellate court whose members may include military officers.

I. COMMAND REVIEW AND EXECUTIVE CLEMENCY

UNITED STATES v. DAVIS
United States Court of Appeals for the Armed Forces
58 M.J. 100 (C.A.A.F. 2003)

JUDGE ERDMANN delivered the opinion of the Court.

We granted review of the following issue:

WHETHER IT WAS ERROR FOR THE CONVENING AUTHORITY TO PERFORM THE POST-TRIAL REVIEW OF APPELLANT'S CASE WHEN THE CONVENING AUTHORITY MADE STATEMENTS THAT DEMONSTRATED AN INELASTIC ATTITUDE TOWARD CLEMENCY.

For the reasons set forth herein, we answer the granted issue in the affirmative and return Appellant's case for a new action by a different convening authority.

Facts

Pursuant to a pretrial agreement with the convening authority, Appellant providently pleaded guilty to using both cocaine and marijuana and to being absent without authority from December 21, 2000 until he was apprehended on February, 16, 2001.

After trial, Appellant's defense counsel submitted a "memorandum for all reviewing authorities" entitled "*Goode* Response and Clemency Petition — *US v. Davis*."[1] The memorandum indicated that Appellant had petitioned the convening authority for clemency and stated the following:

> We object to MajGen [F], 37th TRW/CC, being the convening authority for purposes of taking action on the sentence in this case. During

the early part of this year, MajGen [F] gave several briefings at Lackland Air Force Base, Texas where he discussed illicit drug use by military members as being on the rise. During the briefings, MajGen [F] also publicly commented that people caught using illegal drugs would be prosecuted to the fullest extent, and if they were convicted, they should not come crying to him about their situations or their families['], or words to that effect (Affidavit Attached). MajGen [F]'s comments seriously question his ability to act neutrally and impartially when determining whether AB Davis should receive any clemency on his case as AB Davis was indeed prosecuted and convicted of illegal drug use.

A convening authority should be able to objectively and impartially weigh all the evidence in the Record of Trial and clemency matters submitted by the accused (*US v. Newman*, 14 M.J. 474, C.M.A. 1983). Based on his comments, specifically those regarding 'don't come crying to me about your situation or your families['],' we do not believe MajGen [F] can be fair and impartial in this capacity. In our opinion, these comments illustrate MajGen [F]'s unwillingness to impartially listen to clemency petitions by those convicted of illegal drug use.

Appellant's defense counsel executed the affidavit referenced in the foregoing. In the affidavit defense counsel indicated that several individuals had told him about briefings in which Major General (MG) F stated that "'individuals under his command who were caught using illegal drugs would be prosecuted to the fullest extent, and if they were convicted, they should not come crying to him about their situation or their families['],' or words to that effect."

An addendum to the staff judge advocate's post-trial recommendation, dated September 14, 2001, was silent about the convening authority's alleged comments. Despite Appellant's objections, MG F took action approving Appellant's sentence as adjudged.

Background

A convening authority is vested with substantial discretion when he or she takes action on the sentence of a court-martial. Article 60(c)(2)-(3), UCMJ, 10 U.S.C. § 860(c)(2)-(3) (2002); Rule for Courts-Martial 1107 [hereinafter R.C.M.]. As a matter of "command prerogative" a convening authority "in his sole discretion, may approve, disapprove, commute, or suspend the sentence in whole or in part." Article 60(c)(1)-(2). The convening authority's broad authority is a significant reason that we have noted that the convening authority is an accused's best hope for sentence relief. *United States v. Lee*, 50 M.J. 296, 297 (C.A.A.F. 1999); *United States v. Howard*, 23 C.M.A. 187, 192, 48 C.M.R. 939, 944 (1974).

Action on the sentence is not a legal review. Rather, a convening authority considers numerous factors and reasons in determining a sentence that is "warranted by the circumstances of the offense and appropriate for the accused." R.C.M. 1107(d)(2). The convening authority must consider any mat-

---

1 [n.1] *United States v. Goode*, 1 M.J. 3 (C.M.A. 1975).

ters submitted by the accused pursuant to Article 60(b). Article 60(c)(2), UCMJ; *see also* R.C.M. 1105, 1106(f), 1107(b)(3)(A)(iii).

In the performance of post-trial duties, a convening authority acts in a "role . . . similar to that of a judicial officer." *United States v. Fernandez*, 24 M.J. 77, 78 (C.M.A. 1987) (citing *United States v. Boatner*, 20 C.M.A. 376, 43 C.M.R. 216 (1971)). The requirement for impartiality assures that the convening authority gives full and fair consideration to matters submitted by the accused and determines appropriate action on the sentence. "As a matter of right, each accused is entitled to an individualized, legally appropriate, and careful review of his sentence by the convening authority." *Fernandez*, 24 M.J. at 78. This right is violated where a convening authority cannot or will not approach post-trial responsibility with the requisite impartiality. Under such circumstances, a convening authority must be disqualified from taking action on a record of court-martial. *See Fernandez*, 24 M.J. at 79; *Howard*, 23 C.M.A. at 192, 48 C.M.R. at 944.

Our decisions disqualifying convening authorities from taking post-trial action have fallen into two categories. In the first category, a convening authority will be disqualified if he or she is an accuser, has a personal interest in the outcome of the case, or has a personal bias toward the accused. *See, e.g., United States v. Voorhees*, 50 M.J. 494 (C.A.A.F. 1999); *United States v. Crossley*, 10 M.J. 376 (C.M.A. 1981); *United States v. Conn*, 6 M.J. 351 (C.M.A. 1979); *United States v. Jackson*, 3 M.J. 153 (C.M.A. 1977); *see also* Article 1(9), UCMJ, 10 U.S.C. § 801(9) (2002). In the second category, we have found convening authorities to be disqualified if they display an inelastic attitude toward the performance of their post-trial responsibility. *See, e.g., Fernandez*, 24 M.J. at 79; *Howard*, 23 C.M.A. at 192, 48 C.M.R. at 944. We review de novo claims that a convening authority was disqualified from taking action on a court-martial sentence. *See Conn*, 6 M.J. at 353.

Discussion

Appellant has not argued that MG F was an accuser or possessed a personal, unofficial interest in Appellant's case. Rather, Appellant claims that the convening authority's comments "reflected his animosity toward drug users and his inelastic attitude about the clemency process as a whole." The Government responds that "[w]hile Major General [F's] statements were strong, they do not demonstrate a fixed and inelastic attitude toward dealing with clemency petitions." The Government has not disputed the fact that MG F made the comments attributed to him. Thus, for purposes of this appeal, we will assume that MG F made comments substantially as reported by trial defense counsel. We proceed to review those comments to determine whether MG F possessed an inflexible, disqualifying attitude toward his post-trial responsibilities.

It is not disqualifying for a convening authority to express disdain for illegal drugs and their adverse effect upon good order and discipline in the command. A commanding officer or convening authority fulfilling his or her responsibility to maintain good order and discipline in a military organization need not appear indifferent to crime. Adopting a strong anti-crime position, manifesting an awareness of criminal issues within a command, and taking active steps to deter crime are consonant with the oath to support the Constitution; they do not per se disqualify a convening authority. *See*

Fernandez, 24 M.J. at 78-79; *United States v. Harrison*, 19 C.M.A. 179, 182, 41 C.M.R. 179, 182 (1970); *United States v. Hurt*, 9 C.M.A. 735, 761-62, 27 C.M.R. 3, 44-45 (1958).

In *Fernandez*, the convening authority issued a policy letter to all battalion commanders. That letter characterized illegal drugs as a "threat to combat readiness" and reminded the battalion "commanders that 'detection and treatment of drug abusers' should 'be a primary goal.'" The convening authority directed commanders to "personally screen the names of all court member nominees . . . to ensure that only the most mature officers and NCOs would be detailed for court-martial duty." The policy letter stated that the "full weight of the military justice system must be brought to bear against these criminals." The letter also told commanders to consult with legal advisors before taking action. 24 M.J. at 79.

We found that the policy letter "reveal[ed the convening authority's] serious concern about preventing the illegal distribution of drugs in the force under his command" and that "the letter taken as a whole indicate[d] a flexible mind regarding the legally appropriate ways in which to deal with drug dealers." *Id.*

Although strong, the policy letter in *Fernandez* was balanced, including references to treatment of drug abusers, ensuring the "most mature" court members, and seeking legal advice before disposing of offenses. We held that the record did not demonstrate predisposition to take any particular post-trial action and that the convening authority was not disqualified under Article 60. *Id.*

In the instant case, MG F made direct reference to his post-trial role, asserting that those convicted of using drugs "should not come crying to him about their situations or their families[']." We believe that these words reflect an inflexible attitude toward the proper fulfillment of post-trial responsibilities in cases involving convictions for wrongful use of controlled substances. Unlike the convening authority in *Fernandez*, MG F's comments lacked balance and transcended a legitimate command concern for crime or unlawful drugs.

Regardless of the nature of the offense, a convicted servicemember is entitled to individualized consideration of his case post-trial. That individualized consideration must be by a neutral convening authority capable of fulfilling his or her statutory responsibilities. Statements reflecting an unwillingness to consider each case fully and individually create a perception that a convicted servicemember will be denied the material right to individualized post-trial consideration and action. Where a convening authority reveals that the door to a full and fair post-trial review process is closed, we have held that the convening authority must be disqualified.

In *Howard*, the convening authority issued a letter communicating his views to convicted drug dealers. In that letter, he informed them that their pleas for clemency would be answered in the following manner: "'No, you are going to the Disciplinary Barracks at Fort Leavenworth for the full term of your sentence and your punitive discharge will stand.' Drug peddlers, is that clear?" 23 C.M.A. at 191, 48 C.M.R. at 943. Our Court held that the convening authority was disqualified from taking action on those cases because his statement demonstrated an inelastic attitude toward their clemency requests. *Id.* at 192, 48 C.M.R. at 944.

In *United States v. Wise*, 6 C.M.A. 472, 20 C.M.R. 188 (1955), we found that a convening authority's policy that "he would not consider the retention in the military service of any individual who had been sentenced to a punitive discharge," to be "contrary to the intent and spirit of the Uniform Code of Military Justice and the provisions of the Manual[.]" *Id.* at 474, 476, 20 C.M.R. at 190, 192. In both cases, the convening authority "set[] forth in unmistakable terms" an unwillingness to apply required standards and give individualized consideration during the post-trial review process. *Howard*, 23 C.M.A. 191, 48 C.M.R. at 943. *See also United States v. Walker*, 56 M.J. 617 (A.F. Ct. Crim. App. 2001).

The plain meaning of MG F's words is equally as "unmistakable." He erected a barrier to clemency appeals by convicted drug users who wished to have "their situation or families[']" considered; he said, "Don't come." He revealed his attitude toward the clemency process under such circumstances; he considered pleas for sentence relief as "crying." Finally, his words reflected that the barrier and attitude related directly to his post-trial role as a convening authority: "Don't come crying *to me.*" These words unmistakably reflect an inelastic attitude and predisposition to approve certain adjudged sentences. This attitude is the antithesis of the neutrality required of a "commander's prerogative that is taken in the interests of justice, discipline, mission requirements, clemency, or other appropriate reasons." *Id.* at 618 (citations omitted).

The Government has called to our attention a court-martial order reflecting that MG F provided relief in the form of reducing forfeitures for another Airman convicted, pursuant to his pleas, of using and distributing ecstasy. We need not decide whether the convening authority's action in a separate case would be sufficient to dispel evidence of an inelastic attitude. The bare order in that case does not provide information about the facts and circumstances of that case, including the timing of the convening authority's action in relation to the command briefings at issue here, nor are we privy to any circumstances surrounding the clemency or plea bargaining process in that case. Therefore, we are not persuaded that MG F in fact possessed the required impartiality with regard to his post-trial responsibilities.

Decision

The decision of the United States Air Force Court of Criminal Appeals is reversed, and the action of the convening authority is set aside. The case is returned to the Judge Advocate General of the Air Force for a new review and action before a different convening authority.

Gary D. Solis, *Military Justice, Civilian Clemency: The Sentences Of Marine Corps War Crimes In South Vietnam*

10 TRANSNATIONAL L. & CONTEMPORARY PROCEDURE 59 (2000)

Besides trial, which represents the threat of punishment, an appropriate response to criminality must encompass enforcement — actual punishment —

the "appropriate penal sanctions" spoken of in the 1949 Geneva Conventions. How "appropriate" were the punishments for U.S. war crimes in Vietnam? An answer is suggested by examining the few identifiable war crime prosecutions — limited in the case of the Marine Corps almost exclusively to courts-martial for the murder of Vietnamese noncombatants shown in the following table. No other law of war offense is traceable in sufficient degree to yield meaningful or quantifiable comparisons.

Sentencing of Marines Convicted of the Murder/Manslaughter of Vietnamese Noncombatants, 1965-1971

Individual	Sentence at Trial, in yrs	Sentence approved by CA	Sentence approved by NCMR	Action by USCMA	Sentence after parole (P) or clemency (C), in yrs	Confinement actually served
M. McGee	10	10	7	App.denied	C:6yr, 6 mo	6 yrs, 6 mo.
F.C.Schultz	Life	Life	25	Affirmed	C:6	6 yrs
T.L.Wilson	5	5	5	App.denied	C:denied	5 yrs
S.J.Luczko	Life	Life	3	App.denied	?	unavailable
C. Keenan	Life	25	5	App.denied	C:2yr, 9 mo	2 yrs, ½ mo.
J.H. Boyd	4	4	4	App.denied	C:denied	3 yrs, ½ mo.
J.D. Potter	Life	Life	Life	App.denied	C:12	12 yrs, 1mo.
R.L. Vogel	50	35	10	?	C:8	9 yrs, ½ mo.
C.Ferguson	Life	35	5	App.denied	C:2yr, 5 mo	2yrs, 10 mo.
E.P.Boltik	30	30	Dis.insane	n/a	n/a	n/a
Two Two	10	5	5	No petition	C:4	3yrs, 7½ mo
Wilkerson	Life	30	30	App.denied	C:3	2yrs, ½ mo.
Hamilton	Life	Life	Life	App.denied	C:9	8yrs, 9 mo.
R.E.Wilson	Life	20	20	App.denied	C:7yr, 1 mo	7yrs, 1 mo.
D.R. Allen	Life	20	20	App.denied	C:7	2yrs, 11 mo.
J. Belknap	2	2	2	App.denied	C:denied	1yr, 3 mo.
Licciardo	2	2	2	?	C:denied	1yr, 4 mo.
J. Maushart	2	2	2	App.denied	?	1yr, 4 mo.
S.D. Crider	Life	Life	3	App.denied	?	3yrs, 8½ mo
R.J. Reese	Life	30	3	App.denied	?	2 yrs, 4 mo.
D.W. Parr	4	1 yr, 3 mo.	8 mo.	No petition	C:denied	7 mo. +
F. Sikorski	Life	30	15	10 years	P:3	3 yrs.
M. Stamats	Life	40	15	App.denied	P:3yrs/9mo	3 yrs, 8 mo.
S.G.Green	5	1	1	App.denied	C:denied	8½ mo.
M.Schwarz	Life	1	1	No petition	C:denied	9½ mo.
J.H. Jones	20	20	Dismissed	n/a	n/a	n/a
R.T. Taylor	Life	25	25	App.denied	C:19	7yrs, 8 mo.

a. Sentence at trial = the sentence imposed by the Marine Corps general court-martial in Vietnam that heard case.

b. Sentence approved by CA = the sentence approved by the commanding general (convening authority) who initiated the court-martial and who, with his SJA's (staff judge advocate) written advice, first reviewed the trial and its sentence. CAs have the authority to reduce a court-martial sentence but cannot increase punishment.

c. Sentence approved by NCMR = the sentence approved after a legal review of case by (for sailors and marines) the U.S. Navy Court of Military Review (now the U.S. Navy-Marine Corps Court of Criminal Appeals), in Washington, D.C. Lawyer counsel represents accused throughout this review.

d. Action by USCMA = the action taken following another, *de novo*, appellate review by U.S. Court of Military Appeals, the 3-civilian judge highest military appellate court (now the 5-judge U.S. Court of Appeals for the Armed Forces).

e. Sentence after review by clemency and/or parole boards = sentence reductions awarded upon the periodic, statutory reviews conducted by civilian boards.

f. Confinement actually served = determined by physical review of surviving Naval Clemency and Parole Board records.

g. Dis. Insane = case dismissed when the prisoner was found to be legally insane.

h. ? = instances in which records are incomplete, missing, or not made available.

As the foregoing table illustrates, twenty-seven marines were convicted at courts-martial of murdering noncombatants. In several of those cases there were multiple victims or associated crimes, such as aggravated assault or rape. Did the punishment imposed at trial reflect the seriousness of the offenses? Or were the sentences "wrist slaps" reflective of a dismissive opinion of the Vietnamese victims — the Mere Gook Rule? Do the court-martial results contradict an assertion that American military courts were the effective workings of the law of war and multilateral treaties to which the U.S. is a party? Unlike some of the sentences approved upon appellate review, and some for which clemency were granted, the trial sentences and the sentences approved by the convening authorities — in the combat zone — do not contradict that assertion of effectiveness.

In the twenty-seven cases shown, among attendant punishments such as dishonorable discharge, reduction in grade, and loss of all pay and allowances, the sentences imposed at trial included confinement for life; three cases included confinement for 20, 30, and 50 years. Only in seven of the twenty-seven cases was the confinement imposed less than 10 years. Overall, these are substantial sentences.

Military versus Civilian Sentences, and Appellate Review

Trial-level sentences do not tell the whole story, however. In military practice, unlike civilian forums, appeals are of right,[2] and sentences are often mitigated at the appellate level. That was so in the marine cases involving the murder of noncombatants. After military appellate-level mitigation the 27 sentences were: confinement for life in only two cases; 30 years confinement in another; 20 to 30 years in five others; 10 to 20 years in three others; 5 to 10 in five others; less than 5 years confinement in ten cases; and two convictions set aside, one by reason of procedural error, the other for insanity. Although some sentences were significantly lessened, the range of penalties remained generally high. And one should recall that sentence reductions upon appeal are a result of judicial findings, legal error, or discrepancy in the conviction below. Such reductions are not subjective grants of dispensation.

Case comparisons are suspect, but that range of mitigated court-martial sentence remains comparable to or higher than trial-level sentences in American civilian jurisdictions. In the first half of 1970, for example, when several of the 27 marines were tried, 132 homicide convictions in Pennsylvania state courts resulted in sentences ranging from probation (in 37 cases!), to confinement for life (in 3 cases). Other Pennsylvania sentences for homicide were confinement for 1 year (in 45 cases), 2 years (in 18 cases), 3 to 4 years (in 14 cases), 5 years (in 7 cases), 6 or more years (in 7 cases), and one sentence to death.[3] The mitigated Marine Corps war crime sentences — imposed under active service conditions in a combat zone, one should note — cover a similar, or even higher, span. There is no practical means of determining what, if any, sentence reductions resulted from appellate action in the Pennsylvania cases.

In the federal district courts in 1973, the first year such statistics were compiled, sentences for the twenty-five convicted first and second degree murderers ranged from probation (in two cases), to confinement for 3 to 5 years (in three cases), to 5 years and over — the breakdown is no more specific — in twenty cases.[4] These federal sentences, like the state sentences, are no more harsh than the mitigated sentences imposed upon marines.

Combat Sentences, Stateside Clemency

Whether the military's mitigated court-martial sentences constitute the "appropriate penal sanction" called for by the Geneva Conventions may be

---

[2] [n.72] ". . . The sentences of naval courts-martial are incomplete and cannot lawfully be carried into effect until they have received the approval or confirmation of some revisory power." 5 Op. Att'y Gen. 508 (1852). UCMJ, art. 66(b)(1) requires that a court-martial case be referred to the service's appellate court if the approved sentence extends to death, a dishonorable or bad conduct discharge, or confinement for one year or more. (Except in cases involving the death penalty, UCMJ art. 61 allows an accused to waive or withdraw his right to automatic appellate review.)

[3] [n.75] Franklin E. Zimring, Joel Eigen, and Sheila O'Malley, *Punishing Homicide in Philadelphia: Perspectives on the Death Penalty,* 43 CHI. L. REV. 227, 234, table VI (1976). The table's percentages have been translated into discrete numbers here.

[4] [n76] SOURCEBOOK OF CRIMINAL JUSTICE STATISTICS table 5.38 (Michael J. Hindelang et al. eds. 1973). The rudimentary breakdown lists seven punishment categories: 1 year and under; 1-3 years; 3-5 years; 5 years and over; probation; fine; and other.

arguable. One writer suggests, "it may be concluded, then, that the United States has provided effective penal sanctions for the grave breach involved in willfully killing civilians. . . ."[5] But another contends that the final sentences merely demonstrate that

> The military system is not capable of handling objectively the investigation and punishment of alleged war crimes in Vietnam. . . . [A]n International Criminal Court would be the only acceptable alternative to what is now at best a national embarrassment.[6]

But sentence comparisons, state, federal, and military (general court-martial convictions are federal convictions, of course), suggest not a national embarrassment as much as a sentencing incoherence. The sentences of American soldiers and marines, whether for the murder of Vietnamese or for other Americans, were generally severe, if lacking in discernible pattern. Sentencing results from the same period are similarly mixed when U.S. soldiers murdered other than Vietnamese or fellow-soldiers.[7]

A senior Marine Corps judge advocate who later became counsel to the Assistant Secretary of the Navy, recalled, "It was always disappointing to me . . . how the sentences were just sliced to pieces. . . . That was because of the political climate of the time. . . . There was a feeling in Washington . . . congressional pressure to cut back on a lot of the sentences. . . ."

Such an impression, however, reflects an unawareness of similarly "sliced to pieces" sentences imposed in venues beyond Vietnam. In courts-martial involving the murder of Vietnamese noncombatants — war crimes tried under U.S. military law — the sentences imposed at trial and prior to clemency action were clearly in conformity with or even greater than sentences in similar prosecutions involving both American and other foreign victims. The trial-level military sentences fully reflected not only civilian society's denunciation of the acts involved, and reaffirmed the criminal law. The trial sentences also reflected military society's denunciation. As Professor John Norton Moore has written, "The tradition of judicial review runs deep in the American system. It is not every criminal issue, however, which is constitutionally entrusted to the judiciary or which is suitable for judicial action."[8] Sentence clemency is such an issue.

The Supreme Court held in its Vietnam-era decision, *Parker v. Levy*, "the military establishment is subject to the control of the civilian Commander in

---

[5] [n.82] Alfred P. Rubin, *Legal Aspects of the My Lai Incident*, 49 ORE. L. REV. 260 (1970).

[6] [n.83] Comment, *Punishment for War Crimes: Duty — or Discretion?*, 69 MICH. L. REV. 1312, 1346 n.203 (1971).

[7] [n.84] In the United States, for murdering his wife and her lover, a soldier was sentenced to confinement for 5 years, reduced on appeal to 2 years, *United States v. Griggs*, 41 C.M.R. 541 (A.C.M.R. 1969); for murdering a Canadian soldier in Germany, a U.S. soldier was sentenced to 30 years confinement, *United States v. Stevenson*, 41 C.M.R. 69 (A.C.M.R. 1969); for murdering an Okinawan prostitute, 18 years, *United States v. Nichols*, 46 C.M.R. 1316 (A.C.M.R. 1973); for murdering an American lover, 1 year, reduced to 7 months, *United States v. Small*, 45 C.M.R. 700 (A.C.M.R. 1972).

[8] [n.88] JOHN NORTON MOORE, LAW AND THE INDO-CHINA WAR 598 (1972).

Chief and the civilian departmental heads under him, and its function is to carry out the policies made by those civilian superiors."[9] . . .

Included among those civilian-made policies is the court-martial clemency and parole program, provided for in Federal law,[10] in case law, [11] and promulgated in military regulations.[12] The President of the United States may delegate to the service Secretaries all functions, duties, and powers of confirmation of courts-martial in all cases except those extending to loss of life. Federal law further allows the service Secretaries to "provide a system of parole for offenders who are confined in military correctional facilities. . . ."[13] and directs that the Secretaries shall establish . . . a system for the remission or suspension of the unexecuted part of the sentences of selected offenders.[14] Finally, the U.S. Code allows service Secretaries to further assign their functions, powers, and duties to Under and Assistant service Secretaries.

Each armed service's clemency and parole boards typically consist of five members. The chairperson is a civilian experienced in corrections, with a knowledge of military personnel policies. The four other board members are active duty officers in the grade of major, lieutenant colonel, or colonel. At least one of the officers is a judge advocate — a military lawyer.[15]

Prisoners are eligible for clemency after having served specified periods of their confinement. For example, if the prisoner's sentence is ten years or more, but less than twenty years, by service regulation clemency consideration will be no later than two years from the date confinement began and reconsideration will be annually thereafter. If the sentence is from twenty to thirty years, clemency consideration will be no later than three years into the prisoner's confinement. [If the sentence is] thirty years or more, [clemency consideration occurs] no later than five years into the prisoner's confinement.

Additionally, when "exceptional circumstances exist or for other good cause" the board may consider a prisoner serving a sentence of *any length* for clemency *any time* prior to completing his sentence. In other words, despite pages of specific guidelines, the board has an essentially free hand to act in any case at any time.

Generally, a prisoner is eligible for parole consideration after having served one-third of his period of confinement. But as in clemency regulations, the board "may waive any parole eligibility requirement. . . ." Standards for consideration for both clemency and parole span the factors one might anticipate,

---

[9] [n.89] *Parker v. Levy*, 417 U.S. 733, 751 (1974).

[10] [n.90] 10 U.S.C., §§ 952, Parole; 953, Remission or suspension of sentence; and 871, Execution of sentence; suspension of sentence.

[11] [n.91] *E.g., Sima v. United States*, 96 F. Supp. 932 (Ct. Cl. 1951) (clemency authority of Secretary and Under Secretary of the Navy).

[12] [n.92] UCMJ, art. 74, Remission and suspension; and Army Regulation 27-10, Military Justice, Section V, Post-trial, which is a typical service implementing order.

[13] [n.93] 10 U.S.C. § 952, Parole.

[14] [n.94] 10 U.S.C. § 953, Remission or suspension of sentence.

[15] [n.95] Army Regulation 15-130, Army Clemency and Parole Board ¶ 2-3.

from combat service to prior criminality; from the protection of society to deterrence.

Given such broad authority, it is not surprising that clemency and parole actions injected substantial reductions in many Vietnam war crime convictions — even with the presence of four senior military officers on each board. PFC John Potter, sentenced to confinement for life, served but twelve and-a-half years — a not inconsiderable period, but well below what one might have anticipated, given the horrific nature of his crimes. For the murder of five Vietnamese noncombatants, Lance Corporal Denzil Allen was sentenced by a Marine court-martial to confinement for life; he served but two years and eleven months. These reductions, similar to reductions won by others convicted of Vietnam war crimes, were granted by clemency boards and politically appointed Under Secretaries of the Army, and the Navy.

Court-martial sentences for Vietnam-era war crimes, imposed by officer and enlisted panels in the combat zone, were substantial, even heavy. Compared to sentences imposed in civilian courtrooms, they were *decidedly* heavy. Nor were there discernible differences in sentences levied for the murder of Americans and those imposed for Vietnamese victims. Military courts fully executed their responsibilities under customary law of armed conflict and the 1949 Geneva Conventions.

Once those military sentences were reviewed in the relative calm of the United States, once clemency was exercised by clemency and parole panels, the military sentences were often cut significantly. By 1970, the war had become unpopular. Military confinement facilities were full. The pressures to grant clemency were no doubt significant. But the results remain notable.

There were, it must be said, instances in which the military justice system itself made significant sentence reductions in the appellate process: Vogel's court-imposed fifty-year sentence was cut to ten years; Ferguson's life sentence lessened to five; and Schwarz's life sentence became one year. Two-year sentences resulted for multiple murders in the cases of Belknap, Licciardo, and Maushart. To explain that problems of proof resulted in pre-trial agreements in those cases — plea bargains — is no explanation at all. There were no political appointees or civilians involved in those sentences.

But there were also nine Marine Corps cases — one-third of those considered — wherein clemency and parole boards, far from the sound of guns, granted dramatic reductions in sentences. Among the more obvious examples are Wilkerson's thirty-year sentence, reduced to two years; Hamilton, from life to eight years and nine months; Allen's twenty years reduced to less than three; Sikorski, fifteen years to three years; and Taylor's confinement for twenty-five years to less than eight.

Vietnam was not the first instance of civilian reductions in court-martial sentences, of course. Congress first provided for court-martial review by civilian authorities in 1786, when it revised the Articles of War following a commander's execution of three soldiers without benefit of trial.[16] Civilian control of the military establishment was well-established by the mid-nineteenth century, although it was unclear if that control extended to review of military justice decisions by civilian courts.

Any lack of clarity as to review of courts-martial by civilian courts was resolved in 1858, when the Supreme Court decided *Dynes v. Hoover*, [61 U.S. (20 How.) 65 (1854)]. Odd as it sounds today, the Court held that a court-martial verdict, "when confirmed [through military appellate procedures] is altogether beyond the jurisdiction or inquiry of any civil tribunal whatever. . . ."[17] Accordingly, *Dynes* held, when findings and sentences have been imposed by regularly convened and legally conducted courts-martial, civil courts are in no way involved with such sentences, "nor are they in any way alterable by them."[18]

But there was no such limitation on the power of the President, as commander-in-chief, to confirm, modify, or disapprove court-martial findings and sentences involving general officers, dismissal of any officer or cadet, or death.[19] Before the first modern Articles of War were published,[20] President Abraham Lincoln frequently reduced the penalties imposed by military tribunals.[21] After World War I, 28,000 courts-martial were reviewed by Special Clemency Boards and hundreds of sentences modified or disapproved.[22] These clemency boards were comprised solely of military officers, however.

Before the Uniform Code of Military Justice became law in May 1950, the Articles for the Government of the Navy were the military law of the Navy and, when they were embarked, the Marine Corps. Their source was the Constitution, Article I, section 8, clause 14, giving Congress the power to make rules for the government and regulation of the land and naval forces. Added by Congress in 1909, article 54(b) of the Articles for the Government of the Navy for the first time provided authority for the Secretary of the Navy to "set aside the proceedings or remit or mitigate, in whole or in part, the sentence imposed by any naval court-martial. . . ."[23] After fifty-one years, the *Dynes* decision was overtaken by federal legislation, at least as to civilian

---

[16] [n.100] WILLIAM WINTHROP, MILITARY LAW AND PRECEDENTS 972 (1920). The revision required that no court-martial sentence "in time of peace, extending to the loss of life . . . [or] . . . either in time of peace or war . . . a general officer [shall] be carried into execution until after the whole proceedings shall have been transmitted to the Secretary of War, to be laid before Congress for their confirmation, or disapproval, and their orders on the case."

[17] [n.102] *Id.* at 81.

[18] [n.103] *Id.* at 82.

[19] [n.104] Articles of War, 1917, arts. 48, 49.

[20] [n.105] U.S. War Department, A Manual for Courts-Martial ix (1916). The first Articles of War were passed by the second Continental Congress in 1775. Winthrop, *supra* note 100, at 21-22. The first "modern" Articles of War may be considered those first enacted in the twentieth century, i.e., Articles of War, 1917, which replaced those of 1874.

[21] [n.106] 1 JONATHAN LURIE, ARMING MILITARY JUSTICE 32 n.35 (1992).

[22] [n.107] *Id.* at 83 n.41.

[23] [n.109] Articles for the Government of the Navy, art. 54(b), Feb. 16, 1909, c. 131, § 9, 35 Stat. 621.

government officials. Nine years later, in 1918, similar legislation allowed the Secretary of War to take similar action in regard to Army courts.[24] That legislation was published as article 53, Articles of War, 1917.

The successor to the Articles of War, the UCMJ, replicated both article 54(b), Articles for the Government of the Navy, and article of war 53, in UCMJ article 74's provision for civilian — Secretarial — review of courts-martial. During the Vietnam era, in 1968, Congress further provided for Secretarial parole and clemency authority.[25] Finally, in 1984, Congress passed legislation allowing the appeal of court-martial decisions directly to a civilian tribunal, the United States Supreme Court.[26]

Before that provision, in 1971, Army Lieutenant William Calley was sentenced by court-martial to dismissal from the Army and confinement at hard labor for life. The punishment was reduced to dismissal and twenty years by the court-martial's convening authority. That period of confinement was left undisturbed through two levels of military appellate review. But in 1974 Calley's reduced sentence was considered by the Secretary of the Army, not as a discretionary matter, but as required by UCMJ article 71(b): "If in the case of a commissioned officer . . . the sentence of a court-martial extends to dismissal, that part of the sentence . . . may not be executed until approved by the Secretary concerned. . . ."[27] The same article allows for Secretarial commutation, remission, or suspension of the sentence. The Secretary, Howard W. Calloway, halved Calley's confinement to ten years.[28] Seven months later, Secretary Calloway, now exercising his discretionary authority under UCMJ article 74 ("The Secretary concerned . . . may remit or suspend any part . . ."[29]), paroled Calley, who had completed one-third of his ten-year sentence, virtually all of it served in house arrest.

The UCMJ articles employed in reducing Calley's general court-martial sentence, imposed by Vietnam-experienced Army officers, were only the latest codification of congressionally authorized civilian review of court-martial verdicts and sentences.

The U.S. Code provisions that allowed reduction of Potter's life sentence to twelve years, the lessening of Schultz's life sentence to six years, and Wilkerson's thirty-year sentence to two years, were recognition of the authority of clemency and parole bodies to mitigate military-imposed sentences.

Conclusion

Congressionally authorized clemency action, and civilian political involvement in military sentence review, is entirely appropriate. Civilian control of our military is a constitutionally-mandated concept proven throughout the existence of our Republic.

---

[24] [n.110] War Department, A Manual for Courts-Martial, 1918, 317 (1918).

[25] [n.111] Pub. L. No. 90-377, § 1, July 5, 1968, 82 Stat. 287; that is, 10 U.S.C. §§ 952 and 953.

[26] [n.112] 28 U.S.C. § 1259. *See* UCMJ, art. 67a.

[27] [n.113] UCMJ, art. 71(b), Execution of Sentence; suspension of sentence.

[28] [n.114] *See* HARRY G. SUMMERS, JR., THE VIETNAM WAR ALMANAC 258-59 (1985).

[29] [n.115] UCMJ, art. 74, Remission and suspension.

But it should be borne in mind that the military justice system takes the harshest view of war crimes committed by its own. The Vietnam sentences imposed upon those convicted of war crimes provide ample demonstration of the military jury's recognition of the seriousness of such offenses. While the military record is imperfect, those offenses that are discovered and brought to the court-martial bar are dealt with in severe terms. If there is to be a lessening of the military's punishments, let it be accomplished by those civilian superiors and administrators who oversee our nation's defense.

Finally, even where Vietnam war crimes are concerned, it bears reminding that "war is not a series of case studies that can be scrutinized with objectivity. . . . War is the suffering and death of people you know, set against a background of suffering and death of people you do not."[30]

Letter from Captain Aubrey M. Daniel 3d to President Richard M. Nixon
April 3, 1973, N.Y. TIMES, Apr. 7, 1971, at 12, col. 1

[The trial counsel in the *MyLai* case wrote the following letter after President Nixon released Lt. Calley from the stockade to remain under house arrest at his quarters while the case was on appeal. *Calley prosecutor Asserts Nixon undermines justice*, N.Y., TIMES, Apr. 7.]

It is very difficult for me to know where to begin this letter as I am not accustomed to writing letters of protest. I only hope that I can find the words to convey to you my feelings as a United States citizen, and as an attorney, who believes that respect for the law is one of the fundamental bases upon which this nation is founded.

On November 26, 1969, you issued the following statement through your press secretary, Mr. Ronald Ziegler, in referring to the Mylai incident:

"An incident such as that alleged in this case is in direct violation not only of United States military policy, but is also abhorrent to the conscience of all the American people.

"The Secretary of the Army is continuing his investigation. Appropriate action is and will be taken to assure that illegal and immoral conduct as alleged be dealt with in accordance with the strict rules of military justice.

"This incident should not be allowed to reflect on the some million and a quarter young Americans who have now returned to the United States after having served in Viet-Nam with great courage and distinction."

At the time you issued this statement, a general court-martial had been directed for a resolution of the charges which have been brought against Lieutenant William L. Calley, Jr., for his involvement at Mylai.

On December 8, 1969, you were personally asked to comment on the Mylai incident at a press conference. At that time, you made the following statement:

---

[30] [n.116] JAMES R. MCDONOUGH, PLATOON LEADER 139 (1985).

"What appears was certainly a massacre, and under no circumstances was it justified. One of the goals we are fighting for in Viet-Nam is to keep the people of South Viet-Nam from having imposed upon them a government which has atrocity against civilians as one of its policies. We cannot ever condone or use atrocities against civilians to accomplish that goal."

These expressions of what I believed to be your sentiment were truly reflective of my own feelings when I was given the assignment of prosecuting the charges which had been preferred against Lieutenant Calley. My feelings were generated not by emotionalism or self-indignation but by my knowledge of the evidence in the case, the laws of this nation in which I strongly believe, and my own conscience. I knew that I had been given a great responsibility and I only hoped that I would be able to discharge my duties and represent the United States in a manner which would be a credit to the legal profession and our system of justice.

I undertook the prosecution of the case without any ulterior motives for personal gain, either financial or political. My only desire was to fulfill my duty as a prosecutor and see that justice was done in accordance with the laws of this nation. I dedicated myself to this end from November of 1969 until the trial was concluded.

Throughout the proceedings there was criticism of the prosecution but I lived with the abiding conviction that once the facts and the law had been presented there would be no doubt in the mind of any reasonable person about the necessity for the prosecution of this case and the ultimate verdict. I was mistaken.

The trial of Lieutenant Calley was conducted in the finest tradition of our legal system. It was in every respect a fair trial in which every legal right of Lieutenant Calley was fully protected. It clearly demonstrated that the military justice system which has previously been the subject of much criticism was a fair system.

Throughout the trial, the entire system was under the constant scrutiny of the mass media and the public, and the trial of Lieutenant Calley was also in a very real sense the trial of the military judicial system. However, there was never an attack lodged by any member of the media concerning the fairness of the trial. There could be no such allegation justifiably made.

I do not believe that there has ever been a trial in which the accused's rights were more fully protected, the conduct of the defense given greater latitude, the prosecution held to stricter standards. The burden of proof which the Government had to meet in this case was not beyond a reasonable doubt, but beyond possibility. The very fact that Lieutenant Calley was an American officer being tried for the deaths of Vietnamese during a combat operation by fellow officers compels this conclusion.

The jury selection, in which customary procedure was altered by providing both the defense and the prosecution with three peremptory challenges instead of the usual one, was carefully conducted to insure the impartiality of those men who were selected. Six officers, all combat veterans, five having served in Viet-Nam, were selected. These six men who had served their country well, were called upon again to serve their nation as jurors and to sit in judgment of Lieutenant Calley as prescribed by law.

From the time they took their oaths until they rendered their decision, they performed their duties in the very finest tradition of the American legal system. If ever a jury followed the letter of the law in applying it to the evidence presented, they did. They are indeed a credit to our system of justice and to the officer corps of the United States Army.

When the verdict was rendered, I was totally shocked and dismayed at the reaction of many people across the nation. Much of the adverse public reaction I can attribute to people who have acted emotionally and without being aware of the evidence that was presented and perhaps even the laws of this nation regulating the conduct of war.

These people have undoubtedly viewed Lieutenant Calley's conviction simply as the conviction of an American officer for killing the enemy. Others, no doubt out of a sense of frustration, have seized upon the conviction as a means of protesting the war in Viet-Nam. I would prefer to believe that most of the public criticism has come from people who are not aware of the evidence as it was presented, or having followed it they have chosen not to believe it.

Certainly, no one wanted to believe what occurred at Mylai, including the officers who sat in judgment of Lieutenant Calley. To believe, however, that any large percentage of the population could believe the evidence which was presented and approve of the conduct of Lieutenant Calley would be as shocking to my conscience as the conduct itself, since I believe that we are still a civilized nation.

If such be the case, then the war in Viet-Nam has brutalized us more than I care to believe, and it must cease. How shocking it is if so many people across the nation have failed to see the moral issue which was involved in the trial of Lieutenant Calley — that it is unlawful for an American soldier to summarily execute unarmed and unresisting men, women, children, and babies.

But how much more appalling it is to see so many of the political leaders of the nation who have failed to see the moral issue, or, having seen it, to compromise it for political motive in the face of apparent public displeasure with the verdict.

I would have hoped that all leaders of this nation, which is supposed to be the leader within the international community for the protection of the weak and the oppressed regardless of nationality, would have either accepted and supported the enforcement of the laws of this country as reflected by the verdict of the court or not made any statement concerning the verdict until they had had the same opportunity to evaluate the evidence that the members of the jury had.

In view of your previous statements concerning this matter, I have been particularly shocked and dismayed at your decision to intervene in these proceedings in the midst of the public clamor. Your decision can only have been prompted by the response of a vocal segment of our population who while no doubt acting in good faith, cannot be aware of the evidence which resulted in Lieutenant Calley's conviction. Your intervention has, in my opinion, damaged the military judicial system and lessened any respect it may have gained as a result of the proceedings.

You have subjected a judicial system of this country to the criticism that it is subject to political influence, when it is a fundamental precept of our judicial system that the legal processes of this country must be kept free from any outside influences. What will be the impact of your decision upon the future trials, particularly those within the military?

Not only has respect for the legal process been weakened and the critics of the military judicial system been supported for their claims of command influence, the image of Lieutenant Calley, a man convicted of the premeditated murder of at least 22 unarmed and unresisting people, as a national hero has been enhanced, while at the same time support has been given to those people who have so unjustly criticized the six loyal and honorable officers who have done this country a great service by fulfilling their duties as jurors so admirably.

Have you considered those men in making your decisions? The men who since rendering their verdict have found themselves and their families the subject of vicious attacks upon their honor, integrity and loyalty to this nation.

It would seem to me to be more appropriate for you as the President to have said something in their behalf and to remind the nation of the purpose of our legal system and the respect it should command.

I would expect that the President of the United States, a man whom I believed should and would provide the moral leadership for this nation, would stand fully behind the law of this land on a moral issue which is so clear and about which there can be no compromise.

For this nation to condone the acts of Lieutenant Calley is to make us no better than our enemies and make any pleas by this nation for the humane treatment of our own prisoners meaningless.

I truly regret having to have written this letter and wish that no innocent person had died at Mylai on March 16, 1968. But innocent people were killed under circumstances that will always remain abhorrent to my conscience.

While in some respects what took place at Mylai has to be considered a tragic day in the history of our nation, how much more tragic would it have been for this country to have taken no action against those who were responsible.

That action was taken, but the greatest tragedy of all will be if political expediency dictates the compromise of such a fundamental moral principle as the inherent unlawfulness of the murder of innocent persons, making the action and the courage of six honorable men who served their country so well meaningless.

[Captain Daniel went on to a brilliant career with a leading District of Columbia law firm. President Nixon was re-elected in 1972, but resigned in disgrace following the "Watergate" incident.]

NOTE

For further discussion of *Calley*, see Chapter 9, §II, *supra*.

II. SENTENCE REVIEW

Draft Principles Governing the Administration of Justice through Military Tribunals
UN Commission on Human Rights, E/CN.4/2006/58 (2006)

Principle No. 15, Guarantee of the rights of the defence and the right to a just and fair trial

> The exercise of the rights of the defence must be fully guaranteed in military courts under all circumstances. All judicial proceedings in military courts must offer the following guarantees . . .

> (j) Everyone convicted of a crime shall have the right to have his or her conviction and sentence reviewed by a higher tribunal according to law. . . .

UNITED STATES v. DURANT
United States Court of Appeals for the Armed Forces
55 M.J. 258 (C.A.A.F. 2001)

CHIEF JUDGE CRAWFORD delivered the opinion of the Court.

A military judge sitting as a general court-martial convicted appellant, pursuant to his pleas, of dereliction of duty and two specifications of larceny (totaling $8800) for the improper use of an international merchants purchase authorization card (IMPAC), in violation of Articles 92 and 121, Uniform Code of Military Justice, 10 U.S.C. §§ 892 and 921.

The military judge sentenced appellant to a dishonorable discharge, confinement for 30 months, and reduction to Private E-1. Pursuant to a pretrial agreement, the convening authority approved only so much of the sentence as provided for a bad-conduct discharge, confinement for 12 months, and reduction to E-1. In an act of clemency not required by the pretrial agreement, the convening authority also waived automatic forfeitures imposed pursuant to Article 58b, UCMJ, 10 U.S.C. § 858b, for 6 months.

In his matters submitted to the convening authority under RCM 1105, Manual for Courts-Martial, United States (2000 ed.), appellant requested that his sentence to confinement be reduced to time served (about 5 months at the time of the convening authority action) and that his bad-conduct discharge be disapproved. The basis for this request was that his coactor, Staff Sergeant (SSG) Cochrane, received a sentence that did not include either confinement or a discharge.

Appellant again raised the issue of disproportionately harsh sentencing before the Army Court of Criminal Appeals. Prior to deciding the case, the

Court of Criminal Appeals granted appellant's motion for attachment of an authenticated copy of the record of trial in the general court-martial case of *United States v. Staff Sergeant Garland J. Cochrane*, Army No. 9900228. After review, the lower court affirmed the findings and sentence in appellant's case in an unpublished decision memorandum.

We hold that appellant has failed to show an abuse of discretion or obvious miscarriage of justice.

I. Factual Background

This case presents the unique situation of determining whether Article 66, UCMJ, 10 U.S.C. § 866, requires a Court of Criminal Appeals to mitigate a sentence, which that court otherwise determines to be appropriate, simply because an appellant's coactor receives substantially less punishment at his or her court-martial.[31]

Although charged differently by two separate commands, appellant and SSG Cochrane were essentially coconspirators. The stipulations of fact, introduced at the courts-martial of appellant and SSG Cochrane, show that both noncommissioned officers (NCOs) were IMPAC program cardholders. IMPAC cards are issued in order to buy supplies for a particular military unit efficiently; they are not to be used for personal purchases. SSG Cochrane was the approving official for purchases made by several cardholders, to include appellant, within his 63d Ordnance Battalion. SSG Cochrane was stationed at Fort Dix, New Jersey; appellant was assigned to Fort Monmouth, New Jersey. Each installation had its own general court-martial convening authority.

In January 1996, SSG Cochrane approached appellant, whom he supervised, and initiated a scheme: appellant would make unauthorized purchases of personal items with his IMPAC card for both himself and SSG Cochrane, and SSG Cochrane would approve the purchase of these items and authorize payment with government funds. Over the next 2 years, appellant made over 90 unauthorized purchases totaling more than $30,000 for himself, SSG Cochrane, and others. During this period of time, appellant progressively increased the amount of purchases that he illegally made with his IMPAC credit card, knowing that SSG Cochrane would approve the purchases and cover for him. The record shows that SSG Cochrane received just over $4000 worth of ill-gotten goods, purchased by appellant on his behalf. Appellant illegally purchased for himself, with SSG Cochrane's approval, goods totaling about $6000.

SSG Cochrane was arraigned at Fort Monmouth, New Jersey, on November 24, 1998, the same day that appellant pled guilty to his charges before a military judge sitting as a general court-martial. During SSG Cochrane's arraignment, he requested and was granted the option of deferring his decision on forum selection. SSG Cochrane's next session of his general court-martial was held on February 24, 1999, at Fort Dix, New Jersey. In the interim, he negotiated a pretrial agreement with the Fort Dix general court-martial convening

---

[31] [n.2] The granted issue in this case is:

    WHETHER APPELLANT'S DISPROPORTIONATELY HARSH SENTENCE, COMPARED WITH THE SENTENCE RECEIVED BY HIS CO-ACTOR, WARRANTS APPELLATE RELIEF.

authority that limited his confinement to 15 months and any discharge adjudged to one no more severe than a bad-conduct discharge, and required the Government to dismiss four of the six charges against him.

The presiding judge, Judge Johnston, was the same judge who presided over appellant's trial. SSG Cochrane requested, as was his right, officer and enlisted members to sentence him following his guilty plea to one charge and specification of conspiracy with appellant, and eight specifications of larceny totaling over $4000. The members sentenced SSG Cochrane to be reduced to E-3 and to pay a fine of $4200. SSG Cochrane was discharged from the Army on March 26, 1999, with an honorable discharge, at the expiration of his term of service.

II. Discussion

Congress has vested responsibility for determining sentence appropriateness in the Courts of Criminal Appeals. "The power to review a case for sentence appropriateness, which reflects the unique history and attributes of the military justice system, includes but is not limited to considerations of uniformity and evenhandedness of sentencing decisions." *United States v. Sothen*, 54 M.J. 294, 296 (2001), citing *United States v. Lacy*, 50 M.J. 286, 287-88 (1999).

The role of this Court in cases such as the one at bar is to determine, as a matter of law, whether a Court of Criminal Appeals abused its discretion or caused a miscarriage of justice in carrying out its highly discretionary "sentence appropriateness" role. *See id.; United States v. Fee*, 50 M.J. 290 (1999). In so doing, we examine three questions of law: "(1) whether the cases are closely related . . . ; (2) whether the cases resulted in 'highly disparate' sentences; and (3) . . . whether there is a rational basis for the differences between [these] . . . cases." *See Lacy*, 50 M.J. at 288.

Sentence comparison does not require sentence equation. *See United States v. Ballard*, 20 M.J. 282 (C.M.A. 1985); *United States v. Snelling*, 14 M.J. 267 (C.M.A. 1982).

Both sides agree that *Lacy* controls the disposition of this case, and that the courts-martial of appellant and SSG Cochrane are closely related. Appellate defense counsel maintain that the sentences are highly disparate on their face because one NCO received no punitive discharge and no confinement while the other received a punitive discharge and a year's confinement (after modification in accordance with the pretrial agreement). Citing *Lacy*, the Government contends that the sentences are not highly disparate: "The test in such a case is not limited to a narrow comparison of the relevant numerical values of the sentences at issue, but also may include consideration of the disparity in relation to the potential maximum punishment." 50 M.J. at 289.

In addition to *Lacy*, two other recent cases are instructive. In *Fee, supra*, the appellant received a sentence that included a dishonorable discharge and 6 years' confinement (confinement in excess of 36 months was suspended). Her husband received a sentence that included a bad-conduct discharge and 15 months' confinement. The convictions of both Fee and her husband stemmed from their illegal use and distribution of various controlled substances.

The Navy-Marine Corps Court of Criminal Appeals determined that the cases were closely related but the sentences were not highly disparate. The lower court then found two factors which provided a rational basis for differences in the sentences. *See Fee*, 50 M.J. at 291. This Court found it unnecessary to decide whether the two sentences were highly disparate, thus leaving the lower court's finding that the two sentences were not highly disparate. We found that there was no abuse of discretion or miscarriage of justice in the lower court's judgment because the factors which were used to justify the differences in sentences were indeed logical and rational.

In *United States v. Noble*, 50 M.J. 293 (1999), a case that involved differences in initial disposition of cases rather than sentence uniformity, this Court found no abuse of discretion or miscarriage of justice in the lower court's holding. Noble, a Marine Corps Staff Sergeant, was convicted, among other things, of adultery, obstruction of justice, and fraternization. His coactor in a sexual escapade with lower ranking women Marines was allowed to leave the Marine Corps with an honorable discharge, pursuant to an early-separation program, without ever facing a court-martial. Even though Noble was sentenced to a bad-conduct discharge and 6 months' confinement, both the Court of Criminal Appeals and this Court found that appellant Noble's sentence was appropriate.

Unfortunately, we are forced to examine the issues of sentence disparity and appropriateness in this case without a considered, written opinion from the experienced judges of the Court of Criminal Appeals. *See id.* at 295; *United States v. Hawes*, 51 M.J. 258, 260 (1999); *United States v. Cook*, 46 M.J. 37, 39 (1997). In cases such as the one at hand, involving a unique sentencing issue of first impression, analysis of the facts and the law applicable to those facts by the Courts of Criminal Appeals, with their special expertise, is extremely beneficial. Sound articulation of their rationale by the Courts of Criminal Appeals avoids speculation and promotes judicial economy.

The military justice system promotes sentence uniformity through Article 66 and the requirement that the Courts of Criminal Appeals engage in a sentence appropriateness analysis. While the United States Federal District Courts attempt to control disparate treatment of similarly situated defendants through sentencing guidelines, analogies to the other federal system of criminal justice are helpful.

"[P]rosecutorial charging, plea, and motion practices are . . . a well-spring of sentencing disparity. . . . [P]rosecutors have always enjoyed great discretion in deciding what cases to pursue and what charges to bring." *United States v. Rodriguez,* 162 F.3d 135, 151 (1st Cir. 1998), quoting Kate Stith & José A. Cabranes, *Fear of Judging: Sentencing Guidelines in the Federal Courts* 140-41 (1998). As this case reflects, charging decisions by commanders in consultation with their trial counsel, as well as referral decisions by convening authorities after advice from their Staff Judge Advocates, can certainly lead to differences in sentencing.

Here, appellant was charged with two specifications of larceny covering two distinct periods of time (one for the 18 months prior to appellant's deployment to Bosnia and the other for the 6 months after his return from Bosnia). SSG

Cochrane, on the other hand, was charged with 8 specifications of larceny. Accordingly, appellant was facing a maximum sentence that included 20 years' confinement for his larcenous activity, whereas SSG Cochrane was facing a potential confinement of 80 years for the larceny offenses. *See* para. 46e(1)(c), Part IV, Manual, *supra*. Yet appellant's thefts netted him a higher value of stolen goods.

Neither charging decision was unreasonable, nor the result of some type of invidious, constitutionally impermissible discrimination. Just as "disparity in sentencing among codefendants is not, by itself, a sufficient ground for attacking an otherwise proper sentence under the [federal sentencing] guidelines," the military system must be prepared to accept some disparity in the sentencing of codefendants, provided each military accused is sentenced as an individual. *See United States v. Taylor*, 991 F.2d 533, 536 (9th Cir. 1993), quoting *United States v. Hoy*, 932 F.2d 1343, 1345 (9th Cir. 1991); *see also United States v. Bonnet-Grullon*, 212 F.3d 692 (2d Cir. 2000); *United States v. Torres*, 81 F.3d 900 (9th Cir. 1996); *United States v. Alahmad*, 211 F.3d 538 (10th Cir. 2000).

Similarly, federal courts have held that since the guidelines were enacted to promote uniformity in sentencing among the federal courts trying federal crimes, federal district courts may not depart from sentencing guidelines in order to equalize acknowledged disparities between state and federal sentences for coactors. *See United States v. Snyder*, 136 F.3d 65, 69-70 (1st Cir. 1998); *United States v. Vilchez*, 967 F.2d 1351 (9th Cir. 1992).

Without analysis from the court below as to whether the sentences are highly disparate, we will assume, without deciding, that appellant has met his burden of demonstrating the sentences are highly disparate. *See United States v. Sothen, supra*. Accordingly, we must determine whether or not the Government has presented a rational basis for the assumed high degree of disparity. Since the lower court failed to articulate its rationale for affirmance, we will affirm only where the respective records of trial clearly manifest differences in these two soldiers' cases that explain the respective sentences.

This is not a case where we must decide whether the proverbial scheming Fagin is more culpable than the boy pickpocket Oliver.[32] Appellant presented his sentencing authority with 10 years of credible service, to include tours in both the Gulf War and Bosnia. However, the three witnesses who testified on his behalf, to include the Company First Sergeant and Commander, were lukewarm in their assessment of appellant's future potential. Their testimony was to the effect that "appellant was above average for a supply sergeant"; "I would probably hire him again knowing about the crime"; "His duty performance was pretty good"; "I have known two supply sergeants, appellant was better than the first one." Appellant testified, expressed remorse for his crimes, explained that he committed the thefts because he did not think he would get caught, and admitted that he could "never regain that trust" which he had violated. He did not ask to remain on active duty.

---

[32] [n.4] *See* Charles Dickens's *Oliver Twist* (1838).

The extenuation and mitigation presented at SSG Cochrane's trial, albeit summarized in his record of trial, is more substantive. The defense called four witnesses, ranging in rank from Sergeant First Class to Captain, who had known SSG Cochrane at different locations and times during his 10-year career. Captain Sargent, who was serving as a troop commander in the Third Armored Cavalry Regiment at the time of his trial testimony, described SSG Cochrane's duty performance as "outstanding in every facet." He added: "SSG Cochrane's military character and professional demeanor was impeccable as far as appearance, soldier skills, everything that counts as being a soldier." Command Sergeant Major (CSM) Carey, the CSM of a Ranger training battalion at the time, testified to SSG Cochrane's exemplary military character and noted that SSG Cochrane "accomplished all missions." Significantly, all of the active duty soldiers testifying on SSG Cochrane's behalf said he had either good or outstanding rehabilitative potential.

SSG Cochrane's wife and three children were also present in court. Mrs. Cochrane testified and begged the members not to send her husband to jail. Finally, SSG Cochrane testified that he would welcome a second chance to return to the Army at any rank. In his own summarized words, "there would not be a better soldier if given a second chance."

Our review is limited to the legal questions whether the cases are "closely related," whether the sentences are "highly disparate," and if so, whether there is a "rational basis" for the difference. *Lacy*, 50 M.J. at 288. Having assumed that the cases are closely related and the sentences are highly disparate, the differences in mitigation evidence reviewed above demonstrate that there is a rational basis for the differences in sentences. Therefore, we must, as a court of law, decline to grant relief on the basis of *Lacy*.

While the mitigating evidence in the two cases may well explain why appellant and SSG Cochrane received different sentences, it does not answer appellant's claim that his sentence is neither uniform nor appropriate. Sentence uniformity and appropriateness are matters exclusively within the providence of the Courts of Criminal Appeals. In light of all the evidence, we conclude that the Court of Criminal Appeals did not abuse its discretion in reviewing appellant's sentence for appropriateness and uniformity.

The decision of the United States Army Court of Criminal Appeals is affirmed.

SULLIVAN, JUDGE (concurring):

The Uniform Code of Military Justice provides that an accused may be tried by a court-martial of members or a court-martial composed of a military judge alone. Article 16, UCMJ, 10 U.S.C. § 816. This optional procedure alone may lead to court-martial sentences in closely related cases which are not the same, and that is what happened in this case. Appellant's confederate received from a court of members a sentence consisting of a reduction from E-6 to E-3 and a fine of $4,200. Appellant received from a military judge a sentence of a dishonorable discharge, confinement for 30 months, and reduction from E-5 to E-1. The convening authority, pursuant to a pretrial agreement, reduced this sentence to a bad-conduct discharge, confinement for 12 months, and reduction to E-1.

The Court of Criminal Appeals is statutorily required to ensure that a military accused receives a correct and appropriate sentence. Article 66(c), UCMJ, 10 U.S.C. § 866(c). In *United States v. Lacy*, 50 M.J. 286, 287-88 (1999), we recognized that the Court of Criminal Appeals is primarily responsible for ensuring at least "relative uniformity" in sentencing. We said:

> The power to review a case for sentence appropriateness, including relative uniformity, is vested in the Courts of Criminal Appeals, not in our Court, which is limited to errors of law. *Compare* Art. 66(c) *with* Art. 67(c), UCMJ, 10 U.S.C. § 867(c)(1994); *see United States v. Christopher*, 13 U.S.C.M.A. 231, 236, 32 C.M.R. 231, 236 (1962). With respect to reviewing the actions of the Courts of Criminal Appeals on issues of sentence appropriateness, our review is limited to preventing "obvious miscarriages of justice or abuses of discretion." *United States v. Dukes*, 5 M.J. 71, 73 (C.M.A. 1978); s*ee United States v. Henry*, 42 M.J. 231, 234 (1995).

Nevertheless, in *Lacy*, we further delineated when our Court could find an abuse of discretion by the appellate court below. We said:

> Our review of a decision from a Court of Criminal Appeals in such a case is limited to three questions of law: (1) whether the cases are "closely related" (*e.g.*, coactors involved in a common crime, servicemembers involved in a common or parallel scheme, or some other direct nexus between the servicemembers whose sentences are sought to be compared); (2) whether the cases resulted in "highly disparate" sentences; and (3) if the requested relief is not granted in a closely related case involving a highly disparate sentence, whether there is a rational basis for the differences between or among the cases.

Id. at 288. If evidence exists in the record from which the service appellate court could conclude that a rational basis existed for a "highly disparate" sentence in a closely related case, we must affirm the Court of Criminal Appeals denial of sentence relief.

Turning to the evidence of record in this case, I note that appellant did not request to remain in the Army, but his confederate did. *Compare* Record at 98 (appellant's unsworn statement) *with Cochrane* Record at 32 (SSG Cochrane's unsworn statement). Appellant also had a record of military performance that was obviously inferior to his confederate. *Compare* Record at 85 (appellant's first sergeant noted that he would try to replace appellant as Supply Sergeant if his company went to war) *with Cochrane* Record at 28 (SSG Cochrane's Command Sergeant Major stated, "SSG Cochrane's duty performance during that time [in Hawaii] was excellent. SSG Cochrane's military character was exemplary. . . . SSG Cochrane explained what he did about stealing government property. I believe SSG Cochrane has good rehabilitative potential. I know he can still do great things for the Army."). Appellant also stole merchandise worth more money than SSG Cochrane did. *Compare* Record at 20-21 (stipulating that appellant stole goods valued at at least $30,000) *with Cochrane* Record at Charge Sheet (charging SSG Cochrane with theft of property worth $4,144.44). Finally, SSG Cochrane offered powerful mitigation witness testimony which appellant did not. *See, e.g., Cochrane* Record at 26 (SSG Cochrane's supervisor at the Casualty Mortuary Affairs Office noted his "excellent" duty performance and "positive" attitude, even in light of a pending court-martial). Based on this evidence in the record, I conclude that there is a rational basis for the disparity between the sentences of appellant and SSG Cochrane, per our holding in *Lacy*.

Finally, I personally share Judge Effron's view that articulation by the Court of Criminal Appeals of the basis for its conclusion that highly disparate sentences in closely related cases are rational will promote the interests of fairness in the military justice system. Nevertheless, as I said before, I am "aware of no requirement of law that appellate courts in general or a court of military review in particular must articulate its reasoning on every issue[.]" *United States v. Matias*, 25 M.J. 356, 363 (C.M.A. 1987). And I refuse to do so under the circumstances in this case today. Accordingly, I affirm.

EFFRON, JUDGE (dissenting):

As noted in the majority opinion, our decision in *United States v. Lacy*, 50 M.J. 286 (1999), provides that the issue of sentence appropriateness raises three questions of law: (1) whether the cases are closely related; (2) whether the sentences are highly disparate; and (3) whether there is a rational basis for the disparity.

There is no dispute that appellant's case was closely related to that of his coactor. The highly disparate nature of the sentences is reflected in the fact that the coactor received no discharge, no confinement, a reduction to E-3, and a fine of $4,200, while appellant's sentence included a punitive discharge and confinement for 15 months.

With respect to the question of whether there is a rational basis for the disparity, the responsibility for making such a determination under Article 66, UCMJ, 10 U.S.C. § 866, rests with the Court of Criminal Appeals, not with this Court. I agree that the Courts of Criminal Appeals are not required to articulate reasons for their sentence-appropriateness determinations in all cases. When there are closely related cases involving highly disparate sentences, however, it is particularly critical for the lower court to provide some explanation of its decision on the question of a rational basis for the disparity. This is not an unduly onerous task; there are relatively few cases involving coactors, and even fewer involving highly disparate sentences.

In such a case, a Court of Criminal Appeals possesses a unique expertise that places it in an ideal position to determine whether there exists a rational basis for the sentence disparity. This special expertise is derived from a number of factors, such as the regularity with which the Courts of Criminal Appeals examine cases for sentence appropriateness, relative to the small number of sentence-appropriateness cases decided by our Court; and the active-duty status of most judges on the Courts of Criminal Appeals, which typically affords them recent field experience, including exposure to a broad range of courts-martial and alternative dispositions not within the routine jurisdiction of our Court.

A Court of Criminal Appeals might properly determine that a sentence adjustment is not required where the sentence at issue is found to be objectively appropriate and where it finds that the disparity is largely the result of the coactor's relatively lenient sentence. We cannot assume that the Court of Criminal Appeals made such a determination in this case, particularly in view of factors that heighten concerns about the disparity between appellant's sentence and that of his coactor. For example, factors such as the status of the coactor as the more senior noncommissioned officer — and the fact that the coactor was the person who initiated the crime — underscore the need for a reasoned explanation of the already significant disparity between the sentences. In such as the present appeal, confidence in the fairness of the military justice system requires an articulation by the Court of Criminal Appeals of its reasons for affirming appellant's sentence. I respectfully dissent, and would remand this case to the Court of Criminal Appeals.

R. v. LOVE
Courts-Martial Appeal Court
[1997] EWCA 2903 (1997)

LORD JUSTICE SIMON BROWN:

On 6th June 1997 at a District Court-Martial held at Dover, the appellant pleaded guilty to two charges of sending indecent or obscene material through the post, contrary to section 11(2) of the Post Office Act 1952, for which he was sentenced to be dismissed from Her Majesty's Service and to be reduced to the ranks.

His petition to the defence council for review having failed he now appeals against sentence to this court by leave of the single judge. This, we would note, is the first such appeal against a court martial sentence. The right of appeal was only recently conferred by section 17 of the Armed Forces Act 1996 which amends section 8 of the Courts Martial Appeals Act 1968. In those circumstances we propose, later in this judgment, to make certain observations upon this new and unusual jurisdiction.

First, however, the facts which can be comparatively briefly stated. These offences occurred in early 1996 when the appellant, a divorced man of 35, was a staff sergeant in the military police on a close protection team tour of duty at the British Embassy in Beirut in Lebanon. He sent the obscene material through the post to a man named Copely, a civilian living in Southampton, whom he had contacted through an advertisement, whom he had never met and to whom he gave no indication that he was in the armed forces. Letters, photographs and cartoons of an explicit sexual nature were exchanged between them, using box number addresses.

The first charge related to a letter dated 7th February 1996 which referred to homosexual and heterosexual acts and involved a 14 year old girl, a 14 year old boy and a dog. The second charge related to an undated letter of similar content, together with photographs and cartoons which Copely had sent to the appellant for him to write comments upon and return. This he had done. The girls depicted in the drawings and photographs had the appearance of being under 12 years of age.

This material came to light purely by accident. Copely had been targeted by the police for quite other reasons, notably in relation to computer offences and the supply of drugs, offences for which he was later sent to prison. The letters were found in April 1996 when Copely's house was searched. The police notified the SIB and the appellant came to be interviewed. He immediately admitted the offences and was wholly frank and co-operative throughout.

The appellant has an exemplary record. He had served for 18 years in the force and was highly regarded by all his superiors. His commanding officer Colonel McLean concluded the appellant's 1995 annual review in these terms:

> Staff Sergeant Love is an impressively qualified senior NCO who has proved well above the standard required of his rank and service. He is a first class instructor whose quality of leadership, maturity and experience has enabled him to stand in most effectively for the Close Protection Wing warrant officer on several occasions. I fully endorse the grading and recommendation of the employing officer. Staff Sergeant Love is clearly ready for promotion to WO2 immediately and will make the most effective CSM. I recommend him accordingly.

He was assessed as "outstanding" by Miss Fost, the ambassador whom he was serving in Beirut and whom he had served on an earlier occasion also. She trusted him entirely and regarded him as a friend and confident. Major General Green, the officer commanding the Royal Close Protection Unit was called to give evidence in mitigation. The appellant was under his operational command. The appellant was, General Green explained, the team leader of a 10 man team of British and Lebanese bodyguards with responsibility for the general supervision of 42 other armed guards. He described the appellant as "professional, honest, loyal and a very good example to subordinates." He too assessed him as "outstanding."

At the time the appellant was in Beirut it was being bombed by the Israelis and although he had compassionate leave because of his mother's death, he cut short that leave and returned to Beirut, putting the army first. Major General Green indicated that he would be happy for the appellant to continue in the Royal Military Police despite the charges.

Colonel McLean, we should observe, despite his earlier glowing report on the appellant, had indicated to the court martial that he did not want the appellant back in Beirut. That however was solely because of the embarrassment of having in his unit a staff sergeant whom everyone knew to have been court-martialed.

After his solicitor had mitigated at length on his behalf, the appellant himself addressed the court-martial briefly to express his own deep embarrassment and his sincere apologies for the embarrassment he had caused his corps, the M.O.D, and the foreign office. He asked to be allowed to continue serving.

In giving the reasons for the sentence about to be imposed the Judge Advocate gave the appellant full credit for his immediate admissions to the investigating authorities and his early pleas of guilty, full credit for his exemplary character and having served his country well in a number of areas, and full credit for the strain of having had to wait for something over a year for his trial.

The court took a serious view of the references to sexual acts involving children and animals but fully acknowledged that the materials sent through the post were pure fantasies and not realities. They did not refer to what the appellant was actually intending to do or going to do.

Critically, however, the court in conclusion said this:

> However, you are a Royal Military policeman. You are a senior NCO in the corps. The Army are entitled to a very high standard from somebody in your position. You failed to meet those standards and the court view that failure very seriously indeed. So despite all of the mitigating factors that the court do acknowledge, the court have taken the view that your continued service with Her Majesty's Forces would be impossible. They see no option therefore in due course when the sentence is passed by the president for your dismissal from Her Majesty's Forces to take place with the automatic reduction to the ranks. I shall emphasise that the court do this with a heavy heart because they do recognise that you have performed very well in your career but it would be impossible for the court to take the view for someone having committed offences of this nature and this type to remain serving.

Before turning to the grounds of appeal it is, we think, appropriate at this stage to make certain observations about this new right of appeal and what should be the court's approach to it. In doing so we wish to acknowledge the great assistance we have had from the Ministry of Defence and in particular from a very recently produced publication (so recent indeed that it remains strictly in draft and subject to editorial alteration) which has been compiled and supplied to this Court and which provides a great deal of information about court-martial practices in general and their approach to sentencing in particular.

The first point to make about appeals from court-martial sentences is that the sentences which a court martial can impose are, in many instances, strikingly different from those available to Crown Courts. So far as relevant for present purposes, they are as follows, and we list them in order of gravity:

1. Imprisonment in a civilian prison;

2. Dismissal with disgrace from Her Majesty's Service;

3. Dismissal from Her Majesty's Service;

4. Detention in a corrective training centre for a period not exceeding 2 years;

5. Reduction in rank;

6. Fine;

7. Severe reprimand, or reprimand;

8. Such minor punishments as may from time to time be authorised by the defence council.

As the MOD document makes clear, if, as here, an NCO is dismissed, he is also automatically reduced to the ranks. A further effect of dismissal should also be noted at this stage, namely its effect upon pension rights. Take this appellant. He had served 18 years and, serving a 22 year engagement, as he was, had a further 4 years to serve until, at the age of 40, he would have been entitled to an immediate pension. Upon dismissal, however, this pension right becomes frozen until he is sixty when he will be entitled to 18/22 of the full rate. A calculation in crude terms of his loss of pension rights for the 20 year period between his 40th and 60th birthday reaches a figure in the region of £168,000.

The second point to note about this new appellate jurisdiction is that court-martial sentences are concerned at one and the same time to achieve two things. First, to punish service personnel for the criminality of their conduct; second, to deal with them also on a disciplinary basis. In that they are unique. Members of other professions and occupations who transgress the law of the land are dealt with quite separately, (a) by the civilian criminal courts, followed (b) if appropriate, by disciplinary proceedings before their own professional bodies. This would be so, for example, in the case of lawyers, doctors, nurses, architects and police officers.

These considerations seem to us of some importance when it comes to determining what should be this Court's approach to these appeals. Hitherto this Court has been concerned exclusively with an appellant's criminality and whether his sentence is wrong in principle or manifestly excessive. By contrast, statutory appeals from professional disciplinary bodies have gone traditionally to other courts, generally either the Divisional Court or the Privy Council, where a quite different approach is brought to bear upon them. As Lord Upjohn said in *McCoan and General Medical Council* [1964] 1 WLR 1107 at 1112 to 1113:

> The powers of the Board to correct the determination of the committee on the hearing of such an appeal are in terms unlimited, but in principle, where a professional body is entrusted with a discretion as to the imposition of the sentence of erasure their Lordships should be very slow to interfere with the exercise of that discretion. . . .

> Their Lordships are of the opinion that Lord Parker CJ may have gone too far In re: a Solicitor [[1960] 2 QB 212] when he said that the appellate court would never differ from sentence in cases of professional misconduct, but their Lordships agree with Lord Goddard CJ In re: a Solicitor [[1956] 1 WLR 1312] when he said that it would require a very strong case to interfere with sentence in such a case, because the Disciplinary Committee are the best possible people for weighing the seriousness of the professional misconduct.

> No general test can be laid down, for each case must depend entirely on its own particular circumstances. All that can be said is that if it is

to be set aside the sentence of erasure must appear to their Lordships to be wrong and unjustified.

That passage has frequently been cited with approval and followed, for example in *McEniff and General Dental Council* [1980] 1 WLR 328, and, recently, in the Civil decision of the court of appeal in *Bolton v. the Law Society* [1994] 2 All ER 486. It is well established.

In the present class of appeal therefore it seems to us that this Court is exercising a somewhat hybrid jurisdiction and that whilst we are free and clearly intended by Parliament to correct any injustice which we perceive in a court-martial sentence, we must nevertheless be mindful that those imposing and confirming such sentence are, generally speaking, better placed than we are when it comes to assessing the seriousness of offending in the context of service life, and deciding upon what particular penalty is required to maintain the discipline and efficiency of the armed forces.

These considerations are not surprisingly reflected in the MOD's publication. At paragraph 4 appears this:

> . . . when members of the Services are sentenced for civil offences they are treated, as far as possible, in a similar way to their civilian counterparts. However, whilst a court-martial has, like any criminal court, a duty to consider the general public interest, it must also act in the interests of the Service and for the maintenance of discipline within it. For this reason, there are certain areas where a court-martial may impose a heavier sentence for a civil offence.

Examples of such instances are then given, all of which are to our mind eminently sensible and reasonable. A rape is the more serious if the offender takes advantage of his superior rank or position. Drug offences have to be taken very seriously. As is pointed out:

> The Services are a very close-knit community, particularly when abroad, and such a community is naturally susceptible to the growth of drug abuse. . . . Drug abuse strikes at the heart of the Services' disciplined codes of conduct and is detrimental to the effectiveness of a fighting force in addition to being especially dangerous in the Service environment.

Dishonesty and theft from fellow service personnel clearly take on a more serious complexion:

> . . . in the Service environment people are accommodated and work very closely together, and because the opportunity to steal from one's comrades is always readily available there has to be a mutual feeling of trust. Theft from a colleague in the same barrack room or messdeck . . . erodes that trust and is a aggravating feature.

In all these cases, and certain other cases too, service personnel must expect to be punished more severely than their civilian counterparts and they should not be surprised to find themselves dismissed from the service.

As to dismissal it is convenient at this stage to note what is said about that in the MOD's helpful new publication:

Dismissal is a lesser judicial punishment in the scale than imprisonment but greater than detention and can have far-reaching consequences on the serviceman in civilian life. It is therefore well established that this sentence should not be imposed as a matter of expediency. It would be clearly wrong in principle to impose it purely because the offender is, for some extraneous reason, not fitted for the Service, or states through his counsel or defending officer that he does not wish to remain in the Service. The sole consideration is whether or not the offence is so serious, taking into account the accused's record and any mitigation available to him, as to warrant the imposition of this punishment. If the Service wishes to part company with the serviceman for some other reason there is an administrative procedure whereby personnel can be discharged.

There then follows a paragraph in which it is said:

At a court-martial the prosecution will inform the court whether or not the offender's Commanding Officer actually wishes to retain him in the unit.

It is then, however, pointed out that the CO's view, even if adverse, is not to be regarded as a recommendation for dismissal but merely may be of some use in a borderline case. It was of course pursuant to that practice that the court-martial in the present case was informed that Colonel McLean did not wish to retain the appellant; that, however, ought not to count against him.

With all these considerations in mind, let us now turn back to the circumstances of the present case and the arguments canvassed in support of the appeal. First and foremost amongst these is that the sentence imposed here was quite out of proportion to the criminality of the conduct in question. Dismissal is one of the most severe sentences in the range available and here it necessarily involved too a reduction to the ranks and a huge pension loss. This, frankly, was an offence of limited seriousness which, if dealt with by the civilian courts, would almost certainly have been disposed of by way of a modest fine in the Magistrates' Court. The only precedent of any help which we have been able to discover in the books, is *R v. Littleford* (1984) 6 Cr.App.R (S) 272 where this Court, in a case involving the exchanges by post of video tapes depicting children and adults in sex scenes, held that the appropriate sentences would have consisted not of custody but of financial penalties. Here, as stated, the exchanges in question were merely of personal fantasies, which, whilst no doubt showing some deficiency in character, corrupted no one and hurt no one. Given these facts and given in addition the appellant's full co-operation throughout, his early pleas of guilty, his efforts to avoid any discredit to the service by concealing his service identity from his correspondent, his long wait for trial and his glowing reports and testimonials as a soldier, the penalty imposed here was not merely manifestly excessive but needlessly severe even having full regard to the special interests of the armed services in maintaining high standards of conduct.

In our judgment these arguments are irresistible. Realistically there was nothing about this case which, because the appellant was a serving soldier, made it on that account the more serious. These offences, unlike drug offences or barrack room pilfering, or indeed sexual misconduct with or affecting other service personnel, in no way threatened the trust or discipline within the appellant's unit.

We have, each of us, reached the clear conclusion that the sentence of dismissal from Her Majesty's Service with the inevitable further consequences that that brings about cannot be justified here.

What then should the penalty have been? We have no doubt that this is a case where the appellant should have been treated as far as possible in a way similar to his civilian counterpart. That, as stated, would have involved a fine. Quite what level of fine would have been appropriate here it is for present purposes unnecessary to consider — perhaps something of the order of a month's wages — although we express no concluded view as to that.

The fact here is that this appellant has in the event been unpaid and unemployed since sentence was pronounced on 6th June, some 5 months ago. No doubt the result of our decision today will be to entitle him to retrospective payment of his lost earnings, but we think it right, in all the circumstances, to impose upon him a lesser fine than would otherwise have been appropriate. We would substitute for the sentence passed a fine of £100 on each count (i.e. £200 in total) to be paid within 30 days.

Should the appellant have been reprimanded too — severely or otherwise? These are punishments available only where, as here, the offender is a warrant officer or NCO. Paragraph 96 of the MOD's publication states with regard to these punishments:

> They are a mark of disapproval and may well adversely affect promotion prospects. They are frequently coupled with a financial penalty, but not with reduction in rank because this is a more severe punishment and so renders a reprimand unnecessary.

We express no view as to whether such further punishment should or should not have been added to an appropriate fine. Given the particular circumstances now arising, however, we do not think it necessary to impose it.

There is one other matter which we have not yet touched upon and mention now only by way of footnote. It is this. During the investigation of these offences it came to light that the appellant is a homosexual. As is well-known, the present policy of the MOD is that they will not permit homosexuals to serve with the armed forces. Generally speaking, once such orientation is established administrative discharge follows. That, we recognise, would have been likely to happen in this case. It has, however, nothing whatever to do with this appeal. As the Judge-Advocate himself observed just before the present sentence was passed:

> Finally, I should emphasise of course that you are not being punished in any way for any homosexual acts. That is utterly irrelevant to those proceedings and has formed no basis whatsoever or no part in the decision of the sentence that the court has imposed.

We mention the fact only because it would seem to us unrealistic not to recognise that, despite our judgment, the appellant's days in the army are numbered. Indeed, we have been told today that the appellant now proposes, despite the success of his appeal, to seek his own immediate administrative discharge in recognition of the virtual inevitably of such a result in any event. That administrative discharge, we cannot but note, itself involves the selfsame loss of pension rights as dismissal from the services.

That, however, is for present purposes essentially by the way. For the reasons given earlier, we would allow this appeal, quash the sentences imposed and substitute for them, as indicated, fines of £100 on each of the two counts, with 1 month to pay. To that extent the appeal is allowed.

CASE OF CORPORAL FENI
South African Court of Military Appeals
No. 28/99 (2000)

[A soldier pleaded guilty to common law fraud and was sentenced to be reduced to a lower rank. The court upheld the conviction but commented as follows on the sentence.]

BRIG GEN COETZEE . . . .

6. The applicant has a clean record of service.

7. Counsel, who represented the applicant, submitted very helpful heads of argument. He indicated that in nine (9) other similar cases, the respective Courts Martial only imposed fines. What is of importance is that he, amongst others, referred to the cases of Lt Col Magasela and Col Mineti in which cases fines of R500-00 and R800-00, respectively, were imposed. On account of these cases, he requested the Court to vary the sentence to one of a fine.

8. The prosecutor also submitted very helpful heads of argument in which he, by contrast, indicated that there were also 6 other similar cases in which a reduction of rank had been imposed.

9. This Court is aware of the principle that each and every case should be judged according to its own facts and circumstances. Thus, sentences for the same offence may vary. Every judicial officer has a discretion to impose a sentence within the defined principles of law. In *S v. Giannoulis* 1975(4) SA 867 (AD) the (then) Appellate Division decided that in general, sentence is a matter for the discretion of the trial court. Parity in sentencing should not be raised to a principle because trial courts have a flexible discretion.

10. A further well-established principle is that individualisation is the most important factor in sentencing an offender. A judicial officer should first and foremost look at the offender before him or her and should apply the principles of sentencing to the case under consideration. In this process sentences for the same offences even under more or less similar circumstances may vary.

11. It is also a well-established principle of our law that there should be some measure of parity among sentences imposed for the same offences committed under more or less similar circumstances. Unequal, inconsistent and uneven sentences for equal offenders infringes the general sense of justice. Uniformity and consistency in punishment leads to legal certainty and

confidence in the administration of military justice. It is part and parcel of the well-known principle that justice must not only be done, but it must be seen to be done. *See Du Toit, E., Straf in Suid-Afrika*, p 118e.v.

12. The point to resolve now is how should a judicial officer approach and apply the above-mentioned principles in practice? The Court is of the opinion that the following guidelines may be of assistance:

a. Each case must be dealt with on its own merits.

b. As far as possible, military courts should strive to maintain uniformity and consistency as regards sentence for similar offences and committed under more or less similar circumstances.

c. Uniformity should, however, not be elevated to a rule. It is just a helpful method to determine an appropriate sentence.

d. Disparity in the sentences imposed on offenders who committed the same offence(s) under similar circumstances will not necessarily warrant interference on review or appeal.

e. Where, however, there is a disturbing disparity among such sentences, and the circumstances under which the offences were committed are more or less the same, and there are no personal factors warranting such disparity, interference on review or appeal with the sentence may, depending on the circumstances, be warranted. The ground of interference would be that the sentence is disturbingly inappropriate. *See S v. Giannoulis, supra.*

f. In ameliorating the more severe sentence, the Court does not necessarily equate the sentences: it does what it considers appropriate in the circumstances. *See R v. Fallison* 1969 (1) SA 477 (R, AD).

13. *In casu,* the applicant committed the offence under very similar circumstances to those cases referred to by the defence. The prosecution admitted during argument before the Court, that in 3 of the other (similar) cases referred to by him, there were additional charges involved.

14. The Court is satisfied that there is disparity between the sentence imposed on the applicant and the sentences imposed by other Courts Martial for similar offences committed under more or less similar circumstances referred to by Counsel. A reduction to a lower rank has severe financial implications for a person. There is a vast difference between such a sentence and a mere fine. Such a disparity can only be maintained if it is warranted by the circumstances of the case in which the more severe sentence has been imposed. No such extraordinary circumstances exist and neither could the prosecution refer to same.

15. The Court is satisfied that a fine of R1000-00 is an appropriate sentence. The applicant is a non-commissioned officer and as already said, a first offender. A reduction to a lower rank may be regarded as an appropriate sentence for somebody who has already been convicted for such similar offence.

16. The sentence imposed should, thus, be set aside and substituted with the following:

A fine of R1000-00. In terms of section 130 of the Code he is placed under deduction of pay in the amount of R1000-00 being the amount of the fine.

NOTES AND QUESTIONS

1. Is it, in the end, possible to develop a rigorous standard for sentence review?

2. In *R. v. Drummond*, [1998] EWCA 3875, the Courts-Martial Appeal Court wrote:

> There are, it seems to us, five features in this case which, together, combine to persuade us that this Court should take an exceptional course in varying the sentence which has been hitherto imposed. They are these: first, the offences took place 2 years before the trial; secondly, although all those involved were serving officers, the context was civil rather than military; thirdly, the overwhelming evidence of conspicuous maturity developing since these events; fourthly, the fact that the appellant has already all but served his sentence, and fifthly, that his commanding officer and all those senior and other officers who know him personally want to keep him in the army.

Are these proper factors for appellate review of sentencing? Do they comport with *Love*?

3. In *Ranjit Thakur v. Union of India*, (1987) 4 S.C.C. 611, the Supreme Court of India observed that a sentence "should not be so disproportionate to the offence as to shock the conscience and amount in itself to conclusive evidence of bias. The doctrine of proportionality, as part of the concept of judicial review, would ensure that even an aspect which is, otherwise, within the exclusive province of the court-martial, if the decision of the court even as to sentence is an outrageous defiance of logic, then the sentence would not be immune from correction. Irrationality and perversity are recognised grounds of judicial review." How helpful are these concepts?

4. In some circumstances, the prosecution can appeal from adverse rulings at trial. *See* Article 62, UCMJ, 10 U.S.C. § 862. Should it have a right to appellate review of sentences on grounds of excessive leniency? If so, what should be the test? *Compare State v. Wong Fook Choon*, No. 5 of 1977 (Sing. Mil. App. 1977) (increasing "manifestly inadequate" sentence of detention from 90 days to 18 months; "comprehensive drug rehabilitation programme . . . can only be carried out with a long term of detention"), *with Chief Military Prosecutor v. Then Chee Keong*, No. 17 of 1992 (Sing. Mil. App. 1993) (dismissing government appeal of sentence to one day's detention for homosexual sexual misconduct in light of "strong mitigating circumstances").

III. DIRECT APPELLATE REVIEW

Draft Principles Governing the Administration of Justice through Military Tribunals
UN Commission on Human Rights, E/CN.4/2006/58 (2006)

Principle No. 17, Recourse proceedings in the ordinary courts

In all cases where military tribunals exist, their authority should be limited to ruling in [the] first instance. Consequently, recourse procedures, particularly appeals, should be brought before the civil courts. In all situations, disputes concerning legal issues should be settled by the highest civil court.

Conflicts of authority and jurisdiction between military tribunals and ordinary courts must be resolved by a higher judicial body, such as a supreme court or constitutional court, that forms part of the system of ordinary courts and is composed of independent, impartial and competent judges.

56. While the residual maintenance of first-degree military courts may be justified by their functional authority, there would seem to be no justification for the existence of a parallel hierarchy of military tribunals separate from ordinary law. Indeed, the requirements of proper administration of justice by military courts dictate that remedies, especially those involving challenges to legality, are heard in civil courts. In this way, at the appeal stage, or at the very least, the cassation stage, military tribunals would form "an integral part of the general judicial system." Such recourse procedures should be available to the accused and the victims; this presupposes that victims are allowed to participate in the proceedings, particularly during the trial stage.

CONSTITUTIONAL INTERPRETATION NO. 436
Republic of China Council of Grand Justices, 1997

It states in Article 8, Paragraph 1, of the Constitution that physical freedom shall be guaranteed to the people and that no person shall be tried or punished otherwise than by a court of law in accordance with the procedure prescribed by law. It also provides in Article 16 of the Constitution that the people shall have the right to institute legal proceedings. Active-duty soldiers are also "the people" and thus deserve the above-mentioned protection. In addition, it stipulates in Article 9 of the Constitution: "except for those who are in active military service, no person shall be subject to trial by a military tribunal." Given that active-duty soldiers have the special obligation of protecting the country, a military tribunal is established for crimes committed by said soldiers for the purpose of national security and military necessity. It shall not be interpreted such that military tribunals have exclusive jurisdiction over crimes committed by active-duty soldiers. There is no stipulation in the Constitution concerning military trial; nevertheless, such a system may be established under the law. The initiation and operation of the military trial, which is within the power of punishment of the nation, shall meet the minimum requirements of due process of law, which include an independent and just tribunal and procedure and compliance with constitutional principles as stated in Articles 77 and 80 of the Constitution. The laws governing the procedure of a military trial which limit the rights of active-duty soldiers shall be in compliance with the principle of proportionality (*Verhältnismäßigkeitsprinzip*) as stated in Article 23 of the Constitution. In light of the spirit of protecting physical freedom and the right of instituting legal proceedings and the provision of Article 77, a defendant receiving a sentence of imprisonment in a final and conclusive judgment by a military tribunal in peacetime shall be permitted to appeal directly to a normal court on the ground that the judgment received is in violation of the law. Articles 11, 133, Paragraphs 1 and 3, and 158 of the Military Justice Act and the rest of the Act which state that the defendant is not permitted to appeal to the normal court on the ground that the judgment received from the military tribunal is in violation of the law are unconstitutional and shall be invalidated two years after the announcement of this Interpretation, at the latest. The relevant authority shall, within the two-year period, revise relevant laws based on this principle, adjust the relevant appeal system, improve the separation of prosecution and trial in the military trial system and improve the criteria to appoint army officers to participate in military tribunals and the status protection of military judges to meet the principle of independent trial.

CLINTON v. GOLDSMITH
Supreme Court of the United States
526 U.S. 529 (1999)

JUSTICE SOUTER delivered the opinion of the Court.

The challenge here is to the use of the All Writs Act, 28 U.S.C. § 1651(a), by the Court of Appeals for the Armed Forces, to enjoin the President and various military officials from dropping respondent from the rolls of the Air Force. Because that court's process was neither "in aid of" its strictly circumscribed jurisdiction to review court-martial findings and sentences under 10 U.S.C. § 867 nor "necessary or appropriate" in light of a servicemember's alternative opportunities to seek relief, we hold that the Court of Appeals for the Armed Forces lacked jurisdiction to issue the injunction.

I

Respondent James Goldsmith, a major in the United States Air Force, was ordered by a superior officer to inform his sex partners that he was HIV-positive and to take measures to block any transfer of bodily fluids during sexual relations. Contrary to this order, on two occasions Goldsmith had unprotected intercourse, once with a fellow officer and once with a civilian, without informing either that he was carrying HIV.

As a consequence of his defiance, Goldsmith was convicted by general court-martial of willful disobedience of an order from a superior commissioned officer, aggravated assault with means likely to produce death or grievous bodily harm, and assault consummated by battery, in violation of Articles 90 and 128 of the Uniform Code of Military Justice (UCMJ), 10 U.S.C. §§ 890, 928(b)(1), (a). In 1994, he was sentenced to six years' confinement and forfeiture of

$2,500 of his salary each month for six years. The Air Force Court of Criminal Appeals affirmed his conviction and sentence in 1995, and when he sought no review of that decision in the United States Court of Appeals for the Armed Forces (CAAF), his conviction became final, *see* § 871(c)(1)(A).

In 1996, Congress expanded the President's authority by empowering him to drop from the rolls of the Armed Forces any officer who had both been sentenced by a court-martial to more than six months' confinement and served at least six months. *See* National Defense Authorization Act for Fiscal Year 1996, 110 Stat. 325, 10 U.S.C. § 1161(b)(2), 1167 (1994 ed., Supp. III). In reliance on this statutory authorization, the Air Force notified Goldsmith in 1996 that it was taking action to drop him from the rolls.

Goldsmith did not immediately contest the proposal to drop him, but rather petitioned the Air Force Court of Criminal Appeals for extraordinary relief under the All Writs Act, 28 U.S.C. § 1651(a), to redress the unrelated alleged interruption of his HIV medication during his incarceration. The Court of Criminal Appeals ruled that it lacked jurisdiction to act, and it was in Goldsmith's appeal from that determination that he took the first steps to raise the issue now before us, an entirely new claim that the Air Force's action to drop him from the rolls was unconstitutional. He did not challenge his underlying court-martial conviction (the appeal period for which had expired, *see* Rule 19(a)(1), CAAF Rules of Practice and Procedure). But he charged that the proposed action violated the *Ex Post Facto* Clause, U.S. Const., Art. I, § 9, cl. 3 (arguing that the statute authorizing it had been enacted after the date of his conviction) and the Double Jeopardy Clause, U.S. Const., Amdt. 5 (arguing that the action would inflict successive punishment based on the same conduct underlying his first conviction). 48 M.J. 84, 89-90 (CAAF 1998). The CAAF, on a division of 3 to 2, granted the petition for extraordinary relief and relied on the All Writs Act, 28 U.S.C. § 1651(a), in enjoining the President and various other Executive Branch officials from dropping respondent from the rolls of the Air Force.[33] . . .

II

When Congress exercised its power to govern and regulate the Armed Forces by establishing the CAAF, *see* U.S. Const. Art. I, § 8, cl. 14; 10 U.S.C. § 941; *see generally Weiss v. United States,* 510 U.S. 163, 166-169 (1994), it confined the court's jurisdiction to the review of specified sentences imposed by courts-martial: the CAAF has the power to act "only with respect to the findings and sentence as approved by the [court-martial's] convening authority and as affirmed or set aside as incorrect in law by the Court of Criminal Appeals." 10 U.S.C. § 867(c). *Cf. Parisi v. Davidson,* 405 U.S. 34, 44 (1972) (Court of Military Appeals lacked express authority over claim for discharge based on conscientious objector status). Despite these limitations, the CAAF

---

[33] [n.3] Because respondent had been released from confinement, the CAAF denied respondent's writ-appeal petition concerning his medical treatment claim as moot. *See* 48 M.J. 84, 87-88 (1998). As a result of the CAAF's order, respondent has not been dropped from the rolls, and has returned to active duty status. The Air Force initiated an administrative separation proceeding against respondent, *see* 10 U.S.C. § 1181, which has been deferred pending resolution of this case. *See* Brief for Petitioners 8, n. 2.

asserted jurisdiction and purported to justify reliance on the All Writs Act in this case on the view that "Congress intended [it] to have broad responsibility with respect to administration of military justice," 48 M.J., at 86-87,[34] a position that Goldsmith urges us to adopt. This we cannot do.

While the All Writs Act authorizes employment of extraordinary writs, it confines the authority to the issuance of process "in aid of" the issuing court's jurisdiction. 28 U.S.C. § 1651(a) ("[A]ll courts established by Act of Congress may issue all writs necessary or appropriate in aid of their respective jurisdictions and agreeable to the usages and principles of law"). Thus, although military appellate courts are among those empowered to issue extraordinary writs under the Act, *see Noyd v. Bond,* 395 U.S. 683, 695, n.7 (1969), the express terms of the Act confine the power of the CAAF to issuing process "in aid of" its existing statutory jurisdiction; the Act does not enlarge that jurisdiction, *see, e.g., Pennsylvania Bureau of Correction v. United States Marshals Service,* 474 U.S. 34, 41 (1985). *See also* 16 C. Wright, A. Miller, & E. Cooper, Federal Practice and Procedure § 3932, p. 470 (2d ed. 1996) ("The All Writs Act . . . is not an independent grant of appellate jurisdiction"); 19 J. Moore & G. Pratt, Moore's Federal Practice § 204.02[4] (3d ed. 1998) ("The All Writs Act cannot enlarge a court's jurisdiction").

We have already seen that the CAAF's independent statutory jurisdiction is narrowly circumscribed. To be more specific, the CAAF is accorded jurisdiction by statute (so far as it concerns us here) to "review the record in [specified] cases reviewed by" the service courts of criminal appeals, 10 U.S.C. § 867(a)(2), (3), which in turn have jurisdiction to "revie[w] court-martial cases," § 866(a). Since the Air Force's action to drop respondent from the rolls was an executive action, not a "findin[g]" or "sentence," § 867(c), that was (or could have been) imposed in a court-martial proceeding, the elimination of Goldsmith from the rolls appears straightforwardly to have been beyond the CAAF's jurisdiction to review and hence beyond the "aid" of the All Writs Act in reviewing it.

Goldsmith nonetheless claims that the CAAF has satisfied the "aid" requirement of the Act because it protected and effectuated the sentence meted out by the court-martial. Goldsmith emphasizes that the court-martial could have dismissed him from service, but instead chose to impose only confinement and fines. Hence, he says the CAAF merely preserved that sentence as the court-martial imposed it, by precluding additional punishment, which would incidentally violate the *Ex Post Facto* and Double Jeopardy Clauses. But this is beside the point, for two related reasons. First, Goldsmith's court-martial sentence has not been changed; another military agency has simply taken independent action. It would presumably be an entirely different matter if a military authority attempted to alter a judgment by revising a court-martial finding and sentence to increase the punishment, contrary to the specific provisions of the UCMJ, and it certainly would be a different matter when such a judgment had been affirmed by an appellate court. In such a case, as the

---

[34] [n.6] One judge was even more emphatic: "We should use our broad jurisdiction under the [UCMJ] to correct injustices like this and we need not wait for another court to perhaps act. . . . Our Court has the responsibility of protecting the rights of all servicemembers in court-martial matters." 48 M.J., at 91 (Sullivan, J., concurring).

Government concedes, *see* Tr. of Oral Arg. 15, 19, 52, the All Writs power would allow the appellate court to compel adherence to its own judgment. *See, e.g., United States v. United States Dist. Court for Southern Dist. of N.Y.,* 334 U.S. 258, 263-264 (1948). Second, the CAAF is not given authority, by the All Writs Act or otherwise, to oversee all matters arguably related to military justice, or to act as a plenary administrator even of criminal judgments it has affirmed. Simply stated, there is no source of continuing jurisdiction for the CAAF over all actions administering sentences that the CAAF at one time had the power to review. Thus the CAAF spoke too expansively when it held itself to be "empowered by the All Writs Act to grant extraordinary relief in a case in which the court-martial rendered a sentence that constituted an adequate basis for direct review in [the CAAF] after review in the intermediate court," 48 M.J., at 87.[35]

III

Even if the CAAF had some seriously arguable basis for jurisdiction in these circumstances, resort to the All Writs Act would still be out of bounds, being unjustifiable either as "necessary" or as "appropriate" in light of alternative remedies available to a servicemember demanding to be kept on the rolls.[36] The All Writs Act invests a court with a power essentially equitable and, as such, not generally available to provide alternatives to other, adequate remedies at law. *See, e.g., Carlisle v. United States,* 517 U.S. 416, 429 (1996) ("'The All Writs Act is a residual source of authority to issue writs that are not otherwise covered by statute'") (quoting *Pennsylvania Bureau of Correction,* 474 U.S., at 43). *See also* 19 Moore's Federal Practice § 201.40 ("[A] writ may not be used . . . when another method of review will suffice"). This limitation operates here, since other administrative bodies in the military, and the federal courts, have authority to provide administrative or judicial review of the action challenged by respondent.

In response to the notice Goldsmith received that action was being considered to drop him from the rolls, he presented his claim to the Secretary of the Air Force. *See* Tr. of Oral Arg. 4-5. If the Secretary takes final action to drop him from the rolls (as he has not yet done), Goldsmith will (as the Government concedes) be entitled to present his claim to the Air Force Board of Correction for Military Records (BCMR). This is a civilian body within the military service, with broad-ranging authority to review a servicemember's "discharge or

---

35 [n.10] The court, moreover, was simply wrong when it treated itself as a court of original jurisdiction . . . .

36 [n.11] These remedies are in addition to the review as of right by the military department's Court of Criminal Appeals of any court-martial sentence that includes punitive dismissal or discharge. *See* 10 U.S.C. § 866(b)(1); § 867(a) (decisions of the Court of Criminal Appeals subject to discretionary review by the CAAF). And of course, once a criminal conviction has been finally reviewed within the military system, and a servicemember in custody has exhausted other avenues provided under the UCMJ to seek relief from his conviction, *see Noyd v. Bond,* 395 U.S. 683, 693-699 (1969), he is entitled to bring a habeas corpus petition, *see* 28 U.S.C. § 2241(c), claiming that his conviction is affected by a fundamental defect that requires that it be set aside. *See, e.g., Burns v. Wilson,* 346 U.S. 137, 142 (1953) (opinion of Vinson, C.J.). *See also Calley v. Callaway,* 519 F.2d 184, 199 (5th Cir. 1975); *Gorko v. Commanding Officer, Second Air Force,* 314 F.2d 858, 859 (10th Cir. 1963). In this case, however, respondent chose not to challenge his underlying conviction. . . .

dismissal (other than a discharge or dismissal by sentence of a general court-martial)," 10 U.S.C. § 1553(a), or "to correct an error or remove an injustice" in a military record, § 1552(a)(1).[37]

Respondent may also have recourse to the federal trial courts. We have previously held, for example, that "[BCMR] decisions are subject to judicial review [by federal courts] and can be set aside if they are arbitrary, capricious, or not based on substantial evidence." *Chappell v. Wallace,* 462 U.S. 296, 303 (1983). A servicemember claiming something other than monetary relief may challenge a BCMR's decision to sustain a decision to drop him from the rolls (or otherwise dismissing him) as final agency action under the Administrative Procedure Act (APA), 5 U.S.C. § 551 *et seq.; see* §§ 704, 706. For examples of such challenges entertained in the district courts or courts of appeals, see *Roelofs v. Secretary of Air Force,* 628 F.2d 594, 599-601 (D.C. Cir. 1980) (proceeding in District Court under APA raising due process challenge to administrative discharge based on conviction of civilian offense); *Walker v. Shannon,* 848 F. Supp. 250, 251, 254-255 (D.C. 1994) (suit under APA for review of Army BCMR decision upholding involuntary separation). In the instances in which a claim for monetary relief may be framed, a servicemember may enter the Court of Federal Claims with a challenge to dropping from the rolls (or other discharge) under the Tucker Act, 28 U.S.C. § 1491.[38] *See, e.g., Doe v. United States,* 132 F.3d 1430, 1433-1434 (Fed. Cir. 1997) (suit for backpay and correction of military records following administrative discharge); *Mitchell v. United States,* 930 F.2d 893, 896-897 (Fed. Cir. 1991) (suit for backpay, reinstatement, and correction of records). Or he may enter a district court under the "Little Tucker Act," 28 U.S.C. § 1346(a)(2).[39] *See, e.g., Thomas v. Cheney,* 925 F.2d 1407, 1411, 1416 (Fed. Cir. 1991) (reviewing challenge to action to drop plaintiff from the rolls); *Sibley v. Ball,* 924 F.2d 25, 29 (1st Cir. 1991)

---

[37] [n.12] Respondent argues nonetheless that seeking BCMR review in his case would have been futile (especially in light of his life-threatening illness) since BCMRs lack authority to declare statutes unconstitutional, cannot consider records of courts-martial and related administrative records (with two inapplicable exceptions), and are generally "'unresponsive, bureaucratic extensions of the uniformed services,'" Brief for Respondent 16 (quoting H.R. Conf. Rep. No. 104-450, p. 798 (1996)). In light of the fact that respondent chose to circumvent BCMR review, we need not address whether the Air Force BCMR has the power to correct a record that is erroneous as a result of a constitutional violation. *Cf. Guerra v. Scruggs,* 942 F.2d 270, 273 (4th Cir. 1991) ("The [Army BCMR] has authority to consider claims of constitutional, statutory and regulatory violations"); *Bois v. Marsh,* 801 F.2d 462, 467 (D.C. Cir. 1986) ("[Appellant's] claims based on [the] Constitution, executive orders and Army regulations 'could readily have been made within the framework of this intramilitary procedure'" (quoting *Chappell v. Wallace,* 462 U.S. 296, 303 (1983))). And while it is true that unless specifically authorized a BCMR may not correct a court-martial record, *see* 10 U.S.C. § 1552(f), it may still consider the record, especially where, as here, the court-martial record is relevant in determining the validity of the subsequent dropping from the rolls. Finally, the alleged unresponsive nature of the BCMRs, if true, would in no way alter the fact that BCMRs are legislatively authorized to provide the relief sought by respondent. In any event, it is clear as noted in the text that follows that respondent's constitutional objections could have been addressed by the federal courts.

[38] [n.13] Under the Tucker Act, the Court of Federal Claims has exclusive jurisdiction over non-tort claims against the Government for greater than $10,000. *See* 28 U.S.C. § 1491. Determinations of the Court of Federal Claims may be appealed to the Federal Circuit.

[39] [n.14] The "Little Tucker Act," 28 U.S.C. § 1346(a)(2), confers jurisdiction on district courts for claims of $10,000 or less. Appeals are taken to the Federal Circuit.

(transferring to Federal Circuit case for backpay because within purview of "Little Tucker Act").

In sum, executive action to drop respondent from the rolls falls outside of the CAAF's express statutory jurisdiction, and alternative statutory avenues of relief are available. The CAAF's injunction against dropping respondent from the rolls of the Air Force was neither "in aid of [its] jurisdictio[n]" nor "necessary or appropriate." Accordingly, we reverse the court's judgment. . . .

Eugene R. Fidell, *Guide to the Rules of Practice and Procedure for the United States Court of Appeals for the Armed Forces (12th ed. 2006)*

In the case of the Court of Appeals for the Armed Forces, however, the resolution of procedural issues can be an unexpectedly useful prism through which to examine the pertinent institutional relationships. Those relationships are of special interest because of the Court's unique responsibilities not merely as a dispenser of appellate justice but also as an embodiment of civilian control of the military. If there are themes to be discerned from a study of the Court's rules and manner of conducting its business, these can be distilled into the following broad propositions:

First, questions about the availability of review were long resolved in favor of finding, exercising and preserving the Court's jurisdiction, if fairly arguable. This principle is apparent in its expansive approach to its power under the All Writs Act, 28 U.S.C. § 1651(a) (2000), as well as in a variety of other jurisdictional and procedural rulings the overall effect of which has been the creation of an elaborate network of avenues, not all of equally firm statutory pedigree, by which its jurisdiction may be invoked. Other federal courts labor under a presumption against jurisdiction; subject matter jurisdiction must be affirmatively shown. *E.g., Turner v. Bank of North America*, 4 U.S. (4 Dall.) 8, 10 (1799); *C.F.T.C. v. Nahas*, 738 F.2d 487, 492 & n.9 (D.C. Cir. 1984). Animated by the goal of maximizing civilian review, the Court of Appeals for the Armed Forces has at times seemed to indulge nearly the opposite presumption. This first principle is also reflected in the steps it has taken to ensure that access to it is not thwarted by actions of military commanders and subordinate tribunals that reduce sentences below the statutory jurisdictional threshold and in its hostility to pretrial agreements that preclude appellate review. While somewhat arcane, the Court's claim of authority to act where a service Court of Criminal Appeals has set aside a finding of guilt on the ground of factual insufficiency, *United States v. Leak*, 61 M.J. 234 (2005) (4-1 decision), may also be a manifestation of this first principle.

Second, doubts as to whether an accused desires to invoke the Court's jurisdiction will be resolved in the accused's favor. This policy is manifest in the Court's unwillingness to treat time limits as jurisdictional or to reject petitions for grant of review for errors of form or even for noncompliance with what one would have thought was the congressional demand that the petitioner identify errors showing good cause for a grant of review under Article 67(a)(3). The foundation for this policy is, again, the view that unlike appellate review of other federal criminal convictions, review of courts-martial by the Court of Appeals for the Armed Forces vindicates the distinct constitutional objective of providing civilian oversight of the military. This may explain procedural rulings such as those which, until the tide shifted in *United States v. Rorie*, 58 M.J. 399 (2003) (3-2 decision), required the abatement of proceedings and the dismissal of charges when, by dying before final disposition of a case or expiration of the time for seeking review, an accused had not had the benefit of review by the Court.

Third, the Court will, subject to statutory limits, err on the side of generosity in its efforts to achieve substantial justice and protect the accused from potential lapses on the part of military or civilian defense counsel even where pursuit of these goals has the effect of setting the Court apart from the approach of other appellate courts. This theme is apparent in a reluctance to invoke the doctrine of waiver and in the proposition that the Court's power of review will not be confined to the issues framed by the parties. The reluctance to invoke the doctrine of waiver has been a continuing source of friction with the service Courts of Criminal Appeals. More than any other aspect of its procedural tradition, the practice of specifying issues not asserted by either party, and under circumstances that cannot fairly be considered an exercise of the power to correct plain error, sets it apart from other federal courts of appeals. The specification of issues not assigned by an appellant or certified by a Judge Advocate General subordinates the conventional doctrine of waiver to the interest in treating like cases in like fashion by affording "trailer" case litigants the benefit of rulings in lead cases, even if they have not raised the issue in question.

Fourth, the Court encourages the personal involvement of the accused in the pursuit of appellate remedies, in an effort to overcome the practical difficulties arising from its worldwide territorial jurisdiction and the fact that appellate defense counsel are unlikely ever to meet their clients. Appellate defense counsel consult — it is to be hoped — by mail and telephone with their clients, but face-to-face meetings are rare. The Court's desire to encourage the personal involvement of the accused is illustrated by its insistence that counsel at least identify issues the accused believes may be meritorious and not withdraw untimely petitions for review without the client's consent. Similarly, in the limited category of cases with respect to which the Court exercised its power to establish a procedure for constructive service of decisions of the former Courts of Military Review (now the Courts of Criminal Appeals), it made it clear that constructive notice was to be employed only as a last resort, and even then it required three separate methods for achieving constructive notice.

Fifth, the Court makes a special effort to involve the private bar and other interests outside the military community in order to temper the tendency to insularity that is inherent in the institutional setting in which the Court performs its functions. This is apparent in its reliance on a Rules Advisory Committee that includes civilian and military members, its use of a civilian Court Committee for longer-range institutional assessments, its hospitable attitude toward *amici curiae* and occasional television coverage of hearings, its decision to place audio recordings of oral arguments on its website, and its willingness to conduct hearings at civilian law schools and courthouses away from Washington as part of a public awareness project known as Project Outreach.

Notice of Proposed Rule Change
United States Court of Military Appeals
59 FED. REG. 25622 (May 17, 1994)

This notice announces the following proposed changes (underlined) to Rule 6 and to Rule 21(d) and (e) of the Rules of Practice and Procedure, United States Court of Military Appeals for public notice and comment:

Rule 21. Supplement to Petition for Grant of Review . . .

(d) If no specific errors are assigned in the supplement to the petition, the Clerk will enter an order dismissing the case without awaiting an answer, and the Court will not call for an answer or examine the record. In all other cases, the Court may, in its discretion, examine the record for the purpose of determining whether there is plain error not assigned by the appellant. . . .

Majority Report on Proposed Rule 21(d)

This is to advise the Court that, by a vote of six to five, the Rules Advisory Committee of this Court recommends that Rule 21(d) of the Rules of this Court be revised to read as follows:

> If no specific errors are assigned in the supplement to the petition, the Clerk will enter an order dismissing the case without awaiting an answer, and the Court will not call for an answer or examine the record. In all other cases, the Court may, in its discretion, examine the record for the purpose of determining whether there is plain error not assigned by the appellant.

In addition, Rule 21(e) should be deleted and Rule 21(f) should be renumbered as Rule 21(e).

The purpose of this recommended change is to end the Court's current practice of docketing petition supplements that allege no issues warranting review and then conducting an examination of the record in these cases to determine whether any basis may exist in the record meriting further consideration by the Court. A number of factors support our recommendation.

First, and most fundamentally, the Court's current practice of reviewing, *sua sponte*, cases coming to the Court on petition for review in which no error is alleged by the accused is simply incompatible with the Court's statutory charter. Article 67(a)(3) of the Uniform Code of Military Justice, UCMJ, 10 U.S.C. § 867(a)(3), directs that this Court will review the record "in all cases reviewed by a Court of Military Review * * * upon petition of the accused and on good cause shown * * *." In drafting Article 67 of the Code, Congress demonstrated that, when it wanted this Court to exercise its appellate jurisdiction without requiring particularized claims of error, Congress knew how to say so expressly. *See* Art. 67(a)(1), UCMJ, 10 U.S.C. § 867(a)(1) (granting the

Court jurisdiction to review the record in all cases in which the sentence, as affirmed by a Court of Military Review, extends to death); former Art. 67(a)(3), UCMJ, 10 U.S.C. § 867(a)(3) (Court of Military Appeals shall review the record in all cases involving flag and general officers). The clear implication of the fact that, by contrast with these provisions, Congress included the requirement of a showing of "good cause" in Article 67(a)(3) is that Congress did not intend for this Court *sua sponte* to review the record in cases involving petitions by servicemembers from judgments of the courts of military review.

It has been argued by the members of the Rules Advisory Committee in the minority that this Court's practice of conducting *sua sponte* review of "no issue" petitions is now so well established that Congress has come to expect that this Court will perform that function. The majority finds mistaken the view that Congress can legislate by acquiescence. If Congress intended for this Court to adhere to such a practice, Congress would have expressed that intent in positive law on one of the numerous occasions on which it amended the Code within the last few decades. Absent such a clear expression of legislative intent, this Court does not believe that it lacks the power to revise its internal procedures in order to conform them to its clear statutory mandate.

Second, the Court's practice in conducting *sua sponte* reviews of "no issue" petitions is at odds with the practice of every other appellate court in the federal judicial system, all of which require litigants to present with particularity alleged claims of error. *See, e.g.*, S. Ct. R. 21.1(a) (the petition for writ of certiorari shall contain "[t]he questions presented for review, expressed in the terms and circumstances of the case but without unnecessary detail"); Fed. R. App. P. 28(a)(3); First Cir. R. 28 (incorporating Fed. R. App. P. 28); Second Cir. R. 28 (same); Third Cir. R. 21(d); Fifth Cir. R. 28.3. We are informed by the Office of the Clerk of the Supreme Court that it will not even docket petitions for writs of certiorari that do not present any issues for review. Persistence in this Court's past practice isolates this Court from the mainstream of federal appellate practice and creates the perception that the Court is not truly performing a comparable judicial function but, rather, serves as an inspector general for the military justice system. As Justice (then Judge) Scalia observed in *Carducci* versus *Regan*, 714 F.2d 171, 177 (D.C. Cir. 1983), "[t]he premise of our adversarial system is that appellate courts do not sit as self-directed boards of legal inquiry and research, but essentially as arbiters of legal questions presented and argued by the parties before them."

Those who disagree with our views maintain that, in the context of the armed forces, a different practice from that of the federal judicial system governing civilians is warranted because review by a court composed of civilians ensures and creates the perception that members of the armed forces are being treated fairly by the military justice system. As we explain later, however, other safeguards — including the possibility of Supreme Court review — are more than sufficient to minimize the likelihood that a member of the armed forces will be treated in a manner that is incompatible with accepted standards of justice and also to eliminate the perception that the military justice system is less fair than its civilian counterparts to those who stand accused of crime.

Third, ending the practice of entertaining "no issue" petitions will have the salutary effect of eliminating any risk that defense counsel will rely on this Court to identify legal or factual issues that could be resolved in the service-member's favor, instead of fully canvassing the record to make that determination. The burden of reviewing the record to ensure that a servicemember has received a fair trial properly rests with defense counsel, not with this Court. The proposed rule change reinforces that well-settled principle, while also enabling this Court to perform its role as the arbiter of the legal matters that have been properly brought before the Court for resolution.

Fourth, eliminating the practice of entertaining "no issue" petitions will substantially reduce the workload of this Court's legal staff. We are informed by the Director of this Court's central legal staff, that prior to the recent (and near universal) asserting of constitutional challenges to the selection and assignment of judges in the military justice system, "no issue" cases comprised between 80 and 85 percent of all cases filed with this Court. In response to a query by members of this Committee, the Director estimated that elimination of the practice of reviewing "no issue" cases would reduce the staff's workload by as much as 80 percent, although it is not clear precisely what the net reduction would be. The resulting savings would permit the limited resources of the central legal staff to be directed to cases in which the issues have been identified by the parties through the adversarial process. This will promote the issuance of timely, well-reasoned decisions by this Court.

Fifth, the reasons that appear to have prompted the adoption of the practice of conducting *sua sponte* reviews of "no issue" cases no longer exist. The Director of the Court's central legal staff informed us that the practice began when, shortly after this Court was established, one of the Judge Advocates General stated that he intended to control the cases sent to this Court for its review. In addition, the practice was designed as a check on military appellate counsel, who were frequently perceived to be inexperienced, and as a mechanism to ensure that servicemembers received the benefit of review by a civilian court.

It is highly unlikely that today any of the Judge Advocates General would attempt to restrict the questions presented to this Court by defense appellate counsel, or that the Judge Advocates General could effectively accomplish that end even if they desired to do so. Moreover, the existence of separate defense corps in each branch of the armed forces, as well as independent trial and appellate judiciaries, who are insulated by statute from improper command influence, substantially reduces the risk of any perception that the due process rights of servicemembers can only effectively be protected by a civilian review of courts-martial. Finally, the experience of military appellate counsel, who are all specialists in criminal appeals, is, at least, comparable to that of public defenders in the federal or state systems. And, by contrast to the typical situation in public defender's offices, military appellate counsel are closely supervised in their representational decisions by field grade officers of the

Judge Advocate General's Corps who are invariably highly experienced criminal lawyers. . . .

Minority Report on Proposed Rule 21(d)

Six members of the Court's Rules Advisory Committee have voted to recommend a change to Rule 21(d) of the Court's Rules which would direct the Clerk of the Court to dismiss, without answer or consideration by the judges, any petition for grant of review submitted by an accused which had no specific errors assigned in the supplement filed by counsel. The stated purpose of this recommended change is to end the Court's practice of docketing petition supplements that allege no issues warranting review and then conducting an examination of the record in such cases to determine whether any basis may exist in the record meriting further consideration by the Court. . . .

By way of background, we are today seeing the military justice system at the highest state of its development in its long history. We know it to be a fair system, seemingly in the hands of carefully-selected, well-trained lawyers and judges in adequate numbers in all services and courts, and we believe administration of the system has reached its highest level of competence ever.

Nevertheless, the military justice system is always in danger, both from without and within. From the outside it traditionally appears to be a system of justice that is subject to the control of prosecutorial decisions and outcomes by the command structure of the service involved. Accordingly, no matter what the conditions in today's all-volunteer, relatively peacetime forces, the military justice system must be prepared to meet the suspicions of the families of far greater numbers of servicemembers, perhaps serving involuntarily, and of the Congress, which holds the fate of the UCMJ in its hands.

From the inside, the military justice system always faces a less visible challenge; namely, the impact of budgetary and manpower exigencies on the quality of representation and adjudication. Judge Advocate Generals must compete with others for personnel spaces and money. They don't always win. In short, there is command control, albeit indirect and unintended, over the number of lawyers available (outside factors affect the quality of recruits) and over the funds for educating lawyers and judges and for their continuing training. Even within the sphere of the Judge Advocate Generals, choices must be made as to the assets and efforts to be devoted to various branches of the law, of which military justice is but one.

Those are the reasons why military justice always has had some features we call paternalism. Those are the reasons why we assert that, notwithstanding the triumph of legal professionalism over paternalism reflected in Code and Manual changes and judicial decisions in the last 20 years, some vestiges of paternalism must remain. We regard Rule 21(d) as one of them so long as it does not cause delays that adversely affect justice in other cases.

In addition to those reasons set forth above, the five factors cited by the majority as supporting the recommended rule change will be addressed below.

First Factor. The majority sees the Court's forty-year practice of examining the record in every petitioned case to determine whether good cause exists for further review to be incompatible with Article 67(a)(3), UCMJ. We disagree. Article 67(a)(3) states that: "The Court of Military Appeals shall review the record in * * * all cases reviewed by a Court of Military Review in which, upon petition of the accused and on good cause shown, the Court of Military Appeals has granted a review."

In viewing the Court's practice as contrary to the statute, the majority undoubtedly interprets the phrase "on good cause shown" to mean that good cause must be shown by the accused before the Court may grant review. That interpretation, in our view, is much too narrow. The Court from its inception appears to have seen "good cause shown" as meaning good cause shown by the record. We believe that interpretation to be more reasonable and more in accord with the Congressional grant of discretionary review to this first-time civilian court, created to oversee the military's court-martial system and to protect the rights of the military accused.

In any event, Congress, by its failure to indicate otherwise for over forty years of active oversight of military justice, has accepted the Court's interpretation of the statute as correct. Rather than legislation by acquiescence, as the majority asserts, the inaction of Congress on this matter is simply an affirmation by that body that the law is being applied properly. Accordingly, we believe a change of this magnitude which departs from long-standing interpretation and application of the law, while arguably within the Court's authority to effect as simply a procedural rule change, should more appropriately come from Congress.

With respect to statutory requirements, the majority cites the contrast between the originally drafted mandatory review provisions of Article 67 (death penalty, flag and general officers) and Article 67(a)(3), with its "on good cause shown" phrase, as implying that Congress did not intend the Court to review a case *sua sponte*. The majority mischaracterizes the Court's process as *sua sponte* review. There are only three provisions under Article 67 pertaining to review of a record by the Court, two that make review mandatory — death penalty cases and those cases ordered sent to the Court by the Judge Advocate General — and one that allows discretionary review, upon petition by the accused.

The Court does not have the power to go beyond these three Congressional grants and order a case reviewed on its own initiative. To do so would be truly *sua sponte* review, which is not the situation before us. For that reason we believe it incorrect to term the Court's grant of a petition for review as *sua sponte* review. In any event, the contrast between the provisions calling for mandatory review and the one granting discretionary review, upon petition by the accused, does not reflect an intent by Congress to limit the Court's discretionary review authority to only those cases in which the accused has demonstrated good cause. If an accused petitions for review and the Court finds good cause for such review, the statute is satisfied.

Second Factor. The majority says the Court's procedure is at odds with the practice of every other appellate court in the federal judicial system. If so, there is ample reason for this difference. The military is a closed society with rigorous disciplinary demands and severe limitations on individual rights and freedoms that call for special protections. Furthermore, when needed, individuals have been conscripted to serve in this society, calling for even more protective oversight. To some extent, the majority acknowledges these concerns, but points to other safeguards, including Supreme Court review, as minimizing the likelihood that a member of the armed forces will be treated unfairly or contrary to accepted standards of justice.

In making this argument, the majority overlooks the fact that Congress has authorized the Supreme Court to review only those cases in which the Court of Military Appeals has granted an accused's petition for review. As a result, the proposed rule change calling for automatic dismissal by the Clerk of an accused's petition for review forecloses any possible opportunity for subsequent review by the Supreme Court. The proposed rule thereby denies the accused the very protection cited by the majority in support of the rule change.

Third Factor. The majority focuses on the salutary effect the new rule will have on the professional standards for defense counsel, requiring, as it will, that counsel meet their responsibility to review the record fully for errors. We agree with the premise that Court actions calling for counsel to meet professional standards are salutary. However, we believe there are other means available to the Court for achieving this goal that are just as effective, or more so, without penalizing the accused, as the proposed rule will do. In addition, we view the proposed rule as drafted to create a substantial question as to whether the Clerk is required to dismiss a case in which the only matter presented in the supplement was a *United States v. Grostefon*, 12 M.J. 431 (C.M.A. 1982), assertion by the accused.

Fourth Factor. The majority says that the new rule will result in savings of central legal staff resources from a workload reduction of as much as 80 percent. Suffice it to say that we did not draw the same conclusion from what was said by the Director of the Central Legal Staff when he appeared before the committee. Our recollection is that he saw a minimal reduction in work from the rule change of not more than 10 percent. If so, there appears to be little need for such a rule from a work-savings standpoint.

Fifth Factor. The last point made by the majority is that the reasons for the current practice, while possibly valid forty years ago, are no longer a matter of concern. In answer, we must say that the potential for abuse is still inherent in the system, and that such potential requires constant vigilance. Over the years, this fact has been demonstrated time and time again. The problem of overreaching and undue influence by command authority will always be a possibility that necessitates an unimpeded oversight by the Court of Military Appeals. The procedure that has been in place for over 40 years appears to be working well in that regard and we see no need for a change.

We conclude by urging the Court to reject the proposed change to Rule 21(d).

NOTES AND QUESTIONS

1. The themes identified in the *Rules Guide* seem to suggest that the Court of Appeals believes in either its own exceptionalism or the broader exceptionalism of military justice in general. Is such a belief justified?

2. Without explanation, the Court of Appeals declined to make the change the Rules Advisory Committee's one-vote majority recommended. What would you have done had you been on the Court, and why?

3. Historically, there was no formal appellate review of summary discipline. In 2000, the United Kingdom created a Summary Appeal Court with jurisdiction over summary disposal of charges. For a summary of the legislation and an appraisal of the new court's early work, see Peter Rowe, *A New Court to Protect Human Rights in the Armed Forces of the UK: The Summary Appeal Court*, 8 J. CONFLICT & SECURITY L. 201 (2003). A tri-service Summary Appeal Court was established by the Armed Forces Act 2006, c.52, §§ 140-51.

IV. COLLATERAL REVIEW

UNITED STATES EX REL. NEW v. RUMSFELD
United States Court of Appeals for the District of Columbia Circuit
448 F.3d 403 (D.C. Cir. 2006)

WILLIAMS, SENIOR CIRCUIT JUDGE.

Michael G. New, formerly a medical specialist in the United States Army, was convicted by a court-martial of violating a lawful order to add United Nations insignia — a shoulder patch and a field cap — to his basic uniform. The Army Court of Criminal Appeals ("Court of Criminal Appeals") and the Court of Appeals for the Armed Forces ("Court of Appeals") affirmed. New's collateral attack charges several errors in the military courts' analysis of the lawfulness of the uniform order. Because New fails to identify fundamental defects in the military courts' resolution of his claims, we affirm the district court's denial of relief.

Shortly after he learned during the summer of 1995 that his unit would be deployed to the Republic of Macedonia as part of the United Nations Preventive Deployment Force, New voiced concerns about the lawfulness of the Army's participation in the mission. In particular, he was troubled that wearing U.N. insignia as part of his uniform would manifest an involuntary or fictional shift in his allegiance from the government of the United States to the United Nations. Although his superiors discussed these concerns with him, they failed to alleviate them.

Eventually New's battalion commander issued — and his company commander repeated — an order to begin wearing a special U.N. mission uniform at a battalion formation on October 10, 1995. The uniform consisted of the ordinary United States Army battle dress uniform plus a blue U.N. patch sewn on one shoulder and a blue U.N. cap. New reported for the formation on the scheduled date wearing a uniform that lacked these features, and his superiors immediately removed him from the formation. Although his battalion commander offered him a second chance to comply with the uniform order, New declined.

New was court-martialed and charged with violating Article 92(2) of the Uniform Code of Military Justice (codified at 10 U.S.C. § 892(2)), which provides that any person who, "having knowledge of any . . . lawful order issued by a member of the armed forces, which it is his duty to obey, fails to obey the order . . . shall be punished as a court-martial may direct." New's defense focused on the lawfulness of the order — specifically its consistency with Army Regulation 670-1 (1992) ("AR 670-1"), which permits commanders to require uniform modifications "to be worn within [a] maneuver area," par. 2-6d, or "when safety considerations make it appropriate," par. 1-18, and with Article I, Section 9 of the Constitution, which prohibits any person's acceptance of, inter alia, any emolument from a foreign state without congressional consent. New also argued that the uniform order couldn't be lawful because the Army's participation in the U.N. mission was itself unlawful, asserting various statutory and constitutional grounds discussed below.

The military judge — a law officer presiding over the panel but not serving as one of its members — rejected both sets of arguments: he concluded that the order was consistent with AR 670-1 and that the legality of the deployment was a nonjusticiable political question. The court-martial sentenced New to a bad-conduct discharge.

On appeal to the Court of Criminal Appeals, New argued that the military judge erred in ruling that the lawfulness of the order was a legal question for him to decide rather than an element of the offense to be decided by the "military jury" (the term that we use, following the Court of Appeals, as shorthand for the court-martial panel). *United States v. New*, 55 M.J. 95, 103 (C.A.A.F. 2001) ("CAAF Op."); *see also id.* at 117 & n. 2 (Sullivan, J., concurring). And he argued that the military judge's conclusion on the merits was erroneous. The Court of Criminal Appeals rejected these claims and affirmed New's conviction and sentence. *United States v. New*, 50 M.J. 729 (A.Ct.Crim.App.1999) ("ACCA Op."). The Court of Appeals then granted review and also affirmed. CAAF Op., 55 M.J. at 109.

New had filed a petition for a writ of habeas corpus in federal district court shortly before his court-martial. The district court dismissed that petition on the ground that New had failed to exhaust his remedies in the pending court-martial action, *United States ex rel. New v. Perry*, 919 F.Supp. 491 (D.D.C.1996), and we affirmed, *New v. Cohen*, 129 F.3d 639 (D.C.Cir.1997). After the Court of Criminal Appeals and the Court of Appeals both affirmed his conviction, New returned to the district court. The district court dismissed the petition, finding that each of New's challenges fell outside the scope of collateral review, raised a nonjusticiable political question, or lacked merit as a matter of law. *United States ex rel. New v. Rumsfeld*, 350 F.Supp.2d 80, 102 (D.D.C.2004) ("District Ct. Op."). New appeals.

We begin with jurisdiction and the related issue of the scope and standard of review. New, the government, and the district court have all assumed that jurisdiction rests on 28 U.S.C. § 2241, which authorizes federal courts to grant writs of habeas corpus. . . . But § 2241(c) precludes granting the writ unless the petitioner is in custody. Upon conviction by court-martial New received a bad-conduct discharge; as he is not in custody, § 2241 can't supply subject matter jurisdiction. This is not fatal, however, because the Supreme Court has held that Congress didn't intend to confine collateral attacks on court-martial proceedings to § 2241. *Schlesinger v. Councilman*, 420 U.S. 738, 748-53 (1975).

Thus the district court had subject-matter jurisdiction to hear New's collateral attack under § 1331 (which New's second amended complaint invoked).

The standard of our review is more tangled. In *Councilman*, the Supreme Court not only confirmed jurisdiction in the absence of custody, but also said that collateral relief was barred unless the judgments were "void." *Id.* at 748. And that question "may turn on [1] the nature of the alleged defect, and [2] the gravity of the harm from which relief is sought," *id.* at 753. Specifically, the defect must be "fundamental," for "[a] judgment . . . is not rendered void merely by error." *Id.* at 747. Moreover, "both factors must be assessed in light of the deference that should be accorded the judgments of the carefully designed military justice system established by Congress." *Id.* at 753. Because *Councilman* ultimately denied review pending the court-martial, this standard was not part of the holding, but our circuit later adopted it for non-habeas review of court-martial judgments. *Priest v. Secretary of the Navy*, 570 F.2d 1013, 1016 (D.C.Cir.1977).

The Supreme Court pitched the *Councilman* standard as more deferential than habeas review of military judgments, which it has in turn described as no less deferential than habeas review of state court judgments. This first point was explicit in *Councilman* itself, where the Court said: "[G]rounds of impeachment cognizable in habeas proceedings may not be sufficient to warrant other forms of collateral relief." 420 U.S. at 753. The second point is part of the Court's analysis in *Burns v. Wilson*, 346 U.S. 137 (1953). There, reviewing court-martial death sentences allegedly based on coerced confessions and "an atmosphere of terror and vengeance," *id.* at 138, the Court through a four-justice plurality described military habeas as follows: "It is the limited function of the civil courts to determine whether the military have given fair consideration" to each claim raised by petitioners. *Id.* at 144. As to factfinding, the plurality said that Article III courts should not be in the business of "reexamin[ing] and reweigh[ing] each item of evidence of the occurrence of events which tend to prove or disprove one of the allegations in the applications for habeas corpus." *Id.* The plurality concluded that the petitioners failed to show that the military review process was "legally inadequate" to resolve their constitutional claims and affirmed. *Id.* at 146. (Two additional justices concurred in the result, one of them writing that the Supreme Court's role was limited to assessing the military courts' jurisdiction. *Id.* at 146-48.) In setting out this standard, the plurality explained that the Court must be at least as deferential as it is in the civilian habeas context, for in "military habeas corpus cases themselves, *even more than in state habeas corpus cases*, it would be in disregard of the statutory scheme if the federal civil courts failed to take account of the prior proceedings — of the fair determinations of the military tribunals after all military remedies have been exhausted." *Id.* at 142 (emphasis added).

The uncertainty implied in these rankings of deference level is compounded by the evolution of habeas review over time. Until the Supreme Court's decision in *Johnson v. Zerbst*, 304 U.S. 458 (1938), the scope of habeas corpus review was equally narrow in both military and civilian cases — limited to verifying personal and subject-matter jurisdiction. In *Johnson*, a civilian federal habeas corpus case, the Supreme Court expanded the scope of jurisdictional challenges by holding that the trial court could lose jurisdiction by failing to provide constitutionally-guaranteed counsel to the defendant, *id.* at 468, and this developed into explicit review for constitutional violations. *See Calley v. Callaway*, 519 F.2d 184, 195-96 (5th Cir.1975) (en banc) (citing *Waley v. Johnston*, 316 U.S. 101 (1942), and *House v. Mayo*, 324 U.S. 42 (1945)). *Burns* took military habeas review onto a similar path, though not to the same degree.

As the military habeas standard of review at one time followed review of state court judgments toward less deference, perhaps it (and other collateral review of military decisions) should follow the current path toward more. In light of the *Burns* plurality's view that military habeas review must be at as least as deferential as habeas review of state criminal judgments, the Third Circuit has held that the former enjoy at least as much deference as the latter do now, under the statutory standards adopted in the 1996 Antiterrorism and Effective Death Penalty Act ("AEDPA"). *See Brosius v. Warden*, 278 F.3d 239, 245 (3d Cir.2002) (citing 28 U.S.C. § 2254(d)-(e)). But to the extent that Congress's revision of the standards for state court judgments arose out of special history and circumstances, its decision to tighten in that context may reflect no judgment at all about collateral review of court-martial judgments.

We trace these steps merely as a caution. Except insofar as a standard may be quite specific, such as AEDPA's requirement of a violation of "clearly established Federal law, as determined by the Supreme Court of the United States," *see* 28 U.S.C. § 2254(d)(1), we have serious doubt whether the judicial mind is really capable of applying the sort of fine gradations in deference that the varying formulae may indicate. *See United States v. Boyd*, 55 F.3d 239, 242 (7th Cir.1995). It suffices for our purposes to repeat *Councilman*'s statement that errors must be fundamental to void a court-martial judgment on collateral review. And in light of *Councilman*'s point that non-habeas review is if anything more deferential than habeas review of military judgments, 420 U.S. at 753, a military court's judgment clearly will not suffer such a defect if it satisfies *Burns*'s "fair consideration" test. . . .

McKINNEY v. WHITE
United States Court of Appeals for the District of Columbia Circuit
291 F.3d 851 (D.C. Cir. 2002)

ROGERS, CIRCUIT JUDGE:

Gene C. McKinney, now retired, was a Sergeant Major of the Army who was court martialed in 1998 and found guilty of obstructing justice in violation of Article 134 of the Uniform Code of Military Justice ("UCMJ"), 10 U.S.C. § 934. After unsuccessful attempts to have his conviction set aside under the UCMJ, he sought review in the United States District Court for the District of Columbia under the Administrative Procedure Act ("APA"), 5 U.S.C. §§ 701-706, of the Judge Advocate General's denial of his request to set aside the court martial finding and sentence. The district court dismissed the complaint on the ground that the Judge Advocate General is not an "agency" for purposes of the APA. We hold that the statutory scheme created by Congress for review of courts martial precludes review of the Judge Advocate General's decision under the APA. Accordingly, we affirm the dismissal of the complaint.

I

The relevant facts are undisputed. Pursuant to UCMJ Article 32, 10 U.S.C. § 832, an Army investigation of allegations of sexual harassment and assault by six female military personnel resulted in McKinney's being court martialed. He was charged in 18 counts with violations of military law arising out of alleged sexual harassment and in a separate count with obstruction of justice in violation of UCMJ Article 134, 10 U.S.C. § 934. In March 1998, a jury acquitted him of the 18 sexual harassment counts and convicted him of the obstruction count. He was sentenced to a reprimand and a reduction in grade from Army Sergeant Major to Army Master Sergeant.

McKinney sought a post-trial evidentiary hearing pursuant to UCMJ Article 39(a), 10 U.S.C. § 839(b), to inquire into allegations of prosecutorial misconduct in not disclosing and destroying evidence and attempting to influence witnesses. The Military Trial Judge denied the motion on the papers. The Judge also denied McKinney's renewed Article 39(a) request, to which he had attached the affidavit of his counsel recounting a discussion with a prosecution witness. McKinney then filed a petition for mandamus in the United States Army Court of Criminal Appeals in a further effort to obtain a post-trial evidentiary hearing; the court denied the petition. His writ of appeal to the United States Court of Appeals for the Armed Forces was also denied, without prejudice to his right of review under UCMJ Article 69, 10 U.S.C. § 869. *McKinney v. United States,* 51 M.J. 270 (C.A.A.F. 1998).

Pursuant to UCMJ Article 69, 10 U.S.C. § 869(a), the Commander for the Military District of Washington affirmed the findings and sentence and forwarded the record of the trial to the Judge Advocate General for review. Following an investigation of McKinney's allegations of prosecutorial misconduct that included interviews of several prosecution witnesses, including the witness referred to in McKinney's Article 39(a) affidavit, the Judge Advocate General stated summarily: "The finding and sentence are supported in law and the sentence is appropriate. No modification of the finding or sentence is warranted." The Judge Advocate General did not refer the case to a Court of Criminal Appeals for review as to matters of law. *Id.* § 869(d) & (e).

Having failed to obtain relief from the military justice system, McKinney filed a complaint in the United States District Court for the District of Columbia. He alleged that the decision of the Judge Advocate General was arbitrary and capricious and not based on substantial evidence within the meaning of the APA, 5 U.S.C. § 706, because the Judge Advocate General failed to provide an adequate explanation for rejecting McKinney's claims of prosecutorial misconduct. The Secretary of the Army and the other defendants ("the Secretary") moved to dismiss the complaint for failure to state a cause of action under Federal Rule of Civil Procedure 12(b)(6). The district court granted the motion to dismiss, ruling that the Judge Advocate General is not an "agency" for purposes of the APA.

II

McKinney contends that the district court erred in ruling that the Judge Advocate General's decision is not subject to review under the APA. He maintains that because decisions by the Judge Advocate General under UCMJ

Article 69 are reached independently and constitute final binding decisions affecting the rights of individuals, the Judge Advocate General is an "authority" within the meaning of 5 U.S.C. § 701(b)(1) whose decisions are subject to judicial review under the APA as final agency action. He relies on the broad definition of the word "agency" in the APA, 5 U.S.C. § 701(b)(1), and the presumption favoring review of final agency decisions that is overcome only by clear and convincing evidence that Congress intended to restrict access to the courts. *See Abbott Labs. v. Gardner*, 387 U.S. 136, 141 (1967).

Although the district court addressed McKinney's complaint in terms of whether the Judge Advocate General was an "agency" subject to APA review, we conclude that a threshold jurisdictional issue must be addressed. The APA provides for the non-reviewability of "courts martial and military commissions," 5 U.S.C. § 701(b)(1)(F), but does not expressly preclude review of Judge Advocate General decisions reviewing courts martial pursuant to UCMJ Article 69, 10 U.S.C. § 869. Congress' establishment, pursuant to Article I, Section 8 of the Constitution, of a separate judicial system for courts martial review is, however, convincing evidence that Congress could not have intended Judge Advocate General review of courts martial to fall within APA review of agency decisions.

In *Schlesinger v. Councilman*, 420 U.S. 738, 746 (1975), the Supreme Court stated that it "repeatedly has recognized that of necessity '[m]ilitary law . . . is a jurisprudence which exists separate and apart from the law that governs in our federal judicial establishment.'" 420 U.S. at 746 (quoting *Burns v. Wilson*, 346 U.S. 137, 140 (1953)). The Court also reiterated in *Schlesinger* both the general rule that "the acts of a court martial, within the scope of its jurisdiction and duty, cannot be controlled or reviewed in the civil courts, by writ of prohibition or otherwise," 420 U.S. at 746 (citations omitted), and the limited exception for collateral attack seeking a declaration that a judgment is void, having no res judicata effect, "because of lack of jurisdiction or some other equally fundamental defect." *Id.* at 747. Observing that "[t]he military is 'a specialized society separate from civilian society' with 'laws and traditions of its own [developed] during its long history,'" *id.* at 757 (quoting *Parker v. Levy*, 417 U.S. 733, 743 (1974)), the Court noted that "Congress attempted to balance . . . military necessities against the equally significant interest of ensuring fairness to servicemen charged with military offenses." *Id.* The Court further observed that:

> implicit in the congressional scheme embodied in the [UCMJ] is the view that the military court system generally is adequate to and responsibly will perform its assigned task. We think this congressional judgment must be respected and that it must be assumed that the military court system will vindicate servicemen's constitutional rights.

Id. at 758.

As the proceedings in McKinney's case illustrate, Congress has established a complete and distinct procedure for members of the military who are charged with law violations under the UCMJ. While direct parallels are imprecise, the proceedings in his case suggest a process that begins with a review that serves a function comparable to that of the grand jury for Article III courts. This was followed by a jury trial, imposition of a sentence, and post-trial motions proceedings. Then, in a procedure unique to the military, the finding and sentence were subject to the approval of the Commander of the Military District. 10 U.S.C. § 860. Upon such approval, the trial record was forwarded, in light of the length of McKinney's sentence, to the Judge Advocate General for review instead of a Court of Criminal Appeals. *Id.* §§ 866(b)(1), 869(a). UCMJ Article 69 provides that a soldier who is convicted during a general court martial and sentenced to less than one year of confinement is entitled to an automatic review of the record of the trial by the Judge Advocate General, unless the soldier affirmatively waives review. *Id.* § 869. "If any part of the findings or sentence is found to be unsupported in law or if reassessment of the sentence is appropriate, the Judge Advocate General may modify or set aside the findings or sentence or both." *Id.* § 869(a). Upon referral by the Judge Advocate General, further review of questions of law is available by a Court of Criminal Appeals pursuant to UCMJ Article 69, 10 U.S.C. § 869. UCMJ Article 76 provides that:

> [t]he appellate review of records of trial provided by [Chapter 47, UCMJ] . . . are final and conclusive . . . [and] are binding upon all departments, courts, agencies, and officers of the United States, subject only to action upon a petition for a new trial as provided in section 837 of this title (article 73) and to action by the Secretary concerned as provided in section 847 of this title (article 74) [Remission and suspension], and the authority of the President.

Id. § 876.

The proceedings under the UCMJ demonstrate that the designated reviewing authorities have "heard [McKinney] out on every significant allegation which [he] now urge[s]." *Burns,* 346 U.S. at 144. The Military Trial Judge reviewed McKinney's allegations of prosecutorial misconduct on two occasions and the Court of Appeals for the Armed Forces denied his writ of appeal. The Judge Advocate General reviewed the court martial finding and sentence and also conducted his own investigation into the allegations of prosecutorial misconduct. McKinney makes no claim that the procedures established by Congress in the UCMJ were inadequate to the task, much less "fundamentally defect[ive]." *Schlesinger,* 420 U.S. at 747.

This court has long acknowledged that it lacks jurisdiction of a direct appeal of a court martial. Although McKinney does not seek review of a decision of the Court of Appeals for the Armed Forces, he, like the petitioners in *Shaw v. United States,* 209 F.2d 811, 813 (D.C.Cir. 1954), seeks review of a decision by the military authority that Congress has designated to review his direct appeal and his collateral attack on his general court martial conviction. The fact that he did not receive a more severe sentence, whereby his appeal would have gone to a Court of Criminal Appeals, is a distinction without difference with regard to the jurisdiction of this court. As in *Shaw,* then, "we are clear" that Congress has not granted jurisdiction to this court to review direct appeals from the highest military official of a general court martial. 209 F.2d at 812-13.

Furthermore, Congress has expressly provided that "courts martial" are not subject to review under the APA. 5 U.S.C. § 701(b)(1)(F). While McKinney contends that this prohibition does not extend to the final decision of the Judge Advocate General, the logic of his position is illusive. Congress has provided a separate justice system in the UCMJ for military personnel and it has expressly determined that "courts martial" are not to be subject to APA review. Hence, it is difficult to understand the reasoning that Congress would have utilized in making the final UCMJ review of "courts martial" subject to review by Article III courts under the APA. To adopt that position would not only be contrary to the long-established understanding that "[m]ilitary law, like state law, is a jurisprudence which exists separate and apart from the law which governs in our federal judicial establishment," *Burns,* 346 U.S. at 140, "[i]t is well settled that 'by habeas corpus the civil courts exercise no supervisory or correcting power over the proceedings of a court martial'" and that "[t]he correction of any errors it may have committed is for the military authorities which are alone authorized to review its decision." *Hiatt v. Brown,* 339 U.S. 103, 111 (1950) (citations omitted). In *Shaw,* this court rejected the view that the Court of Military Appeals (now the Court of Appeals for the Armed Forces), was anything other than "a court in every significant respect, rather than an administrative agency." 209 F.2d at 813. Although the Judge Advocate General has independent fact-finding authority under UCMJ Article 69, unlike a Court of Criminal Appeals under UCMJ Article 66 or an Article III appellate court, McKinney points to nothing that would indicate that Congress viewed the UCMJ Article 69 procedures for review of courts martial involving sentences of less than one year to be so inferior as to warrant review by Article III courts under the APA. Although review by the Judge Advocate General is in the nature of a collateral proceeding akin to *coram nobis, Curci v. United States,* 577 F.2d 815, 818 (2d Cir.1978) (citing *inter alia* S. Rep. No. 1601, 90th Cong., 2d Sess. (1968), reprinted in 1968 U.S.C.C.A.N 4501, 4515), for the military justice system where "Congress has taken great care both to define the rights of those subject to military law [] [and to] provide a complete system of review within the military system to secure those rights," *Burns,* 346 U.S. at 140, the Judge Advocate General's decision is properly viewed as what Congress concluded should be the final decision under military law in McKinney's court martial. So understood, Congress' preclusion of APA review of "courts martial" reaches the Judge Advocate General's decision in McKinney's case.

Although McKinney contends only that the Judge Advocate General's summary statement of his decision is inadequate to reveal the basis of his reasoning, and arguably is not seeking review of the underlying court martial finding that he obstructed justice in violation of UCMJ Article 134, by assuming jurisdiction in his case the court would be unable to deny review in later cases where it would be required to review courts martial findings. As framed, moreover, McKinney's allegations of prosecutorial misconduct would effectively require this court to determine whether the alleged misconduct so affected his court martial that he was denied a fair trial. *Cf. United States v. Bagley,* 473 U.S. 667, 678-79 (1985); *Greer v. Miller,* 483 U.S. 756, 765 (1987). Yet this is the type of question that Congress has determined is to be conducted by the Judge Advocate General when a court martial sentence imposes less than one year's confinement. *See Schlesinger,* 420 U.S. at 746-47. Moreover, as the Second Circuit has suggested, the Judge Advocate General's decision to use a short form of response in claims seeking discretionary review is not unexpected where there are a large number of claims. *See Curci,* 577 F.2d at 818 . McKinney's attempt to invoke the APA amounts, then, to an attempt to end run a military justice system wherein Congress has afforded him the direct review procedures it deemed appropriate.

Accordingly, we hold that this court has no jurisdiction under the APA to review the decision of the Judge Advocate General denying McKinney's request to set aside the court martial finding and sentence, and we affirm the dismissal of the complaint.

NOTES AND QUESTIONS

1. Since 1984, United States military personnel have had the right to seek review by the Supreme Court of decisions of the Court of Appeals for the Armed Forces, but only if that court has granted discretionary review or an extraordinary writ. *See* Article 67a(a), UCMJ, 10 U.S.C. § 867a(a). Is there a principled basis for permitting the Court of Appeals to bar the door to direct review by the highest court of the land?

2. Should the availability of Supreme Court review on direct appeal from courts-martial affect the availability of collateral review in the civilian courts? Is there a principled basis for treating collateral review as narrower in military cases than in other kinds of cases?

3. If the highest military court decides a case summarily — *i.e.*, without full briefing and oral argument — should that have any effect on the availability of collateral review?

4. Should collateral review be limited to constitutional issues?

5. For further discussion of *New*, see Chapter 18, § III.B, *infra*.

Chapter 18

MILITARY JUSTICE IN OPERATIONAL SETTINGS

This chapter explores the use of military justice in combat, peacekeeping and humanitarian operations. One of the central purposes of a military justice system is to maintain discipline over armed soldiers in chaotic environments far from the social and moral restraints of home. Military justice serves as a means of enforcing and promoting international humanitarian law. As experience has revealed over the last two decades, the need to restrain servicemembers' conduct toward the civilian population arises in peacekeeping missions as well as combat missions.

Section I assesses the portability of the sending state's military justice system. Portability refers to the extent to which it has the jurisdiction and the capability to function in a deployed setting during a period of heightened operational tempo. Deployments for military operations also raise questions about the extent to which the sending state's military is subject to the receiving state's criminal jurisdiction.

Combat operations can strain the ability of a military justice system to work as designed. Section II explores such strains by examining American courts-martial in and near combat situations. It considers whether the U.S. military justice system is capable of performing as designed in a combat environment and whether military justice effectively protects civilian populations during combat operations.

Peacekeeping operations produce their own unique legal challenges related to tensions over command and control between the sending state and international organizations. Uncertainty may even arise concerning the precise mission that the peacekeeping force is to accomplish and whether soldiers are committing human rights violations. Section III examines these issues through the actions of two individual U.S. soldiers and two Canadian cases from a 1993 peacekeeping mission in Somalia.

I. PORTABILITY

Uniform Code of Military Justice
Article 5. Territorial applicability of this chapter

This chapter applies to all places.

NOTE

The United States' armed forces are often stationed overseas and engage in military operations around the world. Article 5 establishes worldwide jurisdiction of the Uniform Code of Military Justice over those subject to its jurisdiction.

STEVENS v. WARDEN U.S. PENITENTIARY, LEAVENWORTH, KANSAS
United States Court of Appeals for the Tenth Circuit
536 F.2d 1334 (10th Cir.1976)

Appellant Stevens appeals the denial of his petition for a writ of habeas corpus by the United States District Court for the District of Kansas. Stevens is presently serving a thirty-year prison term at Leavenworth, Kansas for being absent without leave (AWOL) and for unpremeditated murder, both offenses having been committed while appellant was a soldier in the United States Army in South Vietnam. He was court-martialled under Articles 86 and 118 of the Uniform Code of Military Justice (UCMJ) in December of 1969. By this action he claims that the court-martial board lacked jurisdiction over him. Several grounds are advanced for the contention that he was triable for the offense only by the government of South Vietnam. The federal district court denied relief. We affirm.

A brief reference to the facts is necessary. In 1969 appellant was a combat soldier in the United States Army stationed in Vietnam. At the time of the incidents for which he was court-martialled, he was off base and AWOL from duty. The victim, a military policeman (MP), was also off base, but since at the time of the killing the latter was attempting to apprehend appellant, the MP was acting within the scope of his military duties. During the struggle between the MP and appellant, a twelve-inch bayonet found its way into the MP. Appellant testified in his own behalf at the court-martial; he claimed that the killing was accidental and that he was trying merely to rid himself of the knife when the MP pulled both appellant and the knife into himself. Based on eye-witness and other testimony, the court-martial board found appellant guilty of being AWOL and of unpremeditated murder. The conviction and sentence were affirmed by the United States Court of Military Appeals.

Appellant claims that because the crime occurred off base and in the civilian community of South Vietnam, that based on various treaty agreements then in effect with Vietnam, the United States had no jurisdiction over him whatsoever for the crime of murder (the AWOL conviction per se is not contested in this action). No authority is cited by appellant that a civilian court was present or available in which appellant's case could have been prosecuted. *See United States ex rel. Jacobs v. Froehlke*, 334 F. Supp. 1107 (D.C. 1971). It further appears that the Republic of Vietnam was not the least bit interested in trying one American serviceman for killing another despite the off-base scene of the crime. *See Wilson v. Girard*, 354 U.S. 524, 1 L. Ed. 2d 1544, 77 S. Ct. 1409. Appellant, being a combat soldier on active duty (i.e., neither a dependent, employee, nor discharged civilian) was subject to the UCMJ. 10 U.S.C. § 802 (Article 2, UCMJ). The Code pursuant to 10 U.S.C. § 805 is applicable to all places, including foreign countries. *Puhl v. United States*, 376 F.2d 194 (10th Cir. 1967). Hence even if an argument can be made that the territorial sovereign (i.e. Vietnam) retained jurisdiction despite the presence of the

United States troops, one who violates the law of two sovereigns is subject to prosecution by both and may not complain of or choose the manner in which each proceeds against him. *Hall v. Looney*, 256 F.2d 59 (10th Cir. 1959). . . .

Affirmed. The mandate shall issue forthwith.

Criminal Expo 2001, 5th International Military Criminal Law Conference
Budapest, Hungary (June 11-13, 2001)

Statement of Mr. Roger Graham Chapple, Assistant Judge Advocate General, United Kingdom

[The protection of individual rights should not be reduced during peacekeeping missions abroad.] [I]t was that important principle that took me to Gorniv Dekuf in Bosnia.

I was the judge conducting the first British court martial in Bosnia. It was the first British court martial that has been held in an operational theatre in many years. Two soldiers were accused of violent assault upon a taxi driver, a Serbian national. It was a serious assault, a knife was used, the taxi driver was left with a broken jaw and permanent facial scaring. There were 3 witnesses, all Serbian nationals. These Serbian nationals were unable and unwilling to leave the country or if they left the country they were unable to return to the country. An application was made to me before the trial that the statements of those witnesses be read at the trial. I refused that application. Perhaps I did not think through the consequences of refusing that application carefully enough. But the defence of both soldiers was that the taxi driver had started the violence, it was him who was trying to kidnap the 2 soldiers and rob them and thus what they did was done in self-defence. I took the view that a fair trial was not possible without a court hearing from the taxi-driver and witnesses. There was no technology for a TV link [to receive] evidence. . . . [T]hus we faced the problem that [either the court must go] to Bosnia or there [would be] no trial.

The third alternative, to hand jurisdiction to the Bosnian authority, was plainly not a viable one because of circumstances that then existed. So . . . [w]e traveled to Bosnia, the Judge Advocate, the military members, the accused, his escort, and many others. It took 2 days to get there through blizzards [and] vehicles breaking down. [I]t took rather shorter to get back because we were flown by helicopter but [we] were shot at on the way back.

Despite all that and the enormous expense, it seems to us we have no alternative at all in similar circumstances but to travel to take justice to the soldiers. That seems to be essential to protect the rule of law and to protect the rights of soldiers.

Statement of Colonel Dr. Ferenc Mátyus, Head of Department, International Law Office, Ministry of the Interior, Hungary

Despite the fact that the history of the Hungarian Army's participation in international peace-keeping missions is only ten years old, unfortunately, we have acquired experience in both the field of discipline and criminal law due to disciplinary deficiencies of varying significance. . . .

According to Hungarian law, military commanders have the power to conduct criminal investigation[s]. This jurisdiction, however, is severely restricted and in practice can only be exercised under the close supervision of a military prosecutor.

Its applicability within the territory of Hungary is beyond doubt, but the same cannot be said of its applicability in an international peace-keeping mission. Even the legal categorization of an offence committed several thousand kilometers from home, in a military zone, can pose a problem for the commander, as for this he would need to be familiar not only with domestic law but also with the entire system of international agreements, as well as the connection, or possibly the distinction, between the two.

To resolve this obvious controversy, we need to examine the disciplinary and criminal jurisdiction of the commander of a Hungarian military contingent abroad. Basically, both are very limited. The so-called Service Act of 1996, which deals with disciplinary jurisdiction in detail, is almost exclusively based on the aspect of application to domestic territory and in peace-time. It is therefore only with great difficulty that the material and procedural provisions can be applied in cases occurring in foreign land, under operative circumstances. . . .

The right to defence of a person against whom procedures have been started is fully guaranteed for domestic circumstances by both the disciplinary [and] criminal law. Offenders regularly exercise this right and often [retain] attorneys, or are . . . provided with a defence counsel in serious cases. The exercise of this right abroad, however, poses problems.

An independent Act is under preparation, which will set out detailed rules of serving abroad. With regard to disciplinary procedures, it will contain provisions concerning the exercise of the right to defence abroad. It should be emphasized that these provisions — similarly to [the] former "Service Act" — are prepared taking into consideration the provisions of the European Convention on Human Rights.

It is obvious, however, that this right cannot be of the same scope as in the case of domestic procedures. It is simply physically impossible for a Hungarian attorney to be at the service of a serviceman under disciplinary procedures upon his request in a short time, possibly in another continent — in order to [comport with] the right to (and requirement for) [a] speedy and fair trial.

NOTE AND QUESTIONS

Compare the United States' and United Kingdom's approach to the military justice system's portability to Hungary's approach. To the Hungarian official, it is "obvious" that military members' right to counsel must be more limited abroad than within Hungary. Britain's Assistant Judge Advocate General, on the other hand, emphasizes that the military justice system must extend the same protections to those who are deployed that it provides domestically.

What explains the differences in the two approaches? Is there room for both in international operations?

Françoise Hampson, *Working Paper on the Accountability of International Personnel Taking Part in Peace Support Operations*
United Nations Commission on Human Rights Sub-Commission
on the Promotion and Protection of Human Rights
E/CN.4/Sub.2/2005/42 (7 July 2005)

IV. Types of Immunity

26. Some measure of immunity serves an important purpose. It is designed to enable a person or organization to discharge its responsibilities independently. It is not supposed to act as a vehicle for impunity.

A. Host State Immunity

27. Different categories of personnel have different types of immunity from the jurisdiction of the host State under the General Convention, bilateral SOFA [Status of Forces Agreement], Model SOFA or MOU [Memorandum of Understanding].

1. Full Immunity

28. Very senior United Nations international civil servants are entitled to full diplomatic immunity. Members of a national military contingent are protected by absolute immunity from the host State jurisdiction, usually as provided in a SOFA.

2. Functional Immunity

29. Functional immunity or provisional immunity is an immunity from legal process in respect of words spoken or written and all acts performed by them in their official capacity or in the course of the performance of their mission in the case of experts on mission.

30. Military observers, CIVPOL [International Civilian Police Program], the majority of United Nations international civil servants and some local personnel working for one of the above are protected by functional immunity, either by the General Convention or by the SOFA. Foreign personnel working for IGOs [inter-governmental organizations] are protected by functional immunity, depending on the agreements between the relevant organization and the host State. Other foreign persons are normally not covered by immunity.

31. There remain uncertainties in the area of functional immunity. The meaning to be given to "during the course of their duty" is determined by the Special Representative of the Secretary-General. This has caused some confusion in the field. For example, in a case of rape involving the United Nations Transitional Authority in East Timor (UNTAET) the alleged perpetrator's immunity was declared inapplicable due to the alleged act being outside of official functions. On the other hand, in a case of murder involving the United Nations Mission in Kosovo (UNMIK), the suspect's immunity was waived. In

the latter case, one would have expected the act to be outside the scope of the immunity.

32. Where immunity is not applicable, foreigners working under contract for one of the components above or foreign staff working for international NGOs [non-governmental organizations] are subject to the host State jurisdiction.

33. In many situations in which [Peace Support Operations (PSOs)] are deployed, there is no national authority with which to negotiate a SOFA (e.g. Somalia) or no agreement. There have been PSOs where the international component has gone in to the territory before negotiating the SOFA with the host State.

34. Even where the exercise of host State jurisdiction is a theoretical possibility, it should be remembered that, in many of the types of situations in which a PSO is deployed, there is no functioning legal system. Impunity in practice is not solely attributable to the existence and exercise of immunity; it may be the product of the lack of a local legal system.

3. Waiver of Immunity

35. The absolute immunity of members of a national contingent is not normally subject to waiver. Apart from that, other immunities can, in theory, be waived.

36. Immunities granted for military observers, CIVPOL, United Nations international civil servants and local personnel can be waived by the Special Representative of the Secretary-General (in the name of the Secretary-General), where he/she considers that immunity would impede the course of justice, and where it can be waived without prejudice to the interests of the United Nations. In the case of his Special Representatives, the Secretary-General has a right and duty to waive.

37. In case of personnel of IGOs, waiver of immunity is normally determined at the headquarters.

38. As previously noted, the function of immunity is not to give impunity. Particular difficulties arise where the United Nations is not simply present in a territory but is, in effect, acting as its Government. Governments do not have immunity. On the contrary, human rights law requires that Governments should be capable of being called to account. Any proposals designed to avoid the risk of immunity giving rise to impunity should distinguish between situations where the United Nations is, in effect, the Government and those in which it is present alongside some form of national Government.

B. Sending States and Immunity

39. Members of national contingents are subject to the exclusive criminal and disciplinary jurisdiction of the sending State. In some States, criminal proceedings against members of armed forces are conducted by court martial. In others, all nationals, including members of the armed forces, are subject to normal (i.e. civil) criminal jurisdiction, even for acts committed abroad. Where that is not the case, special legislation may provide for the possibility of normal criminal proceedings for acts committed abroad specifically in the case of members of armed forces.

40. For military observers and CIVPOL, there is no legal basis for immunity from the sending State's criminal jurisdiction. Military observers are serving officers of a national defence force and should be subject to the criminal and disciplinary jurisdiction of the sending State. For CIVPOL also, there is the possibility of prosecution by the sending State but that depends on whether the State has laws in place which permit the prosecution of all nationals for acts committed abroad or which permit the prosecution of police officers for acts committed abroad. Generally, civil law countries are able to exercise criminal jurisdiction over nationals for acts committed abroad, while common law countries can only do so where there is express legislative provision to that effect. Military observers and CIVPOL, as experts on mission, are not entitled to immunity from their sending State criminal jurisdiction. Wherever functional immunity is based on a SOFA, the sending State immunity question does not arise.

41. There being no legal barrier to the exercise of criminal jurisdiction by the sending State does not, however, mean that such proceedings are likely. There may be a need for express legal provision and, above all, for the necessary practical arrangements to be put in place. There are also likely to be practical difficulties in having access to the victim, witnesses and other evidence.

42. United Nations international civil servants, who are entitled to functional immunity under article V of the General Convention, seem to be protected by the immunity against the exercise of their home State jurisdiction as well. By contrast, some categories of United Nations civilian staff, such as UNVs [United Nations Volunteers] or consultants, do not enjoy functional immunity in their home State, as their immunity is provided on the basis of the SOFA.

43. Some foreign personnel of IGOs appear to have functional immunity from the courts of their national jurisdiction. For those appointed for a short term, immunity derives from an MOU, and immunity in the State of nationality will depend on its provisions.

44. Other foreigners, such as foreign staff of NGOs and foreign contractors, do not enjoy immunity. Depending on national legislation on extraterritorial jurisdiction and practical barriers, there is the possibility of their being prosecuted in their home State.

45. The right and duty to waive immunity in relation to a staff member's home State rests with the Secretary-General.

C. Immunity and Third States

46. In the exceptional case of the alleged misconduct taking the form of an international crime, any State is permitted to exercise jurisdiction in relation to a person located within that State's territory, based on universal jurisdiction, provided that the suspect is not protected by immunity. There is no known example of a third State claiming jurisdiction over a member of a PSO.

47. In addition to the usual questions regarding the applicability of immunity outside the host State, there may be questions of diplomatic immunity. The same practical problems may be expected to arise as in the case of prosecution by the sending State.

D. Jurisdiction of International Criminal Courts

48. Where an international or hybrid court is created under international law to address violations in a particular region or conflict, the scope of its jurisdiction will be determined by the statute of the court. Such courts may have jurisdiction over persons who would otherwise be protected by immunity. The International Criminal Tribunal for the Former Yugoslavia, for example, examined the possibility of war crimes proceedings arising out of the North Atlantic Treaty Organization (NATO) operations in Kosovo. The position is the same in relation to the International Criminal Court (ICC). It would appear that national courts are required to give effect to the personal immunity of senior officials.

49. Practical problems are likely to arise in relation to the collection of evidence and access to the victims and witnesses. Political opposition to the ICC and limited resources may also act as deterrents.

NOTES AND QUESTIONS

1. To promote a disciplined peacekeeping force, is it better to have a portable military justice system? When selecting nations to participate in peace support operations, should UN officials consider the effectiveness of potential sending states' military justice systems? Should the UN continue to rely on sending states to discipline peacekeeping forces? Should the UN adopt its own military justice system that would apply to peacekeeping forces? Would some nations refuse to participate in UN peacekeeping missions if such missions required subjecting the sending states' forces to a UN military justice system?

2. A 2005 letter from United Nations Secretary-General Kofi Annan recognized "sexual exploitation and abuse by a significant number of United Nations peacekeeping personnel in the Democratic Republic of the Congo" in 2004. *See* Letter dated 24 March 2005 from the Secretary-General to the President of the General Assembly, A/59/710. Secretary-General Annan concluded, "As the allegations in the Democratic Republic of the Congo surfaced, it became clear that the measures currently in place to address sexual exploitation and abuse in peacekeeping operations were manifestly inadequate and that a fundamental change in approach was needed." *Id*. A lengthy report by Prince Zeid Ra'ad Zeid Al-Hussein, Permanent United Nations Representative of Jordan, suggested reforms to deter future acts of misconduct by UN peacekeeping forces. A COMPREHENSIVE STRATEGY TO ELIMINATE FUTURE SEXUAL EXPLOITATION AND ABUSE IN UNITED NATIONS PEACEKEEPING OPERATIONS, A/59/710 (24 March 2005).

II.   COMBAT OPERATIONS

UNITED STATES v. BRYANT
United States Army Court of Military Review
35 M.J. 739 (A.C.M.R. 1992)

GRAVELLE, JUDGE:

In this case, we must decide whether the defense counsel's conduct in providing advice to his client regarding choice of forum, advice with which the counsel did not personally agree, amounted to ineffective assistance of counsel. We hold that the defense counsel's conduct amounted to ineffective assistance of counsel.

I.

The appellant's court-martial occurred in Saudi Arabia. On appeal, she initially asserted that her defense counsel, MAJ D [then CPT D], was ineffective during the sentencing proceedings at trial and during the post-trial processing of this case. She has filed an affidavit with this court detailing her reasons for believing that her defense counsel was ineffective. The defense counsel has also filed an affidavit in reply. Based on these affidavits, the government has conceded that MAJ D was ineffective in his representation of the appellant during and after sentencing. In light of our holding, we need not examine the correctness of the government's concession regarding ineffectiveness in the sentencing and post-trial phases of the court-martial process.

The defense counsel's affidavit also raised a troubling issue regarding his effectiveness during the pretrial phase involving a decision made by the appellant at trial. In his affidavit, the trial defense counsel asserted, *inter alia*:

> 4. Prior to trial, I made two trips out to the desert [in Saudi Arabia] where the 1st Armor [sic] Division was encamped to interview my client and prepare the case. I had no means of transportation nor communication and was forced to rely upon transportation provided by the 1st Armor [sic] Division. During these two visits, I focused my investigation on the guilt/innocence portion of the trial and expended a lot of energy attempting to convince the command to dispose of the charges either administratively or through nonjudicial punishment. . . .

> 8. Despite my attempts to make the charges go away, I was notified several days prior to February 23, 1991 that we would be going to trial. I did not arrive at Log Base Echo until the late afternoon of February 22, 1991. The 1st Armor [sic] Division had just moved forward and it was well known that the ground war would be starting in the immediate future. Although I was well prepared for the guilt/innocence phase of the trial, I knew that I had done nothing to put together an extenuation and mitigation case.

> 9. Moreover I was faced with a dilemma that I had never faced before — being torn between my loyalties as an officer and my loyalties as a defense counsel. I knew that the case against PV2 Bryant was full of problems and that there was a chance for acquittal before a

panel. I also knew that the ground war was to about start and that the 1st Armor [sic] Division needed each and every officer and noncommissioned officer to do their part. I am sorry to admit that CPT [D] the officer won over CPT [D] the defense counsel and I convinced PV2 Bryant that she should choose to go judge alone. I knew that this was a classic case which warranted a panel. In fact, after trial the judge questioned me about why I did not go with a panel and indicated that he thought I would have done better with a panel. I gave my client advice which was in the best interest of the war effort and not in her best interest.

Because of these statements, we specified the following issue:

WHETHER THE APPELLANT'S TRIAL DEFENSE COUNSEL WAS INEFFECTIVE AS TO THE MERITS PORTION OF APPELLANT'S TRIAL, BASED UPON ADMISSIONS CONTAINED WITHIN [THE DEFENSE COUNSEL'S] SWORN AFFIDAVIT.

In response to the specified issue, appellate defense counsel, not surprisingly, assert that the trial defense counsel's actions amount to ineffective assistance of counsel under the standards of *Strickland v. Washington*, 466 U.S. 668, (1984), and because the actions involve a conflict of interest, citing *United States v. Cronic*, 466 U.S. 648, (1984). . . .

The government responds that we should not find ineffective assistance of counsel because it is human nature for a defense counsel to second-guess his own decisions and trial tactics after an unfavorable trial result, that "speculation based on hindsight is not the proper standard" for determining whether MAJ D was ineffective, and that the advice was "not unreasonable under the circumstances and was well within professional norms." Assuming, arguendo, that the advice was erroneous, the government further argues that "the appellant was not prejudiced as a result of the counsel's actions because 'the decision regarding forum was ultimately appellant's to make.'" Appellate government counsel argues that the record shows that the appellant knowingly, intelligently, freely, and unequivocally elected trial by military judge alone.

II.

The Sixth Amendment right to counsel includes the right to effective representation of counsel. *Strickland*, 466 U.S. at 690. The appellant is entitled to effective representation of counsel before, during, and after trial. *United States v. Holt*, 33 M.J. 400 (C.M.A. 1991). A counsel's performance is judged under standards set out in *Strickland* which are applicable in the military justice system. *United States v. Scott*, 24 M.J. 186 (C.M.A. 1987). Under *Strickland*, a counsel's performance is presumed to be competent. To overcome this presumption, an appellant must point out specific errors made by his defense counsel that were unreasonable under prevailing professional norms. *Cronic*, 466 U.S. 648. Under *Strickland*, there is a two-part test for showing ineffectiveness of counsel. First, the appellant must show that the counsel's performance was deficient. Second, the appellant must show that the deficient performance prejudiced the defense. *Id.* at 687. However, prejudice may be presumed when the defense counsel is burdened by an actual conflict of in terest, or when an accused has been denied the effective assistance of counsel at a critical stage of trial. *Id.* at 691-92; *Cronic*, 466 U.S. at 659-60; *Cuyler v. Sullivan*, 446 U.S. 335, 345-50, (1980); *United States v. Babbitt*, 26 M.J. 157, 158 (C.M.A. 1988). *See also United States v. Calderon*, 34 M.J. 501, 504 n.5 (A.F.C.M.R. 1991). "Only when the surrounding circumstances justify a presumption of ineffectiveness can a Sixth Amendment claim be sufficient without inquiry into counsel's actual performance at trial." *Cronic*, 466 U.S. 648 at 662.

A defense counsel must "guard the interests of the accused zealously within the bounds of the law" and must "represent the accused with undivided fidelity." R.C.M. 502(d)(6), discussion (B).

III.

We reject the government's arguments summarized in Part I above. We cannot agree that the defense counsel's advice to the appellant before trial was "not unreasonable under the circumstances and was well within professional norms." Nor can we agree that we should treat the contents of the defense counsel's affidavit as merely the product of human nature to second-guess his own performance and as "speculation based on hindsight." Finally, while the record of proceedings may ostensibly show that the appellant's choice of forum was knowingly, intelligently, and freely made, the defense counsel's affidavit shows the contrary. A component of a client's knowing and intelligent decisions prior to and at trial is the counsel's best advice, unencumbered by divided loyalties.

In our system of military justice, it is clear that the interests of the Army are best served when the interests of the defense counsel's client are paramount in that counsel's mind. In the case before us, the defense counsel failed to understand, or lost sight of the fact, that a defense counsel's duty to the Army is to provide his or her client with representation unclouded by the government's operational considerations.

We judicially note that the ground war against Iraq began during Operation Desert Storm on 24 February 1991, and that the First Armored Division was an active participant throughout. We also note that the trial of this case occurred on 23 February 1991. We find that the defense counsel's affidavit is believable, credible, and forthright, and we accept it as accurate. By the defense counsel's own admission, he placed what he perceived to be the Army's interests over those of his client. Utilizing the standards for measuring the effectiveness of counsel set out in *Strickland v. Washington*, we hold that the defense counsel provided ineffective assistance of counsel when he gave advice regarding the critical decision of choice of forum, advice that he himself did not agree with and which he was convinced was not in his client's best interest. Under the unique circumstances of this case, we find the defense counsel was laboring under an actual conflict of interest and will presume prejudice.

The findings of guilty and the sentence are set aside. A rehearing may be ordered by the same or a different convening authority.

NOTES AND QUESTIONS

1. How typical was the *Bryant* case of the military justice system's performance during Operations Desert Shield and Desert Storm? In his invaluable book on military lawyers in combat operations, Army JAG Colonel Frederic L. Borch reviewed the military justice system's performance:

> Did . . . the military justice system function[] well during the Persian Gulf War? Some observers of military criminal law during the war in Vietnam had sharply disagreed over whether the Uniform Code could work in a combat zone. Thus, this was an important question for both commanders and judge advocates. The consensus in the Army was that the Uniform Code did work well during these operations. It is true that the short duration of combat activities may well have obscured problems that might have arisen in a longer war. Moreover, in contrast to Vietnam, units participating in DESERT SHIELD and DESERT STORM consisted overwhelmingly of highly trained and motivated volunteers, rather than draftees, and the Southwest Asia area of operations was free of drugs and alcohol, all of which contributed to the low number of disciplinary problems.
>
> However, when there were violations of the Uniform Code, especially challenges to military authority like those that arose in the 1st Armored Division, the Persian Gulf experience demonstrated that the military criminal justice system not only functioned fairly, but also served an important role in enforcing discipline. In the 1st Armored Division, for example, junior enlisted soldiers "were surprised, if not shocked," upon hearing that a trial by court-martial was being conducted the night before the attack on Iraq was to begin. These young soldiers no doubt assumed that military justice matters would be postponed until combat operations had ended. Holding a trial on the eve of battle, however, demonstrated to every division soldier that the maintenance of discipline was an integral part of preparing for the upcoming attack. High standards of military discipline would remain in place.

FREDERIC L. BORCH, JUDGE ADVOCATES IN COMBAT: ARMY LAWYERS IN MILITARY OPERATIONS FROM VIETNAM TO HAITI 189-90 (2001). Other chapters in the book address the military justice system's performance in various combat operations including Vietnam, Operation Urgent Fury, and Operation Just Cause.

2. In 1984, a Wartime Legislation Team appointed by The Judge Advocate General of the Army assessed whether the military justice system could operate fairly and efficiently during combat operations. *See generally* Lt. Col. E.A. Gates & Maj. Gary V. Casida, *Report to the Judge Advocate General by the Wartime Legislation Team*, 104 MIL. L. REV. 139 (1984). The Team concluded that "although the current system will work with reasonable efficiency during a short, low intensity conflict, several changes are necessary in order to be confident that the system will operate effectively during a general war." *Id.* at 169. The Team proposed a number of military justice reforms, some of which — including court-martial jurisdiction over civilian contractors in combat zones — have been enacted. *See id.* at 147-49; *see also* John Warner National

Defense Authorization Act of 2007, Pub. L. No. 109-364, § 552, 120 Stat. 2217 (2006) (to be codified at 10 U.S.C. § 802(a)(10)).

UNITED STATES v. FINSEL
United States Army Court of Military Review
33 M.J. 739 (A.C.M.R. 1991)

GRAVELLE, JUDGE.

I.

This case arose during military operations in the Republic of Panama, during Operation Just Cause. The evidence at trial showed that the appellant, a light infantry squad leader, deployed with the 7th Infantry Division on 19 December 1989. On the evening of 25 January 1990, his company was located in a business-residential area of Panama City. The appellant and two soldiers were drinking alcoholic beverages in the company area. The appellant suggested they find a brothel for more drinking and an evening of pleasure, despite a no-drinking order issued by the brigade commander and despite an order from the company commander not to leave the company command post area without proper authorization. In order to leave the area, the appellant falsely represented to the platoon sergeant that they were going to a nearby McDonalds restaurant for some food. Having obtained his permission, they instead went to a bar down the street from the company headquarters. They took their weapons with them. The appellant was armed with both an M-16 rifle and a 9mm pistol. [The pistol was the company commander's assigned weapon. Several days prior to the incident, the appellant had been engaged in building clearing operations. Because a pistol was a better weapon in close quarters, the commander had loaned his pistol to the appellant.] At the bar, the appellant ordered a beer and got into a discussion with two Panamanian men. During the discussion, the appellant took the pistol from his holster and placed it on the table in front of himself and the two men. Shortly thereafter, a disturbance arose and the appellant left the table to investigate. When he returned, the pistol and the two Panamanians were gone. A frantic search of the area ensued. When the search proved fruitless, the appellant devised a plan to cover up the loss of the pistol by staging a "firefight." He discussed his plan with one of his two companions. All three went outside and began shooting into the air; shouting that they were being fired upon. [The task force commander had previously published a letter which, in effect, modified the rules of engagement. The letter forbade the chambering of ammunition and the firing of weapons except under specific limited conditions.] A reaction force from their infantry company came to their rescue. A short time later, the appellant began firing wildly at a three-story building, claiming he had seen some men on the roof firing at him. To several of his fellow noncommissioned officers, the appellant appeared to be slurring his words and was "freaked out" or drunk. During this second round of gunfire, a Panamanian woman was fatally wounded by another soldier. A search of the three-story building and the surrounding area revealed no evidence whatsoever of hostile Panamanians or of hostile gunfire, although a number of soldiers and Panamanian witnesses believed they were under hostile fire. The violation of orders, loss of the firearm, and the subsequent coverup led to the charges and the appellant's conviction. . . .

III.

The appellant . . . was convicted of failing to obey a lawful general order of Major General Cavezza, "to wit: to not chamber rounds in his weapon unless necessary for self-defense or the protection of others, by wrongfully chambering rounds in his weapon," in violation of Article 92, UCMJ. The appellant asserts that the evidence is legally insufficient to sustain the finding of guilty of violating a general order under Article 92(1), UCMJ, because there was no evidence that the rules violated were a general order or were punitive.

Under Article 92(1), UCMJ, an order is a general order if generally applicable to the command of the officer issuing it, and if it is issued by:

(1) an officer having general court-martial jurisdiction;

(2) a general or flag officer in command; or

(3) a commander superior to (1) or (2).

Manual for Courts-Martial, United States, 1984, Part IV, para. 16c(1)(a).

The order shows that Major General Cavezza was a general officer in command of Joint Task Force — Panama. Moreover, the court-martial convening order in this case shows that General Cavezza, in his capacity as Commander of the 7th Infantry Division, was a general court-martial convening authority. We hold that he had authority to issue a general order and that the order was in fact a general order. But that does not end our inquiry. We must also determine if the general order had a punitive effect.

To guide us in making this determination, the Court of Military Appeals has set the following standard:

> No single characteristic of a general order determines whether it applies punitively to members of a command. This Court's decisions have established general standards that such an order must meet before a member of the armed forces without actual notice of its provisions can be punished for violating it. The order in its entirety must demonstrate that rather than providing general guidelines for the conduct of military functions it is basically intended to regulate conduct of individual members and that its direct application of sanctions for its violation is self-evident. *United States v. Hogsett*, 8 U.S.C.M.A. 861, 25 C.M.R. 185 (1958); *United States v. Baker*, 18 U.S.C.M.A. 504, 40 C.M.R. 216 (1969); *cf. United States v. Benway*, 19 U.S.C.M.A. 345, 41 C.M.R. 345 (1970). If the order requires implementation by subordinate commanders to give it effect as a code of conduct, it will not qualify as a general order for the purpose of an Article 92 prosecution. *United States v. Tassos*, 18 U.S.C.M.A. 12, 39 C.M.R. 12 (1968), and *United States v. Woodrum*, 20 U.S.C.M.A. 529, 43 C.M.R. 369 (1971).

United States v. Nardell, 45 C.M.R. 101, 103 (C.M.A. 1972) (footnote omitted). . . . With this yardstick, we will measure the punitive effect of the division commander's directive, which is attached as an appendix to this opinion.

The task force commander's letter is titled "Weapons Safety." Despite using the term "guidelines" twice, the letter clearly establishes rules regulating individual conduct. No implementation by subordinate commanders was required to give it effect. All that was required of subordinate commanders was dissemination. [The appellant's company commander perceived the letter as an order and had each of his platoon sergeants read it to their platoons. The appellant's platoon sergeant testified that he read the letter to his platoon with the appellant present.] The letter was in clear and unambiguous "thou shalt not" terms directed to all members of the command. Its meaning is sufficiently lucid to put all members of the command on notice of specific rules of conduct applicable to each member relating to loading and discharge of firearms. We are satisfied that, under the circumstances, the task force commander's letter is directory in nature, and that the appellant's violation of its clear terms is subject to punitive sanctions.

We note that the letter was published under wartime conditions. While some specific references in the letter to the punitive articles of the Uniform Code of Military Justice and to the consequences for violating the order would have been useful, no such warning is required even in peacetime to qualify it as a punitive general order. We certainly will not require such language in wartime. We hold that the evidence is legally and factually sufficient to support the appellant's conviction for violation of its terms. . . .

Appendix

Headquarters, Joint Task Force — Panama, Fort Clayton, Panama

JTF-PM CO (340d)

January 19, 1990

MEMORANDUM FOR ALL SUBORDINATE COMMANDERS

SUBJECT: Weapons Safety

1. Recent accidental discharges of weapons, one of which resulted in a soldier's death, makes it imperative for me to establish the following guidelines:

   a. No one is authorized to maintain a clip in their pistol, a magazine in their rifle (M-16 or AR 203), or a belt of ammunition linked to the feed tray of a M-240 SAW, M-60 MG, or Cal. 50 MG, unless so directed by a commander at the colonel level or higher.

   b. Clips will be placed in pistols, magazines will be placed in rifles, and ammunition belts attached to feed trays only when required by operational necessity, e.g., the knowledge that criminal or enemy contact is probable.

   c. Under no circumstances will U.S. Army forces be authorized to chamber a round of ammunition unless enemy and/or criminal contact is imminent. Even then, the weapon will remain on safe until visual sighting of the target has been made.

   d. Only commanders in the rank of colonel can authorize fragmentation grenades to be carried, and then operational necessity must clearly warrant the carrying and use of those indiscriminate weapons. All fragmentation grenades will be turned in to the ASP and drawn only when colonel-level commanders so direct.

2. These drastic measures are being taken to ensure that we safeguard lives, both U.S. and Panamanian. Our casualties during the last two weeks have all been self-inflicted. This must stop!

3. Commanders at every level must take immediate action to disseminate these guidelines. My intent is simple. I want no one killed or wounded as the result of an accidental discharge of a weapon. I expect everyone's full support.

/s/

CARMEN J. CAVEZZA, Major General
U.S. Army, Commanding General

UNITED STATES v. MANGINELL
United States Air Force Court of Military Review
32 M.J. 891 (A.F.C.M.R. 1991)

Per Curiam

The uncommon crime of looting is at the nub of this appeal. We affirm.

Operation Just Cause

Airman First Class Manginell was a security policeman at Norton Air Force Base, California. He was selected for temporary duty during Operation Just Cause, a military expedition in Panama against hostile forces loyal to General Manuel Noriega.

Manginell was assigned to guard the captured Tocumen International Airport in Panama City. General Noriega's troops in the area continued to resist.

While serving as a night guard to secure a warehouse at Tocumen airport, Manginell appropriated a camera and four watches.

At trial, Manginell pleaded guilty to two specifications of looting under Article 103, UCMJ. The prosecution prepared a detailed brief supporting the providence of Manginell's guilty pleas to looting. After completing his inquiry, the military judge found Manginell guilty in accordance with his pleas.

Before us, Manginell argues that looting requires a taking accompanied by force or violence. Since that requirement was missing here, he insists that his conviction must fall.

Historical Analysis

Looting is a military offense rooted deeply in both the law of chivalry and the law of war. Winthrop calls particular attention to a clearcut prohibition of looting in Article of War XXV of King James II in 1688. His famous treatise also notes American milestones: (1) Brigadier General Wayne's 1779 capture of Stoney Point — Congress approved the division of captured military stores among "the gallant troops;" (2) 1864 Civil War rewards to militiamen dispersing "bushwhackers" — watches and arms were viewed as trophies; and (3) a long history of prize payments in the United States Navy. *See* Winthrop, *Military Law and Precedents* (1920 ed.) 557; *see also* Dudley, *Military Law and the Procedure of Courts-Martial* (1915) 333-334.

In the 1921 and 1928 Manuals for Courts-Martial, looting and similar conduct was punishable under Articles of War 79 and 80. Research reveals few cases under those articles. Among them is an opinion crucial to our analysis, *United States v. Ruppel*, 61 Bd. Rev. 291, 306 (1946). The Board of Review assessed misconduct of an officer in post-war Austria. Reasoning in part from the laws of war, the Board commented that neither force nor violence was necessary to convict of looting.

Good arguments can be made that the *Ruppel* analysis is dicta. Such arguments are academic in light of what occurred next. In the 1951 Manual for Courts-Martial, looting was prohibited by Article 103, a hybrid of old Articles of War 79 and 80. *Ruppel* is specifically cited in the legislative history for the proposition that looting need not necessarily be accompanied by force or violence. *See* Legal and Legislative Basis, Manual for Courts-Martial 1951, 262.

Despite that language, a 1950's Air Force benchbook listed "force or violence" as a necessary predicate to prove looting. *See* Court-Martial Instruction Drafting Guide, Department of the Air Force, Article 103. By 1971, however, "force or violence" was neither listed as an element nor defined. *See* Air Force Manual 111-2, Court-Martial Instructions Guide, Instruction 3-59 (16 October 1971).

In contrast, the Army apparently continued to find force or violence an indispensable requirement. *See, e.g.*, DA Pam 27-9, Military Judges' Guide, Instruction 4-59 (May 1969). That situation remains virtually unchanged in the current Army iteration. *See* DA Pam 27-9, Military Judges' Benchbook, Instruction 3-59 (May 1982). The Army Benchbook "may be used as a procedure guide" for Air Force courts-martial. Air Force Regulation 111-1, Military Justice Guide, para. 12-3 (30 September 1988).

The 1984 Manual for Courts-Martial fails to mention "force or violence" as either an element or part of the definition of looting. Since 1951, a handful of modern courts-martial have included looting as an incidental offense among others but there has been no solid analysis of that crime.

The Manual lists three elements for the sort of looting alleged here: (a) that the accused engaged in the act by unlawfully seizing or appropriating certain property, public or private; (b) that it was located in enemy or occupied territory; and (c) that it was left behind or owned by the enemy, an occupied state, an inhabitant of the occupied state, or the like. *See* MCM, Part IV, para. 27b(4) (1984).

Holding

We hold that the appellant was properly convicted of looting. The current Manual for Courts-Martial lists three elements for this crime. They are found here. The definition of "looting," to mean unlawfully seizing property by force or violence as contained in the Military Judges' Benchbook, need not be followed; the Benchbook is not mandatory for Air Force trials. Freed of that consideration, we may accept the analysis offered in *Ruppel* and adopted by those who created the new Article 103. *See* Legal and Legislative Basis, Manual for Courts-Martial 1951, 262. In addition, the term "looting" is clearly defined at MCM, Part IV para. 27(4)c(4) as "unlawfully seizing or appropriating property." It was further defined for purposes of this case in the trial counsel's brief written to show the propriety of accepting the guilty plea: "to carry off as loot or booty."

We thus view this appellant's guilty plea to looting as intelligent and knowing. He had no quarrel with the Government's definition of the crime, which we find correct.[1]

The approved sentence is a bad conduct discharge, six months confinement, forfeiture of $400.00 per month for six months, and reduction to airman basic. In addition to taking the camera and watches, Manginell was also found guilty (in accord with his pleas) of larceny of a California vehicle registration sticker and a minor dereliction of duty. We think the sentence entirely appropriate . . . perhaps even generous.[2]

The findings of guilty and the sentence are correct in law and fact and, upon the basis of the entire record, are AFFIRMED.

SENIOR JUDGE KASTL (dubitante):

While we affirm, I am not particularly pacific about the ultimate fairness of the result. Yes, Manginell is technically guilty; but I hold considerable reservations about the situation: I say the "wide-open" Air Force definition of looting fails to distinguish between: (a) minor misconduct such as taking a watch or an enemy handgun as a war trophy; and (b) serious crime, such as an unprincipled use of force or violence so outrageous that it merits a possible maximum sentence of life imprisonment.

The decision to prosecute this case as looting fails to rest on a rational standard which separates the serious from the everyday offense. The prosecution convinced the military judge to depart from the Air Force's usual reliance on DA Pam 27-9, Military Judges' Benchbook. Instead, the prosecutor turned to the Manual for Courts-Martial discussion. That omits the requirement for "force and violence."

To my mind, such an approach offers the convening authority unlimited discretion to charge larceny or looting. Without articulable standards, it thus leaves to caprice whether one particular accused will face five years and another a life sentence.

One might respond that several areas of the law give the Government an election — e.g., assault and aggravated assault; or various degrees of homicide. But such examples are grounded in objective degrees of culpability, mea-

---

[1] [n. 4] We have no particular concern with the concept of "time of war" vis-a-vis the Panamanian expedition. See MCM, App 21, Rule 103, A21-5 to 21-6 (1984).

[2] [n. 5] The final prosecution sentencing argument cautioned that the people of Central America were looking to United States combatants to perform honorably. We will presume this argument impermissible under *United States v. Cook*, 11 U.S.C.M.A. 99, 28 C.M.R. 323 (1959) and *United States v. Mamaluy*, 10 U.S.C.M.A. 102, 27 C.M.R. 176 (1959). We also presume that the military judge knew and followed the law. *United States v. Harper*, 22 M.J. 157, 164 (C.M.A. 1986). Even if we were to find error, we would view it as harmless in view of the light sentence approved.

sured by relatively clearcut standards. In contrast, the difference between larceny and looting — if the prosecution argument is correct — is quixotic.

In sum, I think the prosecution's theory sets too low a standard for the Air Force — virtually every appropriation where one can postulate an "enemy" lurking somewhere in the vicinity creates the opportunity to charge looting, with its possible lifetime sentence. Here is a shapeless legal concept which fails to distinguish between the truly egregious and the routine.

I would make three further points:

1. We have decided at least three other cases in recent months concerning security policemen who stole while acting as guards during Operation Just Cause. Specific citations are unnecessary; the point is that all the others passed muster as simple larcenies of private property. I see nothing to distinguish today's case as factually more serious. What logical reason is there to treat similar accuseds in a dissimilar fashion?

2. At the end of the day, a court-martial order should reflect precisely what an accused did, not distort the record. *See United States v. Blucker*, 30 M.J. 690, 691 (A.C.M.R. 1990). Here, others involved with larceny during Operation Just Cause will receive a court-martial order showing they were thieves. Manginell will have an order to inform potential employers that he was guilty of something akin to a war crime. His conduct differs little from the other airmen . . . but his record now is facially far more reprehensible.

3. While Manginell's conduct adds up to "looting" in the Air Force, the definition is chameleonic. In the next contested case, what should a careful military judge do if the accused pleads not guilty and requires the Government to define "looting?" Is the Manual definition all encompassing? Why is the standard different between the Army and the Air Force?

The Bouvier, Ballentine, and Black legal dictionaries contain no definition of "looting." Neither is there useful analysis in American Jurisprudence or Corpus Juris Secundum. We have used the word as a noun, to mean "ill-gotten gains." *See United States v. Weems*, 13 M.J. 609, 610 (A.F.C.M.R. 1981).

Civilian courts often use the word "looting" as a synonym for "larceny." *See Miller v. Alabama*, 405 So.2d 41 (1981); *Arizona v. Gunter*, 100 Ariz. 356, 414 P.2d 734 (1966). Sometimes, it envisions "civil disorder" or vandalism, as in *Shankles v. Costa Armatori*, 722 F.2d 861, 863 (1st Cir. 1983). Still other times, "looting" is taken to mean action occurring during a tumult or riot. *See YMCA v. United States*, 395 U.S. 85, 89 S. Ct. 1511, 23 L. Ed. 2d 117 (1960) (rioting and looting during a prior United States expedition in Panama); Annot., 39 A.L.R. 4th 1170 (1985). Finally, the word sometimes suggests a completely different concept —"insider" skimming of a corporation. *See United States v. Feldman*, 853 F.2d 648 (9th Cir. 1988).[3]

---

[3] [n2] This semantic morass does not technically bar Manginell's conviction. Here, everyone conceded what the word "looting" meant, and the appellant pleaded guilty to that offense.

To repeat for emphasis, it seems irrational that Army and Air Force warriors engaging together in combat operations should be judged by different standards for the same wrongdoing. I suggest that the Code Committee established under Article 67(g), UCMJ reexamine Article 103 and the Manual with an eye to refining for all the definition of "looting." The legislative history is thin. *Ruppel* is scant authority, and I surmise there has been little modern thought to this subject.

NOTE

In a case of a soldier who kept an AK 47 assault rifle that he found in a bunker in Iraq during Operation Desert Storm, the Army Court of Military Review followed *Manginell's* holding that the use of "force and violence" is not a necessary element of looting. *United States v. Mello*, 36 M.J. 1067 (A.C.M.R. 1993). The Army Court, however, also "share[d]" Judge Kastl's "reservations concerning the breadth of the present definition of 'looting,' and concur[ed] in his suggestion that the Code Committee established under Article 146, UCMJ, examine this aspect of Article 103." *Id.* at 1068 n.4.

III. PEACEKEEPING OPERATIONS

A. International Law and Domestic Military Law

UNITED STATES v. ROCKWOOD
United States Army Court of Criminal Appeals
48 M.J. 501 (A. C. C. A. 1998)

CARTER, JUDGE:

On 31 July 1994, the United Nations (U.N.) Security Council determined that the situation in Haiti was a threat to the peace and security of the region. Acting under Chapter VII of the Charter of the United Nations, the Security Council authorized U.N. Member States to form a multinational task force (MNF) "to use all necessary means to facilitate the departure from Haiti of the military leadership, . . . the prompt return of the legitimately elected President [President Aristide] and the restoration of the legitimate authorities of the Government of Haiti, and to establish and maintain a secure and stable environment. . . ." United Nations Security Council Resolution 940, U.N. SCOR, 3413 mtg. (1994) [hereinafter U.N. S.C. Res. 940].

On 19 September 1994, with a MNF invasion of Haiti imminent, a team led by former President Carter negotiated an agreement with the ruling military government in Haiti which permitted the peaceful entry into Haiti of a MNF to accomplish the aims of U.N. S.C. Res. 940. Elements of the 10th Mountain Division immediately began deploying into Haiti on 19 September 1994 as part of Joint Task Force (JTF) 190. The Haitian military government was to remain in place until the agreed return of President Aristide's government on 15 October 1994.

Appellant was a counter intelligence officer with the 10th Mountain Division's Office of the Assistant Chief of Staff for Intelligence (G2). He deployed to Haiti on 23 September 1994. Appellant was personally concerned about intelligence reports which reflected deplorable conditions at the National Penitentiary in Port au Prince. He attempted to initiate a JTF inspection of the National Penitentiary by raising the issue with his superiors on the joint intelligence staff, a captain in the staff judge advocate's office, and the division chaplain. Appellant considered the JTF's inaction toward the National Penitentiary to be contrary to . . . the JTF's obligation under international law to protect human rights.

On 29 September 1994, a grenade attack near the Haitian Presidential Palace killed several Aristide supporters and injured many others. As a result of this attack, Major General (MG) Meade (the 10th Mountain Division commander and the general court-martial convening authority who referred these charges to trial) increased operational and counter intelligence efforts to identify the attackers and to safeguard American forces.

Appellant disagreed with the decision to increase operational security instead of immediately inspecting the National Penitentiary. On the morning of 30 September 1994, he filed a formal complaint with the 10th Mountain Division Inspector General (IG) requesting that the IG "inform the commanding general as soon as possible of facts that may lend the appearance that the JTF is indifferent to probable ongoing human rights violations in PAP [Port au Prince, or National] Penitentiary." . . .

Later that day, appellant decided, without command authorization, to "inspect" the National Penitentiary. Appellant did not go to his appointed place of duty when his shift began that evening because he had gone to the prison without authority. . . .

Appellant asserts that his otherwise criminal acts were justified because . . . he had an affirmative, individual duty under international law to act as he did. . . .

International Law

Appellant contends that the MNF, and hence the United States, became "an occupying power" under international law and thereby assumed control of, and legal responsibility for, the National Penitentiary. He argues that, notwithstanding the permissive nature of the entry of the MNF, the entry was secured under threat of invasion, and therefore duress, so that the rules of occupation should apply.

Whether the MNF and its constituent elements were occupying powers is, in large measure, a nonjusticiable political question. *See generally Gilligan v. Morgan*, 413 U.S. 1, (1973) (review of Ohio National Guard "Use of Force" rules was nonjusticiable); *Oetjen v. Central Leather Co.*, 246 U.S. 297, 301, (1918) (conduct of foreign relations not subject to judicial review); *United States v. Palmer*, 16 U.S. (3 Wheat) 610, (1818) (whether warships of a foreign country engaged in a civil war committed piracy against U.S. vessels on the high seas was a political question). The legality of the employment of military forces is not reviewable by the judiciary. . . .

On matters concerning military operations, courts should defer to the judgments and actions of the President and commanders in the field, at least in the absence of overwhelming facts to the contrary. . . . In this case, the Haitian military government remained in power, the division of responsibilities between it and the MNF was ambiguous, and the degree of control exercised by the MNF was far from absolute. Under these circumstances, this record does not establish a sufficient factual basis to conclude that U.S. forces "occupied" the National Penitentiary.

Even assuming the MNF did constitute an "occupying power," such status imposed no individual legal duty upon appellant to act. Appellant claims that he had a personal legal duty, as a member of the U.S. forces, to prevent human rights violations because he was aware of information which strongly suggested that inhumane conditions existed at the National Penitentiary. Appellant's amorphous argument asserts he would be criminally liable under *In re Yamashita*, 327 U.S. (1946), a "Nuremberg defense," . . . and international law generally, . . . if he failed to act.

Appellant's reliance on General Yamashita's case is misplaced. The legal issue in the prosecution of General Yamashita for war crimes after World War II was

> whether the law of war imposes on an army commander a duty to take such appropriate measures as are within his power to control the troops under his command for the prevention of the specified acts which are violations of the law of war and which are likely to attend the occupation of hostile territory by an uncontrolled soldiery, and whether he may be charged with personal responsibility for his failure to take such measures when violations result.

Yamashita, 327 U.S. at 14-15. General Yamashita was convicted for failing to do his duty to prevent illegal acts that he knew, or should have known, were committed by persons under his command in violation of the law of war. Appellant had no command authority and no one under his control was committing war crimes at the National Penitentiary.

Appellant's purported criminal liability under a "Nuremberg defense" for failing to act is similarly misguided. The Eleventh Circuit, U.S. Court of Appeals, previously rejected this same argument in a prosecution for pouring blood on nuclear missile launchers.

> Defendants here misperceive the persons for whom such a Nuremberg "defense" is appropriate. There the German defendants were in positions which required them to participate in sentencing dissidents to death or in utilizing slave labor because domestic law or superior authority ordered them to do so (citations omitted). The question is whether what they were required to do by domestic law could escape international criminal proscription. The War Crimes Tribunal ruled, however, that in certain circumstances those defendants were charged with a duty not to act in accordance with domestic law to avoid liability under international law. *Defendants in the case before us stand this doctrine on its head in arguing that a person charged*

*with no duty or responsibility by domestic law may voluntarily violate
a criminal law and claim that violation was required to avoid liability
under international law. The domestic law simply did not require
defendants to do anything that could even arguably be criminal under
international law* (emphasis added).

United States v. Montgomery, 772 F.2d 733, 737-38 (11th Cir. 1985). . . .

Appellant cites no case, and we can find none, where a servicemember was
convicted of a war crime for failing to act under facts similar to this case. . . .
Any duty appellant may have had was discharged when he reported the
prison conditions to his superiors. Their failure to act, even assuming they
were required to do so and that their inaction was criminal, could hardly render appellant criminally liable. We hold as a matter of law that appellant had
no personal legal duty to inspect the National Penitentiary to avoid criminal
liability under international law.

NOTES

1. Professor Peter Rowe offers this analysis of the *Rockwood* case and its
implications for other peacekeeping operations:

> [Captain Rockwood's] request to investigate the conditions in the pen-
> itentiary had been expressly rejected by his superior officers. He may
> have been unsure what the mission of the US forces in Haiti was but
> he was able to approach his military superiors with his concerns.
> Other soldiers may not have the same opportunities before acting or
> not acting, or they may witness serious war crimes being committed
> against civilians taking no part in the conflict. There is a difference in
> the legal systems of many countries between being provided with a
> legal justification for acting and failing to act at all. It is therefore
> important to define clearly a soldier's duty in a peace support opera-
> tion, since it is quite unlike his duty when he is engaged in an inter-
> national armed conflict, where he may use proportionate force against
> enemy combatants and military objectives.

Peter Rowe, *Maintaining Discipline in United Nations Peace Support
Operations: The Legal Quagmire for Military Contingents*, 5 J. CONFLICT &
SEC. L. 45, 49 (2000).

2. Professor Rowe asks: Is a soldier required, as a matter of military duty,
"to intervene to prevent serious breaches of international humanitarian law"?
If so, under what circumstances and at what risk to the soldier and others?

3. For further discussion of the *Yamashita* standard and the Nuremberg
defense, see Chapter 9, § II, *supra*.

B. Constitutional Challenges to Disobedience of Domestic Military Law

UNITED STATES v. NEW
United States Court of Appeals for the Armed Forces
55 M.J. 95 (C.A.A.F.)

CHIEF JUDGE CRAWFORD delivered the opinion of the Court. . . .

In 1992, the UN established a Protective Force (UNPROFOR) in the Former Yugoslavian Republic of Macedonia (FYROM). The United States contributed troops to this force in 1993 and, in 1995, this force was redesignated as the UN Preventive Deployment Force (UNPREDEP).

In August of 1995, 1st Battalion, 15th Infantry Regiment, 3d Infantry Division (1/15 Infantry) was ordered to assume the [Former Yugoslavian Republic of Macedonia (FYROM)] UNPREDEP mission as of November 1, 1995. Appellant, a medic, was attached to a squad of Company A, 1/15 Infantry. Appellant expressed concern about wearing the UN accoutrements on his U.S. uniform. . . . Specifically, uniform modifications included in part the UN blue beret and field cap, a UN blue shoulder patch, blue scarf, and UN badge and identification card to be issued in the FYROM. [Appellant later disobeyed an order to wear the UN accoutrements with his uniform.] . . .

Issue III, Legality of the Order

Appellant argues that (1) the UN insignia violates Army uniform regulations (AR 670-1) by transferring his allegiance to the United Nations, . . . and (2) the order stems from an illegal deployment of the Armed Forces because President Clinton misrepresented the nature of the deployment to Congress and failed to comply with the United Nations Participation Act [UNPA]. . . . These arguments fail because they would unacceptably substitute appellant's personal judgment of the legality of an order for that of his superiors and the Federal Government.

The Supreme Court has recognized the importance of the military mission over the beliefs of the individual soldier on the specific issue of uniform requirements. The Court held that Air Force regulations that prohibited wearing a yarmulke are not prohibited by the First Amendment, "even though their effect is to restrict the wearing of the headgear required by his religious beliefs." *Goldman v. Weinberger*, 475 U.S. 503, 510 (1986). The Court reasoned that "the desirability of dress regulations in the military is decided by the appropriate military officials, and they are under no constitutional mandate to abandon their considered professional judgment." *Id.* at 509. The Court stated:

> The considered professional judgment of the Air Force is that the traditional outfitting of personnel in standardized uniforms encourages the subordination of personal preferences and identities in favor of the overall group mission. Uniforms encourage a sense of hierarchical unity. . . . The Air Force considers them as vital . . . because its person-

nel must be ready to provide an effective defense on a moment's notice; the necessary habits of discipline and unity must be developed in advance of trouble.

Id. at 508. Based on this reasoning, we conclude that uniform requirements are considered essential to the military mission for the purpose of determining lawfulness.

Although the *Goldman* decision was overtaken by statute, 10 USC § 774, which now permits wearing religious apparel under certain conditions, its reasoning on uniform requirements is still sound. If uniform requirements relate to military duty, then an order to comply with a uniform requirement meets the "military duty" test set forth in paragraph 14c(2)(a)(iii). . . .

It is not a defense for appellant to claim that the order is illegal based on his interpretation of applicable law. An order is presumed to be lawful and the defense has the burden to prove illegality unless the order is "palpably illegal on its face." *United States v. Kapla*, 22 C.M.R. 825, 827 (AFBR 1956) *quoting* Winthrop's *Military Law and Precedents* 585-76 (2d ed. 1920 Reprint). This does not, however, allow a soldier to disobey an order because he believes it to be palpably illegal. A case remarkably similar to this one is *United States v. Wilson*, 19 U.S.C.M.A. 100, 41 C.M.R. 100 (1969). Private Wilson was denied conscientious-objector status and, after an unauthorized absence, wrote a statement explaining, in part, "I will refuse to wear the uniform of a soldier ever again. I am doing this out of my deeply felt convictions. . . and because the Army has given me no other alternative." 19 U.S.C.M.A. at 100-101, 41 C.M.R. at 100-01. When he later refused to obey an order to wear his uniform, he was charged with willful disobedience. This Court upheld an instruction that personal scruples were not a defense. Citing *United States v. Noyd*, [18 C.M.A. 483, 40 C.M.R. 195 (1969),] the Court in *Wilson* reasoned that personal beliefs could not justify or excuse disobedience by a soldier of a lawful order.

> His position is like that of the civilian whose religion or conscience is in conflict with lawful orders of the Government. . . . To allow scruples of personal conscience to override the lawful command of constituted authority would "in effect . . . permit every citizen to become a law unto himself." *Reynolds v. United States*, 98 U.S. 145, 167, 25 L. Ed. 244 (1879). As *Noyd* indicated, the freedom to think and believe does not excuse intentional conduct that violates a lawful command.

19 U.S.C.M.A. at 101, 41 C.M.R. at 101. The Court in *Noyd* also noted that allowing private judgment by a soldier as to which orders to obey would be "unthinkable and unworkable," and would mean that "the military need for his services must be compromised." 18 U.S.C.M.A. 491, 40 C.M.R. at 203. Appellant's arguments are essentially the same ones that were made there, and they should be rejected on the same basis. . . .

Issue IV, Application of the Political Question Doctrine

The Supreme Court has long recognized the principle of "nonjusticiability": meaning that courts of law should decline to exercise their authority to decide matters where judicial intervention is deemed inappropriate. Based upon the Constitutional principle of separation of powers in the three branches of

Government, judicial review of "a political question" is precluded where the Court finds one or more of the following:

> a textually demonstrable constitutional commitment of the issue to a coordinate political department; or a lack of judicially discoverable and manageable standards for resolving it; or the impossibility of deciding without an initial policy determination of a kind clearly for nonjudicial discretion; or the impossibility of a court's undertaking independent resolution without expressing lack of the respect due coordinate branches of government; or an unusual need for unquestioning adherence to a political decision already made; or the potentiality of embarrassment from multifarious pronouncements by various departments on one question.

Baker v. Carr, 369 U.S. 186, 217, 218 (1962); *see also Flast v. Cohen*, 392 U.S. 83, 95 (1968).

The Constitution assigns specific military responsibilities to the Executive and Legislative branches of the Government. The President is Commander-in-Chief of the Armed Forces, . . . but Congress has the power to declare war and to organize, arm, and govern the military. . . .

While the military judge determined that the order to wear the U.N. insignia was lawful, he properly declined to rule on the constitutionality of the President's decision to deploy the Armed Forces in FYROM as a nonjusticiable political question. Courts have consistently refused to consider the issue of the President's use of the Armed Forces. Two recent examples from the Persian Gulf War era are *Ange v. Bush*, 752 F. Supp. 509 (D.D.C. 1990), and *United States v. Huet-Vaughn*, 43 M.J. 105 (1995). In the *Ange* case, the District Court declined to rule on the legality of deployment of troops in the Persian Gulf despite inconsistent views of Congress and the President. . . . In *Huet-Vaughn*, we reaffirmed the idea that personal belief that an order is unlawful cannot be a defense to a disobedience charge, holding: "The duty to disobey an unlawful order applies only to a positive act that constitutes a crime that is so manifestly beyond the legal power or discretion of the commander as to admit of no rational doubt of their unlawfulness." 43 M.J. at 114 (internal quotation marks omitted). The Court further upheld the military judge's decision not to consider evidence relating to the legality of the decision to deploy the Armed Forces. 43 M.J. at 115.

The basic nature of the separation-of-powers issue was also discussed in a Vietnam-era case where soldiers disobeyed an order to board a sedan for further transportation to Vietnam on the grounds that American involvement there was itself illegal. *United States v. Johnson*, 17 U.S.C.M.A. 246, 247, 38 C.M.R. 44, 45 (1967). This Court noted that the Supreme Court refused to consider challenges to the President's use of the armed forces abroad. In addition, the Court distinguished *Youngstown Sheet and Tube Co. v. Sawyer*, 343 U.S. 579 (1952), since it involved use of military power in a purely domestic dispute. The Court noted Justice Jackson's concurrence in *Youngstown Sheet and Tube Co.*, where he stated: "I should indulge the widest latitude of interpretation to sustain [the President's] exclusive function to command the instruments of national force, at least when turned against the outside world for the security of our society." 343 U.S. at 645.

Under these standards, we hold that this question qualifies as a nonjusticiable political question.

NOTE

Following the completion of his direct appeal, New sought relief from the United States District Court of the District of Columbia. That court "dismissed the petition, finding that each of New's challenges fell outside the scope of collateral review, raised a nonjusticiable political question, or lacked merit as a matter of law. *United States ex rel. New v. Rumsfeld*, 350 F. Supp. 2d 80, 102 (D.D.C. 2004)." *United States ex rel. New v. Rumsfeld*, 448 F.3d 403 (D.C. Cir. 2006). The United States Court of Appeals for the District of Columbia Circuit affirmed the dismissal of the petition. *Id.* The Supreme Court denied certiorari. *New v. Gater* 127 S. Ct. 2096 (2007).

C. Peacekeeping and Military Justice Reform

R. v. LIEUTENANT-COLONEL JOSEPH CAROL ARISTIDE MATHIEU
Court Martial Appeal Court of Canada
CMAC-379, 5 C.M.A.R. 363 (1995)

This is an appeal by the prosecution from a decision of a General Court Martial acquitting the accused of a charge of negligently performing his military duty contrary to section 124 of the National Defense Act [R.S.C. 1985, c. N-5].

The accused was the commanding officer of the Canadian Airborne Regiment Battle Group in Somalia. At the very end of 1992, the Regiment was sent to Somalia to take part in an operation known as Operation Deliverance. The purpose of the operation was to secure the humanitarian aid zone of Belet Huen by means of a military force. This mission involved liberating the zone from the bandits and militias that were occupying it, protecting humanitarian aid convoys, protecting food distribution sites and helping to restore a normal life. The Canadian Forces participated in Operation Deliverance in co-operation with forces from other countries, including the United States. The purpose of the operation was to establish a peaceful environment by force so that the humanitarian organizations could do their work: it was not a traditional peacekeeping operation. . . .

When the Canadian Forces arrived in Belet Huen, the situation was chaotic and dangerous. There was no civil government in place. The position of the Canadian Forces was made perilous by the presence of a number of well-armed militias and technicals (armoured trucks). The main Canadian camp at Belet Huen was set up five kilometers from the town. It was an area of about five hundred metres square surrounded by a perimeter made of rolls of barbed wire. . . . Despite these precautions, however, attempts to infiltrate the

Canadian camps were made, especially by young Somali adults and teenagers, generally unarmed, who slipped under the barbed wire. There were several thefts of soldiers' personal effects and other equipment, such as cans of diesel fuel, binoculars and a barrack box.

However, until the incidents that gave rise to the charge in the instant case, the evidence does not mention any theft of a firearm. Nor were the Canadian camps ever attacked by an armed force or militia. . . .

On January 28, 1993 the accused was very concerned about the security of his camp and the situation created by infiltrations and break-ins. He feared that weapons and ammunition would be stolen. At the meeting of the orders group, he spoke to his subordinates about the use of force against thieves and looters fleeing the camp. It is not clear from the evidence whether he gave an order, directive or authorization (the distinction seems of little importance in the circumstances) or whether it was necessary, before opening fire, to give verbal warnings and fire warning shots rather than simply shooting on sight. However, two things seem clear: the troops under his command could fire at a thief who was running away outside the perimeter as long as they were not certain that the thief was not carrying a firearm in his hands; and if they fired, they had to do so between the feet and the knees ("fire between the skirt and the flip-flops").

Two days later, the accused informed the local tribal kings and elders in the Belet Huen region that the Canadian Forces intended to fire on looters and thieves.

On March 4, 1993 a Somali man was killed by a patrol outside the camp in which the helicopters were kept. Shortly after this incident, the accused changed the position taken at the meeting of the orders group on January 28 and prohibited his troops from using deadly force against looters except where it could be positively ascertained that a thief was fleeing with a firearm in his hands.

The charge against the accused was laid under section 124 of the National Defence Act, which reads as follows:

> 124. Every person who negligently performs a military duty imposed on that person is guilty of an offence and on conviction is liable to dismissal with disgrace from Her Majesty's service or to less punishment.

The indictment was in the following terms:

NEGLIGENTLY PERFORMED A MILITARY DUTY IMPOSED ON HIM

> Particulars: In that, from on or about January 27, 1993 to about mid-March 1993, near Belet Huen in the Republic of Somalia, while he was the officer in command of the Canadian Airborne Regiment Battle Group, he did, by issuing an order to his subordinates to fire on looters/thieves of equipment fleeing Canadian camps, fail to comply with the Canadian rules of engagement issued for Operation Deliverance, even though it was his duty to do so.

The rules of engagement referred to in the indictment were issued under the authority of the Chief of Defence Staff and state that they "constitute orders to Commanders and Commanding Officers." . . .

[The rules of engagement give] the commanders and commanding officers . . . a large degree of discretion. However, [they made] clear that deadly force was to be used only with great care and that only minimum force could be used to repel attacks or threats by unarmed elements. . . .

Lieutenant-Colonel Mathieu is accused of . . . being negligent by failing to correctly observe the rules of engagement. He is thus accused of breaching the duty of care that the Act imposes on all soldiers responsible for performing a military duty. This duty of care is even more important where, as here, the soldier is authorized to use potentially deadly force and to endanger human life. Was the accused negligent in allowing his troops to open fire on looters so long as it had not been ascertained with certainty that they were unarmed?

Since this is a criminal offence, it is of course not sufficient for the prosecution to prove mere civil negligence, what must be shown is penal negligence.

The Crown's appeal in the case at bar principally concerns the directions that the Judge Advocate gave to the Court on the issue of negligence.

In his main closing address, the Judge Advocate gave two definitions of negligence. . . . [The first included the following:]

> To be punishable under this section, the negligence must be culpable. If the negligence is willful, that is, intentional, it is clearly culpable. If it results from an error in judgment made in good faith and does not involve a lack of zeal or a careless or intentional omission to take the appropriate measures, it is equally clear that it is irreproachable and cannot justify a conviction.

Later, just before summarizing the evidence for the benefit of the members of the Court, the Judge Advocate referred again to negligence in the following terms:

> The word "negligently" means that the accused either did or omitted to do something in a manner that would not have been adopted by a reasonably capable and careful officer of his rank in a similar position of responsibility in the service and in the same circumstances.

With respect, I must say that I consider these two definitions incompatible. In the first paragraph cited, the Judge Advocate seems to adopt the theory of subject negligence and open the door to a defence of good faith. However, the second passage is clearly based on an objective standard. It is impossible to reconcile the two texts, and the combination of the two must have confused the members of the Court. . . .

It is now clearly established that, for penal negligence offences, the applicable standard of liability is an objective standard based on the court's assessment of what a reasonable person would have done in the circumstances. Except where the accused claims incapacity, which is not the case here, this standard applies to establish both the *actus reus* and the *mens rea*. Since the standard is objective, it is the act itself that must be assessed; the actor's intention, will and alleged good faith are simply irrelevant. . . .

In my opinion, by espousing and particularly by restating the standard of subjective negligence, the Judge Advocate committed an error that vitiates the verdict and requires that a new trial be held. There was evidence in the record that would have permitted the Court to conclude that the accused had given an order to fire on unarmed thieves fleeing outside the perimeter of the camp. Even if the version of the evidence that is most favourable to the accused is accepted, that is, that it was an authorization rather than an order, that this authorization applied only where it could not be ascertained that the thief was unarmed and that it was necessary to give a verbal warning and fire a warning shot before opening fire, it would be possible for the Court Martial to conclude that the accused's conduct constituted a marked departure from the standard of care of a reasonably prudent person in the same circumstances. I repeat that the rules of engagement require great care before using potentially deadly force and that, like the general law, they prohibit the use of force other than minimum force to repel an unarmed attack . . . . Force that is capable of ending human lives should never be used unless truly necessary. The question that the Court had to ask was whether a reasonable person would have considered such force necessary in the circumstances. This question was never asked.

NOTES

1. At his retrial, Lieutenant-Colonel Mathieu was again acquitted. *See Airborne commander cleared a second time*; TORONTO STAR, Feb. 14, 1996, at A12.

2. A case like *R. v. Mathieu* could not have occurred in the United States. The Supreme Court has construed the Fifth Amendment's Double Jeopardy Clause to bar retrial on a charge that resulted in an acquittal, even if a legal error led to the acquittal. *Arizona v. Rumsey*, 467 U.S. 203, 211 (1984). Also, Article 44(a) of the Uniform Code of Military Justice provides, "No person may, without his consent, be tried a second time for the same offense." 10 U.S.C. § 844(a). In Canada, on the other hand, the Crown has the "right to appeal from an acquittal," but only on "questions of law." Bradley E. Berg, *The 1994 I.L.C. Draft Statute for an International Criminal Court: A Principled Appraisal of Jurisdictional Structure*, 28 CASE W. RES. J. INT'L L. 221, 252-53 (1996). A 1987 report indicated that most common law countries, including New Zealand, India, Ceylon, South Africa, and some Australian states, permit government appeals of acquittals. OFFICE OF LEGAL POLICY OF THE UNITED STATES DEP'T OF JUSTICE, REPORT TO THE ATTORNEY GENERAL: DOUBLE JEOPARDY AND GOVERNMENT APPEALS OF ACQUITTALS 50-53 (1987). The report also indicated that most civil law countries allow such appeals. *Id.* at 2, 53. But a more recent article by a Canadian lawyer maintains that "[i]n England and the majority of the other Commonwealth countries, the Crown is not able to appeal from an acquittal on any ground." Berg, *supra*, at 253.

R. v. BROWN
Court Martial Appeal Court of Canda
CMAC-372 (1995)

HUGESSEN J.A.:

The accused was a member of number 2 Commando, posted to peacekeeping duties near the town of Belet Huen in Somalia in the early months of 1993. By March 16, 1993, the Canadian Forces in Belet Huen had encountered a number of problems with Somalis, mostly young men, breaking into their compounds and stealing. As a result, orders were given for increased security and, in particular, on March 16, 1993, for patrols which would attempt to capture the infiltrators. There was evidence that such orders included a licence to "abuse" or "rough-up" prisoners, at least while in the process of capturing them. On the night of March 16, 1993, the appellant's section was assigned to guard and sentry duty in the compound of number 2 Commando. The appellant's section commander was Sergeant Boland. His section 2 I/C was Master Corporal Matchee, who was the appellant's immediate superior.

Shortly after 9:00 p.m. on March 16, 1993, a 16-year-old Somali male was captured while attempting to infiltrate one of the Canadian compounds and was placed in the custody of the appellant's section. Over the course of the ensuing two and a half to three hours, the prisoner was severely and brutally beaten. By shortly after midnight, he was dead.

The evidence indicated that most of the beating was administered by Matchee. Matchee was charged but, because of a suicide attempt very shortly after the incident, was and is unfit to stand trial and unable to testify. The appellant was present during much but not all of the beating. Other soldiers were also present from time to time while the beating was taking place. The appellant admitted that, at an early stage in the prisoner's ordeal, he had punched him once in the jaw and kicked him twice in the leg. At Matchee's request, the appellant took photographs of Matchee and the prisoner; he also himself posed for two photographs taken by Matchee of him and the prisoner. The photographs leave no room for doubt that the prisoner had, at that time, suffered a very severe beating. There was evidence from other soldiers who visited the bunker where the beating took place that the appellant appeared calm or bored or as if "he didn't want to be there." Matchee, on the other hand, appeared "pumped up." Matchee spoke frequently and expressed satisfaction at what was happening; not so the appellant who appeared, to at least some witnesses, as "upset" or "shocked." There was evidence that the appellant did not like Matchee and was scared of him. Matchee was a violent person with a quick temper and had apparently been drinking that night.

The exact cause of the prisoner's death was never determined since no autopsy was performed. Medical evidence called by the Crown, based on photographs and the descriptions of the beating, was to the effect that death was probably caused by brain swelling resulting from the cumulative effect of blows to the head. Lacerations on the deceased's face were probably caused by blows with a fist and such blows may have had a concussive effect contributing to the victim's death.

[T]he General Court Martial found the appellant not guilty of the charge of murder but guilty of the included offence of manslaughter. It also found him guilty of torture. . . .

The Crown seeks leave to appeal the sentence. The appellant opposes that application on the ground that leave should only be granted where it can be demonstrated that the Judge Advocate has committed an error in his instructions to the Court on the question of sentence. I do not agree. The provisions of the *National Defence Act* subjecting a sentence appeal to a prior requirement of leave contain no such restriction as to the criteria which should guide the Court in deciding whether to grant leave. In this respect, the Court is in the identical situation as a civilian appellate court hearing sentence appeals under the *Criminal Code*. Sentences pronounced by courts martial may require the intervention of this Court for important reasons of public policy quite unrelated to the legality of the instructions given to the court martial by the judge advocate. Indeed, this Court only recently decided a sentence appeal which exemplifies such reasons of public policy. [*R. v. Laflamme* (1993), 5 C.M.A.R. 145.] It should also be remembered that sentence appeals are a two-way street and that if we were to accept the appellant's submissions on this point we might render illusory many sentence appeals by accused persons. Given the importance of this case both nationally and internationally I think it is in the public interest that the sentence should be reviewed in this Court and I would accordingly grant leave.

The Crown submitted that the sentence of five years imposed by the General Court Martial is too low given the objective gravity of both the offence of manslaughter and the offence of torture. In particular the latter offence, containing as it does in its definition a substantial element of breach of public trust and of inhumanity which has given rise to international condemnation, [*see Convention against Torture and Other Cruel, Inhuman or Degrading Treatment or Punishment*, 10 December 1984, Can. T.S. 1987, No. 36] should attract a very substantial sentence.

I agree that at first blush the sentence of five years appears inordinately low. Certainly if the appellant's participation in the beating of the prisoner had been anything approaching what the evidence attributed to Matchee I would feel it incumbent on this Court to intervene. The difficulty I have, however, flows from the very nature of the court martial process and the particular and very complex fact pattern of the present case.

Under military law it is the court martial itself, composed of lay officers, which pronounces the sentence. That sentence, like the finding of guilt which preceded it, is known to the world only by its result. The members of the court are not asked for and may not give any reasons to support the sentence which they impose. Clearly, if an error is made by the judge advocate in his instructions to the court martial, that would provide grounds for appellate intervention. There is no suggestion of that here.

Equally, where the facts of the case admit of only one interpretation, or where the interpretation most favourable to the accused results in a sentence which is manifestly insufficient or disproportionate, a Crown appeal against the sentence may succeed. That was the situation in *Laflamme, supra.* By the same token, an appeal by the accused against sentence would succeed where such sentence was disproportionately heavy on any view of the facts which was open to the Court consistent with the finding of guilt.

In brief, since no reasons are given for the sentence, any error on the part of the members of the court martial must be evident from a reading of the material which is available to the appellate court. In the absence of such error, a sentence must be allowed to stand.

This being a Crown appeal, the question then becomes whether, given the many complexities of the facts of this case, there is at least one view of them which was open to the Court Martial which would justify both the finding of guilt and the sentence imposed. In my opinion there is. If the Court Martial found the accused guilty primarily as a result of his personal actions in hitting the prisoner and kicking him at an early stage of his ordeal and rejected any theory of guilt based on the accused's being an accomplice in Matchee's later terrible actions, the sentences can be supported. Such a view was open to the Court Martial: one of the Crown's alternative theories of guilt for which it advanced evidence and argument was that the blows admittedly struck by the accused contributed to the prisoner's death and caused him intense pain. If that view and that theory of guilt were the only ones accepted by the Court Martial, the sentence imposed would not be inadequate in the light of the many factors weighing in the appellant's favour. There were, of course, many other views which could have been taken of the evidence and many other theories upon which the Court Martial could have found the accused guilty on either or both of the charges which he faced. But since we cannot know the mental processes of the members of the Court it is impossible for us to say that they erred in reaching the sentence that they did.

NOTE

1. The Somali peacekeeping mission in general, and the incident that led to Private Brown's conviction in particular, led to calls for reforming the Canadian Forces, including its military justice system. *See generally* Robert Centa & Patrick Macklem, *Securing Accountability Through Commissions of Inquiry: A Role for the Law Commission of Canada*, 39 OSGOODE HALL L.J. 117 (2001).

2. Again, an appeal such as this would not be possible in the U.S. military justice system. The permissible bases for government appeals are set out in Uniform Code of Military Justice Article 62. 10 U.S.C. § 862. A government appeal against the sentence is not listed.

Statement of Thierry Giet
Belgiun House of Representatives
October 13, 1999

[In 1997 and 1998, a series of Belgian courts-martial tried Belgian soldiers for misconduct during their participation in the United Nations peacekeeping operation in Somalia in 1993. For example, in 1997, a Belgian court-martial acquitted two Belgian paratroopers who were photographed roasting a child over a fire during a United Nations peacekeeping operation in Somalia in 1993. The court-martial accepted the defense that the paratroopers were simply playing with the child, who they claim was not hurt during the episode.

[In 1998, a Belgian paratrooper was convicted and given a three-month suspended sentence for procuring an underage Somali girl for sex with other Belgian soldiers and for tying another child to a moving vehicle during the Belgian peacekeeping mission in Somalia in 1993. The paratrooper was acquitted of feeding a Somali boy pork until he vomited.]

Recent military justice cases reveal the attitude of Belgian soldiers during the humanitarian operation in Somalia. Despite the serious cases presented against them, several defendants were acquitted, received lenient sentences, or were given suspended sentences. Nine of the defendants were discharged, six received suspended sentences, and one officer was sentenced to confinement for eight days, which was suspended for a year.

The public was justifiably outraged to learn than an officer had been sentenced to eight days in prison, which was suspended, for an offense that involved the torture of children.

This sentence also harms Belgium's international reputation.

In this case, as in many others, the military justice system did not enhance good order and discipline. This calls into question the military justice system's continued existence.

Do military professionals need a separate justice system? That separate system has given military members second-class status. Isolated from the rest of society, the military has developed a law unto itself. Making soldiers feel that they do not enjoy the same rights as other citizens can only weaken the effectiveness of our military.

A justice system that engenders mistrust among those it governs cannot be perceived as equitable and impartial.

This problem is not new . . . [but] reforms instituted thus far have been insufficient. . . . The very notion of a military justice system in time of peace must be reconsidered.

Military courts wield disproportionate power, since their procedures represent serious departures from the recognized rights of criminal defendants.

In France, the law of July 22, 1982 eliminated permanent courts for the military. When he presented his report to the National Assembly, the President of the Justice Commission noted: "The legislature affirms its will to eliminate entirely from our legal system those procedures and jurisdictions that, instead of promoting the justice system's mission of protecting freedoms, instead threaten citizens' basic rights."

Abolishing military courts during peacetime does not require the amendment of Article 157 of the [Belgian] Constitution, which recognizes the existence of military courts, since those courts would still be used in wartime.

QUESTIONS

1. Are courts-martial or civilian courts better able to protect good order and discipline in the military? Are courts-martial or civilian courts better able to protect the rights of the accused? Will courts-martial or civilian courts reach more just results?

2. Is allowing military members to be tried by fellow military members consistent with the Anglo-American tradition of a jury of one's peers?

Chapter 19

MILITARY COMMISSIONS

In the wake of the attacks on the United States on September 11, 2001, President George W. Bush authorized military commissions to try non-U.S. citizen members of al Qaeda and others allegedly involved in international terrorism against the United States. The resulting military commission system proved extremely controversial. In *Hamdan v. Rumsfeld*, 126 S. Ct. 2749 (2006), the Supreme Court held the commission system was illegal because it departed from established court-martial procedure without a sufficient showing that applying the court-martial system's procedures were impracticable. The Court also found that it violated the law of war's requirement that punishments for war crimes be imposed only by "a regularly constituted court." Congress responded by passing a statute authorizing a military commission system more similar to the court-martial system, but still with significantly fewer procedural protections.

This chapter begins with a brief look at *Ex parte Milligan*, 71 U.S. 2 (1866), in which the Supreme Court reviewed a military commission conviction of a U.S. citizen, and the World War II case of *Ex parte Quirin*, 317 U.S. 1 (1942), which produced a far different result. After reviewing those two important precedents, we turn to an in-depth look at *Hamdan* followed by notes addressing the Military Commissions Act of 2006.

I. HISTORICAL BACKGROUND

EX PARTE MILLIGAN
Supreme Court of the United States
71 U.S. 2 (1866)

DAVIS, J.

On the 10th day of May, 1865, Lambdin P. Milligan presented a petition to the Circuit Court of the United States for the District of Indiana, to be discharged from an alleged unlawful imprisonment. The case made by the petition is this: Milligan is a citizen of the United States; has lived for twenty years in Indiana; and, at the time of the grievances complained of, was not, and never had been in the military or naval service of the United States. On the 5th day of October, 1864, while at home, he was arrested by order of General Alvin P. Hovey, commanding the military district of Indiana; and has ever since been kept in close confinement.

On the 21st day of October, 1864, he was brought before a military commission, convened at Indianapolis, by order of General Hovey, tried on certain charges and specifications; found guilty, and sentenced to be hanged; and the sentence ordered to be executed on Friday, the 19th day of May, 1865.

On the 2d day of January, 1865, after the proceedings of the military commission were at an end, the Circuit Court of the United States for Indiana met at Indianapolis and empanelled a grand jury, who were charged to inquire whether the laws of the United States had been violated; and, if so, to make presentments. The court adjourned on the 27th day of January, having, prior thereto, discharged from further service the grand jury, who did not find any bill of indictment or make any presentment against Milligan for any offence whatever; and, in fact, since his imprisonment, no bill of indictment has been found or presentment made against him by any grand jury of the United States.

Milligan insists that said military commission had no jurisdiction to try him upon the charges preferred, or upon any charges whatever; because he was a citizen of the United States and the State of Indiana, and had not been, since the commencement of the late Rebellion, a resident of any of the States whose citizens were arrayed against the government, and that the right of trial by jury was guaranteed to him by the Constitution of the United States. . . .

During the late wicked Rebellion, the temper of the times did not allow that calmness in deliberation and discussion so necessary to a correct conclusion of a purely judicial question. Then, considerations of safety were mingled with the exercise of power; and feelings and interests prevailed which are happily terminated. Now that the public safety is assured, this question, as well as all others, can be discussed and decided without passion or the admixture of any element not required to form a legal judgment. We approach the investigation of this case, fully sensible of the magnitude of the inquiry and the necessity of full and cautious deliberation. . . .

The controlling question in the case is this: Upon the facts stated in Milligan's petition, and the exhibits filed, had the military commission mentioned in it jurisdiction, legally, to try and sentence him? Milligan, not a resident of one of the rebellious states, or a prisoner of war, but a citizen of Indiana for twenty years past, and never in the military or naval service, is, while at his home, arrested by the military power of the United States, imprisoned, and, on certain criminal charges preferred against him, tried, convicted, and sentenced to be hanged by a military commission, organized under the direction of the military commander of the military district of Indiana. Had this tribunal the legal power and authority to try and punish this man?

No graver question was ever considered by this court, nor one which more nearly concerns the rights of the whole people; for it is the birthright of every American citizen when charged with crime, to be tried and punished according to law. The power of punishment is, alone through the means which the laws have provided for that purpose, and if they are ineffectual, there is an immunity from punishment, no matter how great an offender the individual may be, or how much his crimes may have shocked the sense of justice of the country, or endangered its safety. By the protection of the law human rights are secured; withdraw that protection, and they are at the mercy of wicked rulers, or the clamor of an excited people. If there was law to justify this military trial, it is not our province to interfere; if there was not, it is our duty to declare the nullity of the whole proceedings. The decision of this question does not depend on argument or judicial precedents, numerous and highly illustrative as they are. These precedents inform us of the extent of the struggle to preserve liberty and to relieve those in civil life from military trials. The founders of our government were familiar with the history of that struggle; and secured in a written constitution every right which the people had wrested from power during a contest of ages. By that Constitution and the laws authorized by it this question must be determined. The provisions of that instrument on the administration of criminal justice are too plain and direct, to leave room for misconstruction or doubt of their true meaning. Those applicable to this case are found in that clause of the original Constitution which says, "That the trial of all crimes, except in case of impeachment, shall be by jury;" and in the fourth, fifth, and sixth articles of the amendments. The fourth proclaims the right to be secure in person and effects against unreasonable search and seizure; and directs that a judicial warrant shall not issue "without proof of probable cause supported by oath or affirmation." The fifth declares "that no person shall be held to answer for a capital or otherwise infamous crime unless on presentment by a grand jury, except in cases arising in the land or naval forces, or in the militia, when in actual service in time of war or public danger, nor be deprived of life, liberty, or property, without due process of law." And the sixth guarantees the right of trial by jury, in such manner and with such regulations that with upright judges, impartial juries, and an able bar, the innocent will be saved and the guilty punished. It is in these words: "In all criminal prosecutions the accused shall enjoy the right to a speedy and public trial by an impartial jury of the state and district wherein the crime shall have been committed, which district shall have been previously ascertained by law, and to be informed of the nature and cause of the accusation, to be confronted with the witnesses against him, to have compulsory process for obtaining witnesses in his favor, and to have the assistance of counsel for his defence." These securities for personal liberty thus embodied, were such as wisdom and experience had demonstrated to be necessary for the protection of those accused of crime. And so strong was the sense of the country of their importance, and so jealous were the people that these rights, highly prized, might be denied them by implication, that when the original Constitution was proposed for adoption it encountered severe opposition; and but for the belief that it would be so amended as to embrace them, it would never have been ratified.

Time has proven the discernment of our ancestors; for even these provisions, expressed in such plain English words, that it would seem the ingenuity of man could not evade them, are now, after the lapse of more than seventy years, sought to be avoided. Those great and good men foresaw that troublous times would arise, when rules and people would become restive under restraint, and seek by sharp and decisive measures to accomplish ends deemed just and proper; and that the principles of constitutional liberty would be in peril, unless established by irrepealable law. The history of the world had taught them that what was done in the past might be attempted in the future. The Constitution of the United States is a law for rulers and people, equally in war and in peace, and covers with the shield of its protection all classes of men, at all times, and under all circumstances. No doctrine, involving more pernicious consequences, was ever invented by the wit of man than that any of its provisions can be suspended during any of the great exigencies of government. Such a doctrine leads directly to anarchy or despotism, but the theory of necessity on which it is based is false; for the government, within the Constitution, has all the powers granted to it, which are necessary to preserve its existence; as has been happily proved by the result of the great effort to throw off its just authority.

Have any of the rights guaranteed by the Constitution been violated in the case of Milligan? and if so, what are they?

Every trial involves the exercise of judicial power; and from what source did the military commission that tried him derive their authority? Certainly no part of the judicial power of the country was conferred on them; because the Constitution expressly vests it "in one supreme court and such inferior courts as the Congress may from time to time ordain and establish," and it is not pretended that the commission was a court ordained and established by Congress. They cannot justify on the mandate of the President; because he is controlled by law, and has his appropriate sphere of duty, which is to execute, not to make, the laws; and there is "no unwritten criminal code to which resort can be had as a source of jurisdiction."

But it is said that the jurisdiction is complete under the "laws and usages of war."

It can serve no useful purpose to inquire what those laws and usages are, whence they originated, where found, and on whom they operate; they can never be applied to citizens in states which have upheld the authority of the government, and where the courts are open and their process unobstructed. This court has judicial knowledge that in Indiana the Federal authority was always unopposed, and its courts always open to hear criminal accusations and redress grievances; and no usage of war could sanction a military trial there for any offence whatever of a citizen in civil life, in nowise connected with the military service. Congress could grant no such power; and to the honor of our national legislature be it said, it has never been provoked by the state of the country even to attempt its exercise. One of the plainest constitutional provisions was, therefore, infringed when Milligan was tried by a court not ordained and established by Congress, and not composed of judges appointed during good behavior.

Why was he not delivered to the Circuit Court of Indiana to be proceeded against according to law? No reason of necessity could be urged against it; because Congress had declared penalties against the offences charged, provided for their punishment, and directed that court to hear and determine them. And soon after this military tribunal was ended, the Circuit Court met, peacefully transacted its business, and adjourned. It needed no bayonets to protect it, and required no military aid to execute its judgments. It was held in a state, eminently distinguished for patriotism, by judges commissioned during the Rebellion, who were provided with juries, upright, intelligent, and selected by a marshal appointed by the President. The government had no right to conclude that Milligan, if guilty, would not receive in that court merited punishment; for its records disclose that it was constantly engaged in the trial of similar offences, and was never interrupted in its administration of criminal justice. If it was dangerous, in the distracted condition of affairs, to leave Milligan unrestrained of his liberty, because he "conspired against the government, afforded aid and comfort to rebels, and incited the people to insurrection," the law said arrest him, confine him closely, render him powerless to do further mischief; and then present his case to the grand jury of the district, with proofs of his guilt, and, if indicted, try him according to the course of the common law. If this had been done, the Constitution would have been vindicated . . . and the securities for personal liberty preserved and defended.

Another guarantee of freedom was broken when Milligan was denied a trial by jury. The great minds of the country have differed on the correct interpretation to be given to various provisions of the Federal Constitution; and judicial decision has been often invoked to settle their true meaning; but until recently no one ever doubted that the right of trial by jury was fortified in the organic law against the power of attack. It is now assailed; but if ideas can be expressed in words, and language has any meaning, this right — one of the most valuable in a free country — is preserved to every one accused of crime who is not attached to the army, or navy, or militia in actual service. The sixth amendment affirms that "in all criminal prosecutions the accused shall enjoy the right to a speedy and public trial by an impartial jury," language broad enough to embrace all persons and cases; but the fifth, recognizing the necessity of an indictment, or presentment, before any one can be held to answer for high crimes, "excepts cases arising in the land or naval forces, or in the militia, when in actual service, in time of war or public danger;" and the framers of the Constitution, doubtless, meant to limit the right of trial by jury, in the sixth amendment, to those persons who were subject to indictment or presentment in the fifth.

The discipline necessary to the efficiency of the army and navy, required other and swifter modes of trial than are furnished by the common law courts; and, in pursuance of the power conferred by the Constitution, Congress has declared the kinds of trial, and the manner in which they shall be conducted, for offences committed while the party is in the military or naval service. Every one connected with these branches of the public service is amenable to the jurisdiction which Congress has created for their government, and, while thus serving, surrenders his right to be tried by the civil courts. All other persons, citizens of states where the courts are open, if charged with crime, are guaranteed the inestimable privilege of trial by jury. This privilege is a vital principle, underlying the whole administration of criminal justice; it is not held by sufferance, and cannot be frittered away on any plea of state or political necessity. When peace prevails, and the authority of the government is undisputed, there is no difficulty of preserving the safeguards of liberty; for the ordinary modes of trial are never neglected, and no one wishes it otherwise; but if society is disturbed by civil commotion — if the passions of men are aroused and the restraints of law weakened, if not disregarded — these safeguards need, and should receive, the watchful care of those intrusted with the guardianship of the Constitution and laws. In no other way can we transmit to posterity unimpaired the blessings of liberty, consecrated by the sacrifices of the Revolution.

It is claimed that martial law covers with its broad mantle the proceedings of this military commission. The proposition is this: that in a time of war the commander of an armed force (if in his opinion the exigencies of the country demand it, and of which he is to judge), has the power, within the lines of his military district, to suspend all civil rights and their remedies, and subject citizens as well as soldiers to the rule of his will; and in the exercise of his lawful authority cannot be restrained, except by his superior officer or the President of the United States.

If this position is sound to the extent claimed, then when war exists, foreign or domestic, and the country is subdivided into military departments for mere convenience, the commander of one of them can, if he chooses, within his limits, on the plea of necessity, with the approval of the Executive, substitute military force for and to the exclusion of the laws, and punish all persons, as he thinks right and proper, without fixed or certain rules.

The statement of this proposition shows its importance; for, if true, republican government is a failure, and there is an end of liberty regulated by law. Martial law, established on such a basis, destroys every guarantee of the Constitution, and effectually renders the "military independent of and superior to the civil power" — the attempt to do which by the King of Great Britain was deemed by our fathers such an offence, that they assigned it to the world as one of the causes which impelled them to declare their independence. Civil liberty and this kind of martial law cannot endure together; the antagonism is irreconcilable; and, in the conflict, one or the other must perish.

This nation, as experience has proved, cannot always remain at peace, and has no right to expect that it will always have wise and humane rulers, sincerely attached to the principles of the Constitution. Wicked men, ambitious of power, with hatred of liberty and contempt of law, may fill the place once occupied by Washington and Lincoln; and if this right is conceded, and the calamities of war again befall us, the dangers to human liberty are frightful to contemplate. If our fathers had failed to provide for just such a contingency, they would have been false to the trust reposed in them. They knew — the history of the world told them — the nation they were founding, be its existence short or long, would be involved in war; how often or how long continued, human foresight could not tell; and that unlimited power, wherever lodged at such a time, was especially hazardous to freemen. For this, and other equally weighty reasons, they secured the inheritance they had fought to maintain, by incorporating in a written constitution the safeguards which time had proved were essential to its preservation. Not one of these safeguards can the President, or Congress, or the Judiciary disturb, except the one concerning the writ of habeas corpus.

It is essential to the safety of every government that, in a great crisis, like the one we have just passed through, there should be a power somewhere of suspending the writ of habeas corpus. In every war, there are men of previously good character, wicked enough to counsel their fellow-citizens to resist the measures deemed necessary by a good government to sustain its just authority and overthrow its enemies; and their influence may lead to dangerous combinations. In the emergency of the times, an immediate public investigation according to law may not be possible; and yet, the peril to the country may be too imminent to suffer such persons to go at large. Unquestionably, there is then an exigency which demands that the government, if it should see fit in the exercise of a proper discretion to make arrests, should not be required to produce the persons arrested in answer to a writ of habeas corpus. The Constitution goes no further. It does not say after a writ of habeas corpus is denied a citizen, that he shall be tried otherwise than by the course of the common law; if it had intended this result, it was easy by the use of direct words to have accomplished it. The illustrious men who framed that instrument were guarding the foundations of civil liberty against the abuses of unlimited power; they were full of wisdom, and the lessons of history informed them that a trial by an established court, assisted by an impartial jury, was the only sure way of protecting the citizen against oppression and wrong. Knowing this, they limited the suspension to one great right, and left the rest to remain forever inviolable. But, it is insisted that the safety of the country in time of war demands that this broad claim for martial law shall be sustained. If this were true, it could be well said that a country, preserved at the sacrifice of all the cardinal principles of liberty, is not worth the cost of preservation. Happily, it is not so.

It will be borne in mind that this is not a question of the power to proclaim martial law, when war exists in a community and the courts and civil authorities are overthrown. Nor is it a question what rule a military commander, at the head of his army, can impose on states in rebellion to cripple their resources and quell the insurrection. The jurisdiction claimed is much more extensive. The necessities of the service, during the late Rebellion, required that the loyal states should be placed within the limits of certain military districts and commanders appointed in them; and, it is urged, that this, in a military sense, constituted them the theatre of military operations; and, as in this case, Indiana had been and was again threatened with invasion by the enemy, the occasion was furnished to establish martial law. The conclusion does not follow from the premises. If armies were collected in Indiana, they were to be employed in another locality, where the laws were obstructed and the national authority disputed. On her soil there was no hostile foot; if once invaded, that invasion was at an end, and with it all pretext for martial law. Martial law cannot arise from a threatened invasion. The necessity must be actual and present; the invasion real, such as effectually closes the courts and deposes the civil administration.

It is difficult to see how the safety of the country required martial law in Indiana. If any of her citizens were plotting treason, the power of arrest could secure them, until the government was prepared for their trial, when the courts were open and ready to try them. It was as easy to protect witnesses before a civil as a military tribunal; and as there could be no wish to convict, except on sufficient legal evidence, surely an ordained and established court was better able to judge of this than a military tribunal composed of gentlemen not trained to the profession of the law.

It follows, from what has been said on this subject, that there are occasions when martial rule can be properly applied. If, in foreign invasion or civil war, the courts are actually closed, and it is impossible to administer criminal justice according to law, then, on the theatre of active military operations, where war really prevails, there is a necessity to furnish a substitute for the civil authority, thus overthrown, to preserve the safety of the army and society; and as no power is left but the military, it is allowed to govern by martial rule until the laws can have their free course. As necessity creates the rule, so it limits its duration; for, if this government is continued after the courts are reinstated, it is a gross usurpation of power. Martial rule can never exist where the courts are open, and in the proper and unobstructed exercise of their jurisdiction. It is also confined to the locality of actual war. Because, during the late Rebellion it could have been enforced in Virginia, where the national authority was overturned and the courts driven out, it does not follow that it should obtain in Indiana, where that authority was never disputed, and justice was always administered. And so in the case of a foreign invasion, martial rule may become a necessity in one state, when, in another, it would be "mere lawless violence." . . .

EX PARTE QUIRIN
Supreme Court of the United States
317 U.S. 1 (1942)

STONE, C.J.

The question for decision is whether the detention of petitioners by respondent for trial by Military Commission, appointed by Order of the President of July 2, 1942, on charges preferred against them purporting to set out their violations of the law of war and of the Articles of War, is in conformity to the laws and Constitution of the United States. . . .

All the petitioners were born in Germany; all have lived in the United States. All returned to Germany between 1933 and 1941. All except petitioner Haupt are admittedly citizens of the German Reich, with which the United States is at war. Haupt came to this country with his parents when he was five years old; it is contended that he became a citizen of the United States by virtue of the naturalization of his parents during his minority and that he has not since lost his citizenship. The Government, however, takes the position that on attaining his majority he elected to maintain German allegiance and citizenship, or in any case that he has by his conduct renounced or abandoned his United States citizenship. *See Perkins v. Elg*, 307 U.S. 325, 334; *United States ex rel. Rojak v. Marshall*, 34 F.2d 219; *United States ex rel. Scimeca v. Husband*, 6 F.2d 957, 958; 8 U.S.C. § 801, and compare 8 U.S.C. § 808. For reasons presently to be stated we do not find it necessary to resolve these contentions.

After the declaration of war between the United States and the German Reich, petitioners received training at a sabotage school near Berlin, Germany, where they were instructed in the use of explosives and in methods of secret writing. Thereafter petitioners, with a German citizen, Dasch, proceeded from Germany to a seaport in Occupied France, where petitioners Burger, Heinck and Quirin, together with Dasch, boarded a German submarine which proceeded across the Atlantic to Amagansett Beach on Long Island, New York. The four were there landed from the submarine in the hours of darkness, on or about June 13, 1942, carrying with them a supply of explosives, fuses, and incendiary and timing devices. While landing they wore German Marine Infantry uniforms or parts of uniforms. Immediately after landing they buried their uniforms and the other articles mentioned, and proceeded in civilian dress to New York City.

The remaining four petitioners at the same French port boarded another German submarine, which carried them across the Atlantic to Ponte Vedra Beach, Florida. On or about June 17, 1942, they came ashore during the hours of darkness, wearing caps of the German Marine Infantry and carrying with them a supply of explosives, fuses, and incendiary and timing devices. They immediately buried their caps and the other articles mentioned, and proceeded in civilian dress to Jacksonville, Florida, and thence to various points in the United States. All were taken into custody in New York or Chicago by agents of the Federal Bureau of Investigation. All had received instructions in Germany from an officer of the German High Command to destroy war industries and war facilities in the United States, for which they or their relatives in Germany were to receive salary payments from the German Government. They also had been paid by the German Government during their course of training at the sabotage school and had received substantial sums in United States currency, which were in their possession when arrested. The currency had been handed to them by an officer of the German High Command, who had instructed them to wear their German uniforms while landing in the United States.

The President, as President and Commander in Chief of the Army and Navy, by Order of July 2, 1942, [7 Federal Register 5103] appointed a Military Commission and directed it to try petitioners for offenses against the law of war and the Articles of War, and prescribed regulations for the procedure of the trial and for review of the record of the trial and of any judgment or sentence of the Commission. On the same day, by Proclamation, [7 Federal Register 5101] the President declared that "all persons who are subjects, citizens or residents of any nation at war with the United States or who give obedience to or act under the direction of any such nation, and who during time of war enter or attempt to enter the United States . . . through coastal or boundary defenses, and are charged with committing or attempting or preparing to commit sabotage, espionage, hostile or warlike acts, or violations of the law of war, shall be subject to the law of war and to the jurisdiction of military tribunals."

The Proclamation also stated in terms that all such persons were denied access to the courts.

Pursuant to direction of the Attorney General, the Federal Bureau of Investigation surrendered custody of petitioners to respondent, Provost Marshal of the Military District of Washington, who was directed by the Secretary of War to receive and keep them in custody, and who thereafter held petitioners for trial before the Commission.

On July 3, 1942, the Judge Advocate General's Department of the Army prepared and lodged with the Commission the following charges against petitioners, supported by specifications:

1. Violation of the law of war.

2. Violation of Article 81 of the Articles of War, defining the offense of relieving or attempting to relieve, or corresponding with or giving intelligence to, the enemy.

3. Violation of Article 82, defining the offense of spying.

4. Conspiracy to commit the offenses alleged in charges 1, 2 and 3.

The Commission met on July 8, 1942, and proceeded with the trial, which continued in progress while the causes were pending in this Court. On July 27th, before petitioners' applications to the District Court, all the evidence for the prosecution and the defense had been taken by the Commission and the case had been closed except for arguments of counsel. It is conceded that ever since petitioners' arrest the state and federal courts in Florida, New York, and the District of Columbia, and in the states in which each of the petitioners was arrested or detained, have been open and functioning normally. . . .

From the very beginning of its history this Court has recognized and applied the law of war as including that part of the law of nations which prescribes, for the conduct of war, the status, rights and duties of enemy nations as well as of enemy individuals. By the Articles of War, and especially Article 15, Congress has explicitly provided, so far as it may constitutionally do so, that military tribunals shall have jurisdiction to try offenders or offenses against the law of war in appropriate cases. Congress, in addition to making rules for the government of our Armed Forces, has thus exercised its authority to define and punish offenses against the law of nations by sanctioning, within constitutional limitations, the jurisdiction of military commissions to try persons for offenses which, according to the rules and precepts of the law of nations, and more particularly the law of war, are cognizable by such tribunals. And the President, as Commander in Chief, by his Proclamation in time of war has invoked that law. By his Order creating the present Commission he has undertaken to exercise the authority conferred upon him by Congress, and also such authority as the Constitution itself gives the Commander in Chief, to direct the performance of those functions which may constitutionally be performed by the military arm of the nation in time of war.

An important incident to the conduct of war is the adoption of measures by the military command not only to repel and defeat the enemy, but to seize and subject to disciplinary measures those enemies who in their attempt to thwart or impede our military effort have violated the law of war. It is unnecessary for present purposes to determine to what extent the President as Commander in Chief has constitutional power to create military commissions without the support of Congressional legislation. For here Congress has authorized trial of offenses against the law of war before such commissions. We are concerned only with the question whether it is within the constitutional power of the National Government to place petitioners upon trial before a military commission for the offenses with which they are charged. We must therefore first inquire whether any of the acts charged is an offense against the law of war cognizable before a military tribunal, and if so whether the Constitution prohibits the trial. We may assume that there are acts regarded in other countries, or by some writers on international law, as offenses against the law of war which would not be triable by military tribunal here, either because they are not recognized by our courts as violations of the law of war or because they are of that class of offenses constitutionally triable only by a jury. It was upon such grounds that the Court denied the right to proceed by military tribunal in *Ex parte Milligan*, [71 U.S. 2 (1866)]. But as we shall show, these petitioners were charged with an offense against the law of war which the Constitution does not require to be tried by jury.

It is no objection that Congress in providing for the trial of such offenses has not itself undertaken to codify that branch of international law or to mark its precise boundaries, or to enumerate or define by statute all the acts which that law condemns. An Act of Congress punishing "the crime of piracy, as defined by the law of nations" is an appropriate exercise of its constitutional authority, Art. I, § 8, cl. 10, "to define and punish" the offense, since it has adopted by reference the sufficiently precise definition of international law. *United States v. Smith*, 5 Wheat. 153; *see The Marianna Flora*, 11 Wheat. 1, 40-41; *United States v. Brig Malek Adhel*, 2 How. 210, 232; *The Ambrose Light*, 25 F. 408, 423-28; 18 U.S.C. § 481. Similarly, by the reference in the 15th Article of War to "offenders or offenses that . . . by the law of war may be triable by such military commissions," Congress has incorporated by reference, as within the jurisdiction of military commissions, all offenses which are defined as such by the law of war (compare *Dynes v. Hoover*, 20 How. 65, 82), and which may constitutionally be included within that jurisdiction. Congress had the choice of crystallizing in permanent form and in minute detail every offense against the law of war, or of adopting the system of common law applied by military tribunals so far as it should be recognized and deemed applicable by the courts. It chose the latter course.

By universal agreement and practice, the law of war draws a distinction between the armed forces and the peaceful populations of belligerent nations and also between those who are lawful and unlawful combatants. Lawful combatants are subject to capture and detention as prisoners of war by opposing military forces. Unlawful combatants are likewise subject to capture and detention, but in addition they are subject to trial and punishment by military tribunals for acts which render their belligerency unlawful. The spy who secretly and without uniform passes the military lines of a belligerent in time of war, seeking to gather military information and communicate it to the enemy, or an enemy combatant who without uniform comes secretly through the lines for the purpose of waging war by destruction of life or property, are familiar examples of belligerents who are generally deemed not to be entitled to the status of prisoners of war, but to be offenders against the law of war subject to trial and punishment by military tribunals. *See* Winthrop, Military Law, 2d ed., pp. 1196-97, 1219-21; Instructions for the Government of Armies of the United States in the Field, approved by the President, General Order No. 100, April 24, 1863, §§ IV and V.

Such was the practice of our own military authorities before the adoption of the Constitution,[1] and during the Mexican and Civil Wars.[2]

Paragraph 83 of General Order No. 100 of April 24, 1863, directed that: "Scouts or single soldiers, if disguised in the dress of the country, or in the uniform of the army hostile to their own, employed in obtaining information, if found within or lurking about the lines of the captor, are treated as spies, and suffer death." And Paragraph 84, that "Armed prowlers, by whatever names they may be called, or persons of the enemy's territory, who steal within the lines of the hostile army, for the purpose of robbing, killing, or of destroying bridges, roads, or canals, or of robbing or destroying the mail, or of cutting the telegraph wires, are not entitled to the privileges of the prisoner of war." These and related provisions have been continued in substance by the Rules of Land Warfare promulgated by the War Department for the guidance of the Army. Rules of 1914, Par. 369-77; Rules of 1940, Par. 345-57. Paragraph 357 of the 1940 Rules provides that "All war crimes are subject to the death penalty, although a lesser penalty may be imposed." Paragraph 8 (1940) divides the enemy population into "armed forces" and "peaceful population," and Paragraph 9 names as distinguishing characteristics of lawful belligerents that they "carry arms openly" and "have a fixed distinctive emblem." Paragraph 348 declares that "persons who take up arms and commit hostilities" without having the means of identification prescribed for belligerents are punishable as "war criminals." Paragraph 351 provides that "men and bodies of men, who, without being lawful belligerents" "nevertheless commit hostile acts of any kind" are not entitled to the privileges of prisoners of war if captured and may be tried by military commission and punished by death or lesser punishment. And paragraph 352 provides that "armed prowlers . . . or persons of the enemy territory who steal within the lines of the hostile army for the purpose of robbing, killing, or of destroying bridges, roads, or canals, of robbing or destroying the mail, or of cutting the telegraph wires, are not entitled to be treated as prisoners of war." As is evident from reading these and related Paragraphs 345-347, the specified violations are intended to be only illustrative of the applicable principles of the common law of war, and not an exclusive enumeration of the punishable acts recognized as such by that law. The definition of lawful belligerents by Paragraph 9 is that adopted by Article 1, Annex to Hague Convention No. IV of October 18, 1907, to which the United

---

[1] [n. 9] On September 29, 1780, Major John Andre, Adjutant-General to the British Army, was tried by a "Board of General Officers" appointed by General Washington, on a charge that he had come within the lines for an interview with General Benedict Arnold and had been captured while in disguise and travelling under an assumed name. The Board found that the facts charged were true, and that when captured Major Andre had in his possession papers containing intelligence for the enemy, and reported their conclusion that "Major Andre . . . ought to be considered as a Spy from the enemy, and that agreeably to the law and usage of nations . . . he ought to suffer death." Major Andre was hanged on October 2, 1780. Proceedings of a Board of General Officers Respecting Major John Andre, Sept. 29, 1780, printed at Philadelphia in 1780.

[2] [n. 10] During the Mexican War military commissions were created in a large number of instances for the trial of various offenses. See General Orders cited in 2 Winthrop, Military Law (2d ed. 1896) p. 1298, note 1. During the Civil War the military commission was extensively used for the trial of offenses against the law of war. . . . For [examples of] cases of violations of the law of war punished by military commissions during the Civil War, see 2 Winthrop, Military Laws and Precedents (2d ed. 1896) 1310-11.

States was a signatory and which was ratified by the Senate in 1909. 36 Stat. 2295. The preamble to the Convention declares:

> Until a more complete code of the laws of war has been issued, the High Contracting Parties deem it expedient to declare that, in cases not included in the Regulations adopted by them, the inhabitants and the belligerents remain under the protection and the rule of the principles of the law of nations, as they result from the usages established among civilized peoples, from the laws of humanity, and the dictates of the public conscience.

Our Government, by thus defining lawful belligerents entitled to be treated as prisoners of war, has recognized that there is a class of unlawful belligerents not entitled to that privilege, including those who, though combatants, do not wear "fixed and distinctive emblems." And by Article 15 of the Articles of War Congress has made provision for their trial and punishment by military commission, according to "the law of war."

By a long course of practical administrative construction by its military authorities, our Government has likewise recognized that those who during time of war pass surreptitiously from enemy territory into our own, discarding their uniforms upon entry, for the commission of hostile acts involving destruction of life or property, have the status of unlawful combatants punishable as such by military commission. This precept of the law of war has been so recognized in practice both here and abroad, and has so generally been accepted as valid by authorities on international law[3] that we think it must be regarded as a rule or principle of the law of war recognized by this Government by its enactment of the Fifteenth Article of War.

Specification 1 of the first charge is sufficient to charge all the petitioners with the offense of unlawful belligerency, trial of which is within the jurisdiction of the Commission, and the admitted facts affirmatively show that the charge is not merely colorable or without foundation.

Specification 1 states that petitioners, "being enemies of the United States and acting for . . . the German Reich, a belligerent enemy nation, secretly and

---

[3] [n. 12] Great Britain, War Office, Manual of Military Law (1929) § 445, lists a large number of acts which, when committed within enemy lines by persons in civilian dress associated with or acting under the direction of enemy armed forces, are "war crimes." The list includes: "damage to railways, war material, telegraph, or other means of communication, in the interest of the enemy. . . ." Section 449 states that all "war crimes" are punishable by death.

Authorities on International Law have regarded as war criminals such persons who pass through the lines for the purpose of (a) destroying bridges, war materials, communication facilities, etc.: 2 Oppenheim, International Law (6th ed. 1940) § 255; Spaight, Air Power and War Rights (1924) 283; Spaight, War Rights on Land (1911) 110; Phillipson, International Law and the Great War (1915) 208; Liszt, Das Volkerrecht (12 ed. 1925), § 58 (B) 4; (b) carrying messages secretly: Hall, International Law (8th ed. 1924) § 188; Spaight, War Rights on Land 215; 3 Merignhac, Droit Public International (1912) 296-97; Bluntschli, Droit International Codifie (5th ed. tr. Lardy) § 639; 4 Calvo, Le Droit International Theorique et Pratique (5th ed. 1896) § 2119; (c) any hostile act: 2 Winthrop, Military Law and Precedents (2nd ed. 1896) 1224. *Cf.* Lieber, Guerrilla Parties (1862), 2 Miscellaneous Writings (1881) 288. These authorities are unanimous in stating that a soldier in uniform who commits the acts mentioned would be entitled to treatment as a prisoner of war; it is the absence of uniform that renders the offender liable to trial for violation of the laws of war.

covertly passed, in civilian dress, contrary to the law of war, through the military and naval lines and defenses of the United States . . . and went behind such lines, contrary to the law of war, in civilian dress . . . for the purpose of committing . . . hostile acts, and, in particular, to destroy certain war industries, war utilities and war materials within the United States."

This specification so plainly alleges violation of the law of war as to require but brief discussion of petitioners' contentions. As we have seen, entry upon our territory in time of war by enemy belligerents, including those acting under the direction of the armed forces of the enemy, for the purpose of destroying property used or useful in prosecuting the war, is a hostile and warlike act. It subjects those who participate in it without uniform to the punishment prescribed by the law of war for unlawful belligerents. It is without significance that petitioners were not alleged to have borne conventional weapons or that their proposed hostile acts did not necessarily contemplate collision with the Armed Forces of the United States. Paragraphs 351 and 352 of the Rules of Land Warfare, already referred to, plainly contemplate that the hostile acts and purposes for which unlawful belligerents may be punished are not limited to assaults on the Armed Forces of the United States. Modern warfare is directed at the destruction of enemy war supplies and the implements of their production and transportation, quite as much as at the armed forces. Every consideration which makes the unlawful belligerent punishable is equally applicable whether his objective is the one or the other. The law of war cannot rightly treat those agents of enemy armies who enter our territory, armed with explosives intended for the destruction of war industries and supplies, as any the less belligerent enemies than are agents similarly entering for the purpose of destroying fortified places or our Armed Forces. By passing our boundaries for such purposes without uniform or other emblem signifying their belligerent status, or by discarding that means of identification after entry, such enemies become unlawful belligerents subject to trial and punishment.

Citizenship in the United States of an enemy belligerent does not relieve him from the consequences of a belligerency which is unlawful because in violation of the law of war. Citizens who associate themselves with the military arm of the enemy government, and with its aid, guidance and direction enter this country bent on hostile acts, are enemy belligerents within the meaning of the Hague Convention and the law of war. *Cf. Gates v. Goodloe*, 101 U.S. 612, 615, 617-18. It is as an enemy belligerent that petitioner Haupt is charged with entering the United States, and unlawful belligerency is the gravamen of the offense of which he is accused.

Nor are petitioners any the less belligerents if, as they argue, they have not actually committed or attempted to commit any act of depredation or entered the theatre or zone of active military operations. The argument leaves out of account the nature of the offense which the Government charges and which the Act of Congress, by incorporating the law of war, punishes. It is that each petitioner, in circumstances which gave him the status of an enemy belligerent, passed our military and naval lines and defenses or went behind those lines, in civilian dress and with hostile purpose. The offense was complete when with that purpose they entered — or, having so entered, they remained upon — our territory in time of war without uniform or other appropriate means of identification. For that reason, even when committed by a citizen, the offense is distinct from the crime of treason defined in Article III, § 3 of the Constitution, since the absence of uniform essential to one is irrelevant to the other. *Cf. Morgan v. Devine*, 237 U.S. 632; *Albrecht v. United States*, 273 U.S. 1, 11-12.

But petitioners insist that, even if the offenses with which they are charged are offenses against the law of war, their trial is subject to the requirement of the Fifth Amendment that no person shall be held to answer for a capital or otherwise infamous crime unless on a presentment or indictment of a grand jury, and that such trials by Article III, § 2, and the Sixth Amendment must be by jury in a civil court. Before the Amendments, § 2 of Article III, the Judiciary Article, had provided, "The Trial of all Crimes, except in Cases of Impeachment, shall be by Jury," and had directed that "such Trial shall be held in the State where the said Crimes shall have been committed."

Presentment by a grand jury and trial by a jury of the vicinage where the crime was committed were at the time of the adoption of the Constitution familiar parts of the machinery for criminal trials in the civil courts. But they were procedures unknown to military tribunals, which are not courts in the sense of the Judiciary Article, *Ex parte Vallandigham*, 1 Wall. 243; *In re Vidal*, 179 U.S. 126; *cf. Williams v. United States*, 289 U.S. 553, and which in the natural course of events are usually called upon to function under conditions precluding resort to such procedures. As this Court has often recognized, it was not the purpose or effect of § 2 of Article III, read in the light of the common law, to enlarge the then existing right to a jury trial. The object was to preserve unimpaired trial by jury in all those cases in which it had been recognized by the common law and in all cases of a like nature as they might arise in the future, *District of Columbia v. Colts*, 282 U.S. 63, but not to bring within the sweep of the guaranty those cases in which it was then well understood that a jury trial could not be demanded as of right.

The Fifth and Sixth Amendments, while guaranteeing the continuance of certain incidents of trial by jury which Article III, § 2 had left unmentioned, did not enlarge the right to jury trial as it had been established by that Article. *Callan v. Wilson*, 127 U.S. 540, 549. Hence petty offenses triable at common law without a jury may be tried without a jury in the federal courts, notwithstanding Article III, § 2, and the Fifth and Sixth Amendments. *Schick v. United States*, 195 U.S. 65; *District of Columbia v. Clawans*, 300 U.S. 617. Trial by jury of criminal contempts may constitutionally be dispensed with in the federal courts in those cases in which they could be tried without a jury at common law. *Ex parte Terry*, 128 U.S. 289, 302-04; *Savin, Petitioner*, 131 U.S. 267, 277; *In re Debs*, 158 U.S. 564, 594-96; *United States v. Shipp*, 203 U.S. 563, 572; *Blackmer v. United States*, 284 U.S. 421, 440; *Nye v. United States*, 313 U.S. 33, 48; *see United States v. Hudson and Goodwin*, 7 Cranch 32, 34. Similarly, an action for debt to enforce a penalty inflicted by Congress is not subject to the constitutional restrictions upon criminal prosecutions. *United States v. Zucker*, 161 U.S. 475; *United States v. Regan*, 232 U.S. 37, and cases cited.

All these are instances of offenses committed against the United States, for which a penalty is imposed, but they are not deemed to be within Article III, § 2, or the provisions of the Fifth and Sixth Amendments relating to "crimes" and "criminal prosecutions." In the light of this long-continued and consistent interpretation we must conclude that § 2 of Article III and the Fifth and Sixth Amendments cannot be taken to have extended the right to demand a jury to trials by military commission, or to have required that offenses against the law of war not triable by jury at common law be tried only in the civil courts.

The fact that "cases arising in the land or naval forces" are excepted from the operation of the Amendments does not militate against this conclusion. Such cases are expressly excepted from the Fifth Amendment, and are deemed excepted by implication from the Sixth. *Ex parte Milligan, supra*, 123, 138-39. It is argued that the exception, which excludes from the Amendment cases arising in the armed forces, has also by implication extended its guaranty to all other cases; that since petitioners, not being members of the Armed Forces of the United States, are not within the exception, the Amendment operates to give to them the right to a jury trial. But we think this argument misconceives both the scope of the Amendment and the purpose of the exception.

We may assume, without deciding, that a trial prosecuted before a military commission created by military authority is not one "arising in the land . . . forces," when the accused is not a member of or associated with those forces. But even so, the exception cannot be taken to affect those trials before military commissions which are neither within the exception nor within the provisions of Article III, § 2, whose guaranty the Amendments did not enlarge. No exception is necessary to exclude from the operation of these provisions cases never deemed to be within their terms. An express exception from Article III, § 2, and from the Fifth and Sixth Amendments, of trials of petty offenses and of criminal contempts has not been found necessary in order to preserve the traditional practice of trying those offenses without a jury. It is no more so in order to continue the practice of trying, before military tribunals without a jury, offenses committed by enemy belligerents against the law of war.

Section 2 of the Act of Congress of April 10, 1806, 2 Stat. 371, derived from the Resolution of the Continental Congress of August 21, 1776, imposed the death penalty on alien spies "according to the law and usage of nations, by sentence of a general court martial." This enactment must be regarded as a contemporary construction of both Article III, § 2, and the Amendments as not foreclosing trial by military tribunals, without a jury, of offenses against the law of war committed by enemies not in or associated with our Armed Forces. It is a construction of the Constitution which has been followed since the founding of our Government, and is now continued in the 82nd Article of War. Such a construction is entitled to the greatest respect. *Stuart v. Laird*, 1 Cranch 299, 309; *Field v. Clark*, 143 U.S. 649, 691; *United States v. Curtiss-Wright Corp.*, 299 U.S. 304, 328. It has not hitherto been challenged, and, so far as we are advised, it has never been suggested in the very extensive literature of the subject that an alien spy, in time of war, could not be tried by military tribunal without a jury.

The exception from the Amendments of "cases arising in the land or naval forces" was not aimed at trials by military tribunals, without a jury, of such offenses against the law of war. Its objective was quite different — to authorize the trial by court martial of the members of our Armed Forces for all that class of crimes which under the Fifth and Sixth Amendments might otherwise have been deemed triable in the civil courts. The cases mentioned in the exception are not restricted to those involving offenses against the law of war alone, but extend to trial of all offenses, including crimes which were of the class traditionally triable by jury at common law. *Ex parte Mason*, 105 U.S. 696; *Kahn v. Anderson*, 255 U.S. 1, 8-9; *cf. Caldwell v. Parker*, 252 U.S. 376.

Since the Amendments, like § 2 of Article III, do not preclude all trials of offenses against the law of war by military commission without a jury when the offenders are aliens not members of our Armed Forces, it is plain that they present no greater obstacle to the trial in like manner of citizen enemies who have violated the law of war applicable to enemies. Under the original statute authorizing trial of alien spies by military tribunals, the offenders were outside the constitutional guaranty of trial by jury, not because they were aliens but only because they had violated the law of war by committing offenses constitutionally triable by military tribunal.

We cannot say that Congress in preparing the Fifth and Sixth Amendments intended to extend trial by jury to the cases of alien or citizen offenders against the law of war otherwise triable by military commission, while withholding it from members of our own armed forces charged with infractions of the Articles of War punishable by death. It is equally inadmissible to construe the Amendments — whose primary purpose was to continue unimpaired presentment by grand jury and trial by petit jury in all those cases in which they had been customary — as either abolishing all trials by military tribunals, save those of the personnel of our own armed forces, or, what in effect comes to the same thing, as imposing on all such tribunals the necessity of proceeding against unlawful enemy belligerents only on presentment and trial by jury. We conclude that the Fifth and Sixth Amendments did not restrict whatever authority was conferred by the Constitution to try offenses against the law of war by military commission, and that petitioners, charged with such an offense not required to be tried by jury at common law, were lawfully placed on trial by the Commission without a jury.

Petitioners, and especially petitioner Haupt, stress the pronouncement of this Court in the *Milligan* case, *supra*, p. 121, that the law of war "can never be applied to citizens in states which have upheld the authority of the government, and where the courts are open and their process unobstructed." Elsewhere in its opinion, at pp. 118, 121-22 and 131, the Court was at pains to point out that Milligan, a citizen twenty years resident in Indiana, who had never been a resident of any of the states in rebellion, was not an enemy belligerent either entitled to the status of a prisoner of war or subject to the penalties imposed upon unlawful belligerents. We construe the Court's statement as to the inapplicability of the law of war to Milligan's case as having particular reference to the facts before it. From them the Court concluded that Milligan, not being a part of or associated with the armed forces of the enemy, was a non-belligerent, not subject to the law of war save as — in circumstances found not there to be present, and not involved here — martial law might be constitutionally established.

The Court's opinion is inapplicable to the case presented by the present record. We have no occasion now to define with meticulous care the ultimate boundaries of the jurisdiction of military tribunals to try persons according to the law of war. It is enough that petitioners here, upon the conceded facts, were plainly within those boundaries, and were held in good faith for trial by military commission, charged with being enemies who, with the purpose of destroying war materials and utilities, entered, or after entry remained in, our territory without uniform — an offense against the law of war. We hold only that those particular acts constitute an offense against the law of war which the Constitution authorizes to be tried by military commission.

Since the first specification of Charge I sets forth a violation of the law of war, we have no occasion to pass on the adequacy of the second specification of Charge I, or to construe the 81st and 82nd Articles of War for the purpose of ascertaining whether the specifications under Charges II and III allege violations of those Articles or whether if so construed they are constitutional. *McNally v. Hill*, 293 U.S. 131.

There remains the contention that the President's Order of July 2, 1942, so far as it lays down the procedure to be followed on the trial before the Commission and on the review of its findings and sentence, and the procedure in fact followed by the Commission, are in conflict with Articles of War 38, 43, 46, 50½ and 70. Petitioners argue that their trial by the Commission, for offenses against the law of war and the 81st and 82nd Articles of War, by a procedure which Congress has prohibited would invalidate any conviction which could be obtained against them and renders their detention for trial likewise unlawful (*see McClaughry v. Deming*, 186 U.S. 49; *United States v. Brown*, 206 U.S. 240, 244; *Runkle v. United States*, 122 U.S. 543, 555-56; *Dynes v. Hoover*, 20 How. 65, 80-81); that the President's Order prescribes such an unlawful procedure; and that the secrecy surrounding the trial and all proceedings before the Commission, as well as any review of its decision, will preclude a later opportunity to test the lawfulness of the detention.

Petitioners do not argue and we do not consider the question whether the President is compelled by the Articles of War to afford unlawful enemy belligerents a trial before subjecting them to disciplinary measures. Their contention is that, if Congress has authorized their trial by military commission upon the charges preferred — violations of the law of war and the 81st and 82nd Articles of War — it has by the Articles of War prescribed the procedure by which the trial is to be conducted; and that, since the President has ordered their trial for such offenses by military commission, they are entitled to claim the protection of the procedure which Congress has commanded shall be controlling.

We need not inquire whether Congress may restrict the power of the Commander in Chief to deal with enemy belligerents. For the Court is unanimous in its conclusion that the Articles in question could not at any stage of the proceedings afford any basis for issuing the writ. But a majority of the full Court are not agreed on the appropriate grounds for decision. Some members of the Court are of opinion that Congress did not intend the Articles of War to govern a Presidential military commission convened for the determination of questions relating to admitted enemy invaders, and that the context of the

Articles makes clear that they should not be construed to apply in that class of cases. Others are of the view that — even though this trial is subject to whatever provisions of the Articles of War Congress has in terms made applicable to "commissions" — the particular Articles in question, rightly construed, do not foreclose the procedure prescribed by the President or that shown to have been employed by the Commission, in a trial of offenses against the law of war and the 81st and 82nd Articles of War, by a military commission appointed by the President.

Accordingly, we conclude that Charge I, on which petitioners were detained for trial by the Military Commission, alleged an offense which the President is authorized to order tried by military commission; that his Order convening the Commission was a lawful order and that the Commission was lawfully constituted; that the petitioners were held in lawful custody and did not show cause for their discharge. . . .

NOTES AND QUESTIONS

1. The Supreme Court issued *Ex parte Quirin* on October 29, 1942. But by that point, most of the petitioners in the case were long since dead. The Court issued a short *per curiam* opinion on July 31, 1942, holding:

> (1) That the charges preferred against petitioners on which they are being tried by military commission appointed by the order of the President of July 2, 1942, allege an offense or offenses which the President is authorized to order tried before a military commission.
>
> (2) That the military commission was lawfully constituted.
>
> (3) That petitioners are held in lawful custody for trial before the military commission, and have not shown cause for being discharged by writ of habeas corpus.

Ex parte Quirin, 63 S. Ct. 1 (1942). On August 8, 1942, six of the convicted saboteurs were executed. *See* Louis Fisher, Nazi Saboteurs on Trial 178 (2003).

2. Justice Frankfurter later famously remarked that *Quirin* "was not a happy precedent." *See id.* at 171 (quoting Memorandum Re: Rosenberg v. United States, Nos. 111 and 687, October Term, 1952, June 4, 1953, at 8, Frankfurter Papers, Harvard Law School, Part I, Reel 70, LC).

3. In his insightful and prescient 1998 book on civil liberties in time of war, Chief Justice Rehnquist addressed the starkly different outcomes in *Milligan* and *Quirin*. William H. Rehnquist, All the Laws But One 218-25 (1998). He noted that the timing of the decision — whether it was rendered during the armed conflict or during time of peace after the conflict — may have affected the outcomes:

> If the decision is made after hostilities have ceased, it is more likely to favor civil liberty than if made while hostilities continue. The contrast between the *Quirin* and the Japanese internment decisions on the one hand and the *Milligan* and *Duncan* [*v. Kahanamoku*, 327 U.S. 304

(1946) (invalidating trial of civilians by military tribunals in Hawaii more than eight months after the Pearl Harbor attack),] decisions on the other show that this . . . is a historically accurate observation about the American system.

Id. at 224.

II. POST-SEPTEMBER 11, 2001, MILITARY COMMISSIONS

HAMDAN v. RUMSFELD
Supreme Court of the United States
126 S. Ct. 2749 (2006)

STEVENS, J., announced the judgment of the Court and delivered the opinion of the Court with respect to Parts I through IV, VI through VI-D-iii, VI-D-v, and VII, in which KENNEDY, SOUTER, GINSBURG, and BREYER, JJ., joined, and an opinion with respect to Parts V and VI-D-iv, in which SOUTER, GINSBURG, and BREYER, JJ., joined. BREYER, J., filed a concurring opinion, in which KENNEDY, SOUTER, and GINSBURG, JJ., joined. KENNEDY, J., filed an opinion concurring in part, in which SOUTER, GINSBURG, and BREYER, JJ., joined as to Parts I and II. SCALIA, J., filed a dissenting opinion, in which THOMAS and ALITO, JJ., joined. THOMAS, J., filed a dissenting opinion, in which SCALIA, J., joined, and in which ALITO, J., joined as to all but Parts I, II-C-1, and III-B-2. ALITO, J., filed a dissenting opinion, in which SCALIA and THOMAS, JJ., joined as to Parts I through III. ROBERTS, C.J., took no part in the consideration or decision of the case.

STEVENS, J., announced the judgment of the Court and delivered the opinion of the Court with respect to Parts I through IV, Parts VI through VI-D-iii, Part VI-D-v, and Part VII, and an opinion with respect to Parts V and VI-D-iv, in which JUSTICE SOUTER, JUSTICE GINSBURG, and JUSTICE BREYER join.

Petitioner Salim Ahmed Hamdan, a Yemeni national, is in custody at an American prison in Guantanamo Bay, Cuba. In November 2001, during hostilities between the United States and the Taliban (which then governed Afghanistan), Hamdan was captured by militia forces and turned over to the U.S. military. In June 2002, he was transported to Guantanamo Bay. Over a year later, the President deemed him eligible for trial by military commission for then-unspecified crimes. After another year had passed, Hamdan was charged with one count of conspiracy "to commit . . . offenses triable by military commission."

Hamdan filed petitions for writs of habeas corpus and mandamus to challenge the Executive Branch's intended means of prosecuting this charge. He concedes that a court-martial constituted in accordance with the Uniform Code of Military Justice (UCMJ), 10 U.S.C. § 801 et seq. (2000 ed. and Supp. III), would have authority to try him. His objection is that the military commission the President has convened lacks such authority, for two principal reasons: First, neither congressional Act nor the common law of war supports trial by this commission for the crime of conspiracy — an offense that,

Hamdan says, is not a violation of the law of war. Second, Hamdan contends, the procedures that the President has adopted to try him violate the most basic tenets of military and international law, including the principle that a defendant must be permitted to see and hear the evidence against him. . . .

[W]e conclude that the military commission convened to try Hamdan lacks power to proceed because its structure and procedures violate both the UCMJ and the Geneva Conventions. Four of us also conclude, *see* Part V, *infra*, that the offense with which Hamdan has been charged is not an "offens[e] that by . . . the law of war may be tried by military commissions." 10 U.S.C. § 821.

I

On September 11, 2001, agents of the al Qaeda terrorist organization hijacked commercial airplanes and attacked the World Trade Center in New York City and the national headquarters of the Department of Defense in Arlington, Virginia. Americans will never forget the devastation wrought by these acts. Nearly 3,000 civilians were killed.

Congress responded by adopting a Joint Resolution authorizing the President to "use all necessary and appropriate force against those nations, organizations, or persons he determines planned, authorized, committed, or aided the terrorist attacks . . . in order to prevent any future acts of international terrorism against the United States by such nations, organizations or persons." Authorization for Use of Military Force (AUMF), 115 Stat. 224, note following 50 U.S.C. § 1541 (2000 ed., Supp. III). Acting pursuant to the AUMF, and having determined that the Taliban regime had supported al Qaeda, the President ordered the Armed Forces of the United States to invade Afghanistan. In the ensuing hostilities, hundreds of individuals, Hamdan among them, were captured and eventually detained at Guantanamo Bay.

On November 13, 2001, while the United States was still engaged in active combat with the Taliban, the President issued a comprehensive military order intended to govern the "Detention, Treatment, and Trial of Certain Non-Citizens in the War Against Terrorism," 66 Fed. Reg. 57833 (hereinafter November 13 Order or Order). Those subject to the November 13 Order include any noncitizen for whom the President determines "there is reason to believe" that he or she (1) "is or was" a member of al Qaeda or (2) has engaged or participated in terrorist activities aimed at or harmful to the United States. *Id.*, at 57834. Any such individual "shall, when tried, be tried by military commission for any and all offenses triable by military commission that such individual is alleged to have committed, and may be punished in accordance with the penalties provided under applicable law, including imprisonment or death." *Ibid.* The November 13 Order vested in the Secretary of Defense the power to appoint military commissions to try individuals subject to the Order, but that power has since been delegated to John D. Altenburg, Jr., a retired Army major general and longtime military lawyer who has been designated "Appointing Authority for Military Commissions."

On July 3, 2003, the President announced his determination that Hamdan and five other detainees at Guantanamo Bay were subject to the November 13 Order and thus triable by military commission. In December 2003, military counsel was appointed to represent Hamdan. Two months later, counsel filed demands for charges and for a speedy trial pursuant to Article 10 of the UCMJ, 10 U.S.C. §810. On February 23, 2004, the legal adviser to the Appointing Authority denied the applications, ruling that Hamdan was not entitled to any of the protections of the UCMJ. Not until July 13, 2004, after Hamdan had commenced this action in the United States District Court for the Western District of Washington, did the Government finally charge him with the offense for which, a year earlier, he had been deemed eligible for trial by military commission.

The charging document, which is unsigned, contains 13 numbered paragraphs. The first two paragraphs recite the asserted bases for the military commission's jurisdiction — namely, the November 13 Order and the President's July 3, 2003, declaration that Hamdan is eligible for trial by military commission. The next nine paragraphs, collectively entitled "General Allegations," describe al Qaeda's activities from its inception in 1989 through 2001 and identify Osama bin Laden as the group's leader. Hamdan is not mentioned in these paragraphs.

Only the final two paragraphs, entitled "Charge: Conspiracy," contain allegations against Hamdan. Paragraph 12 charges that "from on or about February 1996 to on or about November 24, 2001," Hamdan "willfully and knowingly joined an enterprise of persons who shared a common criminal purpose and conspired and agreed with [named members of al Qaeda] to commit the following offenses triable by military commission: attacking civilians; attacking civilian objects; murder by an unprivileged belligerent; and terrorism." There is no allegation that Hamdan had any command responsibilities, played a leadership role, or participated in the planning of any activity.

Paragraph 13 lists four "overt acts" that Hamdan is alleged to have committed sometime between 1996 and November 2001 in furtherance of the "enterprise and conspiracy": (1) he acted as Osama bin Laden's "bodyguard and personal driver," "believ[ing]" all the while that bin Laden "and his associates were involved in" terrorist acts prior to and including the attacks of September 11, 2001; (2) he arranged for transportation of, and actually transported, weapons used by al Qaeda members and by bin Laden's bodyguards (Hamdan among them); (3) he "drove or accompanied [O]sama bin Laden to various al Qaida-sponsored training camps, press conferences, or lectures," at which bin Laden encouraged attacks against Americans; and (4) he received weapons training at al Qaeda-sponsored camps.

After this formal charge was filed, the United States District Court for the Western District of Washington transferred Hamdan's habeas and mandamus petitions to the United States District Court for the District of Columbia. Meanwhile, a Combatant Status Review Tribunal (CSRT) convened pursuant to a military order issued on July 7, 2004, decided that Hamdan's continued detention at Guantanamo Bay was warranted because he was an "enemy combatant."[4] Separately, proceedings before the military commission commenced.

---

[4] [n. 1] An "enemy combatant" is defined by the military order as "an individual who was part of or supporting Taliban or al Qaeda forces, or associated forces that are engaged in hostilities against the United States or its coalition partners." Memorandum from Deputy Secretary of Defense Paul Wolfowitz re: Order Establishing Combatant Status Review Tribunal §a (Jul. 7, 2004), available at http://www.defenselink.mil/news/Jul2004/d20040707review.pdf. . . .

On November 8, 2004, however, the District Court granted Hamdan's petition for habeas corpus and stayed the commission's proceedings. . . . The Court of Appeals for the District of Columbia Circuit reversed. . . . On November 7, 2005, we granted certiorari to decide whether the military commission convened to try Hamdan has authority to do so, and whether Hamdan may rely on the Geneva Conventions in these proceedings. . . .

IV

The military commission, a tribunal neither mentioned in the Constitution nor created by statute, was born of military necessity. *See* W. Winthrop, Military Law and Precedents 831 (rev. 2d ed. 1920) (hereinafter Winthrop). Though foreshadowed in some respects by earlier tribunals like the Board of General Officers that General Washington convened to try British Major John Andre for spying during the Revolutionary War, the commission "as such" was inaugurated in 1847. *Id.*, at 832; G. Davis, A Treatise on the Military Law of the United States 308 (2d ed. 1909) (hereinafter Davis). As commander of occupied Mexican territory, and having available to him no other tribunal, General Winfield Scott that year ordered the establishment of both "*'military commissions'*" to try ordinary crimes committed in the occupied territory and a "*council of war*" to try offenses against the law of war. Winthrop 832 (emphases in original).

When the exigencies of war next gave rise to a need for use of military commissions, during the Civil War, the dual system favored by General Scott was not adopted. Instead, a single tribunal often took jurisdiction over ordinary crimes, war crimes, and breaches of military orders alike. As further discussed below, each aspect of that seemingly broad jurisdiction was in fact supported by a separate military exigency. Generally, though, the need for military commissions during this period — as during the Mexican War — was driven largely by the then very limited jurisdiction of courts-martial: "The *occasion* for the military commission arises principally from the fact that the jurisdiction of the court-martial proper, in our law, is restricted by statute almost exclusively to members of the military force and to certain specific offences defined in a written code." *Id.*, at 831 (emphasis in original).

Exigency alone, of course, will not justify the establishment and use of penal tribunals not contemplated by Article I, § 8 and Article III, § 1 of the Constitution unless some other part of that document authorizes a response to the felt need. *See Ex parte Milligan*, 71 U.S. 2, 4 Wall. 2, 121 (1866) ("Certainly no part of the judicial power of the country was conferred on [military commissions]"); *Ex parte Vallandigham*, 68 U.S. 243, 1 Wall. 243, 251 (1864); *see also* [*Ex parte*] *Quirin*, [317 U.S. 1, 25 (1942)] ("Congress and the President, like the courts, possess no power not derived from the Constitution"). And that authority, if it exists, can derive only from the powers granted jointly to the President and Congress in time of war. *See id.*, at 26-29; *In re Yamashita*, 327 U.S. 1, 11 (1946).

The Constitution makes the President the "Commander in Chief" of the Armed Forces, Art. II, § 2, cl. 1, but vests in Congress the powers to "declare War . . . and make Rules concerning Captures on Land and Water," Art. I, § 8, cl. 11, to "raise and support Armies," *id.*, cl. 12, to "define and punish . . .

Offences against the Law of Nations," *id.*, cl. 10, and "To make Rules for the Government and Regulation of the land and naval Forces," *id.*, cl. 14. The interplay between these powers was described by Chief Justice Chase in the seminal case of *Ex parte Milligan:*

> "The power to make the necessary laws is in Congress; the power to execute in the President. Both powers imply many subordinate and auxiliary powers. Each includes all authorities essential to its due exercise. But neither can the President, in war more than in peace, intrude upon the proper authority of Congress, nor Congress upon the proper authority of the President. . . . Congress cannot direct the conduct of campaigns, nor can the President, or any commander under him, without the sanction of Congress, institute tribunals for the trial and punishment of offences, either of soldiers or civilians, unless in cases of a controlling necessity, which justifies what it compels, or at least insures acts of indemnity from the justice of the legislature." 71 U.S. 2, 139-140, 4 Wall., at 139-140.

Whether Chief Justice Chase was correct in suggesting that the President may constitutionally convene military commissions "without the sanction of Congress" in cases of "controlling necessity" is a question this Court has not answered definitively, and need not answer today. For we held in *Quirin* that Congress had, through Article of War 15, sanctioned the use of military commissions in such circumstances. 317 U.S., at 28. . . . Article 21 of the UCMJ, the language of which is substantially identical to the old Article 15 and was preserved by Congress after World War II, reads as follows:

> "Jurisdiction of courts-martial not exclusive.

> "The provisions of this code conferring jurisdiction upon courts-martial shall not be construed as depriving military commissions, provost courts, or other military tribunals of concurrent jurisdiction in respect of offenders or offenses that by statute or by the law of war may be tried by such military commissions, provost courts, or other military tribunals." 64 Stat. 115.

We have no occasion to revisit *Quirin*'s controversial characterization of Article of War 15 as congressional authorization for military commissions. . . . Contrary to the Government's assertion, however, even *Quirin* did not view the authorization as a sweeping mandate for the President to "invoke military commissions when he deems them necessary." . . . Rather, the *Quirin* Court recognized that Congress had simply preserved what power, under the Constitution and the common law of war, the President had had before 1916 to convene military commissions — with the express condition that the President and those under his command comply with the law of war. *See* 317 U.S., at 28-29.[5] That much is evidenced by the Court's inquiry, *following* its

---

[5] [n. 23] Whether or not the President has independent power, absent congressional authorization, to convene military commissions, he may not disregard limitations that Congress has, in proper exercise of its own war powers, placed on his powers. *See Youngstown Sheet & Tube Co. v. Sawyer*, 343 U.S. 579, 637 (1952) (Jackson, J., concurring). The Government does not argue otherwise.

conclusion that Congress had authorized military commissions, into whether the law of war had indeed been complied with in that case. *See ibid.*

The Government would have us dispense with the inquiry that the *Quirin* Court undertook and find in either the AUMF or the [Detainee Treatment Act of 2005 (DTA) (119 Stat. 2739)] specific, overriding authorization for the very commission that has been convened to try Hamdan. Neither of these congressional Acts, however, expands the President' authority to convene military commissions. First, while we assume that the AUMF activated the President' war powers, *see Hamdi v. Rumsfeld*, 542 U.S. 507 (2004) (plurality opinion), and that those powers include the authority to convene military commissions in appropriate circumstances, *see id.*, at 518; *see also Yamashita*, 327 U.S., at 11, there is nothing in the text or legislative history of the AUMF even hinting that Congress intended to expand or alter the authorization set forth in Article 21 of the UCMJ. *Cf. Yerger*, 8 Wall., at 105, 105 ("Repeals by implication are not favored:").

Likewise, the DTA cannot be read to authorize this commission. Although the DTA, unlike either Article 21 or the AUMF, was enacted after the President had convened Hamdan's commission, it contains no language authorizing that tribunal or any other at Guantanamo Bay. The DTA obviously "recognize[s]" the existence of the Guantanamo Bay commissions in the weakest sense, because it references some of the military orders governing them and creates limited judicial review of their "final decision[s]," DTA § 1005(e)(3), 119 Stat. 2743. But the statute also pointedly reserves judgment on whether "the Constitution and laws of the United States are applicable" in reviewing such decisions and whether, if they are, the "standards and procedures" used to try Hamdan and other detainees actually violate the "Constitution and laws." *Ibid.*

Together, the UCMJ, the AUMF, and the DTA at most acknowledge a general Presidential authority to convene military commissions in circumstances where justified under the "Constitution and laws," including the law of war. Absent a more specific congressional authorization, the task of this Court is, as it was in *Quirin*, to decide whether Hamdan's military commission is so justified. It is to that inquiry we now turn.

V

The common law governing military commissions may be gleaned from past practice and what sparse legal precedent exists. Commissions historically have been used in three situations. *See* Bradley & Goldsmith, *Congressional Authorization and the War on Terrorism*, 118 Harv. L. Rev. 2047, 2132-2133 (2005); Winthrop 831-846; Hearings on H.R. 2498 before the Subcommittee of the House Committee on Armed Services, 81st Cong., 1st Sess., 975 (1949). First, they have substituted for civilian courts at times and in places where martial law has been declared. Their use in these circumstances has raised constitutional questions, *see Duncan v. Kahanamoku*, 327 U.S. 304 (1946); *Milligan*, 4 Wall., at 121-122, but is well recognized. *See* Winthrop 822, 836-839. Second, commissions have been established to try civilians "as part of a temporary military government over occupied enemy territory or territory regained from an enemy where civilian government cannot and does not function." *Duncan*, 327 U.S., at 314; *see Milligan* 4 Wall., at 141-142 (Chase, C.J., concurring in judgment) (distinguishing "martial law proper" from "military government" in occupied territory). Illustrative of this second kind of commission is the one that was established, with jurisdiction to apply the German Criminal Code, in occupied Germany following the end of World War II. *See Madsen v. Kinsella*, 343 U.S. 341, 356 (1952).

The third type of commission, convened as an "incident to the conduct of war" when there is a need "to seize and subject to disciplinary measures those enemies who in their attempt to thwart or impede our military effort have violated the law of war," *Quirin*, 317 U.S., at 28-29, has been described as "utterly different" from the other two. Bickers, *Military Commissions are Constitutionally Sound: A Response to Professors Katyal and Tribe*, 34 Tex. Tech. L. Rev. 899, 902 (2002-2003).[6] Not only is its jurisdiction limited to offenses cognizable during time of war, but its role is primarily a factfinding one — to determine, typically on the battlefield itself, whether the defendant has violated the law of war. The last time the U.S. Armed Forces used the law-of-war military commission was during World War II. In *Quirin*, this Court sanctioned President Roosevelt's use of such a tribunal to try Nazi saboteurs captured on American soil during the War. 317 U.S. 1, 63 S. Ct. 2. And in *Yamashita*, we held that a military commission had jurisdiction to try a Japanese commander for failing to prevent troops under his command from committing atrocities in the Philippines. 327 U.S. 1.

Quirin is the model the Government invokes most frequently to defend the commission convened to try Hamdan. That is both appropriate and unsurprising. Since Guantanamo Bay is neither enemy-occupied territory nor under martial law, the law-of-war commission is the only model available. At the same time, no more robust model of executive power exists; *Quirin* represents the high-water mark of military power to try enemy combatants for war crimes.

The classic treatise penned by Colonel William Winthrop, whom we have called "the 'Blackstone of Military Law,'" *Reid v. Covert*, 354 U.S. 1, 19, n. 38 (1957) (plurality opinion), describes at least four preconditions for exercise of jurisdiction by a tribunal of the type convened to try Hamdan. First, "[a] military commission, [except where otherwise authorized by statute], can legally assume jurisdiction only of offenses committed within the field of the command of the convening commander." Winthrop 836. The "field of command" in these circumstances means the "theatre of war." *Ibid.* Second, the offense

---

[6] [n. 27] So much may not be evident on cold review of the Civil War trials often cited as precedent for this kind of tribunal because the commissions established during that conflict operated as both martial law or military government tribunals and law-of-war commissions. Hence, "military commanders began the practice [during the Civil War] of using the same name, the same rules, and often the same tribunals" to try both ordinary crimes and war crimes. Bickers, 34 Tex. Tech. L. Rev., at 908. "For the first time, accused horse thieves and alleged saboteurs found themselves subject to trial by the same military commission." *Id.*, at 909. The Civil War precedents must therefore be considered with caution; as we recognized in *Quirin*, 317 U.S., at 29, and as further discussed below, commissions convened during time of war but under neither martial law nor military government may try only offenses against the law of war.

charged "must have been committed within the period of the war."[7] *Id.*, at 837. No jurisdiction exists to try offenses "committed either before or after the war." *Ibid.* Third, a military commission not established pursuant to martial law or an occupation may try only "[i]ndividuals of the enemy's army who have been guilty of illegitimate warfare or other offences in violation of the laws of war" and members of one's own army "who, in time of war, become chargeable with crimes or offences not cognizable, or triable, by the criminal courts or under the Articles of war." *Id.*, at 838. Finally, a law-of-war commission has jurisdiction to try only two kinds of offense: "Violations of the laws and usages of war cognizable by military tribunals only," and "[b]reaches of military orders or regulations for which offenders are not legally triable by court-martial under the Articles of war." *Id.*, at 839.[8]

All parties agree that Colonel Winthrop's treatise accurately describes the common law governing military commissions, and that the jurisdictional limitations he identifies were incorporated in Article of War 15 and, later, Article 21 of the UCMJ. It also is undisputed that Hamdan's commission lacks jurisdiction to try him unless the charge "properly set[s] forth, not only the details of the act charged, but the circumstances conferring *jurisdiction*." *Id.*, at 842 (emphasis in original). The question is whether the preconditions designed to ensure that a military necessity exists to justify the use of this extraordinary tribunal have been satisfied here.

The charge against Hamdan, described in detail in Part I, *supra*, alleges a conspiracy extending over a number of years, from 1996 to November 2001.[9] All but two months of that more than 5-year-long period preceded the attacks of September 11, 2001, and the enactment of the AUMF — the Act of Congress on which the Government relies for exercise of its war powers and thus for its authority to convene military commissions.[10] Neither the purported agreement with Osama bin Laden and others to commit war crimes, nor a single overt act, is alleged to have occurred in a theater of war or on any specified date after September 11, 2001. None of the overt acts that Hamdan is alleged to have committed violates the law of war.

---

[7] [n. 28] If the commission is established pursuant to martial law or military government, its jurisdiction extends to offenses committed within "the exercise of military government or martial law." Winthrop 837.

[8] [n. 29] Winthrop adds as a fifth, albeit not-always-complied-with, criterion that "the *trial* must be had within the theatre of war . . .; that, if held elsewhere, and where the civil courts are open and available, the proceedings and sentence will be *coram non judice*." *Id.*, at 836. The Government does not assert that Guantanamo Bay is a theater of war, but instead suggests that neither Washington, D.C., in 1942 nor the Philippines in 1945 qualified as a "war zone" either. . . . [*Cf.*] *Quirin*, 317 U.S. 1; *In re Yamashita*, 327 U.S. 1 (1946).

[9] [n. 30] The elements of this conspiracy charge have been defined not by Congress but by the President. *See* Military Commission Instruction No. 2, 32 CFR § 11.6 (2005).

[10] [n. 31] JUSTICE THOMAS would treat Osama bin Laden's 1996 declaration of jihad against Americans as the inception of the war. *See post*, at 2826-2828 (dissenting opinion). But even the Government does not go so far; although the United States had for some time prior to the attacks of September 11, 2001, been aggressively pursuing al Qaeda, neither in the charging document nor in submissions before this Court has the Government asserted that the President's *war powers* were activated prior to September 11, 2001. . . .

These facts alone cast doubt on the legality of the charge and, hence, the commission; as Winthrop makes plain, the offense alleged must have been committed both in a theater of war and *during*, not before, the relevant conflict. But the deficiencies in the time and place allegations also underscore — indeed are symptomatic of — the most serious defect of this charge: The offense it alleges is not triable by law-of-war military commission. *See Yamashita*, 327 U.S., at 13 ("Neither congressional action nor the military orders constituting the commission authorized it to place petitioner on trial unless the charge proffered against him is of a violation of the law of war").

There is no suggestion that Congress has, in exercise of its constitutional authority to "define and punish . . . Offences against the Law of Nations," U.S. Const., Art. I, § 8, cl. 10, positively identified "conspiracy" as a war crime. As we explained in *Quirin*, that is not necessarily fatal to the Government's claim of authority to try the alleged offense by military commission; Congress, through Article 21 of the UCMJ, has "incorporated by reference" the common law of war, which may render triable by military commission certain offenses not defined by statute. 317 U.S., at 30. When, however, neither the elements of the offense nor the range of permissible punishments is defined by statute or treaty, the precedent must be plain and unambiguous. To demand any less would be to risk concentrating in military hands a degree of adjudicative and punitive power in excess of that contemplated either by statute or by the Constitution. *Cf. Loving v. United States,* 517 U.S. 748, 771 (1996) (acknowledging that Congress "may not delegate the power to make laws"); *Reid,* 354 U.S., at 23-24 ("The Founders envisioned the army as a necessary institution, but one dangerous to liberty if not confined within its essential bounds"); The Federalist No. 47, p 324 (J. Cooke ed. 1961) (J. Madison) ("The accumulation of all powers legislative, executive and judiciary in the same hands . . . may justly be pronounced the very definition of tyranny").

This high standard was met in *Quirin*; the violation there alleged was, by "universal agreement and practice" both in this country and internationally, recognized as an offense against the law of war. 317 U.S., at 30; *see id.,* at 35-36 ("This precept of the law of war has been so recognized in practice both here and abroad, and has so generally been accepted as valid by authorities on international law that we think it must be regarded as a rule or principle of the law of war recognized by this Government by its enactment of the Fifteenth Article of War" (footnote omitted)). Although the picture arguably was less clear in *Yamashita, compare* 327 U.S., at 16 (stating that the provisions of the Fourth Hague Convention of 1907, 36 Stat. 2306, "plainly" required the defendant to control the troops under his command), *with* 327 U.S., at 35 (Murphy, J., dissenting), the disagreement between the majority and the dissenters in that case concerned whether the historic and textual evidence constituted clear precedent — not whether clear precedent was required to justify trial by law-of-war military commission.

At a minimum, the Government must make a substantial showing that the crime for which it seeks to try a defendant by military commission is acknowledged to be an offense against the law of war. That burden is far from satisfied here. The crime of "conspiracy" has rarely if ever been tried as such in this country by any law-of-war military commission not exercising some other form of jurisdiction, and does not appear in either the Geneva Conventions or the Hague Conventions — the major treaties on the law of war. Winthrop explains that under the common law governing military commissions, it is not enough to intend to violate the law of war and commit overt acts in furtherance of that intention unless the overt acts either are themselves offenses against the law of war or constitute steps sufficiently substantial to qualify as an attempt. *See* Winthrop 841 ("[T]he jurisdiction of the military commission should be restricted to cases of offence consisting in *overt acts, i.e.*, in unlawful commissions or actual attempts to commit, and not in intentions merely" (emphasis in original)). . . .

[I]nternational sources confirm that the crime charged here is not a recognized violation of the law of war. . . . [N]one of the major treaties governing the law of war identifies conspiracy as a violation thereof. And the only "conspiracy" crimes that have been recognized by international war crimes tribunals (whose jurisdiction often extends beyond war crimes proper to crimes against humanity and crimes against the peace) are conspiracy to commit genocide and common plan to wage aggressive war, which is a crime against the peace and requires for its commission actual participation in a "concrete plan to wage war." 1 Trial of the Major War Criminals Before the International Military Tribunal: Nuremberg, 14 November 1945-1 October 1946, p 225 (1947). The International Military Tribunal at Nuremberg, over the prosecution's objections, pointedly refused to recognize as a violation of the law of war conspiracy to commit war crimes, *see, e.g.*, 22 *id.*, at 469, and convicted only Hitler's most senior associates of conspiracy to wage aggressive war, *see* S. Pomorski, Conspiracy and Criminal Organization, in the Nuremberg Trial and International Law 213, 233-235 (G. Ginsburgs & V. Kudriavtsev eds. 1990). As one prominent figure from the Nuremberg trials has explained, members of the Tribunal objected to recognition of conspiracy as a violation of the law of war on the ground that "[t]he Anglo-American concept of conspiracy was not part of European legal systems and arguably not an element of the internationally recognized laws of war." T. Taylor, Anatomy of the Nuremberg Trials: A Personal Memoir 36 (1992); *see also id.*, at 550 (observing that Francis Biddle, who as Attorney General prosecuted the defendants in *Quirin*, thought the French judge had made a "'persuasive argument that conspiracy in the truest sense is not known to international law'"). . . .

Because the charge does not support the commission's jurisdiction, the commission lacks authority to try Hamdan.

The charge's shortcomings are not merely formal, but are indicative of a broader inability on the Executive's part here to satisfy the most basic precondition — at least in the absence of specific congressional authorization — for establishment of military commissions: military necessity. Hamdan's tribunal was appointed not by a military commander in the field of battle, but by a retired major general stationed away from any active hostilities. *Cf. Rasul v. Bush*, 542 U.S., at 487 (KENNEDY, J., concurring in judgment) (observing that "Guantanamo Bay is . . . far removed from any hostilities"). Hamdan is charged not with an overt act for which he was caught redhanded in a theater of war and which military efficiency demands be tried expeditiously, but with an *agreement* the inception of which long predated the attacks of September

11, 2001 and the AUMF. That may well be a crime, but it is not an offense that "by the law of war may be tried by military commissio[n]." 10 U.S.C. § 821. None of the overt acts alleged to have been committed in furtherance of the agreement is itself a war crime, or even necessarily occurred during time of, or in a theater of, war. Any urgent need for imposition or execution of judgment is utterly belied by the record; Hamdan was arrested in November 2001 and he was not charged until mid-2004. These simply are not the circumstances in which, by any stretch of the historical evidence or this Court's precedents, a military commission established by Executive Order under the authority of Article 21 of the UCMJ may lawfully try a person and subject him to punishment.

VI

Whether or not the Government has charged Hamdan with an offense against the law of war cognizable by military commission, the commission lacks power to proceed. The UCMJ conditions the President's use of military commissions on compliance not only with the American common law of war, but also with the rest of the UCMJ itself, insofar as applicable, and with the "rules and precepts of the law of nations," *Quirin*, 317 U.S., at 28 — including, *inter alia*, the four Geneva Conventions signed in 1949. *See Yamashita*, 327 U.S., at 20-21. The procedures that the Government has decreed will govern Hamdan's trial by commission violate these laws.

A

The commission's procedures are set forth in Commission Order No. 1, which was amended most recently on August 31, 2005 — after Hamdan's trial had already begun. Every commission established pursuant to Commission Order No. 1 must have a presiding officer and at least three other members, all of whom must be commissioned officers. § 4(A)(1). The presiding officer's job is to rule on questions of law and other evidentiary and interlocutory issues; the other members make findings and, if applicable, sentencing decisions. § 4(A)(5). The accused is entitled to appointed military counsel and may hire civilian counsel at his own expense so long as such counsel is a U.S. citizen with security clearance "at the level SECRET or higher." §§ 4(C)(2)-(3).

The accused also is entitled to a copy of the charge(s) against him, both in English and his own language (if different), to a presumption of innocence, and to certain other rights typically afforded criminal defendants in civilian courts and courts-martial. *See* §§ 5(A)-(P). These rights are subject, however, to one glaring condition: The accused and his civilian counsel may be excluded from, and precluded from ever learning what evidence was presented during, any part of the proceeding that either the Appointing Authority or the presiding officer decides to "close." Grounds for such closure "include the protection of information classified or classifiable . . .; information protected by law or rule from unauthorized disclosure; the physical safety of participants in Commission proceedings, including prospective witnesses; intelligence and law enforcement sources, methods, or activities; and other national security interests." § 6(B)(3). [The accused also may be excluded from the proceedings if he "engages in disruptive conduct." § 5(K).] Appointed military defense counsel must be privy to these closed sessions, but may, at the presiding officer's discretion, be forbidden to reveal to his or her client what took place therein. *Ibid.*

Another striking feature of the rules governing Hamdan's commission is that they permit the admission of *any* evidence that, in the opinion of the presiding officer, "would have probative value to a reasonable person." § 6(D)(1). Under this test, not only is testimonial hearsay and evidence obtained through coercion fully admissible, but neither live testimony nor witnesses' written statements need be sworn. *See* §§ 6(D)(2)(b), (3). Moreover, the accused and his civilian counsel may be denied access to evidence in the form of "protected information" (which includes classified information as well as "information protected by law or rule from unauthorized disclosure" and "information concerning other national security interests," §§ 6(B)(3), 6(D)(5)(a)(v)), so long as the presiding officer concludes that the evidence is "probative" under § 6(D)(1) and that its admission without the accused's knowledge would not "result in the denial of a full and fair trial." § 6(D)(5)(b). Finally, a presiding officer's determination that evidence "would not have probative value to a reasonable person" may be overridden by a majority of the other commission members. § 6(D)(1).

Once all the evidence is in, the commission members (not including the presiding officer) must vote on the accused's guilt. A two-thirds vote will suffice for both a verdict of guilty and for imposition of any sentence not including death (the imposition of which requires a unanimous vote). § 6(F). Any appeal is taken to a three-member review panel composed of military officers and designated by the Secretary of Defense, only one member of which need have experience as a judge. § 6(H)(4). The review panel is directed to "disregard any variance from procedures specified in this Order or elsewhere that would not materially have affected the outcome of the trial before the Commission." *Ibid.* Once the panel makes its recommendation to the Secretary of Defense, the Secretary can either remand for further proceedings or forward the record to the President with his recommendation as to final disposition. § 6(H)(5). The President then, unless he has delegated the task to the Secretary, makes the "final decision." § 6(H)(6). He may change the commission's findings or sentence only in a manner favorable to the accused. *Ibid.*

B

Hamdan raises both general and particular objections to the procedures set forth in Commission Order No. 1. His general objection is that the procedures' admitted deviation from those governing courts-martial itself renders the commission illegal. Chief among his particular objections are that he may, under the Commission Order, be convicted based on evidence he has not seen or heard, and that any evidence admitted against him need not comply with the admissibility or relevance rules typically applicable in criminal trials and court-martial proceedings. . . .

C

In part because the difference between military commissions and courts-martial originally was a difference of jurisdiction alone, and in part to protect against abuse and ensure evenhandedness under the pressures of war, the procedures governing trials by military commission historically have been the same as those governing courts-martial. *See, e.g.,* 1 The War of the Rebellion 248 (2d series 1894) (General Order 1 issued during the Civil War required military commissions to "be constituted in a similar manner and their proceedings be conducted according to the same general rules as courts-martial in order to prevent abuses which might otherwise arise"). Accounts of commentators from Winthrop through General Crowder — who drafted Article of War 15 and whose views have been deemed "authoritative" by this Court, *Madsen,* 343 U.S., at 353 — confirm as much.[11] As recently as the Korean and Vietnam wars, during which use of military commissions was contemplated but never made, the principle of procedural parity was espoused as a background assumption. *See* Paust, *Antiterrorism Military Commissions: Courting Illegality,* 23 Mich. J. Int'l L. 1, 3-5 (2001-2002). . . .

The uniformity principle is not an inflexible one; it does not preclude all departures from the procedures dictated for use by courts-martial. But any departure must be tailored to the exigency that necessitates it. *See* Winthrop 835, n. 81. That understanding is reflected in Article 36 of the UCMJ, which provides:

"(a) The procedure, including modes of proof, in cases before courts-martial, courts of inquiry, military commissions, and other military tribunals may be prescribed by the President by regulations which shall, so far as he considers practicable, apply the principles of law and the rules of evidence generally recognized in the trial of criminal cases in the United States district courts, but which may not be contrary to or inconsistent with this chapter.

"(b) All rules and regulations made under this article shall be uniform insofar as practicable and shall be reported to Congress." 70A Stat. 50.

Article 36 places two restrictions on the President's power to promulgate rules of procedure for courts-martial and military commissions alike. First, no procedural rule he adopts may be "contrary to or inconsistent with" the UCMJ — however practical it may seem. Second, the rules adopted must be "uniform insofar as practicable." That is, the rules applied to military commissions must be the same as those applied to courts-martial unless such uniformity proves impracticable. . . .

Without reaching the question whether any provision of Commission Order No. 1 is strictly "contrary to or inconsistent with" other provisions of the UCMJ, we conclude that the "practicability" determination the President has made is insufficient to justify variances from the procedures governing courts-martial. Subsection (b) of Article 36 was added after World War II, and requires a different showing of impracticability from the one required by subsection (a). Subsection (a) requires that the rules the President promulgates

[11] [n. 45] *See* Winthrop 835, and n. 81 ("military commissions are constituted and composed, and their proceedings are conducted, similarly to general courts-martial"); *id.,* at 841-842; S. Rep. No. 130, 64th Cong., 1st Sess., 40 (1916) (testimony of Gen. Crowder) ("Both classes of courts have the same procedure"); *see also, e.g.,* H. Coppee, Field Manual of Courts-Martial, p. 104 (1863) ("[Military] commissions are appointed by the same authorities as those which may order courts-martial. They are constituted in a manner similar to such courts, and their proceedings are conducted in exactly the same way, as to form, examination of witnesses, etc.").

for courts-martial, provost courts, and military commissions alike conform to those that govern procedures in Article III courts, "so far as *he considers* practicable." 10 U.S.C. § 836(a) (emphasis added). Subsection (b), by contrast, demands that the rules applied in courts-martial, provost courts, and military commissions — whether or not they conform with the Federal Rules of Evidence — be "uniform *insofar as practicable*." § 836(b) (emphasis added). Under the latter provision, then, the rules set forth in the Manual for Courts-Martial must apply to military commissions unless impracticable.

The President here has determined, pursuant to subsection (a), that it is impracticable to apply the rules and principles of law that govern "the trial of criminal cases in the United States district courts," § 836(a), to Hamdan's commission. We assume that complete deference is owed that determination. The President has not, however, made a similar official determination that it is impracticable to apply the rules for courts-martial.[12] And even if subsection (b)'s requirements may be satisfied without such an official determination, the requirements of that subsection are not satisfied here.

Nothing in the record before us demonstrates that it would be impracticable to apply court-martial rules in this case. There is no suggestion, for example, of any logistical difficulty in securing properly sworn and authenticated evidence or in applying the usual principles of relevance and admissibility. Assuming *arguendo* that the reasons articulated in the President's Article 36(a) determination ought to be considered in evaluating the impracticability of applying court-martial rules, the only reason offered in support of that determination is the danger posed by international terrorism. Without for one moment underestimating that danger, it is not evident to us why it should require, in the case of Hamdan's trial, any variance from the rules that govern courts-martial.

The absence of any showing of impracticability is particularly disturbing when considered in light of the clear and admitted failure to apply one of the most fundamental protections afforded not just by the Manual for Courts-Martial but also by the UCMJ itself: the right to be present. *See* 10 U.S.C.A. § 839(c) (Supp. 2006). Whether or not that departure technically is "contrary to or inconsistent with" the terms of the UCMJ, 10 U.S.C. § 836(a), the jettisoning of so basic a right cannot lightly be excused as "practicable."

Under the circumstances, then, the rules applicable in courts-martial must apply. Since it is undisputed that Commission Order No. 1 deviates in many significant respects from those rules, it necessarily violates Article 36(b).

The Government's objection that requiring compliance with the court-martial rules imposes an undue burden both ignores the plain meaning of Article 36(b) and misunderstands the purpose and the history of military commissions. The military commission was not born of a desire to dispense a more summary form of justice than is afforded by courts-martial; it developed,

---

[12] [n. 51] We may assume that such a determination would be entitled to a measure of deference. For the reasons given by JUSTICE KENNEDY, *see post*, at 2801 (opinion concurring in part), however, the level of deference accorded to a determination made under subsection (b) presumably would not be as high as that accorded to a determination under subsection (a).

rather, as a tribunal of necessity to be employed when courts-martial lacked jurisdiction over either the accused or the subject matter. *See* Winthrop 831. Exigency lent the commission its legitimacy, but did not further justify the wholesale jettisoning of procedural protections. That history explains why the military commission's procedures typically have been the ones used by courts-martial. That the jurisdiction of the two tribunals today may sometimes overlap, *see Madsen*, 343 U.S., at 354, does not detract from the force of this history; Article 21 did not transform the military commission from a tribunal of true exigency into a more convenient adjudicatory tool. Article 36, confirming as much, strikes a careful balance between uniform procedure and the need to accommodate exigencies that may sometimes arise in a theater of war. That Article not having been complied with here, the rules specified for Hamdan's trial are illegal.[13]

D

The procedures adopted to try Hamdan also violate the Geneva Conventions. . . .

i

The Court of Appeals relied on *Johnson v. Eisentrager*, 339 U.S. 763 (1950), to hold that Hamdan could not invoke the Geneva Conventions to challenge the Government's plan to prosecute him in accordance with Commission Order No. 1. *Eisentrager* involved a challenge by 21 German nationals to their 1945 convictions for war crimes by a military tribunal convened in Nanking, China, and to their subsequent imprisonment in occupied Germany. The petitioners argued, *inter alia*, that the 1929 Geneva Convention rendered illegal some of the procedures employed during their trials, which they said deviated impermissibly from the procedures used by courts-martial to try American soldiers. *See id.*, at 789. We rejected that claim on the merits because the petitioners (unlike Hamdan here) had failed to identify any prejudicial disparity "between the Commission that tried [them] and those that would try an offending soldier of the American forces of like rank," and in any event could claim no protection, under the 1929 Convention, during trials for crimes that occurred before their confinement as prisoners of war. *Id.*, at 790. [[T]hat is no longer true under the 1949 Conventions.]

Buried in a footnote of the opinion, however, is this curious statement suggesting that the Court lacked power even to consider the merits of the Geneva Convention argument:

> "We are not holding that these prisoners have no right which the military authorities are bound to respect. The United States, by the Geneva Convention of July 27, 1929, 47 Stat. 2021, concluded with forty-six other countries, including the German Reich, an agreement upon the treatment to be accorded captives. These prisoners claim to be and are entitled to its protection. It is, however, the obvious scheme

---

[13] [n. 54] Prior to the enactment of Article 36(b), it may well have been the case that a deviation from the rules governing courts-martial would not have rendered the military commission "*illegal*." *Post*, at 2839-2840 n. 16, (THOMAS, J., dissenting) (quoting Winthrop 841). Article 36(b), however, imposes a statutory command that must be heeded.

of the Agreement that responsibility for observance and enforcement of these rights is upon political and military authorities. Rights of alien enemies are vindicated under it only through protests and intervention of protecting powers as the rights of our citizens against foreign governments are vindicated only by Presidential intervention." *Id.*, at 789, n. 14.

The Court of Appeals, on the strength of this footnote, held that "the 1949 Geneva Convention does not confer upon Hamdan a right to enforce its provisions in court." 415 F.3d at 40.

Whatever else might be said about the *Eisentrager* footnote, it does not control this case. We may assume that "the obvious scheme" of the 1949 Conventions is identical in all relevant respects to that of the 1929 Convention,[14] and even that that scheme would, absent some other provision of law, preclude Hamdan's invocation of the Conventions provisions as an independent source of law binding the Government's actions and furnishing petitioner with any enforceable right.[15] For, regardless of the nature of the rights conferred on Hamdan, *cf. United States v. Rauscher*, 119 U.S. 407 (1886), they are, as the Government does not dispute, part of the law of war. *See Hamdi*, 542 U.S., at 520-521 (plurality opinion). And compliance with the law of war is the condition upon which the authority set forth in Article 21 is granted. . . .

ii

Article 3, often referred to as Common Article 3 because, like Article 2, it appears in all four Geneva Conventions, provides that in a "conflict not of an international character occurring in the territory of one of the High Contracting Parties, each Party to the conflict shall be bound to apply, as a minimum," certain provisions protecting "[p]ersons taking no active part in the hostilities, including members of armed forces who have laid down their arms and those placed *hors de combat* by . . . detention." [6 U.S.T.] at 3318. One such provision prohibits "the passing of sentences and the carrying out of executions without previous judgment pronounced by a regularly constituted court affording all the judicial guarantees which are recognized as indispensable by civilized peoples." *Ibid.*

The Court of Appeals thought, and the Government asserts, that Common Article 3 does not apply to Hamdan because the conflict with al Qaeda, being "'international in scope,'" does not qualify as a "'conflict not of an international character.'" 415 F.3d at 41. That reasoning is erroneous. The term "conflict not

---

[14] [n. 57] *But see, e.g.*, 4 Int'l Comm. of Red Cross, Commentary: Geneva Convention Relative to the Protection of Civilian Persons in Time of War 21 (1958) (hereinafter GCIV Commentary) (the 1949 Geneva Conventions were written "first and foremost to protect individuals, and not to serve State interests"); GCIII Commentary 91 ("It was not . . . until the Conventions of 1949 . . . that the existence of 'rights' conferred in prisoners of war was affirmed").

[15] [n. 58] *But see generally* . . . 1 Int'l Comm. for the Red Cross, Commentary: Geneva Convention for the Amelioration of the Condition of the Wounded and Sick in Armed Forces in the Field 84 (1952) ("It should be possible in States which are parties to the Convention . . . for the rules of the Convention to be evoked before an appropriate national court by the protected person who has suffered a violation"); GCII Commentary 92; GCIV Commentary 79.

of an international character" is used here in contradistinction to a conflict between nations. So much is demonstrated by the "fundamental logic [of] the Convention's provisions on its application." *Id.*, at 44 (Williams, J., concurring). Common Article 2 provides that "the present Convention shall apply to all cases of declared war or of any other armed conflict which may arise between two or more of the High Contracting Parties." 6 U.S.T., at 3318 (Art. 2, ¶ 1). High Contracting Parties (signatories) also must abide by all terms of the Conventions vis-a-vis one another even if one party to the conflict is a nonsignatory "Power," and must so abide vis-a-vis the nonsignatory if "the latter accepts and applies" those terms. *Ibid.* (Art. 2, ¶ 3). Common Article 3, by contrast, affords some minimal protection, falling short of full protection under the Conventions, to individuals associated with neither a signatory nor even a nonsignatory "Power" who are involved in a conflict "in the territory of" a signatory. The latter kind of conflict is distinguishable from the conflict described in Common Article 2 chiefly because it does not involve a clash between nations (whether signatories or not). In context, then, the phrase "not of an international character" bears its literal meaning. . . .

Although the official commentaries accompanying Common Article 3 indicate that an important purpose of the provision was to furnish minimal protection to rebels involved in one kind of "conflict not of an international character," *i.e.*, a civil war, *see* GCIII Commentary 36-37, the commentaries also make clear "that the scope of the Article must be as wide as possible," *id.*, at 36. In fact, limiting language that would have rendered Common Article 3 applicable "especially [to] cases of civil war, colonial conflicts, or wars of religion," was omitted from the final version of the Article, which coupled broader scope of application with a narrower range of rights than did earlier proposed iterations. *See* GCIII Commentary 42-43.

iii

Common Article 3, then, is applicable here and, as indicated above, requires that Hamdan be tried by a "regularly constituted court affording all the judicial guarantees which are recognized as indispensable by civilized peoples." 6 U.S.T., at 3320 (Art. 3, ¶ 1(d)). While the term "regularly constituted court" is not specifically defined in either Common Article 3 or its accompanying commentary, other sources disclose its core meaning. The commentary accompanying a provision of the Fourth Geneva Convention, for example, defines "'regularly constituted'" tribunals to include "ordinary military courts" and "definitely exclud[e] all special tribunals." GCIV Commentary 340 (defining the term "properly constituted" in Article 66, which the commentary treats as identical to "regularly constituted"); *see also Yamashita*, 327 U.S., at 44 (Rutledge, J., dissenting) (describing military commission as a court "specially constituted for a particular trial"). And one of the Red Cross' own treatises defines "regularly constituted court" as used in Common Article 3 to mean "established and organized in accordance with the laws and procedures already in force in a country." Int'l Comm. of Red Cross, 1 Customary International Humanitarian Law 355 (2005); *see also* GCIV Commentary 340 (observing that "ordinary military courts" will "be set up in accordance with the recognized principles governing the administration of justice").

The Government offers only a cursory defense of Hamdan's military commission in light of Common Article 3. . . . As JUSTICE KENNEDY [in his concurring opinion] explains, that defense fails because "[t]he regular military courts in our system are the courts-martial established by congressional statutes." . . . At a minimum, a military commission "can be 'regularly constituted' by the standards of our military justice system only if some practical need explains deviations from court-martial practice." . . . [N]o such need has been demonstrated here.[16]

iv

Inextricably intertwined with the question of regular constitution is the evaluation of the procedures governing the tribunal and whether they afford "all the judicial guarantees which are recognized as indispensable by civilized peoples." 6 U.S.T., at 3320 (Art. 3, ¶ 1(d)). Like the phrase "regularly constituted court," this phrase is not defined in the text of the Geneva Conventions. But it must be understood to incorporate at least the barest of those trial protections that have been recognized by customary international law. Many of these are described in Article 75 of Protocol I to the Geneva Conventions of 1949, adopted in 1977 (Protocol I). Although the United States declined to ratify Protocol I, its objections were not to Article 75 thereof. Indeed, it appears that the Government "regard[s] the provisions of Article 75 as an articulation of safeguards to which all persons in the hands of an enemy are entitled." Taft, *The Law of Armed Conflict After 9/11: Some Salient Features*, 28 Yale J. Int'l L. 319, 322 (2003). Among the rights set forth in Article 75 is the "right to be tried in [one's] presence." Protocol I, Art. 75(4)(e).[17]

We agree with JUSTICE KENNEDY that the procedures adopted to try Hamdan deviate from those governing courts-martial in ways not justified by any "evident practical need," . . ., and for that reason, at least, fail to afford the requisite guarantees. . . . We add only that . . . various provisions of Commission Order No. 1 dispense with the principles, articulated in Article 75 and indisputably part of the customary international law, that an accused must, absent disruptive conduct or consent, be present for his trial and must be privy to the evidence against him. *See* §§ 6(B)(3), (D). That the Government has a compelling interest in denying Hamdan access to certain sensitive information is not doubted. . . . But, at least absent express statutory provision to the contrary, information used to convict a person of a crime must be disclosed to him.

---

[16] [n. 65] Further evidence of this tribunal's irregular constitution is the fact that its rules and procedures are subject to change midtrial, at the whim of the Executive. *See* Commission Order No. 1, § 11 (providing that the Secretary of Defense may change the governing rules "from time to time").

[17] [n. 66] Other international instruments to which the United States is a signatory include the same basic protections set forth in Article 75. *See, e.g.,* International Covenant on Civil and Political Rights, Art. 14, ¶ 3(d), Mar. 23, 1976, 999 U.N.T.S. 171 (setting forth the right of an accused "[t]o be tried in his presence, and to defend himself in person or through legal assistance of his own choosing"). Following World War II, several defendants were tried and convicted by military commission for violations of the law of war in their failure to afford captives fair trials before imposition and execution of sentence. In two such trials, the prosecutors argued that the defendants' failure to apprise accused individuals of all evidence against them constituted violations of the law of war. *See* 5 U.N. War Crimes Commission 30 (trial of Sergeant-Major Shigeru Ohashi), 75 (trial of General Tanaka Hisakasu).

v

Common Article 3 obviously tolerates a great degree of flexibility in trying individuals captured during armed conflict; its requirements are general ones, crafted to accommodate a wide variety of legal systems. But *requirements* they are nonetheless. The commission that the President has convened to try Hamdan does not meet those requirements. . . .

KENNEDY, J., with whom SOUTER, GINSBURG, and BREYER, JJ., join as to Parts I and II, concurring in part.

Military Commission Order No. 1, which governs the military commission established to try petitioner Salim Hamdan for war crimes, exceeds limits that certain statutes, duly enacted by Congress, have placed on the President's authority to convene military courts. This is not a case, then, where the Executive can assert some unilateral authority to fill a void left by congressional inaction. It is a case where Congress, in the proper exercise of its powers as an independent branch of government, and as part of a long tradition of legislative involvement in matters of military justice, has considered the subject of military tribunals and set limits on the President's authority. Where a statute provides the conditions for the exercise of governmental power, its requirements are the result of a deliberative and reflective process engaging both of the political branches. Respect for laws derived from the customary operation of the Executive and Legislative Branches gives some assurance of stability in time of crisis. The Constitution is best preserved by reliance on standards tested over time and insulated from the pressures of the moment.

These principles seem vindicated here, for a case that may be of extraordinary importance is resolved by ordinary rules. The rules of most relevance here are those pertaining to the authority of Congress and the interpretation of its enactments.

It seems appropriate to recite these rather fundamental points because the Court refers, as it should in its exposition of the case, to the requirement of the Geneva Conventions of 1949 that military tribunals be "regularly constituted" . . . — a requirement that controls here, if for no other reason, because Congress requires that military commissions like the ones at issue conform to the "law of war," 10 U.S.C. § 821. Whatever the substance and content of the term "regularly constituted" as interpreted in this and any later cases, there seems little doubt that it relies upon the importance of standards deliberated upon and chosen in advance of crisis, under a system where the single power of the Executive is checked by other constitutional mechanisms. All of which returns us to the point of beginning — that domestic statutes control this case. If Congress, after due consideration, deems it appropriate to change the controlling statutes, in conformance with the Constitution and other laws, it has the power and prerogative to do so. . . .

I

Trial by military commission raises separation-of-powers concerns of the highest order. Located within a single branch, these courts carry the risk that offenses will be defined, prosecuted, and adjudicated by executive officials without independent review. . . . Concentration of power puts personal liberty in peril of arbitrary action by officials, an incursion the Constitution's three-part system is designed to avoid. It is imperative, then, that when military tribunals are established, full and proper authority exists for the Presidential directive.

The proper framework for assessing whether Executive actions are authorized is the three-part scheme used by Justice Jackson in his opinion in *Youngstown Sheet & Tube Co. v. Sawyer*, 343 U.S. 579 (1952). "When the President acts pursuant to an express or implied authorization of Congress, his authority is at its maximum, for it includes all that he possesses in his own right plus all that Congress can delegate." *Id.*, at 635. "When the President acts in absence of either a congressional grant or denial of authority, he can only rely upon his own independent powers, but there is a zone of twilight in which he and Congress may have concurrent authority, or in which its distribution is uncertain." *Id.*, at 637. "[W]hen the President takes measures incompatible with the expressed or implied will of Congress, his power is at its lowest ebb." *Ibid.*

In this case, as the Court observes, the President has acted in a field with a history of congressional participation and regulation. . . . In the Uniform Code of Military Justice (UCMJ), 10 U.S.C. § 801 *et seq.*, which Congress enacted, building on earlier statutes, in 1950, *see* Act of May 5, 1950, ch. 169, 64 Stat. 107, and later amended, *see, e.g.,* Military Justice Act of 1968, 82 Stat. 1335, Congress has set forth governing principles for military courts. The UCMJ as a whole establishes an intricate system of military justice. It authorizes courts-martial in various forms, 10 U.S.C. §§ 816-820 . . .; it regulates the organization and procedure of those courts, *e.g.,* §§ 822-835, 851-854; it defines offenses, §§877-934, and rights for the accused, *e.g.,* §§827(b)-(c), 831, 844, 846, 855 . . .; and it provides mechanisms for appellate review, §§859-876b . . . . [T]he statute further recognizes that special military commissions may be convened to try war crimes. . . . While these laws provide authority for certain forms of military courts, they also impose limitations, at least two of which control this case. If the President has exceeded these limits, this becomes a case of conflict between Presidential and congressional action — a case within Justice Jackson's third category, not the second or first. . . .

III

In light of the conclusion that the military commission here is unauthorized under the UCMJ, I see no need to consider several further issues addressed in the plurality opinion by JUSTICE STEVENS and the dissent by JUSTICE THOMAS.

First, I would not decide whether Common Article 3's standard — a "regularly constituted court affording all the judicial guarantees which are recognized as indispensable by civilized peoples," 6 U.S.T., at 3320 (¶ (1)(d)) — necessarily requires that the accused have the right to be present at all stages of a criminal trial. As JUSTICE STEVENS explains, Military Commission Order No. 1 authorizes exclusion of the accused from the proceedings if the presiding officer determines that, among other things, protection of classified information so requires. *See* §§ 6(B)(3), (D)(5). . . . JUSTICE STEVENS observes that these regulations create the possibility of a conviction and sentence based on evidence Hamdan has not seen or heard — a possibility the plurality is correct to consider troubling. . . .

As the dissent by JUSTICE THOMAS points out, however, the regulations bar the presiding officer from admitting secret evidence if doing so would deprive the accused of a "full and fair trial." MCO No. 1, § 6(D)(5)(b). . . . This fairness determination, moreover, is unambiguously subject to judicial review under the DTA. *See* § 1005(e)(3)(D)(i), 119 Stat. 2743 (allowing review of compliance with the "standards and procedures" in Military Commission Order No. 1). The evidentiary proceedings at Hamdan's trial have yet to commence, and it remains to be seen whether he will suffer any prejudicial exclusion.

There should be reluctance, furthermore, to reach unnecessarily the question whether, as the plurality seems to conclude, . . . , Article 75 of Protocol I to the Geneva Conventions is binding law notwithstanding the earlier decision by our Government not to accede to the Protocol. . . .

I likewise see no need to address the validity of the conspiracy charge against Hamdan . . . . In light of the conclusion that the military commissions at issue are unauthorized Congress may choose to provide further guidance in this area. Congress, not the Court, is the branch in the better position to undertake the "sensitive task of establishing a principle not inconsistent with the national interest or international justice." *Banco Nacional de Cuba v. Sabbatino*, 376 U.S. 398 (1964).

Finally, for the same reason, I express no view on the merits of other limitations on military commissions described as elements of the common law of war in Part V of JUSTICE STEVENS' opinion. . . .

THOMAS, J., with whom SCALIA, J., joins, and with whom ALITO, J., joins in all but Parts I, II-C-1, and III-B-2, dissenting. . . .

I

Our review of petitioner's claims arises in the context of the President's wartime exercise of his commander-in-chief authority in conjunction with the complete support of Congress. Accordingly, it is important to take measure of the respective roles the Constitution assigns to the three branches of our Government in the conduct of war.

As I explained in *Hamdi v. Rumsfeld*, 542 U.S. 507 (2004), the structural advantages attendant to the Executive Branch — namely, the decisiveness, "'activity, secrecy, and dispatch'" that flow from the Executive's "'unity,'" *id.*, at 581 (dissenting opinion) (quoting The Federalist No. 70, p 472 (J. Cooke ed. 1961) (A. Hamilton)) — led the Founders to conclude that the "President ha[s] primary responsibility — along with the necessary power — to protect the national security and to conduct the Nation's foreign relations." 542 U.S., at 580. Consistent with this conclusion, the Constitution vests in the President "[t]he executive Power," Art. II, § 1, provides that he "shall be Commander in Chief" of the Armed Forces, § 2, and places in him the power to recognize foreign governments, § 3. This Court has observed that these provisions confer upon the President broad constitutional authority to protect the Nation's security in the manner he deems fit. *See, e.g., Prize Cases*, 67 U.S. 635, 2 Black 635, 668 (1863) ("If a war be made by invasion of a foreign nation, the President is not only authorized but bound to resist force by force . . . without waiting for any special legislative authority"); *Fleming v. Page*, 50 U.S. 603, 9 How. 603, 615 (1850) (acknowledging that the President has the authority to "employ [the Nation's Armed Forces] in the manner he may deem most effectual to harass and conquer and subdue the enemy").

Congress, to be sure, has a substantial and essential role in both foreign affairs and national security. But "Congress cannot anticipate and legislate with regard to every possible action the President may find it necessary to take or every possible situation in which he might act," and "[s]uch failure of Congress . . . does not, 'especially . . . in the areas of foreign policy and national security,' imply 'congressional disapproval' of action taken by the Executive." *Dames & Moore v. Regan*, 453 U.S. 654, 678 (1981) (quoting *Haig v. Agee*, 453 U.S. 280, 291 (1981)). Rather, in these domains, the fact that Congress has provided the President with broad authorities does not imply — and the Judicial Branch should not infer — that Congress intended to deprive him of particular powers not specifically enumerated. *See Dames & Moore*, 453 U.S., at 678 ("[T]he enactment of legislation closely related to the question of the President's authority in a particular case which evinces legislative intent to accord the President broad discretion may be considered to invite measures on independent presidential responsibility" (internal quotation marks omitted)).

When "the President acts pursuant to an express or implied authorization from Congress," his actions are "'supported by the strongest of presumptions and the widest latitude of judicial interpretation, and the burden of persuasion . . . rest[s] heavily upon any who might attack it.'" *Id.*, at 668 (quoting *Youngstown Sheet & Tube Co. v. Sawyer*, 343 U.S. 579, 637 (1952) (Jackson, J., concurring)). Accordingly, in the very context that we address today, this Court has concluded that "the detention and trial of petitioners — ordered by the President in the declared exercise of his powers as Commander in Chief of the Army in time of war and of grave public danger — are not to be set aside by the courts without the clear conviction that they are in conflict with the Constitution or laws of Congress constitutionally enacted." *Ex parte Quirin*, 317 U.S. 1, 25 (1942).

Under this framework, the President's decision to try Hamdan before a military commission for his involvement with al Qaeda is entitled to a heavy measure of deference. In the present conflict, Congress has authorized the President "to use all necessary and appropriate force against those nations, organizations, or persons *he determines* planned, authorized, committed, or aided the terrorist attacks that occurred on September 11, 2001 . . . in order to prevent any future acts of international terrorism against the United States by such nations, organizations or persons." Authorization for Use of Military Force (AUMF) 115 Stat. 224, note following 50 U.S.C. § 1541 (2000 ed., Supp. III) (emphasis added). As a plurality of the Court observed in *Hamdi*, the "capture, detention, and *trial* of unlawful combatants, by 'universal agreement and practice,' are 'important incident[s] of war,'" *Hamdi*, 542 U.S., at 518 (quoting *Quirin, supra*, at 28, 30) (emphasis added), and are therefore "an exercise of the 'necessary and appropriate force' Congress has authorized the President to use." *Hamdi*, 542 U.S., at 518; *id.*, at 587 (THOMAS, J., dissenting). *Hamdi*'s

observation that military commissions are included within the AUMF's authorization is supported by this Court's previous recognition that "[a]n important
incident to the conduct of war is the adoption of measures by the military commander, not only to repel and defeat the enemy, but to seize and subject to disciplinary measures those enemies who, in their attempt to thwart or impede
our military effort, have violated the law of war." *In re Yamashita*, 327 U.S. 1,
11 (1946); *see also Quirin, supra*, at 28-29; *Madsen v. Kinsella*, 343 U.S. 341,
354, n. 20 (1952) ("'[T]he military commission . . . is an institution of the greatest importance in the period of war and should be preserved'" (quoting S. Rep.
No. 229, 63d Cong., 2d Sess., 53 (1914) (testimony of Gen. Crowder))).

Although the Court concedes the legitimacy of the President's use of military commissions in certain circumstances, . . ., it suggests that the AUMF has
no bearing on the scope of the President's power to utilize military commissions in the present conflict. . . . Instead, the Court determines the scope of this
power based exclusively on Article 21 of the Uniform Code of Military Justice
(UCMJ), 10 U.S.C. §821, the successor to Article 15 of the Articles of War,
which *Quirin* held "authorized trial of offenses against the law of war before
[military] commissions." 317 U.S., at 29. As I shall discuss below, Article 21
alone supports the use of commissions here. Nothing in the language of Article
21, however, suggests that it outlines the entire reach of congressional authorization of military commissions in all conflicts — quite the contrary, the language of Article 21 presupposes the existence of military commissions under
an independent basis of authorization. Indeed, consistent with *Hamdi*'s conclusion that the AUMF itself authorizes the trial of unlawful combatants, the
original sanction for military commissions historically derived from congressional authorization of "the initiation of war" with its attendant authorization
of "the employment of all necessary and proper agencies for its due prosecution." W. Winthrop, Military Law and Precedents 831 (2d ed. 1920) (hereinafter Winthrop). Accordingly, congressional authorization for military
commissions pertaining to the instant conflict derives not only from Article 21
of the UCMJ, but also from the more recent, and broader, authorization contained in the AUMF.[18]

I note the Court's error respecting the AUMF not because it is necessary to
my resolution of this case — Hamdan's military commission can plainly be
sustained solely under Article 21 — but to emphasize the complete congressional sanction of the President's exercise of his commander-in-chief authority
to conduct the present war. In such circumstances, as previously noted, our
duty to defer to the Executive's military and foreign policy judgment is at its
zenith; it does not countenance the kind of second-guessing the Court repeatedly engages in today. Military and foreign policy judgments

> "'are and should be undertaken only by those directly responsible to
> the people whose welfare they advance or imperil. They are decisions
> of a kind for which the Judiciary has neither aptitude, facilities nor

---

[18] [n. 2] Although the President very well may have inherent authority to try unlawful combatants for violations of the law of war before military commissions, we need not decide that question because Congress has authorized the President to do so. *Cf. Hamdi v. Rumsfeld*, 542 U.S. 507,
587 (THOMAS, J., dissenting) (same conclusion respecting detention of unlawful combatants).

responsibility and which has long been held to belong in the domain of political power not subject to judicial intrusion or inquiry.'" *Hamdi, supra*, at 582-583, 587 (THOMAS, J., dissenting) (quoting *Chicago & Southern Air Lines, Inc. v. Waterman S.S. Corp.*, 333 U.S. 103, 111 (1948)).

It is within this framework that the lawfulness of Hamdan's commission should be examined.

II

The plurality accurately describes some aspects of the history of military commissions and the prerequisites for their use. Thus, I do not dispute that military commissions have historically been "used in three [different] situations," . . ., and that the only situation relevant to the instant case is the use of military commissions "'to seize and subject to disciplinary measures those enemies who . . . have violated the law of war,'" . . . (quoting *Quirin, supra*, at 28-29). Similarly, I agree with the plurality that Winthrop's treatise sets forth the four relevant considerations for determining the scope of a military commission's jurisdiction, considerations relating to the (1) time and (2) place of the offense, (3) the status of the offender, and (4) the nature of the offense charged. Winthrop 836-840. The Executive has easily satisfied these considerations here. The plurality's contrary conclusion rests upon an incomplete accounting and an unfaithful application of those considerations.

A

The first two considerations are that a law-of-war military commission may only assume jurisdiction of "offences committed within the field of the command of the convening commander," and that such offenses "must have been committed within the period of the war." *See id.*, at 836, 837. . . . Here, as evidenced by Hamdan's charging document, the Executive has determined that the theater of the present conflict includes "Afghanistan, Pakistan and other countries" where al Qaeda has established training camps, . . ., and that the duration of that conflict dates back (at least) to Usama bin Laden's August 1996 *"Declaration of Jihad Against the Americans," ibid*. Under the Executive's description of the conflict, then, every aspect of the charge, which alleges overt acts in "Afghanistan, Pakistan, Yemen and other countries" taking place from 1996 to 2001, satisfies the temporal and geographic prerequisites for the exercise of law-of-war military commission jurisdiction. . . . And these judgments pertaining to the scope of the theater and duration of the present conflict are committed solely to the President in the exercise of his commander-in-chief authority. *See Prize Cases*, 67 U.S. 635, 2 Black, at 670 (concluding that the President's commander-in-chief judgment about the nature of a particular conflict was "a question to be decided *by him*, and this Court must be governed by the decisions and acts of the political department of the Government to which this power was entrusted").

Nevertheless, the plurality concludes that the legality of the charge against Hamdan is doubtful because "Hamdan is charged not with an overt act for which he was caught redhanded in a theater of war . . . but with an *agreement* the inception of which long predated . . . the [relevant armed conflict]." . . . (emphasis in original). The plurality's willingness to second-guess the

Executive's judgments in this context, based upon little more than its unsupported assertions, constitutes an unprecedented departure from the traditionally limited role of the courts with respect to war and an unwarranted intrusion on executive authority. And even if such second-guessing were appropriate, the plurality's attempt to do so is unpersuasive.

As an initial matter, the plurality relies upon the date of the AUMF's enactment to determine the beginning point for the "period of the war," Winthrop 836, thereby suggesting that petitioner's commission does not have jurisdiction to try him for offenses committed prior to the AUMF's enactment. . . . But this suggestion betrays the plurality's unfamiliarity with the realities of warfare and its willful blindness to our precedents. The starting point of the present conflict (or indeed any conflict) is not determined by congressional enactment, but rather by the initiation of hostilities. *See Prize Cases, supra*, at 668 (recognizing that war may be initiated by "invasion of a foreign nation," and that such initiation, and the President's response, usually *precedes* congressional action). Thus, Congress' enactment of the AUMF did not mark the beginning of this Nation's conflict with al Qaeda, but instead authorized the President to use force in the midst of an ongoing conflict. Moreover, while the President's "war powers" may not have been activated until the AUMF was passed, . . ., the date of such activation has never been used to determine the scope of a military commission's jurisdiction. Instead, the traditional rule is that "[o]ffenses committed before a formal declaration of war or before the declaration of martial law may be tried by military commission." Green, *The Military Commission*, 42 Am. J. Int'l L. 832, 848 (1948) (hereinafter Green); *see also* C. Howland, Digest of Opinions of the Judge-Advocates General of the Army 1067 (1912) (hereinafter Howland) ("A military commission . . . exercising . . . jurisdiction . . . under the laws of war . . . may take cognizance of offenses committed, during the war, *before* the initiation of the military government or martial law" (emphasis in original)); *cf. Yamashita*, 327 U.S., at 13 ("The extent to which the power to prosecute violations of the law of war shall be exercised before peace is declared rests, not with the courts, but with the political branch of the Government"). Consistent with this principle, on facts virtually identical to those here, a military commission tried Julius Otto Kuehn for conspiring with Japanese officials to betray the United States Fleet to the Imperial Japanese Government prior to its attack on Pearl Harbor. Green 848.

Moreover, the President's determination that the present conflict dates at least to 1996 is supported by overwhelming evidence. According to the State Department, al Qaeda *declared war* on the United States as early as August 1996. *See* Dept. of State Fact Sheet: Usama bin Ladin (Aug. 21, 1998); Dept. of State Fact Sheet: The Charges against International Terrorist Usama Bin Laden (Dec. 20, 2000); *cf. Prize Cases*, 67 U.S. 635, 2 Black, at 668 (recognizing that a state of war exists even if "the declaration of it be *unilateral*" (emphasis in original)). In February 1998, al Qaeda leadership issued another statement ordering the indiscriminate — and, even under the laws of war as applied to legitimate nation-states, plainly illegal — killing of American civilians and military personnel alike. *See* Jihad Against Jews and Crusaders: World Islamic Front Statement 2 (Feb. 23, 1998), in Y. Alexander & M. Swetnam, Usama bin Laden's al-Qaida: Profile of a Terrorist Network,

App. 1B (2001) ("The ruling to kill the Americans and their allies — civilians and military — is an individual duty for every Muslim who can do it in any country in which it is possible to do it"). This was not mere rhetoric; even before September 11, 2001, al Qaeda was involved in the bombing of the World Trade Center in New York City in 1993, the bombing of the Khobar Towers in Saudi Arabia in 1996, the bombing of the U.S. Embassies in Kenya and Tanzania in 1998, and the attack on the U.S.S. COLE in Yemen in 2000. *See id.*, at 1. In response to these incidents, the United States "attack[ed] facilities belonging to Usama bin Ladin's network" as early as 1998. Dept. of State Fact Sheet: Usama bin Ladin (Aug. 21, 1998). Based on the foregoing, the President's judgment — that the present conflict substantially predates the AUMF, extending at least as far back as al Qaeda's 1996 declaration of war on our Nation, and that the theater of war extends at least as far as the localities of al Qaeda's principal bases of operations — is beyond judicial reproach. And the plurality's unsupportable contrary determination merely confirms that "'the Judiciary has neither aptitude, facilities nor responsibility'" for making military or foreign affairs judgments. *Hamdi*, 542 U.S., at 585 (THOMAS, J., dissenting) (quoting *Chicago & Southern Air Lines*, 333 U.S., at 111).

B

The third consideration identified by Winthrop's treatise for the exercise of military commission jurisdiction pertains to the persons triable before such a commission, . . . Winthrop 838. Law-of-war military commissions have jurisdiction over "'individuals of the enemy's army who have been guilty of illegitimate warfare or other offences in violation of the laws of war,'" [(plurality opinion)]. They also have jurisdiction over "[i]rregular armed bodies or persons not forming part of the organized forces of a belligerent" "who would not be likely to respect the laws of war." [*Id.*] Indeed, according to Winthrop, such persons are not "within the protection of the laws of war" and were "liable to be shot, imprisoned, or banished, either summarily where their guilt was clear or upon trial and conviction by military commission." [Winthrop] at 784. This consideration is easily satisfied here, as Hamdan is an unlawful combatant charged with joining and conspiring with a terrorist network dedicated to flouting the laws of war. 344 F. Supp. 2d 152, 161 (D.C. 2004). . . .

C

The fourth consideration relevant to the jurisdiction of law-of-war military commissions relates to the nature of the offense charged. As relevant here, such commissions have jurisdiction to try "'[v]iolations of the laws and usages of war cognizable by military tribunals only,'" [(plurality opinion)]. In contrast to the preceding considerations, this Court's precedents establish that judicial review of "whether any of the acts charged is an offense against the law of war cognizable before a military tribunal" is appropriate. *Quirin*, 317 U.S., at 29. However, "charges of violations of the law of war triable before a military tribunal need not be stated with the precision of a common law indictment." *Yamashita*, 327 U.S., at 17. And whether an offense is a violation of the law of war cognizable before a military commission must be determined pursuant to "the system of common law applied by military tribunals." *Quirin, supra*, at 30, *Yamashita, supra*, at 8.

The common law of war as it pertains to offenses triable by military commission is derived from the "experience of our wars" and our wartime tribunals, Winthrop 839, and "the laws and usages of war as understood and practiced by the civilized nations of the world," 11 Op. Att'y Gen. 297, 310 (1865). Moreover, the common law of war is marked by two important features. First, as with the common law generally, it is flexible and evolutionary in nature, building upon the experience of the past and taking account of the exigencies of the present. Thus, "[t]he law of war, like every other code of laws, declares what shall not be done, and does not say what may be done. The legitimate use of the great power of war, or rather the prohibitions upon the use of that power, increase or diminish as the necessity of the case demands." *Id.*, at 300. Accordingly, this Court has recognized that the "jurisdiction" of "our common-law war courts" has not been "prescribed by statute," but rather "has been adapted in each instance to the need that called it forth." *Madsen*, 343 U.S., at 346-348. Second, the common law of war affords a measure of respect for the judgment of military commanders. Thus, "[t]he commander of an army in time of war has the same power to organize military tribunals and execute their judgments that he has to set his squadrons in the field and fight battles. His authority in each case is from the law and usage of war." 11 Op. Att'y Gen., at 305. In recognition of these principles, Congress has generally "'left it to the President, and the military commanders representing him, to employ the commission, *as occasion may require*, for the investigation and punishment of violations of the law of war.'" *Madsen, supra*, at 347, n. 9 (quoting Winthrop 831; emphasis added).

In one key respect, the plurality departs from the proper framework for evaluating the adequacy of the charge against Hamdan under the laws of war. The plurality holds that where, as here, "neither the elements of the offense nor the range of permissible punishments is defined by statute or treaty, the precedent [establishing whether an offense is triable by military commission] must be plain and unambiguous." This is a pure contrivance, and a bad one at that. It is contrary to the presumption we acknowledged in *Quirin*, namely, that the actions of military commissions are "not to be set aside by the courts without the *clear conviction* that they are" unlawful, 317 U.S., at 25 (emphasis added). It is also contrary to *Yamashita*, which recognized the legitimacy of that military commission notwithstanding a substantial disagreement pertaining to whether Yamashita had been charged with a violation of the law of war. *Compare* 327 U.S., at 17 (noting that the allegations were "adequat[e]" and "need not be stated with . . . precision"), *with id.*, at 35 (Murphy, J., dissenting) (arguing that the charge was inadequate). Nor does it find support from the separation of powers authority cited by the plurality. Indeed, Madison's praise of the separation of powers in The Federalist No. 47, . . ., if it has any relevance at all, merely highlights the illegitimacy of today's judicial intrusion onto core executive prerogatives in the waging of war, where executive competence is at its zenith and judicial competence at its nadir.

The plurality's newly minted clear-statement rule is also fundamentally inconsistent with the nature of the common law which, by definition, evolves and develops over time and does not, in all cases, "say what may be done." 11 Op. Att'y Gen., at 300. Similarly, it is inconsistent with the nature of warfare, which also evolves and changes over time, and for which a flexible, evolutionary common-law system is uniquely appropriate. Though the charge against Hamdan easily satisfies even the plurality's manufactured rule, . . . the plurality's inflexible approach has dangerous implications for the Executive's ability to discharge his duties as Commander in Chief in future cases. We should undertake to determine whether an unlawful combatant has been charged with an offense against the law of war with an understanding that the common law of war is flexible, responsive to the exigencies of the present conflict, and deferential to the judgment of military commanders.

1

Under either the correct, flexible approach to evaluating the adequacy of Hamdan's charge, or under the plurality's new, clear-statement approach, Hamdan has been charged with conduct constituting two distinct violations of the law of war cognizable before a military commission: membership in a war-criminal enterprise and conspiracy to commit war crimes. The charging section of the indictment alleges both that Hamdan "willfully and knowingly joined an enterprise of persons who shared a common criminal purpose," . . . and that he "conspired and agreed with [al Qaeda] to commit . . . offenses triable by military commission," *ibid.*

The common law of war establishes that Hamdan's willful and knowing membership in al Qaeda is a war crime chargeable before a military commission. Hamdan, a confirmed enemy combatant and member or affiliate of al Qaeda, has been charged with willfully and knowingly joining a group (al Qaeda) whose purpose is "to support violent attacks against property and nationals (both military and civilian) of the United States." [Charge Sheet.] Moreover, the allegations specify that Hamdan joined and maintained his relationship with al Qaeda even though he "believed that Usama bin Laden and his associates were involved in the attacks on the U.S. Embassies in Kenya and Tazania in August 1998, the attack on the USS COLE in October 2000, and the attacks on the United States on September 11, 2001." [*Id.*] These allegations, against a confirmed unlawful combatant, are alone sufficient to sustain the jurisdiction of Hamdan's military commission.

For well over a century it has been established that "to unite with banditti, jayhawkers, guerillas, or any other unauthorized marauders is a high offence against the laws of war; *the offence is complete when the band is organized or joined. The atrocities committed by such a band do not constitute the offence, but make the reasons, and sufficient reasons they are, why such banditti are denounced by the laws of war.*" 11 Op. Att'y Gen., at 312 (emphasis added). In other words, unlawful combatants, such as Hamdan, violate the law of war merely by joining an organization, such as al Qaeda, whose principal purpose is the "killing [and] disabling . . . of peaceable citizens or soldiers." Winthrop 784; *see also* 11 Op. Att'y Gen., at 314 ("A bushwhacker, a jayhawker, a bandit, a war rebel, an assassin, being public enemies, may be tried, condemned, and executed as offenders against the laws of war"). This conclusion is unsurprising, as it is a "cardinal principle of the law of war . . . that the civilian population must enjoy complete immunity." 4 International Committee of Red Cross, Commentary: Geneva Convention Relative to the Protection of Civilian Persons in Time of War 3 (J. Pictet ed. 1958). "Numerous instances of trials, for 'Violation of the laws of war,' of offenders of this description, are published in the General Orders of the years 1862 to 1866." Winthrop 784, and n 57. Accordingly, on this basis alone, "the allegations of [Hamdan's] charge, tested by any reasonable standard, adequately allege a violation of the law of war." *Yamashita*, 327 U.S., at 17.

The conclusion that membership in an organization whose purpose is to violate the laws of war is an offense triable by military commission is confirmed by the experience of the military tribunals convened by the United States at Nuremberg. Pursuant to Article 10 of the Charter of the International Military Tribunal (IMT), the United States convened military tribunals "to bring individuals to trial for membership" in "a group or organization . . . declared criminal by the [IMT]." 1 Trials of War Criminals Before the Nuernberg Military Tribunals, p XII (hereinafter Trials). The IMT designated various components of four Nazi groups — the Leadership Corps, Gestapo, SD, and SS — as criminal organizations. 22 IMT, Trial of the Major War Criminals 505, 511, 517 (1948); *see also* T. Taylor, The Anatomy of the Nuremberg Trials: A Personal Memoir 584-585 (1992). "[A] member of [such] an organization [could] be . . . convicted of the crime of membership and be punished for that crime by death." 22 IMT, at 499. Under this authority, the United States Military Tribunal at Nuremberg convicted numerous individuals for the act of knowing and voluntary membership in these organizations. For example, in Military Tribunal Case No. 1, *United States v. Brandt*, Karl Brandt, Karl Gebhardt, Rudolf Brandt, Joachim Mrugowsky, Wolfram Sievers, Viktor Brack, and Waldemar Hoven, were convicted and sentenced to death for the crime of, *inter alia*, membership in an organization declared criminal by the IMT; Karl Genzken and Fritz Fischer were sentenced to life imprisonment for the same; and Helmut Poppendick was convicted of no other offense than membership in a criminal organization and sentenced to a 10-year term of imprisonment. 2 Trials 180-300. This Court denied habeas relief, 333 U.S. 836 (1948), and the executions were carried out at Landsberg prison on June 2, 1948. 2 Trials 330.

Moreover, the Government has alleged that Hamdan was not only a member of al Qaeda while it was carrying out terrorist attacks on civilian targets in the United States and abroad, but also that Hamdan aided and assisted al Qaeda's top leadership by supplying weapons, transportation, and other services. . . . These allegations further confirm that Hamdan is triable before a law-of-war military commission for his involvement with al Qaeda. *See* H.R. Doc. No. 65, 55th Cong., 3d Sess., 234 (1894) ("[T]here are numerous rebels . . . that . . . furnish the enemy with arms, provisions, clothing, horses and means of transportation; [such] insurgents are banding together in several of the interior counties for the purpose of assisting the enemy to rob, to maruad and to lay waste to the country. *All such persons are by the laws of war in every civilized country liable to capital punishment*" (emphasis added)); Winthrop 840 (including in the list of offenses triable by law-of-war military commissions "dealing with . . . enemies, or furnishing them with money, arms, provisions, medicines, &c"). Undoubtedly, the conclusion that such conduct violates the law of war led to the enactment of Article 104 of the UCMJ, which provides that "[a]ny person who . . . aids, or attempts to aid, the enemy with arms, ammunition, supplies, money, or other things . . . shall suffer death or such other punishment as a court-martial or military commission may direct." 10 U.S.C. § 904.

2

Separate and apart from the offense of joining a contingent of "uncivilized combatants who [are] not . . . likely to respect the laws of war," Winthrop 784, Hamdan has been charged with "conspir[ing] and agree[ing] with . . . the al Qaida organization . . . to commit . . . offenses triable by military commission. . . ." Those offenses include "attacking civilians; attacking civilian objects; murder by an unprivileged belligerent; and terrorism." *Ibid.* This, too, alleges a violation of the law of war triable by military commission.

"[T]he experience of our wars," Winthrop 839, is rife with evidence that establishes beyond any doubt that conspiracy to violate the laws of war is itself an offense cognizable before a law-of-war military commission. World War II provides the most recent examples of the use of American military commissions to try offenses pertaining to violations of the laws of war. In that conflict, the orders establishing the jurisdiction of military commissions in various theaters of operation provided that conspiracy to violate the laws of war was a cognizable offense. *See* Letter, General Headquarters, United States Army Forces, Pacific (Sept. 24, 1945), Record in *Yamashita v. Styer*, O.T. 1945, No. 672, pp 14, 16 (Exh. F) (Order respecting the "Regulations Governing the Trial of War Criminals" provided that "participation in a common plan or conspiracy to accomplish" various offenses against the law of war was cognizable before military commissions); 1 United Nations War Crimes Commission, Law Reports of Trials of War Criminals 114-115 (1997) (hereinafter U.N. Commission) (recounting that the orders establishing World War II military commissions in the Pacific and China included "participation in a common plan or conspiracy" pertaining to certain violations of the laws of war as an offense triable by military commission). Indeed, those orders authorized trial by military commission of participation in a conspiracy to commit "murder . . . or other inhumane acts . . . against any civilian population," *id.*, at 114, which is precisely the offense Hamdan has been charged with here. And conspiracy to violate the laws of war was charged in the highest profile case tried before a World War II military commission, *see Quirin*, 317 U.S., at 23, and on numerous other occasions. *See, e.g., Colepaugh v. Looney*, 235 F.2d 429, 431 (10th Cir. 1956); Green 848 (describing the conspiracy trial of Julius Otto Kuehn).

To support its contrary conclusion, . . . the plurality attempts to evade the import of *Quirin* (and the other World War II authorities) by resting upon this Court's failure to address the sufficiency of the conspiracy charge in the *Quirin* case. . . . But the common law of war cannot be ascertained from this Court's failure to pass upon an issue, or indeed to even mention the issue in its opinion; rather, it is ascertained by the practice and usage of war. Winthrop 839. . . .

The Civil War experience provides further support for the President's conclusion that conspiracy to violate the laws of war is an offense cognizable before law-of-war military commissions. Indeed, in the highest profile case to be tried before a military commission relating to that war, namely, the trial of the men involved in the assassination of President Lincoln, the charge provided that those men had "combin[ed], confederat[ed], and conspir[ed] . . . to kill and murder" President Lincoln. G.C.M.O. No. 356 (1865), reprinted in H.R. Doc. No. 314, 55th Cong., 3d Sess., 696 (1899) (hereinafter G.C.M.O. No. 356).

In addition to the foregoing high-profile example, Winthrop's treatise enumerates numerous Civil War military commission trials for conspiracy to violate the law of war. Winthrop 839, n. 5. The plurality attempts to explain these examples away by suggesting that the conspiracies listed by Winthrop are best understood as "a species of compound offense," namely, violations both of the law of war and ordinary criminal laws, rather than "stand-alone offense[s] against the law of war." . . . But the fact that, for example, conspiracy to commit murder can at the same time violate ordinary criminal laws and the law of war, so that it is "a combination of the two species of offenses," Howland 1071, does not establish that a military commission would not have jurisdiction to try that crime solely on the basis that it was a violation of the law of war. Rather, if anything, and consistent with the principle that the common law of war is flexible and affords some level of deference to the judgments of military commanders, it establishes that military commissions would have the discretion to try the offense as (1) one against the law of war, or (2) one against the ordinary criminal laws, or (3) both.

In any event, the plurality's effort to avoid the import of Winthrop's footnote through the smokescreen of its "compound offense" theory, . . . , cannot be reconciled with the particular charges that sustained military commission jurisdiction in the cases that Winthrop cites. For example, in the military commission trial of Henry Wirz, Charge I provided that he had been

> "[m]aliciously, willfully, and traitorously . . . *combining, confederating, and conspiring*, together [with various other named and unnamed coconspirators], to injure the health and destroy the lives of soldiers in the military service of the United States, then held and being prisoners of war within the lines of the so-called Confederate States, and in the military prisons thereof, to the end that the armies of the United States might be weakened and impaired, *in violation of the laws and customs of war.*" G.C.M.O. No. 607 (1865), reprinted in H.R. Doc. No. 314, at 785 (emphasis added).

Likewise, in the military commission trial of Lenger Grenfel, Charge I accused Grenfel of "[c]*onspiring, in violation of the laws of war*, to release rebel prisoners of war confined by authority of the United States at Camp Douglas, near Chicago, Ill." G.C.M.O. No. 452 (1865), reprinted in H.R. Doc. No. 314, at 724 (emphasis added); *see also* G.C.M.O. No. 41, at 20 (1864) (indictment in the military commission trial of Robert Louden charged "[c]onspiring with the rebel enemies of the United States to embarrass and impede the military authorities in the suppression of the existing rebellion, by the burning and destruction of steamboats and means of transportation on the Mississippi river"). These examples provide incontrovertible support for the President's conclusion that the common law of war permits military commission trials for conspiracy to violate the law of war. And they specifically contradict the plurality's conclusion to the contrary, thereby easily satisfying its requirement that the Government "make a substantial showing that the crime for which it seeks to try a defendant by military commission is acknowledged to be an offense against the law of war.". . .

The plurality further contends, in reliance upon Winthrop, that conspiracy is not an offense cognizable before a law-of-war military commission because "it is not enough to intend to violate the law of war and commit overt acts in furtherance of that intention unless the overt acts either are themselves offenses against the law of war or constitute steps sufficiently substantial to qualify as an attempt." . . . But Winthrop does not support the plurality's conclusion. The passage in Winthrop cited by the plurality states only that "the jurisdiction of the military commission should be restricted to cases of offence consisting in *overt acts, i.e.* in unlawful commissions or actual attempts to commit, and not in intentions merely." Winthrop 841 (emphasis in original). This passage would be helpful to the plurality if its subject were "conspiracy," rather than the "jurisdiction of the military commission." Winthrop is not speaking here of the requirements for a conspiracy charge, but of the requirements for *all* charges. Intentions do not suffice. An unlawful act — such as committing the crime of conspiracy — is necessary. Winthrop says nothing to exclude either conspiracy or membership in a criminal enterprise, both of which go beyond "intentions merely" and "consis[t] of *overt acts, i.e.* . . . unlawful commissions or actual attempts to commit," and both of which are *expressly* recognized by Winthrop as crimes against the law of war triable by military commissions. *Id.*, at 784; *id.*, at 839, and n. 5, 840. Indeed, the commission of an *"overt ac[t]"* is the traditional requirement for the completion of the crime of conspiracy, and the charge against Hamdan alleges numerous such overt acts. . . . The plurality's approach, unsupported by Winthrop, requires that any overt act to further a conspiracy must *itself* be a completed war crime *distinct from conspiracy* — which merely begs the question the plurality sets out to answer, namely, whether conspiracy itself may constitute a violation of the law of war. And, even the plurality's unsupported standard is satisfied here, Hamdan has been charged with the overt acts of providing protection, transportation, weapons, and other services to the enemy, . . ., acts which in and of themselves are violations of the laws of war. *See* . . . Winthrop 839-840.

3

Ultimately, the plurality's determination that Hamdan has not been charged with an offense triable before a military commission rests not upon any historical example or authority, but upon the plurality's raw judgment of the "inability on the Executive's part here to satisfy the most basic precondition . . . for establishment of military commissions: military necessity." . . . This judgment starkly confirms that the plurality has appointed itself the ultimate arbiter of what is quintessentially a policy and military judgment, namely, the appropriate military measures to take against those who "aided the terrorist attacks that occurred on September 11, 2001." AUMF §2(a), 115 Stat. 224. The plurality's suggestion that Hamdan's commission is illegitimate because it is not dispensing swift justice on the battlefield is unsupportable. . . . Even a cursory review of the authorities confirms that law-of-war military commissions have wide-ranging jurisdiction to try offenses against the law of war in exigent and nonexigent circumstances alike. *See, e.g.,* Winthrop 839-840; *see also Yamashita*, 327 U.S., at 5 (military commission trial after the cessation of hostilities in the Philippines); *Quirin*, 317 U.S. 1 (military commission trial in Washington, D.C.). Traditionally, retributive justice for heinous war crimes is as much a "military necessity" as the "demands" of "military efficiency" touted by the plurality, and swift military retribution is precisely what Congress authorized the President to impose on the September 11 attackers in the AUMF.

Today a plurality of this Court would hold that conspiracy to massacre innocent civilians does not violate the laws of war. This determination is unsustainable. The judgment of the political branches that Hamdan, and others like him, must be held accountable before military commissions for their involvement with and membership in an unlawful organization dedicated to inflicting massive civilian casualties is supported by virtually every relevant authority, including all of the authorities invoked by the plurality today. It is also supported by the nature of the present conflict. We are not engaged in a traditional battle with a nation-state, but with a worldwide, hydra-headed enemy, who lurks in the shadows conspiring to reproduce the atrocities of September 11, 2001, and who has boasted of sending suicide bombers into civilian gatherings, has proudly distributed videotapes of beheadings of civilian workers, and has tortured and dismembered captured American soldiers. But according to the plurality, when our Armed Forces capture those who are plotting terrorist atrocities like the bombing of the Khobar Towers, the bombing of the U.S.S. COLE, and the attacks of September 11 — even if their plots are advanced to the very brink of fulfillment — our military cannot charge those criminals with any offense against the laws of war. Instead, our troops must catch the terrorists "redhanded," . . . in the midst of *the attack itself*, in order to bring them to justice. Not only is this conclusion fundamentally in consistent with the cardinal principal of the law of war, namely protecting non-combatants, but it would sorely hamper the President's ability to confront and defeat a new and deadly enemy. . . .

III

The Court holds that even if "the Government has charged Hamdan with an offense against the law of war cognizable by military commission, the commission lacks power to proceed" because of its failure to comply with the terms of the UCMJ and the four Geneva Conventions signed in 1949. This position is untenable.

A

As with the jurisdiction of military commissions, the procedure of such commissions "has [not] been prescribed by statute," but "has been adapted in each instance to the need that called it forth." *Madsen*, 343 U.S., at 347-348. Indeed, this Court has concluded that "[i]n the absence of attempts by Congress to limit the President's power, it appears that, as Commander in Chief of the Army and Navy of the United States, he may, in time of war, establish and prescribe the jurisdiction and procedure of military commissions." *Id.*, at 348. This conclusion is consistent with this Court's understanding that military commissions are "our common-law war courts." *Id.*, at

346-347.[19] As such, "[s]hould the conduct of those who compose martial-law tribunals become [a] matter of judicial determination subsequently before the civil courts, those courts will give great weight to the opinions of the officers as to what the customs of war in any case justify and render necessary." Birkhimer 534.

The Court nevertheless concludes that at least one provision of the UCMJ amounts to an attempt by Congress to limit the President's power. This conclusion is not only contrary to the text and structure of the UCMJ, but it is also inconsistent with precedent of this Court. Consistent with *Madsen*'s conclusion pertaining to the common-law nature of military commissions and the President's discretion to prescribe their procedures, Article 36 of the UCMJ authorizes the President to establish procedures for military commissions "which shall, *so far as he considers practicable,* apply the principles of law and the rules of evidence generally recognized in the trial of criminal cases in the United States district courts, but which may not be contrary to or inconsistent with this chapter." 10 U.S.C. § 836(a) (emphasis added). Far from constraining the President's authority, Article 36 recognizes the President's prerogative to depart from the procedures applicable in criminal cases whenever *he alone* does not deem such procedures "practicable." While the procedural regulations promulgated by the Executive must not be "contrary to" the UCMJ, only a few provisions of the UCMJ mention "military commissions," . . ., and there is no suggestion that the procedures to be employed by Hamdan's commission implicate any of those provisions.

Notwithstanding the foregoing, the Court concludes that Article 36(b) of the UCMJ, 10 U.S.C. § 836(b), which provides that "[a]ll rules and regulations made under this article shall be uniform insofar as practicable," . . ., requires the President to employ the same rules and procedures in military commissions as are employed by courts-martial *"insofar as practicable."* . . . The Court

---

[19] [n. 15] Though it does not constitute a basis for any holding of the Court, the Court maintains that, as a "general rule," "the procedures governing trials by military commission historically have been the same as those governing courts-martial." . . . While it is undoubtedly true that military commissions have invariably employed most of the procedures employed by courts-martial, that is not a requirement. *See* Winthrop 841 ("[M]ilitary commissions . . . are commonly conducted according to the rules and forms governing courts-martial. These war-courts are indeed more summary in their action than are the courts held under the Articles of war, and . . . their proceedings . . . will not be rendered *illegal* by the omission of details required upon trials by courts-martial" (emphasis in original; footnotes omitted)); 1 U.N. Commission 116-117 ("The [World War II] Mediterranean Regulations (No. 8) provide that Military Commissions shall conduct their proceedings as may be deemed necessary for full and fair trial, having regard for, *but not being bound by,* the rules of procedure prescribed for General Courts Martial" (emphasis added)); *id.,* at 117 ("In the [World War II] European directive it is stated . . . that Military Commissions shall have power to make, as occasion requires, such rules for the conduct of their proceedings consistent with the powers of such Commissions, and with the rules of procedure . . . as are deemed necessary for a full and fair trial of the accused, having regard for, without being bound by, the rules of procedure and evidence prescribed for General Courts Martial"). Moreover, such a requirement would conflict with the settled understanding of the flexible and responsive nature of military commissions and the President's wartime authority to employ such tribunals as he sees fit. *See* Birkhimer 537-538 ("[M]ilitary commissions may so vary their procedure as to adapt it to any situation, and may extend their powers to any necessary degree. . . . The military commander decides upon the character of the military tribunal which is suited to the occasion . . . and his decision is final").

further concludes that Hamdan's commission is unlawful because the President has not explained why it is not practicable to apply the same rules and procedures to Hamdan's commission as would be applied in a trial by court martial. . . .

This interpretation of §836(b) is unconvincing. As an initial matter, the Court fails to account for our cases interpreting the predecessor to Article 21 of the UCMJ — Article 15 of the Articles of War — which provides crucial context that bears directly on the proper interpretation of Article 36(b). Article 15 of the Articles of War provided that:

> "The provisions of these articles conferring jurisdiction upon courts-martial shall not be construed as depriving military commissions, provost courts, or other military tribunals of concurrent jurisdiction in respect of offenders or offences that by statute or by the law of war may be triable by such military commissions, provost courts, or other military tribunals."

In *Yamashita*, this Court concluded that Article 15 of the Articles of War preserved the President's unfettered authority to prescribe military commission procedure. The Court explained, "[b]y thus recognizing military commissions in order to preserve their traditional jurisdiction over enemy combatants unimpaired by the Articles, Congress gave sanction . . . to *any use* of the military commission contemplated by the common law of war." 327 U.S., at 20 (emphasis added); *see also Quirin*, 317 U.S., at 28; *Madsen*, 343 U.S., at 355. In reaching this conclusion, this Court treated as authoritative the congressional testimony of Judge Advocate General Crowder, who testified that Article 15 of the Articles of War was enacted to preserve the military commission as "'our common-law war court.'" *Yamashita, supra*, at 19, n. 7. And this Court recognized that Article 15's preservation of military commissions as common-law war courts preserved the President's commander-in-chief authority to both "establish" military commissions and to "prescribe [their] procedure[s]." *Madsen*, 343 U.S., at 348; *id.*, at 348-349 (explaining that Congress had "refrain[ed] from legislating" in the area of military commission procedures, in "contras[t] with its traditional readiness to . . . prescrib[e], with particularity, the jurisdiction and procedure of United States courts-martial"); *cf.* Green 834 ("The military commission exercising jurisdiction under common law authority is usually appointed by a superior military commander and is limited in its procedure only by the will of that commander. Like any other common law court, in the absence of directive of superior authority to the contrary, the military commission is free to formulate its own rules of procedure").

Given these precedents, the Court's conclusion that Article 36(b) requires the President to apply the same rules and procedures to military commissions as are applicable to courts-martial is unsustainable. When Congress codified Article 15 of the Articles of War in Article 21 of the UCMJ it was "presumed to be aware of . . . and to adopt" this Court's interpretation of that provision as preserving the common-law status of military commissions, inclusive of the President's unfettered authority to prescribe their procedures. *Lorillard v. Pons*, 434 U.S. 575, 580 (1978). The Court's conclusion that Article 36(b) repudiates this settled meaning of Article 21 is not based upon a specific textual reference to military commissions, but rather on a one-sentence subsection providing that "[a]ll rules and regulations made under this article shall be uniform insofar as practicable." 10 U.S.C. § 836(b). This is little more than an impermissible repeal by implication. *See Branch v. Smith*, 538 U.S. 254, 273 (2003). . . . Moreover, the Court's conclusion is flatly contrary to its duty not to set aside Hamdan's commission "without the *clear* conviction that [it is] in conflict with the . . . laws of Congress constitutionally enacted." *Quirin, supra*, at 25 (emphasis added).

Nothing in the text of Article 36(b) supports the Court's sweeping conclusion that it represents an unprecedented congressional effort to change the nature of military commissions from common-law war courts to tribunals that must presumptively function like courts-martial. And such an interpretation would be strange indeed. The vision of uniformity that motivated the adoption of the UCMJ, embodied specifically in Article 36(b), is nothing more than uniformity across the separate branches of the armed services. *See* ch. 169, 64 Stat. 107 (preamble to the UCMJ explaining that the UCMJ is an act "[t]o unify, consolidate, revise, and codify the Articles of War, the Articles for the Government of the Navy, and the disciplinary laws of the Coast Guard"). There is no indication that the UCMJ was intended to require uniformity in procedure between courts-martial and military commissions, tribunals that the UCMJ itself recognizes are different. To the contrary, the UCMJ expressly recognizes that different tribunals will be constituted in different manners and employ different procedures. *See* 10 U.S.C. § 866 (providing for three different types of courts-martial — general, special, and summary — constituted in different manners and employing different procedures). Thus, Article 36(b) is best understood as establishing that, so far as practicable, the rules and regulations governing tribunals convened by the Navy must be uniform with the rules and regulations governing tribunals convened by the Army. But, consistent with this Court's prior interpretations of Article 21 and over a century of historical practice, it cannot be understood to require the President to conform the procedures employed by military commissions to those employed by courts-martial.[20]

Even if Article 36(b) could be construed to require procedural uniformity among the various tribunals contemplated by the UCMJ, Hamdan would not be entitled to relief. Under the Court's reading, the President is entitled to prescribe different rules for military commissions than for courts-martial when he determines that it is not "practicable" to prescribe uniform rules. The Court does not resolve the level of deference such determinations would be owed, however, because, in its view, "[t]he President has not . . . [determined] that it

---

[20] [n. 17] [The Court] . . . makes no citation of the legislative history pertaining to Article 36(b), which contradicts its interpretation of that provision. Indeed, if it were authoritative, the *only* legislative history relating to Article 36(b) would confirm the obvious — Article 36(b)'s uniformity requirement pertains to uniformity between the three branches of the Armed Forces, and no more. When that subsection was introduced as an amendment to Article 36, its author explained that it would leave the three branches "enough leeway to provide a different provision where it is absolutely necessary" because "there are some differences in the services." Hearings on H.R. 2498 before the Subcommittee No. 1 of the House Committee on Armed Services, 81st Cong., 1st Sess., 1015 (1949). A further statement explained that "there might be some slight differences that would pertain as to the Navy in contrast to the Army, but at least [Article 36(b)] is an expression of the congressional intent that we want it to be as uniform as possible." *Ibid.*

is impracticable to apply the rules for courts-martial." . . . This is simply not the case. On the same day that the President issued Military Commission Order No. 1, the Secretary of Defense explained that "the president decided to establish military commissions because he wanted the option of a process that is different from those processes which we already have, namely the federal court system . . . and the military court system," Dept. of Defense News Briefing on Military Commissions (Mar. 21, 2002) (remarks of Donald Rumsfeld) . . ., and that "[t]he commissions are intended to be different . . . because the [P]resident recognized that there had to be differences to deal with the unusual situation we face and that a different approach was needed." *Ibid.* The President reached this conclusion because

> "we're in the middle of a war, and . . . had to design a procedure that would allow us to pursue justice for these individuals while at the same time prosecuting the war most effectively. And that means setting rules that would allow us to preserve our intelligence secrets, develop more information about terrorist activities that might be planned for the future so that we can take action to prevent terrorist attacks against the United States. . . . [T]here was a constant balancing of the requirements of our war policy and the importance of providing justice for individuals . . . and *each* deviation from the standard kinds of rules that we have in our criminal courts was motivated by the desire to strike the balance between individual justice and the broader war policy." *Ibid.* (remarks of Douglas J. Feith, Under Secretary of Defense for Policy (emphasis added)).

The Court provides no explanation why the President's determination that employing court-martial procedures in the military commissions established pursuant to Military Commission Order No. 1 would hamper our war effort is in any way inadequate to satisfy its newly minted "practicability" requirement. On the contrary, this determination is precisely the kind for which the "Judiciary has neither aptitude, facilities nor responsibility and which has long been held to belong in the domain of political power not subject to judicial intrusion or inquiry." *Chicago & Southern Air Lines, Inc. v. Waterman S.S. Corp.*, 333 U.S. 103, 111 (1948). And, in the context of the present conflict, it is exactly the kind of determination Congress countenanced when it authorized the President to use all necessary and appropriate force against our enemies. Accordingly, the President's determination is sufficient to satisfy any practicability requirement imposed by Article 36(b).

The plurality further contends that Hamdan's commission is unlawful because it fails to provide him the right to be present at his trial, as recognized in 10 U.S.C.A. § 839(c) (Supp. 2006). . . . But § 839(c) applies to courts-martial, not military commissions. It provides:

> "When the members of a court-martial deliberate or vote, only the members may be present. All other proceedings, including any other consultation of the members of the court with counsel or the military judge, shall be made a part of the record and shall be in the presence of the accused, the defense counsel, the trial counsel, and, in cases in which a military judge has been detailed to the court, the military judge."

In context, "all other proceedings" plainly refers exclusively to "other proceedings" pertaining to a court-martial. This is confirmed by the provision's subsequent reference to "members of the *court*" and to "cases in which a military judge has been detailed to the *court.*" It is also confirmed by the other provisions of §839, which refer only to courts-martial. *See* §§839(a)(1)-(4) ("[A]ny time after the service of charges which have been referred for trial to a court-martial composed of a military judge and members, the military judge may . . . call the court into session without the presence of the members for the purpose of," hearing motions, issuing rulings, holding arraignments, receiving pleas, and performing various procedural functions). *See also* §839(b) ("Proceedings under subsection (a) shall be conducted in the presence of the accused"). Section 839(c) simply does not address the procedural requirements of military commissions.

B

The Court contends that Hamdan's military commission is also unlawful because it violates Common Article 3 of the Geneva Conventions. . . . Furthermore, Hamdan contends that his commission is unlawful because it violates various provisions of the Third Geneva Convention. These contentions are untenable.

1

As an initial matter, and as the Court of Appeals concluded, both of Hamdan's Geneva Convention claims are foreclosed by *Johnson v. Eisentrager*, 339 U.S. 763 (1950). In that case the respondents claimed, *inter alia*, that their military commission lacked jurisdiction because it failed to provide them with certain procedural safeguards that they argued were required under the Geneva Conventions. *Id.*, at 789-790. While this Court rejected the underlying merits of the respondents' Geneva Convention claims, *id.*, at 790, it also held, in the alternative, that the respondents could "not assert . . . that anything in the Geneva Convention makes them immune from prosecution or punishment for war crimes," *id.*, at 789. The Court explained:

> "We are not holding that these prisoners have no right which the military authorities are bound to respect. The United States, by the Geneva Convention of July 27, 1929, 47 Stat. 2021, concluded with forty-six other countries, including the German Reich, an agreement upon the treatment to be accorded captives. These prisoners claim to be and are entitled to its protection. It is, however, the obvious scheme of the Agreement that responsibility for observance and enforcement of these rights is upon political and military authorities. Rights of alien enemies are vindicated under it only through protests and intervention of protecting powers as the rights of our citizens against foreign governments are vindicated only by Presidential intervention." *Id.*, at 789, n. 14.

This alternative holding is no less binding than if it were the exclusive basis for the Court's decision. . . . While the Court attempts to cast *Eisentrager*'s unqualified, alternative holding as footnote dictum, . . . it does not dispute the correctness of its conclusion, namely, that the provisions of the 1929 Geneva Convention were not judicially enforceable because that Convention contemplated that diplomatic measures by political and military authorities were the exclusive mechanisms for such enforcement. Nor does the Court suggest that the 1949 Geneva Conventions departed from this framework. . . .

Instead, the Court concludes that petitioner may seek judicial enforcement of the provisions of the Geneva Conventions because "they are . . . part of the law of war. And compliance with the law of war is the condition upon which the authority set forth in Article 21 is granted." . . . But Article 21 authorizes the use of military commissions; it does not purport to render judicially enforceable aspects of the law of war that are not so enforceable of their own accord. *See Quirin*, 317 U.S., at 28 (by enacting Article 21, "Congress has explicitly provided, so far as it may constitutionally do so, that military tribunals shall have jurisdiction to try offenders or offenses against the law of war"). The Court cannot escape *Eisentrager's* holding merely by observing that Article 21 mentions the law of war; indeed, though *Eisentrager* did not specifically consider the Court's novel interpretation of Article 21, *Eisentrager* involved a challenge to the legality of a World War II military commission, which, like all such commissions, found its authorization in Article 15 of the Articles of War, the predecessor to Article 21 of the UCMJ. Thus, the Court's interpretation of Article 21 is foreclosed by *Eisentrager*.

In any event, the Court's argument is too clever by half. The judicial non-enforceability of the Geneva Conventions derives from the fact that those Conventions have exclusive enforcement mechanisms, *see Eisentrager, supra*, at 789, n. 14, and this, too, is part of the law of war. The Court's position thus rests on the assumption that Article 21's reference to the "laws of war" selectively incorporates only those aspects of the Geneva Conventions that the Court finds convenient, namely, the substantive requirements of Common Article 3, and not those aspects of the Conventions that the Court, for whatever reason, disfavors, namely the Conventions' exclusive diplomatic enforcement scheme. The Court provides no account of why the *partial* incorporation of the Geneva Conventions should extend only so far — and no further — because none is available beyond its evident preference to adjudicate those matters that the law of war, through the Geneva Conventions, consigns exclusively to the political branches.

Even if the Court were correct that Article 21 of the UCMJ renders judicially enforceable aspects of the law of war that are not so enforceable by their own terms, Article 21 simply cannot be interpreted to render judicially enforceable the particular provision of the law of war at issue here, namely Common Article 3 of the Geneva Conventions. As relevant, Article 21 provides that "[t]he provisions of this chapter conferring jurisdiction upon courts-martial do not deprive military commissions . . . of concurrent jurisdiction with respect to *offenders or offenses* that by statute *or by the law of war* may be tried by military commissions." 10 U.S.C. §821 (emphasis added). Thus, to the extent Article 21 can be interpreted as authorizing judicial enforcement of aspects of the law of war that are not otherwise judicially enforceable, that authorization only extends to provisions of the law of war that relate to whether a particular "offender" or a particular "offense" is triable by military commission. Common Article 3 of the Geneva Conventions, the sole provision of the Geneva Conventions relevant to the Court's holding, relates to neither.

Rather, it relates exclusively to the particulars of the tribunal itself, namely, whether it is "regularly constituted" and whether it "afford[s] all the judicial guarantees which are recognized as indispensable by civilized peoples." Third Geneva Convention, Art. 3, ¶ 1(d), Relative to the Treatment of Prisoners of War, Aug. 12, 1949, [1955] 6 U.S.T. 3316, 3320, T.I.A.S. No. 3364.

2

In addition to being foreclosed by *Eisentrager*, Hamdan's claim under Common Article 3 of the Geneva Conventions is meritless. Common Article 3 applies to "armed conflict not of an international character occurring in the territory of one of the High Contracting Parties." 6 U.S.T., at 3318. "Pursuant to [his] authority as Commander in Chief and Chief Executive of the United States," the President has "accept[ed] the legal conclusion of the Department of Justice . . . that common Article 3 of Geneva does not apply to . . . al Qaeda . . . detainees, because, among other reasons, the relevant conflicts are international in scope and common Article 3 applies only to 'armed conflict not of an international character.'" . . . Under this Court's precedents, "the meaning attributed to treaty provisions by the Government agencies charged with their negotiation and enforcement is entitled to great weight." *Sumitomo Shoji America, Inc. v. Avagliano*, 457 U.S. 176, 184-185 (1982). . . . Our duty to defer to the President's understanding of the provision at issue here is only heightened by the fact that he is acting pursuant to his constitutional authority as Commander in Chief and by the fact that the subject matter of Common Article 3 calls for a judgment about the nature and character of an armed conflict. *See generally United States v. Curtiss-Wright Export Corp.*, 299 U.S. 304, 320 (1936).

The President's interpretation of Common Article 3 is reasonable and should be sustained. The conflict with al Qaeda is international in character in the sense that it is occurring in various nations around the globe. Thus, it is also "occurring in the territory of" more than "one of the High Contracting Parties." The Court does not dispute the President's judgments respecting the nature of our conflict with al Qaeda, nor does it suggest that the President's interpretation of Common Article 3 is implausible or foreclosed by the text of the treaty. Indeed, the Court concedes that Common Article 3 is principally concerned with "furnish[ing] minimal protection to rebels involved in . . . a civil war," . . . precisely the type of conflict the President's interpretation envisions to be subject to Common Article 3. Instead, the Court, without acknowledging its duty to defer to the President, adopts its own, admittedly plausible, reading of Common Article 3. But where, as here, an ambiguous treaty provision ("not of an international character") is susceptible of two plausible, and reasonable, interpretations, our precedents require us to defer to the Executive's interpretation.

3

But even if Common Article 3 were judicially enforceable and applicable to the present conflict, petitioner would not be entitled to relief. As an initial matter, any claim petitioner has under Common Article 3 is not ripe. The only relevant "acts" that "are and shall remain prohibited" under Common Article 3 are "the *passing of sentences* and the *carrying out of executions* without previous judgment pronounced by a regularly constituted court affording all the judicial guarantees which are recognized as indispensable by civilized peoples." Art. 3, ¶ 1(d), 6 U.S.T., at 1318, 1320 (emphases added). As its terms make clear, Common Article 3 is only violated, as relevant here, by the act of "passing of sentenc[e]," and thus Hamdan will only have a claim *if* his military commission convicts him and imposes a sentence. Accordingly, as Hamdan's claim is "contingent [upon] future events that may not occur as anticipated, or indeed may not occur at all," it is not ripe for adjudication. *Texas v. United States*, 523 U.S. 296, 300 (1998) (internal quotation marks omitted). Indeed, even if we assume he will be convicted and sentenced, whether his trial will be conducted in a manner so as to deprive him of "the judicial guarantees which are recognized as indispensable by civilized peoples" is entirely speculative. And premature adjudication of Hamdan's claim is especially inappropriate here because "reaching the merits of the dispute would force us to decide whether an action taken by one of the other two branches of the Federal Government was unconstitutional." *Raines v. Byrd*, 521 U.S. 811, 819-820 (1997).

In any event, Hamdan's military commission complies with the requirements of Common Article 3. It is plainly "regularly constituted" because such commissions have been employed throughout our history to try unlawful combatants for crimes against the law of war. This Court has recounted that history as follows:

> "By a practice dating from 1847 and renewed and firmly established during the Civil War, military commissions have become adopted as authorized tribunals in this country in time of war. . . . Their competency has been recognized not only in acts of Congress, but in executive proclamations, in rulings of the courts, and in the opinions of the Attorneys General." *Madsen*, 343 U.S., at 346, n. 8.

Hamdan's commission has been constituted in accordance with these historical precedents. As I have previously explained, the procedures to be employed by that commission, and the Executive's authority to alter those procedures, are consistent with the practice of previous American military commissions. . . .

The Court concludes Hamdan's commission fails to satisfy the requirements of Common Article 3 not because it differs from the practice of previous military commissions but because it "deviate[s] from [the procedures] governing courts-martial." . . . But there is neither a statutory nor historical requirement that military commissions conform to the structure and practice of courts-martial. A military commission is a different tribunal, serving a different function, and thus operates pursuant to different procedures. The 150-year pedigree of the military commission is itself sufficient to establish that such tribunals are "regularly constituted court[s]." Art. 3, ¶ 1(d), 6 U.S.T., at 3320.

Similarly, the procedures to be employed by Hamdan's commission afford "all the judicial guarantees which are recognized as indispensable by civilized peoples." Neither the Court nor petitioner disputes the Government's description of those procedures.

"Petitioner is entitled to appointed military legal counsel, 32 C.F.R. 9.4(c)(2), and may retain a civilian attorney (which he has done), 32 C.F.R. 9.4(c)(2)(iii)(B). Petitioner is entitled to the presumption of innocence, 32 C.F.R. 9.5(b), proof beyond a reasonable doubt, 32 C.F.R. 9.5(c), and the right to remain silent, 32 C.F.R. 9.5(f). He may confront witnesses against him, 32 C.F.R. 9.5(i), and may subpoena his own witnesses, if reasonably available, 32 C.F.R. 9.5(h). Petitioner may personally be present at every stage of the trial unless he engages in disruptive conduct or the prosecution introduces classified or otherwise protected information for which no adequate substitute is available and whose admission will not deprive him of a full and fair trial, 32 C.F.R. 9.5(k); Military Commission Order No. 1 (Dep't of Defense Aug. 31, 2005) § 6(B)(3) and (D)(5)(b). If petitioner is found guilty, the judgment will be reviewed by a review panel, the Secretary of Defense, and the President, if he does not designate the Secretary as the final decisionmaker. 32 C.F.R. 9.6(h). The final judgment is subject to review in the Court of Appeals for the District of Columbia Circuit and ultimately in this Court. *See* DTA § 1005(e)(3), 119 Stat. 2743; 28 U.S.C. 1254(1)." Brief for Respondents 4.

Notwithstanding these provisions, which in my judgment easily satisfy the nebulous standards of Common Article 3,[21] the plurality concludes that Hamdan's commission is unlawful because of the possibility that Hamdan will be barred from proceedings and denied access to evidence that may be used to convict him. . . . But, under the commissions' rules, the Government may not impose such bar or denial on Hamdan if it would render his trial unfair, a question that is clearly within the scope of the appellate review contemplated by regulation and statute.

Moreover, while the Executive is surely not required to offer a particularized defense of these procedures prior to their application, the procedures themselves make clear that Hamdan would only be excluded (other than for disruption) if it were necessary to protect classified (or classifiable) intelligence, Dept. of Defense, Military Commission Order No. 1, § 6(B)(3) (Aug. 31, 2005), including the sources and methods for gathering such intelligence. The Government has explained that "we want to make sure that these proceedings, which are going on in the middle of the war, do not interfere with our war effort and . . . because of the way we would be able to handle interrogations and intelligence information, may actually assist us in promoting our war aims." News Briefing (remarks of Douglas J. Feith, Under Secretary of Defense for Policy). And this Court has concluded, in the very context of a threat to reveal our Nation's intelligence gathering sources and methods, that "[i]t is 'obvious and unarguable' that no governmental interest is more compelling than the security of the Nation," *Haig*, 453 U.S., at 307 (quoting

---

[21] [n. 20] Notably, a prosecutor before the *Quirin* military commission has described these procedures as "a substantial improvement over those in effect during World War II," further observing that "[t]hey go a long way toward assuring that the trials will be full and fair." National Institute of Military Justice, Procedures for Trials by Military Commissions of Certain Non-United States Citizens in the War Against Terrorism, p. x (2002) (hereinafter Procedures for Trials) (foreword by Lloyd N. Cutler).

Aptheker v. Secretary of State, 378 U.S. 500, 509 (1964)), and that "[m]easures to protect the secrecy of our Government's foreign intelligence operations plainly serve these interests," *Haig, supra*, at 307. . . . According to the Government, "[b]ecause al Qaeda operates as a clandestine force relying on sleeper agents to mount surprise attacks, one of the most critical fronts in the current war involves gathering intelligence about future terrorist attacks and how the terrorist network operates — identifying where its operatives are, how it plans attacks, who directs operations, and how they communicate." Brief for United States in No. 03-4792, *United States v. Moussaoui* (4th Cir.), p. 9. We should not rule out the possibility that this compelling interest can be protected, while at the same time affording Hamdan (and others like him) a fair trial.

In these circumstances, "civilized peoples" would take into account the context of military commission trials against unlawful combatants in the war on terrorism, including the need to keep certain information secret in the interest of preventing future attacks on our Nation and its foreign installations so long as it did not deprive the accused of a fair trial. Accordingly, the President's understanding of the requirements of Common Article 3 is entitled to "great weight." . . .

4

In addition to Common Article 3, which applies to conflicts "not of an international character," Hamdan also claims that he is entitled to the protections of the Third Geneva Convention, which applies to conflicts between two or more High Contracting Parties. There is no merit to Hamdan's claim.

Article 2 of the Convention provides that "the present Convention shall apply to all cases of declared war or of any other armed conflict which may arise between two or more of the High Contracting Parties." 6 U.S.T., at 1318. "Pursuant to [his] authority as Commander in Chief and Chief Executive of the United States," the President has determined that the Convention is inapplicable here, explaining that "none of the provisions of Geneva apply to our conflict with al Qaeda in Afghanistan or elsewhere throughout the world, because, among other reasons, al Qaeda is not a High Contracting Party." . . . The President's findings about the nature of the present conflict with respect to members of al Qaeda operating in Afghanistan represents a core exercise of his commander-in-chief authority that this Court is bound to respect. *See Prize Cases*, 67 U.S. 635, 2 Black, at 670. . . .

NOTES AND QUESTIONS

1. Do you agree with any of the opinions in *Hamdan* in their entirety? Do you agree with the plurality opinion on the issues that Justice Kennedy declined to decide? What issue do you view as the most important in reaching the correct decision in the case? Which opinion offered the most correct answer to that decisional issue?

2. The Notes following the *Quirin* case referred to Chief Justice Rehnquist's theory that where civil liberties clash with perceived military necessity, courts are less likely to protect civil liberties in cases decided during an armed conflict and more likely to protect civil liberties after the end of hostilities, even if the case originated during a time of armed conflict. Does *Hamdan* comport with that theory?

3. Justice Breyer's concurrence, which was joined by Justices Kennedy, Souter, and Ginsburg, observed, "Congress has denied the President the legislative authority to create military commissions of the kind at issue here. Nothing prevents the President from returning to Congress to seek the authority he believes necessary." *Hamdan v. Rumsfeld*, 126 S. Ct. 2749, 2799 (2006) (Breyer, J., concurring). In the wake of the Supreme Court's *Hamdan* ruling, President Bush did just that. In 2006, Congress passed and the President signed the Military Commissions Act of 2006, Pub. L. No. 109-366, 120 Stat. 2600 (to be codified at 10 U.S.C. §§ 948a *et seq.*; 28 U.S.C. § 2241). The Military Commissions Act "establishes procedures governing the use of military commissions to try alien unlawful enemy combatants engaged in hostilities against the United States" and specifies offenses that may be tried by military commissions. 10 U.S.C.A. § 948b(a). Among the controversial aspects of the Military Commissions Act are provisions that: (a) declare that the commissions established under the Act comply with Common Article 3 of the Geneva Convention, 10 U.S.C.A. § 948b(f); (b) prohibit an accused in a military commission proceeding from "invok[ing] the Geneva Conventions as a source of rights," *id.* at § 948b(g); (c) limit the commissions' jurisdiction to aliens, *id.* at § 948c; (d) allow the admissibility of some statements obtained by coercion, *id.* at § 948r; (e) authorize the general admissibility of hearsay evidence, *id.* at 949a(b)(2); and (f) allow the prosecution to prevent the defense from obtaining discovery of classified information, *id.* at § 949j(c).

4. One provision in the Military Commissions Act's "Punitive Matters" subchapter is particularly interesting. 10 U.S.C.A. § 950p provides:

Statement of substantive offenses

(a) Purpose — The provisions of this subchapter codify offenses that have traditionally been triable by military commissions. This chapter does not establish new crimes that did not exist before its enactment, but rather codifies those crimes for trial by military commission.

(b) Effect — Because the provisions of this subchapter (including provisions that incorporate definitions in other provisions of law) are declarative of existing law, they do not preclude trial for crimes that occurred before the date of the enactment of this chapter.

Among the substantive offenses included in the Act is conspiracy "to commit one or more substantive offenses triable by military commission." 10 U.S.C. § 950v(b)(28). Yet the plurality in the *Hamdan* case opined, "The crime of 'conspiracy' has rarely if ever been tried as such in this country by any law-of-war military commission not exercising some other form of jurisdiction, and does not appear in either the Geneva Conventions or the Hague Conventions — the major treaties on the law of war." *Hamdan*, 126 S. Ct. at 2758. Justice Kennedy declined to reach this question, *id.* at 2809 (Kennedy, J., concurring), while Justice Thomas, joined by Justices Scalia and Alito, dissented on the point. *Id.* at 2834-38 (Thomas, J., dissenting). Given Congress' Article I, § 8 power to "define and punish . . . offenses against the law of nations," would retroactive application of the Military Commissions Act's conspiracy article to alleged offenses before the date of that law's enactment violate the Ex Post Facto Clause, U.S. CONST. art. I, § 9, cl. 3? Is Congress' conclusion that it may be applied retroactively entitled to judicial deference despite the *Hamdan* plurality's conclusion that it was not an offense triable by military commission? Does the Ex Post Facto Clause even apply to a statute governing the trial of unlawful enemy alien combatants? If the plurality's conclusion had been the opinion of the full Court, which would prevail: (a) Congress' power to define offenses against the law of nations; or (b) the judiciary's "duty . . . to say what the law is"? *Marbury v. Madison*, 5 U.S. (1 Cranch) 137, 177 (1803).

Chapter 20

LAW REFORM AND GLOBALIZATION

Like any system of justice, military justice cannot be static. It may grow through legislation, or rule making by the Executive Branch, or judicial decisions. Unlike other aspects of the legal system, however, the normal array of interests may be absent or function differently in the case of military justice. Waves of reform have been relatively infrequent in American military justice. When they do arrive, they tend — with exceptions, such as enactment of the Uniform Code of Military Justice itself in 1950 — to be both modest and late. Routine change tends to be a one-way street tending to favor the government; more sweeping change tends to be the product of high-profile cases which, either singly or as a pattern, grip the attention of the public and therefore attract legislative interest. And even when there is political will to effect change, this may not be followed by sustained congressional interest in the form of oversight.

Congress may defer to the Department of Defense on military justice issues more than it might defer to a regulatory agency because of the absence of interest groups with a pocket book or other compelling stake in the subject. To the extent Congress views military justice as highly arcane, that further facilitates domination of the legislative process by the Executive Branch. An additional factor may be the existence of a "revolving door" between the pertinent committees of Congress and the Defense Department, making the two entities' interaction less arm's-length than might otherwise be the case. Congress has explicitly exempted courts-martial from the notice-and-comment procedure for military justice rulemaking such as issuance or amendment of the *Manual for Courts-Martial*. This in itself dramatically alters the dynamics of legal change by making the rulemaking process severely insular — much more so, for example, than is true of the process by which rules are made for the federal courts. Where important or even not-so-important changes are regularly made without hearings or legislative history (the 2006 amendment to Article 2(a)(10) of the UCMJ being but one example, *see* Chapter 6, §§ I and V, *supra*), but rather through informal contacts between the congressional committees and the military services, the chances that the results are wise or fair are needlessly reduced. Legislation on military justice in a democracy ought not to be a private affair to be worked out between the legislature and the military behind closed doors.

As for the courts, there is only so much that can be expected, especially where the vast bulk of the caseload in the military appellate courts is handled by uniformed lawyers in the eight law offices that provide appellate representation to the prosecution and defense, and *amicus curiae* presentations remain the exception. Because the military appellate courts tend to be quite conservative, and there are very few opportunities for public interest litigation over military justice matters in the civilian courts, it is almost immaterial that few federal judges would be willing to tackle institutional issues because of their own unfamiliarity with the basics of the subject.

Because military justice remains a highly specialized field, and because, as a practice area, it lacks the kind of economic incentives needed to attract new entrants that other fields enjoy, the knowledgeable part of the bar is vanishingly small. Nor is the military bar organized in a way that permits practitioners to exert the kind of group influence that is characteristic of the profession. The bar of the highest court of the jurisdiction — the United States Court of Appeals for the Armed Forces — has no organized status; it is a mere list of names. The same is true of the separate bars of the service courts of criminal appeals. While there does exist a voluntary Judge Advocates Association, which is affiliated with the American Bar Association and has a seat in the powerful House of Delegates, its activities have been limited and it tends not to stray from the official position of the armed services. The ABA and a few municipal and state bar associations have military law committees, and these can be potent forces for law reform.

The legal academy is another engine of law reform, but until the military commissions issues washed over the country, there was very little interest in military legal matters beyond the controversy over the "don't ask, don't tell" policy on gays and lesbians in the military and the related question of military recruiting on campus. This lack of interest is probably also a reflection of the simple fact that very few law professors have actually served in uniform. While such service may not be a *sine qua non* for academic involvement with military justice, its absence certainly diminishes the prospect for sustained academic engagement with the entire military justice endeavor.

In short, law reform in the military justice field is a tall order. Nonetheless, the War in Iraq and the military commissions created by President George W. Bush in the aftermath of 9/11 (and later given a statutory framework through the Military Commissions Act of 2006) have certainly helped to focus public, media, bar, and legislative attention on military justice to a greater extent than at any time since the Vietnam War. Whether the subject will remain at the forefront of public concerns for a sustained period remains to be seen, but these events suggest that this is a good time to take a hard look at the process by which military justice reforms take shape.

Military justice law reform can be incremental in the sense of simply keeping pace with legal developments in the larger system of justice, or it can be broader, extending to the institutional arrangements. This chapter will explore some aspects of military justice law reform at the turn of the 21st Century.

I. INTERNATIONAL HUMAN RIGHTS

Draft Principles Governing the Administration of Justice through Military Tribunals
UN Commission on Human Rights, E/CN.4/2006/58 (2006)

Principle No. 20, Review of codes of military justice

Codes of military justice should be subject to periodic systematic review, conducted in an independent and transparent manner, so as to ensure that the authority of military tribunals corresponds to strict functional necessity, without encroaching on the jurisdiction that can and should belong to ordinary civil courts.

64. Since the sole justification for the existence of military tribunals has to do with practical eventualities, such as those related to peacekeeping operations or extraterritorial situations, there is a need to check periodically whether this functional requirement still prevails.

65. Each such review of codes of military justice should be carried out by an independent body, which should recommend legislative reforms designed to limit any unjustified residual authority and thus return, to the greatest extent possible, to the jurisdiction of the civil courts under ordinary law, while seeking to avoid double jeopardy.

66. More generally, this periodic review should ensure that military justice is appropriate and effective in relation to its practical justification. It would also embody the fully democratic nature of an institution that must be accountable for its operations to the authorities and all citizens. In this way, the fundamental discussion concerning the existence of military justice as such can be conducted in a completely transparent way in a democratic society.

II. STATUTORY AND REGULATORY PROVISIONS

Uniform Code of Military Justice
Article 146. Code Committee

(a) *Annual survey.* A committee shall meet at least annually and shall make an annual comprehensive survey of the operation of this chapter.

(b) *Composition of committee.* The committee shall consist of —

(1) the judges of the United States Court of Appeals for the Armed Forces;

(2) the Judge Advocates General of the Army, Navy, and Air Force, the Chief Counsel of the Coast Guard, and the Staff Judge Advocate to the Commandant of the Marine Corps; and

(3) two members of the public appointed by the Secretary of Defense.

(c) *Reports.*

(1) After each such survey, the committee shall submit a report —

>   (A) to the Committees on Armed Services of the Senate and House of Representatives; and

>   (B) to the Secretary of Defense, the Secretaries of the military departments, and the Secretary of Homeland Security.

(2) Each report under paragraph (1) shall include the following:

(A) Information on the number and status of pending cases.

(B) Any recommendation of the committee relating to —

>>   (i) uniformity of policies as to sentences;

>>   (ii) amendments to this chapter; and

>>   (iii) any other matter the committee considers appropriate.

(d) *Qualification and terms of appointed members.* Each member of the committee appointed by the Secretary of Defense under subsection (B)(3) shall be a recognized authority in military justice or criminal law. Each such member shall be appointed for a term of three years.

(e) *Applicability of Federal Advisory Committee Act.* The Federal Advisory Committee Act (5 U.S.C. App. I) shall not apply to the committee.

NOTES AND QUESTIONS

1. The annual reports prepared by the "Code Committee on Military Justice" are available on the website of the United States Court of Appeals for the Armed Forces, www.armfor.uscourts.gov. Do they satisfy the requirements of Article 146? If you were on the Code Committee, how would you change the reports?

2. Is the Code Committee workable given its statutory membership? Are there constraints on the judges of the Court of Appeals that prevent them from performing the role Congress contemplated? How likely is it that the Judge Advocates General will act independently in their capacity as Code Committee members?

3. Should the Code Committee make decisions by formal vote or consensus?

4. The Code Committee typically meets once a year. Is that sufficient? Why is it exempt from the requirements of the Federal Advisory Committee Act?

5. What use do you think Congress has made of the annual reports?

6. What criteria would you apply when deciding who should be appointed as a public member of the Code Committee? Political affiliation?

Review of the Manual for Courts-Martial
Department of Defense, 32 C.F.R. Part 152 (2006)

Section 152.3. Policy

To assist the President in fulfilling his responsibilities under the UCMJ, and to satisfy the requirements of Executive Order 12473, the Department of Defense shall review the Manual for Courts-Martial annually, and, as appropriate, propose legislation amending the UCMJ to ensure that the MCM and the UCMJ fulfill their fundamental purpose as a comprehensive body of military criminal law and procedure. The role of the JSC [Joint Service Committee on Military Justice] furthers these responsibilities. Under the direction of the General Counsel of the Department of Defense, the JSC is responsible for reviewing the MCM and proposing amendments to it and, as necessary, to the UCMJ.

Section 152.4. Responsibilities

(a) The General Counsel to the Department of Defense shall:

(1) Administer this part, to include coordination on and approval of legislative proposals to amend the UCMJ, approval of the annual review of the MCM, and coordination of any proposed changes to the MCM under OMB [Office of Management and Budget] Circular A-19.

(2) Designate the Secretary of a Military Department to serve as the joint Service provider for the JSC. The joint Service provider shall act on behalf of the JSC for maintaining the JSC's files and historical records, and for publication of the updated editions of the MCM to be distributed throughout the Department of Defense, as appropriate.

(3) Invite the Secretary of Homeland Security to appoint representatives to the JSC.

(4) Invite the Chief Judge of the United States Court of Appeals for the Armed Forces to provide a staff member to serve as an advisor to the JSC.

(5) Invite the Chairman of the Joint Chiefs of Staff to provide a staff member from the Chairman's Office of Legal Counsel to serve as an advisor to the JSC.

(6) Ensure that the Associate Deputy General Counsel (Military Justice and Personnel Policy), Office of the General Counsel, Department of Defense, shall serve as the General Counsel's representative to the JSC in a non-voting capacity. In addition, the United States Court of Appeals for the Armed Forces (USCAAF) and the Legal Counsel to the Chairman of the Joint Chiefs of Staff shall be invited to provide a staff member to serve as an advisor to the JSC in a non-voting capacity.

(b) The Secretaries of the Military Departments shall ensure that the Judge Advocates General of the Military Departments and the Staff Judge Advocate to the Commandant of the Marine Corps appoint representatives to the JSC.

(c) The JSC shall further the DoD policy established in section 3 of this part and perform additional studies or other duties related to the administration of military justice, as the General Counsel of the Department of Defense may direct. (See DoD Directive 5105.18, "DoD Committee Management Program.") The membership of the JSC shall consist of one representative of each of the following, who shall comprise the JSC Voting Group:

(1) The Judge Advocate General of the Army.

(2) The Judge Advocate General of the Navy.

(3) The Judge Advocate General of the Air Force.

(4) The Staff Judge Advocate to the Commandant of the Marine Corps; and

(5) By agreement with the Department of Homeland Security, the Chief Counsel, United States Coast Guard.

(d) The JSC Working Group (WG) shall assist the JSC Voting Group in fulfilling its responsibilities under this part. The WG consists of non-voting representatives from each of the Services and may include the representatives from the USCAAF, and the Office of the Legal Counsel to the Chairman of the Joint Chiefs of Staff.

(e) The JSC chairmanship rotates biennially among the Services in the following order: The Army, the Air Force, the Marine Corps, the Navy, and the Coast Guard. Due to its size and manning constraints, a Coast Guard's request not to be considered for JSC chairmanship shall be honored. The Military Service of the JSC Chairman shall provide an Executive Secretary for the JSC.

Section 152.5. Implementation

The foregoing policies and procedures providing guidelines for implementation of this part, as well as those contained in the appendix, are intended exclusively for the guidance of military personnel and civilian employees of the Department of Defense, and the United States Coast Guard by agreement of the Department of Homeland Security. These guidelines are intended to improve the internal management of the Federal Government and are not intended to create any right, privilege, or benefit, substantive or procedural, to any person or enforceable at law by any party against the United States, its agencies, its officers, or any person.

Appendix A to Part 152 — Guidance to the Joint Service Committee (JSC)

(a) Review the Manual for Courts-Martial.

(1) The Joint Service Committee (JSC) shall conduct an annual review of the Manual for Courts-Martial (MCM), in light of judicial and legislative developments in military and civilian practice, to ensure:

(i) The MCM implements the Uniform Code of Military Justice (UCMJ) and reflects current military practice and judicial precedent.

(ii) The rules and procedures of the MCM are uniform insofar as practicable.

(iii) The MCM applies, to the extent practicable, the principles of law and the rules of evidence generally recognized in the trial of criminal cases in United States district courts, but which are not contrary to or inconsistent with the UCMJ.

(iv) The MCM is workable throughout the worldwide jurisdiction of the UCMJ; and,

(v) The MCM is workable across the spectrum of circumstances in which courts-martial are conducted, including combat conditions.

(2) During this review, any JSC voting member may propose for the Voting Group's consideration an amendment to the MCM. Proposed amendments to the MCM shall ordinarily be referred to the JSC Working Group (WG) for study. The WG assists the JSC in staffing various proposals, conducting studies of proposals and other military justice related topics at the JSC's direction, and making reports to the JSC. Any proposed amendment to the MCM, if approved by a majority of the JSC voting members, becomes a part of the annual review.

(3) The JSC shall prepare a draft of the annual review of the MCM and forward it to the General Counsel of the Department of Defense, on or about December 31st. The General Counsel of the Department of Defense may submit the draft of the annual review to the Code Committee established by Article 146 of the UCMJ, with an invitation to submit comments.

(4) The draft of the annual review shall set forth any specific recommendations for changes to the MCM, including, if not adequately addressed in the accompanying discussion or analysis, a concise statement of the basis and purpose of any proposed change. If no changes are recommended, the draft review shall so state. If the JSC recommends changes to the MCM, the draft review shall so state. If the JSC recommends changes to the MCM, the public notice procedures of paragraph (d)(3) of this appendix are applicable.

(b) Changes to the Manual for Courts-Martial.

(1) By January 1st of each year, the JSC voting members shall ensure that a solicitation for proposed changes to the MCM is sent to appropriate agencies within their respective Services that includes, but is not limited to, the judiciary, the trial counsel and defense counsel organizations, and the judge advocate general schools.

(2) The Federal Register announcement of each year's annual review of proposed changes to the MCM shall also invite members of the public to submit any new proposals for JSC consideration during subsequent JSC annual reviews.

(3) When the JSC receives proposed changes to the MCM either by solicitation or Federal Register notice, the JSC shall determine whether the proposal should be considered under paragraph (a)(2) of this appendix by determining if one or more of the JSC voting member(s) intends to sponsor the proposed change. The JSC shall determine when such sponsored proposals should be considered under the annual review process, taking into account any other proposals under consideration and any other reviews or studies directed by the General Counsel of the Department of Defense.

(4) Changes to the MCM shall be proposed as part of the annual review conducted under paragraph (a) of this appendix. When earlier implementation is required, the JSC may send proposed changes to the General Counsel of the Department of Defense, for coordination under DoD Directive 5500.1.

(c) Proposals to Amend the Uniform Code of Military Justice. The JSC may determine that the efficient administration of military justice within the Armed Services requires amendments to the UCMJ, or that a desired amendment to the MCM makes necessary an amendment to the UCMJ. In such cases, the JSC shall forward to the General Counsel of the Department of Defense, a legislative proposal to change the UCMJ. The General Counsel of the Department of Defense may direct that the JSC forward any such legislative proposal to the Code Committee for its consideration under Article 146, UCMJ.

(d) Public Notice and Meeting.

(1) Proposals to amend the UCMJ are not governed by the procedures set out in this paragraph. (See DoD Directive 5105.18. This paragraph applies only to the JSC recommendations to amend the MCM.)

(2) It is DoD policy to encourage public participation in the JSC's review of the MCM. Notice that the Department of Defense, through the JSC, intends to propose changes to the MCM normally shall be published in the Federal Register before submission of such changes to the President. This notice is not required when the Secretary of Defense in his sole and unreviewable discretion proposes that the President issue the change without such notice on the basis that public notice procedures, as set forth in this part, are unnecessary or contrary to the sound administration of military justice, or a MCM change corresponding to legislation is expeditiously required to keep the MCM current and consistent with changes in applicable law.

(3) The Office of General Counsel of the Department of Defense shall facilitate publishing the Federal Register notice required under this paragraph.

(4) The notice under this paragraph shall consist of the publication of the full text of the proposed changes, including discussion and analysis, unless the General Counsel of the Department of Defense determines that such publication in full would unduly burden the Federal Register, the time and place where a copy of the proposed change may be examined, and the procedure for obtaining access to or a copy of the proposed change.

(5) A period of not fewer than 60 days after publication of notice normally shall be allowed for public comment, but a shorter period may be authorized when the General Counsel of the Department of Defense determines that a 60-day period is unnecessary or is contrary to the sound administration of military justice. The Federal Register notice shall normally indicate that public comments shall be submitted to the Executive Secretary of the JSC.

(6) The JSC shall provide notice in the Federal Register and hold a public meeting during the public comments period, where interested persons

shall be given a reasonable opportunity to submit views on any of the proposed changes contained in the annual review. Public proposals and comments to the JSC should include a reference to the specific provision to be changed, a rational for the proposed change, and specific and detailed proposed language to replace the current language. Incomplete submissions might be insufficient to receive the consideration desired. The JSC shall seek to consider all views presented at the public meeting as well as any written comments submitted during the 60-day period when determining the final form of any proposed amendments to the MCM.

(e) Internal Rules and Record-Keeping.

(1) In furthering DoD policy, studying issues, or performing other duties relating to the administration of military justice, the JSC may establish internal rules governing its operation.

(2) The JSC shall create a file system and maintain appropriate JSC records.

NOTES AND QUESTIONS

1. The Administrative Procedure Act exempts courts-martial from the definition of "agency," 5 U.S.C. §§551(1)(F), 701(b)(1)(F), and contains a sweeping exemption for military and foreign affairs functions. 5 U.S.C. §§553(a)(1), 554(a)(4). Should the APA apply to rulemaking for courts-martial?

2. In 1997, the American Bar Association's House of Delegates adopted a resolution calling for reform of the Manual for Courts-Martial rule making process through:

(1) a broadly constituted advisory committee, including public membership and including representatives of the bar, the judiciary, and legal scholars, to consider and recommend rules of procedure and evidence at courts-martial;

(2) a method of adopting rules of procedure and evidence at courts-martial which is generally consistent with court rule-making procedures in Federal civilian courts;

(3) requirements for reporting to Congress [and] a waiting period for rules of procedure and evidence at courts-martial.

See ABA Recommendation 100 (Feb. 1997), *in* Kevin J. Barry, *Modernizing the Manual for Courts-Martial Rule-Making Process: A Work in Progress*, 165 MIL. L. REV. 237, 264-65 & n.100 (2000). Are there cogent reasons not to replicate civilian federal rule making procedures in the case of military justice? Captain Barry's article also includes an excellent summary of military justice reform proposals over the years.

3. The continuing evolution of military justice rules and jurisprudence has made it an administrative challenge to keep the Manual for Courts-Martial current:

[W]hy are we continuing to use a Manual for Courts-Martial that has been out of date for well more than a year? . . .

When DOD switched from the three-ring binder version of the 1984 Manual to complete reprints, the expectation was that a new Manual would come out with each Executive Order amending the Manual. A 1994 Army Lawyer article explained: "Change 6 and recent legislative (UCMJ) changes have been incorporated into the Manual scheduled for publication in 1994. The reprinted Manual will be a single, soft-bound volume and will be republished annually or as changes are required." Lt. Col. Eugene R. Milhizer & Lt. Col. Thomas W. McShane, *Analysis of Change 6 to the 1984 Manual for Courts-Martial*, Army Law., May 1994, at 40, 47.

Things sure haven't worked out that way. Only six soft-bound Manuals have been issued: 1994, 1995, 1998, 2000, 2002, and 2005. Consider what is not in the current Manual: the 2005 Amendments to the Manual for Courts-Martial, published on 18 October 2005, 70 Fed. Reg. 60,697; the UCMJ amendments made by the the the FY 2006 DOD Authorization Act, Pub L. No. 109-163; and the UCMJ amendments made by the FY 2007 DOD Authorization Act, Pub. L. No. 109-364.

Maybe the concept of publishing an entire new Manual and throwing away the old one is dated. Maybe it was a bad idea even in 1994 when it was originally hatched. But many years ago Al Gore invented this wonderful new device called the Internet. You know, that thing that allows me to post this rant and allows you to read it. Can't DOD at least post an annual updated version of the MCM, even if it doesn't want to devote the expense and cause the deforestation necessary to print it? . . .

Dwight H. Sullivan, *Annual Manual*, http://www.caaflog.blogspot.com/ (Feb. 4, 2007).

III. VOICES OF REFORM

Report of the Commission on the 50th Anniversary of the Uniform Code of Military Justice
National Institute of Military Justice, 2001

I. Statement of Purpose

Sponsored by the National Institute of Military Justice, a private non-profit organization dedicated to the fair administration of military justice, this Commission was formed on the occasion of the 50th anniversary of the Uniform Code of Military Justice, the greatest reform in the history of United States military law. The UCMJ was drafted in the aftermath of World War II, at a time when protecting the rights of military personnel was foremost in the minds of lawmakers. The outcry of veterans' organizations and bar associations made legislators aware of the arbitrary and summary nature of many of the two million courts-martial held during the war. By setting a higher standard of due process for servicemembers accused of crimes, the UCMJ, augmented by significant revisions in 1968 and 1983, became a model for criminal justice. It protected accused servicemembers against self-incrimination fifteen years before *Miranda v. Arizona*, provided for extensive pretrial screening investigations, permitted relatively broad access to free counsel, and incorporated many of the best features of federal and state criminal justice systems.

This landmark legislation created the fairest and most just system of courts-martial in any country in 1951. But the UCMJ has failed to keep pace with the standards of procedural justice adhered to not only in the United States, but in a growing number of countries around the world, in 2001. The UCMJ governs a criminal justice system with jurisdiction over millions of United States citizens, including members of the National Guard, reserves, retired military personnel, and the active-duty force, yet the Code has not been subjected to thorough or external scrutiny for thirty years. The last comprehensive study of courts-martial took place in 1971, when Secretary of Defense Melvin Laird, troubled by allegations of racism at courts-martial, appointed a task force to study the administration of military justice. This legislative and executive inattention is a new phenomenon; between 1951 and 1972, military justice was the focus of dozens of congressional hearings and the subject of countless official reports from government agencies.

Based on the response to the Commission's request for comments on the current military justice system, a "bottom-up" review of military justice is long overdue. In recent years, countries around the world have modernized their military justice systems, moving well beyond the framework created by the UCMJ fifty years ago. In contrast, military justice in the United States has stagnated, remaining insulated from external review and largely unchanged despite dramatic shifts in armed forces demographics, military missions, and disciplinary strategies. Since the Tailhook episode in 1991, the armed forces have faced a near-constant parade of high-profile criminal investigations and courts-martial, many involving allegations of sexual misconduct, each a threat to morale and a public relations disaster. As a result of the perceived inability of military law to deal fairly with the alleged crimes of servicemembers, a cottage industry of grassroots organizations devoted to dismantling the current court-martial system has appeared, aided by the reach of the worldwide web and driven by the passions of frustrated servicemembers, their families, and their counsel. The Commission — which could not pay for the travel of witnesses, and which publicized its hearings largely by word-of-mouth — heard testimony from citizens who traveled to Washington, D.C., from states around the country, including those who came from Washington, Colorado, Massachusetts, and Louisiana to make their voices heard, joining hundreds who submitted written comments.

In order to address this need for public scrutiny and reform, the Commission began its work by soliciting comments in order to formulate a list of topics to be addressed. Thereafter, a public hearing was held on Tuesday, March 13, 2001, at The George Washington University Law School. More than 250 individuals, representing themselves and more than a dozen organizations, submitted written comments to the Commission. Nineteen testified in person. This Report, intended for submission to the House and Senate Committees on Armed Services, the Secretary of Defense, the Service Secretaries, and the Code Committee, was prepared to convey the results of the hearing and the

Commission's deliberations about military justice to those who can help the UCMJ live up to its promise when it was implemented in 1951.

In this Report, the Commissioners seek to:

(1) Provide a record of submissions and testimony;

(2) Make specific recommendations for improvement; and

(3) Identify issues warranting further study and consideration.

The Commission's work is not intended to substitute for congressional hearings or officially sponsored government studies of military justice, both of which the Commissioners would heartily welcome. However, the depth and breadth of the Commission's experience should make any observer pause before dismissing its recommendations. Chaired by the Honorable Walter T. Cox III, the Commission's cumulative experience with the armed forces and the law exceeds 150 years. Its members have served in the uniforms of the United States Army, Navy, Air Force, and Coast Guard and are members of multiple bars. They have practiced, studied, taught — and made — military law under the UCMJ. . . .

Before setting forth its recommendations, the Commission wishes to acknowledge the unique atmosphere in which military justice operates. During hostilities or emergencies, it is axiomatic that commanders must enjoy full and immediate disciplinary authority over those placed under their command. The Commission believes that none of its suggestions will interfere with the recognized need of commanding officers to function decisively and effectively during times of war as well as peace.

II. Executive Summary

The Commission recommends immediate action to address four problem areas of court-martial practice and procedure. These recommendations, addressed at length in Part III below, are:

1. Modify the pretrial role of the convening authority in both selecting court-martial members and making other pre-trial legal decisions that best rest within the purview of a sitting military judge.

2. Increase the independence, availability, and responsibilities of military judges.

3. Implement additional protections in death penalty cases.

4. Repeal the rape and sodomy provisions of the Uniform Code of Military Justice, 10 U.S.C. §§ 920 & 925, and the offenses specified under the general article, 10 U.S.C. § 134, that concern criminal sexual misconduct. Replace them with a comprehensive Criminal Sexual Conduct Article, such as is found in the Model Penal Code or Title 18 of the United States Code.

Other issues warrant consideration as well. Part IV lists several concerns of the Commission, including the proper role of the staff judge advocate, the question of fairness in administrative processes, the wisdom of the *Feres* doctrine in light of present-day tort practice, the sentencing authority of military judges, the trial instructions used in cases of conscientious objection, and the jurisdiction of military appellate courts. Further study and more extensive hearings would help to resolve the many questions that plague servicemembers and military legal practitioners who confront these important areas of military law.

Consistent with its emphasis on enhancing the perceived and actual fairness of military justice under the UCMJ, the Commission also urges the adoption of a more open process for studying and altering the UCMJ as necessary. The current system of recommending changes to the Code, which involves closed meetings and little opportunity for input from civilian and military practitioners, has failed to encourage much-needed reform while contributing to a public image of courts-martial as immune from external scrutiny. Implementing a more transparent process to consider changes to court-martial rules and procedures would correct the impression that the military justice system is unresponsive to the legitimate concerns of the public.

III. Recommendations

The Commission identified four areas in need of immediate attention, based on its first-hand observations as well as the submissions received and the testimony heard. We recommend the following changes be effected as soon as possible:

A. Modify the pretrial role of the convening authority in both selecting court-martial members and making other pre-trial legal decisions that best rest within the purview of a sitting military judge.

As many witnesses before the Commission pointed out, the far-reaching role of commanding officers in the court-martial process remains the greatest barrier to operating a fair system of criminal justice within the armed forces. Fifty years into the legal regime implemented by the UCMJ, commanding officers still loom over courts-martial, able to intervene and affect the outcomes of trials in a variety of ways. The Commission recognizes that in order to maintain a disciplinary system as well as a justice system commanders must have a significant role in the prosecution of crime at courts-martial. But this role must not be permitted to undermine the standard of due process to which servicemembers are entitled.

The submissions that appear in Appendix B describe many possible ways to reduce the impression of unfairness created by the role of convening authorities in military criminal justice. The question of what role such authorities should play in the disciplinary and criminal structure of the modern armed forces warrants further study. But based on the Commission's experience, and on the input received in submissions and testimony, there is one action that should be taken immediately: Convening authorities must not be permitted to select the members of courts-martial.

There is no aspect of military criminal procedures that diverges further from civilian practice, or creates a greater impression of improper influence, than the antiquated process of panel selection. The current practice is an invitation to mischief. It permits — indeed, requires — a convening authority to choose the persons responsible for determining the guilt or innocence of a servicemember who has been investigated and prosecuted at the order of that same authority. The Commission trusts the judgment of convening authorities as well as the officers and enlisted members who are appointed to serve on courts-martial. But there is no reason to preserve a practice that creates such a strong impression of, and opportunity for, corruption of the trial process by commanders and staff judge advocates. Members of courts-martial should be chosen at random from a list of eligible servicemembers prepared by the convening authority, taking into account operational needs as well as the limitations on rank, enlisted or officer status, and same-unit considerations currently followed in the selection of members. Article 25 of the UCMJ should be amended to require this improvement in the fundamental fairness of court-martial procedure.

While the selection of panel members is clearly the focal point for the perception of improper command influence, the present Code entrusts to the convening authority numerous other pretrial decisions that also contribute to a perception of unfairness. For example, the travel of witnesses to Article 32 hearings, pretrial scientific testing of evidence, and investigative assistance for both the government and the defense are just a few of the common instances in which the convening authority controls the pretrial process and can withhold or grant approval based on personal preference rather than a legal standard. While the responsibility for such matters shifts to the military judge upon referral to court-martial, the delays created before the trial begins undermine due process for both sides at a court-martial. The need for the availability of a sitting judge, from at least the moment of preferral of the charges, is discussed at length in III.B. below, but it is the perception that the convening authority can manipulate the pretrial process to the advantage of either side that mandates this change in authority over pretrial legal matters. This issue goes to the core of a serviceperson's rights to due process and equal protection under the law. Pretrial decisions involve legal judgments that can — and often do — affect the outcome of trials. For that reason, like the selection of panel members, decisions on pretrial matters should be removed from the purview of the convening authority and placed within the authority of a military judge.

The Commission is aware of the 1999-2000 comprehensive study completed by the Joint Service Committee on Military Justice of the Department of Defense, which concluded that the present allocation of responsibility among convening authorities and military judges should be retained. We respectfully disagree with the conclusions reached by that body. The combined power of the convening authority to determine which charges shall be preferred, the level of court-martial, and the venue where the charges will be tried, coupled with the idea that this same convening authority selects the members of the court-martial to try the cases, is unacceptable in a society that deems due process of law to be the bulwark of a fair justice system.

B. Increase the independence, availability and responsibilities of military judges.

Complaints against the military justice system have long been fueled by allegations that military judges are neither sufficiently independent nor empowered enough to act as effective, impartial arbiters at trial. Since the adoption of the UCMJ, the authority of military judges (initially "law officers" under the 1950 UCMJ) has gradually increased, to the point where many judges now possess, either by regulation or by custom and tradition of the services, at least some modicum of judicial independence. The Commission is convinced that further and innovative change is needed to complete the process of making military trial and appellate judges full-fledged adjudicators of criminal law and procedure.

The Commission believes that three immediate changes would enhance the military judiciary and its ability to accomplish its mission and, at the same time, provide greater protections for accused persons. The changes would also enhance the prosecutors' ability to process courts-martial in an orderly and effective fashion. First, the Commission recommends the creation of standing judicial circuits, composed of tenured judges and empowered to manage courts-martial within geographic regions. Variants of this system are already in use in some regions and branches of the service, but it is crucial that a judge be identified and made available to all accused servicemembers, as well as to the prosecution, after charges are preferred. Under the current system, neither defense counsel nor prosecutors have a judicial authority to whom to turn until very close to the date of trial. This creates delay, inefficiency, and injustice, or at a minimum, the perception of injustice, as described in III.A. above.

Second, establishing fixed terms of office for military judges would also enhance the overall independence of the military judiciary. The Joint Service Committee of the Department of Defense in a recent report to the Code Committee recognized that this was desirable and feasible, but stopped short of recommending a legislative fix. The Commission believes that increased judicial independence is critical, given the central role of judges in upholding the standards of due process, preserving public confidence in the fairness of courts-martial, and bringing United States military justice closer to the standards being set by other military criminal justice systems around the world.

Third, either the President through his rule making authority, or Congress through legislation, should establish clear processes and procedures for collateral attack on courts-martial and authorize appellate military courts to both stay trial proceedings and to conduct hearings on said matters within their jurisdiction. The present ad hoc system of appellate courts ordering post-trial hearings without any clear guidelines or procedures is contrary to the practice of the United States District Courts and state trial courts throughout the land.

C. Implement additional protections in death penalty cases.

Given the increased scrutiny focused on capital litigation in the United States, the operation of the death penalty in the armed forces deserves close attention. Opponents of capital punishment have raised substantial questions of whether the modern military needs a death penalty, particularly during peacetime (an issue that the Commission feels deserves further study), but even the most ardent supporters of the death penalty accept the critical need for procedural fairness in capital cases. The Commission recommends that three steps be taken to improve capital litigation in the military:

1. Require a court-martial panel of 12 members.

2. Require an anti-discrimination instruction.

3. Address the issue of inadequate counsel by studying alternatives to the current method of supplying defense counsel.

Among all of the United States criminal jurisdictions that may impose a sentence of death, only at a court-martial does that sentence not require the verdict of a twelve-person jury. A general court may adjudge death with as few as five members, an anomaly that corrupts the legitimacy of both panel selection and the verdict itself. Because citizens in uniform deserve no less consideration than their civilian peers, the UCMJ should be amended to require twelve members in capital cases. Already the Manual for Courts-Martial requires special procedures for capital courts-martial, and the Court of Appeals for the Armed Forces has recognized the burdens that capital litigation imposes on both accused servicemembers and the resources of military justice. Requiring twelve members to serve on capital courts-martial (and implementing our first recommendation overall, calling for random selection of eligible members) would raise the standard of procedural justice for accused servicemembers to the level already established in civilian capital litigation.

Like requiring twelve-member panels in capital cases, our second recommendation could be implemented without major cost or change in existing procedures. We recommend that military judges instruct panels in capital cases that they may not consider the race of the accused servicemember or the victim(s) in deciding whether to impose death. The racial disparities of military death row mirror the disparities evident in civilian criminal jurisdictions that impose death. Of the six servicemembers currently on military death row, four are African American, one is a native Pacific Islander, and one is white; all were convicted for killing white victims. An explicit instruction prior to sentencing would remind courts-martial of the importance of ensuring racial justice amid the high stakes and emotions of capital cases.

Addressing the Commission's third concern is more difficult, but no less important, than addressing the issues of panel size and racial disparities in the administration of the military death penalty. Inadequate counsel is a serious threat to the fairness and legitimacy of capital courts-martial, made worse at court-martial by the fact that so few military lawyers have experience in defending capital cases. The current system of providing and funding defense counsel shortchanges accused servicemembers who face the ultimate penalty. It has been long recognized by every U.S. jurisdiction with a death penalty that only qualified attorneys may conduct death penalty cases. The paucity of military death penalty referrals, combined with the diversity of experience that is required of a successful military attorney, leaves the military's legal corps unable to develop the skills and experience necessary to represent both sides properly. The Commission believes that Congress should study and consider the feasibility of providing a dedicated source of external funding for experienced defense counsel if military capital litigation continues to be a feature of courts-martial in the 21st century.

D. Repeal the rape and sodomy provisions of the Uniform Code of Military Justice, 10 U.S.C. §§ 920 & 925, and the offenses specified under the general article, 10 U.S.C. § 134, that concern criminal sexual misconduct. Replace them with a comprehensive Criminal Sexual Conduct Article, such as is found in the Model Penal Code or Title 18 of the United States Code.

Of all of the topics that appeared on the Commission's long list of possible areas for consideration, the issue of prosecuting consensual sex offenses attracted the greatest number of responses from both individuals and organizations. The Commission concurs with the majority of these assessments in recommending that consensual sodomy and adultery be eliminated as separate offenses in the UCMJ and the Manual for Courts-Martial. Although popular acceptance of various sexual behaviors has changed dramatically in the fifty years since the UCMJ became effective, the Commission accepts that there remain instances in which consensual sexual activity, including that which is currently prosecuted under Articles 125 and 134, may constitute criminal acts in a military context. Virtually all such acts, however, could be prosecuted without the use of provisions specifically targeting sodomy and adultery. Furthermore, the well-known fact that most adulterous or sodomitical acts committed by consenting and often married (to each other) military personnel are not prosecuted at court-martial creates a powerful perception that prosecution of this sexual behavior is treated in an arbitrary, even vindictive, manner. This perception has been at the core of the military sex scandals of the last decade.

Because it is crucial that servicemembers are both made aware of and held accountable for sexual activities that interfere with military missions, undermine morale and trust within military units, or exploit the hierarchy of the military rank structure, the Commission recommends that a new statute be drafted to replace the current provisions. Many issues presented in the modern context simply do not fit the current statutes. For example, adultery, indecent exposure, indecent acts, unprotected sexual intercourse by an HIV-positive servicemember, wrongful cohabitation, fraternization, and numerous other offenses are not specified in the Uniform Code of Military Justice but are instead prosecuted under the general article of the Code as "conduct prejudicial to good order and discipline or service discrediting conduct." The same is true of incest, the sexual abuse of minors, pandering or pornography.

A comprehensive Criminal Sexual Conduct statute would more realistically reflect the offenses that should be proscribed under military law. The new statute would reconfigure the entire field of "Criminal Sexual Conduct" in the military context, replacing the outdated "rape and carnal knowledge," "sodomy," and general article offenses with a modern statute similar to the laws adopted by many states and in Title 18 of the United States Code. The Commission urges that the new statute recognize that military rank and organization may produce an atmosphere where sexual conduct, although apparently consensual on its face, should be proscribed as coercive sexual misconduct. There are many models from civilian life that make similar legal distinctions, including laws that govern sexual activity between teachers and students, doctors and patients, probationers and counselors, and corrections officers and prisoners. The Commission believes that this type of statute is appropriate and relevant in a military organization with its attendant subordinate-superior and special trust relationships.

IV. Discussion of Additional Issues

The Commission stands ready to assist in the implementation of the recommendations set forth above. These proposals, however, do not exhaust the need for reform within the military justice system. Additional matters worthy of further consideration include:

A. *Staff Judge Advocates*. The impression that staff judge advocates (SJA's) possess too much authority over the court-martial process is nearly as damaging to perceptions of military justice as the over-involvement of convening authorities at trial. The broad authority granted some staff judge advocates creates a number of unwanted, contradictory images of courts-martial: that over-zealous prosecutors can pursue charges at will and are rewarded for aggressive prosecution, that convening authorities routinely disregard the legal advice of their SJA's in order to pursue unwarranted or even vindictive prosecutions, and that lawyers, rather than line officers, control the military justice apparatus. Staff judge advocates, who act as counsel to commanding officers and not as independent authorities, should not exert influence once charges are preferred, should work out plea bargains only upon approval of the convening authority, and deserve a clear picture of what their responsibilities are.

It has been recognized since the adoption of the UCMJ that the invidiousness of command influence strikes at the heart of the fairness of the process. Too often, however, critics have focused exclusively on the inappropriate actions of convening authorities in pointing out instances of command influence that violate Article 36 of the UCMJ. In reality, the threat is as likely to come from SJAs and "others subject to the Code," *see* Article 36(b), as from convening authorities. The Code and the Manual for Courts-Martial should be amended to stress the need for impartiality, fairness and transparency on the part of staff judge advocates as well as all attorneys, investigators, and other command personnel involved in the court-martial process. These amendments should be drafted so as to make clear that violation of these principles as well as the trust inherent in these tasks is punishable under the UCMJ.

B. *Administrative processes*. The Commission's focus is on military criminal justice, but we would be remiss in ignoring the impression of unfairness created by the growing use of administrative discharge action in lieu of court-martial. While the services must be afforded considerable latitude to manage their personnel, there is no denying that administrative action, from non-judicial punishment to administrative withdrawal of qualifications, certifications, and promotion opportunities, can have a devastating effect on an individual's enlistment or career. The misuse, or the perception of misuse, of these administrative processes subverts the fundamental protections of the UCMJ, destroying the notion of fundamental fairness that is so critical to a professional military force. The Commission recognizes that an aggrieved servicemember may seek administrative redress at either the appropriate military administrative appeal board or in federal court, but in most instances these processes cannot make these individuals whole. Rarely can servicemembers be returned to normal career tracks once they have been unfairly administratively sanctioned and fallen behind their career peer groups. Thus, the Commission recommends an overall review of the military disciplinary system should consider, and, where necessary, reform, the administrative disciplinary and sanctioning process.

Three aspects of the current system in particular concern the Commission. First, the manner in which discharges are characterized is a relic of the past and should be updated to reflect contemporary realities. The current U.S. military is a volunteer-mercenary force, not a conscripted armed force. It may be sufficient simply to "fire" a servicemember who does not conform to the standards and norms of military service rather than stigmatizing that person with a negative discharge. This shift in the characterization of military discharges would permit servicemembers to receive veterans' entitlements based on criteria such as their length of good service and whether they were medically disabled while on active duty, rather than relying on an arcane hierarchy of discharge categories.

Second, the current system encourages disparate treatment of servicemembers: One member may be administratively discharged for felonious conduct, such as use of controlled substances, and another subjected to court-martial for the same offense. The member who is tried by a court-martial ends up with a federal criminal felony record, the other none. Such widely varying punishments are inconsistent with the UCMJ's fundamental goal of standardizing and modernizing criminal sanctions in the armed forces and should be corrected.

Finally, the current system does not provide ready access to the federal courts or other appellate review. Consideration should be given to providing for military appellate review of administrative discharges. The military appellate courts are already in place and are capable of reviewing administrative discharges in a manner similar to their current review of court-martial convictions. Likewise, the United States Court of Appeals for the Armed Forces could review the military appellate courts upon petition in the same way that it currently reviews courts-martial convictions.

C. *Feres* Doctrine. The Commission was not chartered with the idea that our study would include matters such as the *Feres* Doctrine. [*Feres v. United States*, 340 U.S. 135 (1950) (U.S. not liable under Federal Tort Claims Act for injuries to service members sustained while on active duty resulting from negligence of others in armed forces) — Eds.] However, given that it was articulated the same year that the UCMJ was adopted, and that many former servicemembers have been frustrated by its constraints on their ability to pursue apparently legitimate claims against the armed forces, many of which bear little if any relation to the performance of military duties or obedience to orders on their merits, the Commission believes that a study of this doctrine is warranted. An examination of the claims that have been barred by the doctrine, and a comparison of servicemembers' rights to those of other citizens, could reform military legal doctrine in light of present day realities and modern tort practice. Revisiting the *Feres* Doctrine would also signal to servicemembers that the United States government is committed to promoting fairness and justice in resolving military personnel matters.

D. *Sentencing.* The Commission believes the sentencing process at court-martial deserves further review. Suggestions for reform have ranged from the use of sentencing guidelines to making military judges responsible for all sentencing. An anomaly of the court-martial sentencing process is that a military accused may request to be sentenced by military judge alone only if he or she elects to be tried without court members. The Commission urges Congress to authorize a military accused to permit the military judge to pass on a sentence even if a trial has proceeded before court members. Further, the Commission recommends that serious consideration and study be given to making military judges responsible for all sentencing in all cases, and to granting military judges the authority to suspend all or part of a court-martial sentence. Such judicial powers are closely related to the Commission's suggestion that the military judges be given enhanced independence and authority to manage pretrial matters.

E. *Instruction on conscientious objection.* The armed forces' current management of conscientious objectors is hindered by inadequate trial instructions and administrative shortcomings, both of which the Commission believes should be addressed. Protecting the rights of conscientious objectors is a particular concern at court-martial, where an individual who has professed principled opposition to military service is judged by persons who have embraced that very service. Military judges should issue clear instructions explaining the legal status and responsibilities of a servicemember who has made a claim of conscientious objection but is awaiting a decision on his or her status. The services should also study ways to coordinate better the criminal and administrative processes in these cases, particularly when criminal charges are brought against a servicemember whose discharge for conscientious objection is pending.

F. *Jurisdiction of the military appellate courts.* In the aftermath of the Supreme Court's decision to limit the authority of the United States Court of Appeals for the Armed Forces in *Clinton v. Goldsmith*, the Commission believes that further study to clarify the jurisdiction of appellate courts should be undertaken. However, if the authority of military judges were enhanced as suggested above in III.B., the question of appellate jurisdiction would begin to resolve itself, since military appeals courts clearly possess authority under the UCMJ to review the rulings of military judges at trial.

G. *Pre-trial and trial procedures.* The Commission received a number of suggestions concerning improvements to the actual trial process. For example, many submissions suggested that the Article 32 officer should be either a military judge or a field grade judge advocate with enhanced powers to issue subpoenas, and to make binding recommendations to dismiss charges where no probable cause was found. Others recommended increasing the number of peremptory challenges for both the government and the defense, permitting lawyer voir dire, granting military judges contempt power over both military personnel and civilians during trial, and allowing witnesses to be sworn by either military judges or clerks. The Commission takes no position regarding these suggestions, but believes that like many of the other issues presented, these comments are worthy of further study and full consideration.

Kevin J. Barry, *A Face Lift (and Much More) for an Aging Beauty: The Cox Commission Recommendations to Rejuvenate the Uniform Code of Military Justice*
L. Rev. Mich. State U. — Detroit C.L. 57 (2002)

My thesis is that the Cox Commission recommendations can be understood fully only if viewed in the context of the historical development of the military justice system, and by one cognizant of the *systemic flaws* in that system — flaws which derive from the nature and purpose of the original courts-martial as simply tools of command intended to ensure discipline, and not as courts of justice. The UCMJ was a large step forward in transforming courts-martial into instruments of justice, but it was an incomplete reform, and it has been overtaken by advances in concepts of fundamental fairness both here and abroad in the intervening fifty years. Only if the vestiges of inappropriate command control are eliminated will the system be free to function as a true and fully effective system of criminal justice.

My conclusion is that substantial structural reforms *must* be implemented if the U.S. military justice system is to be allowed to continue to function, for it no longer meets the standards which today define due process and fundamental fairness. As it now exists, if any conviction under the UCMJ were appealable to an appellate court applying the constitutional standards applicable to every other criminal justice system in the United States, federal or state, that conviction almost certainly would be set aside. Its defenders may argue, however, that this is not a *civilian* justice system, and therefore is properly subject to different standards. Even if we assume this argument to be valid, however, it must nevertheless fail on a comparative law analysis, for if any UCMJ conviction were appealable to a court applying the standards applicable to the *military* justice systems of most of our major allies, the conviction would be similarly suspect and likely would be overturned as violating fundamental fairness doctrines. No criminal justice system with the inherent deficiencies of the current UCMJ system would survive a constitutional challenge and be permitted to adjudicate such important issues involving criminal culpability. The several million Americans who volunteer to serve in our armed forces deserve better. The military justice system must be changed, or it should be abolished.

The small peacetime army was vastly expanded during World War I, and the operation of the system in this war revealed substantial weakness in the 1916 Articles. "Troops, officers, and soldiers alike returned with bitter complaints about military justice." General Samuel T. Ansell, the Acting Judge Advocate General of the Army, became the system's severest critic. He opened his 1919 article:

> I contend — and I have gratifying evidence of support not only from the public generally but from the profession — that the existing system of Military Justice is un-American, having come to us by inheritance and rather witless adoption out of a system of government which we regard as fundamentally intolerable; that it is archaic, belonging as it does to an age when armies were but bodies of armed retainers and bands of mercenaries; that it is a system arising out of and regulated

by the mere power of Military Command rather than Law; and that it has ever resulted, as it must ever result, in such injustice as to crush the spirit of the individual subjected to it, shock the public conscience and alienate public esteem and affection from the Army that insists upon maintaining it. Intemperate criticism of those who have pointed out these defects will not serve to conceal them.

Ansell's criticisms resulted in a re-examination of the system, and new articles, imposing additional procedural safeguards, were enacted in 1920. Among the changes were the requirement of a pre-trial investigation at which the accused had a right to be present, to examine and cross-examine witnesses, and to present evidence in defense or in mitigation; the requirement for a unanimous vote, versus the prior two thirds vote, to impose the death penalty; and the establishment of a board of review within the office of the judge advocate general to review courts-martial.

While these 1920 changes did, in some measure, further conform the military justice system to the changing perception of the requirements of due process, they did not fundamentally alter the system, or the role and ability of the commander, as convening authority, to exercise overarching control over the entire process. "A single commander could prefer charges, convene the court, select the members and counsel, and review the case," with the result that "[t]he spectre of unlawful command influence lingered." So it would, since the Articles of War would remain unchanged in any material way for the next thirty years. However, when the military services saw their largest expansion in history during World War II, the perceptions of unlawful command influence and of a fundamentally unfair system became so widespread that the clamor for reform became overwhelming. Many returning service members reached positions of influence, and added their voices to those calling for change. One example was the 1949 testimony of then Congressman Gerald Ford, a World War II Naval officer who would later become President. He testified that he

> recalled hearing conversations among members of courts-martial during his several years in the navy "along this line: What does the Old Man . . . want us to do?" Ford concluded that all too often such individuals were concerned less with determining guilt or innocence, than "with what the captain of a ship, or the commanding officer of a station, wants done with the man. . . . I also participated in various courts martial; and the whole system is fundamentally wrong; and I am particularly pleased to see something being done about it."

In fact, in the 175 years from the adoption of the first Articles of War in 1775 to the adoption of the Uniform Code of Military Justice in 1950, little had changed in the fundamental nature of the military justice system in the United States. It remained a tool of the commander, and its purpose was to enforce discipline as prescribed by the commander. Perhaps the most aggressively caustic, yet largely accurate, assessment of the flaws in the military justice system remains that of General Ansell in 1919. He viewed the entire process as antithetical to the rule of law.

Out of these opposite basic theories — on the one side that Military
Justice is to be controlled by the power of Military Command and on
the other that it is to be regulated by established principles of Law —
arise the two antagonistic views as to the character of courts-martial.
One is that a court-martial is an executive agency belonging to and
under the control of the military commander; is, indeed, but a board of
officers appointed to investigate the accusation and report their findings to the commander for his approval. Under such a theory, a commander exercises an almost unrestrained and unlimited discretion in
determining (1) who shall be tried, (2) the prima facie sufficiency of the
proof, (3) the sufficiency of the charge, (4) the composition of the court,
(5) all questions of law arising during the progress of the trial, (6) the
correctness of the proceedings and their sufficiency in law and in fact.
Under such a theory all these questions are controlled not by law but
by the power of Military Command.

Thus it is said by Winthrop, the greatest departmental authority
upon Military Law:

> "Courts-martial are not courts, but are, in fact, simply instru-
> mentalities of the executive power provided by Congress for
> the President as Commander-in-Chief to aid him in properly
> commanding the army and enforcing discipline therein, and
> utilized under his orders or those of his authorized military
> representative; they are, indeed, creatures of orders and
> except in so far as an independent discretion may be given
> them by statute, they are as much subject to the orders of a
> competent superior as is any military body of persons."

This, of course, is in accordance with the old monarchical view. At
the time of our separation, the King was not only the commander of
the Army, he was the legislator of the Army; he prescribed the Articles
of War, the offenses and the penalty; he prescribed both the substantive and procedural law; he prescribed the courts-martial, their jurisdiction and their procedure. He controlled the entire system of
discipline and the methods of its administration. The Army was his,
the officers were his officers and from him drew their authority.
Courts-martial were courts-martial of the King and of the officers representing him and his power of command. The courts-martial, therefore, applied his law, his penalties, followed his procedure and were
subject to his command. Under such a scheme, a court-martial was but
an agency of command, nowhere in touch with the popular will,
nowhere governed by laws established by the people to regulate the
relation between sovereign and subject. It was not a judicial body. Its
functions were not judicial functions. It was but an agency of the
power of military command to do its bidding.

Basically, such is our system today. It does not contemplate that a
court-martial shall be a court doing justice according to established
principles of jurisprudence and independently of all personal power.
Quite the contrary. It regards the court-martial simply as the right
hand of the commanding officer to aid him in the maintenance of

discipline. It is his agent; he controls it. It is answerable not to the law but to him. The court-martial is not a court at all; it is but an agency of military command governed and controlled by the will of the commander. Under such a system an officer, of course, belongs to a caste. Any officer can prefer charges against a man and at his will can succeed in getting him tried. The statute requires no preliminary investigation to determine whether or not the accused should be tried, and such investigation as is required by regulation is also controlled by the military commander, and is neither thorough nor effective. From then on everything is governed not by law but by the power of military command. The detail of counsel, the membership of the court, the question of the validity of the charge, the sufficiency of the evidence, the correctness of the procedure, the validity of the judgment and sentence and the thousand and one questions arising in the progress of a criminal trial are all left finally to the judgment of the commanding general. Even the ultimate conclusion of guilt or innocence is subject to his control. There is no right of review; there is no legal supervision. All is to be determined by the commanding general. Whatever he says is right; is right and becomes right as his *ipse dixit* regardless of general principles of jurisprudence, and right beyond any power of review. He is the law. No matter how great the departures are from the well established principles of law and right and justice, these departures become error or not, just as the commanding officer may choose to regard them. There is no legal standard to which court-martial procedure must conform and, therefore, there can be no error adjudged according to a legal standard. In other words, military justice is administered not according to a standard of law at all, but under the authority of a commanding officer. The results are as might be expected when one man is left to be judged at the will of another — the penalties and sentences are shockingly harsh, and frequently shamefully unjust.

Such is our system conceded to be; and such, according to the militaristic view, ought to be. The departmental view, as expressed in the hearing before the Committees in 1912, is that "the introduction of fundamental principles of civil jurisprudence into the administration of military justice is to be discouraged."[1]

The harshness of General Ansell's assessment does not detract from its importance. General Ansell has been described as one whose "views were a generation ahead of their time."[2] That is probably an understatement — he was in fact several generations ahead. Judge Cox considered him "the father

---

[1] [n.206] Ansell, [*Military Justice*, 5 CORNELL L.Q. 1 (1919)], at 5-7 (citations omitted). Two of his complaints, those regarding the lack of a pre-trial investigation, and the need for some system of post-trial review, were addressed, though with doubtful effectiveness, in the 1920 legislation. The other flaws continued, some until 1950 or beyond, others in varying degrees remain even today.

[2] [n.207] [DAVID A.] SCHLUETER, [MILITARY CRIMINAL JUSTICE: PRACTICE AND PROCEDURE (5th ed. 1999)], at 24 n.1.

of modern American military law."[3] His perceptions were clearly at odds with the common view in 1917, and were only partially accepted even in 1950. Indeed, it was not until the 1970s, when General Kenneth J. Hodson offered his own visionary recommendations, that many of General Ansell's views were seemingly validated.[4] It is worth noting, however, that even today — almost thirty years after he wrote — most of General Hodson's recommendations still have not been adopted.

There was, in 1919, and there still exists today, a palpable tension between the demands of discipline and the requirements of justice under law. What Ansell referred to as the "militaristic" point of view tends to demand strict discipline, and argues for a military justice system which will ensure that the commander can — through "legal" command influence — retain some significant control over the system which effects that discipline. Those such as General Ansell and General Hodson, who put the demands of justice and the rule of law as equally important priorities along with "discipline," have severely criticized the system — a system that has allowed for unlawful command influence, sometimes to the detriment of a just and fair result, to continue. The enactment of the Uniform Code in 1950 was an effort to change 175 years of history. It has proved to be a significant, yet still only a partial and incomplete, success.

In 1991, the National Institute of Military Justice (NIMJ) was established as a nonprofit, nongovernmental organization "for the purpose of advancing the administration of military justice within the Armed Services of the United States." In support of this generic goal, NIMJ has indicated that it is available

> to foster coordination and cooperation between military and civilian practitioners and among the various Armed Services; to appear as a friend of the court in cases involving issues of military law; to cooperate with individuals, agencies and organizations involved in the study or administration of military justice in other countries; to work with military lawyers to fashion litigation and appellate strategies; to work with the news media to ensure proper, balanced, and accurate coverage of newsworthy events in military justice, in order to improve public understanding of this important, specialized and little-known field of the law; to encourage, conduct and cooperate with studies relating to judicial administration, criminal justice and correctional practices within the military; and to furnish general backup legal assistance to civilian and military defense counsel in courts-martial and appeals and collateral litigation.

In pursuing its goals, NIMJ has engaged in a variety of activities, including publishing the *Military Justice Gazette*, a monthly newsletter on military

---

[3] [n.208] [Walter T.] Cox, [*The Army, the Courts, and the Constitution: The Evolution of Military Justice,*118 MIL. L. REV. 1 (1987)], at 9.

[4] [n.209] In 1973, Major General Kenneth J. Hodson, former Judge Advocate General of the Army and former Chief Judge of the Army Court of Military Review, recommended a number of changes to the military justice system. *See* Kenneth J. Hodson, *Military Justice: Abolish or Change?*, 22 KAN. L. REV. 31 (1973). The author is aware of no other U.S. military lawyer in the modern era who has contributed as much to the profession or who is more highly respected.

justice events, and the *Guide to the Rules of Practice and Procedure for the United States Court of Appeals for the Armed Forces*; sponsoring a number of meetings or training programs, including an international military justice program in London in 1998; filing amicus curiae briefs at the Supreme Court of the United States, the Court of Appeals for the Armed Forces, and the Coast Guard Court of Criminal Appeals; and participating in a variety of congressional hearings or court rulemaking proceedings.

NIMJ was established to fill a void, and is the only nongovernmental organization in the United States dedicated to the enhancement of the operation of the military justice system, and which has remained active in an ongoing review and oversight of that system. NIMJ's focus extends beyond the United States, as it attempts to monitor military justice developments worldwide. It is a nonmember organization, operated by its board of directors with the assistance of an Advisory Committee. It is not in any way affiliated with or supported by the armed forces or the government of the United States, and thus is able to maintain independence from, and has established credibility with, the armed services and the various other entities such as bar associations and bar committees, which also have an interest in military law.

The military justice system in the United States has been evolving for more than 225 years, and during the entire period, the tension between the desire of commanders to be able to use the system to ensure "discipline," and the goal of having courts-martial be true courts of justice, has lessened but has never been fully resolved. The UCMJ was a huge advance, marking the U.S. military justice system as a "model" in its day, well ahead not only of other nations' military justice systems, but also of civilian justice systems in the United States in a number of important areas. However, the world has moved forward significantly in the last fifty years, and particularly in the last decade there have been dramatic advances in what other nations view as "fair," and consider to be the minimum requirements of due process and fundamental fairness in military justice systems. Virtually every one of these changes resolves the "discipline versus justice" debate in favor of enhanced due process protections, and limits the potential for, and the appearance of, inappropriate command influence. While these other nations have recognized and have responded aggressively to changed circumstances and perspectives, the Cox Commission found that the United States has not kept pace with these developments.

The National Institute of Military Justice took a giant step forward by sponsoring the Commission on the Fiftieth Anniversary of the UCMJ, and that Commission, based on limited but diverse input, made dramatic and dynamic proposals, and has recommended substantial procedural and substantive changes to the UCMJ and the MCM. If implemented, the Commission's primary recommendations, standing alone, would help to restore a significantly higher level of systemic fairness to the U.S. military justice system, and help toward achieving again its former status as a model for military justice systems around the world.

The Cox Commission was a broad and comprehensive review, which showed the tip of the iceberg as far as what problems exist. To reach its full potential, however, the Cox Commission will need to be followed by larger studies, for the Cox Commission had neither the resources nor the access to accomplish the extended reviews needed. The breadth of the Cox Commission review now must be fleshed out with the depth which will be provided by a well-staffed and funded "bottom-up" review of the entire system. What is now needed is the kind of attention and effort which followed World War II, and the dedication to systemic review and reform which were evidenced in the appointment and functioning of the Morgan Committee.

Is the United States up to that challenge? One would hope so. But history would suggest that adequate further studies and reports are likely to be forthcoming only if Congress becomes directly involved, abandons the "inattention" it has shown for too long, and mandates studies to be performed by broadly constituted, diverse commissions, including substantial "outside" membership, in addition to full participation by the services and the Department of Defense. The Congress thereafter should hold hearings on the substantive and procedural issues bound to be raised. NIMJ and the Cox Commission have started the process; it now is up to Congress and the Administration to realize the potential of that beginning. America servicemen and women volunteer to put their lives on the line to defend constitutional rights for all others privileged to live in this great nation. It is somehow unseemly to think that, as a consequence, they must give up basic rights which are seen as essential not only for those not in uniform, but also for those who wear similar uniforms in our allies' armed forces.

It is a matter of right, of fairness, and of justice. General Ansell found the military justice system to be "un-American" in 1919, and if he were here today he likely would be similarly offended by today's system. General Hodson opined in 1973 that the system was sufficiently flawed that it either should be changed or the American military should cease to operate a separate system of justice. Almost none of his recommendations have yet been implemented, and the most important have not even been seriously considered. The U.S. military justice system today so far deviates from the norms of fundamental fairness that it is improbable that any UCMJ conviction could be upheld if measured against the minimum standards applicable to every other U.S. criminal justice system and virtually all of our allies' military justice systems. No system so deficient in fundamental fairness should be tolerated or allowed to continue to operate.

General Ansell and General Hodson, along with many others, are watching. The question is whether we will measure up to the standards they have set. They may have been generations ahead of their time, and many agree they were. But Judge Cox and the others on the Fiftieth Anniversary Commission would hardly claim such prescience. The test is for the rest of us to respond to the vision long ago set forth, and now embodied in the findings and recommendations of the Cox Commission. General Hodson's challenge to his generation was "abolish or change." It is our challenge as well. As recommended by so many, most recently by the Cox Commission, we should, we must, choose change.

NOTES AND QUESTIONS

1. How would you have structured the membership of the Cox Commission?

2. Copies of the Cox Commission report were provided to the House and Senate Committees on Armed Services, but no hearings were ever held on its recommendations. Nonetheless, Congress thereafter amended the UCMJ to require 12 member juries in capital courts-martial and has since thoroughly revised the law regarding the prosecution of sex offenses.

3. The armed forces did not participate in the Cox Commission's hearing, submitted no comments during its proceedings, and did not support its recommendations. Why might that have happened?

4. Lt. Col. Theodore Essex & Maj. Leslea Tate Pickle, *A Reply to the Report of the Commission on the 50th Anniversary of the Uniform Code of Military Justice (May 2001): "The Cox Commission,"* 52 A.F. L. REV. 233 (2002):

> It is encouraging that, after all the evidence was examined, the commission, with its 150 years of collective experience, could find no actual problems with the UCMJ and MCM. It is disturbing that a commission with such a depth of experience would suggest changes based solely on perceptions. The better course of action would be to determine whether the perceptions were accurate, and if not, suggest ways to correct them.
>
> This article will examine the Cox Commission's recommendations for changing the current military justice system. Our position is that the changes suggested by the Commission are not needed because there are no actual systemic problems with the UCMJ or the military justice system. The UCMJ should only be modified when the change will correct a real problem. This article will show that the current system already includes checks and balances that adequately address the Commission's concerns. . . .
>
> The CCR [Cox Commission Report] states, "The UCMJ governs a criminal justice system with jurisdiction over millions of United States citizens, including members of the National Guard, reserves, retired military personnel, and the active-duty force, yet the Code has not been subjected to thorough or external scrutiny for thirty years." This statement makes it appear that there are no provisions in place for reviewing the UCMJ. This is simply not the case. The UCMJ, as federal law, is subject to the oversight of the legislature. If the President proposes amendments to the UCMJ, there will be congressional oversight. Additionally, both the judiciary and the armed services committees have jurisdiction to review matters of military justice. There is even a Department of Defense directive that establishes a Joint Service Committee on Military Justice that is required to report to the President annually and to propose legislation to improve military justice. The committee's annual review of the UCMJ is both thorough and extensive.

Another check is in the U.S. code itself. Article 146 provides: "A committee shall meet at least annually and shall make an annual comprehensive survey of the operations of this chapter." The term "this chapter" refers to 10 U.S.C. Chapter 47, which is the UCMJ. The committee consists of the judges of the United States Court of Appeals for the Armed Forces (USCAAF), who are all civilians, the Judge Advocate Generals (TJAGS) for each of the services, and the Commandant of the Marine Corps, along with two civilians appointed by the Secretary of the Air Force (SECAF). Moreover, another oversight is the American Bar Association which has a standing committee on Armed Forces Law that produces reports, recommendations, and investigations. Finally, in cases brought under the UCMJ, virtually all hearings are public hearings, including Article 32 investigations and appellate procedures. Indeed, it would be hard to identify a system of criminal justice that is more open or more carefully examined than the UCMJ. . . .

The Cox Commission stated that there are systemic problems with the military justice system. Throughout the CCR, however, there is no evidence presented that supports the claim of "systemic problems." The UCMJ provides for greater procedural protection that an accused would receive under the federal criminal court system such as are present within the Article 32 hearing process. The military justice system already includes checks and balances within it to address all of the Commission's concerns. . . .

In the end, what the Commission ultimately proposes, is to change the military justice system simply because of the perceptions of some individuals, many of whom are biased and motivated by their opposition to particular results in their loved ones' cases. As stated previously, there will always be those who have a bias against the military justice system because of a result with which they disagree. If changes are made based solely on perceptions rather than evidence, then the military justice system will be forever at the mercy of anyone who doesn't agree with a particular result.

We will close with the timely remarks of Judge J. De Meyer, in a concurring opinion in the *Findlay* case cited by the Commission:

> To this judgment, the result of which I fully approve, I would add a brief remark. Once again reference is made in its reasoning to "appearances" (paragraphs 73 and 76). First of all, I would observe that the Court did not need to rely on "appearances", since there were enough convincing elements to enable it to conclude that the court-martial system, under which Lance-Sergeant Findlay was convicted and sentenced in the present case, was not acceptable. Moreover, I would like to stress that, as a matter of principle, we should never decide anything on the basis of "appearances", and that we should, in particular, not allow ourselves to be impressed by them in determining whether or not a court is independent and

impartial. We have been wrong to do so in the past, and we should not do so in the future.

Nor should the UCMJ be changed based on perceptions. We may need a campaign to educate the public and military members, but we do not need to change the law because of perceptions. In the end, we believe a cautious approach to change, rather than a preference for the new, simply because it is new, will best serve the needs of the military and its members in the new century.

See also Chapter 13, §III, *supra.* Do you agree with the authors' analysis of the Cox Commission report? Why would proposals for study and reform provoke such negative responses from judge advocates? Despite the chilly reception the Cox Commission received from the military, *e.g.,* Maj. Gen. William A. Moorman, *Fifty Years of Military Justice: Does the Uniform Code of Military Justice Need to be Changed?*, 48 A.F. L. REV. 185, 194 (2000) (fiftieth anniversary as "least compelling argument" for complete review of UCMJ), there has been no shortage of thoughtful commentary from defenders of the military justice system as to ways in which that system might be improved. Excellent examples include Brig. Gen. John S. Cooke, *The Twenty-Sixth Annual Kenneth J. Hodson Lecture: Manual for Courts-Martial 20X*, 156 MIL. L. REV. 1 (1998), and H.F. "Sparky" Gierke, *Five Questions About the Military Justice System*, 56 A.F. L. REV. 249 (2005).

IV.   INTERNATIONAL ASSISTANCE IN REFORM

Lt. Col. J. McClelland MBE, *Starting from Scratch: The Military Discipline System of the East Timor Defence Force*
7 J. CONFLICT & SEC. L. 253, 253-73 (2002)

1. Introduction

On 1 February 2001 at a ceremony in Aileu, East Timor, the Forcas de Defesa de Timor Lorosa'e (FDTL or East Timor Defence Force) was created. The 650 soldiers who formed that first batch were drawn from ex-members of FALINTIL [Forcas Armadas De Libertacão National De Timor Leste (National Liberation Armed Forces of East Timor)], the guerilla army that had fought against the Indonesian army (TNI) in the period 1975-1999. Over the next few months and under the command of Brig Gen Taur Matan Ruak the FDTL began the slow and sometimes painful transition to a peacetime regular army.

One of the areas that the Defence Force would need to address was the creation and implementation of a discipline system that would be both appropriate to its size and reflective of its military culture whilst at the same time guaranteeing the fundamental rights of those soldiers accused of breaching service discipline.

2. Background

A very brief review of the recent history of the newly independent East Timor, and the role of FALINTIL in it, warrants some consideration in understanding the nature of the members of the FDTL and therefore the system of military justice that would best serve them.

2.1 Indonesian Repression

Indonesia governed in East Timor in the period 1975-1999 during which many East Timorese died at the hands of the oppressive regime. It was in response to this oppression that FALINTIL was raised as the armed wing of the political party, FRETILIN [Frente Revolucionaria do Timor Leste Independente (Revolutionary Front for an Independent East Timor)] on 20 August 1975. In its first few years, it enjoyed success disproportionate to its size and organization but by early 1979 it was reported to have lost 80 per cent of its manpower. Following a reorganization under its charismatic leader, Alexandre "Xanana" Gusmao, it again made its presence felt. This successful reorganization under difficult conditions inevitably required a system of discipline that was swift, rough and ready.

2.2 UNAMET, INTERFET, UNTAET and Independence

A changed economic and political landscape in the late 1990s allowed for the organization, under the auspices of the United Nations Assistance Mission in East Timor (UNAMET), of the so-called "Popular Consultation" in which the East Timorese people were able to vote on whether to become independent or retain autonomy within Indonesia. The emphatic vote for independence was followed by widespread violence which prompted the UN to mandate an International Force for East Timor (INTERFET). As INTERFET restored order in East Timor, the UN Transitional Administration in East Timor (UNTAET) came into being on 25 October 1999 with the role of governing East Timor whilst at the same time preparing it for independence. Independence was finally achieved on 20 May 2002.

The defence of East Timor in this period was the responsibility of the UNTAET Peace Keeping Force (PKF). However, in due course the PKF would leave and by that point East Timor needed to have developed a defence force capable of defending its hard won sovereignty. This would require the raising and development of a force in a relatively short space of time.

2.3 FALINTIL to FDTL

The role of FALINTIL in the period 1975-1999 was considered key in its being favoured as the basis for the FDTL. The transition from a guerilla force to a conventional defence force was envisaged as resulting in a force of 3000 personnel comprising 4 battalions (2 regular and 2 reservist) based near major population centres, an independent company in the Oecussi enclave and a small maritime element. The development of the Defence Force was to be assisted by an international staff of advisors.

The creation the FDTL, in law, was effected by a regulation promulgated by UNTAET on 31 January 2001. This laid down the mission of the FDTL, its duty to observe international humanitarian law and terms and conditions of service. Importantly in the context of this paper, it stated (section 6) that a Code of Military Discipline could be created by UNTAET regulations that would bind FDTL members.

The task, or mission, of the FDTL post-independence is threefold:

(i) To defeat incursions.

(ii) To deter aggressors, and delay and harass an invader until external assistance arrives; and

(iii) To support the government during natural disasters and other emergencies.

The size of the FDTL and its mission will ensure that it remains within East Timor for the foreseeable future. It is not expected that it will deploy overseas in a formed body.

3. Creating the Military Legal System

3.1. Approach

In creating a system of discipline for the FDTL it was important to avoid any temptation simply to "cut and paste" a system from another state. Such an approach would have ignored the cultural and military experiences that the FDTL clearly valued as well as the structure of the FDTL.[5] Additionally, the system needed to be created on the premise not of what was desirable nor politically correct but what was essential for the FDTL. This would ensure that the system was as streamlined and viable as possible. An assessment of the needs of the FDTL from the system was therefore necessary. In approaching this assessment 3 factors were pivotal.

3.1.1 Political

The experience of the East Timorese at the hands of a highly political Indonesian military (TNI) was one that they did not wish to replicate. Central in this view was the fact that the Indonesian military were not seen to be accountable for their actions. There therefore had to be some element of civil control that was clear and unambiguous to both military personnel and civilians from the way in which the military discipline system operated. It was also necessary to show that the military was subject to ultimate civil judicial control. At the same time however, in the interests of military discipline, it was important that the FDTL had the ability to deal internally in a swift and effective manner with breaches of discipline.

---

[5] [n.15] On independence in 1984, Brunei enacted the Royal Brunei Armed Forces Act (RBAFA), an act that very closely resembled the British Army Act 1955. This "cut and paste" of the British system created a system that was unworkable in practice in Brunei as the structure of the RBAF differed significantly from that of the British army. One example of the "mismatch" of systems was the requirement for the Commander of RBAF or Colonel in Chief to be the Appropriate Superior Authority (ASA) (s 83(2) RBAFA). As the Colonel in Chief was His Majesty, the Sultan, it created difficulties in reviewing any of the decisions of the ASA as allowed for under s 107(2)(c). A similar problem arose in relation to the convening of courts martial (s 85).

3.1.2 Military

The projected size of FDTL meant that it was too small to support the bureaucracy of a court-martial system. It would therefore need a one-tier system that could be operated at battalion level. However, as the system would be one-tier only it had to have an effective system of review/appeal from that level in order to be seen as fair.

As the force would not be deploying overseas the need to have a system of military discipline that would allow for civil matters to be dealt with by the military did not arise. Civil matters could be dealt with in the civil system, thereby imbuing an element of reassurance of FDTL accountability. Accordingly, the scope of jurisdiction *vis à vis* offences could be limited to military breaches of discipline.

The system of discipline would need to be relatively simple to operate in order for there not to be too great a gap between the informal and *ad hoc* system of FALINTIL and the new system. In approaching the establishment of procedures the key aspect was to avoid complexity.

It is important to note that at all stages of the development of the discipline system, Brig Gen Taur Matan Ruak was briefed. This was essential if the system was to be considered that of the FDTL and not one that had been imposed on them.

3.1.3 Legal

At the time of the system being created a civil legal system was in existence in East Timor. It had been created by a series of UNTAET regulations and had been in operation since mid-2000. This system was likely to form the basis of the future system of justice for East Timor, at least insofar as the District Courts remained. The existence of this system, coupled with the likely proximity of FDTL battalions to towns and therefore to District Courts, reinforced the possibility of the soldiers being subject to civil law for civil offences.

It was important if the soldiers were to be subject to both the military and civil systems that the military system was compatible with the civil system, the latter clearly having primacy. Time limits for military arrest for instance would need to "dovetail" with the civil time limits in order that, in those cases in which the military breach could also amount to a civil offence (e.g. fighting and assault), the operation of the military system did not prejudice the civil system.

As the system would be created under an UNTAET regulation it would need also to be approved by the Office of the Principal Legal Adviser, the Human Rights Department and the Gender Affairs Department, all departments within UNTAET.

A reduction in the complexity of the system could be achieved by making it inquisitorial rather than adversarial. This would also assist in the perception that the disciplinary officer was intent on getting to the truth of a matter rather than the unit turning against a soldier and prosecuting him. Such a system would not have been welcomed by the FDTL as it would have been alien to their guerilla background.

In recent years the military discipline systems of more developed states have been subject to increased levels of scrutiny. The remedial responses to such scrutiny have involved increased levels of complexity as additional safeguards against the risk of unfairness are provided. When approaching the creation of the FDTL Code, the rights provided by such instruments as the European Convention on Human Rights and Fundamental Freedoms 1950 and the International Covenant on Civil and Political Rights 1966, formed a foundation upon which a simple but workable system could be built.

Indeed, foremost in approaching the creation of the system was one factor that could not be compromised: the guarantee of the fundamental rights of the accused within the military discipline system.

3.1.4 Military Legal Systems in Concept

The system of military discipline should always begin within the unit. It may in some systems move out of the unit to either a more senior officer or to a court martial but it must at least start with the unit as it is essential that this disciplinary control is exercised by those who will lead the soldiers in conflict. Therefore it is necessary for those who are not legally qualified to exercise disciplinary power.

If this is accepted then some compromises are necessary: the rules of evidence cannot apply as the officer would be unfamiliar with them; lawyers should take no part as it is not a court of law; it is not open to the public as it would render operational discipline unworkable. These compromises are offset by the accused having the right to have witnesses present to give their evidence in front of him or her, having the right to an officer or senior non-commissioned officer to assist him or her and having a record made of the hearing. Accordingly, the aim is that the fairness of the system is not compromised even though certain aspects of the legal process might be.

3.2 Analysis of the Code of Military Discipline

In order to analyze the operation of the Code of Military Discipline it is necessary to consider its constituent parts. In short the system provides that an allegation be investigated and the evidence then considered by an officer to assess its susceptibility to military jurisdiction. The appropriate charge is then considered and the evidence disclosed to the accused prior to a hearing taking place. Indeed, it represents the basic elements of any legal system, shed of its legalistic complexity.

This system will be considered in relation to its component parts and the decision making process followed in creating it.

3.2.1 Jurisdiction

The starting point of any system is establishing who is subject to it and when. As with most military discipline systems, regular (i.e. full time) members of FDTL are subject to military law at all times, regardless of whether they are "on duty." For former guerillas the notion of never being "off duty" was one with which they were familiar. The soldiers' difficulty lay in distinguishing their liability to civil and military law. There was a perception with some that they should be subject to military law alone.[6]

The debates in the National Council exposed a fear that civilians would fall within the scope of the code simply by working on military camps. This view exposed a need to educate those involved with the system on the very basics of a military legal system.

3.2.2 Breaches of Military Discipline

As indicated, it was important to ensure that civil primacy was apparent. Jurisdiction was therefore limited to military matters with civil offences being left to the civil system. The term "breach of service discipline" was deliberately used in the Code of Military Discipline to make this distinction. There was clearly some scope for overlap of breaches and offences but this was minimized as much as possible.

All breaches were given a military context. In some cases this was obvious, for example absence without leave, but in others such as fighting, the *actus reus* was qualified to add the military context.

The breaches of discipline themselves were drawn from those common to many military forces around the world. The situation regarding the FDTL did not require the addition of any new types of breaches although it did require the omission of some (e.g. offences relating to flying as the FDTL did not have an air component). In all, the breaches numbered fourteen. Most notable were absence without leave, drunkenness, insubordinate behaviour, disobeying orders (written and verbal), damaging or losing FDTL property, avoiding duty and fighting.

The absence of a court-martial level necessarily limited the seriousness of cases that could be dealt with within the military system as the disciplinary officers would not be legally qualified. The consequent limitation on the powers of punishment therefore meant that offences such as mutiny and desertion will need to be created as civil offences.

The elements of the breaches were initially intended to be included in the secondary legislation (i.e. Administrative Instruction). However, it was decided that they should be included in the UNTAET regulation as an annex. The format used mirrored that of the elements of crimes in the Rome Statute on the International Criminal Court.[7] It was important that the elements of breaches were laid down from the outset as the absence from the discipline system of a Court Martial level meant that "caselaw" regarding the elements would not develop.

---

[6] [n.29] This attitude was symptomatic of the length of the struggle of FALINTIL with the Indonesian military (TNI). The rigorous maintenance of discipline by FALINTIL alone over its 24 years meant that the concept of now being subject to both civil and military jurisdictions (with civil having primacy) was one that sat uneasily with the soldiers.

[7] [n.32] This was deliberate. The timing of the submission of the Code of Military Discipline as an UNTAET regulation to the National Council meant that there was little time for manoeuvre. Accordingly, it was important that when the Office of the Legal Adviser in New York reviewed the code they were familiar with the format. This would smooth its passage.

The incorporation of the elements of the breaches into the procedures for the system was accomplished by a check-list being created for the disciplinary officer to have in front of him when considering a case. The officer could simply "tick off" the elements if sure about them and if they were all "ticked" then the accused's guilt was established.

3.2.3 Arrest

A system of military arrest would undoubtedly increase the complexity of the system: the issue was whether it added any value. The reality was that, as with any defence force, regardless of whether a formal system would be implemented, the retention of soldiers in some form of "arrest" would take place. Accordingly, some mechanism to control that would be necessary.

In order to maintain the chain of command, the power to arrest was confined to those superior in rank to the accused. Reasons for the arrest (which could be verbal) must be given within 24 hours, by which time the disciplinary officer must also have been informed. The officer would then assess the requirement for further arrest up to a maximum total of 48 hours. This additional complexity caused some concern. In order to lessen the problem no requirement for paperwork was included in the regulation.

The criteria for arrest were drawn from the civil system as were the time limits. In the circumstances of an allegation of a military breach of discipline being considered by the disciplinary officer to be a civil matter, it was important that the civil prosecution was not prejudiced by unlawful military arrest. The review within 72 hours required by the civil system could quite easily be carried out following the elapse of the military arrest at the 48-hour point.

3.2.4 Investigation

Criminal investigations within most military forces are carried out by specially trained investigators (military police). However, investigations for military breaches of discipline are invariably carried out within the unit of the accused. The rules of evidence are not followed but then the rules of evidence are difficult to apply at the unit level as the officer hearing the case is usually not legally qualified. The unit investigation is necessarily limited and straightforward but gives the officer sufficient information to assess how best to deal with the matter, for example by formal disciplinary action or an informal rebuke.

The size of the FDTL did not lend itself to the creation of a military police component. Nonetheless, Brig Gen Taur Matan Ruak was keen to ensure that any investigation to be carried out by someone relatively experienced. It was decided that the rank of the investigator should be at least Chief Sergeant.

The investigation itself was intended to be simple. A proposed set of Codes for Investigators was abandoned as being too ambitious. Nonetheless certain rights of an accused had to be protected. In teaching the system, emphasis was placed on the need to respect the "basic rights" during any investigation. During the investigation phase, this was most important in "interview" with the accused.

The rights in question were:

- the right of silence;

- the right to have a "defending officer" present in any interview;

- the right to give his account of events in any interview;

- the right not to be bulled by the investigating officer in any interview;

- the right to be considered innocent until proven guilty.

These rights were outlined in a one-page explanation that was handed to the accused once he was charged with an offence. These rights were translated into Tetun, Bahasa Indonesian, and Portugese.[8]

The requirement for the accused to have copies of all the evidence and the charge sheet, meant that all investigations had to be written. This would assist in creating a record of the investigation that could be used in any subsequent review. Standard forms were produced to ensure an element of uniformity in the format of the investigations.

3.2.5 Charging

In several systems around the world, both civil and military, the point of charging has consequences for the investigation, for example the accused may not be further interviewed following his being charged. Accordingly, in those systems it is important to establish the point of charge. The straightforward nature of the FDTL system did not require such a definite point as the investigation would continue through to the disciplinary hearing itself. This would be consistent with the inquisitorial nature of the whole process.

Accordingly, the only requirements imposed regarding charging were that the decision be that of the disciplinary officer and that any charge be reduced into writing.

3.2.6 Disciplinary Officers

Within any legal system it is important to identify clearly the persons who are to exercise disciplinary power. In a military legal system the connection between command and authority is similarly important. In several military forces, the exercise of disciplinary power is predicated on being in command and a series of criteria are laid down that the officer must fulfil. In military forces larger than the FDTL such a system, based on criteria related to command, is necessary as it would be practically impossible to appoint individuals by name with the movement of such a large number of officers being so frequent.

That problem did not arise in the FDTL as there would only be two regular and two reserve battalions when at full strength. Accordingly, it was possible

---

[8] [n.39] Language became a significant problem in both the creation and implementation of the system. The official language of UNTAET was English whilst the official language of East Timor was Portuguese. However, the majority of the FDTL spoke either Tetun or Bahasa. The only members to speak Portuguese were the senior officers (Lieutenant Colonels and above). The absence of a universal official language meant that all documents were translated into 3 languages and some into all 4 languages, a time consuming process.

simply to require that before an officer could exercise disciplinary power he must be "appointed" as a "disciplinary officer" by the Chief of the Defence Force (CDF). The disadvantage of this was that it meant that, on paper, the link between command and the exercise of disciplinary power was not maintained. However, in practice only those in command would exercise disciplinary power. The remaining disciplinary officers acted as "spare" capacity in the event of the battalion or company commander being absent.

The jurisdiction of the disciplinary officers was limited to those below them in rank. This was common sense. A limitation was imposed that the disciplinary officer must be at least a Major in rank. Provision was made for the Chief of the Defence Force to further limit the power of the disciplinary officers if he felt it was necessary.

3.2.7 Disciplinary Hearing

The disciplinary hearing, as the culmination of the system, would inevitably act as a litmus test for how fair it was perceived to be by the soldiers subject to it. Disciplinary officers would similarly use it as the gauge of how workable it was. The procedures therefore needed to tread a middle line between fairness and simplicity.

One of the first considerations was the format of the hearing. An inquisitorial as opposed to an adversarial system was adopted as this would be less encumbered with procedures. The absence of qualified lawyers would also make it difficult to implement an adversarial system. In addition, the inquisitorial system, with the disciplinary officer as the person "running" the proceedings, had the advantage of underlining his position in command.

Safeguards in respect of the suitability of the particular disciplinary officer to hear the case were provided for. The disciplinary officer had to actively consider whether there was any reason why he or she should not hear the case. Further, on preliminary matters, the need to obtain confirmation that the accused had received copies of the charge sheet, the evidence in support of the charge and an explanation of the accused's rights was inserted.

The accused was given the right to plead guilty. This had obvious advantages in that the witnesses would not be required. However, it was clear that, as the accused was not going to be advised by a lawyer, a safeguard needed to be provided to verify that the plea of guilty was correct. The disciplinary officer in those circumstances would be required to read out the elements of the breach from the Code of Discipline and be satisfied that the accused accepted guilt on all the elements.

The hearing of evidence was to take place in a form familiar to most trials, with the evidence in support of the prosecution being called first and then the accused being given an opportunity to give or call evidence. All evidence would be given on oath or affirmation.

As indicated above, a defending officer was to be provided for the accused. That officer's role at the disciplinary hearing would include questioning witnesses and giving a "plea in mitigation" on behalf of any soldiers convicted.

With the system not having a court martial level it was not possible to insert a right to elect trial by court martial as exists in other systems. This was not considered to be a problem as the level of matters dealt with by the military system was limited. Similarly the level of punishments was restricted. For the same reasons the right to elect to be tried by the civil courts was not considered appropriate.

3.2.8 Punishments

Of all the aspects of the system, decisions regarding the types and level of punishments caused the greatest difficulty. FALINTIL had exercised discipline rigorously and ruthlessly when in the mountains.[9] The soldiers were familiar with and understood such discipline. Reaching a compromise between these previously unregulated practices and the new system that would be scrutinized by the UNTAET National Council as well as the UN Office of the Principal Legal Adviser proved difficult. The system had to be accepted by members of the FDTL as sufficiently severe to act as a deterrent. When viewed against the punishments meted out in the mountains it remains to be seen whether this has been achieved.

In deciding on the types of punishments to be imposed the views of senior officers in the FDTL were clearly central. Whilst there was a temptation to be creative,[10] there was also a sense of security in adopting punishments that had been tried and tested in military forces around the world. Following consultation with FDTL officers, this latter view was adopted.

Accordingly, the punishments available will be familiar to most military forces. The most severe punishment is detention and the least severe is a reprimand. The maximum amount of detention that can be imposed for each breach is limited to seven days with a cumulative total per hearing of 28 days. This presupposed that punishments imposed would be consecutive and not concurrent. The factor of four was applied as the maximum amount of any punishment to be imposed at any one hearing. The combination of punishments was regulated by an Administrative Instruction.

One punishment excluded from the list was that of compensation, either to the service for damaged property or to a victim for an injury. There were several difficulties related to such a punishment. The salaries of FDTL soldiers were low and would not have allowed for large amounts of money to be taken

---

[9] [n.52] A conversation between the author and a former FALINTIL commander took place when deciding on the punishments to be imposed. The commander was asked what the punishment would be for a soldier who disobeyed a command when in the mountains with FALINTIL. The response was a smile and a finger drawn across the throat. This would not appear to have been an example of bravado as this form of punishment is also recorded in the UNICEF Case Studies Report on East Timorese Children in Armed Conflict released 12 September 2001, 18 ("Extra-judicial killings by FALINTIL have also been reported . . .").

[10] [n.53] Just prior to the implementation of the system an account was heard of an informal punishment imposed on two soldiers caught fighting at Metinaro Training Camp. Both were handed a flag (red and blue) and told to climb the mountain behind their camp in the morning and hide the flag that they had been given. That evening both were sent up the mountain again and told to retrieve the other's flag. It is submitted that this type of *ad hoc*, convenient punishment has only superficial attractions as it overlooks the importance of there being equality of punishments across the FDTL. Only strictly controlled punishments offer this fairness.

from them. The fine was limited to 2 days pay for this reason. Initially, it was felt that such a punishment would have added undue complexity to the system regarding an assessment of the money to be taken from the soldier. In relation to injuries, assaults would have to be dealt with in the civil courts. In other circumstances, for example negligent discharge of a round injuring another soldier, the disciplinary officer was not qualified to make an assessment of liability and quantum.

However, in retrospect the inclusion of a system of compensation could have been achieved without creating difficulties regarding the financial allocation of monies from fines post-hearing. This could also have been achieved in such a way as to reflect the cultural approach of the East Timorese people. It was common in the *suco* (or village) system of justice for an accused to be "fined" an animal of some sort and some refreshment in relation to an offence by the *chef de suco*. The animal would be slaughtered and the food and drink used in a feast that would act both as the punishment and reconciliation of the accused with the *suco* that he had offended.

Dismissal and discharge were also excluded from the punishments available to disciplinary officers. Provision for the termination of the appointment of officers and for the discharge of soldiers was included as an administrative procedure in the regulation creating the defence force and this was considered sufficient.

In order to assist the disciplinary officer in navigating the various options for punishments, a Guide to Punishments was created. Initially, a set tariff of punishments was requested that would apply regardless of the specific circumstances of the breach. This was resisted and instead a scale of punishments was produced. This preserved the discretion of the disciplinary officer but also guaranteed some element of parity in the punishments imposed.

3.2.9 Review

The perception of fairness that the system enjoyed depended in part on there being a formal mechanism of scrutiny within it. The review procedure provided that. Albeit that review was internal (i.e. to the Chief of the Defence Force),[11] in a discipline system as small as that in the FDTL the perception of fairness would be dependent on personalities rather than the system itself. A right to seek a review of a decision by the Chief of the Defence Force to the Transitional Administrator existed. The basis upon which a decision would be reviewed would be what was "deem[ed] proper in the interests of justice."

The power of Review is to confirm the finding and punishment, overturn the finding or reduce the punishment. There is no power to increase the punishment. The procedure for the review is not proscribed as it was felt that the system would need to develop its own procedures for this.

4. Implementation

In order to ensure the most favourable acceptance, it was considered important to use the system quickly and frequently. Too great a gap between the

---

[11] [n.61] But see *Morris v. UK*, Case No. 38784/97 dated 26 Feb 2002 in the European Court of Human Rights.

teaching of the system and its practice would undermine the initial enthusiasm that the soldiers had shown for it. No less important was the need to persuade the disciplinary officers that the system was workable.

In adopting this approach, compromises were made. Inevitably, in the initial stages, mistakes were made in the investigation of breaches and in the procedure at the disciplinary hearings. A conscious decision was taken not to concentrate on these but to develop an adherence to the "spirit" of the law before emphasizing the "letter" of the law. Whilst this would be considered unacceptable in other developed military forces, the reality was that if the system was perceived as cumbersome from the outset then it would fail. The result would have been its replacement by an unofficial, more malleable system that was less subject to scrutiny. Accordingly, so long as fairness to the accused was not adversely affected then any mistakes were merely noted for action during subsequent cases.

In this way the system developed pragmatically. Delays were reduced and its simplicity highlighted, both of which were intended to add to its attraction. The corollary to this approach was the fear that "bad habits" would be learned; this was not realized.

Notwithstanding this the system developed slowly. There were two main reasons for this:

(i) *Introduction of Formality:* The introduction of a requirement for evidence to be reduced to writing (a safeguard for the accused soldier) added bureaucracy. The opportunity to simply "get to the bottom" of the allegation therefore appeared at first glance to be hindered by the system's structure. To the disciplinary officers who were unfamiliar with set procedures of a legal nature this was a significant barrier to their acceptance of the system.

This discomfort translated into an unwillingness to use the system and some gentle encouragement was required to overcome this. Further, the initial hearings were heavily "choreographed." This involved rehearsals immediately prior to the hearing and then a close monitoring of the procedures as the hearing progressed. Over time the "fear" of the procedure began to subside.

(ii) *Paperwork:* Statements, charge sheets, notices to the accused and records of proceedings caused a similar feeling of discomfort. Of necessity, FALINTIL had not kept records and therefore the regimen of creating and retaining documents was alien.

In order to address this point a course on unit administration was created. It dealt with the purpose of record keeping and the processes involved. It was difficult to see an alternative to the need for such paperwork as this provided for an element of scrutiny.

As well as using the system quickly in order to engender familiarity and acceptance, the deterrent factor was also important. Problems with poor attendance (both AWOL[12] and not attending parades on time), which were common

---

[12] [n.62] One of the difficulties with the amount of AWOL was the absence of any formalized system of leave. This was symptomatic of the sheer scale of the task facing the FDTL in starting from scratch. These basic issues impacted upon the discipline system at all stages of its implementation.

in the early stages of training, would benefit from several cases being dealt with early on and punishments publicized. In order to extend this deterrent factor the cases chosen in the early stages involved as wide a range of breaches of discipline as possible. This also prevented a "tunnel vision" approach developing in relation to the types of breaches that could be committed.

A further facet of the deterrent factor was ensuring that it was seen to apply to all ranks. The second case was chosen to reflect this. It involved six Capitaos who were alleged to have failed to attend a parade. Although they were acquitted, the informal rebuke that the Chief of the Defence Force gave them in respect of their future behaviour reinforced his support of the system.

Regarding the operation of the system itself the following points were noted in the initial stages:

(i) *Breaches of Discipline:* One issue that was encountered from the outset and will continue to be an issue for some time to come was the concept of a "reasonable excuse" for being absent without leave. Several soldiers claimed that they left owing to their duty to provide food for their families.[13] Each case will clearly need to be considered on its own merits by the disciplinary officers in light of their experience of East Timorese life.

(ii) *Investigations (Witness statements):* The taking of statements was a time consuming process as they needed to be translated into/from Tetun and English. Without such translation there would be no way of monitoring the system. This was a short-term problem.

(iii) *Investigations (Interview with suspects)*: Interviews were conducted in a fair manner despite the absence of any set procedures. This was particularly encouraging. Use of the defending officer was limited at first but this did not undermine the rights of the accused.

(iv) *Charge Sheets:* An FDTL reliance on the international legal adviser in drafting charges took some time to break. This was understandable. The specimen charges, once translated into Tetun, began to assist in this regard.

(v) *Hearings (Procedures):* The speed of hearings increased as familiarity with the system increased. Again, assisting this was the translation of the procedural guidance into Tetun. Initially, it had only been in English and Portuguese. The Tetun version avoided the need to translate for the benefit of the soldiers who could not understand Portuguese.

(vi) *Hearings (Recorder):* The viability of the review process was dependent on the quality of the evidence recorded at the hearing. There was a reluctance to take on the role of recorder that proved difficult to resolve. Accordingly, in the initial stages the international legal adviser took on the role in a tutor capacity.

---

13 [n.65] Such an excuse on a frequent basis augurs badly for the FDTL. One soldier left his duty to work on a coffee plantation to earn extra money for his family. He was unable to understand why his pay for the time he was absent was forfeited (via UNTAET Regulation 2001/1 as amended by 2001/9, s.23) as this cancelled out the financial benefit of his going absent in the first place. This lesson will no doubt need to be learned many times in the progress to a peacetime regular army.

(vii) *Hearings (Defending Officer):* This was the real surprise of the system. Young officers grew into the role of defending officers at the hearings.

(viii) *Punishments (Types):* Several of the punishments were, to all intents and purposes, redundant as a result of the stage of FDTL development. For instance, the concept of "extra duties" only works when there is a system of duties to which "extras" can be added. Similarly, the stopping of leave can only operate once a structured leave system is in operation. This should change upon the FDTL developing such systems.

The use of detention proved an effective deterrent. So small was the cell that any period over two days in it was extremely uncomfortable, especially in the heat of the wet season in East Timor. Careful managing of the state of the prisoner was needed in order to ensure the safe use of the cell.

(ix) *Punishments (Severity)*: The imposition of fines was limited in severity. The pay for a private soldier was US$85 per month. There was a feeling amongst many soldiers that this was insufficient. This was a view that the disciplinary officers had some sympathy with as they were loathe to impose fines. The deterrent effect of the punishment was therefore high but it remains to be seen whether it is a punishment that is used.

(x) *Review*: The review process was not used in the initial stages. The decision to find an accused guilty was reached with a reassuring abundance of caution and the punishments imposed were initially lenient. This diminished the practical requirement for the review process.

5. Review of Implementation

It would be naïve to suggest that the system will not need to be changed. The speed with which the system was created is such that there will be issues that have been overlooked. In time these will become apparent and appropriate action to remedy the deficiencies can be taken.

The temptation to alter the system as and when issues arise has been resisted. Only once the system is established can the real inadequacies be identified. Until initial scepticism and unfamiliarity have been overcome, it will be difficult to differentiate between the problems with the system and the problems with the intransigence of its operators. Inevitably changes will be driven by the operators but care will need to be taken that such changes address flaws in the system and not in the operators.

A particular decision that has been revisited concerns the absence of a compensatory punishment. The creation of a fund for the benefit of the FDTL into which the money from fines could be directed provided a resonance between the new system and the more established local systems of justice. This assisted acceptance by the soldiers.

As regards "lessons learned" so far, in retrospect, the failure to have all of the disciplinary documents translated into Tetun from the outset was a key oversight that retarded the acceptance of the system. Reliance had been placed on Portuguese (the "official" language) and not Tetun (the "universal" language) being the common form of parlance. This misunderstood the reality of the language abilities within the FDTL. This absence of Tetun documents initially necessitated the translation of proceedings that added to the delay and perception of complexity.

A further issue regarding language was the use of specific terms. The term "detention" in English was translated into Portuguese as "detencao." However, this had a specific meaning in the Portuguese military disciplinary system of "arrest whilst awaiting trial." The confusion that this initially caused to officers and soldiers who had been influenced and, in some cases, trained by the Portuguese can be imagined. Gradually an understanding of the new meaning grew.

As the disciplinary officers became more familiar with the system, the procedural guidance within the Administrative Instructions became too prescriptive and prevented the FDTL from developing its own approach to the running of the disciplinary hearing. Accordingly, a strict adherence to what was intended as a useful guide was abandoned by the time a dozen cases had been heard. Instead the general procedures were followed. The method of hearing evidence for instance become more traditional with all the witnesses being present in the hearing at the same time.[14]

6. The Future

The task of implementation is far from over and will need careful management for several years to come. In that time it will be subject to many external influences that could alter it. The very recent independence of East Timor has not seen any changes being made to the system as yet.

In the immediate future there are some developments that will require attention. The availability of an East Timorese legally qualified adviser will be essential. The size of the FDTL would make it impractical to create a legal department within it. It may be advisable nonetheless to have a civilian lawyer as part of the reserve in order to have a lawyer, familiar with the military legal system, from whom advice could be sought on an *ad hoc* but regular basis. Additionally, a Discipline Sergeant based in the Battalion headquarters would provide a more readily available source of advice. Both would ensure that the FDTL took complete ownership of "their" system.

Conclusion

The continuing transition from a guerilla force to a peacetime conventional army involves many changes to the way in which FALINTIL operated. The absence of an enemy with which they are engaged as the FDTL means that the maintenance of discipline will be determined not so much by an innate sense of survival but by the instilling of conventional military discipline in its members. The traditional rank structure provides the legitimate framework for this discipline but this occasionally requires enforcement.

The discipline system created under the authority of UNTAET Regulation 2001/12 on 20 July 2001 represents a start: a tailored system intended to

---

14 [n.67] This may sound odd to practitioners in Western legal systems. However, the presence of all the witnesses in court during the giving of evidence was apparently common in some courts in East Timor. It certainly accords with the author's experience of representing an FTDL solder in the District Court in Dili.

reflect both the culture of FALINTIL and the fairness demanded for an accused. It will evolve over time as it should. But it is hoped that the delicate balance between pragmatism and justice is maintained as only then will the FDTL retain the confidence of its members at all levels as well as that of the sovereign state that it exists to serve.

Maj. Steve Cullen, *Starting Over — The New Iraqi* **Code of Military Discipline**
ARMY LAW., Sept. 2004, at 44

Introduction

Operation Iraqi Freedom ended Saddam Hussein's regime and with it the Ba'ath party's control of the Iraqi government. To achieve the goal of eradicating the Ba'athist influence in Iraqi government institutions, the Coalition Provisional Authority (CPA) dissolved many government entities previously controlled by the Ba'athists, including the Iraqi Armed Forces. Noting that United Nations Security Resolution 1483 called for member states to assist the people of Iraq in order to contribute to the stability and security in their country, the CPA, on 18 August 2003, created an all volunteer Iraqi Army. With the creation of a new Iraqi Army, commanders required a new discipline code to fill the gap created by the suspension of the old regime's military laws. To help maintain good order and discipline in the new Iraqi Armed Forces (IAF), the CPA promulgated a *Code of Military Discipline* (*Code*) that was immediately applicable[15] to all IAF members. Not surprisingly, the Code bears similarities to the American military justice system. This note describes the Code, comparing it with its American counterpart, and suggests possible improvements for a more complete, permanent Iraqi military law.

The *Code* details the jurisdictions and conditions under which IAF members may be prosecuted. It states that IAF members are subject to the *Code* from the date of attestation into the IAF until the date of termination of service. Iraqi Armed Forces members also remain subject to the jurisdiction of the civilian courts, though they are immune from civil prosecution and liability "for acts or omissions arising within the scope of their duties and authorized operations." These provisions have familiar counterparts in the American military justice system.

The *Code* also creates a substantive military criminal law and discipline system. The substantive law enumerates a number of military offenses, which are grouped into three categories. The first category, discussed in detail below, might be thought of as "true" military offenses, as they have no criminal counterpart in civilian society (e.g., absence without leave, disobeying lawful orders, and dereliction of duty). The second category of military offenses is civilian criminal offenses. The *Code* adopts, by reference, the entire Iraqi civilian criminal code and re-labels the offenses as "military offenses." The *Code*

---

[15] [n.7] COALITION PROVISIONAL AUTHORITY, ORDER 23, CREATION OF A CODE OF MILITARY DISCIPLINE FOR THE NEW IRAQI ARMY (Aug. 20, 2003), *available at* www.cpa-iraq.org/regulations/#Orders [hereinafter CPA ORDER 23].

states that "[a]ny member of the Iraqi Armed Forces . . . who commits a civilian criminal offense shall be guilty, by reason of so doing, of a Military Offense. . . ." The third and final category of military offenses is crimes or offenses against the law of war as adopted by Iraq or recognized as customary international law.

In order to help Iraqi commanders maintain good order and discipline in their units, the *Code*, like the *Uniform Code of Military Justice* (UCMJ), incorporates a number of military offenses that have no counterpart in civilian society. . . .

Enforcement of the *Code of Military Discipline*

The *Code*'s enforcement mechanism for the true military offenses is similar to the American military nonjudicial punishment (NJP) process. A number of differences make a comparison to the American military justice system a worthwhile exercise in exploring features of the new Iraqi system and considering possible amendments for the future.

The *Code*'s determination concerning who may administer military discipline is similar to the American military company and field grade NJP authorities. In the Iraqi system, authority is divided between junior and senior disciplinary officers. Junior disciplinary officers are defined as officers at least a captain in rank who either command a company or an equivalent-size unit of which an accused is a member or are appointed in writing by a brigade commander to be the junior disciplinary officer of an accused. Senior disciplinary officers are defined as officers at least lieutenant colonel in rank who either command the battalion of which the accused is a member or are appointed by the commander of the IAF to be the senior disciplinary officer of the accused.

Junior disciplinary officers have jurisdiction over members of the IAF below the rank of lieutenant for true military offenses. For company commanders, this includes all enlisted members of the command. The *Code* does not provide a mechanism for superior commanders to withhold authority to dispose of specific cases or certain types of cases, as American commanders often do for senior noncommissioned officer misconduct. Brigade commander authority to appoint junior disciplinary officers has definite merit. In the American military justice system, NJP authority is tied to command; therefore, disputes occasionally arise over whether the NJP-imposing officer has proper command authority. The Army's governing regulation states, "[w]hether [the] officer is a commander is determined by the duties he or she performs, not necessarily by the title of the position." In the *Code*, a brigade commander can appoint, in writing, junior disciplinary officers to administer discipline in separate and other units that may not have a company commander available to fill this role. Additionally, the Iraqi system clearly contemplates appointing junior disciplinary officers after the commission of an offense. In the event that a company commander is unavailable or disqualified from administering NJP, it is unnecessary to resort to the next superior commander, because a junior disciplinary officer can be appointed to administer the case.

A senior disciplinary officer's authority is considerably different than that of a field grade's NJP authority in the American military system. Senior disciplinary officers only have original jurisdiction over true military offenses concerning members of the IAF in the rank of lieutenant and above, as long as the senior disciplinary officer is at least one rank above the accused. Senior disciplinary officers also have jurisdiction over appeals of junior disciplinary officer's decisions. The jurisdiction of Iraqi battalion commanders as senior disciplinary officers is much more limited than that of their American counterparts. American field grade NJP authorities have jurisdiction over all members of their command. Although there are arguably many drawbacks to this limitation in a senior disciplinary officer's jurisdiction, it enforces a strict application of the American military policy to dispose of offenses at the lowest appropriate level.

Maximum Punishments

For true military offenses, the *Code* shares many similarities with the American military NIP system. As with the commanders' jurisdiction, however, the *Code* also contains significant differences, including available punishments for military offenses.

In the Iraqi system, a junior disciplinary officer can administer the following punishments in respect to each military offense of which he finds an enlisted IAF member guilty:

(a) detention for a period not longer than seven days;

(b) [a] fine not exceeding fourteen days' pay;

(c) a reprimand;

(d) extra duties to a maximum of seven days;

(e) in respect of a private first class, corporal, or sergeant, reduction by one rank;

(f) stoppages of pay in respect [to] damage or loss caused by the act or acts which formed the basis of the Offense charged, not exceeding fourteen days' pay.

Similar to American military company grade NJP, a junior disciplinary officer may combine certain punishments; however, there are clear distinctions. . . .

The maximum punishments available to the senior disciplinary officer also differ significantly from those of the American field grade NJP authority. As the senior disciplinary officer's non-appeal jurisdiction is limited to IAF commissioned officers, the punishments available are very different from those of the American field grade NJP authority. The senior disciplinary officer's punishments, however, are very similar to the junior disciplinary officer's punishment, though detention is not authorized. The rules for senior disciplinary officers combining punishments are otherwise identical to those of the junior disciplinary officers.

The punishments available to Iraqi commanders do not appear as nuanced as the American military justice system. The most notable demonstration of this is that unlike field grade NJP, senior disciplinary officers do not expose Soldiers to greater maximum punishments. Additionally, Iraqi commanders do not have the variety of punishments available as their American counterparts (e.g., restriction to specified limits). More importantly, unlike the American military NJP process, the *Code* lacks provisions to suspend, mitigate, remit, or set aside punishments. These tools introduce an enormous amount of flexibility into the American military NJP system. They permit commanders to individualize NJP for Soldiers and meet the NJP purpose of promoting positive behavior changes in service members. The addition of a suspension procedure may be one of the first areas for reform in the *Code*.

Despite these differences, a fair argument can be made that the Iraqi Discipline System has advantages over the American military justice system. As a junior disciplinary officer, an Iraqi company commander has a wider range of punishments available than his American counterpart. The American company commander's punishments are limited primarily to seven days confinement, seven days forfeiture, fourteen days extra duty, and a one rank reduction for enlisted, however, an Iraqi company commander can administer seven days detention, seven days extra duty, up to twenty-eight days loss of pay, and reduction of IAF corporals and below to the lowest enlisted grade. Perhaps an even more persuasive argument for the advantages of the Iraqi system is its relative simplicity. Providing accurate training on the *Code* to IAF members is a simpler task than teaching the rules of NJP to American service members, because only one set of punishments is available.

Disciplinary Hearings

The procedure for Iraqi disciplinary hearings is also similar to the procedures for American military NJP hearings. . . .

For the most part, each procedure's design is very similar. Both provide the accused fair notice of the proceeding, respect an accused's right to avoid self-incrimination, and permit the accused to present evidence on the merits and in mitigation of their punishment.

The differences between these procedures are nevertheless apparent. Unlike an American accused, an IAF member has the right to request the assistance of an officer of his choice to prepare for a disciplinary hearing. This is a significant protection afforded to IAF members. The most similar right in the American military system permits a Soldier to have a spokesperson present at his disciplinary hearing. The right to request assistance of a specific officer in preparing for a disciplinary hearing may not be as effective as having trial defense counsel representation, but this officer could influence the commander and serve as a highly effective advocate for the accused.

A clear advantage to an accused Soldier in the American military justice system is that an accused may refuse NJP and demand trial by court-martial. This right effectively enforces a standard of guilty only beyond a reasonable doubt for NJP, and it gives the accused an alternate forum if he believes he will not receive a fair hearing from the NJP authority.

One last important distinction between the two systems is the appeals process. In American military NJP "any service member punished under Article 15 who considers the punishment to be unjust or disproportionate to the offense may appeal through the proper channels to the next superior authority." The *Code*'s appeal system is different and possibly less likely to be used by members of the IAF, particularly those convicted by senior disciplinary officers. Under the *Code*, accused who are convicted by junior disciplinary officers may appeal their case in writing within fourteen days to the senior disciplinary officer. This process is nearly identical to the American military system, except the accused can appeal the conviction and punishment imposed by the junior disciplinary officer. Accuseds convicted by senior disciplinary officers have a more intimidating appeals process. The only appeal available is to the IAF commander.

Military Courts

The *Code*'s lack of a military court-martial procedure is the most significant divergence from the UCMJ. Under the *Code*, a military court is one in name only and is defined as "a civilian court with a civilian judge who has been appointed as a military judge." These "military courts" have jurisdiction over all military offenses and exclusive jurisdiction over many military offenses. Their exclusive jurisdiction includes military offenses that are also civilian offenses and war crimes. These cases will be investigated and tried in accordance with the Iraqi civilian law of criminal procedure. This arrangement demonstrates the ingenuity of CPA Order 23. Without re-writing the Iraqi military discipline code, CPA Order 23 established a system of military justice capable of disciplining the entire range of offenses, from simple military disorders to major felonies.

The present system of Iraqi military justice created by CPA Order 23 has apparent shortcomings. A paramount problem is that a military commander loses control of any offense that is not a "true" military offense, but a crime under the Iraqi civilian criminal code. In the American military discipline system, commanders are encouraged to dispose of allegations of offenses at the lowest appropriate level. Accordingly, commanders often dispose of minor non-military specific offenses (e.g., wrongful use of marijuana) using NJP procedures. In maintaining good order and discipline, American commanders have the discretion to keep otherwise good Soldiers at their duties by punishing minor misconduct using NJP procedures. Iraqi commanders do not have this flexibility or discretion. An Iraqi commander cannot use *Code* NJP procedures to punish any offense other than the military-unique offenses listed in CPA Order 23. Any other offense must be referred to the civilian criminal system acting as a military court.

Conclusion

After the fall of the previous Iraqi regime, CPA Order 23 established a military discipline system for the new IAF. Coalition Provisional Authority Order 23 supports the command's obligation to maintain good order and discipline by enumerating true military offenses and creating a non-judicial system to enforce them. The military discipline system created by CPA Order 23 relies on the existing Iraqi civilian criminal justice system for disposition of all other criminal offenses, including disposition of minor criminal misconduct committed by IAF members. The current Iraqi Ministry of Defense recognizes the shortcomings of the present military discipline system and understands the *Code* established by CPA Order 23 is a useful interim system between the military justice system enforced by Saddam Hussein's regime and the future Iraqi government. The Iraqi Ministry of Defense General Counsel's office has already begun addressing the need for a more complete military justice system and is in the process of drafting a new Iraqi *Code of Military Justice*. The Iraqi Ministry of Defense intends to borrow heavily from the Iraqi 1941 Military Code for Substantive Crimes and from the American UCMJ for procedures to protect IAF members. This new system will propose assigning military attorneys to all the field commands in order to provide free legal representation to all accused and also appoint independent military judges in each governorate. The new Iraqi *Code of Military Justice*'s goal is to preserve a commander's inherent right to maintain good order and discipline over the entire spectrum of misconduct and simultaneously preserving the rights of members of the new IAF.

Maj. Sean M. Watts & Capt. Christopher E. Martin, *Nation-Building in Afghanistan: Lessons Identified in Military Justice Reform*,
ARMY LAW., May 2006, at 1, 10-11

We also observed that vigorous coordination, both horizontally and vertically, is absolutely essential to making effective progress in something as multi-faceted as military justice reform. Military justice reform cannot happen in a passive environment, and changes made by U.S. mentors will never take root unless they are closely coordinated with the Afghans and other parties involved. We observed that critical coordination was needed at several levels: with the Afghans themselves, within the U.S. military effort, and with the international community. Without such coordination, military justice reform may repeat many of the mistakes made in the parallel civil justice reform effort.

> Do not try to do too much with your own hands. Better the Arabs do it tolerably than that you do it perfectly. It is their war, and you are to help them, not to win it for them.[16]

Lawrence of Arabia's words of wisdom, popular among U.S. military commanders, could just as easily apply to development efforts in Afghanistan or anywhere else in the world. After discovering how foreign a transplanted common law system could be to experienced afghan lawyers, we quickly realized that any new legal system would have to be recognizable to Afghan practitioners if it were to have any lasting value. This illustrates the final and most important lesson learned: ownership ultimately has to be in the hands of the reformed, not the reformers. This observation, while perhaps obvious, is nonetheless easy to overlook.

There is perhaps a cliché among the international community in Afghanistan, prevalent in the legal as well as other reform sectors, that because Afghanistan suffered under a succession of oppressive, destructive

---

[16] [n.91] JEREMY WILSON, LAWRENCE OF ARABIA: THE AUTHORIZED BIOGRAPHY OF T.E. LAWRENCE 962 (1989). This excerpt comes from T.E. Lawrence's famous *Twenty Seven Articles*, published in the *Arab Bulletin* on 20 August 1917 to offer tips on relating to Arabs. *See 27 Articles of T.E. Lawrence*, http://www.lib.byu.edu/~rdh/wwi/1917/27arts.html (last visited Mar. 23, 2006).

regimes, good law, government organizations, or even societal norms simply
do not or cannot exist. The logic continues that even if these resources do exist,
they must be categorically "bad," since they emerged from "bad" regimes. At
least with respect to military justice, this could not be further from the truth.
We discovered that Afghanistan enjoys a great wealth of knowledge, experience, and even written laws to govern military justice. It is an equally great
challenge to pull together this knowledge from its scatterings over decades of
war, but the results will be rewarding. Given that it targets a finite group of
individuals, reflecting a population that tends to be more educated than the
average for Afghan society, with highly trained judges, defense counsel, and
prosecutors, the Afghan military justice system stands to be a huge success
story in the modern reform taking place in Afghanistan. . . .

Military justice reform in Afghanistan is well under way. Currently, the
U.S. units charged with this mission enjoy a number of conditions conducive
to success, including prepared partners, talented support staff, and relatively
good security conditions. Above all, owing to their unfortunate political history, the Afghan military legal community possesses a wealth of experience at
learning from other legal systems. Leveraging these advantages, while mindful of shortcomings associated with past legal reforms and even the present
effort, will ensure a lasting and successful transition. Readers with previous
international justice reform experience have likely found similarities between
their own experience and that related in this article. To be sure, the lessons
identified in this article — appreciation of history, the value of embedding oneself in advisee operations, and fostering a sense of ownership in reform —
apply to nation-building efforts elsewhere.

NOTES AND QUESTIONS

1. Foreign involvement in military justice reform has a long history. After
all, most current national military justice systems have been inspired to a
greater or lesser degree by foreign sources, whether as a result of a shared
legal heritage, cultural affinity, or purely elective choice. Sometimes, as in the
case of the Coalition Provisional Authority effort described by Major Cullen,
new arrangements may be imposed by an occupying power. At other times,
several countries with a common legal heritage may collaborate in an effort to
break out of past patterns in upgrading their systems, as in the case of the
"Model Code of Military Justice" published in 1998 by the eight Latin
American countries and the United States that made up the "American
Military Legal Committee." *See generally* Colonel Enrique Arroyo, *The
Cojuma Story*, 52 A.F. L. Rev. 169 (2002).

2. Based on the experience in Iraq and Afghanistan, as described in these
readings, how would you structure foreign assistance to a country that was
interested in reforming its military justice system? Who would you have
involved in the process, on both sides? For one model, consider the Military
Law Development Program conducted by the United States' Defense Institute
for International Legal Studies, www.dsca.osd.mil/diils/catalog/Catalog_06.
pdf, which "is designed to assist international officers and civilian officials in

the development and improvement of their own military legal systems through a comparative study of U.S. military law. Participants attend classes at the Naval Justice School, including parts of the Basic Lawyer, Legal Officer and Senior Officer courses. They also attend [among others] the course on Conducting Military and Peacekeeping Operations in Accordance with the Rule of Law. . . . After exposure to the U.S. military justice system, training, and institutions, participants conduct research based on a comparison of their own legal system and that of the United States, with an emphasis on recommendations for their own governments." *See generally The Defense Institute for International Legal Studies*, DEF. INST. OF SEC. ASSISTANCE MGT. J., Fall 1997, at www.dsca.osd.mil/diils/images/disam-article.pdf; *see also* Chris Martin, *A Day in Court: Afghan Army Puts Legal System into Action*, Defense Security Cooperation Agency, PARTNERS, Jan. 2007, at 4 (describing DIILS assistance to Afghanistan).

V. GLOBALIZATION

It is a central premise of this book that national military justice systems cannot be considered in a vacuum. Advances in communication, such as the internet, have accelerated and improved our ability simply to know about events in other legal systems. Can a court-martial in one country order internet uses elsewhere not to disseminate the photographs of persons who stand accused of war crimes? *See R. v. Payne*, (UK Sept. 19, 2006) (McKinnon, J.A.), slip op. at 52 [¶ 58] ("publication abroad and on the internet by people outside this jurisdiction cannot be prevented by the court's order"). Legal education has also increasingly viewed comparative studies as useful for understanding our own system of law. These considerations are, if anything, even more salient in military justice, since national military forces increasingly interact with one another, either as part of peacekeeping operations under UN or NATO auspices, as in Afghanistan, or in joint or coalition operations, as in Iraq. Additionally, as noted throughout this book, transnational standards increasingly find their way into the analysis of military justice issues as a result of decisions under a variety of human rights conventions. International cooperative programs for military law reform, discussed in earlier parts of this Chapter, are a further manifestation of the globalization of military justice. Finally, although ensuring good order and discipline in the armed forces remains a national responsibility, for parties to the Rome Statute the potential for the International Criminal Court to exercise jurisdiction if the state is unwilling or unable to prosecute provides a further reason to look beyond national borders and national statute books in framing an approach to the administration of military justice.

Eugene R. Fidell, *A Worldwide Perspective on Change in Military Justice*

48 A.F. L. REV. 195 (2000) and EVOLVING MILITARY JUSTICE (2004)

Introduction

Military justice is going through a period of ferment that is both rare and broad. In country after country, dramatic change either has occurred in the recent past or is under active consideration. Nothing like this has happened since the years just after World War II. There is no way of telling how long this phase will last, but there can be no question that it exists and is worthy of our careful attention.

Examples of the ferment I have in mind include the enactment of major reforms both in the United Kingdom,[17] hastened by a series of cases in the European Court of Human Rights,[18] and in Canada,[19] where decisions of the Supreme Court and Court Martial Appeal Court have played a major role.[20] In South Africa, new military justice legislation[21] was required when the government conceded that the former system, dating to the era of apartheid, was unconstitutional.[22] Australia has been considering the need for reform in light of a report prepared by Mr. Justice Abadee of the Supreme Court of New South Wales.[23] In India, the Law Commission has recommended creation of an Armed Forces Appellate Tribunal.[24] In Mexico, disaffected personnel have taken to the streets to demand a fresh look at the military justice system.[25] In the United States, the American Bar Association's Standing Committee on Armed Forces Law has under consideration a proposal to recommend

---

[17] [n.1] Armed Forces Act 1996, ch. 46 (Eng.).

[18] [n.2] *Findlay v. United Kingdom*, 24 E.H.R.R. 221 (1997) (British Army); *Coyne v. United Kingdom*, 1997-v Eur. Ct. H.R. 1842 (RAF); *see also Lane v. United Kingdom*, No. 27347/95 (Comm. of Ministers, Council of Eur. June 9, 1999) (interim resolution) (Royal Navy). For a perceptive summary of the *Findlay* fallout through 1998, see Ann Lyon, *After Findlay: A Consideration of Some Aspects of the Military Justice System*, [1998] CRIM. L. REV. 109.

[19] [n.3] Act of Dec. 10, 1998, S.C. 1998, c. 35 (Can.), *proclaimed in force*, Stat. Inst. No. 99-74, 133 C. GAZ. 1959 (1999).

[20] [n.4] *E.g., R. v. Généreux*, [1992] 1 S.C.R. 259, 88 D.L.R.4th 100 (1992); *Lauzon v. The Queen*, 56 C.R.R.2d 30, 129 C.C.C.3d 399 (C.M.A.C. 1998); *see also R. v. Edwards*, [1995] C.M.A.J. No. 10 (Q.L.) (Can.); *Bergeron v. The Queen*, 62 C.R.R.2d 322, 136 C.C.C.3d 327 (C.M.A.C. 1999) (Can.); *Boivin v. The Queen*, [1998] C.M.A.J. No. 7 (Q.L.), 1998 F.C.A.D.J. 67 (Can.); *see generally* Department of National Defence, *Minister's Monitoring Committee on Change in the Department of National Defence and the Canadian Forces, Interim Report* ch. 6 (1998), <http:www.dnd.ca/menu/press/Reports/Changes/Eng/justice.htm>; and Dep't of National Defence, *Minister's Monitoring Committee on Change in the Dep't of National Defence and the Canadian Forces, Final Report* ch. 5 (1999), <http://www.dbd.ca.menu/press/Reports/monitor_final/eng/cov.htm>.

[21] [n.5] Military Discipline Supplementary Measures Act, No. 16 of 1999 (S. Afr.). The new legislation took effect on May 28, 1999. Proc. R. 67, Gov't Gaz. No. 20,101 (S. Afr. 1999).

[22] [n.6] *Freedom of Expression Institute v. President of the Ordinary Court-Martial*, Nos. 7057/97, 7058/97 (Cape High Ct. Dec. 18, 1998). Because of the legislation enacted following the decision of the High Court, the Constitutional Court decided that there was no reason for it to address the merits of the case. *President of the Ordinary Court-Martial v. Freedom of Expression Institute*, No. 5/99, 1999 (4) S.A. 682 (Const. Ct.).

[23] [n.7] In addition to the Abadee Report, the Australian Parliament's Defence Subcommittee of the Joint Standing Committee on Foreign Affairs, Defence and Trade began military justice hearings in 1998.

[24] [n.8] 15th Law Comm'n of India, Report No. 169 (1999); *see Armed Forces Tribunal to be Set Up Soon*, THE HINDU, May 22, 1999, <www.indiaserver.com/thehindu/1999/05/22/stories/0222000i.htm>.

[25] [n.9] Julia Preston, *Mexican Military Arrests Dissident Army Officer*, N.Y. TIMES, Mar. 18, 1999, at A3; Ginger Thompson, *Mexican Army Protester Goes Loudly Into Hiding*, N.Y. TIMES, Dec. 29, 1998, at A3.

legislation creating a commission to study military justice in connection with the fiftieth anniversary of enactment of the Uniform Code of Military Justice.[26] Beyond the legislative developments, a spate of individual cases in many countries has attracted broad public attention to what is ordinarily quite an obscure and overlooked field.

In addition to these legal developments, there is a growing awareness on the part of military justice specialists of the need for collaborative efforts and exchange of information across national boundaries.

Why is any of this noteworthy? There are two reasons. First, the mere fact that we are even aware of global military justice developments is remarkable because, even though "Breaker Morant," "Billy Budd," and "The Caine Mutiny Court-Martial" resonate across borders, little information on military justice developments has historically flowed across national borders, and when it has, it has done so at a snail's pace. Even then, it has been of interest only to a few professionals (almost exclusively serving officers or ministerial officials). Second, a number of themes emerge from the new flood of information and activity. Both of these factors have cultural, public policy, and institutional implications that deserve our attention.

1

It is an unfortunate but undeniable fact that historically, American military justice jurisprudence has shown little interest in foreign military justice developments. The bar and the bench can share responsibility for arguments not made, or, if made, disregarded.

To be sure, there have long been foreign students at the Judge Advocate General's School of the Army, and that institution's estimable *Military Law Review* has run articles about foreign systems.[27] Such articles have become infrequent, a notable exception being the valuable recent contribution by the Judge Advocate General of the United Kingdom, Judge James W. Rant,[28] whose work has also been published by the United States Air Force.[29]

But as far as the courts are concerned, the American military justice system pays precious little attention to developments in other countries' systems. To its credit, in *United States v. Graf*,[30] the United States Court of Military

---

26 [n.10] ABA, Standing Comm. on Armed Forces Law, *Draft Report and Recommendation* (1999), <www.jaa.org/Ucmj-01u.htm#N_18>; *see* MIL. J. GAZ. No. 69 (Sept. 1999).

27 [n.11] *E.g.*, Mohammad Anwar, *The Administration of Military Justice in the Pakistan Air Force*, 61 MIL. L. REV. 41 (1973); George C. Ryker, *The New French Code of Military Justice*, 44 MIL. L. REV. 71 (1969). Foreign military law has also been examined from time to time in civilian law reviews. *E.g.*, Edward F. Sherman, *Military Justice Without Military Control*, 82 YALE L.J. 1398 (1973).

28 [n.12] James W. Rant, *The British Courts-Martial System: It Ain't Broke, But It Needs Fixing*, 152 MIL. L. REV. 179 (1996). A short description of the German system appeared in Kenneth S. Kilimnik, *Germany's Army After Reunification: The Merging of the* Nationale Volksarmee *Into the* Bundeswehr, 145 MIL. L. REV. 113, 131-33 (1994).

29 [n.13] James W. Rant, *Findlay, The Consequences: Remarks Given at the Judge Advocate General School, November 1997*, 25 A.F. L. RPTR. 3 (Sept. 1998).

30 [n.14] 35 M.J. 450 (1992).

Appeals at least took the time to address the Canadian jurisprudence on military judicial independence, although ultimately it concluded that "our application of these principles to the military justice system of the United States and its military judges does not necessarily lead to the same result."[31] The court went on to test the United States arrangements against the Canadian Supreme Court's *Généreux* analytical framework.[32] When Graf sought review in the Supreme Court on the ground that due process requires fixed terms of office for military judges, his petition for a writ of certiorari cited Canadian and Soviet arrangements,[33] and argued

> If nations with such divergent legal traditions and military postures as these can accom[m]odate fixed terms for military judges, it is difficult to treat seriously the notion that there is anything inherent in military affairs that precludes them for this country's soldier- and sailor-judges.[34]

In the end, the Supreme Court denied certiorari,[35] and although it granted review on the terms-of-office issue in the companion case of *Weiss v. United States*,[36] no Justice thought the evolving modern foreign experience worth mentioning.

Foreign military justice arrangements were also invited to the attention of the Supreme Court in *Solorio v. United States*,[37] where the Court overturned the requirement of *O'Callahan v. Parker*[38] that military offenses be service-connected. One amicus argued that "the experience of other countries teaches that a service connection requirement is workable and appropriate."[39] "The purpose of presenting these foreign materials," the brief stated,

> is to suggest, not that these are matters to be decided by a "show of hands" among the legal systems of the world, but rather that the approach adopted by this Court a generation ago [in *O'Callahan*] is well within the experience of other nations — including some with substantial defense establishments — and, from a comparative

---

[31] [n.15] *Id.* at 466.

[32] [n.16] *Id.* at 465-66. *See* Andrew M. Ferris, *Military Justice: Removing the Probability of Unfairness*, 63 U. Cin. L. Rev. 439, 476-77 (1994).

[33] [n.17] Petition for Writ of Certiorari 25-26, *Graf v. United States*, 510 U.S. 1085 (1994) (denying cert.), citing *R. v. Généreux*, [1992] 1 S.C.R. 259, 70 C.C.C.3d 1 (1992); Jody M. Prescott, *Soviet Military Justice and the Challenge of Perestroika*, 123 Mil. L. Rev. 129, 131-32 (1989); Michael N. Schmitt & James E. Moody, *The Soviet Military Justice System*, 34 A.F. L. Rev. 1, 28 & nn.235, 238 (1991); Michael N. Schmitt, *The Judicial and Non-Judicial Punishment Systems of the Soviet Armed Forces*, 4 J. Sov. Mil. Studies 87, 102 & n.50 (1991).

[34] [n.18] *Graf* Pet. at 26.

[35] [n.19] 510 U.S. 1085 (1994).

[36] [n.20] 510 U.S. 163 (1994).

[37] [n.21] 483 U.S. 435 (1987).

[38] [n.22] 395 U.S. 258 (1969).

[39] [n.23] ACLU Br. as Amicus Curiae in Support of Petitioner 11-24, *Solorio v. United States*, *supra* (collecting authorities from U.K., U.S.S.R., Canada, Australia, New Zealand, Israel, Philippines, Pakistan, France, South Korea).

standpoint, anything but a "sport in the law." *Screws v. United States*, 325 U.S. 91, 112 (1945) (plurality opinion).

The Court deemed this line of argument unworthy of comment.[40]

I hasten to add that resort to foreign legal developments generally is not without controversy in the American judicial system,[41] so no one should imagine that military justice is being singled out in this regard. For example, in *Printz v. United States*,[42] which concerned the power of Congress to compel state and local police to help enforce federal gun control legislation, Justice Breyer (in a dissent in which Justice Stevens joined) referred to the federal systems of Switzerland, Germany and the European Union, and commented:

> Of course, we are interpreting our own Constitution, not those of other nations, and there may be relevant political and structural differences between their systems and our own. *Cf.* THE FEDERALIST No. 20, pp. 134-138 (C. Rossiter ed. 1961) (J. Madison and A. Hamilton) (rejecting certain aspects of European federalism). But their experience may nonetheless cast an empirical light on the consequences of different solutions to a common legal problem — in this case the problem of reconciling central authority with the need to preserve the liberty-enhancing autonomy of a smaller constituent governmental entity. *Cf. id.*, No. 42, p. 268 (J. Madison) (looking to experiences of European countries); *id.*, No. 43, pp. 275, 276 (J. Madison) (same). . . .[43]

In reply, Justice Scalia, writing for the majority, observed:

> Justice Breyer's dissent would have us consider the benefits that other countries, and the European Union, believe they have derived from federal systems that are different from ours. We think such comparative analysis inappropriate to the task of interpreting a constitution, though it was of course quite relevant to the task of writing one. . . .[44]

Judging by Justice Ginsburg's later Cardozo Lecture to the Association of the Bar of the City of New York, she is plainly in the Breyer camp.[45] Speaking of affirmative action and human rights, she cited comparative developments in India, Germany and the European Union, and argued that "[e]xperience in one nation or region may inspire or inform other nations or regions in this area, as generally holds true for human rights initiatives." In her view,

---

[40] [n.24] It is a curious fact that our legal system at times seems to take a greater interest in foreign military justice developments that occurred hundreds of years ago than it does in those that have occurred in the last decade. *See, e.g., Loving v. United States*, 517 U.S. 748, 761 (1996) (quoting 1190 ordinance of Richard I).

[41] [n.25] *See generally* Vicki C. Jackson, *Ambivalent Resistance and Comparative Constitutionalism: Opening Up the Conversation on "Proportionality," Rights and Federalism*, 1 U. PA. J. CONST. L. 583 (1999).

[42] [n.26] 521 U.S. 898 (1997).

[43] [n.27] *Id.* at 977.

[44] [n.28] *Id.* at 921 n.11.

[45] [n.29] Ruth Bader Ginsburg & Deborah Jones Merritt, *Affirmative Action: An International Human Rights Dialogue*, 54 REC. OF ASS'N OF B. OF CITY OF NEW YORK 278, 308-09 (1999).

[t]he same readiness to look beyond one's own shores has not marked the decisions of the court on which I serve. The United States Supreme Court has mentioned the Universal Declaration of Human Rights a spare five times, and only twice in a majority decision. The most recent citation appeared twenty-eight years ago, in a dissenting opinion by Justice Marshall. Nor does the U.S. Supreme Court invoke the laws or decisions of other nations with any frequency. . . .

In my view, comparative analysis emphatically *is* relevant to the task of interpreting constitutions and enforcing human rights. We are the losers if we neglect what others can tell us about endeavors to eradicate bias against women, minorities, and other disadvantaged groups. For irrational prejudice and rank discrimination are infectious in our world. In this reality, as well as the determination to counter it, we all share.[46]

Do the kinds of issues that have emerged in the field of military justice rise to the level of the human rights issues about which Justice Ginsburg spoke with such obvious conviction? Some, at least, of those who concern themselves with capital punishment or the role of women in the military[47] would likely say so. I suggest, however, that even aspects of military justice that have not engaged our society or our legal system as deeply would fall within the sphere where comparative information can be instructive.

Some countries are less jurisprudentially xenophobic than others.[48] Foreign legal institutions and policy judgments cannot simply be transplanted.[49] As Chief Judge Posner warns, "[w]e must be cautious . . . about basing policy on

---

46 [n.30] *Id.* at 308-09 (emphasis in original; footnotes omitted).

47 [n.31] There is a rich and growing literature in this area. *E.g.,* Diane H. Mazur, *A Call to Arms*, 22 HARV. WOMEN'S L.J. 39 (1999); Elizabeth Lutes Hillman, *The "Good Soldier" Defense: Character Evidence and Military Rank at Courts-Martial*, 108 YALE L.J. 879, 908-10 (1999); Diane H. Mazur, *Women, Responsibility, and the Military*, 74 NOTRE DAME L. REV. 1 (1998); Madeline Morris, *By Force of Arms: Rape, War, and Military Culture*, 45 DUKE L.J. 651 (1996); Michael F. Noone & Mary Jo Wiley, *Sticks, Stones and Broken Bones: Military Law's Criteria for Aggravated Assault*, 14 FEMINIST ISSUES 67 (1994).

48 [n.32] *E.g., S. v. Makwanyane*, 1995 (3) S.A. 391 (S.A. Const. Ct.) (invalidating death penalty; broadly surveying international and foreign comparative law). Section 39(1) of the 1996 South African Constitution provides that "[w]hen interpreting the Bill of Rights, a court, tribunal or forum — . . . may consider foreign law." President Chaskalson wrote: "We can derive assistance from public international law and foreign case law, but we are in no way bound by it." *Makwanyane, supra,* § 39. The Cape High Court cited Canadian cases, including *Généreux,* and the European Court of Human Rights' decision in *Findlay* in determining that the South African military justice system did not provide an impartial and independent tribunal. *Freedom of Expression Institute, supra* note 6, slip op. at 15-18.

49 [n.33] As one group of commentators noted,

When comparatists devote their attention to a vexing or unsolved problem, it is not with the idea that they will find in some foreign land a "solution" which, like a new electrical appliance, can be fitted with an adaptor and plugged into the system back home. What they are usually looking for is, initially, a deepened understanding of the problem, and, if they are lucky, a source of inspiration.

MARY ANN GLENDON, MICHAEL WALLACE GORDON & CHRISTOPHER OSAKWE, COMPARATIVE LEGAL TRADITIONS 10 (2d ed. 1994).

the practices of other nations."[50] But even cautious lawmakers and regulation-issuers can still cast their net broadly, seeking useful insight *wherever* it can be found. In an earlier age, this, indeed, was one of the cornerstones of the jurisprudence of the United States Court of Military Appeals.[51] I have argued — and perhaps a little grumpily continue to believe — that the court's early declaration of doctrinal independence had unanticipated adverse consequences (especially in conjunction with other institutional weaknesses in the American military justice system).[52] Nonetheless, the experience of the last several years suggests that there will be occasions when the Court of Appeals can gain valuable perspective from foreign military justice developments and that doing so would not give rise to the kind of institutional concerns that, to my mind, made the "Brosman Doctrine"[53] questionable. In any event, those concerns in no way bear on Legislative and Executive Branch decision making. Whether or not the Court of Appeals should from time to time take foreign developments into account, nothing prevents Congress and the Executive Branch, whose opportunities to influence the administration of military justice far exceed those of the court, from informing themselves of and drawing appropriate lessons from such developments as they exercise their high responsibilities.

2

It is hard to imagine a clearer case of preaching to the choir than to argue the virtues of comparative studies to an international audience such as the Inter-University Seminar on Armed Forces and Society. Nonetheless, because there is reason to fear that the value of such studies may not be as fully accepted as one might hope within the military legal community, a few words on the point may be in order.

Assimilators of esoterica need no greater reason to concern themselves with foreign military justice developments, which make for scintillating conversation (or at least so some mavens believe). More seriously, this kind of learning is of value not simply for its own sake or to better understand events elsewhere. It is of practical value because — by showing that what we do is not necessarily the only way to do things — it helps us to understand our own system and to conduct what ought to be a periodic, if not continual, conscious process of reevaluation so that we can be sure our system reflects the best thinking in order to achieve our national goals. The same impulse that leads us to view the States' role as laboratories for testing new ideas as part of the genius of the

---

50 [n.34] Richard A. Posner, *Ask, Tell*, NEW REPUBLIC, Oct. 11, 1999, at 52, 54.

51 [n.35] Paul W. Brosman, *The Court: Freer than Most*, 6 VAND. L. REV. 166 (1953).

52 [n.36] Eugene R. Fidell, *"If a Tree Falls in the Forest . . .": Publication and Digesting Policies and the Potential Contribution of Military Courts to American Law*, 32 JAG J. 1, 9 n.55 (1982); *see also* Eugene R. Fidell, *Going on 50: Evolution and Devolution in Military Justice*, 32 WAKE FOREST L. REV. 1213, 1214-19 (1997). Where legal institutions are newborn, a broader perspective is to be expected. For example, in *Makwanyane*, President Chaskalson commented that "[c]omparative 'bill of rights' jurisprudence will no doubt be of importance, particularly in the early stages of the transition when there is no developed indigenous jurisprudence in this branch of the law on which to draw." *Makwanyane, supra* note 32, § 37.

53 [n.37] *See* Brosman, *supra* note 35; Fidell, *supra* note 36.

American federal system,[54] or to view the various branches of the service in something of the same light,[55] ought to cause us to welcome any opportunity to know and potentially learn from the experience of other democratic countries in the administration of military justice. That experience should be discounted where the other country's political or value system, strategic role, or other distinguishing features suggest a poor fit. But that discount can only be applied intelligently if we have first considered the pertinent data.

There are ample reasons for lawyers to pay attention to foreign law. Justice O'Connor has cited three: the need to apply foreign law in domestic courts, the ability to borrow beneficial ideas, and the enhancement of cross-border cooperation.[56] The practical arguments for a global perspective are obvious in areas such as commercial transactions, securities regulation or intellectual property.[57] I submit that the current era of joint and United Nations-sponsored humanitarian and peacekeeping military operations in widely separated parts of the planet argues equally strongly for a global approach — not one of edicts, but rather one in which common themes are identified and viewed as a source of strength and as a stimulus to creative thinking on the national level. Indeed, in what other contemporary area of law could international perspectives be *more* welcome than in the field of military justice? Given the extraordinarily delicate situations the military faces around the world, anything that fosters foreign confidence in the integrity and intellectual rigor of our system eases the task of preserving the primacy of United States military jurisdiction over deployed personnel. Even merely acknowledging foreign approaches is a way to show respect for other nations in an area where sources of friction may be all too real.

3

I have suggested that a variety of common themes emerges from a review of foreign military justice developments. Let me offer some examples. Then let us consider the implications if my hypothesis is correct.

Judicial Independence. One country after another has in recent times focused on issues of independence and impartiality in the administration of military justice. Canada[58] and the United States Army,[59] for example, have instituted fixed terms of office for military judges.

---

[54] [n.38] *New State Ice Co. v. Liebman*, 285 U.S. 262, 311 (1932) (Brandeis, J., dissenting).

[55] [n.39] *See* EUGENE R. FIDELL, GUIDE TO THE RULES OF PRACTICE AND PROCEDURE FOR THE UNITED STATES COURT OF APPEALS FOR THE ARMED FORCES 131 (10th ed. 2001).

[56] [n.40] Sandra Day O'Connor, *Broadening Our Horizons: Why American Lawyers Must Learn About Foreign Law*, 45 FED. LAW., No. 8, 20 (Sept. 1998).

[57] [n.41] "The major distinguishing characteristic of global activities is that the areas of integration are largely oblivious to state boundaries, and that the processes of globalization usually occur without or with little direct agency of the state." Alfred C. Aman, Jr., *The Globalizing State: A Future-Oriented Perspective on the Public/Private Distinction, Federalism, and Democracy*, 31 VAND. J. TRANS. L. 769, 780 & n.34 (1998).

[58] [n.42] Act of Dec. 10, 1998, S.C. 1998, c. 35, § 42 (Can.) (National Defence Act § 165.21[2]).

[59] [n.43] Dep't of the Army, *Legal Services: Military Justice*, Army Reg. 27-10, ch. 1. Chief Judge Cox has described the new regulation as "a giant step forward." Walter T. Cox, III, *The 27th Annual Kenneth J. Hodson Lecture: Echoes and Expectations: One Judge's View*, 159 MIL. L. REV. 183, 201 (1999).

Unlawful Command Influence. This has been justly described as the "mortal enemy of military justice" in American military jurisprudence.[60] Concerns over the excessive involvement of command have surfaced in the United Kingdom and were central to the hammer blows applied by the European Court of Human Rights. Even on a subtler level, uneasiness over command influence is a transnational phenomenon, as suggested by a case in which the New Zealand Court Martial Appeal Court declined to establish a hard-and-fast rule, but cautioned that it would have been prudent for the convening authority not to be present at trial.[61] On the other hand, an Australian judge recognized a national characteristic in observing, in a case involving the required sequence of voting by court-martial members, that once upon a time "there was greater deference to authority than is typically the case in Australia today."[62] "Crocodile Dundee" aficionados take note.[63]

Fraternization. Many countries' military justice systems have recently had to address issues relating to social relations across the officer/enlisted divide or between officer or enlisted pay grades.

Adultery. Various systems have wrestled with the status of adultery as a military crime. Should it be prosecuted in isolation? Military juries may be reluctant to convict on such charges. Stay tuned.

Capital Punishment. Canada has abolished the military death penalty;[64] in the United States, where the last military execution occurred in 1961,[65] capital cases are inexorably moving towards the President's desk.[66]

Prosecution by Court-Martial of Offenses Under Civilian Criminal Law. May conduct that is an offense under civilian law be tried by court-martial?[67] Must there be a nexus to military service in order for an offense known to civilian criminal law to be prosecuted by court-martial? The United States is far from the only democracy to have addressed this issue.[68]

---

[60] [n.44] *E.g., United States v. Thomas,* 22 M.J. 388, 393 (1986).

[61] [n.45] In *R. v. Sullivan* (N.Z.C.M.A.C. 1994), the convening authority was in the vicinity of the courtroom for part of the trial, and during argument and deliberations, and was apparently in the courtroom when the verdict was announced and during the sentencing phase.

[62] [n.46] *Hembury v. Chief of the General Staff,* 155 A.L.R. 514, 193 C.L.R. 641 (1998) (?¶ 58(2)) (Kirby, J.). Notably, the High Court referred to the voting practices of courts-martial in the United Kingdom, United States, Canada and New Zealand.

[63] [n.47] Jury selection is one area in which command has traditionally played a key role. In 1998, Congress directed the preparation of a report on the method of selection of court-martial members, including an examination of alternatives. Strom Thurmond National Defense Authorization Act for Fiscal Year 1999, § 552, 112 Stat. 2023 (1998). Among the alternatives considered by the Joint Service Committee on Military Justice are the British and Canadian systems.

[64] [n.48] Act of Dec. 10, 1998, S.C. 1998, c. 35, §§ 24 *et seq.* (Can.).

[65] [n.49] *United States v. Bennett,* 7 C.M.A. 97, 21 C.M.R. 223 (1956).

[66] [n.50] *E.g., Loving v. United States,* 517 U.S. 749 (1996); *United States v. Gray,* 51 M.J. 1 (1999) (3-2 decision).

[67] [n.51] *See, e.g., R. v. Marsaw,* 151 D.L.R.4th 667, 686-89, 119 C.C.C.3d 3, 21-25 (C.M.A.C. 1997).

[68] [n.52] *See Solorio v. United States, supra; Ionson v. The Queen,* 4 C.M.A.R. 433 (C.M.A.C. 1987) (Can.), *app. dism.,* [1989] 2 S.C.R. 1073; *Brown v. The Queen,* 26 C.R.R.2d 325 (C.M.A.C. 1995) (Can.); *Re Nolan; Ex parte Young,* [1991] 172 C.L.R. 460 (Austl.).

Summary Discipline. In what circumstances, if any, should personnel be permitted to refuse summary (nonjudicial) punishment? This question was at issue in *United States v. Edwards*[69] and *Robinson v. Dalton.*[70] In preparing the latter case as counsel for Commander Robinson, it proved illuminating to explore the right to reject mast (or "captain's table") under other military justice systems.[71]

Jurisdiction over Dependents. We resolved this, at least until now,[72] in *Reid v. Covert.*[73] In *R. v. Martin,*[74] the United Kingdom — unencumbered by a written constitution that could trump a statute — came out the other way.

Good Military Character as a Defense. A recent law review article has penetratingly explored this defense under American military law.[75] One would expect such a defense to be accepted in other systems that share the same historical roots as ours.[76] Perhaps an enterprising law review editor or faculty member or student at one of the service law schools will find the comparative law question worth pursuing.

---

[69] [n.53] 46 M.J. 41 (1997).

[70] [n.54] 45 F. Supp. 2d 1 (D.D.C. 1998) (Robertson, J.). It was critical that the district judge in *Robinson* had once served as a naval officer. The shrinking percentage of veterans on the bench, Donald N. Zillman, *Where Have All the Soldiers Gone: Observations on the Decline of Military Veterans in Government,* 49 ME. L. REV. 85, 100 (1997); Posner, *supra* note 34 — a phenomenon also noted in Canada, CHRIS MADSEN, ANOTHER KIND OF JUSTICE: CANADIAN MILITARY LAW FROM CONFEDERATION TO SOMALIA 133 (1999) — makes the litigation of peculiarly military legal issues in the federal courts even more challenging than in the past.

[71] [n.55] *E.g.,* Armed Forces Discipline Amendment Act, 1988, ch. 89, § 21 n.4 (N.Z.) ("[f]or the purposes of the application of this punishment, a person is on sea service if that person is a member of the crew of a ship that is at sea or of a ship whose commanding officer has been ordered to keep the ship at less than 48 hours' notice for sea"); *see also* Q.R. & O. § 108.31 (Can.); Naval Summary Discipline Regulations 1997, Regulations 54-58 (U.K.); JAMES W. RANT, COURTS-MARTIAL HANDBOOK: PRACTICE AND PROCEDURE § § 9.12, 9.16 (1998); The Military Justice Law, 1955, S.H. 189, § 150 (Isr.); HERMAN MELVILLE, WHITE-JACKET, OR THE WORLD IN A MAN-OF-WAR 302 (Northwestern-Newberry ed. 1988).

[72] [n.56] The question of jurisdictional gaps remains in play in the United States. The report prepared in response to § 1151 of the National Defense Authorization Act for Fiscal Year 1996, 110 Stat. 186 (1996), addressed British and Canadian experience. OVERSEAS JURISDICTION ADVISORY COMMITTEE, REPORT OF THE ADVISORY COMMITTEE ON CRIMINAL LAW JURISDICTION OVER CIVILIANS ACCOMPANYING THE ARMED FORCES IN TIME OF ARMED CONFLICT 30-32 (1997). Legislation was finally enacted in 2000. *See* Military and Extraterritorial Jurisdiction Act of 2000, Pub. L. No. 106-523, 114 Stat. 2488 (2000) (to be codified at 18 U.S.C. § § 3261-67).

[73] [n.57] 354 U.S. 1 (1957).

[74] [n.58] [1998] 1 All E.R. 193, [1998] 2 W.L.R. 1, [1998] 1 Cr. App. Rep. 347 (1997), <www.parliament.the-stationery-office.co.uk/pa/ld199798/ldjudgment/jd971216/mart01.htm>.

[75] [n.59] Hillman, *supra* note 31. For a very different view see Paul A. Capofari, *Military Rule of Evidence 404 and Good Military Character,* 130 MIL. L. REV. 171, 189 (1990) (urging admissibility of evidence of good military character at all courts-martial).

[76] [n.60] *See, e.g., R. v. Marsaw, supra,* 151 D.L.R.4th at 676-79, 119 C.C.C.3d at 12-15 (discussing application of Can. Mil. R. Evid. 20-21).

Civilian Review of Courts-Martial. Should civilian courts review courts-martial directly, collaterally, or not at all?[77] Should there be a specialized appellate court for military cases, and if so, should its membership include military personnel (including nonlawyers), as the recent South African legislation and current Indian proposal provide?[78] Should its membership rotate from a larger body of judges?[79] United States law requires only that the judges of the Court of Appeals for the Armed Forces be drawn from civilian life and not have served on active duty for 20 years.[80]

We should not be surprised that so many themes are familiar to the common law democracies. After all, these countries' military justice systems can be traced to the British Articles of War.[81] Like Darwin's finches, they evolved differently, and the process by which they came to differ from one another may lead to useful insights into the development of law and legal institutions. For present purposes, however, it suffices to observe that they spring from a common source — further reason, rooted in history, to look past our borders.

4

Now let me shift gears to American legal doctrine for a moment. It is a commonplace that military law stands separate and distinct from the remainder of American law because military society is a "specialized society separate from civilian society." The Supreme Court has told us this numerous times,[82]

---

[77] [n.61] A recent decision of the Supreme Court of India held that the Bombay High Court had no writ jurisdiction over a naval court-martial. T. Padmanabha Rao, *Supreme Court Dismisses Plea Against Court-Martial*, THE HINDU, July 8, 1999, <www.indiaserver.com/the-hindu/1999/07/08/stories/0208000f.htm>. Similarly, the High Court of Singapore has held that it lacks authority to review decisions of the Military Court of Appeal by prerogative writ. *Abdul Wahab bin Sulaiman v. Commandant, Tanglin Detention Barracks*, 1985-1 Malayan L.J. 418, 1985 MLJ LEXIS 37 (Sing. 1985).

[78] [n.62] Military Discipline Supplementary Measures Act, No. 16 of 1999 7(1) (S. Afr.); 15th Law Comm'n of India, Report No. 169 (1999) (Armed Forces Appellate Tribunal to include retired flag or general officers). Israeli law also permits nonlawyers to sit, in exceptional cases, on the Appeal Court Martial. *See* The Military Justice Law, 1955, S.H. 189, § 216 (Isr.).

[79] [n.63] "By 1982, forty judges from the Federal Court of Canada and other superior courts of criminal jurisdiction appointed by the governor-in-council belonged to the Court Martial Appeal Court. . . . The court grew to fifty-five judges in 1986." CHRIS MADSEN, ANOTHER KIND OF JUSTICE: CANADIAN MILITARY LAW FROM CONFEDERATION TO SOMALIA, *supra*, at 133-34. In the United States, judges of the Article III courts may sit by designation on military appeals, 10 U.S.C. § 942(f) (1994), but these cases remain the exception; ordinarily, only judges appointed to the United States Court of Appeals for the Armed Forces sit on that court.

[80] [n.64] 10 U.S.C. § 942(b)(1), -(4) (1994).

[81] [n.65]

> In nearly all fields of law, however, we observe that — even in the absence of organized unification efforts — there exists a common core of legal concepts and precepts shared by some, or even by a multitude, of the world's legal systems. To explain this phenomenon in terms of the underlying historical and social causes, is a task of considerable complexity; the explanations will differ from subject to subject and from continent to continent. In spite of the difficulty of establishing its etiology, however, the existence and vast extent of this common core of legal systems cannot be doubted.

RUDOLPH B. SCHLESINGER, HANS W. BAADE, MIRJAN R. DAMASKA & PETER E. HERZOG, COMPARATIVE LAW: CASES — TEXT — MATERIALS 34-35 (5th ed. 1988) (footnotes omitted). The known British roots of many military justice systems obviate the need for etiological guesswork.

[82] [n.67] *E.g., Parker v. Levy*, 417 U.S. 733, 743 (1974); *see also Weiss v. United States*, *supra*, 510 U.S. at 174.

and "the concept . . . has had extensive historical recognition."[83] Whether you agree with the proposition or not — and a few authors have attempted to call it into question[84] — it is interesting to consider that it may find confirmation in the existence of the common themes I have previously identified. Arguably, the very distinctiveness that takes military justice out of the mainstream of national law places it in a broader, but clearly international, way of thinking about how to maintain good order and discipline within organized military forces. That is, if military society is separate from the rest of American society, do the characteristics that make it separate also manifest themselves in military society in other countries. If so, does that suggest an *international* military society, or a collection of military societies that have nearly as much in common with one another as each does with its larger national society? Given this, can the Supreme Court's concept that the military is a separate society be reconciled with its apparent unwillingness to consider foreign military legal developments?

5

Assuming there is merit to the notion that we ought to be more attentive to current military justice developments overseas, what is to be done? Happily, the answers here are fairly obvious, and not particularly difficult to achieve.

First, the flow of information should be encouraged. Commander Philip D. Cave of the United States Navy and Colonel Anthony S. Paphiti of the British Army have rendered exceptional service to the global military legal community through their extraordinary, internationally-oriented military justice websites.[85]

Second, all who are responsible on a national level for the administration of military justice should strive to identify and promptly upload or disseminate in "hard copy" all major decisions, statutes and regulations in the area.

Third, military justice experts, including judges,[86] civilian practitioners and academics, should meet more often. One such meeting was convened by the National Institute of Military Justice, a United States-based nonprofit organization, in London in 1998. A follow-on meeting will probably be held next year, venue to be determined. The London meeting drew attendance from countries in the common law tradition. In time, the constituency should be expanded to countries whose military justice systems are not descended from the British

---

[83] [n.68] C. Thomas Dienes, *When the First Amendment is Not Preferred: The Military and Other "Special Contexts,"* 56 U. CIN. L. REV. 779, 802 n.73 (1987).

[84] [n.69] *E.g.,* Hillman, *supra* note 31, at 899-90; Karen A. Ruzic, Note and Comment, *Military Justice and the Supreme Court's Outdated Standard of Deference:* Weiss v. United States, 70 CHI.-KENT L. REV. 265 (1994); Ferris, *supra* note 16, at 485. For the other side of the argument see James M. Hirschhorn, *The Separate Community: Military Uniqueness and Servicemen's Constitutional Rights*, 62 N.C. L. REV. 177 (1984).

[85] [n.70] Commander Cave's site may be found at <http://www.court-martial.com>; Colonel Paphiti's may be found at <http://www.aspals.com>. They have received thousands of "hits."

[86] [n.71] Professor Jackson has reported "an increase in U.S. judges' travel abroad to meet with their counterparts, and likewise a substantial influx in the other direction, fueled in some measure by the emergence of new regimes in Eastern and Central Europe and the constitutional revolution in South Africa." Jackson, *supra* note 25, at 596 n.49.

model. It is also to be hoped that non-Commonwealth observers will in time be invited to attend the periodic meetings of the Commonwealth Association of Armed Forces Lawyers.

Fourth, and without in any way detracting from either the excellent foreign works on military law that have become available[87] or the critical importance of the Internet as a means of disseminating information, there is a need for a "hard copy" *International Military Legal Materials*, by analogy to the American Society of International Law's long-running *International Legal Materials*. *The Military Law and Law of War Review*, published by the International Society for Military Law and Law of War, has included articles on national systems[88] and synopses of decisions,[89] but a more systematic and timely process is called for.

There is also a clear need for military justice teaching materials that include a broad range of comparative law documents. One such set of materials was developed for use at the London conference referred to above.[90] More work needs to be done so that the materials can be kept current and made available broadly and at reasonable cost. This, in turn, will facilitate civilian instruction in military law, which must be a high priority in any democracy. . . .

Conclusion

It will be a worthy achievement if, consistent with the military justice legislation passed by Congress and the regulations prescribed by the President, our generation can foster bidirectional creative interaction between military justice and general American jurisprudence. Similarly, and subject to the same constraints, those responsible for the framing and administration of American military justice legislation, should, with the encouragement of the bar and the academy, be alert to opportunities for the same kind of interaction with our "separate society" counterparts globally. If they are, there is every reason to hope that both realms will be enriched.

---

[87] [n.73] Oded Mudrik, Sh'fita Tzava'it [Military Judging] (1993) (Isr.); James W. Rant, Courts-Martial Handbook: Practice and Procedure (1998) (U.K.); Gerard Humphreys & Ciaran Craven, Military Law in Ireland (1997); G.K. Sharma, Study and Practice of Military Law (4th ed. 1996) (India); D.C. Jain, N.K. Indrayan & C.G. Goel, Military Law in India (1984); Chris Madsen, Another Kind of Justice: Canadian Military Law from Confederation to Somalia (1999). For two notable recent contributions to the American military justice literature see Jonathan Lurie, Arming Military Justice: The Origins of the United States Court of Military Appeals, 1775-1950 (1992); Jonathan Lurie, Pursuing Military Justice: The History of the United States Court of Appeals for the Armed Forces, 1951-1980 (1998).

[88] [n.74] *E.g.*, Vladislav Lavochkin, *Military Justice System in Russia Today: Organization and Functions*, 33 Mil. L. & L. of War Rev. 9 (1994).

[89] [n.75] *E.g.*, M.M. Oosthuizen, *South African Court Cases on Military Law: 1980-1990*, 33 Mil. L. & L. of War Rev. 405 (1994).

[90] [n.76] National Institute of Military Justice, Sourcebook on Contemporary Comparative Military Justice (1998).

Lord Chief Justice of England and Wales
Practice Direction on the Citation of Authorities,
[2001] 1 W.L.R. 1001, [2001] 2 All E.R. 510 (April 9, 2001)

1. In recent years, there has been a substantial growth in the number of readily available reports of judgments in this and other jurisdictions, such reports being available either in published reports or in transcript form. Widespread knowledge of the work and decisions of the courts is to be welcomed. At the same time, however, the current weight of available material causes problems both for advocates and for courts in properly limiting the nature and amount of material that is used in the preparation and argument of subsequent cases.

2. The latter issue is a matter of rapidly increasing importance. Recent and continuing efforts to increase the efficiency, and thus reduce the cost, of litigation, whilst maintaining the interests of justice, will be threatened if courts are burdened with a weight of inappropriate and unnecessary authority, and if advocates are uncertain as to the extent to which it is necessary to deploy authorities in the argument of any given case.

3. With a view to limiting the citation of previous authority to cases that are relevant and useful to the court, this Practice Direction lays down a number of rules as to what material may be cited, and the manner in which that cited material should be handled by advocates. These rules are in large part such as many courts already follow in pursuit of their general discretion in the management of litigation. However, it is now desirable to promote uniformity of practice by the same rules being followed by all courts. . . .

9.1 Cases decided in other jurisdictions can, if properly used, be a valuable source of law in this jurisdiction. At the same time, however, such authority should not be cited without proper consideration of whether it does indeed add to the existing body of law.

9.2 In future therefore, any advocate who seeks to cite an authority from another jurisdiction must . . .

ii. indicate in respect of each authority what that authority adds that is not to be found in authority in this jurisdiction; or, if there is said to be justification for adding to domestic authority, what that justification is;

iii. certify that there is no authority in this jurisdiction that precludes the acceptance by the court of the proposition that the foreign authority is said to establish.

9.3 For the avoidance of doubt, paragraphs 9.1 and 9.2 do not apply to cases decided in either the European Court of Justice or the organs of the European Convention of Human Rights. Because of the status in English law of such authority, as provided by, respectively, section 3 of the European Communities Act 1972 and section 2(1) of the Human Rights Act 1998, such cases are covered by the earlier paragraphs of this Direction.

NOTES AND QUESTIONS

1. If anything, the ferment refered to in the *Worldwide Perspective* essay has accelerated in the intervening years. In 2006 alone, the United Kingdom and Australia enacted important new military justice legislation, including, for the first time, a single disciplinary statute covering all branches of the British armed forces. Armed Forces Act 2006, c. 52 (Eng.). Important military justice legislation is also in the works in Canada and New Zealand. The pace of developments underscores the tremendous value of online resources such as the various legal information institutes and international forums such as those provided by the International Society for Military Law and Law of War and human rights organizations that have increasingly come to focus on military justice. Compendia of national studies such as the 2002 "Military Justice International Comparative Edition" that filled an entire volume of the *Air Force Law Review* and analyses such as Georg Nolte & Heike Krieger, *European Military Law Systems — Summary and Recommendations* 1-17, *in* EUROPEAN MILITARY LAW SYSTEMS (Georg Nolte ed. 2003) (discussing harmonization, including Draft Common Disciplinary Code of European Defence Community), are dramatic proof that there is a broad recognition of the utility of attepting a global or at least a transnational understanding of trends in military justice.

2. In 2006, Dean Harold Hongju Koh reported that Yale Law School had made a decision to educate its students about law and globalization. "This means that we teach them about three aspects of law and globalization. First, the law *of* globalization: globalization as a legal subject, a mixed international-domestic subject, like human rights and international business transactions. Second, we teach them about law *as* globalization. We understand the globalization of culture, the globalization of the economy — we need similarly to understand law as itself a phenomenon that is being globalized. Third, we teach them about the role that law plays in globalization, law *in* globalization. We teach the students that, as lawyers, they can promote a process of humane globalization or they can be the tools of a process of inhumane globalization, with our main goal being to train lawyers to recognize and act on global trends." Harold Hongju Koh, *On Law and Globalization*, American Law Institute, Remarks and Addresses at the 83d Annual Meeting 68, 83 (2006). Which, if any, of these aspects applies to military justice?

3. As long as nations remain autonomous in legal and military affairs, there will be debate over the utility of foreign legal developments in the resolution of domestic military legal and policy issues. Do you agree with Justice Scalia's skepticism? Or is military justice one of the rare fields — can you think of another? — in which what one might call "transnational legal curiosity" is particularly appropriate if one embraces the notion that military forces represent a "separate society"? But does that also mean that the less a country embraces that notion, the less heed others should pay to its military justice arrangements and jurisprudence?

4. It has been said that "comparative constitutional law can deepen our understanding in three principal ways: (1) it pushes us to evaluate the foundations of individual legal systems: the assumptions, choices, trade-offs, and values that have formed them; (2) it gives us a better purchase on our own systems and legal cultures by revealing how other constitutional democracies address similar problems; and (3) it helps us to comprehend the nature and problems of regional and international institutions and adjudicatory bodies." NORMAN DORSEN, MICHEL ROSENFELD, ANDRÁS SAJÓ & SUSANNE BAER, COMPARATIVE CONSTITUITIONALISM: CASES AND MATERIALS iv (2003). Do these benefits also apply to the comparative study of military justice?

5. There is no question that reference to foreign law is a hazardous practice, despite the fact that foreign legal materials have never been as readily accessible as they are now. *See* Diane Marie Amann, *International Law and Rehnquist-Era Reversals*, 94 GEO. L.J. 1319, 1342-43 & n.146 (2006) (noting difficulty of task of consulting foreign law). At times, these references seem easy and useful in analyzing a domestic issue. *E.g., White v. Director of Military Prosecutions*, No. S312 of 2006, [2007] HCATrans 26 (Austl. 2007) ("If it were said that the maintenance of a defence force requires a military justice system separate from Chapter III, would it be relevant for us to look at what goes on in other parts of the world today in relation to military justice?") (Gleeson, C.J.). When counsel in *White* referred to a worldwide summary of national constitutional provisions on court-martial subject-matter jurisdiction — 1 FEDERICO ANDREU-GUZMÁN, MILITARY JURISDICTION AND INTERNATIONAL LAW: MILITARY COURTS AND GROSS HUMAN RIGHTS VIOLATIONS (Int'l Comm'n of Jurists 2004) — Justice Gummow acidly observed, "I am beginning to understand why Justice Scalia gets irritated when these sort of things are put to his court." *Id.* An example of the dangers is the decision in *Uganda Law Society v. Attorney General*, Const. Pet. No. 18 of 2005 (Uganda Const. Ct. 2006), concerning, among other things, the amenability of civilians to trial by court-martial. The opinions quoted incorrectly from the United States Manual for Courts-Martial and drew inferences from jurisdictional provisions of the Uniform Code of Military Justice that had been materially narrowed if not entirely invalidated by decisions of the Supreme Court of the United States. How can a court be sure that its legal resources are equal to the task before sailing into such shoal water?

6. The 2001 Practice Direction adopts a high threshold for referring to foreign sources of law. Can you think what led to its issuance? What effect do you think it has had? Would you modify it? If so, how?

Table of Cases

Principal case names are cited in bold. Cases cited in principal cases and other excerpted materials are not included.

A

A.D. v. Turkey **148**
ABC, Inc. v. Powell
. . . . 131-32, **758**, 761
Ainsworth v. United Kingdom 419
Aird, Re Colonel; Ex parte
Albert **347**, 380
Anderson v. Laird 514
Anning, Re **437**
Arden v. State Bar 796
Arizona v. Rumsey 938
Asch v. State 217
Ashcroft v. Free Speech
Coalition 502
Attorney General ex rel.
Royal N.Z. Navy v.
Lawrence **476**, 477
Averette, United States v. 319
Avrech v. Secretary of the Navy . . . 501

B

Ballew v. Georgia 725-26
Barraza Rivera v. Immigration
and Naturalization
Service **11**
Barry v. Chief of Naval Staff . . **743**
Bartley, United States v. 119
Bell, State v. 217
Biagase, United States v. 119
Bivins, United States v. 440
Brady, H.M. The Queen v. **295**
Bolling v. Sharpe 658
Boyd v. Army Prosecuting
Authority **94**
Boyd, United States v. 850
Broadnax, United States v.
. . . . **807**, 812
Brown v. Dep't of the Navy 381
Brown, R. v. **939**
Brown, United States v.
. . . . 501-02, 609-10
Bryant, United States v. . **917**, 920

Burch v. Louisiana 725-26
Burry, United States v. **507**

C

Cain, United States v. **218**
Calley v. Callaway 118
Calley, United States v. . . **465**, 472
Canády v. Slovakia **150**
Captain . . . . See name of Captain
Captain Wong Chee Wai v. State 410
Carlos Alfredo Villalba Zapata . . 303
Carson, United States v. . **413**, 419
Case of . . . . See name of party
Chadwell, United States v. 511
Chief Military Prosecutor v
3SG (RES) Then
Chee Keong 610, 885
Choate, United States v. 440
Christian, United States v. 823
Clay, United States v. 55
Clemons, United States v. **485**
Clinton v. Goldsmith 813, **847**, 887
Cohen, United States v. 783
Commonwealth of Australia v.
Vance 204
Commonwealth v. Via 218
Convening Authority v.
Private Doyle **405**
Cook v. Gates 595, 608
Cooper v. United Kingdom
. . . . **672**, 679
Corporal . . . . . See name of Corporal
Correa Belisle v. Argentina . . 398-99
Courtney v. Williams 56
Creek, United States v. 92
Cupp, United States v. 511
Curtin, United States v. 462
Curtis, United States v. 846
Cuthbert, CPL Cornelius Colin,
v. State 574

D

Daniels, People v. 217

Davis v. United States **43**, 773
Davis, United States v.
.... 132, 440, **851**
Diaz v. Judge Advocate
  General of the Navy **733**
Dinges, United States v. **104**
Doe, In re 210
Doe v. Rumsfeld 462
Dorman, United States v. 207
Drummond, R. v. 885
Duncan v. Kahanamoku
.... **304**, 317, 963-64
Duncan, United States v. **794**
Dunlap v. Convening Authority . 741
Dunphy v. Her Majesty the
  Queen **645**
Durant, United States v. **868**
Durkin, R. v. 68

E

Edwards, United States v. **191**
Engel v. The Netherlands **133**
Engle, United States v. 262
Espinoza v. Rogers 218
Ex parte .... See name of party

F

Feni, Case of Corporal **883**
Ferguson v. City of Charleston .. 574
Ferrara, United States v. 210
Findlay v. United Kingdom
.... **659**, 679, 699, 702-05
Finsel, United States v. **921**
Free, United States v. 606-08

G

Gardner, United States v. **786**
Gatlin, United States v. 319
Généreux, R. v.
.... **626**, 656, 699-702, 705
Gentile v. State Bar of Nevada .. 207
Goldman v. Weinberger 511
Good, United States v. 783
Gore, United States v. 118
Graves v. State 217
Gray, United States v. 845-46
Greaves, United States v. 850
Green, United States v. . 448, **815**
Griggs, United States v. 829
Grunden, United States v. 745
Guilford, United States v. **724**

H

Hamdan v. Rumsfeld .. **57**, 60, 62,
..... 261, 804, 945, 964, 1006-08
Harness, United States v. 205

Harvey, United States v. 118
Hatfield, State v. 218
Hay, United States v. 574
H.C.M.A. v. The Netherlands ... 103
Henderson, United States v. 129
Hickson, United States v. 455
Hill v. State 218
Hlongwane, In re **458**
H.M. The Queen
.... See name of defendant
Hooper v. United States 303
Howe, United States v. 502
Howes, In the Matter of 210
Huet-Vaughn, United
  States v. 474-75, 483
Hutchinson, United States v. ... 347

I

In re .... See name of party
In the Matter of .. See name of party

J

Jackson v. State 217
Jackson, United States v. 205
Jacoby, United States v. 55
Jaffee v. Redmond 792
Jameson, United States v. **575**
Jeffers, United States v. 474
Jobson, United States v. **819**
Johanns v. United States 67
Johanns, United States v. 443, 456
Johnston's Appeal, Re 68

K

Kipling, R. v. **459**
Kirkland, United States v. 683, 686
Kitchens, United States v. 119

L

Lania, United States v. **816**
Le Petit v. United Kingdom .. **750**
Lentz, State v. 217
Lieutenant . See name of Lieutenant
Littrice, United States v. **119**
Lonetree, United
  States v. 744, 794-95
Lopez, United States v. **785**
Lord Sackville's Case **244**
Loukas, United States v. . 773, 783
Love, R. v. 876, 885
Loving v. Hart 687, 845
Loving v. United States .. 813, 834
Loving, United States v. 846
Luster, United States v. 850
Lustig-Prean & Beckett v.
  United Kingdom **581**

Lwin, United States v. 523

M

MacDonald v. Hodson . . . **130**, 132
MacDonald, United States v. 131
MacKay v. Regina 380
Maher, United States v. 204
Manginell, United States v. . . **924**
Marbury v. Madison 1008
Marsaw v. H.M. The Queen . . 380-81
Martin v. Mott 68
Martin, The Queen v. **271**
Martin v. United Kingdom 278, 280
Martin v. Ver 262
Mason, United States v. **502**
**Mathieu, Lieutenant-Colonel
    Joseph Carol Aristide,
    R. v.** **935**, 938
Matthews, United
    States v. 820, 844, 846
McCall v. District Court for
    Twenty-First Judicial Dist. 217-18
McCants, United States v. **818**
McKinney v. White **903**
Meek, United States v. **231**
Mellon, United States v. 928
Mendrano v. Smith 726
Middendorf v. Henry **157**
Middleton, United States v. . . 573-74
Miller, People v. 217
Milligan, Ex parte **945**, 963
Mills v. State 656
Miranda v. Arizona 772-73
Mizgala, United States v. . . **48**, 56
Mora v. Colombia **383**
Morales v. Bridgforth 217
Moreno, United States v. 741
Morris, United States v. 204
Moses, United States v. 783
Murray, United States v. 785

N

Naduaniwai v. Commander, Republic
    of Fiji Military Forces 656
Navales v. Abaya; In re Reaso 375
**Neiman v. Military Governor
    of the Occupied Area of
    Jerusalem** **245**
New v. Gater 935
New, United States v. . 473-74, **932**
**New, United States ex rel., v.
    Rumsfeld** **900**, 908, 935
**Nineteen Merchants v.
    Colombia** **389**

Nguyen, United States v. 229
Nwaoga v. State **463**, 472

O

O'Callahan v. Parker 498-99
Öcalan v. Turkey 321-22
O'Connor, United States v. 502
Okeani v. Arizona 217
O'Keefe, United States ex rel., v.
    McDonnell Douglas Corp. 210
Olinger, United States v. 483-84

P

Pacheco, United States v. 475
Padgett, United States v. 440
Parker v. Levy . **420**, 432, 439, 491,
    . . . . **492**, 499, 502, 507
Parker, United States v. **769**
Payne, R. v. 1060
People v. . . . . See name of Defendant
Perkins v. State 217
Piersack v. Belgium 322
Piersall v. Winter 197
Pitt, State v. 217
Pratt, United States v. **62**
**Poon Chee Seng, Lance
    Corporal (Res), State v.** **403**, 407
**Potsane v. Minister of
    Defence** **97**
PTE Tee Lian Seng v. State 574

Q

Quilona v. General Court-
    Martial 244
Quinn v. Chief of Army . . **410** 419
**Quirin, Ex
    parte** 945, **952**, 963, 1006

R

R. v. . . . . See name of Defendant
Rankin, United States v. 812
Rasnick, United States v. 827
Re . . . . See name of party
Reid v. Covert **262**, 319
Repp v. United States **562**
Roberts, United States v. **569**
Robinson, United States v. 462
**Rockwood, United
    States v.** 482-83, **928**
Rodriguez, United States v. . . **789**
Rodriguez-Rivera, United States v. 234
Rogers, United States v. . **435**, 440
Rome, United States v. 719
Ronghi, United States v. 823
Rush, United States v. 823, 827-28

S

Sadinsky, United States v. . . . 438-39
Saunders, United States v. 440
Scheffer, United States v. 796
Scott, Lieutenant (N) G.D. ,
  v. Her Majesty the
  Queen **511,** 514
Sekoati v. President of the
  Court Martial 656
Selsor v. Kaiser 218
Shearer, United States v. 89
Simmons, United States v. 67
Simpson, United States v. 119
Smith v. Phillips 234
Smith, State v. 218
Smith, United States v. 689
Solorio v. United States . . . .
  . . . . 121, **330,** 343, 347
Sommacal v. Chief Auditor
  of the Army and Confederal
  Military Department . . **299,** 303
Soriano v. Hosken 205
South African National Defence
  Union v. Minister of Defence 555-56
State v. . . . . . See name of defendant
Stebbins, United States v. 823
Steele, United States v. 201
Stephens, United States v. 119
Stevens v. Warden, U.S.
  Penitentiary, Leavenworth,
  Kansas 910
Stevenson, United States v. . . 564
Stoneman, United States v.119
Stuart v. Chief of General
  Staff 431
Sulaiman v. Commandant,
  Tanglin Detention Barracks . . . 262
Sulaiman, State v. 262
Sullivan, R. v. 118
Sullivan, United States v. . . 440, 783
Sutter, Case of, v.
  Switzerland 752, 761

T

Tardiff, United States v. 727
Taylor, United States v. . . 406, 812
Tempia, United States v. 773
Thakur v. Union of India 457, 885
The Queen . . See name of defendant
Thomas, United States v. 112
Thompkins, United States v. 234
Tolkach, United States v. 66, 462
Toohey v. United States 739

Toth, United States ex rel., v.
  Quarles **251**
Truskoski v. The Queen 756
Tullock, United States v. 44
Turner v. Department of the
  Navy 189
Tzufan v. Judge Advocate
  General 103, **173**

U

Uganda Law Society v. Attorney
  General 1075
Union of India v. Sharma 399
United States ex rel. . . . .
  . . . . See name of plaintiff
United States v.
  . . . . See name of defendant

V

Vaughan, United States v. 439

W

Walker, United States v. . 514, 523
Ward v. State 217
Warner, United States v. 828
Washington, United States v. . 478
Watson, State v. 217
Weiss v. United States **648**
Wiesen, United States v.
  . . . . **708,** 719-22
Whelchel v. McDonald 686
White v. Director of Military
  Prosecutions 380, 1075
Wolff, United States v. 726
Wilkens, People v. 217
Willenbring v. Neurauter 280
Williams v. Warden 217
Wilson, United States v. . . . .
  . . . . 67, **499,** 829
Wisely, R. v. 462
Wong Chee Wai, Captain, v.
  State 410
Woods, United States v. 262

Y

Yamashita, In re . . 79, 89, 473, 931
Yarchak, United States v. 829
Yoon v. Republic of Korea . . . 530

Z

Zimmerman, United States v. 560-62
Zonschein v. Judge
  Advocate General **523**

INDEX

A

ABSENCE OFFENSES
Convening Authority v. Doyle . . . 405
Dereliction, disobedience, and negligence (See DERELICTION, DISOBEDIENCE, AND NEGLIGENCE)
Disorderly and service-discrediting acts (See DISORDERLY AND SERVICE-DISCREDITING ACTS)
National Defence Act (Canada) . . . 401; 403
State v. Seng . . . 403
Taylor, United States v. . . . 406

ADULTERY
Green, United States v. . . . 448
Johanns, United States v. . . . 443
Manual for Courts-Martial, United States, Part IV, ¶ 62(C) (2002) . . . 441
National Institute of Military Justice comments to Department of Defense on adultery policy . . . 442

AFGHANISTAN
Reform of military justice . . . 1058

ANGOLA
Personal jurisdiction under Military Jurisdiction Act . . . 243

ASSOCIATION, FREEDOM OF
Dissident and protest activities . . . 553
Major Walter M. Hudson, Racial Extremism in Army . . . 556
Military unions . . . 543
Professional interests, right to create associations protecting . . . 545

AUSTRALIA
Disorderly and service-discrediting acts . . . 437
Negligence under Naval Discipline Act . . . 408
Public access . . . 742; 743
Service-connection of offenses . . . 347

AUSTRIA
Superior orders, defense of obedience to . . . 463

AWOL (ABSENT WITHOUT LEAVE) (See ABSENCE OFFENSES)

B

BELGIUM
Military justice reform and peacekeeping . . . 941

BOLIVIA
Offense, jurisdiction over . . . 395

C

CAMBODIA
Offense, jurisdiction over . . . 328

CANADA
Absence offenses
    Desertion . . . 401
    Without leave, absence . . . 403
Condonation by commanding officer . . 475
Disobedience, defenses to crimes of . . . 459
Military judges . . . 626; 645
Offense, jurisdiction over . . . 329
Peacekeeping and military justice reform . . . 935; 939
Personal jurisdiction under National Defence Act . . . 238
Public access . . . 756

CHINA
Direct appellate review . . . 886
Personal jurisdiction under Interim Regulations . . . 243

CIVILIANS
Court-martial panel and civilian jury contrasted . . . 687
Gary D. Solis, Military Justice, Civilian Clemency . . . 855
Personal jurisdiction
    Duncan v. Kahanamoku . . . 304
    Military Extraterritorial Jurisdiction Act . . . 317

CLASSIFIED EVIDENCE
Duncan, United States v. . . . 794

CLEMENCY (See REVIEW AND APPEAL, subhead: Command review and executive clemency)

COLLATERAL REVIEW
McKinney v. White . . . 903
Rumsfeld, United States ex rel. New v. . . . 900

COLOMBIA
Offense, jurisdiction over
    Colombia Human Rights Certification II, 2004 . . . 384
    Mora v. Colombia, Inter-American Court of Human Rights . . . 383
    Nineteen Merchants v. Colombia . . 389

[References are to pages.]

COMBAT OPERATIONS
Portability of military justice system
    Bryant, United States v. . . . 917
    Finsel, United States v. . . . 921
    Manginell, United States v. . . . 924

COMMANDING OFFICERS
Accountability and liability
    Criminal Code, Ukraine . . . 88
    In re Yamashita . . . 79
    Manual of Law of Armed Conflict, UK
      Ministry of Defense . . . 87
    Shearer, United States v. . . . 89
Command review (See REVIEW AND AP-
  PEAL)
Defenses (See DEFENSES)
Disobedience to commanding officer (See DER-
  ELICTION, DISOBEDIENCE, AND NEGLI-
  GENCE)
Executive clemency (See REVIEW AND AP-
  PEAL, subhead: Command review and exec-
  utive clemency)
Influence over proceedings, improper
    Manual for Legal Administration, United
      States Marine Corps . . . 110
    Thomas, United States v. . . . 112
    Uniform Code of Military Justice, Article
      37 . . . 109
Liability (See subhead: Accountability and
  liability)
Prosecutorial authority
    Boyd v. Army Prosecuting Authority
      . . . 94
    Dinges, United States v. . . . 104
    Potsane v. Minister of Defence . . . 97
    Queen's Regulations for Army, United
      Kingdom . . . 92
    Uniform Code of Military Justice, Articles
      1, 22-25, 60 . . . 98
Review and appeal (See REVIEW AND
  APPEAL)

COMMISSIONS, MILITARY (See MILI-
  TARY COMMISSIONS)

**CONDONATION BY COMMANDING OF-
  FICER**
Armed Forces Act, Malaysia . . . 475
Lawrence, *Attorney General* ex rel. *Royal N.Z.
  Navy v.* . . . 476
Queen's Regulations and Orders for Canadian
  forces . . . 475

CONSCIENTIOUS OBJECTION
Walker, United States v. . . . 514
Yoon v. Republic of Korea . . . 530
Zonschein v. Judge Advocate General . . . .
  523

**CONSTITUTION AND MILITARY JUS-
  TICE**
Association, freedom of (See ASSOCIATION,
  FREEDOM OF)
Bill of Rights and service members . . . 129
Conscience, freedom of (See CONSCIENTIOUS
  OBJECTION)
Davis v. United States . . . 43
Domestic military law, challenges to disobedi-
  ence of . . . 932
Earl Warren, The Bill of Rights and the Mili-
  tary . . . 40
Evidentiary issues (See EVIDENCE)
Mizgala, United States v. . . . 48
Pretrial investigations . . . 121
Religion, freedom of (See RELIGION, FREE
  EXERCISE OF)
Speech, freedom of (See SPEECH, FREEDOM
  OF)
Tulloch, United States v. . . . 44
United States Constitution, Article I, §§ 8 and
  9; Article II, § 2; Amend. II, III, V . . 37

COURTS-MARTIAL
Cold War . . . 10
Commanding officers
    Influence over proceedings, improper (See
      COMMANDING OFFICERS, subhead:
      Influence over proceedings, improper)
    Prosecutorial authority (See COMMAND-
      ING OFFICERS, subhead: Prosecu-
      torial authority)
Panel
    Generally . . . 681
    Civilian jury, differences between panel
      and . . . 687
    Kirkland, United States v. . . . 683
    Selection of members . . . 689
    Size and voting requirements
      Guilford, United States v. . . . 724
      Uniform Code of Military Justice,
        Article 16 . . . 723
    Uniform Code of Military Justice, Article
      25 . . . 682
Prosecutorial authority of commanding officers
  (See COMMANDING OFFICERS, subhead:
  Prosecutorial authority)
Rules of procedure, promulgation of . . . 57
Summary courts-martial (See SUMMARY
  COURTS-MARTIAL)

CUSTOM OF SERVICE
Pratt, United States v. . . . 62

D

DEATH PENALTY
Loving v. Hart . . . 845
Loving v. United States . . . 834

[References are to pages.]

DEFENSES
Condonation by commanding officer
  Armed Forces Act, Malaysia . . . 475
  Lawrence, *Attorney General* ex rel. *Royal N.Z. Navy v.* . . . 476
  Queen's Regulations and Orders for Canadian forces . . . 475
Disobedience, defenses to crimes of
  In re Hlongwane . . . 458
  R. v. Kipling . . . 459
  Thakur v. Union of India . . . 457
Duress . . . 478
Good soldier defense . . . 485
Necessity . . . 478
Superior orders, defense of . . . 463; 465

DENMARK
Superior orders, defense of obedience to . . . 463

DEPENDENTS
Personal jurisdiction
  Martin v. United Kingdom . . . 278
  Queen v. Martin . . . 271
  Reid v. Covert . . . 262

DERELICTION, DISOBEDIENCE, AND NEGLIGENCE
Carson, United States v. . . . 413
Defence Force Discipline Act, New Zealand . . . 408
Defenses to crimes of disobedience
  In re Hlongwane . . . 458
  R. v. Kipling . . . 459
  Thakur v. Union of India . . . 457
Domestic military law, constitutional challenges to disobedience of . . . 932
Military Discipline Code, South Africa . . . 408
Naval Discipline Act, Australia . . . 408
Quinn v. Chief of Army . . . 410
Uniform Code of Military Justice, Article 90 . . . 408

DESERTION (See ABSENCE OFFENSES)

DETENTION
Colonel Paul E. Kantwill and Major Sean Watts, Hostile Protected Persons or "Extra-Conventional Persons" . . . 27
Raymond Lech, Broken Soldiers . . . 24

DISCHARGED SOLDIERS (See FORMER SOLDIERS)

DISOBEDIENCE TO SUPERIOR OFFICER (See DERELICTION, DISOBEDIENCE, AND NEGLIGENCE)

DISORDERLY AND SERVICE-DISCREDITING ACTS
Defence Force Discipline Act, New Zealand . . . 419

DISORDERLY AND SERVICE-DISCREDITING ACTS—Cont.
Parker v. Levy . . . 420
Re Anning . . . 437
Rogers, United States v. . . . 435
Stuart v. Chief of General Staff . . . 431
Uniform Code of Military Justice, Article 134 . . . 419

DURESS
Defense, as . . . 478

E

EVIDENCE
Adopting Military Rules of Evidence
  Generally . . . 767
  Stephen A. Saltzburg, Lee D. Schinasi and David A. Schlueter, Military Rules of Evidence Manual . . . 768
Amending Military Rules of Evidence
  Military Rule of Evidence 1102 . . 768
  Parker, United States v. . . . 769
Classified evidence . . . 794
Hearsay
  Broadnax, United States v. . . . 807
  Military Rule of Evidence 803 . . . 804
Polygraph examinations . . . 795
Privileges
  Rodriguez, United States v. . . . 789
  Stephen A. Saltzburg, Lee D. Schinasi and David A. Schlueter, Military Rules of Evidence Manual . . . 792
Search and seizure
  Gardner, United States v. . . . 786
  Military Rules of Evidence 315 and 313 . . . 784
Self-incrimination
  Loukas, United States v. . . . 773
  Uniform Code of Military Justice, Article 31 . . . 771

EXECUTIVE CLEMENCY (See REVIEW AND APPEAL, subhead: Command review and executive clemency)

"EXTRA-CONVENTIONAL PERSONS"
Detainees . . . 27

F

FORMER SOLDIERS
Lord Sackville's Case . . . 244
Neiman v. Military Governor of the Occupied Area of Jerusalem . . . 245
Quarles, United States ex rel. *Toth v.* . . . 251

FRANCE
Personal jurisdiction under Code of Military Justice . . . 241

[References are to pages.]

G

GLOBALIZATION
Eugene R. Fidell, Worldwide Perspective on Change in Military Justice . . . 1060
Lord Chief Justice of England and Wales, Practice Direction on Citation . . . 1073

GOOD SOLDIER DEFENSE
Generally . . . 485

H

HAWAII
Harry N. Scheiber and Jane L. Scheiber, Bayonets in Paradise . . . 15

HEARSAY
Broadnax, United States v. . . . 807
Military Rule of Evidence 803 . . . 804

HISTORICAL BACKGROUND
Code of Articles of King Gustavus Adolphus of Sweden . . . 31
Elizabeth Lutes Hillman, Defending America . . . 34
Joseph W. Bishop, Jr., Justice Under Fire . . . 33
Native Americans . . . 1; 2
Robert C. Stacey, Age of Chivalry . . . 29

HOMOSEXUALITY (See SEXUAL ORIENTATION)

HOSTILE PROTECTED PERSONS
Detainees . . . 27

HUMAN RIGHTS, INTERNATIONAL (See INTERNATIONAL HUMAN RIGHTS)

I

IDENTITY, RIGHT OF
Sexual orientation (See SEXUAL ORIENTATION)

INDEPENDENCE OF JUDICIARY (See JUDICIAL INDEPENDENCE)

INDIA
Disobedience, defenses to crimes of . . . 457

INTERNATIONAL HUMAN RIGHTS
Draft Principles Governing Administration of Justice . . . 1011
Judicial independence
    Cooper v. United Kingdom . . . 672
    Draft Principles Governing Administration of Justice . . . 658
    Findlay v. United Kingdom . . . 659

INTERNATIONAL HUMAN RIGHTS— Cont.
Offense, jurisdiction over
    Colombia Human Rights Certification II, 2004 . . . 384
    Draft Principles Governing Administration of Justice . . . 381
    Letter to Bolivian President Carlos Mesa Gisbert . . . 395
    Mora v. Colombia, Inter-American Court of Human Rights . . . 383
    Nineteen Merchants v. Colombia . . 389
Personal jurisdiction
    Human Rights Report on Terrorism and Human Rights . . . 320
    Office of High Commissioner for Human Rights . . . 319
Review of Manual for Courts-Martial 1013
Summary courts-martial
    A.D. v. Turkey . . . 148
    Canády v. Slovakia . . . 150
    Engel v. Netherlands . . . 133
Uniform Code of Military Justice, Article 146 . . . 1011

INTERNATIONAL LAW
Federico Andreu-Guzmán, Military Jurisdiction and International Law . . . 68
Nuremberg Principles . . . 69
Patricia M. Wald, General Radislav Krstic: A War Crimes Case Study . . . 70

IRELAND
Absence offenses . . . 405

ISRAEL
Former soldiers, jurisdiction over . . . 245
Offense, jurisdiction over . . . 329
Summary courts-martial . . . 173

J

JUDGES, MILITARY (See MILITARY JUDGES)

JUDICIAL INDEPENDENCE
Eugene R. Fidell, Military Judges and Military Justice . . . 613
International human rights
    Cooper v. United Kingdom . . . 672
    Draft Principles Governing Administration of Justice . . . 658
    Findlay v. United Kingdom . . . 659
Model Code of Military Justice, Article 2 . . . 613
Rule for Courts-Martial 109 . . . 612
Uniform Code of Military Justice, Article 6a and 37 . . . 611

JURISDICTION
Federico Andreu-Guzmán, Military Jurisdiction and International Law . . . 68
Occupational jurisdiction . . . 23
Offense, over the (See OFFENSE, JURISDICTION OVER)
Person, over the person (See PERSONAL JURISDICTION)
Portability of military justice system (See PORTABILITY OF MILITARY JUSTICE SYSTEM)
Preamble, Manual for Courts-Martial, United States (2005 Ed.) . . . 39
Uniform Code of Military Justice, Article 36 . . . 39

JURY (See COURTS-MARTIAL, subhead: Panel)

K

KOREA
Conscientious objection . . . 530

L

LICENSING OF MILITARY JUSTICE PERSONNEL
Judge Advocate General of Army, Standards of Conduct Office . . . 200
Steele, United States v. . . . 201
Uniform Code of Military Justice, Articles 26 and 27 . . . 199

LIE-DETECTOR TESTS
Admissibility . . . 795

LUXEMBOURG
Personal jurisdiction under Revised Code of Military Procedure . . . 242

M

MALAYSIA
Condonation by commanding officer . . 475

MARITIME JUSTICE
Edwards, United States v. . . . 191
Herman Melville, *White-Jacket, or The World in a Man-of-War* . . . 190
Negligence under Australia Naval Discipline Act . . . 408
Public access . . . 743

MILITARY COMMISSIONS
Ex parte Milligan . . . 945
Ex parte Quirin . . . 952
Post-September 11, 2001 Military Commissions . . . 964
Rules of procedure, promulgation of . . . 57

MILITARY JUDGES
Army Regulation 27-10, Legal Services: Military Justice . . . 655
Dunphy v. Her Majesty Queen . . . 645
Eugene R. Fidell, Military Judges and Military Justice . . . 613
Regina v. Généreux . . . 626
Weiss v. United States . . . 648

MOROCCO
Personal jurisdiction under Code of Military Justice . . . 241

N

NAVAL JUSTICE (See MARITIME JUSTICE)

NECESSITY
Defense, as . . . 478

NEGLIGENCE (See DERELICTION, DISOBEDIENCE, AND NEGLIGENCE)

NETHERLANDS
Summary courts-martial . . . 133

NEW ZEALAND
Condonation by commanding officer . . 476
Disorderly and service-discrediting acts . . . 419
Negligence in performance of a duty . . 408

NIGERIA
Superior orders, defense of obedience to . . . 463

O

OCCUPATION
Harry N. Scheiber and Jane L. Scheiber, Bayonets in Paradise . . . 15
Ry Swift, Occupational Jurisdiction . . . 23

OFFENSE, JURISDICTION OVER
Alaska Statutes, Statement of Policy on Military Justice . . . 328
Cambodia, Law of Feb. 8, 1993 . . . 328
Canada . . . 329
Connection to service (See subhead: Service-connection of offenses)
International human rights
    Colombia Human Rights Certification II, 2004 . . . 384
    Draft Principles Governing Administration of Justice . . . 381
    Letter to Bolivian President Carlos Mesa Gisbert . . . 395
    Mora v. Colombia, Inter-American Court of Human Rights . . . 383
    Nineteen Merchants v. Colombia . . 389

[References are to pages.]

OFFENSE, JURISDICTION OVER—Cont.
Latin American Model Code of Military Justice, Article 4 . . . 327
Philippines, Republic Act . . . 328
Rules for Courts-Martial 203 . . . 327
Service-connection of offenses
    Navales v. Abaya; In re Reaso . . . 375
    Re Colonel Aird; Ex parte Alpert 347
    Solorio v. United States . . . 330
South Africa, Military Discipline Supplementary Measures Act . . . 329

P

PANEL, COURT-MARTIAL (See COURTS-MARTIAL, subhead: Panel)

PEACEKEEPING OPERATIONS
Constitutional challenges to disobedience of domestic military law . . . 932
International law and domestic military law . . . 928
Military justice reform and peacekeeping
    R. v. Brown . . . 939
    R. v. Mathieu . . . 935
    Statement of Thierry Giet, Belgium House of Representatives . . . 941

PERSONAL JURISDICTION
Angola, Military Jurisdiction Act . . . 243
Canada, National Defence Act . . . 238
China, Interim Regulations of People's Republic of . . . 243
Civilians (See CIVILIANS, subhead: Personal jurisdiction)
Dependents (See DEPENDENTS)
Former soldiers (See FORMER SOLDIERS)
France, Code of Military Justice . . . 241
International human rights
    Human Rights Report on Terrorism and Human Rights . . . 320
    Office of High Commissioner for Human Rights . . . 319
Luxembourg, Revised Code of Military Procedure . . . 242
Morocco, Code of Military Justice . . . 241
Reservists (See RESERVISTS)
Singapore, Armed Forces Act . . . 239
Switzerland, Military Penal Code . . . 241
Uganda People's Defence Forces Act . . 243
Uniform Code of Military Justice, Articles 2 and 3 . . . 235
United Kingdom, Armed Forces Act 2006 . . . 244

PHILIPPINES
Offense, jurisdiction over . . . 328
Service-connection of offenses . . . 375

POLYGRAPH EXAMINATIONS
Admissibility . . . 795

PORTABILITY OF MILITARY JUSTICE SYSTEM
Combat operations
    Bryant, United States v. . . . 917
    Finsel, United States v. . . . 921
    Manginell, United States v. . . . 924
Criminal Expo 2001, 5th International Criminal Law Conference . . . 911
Françoise Hampson, Working Paper . . 913
Peacekeeping operations (See PEACEKEEPING OPERATIONS)
Stevens v. Warden, U.S. Penitentiary, Leavenworth, Kansas . . . 910
Uniform Code of Military Justice, Article 5 . . . 909

POST-TRIAL DELAYS
Diaz v. Judge Advocate General of Navy . . 733
Tardif, United States v. . . . 727
Toohey v. United States . . . 739

PRETRIAL AGREEMENTS
Jobson, United States v. . . . 819
McCants, United States v. . . . 819
Rule for Courts-Martial 901(f) . . . 818

PRETRIAL INVESTIGATIONS
Bill of Rights and service members . . . 129
MacDonald v. Hodson . . . 130
Rule for Courts-Martial 405 . . . 122
Uniform Code of Military Justice, Article 32 . . . 121
United States Constitution, Amend. V 121

PRIVACY, RIGHT TO
Repp v. United States . . . 562
Roberts, United States v. . . . 569
Stevenson, United States v. . . . 564

PRIVILEGES, EVIDENTIARY
Rodriguez, United States v. . . . 789
Stephen A. Saltzburg, Lee D. Schinasi and David A. Schlueter, Military Rules of Evidence Manual . . . 792

PROFESSIONAL RESPONSIBILITY
Judge Advocate General of Army, Standards of Conduct Office . . . 200
Licensing
    Judge Advocate General of Army, Standards of Conduct Office . . . 200
    Steele, United States v. . . . 201
    Uniform Code of Military Justice, Articles 26 and 27 . . . 199
Regulation
    Army Rules of Professional Conduct for Lawyers . . . 210

[References are to pages.]

PROFESSIONAL RESPONSIBILITY—Cont.

Regulation—Cont.

    Cain, United States v. . . . 218

    Informal Opinion, American Bar Association Committee . . . 213

    Meek, United States v. . . . 231

    Professional Responsibility for Lawyers . . . 205

PROSECUTORIAL AUTHORITY OF COMMANDING OFFICERS

Boyd v. Army Prosecuting Authority . . . 94

Dinges, United States v. . . . 104

Potsane v. Minister of Defence . . . 97

Queen's Regulations for Army, United Kingdom . . . 92

Uniform Code of Military Justice, Articles 1, 22-25, 60 . . . 98

PUBLIC ACCESS

ABC, Inc. v. Powell . . . 758

Armed Forces Act, Singapore . . . 758

Barry v. Chief of Naval Staff . . . 743

Le Petit v. United Kingdom . . . 750

Lonetree, United States v. . . . 744

Sutter v. Switzerland . . . 752

Truskoski v. Queen . . . 756

R

REFORM OF MILITARY LAW

Generally . . . 1009

International assistance

    Lieutenant Colonel J. McClelland MBE, Starting From Scratch . . . 1038

    Major Sean M. Watts and Captain Christopher E. Martin, Nation-Building in Afghanistan . . . 1058

    Major Steve Cullen, Starting Over – The New Iraqi Code of Military Discipline . . . 1053

Kevin J. Barry, A Face Lift (and Much More) for an Aging Beauty . . . 1029

Peacekeeping operations

    R. v. Brown . . . 939

    R. v. Mathieu . . . 935

    Statement of Thierry Giet, Belgium House of Representatives . . . 941

Report of Cox Commission . . . 1018

RELIGION, FREE EXERCISE OF

Burry, United States v. . . . 507

Conscientious objection (See CONSCIENTIOUS OBJECTION)

Manual for Courts-Martial, Pt. IV, ¶14 . . . 507

Scott v. Her Majesty the Queen . . . 511

RESERVISTS

Personal jurisdiction over

    H.M. The Queen v. Brady . . . 295

    Sommacal v. Chief Auditor of the Army and Confederal Military Department . . . 299

    Willenbring v. Neurauter . . . 280

REVIEW AND APPEAL

Collateral review

    McKinney v. White . . . 903

    Rumsfeld, United States ex rel. *New v.* . . . 900

Command review and executive clemency

    Davis, United States v. . . . 851

    Gary D. Solis, Military Justice, Civilian Clemency . . . 855

    Letter From Captain Aubrey M. Daniel 3d to President Richard M. Nixon 864

Direct appellate review

    Clinton v. Goldsmith . . . 887

    Constitutional Interpretation, Republic of China Council of Grand Justices . . . 886

    Draft Principles Governing Administration of Justice . . . 886

    Eugene R. Fidell, Guide to Rules of Practice and Procedure . . . 892

    Notice of Proposed Rule Change . . 894

Public access . . . 742

Sentence review

    Case of Corporal Feni . . . 883

    Draft Principles Governing Administration of Justice . . . 868

    Durant, United States v. . . . 868

    Regina v. Love . . . 876

S

SEARCH AND SEIZURE

Gardner, United States v. . . . 786

Military Rules of Evidence 315 and 313 . . . 784

SELF-INCRIMINATION

Loukas, United States v. . . . 773

Uniform Code of Military Justice, Article 31 . . . 771

SENTENCE AND PUNISHMENT

Administrative sanctions and collateral consequences . . . 847

Adversarial sentencing

    Green, United States v. . . . 815

    Lania, United States v. . . . 816

    Rule for Courts-Martial 1001, Drafters' Analysis . . . 815

Authorized punishments . . . 821

SENTENCE AND PUNISHMENT—Cont.

Death penalty
  Loving v. Hart . . . 845
  Loving v. United States . . . 834
Pretrial agreements
  Jobson, United States v. . . . 819
  McCants, United States v. . . . 819
  Rule for Courts-Martial 901(f) . . . 818
Review of sentence (See REVIEW AND
  APPEAL)
Sentencing authority . . . 813
Summary courts-martial, nonjudicial punish-
  ment and (See SUMMARY COURTS-
  MARTIAL, subhead: Nonjudicial punish-
  ment and)
Unique military punishments
  Eugene R. Fidell and Jay M. Fidell, Loss
    of Numbers . . . 831
  Rush, United States v. . . . 823
  Uniform Code of Military Justice, Article
    55 . . . 829
  Yatchak, United States v. . . . 829

SERVICE-DISCREDITING ACTS (See DIS-
  ORDERLY AND SERVICE-DISCREDITING
  ACTS)

SEXUAL ORIENTATION
Armed Forces Code of Social Conduct . . . .
  591
Brief of *amici curiae, Cook v. Gates* . . 595
Homosexuality and Armed Forces, United
  Kingdom Ministry of Defence . . . 589
Jameson, United States v. . . . 575
Lustig-Prean and Beckett v. United Kingdom
  . . . 581
Policy Concerning Homosexuality . . . 592

SINGAPORE
Personal jurisdiction under Armed Forces Act
  . . . 239
Public access . . . 758

SLOVAKIA
Summary courts-martial . . . 150

SOUTH AFRICA
Dereliction of duty . . . 408
Disobedience, defenses to crimes of . . . 458
Offense, jurisdiction over . . . 329
Sentence review . . . 883

SPEECH, FREEDOM OF
Generally . . . 491
Brief of *amici curiae, Cook v. Gates* . . 595
Mason, United States v. . . . 502

SPEECH, FREEDOM OF—Cont.
Parker v. Levy . . . 492
Wilson, United States v. . . . 499

SUMMARY COURTS-MARTIAL
International human rights
  A.D. v. Turkey . . . 148
  Canády v. Slovakia . . . 150
  Engel v. Netherlands . . . 133
Nonjudicial punishment and
  Middendorf v. Henry . . . 157
  Tzuf v. Judge Advocate General . . 173
  Uniform Code of Military Justice, Articles
    15 and 20 . . . 153

SWEDEN
Code of Articles of King Gustavus Adolphus
  . . . 31

SWITZERLAND
Personal jurisdiction . . . 241; 299
Public access . . . 752

T

TURKEY
Summary courts-martial . . . 148

U

UGANDA
Personal jurisdiction under People's Defence
  Forces Act . . . 243

UKRAINE
Military authorities, omissions of . . . 88

UNITED KINGDOM
Citation, Practice Direction on . . . 1073
Commanding officers
  Prosecutorial authority of . . . 92
  Responsibility of . . . 87
Criminal responsibility . . . 87
Dependents, jurisdiction over . . . 271; 278
Judicial independence . . . 659; 672
Personal jurisdiction
  Lord Sackville's Case . . . 244
  Reservists . . . 295
  United Kingdom, Armed Forces Act 2006
    . . . 244
Prosecutorial authority of commanding officers
  . . . 92
Public access . . . 750
Religion, free exercise of . . . 511
Sexual orientation . . . 581; 589; 591